The Greek Islands

THE ROUGH GUIDE

There are more than one hundred and fifty Rough Guide titles
covering destinations from Amsterdam to Zimbabwe

Forthcoming titles include

Beijing • Cape Town • Croatia • Ecuador • Switzerland

Rough Guide Reference Series

Classical Music • Drum 'n' Bass • English Football • European Football
House • The Internet • Jazz • Music USA • Opera • Reggae
Rock Music • World Music

Rough Guide Phrasebooks

Czech • Dutch • Egyptian Arabic • European Languages • French • German
Greek • Hindi & Urdu • Hungarian • Indonesian • Italian • Japanese
Mandarin Chinese • Mexican Spanish • Polish • Portuguese • Russian
Spanish • Swahili • Thai • Turkish • Vietnamese

Rough Guides on the Internet

www.roughguides.com

ROUGH GUIDE CREDITS

Text editor: Claire Fogg
Series editor: Mark Ellingham
Editorial: Martin Dunford, Jonathan Buckley, Jo Mead, Kate Berens, Amanda Tomlin, Ann-Marie Shaw, Paul Gray, Helena Smith, Judith Bamber, Orla Duane, Olivia Eccleshall, Ruth Blackmore, Sophie Martin, Geoff Howard, Claire Saunders, Gavin Thomas, Alexander Mark Rogers, Polly Thomas, Joe Staines, Lisa Nellis, Andrew Tomičić, Richard Lim, Duncan Clark, Peter Buckley (UK); Andrew Rosenberg, Mary Beth Maioli (US)
Production: Susanne Hillen, Andy Hilliard, Link Hall, Helen Ostick, Julia Bovis, Michelle Draycott, Katie Pringle, Robert Evers, Neil Cooper
Cartography: Melissa Baker, Maxine Repath, Nichola Goodliffe, Ed Wright
Picture research: Louise Boulton, Sharon Martins
Online editors: Kelly Cross, Loretta Chilcoat (US)
Finance: John Fisher, Gary Singh, Edward Downey, Mark Hall, Tim Bill
Marketing & Publicity: Richard Trillo, Niki Smith, David Wearn, Jemima Broadbridge (UK); Jean Marie Kelly, Myra Campolo, Simon Carloss (US)
Administration: Tania Hummel, Charlotte Marriott, Demelza Dallow

ACKNOWLEDGEMENTS

Lance Chilton thanks wife Hilary; David and Vanessa Grant in Éyina; Nik Panou in Angístri; Catherine Protopapa and Nektarios Stavrou in Póros; Chris and Dave Windell in Pyrgiótika; Julia Tzanidou-Zuberer of Porfyra Travel in Kýthira; Babis Doufexis, Nicola Dyas and Heike Johnson of Doufexis Travel of Stoupa; Maggie Price, Andrew Fielding and Vasso Tavoularea in Stoúpa; the NTOG staff in Olymbía, and the town tourist office in Loutráki.

Marc Dubin thanks Persephone Papakyriakou on Thássos; George and Barbara Ballis on Lésvos; Markos Kostalas and Theodhore and Güher Spordhilis on Híos; Michael and Avra Ward on Sámos; Alexis and Dhionysia Zikas on Kós; Baz Ward, Nigel Gardner and Joanna on Tílos; Nikos, Wendy and Jean on Sými; Sotiris and Marianne Nikolis in Rhodes Town, and Willard and Mavis Manus in Líndhos; and last but not least Pamela for eating far more than she'd like in the interests of science, and tolerating 150km driving days on Lésvos.

Nick Edwards thanks the countless people who helped along the way with info, drinks, winks and smiles. *Efharistó* to the staff of EOT offices in Athens and elsewhere. Special thanks to the following: Jonathan Sim for friendship and a nest in Athens; Yiannis Karapapas for continuing brotherhood; Debbie Spanoudaki for the fine tour of Attikí; Pete Birch and Steve Thompson for joint legwork in parts of the metropolis; Maria Zygouraki for expert driving in Évvia; Mariana, Petros, Orestis and Orpheas Zoupanos, Spyros Hytiris and Hilary Whetton-Paipeti for hospitality and invaluable help in Corfu; Efi and Antonio for introducing me to the Perdika turtle; Captain Elias Vernikos for making me first mate in Lefkádha and the Kálamos trip; Panayiotis of Hotel Chara, Argostóli; June and Angie Kalogeratou for hospitality in Zákynthos. Last but not least, to Maria Edwards née Viskochil for lasting the RG pace in the Sporades and continuing inspiration.

Chris Nicholas thanks Susanna in Porto Tango; Tínos for getting me off to a good start; Sarah Adams in Skhinoússa for sharing major insider tips on the minor Cyclades islands; John van Lerberghe of Mýkonos Accommodation Centre for providing ongoing advice and support throughout my trip; Dimitri and Chrisoula Ghikas in Páros; John Gregory who helped me unwind when things got hectic; Tobias Schweitzer for his unfailing encouragement; Alexia Mantoudis and Bianca Kokkolas for imparting a love of Greece to me; and my parents in Ándhros for sharing my enthusiasm.

The Editor thanks Jennifer Speake for proofreading, Robert Mackey and Silke Kerwick for additional updating, and Melissa Baker and Stratigraphics for cartography. At the Rough Guides thanks go to Paul Gray for help and support; to Susanne Hillen, Katie Pringle, Julia Bovis, Maxine Repath and Ed Wright for their patience and efficiency.

PUBLISHING INFORMATION

This third edition published March 2000 by Rough Guides Ltd, 62–70 Shorts Gardens, London, WC2H 9AB.
Distributed by the Penguin Group:
Penguin Books Ltd, 27 Wrights Lane, London W8 5TZ
Penguin Books USA Inc., 375 Hudson Street, New York 10014, USA
Penguin Books Australia Ltd, 487 Maroondah Highway, PO Box 257, Ringwood, Victoria 3134, Australia
Penguin Books Canada Ltd, 10 Alcorn Avenue, Toronto, Ontario, Canada M4V 1E4
Penguin Books (NZ) Ltd, 182–190 Wairau Road, Auckland 10, New Zealand
Typeset in Linotron Univers and Century Old Style to an original design by Andrew Oliver.
Printed in England by Clays Ltd, St Ives PLC
Illustrations in Part One and Part Three by Edward Briant.
Illustration on p.1 by Henry Iles

544pp – Includes index
A catalogue record for this book is available from the British Library
ISBN 1-85828-523-2

The Greek Islands

THE ROUGH GUIDE

written and researched by

Mark Ellingham, Marc Dubin,
Natania Jansz and John Fisher

additional contributions by

Lance Chilton, Nick Edwards, Geoff Garvey
and Chris Nicholas

THE ROUGH GUIDES

THE ROUGH GUIDES

TRAVEL GUIDES • PHRASEBOOKS • MUSIC AND REFERENCE GUIDES

We set out to do something different when the first Rough Guide was published in 1982. Mark Ellingham, just out of university, was travelling in Greece. He brought along the popular guides of the day, but found they were all lacking in some way. They were either strong on ruins and museums but went on for pages without mentioning a beach or taverna. Or they were so conscious of the need to save money that they lost sight of Greece's cultural and historical significance. Also, none of the books told him anything about Greece's contemporary life – its politics, its culture, its people, and how they lived.

So with no job in prospect, Mark decided to write his own guidebook, one which aimed to provide practical information that was second to none, detailing the best beaches and the hottest clubs and restaurants, while also giving hard-hitting accounts of every sight, both famous and obscure, and providing up-to-the-minute information on contemporary culture. It was a guide that encouraged independent travellers to find the best of Greece, and was a great success, getting shortlisted for the Thomas Cook travel guide award, and encouraging Mark, along with three friends, to expand the series.

The Rough Guide list grew rapidly and the letters flooded in, indicating a much broader readership than had been anticipated, but one which uniformly appreciated the Rough Guide mix of practical detail and humour, irreverence and enthusiasm. Things haven't changed. The same four friends who began the series are still the caretakers of the Rough Guide mission today: to provide the most reliable, up-to-date and entertaining information to independent-minded travellers of all ages, on all budgets.

We now publish more than 150 titles and have offices in London and New York. The travel guides are written and researched by a dedicated team of more than 100 authors, based in Britain, Europe, the USA and Australia. We have also created a unique series of phrasebooks to accompany the travel series, along with an acclaimed series of music guides, and a best-selling pocket guide to the Internet and World Wide Web. We also publish comprehensive travel information on our web site:

www.roughguides.com

HELP US UPDATE

We've gone to a lot of effort to ensure that the third edition of *The Rough Guide to The Greek Islands* is accurate and up-to-date. However, things change – places get "discovered", opening hours are notoriously fickle, restaurants and rooms raise prices or lower standards. If you feel we've got it wrong or left something out, we'd like to know, and if you can remember the address, the price, the time, the phone number, so much the better.

We'll credit all contributions, and send a copy of the next edition (or any other Rough Guide if you prefer) for the best letters. Please mark letters: "Rough Guide Greek Islands Update" and send to:

Rough Guides, 62–70 Shorts Gardens, London WC2H 9AB, or
Rough Guides, 375 Hudson St, New York NY 10014.
Or send email to: mail@roughguides.co.uk
Online updates about this book can be found on Rough Guides' Web site at www.roughguides.com

THE AUTHORS

Mark Ellingham and Natania Jansz wrote the original edition of this book – the first ever Rough Guide – in 1981. They couldn't believe their good fortune in being paid by a publisher to spend time roaming around Classical ruins and medieval castles, and island-hopping in the Aegean. Mark continued writing Rough Guides and still works for the company as Series Editor. He is currently spending most of his time developing publication of the guides on the Internet but would be happier roaming the ruins, etc. Natania divides her time between Clinical Psychology and writing; she has edited the Rough Guide special, *More Women Travel*. Natania and Mark have a toddler, Miles, who rates Greek food (and sand) high on his list of life's good things.

John Fisher has also been involved with Rough Guides from the start. One of the original authors of the Greek guide, he has since written numerous other Rough Guide titles including the *Rough Guide to Crete*. Between travels, John can usually be found chained to a desk at Rough Guide HQ in London. He lives in south London with his wife and two young sons.

Marc Dubin first arrived in Greece in 1978, able to ask only for yoghurts, and the loo, in the local tongue. Since 1981 he has returned yearly, thereby acquiring fluency in Greek, and from 1989 onwards has lived part-time on the island of Sámos, where he recently restored an old cottage. Marc writes regularly for various publications on topics as diverse as Greek cuisine, music and backcountry trekking. When not in Greece, he lives in London or ranges across the Mediterranean in the course of updating his other Rough Guides: Turkey, Cyprus, and the Pyrenees

READERS' LETTERS

We'd like to thank the readers of previous editions, who took time to write in with comments and suggestions. For this edition, we were helped by letters from:

George Androvik, Chris Arthur, David Authers, Judith Azrael, Kate Bennett, Beth Bornstein, Rev. & Mrs R. J. Blakeway-Phillips, Fred Bohrer, Roland Chapman, Vickie Chatzigeorgiou, Clare Clarke, Dennis Cunningham, Joanne Davies, Michael Davies, Gary Eastwood, Imogen Edwards, Samantha Evans, Sally Fairns, Rev Alan Everett, Henry Fan, Frances Faux, Gilian Foxon, Richard Francis, John Garratt & Monica Mackaness, C. Gipson, Benita Goldman, Ceri Greenwood, Judy Greenwood, Emanuele Habib, B. Halatas & E. Molla, Elizabeth Halliday, Janet & Harry Hannaby, Paul Hargrave & Ashleigh Rinchay, Annabel Hayward, John Holden, Lynne Kelly, Andreas Kitidis, Kate Lackie, Rebecca Lisle-Taylor, Linda & Peter Ludlow, Katy Lumb, Deborah Lyons, Ellie McKinlay, Allegra Madgewick, Carles Manton, K. M. Marriott, Gareth Morris Jones, Emilie Nangle, Richard Nelsson, Carla & John Nesbitt, Christopher Nicholas, Raphaella Nicol, David Phillips, Martin Potter, E. Randall, Caroline Ray, David Reilly, John H. Rose, Joyce B. Siegel, Murray Sugden, Carole Supham, Ed & Brenda Swidler, Franka Van Der Loo Bno, Peter Verity, Simon Whittaker, Stuart Wilson, Peggy A. Wright, Laura Wyatt, Lisa Wycherley, Rhea Zambellas.

CONTENTS

• CHAPTER 4: THE DODECANESE 234–308

• CHAPTER 5: THE EAST AND NORTH AEGEAN 309–373

• CHAPTER 6: THE SPORADES AND ÉVVIA 374–401

• CHAPTER 7: THE IONIAN ISLANDS 402–453

PART THREE CONTEXTS 455

LIST OF MAPS

MAP SYMBOLS

Railway	Waterfall
Major paved road	Spa/spring
Minor paved road	Cave
Unpaved road	Viewpoint
Footpath	Campsite
Steps	Accommodation
Ferry route	Restaurant
Waterway	Airport
Chapter division boundary	Bus stop
International boundary	Lighthouse
Point of interest	Information office
Mosque	Post office
Synagogue	Building
Church	Church
Monastery or convent	Christian cemetery
Castle	Park
Hill	National park
Archeological site	Pedestrianized area
Peak	Beach
Marshland	

PLACE NAMES: A WARNING!

The art of rendering Greek words in Roman letters has always been in a state of uproar. It's a major source of confusion with **place names**, for which each local authority and map-maker apparently uses a different system. The word for "saint", for instance, one of the most common prefixes, can be spelt Áyios, Ágios, or Ághios. And, to make matters worse, there are often two forms of a name in Greek – the popularly used *dhimotikí*, and the old "classicizing" *katharévoussa*. Thus you will see the island of Spétses written also as Spétsai, or Halkídha, the capital of Évvia, as Chalkida, Halkís (or even Chalcís, on more traditional maps). Throw in the complexities of Greek grammar – with different case-endings for names – and the fact that there exist long-established English versions of Classical place names, which bear little relation to the Greek sounds, and you have a real tangle.

In this book, we've used a modern and largely phonetic **system**, with Y rather than G for the Greek gamma when preceding I or E; Y also for ypsilon whenever possible; H or KH (not CH) for Greek chi; and DH rather than D for delta, in the spelling of all modern Greek place names. We have, however, retained the accepted "English" or classicized spellings for the **ancient sites**, and for familiar places like Athens (Athiná in modern Greek), Crete (Kríti) or Corfu (Kérkyra). We have also accented (with an acute or sometimes a dieresis) the stressed letter of each word; getting this right in pronunciation is vital for being understood.

INTRODUCTION

It would take a lifetime of island-hopping to really get to know the more than 160 permanently inhabited Greek **islands**, let alone the countless smaller gull-roosts which dot the Aegean and Ionian seas. At the right time of year or day, they conform remarkably well to their fantastic travel-poster image; any tourist board would give their eyeteeth for the commonplace vision of purple-shadowed island silhouettes floating on a cobalt-and-rose horizon.

Closer to hand, island **beaches** come in all shapes, sizes and consistencies, from discrete crescents framed by tree-fringed cliffs straight out of a Japanese screen painting, to deserted, mile-long gifts deposited by small streams, where you could imagine enacting Crusoe scenarios among the dunes. But inland there is always civilization, whether the tiny cubist villages of the remoter outposts, or burgeoning resorts as cosmopolitan – and brazen – as any in the Mediterranean.

What amazes most first-time visitors is how, despite the strenuous efforts of developers and arsonists, this **environment** has not yet been utterly destroyed. If you're used to the murky waters of the open Mediterranean as sampled in Spain, Israel or southern France, then the Aegean will come as a revelation, with thirty to forty-foot visibility the norm. This relative lack of pollution is proclaimed at certain beachfronts by tourist-board signs bestowing "Golden Starfish" or EU-ratified "Blue Flag" awards on the place: patently self-congratulatory, but with basis in fact at many coves, where live starfish or octopi curl up to avoid you, and dover sole, cuttlefish or rays skitter off across the bottom.

The sea is also a **water-sports** paradise: the joys of snorkelling and kayaking are on offer to the untrained, and some of the best windsurfing areas in the world beckon. Yacht charter, whether bare-boat or skippered, is big business, particularly out of Rhodes, Kálymnos, Lefkádha, Póros and Pireás; indeed,the Greek islands are rated on a par with the Caribbean for quality sailing itineraries. And during the months when the sea is too cold or the weather too blustery, many islands – not necessarily the largest ones – offer superb **hiking** on surviving mule-trails between hill villages, or up the highest summits.

Although more protected than the Greek mainland from invasions, the various island groups have been subjected to a staggering variety of **foreign influences**. Romans, Arabs, Byzantines, crusading Knights of St John, Genoese, Venetians, French, English, Italians and Ottomans have all controlled various islands since the time of Alexander the Great. The high tide of empire has left behind countless **monuments**: frescoed Byzantine churches and monasteries, the fortified Venetian towns of the Cyclades and the Ionians, the more conventional castles of the Genoese and Knights in the northeast Aegean and Dodecanese, Ottoman bridges and mosques, and the Art Deco or mock-Renaissance edifices of the Italian Fascist administration.

Constructions from many of these eras are often juxtaposed with – or even superimposed on – the cities and temples of ancient Greece, which provide the foundation in all senses for claims of an enduring Hellenic **cultural identity** down the centuries; museums, particularly those on Crete, Sámos, Rhodes and Límnos, amply document the archeological evidence. But it was medieval Greek peasants, fisherman and shepherds, working without a local ruling class or formal Renaissance to impose models of taste or patronize the arts, who most tangibly and recently contributed to our idea of Greekness with their songs and dances, costumes, weaving and vernacular architecture, some unconsciously drawing on ancient antecedents. Much of this has vanished in recent decades, replaced by an avalanche of bouzouki cassettes, "genuine museum copies"

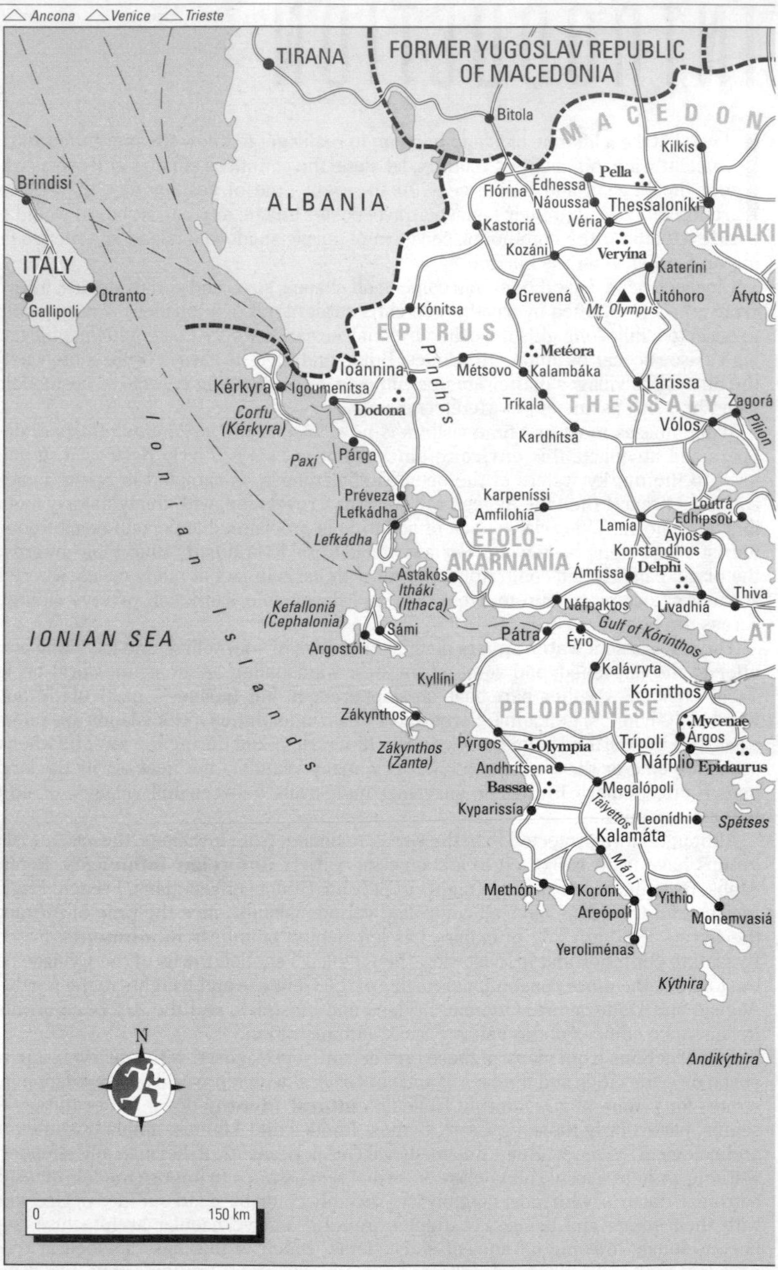
Ancona
Venice
Trieste
Bari
TIRANA
FORMER YUGOSLAV REPUBLIC OF MACEDONIA
MACEDON
Bitola
Kilkís
Pella
Édhessa
Flórina
Náoussa
Thessaloníki
Véria
KHALKI
Kastoriá
Kozáni
Veryína
Kateríni
ALBANIA
Brindisi
ITALY
Otranto
Gallipoli
Grevená
Mt. Olympus
Litóhoro
Áfytos
Kónitsa
EPIRUS
Píndhos
Metéora
Ioánnina
Métsovo
Kalambáka
Lárissa
Kérkyra
Igoumenítsa
Dodona
Tríkala
THESSALY
Zagorá
Corfu (Kérkyra)
Vólos
Pílion
Kardhítsa
Ionian Islands
Párga
Paxí
Préveza
Karpeníssi
Lefkádha
Amfilohía
Loutrá Edhípsou
Lamía
Lefkádha
ÉTOLO-AKARNANÍA
Áyios Konstandínos
Astakós
Ámfissa
Delphi
Itháki (Ithaca)
Thiva
Kefalloniá (Cephalonia)
Náfpaktos
Livadhiá
Sámi
Pátra
Éyio
Gulf of Kórinthos
AT
IONIAN SEA
Argostóli
Kalávryta
Kyllíni
Kórinthos
PELOPONNESE
Zákynthos
Mycenae
Árgos
Zákynthos (Zante)
Pýrgos
Olympia
Trípoli
Náfplio
Epidaurus
Andhrítsena
Megalópoli
Bassae
Taïyettos
Kyparissía
Leonídhi
Spétses
Kalamáta
Máni
Methóni
Koróni
Yíthio
Areópoli
Monemvasiá
Yerolíménas
Kýthira
Andikýthira
N
0
150 km

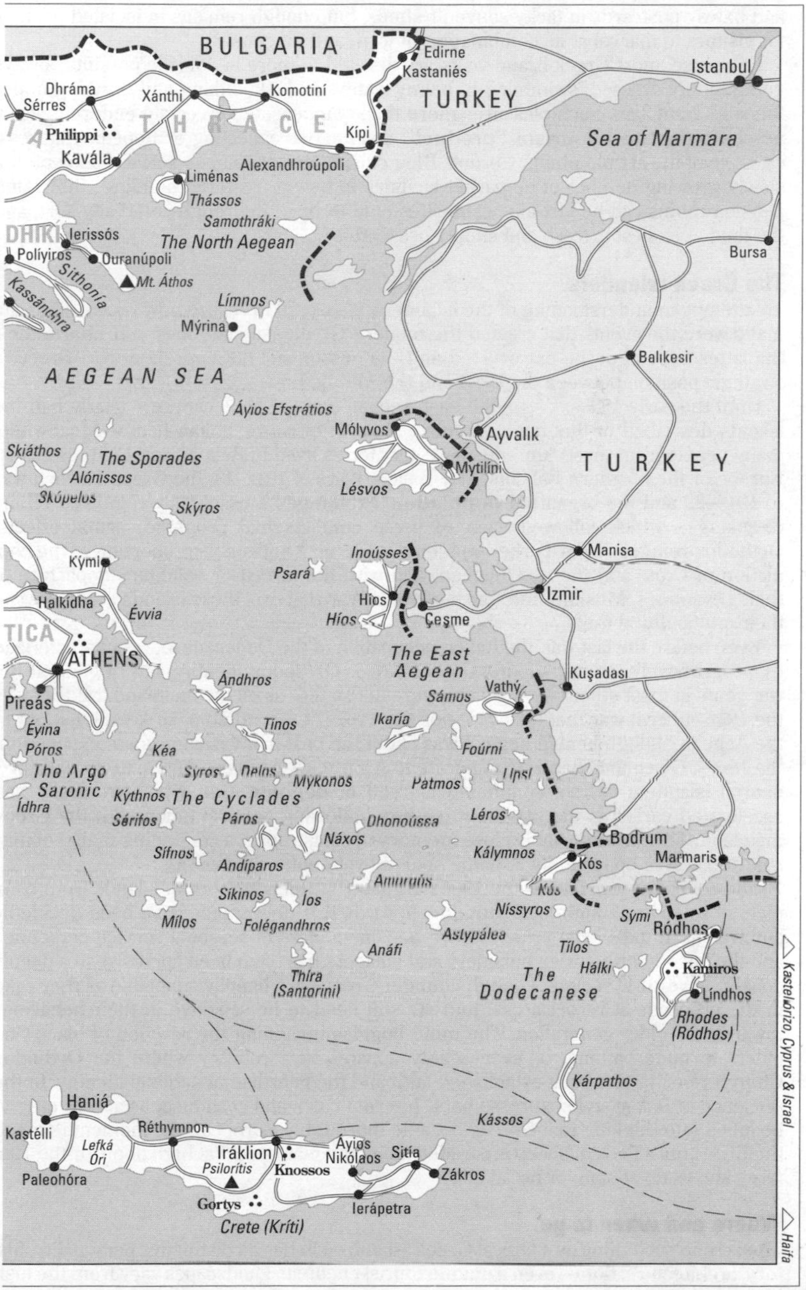
BULGARIA
Edirne
Kastaniés
Istanbul
Dhráma
Sérres
Xánthi
Komotiní
TURKEY
Philippi
THRACE
Kípi
Sea of Marmara
Kavála
Alexandhroúpoli
Liménas
Thássos
Samothráki
Ierissós
The North Aegean
Bursa
Políyiros
Ouranúpoli
Sithonía
Mt. Áthos
Kassándhra
Límnos
Mýrina
Balıkesir
AEGEAN SEA
Áyios Efstrátios
Mólyvos
Ayvalık
Skiáthos
The Sporades
Mytilíni
TURKEY
Alónissos
Skópelos
Lésvos
Skýros
Inoússes
Manisa
Kými
Psará
Izmir
Halkídha
Híos
Évvia
Híos
Çeşme
ATHENS
The East Aegean
Kuşadası
Ándhros
Vathý
Pireás
Sámos
Éyina
Tínos
Ikaría
Póros
Kéa
Foúrni
The Argo Saronic
Sýros
Delos
Mýkonos
Pátmos
Lipsí
Ídhra
Kýthnos
The Cyclades
Sérifos
Páros
Dhonoússa
Léros
Bodrum
Náxos
Sífnos
Kálymnos
Marmaris
Kós
Andíparos
Amorgós
Kós
Síkinos
Íos
Níssyros
Sými
Mílos
Folégandhros
Astypálea
Ródhos
Anáfi
Tílos
Kameiros
Thíra (Santoríni)
The Dodecanese
Hálki
Líndhos
Rhodes (Ródhos)
Kastellórizo, Cyprus & Israel
Kárpathos
Haniá
Kássos
Kastélli
Réthymnon
Lefká Óri
Iráklion
Áyios Nikólaos
Sitía
Paleohóra
Psiloríti
Knossos
Zákros
Gortys
Ierápetra
Crete (Kríti)
Haifa

and bawdy postcards in tacky souvenir shops, but enough remains in isolated pockets for visitors to marvel at its combination of form and function.

Of course, most Greek-island visits are devoted to more hedonistic pursuits: always going lightly dressed, swimming in balmy waters at dusk, talking and drinking under the stars until 3am. Such pleasures more than compensate for certain enduring weaknesses in the Greek **tourism "product"**: don't arrive expecting orthopedic mattresses, state-of-the-art plumbing, Cordon Bleu cuisine or obsequious service. Except at a slowly growing number of upmarket facilities in new or restored buildings, hotel and pension rooms can be box-like, campsites tend to be of the rough-and-ready sort, and the food at its best is fresh and simply presented.

The Greek islanders

To attempt an understanding of the islanders, it's useful to realize how recent and traumatic were the events that created the modern Greek state and **national character** – the latter a blend of the extroverted and the pessimistic not entirely due to Greece's strategic position between the West and the Middle East.

Until the early 1900s, Crete, the east Aegean and the Dodecanese – nearly half the islands described in this book – remained in Ottoman or Italian hands. Meanwhile, many people from these "unredeemed" territories lived in Asia Minor, Egypt, western Europe or the northern Balkans. The Balkan Wars of 1912–13, the Greco-Turkish war of 1919–22 and the organized **population exchanges** – essentially regulated ethnic cleansing – which followed each of these conflicts had profound, brutal effects. Orthodox refugees from Turkey suddenly made up a noticeable proportion of the population of Crete and the east Aegean, and with the forced or voluntary departure of their Levantines, Muslims and (during World War II) Jews, these islands gradually lost their multicultural traits.

Even before the last war, the Italian occupation of the Dodecanese was characterized by progressively stricter suppression of Greek Orthodox identity, but in general the war years in most other island groups were not so dire as on the mainland. Neither was the 1946–49 civil war that followed, nor the 1967–74 dictatorship, so keenly felt out in the Aegean, though benign neglect was about the best many islands could expect until the 1960s. Given the chance to emigrate to Australia, Canada or Africa, many entrepreneurial islanders did so, continuing a trend of **depopulation** which ironically had accelerated earlier in the twentieth century, following political union with the Greek mainland. The uncomfortably close memory of catastrophe, a continuing reality of misrule and scarce opportunity at home spurred yet another diaspora.

The advent of **tourism** in the 1960s arguably saved a number of islands from complete desolation, though local attitudes towards this deliverance have been decidedly ambivalent. It galls local pride to have become a class of seasonal service personnel, and the encounter between outsiders and villagers has often been corrosive to a deeply conservative rural society. Though younger Greeks are happily adaptable as they rake in the proceeds at resort areas, tourists still need to be sensitive in their behaviour towards the older generation. The mind boggles imagining the reaction of black-clad elders to nude bathing, or even scanty apparel, in a country where the Orthodox Church remains an all-but-established faith and the guardian of national identity. In the presence of Italian-style expresso bars, Internet cafés and cash dispensers, it's easy to be lulled into thinking that Greece became thoroughly European the moment it joined the EU – until a flock of sheep is paraded along the main street at high noon, or the 1pm ferry shows up at 3pm, or not at all.

Where and when to go

There is no such thing as a typical Greek island; each has its distinctive personality, history, architecture, flora – even a unique tourist clientele. Landscapes vary from the lush cypress and olive-swathed Ionians to the bare, minimalist ridges of the Cyclades and Dodecanese, by way of subtle gradations between these extremes in the Sporades and northeast Aegean. Setting aside the scars from a few unfortunate man-made developments, it would be difficult to single out an irredeemably ugly island; all have their adherents and individual appeal, described in the chapter or section introductions.

Most islands and their inhabitants are far more agreeable, and resolutely Greek, outside the **busiest period** of early July to late August, when crowds of foreigners or locals, soaring temperatures and the effects of the infamous *meltémi* can detract considerably from enjoyment. The **meltémi** is a cool, fair-weather wind which originates in high-pressure systems over the far north Aegean, gathering steam as it travels southwards and assuming near-gale magnitude by the time it reaches Crete. North-facing coasts there, and throughout the Cyclades and Dodecanese, bear the full brunt; its howling is less pronounced in the north or east Aegean, where continental landmasses provide some shelter for the islands just offshore.

You won't miss out on **warm weather** if you come between late May and mid-June – when a wide variety of garden produce and fish is still available – or September, when the sea is warmest for swimming, though at these times you'll find little activity on the northernmost islands of Thássos and Samothráki. During October you will probably hit a week's stormy spell anywhere, but for much of that month the "little summer of Áyios Dhimítrios", the Greek equivalent of **Indian summer**, prevails. While the choice of restaurants and nightlife in autumn can be limited, the light is softer, and going out at midday becomes a pleasure rather than an ordeal. The most reliable venues for late autumn or early winter breaks are Rhodes and relatively balmy southeastern Crete, where swimming in December is not unheard of.

December to March are the **coldest** and least comfortable months, particularly on the Ionian islands, simply the rainiest patch in Greece from November onwards. The high peaks of northerly or lofty islands wear a brief mantle of **snow** around the turn of the year, with Crete's mountainous spine staying partly covered into April. Between January and April the glorious lowland wildflowers begin to bloom, beginning in the

AVERAGE TEMPERATURES AND RAINFALL

	Jan			March			May			July			Sept			Nov		
	°F		Rain	°F		Rain	°F		Rain	°F		Rain	°F		Rain	°F		Rain
	Max	Min	days	Max	Min	days	Max	Min	days	Max	Min	days	Max	Min	days	Max	Min	days
Crete (Haniá)	60	46	17	64	48	11	76	56	5	86	68	0	82	64	3	70	54	10
Cyclades (Mýkonos)	58	50	14	62	52	8	72	62	5	82	72	0.5	78	68	1	66	58	9
North Greece (Halkidhikí)	50	36	7	59	44	9	77	58	10	90	70	4	83	64	5	60	47	9
Ionian (Corfu)	56	44	13	62	46	10	74	58	6	88	70	2	82	64	5	66	52	12
Dodecanese (Rhodes)	58	50	15	62	48	7	74	58	2	86	70	0	82	72	1	68	60	7
Sporades (Skiáthos)	55	45	12	58	47	10	71	58	3	82	71	0	75	64	8	62	53	12
East Aegean (Lésvos)	54	42	11	60	46	7	76	60	6	88	70	2	82	66	2	64	50	9

southeast Aegean. Early arrivals should keep in mind that travelling a few islands north or south often means the difference between tourist facilities open or still shut, as well as blossoms gone or yet to bloom. April weather is notoriously unreliable, though the air is crystal-clear and the landscape **green** – a photographer's dream. May is more settled, though the sea is still a bit cool for prolonged dips.

Other factors that affect the timing of a Greek island visit have to do with the level of tourism and the related **amenities** provided. Service standards, particularly in tavernas, invariably slip under peak-season pressures, and room rates are at their highest from July to September. If you can only visit during mid-summer, reserve a package well in advance, or plan an itinerary off the beaten track, gravitating towards islands with sparser ferry connections and/or no airport. Between November and April, you have to contend with pared-back ferry schedules (and almost nonexistent hydrofoil departures), plus skeletal facilities when you arrive. However, you will find fairly adequate services to the more populated islands, and at least one hotel and taverna open in the port or main town of all but the tiniest isles.

PART ONE

THE BASICS

GETTING THERE FROM BRITAIN

It's close on 2000 miles from London to most points in Greece, so for many visitors flying is the only viable option. There are direct flights to a variety of Greek destinations from all the major British airports. Flying time varies from three hours (to Corfu) to almost four hours (to Rhodes), and the cost of charter flights is reasonable – sample return fares to Athens from London in midsummer start from around £160 (Manchester £180, Glasgow £200), but there are always bargains to be had. Easter and Christmas are also classed as high season, but outside these periods flights can be snapped up for as little as £120 return. Costs can often be highly competitive too if you buy a flight as part of an all-in package; see pp.6–7 for details of holiday operators.

Road or **rail** alternatives take a minimum of three days, and are only worth considering if you plan to visit Greece as part of an extended trip through Europe. The most popular route is down through Italy, then across to Greece by ferry, with (in summer) stopovers available on many of the Ionian islands.

BY PLANE

Most of the cheaper flights from Britain to Greece are **charters**, which are sold either with a package holiday or as a flight-only option. The flights have fixed and unchangeable outward and return dates, and often a maximum stay of one month.

For longer stays or more flexibility, or if you're travelling out of season (when few charters are available), you'll need a **scheduled** flight. As with charters, these are offered under a wide variety of fares, and are again often sold off at discount by agents. Useful sources for discounted flights are the classified ads in the travel sections of newspapers like the *Independent*, *Guardian*, *Observer* and *Telegraph*, as well as weekly listings magazines such as *Time Out*. Teletext is also worth checking, as are **Internet sites** such as:

www.deckchair.com
www.travelocity.co.uk
www.lastminute.com
www.travelselect.com
www.bargainholidays.com
www.cheapflights.co.uk

Although **Athens** remains the prime destination for cheap fares, there are also **direct flights** from Britain to **Thessaloníki**, **Kalamáta**, **Kavála** and **Préveza** on the Greek mainland (all of these are either ports for various islands, or close to such), and to the islands themselves of **Crete**, **Rhodes**, **Kós**, **Kárpathos**, **Corfu**, **Páros**, **Mýkonos**, **Santoríni**, **Zákynthos**, **Kefalloniá**, **Skiáthos**, **Sámos, Lésvos** and **Límnos.** And with any flight to Athens, you can buy a **domestic connecting flight** (on the national carrier, Olympic) to one of three dozen or so additional Greek mainland and island airports.

CHARTER FLIGHTS

Travel agents throughout Britain sell **charter flights** to Greece, which usually operate from late April or May to late October or mid-November (depending on destination); late-night departures and early-morning arrivals are common, though you usually have a choice of more civilized hours. Even the high-street chains frequently promote "flight-only" deals, or discount all-inclusive holidays, when their parent companies need to offload their seat allocations. In any case, phone around for a range of offers. Charter airlines include Air 2000, Flying Colours, Britannia, Caledonian, Sabre and Monarch, but you can often only book tickets on these through travel agents.

The greatest variety of **flight destinations** tends to be from London and Manchester. In summer, if you book in advance, you should have a choice of most of the Greek regional airports listed above. Flying from elsewhere in Britain (Birmingham, Cardiff, Glasgow or Newcastle), or looking for last-minute discounts, you'll find options more limited, most commonly to Athens, Corfu, Rhodes, Kós and Crete.

It's worth noting that **non-EU nationals** who buy charter tickets to Greece must buy a return ticket, coming back after no fewer than three days and no more than four weeks, and must accompany it with an **accommodation voucher** for at least the first few nights of their stay – check that the ticket satisfies these conditions or you could be refused entry. In practice, the accommodation voucher has become a formality; it has to name an existing hotel but you're not expected to use it (and probably won't be able to if you try).

The other important condition regards travel to **Turkey** (or any other neighbouring country). If you travel to Greece on a charter flight, you may visit another country only as a day-trip; if you stay overnight, you will invalidate your ticket. This rule is justified by the Greek authorities because they subsidize charter airline landing fees, and are therefore reluctant to see tourists spending their money outside Greece. Whether you go along with that rationale or not, there is no way around it, since the Turkish authorities clearly stamp all passports, and the Greeks usually check them. The package industry on the east Aegean and Dodecanese islands bordering Turkey, however, does sometimes prevail upon customs officials to back-date re-entry stamps when bad weather strands their tour groups overnight in Anatolia.

Student/youth charters are allowed to be sold as one-way flights only. By combining two one-way charters you can, therefore, stay for over a month. Student/youth charter tickets are available to anyone under 26, and to all card-carrying full-time students under 32.

Finally, remember that **reconfirmation** of return charter flights is vital and should be done at least 72 hours before departure. If you've travelled out with a package company, this service will usually be included as part of the rep's duties, but you should not assume that it has been done. Personal visits to the airline's representative office are best, as phone numbers given on ticket wallets are usually engaged.

SCHEDULED FLIGHTS

The advantages of **scheduled flights** are that they can be booked well in advance, have longer ticket validities (30, 60, 90 or even 180 days), involve fewer or none of the typical restrictions applicable to charters, and often leave at more sociable hours. However, many of the cheaper, shorter-duration SuperPEX or APEX fares do have advance-purchase and/or minimum-stay requirements, and also severe restrictions on date changes or refunds. As with charters, discount fares on scheduled flights are available from most high-street travel **agents**, as well as from a number of specialist flight and student/youth agencies – though it's always well worth contacting the airlines direct, using the telephone numbers in the box opposite. Like charters, they must be reconfirmed within 72 hours of the return leg.

The widest choice of scheduled flights is with the Greek national carrier **Olympic Airways** and with **British Airways**, who both fly from London Heathrow to Athens (twice daily on BA, three times daily on Olympic), mostly direct, but on Olympic stopping four times weekly in Thessaloníki. BA also offers one daily Athens service from Gatwick, but nothing to Thessaloníki. Both airlines have a range of special fares, and even in July and August, discount flight agents can come up with deals, valid for sixty days away, for as low as £190 return, including tax; more realistically, you'll pay around £250 return during high season. It may be worth avoiding absolutely rock-bottom fares, as Olympic no longer allows changes to your return date on tickets of under ninety days' validity. In the spring or autumn, return fares to Athens run to about £160 including taxes, and in winter dip to about £140. As this route is common-rated between these airlines, you'll also be able to book onward connections simultaneously to domestic Greek airports, though discounts will apply only if using Olympic on all legs of the journey.

Virgin Atlantic Airways also has a near-daily service from Gatwick to Athens, arriving in the late afternoon, plus daily (in summer) departures from Heathrow to Athens, though that flight arrives in the small hours. Fares, in a bewildering array of structures and limited-time special offers, tend to work out slightly pricier than BA or Olympic. A sixty-day midweek ticket, tax inclusive, might set you back £220 during low season, £235 in summer; changing your return date will incur a small charge, but at least (unlike at Olympic) it's allowed.

Cronus Airlines, so far the only Greek scheduled airline to challenge Olympic on inter-

FLIGHT AGENTS

Argo Holidays, 100 Wigmore St, London W1H 9DR (☎020/7331 7000). *Designated consolidator for Olympic, BA and Virgin Atlantic; consistently some of the lowest fares, and good service.*

Avro, 1 Weir Rd, London SW19 8UX (☎020/8715 1999). *Seat-only sales of all Monarch charter flights to Athens, Corfu, Iráklion (Crete) and Rhodes from a selection amongst Gatwick, Luton, Manchester and Glasgow.*

Campus & Travel, 52 Grosvenor Gardens, London SW1 0AG (☎020/7730 3402); 541 Bristol Rd, Selly Oak, Birmingham B29 6AU (☎0121/414 1848); 39 Queens Rd, Clifton, Bristol BS8 1QE (☎0117/929 2494); 5 Emmanuel St, Cambridge CB1 1NE (☎01223/324283); 53 Forest Rd, Edinburgh EH1 2QP (☎0131/668 3303); 166 Deansgate, Manchester M3 3FE (☎0161/273 1721); 105–106 St Aldates, Oxford OX1 1DD (☎01865/242067). *Student/youth travel specialists, with branches also in YHA shops and on university campuses all over Britain, and its own student/youth charter flights to Athens during the summer.*

Eclipse Direct ☎0161/742 2277 or 0990/010203. *Seat-only deals on Air 2000, and fly-drives to Rhodes and Kós from various UK airports.*

Greece & Cyprus Travel Centre, 44 Birmingham Rd, Sutton Coldfield, West Midlands B72 1QQ (☎0121/355 6955). *Flight consolidator and general Greek packages specialist.*

Mondial Travel, 8 Moscow Rd, London W2 4BT (☎020/7792 3333). *Good ticketing agency for scheduled flights to Greece.*

North South Travel, Moulsham Mill Centre, Parkway, Chelmsford, Essex CM2 7PX (☎01245/492882). *Discount flight agency, with added bonus in a portion of profits going to aid Third World development projects.*

STA Travel, 86 Old Brompton Rd, London SW7 3LH (☎020/7361 6161); 25 Queens Rd, Bristol BS8 1QE (☎0117/929 4399); 38 Sidney St, Cambridge CB2 3HX (☎01223/366966); 75 Deansgate, Manchester M3 2BW (☎0161/834 0668); and personal callers at 117 Euston Rd, London NW1 2SX; 88 Vicar Lane, Leeds LS1 7JH; 36 George St, Oxford OX1 2OJ; and branches at the universities of Birmingham, Kent, London and Loughborough. *Discount fares, particularly good for students and under-26s.*

Sunset Air Fares, Sunset Business Centre, Manchester Rd, Bolton BL4 8RT (☎0870/607 5085). *Flight-only and fly-drive deals from regional airports to Kalamáta, Préveza and Kavála (for Thássos) in addition to the usual destinations; typically uses Flying Colours.*

Thomson/Britannia Flights ☎0990/502555. *Limited number of flight-only deals to Corfu, Rhodes, Iráklion (Crete), Thessaloníki, Zákynthos, Kós, Sámos, Kefalloniá, Skiáthos and Kavála (for Thássos) on Britannia Airways.*

Trailfinders, 42–50 Earls Court Rd, London W8 6FT (☎020/7937 5400); 194 Kensington High St, London W8 7RG (☎020/7938 3939); 22–24 The Priory, Queensway, Birmingham B4 6BS (☎0121/236 1234); 48 Corn St, Bristol BS1 1HQ (☎0117/929 9000); 254–284 Sauchiehall St, Glasgow G2 3FH (☎0141/353 2224); 58 Deansgate, Manchester M3 2FF (☎0161/839 6969). *One of the best-informed and most efficient agents, for scheduled flights only; all branches open daily until 6pm, Thurs until 7pm.*

AIRLINES

British Airways ☎0345/222111.
Cronus Airlines ☎020/7580 3500.
EasyJet ☎0870/600 0000 or *www.easyjet.com.*
Olympic Airways ☎020/7409 3400.
Virgin Atlantic Airways ☎01293/747747.

national routes, offers daily late-evening services to Athens, arriving at dawn the next day. Advertised flights to Thessaloníki all currently go via Athens, with a whopping three-hour layover, but Cronus plans to introduce three weekly direct services to Thessaloníki in 2000. Fares to either city weigh in at about £160 low season, tax included, or £235 high season, though between these two seasons they frequently offer specials of about £180.

Note that flights from **British regional airports** route through Heathrow in the first instance, with a supplement applicable. Olympic has a code-sharing partnership with British

Midland, which should ease the pain (and possibly the cost) of connections from Leeds and Manchester in particular.

Potentially the cheapest, no-frills service is provided by **EasyJet**, out of London Luton to Athens only; fares vary from £49 to £159 **one way**, tax included, with the exact amount depending on the season, how far in advance you book, whether you use their Web site (a couple of quid cheaper) and availability for the particular flight. Departures also vary with time of year, but typically there are two flights daily, at around noon and late in the evening. The cheaper tickets are obviously very restrictive, and there's no on-board meal service. On the plus side, EasyJet usually offers special train fares from central London to Luton in co-operation with Thameslink.

PACKAGES AND TOURS

Virtually every British **tour operator** includes Greece in its programme, though with many of the

SPECIALIST PACKAGE OPERATORS

VILLA OR VILLAGE ACCOMMODATION

Argo Holidays, 100 Wigmore St, London W1H 9DR (☎020/7331 7070). *Packages to luxury hotels and top villas on more than thirty islands; special strengths the Argo-Saronic, northeast Aegean and Dodecanese (including "Winter Sun" on Rhodes).*

CV Travel, 43 Cadogan St, London SW3 2PR (☎020/7591 2800). *Quality villas on Corfu and Paxí.*

Direct Greece, Granite House, 31–33 Stockwell St, Glasgow G1 4RY (☎0141/5597111); also in Manchester (☎0161/236 2838). *Moderately priced villas, apartments and restored houses on Rhodes, Hálki, Lésvos, Corfu, Crete, Lefkádha and Zákynthos.*

Elysian Holidays, 16 High St, Tenterden, Kent TN30 6AP (☎01580/766599). *Began as Híos restored-house specialists, now have a wide programme of quality premises on Páros, Sýros, Spétses, Mýkonos, Pátmos and the Candili Estate on Évvia.*

Filoxenia/Grecofile, Sourdock Hill, Barkisland, Halifax, West Yorkshire HX4 0AG (☎01422/375999). *Tailor-made itineraries and bespoke packages to several less visited islands; flight arrangements on scheduled or charter airlines.*

Greek Islands Club, 10–12 Upper Square, Old Isleworth, Middlesex TW7 7BJ (☎020/8232 9780). *Extremely high-quality villas throughout the Ionian and Sporades islands; also Kýthira and Crete.*

Greek Sun Holidays, 1 Bank St, Sevenoaks, Kent TN13 1UW (☎01732/740317). *Good-value package holidays, including some fly-drive options, in the Dodecanese, northeast Aegean or the Cyclades; also tailor-made island-hopping itineraries.*

Hidden Greece ☎020/8766 7868. *A bespoke agency running for forty years now, arranging accommodation on and transport to thirty less-visited islands, mostly in the Cyclades and Dodecanese.*

Laskarina Holidays, St Marys Gate, Wirksworth, Derbyshire DE4 4DQ (☎01629/822203). *Top-end villas, quality hotels and restored houses on Spétses, Skópelos, Alónissos, Hálki, Sými, Tílos, Kálymnos, Télendhos, Léros, Lipsí, Pátmos, Ikaría and Sámos; consistently high marks for customer service.*

Pure Crete, 79 George St, Croydon CR10 1LD (☎020/8760 0879, *info@pure-crete.com*). *Characterful, converted cottages and farmhouses in western Crete.*

Simply Simon Holidays, 45 Nevern Square, London SW5 9PF (☎020/7373 1933). *Cyclades specialist, focusing on small hotels and studios; direct charters to Mýkonos and Santoríni.*

Simply Travel, Kings House, Wood Street, Kingston-upon-Thames, Surrey KT1 1UG. Administers two separate programmes: Simply Ionian (☎020/8541 2202) and Simply Crete (☎020/8541 2201). *Offers top-quality apartments, villas, restored houses and small hotels for each area.*

Skiathos Travel, 4 Holmesdale Rd, Kew Gardens, Richmond, Surrey TW9 3J2 (☎020/8940 5157). *Long-running Sporades specialist; also a small Cyclades programme, and some flight-only deals.*

Sunvil Holidays, Sunvil House, 7–8 Upper Square, Old Isleworth, Middlesex TW7 7BJ (☎020/8568 4499). *Durable and consistently high-quality outfit specializing in upmarket hotels and villas in the Ionian islands, the Sporades, select Cyclades, western Crete and Límnos. Also sailing holidays in the Ionian islands.*

larger groups you'll find choices limited to the established resort islands of Rhodes, Kós, Crete, Skiáthos, Zákynthos and Corfu. If you buy one of these at a last-minute discount, especially in spring or autumn, you may find it costs little more than a flight – and you can use the accommodation offered as much or as little as you want.

For a more low-key and genuinely "Greek" resort, however, it's better to book your holiday through one of the **specialist agencies** listed below. Most of these are fairly small-scale operations, providing competitively priced packages with flights (unless otherwise stated) and often more traditional village-based accommodation. They also make an effort to offer islands without overdeveloped tourist resorts. Such agencies tend to divide into two types: those which, like the major chains, contract a block of accommodation and flight seats (or even their own plane) for a full season, and an increasing number of bespoke agencies which tailor holidays at your request, making all transport and accommodation arrange-

Tapestry Holidays, 24 Chiswick High Rd, London W4 1TE (☎020/8235 7788). *Top-rated Turkey specialists, now branched out into quality apartments and studios on Kefalloniá.*

Travel à la Carte, The Whitehouse, Bucklebury Alley, Cold Ash, Newbury, Berks RH16 9NN (☎01635/201140, *www.travelalacarte.co.uk*). *Established Corfu specialist, now branched out to beach and rural villas on Alónissos, Hálki, Paxí, Skiáthos, Skópelos and Sými as well.*

Travelux, 40 High St, Tenterden, Kent TN30 6AR (☎01580/765000, *www.travelux.co.uk*). *Long-established Lefkádha villa specialists.*

WALKING HOLIDAYS

Alternative Travel Group, 69–71 Banbury Rd, Oxford OX2 6PE (☎01865/315678). *Somewhat pricey guided walks on Ándhros and Náxos.*

Headwater, 146 London Rd, Northwich, Cheshire CW9 5HH (☎01606/813399). *Treks on Amorgós island.*

Ramblers Holidays, Longcroft House, Fretherne Rd, Welwyn Garden City, Herts AL8 6PQ (☎01707/331133). *An outfit which has shed its former fusty image and now offers fairly challenging treks in Crete, plus easier outings on Sámos, Pátmos, Náxos and Amorgos.*

Waymark Holidays, 44 Windsor Rd, Slough SL1 2EJ (☎01753/516477). *Spring and autumn walking holidays on Sámos, Mílos and Crete.*

NATURE AND WILDLIFE

Limosa ☎01263/578143. *Birding on Lésvos.*

Marengo Guided Walks, 17 Bernard Crescent, Hunstanton P36 6ER (☎01485/532710, *marengopub@supanet.com*). *Annually changing programme of easy walks guided by ace botanist Lance Chilton; past one-week offerings have included Sámos, Sými, northern Lésvos, Crete and Thássos.*

Naturetrek, The Cadcam Centre, Bighton, near Alresford, Hampshire SO24 9RE (☎01962/733051, *www.naturetrek.co.uk*). *Fairly pricey but expertly led one-week birdwatching expeditions on Sámos and Lésvos.*

SAILING HOLIDAYS

Explore Worldwide, 1 Frederick St, Aldershot, Hampshire GU11 1LQ (☎01252/760 1000). *Kaïki-based island-wanderer trips, mostly in the Cyclades, with light walking ashore.*

The Moorings, Bradstowe House, Middle Wall, Whitstable, Kent CT5 1BF (☎01227/776677). *Operates bareboat charters out of Athens, Corfu and Kós Town.*

Nautilus Yachting ☎01732/867445. *Bareboat yacht charter out of Corfu, Lefkádha, Kós, Rhodes and Skiáthos, also flotilla holidays from Lefkádha and Póros.*

Sunsail, The Port House, Port Solent, Portsmouth, Hampshire, PO6 4TH (☎02392/222222). *Resort-based tuition in dinghy sailing, yachting and windsurfing at several locations in Greece; one- or two-week flotilla sailings northward out of Kós Town, Lefkádha, Kefalloniá and the Sporades.*

Top Yacht Charter, Andrew Hill Lane, Hedgerley, Bucks SL2 3UW (☎01753/646636). *Bareboat charters from six bases around Greece, including Kós and Rhodes.*

MIND AND BODY

Skyros Centre, 92 Prince of Wales Rd, London NW5 3NE (☎020/7267 4424). *Holistic health, fitness and "personal growth" holidays at two centres on the island of Skýros, as well as prestigious writers' workshops tutored by big names.*

ments on the spot. These can work out somewhat more expensive, but the quality of flights and lodging is often correspondingly higher.

The **walking** holiday operators listed in the box on p.7 run trekking groups of ten to fifteen people plus an experienced guide. Walks tend to be day-long hikes from one or more bases, or (on the largest islands) point-to-point treks staying in village accommodation en route. Camping out is not usually involved.

Sailing holidays usually involve small flotillas of four- to eight-berth yachts, and can be based on shore or at sea. All levels of experience are catered for. Prices start at around £520 per person, flights included, in a group of four on a two-week flotilla. Alternatively, confident sailors can simply arrange to charter a yacht from a broker; the Greek National Tourist Organization has lists of companies.

BY TRAIN

Travelling by **train** from Britain to Greece takes around three and a half days and fares work out much more expensive than flights. However, with a regular ticket, stopovers are possible – in France, Switzerland and Italy – while with an InterRail or Eurail train pass you can take in Greece as part of a wider rail trip around Europe.

ROUTES

The most practical route from Britain takes in France, Switzerland and Italy before crossing on the ferry from Bari or Brindisi to Pátra (Patras). Book seats well in advance, especially in summer (for ferry information, see the box on pp.10–11).

Until 1990, the route through **former Yugoslavia** was the most popular; for obvious reasons this is a non-starter for the foreseeable future. A more rambling alternative from Budapest runs via **Bucharest** and **Sofia** to **Thessaloníki**, which is advised as your first stop, since Athens is nearly nine hours further on the train.

TICKETS AND PASSES

Regular train tickets from Britain to Greece are not good value; London to Athens costs at least £380 return. If you are **under 26**, you can get a **BIJ ticket**, discounting these fares by around 25 percent; these are available through Eurotrain and Wasteels (see box above for addresses). Both regular and BIJ tickets have two months' return validity, or can be purchased as one ways, and the Italy routes include the ferry crossing. The tickets also allow for stopovers, so long as you stick to the route prescribed.

Better value by far is to buy an **InterRail youth pass** which is available to European residents and offers unlimited travel on a zonal basis on up to 25 European rail networks. The only extras you pay are supplements on certain express trains, plus half-price fares in Britain (or the country of issue) and on the cross-Channel ferries. The pass includes the ferry from Brindisi in southern Italy to Pátra in Greece. There are several types: to reach Greece from the UK you'll need a pass valid for at least two zones (£209 for 22 days), though if you're intending to travel further in Europe you might invest in an all-zone card for £259; Greece is zoned with Italy, Turkey and Slovenia. The **Adult InterRail pass**, dubbed the 26+, operates on a similar basis, costing £279 for one zone and £359 for an all-zone card.

Finally, anyone over sixty and holding a British Rail Senior Citizen Railcard, can buy a **Rail Europe Senior Card** (£5 for a year). This gives up to thirty percent reductions on rail fares throughout Europe and thirty percent off sea crossings.

RAIL TICKET OFFICES

Eurotrain, 52 Grosvenor Gardens, London SW1 (☎020/7730 3402).

Rail Europe, 179 Piccadilly, London W1 (☎0990/848848).

Wasteels, Victoria Station, London SW1 (☎020/7834 7066).

BUS TICKET OFFICES

National Express Eurolines, 52 Grosvenor Gardens, London SW1 (☎0990/808080).

BY BUS

With charter flights and no-frills airlines like EasyJet offering such competitive rates, it's hard to find good reasons for wanting to spend three or four days on a bus to Greece. However, it's still a considerably cheaper option than taking the train.

National Express Eurolines (bookable through any National Express office; see box above) is the only coach company still offering this line, and only during summer. The **route** is either Belgium, Germany and Austria, or via France, to Italy, and then a ferry across to Greece. Stops of about twenty minutes are made every five or six hours, with the odd longer break for roadside café meals.

BY CAR

If you have the time and inclination, **driving to Greece** can be a pleasant proposition. Realistically, though, it's really only worth considering if you have at least a month to spare, are going to stay in Greece for an extended period or want to take advantage of various stopovers en route.

It's important to plan ahead. The **Automobile Association** (AA) provides a comprehensive service offering general advice on all facets of driving to Greece and the names and addresses of useful contact organizations. Their European Routes Service (contact the AA on ☎01256/20123) can arrange a detailed print-out of a route to follow.

The most popular **route** is down through France and Italy to catch one of the Adriatic ferries. A longer alternative through Eastern Europe (Hungary, Romania and Bulgaria) is just about feasible.

THE SHUTTLE AND THE FERRIES

The **Shuttle** train operates trains 24 hours a day, carrying cars, motorcycles, buses and their passengers, and taking 35 minutes between Folkestone and Calais. At peak times, services operate every fifteen minutes, making advance bookings unnecessary; during the night, services still run hourly. Through trains connect London with Paris in just over three hours. Return fares from May to August cost around £280–310 per vehicle (passengers included), with discounts in the low season; passenger fares from London to Paris cost £95–135 return, depending on when you book.

CROSS-CHANNEL INFORMATION

Hoverspeed ☎01304/240101. To Boulogne and Calais.

P&O European Ferries Dover (☎01304/203388); Portsmouth (☎02392/772244); London (☎0990/980980). To Calais.

Sally Line ☎01843/595522. To Dunkerque.

Shuttle ☎0990/353535 (Customer Services Centre Information and ticket sales).

Stena Sealink Line Ashford (☎01233/647047). To Calais and Dieppe.

The alternative **cross-Channel** options for most travellers are the **ferry** or **hovercraft** links between Dover and Calais or Boulogne (the quickest and cheapest routes), Ramsgate and Dunkerque, or Newhaven and Dieppe.

Ferry **prices** vary according to the time of year and, for motorists, the size of your car. The Dover–Calais/Boulogne runs, for example, start at about £180 return low season, £220 return high season for a car with up to five passengers. **Foot passengers** should be able to cross for about £50 return year-round; taking a **motorbike** costs from £80–90 return.

VIA ITALY

Heading for the Ionian islands, it has always made most sense to drive **via Italy** – and whatever your final destination, taking a ferry on the final leg makes for a more relaxed journey. Initial routes down to Italy through **France** and **Switzerland** are very much a question of personal taste. One of the most direct is Calais–Reims–Geneva–Milan and then down the Adriatic coast to the Italian port of your choice. Even on the quickest autoroutes (with their accompanying tolls), the journey will involve two overnight stops.

Once in Italy, there's a choice of five **ports**. Regular car and passenger ferries link **Ancona**, **Bari** and **Brindisi** with **Igoumenítsa** (a port in western Greece, just opposite Corfu) and/or **Pátra** (at the northwest tip of the Peloponnese, and the closest major port to Athens or the islands of Kefalloniá or Zákynthos). Most actually sail via the island of **Corfu**, and a very few companies call at other Ionian islands such as **Paxí**, **Itháki** or **Kefalloniá** en route to Pátra during the summer; you can stop over at no extra charge if you get these halts specified on your ticket. Generally, these ferries run almost year-round, but services are greatly reduced out of season. Ferries also sail regularly from **Venice** and less frequently from **Trieste**. For more details see the box on pp.10–11.

The crossing to Igoumenítsa is usually, but not always, substantially cheaper than to Pátra; the cheapest of all the crossings is from Brindisi to Igoumenítsa. However, drivers will discover that the extra cost in Italian motorway tolls and fuel offsets the Brindisi route's savings over those from Bari, Ancona or Venice; the shipping companies are well aware of this and set their prices accordingly.

FERRIES FROM ITALY

Note: all timings are approximate.

From Ancona Strintzis, ANEK and Minoan to Igoumenítsa (16–23hr) or Pátra (20–31hr); daily or nearly so year-round. Strintzis via Corfu and Igoumenítsa or direct to Pátra; Minoan and ANEK via Igoumenítsa only. Most sailings 8–10pm, but there are a number of afternoon departures. Also Superfast direct to Pátra in 19hr almost daily year-round.

From Bari Ventouris to Igoumenítsa direct (11hr 30min), roughly every other day March–Sept; late June–early Sept calls at Corfu (10hr) en route; Marlines to Igoumenítsa (13hr) daily late June–mid-Sept; Superfast heads almost daily year-round for Igoumenítsa (9hr) and then Pátra (15hr 30min). All sailings 6–9pm.

From Brindisi Adriatica to Corfu (7hr 30min), Igoumenítsa (9hr 30min) and Pátra (19hr) every other day year-round; direct to Pátra (14hr) summer only. Fraglines to Corfu/Igoumenítsa (10hr) almost daily March–Oct; Agoudimos to Igoumenítsa most days June–Dec (12hr); Diler to Igoumenítsa (7–8hr 30min) almost daily May–Sept, via Corfu Aug. Hellenic Mediterranean Lines to Corfu/Igoumenítsa (8hr/9hr 30min), 3–7 weekly April–Oct; to Kefalloniá (15hr), most days late June–early Sept; Paxí and Zákynthos, several weekly early July–early Sept. European Seaways, 4 to 6 weekly April–Sept to Corfu and usually Igoumenítsa (10hr). Med Link Lines, daily to Pátra (13hr) April–Sept; via Kefalloniá (11hr) 4–7 weekly July–Aug. Strintzis almost daily late March–Oct to Corfu (7hr) and Igoumenítsa (8hr 30min); Ventouris, every other day May–June & Sept, daily July–Aug to Igoumenítsa (8hr), via Corfu (6hr) July–Aug. Most ferries leave Brindisi 8–11pm, but Ventouris, Fragline, Agoudimos and European Seaways offer 9–10am departures at peak season, Strintzis and Diler consistently so across the year. There's usually at least one daily boat in winter, except between Christmas and New Year's Eve.

From Trieste ANEK to Igoumenítsa (24–28hr), 2–5 weekly almost year-round; continues to Corfu 1–2 times weekly April–Oct, to Pátra (32–35hr) 3–4 weekly April–Oct. Departs mid- to late afternoon.

From Venice Strintzis, 2–3 weekly Nov–March, 4 weekly otherwise to Igoumenítsa (28hr), Corfu and Pátra (38hr); Minoan 4–5 weekly late Oct–late March, daily otherwise to the same ports (25hr & 36hr respectively). Note that, along with Ancona, this is one of the more reliable departure ports out of season. Departures about 5pm.

SAMPLE FARES

Prices below are one-way high/low season fares; port taxes (£3–5 per person in each direction) are not included. Substantial reductions apply on many lines for both InterRail or Eurail pass-holders, and for those under 26. Slight discounts are usually available on return fares. Many companies allow you to sleep in your van on board, sparing you the cost of a cabin berth; ask about reduced "camping" fares.

Igoumenítsa from Bari or Brindisi: deck class £18–£24/£12–£20; car from £24–£32/£13–£20. Superfast fares are £32/£22 (deck) and £32/£19 (car), also valid all the way to **Pátra**.

Pátra from Ancona: deck class £42/£28; car from £65/£35. Superfast fares £52/£36 (deck) & £74/£40 (car).

Pátra from Brindisi: deck class £25–£35/£15–£24; car from £28–£46/£18–£25.

In summer, it is essential to **book tickets** a few days ahead, especially in the peak July–August season. During the winter you can usually just turn up at the main ports (Ancona and Venice have the most reliable departures at that time of year), but it's still wise to book in advance, certainly if you are taking a car or want a cabin. A few phone calls or Internet searches before leaving are, in any case, advisable, as the range of fares and operators (from Brindisi especially) is considerable; if you do just turn up at the port, spend some time shopping around the agencies.

VIA HUNGARY, ROMANIA AND BULGARIA

Avoiding former Yugoslavia involves a pretty substantial diversion through Hungary, Romania and Bulgaria. This is not a drive to contemplate unless you actively want to see some of the countries en route – too exhausting and too problematic. However, it's all simpler than it was, with visas easier to obtain at the borders, if you haven't fixed them in advance.

From **Budapest**, the quickest route **through Romania** is via Timisoara, then to head towards Sofia in Bulgaria and on across the Rila moun-

Pátra from Trieste: deck class £39/£29; car from £79/£39.

Pátra from Venice: deck class £43/£32; car from £86/£43.

ITALIAN AGENTS

The dialling code for Italy is ☎39.

Adriatica, c/o Adria Shipping, Corso Garibaldi 85/87, Brindisi (☎0831/523825, fax 590758).

Agoudimos, c/o Hellas Ferry Lines, Corso Garibaldi 81, Brindisi (☎0831/529091, fax 529217).

ANEK, Ancona: Stazione Marittima (☎071/205959); Trieste, Stazione Marittima (☎040/302888, fax 311881).

Diler, c/o Italian Ferries, Corso Garibaldi 96/98, Brindisi (☎0831/590305, fax 590191).

European Seaways, c/o Adriatico, Corso Garibaldi 54, Brindisi (☎0831/523355, fax 561014).

Fraglines, Corso Gariboldi 00, Brindisi (☎0831/590196, fax 590181).

Hellenic Mediterranean Lines, Corso Garibaldi 8, Brindisi (☎0831/528531, fax 526872)

Marlines, c/o Pier Paolo Santelia, Stazione Marittima, Bari (☎080/52 31 824, fax 52 30 287).

Med Link Lines, c/o Discovery Shipping, Corso Garibaldi 49, Brindisi (☎0831/527667, fax 564070) .

Minoan Lines, Ancona: Via Astagno 1 (☎071/201708, fax 201933); Venice, Santa Marta (San Basilio) Magazzino 17 (☎041/27 12 345, fax 52 12 929).

Strintzis Lines, Brindisi: Corso Garibaldi 65 (☎0831/562200, fax 568300); Ancona: Stazione Marittima (☎071/20 71 068, fax 20 70 874); Venice: Stazione Marittima 103 (☎041/27 70 559, fax 27 70 367).

Superfast Ferries, Ancona: Morandi & Co, Via XXIX Settembre 2/0 (☎071/202033, fax 202219); Bari, c/o Portrans, Corso A. de Tullio 6 (☎080/52 11 416, fax 57 20 427) .

Ventouris, Bari: c/o P. Lorusso & Co, Stazione Marittima Booths 3–4 (☎080/52 17 118, fax 52 17 734); Brindisi, c/o Venmare, Corso Garibaldi 56 (☎0831/5212614, fax 521654).

UK AGENTS

The following are UK agents for advance bookings:

Serena Holidays, 40 Kenway Rd, London SW5 (☎020/7373 6548). For Adriatica Lines.

Viamare Travel Ltd, Graphic House, 2 Sumatra Rd, London NW6 (☎020/7431 4560). Agents for Agoudimos, ANEK, Fragline, Marlines, Med Link, Strintzis, Superfast, Ventouris.

DIRECT CONTACTS

Most of the more durable shipping companies have Web sites or email addresses for making bookings. They include:

Adriatica *www.adriatica.it*
adrnav@interbusiness.it

ANEK *www.anek.gr*

Hellenic Mediterranean Lines
hml@mail.otenet.gr

Marlines *www.marlines.gr*
info@marlines.gr

Minoan Lines *www.minoan.gr*
booking-eta@minoan.gr

Strintzis Lines *www.strintzis.gr*
sales@strintzis.gr

Superfast *www.superfast.com*
superfast@superfast.com

tains to the border at Kulata. Once at the Greek border, it's a three- to four-hour drive to Thessaloníki or Kavála. Bear in mind that road conditions are often poor and border crossings difficult. Contact the respective embassies and the AA for more advice.

GETTING THERE FROM IRELAND

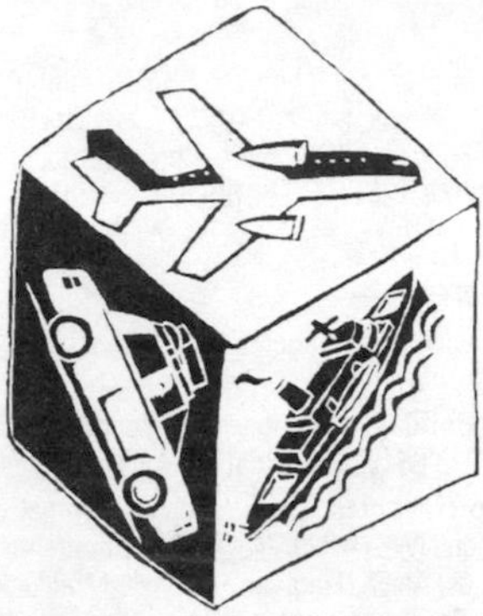

Summer charters operate from Dublin and Belfast to Athens and there are additional services to Mýkonos, Rhodes, Crete and Corfu. A high-season charter from Dublin to Athens costs upwards of IR£200 return, while a week's package on one of the above islands costs from IR£440 per person for two weeks.

Year-round **scheduled services** with Aer Lingus and British Airways operate from both Dublin and Belfast via Heathrow to Athens, or from Dublin via Heathrow on British Midland and Olympic, but you'll find them pricey compared to charters. Youth and student fares are offered by USIT (see box below for address).

Travelling **via London** is an alternative if flights are in short supply, and may sometimes save you a little money, but on the whole it's rarely worth the time and effort. For the record, budget flights to London are offered by British Midland, Aer Lingus and Ryanair.

TRAVEL AGENTS IN IRELAND

Balkan Tours, 37 Ann St, Belfast (☎02890/246795). *Direct charter flights.*

Joe Walsh Tours, 8–11 Baggot St, Dublin (☎01/676 3053). *General budget fares agent.*

Thomas Cook, 118 Grafton St, Dublin (☎01/677 1721). *Package holiday and flight agent, with occasional discount offers.*

Trailfinders, 4–5 Dawson St, Dublin 2 (☎01/677 7888). *Branch of the reliable scheduled-flight discount agents.*

USIT, Fountain Centre, Belfast (☎02890/324073); 10–11 Market Parade, Patrick St, Cork (☎021/270900); 33 Ferryquay St, Derry (☎01504/371888); Aston Quay, O'Connell Bridge, Dublin (☎01/679 8833); Victoria Place, Eyre Square, Galway (☎091/565177); Central Buildings, O'Connell St, Limerick (☎061/415064); 36–37 Georges St, Waterford (☎051/72601). *Student and youth specialist.*

AIRLINES IN IRELAND

Aer Lingus, 46–48 Castle St, Belfast (☎02890/245151); 2 Academy St, Cork (☎021/274331); 41 Upper O'Connell St, Dublin (☎01/844 4777).

British Airways, 9 Fountain Centre, College St, Belfast (☎02890/899131). British Airways does not have a Dublin office; for reservations from Eire, call ☎0141/222 2345, or contact Aer Lingus.

British Midland, Suite 2, Fountain Centre, College St, Belfast (☎02890/241188); Nutley, Merrion Rd, Dublin (☎01/283 8833).

Olympic Airways, c/o Travel Cuts, Frankin House, 142 Pembroke Rd, Dublin (☎01/608 0090).

Ryanair, Phoenix House, Conyngham Rd, Dublin (☎01/609 7800).

GETTING THERE FROM NORTH AMERICA

Only a few carriers fly directly to Greece from North America, so most North Americans travel to a gateway European city and pick up a connecting flight on from there with an associated airline. If you have time, you may well discover that it's cheaper to arrange the final Greece-bound leg of the journey yourself, in which case your only criterion will be finding a suitable and good-value North America–Europe flight; for details of onward flights from the UK, see "Getting There from Britain" above.

The **Greek national airline**, Olympic Airways, flies out of New York (JFK), Boston, Montréal and Toronto, though the airline can offer reasonably priced add-on flights within Greece, especially to the Greek islands, leaving from the same Athens terminal that you will fly into.

Another option to consider is picking up a flight to Europe and making your way to Greece by train, in which case a **Eurail Pass** makes a reasonable investment – all the details are covered below. For details of train routes, see "Getting There from Britain".

SHOPPING FOR TICKETS

Discount ticket outlets – advertised in the Sunday travel sections of major newspapers – come in several forms. **Consolidators** buy up blocks of tickets that airlines don't think they'll be able to sell at their published fares, and unload them at a discount. Many advertise fares on a one-way basis, enabling you to fly into one city and out from another without penalty. Consolidators normally don't impose advance purchase requirements (although in busy times you should book ahead just to be sure of getting a ticket), but they do often charge very stiff fees for date changes. **Discount agents** also deal in blocks of tickets offloaded by the airlines, but they typically offer a range of other travel-related services like insurance, rail passes, youth and student ID cards, car rentals and tours. These agencies tend to be most worthwhile for students and under-26s, who can

AIRLINES IN NORTH AMERICA

Air Canada Canada, call directory enquiries, ☎1-800/555-1212, for local toll-free number; US, ☎1-800/776-3000.

Air France US, ☎1-800/237-2747; Canada, ☎1-800/667-2747.

Alitalia ☎1-800/223-5730.

British Airways US, ☎1-800/247-9297; Canada, ☎1-800/AIRWAYS or 1-800/668-1055.

Canadian Airlines Canada, ☎1-800/665-1177; US, ☎1-800/426-7000.

Czech Airlines ☎1-800/223-2365 or 212/765-6022; Montreal ☎1-800/561-5171; Toronto ☎1-800/641-0641.

Delta Airlines ☎1-800/241-4141.

Iberia ☎1-800/772-4642.

KLM US, ☎1-800/374-7747; Canada, ☎1-800/361-5073.

LOT Polish Airlines ☎1-800/223-0593.

Lufthansa ☎1-800/645-3880.

Olympic Airways ☎1-800/223-1226 or 212/838-3600.

Sabena ☎1-800/955-2000.

Swissair ☎1-800/221-4750.

United Airlines ☎1-800/538-2929.

benefit from special fares and deals. **Travel clubs** are another option – most charge an annual membership fee, which may be worth it for their discounts on air tickets and car rental. Some agencies specialize in **charter flights**, which may be even cheaper than anything available on a scheduled flight, but again there's a trade-off: departure dates are fixed, and withdrawal penalties are high (check the refund policy). Student/youth fares can sometimes save you money, though again the best deals are usually those offered by seat consolidators advertising in Sunday newspaper travel sections.

Don't automatically assume that any tickets purchased through a travel specialist will be the cheapest – once you get a quote, check with the airlines and you may turn up an even better deal. In addition, exercise caution and never deal with a company that demands cash up front or refuses to accept payment by credit card.

For destinations not handled by discounters – which applies to most regional airports – you'll

DISCOUNT TRAVEL COMPANIES

Air Brokers International, 323 Geary St, Suite 411, San Francisco, CA 94102 (☎1-800/883-3273, *www.airbrokers.com*). *Consolidator.*

Air Courier Association, 191 University Boulevard, Suite 300, Denver, CO 80206 (☎303/278-8810). *Courier flight broker.*

Airhitch, 2472 Broadway, Suite 200, New York, NY 10025 (☎212/864-2000). *Standby-seat broker. For a set price, they guarantee to get you on a flight as close to your preferred destination as possible, within a week.*

Council Travel, Head Office: 205 East 42nd St, New York, NY 10017 (☎1-800/226-8624, 1-888 COUNCIL, 212/822-2700, *www.counciltravel.com*). *Student travel organization with sixty branches in the US.*

Educational Travel Center, 438 North Frances St, Madison, WI 53703 (☎1-800/747-5551 or 608/256-5551). *Student/youth discount agent.*

Encore Travel Club, 4501 Forbes Blvd, Lanham, MD 20706 (☎1-800/444-9800). *Discount travel club.*

Interworld Travel, 800 Douglass Rd, Miami, FL 33134 (☎305/443-4929). *Consolidator.*

Last Minute Travel Club, 100 Sylvan Rd, Suite 600, Woburn, MA 01801 (☎1-800/LAST-MIN). *Travel club specializing in standby deals.*

Moment's Notice, 7301 New Utrecht Ave, Brooklyn, NY 11204 (☎212/486-0500). *Discount travel club.*

New Frontiers/Nouvelles Frontières, 12E 33rd St, New York, NY 10016 (☎1-800/366-6387); 1001 Sherbrook East, Suite 720, Montréal, H2L 1L3 (☎514/526-8444) and other branches in LA, San Francisco and Québec City. *French-originated discount travel firm.*

Now Voyager, 74 Varick St, Suite 307, New York, NY 10013 (☎212/431-1616). *Courier flight broker and consolidator.*

STA Travel, 10 Downing St, New York, NY 10014 (☎1-800/781-4040 or 212/627-3111) and other branches in the Los Angeles, San Francisco and Boston areas. *Worldwide specialist in independent travel.*

TFI Tours International, Head Office: 34 West 32nd St, New York, NY 10001 (☎1-800/745-8000). *Consolidator; other offices in Las Vegas, San Francisco, Los Angeles and Miami.*

Travac, 989 6th Ave, New York, NY 10018 (☎1-800/872-8800 or 212/563-3303). *Consolidator and charter broker. If you have a fax machine you can have a list of fares faxed to you by calling toll-free* ☎1-888/872-8327.

Travel Avenue, 10 South Riverside, Suite 1404, Chicago, IL 60606 (☎1-800/333-3335 or 312/876-6866). *Discount travel agent.*

Travel CUTS, 243 College St, Toronto, ON M5T 1P7 (☎1-800/667-2887), and other branches all over Canada. *Student/youth travel organization with branches all over the country.*

Travelers Advantage, 801 Royal Parkway, Suite 200, Nashville, TN 37214 (☎1-800/548-1116). *Discount travel club; annual membership required.*

UniTravel, 1177 North Warson Rd, St Louis, MO 63132 (☎1-800/325-2222). *Consolidator.*

Worldtek Travel, 111 Water St, New Haven, CT 06511 (☎1-800/243-1723). *Discount travel agency.*

Worldwide Discount Travel Club, 1674 Meridian Ave, Miami Beach, FL 33139 (☎305/534-2082). *Discount travel club.*

have to deal with airlines' published fares. The cheapest of these is an **APEX** (Advance Purchase Excursion) ticket. This carries certain restrictions. For instance, you may be expected to book – and pay – at least 21 days before departure, keep to a minimum/maximum limit on your stay and be liable to penalties if you change your schedule. On transatlantic routes there are also winter **Super APEX** tickets, sometimes known as "Eurosavers"; slightly cheaper than ordinary Apex, they limit your stay to between seven and 21 days. Some airlines also issue **Special APEX** tickets to those under 24, often extending the maximum stay to a year.

Note that fares are heavily dependent on **season**, and are highest from June to September; they drop either side of this, and you'll get the best deals during the low season (November–February, excluding Christmas). Note that flying on weekends ordinarily adds $50 or so to the round-trip fare; price ranges quoted in the sections below assume midweek travel.

FLIGHTS FROM THE US

The twice-weekly non-stop flights to Athens out of **New York** and **Boston** on Olympic start at around US$500 round-trip in winter, rising to around $950 in summer for a maximum thirty-day stay with seven-day advance purchase. Delta has a daily direct service from New York to Athens for the same APEX fare. Prices are usually similar on British Airways, Lufthansa, Swissair, Sabena and United, although their flights are via European gateway cities. However, it is worth checking for discounts with these carriers. Swissair for example was offering a summer fare of $730 from New York at time of writing and Lufthansa and Sabena were even lower at $649. LOT Polish Airlines had special deals on their round-trip high season APEX fares from several US cities to Athens, via Warsaw ($749 from New York, $739 from Chicago, $879 from LA). United also flies to Athens from **Washington DC** for a high/low season rate of around $1140/$560. Flying in the "mid season" of September or October can make for significant savings. United's fare from Washington DC, for instance, falls from the summer high to about $790 on September 5 and Olympic will bring you from New York to Athens for $730 in the same period.

EUROPEAN CONNECTIONS

There are direct flights to:

Thessaloníki from Amsterdam, Brussels, Copenhagen, Dusseldorf, Frankfurt, London, Munich, Stuttgart, Vienna, Zürich.

Corfu from Amsterdam, Dusseldorf, Frankfurt, Geneva, London, Milan, Stuttgart.

As with the service from the Eastern cities, the stiff competition between the different airlines dictates that fares to Athens from the **Mid-West** or **West Coast** are virtually identical: high/low season fares on Olympic, Delta, United, Iberia and so on start at $1040/$600 from Chicago or $1310/$1010 from LA, San Francisco or Seattle. With little else to choose between the major carriers, you might look into the stopover time at the different European gateway cities, as these can sometimes be overnight; check with your ticket agent.

FLIGHTS FROM CANADA

As with the US, air fares from **Canada** to **Athens** vary tremendously depending upon where you start your journey. Olympic flies non-stop out of Montréal and Toronto twice a week for a scheduled fare of CDN$1380 round-trip in winter or CDN$1540 in summer.

Northwest/KLM operates several flights a week to Athens via Amsterdam, from Toronto, Montréal, Vancouver and Edmonton. From Toronto, expect to pay around CDN$1850 in low season, CDN$2050 in high season; and from Vancouver CDN$2100 (low) or CDN$2400 (high). Travellers from Montréal can also try the European carriers Air France, Alitalia, British Airways, Iberia, Lufthansa and Swissair, all of which operate several flights a week to Athens via major European cities. One unlikely source for good deals is Czech Airlines, which flies out of Montreal to Athens via Prague for CDN$880 (low) or CDN$1285 (high).

Air Canada, flying in conjunction with Lufthansa, quotes the following low/high season fares to Athens: from Toronto/Montréal around CDN$1360/CDN$1540, and from Vancouver around CDN$1740/CDN$1970. Canadian Airlines offers a much cheaper option from Toronto at about CDN$950/CDN$1320.

SPECIALIST TOUR OPERATORS

US

Astro Tours, 2359 East Main St, Columbus, OH 43209 (☎1-800/543-7717 or 614/237-7798). *Cruise packages to the Greek islands.*

Avenir Travel, 2029 Sidewinder Dr, POB 2730, Park City UT 84060 (☎1-800/367-3230, *www.avenirtravel.com*). *Small-group, spring/autumn tours, personally led by Shirley Smith, in and around Sými and Samos.*

Brendan Tours, 15137 Califa St, Van Nuys, CA 91411 (☎1-800/421-8446). *City highlights, cruise packages and car rental.*

Caravan Tours Inc, 401 North Michigan Ave, Suite 2800, Chicago, IL 60611 (☎1-800/621-8338). *All kinds of packages covering the entire country.*

Classic Adventures, PO Box 153, Hamlin, NY 14464-0153 (☎1-800/777-8090, *www.classicadventures.com*). *Trekking, biking and walking tours in May–June and Sept–Oct, covering archeological sites and coastal trips.*

Classic Holidays, 350 Park St, Suite 204, North Reading, MA 01864 (☎1-800/752-5055). *Packages from eight to 21 days, group tours and cruises.*

Classic Journeys, 5580 La Jolla Blvd. No. 104, La Jolla, CA 92037 (☎1-800/200-3887). *Walking tours of the Greek isles.*

Cloud Tours Inc, 645 Fifth Ave, New York, NY 10022 (☎1-800/223-7880 or 212/753-6104). *Affordable escorted tours and Mediterranean cruises.*

Educational Tours and Cruises, 9 Irving St, Medford, MA 02155 (☎1-800/275-4109). *Custom-designed tours to the islands, specializing in art, history, food and wine, ancient drama, painting and birdwatching.*

Elderhostel, 75 Federal St, Boston, MA 02110 (☎877/426-8056). *Educational and activity programmes for senior travellers (companions may be younger).*

Globus and Cosmos, Littleton,CO (☎1-800/221-0090, *www.cosmostours.com*). *Group tours and packages.*

Guaranteed Travel, 83 South St, Morristown, NJ 07963 (☎973/540-1770). *Specializes in "Greece-Your-Way" independent travel.*

Hellenic Adventures, 4150 Harriet Ave South, Minneapolis, MN 55409 (☎1-800/851-6349 or 612/827-0937). *A vast range of small group and independent tours: cultural, historical, horseback riding, hiking, wilderness, culinary and family-oriented.*

Homeric Tours, 55 East 59th St, New York, NY 10017 (☎1-800/223-5570). *All-inclusive tours from nine to 23 days, as well as cruises and charter flights.*

Insight International Tours, 745 Atlantic Ave, Suite 720, Boston, MA 02111 (☎1-800/582-8380). *General Greek vacations.*

ST Cultural Tours, 225 West 34th St, New York, NY 10122 (☎1-800/833-2111 or 212/563-1202). *A wide range of package and independent educational tours.*

Valef Yachts, Box 391, Ambler, PA 19002 (☎1-800/223-3845 or 215/641-1624). *Yachting trips and charters.*

CANADA

Adventures Abroad, 20800 Westminter Highway, Suite 2148, Richmond, BC V6V 2W3 (☎1-800/665-3998 or 604/303-1099). *General operator, offering group and individual tours and cruises.*

Auratours, 1470 Peel St, Suite 252, Montréal, Quebec H3A 1TL (☎1-800/363-0323 or 514/282-9056). *General operator, offering group and individual tours and cruises.*

GETTING THERE FROM AUSTRALIA & NEW ZEALAND

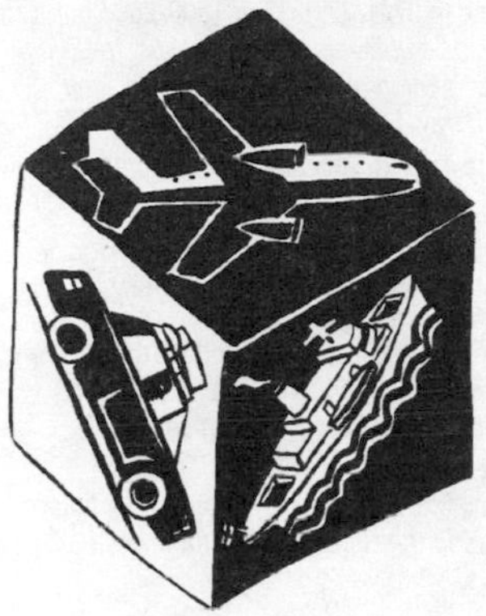

It's fairly easy to track down flights from Australia to Athens, less so from New Zealand, but given the prices and most people's travel plans, you'll probably do better looking for some kind of Round-the-World (RTW) ticket that includes Greece. If London is your first destination in Europe, and you've picked up a reasonably good deal on a flight there, it's probably best to wait until you reach the UK before arranging your onward travel to Greece; see "Getting There from Britain" for all the details.

Fares are seasonally adjusted, with low season from mid-January to the end of February and October–November; high season mid-May to August, December to mid-January; and shoulder seasons the rest of the year. Tickets purchased direct from the airlines tend to be expensive; travel agents offer much better deals on fares and have the latest information on limited specials, Round-the-World fares and stopovers. Some of the best discounts are through **Flight Centres** and **STA**, who can also advise on visa regulations.

AGENTS AND AIRLINES IN AUSTRALIA AND NEW ZEALAND

DISCOUNT TRAVEL AGENTS

Anywhere Travel, 345 Anzac Parade, Kingsford, Sydney (☎02/9663 0411, *anywhere@ozemail.com.au*).

Budget Travel, 16 Fort St, Auckland, plus branches around the city (☎09/366 0061 or 0800/808 040).

Destinations Unlimited, 3 Milford Rd, Auckland (☎09/373 4033).

Flight Centres Australia: 82 Elizabeth St, Sydney, plus branches nationwide (☎13 1600). 205 Queen St, Auckland (☎09/309 6171), plus branches nationwide. *Good discounts on fares.*

STA Travel, Australia: 702 Harris St, Ultimo, Sydney; 256 Flinders St, Melbourne; other offices in state capitals and major universities (nearest branch ☎13 1776, fastfare telesales ☎1300/360 960); New Zealand: 10 High St, Auckland (☎09/309 0458, fastfare telesales ☎09/366 6673), plus branches in Wellington, Christchurch, Dunedin, Palmerston North, Hamilton and at major universities (*www.statravelaus.com.au*). *Fare discounts for students and under-26s.*

Status Travel, 22 Cavenagh St, Darwin (☎08/8941 1843).

Student Uni Travel, 92 Pitt St, Sydney (☎02/9232 8444) plus branches in Melbourne, Darwin, Brisbane, Cairns and Perth. *Special backpacker and student rates.*

Thomas Cook, Australia: 175 Pitt St, Sydney; 257 Collins St, Melbourne plus branches in other state capitals (nearest branch ☎13 1771; telesales 1800/063 913). New Zealand: Level 5, Telstra Business Centre, Auckland (☎09/359 5200, *www.thomascook.com.au*). *Travellers' cheques and airfares.*

Trailfinders, 8 Spring St, Sydney (☎02/9247 7666). *Australian branch of UK-based fare discounter.*

Travel.com.au, 80 Clarence St, Sydney (☎02/9290 1500, *www.travel.com.au*). *Web-based travel agency, with special discounts for booking online.*

USIT Beyond, corner of Shortland and Jean Batten Place, Auckland (☎09/379 4224) plus branches in Christchurch, Hamilton, Palmerston North and Wellington (*www.usitbeyond.co.nz*). *Specialists in student and independent travel.*

continued overleaf

continued from previous page

SPECIALIST AGENTS

Adventure Travel Company, 164 Parnell Rd, Parnell, Auckland (☎09/379 9755). *New Zealand agent for Peregrine Adventures.*

Adventure World, 73 Walker St, North Sydney; plus branches in Adelaide, Brisbane, Melbourne and Perth (☎02/956 7766 or 1800/221 931). *Agents for a vast array of international adventure travel companies that operate trips to the islands.*

Australians Studying Abroad, 1/970 High St, Armadale, Melbourne (☎03/9509 1955 or 1800/645 755, *www.asatravinfo.com.au*). *Study tours exploring Greek culture and art; Anatolian tour includes Turkey too.*

Grecian Tours Travel, 237a Lonsdale St, Melbourne (☎03/663 3711). *Offers a variety of accommodation, and sightseeing tours.*

House of Holidays, 539 Main St, Mordialloc, Victoria (☎03/9580 4488). *Wholesalers with a wide selection of Greek holidays.*

Kompas Holidays, 232 Boundary St, Spring Hill, Brisbane (☎07/3222 3333 or 1800/269 968). *City stopovers, sightseeing tours, cruises, traditional accommodation and yacht charter. Booking through travel agents only.*

Kyrenia Travel Services, 92 Goulburn St, Sydney (☎02/9283 2144). *Island accommodation and island-hopping.*

Peregrine Adventures, 258 Lonsdale St, Melbourne (☎03/9663 8611), plus offices in Brisbane, Sydney, Adelaide and Perth (*www.peregrine.net.au*). *Walking and cycling trips, visiting historic towns and monuments.*

Travel Market,11th floor, 141 Queen St, Brisbane (☎07/3210 0323). *Individually tailored holidays in the Greek islands, for a range of budgets.*

AIRLINES

Aeroflot, Australia (☎02/9262 2233). *Once-a-week flight from Sydney to Athens via transfers in Moscow and Singapore.*

Air New Zealand, Australia (☎02/9223 4666); New Zealand (☎09/357 3000). *Several flights weekly to Athens via LA or Bangkok from major Australian and New Zealand cities (in partnership with the "Star Alliance" and other code-share arrangements).*

Alitalia, Australia (☎1300/653 747); New Zealand (☎09/379 4455). *Three flights per week from Sydney (plus Brisbane, Canberra and Melbourne under code-share agreements with other airlines) to Athens via Milan.*

British Airways, Australia (☎02/8904 8800); New Zealand (☎09/356 8690). *Daily flights to London from major Australasian cities: code-share with Qantas to offer their "Global Explorer" and "One World" RTW fares.*

Garuda, Australia (☎1300/365 330); New Zealand (☎09/366 1855). *Several flights weekly from Australian and New Zealand cities to London, Frankfurt and Amsterdam via either a transfer or stopover in Denpasar/Jakarta.*

Gulf Air, Australia (☎02/9244 2199). *Once-weekly flight to Athens via Singapore and Bahrain.*

Olympic Airways, Australia (☎02/9251 2044); no New Zealand office. *Thrice-weekly flights to Athens from Sydney and Melbourne, with quick onward connections to other Greek destinations.*

Qantas Australia (☎13 1313); New Zealand (☎09/357 8900 and 0800/808 767). *Daily flights to London from major Australasian cities; code-share with British Airways in their "Global Explorer" and "One World" RTW fares.*

Singapore Airlines, Australia (☎13 1011); New Zealand (☎09/379 3209). *Daily flights to Athens from Brisbane, Sydney, Melbourne, Perth and Auckland via Singapore.*

Thai Airways Australia (☎1300/651 960); New Zealand (☎09/377 3886). *Three flights a week to Athens via either a transfer or stopover in Bangkok from Brisbane, Sydney, Melbourne, Perth and Auckland.*

FLIGHTS FROM AUSTRALIA

Cheapest fares to Athens **from Australia** are with Gulf Air or Olympic Airways from A$1450 low season, while Alitalia via Milan, Aeroflot via Moscow and Thai Airways via Bangkok all start around A$1540. In addition, Singapore Airlines has a good connecting service to Athens from $1750. Qantas and British Airways offer a free return flight within Europe for A$1850–2300 which differs only slightly from their "Global Explorer" Pass (A$2000–3000), a **Round-the-**

World fare that allows six stopovers worldwide wherever these two airlines fly to. An alternative covering more destinations is the BA/Qantas "One World" deal in conjunction with American Airlines and Cathay Pacific, costing A$2400–3500. Also worth considering is Garuda's A$1600 fare from Sydney, Brisbane or Cairns via Jakarta or Denpasar to various European cities, from where you could pick up a cheap onward flight or continue **overland** to Athens.

FLIGHTS FROM NEW ZEALAND

From New Zealand, the best deals to Athens are with Thai Airlines via Bangkok from $1999, and Singapore Airlines via Singapore and Alitalia via Milan, both for around NZ$2275. There's also a very versatile offer with Lufthansa from $2299, who can route you through anywhere that Air New Zealand or Qantas flies – including Los Angeles, Singapore, Sydney, Hong Kong or Tokyo – for a stopover. Lufthansa are also partners in the "Star Alliance" **RTW fare**, starting at NZ$3299. British Airways/Qantas can get you to a variety of European destinations, including Athens for $2475, but you may be better off with their "Global Explorer" or "One World" RTW fares from NZ$2999.

DEPARTURE POINTS: ATHENS, PIREÁS & MAIN PORTS

As detailed in the "Getting There" sections, you may well find yourself travelling to the islands via Athens. This is not necessarily a hardship. The Greek capital is, admittedly, no holiday resort, with its concrete architecture and air pollution, but it has modern excitements of its own, as well as superlative ancient sites. A couple of nights' stopover will allow you to take in the Acropolis, the ancient Agora and major museums, wander around the old quarter of Pláka and the bazaar area, and sample some of the country's best restaurants and clubs. And a morning flight into Athens would allow you time to take a look at the Acropolis and Pláka, before heading down to the port of Pireás (Piraeus) to catch one of the overnight ferries to Crete or the Dodecanese.

Not all the islands are accessible from Pireás, so we've given brief accounts of other useful mainland ports below.

ATHENS

Although a new airport, east of town at Spáta, is scheduled to open in March 2001, for the moment Athens **airport** lies south of the centre at Ellinikón. This has two separate terminals: west (*dhytikó*), which is used by Olympic Airways (both national and international), and east (*anatolikó*), which is used by all other international flights and adjoins the charter-flight terminal. The east and west terminals are on opposite sides of the runway, so you have to drive halfway round the perimeter fence to get from one to the other. Public buses connect the two regularly from around 6am to midnight, much less frequently in the small hours; taxis are available, too, and should cost no more than 1500dr at day rates for the trip. Both terminals have money exchange facilities, open 24 hours at the east terminal, 7am to 11pm at the west one; the west terminal also has cash dispensers that accept Visa, Mastercard, Cirrus and Plus cards. Insist on some small denomination notes for paying for your bus ticket or taxi ride.

It's about 9km to **central Athens** or to the ferry port of **Pireás** (Piraeus). The easiest way to travel is by **taxi**, which should cost around 1500–2100dr, depending on your destination and how many bags you have. Make sure that the meter is switched on, as new arrivals are often charged well over the odds. You may find that you have fellow passengers in the cab: this is permitted, and each drop-off will pay the full fare.

If you're happy to carry your bags around, you could also travel in by **bus**. Bus #92 connects the west terminal and Omónia square via Syngroú and Sýndagma squares; bus #93 shuttles between the west, east and charter terminals only; bus #91 between the east/charter terminal and the city centre; and bus #19 between Pireás and the west, east and charter terminals, allowing you to get straight to the ferries. Take the #19 to the end of the route, Platía Karaïskáki, which fronts the main harbour, and a line of ferry agencies. At some times of the year #93 may be eliminated, and lines #91/92 amalgamated. In theory, the #91/92 bus runs every 30 minutes from 5am to midnight, and every hour from midnight to 5am. Bus #19 runs about every hour between 6am and 8pm; #93 roughly every 40 minutes. Tickets on each of these routes cost 250dr (500dr from midnight to 5.30am).

All international **trains** arrive at the Stathmós Laríssis, just to the northwest of the city centre. There are hotels in this area or you can take yellow trolley bus (#1) immediately outside to reach Sýndagma square.

If you are just spending the day in Athens, and want to **store your baggage**, you can do so at all three airport terminals for a reasonable fee (about 1000dr per bag for 24hr).

ACCOMMODATION AND EATING

Finding **accommodation** in Athens is not a problem except at the very height of summer – though it's always best to phone ahead. A small selection of places is listed below, or you can book more upmarket rooms through the main EOT tourist office (Mon–Fri 9am–7pm, Sat 9am–2pm; ☎33 10 437 or 33 10 562 or 33 10 565) at Amerikís 2, just up from Stadhíou, which can also supply you with maps of the city.

For a quick stay, **Pláka**, the oldest quarter of the city, is the best area. It spreads south of Sýndagma square, is in easy walking range of the Acropolis and has lots of outdoor restaurants and cafés. It's possible to stay in the port of Pireás, too, though there's no real need, and you might as well make the most of your time in Athens. All the listings below are in Pláka, except for *Marble House*, which is just south in Koukáki district; price categories are for a double room in high season.

5000–8000dr
George's Guest House, Níkis 46 (☎32 26 474).
Thisseus Hostel, Thisséos 10 (☎32 45 960).

8000–11,000dr
Dioskouri, Pittákou 6 (☎32 48 165).
Marble House, Zínni 35 (☎92 34 058).
Kouros, Kódhrou 11 (☎32 27 431).
Student Inn, Kidhathinéon 18 (☎32 44 808).

11,000–16,000dr
Acropolis House, Kódhrou 6 (☎32 22 344).
Adonis, Kódhrou 3 (☎32 49 737).
Nefeli, Iperídhou 16 (☎32 28 044).

Pláka is bursting with touristy **restaurants**, most very pleasantly situated but poor value. Three with nice sites and good food are *Yerani/Skholarhio* (Tripódhon 14), *O Platanos* (Dhioyénous 4) and *Iy Klimataria* (Klepsídhras 5). *Eden* (Liossíou 12) is one of the city's few vegetarian restaurants.

THE CITY AND SIGHTS

Central Athens is a compact, easily walkable area. Its hub is **Sýndagma square** (Platía Sintágmatos), flanked by the Parliament buildings, banks and airline offices, and the National Bank with the tourist office. Pretty much everything you'll want to see in a fleeting visit – the Acropolis, Pláka, the major museums – is within 20–30 minutes' walk of here. Just east of the square, too, are the **National Gardens** – the nicest spot in town for a siesta.

Walk south from Sýndagma, along Níkis or Filellínon streets, and you'll find yourself in Pláka, the surviving area of the nineteenth-century, pre-Independence village. Largely pedestrianized, it is a delightful area just to wander around – and it is the approach to the Acropolis. For a bit of focus to your walk, take in the fourth-century BC **Monument of Lysikrates**, used as a study by Byron, to the east, and the Roman-era **Tower of the Winds** (Aéridhes), to the west. The latter adjoins the Roman Forum. Climb north from the Tower of the Winds and you reach **Anafiótika**, with its whitewashed Cycladic-style cottages (built by workers from the island of Anáfi) and the eclectic **Kanellópoulos Museum** (Tues–Sun 8am–2.30pm; 500dr).

Head north from the Roman Forum, along Athinás or Eólou streets, and you come to an equally characterful part of the city – the **bazaar** area, which shows Athens in its Near Eastern lights. **Monastiráki square** is worth a look, too, with its Turkish mosque. On Sundays a genuine **flea market** sprawls to its west, out beyond the tourist shops promoted as "Athens Flea Market".

Even with a few hours to spare between flight and ferry, you can take in a visit to the **Acropolis** (April–Sept daily 8am–7pm; Oct–March Mon–Fri 8am–4.30pm, Sat & Sun 8am–2.30pm; site and museum 2000dr, Oct–March free on Sun). The complex of temples, rebuilt by Pericles in the Golden Age of the fifth century BC, is focused on the famed Parthenon. This, and the smaller Athena Nike and Erechtheion temples are given context by a small museum housing some of the original statuary left behind by Lord Elgin.

If you have more time, make your way down to the **Theatre of Dionysos**, on the south slope (summer daily 8am–7pm; winter daily 8.30am–2.45pm; 500dr), and/or to the Ancient (Classical Greek era) **Agora** (southeastern entrance down the path from the Areopagus; northern entrance on Adhrianoú; Tues–Sun 8.30am–2.30pm; 1200dr), presided over by the Doric **Thiseion**, or Temple of Hephaestus.

Athens' major museum is the **National Archeological Museum** (Patissíon 28; Mon 12.30–7pm, Tues–Sun 8am–7pm; 2000dr). Its highlights include the Mycenaean (*Odyssey*-era) treasures, Classical sculpture and, upstairs, the brilliant Minoan frescoes from Thíra (Santoríni).

Two other superb museums are the **Benáki** (scheduled to reopen in 2000), a fascinating personal collection of ancient and folk treasures, and the **Goulandris Museum of Cycladic and Ancient Greek Art** (Mon, Wed–Fri 10am–4pm, Sat 10am–3pm; 1000dr, 500dr Sat), with its wonderful display of figurines from the Cycladic island civilization of the third millennium BC.

PIREÁS

Pireás (Piraeus), the port of Athens, is the last stop on the single-line **metro** (currently being expanded to three lines), which you can board at Platía Viktorías, Omónia or Monastiráki squares. The journey takes about 25 minutes – trains run from 6am to midnight – and fares vary from 120dr to 180dr depending on how many "zones" you cross. If you're travelling by rail from Pátra, the train continues through Athens down to Pireás. **Taxis** cost 1500–2100dr from the city centre or the airport.

You can buy **ferry tickets** from agencies at the harbour in Pireás, or in central Athens (there are several outlets on Leóforos Amalías, which runs south of Sýndagma square). Wherever you buy tickets, make sure you ask around the agencies and get a ferry that makes a reasonably direct run to your island destination. There may be little choice to obscure islands, but ferries to the Cyclades and Dodecanese can take very different routes.

For the Argo-Saronic islands, you may prefer to take a "Flying Dolphin" **hydrofoil** from the Zéa Marina – a taxi ride (or bus #8) from the metro. These are twice as fast and around twice the cost. Tickets can be bought in advance in Athens – worth doing in high season – or an hour before departure at the quay.

OTHER MAINLAND PORTS

Although Pireás has a wide choice of ferry and hydrofoil connections, certain islands can (or must) be reached from other ports on the mainland. Below is a quick run-through of the more important and useful.

Note also that there are two islands – **Évvia** (northeast of Athens) and **Lefkádha** in the Ionian islands – that require no ferry, and can be reached by bus, and in Évvia's case also by train.

ALEXANDRHÓUPOLI

The third northern port (6hr by bus from Thessaloníki) has regular ferries and summer-only hydrofoils to Samothráki. It's a somewhat unenticing place to stay, though if you get stuck the *Lido* at Paleológou 15 (☎0551/28 808) represents by far the best budget-hotel value.

IGOUMENÍTSA

Many ferries from Italy call at Igoumenítsa, stopping at Corfu en route. There are regular shuttles across to **Corfu**, to both the main town and also Lefkími in the south, plus an unreliable service to **Paxí**. Hotel vacancies are plentiful as nobody stays more than a night; the *Stavrodhromi* (☎0665/22 343) is a reliable, friendly cheapie, 500m inland at Soulíou 14.

KAVÁLA

The second port of northern Greece (3hr by bus from Thessaloníki) offers fast access to **Thássos**, either direct by hydrofoil, or from the nearby ro-ro shuttle point at Keramotí. There are also links to **Límnos** and other **northeast Aegean** islands, as well as (seasonally) to **Samothráki**. The city has a line of good tavernas in the old quarter below the castle, but pleasant, affordable hotels are in short supply. In ascending order of comfort and price, try the *Akropolis* (☎051/223 543) at Venizélou 29, the *Panorama* (☎051/228 412) at Venizélou 26/c or the *Esperia* (☎051/229 621) on Erythroú Stavroú, opposite the archeological museum.

KYLLÍNI

This small port, south of Pátra (buses), is the main departure point for the Ionian island of **Zákynthos**, and in summer has boats to **Kefalloniá**. Little point in staying, if you time things right.

KÝMI

This is technically an island port – on Évvia (see Chapter 6) – but is mentioned here as it is the main port for the island of **Skýros** in the Sporades. Kými can be reached from Athens by bus, which should be timed to dovetail with ferry departures. If you miss the connection, staying options are limited to two fairly expensive hotels.

LÁVRIO

This tiny port, south of Athens (and reachable by bus from the Mavromatéon terminal; 1hr 15min) has daily ferries to **Kéa**, the closest of the Cyclades.

NEÁPOLI

A small, undistinguished port at the southern foot of the Peloponnese, with ferry and hydrofoil connections to **Kýthira**, and local boats to the islet of **Elafónissos**. It can be reached by hydrofoil in summer from the Argo-Saronic islands.

PÁRGA AND ASTAKÓS

These two small ports, south of Igoumenítsa, have daily ferries to, respectively, **Paxí** and **Itháki** in the Ionian. Párga is a popular, crowded resort, more pleasant (and with more accommodation vacancies, mostly studios) off-season; Astakós is rarely busy but has few places to stay – buses from Athens tend to dovetail with ferry departures.

PÁTRA (PATRAS)

Pátra is the major port of the Peloponnese, and the main jump-off for Italy and most of the **Ionian islands**. Easiest access from Athens is on the train (Statmós Peloponíssou terminal; 4hr), since the Pátra station is right by the boat terminals. The city itself is uninteresting, so plan on moving out the same day, if possible. Reasonable budget hotels include the *El Greco*, Ayíou Andhréou 145 (☎061/272 931) or the *Atlanta* at Ayíou Andhréou 16 (☎061/277 502).

RÁFINA

Another small port near Athens (again reachable by bus from the Mavromatéon terminal; 40min). Connections are to the **Cyclades**, **northeast Aegean** and nearby **Évvia**.

THESSALONÍKI

The northern capital is a busy mainland port. There are useful long-haul **ferries** to the major Dodecanese via Sámos; to the northeastern Aegean islands; and to Crete via select Sporades and Cyclades. There are useful if pricey hydrofoils to **Skíathos**, **Skópelos** and **Alónissos** in the Sporades. It's worth exploring the Byzantine churches, especially the Áyios Yeóryios Rotunda and tiny Ósios David, as well as the Archeological Museum. Hotels are plentiful if mostly uninspiring, noisy and often vastly overpriced; worthwhile exceptions include the *Tourist* on Mitropóleos 21 (☎031/276 335), the *Nea Mitropolis* at Syngroú 22 (☎031/525 540), the *Bill* at Syngroú 29 (☎031/537 666) and the *Orestias Kastorias* at Agnóstou Stratiótou 14 (☎031/276 517).

VÓLOS AND ÁYIOS KONSTANDÍNOS

Vólos is a large port city – modern and rather grim – in Thessaly, in central Greece. It is easiest reached from Athens by bus (Mavromatéon terminal; 4hr) though there are also a couple of through express trains daily. Ferries and hydrofoils run regularly to the Sporades – **Skiáthos**, **Skópelos**, **Alónissos** and **Skýros**. Try to complete your journey the same day; failing that, pleasantly situated budget hotels include the *Roussas* (☎0421/21 732) or the *Iasson* right by the dock (☎0421/26 075). **Áyios Konstandínos** is an alternative port for the **Sporades**, again with buses from Athens (Mavromatéon terminal; 2hr 30min).

YÍTHIO

This elegant Peloponnese town has ferries most days to the isolated island of **Kýthira**. It's a 5–6hr haul here by bus (Kifissóu 100 terminal) from Athens, changing at Spárti. Budget hotels or pensions in town include the *Kondoyannis*, Vassiléos Pávlou 19 (☎0733/22 518); the *Saga* on Tzanetáki, opposite Kranae islet (☎0733/23 220); or the *Kranae*, Vassiléos Pávlou 15 (☎0733/22 011).

TRAVELLERS WITH DISABILITIES

It is all too easy to wax lyrical over the attractions of Greece: the stepped, narrow alleys, the ease of travel by bus and ferry, the thrill of clambering around the great archeological sites. It is almost impossible, on the other hand, for the able-bodied travel-writer to see these attractions as potential hazards for anyone who has difficulty in walking, is wheelchair-bound or suffers from some other disability.

However, don't be discouraged. It is possible to enjoy an inexpensive and trauma-free holiday in Greece if some time is devoted to gathering **information** before arrival. Much existing or

USEFUL CONTACTS

National Tourist Organization of Greece: See box on p.33 for addresses. *Offers general advice on terrain and climate. They have nothing specific for disabled visitors except a brief list of hotels which may be suitable.*

GREECE

Association Hermes, Patriárhou Grigoríou toú Pémptou 13, 165 42 Aryiroúpolis, Athens (☎01/99 61 887). *Can advise disabled visitors to Greece.*

Lavinia Tours, Egnatía 101, 541 10 Thessaloníki (☎031/232 828). *Evyenia Stravropoulou will advise disabled visitors and has tested many parts of Greece in her wheelchair. She also organizes tours within Greece.*

UK and IRELAND

Holiday Care Service, 2nd floor, Imperial Buildings, Victoria Rd, Horley, Surrey RH6 7PZ (☎01293/774535). *Publishes a fact sheet, and also runs a useful "Holiday Helpers" service for disabled travellers.*

Mobility International, 228 Borough High St, London SE1 1JX (☎020/7403 5688). *Issues a quarterly newsletter on developments in disabled travel.*

Opus 23, Sourdock Hill, Barkisland, Halifax, West Yorkshire HX4 0AG (☎01422/375999). *Part of Grecofile (see box on p.6); will advise on and arrange independent holidays, or trips for those with carers.*

RADAR, 12 City Forum, 250 City Rd, London EC1V 8AF (☎020/7250 3222). *They publish fact sheets and an annual guide to international travel for the disabled.*

Tripscope, The Courtyard, Evelyn Rd, London W4 5JL (☎020/8994 9294). *Transport advice to most countries for all disabilities.*

NORTH AMERICA

Directions Unlimited, 720 North Bedford Rd, Bedford Hills, NY 10507 (☎1-800/533-5343). *Tour operator specializing in custom tours for people with disabilities.*

Jewish Rehabilitation Hospital, 3205 Place Alton Goldbloom, Montreal, PQ H7V 1R2 (☎514/688-9550, ext 226). *Guidebooks and travel information.*

Mobility International USA, PO Box 10767, Eugene, OR 97440 (Voice & TDD: ☎503/343-1284). *Information and referral services, access guides, tours and exchange programmes. Annual membership $20 (includes quarterly newsletter).*

Society for the Advancement of Travel for the Handicapped (SATH), 347 5th Ave, New York, NY 10016 (☎212/447-7284). *Non-profit travel-industry referral service that passes queries on to its members as appropriate; allow plenty of time for a response.*

Travel Information Service, Moss Rehabilitation Hospital, 1200 West Tabor Rd, Philadelphia, PA 19141 (☎215/456-9600). *Telephone information and referral service.*

Twin Peaks Press, Box 129, Vancouver, WA 98666 (☎206/694-2462 or 1-800/637-2256). *Publisher of the* Directory of Travel Agencies for the Disabled *($19.95), listing more than 370 agencies worldwide;* Travel for the Disabled *($14.95); and the* Directory of Accessible Van Rentals and Wheelchair Vagabond *($9.95), loaded with personal tips.*

AUSTRALIA AND NEW ZEALAND

ACROD (Australian Council for Rehabilitation of the Disabled), PO Box 60, Curtin, ACT 2605 (☎02/6282 4333).

Disabled Persons Assembly, 173–175 Victoria St, Wellington (☎04/811 9100).

readily available information is out of date – you should always try to double-check. A number of addresses of contact organizations are published in the box on p.23. The Greek National Tourist Office is a good first step as long as you have specific questions to put to them; they publish a useful questionnaire which you could send to hotels or owners of apartment/villa accommodation.

PLANNING A HOLIDAY

There are **organized tours** and **holidays** specifically for people with disabilities; many companies in Britain will advise on the suitability of holidays or villas advertised in their brochures. If you want to be more independent, it's perfectly possible, provided that you do not leave home with the vague hope that things will turn out all right, and that "people will help out" when you need assistance. This cannot be relied on. You must either be completely confident that you can manage alone or travel with an able-bodied friend (or two).

It's important to become an authority on where you must be self-reliant and where you may expect help, especially regarding transport and accommodation. For example, to get between the terminals at Athens airport, you will have to fight for a taxi; it is not the duty of the airline staff to find you one.

It is also vital to **be honest** – with travel agencies, insurance companies, companions and, above all, with yourself. Know your limits and make sure others know them. If you do not use a wheelchair all the time but your walking capabilities are limited, remember that you are likely to need to cover greater distances while travelling (often over tougher terrain and in hotter weather) than you are used to. If you use a wheelchair, have it serviced before you go, and carry a repair kit.

Read your travel **insurance** small print carefully to make sure that people with a pre-existing medical condition are not excluded. And use your travel agent to make your journey simpler: **airlines** or bus companies can cope better if they are expecting you, with a wheelchair provided at airports and staff primed to help. A **medical certificate** of your fitness to travel, provided by your doctor, is also extremely useful; some airlines or insurance companies may insist on it.

Make a **list** of all the facilities that will make your life easier while you are away. You may want a ground-floor room, or access to a large elevator; you may have special dietary requirements, or need level ground to enable you to reach shops, beaches, bars and places of interest. You should also keep track of all your other special needs, making sure, for example, that you have extra supplies of drugs – carried with you if you fly – and a prescription including the generic name in case of emergency. Carry spares of any kind of drug, clothing or equipment that might be hard to find in Greece; if there's an association representing people with your disability, contact them early in the planning process.

VISAS AND RED TAPE

UK and all other EU nationals need only a valid passport for entry to Greece; you are no longer stamped in on arrival or out upon departure, and in theory at least enjoy uniform civil rights with Greek citizens. US, Australian, New Zealand, Canadian and most non-EU Europeans receive mandatory entry and exit stamps in their passports and can stay, as tourists, for ninety days. If you arrive on a flight or boat from another EU state, such nationals may not be stamped in routinely – make sure this is done to avoid unpleasantness on exit.

If you are planning to **travel overland**, you should check current visa requirements for Hungary, Romania and Bulgaria at their closest consulates; transit visas for most of these territories are at present issued at the borders, though at a higher price than if obtained in advance at a local consulate.

VISA EXTENSIONS

If you wish to remain in Greece for longer than three months, you should officially apply for an **extension**. This can be done in the larger cities like Rhodes and Iráklio (Crete) through the *Ypiresía Allodhapón* (Aliens' Bureau); prepare yourself for concerted bureaucracy. In other locations you visit the local police station, where the staff are apt to be more co-operative.

Unless they are of Greek descent, visitors from **non-EU** countries are currently allowed only one six-month extension to a tourist visa, which costs 11,000dr. In theory, **EU nationals** are allowed to stay indefinitely but, at the time of writing, must still present themselves every six months or every year, according to whether they have a non-employment resident visa or a work permit; the first extension is free, but you will probably be charged for subsequent extensions. In all cases, the procedure should be set in motion a couple of weeks before your time runs out. If you don't have a work permit, you will be required to present pink, personalized bank **exchange receipts** (see "Currency Regulations", p.32) totalling at least 500,000dr for the preceding three months, as proof that you have sufficient funds to support yourself without working. Possession of unexpired credit cards, a Greek savings account passbook or travellers' cheques can to some extent substitute for the pink receipts.

Certain individuals get around the law by leaving Greece every three months and re-entering a few days later, ideally via a different frontier post, for a new, ninety-day tourist stamp. However, with the recent flood of Albanian and eastern European refugees into the country, all looking for work, security and immigration personnel don't always look very kindly on this practice.

If you **overstay** your time and then leave under your own power – ie are not deported – you'll be given a 22,000dr spot fine upon departure, effectively a double-priced retroactive visa extension; no excuses will be entertained except perhaps a doctor's certificate stating you were immobilized in hospital. It cannot be overemphasized just how exigent Greek immigration officials often are on this issue.

GREEK EMBASSIES ABROAD

Australia 9 Turrana St, Yarralumla, Canberra, ACT 2600 (☎02/6273 3011).

Britain 1a Holland Park, London W11 3TP (☎020/7221 6467).

Canada 80 Maclaren St, Ottawa, ON K2P 0K6 (☎613/238-6271).

Ireland 1 Upper Pembroke St, Dublin 2 (☎01/676 7254).

New Zealand 5–7 Willeston St, Wellington (☎04/473 7775).

USA 2221 Massachusetts Ave NW, Washington DC 20008 (☎202/939-5800).

INSURANCE

British and other EU nationals are officially entitled to free medical care in Greece (see "Health Matters", p.28) upon presentation of an E111 form, available from most post offices. "Free", however, means admittance only to the lowest grade of state hospital (known as a *yenikó nosokomío*), and does not include nursing care or the cost of medication. Occasionally, hospital staff greet E111s with uncomprehending looks, in which case you may have to request reimbursal by the NHS upon your return home. If you need prolonged medical care, you should make use of private treatment, which is expensive – 8000dr minimum for a brief clinic consultation.

Some form of **travel insurance**, therefore, is advisable – and essential for **North Americans** and **Australasians**, whose countries have no formal health-care agreements with Greece (other than allowing for free emergency trauma treatment). For **medical claims**, keep receipts, including those from pharmacies. You will have to pay for all private medical care on the spot (insurance claims can be processed if you have hospital treatment) but it can all be (eventually) claimed back.

A typical travel insurance policy provides cover for the **loss** of baggage, tickets and – up to a certain limit – cash or cheques, as well as **cancellation or curtailment** of your journey. Most of them exclude "**dangerous sports**" unless an extra premium is paid: in the Greek islands this means motorbiking, windsurfing, paragliding and possibly sailing, with most visitors engaging in one or the other at some point. Read prospective policies carefully; coverage can vary wildly for roughly similar premiums and many policies can be adapted to exclude cover you don't need. If you take medical coverage, ascertain whether benefits will be paid as treatment proceeds or only after return home, and whether there is a **24-hour medical emergency number**. When securing baggage cover, make sure that the **per-**

TRAVEL INSURANCE COMPANIES

AUSTRALIA

Cover More ☎02/9202 8000 or ☎1800/251881
Ready Plan ☎03/9791 5077 or ☎1300/557 017

BRITAIN

Columbus Direct Insurance ☎020/7375 0011
Endsleigh Insurance ☎020/7436 4451
Marcus Hearne & Co Ltd ☎020/7739 3444
STA Travel ☎020/7361 6161
USIT Campus ☎0870/240 1010 (national call centre)
Worldwide Travel Insurance Services Ltd ☎01892/833 338

IRELAND

USIT Now ☎01/602 1600 or 679 8833

NEW ZEALAND

Ready Plan ☎09/300 5333

NORTH AMERICA

Access America ☎1-800/284 8300; Canada, ☎1-800/654-1908
Carefree Travel Insurance ☎1-800/323 3149
STA Travel ☎1-800/777 0112
Travel Guard ☎1-800/826 1300; Canada, ☎715/345-0505
Travel Insurance Services ☎1-800/937 1387
Worldwide Assistance ☎1-800/821 2828

article limit (typically under £500 equivalent) will cover your most valuable possession.

EUROPEAN COVER

In **Britain and Ireland**, travel insurance schemes (from around £25 for three weeks) are sold by a number of specialist insurance companies and travel agents, listed in the box opposite, as well as by banks or credit-card companies (such as American Express). Policies issued through the specialist companies listed are all good value; annual, multi-trip policies are available from about £90.

Most **banks** and **credit-card** issuers also offer some sort of vacation insurance, which is often automatic if you pay for the holiday with their card. However, it's vital to check just what these policies cover – usually only death or dismemberment.

Travel agents and tour operators are likely to **require** some sort of insurance when you book a package holiday, though after a change in the UK law in late 1998 they can no longer require you to buy their own. If you have a good "all risks" **home insurance policy** it *may* cover your possessions against loss or theft even when overseas. Many **private medical schemes** (such as BUPA or PPP) also offer coverage plans for abroad, which include baggage loss, cancellation or curtailment and cash replacement as well as sickness or accident.

NORTH AMERICAN COVER

Before buying an insurance policy, check that you're not already covered. **Canadians'** provincial health plans usually provide partial cover for medical mishaps overseas. Holders of official **student/teacher/youth cards** are entitled to (admittedly very meagre) accident coverage and hospital in-patient benefits. Students will often find that their student health coverage extends during the vacations and for one term beyond the date of last enrolment. **Bank and credit cards** often have certain levels of medical or other insurance included – as in the UK, check their limitations – and you may automatically get travel insurance if you use a major credit card to pay for your trip. **Homeowners' or renters' insurance** often covers theft or loss of documents, money and valuables while overseas, though conditions and maximum amounts vary from company to company.

After exhausting the possibilities above, you might want to contact a specialist **travel insurance company**; your travel agent can usually recommend one, or see the box opposite. The best deals are usually to be had through student/youth travel agencies – ISIS now offers STA Travel Insurance for travellers under the age of sixty. Coverage is worldwide and comes in packages covering seven days ($35), fifteen days ($55), one month ($115), 45 days ($155), two months ($180) and one year ($730) – add an extra $35–50 for each additional month on longer stays.

Most North American travel policies apply only to items lost, stolen or damaged while in the custody of an identifiable, responsible third party such as a hotel porter, an airline or a luggage consignment. Note also that very few insurers will arrange on-the-spot payments in the event of a major expense or loss; you will usually be **reimbursed** only after you've returned home.

AUSTRALIAN AND NEW ZEALAND COVER

In Australasia, travel insurance is put together by the airlines and travel agent groups (see box opposite) in conjunction with insurance companies. Policies are all comparable in cost and coverage; a typical one costs A$110/NZ$130 for two weeks, A$180/NZ$215 for one month, A$260/NZ$315 for two months.

INSURANCE REPORTS

In all cases of theft or loss of goods, you must contact the local police within a certain time limit to have a **report** made out so that your insurer can process the claim. This can occasionally prove tricky in Greece, since many officials simply won't accept that anything could be stolen on their turf, or at least don't want to take responsibility for it. Moreover, there have been enough fraudulent claims in recent years to make the police justifiably wary. Be persistent, and if necessary enlist the support of the local **tourist police** or tourist office.

HEALTH MATTERS

There are no required inoculations for Greece, though it's wise to ensure that you are up to date on tetanus and polio. Don't forget to take out travel insurance (see "Insurance", p.26), so that you're covered in case of serious illness or accidents.

The **water** is safe pretty much everywhere, though you will come across shortages or brackish supplies on some of the drier and more remote islands. Bottled water is widely available if you're feeling cautious.

SPECIFIC HAZARDS

The main health problems experienced by visitors have to do with **overexposure to the sun**, and the odd nasty from the sea. To combat the former, don't spend too long in the sun, cover up limbs, wear a hat and drink plenty of fluids in the hot months to avoid any danger of **sunstroke**; remember that even hazy sun can burn. For sea-gear, goggles or a dive mask for swimming and rubber footwear for walking over wet or rough rocks are useful.

HAZARDS OF THE DEEP

In the sea, you may have the bad luck to meet an armada of **jellyfish** (*tsoúkhtres*), especially in late summer; they come in various colours and sizes ranging from purple "pizzas" to invisible, minute creatures. Various over-the-counter remedies are sold in resort pharmacies; baking soda or diluted ammonia also help to lessen the sting. The welts and burning usually subside of their own accord within a few hours; there are no deadly man-of-war species in Greek waters.

Less vicious but more common are black, spiky **sea urchins** (*ahiní*), which infest rocky shorelines year-round; if you step on or graze one, a sewing needle (you can crudely sterilize it by heat from a cigarette lighter) and olive oil are effective for removing spines; if you don't extract them they'll fester. You can take your revenge by eating the roe of the reddish-purple ones, which is served as a delicacy in a few seafood restaurants.

The worst maritime danger – fortunately very rare – is the **weever fish** (*dhrákena*) which buries itself in tidal-zone sand with just its poisonous dorsal and gill spines protruding. If you tread on one, the sudden pain is excruciating, and the exceptionally potent venom can cause permanent paralysis of the affected area. Imperative first aid is to immerse your foot in water as hot as you can stand, which degrades the toxin and relieves the swelling of joints and attendant pain, but you should still seek medical attention as soon as possible.

Somewhat more common are **stingrays and skates** (Greek names include *platý*, *seláhi*, *vátos* or *trígona*), which frequent bays with sandy bottoms where they can camouflage themselves. Though shy, they can give you a nasty lash with their tail if trodden on, so shuffle your feet a bit when entering the water.

When snorkelling in deeper water, especially around Crete or the Dodecanese, you may happen upon a brightly coloured **moray eel** (*smérna*) sliding back and forth out of its rocky lair. Keep a respectful distance – their slightly comical air and clown-colours belie an irritable temper and the ability to inflict nasty bites or even sever fingers.

SANDFLIES, DOGS AND MOSQUITOES

If you are sleeping on or near a **beach**, it's wise to use insect repellent, either lotion or wrist/ankle bands, and/or a tent with a screen to guard against **sandflies**. Their bites are potentially dangerous, as these flies spread leishmaniasis, a parasitic infection characterized by chronic fever, listlessness and weight loss. It's difficult to treat, requiring long courses of medication.

In Greece, the main reservoirs for leishmaniasis are **dogs**. Transmission of the disease to humans by fleas has not been proven, but it's wisest not to befriend strays as they also carry echinococcosis, a debilitating liver fluke. In humans these form nodules and cysts which can only be removed surgically.

Mosquitoes (*kounóupia*) in Greece carry nothing worse than a vicious bite, but they can be infuriating. One solution is to burn pyrethrum incense coils (*spíres* or *fidhákia*), which are widely and cheaply available, if pungently malodorous. Better, if you can get them, are the small electrical devices (trade names Vape-Net or Bay-Vap) that vaporize an odourless insecticide tablet; many accommodation proprietors supply them routinely. Insect repellents such as Autan are available from most general stores and kiosks.

CREEPY-CRAWLIES

Adders (*ohiés*) and **scorpions** (*skorpií*) are found throughout Greece; both creatures are shy, but take care when climbing over dry-stone walls where snakes like to sun themselves, and don't put hands or feet in places, like shoes, where you haven't looked first.

Snakebites cause very few deaths in Europe. Many snakes will bite if threatened, whether they are venomous or not. If a bite injects venom, then swelling will normally occur within thirty minutes. If this happens, get medical attention; keep the bitten part still; and make sure all body movements are as gentle as possible. If medical attention is not nearby then bind the limb firmly to slow the blood circulation, but not so tightly as to stop the blood flow.

Many reptiles, including snakes, can harbour *Salmonella* bacteria, so should be handled cautiously and preferably not at all. This applies particularly to **tortoises**.

In addition to munching its way through a fair fraction of Greece's surviving pine forests, the **pine processionary caterpillar** – taking this name from the long, nose-to-tail convoys which individuals form at certain points in their life cycle – sports highly irritating hairs, with a poison worse than a scorpion's. If you touch one, or even a tree-trunk they've been on recently, you'll know all about it for a week, and the welts may require antihistamine to heal.

PHARMACIES AND DRUGS

For **minor complaints** it's enough to go to the local **farmakío**. Greek pharmacists are highly trained and dispense a number of medicines which elsewhere could only be prescribed by a doctor. In the larger towns and resorts there'll usually be one who speaks good English. Pharmacies are usually closed evenings and Saturday mornings, but all should have a monthly schedule (in both English and Greek) on their door showing the complete roster of night and weekend duty pharmacists in town. **Homeopathic and herbal remedies** are quite widely available too, and the largest towns have dedicated homeopathic pharmacies, identified by the characteristic green cross.

If you regularly use any form of **prescription drug**, you should bring along a copy of the prescription, together with the generic name of the drug; this will help should you need to replace it, and also avoids possible problems with customs officials. In this regard, it's worth being aware that **codeine is banned** in Greece. If you import any you might find yourself in serious trouble, so check labels carefully; it's the core ingredient of Panadeine, Veganin, Solpadeine, Codis and Empirin-Codeine, to name just a few common compounds.

Contraceptive pills are more readily available every year, but don't count on getting these – or spermicidal jelly/foam – outside of a few large island towns, over-the-counter at the larger *farmakía*; Greek women tend not to use any sort of birth control systematically, and have an average of four abortions during their adult life. **Condoms**, however, are inexpensive and ubiquitous – just ask for *profylaktiká* (the slangy terms *plastiká* or slightly vulgar *kapótes* are even better understood) at any pharmacy or corner *períptero* (kiosk).

Women's hygienic supplies are sold in pharmacies (*farmakía*), or in supermarkets near the toilet paper and diapers. Napkins ("Always" brand) are ubiquitous; tampons, known by the trademark catch-all of "Tampax", can be trickier to find in remoter spots, especially on the smaller islands. Where there are no Tampax as such you may have to make do with "OB".

Lastly, **hayfever** sufferers should be prepared for the early Greek pollen season, at its height from April to June. If you are taken by surprise, pharmacists stock tablets and creams, but it's cheaper to come prepared. Commercial antihistamines like Triludan are difficult to find in smaller towns, and local brands can cost upwards of £10/$16 equivalent for a pack of ten.

DOCTORS AND HOSPITALS

You'll find English-speaking **doctors** in any of the bigger towns or resorts; the tourist police, hotel staff or even your consulate should be able to come up with some names if you have any difficulty.

For **an ambulance**, phone ☎166. In **emergencies** – cuts, broken bones, etc – treatment is given free in **state hospitals**, though you will only get the most basic level of nursing care. Greek families routinely take in food and bedding for relatives, so as a tourist you'll be at a severe disadvantage. Somewhat better are the ordinary state-run **out-patient clinics** (*yiatría*) attached to most public hospitals and also found in rural locales. These operate on a first-come, first-served basis, so go early; usual hours are 8am to noon.

Don't forget to obtain **receipts** for the cost of all drugs and medical treatment; without them you won't be able to claim back the money on your travel insurance.

COSTS, MONEY AND BANKS

The cost of living in Greece has spiralled since full EU membership in 1981: the days of renting an island house for a few thousand drachmas a week are long gone, and food prices at corner shops now differ little from those of other member countries. However, outside the established resorts, travel between and around the islands remains reasonably priced, with the cost of restaurant meals, short-term accommodation and public transport still cheaper than anywhere in northern or western Europe except parts of Portugal.

Prices depend on where and when you go. Island capitals, larger tourist resorts and the trendier small islands (such as Sými, Sífnos and Pátmos) are more expensive, and costs everywhere increase sharply during July, August or Easter week. **Students** with an International Student Identity Card (ISIC) can usually get fifty percent discount off admission fees at many archeological sites and museums; those over 65 can rely on site-admission discounts of 25 to 30 percent. These, and other occasional discounts, tend to be more readily available to EU nationals.

SOME BASIC COSTS

On most islands a **daily per-person budget** of £21–24/US$34–39 will get you basic accommodation, breakfast, picnic lunch, a ferry or bus ride and a simple evening meal, as one of a couple. Camping would cut costs marginally. On £33–36/$54–59 a day you could be living quite well, plus sharing the cost of renting a large motorbike or small car.

Inter-island **ferries**, a main unavoidable expense, are reasonably priced, subsidized by the government in an effort to preserve remote island communities. A deck-class ticket for the four-hour trip from Rhodes to Kós costs about £7/US$10.50, while Sámos to Híos, another four- or five-hour journey, runs to just £6/US$10. For even less you can catch a ferry to the numerous small islands that lie closer to Rhodes, Kós and Sámos, the most likely touchdown points if you're flying in on a direct charter.

The simplest double **room** generally costs around £11–15/$18–25 a night, depending on the location and the plumbing arrangements. Bona fide single rooms are rare, and cost about seventy percent of double rates. Organized **campsites** are little more than £2.50/US$3.75 per person, with similar charges per tent and perhaps 25 percent more for a camper van. With discretion you can camp for free in the more remote, rural areas.

A basic taverna **meal** with local wine can be had for around £6/US$10 a head. Add a better bottle of wine, seafood or more careful cooking, and it could be up to £10/US$16 a head; you'll rarely pay more than that except in Ródhos Town. Sharing seafood, Greek salads and dips is a good way to keep costs down in the better restaurants, and even in the most developed of resorts, with inflated "international" menus, you'll often be able to find a more earthy but decent taverna where the locals eat.

CURRENCY

The Greek currency is the **drachma** (*dhrakhmí*), and the exchange rate is currently around 500dr to the pound sterling, or 300dr to the US dollar.

The most common **notes** in circulation are those of 100, 500, 1000, 5000 and 10,000 drachmas (*dhrakhmés*), while **coins** come in denominations of 5, 10, 20, 50 and 100dr; you might come across 1dr and 2dr coins, and 50dr bills, too, though they're rarely used these days. In 1998 a new, compact 5000dr note was introduced which is very easily confused with the 500dr one, so beware. In practice, shopkeepers rarely bother with differences of under 20dr – whether in your favour, or theirs.

BANKS AND EXCHANGE

Greek **banks** are normally open Monday to Thursday 8.30am–2pm, Friday 8.30am–1.30pm. Certain branches in the major towns or tourist centres are open extra hours in the evenings and on Saturday mornings for exchanging money. Always take your passport with you as proof of identity and be prepared for at least one long line; sometimes you have to line up once to have the transaction approved, and again to pick up the cash.

Outside these times, the largest hotels and **travel agencies** can often provide this service, albeit sometimes with hefty commissions. On small islands with no full-service bank, "authorized" bank agents will charge yet another extra fee (1–2 percent) to cover the cost of posting a travellers' cheque or Eurocheque to the main branch.

The safest way to carry money is in **travellers' cheques**. These can be obtained from banks (even if you don't have an account) or from offices of Thomas Cook and American Express; you'll usually pay a commission of between one and two percent, though it pays to be aware of any special commission-free deals. You can cash the cheques at most banks, though rarely elsewhere. Each travellers' cheque transaction in Greece will incur a **commission** charge of 400–800dr, so you won't want to change too many small amounts.

Small-denomination **foreign bank notes** are also extremely useful, and relatively unlikely to be stolen in Greece (see "Police and Trouble", p.67). Since the freeing up of all remaining currency controls in 1994, a number of authorized brokers for exchanging foreign cash have emerged in major tourist centres. When changing small amounts, choose those bureaux that charge a flat percentage commission (usually one percent) rather than a high minimum. There also a small number of 24-hour automatic **foreign-note-changing machines** in a few resorts, but again a high minimum commission tends to be deducted.

Alternatively, most British banks can issue current account holders with a **Eurocheque** card and chequebook, with which you can pay for expensive items in certain shops, and withdraw money from cash dispensers (if the card has a PIN number) or at bank counters. An annual or biennial fee is charged for issuing the card, while each cheque attracts a two percent processing charge on the debit facility subject to a minimum of £1.75, but there's no on-the-spot commission levied on transactions. Indeed, if you use this scheme to obtain over £85 equivalent, it is one of the cheaper ways of getting money abroad, and unlike with travellers' cheques the money stays in your account until the Eurocheque is presented from Greece, usually three weeks later. The current limit is 50,000dr per cheque, and the bank or merchant does not need to know the prevailing exchange rate – useful if bank computers have gone down.

In 1998, the Greek **post office** abandoned the business of changing money – a nuisance, as many tiny islands have a post office but no bank. If you have a UK-based Girobank account, you can, however, use your chequebook to get money at remote post offices.

Finally, there is no need to purchase drachmas **before arrival** unless you're coming in at some ungodly hour to one of the remoter land or sea frontier posts, or on a Sunday. Airport arrival lounges will always have an exchange booth or cash dispenser for passengers on incoming international flights.

CREDIT CARDS AND CASH DISPENSERS

Major **credit cards** are not usually accepted by cheaper tavernas or hotels, but they're almost essential for renting cars, for buying Olympic Airways tickets and for expensive souvenirs. If you run short of money, you can get an over-the-counter **cash advance** on a credit card, but be warned that the minimum amount is 15,000dr. The Emboriki Trapeza (Commercial Bank) handles Visa, while the Ethniki Trapeza (National Bank) services Access/Mastercard customers. However, there is usually a two-percent charge on the total, high additional transaction fees and always interminable delays while approval is sought by telex.

It is far simpler to use the growing network of Greek **cash dispensers**, by learning the PIN numbers for your debit/credit cards. Larger airports (such as Athens, Crete, Rhodes and Thessaloníki) have at least one of these in the arrivals hall, and almost any island with a population larger than a few thousand (or a substantial tourist traffic) also has at least one. The most well distributed are those of the National Bank/Ethniki Trapeza and the Commercial Bank/Emboriki Trapeza, which happily and interchangeably accept Visa, Mastercard, Plus, Cirrus and Eurocheque cards; those of the Alfa Trapeza Pisteos/Alpha Credit Bank and its subsidiary the Ionian Bank/Ioniki Trapeza are less widespread and somewhat more restrictive – for example, Alpha Credit cash dispensers accept only American Express and Visa cards.

Cash dispenser transactions with **debit cards** linked to a cheque account via the Plus/Cirrus systems attract charges of two percent on the sterling transaction value, subject to a minimum of £1.50, making them slightly cheaper than Eurocheques, and indeed the **least expensive** way of getting money in Greece as long as you withdraw more than £75 equivalent. By contrast, using **credit cards** at a cash dispenser is one of the **dearest** ways of obtaining cash: a cash advance per-transaction fee of £1.50 minimum, plus a "foreign transaction" fee of up to 2.75 percent on the total, depending on the card issuer.

EMERGENCY CASH

All told, learning and using the PIN numbers for any debit or credit cards you have is the quickest and least expensive way of securing moderate amounts of emergency funds from abroad. In an emergency, however, you can arrange to have **money sent** from home to a bank in Greece. Receiving funds via telex takes a minimum of three days and often up to seven days, so be prepared for delays. From the UK, a bank charge of three percent, or minimum £17, maximum £35, is levied. Bank drafts can also be sent, with higher commission rates. You can retrieve the amount in foreign currency, or even as travellers' cheques, but still more onerous commissions will apply.

Funds can also be sent via Western Union Money Transfer (☎0800/833833 in the UK, 1-800/325-6000 in North America). Exact fees depend on the amount being transferred and the destination, but as examples, wiring £400–500 should cost around £37, while $1000 will cost around $75. The American Express MoneyGram (☎0800/894887 in the UK, 1-800/543-4080 in North America) is now only available to American Express cardholders. Funds should be available for collection at Amex's or Western Union's local office within minutes of being sent.

CURRENCY REGULATIONS

Since 1994, Greek **currency restrictions** no longer apply to Greek nationals and other EU member citizens, and since Greece's entry into the European ERM in 1998, the drachma is totally convertible. Arcane rules may still apply to arrivals from North America, Australia or non-EU nations, but you would have to be extremely unlucky to run foul of them.

If you have reason to believe that you'll be acquiring large quantities of drachmas – from work or sale of valuables (though the latter is officially illegal) – declare all monetary devices on arrival, then request (and save) pink, personalized receipts for all **bank exchange transactions**. Otherwise you may find that you can only re-exchange a limited sum of drachmas on departure; even at the best of times many banks stock a limited range of foreign notes – your best bet is often the exchange booth in airport arivals (not departures). These pink receipts are also essential for obtaining a non-employment resident visa (see p.25).

INFORMATION AND MAPS

The National Tourist Organization of Greece (*Ellinikós Organismós Tourismoú*, or EOT; GNTO abroad) maintains offices in most European capitals, plus major cities in North America and Australia (see box below for addresses). It publishes an impressive array of free, glossy, regional pamphlets, which are good for getting an idea of where you want to go, even if the actual text should sometimes be taken with an occasional pinch of salt. Also available from the EOT are a reasonable fold-out map of the country and a large number of brochures on special interests and festivals.

TOURIST OFFICES

In Greece, you will find official **EOT offices** in most of the larger towns and resorts. The principal Athens office is at Amerikís 2, just up from Stadhíou. Here, in addition to the usual leaflets, you can pick up weekly **schedules** for the inter-island **ferries** – not one hundred percent reliable, but useful as a guideline. The EOT staff are themselves very helpful for advice on **ferry**, **bus** and **train** departures as well as new opening hours for sites and museums, and occasionally can give assistance with accommodation.

Where there is no EOT office, you can get information (and often a range of leaflets) from municipally run tourist offices, for example in Kós Town, Argostóli (Kefalloniá) and Mólyvos (Lésvos) – these are often very good and highly motivated. In the absence of any of these, you can visit the **tourist police**, essentially a branch (often just a single delegate) of the local police. They can sometimes provide you with lists of rooms to let, which they regulate.

GREEK NATIONAL TOURIST OFFICES ABROAD

Australia
51 Pitt St, Sydney NSW 2000 (☎02/9241 1663)

Britain
4 Conduit St, London W1R 0DJ (☎020/7734 5997)

Canada
1300 Bay St, Upper Level, Toronto, ON M5R 3K8 (☎416/968-2220); 1233 rue de la Montagne, H3G 1Z2, Montréal, Quebec (☎514/871-1535)

Denmark
Copenhagen Vester Farimagsgade 1, 2 DK 1606-Kobenhavn V (☎325-332)

Netherlands
Leidsestraat 13, NS 1017 Amsterdam (☎20/254-212)

Norway
Ovre Stottsgate 15B, 0157 Oslo 1 (☎2/426-501)

Sweden
Grev Turigatan 2, PO Box 5298, 10246 Stockholm (☎8/679 6480)

US
645 Fifth Ave, New York, NY 10022 (☎212/421-5777); 168 North Michigan Ave, Chicago, IL (☎312/782-1084); 611 West 6th St, Suite #2198 Los Angeles, CA (☎213/626-6696)

If your home country isn't listed here, apply to the embassy.
Note that there are no Greek tourist offices in Ireland or New Zealand.

MAPS

No authoritative, authentic maps . . . . Well, isn't that as it should be? Why does anybody need maps? If an individual wants them he's a spy. If a country needs maps it's moribund. A well-mapped country is a dead country. A complete survey is a burial shroud. A life with maps is a tyranny!

That extract from Alan Sillitoe's 1971 satire, *Travels in Nihilon*, pretty much sums up the prevailing attitude towards **maps** in Greece, which are an endless source of confusion and often outright misinformation. Each cartographic company seems to have its own peculiar system of transcribing Greek letters into English – and these, as often as not, do not match the semi-official transliterations on the road signs. Maps of **individual islands** are more easily available on the spot, and while most are wildly inaccurate or obsolete, a rare few are reliable and up to date.

The most reliable **general touring maps** of Greece are those published by Athens-based Road Editions (*www.road.gr*). They're available in Greece at selected bookstores, including their own retail outlet in Athens, or in Britain at Stanfords and other quality travel shops. In case of difficulty, contact (in Britain) Portfolio, Unit 1C, West Ealing Business Centre, Alexandria Road, London W13 0NJ (☎020/8579 7748). In the US, they're sold exclusively through Map Link (see address in box below) or Omni Resources, PO Box 2096, Burlington NC 27216 (☎910/227-8300). These are not perfect – no Greek map is – but, based on large-scale military maps not available to the public, they're the best you will find. To date their island products

MAP OUTLETS

AUSTRALIA

Adelaide

The Map Shop, 16a Peel St, Adelaide (☎08/8231 2033).

Brisbane

Worldwide Maps & Guides, 187 George St, Brisbane (☎07/3221 4330).

Melbourne

Mapland, 372 Little Bourke St, Melbourne (☎03/9670 4383).

Perth

Perth Map Centre, 891 Hay St, Perth (☎08/9322 5733).

Sydney

Travel Bookshop, 3/175 Liverpool St, Sydney (☎02/9261 8200).

CANADA

Montréal

Ulysses Travel Bookshop, 4176 St-Denis, Montréal, PQ H2W 2M5 (☎514/289-0993).

Toronto

Open Air Books and Maps, 25 Toronto St, Toronto ON M5R 2C1 (☎416/363-0719).

Vancouver

International Travel Maps and Books, 552 Seymour St, Vancouver V6Z 1G3 (☎604/687-3320).

World Wide Books and Maps, 1247 Granville St, Vancouver, BC V6Z 1E4 (☎604/687-3320).

IRELAND

Easons Bookshop, 40 O'Connell St, Dublin 1 (☎01/873 3811).

Fred Hanna's Bookshop, 27–29 Nassau St, Dublin 2 (☎01/677 1255).

Hodges Figgis Bookshop, 56–58 Dawson St, Dublin 2 (☎01/677 4754).

Waterstone's, Queens Building, 8 Royal Ave, Belfast BT1 1DA (☎02890/247355); 69 Patrick St, Cork (☎021/276522); 7 Dawson St, Dublin 2 (☎01/679 1415).

NEW ZEALAND

Specialty Maps, 58 Albert St, Auckland (☎09/307 2217).

BRITAIN

London

Daunt Books, 83 Marylebone High St, London W1M 3DE (☎020/7224 2295).

National Map Centre, 22–24 Caxton St, London SW1H 0QU (☎020/7222 2466).

Stanfords, 12–14 Long Acre, London WC2E 9LP (☎020/7836 1321); inside Campus Travel at 52 Grosvenor Gardens, London SW1W 0AG (☎020/7730 1314); inside British Airways at 156 Regent St, London W1R 5TA (☎020/7434 4744). Maps available by mail or phone order.

include Crete at 1:250,000, plus a steadily growing number of titles for smaller ones, including Rhodes, Kós, Sýros, Corfu, Thíra, Kéa, Mílos, Zákynthos, Ándhros, Náxos, Páros, Mýkonos, Sámos, Kefalloniá–Itháki, Kýthira, Paxí and Lefkádha.

If Road products are unavailable, good second choices are the GeoCenter maps *Greece and the Islands* and *Greek Islands/Aegean Sea*, which together cover the country at a scale of 1:300,000. The single-sided fold-up Freytag-Berndt 1:650,000, with an index, is very nearly as good, and easier to use when driving. Despite recent revisions and updating, Michelin #980 remains a fourth choice. All these are widely available in Britain and North America, though less easily in Greece; see the list of overseas map outlets in the box below. Freytag-Berndt also publishes a series of more detailed maps on various regions of Greece, such as the Cyclades and the northeast Aegean islands (in two sheets); these are best bought overseas from specialist outlets, though in Greece they are re-jacketed and distributed by Efstathiadis.

HIKING/TOPOGRAPHICAL MAPS

Hiking/topographical maps, subject to uneven quality and availability, are gradually improving, but understandably devoted only to mainland mountain areas. Most of these commercial products (issued by Road, Korfes magazine or Anavisi) are based on the older maps of the **Yeografikí Ipiresía Stratoú** (Army Geographical Service, or YIS). If you want to obtain these for islands, visit the YIS at Evelpídhon 4, north of Aréos Park in Athens, on Monday, Wednesday or Friday from

The Travel Bookshop, 13–15 Blenheim Crescent, London W11 2EE (☎020/7229 5260).

John Smith and Sons, 57–61 St Vincent St, Glasgow G2 5TB (☎0141/221 7472).

THE REST OF ENGLAND AND WALES

Austick's City Bookshop, 91 The Headrow, Leeds LS1 6OJ (☎0113/243 3099).

Blackwell's, 156–160 West St, Sheffield S1 3ST (☎0114/273 8906); 13–17 Royal Arcade, Cardiff CF1 2PR (☎029/2039 5036); 32 Stonegate, York YO1 2AP (☎01904/624531); also trading as Blackwell's University Bookshop, Alsop Building, Brownlow Hill, Liverpool L3 5TX (☎0151/709 8146) and Blackwell's Map and Travel Shop, 53 Broad St, Oxford OX1 3BQ (☎01865/568467).

Heffers Map Shop, 20 Trinity St, Cambridge, and 19 Sidney St, 3rd Flr, Cambridge CB2 3HL (☎01223/568467).

The Map Shop, 30a Belvoir St, Leicester LE1 6QH (☎0116/247 1400).

Newcastle Map Centre, 55 Grey St, Newcastle upon Tyne NE1 6EF (☎0191/261 5622).

Stanfords, 29 Corn St, Bristol BS1 1HT (☎0117/929 9966).

Waterstone's, 91 Deansgate, Manchester M3 2BW (☎0161/832 1992).

SCOTLAND

Aberdeen Map Shop, 74 Skene St, Aberdeen AB10 1QE (☎01224/637999).

James Thin Melven's Bookshop, 29 Union St, Inverness IV1 1QA (☎01463/233500).

US

Book Passage, 51 Tamal Vista Blvd, Corte Madera, CA 94925 (☎415/927-0960).

The Complete Traveler Bookstore, 199 Madison Ave, New York, NY 10016 (☎212/685-9007); 3207 Fillmore St, San Francisco, CA 92123 (☎415/923-1511).

Eliot Bay Book Company, 101 S Main St, Seattle, WA 98104 (☎206/624-6600).

Forsyth Travel Library, 226 Westchester Ave, White Plains, NY 10604 (☎1-800/367-7984).

Map Link Inc, 30 S La Patera Lane, Unit 5, Santa Barbara, CA 93117 (☎805/692-6777).

Phileas Fogg's Books & Maps, #87 Stanford Shopping Center, Palo Alto, CA 94304 (☎1-800/533-FOGG).

Rand McNally, 444 N Michigan Ave, Chicago, IL 60611 (☎312/321-1751); 150 E 52nd St, New York, NY 10022 ☎(212/758-7488); 595 Market St, San Francisco, CA 94105 (☎415/777-3131); 1201 Connecticut Ave NW, Washington, DC 20003 (☎202/223-6751). Or call ☎1-800/333-0136 (ext 2111) for the address of your nearest store/direct mail order.

Sierra Club Bookstore, 6014 College Ave, Oakland, CA 94618 (☎510/658-7470).

Traveler's Choice Bookstore, 22 W 52nd St, New York, NY 10019 (☎212/664-0995).

8am to noon only. All foreigners must leave their passport with the gate guard; EU citizens may proceed directly to the sales hall, where efficient, computerized transactions take just a few minutes. Other nationals will probably have to go upstairs for an interview; if you don't speak reasonably good Greek, it's best to have a Greek friend get them for you.

As of writing, YIS maps covering Crete, the Dodecanese, the east Aegean, Skýros, most of Corfu and much of Epirus, Macedonia and Thrace are still off-limits to all foreigners and Greeks alike. With matters unsettled across the Balkans, previous plans to lift such restrictions have been shelved indefinitely. A German company, **Harms**, has released a series of five maps at 1:80,000 scale which cover Crete from west to east and show, with about fifty percent accuracy, many hiking routes; despite these defects, they're invaluable until and unless the YIS declassifies this area, and are available overseas at specialist map outlets.

Finally, for hiking in particular areas of Crete, Corfu, Sámos, Rhodes, Sými, Thássos and Lésvos, **maps-with-guide-booklets** published by Marengo Publications in Britain also prove very useful. Stanfords keeps a good stock of these, or order from Marengo direct at 17 Bernard Crescent, Hunstanton PE36 6ER (☎01485/532710, *marengo@supanet.com*).

GETTING AROUND

Island-hopping is an essential feature of a Greek holiday; the ferry network – supplemented in season by hydrofoils – is extensive, and will eventually get you to any of the 166 inhabited isles. Planes are relatively expensive, at three to four times the cost of a deck-class ferry ticket and almost twice as much as first or cabin class. They are, however, useful for saving time at the start or finish of a visit, providing critical links between smaller islands and Athens, Thessaloníki, Rhodes and Crete. Once on the islands themselves, buses provide skeletal connections, which most tourists choose to supplement by renting a scooter, motorbike or car.

FERRIES

There are three different varieties of vessel carrying passengers (and often vehicles): medium-sized to large **ordinary ferries** (which operate the main services), **hydrofoils** (run by Minoan "Flying Dolphins", Samos Hydrofoils and Dodecanese Hydrofoils, among several companies) and local **kaïkia** (small boats which do short hops and excursions in season). Costs are very reasonable on the longer journeys, though proportionately more expensive for shorter, inter-island connections. Short-haul lines with monopolies – for example Alexandhroúpoli–Samothráki and Kými–Skýros – are invariably overpriced for the distance involved.

We've indicated most of the **ferry connections**, both on the maps (see pp.72–73 for a general pattern) and in the "Travel Details" at the end of each chapter. Don't take our listings as exhaustive or wholly reliable, however, as schedules are notoriously erratic, and must be verified each year; details given are essentially for departures between June and September. **Out of season**, departure frequencies are severely reduced, with many islands connected only once or twice a week. However, in spring or autumn those ferries that do operate are often compelled by the transport ministry to call at extra or unusual islands, making possible some interesting connections.

The most reliable, up-to-date information is available from the local **port police** (*limenarhío*), which maintains offices at Pireás (☎01/42 26 000) and on or near the harbours of all fair-sized islands. Smaller places may only have a *limenikós stathmós* (marine post), often just a single room with a VHF radio. Their officers rarely speak much English, but keep complete schedules posted – and, meteorological report in hand, are the final arbiters of whether a ship will sail or not in stormy weather conditions. *Apagorevtikó*, or obligatory halt of all seaborne traffic, is applied for weather in excess of force 7 on the Beaufort scale; hydrofoils are confined to port at force 6 or above.

Few domestic ferry or hydrofoil companies, with the exceptions of Miniotis Lines, NEL Lines and Samos Hydrofoils, produce regular **schedule** sheets. The only attempt at an all-inclusive Greek ferry guide is the yearly "Greek Travel Routes, Domestic Sea Schedules", co-produced by the GNTO and the Greek travel agents' manual the GTP; be prepared to master an array of bewildering abbreviations for ports and shipping companies. The printed guide is usually available at GNTO/EOT offices, but you'll find a more reliable, regularly updated version at *www.gtpnet.com*.

REGULAR FERRIES

On most **ferry** routes, your only consideration will be getting a boat that leaves on the day, and for the island, that you want. However, when sailing from **Pireás**, the port of Athens, to the Cyclades or Dodecanese islands, you should have a choice of at least two, often three, sailings and may want to consider a few of the factors below.

Most importantly, bear in mind that **routes** taken and the speed of the boats vary enormously. A journey from Pireás to Thíra (Santoríni), for instance, can take anything from nine to fourteen hours. Prior to buying a ticket it's wise to establish how many stops there will be before your island, and the estimated time of arrival. Many agents act just for one specific boat (they'll blithely tell you that theirs is the only available service), so you may have to ask around to uncover alternatives. Especially in high season, early arrival is critical in getting what may be a very limited stock of accommodation.

The **boats** themselves have improved somewhat since the early 1990s, with a fair number of elderly rustbuckets consigned to the scrap heap or dumped overseas. Just about the only ferries you might want to avoid if you have the choice, especially for overnight journeys, is Agapitos Lines' *Golden Vergina* (on the line to Páros, Ikaría and Sámos) and the *Ayios Rafael*, run by NEL in the northeast Aegean. You will more often than not be surprised to encounter a former English Channel or Scandinavian fjord ferry, rechristened and enjoying a new lease of life in the Aegean.

Regular ferry **tickets** are, in general, best bought on the day of departure, unless you need to reserve a cabin berth or space for a car. Buying tickets in advance will tie you down to a particular ferry at a particular time – and innumerable factors can make you regret that. Most obviously there's bad weather; particularly off-season, it can play havoc with the schedules, causing some small boats to remain at anchor and others to alter their routes drastically. (The ticket price is refunded if a boat fails to sail.) There are only three periods of the year – March 23–25, the week before and after Easter, and mid-August – when ferries need to be booked at least a couple of days in advance.

Following cases in 1996 of captains loading ferries to double their rated capacity, **obligatory advance ticketing** was universally introduced in 1998. Larger, reputable companies such as ANEK and DANE have been computerized for some years anyway. Staff at the gangway may bar you from embarking if you don't have a ticket, and should you succeed in sneaking aboard, you will find that tickets sold at the *loyistírio* (purser's office) will have a stiff surcharge attached (usually 20–30 percent). **Fares** for each route are currently set by the transport ministry and should not differ among ships or agencies, though curiously, tickets for journeys towards Athens are marginally more expensive than those in the opposite direction.

The cheapest class of ticket, which you'll probably automatically be sold, is **deck class**, variously called *tríti* or *gámma*. This gives you the run of most boats except for the upper-class restaurant and bar. On the shorter, summer journeys the best place to be, in any case, is on deck – space best staked out as soon as you get on board. However, boats fitted out recently seem, with their glaring overhead lights and moulded-plastic bucket seats, expressly designed to frustrate those attempting to sleep on deck. In such cases it's well worth the few thousand extra drachmas for a cabin bunk, especially if you can share with friends (cabins are usually quadruple). Class consciousness has increased of late, so deck-class passengers may find themselves firmly locked out of second-class facilities at night to prevent them from crashing on the plush sofas, and may have to make do with pullman-type seats. First-class cabins usually cost scarcely less than a plane flight and are not terrific value – the main difference between first and second being the presence of a bathroom in the cabin, and sometimes two bunks rather than four. Most cabins, incidentally, are overheated or overchilled, and pretty airless; ask for an *exoterikí* (outer) cabin if you want a porthole (though these are always bolted shut).

Occasionally, with non-computerized companies, you will be sold a cabin berth at an intermediate port only to find that they are "full" when the boat arrives. Pursers will usually not refund you the difference between a cabin and third class. Your first- or second-class fare entitles you to a bunk, and this is clearly stated (in Greek) on the verso of your ticket. Make a scene if necessary until you are accommodated – there are often cabins in the bilge, set aside for the crew but generally unused, where you can sleep.

Motorbikes and **cars** get issued extra tickets, in the latter case up to four times the passenger fare. This obviously limits the number of islands you'll want to drag a car to from the mainland – it's really only worth it for the larger ones like Crete, Rhodes, Híos, Lésvos, Sámos, Corfu or Kefalloniá. Even with these, unless you're planning a stay of more than four days, you may find it cheaper to leave your car on the mainland and rent another on arrival. Technically, written permission is required to take rental motorbikes and cars on ferries, though in practice few crew will bother to quiz you on this.

Long-haul ferries sell a limited range of **food on board**, though it tends to be overpriced and mediocre. Honourable exceptions are the meals served by DANE, NEL and all ferries to Crete on their overnight sailings. On the short, daytime hops between the various islands of the Argo-Saronic, Cyclades and Sporades, it's a good idea to stock up beforehand with your own provisions; most ferries on these lines offer nothing other than biscuits, coffee and soft drinks.

HYDROFOILS

Hydrofoils – commonly known as *dhelfínia* (after the Minoan "Flying Dolphins") – are roughly twice as fast (and at least twice as expensive) as ordinary ferries. However, they're a useful alternative to regular ferries if you are pushed for time, and their network can also neatly fill gaps in ferry scheduling. Their main drawback is that they were originally designed for cruising on placid Russian or Polish rivers, and are quite literally out of their depth on the open sea; thus they are extremely sensitive to bad weather, and even in a moderate swell are not for the seasick-prone. Most of these services don't operate – or are heavily reduced – from October to June and are prone to arbitrary cancellation if not enough passengers turn up.

At present, hydrofoils operate among the **Argo-Saronic islands** close to Athens, down the east coast of the **Peloponnese** to Monemvassiá and **Kýthira**, among the **northern Sporades** (Évvia, Skýros, Skiáthos, Skópelos and Alónissos), between Kavála and **Thássos**, between Alexandhroúpoli and Samothráki (occasionally out to Límnos), among certain of the **Cyclades** (Ándros, Tínos, Mýkonos, Páros, Náxos, Amorgós, the minor islets, Íos, Thíra), and in the **Dodecanese** and east Aegean among Rhodes, Kós, Kálymnos, Léros and Pátmos, with regular forays up to Sámos, Ikaría and Foúrni, or over to Tílos and Níssyros. The principal **mainland ports** are Zéa and Flísvos marinas in Pireás, Rafína, Vólos, Áyios Konstandínos and Thessaloníki, as well as Kavála and Alexandhroúpoli.

Schedules and **tickets** for the Minoan Flying Dolphins company, which also operates high-speed catamarans to the Cyclades, are available from their head office in Athens at Filellínon 3, off Platía Sýndagma (☎01/32 44 600); in Pireás at Aktí Themistokléous 8 (☎01/42 80 001); in Vólos from Andonopoúlou 9–11 (☎0421/39 786); and in Thessaloníki from Kriti Travel, Íonos Dhragoúmi 1 (☎031/547 454). The Cyclades catamarans have separate booking numbers (☎01/75 12 356, fax ☎01/68 98 344). Samos Hydrofoils, based on Sámos in Vathý, tends to be more reliable than Dodecanese Hydrofoils, which has hubs on Kós and Rhodes. You may see craft with other livery, but we have excluded them, as they are chartered by tour agencies and do not offer scheduled services controlled by the ministry of transport.

KAÏKIA AND OTHER SMALL FERRIES

In season **kaïkia** (caiques) and small ferries of a few hundred tonnes' displacement sail between adjacent islands and to a few of the more obscure ones. These can be extremely useful and often very pleasant, but are no cheaper than mainline services. In fact, if they're classified as **tourist**

agency charters, and not passenger lines controlled by the transport ministry, they tend to be quite expensive, with pressure to buy return fares (one-ways almost always available). The more consistent kaïki links are summarized in the "Travel Details" section of each island chapter, though inevitably departures depend on the whims of local boat-owners, so the only firm information is to be had on the quayside. Kaïkia and small ferries, despite appearances, have a good safety record; indeed it's the larger, overloaded carferries that have in the past run into trouble.

DOMESTIC FLIGHTS

Olympic Airways and its subsidiary Olympic Aviation operate most of the **domestic flights** within Greece. They cover a fairly wide network of islands and larger mainland towns, though most routes are to and from Athens or Thessaloníki. Airline operation has been officially deregulated in Greece since 1993, but few private airlines have successfully challenged the state-run carrier. Air Greece and Cronus both serve the high-volume routes between Crete, Rhodes, Athens and Thessaloníki, while Air Manos has about a dozen routes to and between the central and southeast Aegean, but only reliably operates from June to October – with booking via designated local travel agents. All three airlines undercut Olympic prices by a fair margin, though frequencies tend to be relatively sparse.

For the moment, Olympic **schedules** can be picked up at their offices abroad (see "Getting There" sections) or from their branches and representatives in Greece, which are found in almost every town or island of any size; Greek-only booklets, which include prices for domestic routes, are published twice yearly (early April and late June), as are English-language books geared towards an international readership (March and October).

Fares for flights to and between the islands, including the domestic airport tax of about £7/$11, work out around three to four times the cost of a ferry journey, but on inter-island hauls that are poorly served by boat (Rhodes–Kastellórizo or Kárpathos–Kássos, for example), you can consider this time well bought. Flights between Athens and Mílos, Kýthira and Préveza (for Lefkádha) are slightly better value per air mile, so take advantage.

Island flights are often full in peak season; if they're an essential part of your plans, it is worth trying to make a **reservation** at least a week to ten days in advance. Domestic air tickets are non-refundable, but you can change your flight, space permitting, without penalty as late as a day before your original departure.

The only surviving Olympic-run **shuttle buses** between the main town and the airport are on Kós and Kastellórizo. In other places (Corfu, Híos, Rhodes), municipally run services have picked up the slack, but elsewhere you're at the mercy of the taxi-drivers who congregate outside the arrivals gate.

Like ferries, flights are subject to **cancellation** in bad weather, since many services are on small, 50- or 68-seat ATR prop planes that won't fly in strong winds. A flight on a Dornier puddle-jumper is recommended at least once; you can watch the crew flicking switches in the cockpit and you fly low enough to pick out every island feature.

Size restrictions mean that the 15-kilo **baggage weight limit** is fairly strictly enforced; if, however, you've just arrived from overseas or purchased your ticket outside Greece, you are allowed the 23-kilo standard international limit. All services operated on the domestic network are **non-smoking**.

ISLAND GROUND TRANSPORT

Most islands have some kind of bus service, but many visitors prefer to rent a two- or four-wheeler. Even if you just do this for a day, you can get the measure of a small or medium-sized island and work out where you'd like to be based.

BUSES

Bus services on the **major routes** are highly efficient and frequent. On **secondary roads** they're less regular, but even the most remote villages will be connected – at least on weekdays – by a school or market bus to the island capital. As these often leave shortly after dawn, an alarm clock may come in useful. Coming in the opposite direction, these local buses generally leave the county town (or on Crete, the provincial) at about 2pm. There are usually buses to connect the port and main town for ferry arrivals or departures.

The network is nationally run by a single syndicate known as the **KTEL** (Kratikó Tamío Ellinikón Leoforíon). In medium-sized towns there can be several scattered terminals for services in different directions (as at Iráklion, Crete) or separate terminals for suburban and long-distance routes (Híos, Mytilíni), so make sure you have the right station for your departure.

Buses are usually amazingly **prompt**, so be there in plenty of time for scheduled departures. On smaller island routes, it's generally first come, first served, with some standing allowed; tickets are dispensed on board by an *ispráktoros*, or conductor.

MOTORBIKES, SCOOTERS AND MOPEDS

The cult of the **motorcycle** is highly developed in Greece, presided over by a jealous deity apparently requiring regular human sacrifice. Accidents among bikers are routine occurrences, with annual fatalities edging into two figures on the busier islands. Some package companies have taken to warning clients in print against renting motorbikes (thereby making extra on organized excursions), but with caution and common sense – and an eye to increasingly enforced regulations – piloting a two-wheeler through a resort should be a lot safer than in London or New York.

Many tourists come to grief on rutted dirt tracks or astride mechanically dodgy machines. In other cases **accidents** are caused by riding two on a scooter underpowered to propel such a load. Don't be tempted by the apparent economy – you won't regret getting two separate machines, or one powerful bike to share – and remember that you're likely to be charged an exorbitant sum for any repairs if you do have a wipeout. Above all, verify that your travel insurance policy covers motorcycle accidents.

One worthwhile precaution is to wear a **crash helmet** (*kránio*); most rental outfits will offer you one, and some will make you sign a waiver of liability if you refuse it. Helmet-wearing is required by law, but few riders (except army conscripts) wear them – though compliance is increasing as police set up random roadblocks to catch offenders. Reputable establishments demand a full motorcycle driving licence for any engine over 90cc (the law actually stipulates "over 50cc"), and you will usually have to leave your passport as security. For smaller models, any driving licence will do.

Mopeds and small **motor scooters**, known in Greek as **papákia** (little ducks) after their characteristic noise, are good transport for all but the hilliest islands. They're available for rent on most islands for 3000dr a day (mopeds) or 4000–5500dr (scooters and small motorbikes). These specimen rates can be bargained down out of peak season, or if you negotiate for a longer period of rental.

Before riding off, make sure you check the bike's mechanical state, since many are only cosmetically maintained. Bad brakes and worn or oil-fouled spark plugs are the most common defects; dealers often keep the front brakes far too loose, with the commendable intention of preventing you going over the handlebars. If you break down it's your responsibility to return the machine, so take down the phone number of the rental agency in case it gives out in the middle of nowhere. Better outlets often offer a free retrieval service.

Mopeds are increasingly on the way out. Those models still on offer tend to be the surprisingly powerful Piaggio Si or Piaggio Monte Carlo, which can take one person only along almost any road, carry two baskets or bags and are automatic with a pedal or push-start. Bungee cords (*khtapódi* in slang) are supplied on request.

As far as increasingly popular **scooters** go, the Piaggio Typhoon, Suzuki Address and their numerous Japanese clones are more comfortable than mopeds for long trips, with capacious baskets, but have much less stability on unpaved surfaces. The latest generation of these models are ultra-trendy and practical enough, but thirsty on fuel and a few don't have kick-starts as battery backups.

In the family of true **motorbikes**, the favourites are the Honda 50, Yamaha Townmate and Suzuki FB Birdie; gears are shifted with an easy-to-learn pedal action, and these can all be push-started if the battery fails. They can just carry two, though if you have a choice, the Honda Cub 70–90cc series give more power at nominal extra cost, as does the Yamaha 80 Townmate. Best of all is the Honda Astrea 100, very powerful but scarcely bigger than older models.

CYCLING

Cycling in Greece is not such hard going as you might imagine (except in mid-summer), especially on one of the mountain bikes that are rapidly supplanting the old bone-shakers at rental outfits; they rarely cost more than 1500dr a day. You do, however, need steady nerves, as roads are generally narrow with no verges or bike lanes (except on Kós), and many Greek drivers consider bicyclists a low form of life.

If you have your own mountain or touring bike, you might consider taking it along by plane (free if within your 23kg international allowance). Once in Greece you should be able to take a bike for free on most of the **ferries**, and with a little persuasion on the roof of **buses**. Any small spare parts you might need, however, are best brought along, since **specialist bike shops** are only found in the largest island towns.

DRIVING

Cars have obvious advantages for getting to the more inaccessible parts of larger islands, but this is an expensive part of Europe to **rent a car**. If you drive **your own vehicle** to and through Greece, via EU member states, you no longer require a Green Card. In accordance with recent directives, **insurance** contracted in any EU member state is valid in any other, but in many cases this is only third-party cover – the statutory legal minimum. Competition in the industry is so intense, however, that many UK insurers will throw in full, pan-European cover for free or for a nominal sum, up to sixty days; shop around if necessary.

Upon arrival with EU number plates, the car is in theory free to circulate in the country until its road tax or insurance expires. Beware, however, that the rules governing car import are in a constant state of flux, and there have been reports of people being only allowed to use their cars for six-month periods each year (you choose the time period), and of customs officials looking for foreign number plates, and demanding proof of when you brought the car into Greece. Nationalities from outside the EU will get a **carnet** stamp entered in their passport; this normally allows you to keep a non-EU vehicle in Greece for up to six months, exempt from road tax. It is difficult, though not impossible, to leave the country without the vehicle; the nearest customs post will seal it for you (while you fly back home for a family emergency, for example) but you must find a Greek national to act as your guarantor, and possibly pay storage. This person will assume ownership of the car should you ultimately abandon it.

CAR RENTAL

Car rental on the islands starts at £190/$305 a week in high season for the smallest, A-group vehicle, including unlimited mileage, tax and insurance. Tour operators' and local agents' brochures threaten alarming rates of £230/$370 for the same period but, except in August, no rental company expects to fetch that price for a car. Outside peak season, at the smaller local outfits, you can often get terms of about £22/$36 per day, all inclusive, with slightly better rates for three days or more. **Comparison shopping** among agencies in the larger resorts can yield a variation in quotes of up to fifteen percent for the same conditions over a four-to-seven-day period; the most negotiable variable is whether or not kilometres in excess of one hundred per day (a common hidden catch) are free. Open **jeeps**, an increasingly popular extravagance, begin at about £45/$72 per day, rising to as much as £60/$96 at busy times and places.

Note that brochure prices in Greece almost never include tax, **collision damage waiver** (CDW) and personal insurance. CDW in particular is absolutely vital, as the coverage included by law in the basic rental fee is generally inadequate, so check the small print on your contract. Be careful of the hammering that cars get on dirt tracks; tyres, windshield and the underside of the vehicle are almost always excluded from even supplementary insurance policies. All agencies will want either a credit card or a large **cash deposit** up front; minimum age requirements vary from 21 to 25. Driving licences issued by any European Union state are honoured, but in theory (and increasingly, in practice) an **International Driving Licence** is required by all other drivers. This must be arranged before departure, as ELPA (the Greek motoring association) no longer issues IDLs to foreign nationals.

In peak season, you may get a better price through one of the **overseas booking companies** that deal with local firms than if you negotiate for rental in Greece itself; this may also be the only way to get hold of a car, at any price, at such times. Competitive companies in Britain include Holiday Autos, Suncars and Transhire (see box on p.42). Payless, European, Kosmos, Alamo, Reliable, Thrifty, Eurodollar and Just are dependable Greek, or smaller international, chains with branches in many towns; all are considerably cheaper than the biggest international operators Budget, Europcar, Hertz and Avis. Specific local recommendations are given in the guide.

In terms of **models**, the more competitive companies tend to offer the Subaru M80 or Vivio, the Fiat Cinquecento or Seisento and the Suzuki Alto 800 as A-group cars, and Opel (Vauxhall) Corsa 1.2, Fiat Uno/Punto or Nissan Micra in the B-group. Any more than two adults, with luggage, will generally require a B-category car. The Suzuki Alto 600, Fiat

Panda 750/900 and Seat Marbella should be avoided if at all possible, and are being phased out by the more reputable agencies. The standard four-wheel-drive option is a Suzuki open jeep – great for bashing down rutted tracks to remote beaches.

DRIVING IN GREECE

Greece has the highest **accident rate** in Europe after Portugal, and on the larger tourist islands it's easy to see why. **Driving habits** amongst locals can be atrocious: overtaking is erratic, lane lines and turn signals may as well not exist, and motorbikes hog the road or weave from side to side. **Drunk driving** has also become a major problem; Sunday afternoons in rural areas are particularly bad, and for the same reason you should avoid driving late at night on weekends or holidays.

Matters are made worse by poor **road conditions**: signposting is absent or badly placed, pavement markings are faded, asphalt can turn into a one-lane surface or a dirt track without warning on secondary routes, and you're heavily dependent on magnifying mirrors at blind intersections in congested villages. Uphill drivers insist on their **right of way**, as do those first to approach a one-lane bridge; **flashed headlights** mean the opposite of what they do in the UK or North America, here signifying that the other driver insists on coming through or overtaking.

On so-called motorways, as found on Rhodes or Kós, there may be no proper far-right lane for slower traffic, which is expected to straddle the solid white line at the verge and allow rapid traffic to pass.

Wearing a **seatbelt** is compulsory; if you don't, you risk a 50,000dr spot fine at random checkpoints. Other legal requirements include keeping a first-aid kit in the boot, and not allowing children under the age of 10 to sit in the front seats. It's illegal to drive away from any kind of **accident**, and you can be held at a police station for up to 24 hours. If this happens, you have the right to ring your consulate immediately to summon a lawyer; don't make a statement to anyone who doesn't speak, and write, very good English. In practice, once police are informed that there was no personal injury, they rarely come out to investigate.

Tourists with proof of AA/RAC/AAA membership are given free road assistance from ELPA, the Greek equivalent, which runs **breakdown services** on several of the larger islands; in an emergency ring their road assistance service on ☎104. Many car rental companies have an agreement with ELPA's equally widespread competitors Hellas Service and Express Service, but they're prohibitively expensive to summon on your own – over 40,000 drachmas to enrol as an "instant member".

CAR RENTAL AGENCIES

UK

Alamo ☎0990/993000
Avis ☎0990/900500
Budget ☎0800/181 181
Eurodollar ☎0990/365365
Europcar/InterRent ☎0345/222 525
Hertz ☎0990/996699
Holiday Autos ☎0990/300400
Suncars ☎0990/335588
Transhire ☎020/7978 1922

NORTH AMERICA

Alamo ☎1-800/522-9696; Canada, ☎1-800/GO-ALAMO
Auto Europe ☎1-800/223-5555
Avis ☎1-800/331-1084; Canada, ☎1-800/879-2847
Budget ☎1-800/527-0700; Canada, ☎1-800/268-8900
Camwell Holiday Autos ☎1-800/422-7737; Canada, ☎1-800/678-0678
Dollar ☎1-800/800-6000
Europe by Car ☎1-800/223-1516 or 212/245-1713
Hertz ☎1-800/654-3001
National ☎1-800/CAR RENT

AUSTRALIA

Avis ☎1800/225 533
Budget ☎1300/362 848
Hertz ☎1800/550 067

NEW ZEALAND

Avis ☎09/526 2847
Budget ☎09/375 2222
Hertz ☎09/367 6350

RUNNING A VEHICLE

Petrol currently costs 215–245dr a litre for either regular unleaded (*amólyvdhi*) or super unleaded; as throughout the EU, leaded four-star is to become unavailable after January 1, 2000. It is easy to run out of fuel after dark or on weekends in both rural and urban Greece; most stations close at some point between 7pm and 9pm, and nearly as many are shut all weekend. There will always be at least one pump per district open on a rota basis, but it's not always apparent which one it is. This is not so much of a problem on the major highways, but it is a factor everywhere else. So always fill up, or insist on full rental vehicles at the outset, and if you've brought your own car, keep a full jerrycan at all times. Filling stations run by international companies (BP, Mobil and Texaco) often take credit cards; Shell, and Greek chains like EKO, Mamidhakis, Jetoil, Revoil and Elinoil usually don't (except in tourist areas).

Incidentally, the smallest grade of **mopeds** and **scooters** consume **mix** – a red- or green tinted fuel dispensed from a transparent cylindrical device. This contains a minimum of three percent two-stroke oil by volume; when unavailable, you brew it up yourself by adding to super-grade fuel the necessary amount of separately bottled two-stroke oil (*ládhi dhýo trohón* in Greek). It's wise to err on the generous side – say five percent – or you risk the engine seizing up.

In terms of **maintenance**, the easiest models to have serviced and buy parts for in Greece are VWs (including combi and Transporter vans), Mercedes, Opels, Ladas, Skodas and virtually all French, Italian, Korean and Japanese makes. British models are a bit more difficult, but you should be fine as long as you haven't brought anything too esoteric.

In general, both mechanics' **workshops** and **parts retailers** are clustered at the approach and exit roads of all major towns, usually prominently signposted. For the commonest makes, emergency spares like fan belts and cables are often found at surprisingly remote service stations, so don't hesitate to ask at an unlikely-looking spot. Rural mechanics are okay for quick patch-up jobs like snapped clutch cables, but for major problems it's best to limp into the nearest sizable town to find a mechanic who is factory-trained for your make.

HITCHING

Hitching carries the usual risks and dangers, and is inadvisable for women travelling alone, but overall Greece is one of the safer countries in which to do it. It's fairly reliable, too, as a means of getting around, so long as you're not overly concerned about time; lifts are fairly frequent but tend to be short.

Hitching is easiest in remote areas of the larger islands; at best, it's a wonderful method of getting to know the country – there's no finer way to take in Crete than from the back of a motorized tricycle that looks like it's been converted from a lawnmower – and a useful way of picking up some extra Greek. While you'll often get lifts from Greeks eager to display or practise their English, there will be as many where to communicate you're forced to try the language.

TAXIS

Greek **taxis** are among the cheapest in western Europe – so long as you get an honest driver who switches the meter on, and zeroes it. Use of the meter is mandatory within city or town limits, where Tariff "1" applies, while in rural areas or between midnight and 5am, Tariff "2" is in effect. On certain islands, such as Kálymnos and Léros, set rates apply on specific fixed routes for "collective" taxis – these only depart when full. Otherwise, throughout Greece the flag falls at 200dr (though you can expect this figure to inch up); any baggage not actually on your lap is charged at 50dr apiece. Additionally, there are **surcharges** of 200dr for leaving (but not entering) an airport, and 100dr for leaving a harbour area. If you summon a taxi by phone on spec, there's a 400dr charge, while a pre-arranged rendevous is 500dr; in either case the meter starts running from the moment the driver begins heading towards you. For a week or so before and after Orthodox Easter, and Christmas, a *filodhórima* or gratuity of about ten percent is levied. Any or all of these extras will legitimately bump up the basic meter reading of about 1300dr for ten rural kilometres.

ACCOMMODATION

There are huge numbers of beds for tourists on the Greek islands, so most of the year you can rely on turning up pretty much anywhere and finding a room – if not in a hotel, then in a private house or block of rooms (the standard island accommodation). Only from mid-July to early September, the country's high season, are you likely to experience problems. At these times, if you don't have accommodation reserved well in advanced, you'd be wise to keep well off the main tourist trails, turning up at each new place early in the day and taking whatever is available – you may be able to exchange it for something better later on.

Out of season, you face a slightly different problem: most private rooms – and campsites – operate only from late April or early May to October, leaving hotels your only option. During winter you may have no choice but to stay in the main port towns. There will often be very little life outside these places anyway, with all the seasonal beach bars and restaurants closed. On many smaller islands, you may find just one hotel – and perhaps one taverna – staying open year-round.

HOTELS

Hotels in the larger resorts are often contracted out on a seasonal basis by foreign package holiday companies, though there are often vacancies available (especially in spring or autumn) for walk-in trade. The tourist police set official **categories** for hotels, which range from De Luxe down to the rarely encountered E-class; all except the top category have to keep within set price limits. Letter ratings are supposed to correspond to **facilities** available, though in practice categorization often depends on location within a resort and influence with the tourism authorities. It is mandatory for D-class rooms to have attached baths; C-class must additionally have a bar or designated breakfast area. The presence of a pool and/or tennis court will attract a B-class rating, while A-category hotels should have a restaurant, bar and extensive common areas. Often these and the De Luxe outfits (the latter essentially self-contained complexes) back onto a quasi-private beach.

In terms of **food**, C-class hotels are required only to provide the most rudimentary of continental breakfasts – you may choose not to take, or pay for, it – while B-class and above will usually offer some sort of buffet breakfast including cheese, cold cuts, sausages, eggs and so on. With some outstanding exceptions, noted in the guide, lunch or supper at hotel-affiliated restaurants is bland and poor value.

PRIVATE ROOMS

The most common island accommodation is **privately let rooms** (*dhomátia*). Like hotels, these

HOT WATER

A key variable in both rooms and hotels is the type of water heating. Rooftop **solar units** (*iliaká*), with their nonexistent running costs, are more popular than electric **immersion heaters** (*thermosífona*). Under typical high-season demand, however, solar-powered tanks tend to run out of hot water with the post-beach shower crunch at 6pm, with no more available until the next day. A heater, either as a backup or primary source, is more reliable; proprietors may either jealously guard the **boiler controls** or entrust you with its workings, which involves either a circuit breaker or a rotary switch turned to the "I" position for fifteen minutes. You should never shower with a *thermosífono* powered up (look for the glow-lamp indicator on the tank) – besides the risk of shock from badly earthed plumbing, it would be fairly easy to empty smaller tanks and burn out the heating element.

ROOM PRICES

Establishments listed in this book have been **price-coded** according to the scale outlined below. The rates quoted represent the **cheapest available double room** in high season. Out of season, rates can drop by up to fifty percent, especially if you negotiate for a stay of three or more nights. Bona fide single rooms, where available, cost around seventy percent of the price of a double. The limited number of **youth hostels** typically charge 2000–2500dr for a dormitory bed, and are excluded from the category scheme following.

① up to 6000dr	③ 9000–12,000dr	⑤ 16000–20,000dr
② 6000–9000dr	④ 12000–16,000dr	⑥ above 20,000dr

£1=500dr; $1=300dr

Old-fashioned, 1970s-vintage rooms on the remoter islets, occasionally still without private bath, tend to fall into the ① price category. Standard, en-suite rooms without cooking facilities weigh in at ②; newer, state-of-the-art rooms and self-catering studios occupy the top end of the ③ niche, along with the more modest government-rated C-class hotels, the better among these edging into ④. The top half of ④ corresponds fairly well to the better-value B-class hotels, while ⑤ tallies with most of B-class, and ⑥ with A- and De Luxe class.

Prices in any establishment should by law be displayed on the back of the door of your room, or over the reception desk. If you feel you're being overcharged at a place which is officially registered, threaten to report it to the tourist office or police, who will generally adopt your side in such cases. Small amounts over the posted price may be legitimately explained by municipal tax or out-of-date forms. More commonly you will find that you have bargained so well, or arrived so far out of high season, that you are actually paying less than you're supposed to.

are regulated and officially divided into three classes (A down to C), according to facilities. These days the bulk of them are in new, purpose-built, low-rise buildings, but a few are still actually in people's homes, where you'll occasionally be treated to disarming hospitality.

Rooms are almost always scrupulously clean, whatever their other amenities. At their simplest, you'll get a bare, concrete room, with a hook on the back of the door and toilet facilities outside in the courtyard. At the fancier end of the scale, they are modern, fully furnished places with an en-suite, marble-clad bathroom and a fully equipped kitchen shared by guests. Cheap places may have more expensive rooms with en-suite facilities – and vice versa, with singles often tucked under stairways or in other less desirable corners of the building; owners will usually show you the most expensive first. Price and quality are not necessarily directly linked, so always ask to see the room before agreeing to take it.

Areas to **look for rooms**, along with recommendations of the best places, are included in the guide. As often as not, however, the rooms find you: owners descend on ferry or bus arrivals to fill any space they have, sometimes waving photos of the premises. In smaller places you'll often see rooms advertised, sometimes in German (*Zimmer*); the Greek signs to look out for are "ENIKIAZÓMENA DHOMÁTIA" or "ENIKIÁZONTEH DHOMÁTIA". In the more developed island resorts, where package holidaymakers predominate, *dhomátia* owners will often require you to stay for at least three days, or even a week.

It has become standard practice for rooms proprietors to ask to keep your **passport** – ostensibly "for the tourist police", who do require customer particulars – but in reality to prevent you skipping out with an unpaid bill. Some owners may be satisfied with just taking down your details, as is done in hotels, and they'll almost always return the documents once you get to know them, or if you need them for another purpose.

If you are **stranded**, or arrive very late in a remote island village, you may very well find that there is someone prepared to earn extra money by putting you up. This should not be counted on, but things work out more often than not. Otherwise, the most polite course is to have a meal or drink at the taverna or kafenío and then, especially in summer, enquire as to the possibility of sleeping either in the vacant schoolhouse or in a spare room at the *kinotikó grafío* (community records office).

In **winter**, officially from November until early April, private rooms – except in Ródhos Old Town

– are closed to keep the hotels in business. There's no point in traipsing about hoping to find exceptions; most owners obey the system very strictly. If they don't, the room-owners will find you themselves and, watching out for hotel rivals, guide you back to their place.

VILLAS AND LONG-TERM RENTALS

The easiest – and usually most economical – way to arrange a **villa rental** is through one of the package holiday companies in the box on p.6. They represent some superb places, from fairly simple to luxurious, and costs can be very reasonable, especially if shared between a few people. Several of the companies we list will arrange "**multi-centre**" stays on two or more islands.

On the islands, a few local travel agents arrange villa rentals, though they are often places the overseas companies could not fill. **Out of season**, you can sometimes get a good deal on villa or apartment rental for a month or more by asking around locally, though in these days of EU convergence and the increasing desirability of the islands as year-round residences, "good deal" means anything under 50,000dr for a large studio (*garsoniéra*) or 60,000dr for a small one-bedroom flat.

HOSTELS AND MONASTERIES

The Greek islands are not exactly packed with **youth hostels** (*xenón neótitos* in the singular) – just a half-dozen or so on Thíra and Crete, mostly not IYHF-affiliated. Of those that do exist the majority are very run-down and/or filthy, and thus a far cry from similar north European institutions. Some offer **roofspace**, providing a mattress and a pleasantly cool night under the stars. Competition from inexpensive rooms means that they are not nearly as cost-effective as elsewhere in Europe. It's best to have a valid IYHF card, but you can often buy one on the spot, or maybe just pay a little extra for your bed. Charges for a dormitory bed are around £4–5/$6.50–8 a night; most hostels have a curfew at 11pm or midnight and many places only open in spring and summer.

Greek **monasteries** and **convents** have a tradition of putting up travellers (of the appropriate sex). On the largest islands, this is still a customary – if steadily decreasing – practice, used mostly by villagers on pilgrimage; on the smaller islands dominated by tourism, monasteries tend to be unstaffed, and rarely provide cell-keys, even for a fee. Accordingly you should always ask locally about the prevailing policy before heading out to a monastery or convent for the night. Also, dress modestly – shorts for men and women, and short skirts are total anathema – and try to arrive early in the evening, not later than 8pm or sunset (whichever is earlier).

CAMPING

Officially recognized campsites on the islands range from ramshackle compounds to highly organized and rather soulless complexes, formerly run by the EOT (Greek Tourist Organization) prior to privatization. Most places cost 900dr a night per person, slightly less per tent and 1500dr per camper van, but at the fanciest sites, rates for two people plus a tent can almost add up to the price of a basic room. Generally, you don't have to worry about leaving tents or other equipment unattended at wardened campsites; Greeks are very honest about such things. The main risk, alas, comes from other campers. The Greek Camping Association, Solonós 102, 106 80 Athens (☎01/36 21 560), publishes a sporadically updated booklet covering most officially recognized Greek campsites and the facilities they offer; it's available from EOT offices.

Camping rough – outside authorized campsites – is such an established element of Greek travel that few people realize that it's officially illegal. Since 1977 "free" camping, as EOT calls it, has actually been forbidden by a law originally enacted to harass gypsies, and regulations are increasingly enforced. Another drawback is the increased prevalence of theft in rural areas, often from marauding bands of refugees from Albania and other north Balkan states. All told, you will feel less vulnerable inside a tent, camper van or even a rock-cave – not that rain is likely during the long Greek summer, but some protection is essential from wind, sun, insects (see "Health", p.28) and stray animals raiding your food. You will always need at least a light sleeping bag, since even summer nights can get cool and damp; a foam pad is also recommended for pitching on harder ground.

If you do camp rough, it's vital to exercise sensitivity and discretion. Police will crack down on people camping (and especially littering) around popular tourist beaches, particularly when a large community of campers develops. Off the beaten track, however, nobody is very bothered, though it is always best to ask permission locally in the village taverna or café. During high season, when everything – even the authorized campsites – may be full, attitudes towards freelance camping are more relaxed, even in the most touristed places. At such times the best strategy is to find a sympathetic taverna, which in exchange for regular patronage will probably be willing to guard small valuables and let you use their facilities.

EATING AND DRINKING

Greeks spend a lot of time socializing outside their homes, and sharing a meal is one of the chief ways of doing it. The atmosphere is always relaxed and informal, and pretensions (plus expense-account prices) are rare outside of the more chi-chi parts of major resorts. Greeks historically have not been prodigious drinkers – tippling is traditionally meant to accompany food – although since the mid-1990s a whole range of bars and pubs have sprung up, both in tourist resorts and as pricey "music halls" at the outskirts of the major towns.

BREAKFASTS, PICNIC FARE AND SNACKS

Greeks don't generally eat **breakfast**, so the only egg-and-bacon kind of places are in resorts where foreigners congregate, or where there are returned North American or Australian Greeks. Such spots can sometimes be fairly good value (1200–1900dr for the works, with coffee), especially if there's competition. More indigenous alternatives are yoghurts at a **galaktopolío** (milk bar), or cheese pies and pretzel rings from a street stall (see "Snacks", p.48).

PICNIC FARE

Picnic fare is good, cheap and easily available at bakeries and *manávika* (fruit-and-veg stalls). **Bread**, alas, is often of minimal nutritional value and inedible within a day of purchase. It's worth paying extra at the bakery (*foúrnos* or *psomádhiko*) for *olikís* (wholemeal), *sikalísio* (rye bread), *oktásporo* (eight-grain) or even *enneásporo* (nine-grain), the latter types most commonly baked where large numbers of Germans or Scandinavians are about. When buying **olives**, go for the fat Kalamáta or Ámfissa ones; they're more expensive, but tastier. The best **honey** is reckoned to be the pure-thyme variety from the more barren islands (such as Límnos, Náxos, Pátmos and Astypálea), although it's about double the price of ordinary pine-flower honeys.

Honey is an ideal topping for the famous local **yoghurt**, which is not confined to the bland Fage-brand stuff of the UK supermarket. All of the larger island towns have at least one dairy shop where locally produced yoghurts are sold in plastic or (better) clay containers of various sizes. Sheep-milk yoghurt is richer and sweeter, scarcely requiring honey; cow-milk yoghurt is tarter but more widely available. Side by side with these will be *krémes* (custards) and *ryzógala* (rice puddings) in one-serving plastic containers.

Féta cheese is ubiquitous – often, ironically, imported from Holland or Denmark, though local brands are usually better and not much more expensive. The goat's-milk variety can be very dry and salty, so ask for a taste before buying. If you have access to a fridge, leaving the cheese overnight in a plastic container filled with water will solve both problems. This sampling advice goes for other indigenous cheeses as well, the most palatable of which are the expensive gruyère-type *graviéra*.

Despite membership of the EU, plus growing personal incomes and exotic tastes, Greece imports very little garden produce from abroad, aside from bananas and a few mangoes. **Fruit** in particular is relatively expensive and available only by season, though in the more cosmopolitan spots it is possible to find such things as **avocados** (light-green ones from Crete are excellent). Reliable picnic fruits include *yiarmádhes*, a variety of giant **peach** available during August and September; *krystália*, tiny, hard green **pears** that ripen a month or two later and are heavenly; and the *himoniátiko* **melon** (called casava in North America) which appears at the same time, in its yellow, puckered skin with green flecks. Greece also has a burgeoning **kiwi** industry, and while the first crop in October coincides with the end of the tourist season, the harvest carries over into the following April. Less portable, but succulent, are **figs** (*sýka*); there's a crop of large fruits in May, followed by smaller ones in August. Salad vegetables are more reasonably priced; besides the famous, enormous tomatoes (June to September), there is a bewildering variety of springtime greens, including rocket, dill, enormous spring onions and lettuces. Useful expressions for shopping are *éna tétarto* (250g) and *misó kiló* (500g).

SNACKS

Traditional **snacks** can be one of the distinctive pleasures of Greek eating, though they are being increasingly edged out by an obsession with *tóst* (toasted sandwiches) and other Western junk/fast food at nationwide chains such as Goody's (burgers), Roma Pizza and Theios Vanias (baked pastries) – somewhat less insipid for being home-grown. However, independently produced kebabs (*souvlákia*) are widely available, and in most larger resorts and towns you'll find *yíros* – doner kebab with garnish in thick, doughy *píta* bread that's closer to Indian naan bread.

Other common snacks include *tyrópites* (cheese pies) and *spanokópites* (spinach pies), which can usually be found at the baker's, as can *kouloúria* (crispy pretzel rings sprinkled with sesame seeds) and *voutímata* (dark biscuits heavy on the molasses, cinnamon and butter).

RESTAURANTS

Greek cuisine and **restaurants** are simple and straightforward. There's usually no snobbery about eating out; everyone does it regularly, and it's still reasonable – around 2900–3800dr per person for a substantial meal with a measure of house wine. That said, there's a lot of lazy cooking about – especially in resorts, menus are dominated by pizza, spaghetti and chops – and you'll now find growing numbers of what the Greeks call **"kultúra" restaurants**, often pretentious attempts at Greek nouvelle cuisine which tend to be long on airs and graces, and (at 5000–7000dr a head) short on value. The exceptions which succeed have been singled out in the text.

In choosing a restaurant, the best strategy is to go where the Greeks go. And they go late: 2pm to 3pm for **lunch**, 9pm to 11pm for **supper**. You can eat earlier, but you're likely to get indifferent service and cuisine if you frequent establishments catering to the tourist schedule. Chic appearance is not a reliable guide to quality; often the more ramshackle, traditional outfits represent the best value. One good omen is the waiter bringing a carafe of refrigerated water, unbidden, rather than pushing you to order bottled stuff.

In busy resort areas, it's wise to keep a wary eye on the **waiters**, who are inclined to urge you into ordering more than you want, then bring things you haven't ordered. They often don't actually write anything down and may work out the **bill** by examining your empty plates. Although cash-register receipts are now required in all establishments, these are often only for the grand total, and itemized tabs will be in totally illegible Greek script. Where prices are printed on menus, you'll be paying the right-hand (higher) of the two columns, inclusive of all taxes and usually **service charge**, although a small extra tip of about ten percent directly to the waiter is hugely appreciated – and usually not expected.

Bread costs extra, but consumption is not obligatory; unless it is assessed as part of the cover charge, you have the right to send it back without paying for it. You'll be considered deviant for refusing it, but so much Greek bread is inedible sawdust that there's little point in paying extra unless you actually want to use it as a scoop for dips.

Children are always welcome, day or night, at family tavernas, and Greeks don't mind in the slightest if they play tag between the tables or chase the **cats** running in mendicant packs – which you should not feed, as signs often warn you.

ESTIATÓRIA

There are two basic types of restaurant: the **estiatório** and the **taverna**. Distinctions between the two are slight, though the former is more commonly found in towns and tends to have the slightly more complicated dishes termed **mayireftá** (literally, "cooked").

An estiatório will generally feature a variety of such oven-baked **casserole** dishes: *moussakás*, *pastítsio*, meat or game stews like *kokinistó* and *stifádho*, *yemistá* (stuffed tomatoes or peppers), the oily vegetable casseroles called *ladherá* and oven-baked meat and fish. Usually you go into the kitchen and point at the desired steam trays to choose these dishes.

Batches are cooked in the morning and then left to stand, which is why this *mayireftá* food is often **lukewarm** or even cold. Greeks don't mind this (most actually believe that hot food is bad for you), and dishes like *yemistá* are actually enhanced by being allowed to cool off and stand in their own juice. Similarly, you have to specify if you want your food with little or no oil (*horís ládhi*), but once again you will be considered a little strange since Greeks regard olive oil as essential to digestion (and indeed it is the healthiest of the vegetable oils, even in large quantities).

Desserts (*epidhórpia* in formal Greek) of the pudding-and-pie variety don't exist at estiatória, and yoghurt or cheese only occasionally. Fruit, however, is always available in season; watermelon (often on the house), melon and grapes are the summer standards. Autumn treats worth asking after include *kydhóni* or *akhládhi stó foúrno*, baked quince or pear with some sort of syrup or nut topping.

TAVERNAS AND PSISTARIÉS

Tavernas range from the glitzy and fashionable to rough-and-ready huts set up under a reed canopy, behind a beach. Really primitive ones have a very limited (often unwritten) menu, but the more established will offer some of the main *mayireftá* dishes mentioned above, as well as the standard taverna fare. This essentially means **mezédhes** (hors-d'oeuvres) or **orektiká** (appetizers) and *tís óras* (meat and fish, fried or grilled to order).

Psistariés or grill-houses serve spit-roasted lamb, pork or goat (generically termed *kondosoúvli*), grilled chicken (*kotópoulo skáras*) or *kokorétsi* (grilled offal roulade) – in remote villages, often plonked straight on your table upon a sheet of waxed paper. They will usually have a limited selection of mezédhes, but no *mayireftá* at all.

Since the idea of courses is foreign to Greek cuisine, starters, main dishes and salads often arrive together unless you request otherwise. The best thing is to order a selection of mezédhes and salads to share, in true Greek fashion. Waiters encourage you to take the *horiátiki* **salad** – the so-called Greek salad, including *féta* cheese – because it is the most expensive. If you only want tomato, or tomato and cucumber, ask for *domatosaláta* or *angourodomáta*. *Láhano* (cabbage) and *maroúli* (lettuce) are the typical winter and spring salads, respectively.

The most interesting **mezédhes** are *tzatzíki* (yoghurt, garlic and cucumber dip), *melitzanosaláta* (aubergine/eggplant dip), *kolokythákia tiganitá* (courgette/zucchini slices fried in batter) or *melitzánes tiganités* (aubergine/eggplant slices fried in batter), *yígandes* (white haricot beans in vinaigrette or hot tomato sauce), *tyropitákia* or *spanakópittes* (small cheese and spinach pies), *revythókeftedhes* or *pittaroúdhia* (chickpea patties similar to falafel), *okhtapódhi* (octopus) and *mavromátika* (black-eyed peas).

Among **meats**, *souvláki* (shish kebab) and *brizóles* (chops) are reliable choices. In both cases, pork (*hirinó*) is usually better and cheaper than veal (*moskharísio*). The best *souvláki*, though not often available, is lamb (*arnísio*). At *psistariés*, meaty lamb shoulder chops (*kopsídha*) are more substantial than the scrawny rib chops called *païdhákia*; roast lamb (*arní psitó*) and roast kid (*katsíki stó fournó*) are considered estiatório fare. *Keftédhes* (breadcrumbed meatballs), *biftékia* (similar, but meatier) and the spicy, home-made sausages called *loukánika* are cheap and good. *Kotópoulo* (chicken), especially grilled, is also usually a safe bet.

Seaside *psarotávernes* offer **fish**, though for the inexperienced, ordering can be fraught with peril. Summer visitors get a relatively poor choice of fish, most of it frozen, farmed or imported from Egypt and North Africa. Drag-net-trawling is prohibited from the end of May until the beginning of October, when only line methods are allowed. During these warmer months, such few fish as are caught tend to be smaller and dry-tasting, and are served with butter sauce. Taverna owners often comply only minimally with the requirement to indicate when seafood is **frozen** (look for the abbreviation "kat." on the Greek-language side of the menu). Given these considerations, it's often best to set your sights on the **humbler**, seasonally migrating or perennially local species. The

A FOOD AND DRINK GLOSSARY

BASICS

Alát	Salt	*Lahaniká*	Vegetables	*Olikís*	Wholemeal bread
Avgá	Eggs	*O logariasmós*	The bill	*Sikalísio*	Rye bread
(Horís) ládhi	(Without) oil	*Méli*	Honey	*Thalassiná*	Seafood
Hortofágos	Vegetarian	*Neró*	Water	*Tyrí*	Cheese
Katálogo/lísta	Menu	*Psári(a)*	Fish	*Yiaoúrti*	Yoghurt
Kréas	Meat	*Psomí*	Bread	*Zákhari*	Sugar

COOKING TERMS

Akhnistó	Steamed	*Sto foúrno*	Baked
Pastó	Marinated in salt	*Tiganitó*	Pan-fried
Psitó	Roasted	*Tis óras*	Grilled/fried to order
Saganáki	Rich red sauce	*Yakhní*	Stewed in oil and tomato sauce
Skáras	Grilled	*Yemistá*	Stuffed (squid, vegetables, etc)
Sti soúvla	Spit roasted		

SOUPS AND STARTERS

Avgolémono	Egg and lemon soup	*Mavromátika*	Black-eyed peas
Dolmádhes	Stuffed vine leaves	*Melitzanosaláta*	Aubergine/eggplant dip
Fasoládha	Bean soup	*Revythókeftedhes*	Chickpea/garbanzo patties
Florínes	Canned red Macedonian peppers	*Skordhaliá*	Garlic dip
		Soúpa	Soup
Kápari	Pickled caper leaves	*Taramosaláta*	Cod roe paté
Kopanistí, khtypití	Spicy cheese purée	*Tzatzíki*	Yoghurt and cucumber dip
Krítamo	Rock samphire	*Tzirosaláta*	Slightly "high" mackerel dip

VEGETABLES

Anginares	Artichokes	*Koukiá*	Broad fava beans
Angoúri	Cucumber	*Maroúli*	Lettuce
Ánitho	Dill	*Melitzána*	Aubergine/eggplant
Bámies	Okra, ladies' fingers	*Papoutsákia*	Stuffed aubergine/eggplant
Bouréki, bourekákia	Courgette/zucchini, potato and cheese pie	*Patátes*	Potatoes
		Piperiés	Peppers
Briám	Ratatouille	*Pligoúri, pinigoúri*	Bulgur wheat
Domátes	Tomatoes	*Radhíkia*	Wild chicory
Fakés	Lentils	*Rízi/Piláfi*	Rice (usually with *sáltsa* – sauce)
Fasolákia	French beans		
Horiátiki (saláta)	Greek salad (with olives, féta etc)	*Rókka*	Rocket greens
		Saláta	Salad
Hórta	Greens (usually wild)	*Spanáki*	Spinach
Kolokythákia	Courgette/zucchini	*Yígandes*	White haricot beans

FISH AND SEAFOOD

Astakós	Aegean lobster	*Gávros*	Mild anchovy	*Koutsomoúra*	Goatfish (small barboúni)
Atherína	Sand smelt	*Glóssa*	Sole		
Bakaliáros	Cod	*Gópa*	Bogue	*Kydhónia*	Cherrystone clams
Barbóuni	Red mullet	*Kalamarákia*	Baby squid		
Fangrí	Common bream	*Kalamária*	Squid	*Lakérdha*	Light-fleshed premium tuna
Galéos	Dogfish, hound shark	*Karavídhes*	Crayfish		
		Kefalás	Axillary bream	*Lavráki*	Sea bass
Garídhes	Shrimp, prawns	*Koliós*	Chub mackerel	*Marídhes*	Whitebait

Melanoúri	Saddled bream	*Sargós*	White bream	*Synagrídha*	Dentex
Mýdhia	Mussels	*Seláhi*	Skate, ray	*Tsipoúra*	Gilt-head bream
Okhtapódhi	Octopus	*Skathári*	Black bream	*Vátos*	Skate, ray
Platý	Skate, ray	*Skoumbrí*	Atlantic mackerel	*Xifías*	Swordfish
Sardhélles	Sardines	*Soupiá*	Cuttlefish		

MEAT AND MEAT-BASED DISHES

Arní	Lamb	*Moussakás*	Aubergine, potato and meat pie with bechamel topping
Biftéki	Hamburger	*Païdhákia*	Lamb rib chops
Brizóla	Pork or beef chop	*Pastítsio*	Macaroni baked with meat
Hirinó	Pork	*Patsás*	Tripe and trotter soup
Keftédhes	Meatballs	*Salingária*	Garden snails
Kokorétsi	Liver/offal roulade, spit-roasted	*Soutzoukákia*	Mincemeat rissoles/beef patties
Kopsídhia	Lamb shoulder chops	*Stifádho*	Meat stew with tomato
Kotópoulo	Chicken	*Sykóti*	Liver
Kounélli	Rabbit	*Youvétsi*	Baked clay casserole of meat and short pasta
Loukánika	Spicy homemade sausages		
Moskhári	Veal		

SWEETS AND DESSERT

Baklavás	Honey and nut pastry	*Karydhópita*	Walnut cake
Bougátsa	Salt or sweet cream pie served warm with sugar and cinnamon	*Kréma*	Custard
		Loukoumádhes	Dough fritters in honey syrup and sesame seeds
Galaktobóureko	Custard pie	*Pagotó*	Ice cream
Halvás	Sweetmeat with sesame or semolina	*Pastélli*	Sesame and honey bar
		Ryzógalo	Rice pudding

FRUIT AND NUTS

Akhládhia	Big pears	*Krystália*	Miniature pears	*Rodhákino*	Peach
Aktinídha	Kiwis	*Kydhóni*	Quince	*Stafýlia*	Grapes
Fistíkia	Pistachio nuts	*Lemóni*	Lemon	*Sýka*	(Dried) figs
Fráoules	Strawberries	*Míla*	Apples	*Yiarmádhes*	Giant autumn peach
Karpoúzi	Watermelon	*Pepóni*	Melon		
Kerásia	Cherries	*Portokália*	Oranges		

CHEESE

Féta	Salty, white cheese	*Kasséri*	Medium-sharp cheese
Graviéra	Gruyère-type hard cheese	*Myzíthra*	Sweet cream cheese
Katsikísio	Goat cheese	*Próvio*	Sheep cheese

DRINKS

Alisfakiá	"Island" (sage) tea	*Krasí*	Wine	*Portokaládha*	Orangeade
Bíra	Beer	*áspro*	white	*Potíri*	Glass
Boukáli	Bottle	*kokkinélli/rozé*	rosé	*Stinyássas!*	Cheers!
Gála	Milk	*kókkino/mávro*	red	*Tsáï*	Tea
Galakakáo	Chocolate milk	*Limonádha*	Lemonade	*Tsáï vounoú*	"Mountain" (sage) tea
Gazóza	Generic fizzy drink	*Metalikó neró*	Mineral water		
Kafés	Coffee				

cheapest consistently available fish are *gópes* (bogue), *atherína* (sand smelts) and *marídhes* (picarel), the latter eaten head and all, best rolled in salt and sprinkled with lemon juice. In autumn especially you may encounter *psarósoupa* or *kakaviá* (fish stew).

The **choicer** varieties, such as *barboúni* (red mullet), *tsipoúra* (gilt-head bream), *lavráki* (sea bass) or *fangrí* (common bream), will be expensive; if the price seems too good to be true, it's probably farmed. Prices are usually quoted by the kilo, and should not be more than double the street market rate, so if squid is 2500dr a kilo at the fishmongers, that sum should fetch you two 250-gramme portions. Standard procedure is to go to the glass-fronted cooler, pick your own specimen and have it weighed in your sight.

Cheaper **seafood** (*thalassiná*) such as *kalamarákia* (fried baby squid) and *okhtapódhi* (octopus) are a summer staple of most seaside tavernas, and occasionally *mýdhia* (mussels), *kydhónia* (cockles) and *garídhes* (small prawns) will be on offer at reasonable prices. Keep an eye out, however, to freshness and season – mussels in particular are a common cause of stomach upsets or even mild poisoning.

As the more favoured species have become overfished, **unusual seafoods**, formerly the exclusive province of the poor, are putting in a greater appearance on menus. Ray or skate (variously known as *platý*, *seláhi*, *trígona* or *vátos*) can be fried or used in soup, and is even dried for decoration. Sea urchins (*ahiní*) are also a humble favourite, being split and emptied for the sake of their (reputedly aphrodisiac) roe that's eaten raw. Only the reddish ones are gravid; special shears are sold for opening them if you don't fancy a hand full of spines.

As in estiatória, traditional tavernas offer fruit rather than sticky **desserts**, though nowadays these are often available, along with coffee, in tavernas frequented by foreigners.

WINES

Both estiatória and tavernas will usually offer you a choice of bottled **wines**, and many still have their own house variety: kept in barrels, sold in bulk by the quarter-, half- or full litre, and served either in glass flagons or the brightly coloured tin "monkey-cups" called *kantária*. Not as many tavernas stock their own wine as once did, but it's worth asking whether they have wine *varelísio* (barrelled) or *hýma* (in bulk). You should expect to pay no more than about 1200dr per litre, with smaller measures priced proportionately. Non-resinated wine is almost always more than decent. **Retsína** – pine-resinated wine, a slightly acquired taste – is also usually better straight from the barrel, though the bottled Yeoryiadhi brand from Thessaloníki is excellent.

Among the **bottled wines** available **nationwide**, Cambas, Boutari Lac de Roches, Calliga and the Rhodian CAIR products (especially the Moulin range) are good, **inexpensive** whites, while Boutari Nemea or Naoussa are decent, **mid-range** reds. If you want something better but still moderately priced, Tsantali Agioritiko is an excellent white or red. But especially if you're travelling around wine-producing islands, you may as well go for **local bottlings**. Almost anything produced on **Límnos** is decent; the Alexandrine muscat is used for whites, the local *límnio* grape for reds and rosés. **Santoríni**, another volcanic island, has a number of premium products such as Nykhteri and Vysanto, and the Robola white of **Kefalloniá** is justly esteemed. **Páros** and **Náxos** also both have acceptable local vintages, while **Crete** is now beginning to have labels superior to the bog-standard Logado. On **Rhodes**, Alexandhris products from Émbonas are well thought of, as is the Emery label with its Villaré white.

Curiously, island red wines (except for Rhodes's CAIR Moulin and Emery Mythiko) are almost uniformly mediocre; in this respect you're better off pushing the boat out for **reds from the mainland**. The Halkidhikí peninsula vintner Carras does the excellent Porto Carras, and Ktima Papaïoannou Nemea (Peloponnese), Averof Katoï (Métsovo, Epirus) and Tsantali Rapsani (Thessaly) are all superb, velvety reds – and likely to be

VEGETARIANS

If you are **vegetarian**, you may be in for a hard time, and will often have to assemble a meal from various mezédhes. Even the excellent standbys of yoghurt with honey, tzatzíki and Greek salad begin to pall after a while, and many of the supposed "vegetable" dishes on menus are cooked in stock or have pieces of meat added to liven them up. Wholly or largely vegetarian restaurants are slowly on the increase in touristy areas; this guide highlights them where appropriate.

found only in the better *kultúra* tavernas or *káves* (**bottle shops**). Other **premium micro-wineries** on the mainland whose products have long been fashionable, in both red and white, include Hatzimihali (Atalánti, central Greece), Spyropoulos Mantinia (central Peloponnese), Athanasiadhi (central Greece), Skouras and Lazaridhi (east Macedonia). For any of these you can expect to pay 2000–3000dr per bottle in a shop, double that at a taverna.

Last but not least, CAIR on Rhodes makes its very own "**champagne**" ("naturally sparkling wine fermented *en boteille*", says the label), in both brut and demi-sec versions. It's not Moet & Chandon quality by any means, but at about £4 equivalent per bottle, who's complaining....

CAFÉS, CAKE SHOPS AND BARS

The Greek eating and drinking experience encompasses a variety of other places beyond restaurants. Most importantly, there is the institution of the **kafenío**, found in every town, village and hamlet in the country. In addition, you'll come across **ouzerís**, **zaharoplastía** (Greek patisseries) and **barákia**.

THE KAFENÍO

The **kafenío** (plural, kafenía) is the traditional Greek coffee shop or café. Although its main business is "Greek" (Middle Eastern) coffee – prepared *skéto* or *pikró* (unsweetened), *métrio* (medium) or *glykó* (sweet) – it also serves spirits such as oúzo (see below), brandy (usually Metaxa or Botrys brand, in three grades), beer, tea (either sage-based tea known variously as *alisfakiá* or *tsái vounoú*, or British-style) and soft drinks. Another refreshing drink sold in cafés is *kafés frappé*, a sort of iced instant coffee with or without milk and sugar – uniquely Greek despite its French-sounding name. Like Greek coffee, it is always accompanied by a welcome glass of cold water. Standard fizzy soft drinks are also sold in all kafenía.

Usually the only **edibles** available are *glyká koutalioú* (sticky, syrupy preserves of quince, grape, fig, citrus fruit or cherry) and the traditional *ipovrýhio*, a piece of mastic submerged in a glass of water like a submarine – which is what the word means in Greek.

Like tavernas, kafenía range from the plastic and sophisticated to the old-fashioned, spit-on-the-floor variety, with marble or brightly painted metal tables and straw-bottomed chairs. An important institution anywhere in Greece, they form the pivot of life in the country villages. You get the impression that many men spend most of their waking hours there. Greek women are rarely to be seen in the more traditional places – and foreign women may sometimes feel uneasy or unwelcome in these establishments. Even in holiday resorts, you will find that there is at least one coffeehouse that the local men have reserved for themselves.

Some kafenía close at siesta time, but many remain open from early in the morning until late at night. The chief summer socializing time is 6–8pm, immediately after the siesta. This is the time to take your pre-dinner oúzo, as the sun begins to sink and the air cools down.

OÚZO, MEZÉDHES AND OUZERIS

Oúzo and the similar *tsípouro* (mainland) and *tsikoudhiá* (Crete), are simple **spirits** of up to 48 percent alcohol, distilled from grape-mash residue left over from wine-making, and then flavoured with herbs such as anise or fennel. There are nearly a score of brands, with the best reckoned to be from Lésvos, Sámos and Týrnavos on the mainland; inferior ones are either weak (such as the Rhodian Fokiali, at 40 percent) or spiked with molasses or grain alcohol to "boost" them.

When you order, you will be served two glasses: one with the oúzo, and one full of water to be tipped into your oúzo until it turns a milky white. You can drink it straight, but the strong, burning taste is hardly refreshing if you do. It is increasingly common to add **ice cubes** (*pagáki*), a bowl of which will be provided upon request.

A much smoother variant of oúzo is **soúma**, found chiefly on Rhodes and Sámos, but in theory anywhere grapes are grown. The smoothness is deceptive – two or three glasses of it and you had better not have any other firm plans for the afternoon.

Until the 1980s, every oúzo you ordered was automatically accompanied by a small plate of **mezédhes**, on the house: bits of cheese, cucumber, tomato, a few olives, sometimes octopus or even a couple of small fish. Unfortunately these days you usually have to ask, and pay, for this.

Though they are confined to the better resorts and select neighbourhoods of the larger islands and towns, one kind of drinking establishment specializes in oúzo and mezédhes. These are called **ouzerí** (same in the Greek plural, we've added 's' to the hybrid), and are well worth trying for the marvellous variety of mezédhes they serve (though lately numbers of mediocre tavernas have counterfeited the name). At the genuine article, several plates of mezédhes plus drinks will effectively substitute for a more involved meal at a taverna (though it usually works out more expensive if you have a healthy appetite). Faced with an often bewilderingly varied menu, you might opt for the *pikilía* (medley, assortment) available in several sizes, the largest and most expensive one usually heavy on the seafood. At other ouzeris the language barrier may be overcome by the waiter wielding an enormous **dhískos** or tray laden with all the current cold offerings – you pick the ones you like the looks of.

SWEETS AND BREAKFAST

Similar to the kafenío is the **zaharoplastío**, a cross between café and patisserie, serving coffee, alcohol, yoghurt with honey and sticky cakes.

The better establishments offer an amazing variety of pastries, cream-and-chocolate confections, honey-soaked Greco-Turkish sweets like *baklavás*, *kataïfi* (honey-drenched "shredded wheat"), *loukoumádhes* (deep-fried batter puffs dusted with cinnamon and dipped in syrup), *galaktoboúreko* (custard pie) and so on.

If you want a stronger slant towards the dairy products and away from the pure sugar, seek out a **galaktopolío**, where you'll often find *ryzógalo* (rice pudding – rather better than the English canned variety), *kréma* (custard) and locally made *yiaoúrti* (yoghurt), best if it's *próvio* (from sheep's milk).

Ice cream, sold principally at the gelaterie which have swept over Greece of late (Dhodhoni is the posh chain), can be very good and almost indistinguishable from Italian prototypes. A scoop (*baláki*) costs 250–400dr; you'll be asked if you want it in a cup (*kypelláki*) or a cone (*konáki*), and whether you want toppings like *santí* (whipped cream). By contrast, the mass-produced brands like Delta or Evga are pretty average, with the exception of Floca Poème and Nirvana labels; Häagen-Dazs is also widely available. A sign reading "PAGOTÓ POLÍTIKO" or "KAÏMÁKI" means that the shop concerned makes its own Turkish-style ice cream – as good as or better than the usual Italian version – and the proprietors are probably of Asia Minor or Constantinopolitan descent.

Both zaharoplastía and galaktopolía are more family-oriented places than the kafenío, and many also serve a basic **continental breakfast** of *méli me voútyro* (honey poured over a pat of butter) or jam (all kinds are called *marmeládha* in Greek; ask for *portokáli* – orange – if you want proper marmalade) with fresh bread or *friganiés* (melba-toast-type slivers). You are also more likely to find proper (*evropaïkó*) tea and non-Greek coffee. *Nescafé* has become the generic term for all instant coffee, regardless of brand; it's generally pretty vile, and in resort areas smart proprietors have taken to offering filter coffee, dubbed *gallikós* (French).

BARS – AND BEER

Bars (*barákia* in the plural), once confined to towns, cities and holiday resorts, are now found all over Greece, especially in pedestrian areas. They range from clones of Parisian cafés or Spanish *bodegas* to seaside cocktail bars, or imitation English "pabs" (sic), with videos running all day. At their most sophisticated, however, they are well-executed theme venues in ex-industrial premises or Neoclassical houses that can hold their own against close equivalents in Spain or London, with Western (currently techno) soundtracks.

For this and other reasons, drinks are invariably more expensive than in a café. Bars are, however, most likely to stock a range of **beers**, mostly foreign labels made locally under licence. However, since 1996 three new **homegrown brews** have appeared, rapidly capturing a big slice of market: Mythos, a smooth lager in a green bottle, put out by the Boutari vintners; Veryina, brewed in Komotiní and common in eastern Macedonia and Halkidhikí; and Fisher, a sharp pilsner. Kronenberg 1664 and Kaiser are two of the more common quality **foreign-licence** varieties, with the latter available in both light and dark. Bland, inoffensive Amstel and the increasingly rare, yeasty Henninger are the two ubiquitous cheapies; the Dutch themselves claim that Amstel is better than the one available in Holland, and Amstel also makes a very palatable, strong (seven percent) **bock**. Heineken, still referred to as a "*prássini*" by bar and taverna staff after its green bottle, despite the advent of Mythos, is too harshly sharp for many. Since 1993 a tidal wave of even pricier, genuinely imported German beers, such as Bitburger and Warstein (plus a few British ones), has washed over the fancier resorts.

Incidentally, try not to get stuck with the one-third litre cans, vastly more expensive (and more of a rubbish problem) than the returnable half-litre bottles.

COMMUNICATIONS

POSTAL SERVICES

Post offices (*tahydhromía*) are open Monday to Friday from 7.30am to 2pm, though certain main branches have hours through the evening and on Saturday morning.

Airmail letters from the mainland take three to seven days to reach the rest of Europe, five to twelve days to get to North America, and a bit longer for Australia and New Zealand. Generally, the larger the island (and the planes serving its airport), the quicker the service. Postal rates fall within the normal EU range: 170dr (35p equivalent) for postcards or letters to Europe, 200dr (42p equivalent) to North America or Australasia. For a modest fee (about 500dr), you can shave a day or two off delivery time to any destination by using the **express service** (*katepígonda*). **Registered** (*systiméno*) delivery is also available for a similar amount, but proves quite slow unless coupled with express service. If you are sending large purchases home, note that **parcels** should and often can only be handled in the main provincial or county capitals. This way, your bundle will be in Athens, and on an international flight, within a day.

For a simple letter or card, a **stamp** (*grammatósima*) can also be purchased at a *períptero* (kiosk). However, the proprietors charge ten percent commission on the cost of the stamp, and never seem to know the current international rates.

Ordinary **post boxes** are bright yellow, express boxes dark red, but it's best to use only those by the door of an actual post office, since days may pass between collections at other street-corner or wall-mounted boxes. If you are confronted by two slots, "FSOTERIKÓ" is for domestic mail, "EXOTERIKÓ" for overseas.

The **poste-restante** system is reasonably efficient, especially at the post offices of larger towns. Mail should be clearly addressed and marked "poste restante", with your surname underlined, to the main post office of whichever town you choose. It will be held for a month and you'll need your passport to collect it.

PHONES

Making **telephone calls** is relatively straightforward, though the **OTE** (*Organizmós Tiliepikinoníon tís Elládhos*, the state-run telecom) has historically provided some of the worst service in the EU. However, since the mid-1990s this has improved drastically, and rates have dropped dramatically, under the twin threats of privatization and thriving competition from local mobile networks.

In theory, all exchanges are to become **digital** (*psifiakó*) by the year 2002, but in the meantime you may still encounter a few **pulse-analogue** (*palmikó*) exchanges. When ringing long-distance on such circuits, you must wait for a critical series of six electrical crunches on the line after dialling the country or Greek area code, before proceeding.

Call boxes, invariably sited at the noisiest street corners, work only with phone cards; these come in two denominations – 100 and 1000 units – and are available from kiosks, OTE offices and newsagents. Not surprisingly, the more expensive cards are the best value, though the 500 unit one tends to be rare. Despite numbers hopefully scribbled on the appropriate tabs, call boxes **cannot be rung back**, certainly not from abroad.

If you won't be around long enough to use up a phone card – the cheapest one costs £2 equivalent – it's probably easier to make **local calls** from a *períptero* or **street kiosk**. Here the phone may be connected to a meter (if not, there'll be a sign saying *móno topikó*, "local only"), and you pay after you have made the call. Local, one-unit calls are reasonable enough (30dr for the first three minutes), but long-distance ones add up quickly.

Other options for calling include **counter coin-op phones** in bars, kafenía and hotel lobbies; these take 10-, 20-, 50- and 100-dr coins and, unlike kerbside phone boxes, can be rung back. Most of them are made in northern Europe and bear instructions in English. Avoid making long-distance calls from hotel rooms, as a hundred percent surcharge will be slapped on.

For **international** (*exoterikó*) **calls**, it's better to use either kerbside card-phones or the very few remaining inside the premises of the nearest OTE office. As of writing, most OTE branches have withdrawn from the business of providing call facilities, with opening hours drastically shortened, and now generally resemble a UK high-street BT Phone Store with their array of phones and fax machines for sale. **Faxes** are best sent from post offices and some travel agencies – at a price; receiving a fax may also incur a small charge.

Overseas phone calls with a 100-unit card will **cost**, approximately, £2 for six minutes to all EU countries and much of the rest of Europe, and $5

PHONING GREECE FROM ABROAD

Dial the international access code (given below) + 30 (country code) + area code (minus initial 0) + number

Australia ☎0011	Ireland ☎010	UK ☎0
Canada ☎011	New Zealand ☎00	US ☎011

PHONING ABROAD FROM GREECE

Dial the country code (given below) + area code (minus any initial 0) + number

Australia ☎0061	Ireland ☎00353	UK ☎0044
Canada ☎001	New Zealand ☎0064	US ☎001

GREEK PHONE CODES

Athens ☎01	Páros ☎0284
Corfu ☎0661	Pátra ☎061
Iráklion ☎081	Rhodes ☎0241
Kós ☎0242	Santoríni ☎0286
Mobiles ☎093, ☎094, ☎095, ☎097	Skiáthos ☎0427
	Thessaloníki ☎031
Mýkonos ☎0289	Zákynthos ☎0695

USEFUL GREEK TELEPHONE NUMBERS

Ambulance ☎166	Forest fire reporting ☎191	Police/Emergency ☎100
ELPA Road Service ☎104	Operator (domestic) ☎132	Speaking clock ☎141
Fire brigade, urban ☎199	Operator (international) ☎161	Tourist police ☎171

CREDIT CARD OPERATOR ACCESS NUMBERS FROM GREECE

AT&T USA Direct ☎00 800 1311	British Telecom ☎00 800 4411
Australia ☎00 800 61 11	Cable & Wireless ☎00 800 4422
Australia (Ortus) ☎00 800 6121	Canada ☎00 800 1611
Bell Atlantic ☎00 800 1821	MCI ☎00 800 1211
Bell South ☎00 800 1721	Sprint ☎00 800 1411

for the same time to North America or Australia – more than double what you'd pay at night rates on a private line, whose economy is only approached if you buy the 1000-unit card. **Cheap rates**, a reduction of ten to fifty percent depending on call distance, apply from 10pm to 8am daily, plus all day Sunday, for calls **within Greece**; calling **internationally**, cheap rates take effect from 10pm to 6pm for Europe, 11pm to 8am for North America, and 8pm to 6am for Australia. Discounts for other destinations are minimal. With access to a subscriber line, night rates to any EU country are about 19p per minute equivalent.

British Telecom, as well as North American long-distance companies like AT&T, MCI and Sprint, provide **credit-card call** services from Greece, but only back to the home country. There are now a few local-dial numbers with some providers (given in the box opposite) which enable you to connect to the international network for the price of a one-unit call, and then charge the call to your home number – usually cheaper than the alternatives.

Mobile phones are an essential fashion accessory in Greece, which has the highest per-capita usage in Europe outside of Italy. There are three networks at present: Panafon, Telestet and Cosmote. Ringing any of them from Britain, you will find that costs are exactly the same as calling a fixed phone, though of course such numbers are pricey when rung locally. UK based users should note that only GSM phones will work in Greece. Coverage country-wide is fairly good, though there are a number of "dead" zones in the shadows of mountains, or on really remote islets. Pay-as-you-go, contract-free plans (such as Telestet B-Free and Panafon À La Carte) are being heavily promoted in Greece, and if you're going to be around for a while – for example, working a season in the tourist industry – an outlay of £80 or less will see you to a decent apparatus and your first calling card, which lasts six months rather than the sixty-day norm in Britain.

Email and **Internet** use is catching on slowly but surely in Greece; electronic addresses or Web sites are given for the few travel companies and hotels that have them. For your own email needs, you're best off using the various Internet cafés which have sprung up in the larger towns – street addresses are given where appropriate.

THE MEDIA

Although the Greek press and airwaves have been relatively free since the fall of the colonels' dictatorship in 1974, nobody would ever put forth the Greek media as a paradigm of responsible or objective journalism. Papers are almost uniformly sensational, state-run radio and TV often biased in favour of the ruling party, and private channels imitative of the worst American programming. Most visitors will tune all this out, however, seeking solace in the music of private radio stations, or the limited number of English-language publications.

British **newspapers** are fairly widely available in Greece at a cost of 500–700dr for dailies, or 900–1000dr for Sunday editions. You'll find day-old copies of *The Independent* and *The Guardian*'s European edition, plus a few of the tabloids, in all the resorts as well as in major towns. American and international alternatives include the turgid *USA Today* and the more readable *International Herald Tribune*, the later including as a major bonus a free, somewhat abridged English translation of the respected Greek daily *Kathemerini* (see below). *Time* and *Newsweek* are also widely available.

Among locally produced monthly **English-language magazines**, the late lamented *The Athenian* folded in 1997 after 23 years, with a rather sloppy successor, *Atlantis*, rising less than phoenix-like from the ashes. Slightly better is the expensive, glossy *Odyssey*, produced every other month by and for wealthy diaspora Greeks, and little different from the average in-flight magazine. **English-language newspapers** are the *Athens News* (daily except Monday, 300dr) in colour with good features and Balkan news, plus entertainment listings on Friday, available in most resorts, and the less commonly encountered rival weeklies *Hellenic Times* (Fridays, 300dr) and *Hellenic Star* (Thursdays, 400dr).

Before setting out from Britain, there are two **newsletters** worth consulting. One is *Greek-o-File*, a quarterly available only by annual subscription; contact Sylvia Stephenson at ☎01753/544475, fax 711554 or *greekofile@aol.com*. It's a mixed bag, with useful adverts, book or music reviews, Greek language lessons and travelling updates along with perhaps too many first-person touristic accounts, but recommended nonetheless. At the opposite end of the spectrum is the Greek London Embassy's newsletter, *Greece: Background-News-Information*. It's well-written, often witty, and gives a lively overview of events in the country over the past month. To register on their mailing list, contact Yiota Politis at ☎020/7727 3071 or fax 727 8960.

GREEK PUBLICATIONS

Many papers are funded by **political groups**, which tends to decrease the already low quality of Greek dailies. Among these, only the **centrist** *Kathemerini* – whose former proprietress Helen Vlahos attained heroic status for her defiance of the junta – approaches the standards of a major European newspaper. *Eleftherotypia*, once a PASOK mouthpiece, now aspires to more independence, and has links with the UK's *Guardian*; *Avriani* has taken its place as the PASOK cheerleading section. *Ta Nea* is mostly noted for its extensive small ads. On the far **Left**, *Avyi* is the Eurocommunist/Synaspizmós forum with literary leanings, while *Rizospastis* acts as the organ of the KKE (unreconstructed Communists). *Ethnos* became notorious some years back by receiving covert funding from the KGB to act as a disinformation bulletin. At the other end of the political spectrum, *Apoyevmatini* generally supports the **centre-right** Néa Dhimokratía party, while *Estia*'s no-photo format and reactionary politics are both stuck somewhere at the turn of the century. The **ultra-nationalist**, lunatic fringe is staked out by paranoid *Stohos* ("Our Goal: Greater Greece; Our Capital: Constantinople").

Among **magazines** not merely translations of overseas titles, *Takhydhromos* is the respectable news-and-features weekly; *Ena* is more sensationalist, *Klik* a crass rip-off of *The Face*, while *To Pondiki* (The Mouse) is a satirical weekly revue in the same vein as Britain's *Private Eye*; its famous covers are spot-on and accessible to anyone with minimal Greek. More specialized niches are occupied by low-circulation titles such as *Adhesmatos Typos* (a slightly rightist, muckraking journal) and *Andi*, an intelligent bi-weekly somewhat in the mould of Britain's *New Statesman and Society*.

RADIO

If you have a **radio** on your personal stereo, playing dial roulette can be rewarding. Greek music programmes are always accessible (if variable in quality), and since abolition of the government's former monopoly of wavelengths, regional stations have mushroomed; indeed the airwaves are now positively cluttered as every island town sets up its own studio and transmitter.

On Rhodes, 102 FM International (also on 104.3FM) features foreign DJs and mostly rock, as well as regular news bulletins in English. The Turkish state radio's third channel is also widely (if somewhat unpatriotically) listened to on border islands for its classical, jazz and blues programmes. The **BBC World Service** broadcasts on short wave throughout Greece; 9.41, 15.07 and 12.09 MHz are the most common frequencies. The **Voice of America**, with its transmitters on Rhodes, can be picked up in most of the Dodecanese on medium wave.

TV

Television first appeared in Greece in 1965, but it only became dominant during the 1967–74 junta, with the ruling colonels using it as a means of social control and to purvey anodyne variety revues, sports events and so on. As in many countries, it transformed the Greeks from a nation of live performers and coffee-house habitués to introverted stay-at-homes, which dovetailed nicely with the junta's "family values".

Greece's centralized, government-controlled **TV stations**, ET1, NET and (out of Thessaloníki) ET3, nowadays lag behind private, decidedly right-wing channels – Mega, Antenna, Star, Skaï and Seven-X – in the ratings. On NET, news summaries in English are broadcast daily at 6pm. Programming on all stations has evolved little since junta days, tending to be a mix of soaps (especially Italian, Spanish and Latin American), game shows, westerns, B-movies and sports. All foreign films and serials are broadcast in their original language, with Greek subtitles. Except for the round-the-clock channels Mega, Skaï and Antenna, channels broadcast from breakfast time, or just after, until the small hours. Numerous **cable and satellite** channels are received, including CNN, MTV, Filmnet, Euronews (in English), French TV5 and Italian Rai Due. The range available depends on the area (and hotel) you're in.

OPENING HOURS AND PUBLIC HOLIDAYS

It is virtually impossible to generalize about Greek opening hours, except to say that they change constantly. The traditional timetable starts at a relatively civilized hour, with shops opening between 8.30 and 9.30am, then runs through until lunchtime, when there is a long break for the hottest part of the day. Things (except banks and government offices) may then reopen in the mid- to late afternoon.

Tourist areas tend to adopt a slightly more northern timetable, with shops and offices, as well as the most important archeological sites and museums, usually open throughout the day.

BUSINESS AND SHOPPING HOURS

Most **government agencies** are open to the public on weekdays from 8am to 2pm. In general, however, you'd be optimistic to show up after 1pm expecting to be served the same day. Private businesses, or anyone providing a service, frequently operate a 9am to 6pm schedule. If someone is actually selling something, then they are more likely to follow a split shift as detailed below.

Shopping hours during the hottest months are theoretically Monday, Wednesday and Saturday from approximately 9am to 2.30pm, and Tuesday, Thursday and Friday from 8.30am to 2pm and 6 to 9pm. During the cooler months the morning schedule shifts slightly forward, the evening trade a half or even a full hour back. In Athens recently many enterprises have taken to keeping continuous hours (*synéhies óres*) during the winter, but this is by no means universally observed. Thus, there are so many exceptions to these rules by virtue of holidays and professional idiosyncrasy that you can't count on getting anything done except from Monday to Friday, between 9.30am and 1pm. It's worth noting that **delis** and **butchers** are not allowed to sell fresh meat during summer afternoons (though some flout this rule); similarly **fishmongers** are only open in the morning until they sell out (usually by noon), as are **pharmacies**, which additionally are shut on Saturday (except for the duty pharmacist).

All of the above opening hours will be regularly thrown out of sync by the numerous **public holidays and festivals**. The most important, when almost everything will be closed, are listed in the box below.

ANCIENT SITES AND MONASTERIES

All the major **ancient sites** are now fenced off and, like most **museums**, charge admission fees ranging from a token 500dr to a whopping 2000dr, with an average fee of around 800dr. At most of them reductions of twenty-five to thirty percent apply to senior citizens, and fifty percent to students with proper identification. In addition, entrance to all state-run sites and museums is **free** to all EU nationals on Sundays and public holidays outside of peak season – non-EU nationals are unlikely to be detected as such unless they go out of the way to advertise the fact.

PUBLIC HOLIDAYS

January 1
January 6
March 25
First Monday of Lent
(variable Feb/March; see below)
Easter weekend (variable April/May; see below)
May 1
Pentecost or Whit Monday
(50 days after Easter; see below)
August 15
October 28
December 25 & 26

VARIABLE RELIGIOUS FEASTS

	Lenten Monday	Easter Sunday	Whit Monday
2000	March 13	April 30	June 19
2001	February 26	April 15	June 4
2002	March 18	May 5	June 24

Opening hours vary from site to site. As far as possible, individual times are quoted in the text, but bear in mind that these change with exasperating frequency, and at smaller sites may be subject to the whim of a local keeper. Unless specified, the times quoted are generally summer hours, in effect from around late April to the end of September. Reckon on similar days but later opening and earlier closing in winter.

Smaller sites generally close for a long lunch and **siesta** (even where they're not supposed to), as do **monasteries**. The latter are generally open from 9am to 1pm and 5 to 8pm (3.30 to 6.30pm in winter) for limited visits. Most monasteries impose a fairly strict **dress code** for visitors: no shorts on either sex, with women expected to cover their arms and wear skirts; the necessary wraps are sometimes provided on the spot.

It's free to take **photos** of open-air sites, though museum photography and the use of videos or tripods anywhere requires an extra fee and written permit. This usually has to be arranged in writing from the nearest Department of Antiquities (*Eforía Arheotíton*). It's also worth knowing that Classical studies students can get a free annual pass to all Greek museums and sites by presenting themselves at the office on the rear corner (Tossítsa/Bouboulínas) of the National Archeological Museum in Athens – take documentation, two passport-sized photographs and be prepared to say you're a teacher.

FESTIVALS AND CULTURAL EVENTS

Many of the big Greek popular festivals have a religious basis so they're observed in accordance with the Orthodox calendar. Give or take a few saints, this is similar to the regular Catholic liturgical year, except for Easter, which can fall as many as five (but usually one or two) weeks to either side of the Western festival. Other festivals are cultural in nature, with the highlight for most people being to catch a performance of Classical drama in one of the country's ancient theatres. There's also a full programme of cinema and modern theatre, at its best in Athens, but with something on offer in even the smallest town at some point during the year.

EASTER

Easter is by far the most important festival of the Greek year – infinitely more so than Christmas – and taken much more seriously than it is anywhere in western Europe. From Wednesday of Holy Week until the following Monday, the state radio and TV networks are given over solely to religious programmes.

The **festival** is an excellent time to be in Greece, both for its beautiful religious ceremonies and for the days of feasting and celebration that follow. The mountainous island of **Ídhra** with its alleged 360 churches and monasteries is the prime Easter resort, but unless you plan well in advance you have no hope of finding accommodation at that time. Other famous Easter celebrations are held at Corfu, Pyrgí on Híos, Ólymbos on Kárpathos and St John's monastery on Pátmos.

The first great public ceremony takes place on **Good Friday** evening as the Descent from the Cross is lamented in church. At dusk the Epitáfios, Christ's funeral bier, lavishly decorated by the women of the parish (in large villages there will be more than one, from each church), leaves the sanctuary and is paraded solemnly through the streets. In many places, Crete especially, this is accompanied by the burning of effigies of Judas Iscariot.

Late **Saturday** evening sees the climax in the majestic Anástasis Mass to celebrate Christ's triumphant return. At the stroke of midnight all the lights in every crowded church are extinguished, and the congregation plunged into the darkness which envelops Christ as He passes through the underworld. Then there's a faint glimmer of light behind the altar screen before the priest appears, holding aloft a lighted taper and chanting *"Avtó to Fós . . ."* (This is the Light of the World). Stepping down to the level of the parishioners, he touches his flame to the unlit candle of the nearest worshippers, intoning *"Dévteh, léveteh Fós"* (Come, take the Light). Those at the front of the congregation and on the aisles do the same for their neighbours until the entire church – and the outer courtyard, standing room only for latecomers – is ablaze with burning candles and the miracle reaffirmed.

Even the most committed agnostic is likely to find this moving. The traditional greeting, as fireworks explode all around you in the street, is *"Khristós Anésti"* (Christ is risen), to which the response is *"Alithós Anésti"* (Truly He is risen). In the week up to Easter Sunday you should wish people a Happy Easter: *"Kaló Páskha"*; on or after the day, you say *"Khrónia Pollá"* ("Many years" as in "Many happy returns").

Worshippers then take the burning **candles** home through the streets; they are said to bring good fortune to the house if they arrive still burning. On reaching the front door it is common practice to make the sign of the cross on the lintel with the flame, leaving a black smudge visible for the rest of the year. The **Lenten fast** is traditionally broken early on Sunday morning with a meal of **mayerítsa**, a soup made from lamb tripe, rice, dill and lemon. The rest of the lamb will be roasted on a spit for Sunday lunch, and festivities often take place through the rest of the day.

THE FESTIVAL CALENDAR

Most of the other Greek festivals are celebrations of one or other of a multitude of **saints**; the most important are detailed below. A village or church bearing the saint's name is a fair guarantee of some sort of observance – sometimes right across the town or island, otherwise quiet, local and consisting of little more than a special liturgy and banners adorning the chapel in question. Saints' days are also celebrated as **name days**; if you learn that it's an acquaintance's name day, you wish them *"Khrónia Pollá"* ("Many happy returns"). Also listed are a few more **secular** holidays, most enjoyable of which are the pre-Lenten carnivals.

In addition to the specific dates mentioned, there are literally scores of **local festivals**, or **paniyíria**, celebrating the patron saint of the main village church. With hundreds of possible name-saints' days (calendars list two or three, often arcane, for each day) you're unlikely to travel around Greece for long without stumbling on something.

It is important to remember the concept of the **paramoní**, or **eve of the festival**. Most of the events listed below are celebrated on the night before, so if you show up on the morning of the date given you will very probably have missed any music, dancing or drinking.

January 1

New Year's Day (*Protokhroniá*) in Greece is the feast day of Áyios Vassílios, and is celebrated with church services and the baking of a special loaf, the *vasilópitta*, in which a coin is baked which brings its finder good luck throughout the year. The traditional New Year greeting is *"Kalí Khroniá"*.

January 6

Epiphany (*Ayía Theofánia*, or *Fóta* for short), when the *kalikántzari* (hobgoblins) who run riot on earth during the twelve days of Christmas are rebanished to the nether world by various rites of the Church. The most important of these is the blessing of baptismal fonts and all outdoor bodies of water. At seaside locations, the priest traditionally casts a crucifix into the deep, with local youths competing for the privilege of recovering it.

Pre-Lenten carnivals

These – known in Greek as *Apokriátika* – span three weeks, climaxing during the seventh weekend before Easter. *Katharí Dheftéra* (Lenten Monday) of the first carnival week is always seven weeks before Easter Sunday. **Pátra Carnival**, with a chariot parade and costume parties, is one of the largest and most outrageous in the Mediterranean, with events from January 17 until "Clean Monday", the last day of Lent; on the last Sunday before Lent there's a grand parade, with the city's large **gay population** in conspicuous participation. The Ionian islands, especially Kefalloniá, are also good for carnival, while the outrageous **Goat Dance** is enacted on Skýros in the Sporades.

March 25

Independence Day and the feast of the **Annunciation** (*Evangelismós* in Greek) is both a religious and a national holiday, with, on the one hand, military parades and dancing to celebrate the beginning of the revolt against Turkish rule in 1821, and on the other church services to honour the news being given to Mary that she was to become the Mother of Christ. There are major festivities on Tínos, Ídhra (Hydra) and any locality with a monastery or church named Evangelístria or Evangelismós.

April 23

The feast of **Áyios Yeóryios** (St George), the patron of shepherds, is a big rural celebration, with much feasting and dancing at associated shrines and towns. Good island venues include Skýros, of which George is patron saint, and Asigonía, a major pastoral centre in the mountains of Crete. If April 23 falls before Easter, ie during Lent, the festivities are postponed until the Monday after Easter.

May 1

May Day is the great urban holiday when townspeople traditionally make for the countryside to picnic, returning with bunches of wild flowers. Wreaths are hung on their doorways or balconies until they are burnt in bonfires on St John's Eve (June 23). There are also large demonstrations by the Left, claiming the *Ergatikí Protomayiá* (Working-Class First of May) as their own.

May 21

The feast of **Áyios Konstandínos** (St Constantine) and his mother, Ayía Eléni (St Helen), the first pro-Orthodox Byzantine rulers. It's widely celebrated as the name day for two of the more popular Christian names in Greece.

May/June

The Monday of **Áyio Pnévma** (the Holy Spirit) marks the descent of same to the assembled disciples, fifty days after Easter. Usually a modest liturgy at rural chapels of the Holy Spirit, gaily decked out with pennants.

June 29

The joint feast of **Áyios Pétros and Áyios Pávlos** (Peter and Paul), two of the more widely celebrated name days.

July 17

The feast of **Ayía Marína**: a big event in rural areas, as she's an important protector of crops. The eponymous port town on Léros will be en fête, as will Ayía Marína village on Kássos. Between mid-July and mid-September there are religious festivals every few days, especially in the rural areas, and between these and the summer heat, ordinary business comes to a virtual standstill.

July 20

The feast of **Profítis Ilías** (the Prophet Elijah) is widely celebrated at the countless hill- or mountain-top shrines of Profítis Ilías.

July 26

Ayía Paraskeví is celebrated in parishes or villages bearing that name, especially common across the northeast Aegean.

August 6

Metamórfosis toú Sotíros (Transfiguration of the Saviour) provides another excuse for celebrations, particularly at Khristós Ráhon village on Ikaría, and at Plátanos on Léros. On Hálki the date is marked by messy food fights with flour, eggs and squid ink (!), so beware.

August 15

Apokímisis tis Panayías (Assumption or Dormition of the Blessed Virgin Mary). This is the day when people traditionally return to their home village, and in most places there will be no accommodation available on any terms. Even some Greeks will resort to sleeping in the streets. There is a great pilgrimage to Tínos, and major festivities at Páros, at Ayiássos on Lésvos, on Lipsí and at Ólymbos on Kárpathos.

August 29

Apokefálisis toú Prodhromou (Beheading of John the Baptist). Popular pilgrimages and celebrations at Vrykoúnda on Kárpathos.

September 8

Yénisis tis Panayías (Birth of the Virgin Mary) sees special services in churches dedicated to the event, and a double cause for rejoicing on Spétses where they also celebrate the anniversary of the battle of the straits of Spétses, which took place on September 8, 1822. A re-enactment of the battle takes place in the harbour, followed by fireworks and feasting well into the night. Elsewhere, a lively festival at Vourliótes, Sámos, and a pilgrimage of childless women to the monastery at Tsambíka, Rhodes.

September 14

A last major summer festival, the **Ípsosis toú Stavroú** (Exaltation of the Cross), keenly observed on Hálki.

September 24

The feast of **Áyios Ioánnis Theológos** (St John the Divine), observed on Níssyros and Pátmos.

October 26

The feast of **Áyios Dhimítrios** (St Demetrius) is another popular name day. In rural areas the new wine is traditionally broached on this day, a good excuse for general inebriation.

October 28

Óhi Day, the year's major patriotic shindig – a national holiday with parades, folk-dancing and speeches to commemorate Metaxas's apocryphal one-word reply to Mussolini's 1940 ultimatum: "*Ohi!*" (No!).

November 8

Another popular name day, the feast of the **Archangels Michael and Gabriel** (Mihaïl and Gavriïl, or *tón Taxiárhon*), marked by rites at the numerous churches named after them, particularly at the rural monastery of Taxiárhis on Sými, and the big monastery of Mandamádhos, Lésvos.

December 6

The feast of **Áyios Nikólaos** (St Nicholas), the patron of seafarers, who has many chapels dedicated to him.

December 25

A much less festive occasion than Greek Easter, **Christmas** (*Khristoúyenna*) is still an important religious feast celebrating the birth of Christ, and in recent years it has started to take on more of the trappings of the Western Christmas, with decorations, Christmas trees and gifts. December 26 is not Boxing Day as in England but the **Sýnaxis tis Panayías**, or Assembly of the Virgin's Entourage.

December 31

New Year's Eve (Paramoní Protokhroniá), when, as on the other twelve days of Christmas, children go door-to-door singing the traditional *kálanda* (carols), receiving money in return. Adults tend to sit around playing cards, often for money. The *vassilópitta* is cut at midnight (see January 1).

CULTURAL FESTIVALS

As well as religious festivals, Greece has a full range of **cultural festivals**, including a few on the more popular islands. A leaflet entitled "Greek Festivals", available from GNTO offices abroad, includes details of these smaller, local festivals of music, drama and dance. The most durable are listed below:

Itháki Music Festival (July)
Ippokrateia Festival, Kós (July–Aug)
Manolis Kalomiris Festival, Sámos (July–Aug)
Réthymnon Renaissance Fair (July–Aug)
Sými Festival (July–Sept)
Lefkádha Arts Jamboree (Aug)
Iráklion Festival (early Aug)
Santoríni Music Festival (Aug–Sept)
Rhodes Festival (Aug–Oct)

CINEMA

Greek **cinemas** show a large number of American and British movies, always in the original soundtrack with Greek subtitles, though flyposters tend to be Greek-only. **Indoor screenings** are highly affordable, currently 1700–2000dr depending on location and plushness of facilities; they shut from mid-May to late September unless they have air conditioning or a roll-back roof. Accordingly in summer numbers of outdoor cinemas operate on the larger islands; an **outdoor movie** (marginally cheaper) is worth catching at least once for the experience alone, though it's best to opt for the early screening (about 9pm) since the sound on the 11pm show gets turned right down or even off to avoid complaints of noise from adjacent residences.

SPORTS AND OUTDOOR PURSUITS

The Greek seashore offers endless scope for water sports, with windsurfing-boards for rent in most resorts and, less reliably, water-skiing and parasailing facilities. Inland, the greatest attraction lies in hiking; often the smaller, less developed islands are better for this than the larger ones criss-crossed by roads.

As far as spectating goes, the twin Greek obsessions are **football** (soccer) and **basketball**, with **volleyball** a close third in popularity.

WATER SPORTS

The years since the mid-1980s have seen a massive growth in the popularity of **windsurfing** in Greece. The country's bays and coves are ideal for beginners, and boards can be rented in literally hundreds of resorts. Particularly good areas, with established schools, include Vassilikí on Lefkádha island, Prassoníssi on Rhodes, Kéfalos on Kós, Zákynthos, western Náxos, Kokkári on Sámos, Paleohóra on Crete, Skáka Kalloní on Lésvos and various spots on Corfu. You can almost always pay for an initial period of instruction, if you've not tried the sport previously. Board rental rates are very reasonable – about £6/$10 an hour.

Waterskiing is available at a number of the larger resorts, and a fair few of the smaller ones too. By the crippling rental standards of the ritzier parts of the Mediterranean it is a bargain, with twenty minutes' instruction often available for around £8–10/$13–16. At many resorts, **parasailing** (*parapént* in Greek) is also possible; rates start at £10/$16 a go.

A combination of steady winds, appealing seascapes and numerous natural harbours have long made Greece a tremendous place for **sailing**. Holiday companies offer all sorts of packaged and tailor-made cruises (see pp.6–7, 16 & 18 in "Getting There"). In Greece, small boats and motorized dinghies are rented out by the day at a few resorts. Spring and autumn are the most pleasant and least expensive seasons; *meltémi* winds make for pretty nauseous sailing between late June and early September, and summer rates for the same craft can be three times as high as shoulder-season prices. For more details, pick up the informative brochure "Sailing the Greek Sea" from GNTO offices, or contact the Hellenic Yachting Federation, Aktí Navárhou Koundourióti 7, 185 34 Pireás (☎01/41 37 351, fax 01/41 31 119).

Because of the potential for pilfering submerged antiquities, **scuba diving** is severely restricted, its legal practice confined in the islands to certain coasts around Kálymnos, Rhodes, Skiáthos, Corfu, Zákynthos and Mýkonos. For more information and an update on new, approved sites, contact the Union of Greek Diving Centres (☎01/92 29 532 or 41 18 909), or request the information sheet "Regulations Concerning Underwater Activities" from the nearest branch of the GNTO/EOT.

WALKING

Greeks are just becoming used to the notion that anyone should want to **walk** for pleasure, yet if you have the time and stamina it is probably the single best way to see the quieter islands. This guide includes descriptions of the best walking routes on a number of islands; for more detail, you may want to acquire specific hiking guidebooks – see p.503. See also pp.35–6 for details of hiking maps available, and pp.7, 16 and 18 for details of companies offering walking holidays on the islands.

FOOTBALL AND BASKETBALL

Football (soccer) is far and away the most popular sport in Greece – in terms of both participating and watching. The most important (and most heavily sponsored) teams are Panathanaïkós and AEK of Athens, Olympiakós of Pireás and PAOK of Thessaloníki. The only major team on the islands is the Cretan Ofí. If you're interested, matches (usually played on Wednesday nights and Sunday afternoons) are easy enough to catch from September to May; in mid-autumn you might even see one of the Greek teams playing European competition.

The nation's **basketball** team, by contrast, is one of the continent's strongest and won the European Championship in 1987 – cheered all the way with enormous enthusiasm. At club level, many of the football teams maintain basketball squads.

FINDING WORK

Since Greece's full accession to the European Union in early 1993, a citizen of any EU state has (in theory) the right to work in Greece. In practice, however, there are a number of bureaucratic hurdles to overcome. Formerly, the most common job for foreigners was teaching English in the numerous private cramming academies (*frondistíria*), but lately severe restrictions have been put on the availability of such positions for non-Greeks, and you will more likely be involved in a commercial or leisure-oriented trade. Similarly, that other long-standing fall-back of long-haul backpackers, picking fruit or greenhouse vegetables, is now the exclusive province of Albanian males.

SHORT-TERM WORK

EU membership notwithstanding, short-term work in Greece is always on an unofficial basis and for this reason it will generally be where you can't be seen by the police or you're badly paid – or, more often, both. The recent influx of between 500,000 and a million Albanians, Serbs, Bulgarians and Russians has resulted in a surplus of unskilled labour and severely depressed wages. Note that **youth hostels** are a good source of information on temporary work – indeed a few may even offer you a job themselves, if you turn up at the right time.

TOURISM-RELATED WORK

Most women working casually in Greece find jobs in **bars** or **restaurants** around the main resorts. Men, unless they are "trained" chefs, will be edged out by Albanians even when it comes to washing up.

If you're waiting or serving, most of your wages will probably have to come from tips but you may well be able to get a deal that includes free food and lodging; evening-only hours can be a good shift, leaving you a lot of free time. The main drawback may be the machismo and/or chauvinist attitudes of your employer. (Ads in the local press for "girl bar staff" are certainly best ignored; see "Sexual Harassment" on p.68)

Corfu, with its big British slant, is an obvious choice for bar work; Rhodes, Crete, Skiáthos, Páros, Íos and Santoríni are also promising. Start looking, if you can, around April or May; you'll get better rates at this time if you're taken on for a season.

On a similar, unofficial level you might be able to get a sales job in **tourist shops** on Corfu, Ídhra, Rhodes or Crete, or (if you've the expertise) helping out at one of the **windsurfing** schools that have sprung up all around the coast. **Yacht marinas** can also prove good hunting-grounds though less for the romantic business of crewing, than scrubbing down and repainting. Again, the best possibilities are likely to be on Rhodes, Corfu or Kálymnos; the Zéa port at Piréas is actually the biggest marina, but non-Greek owners don't tend to rest up there for long.

Perhaps the best type of tourism-related work, however, is that of courier/greeter/group co-ordinator for a **package holiday company**. All you need is EU nationality and language proficiency compatible with the clientele, though knowledge of Greek is a big plus. English-only speakers are pretty well restricted to places with a big British package trade, namely Crete, Rhodes, Skiáthos and the Ionian islands.

Many such staff are recruited through ads in newspapers issued outside Greece, but it's by no means unheard of to be hired on the spot in April or May. A big plus, however you're taken on, is that you're usually guaranteed about six months of steady work, and that if things work out you may be re-employed the following season with contract and foreign-currency wages from the home company, not from the local affiliate.

SELLING AND BUSKING

You may do better by working for yourself. Travellers report rich pickings during the tourist season from **selling jewellery** on island beaches, or on boats – trinkets from Asia are especially popular with Greeks. Once you've managed to get the stuff past the customs officials (who will be sceptical, for instance, that all those trinkets are presents for friends), there rarely seem to be problems with the local police, though it probably pays to be discreet.

Busking can also be quite lucrative. Playing on the Athens metro or the city's streets, it's possible to make around 3000dr in a two-hour session.

DOCUMENTATION FOR LONG-TERM EMPLOYMENT

If you plan to work professionally for someone else, you first visit the nearest Department of Employment and collect two forms: one an **employment application** which you fill in, the other for the formal offer of work by your prospective employer. Once these are vetted, and revenue stamps (*hartósima*, purchased at kiosks) applied, you take them to the Alien's Bureau (*Ypiresía Allodhapón*) or, in its absence, the central police station, to support your application for a **residence permit** (*ádhia paramonís*). For this, you will also need to bring your passport, six photographs, a blank *ipefthyní dhílosi* (declaration) form, more *hartósima* and a stable address (not a hotel). Permits are given for terms of one year (green triptych booklets), or five years (blue booklets) if they've become well acquainted with you. A **health examination** at the nearest public hospital is required, to screen for TB, hepatitis and HIV.

As a **self-employed professional**, you must satisfy the requirements of the Greek state with equivalent qualifications to native Greeks plying the same trade. You should also befriend a good accountant, who will advise you on which of the several varieties of incorporation are to your advantage; trading under a fictitious name is vastly more expensive tax-wise than doing business as a private person. You will need to sign on with **TEBE**, the Greek National Insurance scheme for self-employed people (analogous to Class 4 National Insurance contributions in the UK). If you are continuing to contribute to a social insurance scheme in a country which has reciprocal agreements with Greece (all EU states do), this must be proved in writing – a tedious and protracted process.

Once you're square with TEBE, visit the tax office or *eforía* to be issued a **tax number** (abbreviated "ah-fi-mi" in Greek, similar to a UK Schedule D number) which must be cited in all transactions. You will be required to prepare receipt and invoice books with your tax number professionally printed on them, or have a rubber stamp made up for applying that number to every sheet. The tax office will also determine which rate of VAT (the "fi-pi-ah") you should pay for each kind of transaction; VAT returns must be filed every two months, which is where the friendly accountant who chose your incorporation type comes in handy again.

The self-employed tend to be issued one- or five-year residence permits, and these are supposed to be free of charge. **EU nationals** who do not wish to work in Greece but still need a residence permit (such as property-owners needing to set up a bank account) will still get a "white" pass gratis, but must present evidence of financial solvency; personalized pink exchange receipts, travellers' cheques or credit cards are all considered valid proofs.

At the present time, **non-EU nationals** who wish to work in Greece do so surreptitiously, with the ever-present risk of denunciation to the police and instant deportation. Having been forced to accept large numbers of EU citizens looking for jobs in a climate of rising unemployment, Greek immigration authorities are cracking down hard on any suitable targets, be they Albanian, African, Swiss or North American. That old foreigners' standby, teaching English, is now available only to TEFL certificate-holders, preferably Greek, non-EU nationals of Greek descent and EU nationals in that order. If you are a non-EU foreign national of Greek descent, you are termed *omólogos* (returned Greek diaspora member) and in fact have tremendous employment and residence rights – you can, for example, open your very own *frondistírio* without any qualifications.

POLICE AND TROUBLE

As in the past, Greece remains one of Europe's safest countries, with a low crime rate and a deserved reputation for honesty. If you leave a bag or wallet at a café, you'll most likely find it scrupulously looked after, pending your return. Similarly, Greeks are relatively relaxed about leaving possessions unlocked or unattended on the beach, in rooms or on campsites.

However, in recent years there has been a large increase in **theft** and **crimes against persons** (blamed largely on Albanian and Romanian refugees) in towns, remote villages and resorts, so it's wisest to lock things up and treat Greece like any other European destination. Following are also a few pointers on offences that might get you into trouble locally, and some advice on the steadily dwindling practice of **sexual harassment**.

SPECIFIC OFFENCES

The most common causes of a brush with authority are nude bathing or sunbathing, and camping outside an authorized site.

Nude bathing is legal on only a very few beaches (most famously on Mýkonos), and is deeply offensive to the more traditional Greeks – exercise considerable sensitivity to local feeling and the kind of place you're in. It is, for example, very bad etiquette to swim or sunbathe nude within sight of a church. Generally, if a beach has become fairly well established as naturist, or is well secluded, it's highly unlikely that the police are going to come charging in. Where they do get bothered is if they feel a place is turning into a "hippie beach" or nudity is getting too overt on mainstream tourist stretches. Most of the time, the only action will be a warning, but you can officially be arrested straight off – facing up to three days in jail and a stiff fine.

Topless (sun)bathing for women is technically legal nationwide, but specific locales often opt out of the "liberation" by posting signs, which should be heeded.

Very similar guidelines apply to **camping rough**, which has been theoretically illegal nationwide since 1977 (see "Accommodation", p.46). Even for this you're still unlikely to incur anything more than a warning to move on. The only real risk of arrest is if you are told to clear off and fail to do so. In either of the above cases, even if the police do take any action against you, it's more likely to be a brief spell in their cells than any official prosecution.

Incidentally, any sort of **disrespect** towards the Greek state or Orthodox Church in general, or Greek civil servants in particular, may be construed as offences in the most literal sense, so it's best to keep your comments on how things are working (or not) to yourself. Every year a few foreign louts find themselves in deep trouble over a drunken indiscretion. This is a society where verbal injuries count, with a consistent backlog of court cases dealing with the alleged public utterance of *malákas* (wanker). In the non-verbal field, ripped or soiled clothes and untucked-in shirts are considered nearly as insulting. Don't expect a uniformly civil reception if dressed in grunge attire, since many Greeks – for whom poverty is an uncomfortably close memory – may consider that you're making light of hard times.

Drug offences are treated as major crimes, particularly since there's a mushrooming local use and addiction problem. The maximum penalty for "causing the use of drugs by someone under 18", for example, is life imprisonment and an astronomical fine. Theory is by no means practice, but

> In an emergency, dial ☎100 for the police; ☎171 for the tourist police in Athens, ☎01-171 outside of it; ☎166 for an ambulance; and ☎199 for the fire brigade.

CONSUMER PROTECTION ON HOLIDAY

In a tourist industry as developed as in Greece there are inevitably a number of cowboys and shady characters amongst the taxi-drivers, hoteliers and car rental agencies in particular. **EKPIZO**, the **Greek Consumers' Association**, has established a "Legal Information and Assistance for Tourists" programme, to be run yearly from June to September. Their main branch is in Athens (☎01/33 04 444), with offices also in Vólos, Pátra, Crete and Kavála. EKPIZO issues a pamphlet about holidaymakers' rights, available in airports and tourist offices. They are always prepared to pursue serious cases, by friendly persuasion or court action if necessary.

foreigners caught in possession of even small amounts of grass do get long jail sentences if there's evidence that they've been supplying the drug to others.

If you get arrested for any offence, you have a right to contact your **consulate**, who will arrange a lawyer for your defence. Beyond this, there is little they can, or in most cases will, do. There are honorary British consulates on Rhodes, Crete and Corfu, but full-ranking diplomats only in Athens and Thessaloníki.

SEXUAL HARASSMENT

Thousands of women travel independently in Greece without being **harassed** or feeling intimidated. Greek machismo, however, is strong, if far less upfront than in, for example, southern Italy. Most of the hassle you may get is from a dwindling minority of Greek men, known as *kamákia* (fish harpoons), who migrate in summer to the beach bars and discos of the main resorts and towns, specifically in pursuit of "liberated, fun-loving" tourists.

Indigenous Greeks, who become increasingly protective of you as you become more of a fixture in any one place, treat these outsiders with contempt; their obvious stakeouts are waterfront cafés, beach bars and dance clubs. Words worth remembering as unambiguous responses include "*pápsteh*" (stop it), "*afístemeh*" (leave me alone) and "*fíyeteh*" (go away), the latter intensified if followed by "*dhrómo*"! (road, as in "Hit the road!").

Hitching is not advisable for lone women travellers, but **camping** is generally not a problem, though away from recognized sites it is often wise to attach yourself to a local family by making arrangements to use nearby private land. In the more remote mountains and islands you may feel more uncomfortable travelling alone. The intensely traditional Greeks may have trouble understanding why you are unaccompanied, and might not welcome your presence in their exclusively male kafenía – often the only place where you can get a drink. Travelling with a man, you're more likely to be treated as a *xéni*, a word meaning both (female) stranger and guest.

Lone men need to be aware of one long-established racket in the largest island port towns. You may be approached by dubious gents asking the time or your origins, and then offering to take you for a drink in a nearby bar. This is invariably staffed with hostesses (who may also be on the game) whose main job is to convince you to treat them to drinks. At the end of the night you'll be landed with an outrageous bill, some of which goes for the hostess's "commission"; physical threats are brought to bear on reluctant payers.

DIRECTORY

BARGAINING This isn't a regular feature of life, though you'll find it possible with private rooms and some hotels out of season. Similarly, you may be able to negotiate discounted rates for vehicle rental, especially for longer periods. Services such as shoe, watch and camera repair don't have iron-clad rates, so use common sense when assessing charges (advance written estimates are not routine practice).

CHILDREN Kids are worshipped and indulged in Greece, arguably to excess, and present few problems when travelling. Baby foods and nappies/diapers are ubiquitous and reasonably priced, plus concessions are offered on most forms of transport. Private rooms establishments and luxury hotels are more likely to offer some kind of babysitting service than the mid-range, C-class hotels.

DEPARTURE TAX This is levied on all international ferries – currently 1500dr per person *and* per car or motorbike, often included in quoted fares. To non-EU states (Turkey, Cyprus and Israel), it's 4000–5000dr per person, sometimes arbitrarily levied twice (on entry and exit). There's also an airport departure tax of £7 equivalent (currently 3400dr) for destinations less than 750 miles away, £13.50/6600dr if it's further, but this is always included in the price of the ticket – there's no collection at the airport itself. This tax, nicknamed the *spatósima* locally, is supposed to fund ongoing construction of the new Athens airport at Spáta, so it may be abolished upon completion in March 2001.

ELECTRICITY Voltage is 220 volt AC throughout the country. Wall outlets take double round-pin plugs as in the rest of continental Europe. Three-to-two-pin adapters should be purchased beforehand in the UK, as they can be difficult to find locally; the standard 5, 6 or 7.5 amp models permit operation of a hair dryer or travel iron. North American appliances will require both a step-down transformer and a plug adapter (the latter easy to find in Greece).

FILMS Fuji and Kodak print films are reasonably priced and easy to have processed – you practically trip over "One Hour Foto" places in resorts. Kodak and Fuji slide films can be purchased, again at UK prices or better, in larger towns, but cannot be processed there – whatever you may be told, exposed rolls will be sent to Athens for handling, so wait until you get home.

GAY LIFE For men, overtly gay behaviour in public remains taboo in rural areas, and only visible at certain resorts like Ídhra, Rhodes or Mýkonos, still the most popular European gay resort after Ibiza in Spain. Fressós on Lésvos, the birthplace of Sappho, is (appropriately) an international mecca for lesbians. Homosexuality is legal over the age of 17, and (male) bisexual behaviour common but rarely admitted. Greek men are terrible flirts, but cruising them is a semiotic minefield and definitely at your own risk – references in gay guides to male cruising grounds should be treated sceptically. "Out" gay Greeks are rare, and "out" local lesbians rarer still; foreign same-sex couples will be regarded in the provinces with some bemusement but accorded the standard courtesy as foreigners.

LAUNDRIES *Plindiria*, as they're known in Greek, are beginning to crop up in most of the main resort towns; sometimes an attended service wash is available for little or no extra charge over the basic cost of 1500–1700dr per wash and dry. Otherwise, ask rooms owners for a *skáfi* (laundry trough), a bucket (*kouvás*) or the special laundry area often available; they freak out if you use bathroom washbasins, Greek plumbing and wall-mounting being what they are.

PERÍPTERA These are street-corner kiosks, or sometimes a hole-in-the-wall shopfront. They sell everything from pens to disposable razors, stationery to soap, sweets to condoms, cigarettes to plastic crucifixes, yoghurts to milk-in-cartons – and are often open when nothing else is.

TIME As throughout the EU, Greek summer time begins at 2am on the last Sunday in March, when the clocks go forward one hour, and ends at 2am the last Sunday in October when they go back. Be alert to this, as the change is often not well publicized, leading scores of visitors to miss planes and ferries every year. Greek time is thus always two hours ahead of Britain. For North America, the difference is seven hours for Eastern Standard Time, ten hours for Pacific Standard Time, with an extra hour plus or minus for those weeks in April and October when one place is on daylight saving and the other isn't. A recorded time message (in distinctly slow Greek, 24-hour convention) is available by dialling ☎141.

TOILETS Public toilets are usually in parks or squares, often subterranean; otherwise try a bus station. Except in areas frequented by tourists, public toilets tend to be pretty filthy – it's best to use those in restaurants and bars. Remember that throughout Greece, you drop paper in the adjacent wastebins, *not* in the bowl.

USEFUL THINGS TO BRING A high-quality, porcelain-lined canteen or drinking-water bottle; a small alarm clock for early buses and ferries; a flashlight even if you're not camping out (for power cuts); sunscreen of high SPF (25 or above, generally unavailable in Greece); pocket knife (Swiss Army type or similar), with tweezers, mini-screwdriver and other similar accessories; teabags (though good coffee is easy to find); and ear plugs for noisy ferries or hotels.

PART TWO

THE GUIDE

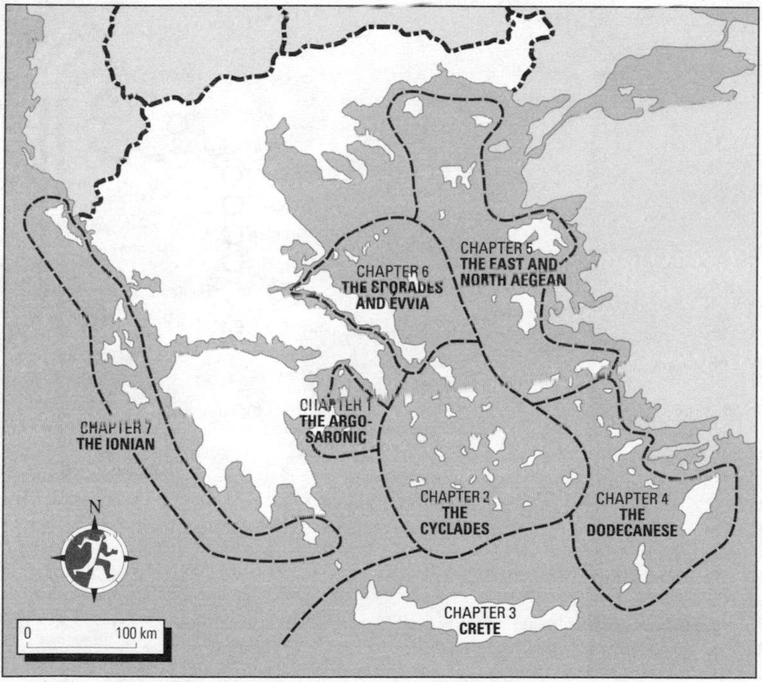

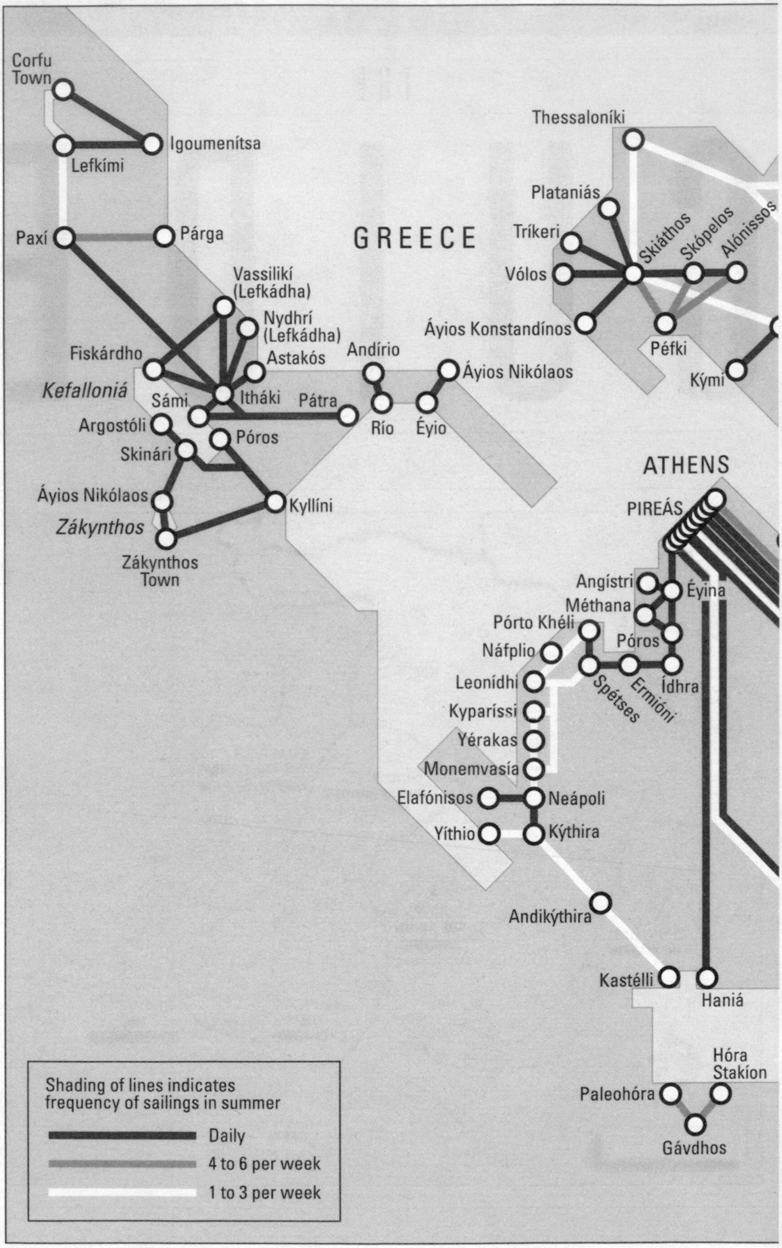
Corfu Town
Igoumenítsa
Lefkími
Paxí
Párga
GREECE
Thessaloníki
Plataniás
Tríkeri
Vólos
Skiáthos
Skópelos
Alónissos
Áyios Konstandínos
Péfki
Kými
Vassilikí (Lefkádha)
Nydhrí (Lefkádha)
Astakós
Fiskárdho
Kefalloniá
Sámi
Itháki
Pátra
Andírio
Río
Éyio
Áyios Nikólaos
Argostóli
Skinári
Póros
Áyios Nikólaos
Zákynthos
Kyllíni
Zákynthos Town
ATHENS
PIREÁS
Angístri
Éyina
Méthana
Pórto Khéli
Póros
Náfplio
Spétses
Ermióni
Ídhra
Leonídhi
Kyparíssi
Yérakas
Monemvasía
Elafónisos
Neápoli
Yíthio
Kýthira
Andikýthira
Kastélli
Haniá
Hóra Stakíon
Paleohóra
Gávdhos
Shading of lines indicates frequency of sailings in summer
Daily
4 to 6 per week
1 to 3 per week

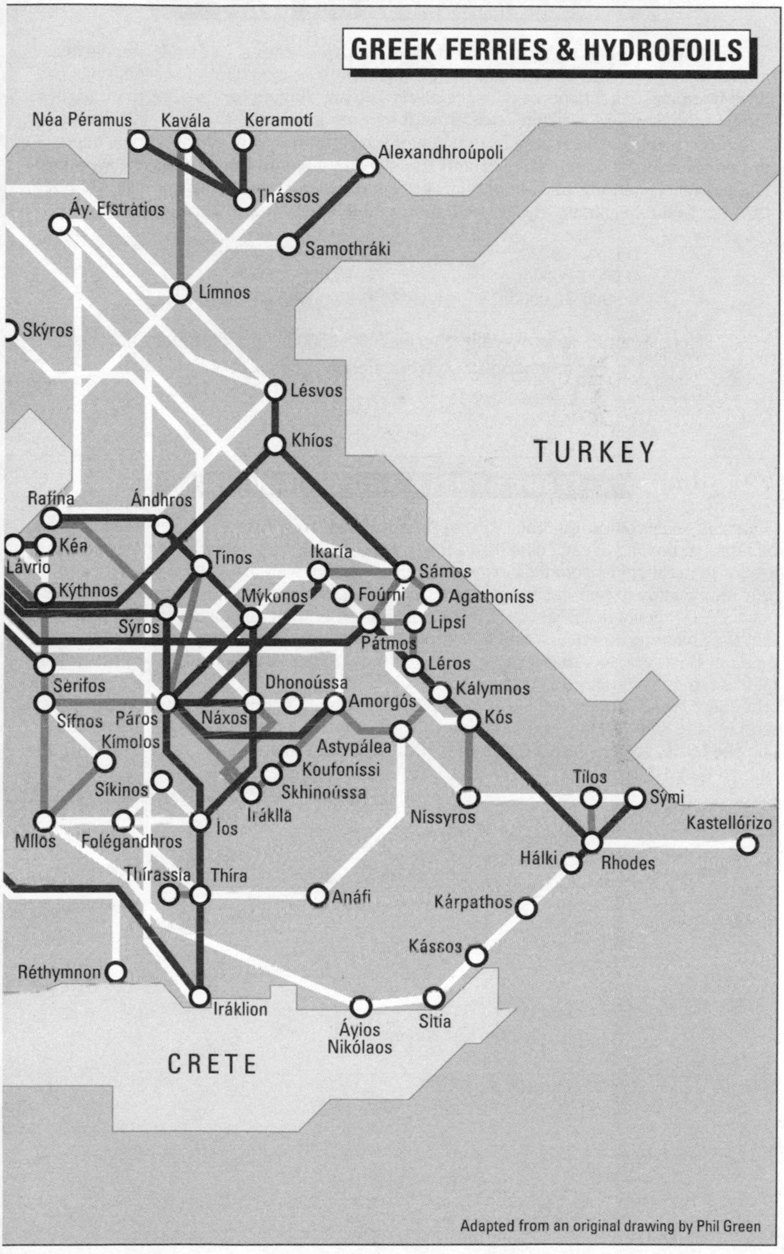
GREEK FERRIES & HYDROFOILS
Néa Péramus
Kavála
Keramotí
Alexandhroúpoli
Thássos
Áy. Efstrátios
Samothráki
Límnos
Skýros
Lésvos
Khíos
TURKEY
Rafína
Ándhros
Kéa
Lávrio
Tínos
Ikaría
Sámos
Kýthnos
Mýkonos
Foúrni
Agathoníss
Sýros
Lipsí
Pátmos
Léros
Sérifos
Dhonoússa
Kálymnos
Sífnos
Páros
Náxos
Amorgós
Kós
Kímolos
Astypálea
Koufoníssi
Síkinos
Skhinoússa
Tílos
Sými
Iráklia
Níssyros
Mílos
Folégandhros
Íos
Kastellórizo
Rhodes
Hálki
Thírassia
Thíra
Anáfi
Kárpathos
Kássos
Réthymnon
Iráklion
Áyios Nikólaos
Sitía
CRETE
Adapted from an original drawing by Phil Green

ACCOMMODATION PRICE CODES

Throughout the book we've used the following **price codes** to denote the cheapest available double room in each establishment in high season. Out of season, rates can drop by more than fifty percent, especially if you are staying for three or more nights. Single rooms, where available, cost around seventy percent of the price of a double.

Rented private rooms on the islands usually fall into the ② or ③ categories, depending on their location and facilities, and the season; a few in the ④ category are more like plush self-catering apartments. They are not generally available from late October through to the beginning of April, when only hotels tend to remain open.

① Up to 6000dr	④ 12,000–16,000dr
② 6000–9000dr	⑤ 16,000–20,000dr
③ 9000–12,000dr	⑥ 20,000dr and upwards

Note: Youth hostels typically charge 2000–2500dr for a dormitory bed.

For more accommodation details, see pp.44–47.

FERRY ROUTES AND SCHEDULES

Details of ferry routes, together with approximate journey times and frequencies, are to be found at the end of each chapter in the "Travel details" section. Please note that these are for general guidance only. Ferry schedules change with alarming regularity and the only information to be relied upon is that provided by the port police in each island harbour. Ferry agents in Pireás and on the islands are helpful, of course, but keep in mind that they often represent just one ferry line and won't necessarily inform you of the competition. Be aware, too, that ferry services to the smaller islands tend to be pretty skeletal from mid-September through to April.

In many island groups, ferries are supplemented by Flying Dolphin hydrofoils – which tend to take half the time and be twice the price. Most of the major hydrofoil routes are operated from May to early September, with lesser ones sometimes running in July and August only.

CHAPTER ONE

THE ARGO-SARONIC

The rocky, volcanic chain of **Argo-Saronic** islands, most of them barely an olive's throw from the Argolid, differs to a surprising extent not just from the mainland but from one another. Less surprising is their massive popularity, with Éyina (Aegina) almost becoming an Athenian suburb at weekends. Ídhra (Hydra),

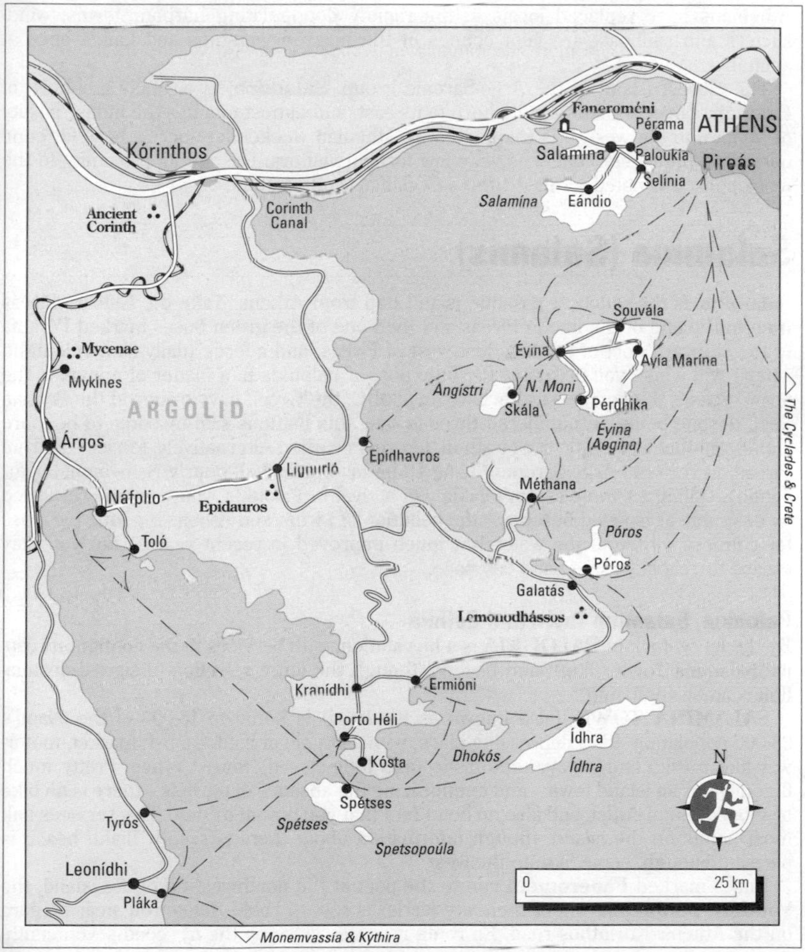

Póros and Spétses (Spetsai) are not far behind in summer, though their visitors tend to be predominantly cruise- and package-tourists. More than any other group, these islands are at their best out of season, when populations fall dramatically and the port towns return to a quieter, more provincial life.

Éyina, important in antiquity and more or less continually inhabited since then, is the most fertile of the group, famous for its pistachio nuts, as well as for one of the finest ancient temples in Greece. Its main problem – the crowds – can be escaped by avoiding weekends, or taking the time to explore its satellite isle, **Angístri**.

The three southerly islands, **Spétses**, **Ídhra** and **Póros**, are pine-cloaked and comparatively infertile. They were not extensively settled until medieval times, when refugees from the mainland – principally Albanian Christians – established themselves here. In response to the barrenness of their new homes the islanders adopted piracy as a livelihood. The seamanship and huge fleets thus acquired were placed at the disposal of the Greek nation during the War of Independence. Today, foreigners and Athenians have replaced locals in the rapidly depopulating harbour towns; windsurfers and sailboats are faint echoes of the massed warships and kaïkia once at anchor.

The closest island of the Argo-Saronic group, **Salamína**, is virtually a suburb of Pireás, just over a kilometre offshore to its east, and almost touches the industrial city of Mégara to the west. It is frequented by Athenian weekenders or is a base for commuting to the capital, but sees very few foreign visitors. Despite its proximity to the metropolis, it is noted for its distinct folk dances and costumes.

Salamína (Salamis)

Salamína is the quickest possible island hop from Athens. Take the Kifissiá–Pireás train to the end of the line in Pireás and then one of the green buses marked Pérama to the shipyard port of Pérama, just west of Pireás, and a ferry (daily 5am–midnight; 140dr) will whisk you across to the little port of Paloukía in a matter of minutes. The ferry crosses the narrow strait where, in 480BC, the Greek navy trounced the Persian fleet, despite being outnumbered three to one; this battle is said by some to be more significant than the Battle of Marathon, ten years earlier. Alternatively, ferries run from Pireás, next to the Argo-Saronic Flying Dolphins berth (half-hourly, 8am–5pm; 360dr; 45min), calling en route at Ambelákia. On arrival in Paloukía, you won't be rewarded by desirable or isolated beaches – the pollution of Pireás and Athens is a little too close for comfort, although the water has much improved in recent years – but you may escape the capital's smog and city pace.

Paloukía, Salamína Town and Selínia

By the ferry dock in **PALOUKÍA** is a bus station, with services to the contiguous capital Salamína Town (3km), and beyond, though the large selection of signed destinations can be confusing.

SALAMÍNA TOWN (also known as Kouloúri) is home to 18,000 of the island's 23,000 population. It's a depressing place, with a couple of banks, a fish market, motorway-like traffic, and an over-optimistic (and long-closed) tourist office. Pretty much uniquely for an island town – and emphasizing the absence of tourists – there is no bike or moped rental outlet, and also no hotel (not that you'd want to stay). Bus services link most points on the island, though information about them is scanty. Iliaktí beach is pleasant enough, some 5km to the west.

Buses marked **Faneroméni** run to the port at the northwest tip of the island, the **Voudóro peninsula**, where there are ferries across to Lákki Kalomírou, near Mégara on the Athens–Kórinthos road. En route it passes close by the frescoed seventeenth-century **monastery of Faneroméni** (6km from Salamína), rather majestically sited above the gulf.

Around 6km to the south of Paloukía is a third island port, **SELÍNIA**, which has connections direct to the Pireás ferry dock (winter 9.30am, summer five crossings daily between 8am–2.30pm; 380dr; 30min). It can also be reached direct by bus from Paloukía. This is the main summer resort, with a pleasant waterfront, a bank, several tavernas and two inexpensive hotels, the *Akroyali* (☎01/46 73 263; ③) and *Votsalakia* (☎01/46 71 334; ③).

Eándio and the south

South from Salamína Town, the road edges the coast towards Eándio (6km; regular buses). There are a few tavernas along the way, but the sea vistas are not inspiring. **EÁNDIO**, however, is quite a pleasant village, with a little pebble beach and the island's best **hotel**, the *Gabriel* (☎01/46 62 275; ④), owned by poet and journalist Giorgos Tzimas, who can be prevailed upon to recite a poem or two. The hotel overlooks the bay, whose waters are said to be returning to health, although the Salamína waterfront opposite can be less than sweet-smelling.

Two roads continue from Eándio. The one to the southeast runs to the unassuming village resorts of Peráni and Paralía (both around 4km from Eándio). The more interesting route is southeast towards Kanákia (8km from Eándio; no buses), over the island's pine-covered mountain, and passing (at around 5km) a monastery – dedicated, like most Salamína churches, to Áyios Nikólaos. At the monastery, turn off left to the harbour and small-scale resort of Peristéria (5km). This is a much more attractive settlement than the littered beach and scruffy huts of Kanákia itself.

Éyina (Aegina)

Given its current population of a little over 10,000, it seems incredible that **Éyina** (Aegina, Aigina) was a major power in Classical times, rivalling Athens. It carried trade to the limits of the known world, maintained a sophisticated silver coinage system (the first in Greece) and had prominent athletes and craftsmen. During the fifth century BC, however, the islanders made the political mistake of siding with their fellow Dorians, the Spartans. Athens seized on this as an excuse to act on a long-standing jealousy; her fleets defeated those of the islanders in two separate sea battles and, after the second, the population was expelled and replaced by more tractable colonists.

Subsequent history was less distinguished, with the pattern of occupation familiar to central Greece – by Romans, Franks, Venetians, Catalans and Turks – before the War of Independence brought a brief period as seat of government for the fledgling Greek nation. For a time it was, like Salamína, a prison island; only comparatively recently has it shaken off the consequent unfavourable reputation. The grim Éyina prison still stands, behind the stadium, but is currently used as a stray-dog shelter. These days, the island is most famous for its **pistachio orchards**, whose thirsty trees lower the water table several feet annually – hence the notices warning you of the perennial water crisis.

Athenians regard Éyina as a beach annexe for their city, being the closest place to the capital most of them would swim at, though for tourists it has a monument as fine as any in the Aegean in its beautiful fifth-century BC **Temple of Afaia**. This is located on the east coast, close to the port of **Ayía Marína**, and if it is your primary goal, you'd do best to take one of the ferries or hydrofoils which run directly to that port in season. If you plan to stay, then make sure your boat will dock at **Éyina Town**, the island capital. Ferries and hydrofoils also stop at **Souvála**, a Greek weekend retreat between the two ports devoid of interest to outsiders. Hydrofoils are far more frequent than ferries,

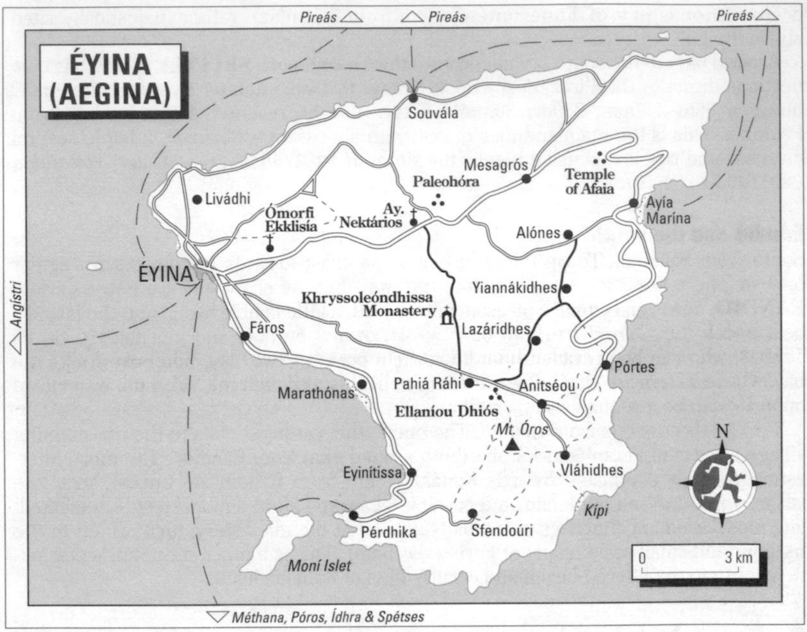

run from the same quay in Pireás as the conventional boats, and cost hardly any more for this particular destination.

Éyina Town

A solitary column of the Temple of Apollo beckons as your ferry or hydrofoil steams around the point into the harbour at **ÉYINA TOWN**. The island's capital, it makes an attractive base, with some grand old buildings from the time (1826–28) when it served as the first capital of Greece during the War of Independence. And for somewhere so close to Athens, it isn't especially overrun by foreign tourists, although accommodation prices are high, particularly at weekends.

The **long harbour** waterfront combines the workaday with the picturesque, but is nonetheless appealing: fishermen talk and tend their nets, and kaïkia selling produce from the mainland bob at anchor. North of the port, behind the small town beach, the rather weather-beaten Apollo temple column stands on a low hill that was the ancient acropolis and is known, logically enough, as **Kolóna** (Column). Around the temple are **ruins** (daily 8.30am–3pm; 500dr), but unlike at Afaia (see below), extensive excavation has been possible, revealing five thousand years of settlement and ten layers of city life. There is a small museum in the grounds. On the north flank of Kolóna hill there's an attractive bay with a very small, sandy **beach** – the best spot for swimming in the immediate vicinity of the town.

The town's other sights, such as they are, are the frescoed thirteenth-century church of **Ómorfi Ekklisía**, fifteen minutes' walk east of the port, and a house in the suburb of Livádhi, just to the north, where a plaque recalls the residence of **Nikos Kazantzakis**, when he was writing his most celebrated book, *Zorba the Greek*.

Arrival and accommodation

The **bus station** is on the over-ambitiously refurbished Platía Ethneyersías, just north of the ferry arrival point, with excellent services to most villages; buy your tickets before you get on the bus. Horse buggies and taxis go from nearby, the **post office** is here, and most accommodation is in the area immediately behind the square. Several offices on and behind the main waterfront rent cars, mopeds, motorbikes and mountain bikes, though Éyina is large and hilly enough to make a motor worthwhile for anything other than a pedal to the beaches towards Pérdhika. Four **banks** line the main waterfront. There's a **tourist police** post (☎0297/23 333) in the same building as the regular police, immediately behind the post office but reached from Leonárdhou Ladhá. Aegina Island Holidays (☎0297/26 430) on the waterfront, offers excursions to the Epidaurus theatre festival and handles tickets for the Sea Falcon Hydrofoils to Souvála and Ayía Marína.

Good inexpensive **accommodation** can be found in the *Electra* rooms (☎0297/23 360, fax 26 715; ③) on Leonárdhou Ladhá. The Scottish-run *House of Peace* (☎0297/28 726, fax 24 742; *houseofpeace@aig.forthnet.gr*; ③) is an old villa with charming, inexpensive self-catering rooms set in a large, quiet garden behind the bus station. Computer and email links are available, and the owner acts as an agent for other accommodation on Éyina and Angístri. On the seafront between Platía Ethneyersías and Kolóna are the *Areti* (☎0297/23 593; ⑤) and *Avra* (☎0297/22 303, fax 23 917; ⑤) hotels, where sea views for both of them compensate for the traffic noise. Next to the *Avra* is the friendly *Plaza Hotel* (☎0297/25 600; ④), while inland, near the cathedral, is the attractively restored *Traditional Pension* (*Eyinitiko Arhondiko*; ☎0297/24 968, fax 24 156; ④).

Eating and entertainment

Directly behind the fish market on P. Irióti is a particularly good and inexpensive seafood **taverna**, the *Psarotaverna Agora*, with outdoor seating on the cobbles in summer. Next to the *Areti* hotel, the small *Lekkas* is excellent for no-nonsense meat grills by the waterside, and near the *Plaza Hotel* is *Floisvos*, also offering charcoal-grilled food by the sea. Further south along the main quay, near the Ionian Bank, the *Economou* fish taverna-ouzeri serves good traditional food, while a couple of kilometres south, in the suburbs, the *Stratigos* serves straightforward but well-prepared food overlooking the little harbour at Fáros. Self-caterers will find good prices at the Kritikou supermarket on the Ayía Marína road, just beyond the stadium and prison.

In terms of **nightlife**, Éyina Town boasts two summer **cinemas**: the Olympia near the football grounds before the *Miranda* hotel and the new Akroyiali at the end of Eyina harbour on the Pérdhika road, which shows quality foreign films; the winter cinema, the Titina, is by the park of the medieval tower-house, a block below the OTE. The young and lively might try the *Apocalypse* or *Perdiotika* bars, or Petros' *Tropic* all-night café. The well-heeled can sample genuine live *bouzoúki* at Athenian prices at *Kanellas*, also on the waterfront. Most discos are across the island in Ayía Marína, but the vast *Vareladiko* disco is in Fáros, just beyond the *Stratigos* taverna.

The free *Essential Aegina* is a useful **listings** booklet, updated regularly during the summer season.

The Temple of Afaia

The Doric **Temple of Afaia** (Mon–Fri 8.00am–7pm, Sat & Sun 8.00am–3pm; 800dr) lies 12km east of Éyina Town, among pines that are tapped to flavour the local retsina, and beside a less aesthetic radio mast. It is one of the most complete and visually complex ancient buildings in Greece, its superimposed arrays of columns and lintels evocative of an Escher drawing. Built in the fifth century BC to replace a destroyed sixth century original, it slightly predates the Parthenon. The dedication is unusual: Afaia was a Cretan nymph who had fled from the lust of King Minos, and seems to have been worshipped almost exclusively on Éyina. As recently as two centuries ago the temple's pediments were intact and virtually perfect, depicting two battles at Troy. However, like the Elgin marbles they were "purchased" from the Turks – this time by Ludwig I of Bavaria, which explains their current residence in the Munich Glyptothek museum.

Buses from Éyina Town to Ayía Marína stop at the temple, or you could walk from Ayía Marína along the path that takes up where Kolokotróni leaves off, but rented transport allows you to stop at the monastery of Áyios Nektários and at the island's former capital of Paleohóra.

Áyios Nektários and Paleohóra

Áyios Nektários, a whitewashed modern convent situated around halfway to the Temple of Afaia, was named in honour of the Greek Orthodox Church's most recent and controversial saint, Anastasios Kefalas, a rather high-living monk who died in 1920 and was canonized in 1962. An oversized church – the largest in Greece – was recently completed on the main road below. Opposite the convent car park a partly paved road leads up into the hills towards the seventeenth-century convent of Khryssoleóndissa – primarily worth seeing for its views.

Paleohóra, a kilometre or so further east, was built in the ninth century as protection against piracy, but failed singularly in this capacity during Barbarossa's 1537 raid. Abandoned in 1827 following Greek independence, Paleohóra is now utterly deserted, but possesses the romantic appeal of a ghost village. You can drive right up to the site: take the turning left after passing the new large church and keep going about 400m. Some twenty of Paleohóra's reputed 365 churches and monasteries – one for every saint's day – remain in recognizable state, and can be visited, but only those of Episkopí (locked), Áyios Yeóryios and Metamórfosis (on the lower of the two trails) retain frescoes of any merit or in any state of preservation. Little remains of the town itself; when the islanders left, they simply abandoned their houses and moved to Éyina Town.

The East: Ayía Marína and Pórtes

The island's major package resort of **AYÍA MARÍNA**, 15km from Éyina Town, lies on the east coast of the island, south of the Afaia temple ridge. The concentrated tackiness of its jam-packed high street is something rarely seen this side of Corfu: signs abound for Guinness and cider, burger bars, and salaciously named cocktails. The beach is packed and overlooked by constantly sprouting, half-built hotels, and the water is not clean. It's really only worth coming here for connections to Pireás. There are some five ferries a day in season, with departures in the morning and late in the afternoon, and the Sea Falcon Line hydrofoils (☎0297/26 430) link both Ayía Marína and Souvála with Pireás.

Beyond the resort, the paved road continues south 8km to **PÓRTES**, a low-key shore hamlet. Among the uneasy mix of new summer villas-in-progress (no short-term accommodation) and old basalt cottages are scattered a few tiny fish **tavernas** and snack bars, with a functional beach between the two fishing anchorages. The road climbs to the village of Anitséou, just below a major saddle on the flank of Mount Óros, and then forges west towards the scenic village of **Pahiá Ráhi**, almost entirely rebuilt in traditional style by foreign owners. From here, a sharp, winding descent leads to the main west-coast road at Marathónas (for which see opposite), or a longer, paved and tree-lined route back to Éyina Town.

Mount Óros

Just south of the saddle between Pahiá Ráhi and Anitséou, mentioned above, are the foundations of the shrine of **Ellaníou Dhiós**, with the monastery of Taxiárhis squatting amid the massive masonry. The 532-metre summit cone of **Mount Óros**, an hour's walk from the highest point of the road, is capped by the modern chapel of Análipsi (the Ascension) and has views across the entire island and much of the Argo-Saronic Gulf.

A few other **paths** cross the largely roadless, volcanic flanks of Óros from Vláhidhes. Amazingly in this bulldozer-mad country, one to **Sfendoúri** hamlet still mostly survives, spasmodically marked by white paint blobs. The unmarked but well-used path, down to the sea at Kípi, may look tempting, but the litter-strewn boulder beach is far less appealing close to. Gerald Thompson's *A Walking Guide to Aegina*, available locally, describes in detail a series of walks across the range of mountains and wooded valleys between Mount Óros and the Afaia temple and down to the port of Souvála, all avoiding main roads.

The West: Marathónas, Pérdhika and Moní islet

The road due south of Éyina Town running along the west coast of the island is served by regular buses (8–10 daily). Small but sprawling **MARATHÓNAS**, 5km from Éyina, has the biggest of the west coast's small and rather scruffy sand beaches, and is tolerable enough, with a scattering of rooms, tavernas and cafés along the shore.

PÉRDHIKA, 9km along and the end of the coastal line, is more scenically set on its little bay and certainly has the best range of non-packaged accommodation on the island, outside Éyina Town. There are **rooms** on the main road, and just off it, immediately before the waterfront, the well-priced *Hotel Hippocampus* (☎0297/61 363; ②). On first sight the elongated village can appear characterless; however, further exploration reveals a relaxed, seaside-holiday atmosphere, very different from the rest of the island. On the attractive, pedestrianized waterfront esplanade, overlooking a panorama of Moní islet and the Peloponnese, are a dozen **tavernas** and cafés; probably the best food is at the first, *Nondas*.

The only other diversion at Pérdhika is a trip to the pale limestone offshore islet of **Moní** (500dr one way; 10min; several departures daily). There was once an EOT-run campsite on Moní, but this is now abandoned and derelict. There are no facilities on the island and most of it is fenced off as a nature conservation area. It's really only worth the trip for a swim in wonderfully clear water, as Pérdhika bay itself is of questionable cleanliness and has very small beach areas.

Angístri

Angístri, a quarter-hour by catamaran from Éyina, is small enough to be overlooked by most island-hoppers, though it is now in many foreign holiday brochures. The island fosters an uneasy coexistence between Athenian and German old-timers, who bought property here years ago, and British newcomers on package trips. Beaches, however, remain better and less crowded than on Éyina, and out of season the pine-covered island succumbs to a leisurely village pace, with many islanders still making a living from fishing and farming. Headscarves worn by the old women indicate the islanders' Albanian ancestry, and until recently they still spoke Arvanítika – a dialect of medieval Albanian with Greek accretions – amongst themselves.

The Angístri dock in Éyina Town is immediately south of the main harbour. **Boats and catamarans** from Éyina and Pireás call at Skála, and possibly at Mýlos. **From Pireás**, a direct ferry runs at least twice daily in season, once a day out of season, tak-

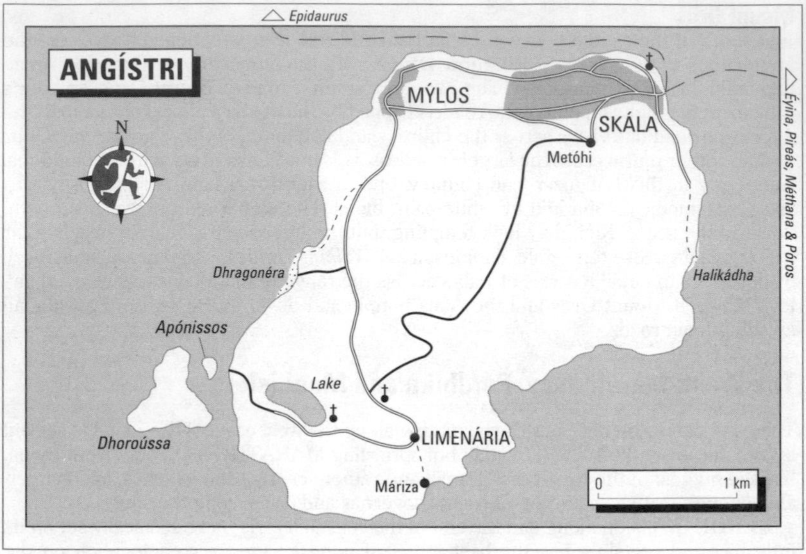

ing two hours; the fast catamaran three times a day, via Éyina, takes one hour. A water taxi is based in Angístri, but will be more expensive.

Skála and Mýlos

The essentially modern resort of **SKÁLA** is dominated by many new apartment buildings and hotels with little to distinguish them; they tend to face either inland or the windswept northeast corner of the island, over which Skála is rapidly spreading. The popular town beach, Angístri's only sandy one, nestles against the protected south shore of this headland, below an enormous church that is the local landmark. Just inland of the ferry dock is the attractive hotel *Yanna* (☎0297/91 228; ③), sharing a pool with the *Alter Ego* self-catering apartments; both are run by the helpful Nektarios Panou of Skala Travel (☎0297/91 356, fax 91 342; *nik.panou@otenet.gr*), who can arrange reservations for other accommodation. On summer weekends you would be well advised to reserve ahead. The *Neptune* taverna in Skála and the *Sailor* and *Konaki* in Mýlos are recommended.

Both **mopeds** and **mountain bikes** are available for rent; Limenária, near the end of the trans-island road, is less than 8km distant, so in cooler weather you can comfortably cross Angístri on foot or by bike. A road to the left of the harbour leads within fifteen minutes to the *Angistri Club*, with a disco-bar on the rocks above the sea, and the nearby *Alkyoni* taverna. From there, it's another ten minutes' walk to the secluded **Halikádha** pebble beach backed by crumbling cliffs and pine-covered hills; along with Dhragonéra (see opposite), this is the best that the island has to offer, and is clothing-optional.

Metóhi, the hillside hamlet just above Skála, was once the main village, and in recent years has been completely bought up and restored by foreigners and Athenians; there are no facilities.

Ever-spreading Skála threatens in the future to merge with **MÝLOS** (Megalohóri), just 1500m west along the north coast. Once you penetrate a husk of new construction, you find an attractive, traditional Argo-Saronic-style village centre. Although there's no decent beach nearby, it makes an alternative base to Skála, with plenty of rented **rooms** and some **hotels**. The *Milos Hotel* (☎0297/91 241; ③) is a good, well-positioned choice.

The rest of the island

A regular bus service, designed to dovetail with the ferry schedule, connects Skála and Mýlos with Limenária on the far side of the island – or you could hike from Metóhi along a winding dirt road through the pine forest, with views across to Éyina and the Peloponnese. The paved west-coast road takes you past the turning for **Dhragonéra**, a broad pebble beach with a dramatic panorama across to the mainland.

LIMENÁRIA is a small farming community set at the edge of a fertile plateau in the southeast corner of the island, and still largely unaffected by tourism. There are two tavernas – *Tasos* is very good – and a few rooms. A sign points to a misleadingly named "beach", really just a spot, often monopolized by male naturists, where you can swim off the rocks. A half-hour walk west of Limenária, on the old path which parallels the road, will bring you past a shallow salt lake, to a seasonal taverna overlooking the tiny islet of Apónissos and larger Dhoroússa beyond.

Póros

Separated from the mainland by a 450-metre strait, **Póros** ("the ford") only just counts as an island – but qualify it does, and far more than any other Argo-Saronic islands it is package-tour territory – its proximity to Pireás also means a weekend Athenian invasion. The island town has character though, and the topography is interesting. Póros is in fact two islands, **Sferiá** (Póros Town) and the much more extensive **Kalávria**, separated from each other by a shallow engineered canal, which is now silting up.

In addition to its regular ferry and hydrofoil connections with Pireás and the other Argo-Saronics, Póros has frequent boats shuttling across from the workaday mainland port of **Galatás** in the Peloponnese, and there's a car ferry every twenty minutes from near the Naval Academy. These allow for some interesting excursions – locally to the lemon groves of Lemonodhássos, ancient Troezen near Trizína, and the nearby Devil's Bridge. Further afield, day-trips to Náfplio or to performances of ancient drama at the great theatre of Epidaurus are possible by car, or by taking an excursion, available through travel agents in Póros Town (see below).

Póros Town

Ferries from the Argo-Saronics or from Galatás drop you at **PÓROS**, the main town on the island, which rises steeply on three sides of the tiny volcanic Sferiá. The harbour and town are picturesque, and the cafés and waterfront lively. Fishermen sell their catches direct from the boat and it is possible to arrange fishing trips. Particular sights are the hill-top clocktower and a small, well-labelled **archeological museum** (Mon–Sat 9am–3pm; free), with items from the mainland site of Troezen and elsewhere.

Near the main ferry dock is the helpful Family Tours (☎0298/23 743, fax 24 480) which has a variety of rooms available. Also on the waterfront are three other **travel agents**: Marinos Tours (☎0298/23 423), sole agents for the Flying Dolphin hydrofoils and with well-priced local maps, Hellenic Sun Travel (☎0298/25 901) and Saronic Gulf Travel (☎0298/24 555). All these agencies **exchange** money, arrange **accommodation** in rented rooms and handle **tours** off the island. If you want to look around on your own, the quieter places are up on the hill behind the clocktower, although prices are generally on the high side. To the right of the road to Kalávria

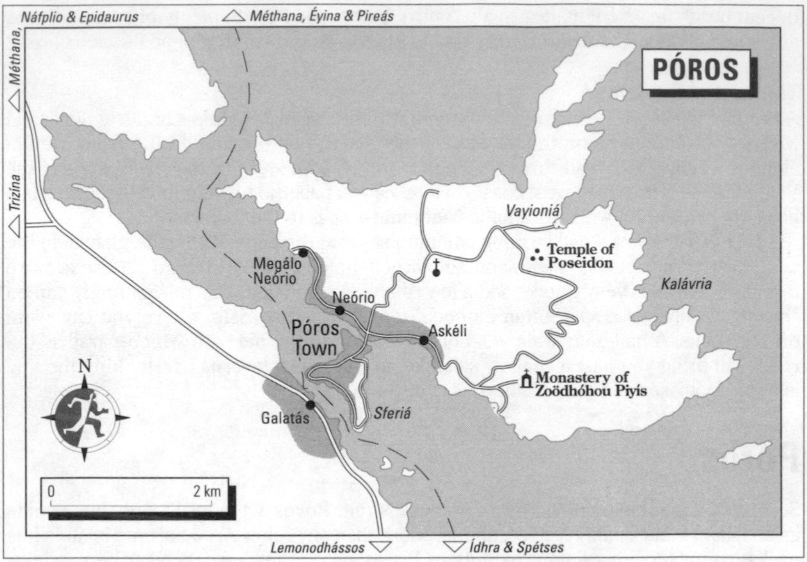

you'll find two reasonable hotels: *Dimitra* (☎0298/25 902, fax 25 653; ③) and *Latsi* (☎0298/22 392; ③). Most of the other hotels are across the canal. Camping is not encouraged anywhere on the island and the nearest official campsite, *Kyrayelo*, is just west of Galatás.

Down on the quayside, among the cafés, bars, creperies and souvenir shops facing Galatás, good-value **restaurants** include *Grill Oasis* and *Mouragio*, at the far end away from the ferry dock. *Moskhoyiannis* has traditional Greek food in the souvenir lane which runs between the Alpha Pistos (Alpha Credit) bank and the post office square. A well-signed lane, between the *Latsi* and the school, leads gently up, past the police station and Ergani weaving shop, to the upper square. Here, by the Áyios Yeóryios cathedral are a cluster of good tavernas: *Platanos*, *Perasma*, *Dimitris* – the last run by a local butcher, so excellent meat – and, just beyond, the *Kipos (Garden)*. The *Lithos* bar is nearby. The *Korali* and *Sirocco* **discos** provide nightlife, with both Greek and foreign music.

Additional facilities around the waterfront include **moped** and **bicycle** rental outlets (you can take either across on boats to the mainland), four **banks**, the **post office**, the summer-only Diana **cinema** and the helpful **tourist police** (☎0298/22 462; mid-May to Sept).

Kalávria

Most of Póros's **hotels** are to be found on Kalávria, the main body of the island, just across the canal beyond the Naval Cadets' Training School. They stretch for a couple of kilometres on either side of the bridge, with some of those to the west in Neório ideally situated to catch the dawn chorus – the Navy's marching band. If you'd rather sleep on, head beyond the first bay where the fishing boats tie up. Two kilometres from the bridge, in **Megálo Neório**, is the pleasant *Pavlou* hotel (☎0298/22 734, fax 22 735; ⑤), a larger beach and a watersports centre.

Alternatively, turn right through **Askéli**, where posh hotels and villas face good clear water. Two **bus** routes run half-hourly from Poros Town waterfront to Askéli and Zoödhóhou Piyís, and to Neório.

The monastery of Zoödhóhou Piyís and Temple of Poseidon

At the end of the four-kilometre stretch of road through Askéli lies the eighteenth-century **monastery of Zoödhóhou Piyís**, whose monks have fled the tourists and been replaced by a caretaker. It's a pretty spot, with a couple of summer tavernas at the beach below.

From here you can either walk up across to the northern side of the island through the pines, or bike along the road. Initially, Kalávria appears to be mostly pine forest, but the far side has fertile plateaus, olive terraces, small deserted beaches in narrow inlets and magnificent panoramic views. Foot or bike routes should lead you to a saddle in the hills and the few columns and ruins that make up the sixth-century BC **Temple of Poseidon** – though keep your eyes open or you may miss them; look for a small blue caretaker's hut. It was here that Demosthenes, fleeing from the Macedonians after taking part in the last-ditch resistance of the Athenians, took poison rather than surrender. The road leads on, back down in a circular route to the canal and Sferiá.

Ídhra (Hydra)

The port and town of **Ídhra**, with tiers of substantial greystone mansions and white-walled, red-tiled houses climbing up from a perfect horseshoe harbour, are a beautiful spectacle. Unfortunately, thousands of others think so too, and from Easter until September it's packed to the gills. The front becomes one long outdoor café and souvenir stall, the hotels are full and the discos flourish. Once a fashionable artists' colony, established in the 1960s as people restored the grand old houses, it has experienced a predictable metamorphosis into one of the more popular (and expensive) resorts in Greece. But this acknowledged, a visit is still recommended, especially out of peak season.

Ídhra Town

The waterfront of **ÍDHRA TOWN** is lined with mansions, most of them built during the eighteenth century, on the accumulated wealth of a remarkable merchant fleet of 160 ships which traded as far afield as America and, during the Napoleonic Wars, broke the British blockade to sell grain to France. Fortunes were made and the island also enjoyed a special relationship with the Turkish Porte, governing itself and paying no tax, but providing sailors for the sultan's navy. These conditions naturally attracted Greek immigrants from the less-privileged mainland, and by the 1820s the town's population was nearly 20,000 – an incredible figure when you reflect that today it is under

ÍDHRA FESTIVALS

On the second or third weekend in June, Ídhra Town celebrates the **Miaoulia**, in honour of Admiral Andreas Miaoulis whose **fire boats**, packed with explosives, were set adrift upwind of the Turkish fleet during the War of Independence. The highlight of the celebrations is the burning of a boat at sea as a tribute to the sailors who risked their lives in this dangerous enterprise.

On an altogether more peaceful note, the **International Puppet Theatre Festival** takes place here at the end of July and appeals to children of all ages.

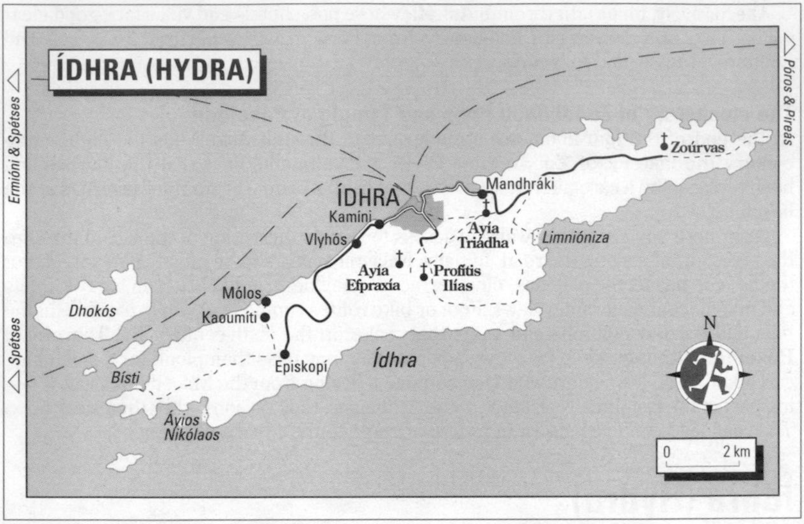

3000. During the War of Independence, Hydriot merchants provided many of the ships for the Greek forces and consequently many of the commanders.

The **mansions** (*arhóndika*) of these merchant families, designed by Venetian and Genoese architects, are still the great monuments of the town. A town map is available locally, if you are interested in seeking them out – some are labelled at the entrance with "*Oikía*" (home) and the family name. On the western waterfront, and the hill behind, are the **Voulgaris** mansion, with its interesting interior, and the **Tombazis** mansion, used as a holiday hostel for arts students. Set among pines above the restored windmill on the western point, the **Koundouriotis** mansion was the home of George Koundouriotis, a wealthy shipowner who fought in the War of Independence and whose great grandson, Pavlos Koundouriotis, was president of republican Greece in the 1920s. It is being refurbished as a museum with EU funding. On the eastern waterfront are the **Kriezis** mansion, the **Spiliopoulos** mansion and the **Tsamados** mansion – now the national merchant navy college which you can sometimes visit between lectures. The **historical archives museum** is also on the eastern waterfront (Tues–Sun 9am–2.30pm; 500dr).

Ídhra is also reputedly hallowed by no fewer than 365 churches – a total claimed by many a Greek island, but here with some justice. The most important is the church of **Panayía Mitropóleos**, set in a monastic courtyard by the port, with a distinctive clock-tower and a **Byzantine museum** of uncertain opening hours.

Practicalities

The town is small and compact, but away from the waterfront the streets and alleyways are steep and maps slightly ambiguous, so finding your way around can be difficult. There are several **banks** along the waterfront, and the **tourist police** (daily mid-May to mid-Oct, 9am–10pm; ☎0298/52 205) are on Vótsi. The **post office** and a **laundry** are on the small market square, behind the National Bank. The ferry office, Hydreoniki Travel (☎0298/54 007) is upstairs on a side-street to the left of the Bank, while the new Minoan hydrofoil office is through a doorway on the eastern waterfront, about 10m beyond the Studio Hydra shop.

There are a number of **pensions** and **hotels** along, or just behind, the waterfront in Ídhra Town, often charging up to a third more than usual island rates. Some of the restaurants along the waterfront act as agents for the outlying pensions and hotels, which could save you time and footwork; better still, phone ahead and book – certainly for any weekend. The *Amarillis* at Tombázi 15 (☎0298/53 611; ③) is a small hotel with comfortable rooms and private facilities; or there are a couple of old mansions beautifully converted into hotels, *Angelika*, Miaoúli 42 (☎0298/53 202; ⑥), and *Hydra*, steeply uphill at Voulgari 8 (☎0298/52 102; ③–④). Of the pensions, try the *Theresia*, further up Tombázi (☎0298/53 984; ③).

There's no shortage of **restaurants** and cafés around the waterfront, but for good tavernas you would do well to head a little inland. The *Garden* taverna, known for good meat, is on the road heading up from the hydrofoil dock, with the equally good *Xeri Elia* down the narrow street outside The *Garden*'s wall. Above the *Amarillis Hotel* is the small *Barba Dimas* taverna, which has wonderful mezédhes, snails and fish. Farther up on the same road, *To Kryfo Limani* is a pleasant taverna in a small garden, while farther yet will bring you good home cooking at the *Yeitoniko* (also known as *Manolis & Christina's*), which has tables on its small veranda. For light snacks and refreshments, try the small and friendly *Pigadi* café, below the *Amarillis*.

For **nightlife** go west; the long-established *Kavos* above the harbour is the best disco, while *Heaven* has impressive views from its hillside site. *Hydronetta*, above the sea at the edge of town, towards Kamíni, is lively and plays foreign music.

Beaches around Ídhra Town

The town's only sandy beach is at **MANDHRÁKI**, 1.5km east of the harbour along a concrete track; it's the private domain of the *Miramare Hotel* (☎0298/52 300; ⑤), although the windsurfing centre is open to all.

On the opposite side of the harbour, to the southwest, a broad coastal path leads around to **KAMÍNI**, about a twenty-minute walk. Just as you reach Kamíni on the right is a small pension, *Antonia* (☎0298/52 481; ③) On the left, across the street, Eléni Petrolékka has a popular rival pension and apartments (☎0298/52 701; ③). Also on the left is the *Kodylenia* restaurant, with fresh fish and wonderful views of the sunset. About 100m up the dry, paved streambed to the left is *Christina's*, a fine traditional Greek fish taverna.

Thirty minutes' walk beyond Kamíni (or a boat ride from the port) will bring you to **VLYHÓS**, a small hamlet with three tavernas, rooms, a small **beach** and a restored nineteenth-century bridge. The *Iliovasilema* taverna enjoys sunset views from the water's edge, near the small jetty, while just beyond are the attractive *Antigone* rooms (☎0298/53 228, fax 53 042; ⑤) and café. Any of these establishments can call a water taxi to whisk you back to town. **Camping** is tolerated here (though nowhere else closer to town) and the swimming in the lee of an offshore islet is good. Further out is the steep-sided island of **Dhokós**, large but only seasonally inhabited by goatherds and people tending their olives.

The interior and south coast

There are no motor vehicles on Ídhra, except for a few lorries to cart away rubble and rubbish, and no surfaced roads away from the port: the island is mountainous and its interior accessible only by foot or hoof. The net result is that most tourists don't venture beyond the town, so by a little walking you can find yourself in a dramatically different kind of island. The pines devastated by forest fires in 1985 are now regenerating.

Following the streets of the town upwards and inland behind the *Angelica* you reach a path which winds up the mountain, in about an hour's walk, to the **monastery of Profítis Ilías** and the **convent of Ayía Efpraxía**. Both are beautifully situated; the nuns at the convent (the lower of the two) offer hand-woven fabrics for sale. A path continues behind Profítis Ilías to a saddle overlooking the south coast and a steeply descending *kalderími* onwards to scattered houses and chapels near the sea. From the saddle, a faint path climbs to the right in twenty minutes to the 588-metre summit of Mount Éros, the Argo-Saronic islands' highest viewpoint. To the east of Profítis Ilías are three more monasteries, the nearest to town being **Ayía Triádha**, occupied by a few monks (no women admitted). From here a path continues east for two more hours to the cloister of **Zourvás** in the extreme east of the island.

A dirt road continues west of Vlyhós, past a busy boat repair yard, to **Episkopí**, a high plateau planted with olives and vineyards and dotted by a scattering of homes (no facilities), and then climbs above Mólos Bay, the property of an Athenian hospital owner, and closed to the public. From Episkopí itself, vague tracks lead to the southwestern extreme of the island, on either side of which the bays of **Bísti** and **Áyios Nikólaos** offer solitude and good swimming. Bísti has a pebble beach with good rocks for swimming off at one side; Ayios Nikólaos has a small sand beach. Points on the coast can be reached much more easily by water taxis, which will drop you off and then pick you up again at any time you arrange.

The best cove of the many on the south coast is **Limnióniza** (beyond Ayía Triádha), with a pebble beach and pine trees – though the overland access path is long (a half hour plus from town) and rough, and arrival by sea is recommended.

Spétses (Spetsai)

Spétses was the island where John Fowles once lived and which he used, thinly disguised as Phraxos, as the setting for *The Magus*. It is today very popular with well-to-do Athenians and with foreigners, and seems to have risen above the bad 1980s reputation earned by an unhealthy proportion of cheap package tours and lager louts. The architecture of Spétses Town is distinct and distinguished, though less photogenic than that

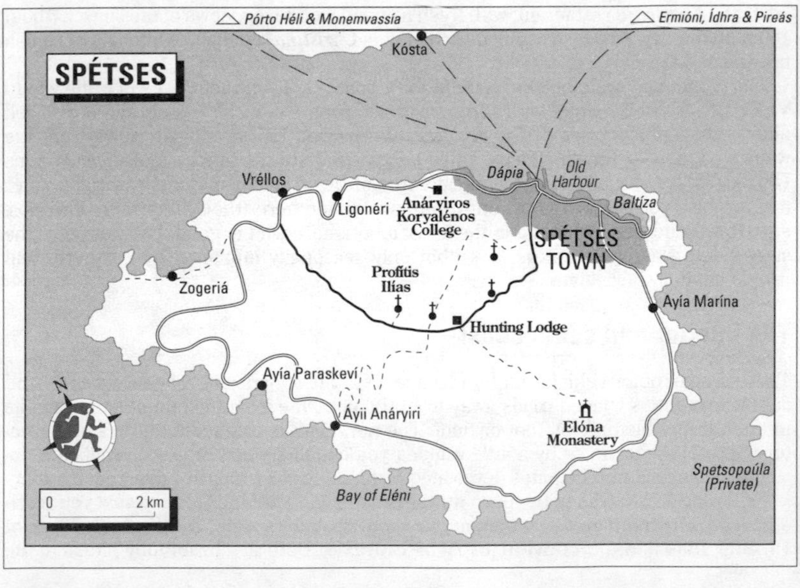

of Ídhra. Lacking any dramatic topography, and despite a bout of forest-fire devastation in 1990, hints of the landscape described by Fowles are still to be seen: "away from its inhabited corner [it is] truly haunted . . . its pine forests uncanny". Remarkably, at Áyii Anáryiri, Spétses' best beach, development has been restrained to a scattering of holiday villas.

Spétses Town

SPÉTSES TOWN is the island's port – and its only settlement. It shares with Ídhra the same history of late eighteenth-century mercantile adventure and prosperity, and the same leading role in the War of Independence, which made its foremost citizens the aristocrats of the newly independent Greek state. Pebble-mosaic courtyards and streets sprawl between 200-year-old mansions, whose architecture is quite distinct from the Peloponnesian styles across the water. Though homeowners may bring private cars onto the island, their movement inside the town limits is prohibited. A few taxis supplement the horse-drawn buggies, whose bells ring cheerfully night and day along the long waterfront, though animal welfare activists are justifiably worried by the condition of some of the horses by summer's end. Motorbikes, mopeds and noisy three-wheel mini-trucks are the preferred mode of transport, and career continuously through the town streets, making life almost as difficult for pedestrians as if cars had been allowed.

The sights are principally the majestic old houses and gardens, the grandest of which is the magnificent Mexis family mansion, built in 1795 and now used as the **local museum** (Tues–Sun 8.30am–2.15pm; 500dr), housing displays of relics from the War of Independence that include the bones of the Spetsiot admiral-heroine **Laskarina Bouboulina**. One of Bouboulina's homes, to the rear of the cannon-studded main harbour known as the **Dápia**, has been made into a **museum** (daily morning & late afternoon; 1000dr) by her descendants and is well worth visiting. Guided tours (30min) are given in English several times a day.

Just outside the town, Fowles aficionados will notice **Anáryiros Koryalénos College**, a curious Greek re-creation of an English public school where the author was employed and set part of his tale; it is now vacant, save for the occasional conference or kids' holiday programme. Like the massive waterfront **Hotel Posidonion** – now no longer a hotel – where kings and presidents once slept, the college was endowed by Sotirios Anaryiros, the island's great nineteenth-century benefactor. An enormously rich self-made man, he was also responsible for replanting the pine forest that now covers the island. His former residence, behind the *Hotel Roumani*, is a Pharaonic monument to bad taste.

Walking east from the Dápia, you pass the **Old Harbour** inlet, still a well-protected mooring, and the church of **Áyios Nikólaos** – with its graceful belfry, "*Freedom or Death*" memorial and some giant pebble mosaics. At the end of the road you reach the **Baltíza** inlet where, among the sardine-packed yachts, half a dozen boatyards continue to build kaïkia in the traditional manner; it was one of these that recreated the *Argo* for Tim Severin's re-enactment of the "Jason Voyage". An extensive new housing development behind Baltíza will probably edge local prices even higher.

Practicalities

A good way to get around the island is by bike, and, despite the hills, you can reach most points or make the 25km circuit without too much exertion. Several reliable **bike** and **moped** rental outlets are scattered through town.

All kinds of **accommodation** are available in Spétses Town, but be warned that prices are inflated in high season, although the town is smaller and less steep than Ídhra, so hunting around for a good deal is not such hard work. If you don't fancy pounding the streets yourself, try Alasia Travel (☎0298/74 098) or Melédon Tourist and Travel Agency (☎0298/74 497), both by the Dápia. Two simple but comfortable hotels are *Faros* (☎0298/72 613, fax 72 614; ④) on Platía Oroloyíou ("Clocktower Square") and *Stelios* (☎0298/72 971; ③) on the waterfront. A few hotels – the *Faros*, the *Alexandris* (☎0298/72 211; ④), above the petrol station, and the waterfront *Klimis* (☎0298/72 334; ④) stay open all winter. Inland and uphill from the centre, near the *Lazaros* taverna, rooms at the *Villa Orizontes* (☎0298/72 509; ③) have a fridge and extensive sea views.

In Spétses Town, **food** and **drink** tend to be overpriced. Among the better options are *Roussos*, 300m east of the Dápia, just beyond the *Klimis*; or the *Lazaros* taverna, about 400m up from the Dápia. For fish, go to the *Bouboulina* ouzerí opposite the fish market, which is before *Klimis*, or the long-established *Patralis* near the water in Kounoupítsa, west towards the *Spetses* hotel. The ouzerí *Byzantino* is popular, characterful, but expensive, as are many other places around the Old Harbour.

By day, *To Kafenio*, near the Flying Dolphin office at the Dápia, remains steadfastly traditional, with drinks and lunchtime mezedhes – a good place to watch and wait for your ferry. By night, clubbers head for *Figaro*, in the Old Harbour, and the places at the other end of town around Kounoupítsa. Few of these places shut until the fishermen are setting out.

The **post office** is near the *Roussos* taverna, while a couple of **banks** are behind the Dápia, near the *Roumani* hotel. There is a **laundry** behind Platía Oroloyíou.

Around the island

For **swimming** you need to get clear of the town. Beaches within walking distance are at **Ayía Marína** (twenty minutes east, with the very pleasant *Paradise* restaurant), at various spots beyond the **Old Harbour**, and several other spots half an hour away in either direction. The tempting smaller isle of **Spetsopoúla**, just offshore from Ayía Marína, is off-limits: it's the private property of the heirs of shipping magnate Stavros Niarchos.

For heading further afield, you'll need to hire a **bike** or **moped**, or use the **kaïkia** rides from the Dápia, which run to beaches around the island in summer. A very expensive alternative are **water taxis**, though they can take up to ten people. **Walkers** might want to go over the top of the island to Áyii Anáryiri; forest fire has ravaged much of the southern side's pines between Ayía Marína and Áyii Anáryiri, though happily they are growing back. Routes out of town start from beyond the *Lazaros* taverna, and pass the forest service firewatch tower. Brave the precariously attached steps and you're rewarded with the island's highest and best viewpoint.

West from Spétses Town

Heading west from the Dápia around the coast, the road is paved or in good condition almost all around the island. The forest that survived the fires stretches from the central hills right down to the western shores and makes for a beautiful coastline with little coves and rocky promontories, all shaded by trees. *Panas Taverna* at Ligonéri, run by a Greek-American woman, provides wonderful respite from the bustle of town. You can swim below and then have lunch or dinner under the pines. A regular bus service runs to Ligonéri in season, from in front of the *Hotel Posidonion*.

Vréllos is the next place you come to, at the mouth of a wooded valley known locally as "Paradise", which would be a fairly apt description, except that, like so many of the beaches, it becomes littered every year with windblown rubbish. However, the entire shore is dotted with coves and in a few places there are small, seasonal tavernas – there's a good one at **Zogeriá**, for instance, where the scenery and rocks more than make up for the small beach.

Working your way anti-clockwise around the coast towards Áyii Anáryiri you reach **Áyia Paraskeví** with its small church and beach – one of the most beautiful coves on

Spétses and an alternate stop on some of the kaïki runs. There's a basic beach café and watersports here in summer. On the hill behind is the house John Fowles used as the setting for *The Magus*, the **Villa Yasemiá**. It was owned by the late Alkis Botassis, who claimed to be the model for the *Magus* character – though Fowles denies "appropriating" anything more than his "outward appearance" and the "superb site" of his house.

Áyii Anáryiri

Áyii Anáryiri, on the south side of the island, is the best, if also the most popular, beach: a beautiful, long, sheltered bay of fine sand. Gorgeous first thing in the morning, it fills up later in the day, with bathers, windsurfers and, at one corner, speedboat-driving waterski instructors. On the right-hand side of the bay, looking out to sea, there's a sea cave, which you can walk or swim to and explore, if you're not discouraged by the ominous rockfall on the access steps. There's a good seafront taverna and another just behind, *Tassos*, run by one of the island's great eccentrics.

travel details

Ferries

From the central harbour at **Pireás** at least 4 boats daily run to Ayía Marína (1hr) and 11 to Éyina (1hr 30min); 1–2 daily to Skála and Mýlos (2hr); 4 daily to Póros (3hr 30min); 1–2 daily to Ídhra (4hr 30min) and Spétses (5hr 30min). About 4 connections daily between Éyina and Póros; 4–5 daily between Éyina and Angístri; from Angístri about 4 weekly to Paleá Epídhavros, far less frequently to Póros and Méthana.

Most of the ferries stop on the Peloponnesian mainland at Méthana (between Éyina and Póros) and Ermióni (between Ídhra and Spétses); it is possible to board them here. Some continue from Spétses to Pórto Héli. There are also constant boats between Póros and Galatás (10min) from dawn until late at night, boat-taxis between Spétses and Pórto Héli, and 4 daily ferries between Spétses and Kósta.

NB There are more ferries at weekends and fewer out of season (although the service remains good); for Éyina and Póros they leave Pireás most frequently between 7.30am and 9am, and 2pm and 4pm. Do not buy a return ticket as it saves no money and limits you to one specific boat. The general information number for the Argo-Saronic ferries is ☎01/41 75 382.

Flying Dolphin hydrofoils

Approximately hourly services from the central harbour at Pireás to **Éyina** only 6am–8pm in season, 7am–7pm out of season (40min).

All hydrofoils going beyond Éyina leave from the **Zéa Marina**: 4–15 times daily to Póros (1hr), Ídhra (1hr 40min) and Spétses (2hr–2hr 30min). All these times depend upon the stops en route, and frequencies vary with the season.

Éyina is connected with Méthana and Póros 1–3 times a day; Póros, Ídhra and Spétses with each other 5–7 times daily. Some hydrofoils also stop at Méthana and Ermióni and most of those to Spétses continue to Porto Héli (15min more). This is a junction of the hydrofoil route – in season there is usually one a day onwards to Toló and Náfplio (and vice versa; 30 and 45min) and another to Monemvassía (2hr). The Monemvassía hydrofoil continues 2–4 days a week (Friday to Sunday) to the island of Kýthira.

NB Services are heavily reduced out of season, though all the routes between Pórto Héli and Pireás still run. Hydrofoils are usually twice as fast and twice as expensive as ordinary boats, though to Éyina the price is little different. You can now buy round-trip tickets to destinations in the Argo Saronic Gulf. In season, it's not unusual for departures to be fully booked for a day or so at a time.

Details and tickets available from the Minoan Pireás Flying Dolphins office at Ákti Themistokléous 8 (☎01/42 80 001, number perennially engaged). Their Ceres Athens office at Filellínon 3 (☎01/32 44 600) is more convenient if you are in Athens. Tickets can also be bought at the departure quays on Aktí Tselépi in Pireás and at Zéa.

CHAPTER TWO

THE CYCLADES

Named after the circle they form around the sacred island of Delos, the **Cyclades** (Kykládhes) is the most satisfying Greek archipelago for island-hopping. On no other group do you get quite such a strong feeling of each island as a microcosm, each with its own distinct traditions, customs and path of modern development. Most of these self-contained realms are compact enough to walk around in a few days, giving you a sense of completeness and identity impossible on, say, Crete or most of the Ionian islands.

The islands do share some features however, the majority of them (Ándhros, Náxos, Sérifos and Kéa excepted) being arid and rocky; most also share the "Cycladic" style of brilliant white, cubist architecture. The extent and impact of tourism, though, is markedly haphazard, so that although some English is spoken on most islands, a slight detour from the beaten track – from Íos to Síkinos, for example – can have you groping for your Greek phrasebook.

But whatever the level of tourist development, there are only two islands where it has come completely to dominate their character: **Íos**, the original hippie-island and still a paradise for hard-drinking backpackers, and **Mýkonos**, by far the most popular of the group, with its teeming old town, selection of nude beaches and sophisticated clubs and gay bars. After these two, **Páros**, **Sífnos**, **Náxos**, and **Thíra** (Santoríni) are currently the most popular, with their beaches and main towns drastically overcrowded at the height of the season. To avoid the hordes altogether – except in August, when nearly everywhere is overrun and escape is impossible – the most promising islands are **Síkinos**, **Kímolos** or **Anáfi**, or the minor islets around Náxos. For a different view of the Cyclades, visit **Tínos** and its imposing pilgrimage church, a major spiritual centre of Greek Orthodoxy, or **Sýros** with its elegant townscape, and (like Tínos), large Catholic minority. Due to their closeness to Athens, adjacent **Kýthnos** and **Kéa** are predictably popular – and relatively expensive – weekend havens for Greeks. The one major ancient

ACCOMMODATION PRICE CODES

Throughout the book we've used the following **price codes** to denote the cheapest available double room in each establishment in high season. Out of season, rates can drop by more than fifty percent, especially if you are staying for three or more nights. Single rooms, where available, cost around seventy percent of the price of a double.

Rented private rooms on the islands usually fall into the ② or ③ categories, depending on their location and facilities, and the season; a few in the ④ category are more like plush self-catering apartments. They are not generally available from late October through to the beginning of April, when only hotels tend to remain open.

① Up to 6000dr	④ 12,000–16,000dr
② 6000–9000dr	⑤ 16,000–20,000dr
③ 9000–12,000dr	⑥ 20,000dr and upwards

Note: Youth hostels typically charge 2000–2500dr for a dormitory bed.

For more accommodation details, see pp.44–47.

site is **Delos** (Dhílos), certainly worth making time for; the commercial and religious centre of the Classical Greek world, it's visited most easily on a day-trip, by kaïki or jet boat from Mýkonos.

When it comes to **moving on**, many of the islands – in particular Mílos, Páros, Náxos and Thíra – are handily connected with Crete (easier in season), while from Tínos, Mýkonos, Sýros, Páros, Náxos, Thíra or Amorgós you can reach many of the Dodecanese by direct boat. Similarly, you can regularly get from Mýkonos, Náxos, Sýros and Páros to Ikaría and Sámos (in the eastern Aegean – see p.323 and p.311).

One consideration for the timing of your visit is that the Cyclades often get frustratingly **stormy**, particularly in early spring or late autumn, and it's also the group worst affected by the *meltémi*, which blows sand and tables about with ease throughout much of July and August. Delayed or cancelled ferries are not uncommon, so if you're heading back to Athens to catch a flight leave yourself a day or two's leeway.

Kéa (Tziá)

Kéa is the closest of the Cyclades to the mainland and is extremely popular in summer, and at weekends year-round, with Athenians. Their impact is mostly confined to certain small coastal resorts, leaving most of the interior quiet, although there is a preponderance of expensive apartments and villas and not as many good tavernas as you might expect because so many visitors self-cater. Midweek, or outside peak season, Kéa is a more enticing destination, with its rocky, forbidding perimeter and inland oak and almond groves.

As ancient Keos, the island and its strategic, well-placed harbour supported four cities – a pre-eminence that continued until the nineteenth century when Sýros became the main Greek port. Today, tourists account for the sea traffic: regular (in season) ferry connections with Lávrio on the mainland (only a ninety-minute bus ride from Athens), plus useful hydrofoils and ferries to and from Pireás, Sýros, and Kýthnos.

The northwest coast: Korissía to Otziás

The small northern ferry and hydrofoil port of **KORISSÍA** has fallen victim to uneven expansion and has little beauty to lose; if you don't like its looks upon disembarking, try to get a bus to Písses (16km), Otziás (6km) or Ioulídha (6km). Buses usually meet the boats; from July until August there's a regular fixed schedule around the island, but at other times they can be very elusive. There are just four **taxis** on Kéa, and two motorbike rental outfits: Antonis (☎0288/21 097), close to the *Karthea* hotel, and Moto Center (☎0288/21 844), a little inland near the **OTE**, both of them being more expensive than on most islands.

There's a list of rooms in the seafront tourist information office, and the kindly agents for the Flying Dolphin hydrofoils (To Stegadhi bookshop) sell maps and guides, and can phone around in search of **accommodation**. The best choices are the *Nikitas* pension (☎0288/21 193; ③), open all year and very friendly; *Hotel Korissia* (☎0288/21 484; ④), well inland along the stream bed; *Hotel Tzia* (☎0288/21 305; ④), right behind the best end of the otherwise uninspiring port beach; and the somewhat noisy *Karthea* (☎0288/21 204; ④), which does, however, boast single rooms and year-round operation – and a cameo appearance in recent Greek history. When the junta fell in July 1974, the colonels were initially imprisoned for some weeks in the then-new hotel, while the recently restored civilian government pondered what to do with them; Kéa was then so remote and unvisited that the erstwhile tyrants were safely out of reach of a vengeful populace. For **eating**, *Iy Akri* and *Angyrovoli* near the *Karthea* hotel have standard fare, while near the jetty *Apothiki* seems more popular than its smarter neighbour,

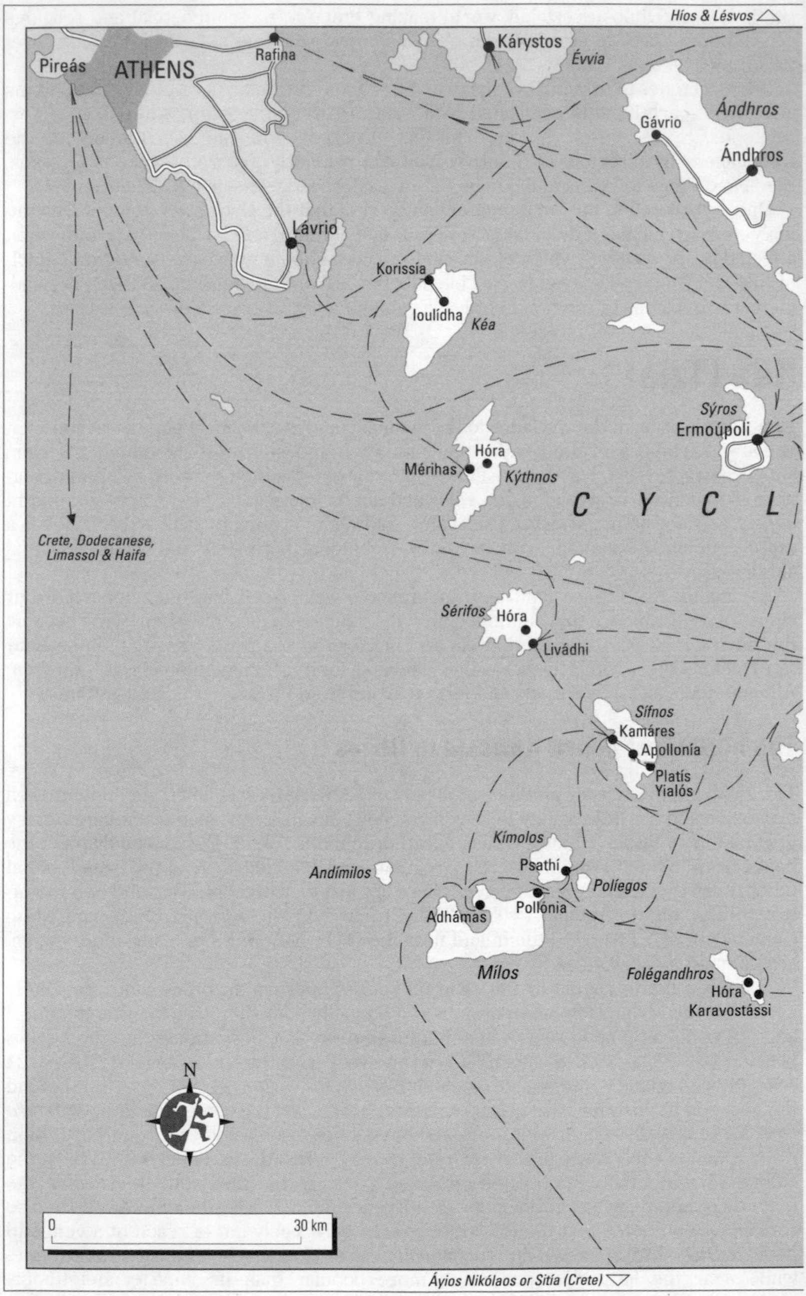
Híos & Lésvos
Pireás
ATHENS
Rafina
Kárystos
Évvia
Ándhros
Gávrio
Ándhros
Lávrio
Korissía
Ioulídha
Kéa
Sýros
Ermoúpoli
Hóra
Mérihas
Kýthnos
C Y C L
Crete, Dodecanese,
Limassol & Haifa
Sérifos
Hóra
Livádhi
Sífnos
Kamáres
Apollonía
Platís
Yialós
Kímolos
Psathí
Andímilos
Políegos
Adhámas
Pollónia
Mílos
Folégandhros
Hóra
Karavostássi
N
0
30 km
Áyios Nikólaos or Sitía (Crete)

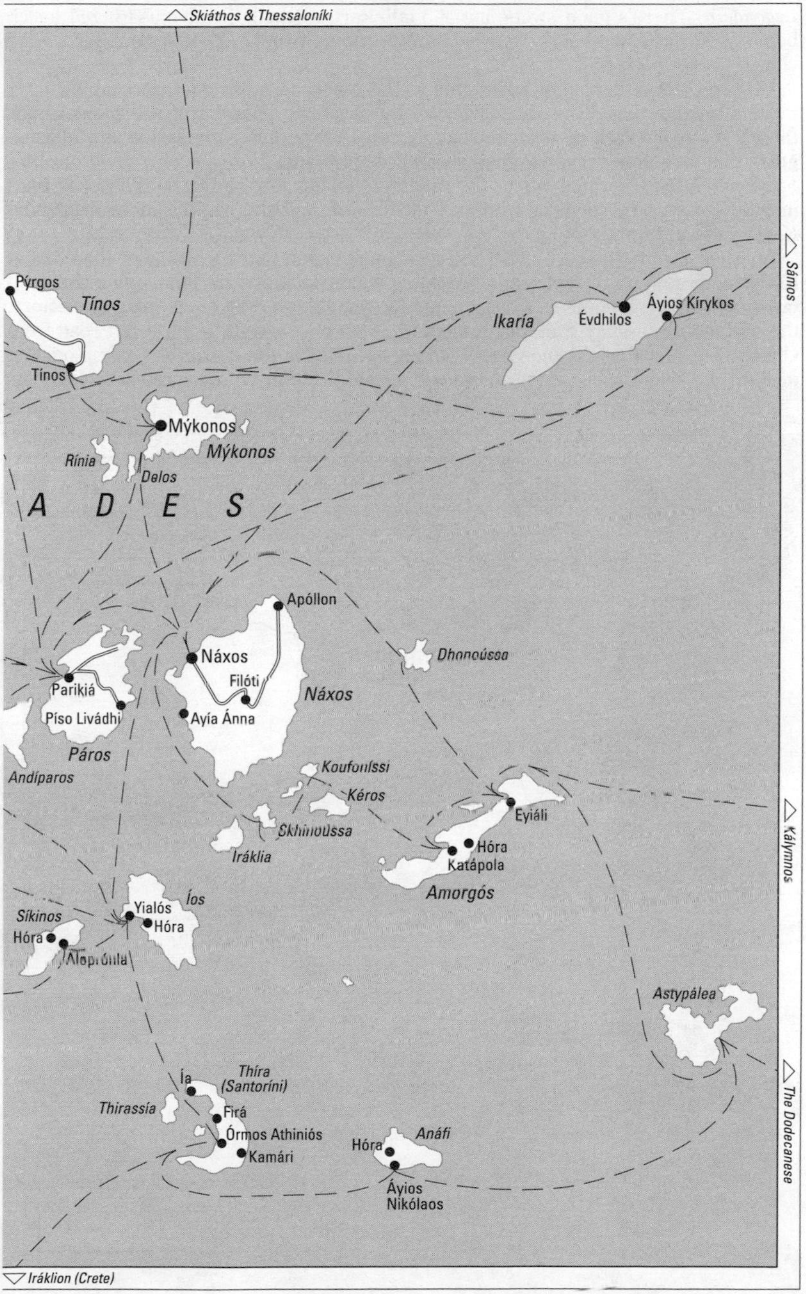
Skiáthos & Thessaloníki
Sámos
Pýrgos
Tínos
Tínos
Ikaría
Évdhilos
Áyios Kírykos
Mýkonos
Mýkonos
Rínia
Delos
A D E S
Apóllon
Dhonoússa
Náxos
Filóti
Náxos
Parikiá
Píso Livádhi
Ayía Ánna
Páros
Andíparos
Koufonissi
Kéros
Eyiáli
Kálymnos
Skhinoussa
Iráklia
Hóra
Katápola
Amorgós
Íos
Síkinos
Yialós
Hóra
Hóra
Aloprónia
Astypálea
Ía
Thíra
(Santoríni)
The Dodecanese
Thirassía
Firá
Órmos Athiniós
Kamári
Anáfi
Hóra
Áyios
Nikólaos
Iráklion (Crete)

Lagoudera. There's good swimming at **Yialiskári**, a small, eucalyptus-fringed beach between Korissía and Vourkári; the *Yialiskari* rooms (☎0288/21 197; ③) enjoy a good view.

VOURKÁRI, a couple of kilometres to the north, is more compact and arguably more attractive than Korissía, serving as the favourite hangout of the yachting set; there's no real beach or accommodation here. Three fairly expensive and indistinguishable **tavernas** serve up good seafood dishes, and there's a very good ouzerí – *Strofi tou Mimi* – located where the road cuts inland towards Otziás. The few **bars** include *Vourkariani*, popular with an older crowd, and the slightly more happening *Kokko Cafe* and *Emage*.

Another 4km to the east, **OTZIÁS** has a small beach that's a bit better than that at Korissía, though more exposed to prevailing winds; facilities are limited to a couple of tavernas and a fair number of apartments for rent. Kéa's only functioning monastery, the eighteenth-century **Panayía Kastrianí**, is an hour's walk along a dirt road from Otziás. The hostel at the monastery (☎0288/21 348) is the cheapest accommodation deal on the island, albeit rather basic and isolated. Although more remarkable for its

fine setting on a high bluff than for any intrinsic interest, from here you can take the pleasant walk on to the island capital, Ioulídha, in another two hours.

Ioulídha

IOULÍDHA (ancient Ioulis) was the birthplace of the renowned early fifth-century BC poets Simonides and Bacchylides. With its numerous red-tiled roofs, Neoclassical buildings and winding flagstoned paths, it is by no means a typical Cycladic village, but, beautifully situated in an amphitheatric fold in the hills, it is architecturally the most interesting settlement on the island. Accordingly it has "arrived" in recent years, with numerous trendy bars and bistros much patronized on weekends. The **archeological museum** (Tues–Sun 8.30am–3pm; free) displays finds from the four ancient city-states of Kéa, although the best items were long ago spirited away to Athens. The lower reaches of the town stretch across a spur to the **Kástro**, a tumbledown Venetian fortress incorporating stones from an ancient temple of Apollo. Fifteen minutes' walk northeast, on the path toward Panayía Kastrianí, you pass the **Lion of Kea**, a sixth-century BC sculpture carved out of the living rock. Six metres long and two metres high, the imposing beast has crudely powerful haunches and a bizarre facial expression. There are steps right down to the lion, but the effect is most striking from a distance.

Currently there is only one **hotel** in Ioulídha: the somewhat pokey *Filoxenia* (☎0288/22 057; ③), perched above a shoe shop, with no en-suite plumbing and saggy beds; the more comfortable *Ioulis* up in the kástro is due to reopen its doors under new management in the near future.

You're spoiled for choice in the matter of **eating** and **drinking** though, with quality generally higher here than near Korissía. *Iy Piatsa*, just as you enter the lower town from the car park, has a variety of tasty dishes, while *Iy Dafni*, reached by a path from the bus stop, and *To Kalofagadhon*, up on the platía, both enjoy great views, the latter being the best place for a full-blown meat feast. Further up there is good standard fare on the terrace of *To Steki tis Tzias*. The aptly named *Panorama* serves up pastries and coffee and is a good place to watch the sun set, while after-dark action seems to oscillate between such bars as *Kamini*, *Leon* and, best of all, *Mylos*. *Ta Pedhia Pezi* (which means "the guys are playing"), is a lively hangout a few kilometres out off the road towards Písses and is terrific for a full-on *bouzoúki* night. A **post office** and **bank agent** round up the list of amenities.

The south

About 8km southwest of Ioulídha, reached via a mix of tracks and paths, or by mostly paved road, the crumbling Hellenistic watchtower of **Ayía Marína** sprouts dramatically from the grounds of a small nineteenth-century monastery. Beyond, the paved main road twists around the startling scenic head of the lovely agricultural valley at **PÍSSES**, emerging at a large and little-developed beach. There are two tavernas, plus a pleasant **campsite**, *Camping Kea*, which has good turfy ground and also runs the studios (☎0288/31 302; ③) further inland. Of the tavernas, the best is *To Akroyiali*, with a good range of dishes and excellent rosé wine, as well as rooms to rent upstairs (☎0288/31 301 or 31 327; ③).

Beyond Písses, the asphalt – and the bus service – peters out along the 5km south to **KOÚNDOUROS**, a sheltered, convoluted bay popular with yachters; there's a taverna behind the largest of several sandy coves, none cleaner or bigger than the beach at Písses. The luxury *Kea Beach* hotel (☎0288/31 230; ⑤) sits out on its own promontory with tennis courts and pool, and there is a hamlet of dummy windmills; built as holiday homes, they are "authentic" right down to their masts, thatching and stone cladding. At the south end of the bay, *St George Bungalows* (☎0288 31 277; ④) has smart rooms at very reasonable prices, as well as its own taverna which is recommended. Admittedly, *Manos* taverna and rooms (☎0288/31 214; ②), a little further south, is cheaper; however the place looks as if it is on its last legs. A further 2km south at **Kambí**, there's a nice little beach and a good taverna, *To Kambi*.

Besides the very scant ruins of ancient Poiessa near Písses, the only remains of any real significance from Kéa's past are fragments of a temple of Apollo at **ancient Karthaia**, tucked away on the southeastern edge of the island above Póles Bay, with an excellent deserted twin beach that's easiest reached by boat. Otherwise, it's a good three-hour round-trip walk from the hamlet of Stavroudháki, some way off the lower road linking Koúndouros, Hávouna and Káto Meriá. Travelling by motorbike, the upper road, which more directly plies between Písses and Káto Meriá, is worth following as an alternative return along the island's summit to Ioulídha; it's paved between Ioulídha and Káto Meriá, and the entire way affords fine views, over the thousands of magnificent oaks which constitute Kéa's most distinctive feature.

Kýthnos (Thermiá)

Though perhaps the dullest and certainly the most barren of the Cyclades, a short stay on **Kýthnos** is a good antidote to the exploitation likely to be encountered elsewhere. Few foreigners bother to visit – the island is much quieter than Kéa. It's a place where Athenians come to buy land for villas, go spear-fishing and sprawl on generally mediocre beaches without having to jostle for space. You could use it as a first or, better, last island stop; in season there are several ferry connections a week with Kéa and Lávrio, a frequent ferry and hydrofoil service to and from Sérifos, Sífnos and Pireás, plus further direct ferry and hydrofoil connections with Mílos and Kímolos.

Mérihas and around

In good weather boats dock on the west coast at **MÉRIHAS**, a rather functional ferry and fishing port with most of the island's facilities. This fact almost obliges you to stay here, and makes Mérihas something of a tourist ghetto, but it's redeemed by proximity to the island's best beaches. The closest beach of any repute is **Episkopí**, a 500m stretch of averagely clean grey sand with a single taverna, thirty minutes' walk north of the town; you can shorten this considerably by sticking to coast-hugging trails and tracks below the road. Far better are the adjacent beaches of **Apókroussi**, which has a canteen, and **Kolóna**, the latter essentially a sandspit joining the islet of Áyios Loukás to Kýthnos. These lie about an hour's walk northwest of Episkopí, and are easiest reached by boat-trip from the harbour. Camping is generally tolerated, even on Martinákia beach, the nearest to Mérihas, which has an eponymous taverna.

Owners of **accommodation** often meet the ferries in high season, and a relative abundance of rooms makes for good bargaining opportunities. Few places have sea views, one exception being the *Kythnos Hotel* (☎0281/32 247; ②), near the ferry dock, which has the added bonus of being open all year round. A little inland, behind the small bridge on the seafront, *Panayiota* (☎0281/32 268; ③) is a decent choice; and there are plenty of other rooms and studios of similar price and quality along the same road. The best **restaurants** are *To Kandouni*, furthest from the ferry, a tasty grill with tables right by the water and specialities like *sfougáto*, and *Kissos*, a little inland, where you are paying for the food rather than the setting. Among purveyors of a modest nightlife, by far the friendliest and liveliest place is *To Vyzantio*, just back from the water, whose animated owner plays varied rock music. *Remezzo* behind the beach has a fine location and plays good music, while eclectic Greek folk can be heard at the mod-

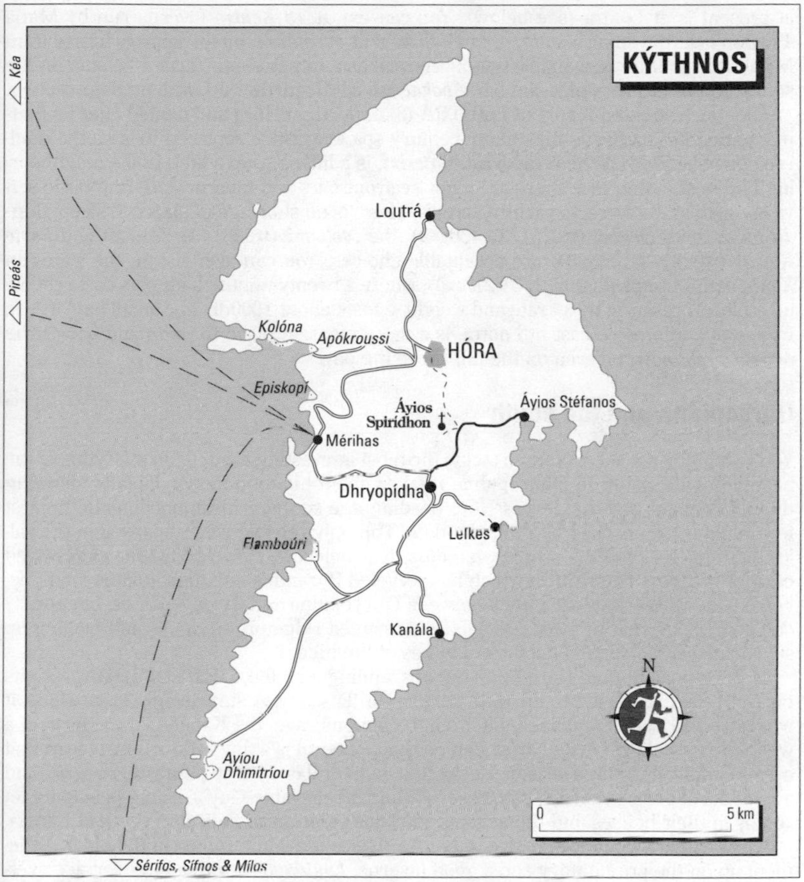

ern *New Corner*, 100m along the road to Dhryopídha. The latest addition of any significance is *Akrotiri Club*, perched up on the headland past *To Kundouni* (see above), playing that popular island blend of summer hits and Greek music.

The **bus service**, principally to Loutrá, Hóra, Dhryopídha and Kanála, is reasonably reliable, in season at least; the only motorbike rental is through the main Mílos Express ticket agency and is noticeably more expensive than on many islands. The Cava Kythnos shop doubles as the official **National Bank** outlet (exchange all day), and is the agent for hydrofoil tickets and the boat to Kéa.

Hóra and Loutrá

HÓRA lies 6km northeast of Mérihas, set in the middle of the island. Tilting south off an east–west ridge, and laid out to an approximate grid plan, it's an awkward blend of Kéa-style gabled roofs, Cycladic churches with dunce-cap cupolas, and concrete monsters. Hóra supports a **post office** (open only until noon); the closest accommodation at present is at Loutrá (see below). You can **eat** at *To Kentro* taverna run by Maria Tzoyiou near the small square, or at *To Steki* grill; *Paradisos*, on the approach road from Mérihas is another reasonable option. As well as a rather sophisticated kafenío on the square, there is a very pleasant bar, *Apokalypsi*, a little further up, with outdoor seating.

The much-vaunted resort of **LOUTRÁ** (3km north of Hóra and named after its thermal baths) is scruffy, its nineteenth-century spa long since replaced by a sterile modern construction. The best **taverna**, *Katerini*, is a little out on a limb in the neighbouring bay west. Otherwise there are a few seafront bars and tavernas offering basic services, such as showers, to yachting crews. There is no shortage of places to sleep; **pensions** such as *Delfini* (☎0281/31 430; ②), the *Meltemi* (☎0281/31 271; ③) and *Porto Klaras* (☎0281/31 276; ④) are acceptable choices. You can also stay in the state-run *Xenia* baths complex (☎0281/31 217; ③), where a twenty-minute bath plus basic check-up – blood pressure, heart rate and weight – costs about 1000dr. The small bay of Ayía Iríni, just a kilometre east of Loutrá, is a more pleasant place to swim and boasts the decent *Trehandiri* taverna on the hill above the bay.

Dhryopídha and the south

You're handily placed in Hóra to tackle the most interesting thing to do on Kýthnos: the beautiful **walk** south to Dhryopídha. It takes about ninety minutes, initially following the old cobbled way that leaves Hóra heading due south; critical junctions in the first few minutes are marked by red paint dots. The only reliable water is a well in the valley bottom, reached after thirty minutes, just before a side-trail to the triple-naved **chapel of Áyios Spyrídhon** which has recycled Byzantine columns. Just beyond this, you collide with a bulldozed track between Dhryopídha and Áyios Stéfanos, but purists can avoid it by bearing west towards some ruined ridgetop windmills and picking up secondary paths for the final forty minutes of the hike.

More appealing than Hóra by virtue of spanning a ravine, **DHRYOPÍDHA**, with its pleasing tiled roofs, is reminiscent of Spain or Tuscany. A surprisingly large place, it was once the island's capital, built around a famous cave, the Katafíki, at the head of a well-watered valley. Tucked away behind the cathedral is a tiny **folklore museum** that opens erratically in high season. Beside the cathedral is a cheap psistariá, *To Steki*, and a good local ouzerí called *O Apithanos* ("The Unbelievable Guy"). Some people do let rooms in their houses, but the nearest official accommodation is 6km south at Kanála.

KANÁLA is a good alternative to Loutrá. There are some rooms in the older settlement up on the promontory and a good taverna, *Louloudhas*, with a huge terrace overlooking the larger western beach, **Megáli Ámmos**, which also has rooms and a combination snack bar and taverna. Two adjacent pensions on the beach are *Anna* (☎0281/32 035; ②) and the B&B *Margarita* (☎0281/32 265; ② & ④), with the latter warmly recommended.

From Kanála, a succession of small coves extends up the east coast as far as **ÁYIOS STÉFANOS**, a small coastal hamlet with two high-season tavernas opposite a chapel-crowned islet linked by a causeway to the body of the island. Southwest of Dhryopídha, reached by a turning off the road to Kanála, **Flamboúri** is the most presentable beach on the west coast. The recent extension of the asphalted road southwards makes the double bay of **Ayíou Dhimitríou** more accessible than before; although not too exciting, there are however a couple of tavernas and rooms to rent in high season.

Sérifos

Sérifos has long languished outside the mainstream of history and modern tourism. Little has happened here since the legendary Perseus returned with the Gorgon's

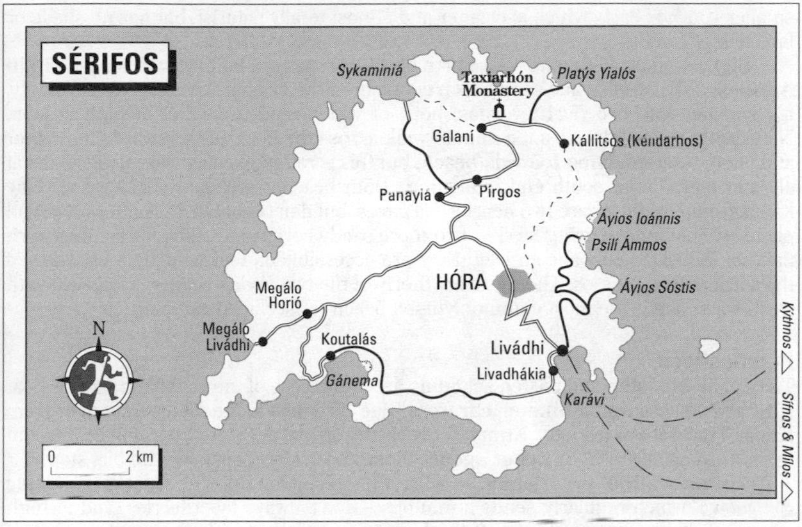

head, in time to save his mother Danaë from being ravished by the local king Polydectes. Many would-be visitors are deterred by the apparently barren, hilly interior which, with the stark, rocky coastline, makes Sérifos appear uninhabited until your ferry turns into Livádhi bay. The island is recommended for serious **walkers**, who can head for several small villages in the little-explored interior, plus some isolated coves. Modern Serifots love seclusion, and here, more than anywhere else in the Cyclades, you will find farmsteads miles from anywhere, with only a donkey path to their door. Everyone here seems to keep livestock, and to produce their own wines, and many also cultivate the wild **narcissus** for the export market.

Few islanders speak much English; even a few select words of amateur Greek will come in handy and will be warmly received. American yachties drop anchor here in some numbers as well, to take on fresh water which, despite appearances, Sérifos has in abundance.

Livádhi and the main beaches

Most visitors stay in the port, **LIVÁDHI**, set in a wide greenery-fringed bay and handy for most of the island's beaches. The usually calm bay here is a magnet for island-hopping yachts, whose crews chug to and fro in dinghies all day and night. It's not the most attractive place on Sérifos – and to stay here exclusively would be to miss some fine walks – but Livádhi and the neighbouring cove of Livadhákia are certainly the easiest places to find rooms and any other amenities you might need, all of which are very scarce elsewhere.

Unfortunately, the long **beach** at Livádhi is nothing to write home about: the sand is hard-packed and muddy, and the water weedy and prone to intermittent jellyfish flotillas – only the far northeastern end is at all usable. Walk uphill along the street from the *Mylos* bakery, or over the southerly headland from the cemetery, to reach the neighbouring, far superior **Livadhákia**. This golden-sand beach, shaded by tamarisk trees, offers snorkelling and other watersports, as well as an acceptable taverna. If you prefer more seclusion, five minutes' stroll across the headland to the south brings you to the smaller **Karávi** beach, which is cleaner and almost totally naturist, but has no shade or facilities.

A slightly longer 45-minute walk north of the port along a bumpy track leads to **Psilí Ámmos**, a sheltered, white-sand beach considered the best on the island. Accordingly, it's popular, with two rival tavernas, both of which tend to be full in high season. Naturists are pointed – via a ten-minute walk across the headland – towards the larger and often deserted **Áyios Ioánnis** beach, but this is rather exposed with no facilities at all, and only the far south end is inviting. Both beaches are theoretically visited by kaïkia from Livádhi, as are two nearby sea caves, but don't count on it. Additionally, and plainly visible from arriving ferries, two more sandy coves hide at the far southeastern flank of the island opposite an islet; they are accessible on foot only, by a variation of the track to Psilí Ámmos. The more northerly of the two, **Áyios Sóstis**, has a well with fresh water and is the most commonly used beach for secluded camping.

Practicalities

The public **bus stop** and posted schedule are at the base of the yacht and fishing-boat jetty, and you can rent a **bike** or **car** from Blue Bird next to the filling station, or from Krinas Travel above the jetty. Krinas Travel is the official agent for hydrofoil tickets and there are a couple of **boat-ticket agents** along the seafront opposite the bus stop.

Accommodation proprietors – with the exception of the *Coralli Camping Bungalows*, which regularly sends a minibus – don't always meet ferries, and in high season you'll have to step lively off the boat to get a decent bed. The most rewarding hunting grounds are on the headland above the ferry dock, or Livadhákia beach (see below); anything without a sea view will be a notch cheaper. Up on the headland, the *Pension Cristi* (☎0281/51 775; ④) has an excellent, quiet position overlooking the bay; the nearby *Areti* (☎0281/51 479; ④) is a little smarter for the same price. Alternatively, down in the flatlands, the inexpensive seafront rooms of *Anna* (☎0281/51 263; ③) and *Fani* (☎0281/51 746; ③) are friendly and spotlessly clean, though the rooms at the front get some traffic noise. The *Hotel Anna* (☎0281/51 666; ③) above the pizzeria by the yacht harbour is another fall-back, while the cheapest rooms in Livádhi are next to each other at the far end of the bay: *Margarita* (☎0281/51 321; ②) and *Adonios Peloponnisos* (☎0281/51 113; ②).

Livadhákia, ten to fifteen minutes' walk south, offers more nocturnal peace, choice and quality, though it has a more touristy feel and the mosquitoes are positively ferocious – bring insecticide coils or make sure your room is furnished with electric vapour pads. One of the oldest and largest complexes of rooms and apartments, close to the beach and with verdant views, is run by Vaso Stamataki (☎0281/51 346; ③). Newer and higher-standard choices include the *Helios Pension* (☎0281/51 066; ③), just above the road as you arrive at Livadhákia, and, further along, the *Medusa* (☎0281/51 127; ③). Cheaper are the rooms in adjacent buildings just after *Helios*, run by two sisters, Yioryia (☎0281/51 336; ②) and Mina (☎0281/51 545; ②–③) – the latter place has sea views. Further along are *Dhorkas* (☎0281/51 422; ④) and, right by the beach above a restaurant, *O Alexandros* (☎0281/51 119; ④). Near the built-up area, beside one of only two public access tracks to the beach and behind the best patch of sand, *Coralli Camping Bungalows* (☎0281/51 500; ④) has a restaurant, bar, shop and landscaped camping area.

A makeshift road runs the length of the Livádhi seafront, crammed with restaurants, shops and all the services you might need. At the strategic southerly crossroads, the *Mylos* bakery has exceptionally good cheese pies and wholegrain bread; a butcher and a handful of fruit shops and **supermarkets** are scattered along the beach, while there's a **pharmacy** at the foot of the quay.

Like most islands, tavernas near the quay tend to be slightly pricier, but *Mokkas* fish taverna is recommended nonetheless. Walk up the beach, and meals get less expensive; the two best traditional tavernas are the busy *Perseus* and the welcoming restaurant under the *Hotel Cyclades*. At the extreme far northeast end of the beach, *Sklavenis* (aka *Margarita's*) has loyal adherents to its down-home feel and courtyard seating, but many find the food overly deep-fried and too pricey. Closer to the yacht harbour, *Meltemi* is a good – if slightly expensive – ouzerí, something out of the ordinary for the island. For crepes and ice cream, try *Meli*, in the commercial centre by the port police.

Nightlife is surprisingly lively, though few establishments stay in business more than two consecutive seasons. The main cluster is about a third of the way along the seafront and includes a mini-mall type affair housing several bars, clubs and eateries. Of the clubs, *Agria Menta* plays a mix of dance music and *bouzoúki*, whereas *Astra Club* upstairs is a conventional disco and *Mythos* has a pool table. *Vitamin C* and *Karnayio* are two popular bars next door, and further along towards the beach is the *Sérifos Yacht Club*, which is actually just a dolled-up kafenío. *Captain Hook* is a new, loud soundproofed club under Krinas Travel.

Buses connect Livádhi with Hóra, 2km away, some ten times daily, but only manage one or two daily trips to Megálo Livádhya, Galaní, and Kállitsos. You may well want to walk, if you're travelling light; it's a pleasant if steep forty minutes up a cobbled way to Hóra, with the *kalderími* leading off from a bend in the road about 300m out of Livádhia. By the beginning of October, you'll have no choice, since the bus – like nearly everything else – ceases operation for the winter.

Hóra

Quiet and atmospheric **HÓRA**, teetering precariously above the harbour, is one of the most spectacular villages of the Cyclades. The best sights are to be found on the town's borders: tiny churches cling to the cliff-edge, and there are breathtaking views across the valleys below. At odd intervals along its alleyways you'll find part of the old castle making up the wall of a house, or a marble statue leaning incongruously in one corner. A pleasant diversion is the hour-long **walk** down to **Psilí Ámmos**: start from beside Hóra's cemetery and aim for the lower of two visible pigeon towers, and then keep close to the phone wires, which will guide you towards the continuation of the double-walled path descending to a bend in the road just above the beach.

Among two or three **tavernas**, the nicest place is *Zorbas*, near the church on the upper square, serving local dishes such as wild fennel fritters; *Stavros*, just east of the bus-stop platía, is consistent and can arrange beds too (☎0281/51 303; ②). The island's **post office** is found in the lowest quarter, and a few more expensive **rooms** for rent lie about 200m north of town, on the street above the track to the cemetery.

The north

North of Hóra, the island's high water-table sometimes breaks the surface to run in delightful rivulets swarming with turtles and frogs, though in recent years many of the open streams seem to have dried up. Reeds, orchards and even the occasional palm tree still take advantage of the unexpected moisture, even if it's no longer visible. This is especially true at **KÁLLITSOS** (Kéndarhos), reached by a ninety-minute path from Hóra, marked by fading red paint splodges along a donkey track above the cemetery. Once at Kállitsos (no facilities), a paved road leads west within 3km to the fifteenth- to seventeenth-century **monastery of Taxiarhón**, designed for sixty monks but presently home only to one of the island's two parish priests, one of a dying breed of farmer-fisherman monks, If he's about, the priest will show you treasures in the monastic church, such as an ivory-inlaid bishop's throne, silver lamps from Egypt (to where many Serifots emigrated) and the finely carved *témblon*.

As you loop back towards Hóra from Kállitsos on the asphalt, the fine villages of Galaní and Panayía (named after its tenth-century church) make convenient stops. In **GALANÍ** you can sometimes get simple **meals** at the central store, which also sells excellent, tawny-pink, sherry-like wine; its small-scale production in the west of the island is highly uneconomic, so you'll find it at few other places on Sérifos. Below the village, trails lead to the remote and often windswept beach of **Sykaminiá**, with no facilities and no camping allowed; a better bet for a local swim is the more sheltered cove of **Platýs Yialós** at the extreme northern tip of the island, reached by a partly paved track (negotiable by moped) that branches off just east of Taxiarhón. The neighbouring beach has a taverna, *Nikoulias*, with a couple of very basic rooms (☎0281/52 174; ②), which nonetheless have great views. The church at **PANAYIÁ** is usually locked, but comes alive on its feast day of Xilopanayía (August 16). Traditionally the first couple to dance around the adjacent olive tree would be the first to marry that year, but this led to unseemly brawls – so the priest always goes first these days.

The southwest

A little way south of Panayía, you reach a junction in the road. Turn left to return to Hóra, or continue straight towards **Megálo Horió** – the site of ancient Sérifos, but with little else to recommend it. **Megálo Livádhi**, further on, is a remote and quiet beach resort 8km west of Hóra, with two lovely tavernas whose tables are practically on the beach. *Iy Mardhitsa* taverna has some simple rooms behind the beach (☎0281/51 003; ②). Iron and copper ore were once exported from here, but cheaper African deposits sent the mines into decline and today most of the idle machinery rusts away, though some gravel-crushing still goes on. There is a monument at the north end of the beach to four workers killed during a protest against unfair conditions in 1916. An alternate turning just below Megálo Horió leads to the small mining and fishing port of **Koutalás**, a pretty sweep of bay with a church-tipped rock, and a long if narrow beach – it has become rather a ghost settlement and the workers' restaurants have all closed down. There is however one snack bar/taverna, catering mainly for yachting crews, which has sprung up recently. The winding track above the village leads to Livádhi, and apart from the pleasant **Gánema** beach, which has a taverna of the same name, there are no places to rest or buy refreshments on the long journey back.

Sífnos

Sífnos is a more immediately appealing island than its northern neighbours: prettier, more cultivated and with some fine architecture. This means that it's also much more popular, and extremely crowded in July or August, when rooms are very difficult to find. Take any offered as you land, come armed with a reservation or, best of all, time your visit for June or early in September, though bear in mind that most of the trendier bars and the souvenir shops will be shut for the winter by the middle of the latter month. In keeping with the island's somewhat upmarket clientele, freelance camping is forbidden (and the two designated sites are substandard), while nudism is tolerated only in isolated coves. The locals tend, if anything, to be even more dour and introverted than on Sérifos.

On the other hand, Sífnos's modest size – no bigger than Kýthnos or Sérifos – makes it eminently explorable. The **bus service** is excellent, most of the roads quite decent, and there's a network of paths that are fairly easy to follow. Sífnos has a strong tradition of pottery and was long esteemed for its distinctive cuisine, although most tourist-orientated cooking is average at best. However, the island's shops and greengrocers are well stocked in season.

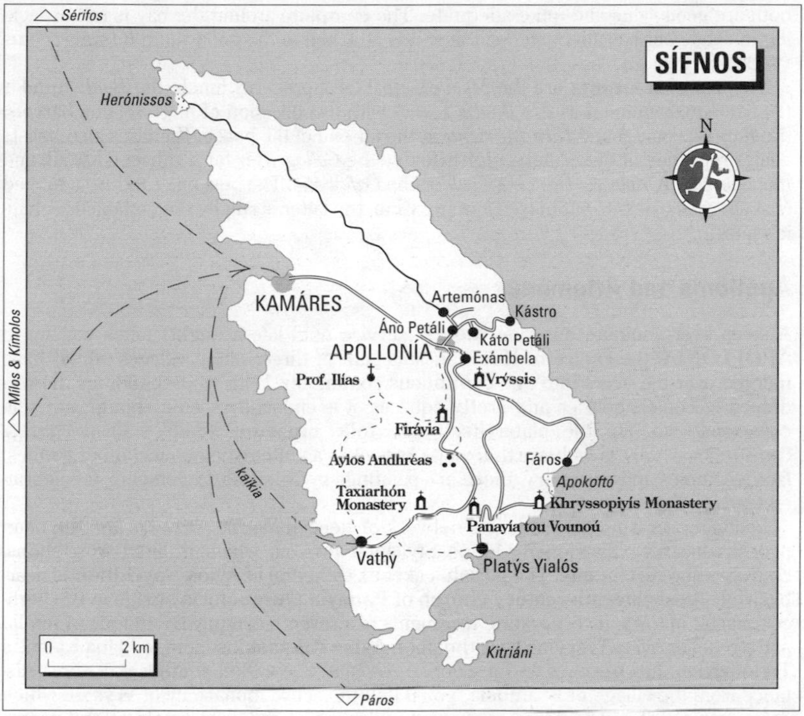

Ferry connections have improved in recent years, keeping pace with the island's increasing popularity. The main lines head south, via Kímolos to Mílos, with occasional extensions to Thíra, Crete and select Dodecanese, or north, via Sérifos and Kýthnos to Pireás. Links with the central Cyclades are provided by the infrequent visits of the Georgios Express to Páros or Sýros and backed up by an almost daily hydrofoil service which also goes to Náxos and Mýkonos several times a week.

Kamáres

KAMÁRES, the island's port, is tucked away at the foot of high, bare cliffs in the west, which enclose a beach. A busy, fairly downmarket resort with concrete blocks of villas edging up to the base of the cliffs, Kamáres' seafront is crammed with bars, travel agencies, ice-cream shops and fast-food places. You can store luggage at the Aegean Thesaurus **travel agency** while hunting for a room (proprietors tend not to meet boats); they also change money and can advise on bed availability throughout the island.

Accommodation is relatively expensive, though bargaining can be productive outside peak season. Try the rooms above the Katzoulakis Tourist Agency near the quay(☎0284/32 362; ③), as well as the reasonable *Hotel Stavros* (☎0284/31 641; ③), a little further along; the good but slightly pricier *Boulis Hotel* (☎0284/32 122; ⑤) is on the beach, across the bay, and has very friendly management. *Ekaterinis* (☎0284/32 392; ④), a short hike up the hill behind the main road leading out of town, consists of rooms in two buildings, one is much newer and more modern than the other; however both are good value and quite adequate. The **campsite** around the bay is rather lacking in shade but has adequate facilities; it is attached to the good-value *Korakis* rooms (☎0284/32 366; ③).

The best **restaurants** are the *Meropi*, ideal for a pre-ferry lunch, the *Boulis* (under the same management as the *Boulis Hotel*) with its collection of huge retsina barrels, the *Kamares* ouzerí and *Kira Mariena* at the far end of the beach. Kamáres also boasts a fair proportion of the island's **nightlife**: try the *Collage Bar* for a sunset cocktail, and move on to the *Mobilize Dancing Club* or the *Cafe Folie*. The best place to hire a moped is at Dionysos, next to Mobilize Dancing Club, the latter is run by the amiable mechanic's son.

Apollonía and Artemónas

A steep twenty-minute bus ride (hourly service until late at night) takes you up to **APOLLONÍA**, the centre of Hóra, an amalgam of three hilltop villages which have merged over the years into one continuous community. With white buildings, flower-draped balconies, belfries and pretty squares, it is eminently scenic, though not self-consciously so. On the platía itself, the **folk museum** (daily 9.30am–2pm & 6pm–10pm; 300dr) is well worth a visit. As well as an interesting collection of textiles, lace, costumes and weaponry, there are paintings by Nikolaos Tselemendi, a celebrated teacher of cookery.

Radiating out from the platía is a network of stepped marble footways and the main pedestrian street, flagstoned Odhós Styliánou Prókou, which is lined with shops, churches and restaurants. The garish, cakebox cathedral of **Áyios Spyrídhon** is nearby, while the eighteenth-century church of **Panayía Ouranoforía** stands in the highest quarter of town, incorporating fragments of a seventh-century BC temple of Apollo and a relief of Áyios Yeóryios over the door. **Áyios Athanásios**, next to Platía Kleánthi Triandafýlou, has frescoes and a wooden *témblon*. Some 3km southeast, a short distance from the village of Exámbela, you'll find the active monastery of **Vrýssis** which dates from 1612 and is home to a good collection of religious artefacts and manuscripts.

ARTEMÓNAS, fifteen minutes south of Apollonía on foot, is worth a morning's exploration for its churches and elegant Venetian and Neoclassical houses alone. **Panayía Gourniá** (key next door) has vivid frescoes; the clustered-dome church of **Kohí** was built over an ancient temple of Artemis (also the basis of the village's name); and seventeenth-century **Áyios Yeóryios** contains fine icons. Artemónas is also the point of departure for **Herónissos**, an isolated hamlet with two tavernas and a few potteries behind a deeply indented, rather bleak bay at the northwestern tip of the island. There's a motorable dirt track there – and occasional boat trips from Kamáres, though these are only worth the effort on calm days.

Practicalities

The **post office** and **bus stop** edge onto Apollonía's central platía. The **bank** and **police station** are located on the main road leading north out of town. There are rooms scattered all over the village, making them hard to find; however, there are some obvious choices along the road towards Fáros (thus a bit noisy), the *Margarita* (☎0284/31 032; ②) being fairly representative. If you want quieter premises with a better view, be prepared to pay more: *Margarita Kouki* (☎0284/33 152; ③), above the luxurious *Hotel Petali* (☎0284/33 024; ⑥), is a welcome exception. Probably your best bet is to look on the square for the main branch of the excellent travel agency, Aegean Thesaurus (☎0284/31 151, fax 32 190), which can book you into rooms of all categories. They also sell a worthwhile package consisting of an accurate topographical map, bus/boat schedules and a short text on Sífnos for a few hundred drachmas.

In Hóra there are still a bare handful of quality **tavernas**, the doyen of which is the *Liotrivi* up in Artemónas, which has moved from the old oil-press suggested by its name to extended new premises on the village square. Next to the post office in Apollonía, *Iy Orea Sifnos* has standard fare and a flower-decked garden; there are several tavernas up in the backstreets, of which *To Apostoli to Koutouki* is very reasonable.

Nightlife in Apollonía tends to be dominated by the thirty-something crowd which, having dined early by Greek-island standards, lingers over its oúzo until late. Starting with *Isidora*, a trendy bar at the foot of Odhós Styliánou Prókou, there are several bars further up this street worth visiting. The central *Argo* music bar features the currently fashionable mix of dance music early on and Greek pop later, and *To Doloma* plays an interesting mix of jazz and classic rock; the *Camel Club* on the edge of town has become a new favourite late night hangout.

The east coast

Most of Sífnos's coastal settlements are along the less precipitous eastern shore, within a modest distance of Hóra and its surrounding cultivated plateau. These all have good bus services, and a certain amount of food and accommodation, Kástro being far more appealing than the touristy resorts of Platýs Yialós and Fáros.

Kástro

An alternative east-coast base which seems the last place on Sífnos to fill up in season, **KÁSTRO** can be reached on foot from Apollonía in 35 minutes, all but the last ten on a clear path beginning at the fork in the road to Kástro, threading its way via Káto Petáli hamlet. Built on a rocky outcrop with an almost sheer drop to the sea on three sides, the ancient capital of the island retains much of its medieval character. Parts of its boundary walls survive, along with a full complement of sinuous, narrow streets graced by balconied, two-storey houses and some fine sixteenth- and seventeenth-century churches with ornamental floors. Venetian coats of arms and ancient wall-fragments can still be seen on some of the older dwellings; there are the remains of the ancient acropolis (including a ram's head sarcophagus by one of the medieval gates), as well as a small **archeological museum** (Tues–Sun 8am–2.30pm; free), which does not always stick closely to the official opening hours, installed in a former Catholic church in the higher part of the village.

Among the several **rooms**, the modernized *Aris* apartments (☎0284/31 161; ③–④) have something for most budgets and are open all year. More rooms are available at the lower end of the village, of which the friendly *Marianna* (☎0284/33 681; ③) is a good basic option. The *Star* and *Leonidas* are the obvious tavernas to try out, while the *Cavos Sunrise* café-bar, run by an old hippy, is suitably laid back and has a fantastic view. On the edge of town, the *Castello* disco-bar is a livelier hang-out. There's nothing approximating a beach in Kástro; for a swim you have to walk to the nearby rocky coves of **Serália** (to the southeast, and with more rooms) and **Paláti**. You can also hike – from the windmills on the approach road near Káto Petáli – to either the sixteenth-century monastery of **Khryssostómou**, or along a track opposite to the cliff-face that overlooks the church of the **Eptá Martíres** (Seven Martyrs); nudists sun themselves and snorkel on and around the flat rocks below.

Platýs Yialós

From Apollonía there are almost hourly buses to the resort of **PLATÝS YIALÓS**, some 12km distant, near the southern tip of the island. Despite claims to be the longest beach in the Cyclades, the sand can get very crowded at the end near the watersport facilities rental. Diversions include a pottery workshop, but many are put off by the continuous row of snack bars and rooms to rent, which line the entire stretch of beach, and the strong winds which plague it. **Rooms** are expensive, although the comfortable *Pension Angelaki* (☎0284/71 288; ④), near the bus stop, is more reasonably priced, while the *Hotel Eurosini* (☎0284/71 353; ⑤) next door is comfortable, and breakfast is included in the price. The local **campsite** is rather uninspiring: a stiff hike inland, shadeless and on sloping, stony ground. Among several fairly pricey **tavernas** are the straightforward *To Steki* and *Bus Stop*.

A more rewarding walk uphill from Platýs Yialós brings you to the convent of **Panayía toú Vounoú** (though it's easy to get lost on the way without the locally sold map); the caretaker should let you in, if she's about.

Fáros and around

Less crowded beaches are to be found just to the northeast of Platýs Yialós (though unfortunately not directly accessible along the coast). **FÁROS**, again with regular bus links to Apollonía, makes an excellent fall-back base if you don't strike it lucky elsewhere. A small and friendly resort, it has some of the cheapest **accommodation** on the island, as well as a couple of smarter places, including the recommended *Apéranto* guesthouse (☎0284/71 473; ④) at the far end of the bay. *To Kyma* is a pleasant seafront **taverna**, and the smart *On the Rocks*, perched on the headland at the far end of the beach, serves a tasty selection of snacks as well as full meals. The closest beaches are not up to much: the town strand itself is muddy, shadeless and crowded, and the one to the northeast past the headland not much better. Head off in the opposite direction, however, through the older part of the village, and things improve at **Glyfó**, a longer, wider family beach.

Continuing from Glyfó, a fifteen-minute cliffside path leads to the beach of **Apokoftó**, with a couple of good tavernas, and, up an access road, the *Hotel Flora* (☎0284/71 278; ③), which has superb views. The shore itself tends to collect seaweed, however, and a rock reef must be negotiated to get into the water. Flanking Apokoftó to the south, marooned on a sea-washed spit and featuring on every EOT poster of the island, is the disestablished, seventeenth-century **Khryssopiyís monastery**, where until recently cells were rented out as tourist accommodation. According to legend, the cleft in the rock appeared when two village girls, fleeing to the spit to escape the attentions of menacing pirates, prayed to the Virgin to defend their virtue.

The interior and Vathý

Apollonía is a good base from which to start your explorations of remoter Sífnos. You can rent **bikes** at Moto Apollo, beside the petrol station on the road to Fáros, but the island is best explored on foot.

Taking the path out from Katavatí (the district south of Apollonía) you'll pass, after a few minutes, the beautiful empty **monastery of Firáyia** and – fifteen minutes along the ugly new road – the path climbing up to **Áyios Andhréas**, where you'll be rewarded with tremendous views over the islands of Sýros, Páros, Íos, Folégandhros and Síkinos. Just below the church is an enormous Bronze Age archeological site.

Even better is the all-trail walk to Vathý, around three hours from Katavatí and reached by bearing right at a signed junction in Katavatí. Part way along you can detour on a conspicuous side-trail to the **monastery of Profítis Ilías**, on the very summit of the island, with a vaulted refectory and extensive views.

Vathý

A fishing village on the shore of a stunning funnel-shaped bay, **VATHÝ** is the most attractive and remote base on the island and, remarkably, the 1933-vintage road hasn't promoted much extra development. There are, however, an increasing number of **rooms**, the best deals probably being at *Manolis* taverna (☎0284/71 111; ③), or those attached to the tiny **monastery of the Archangel Gabriel**. Unusually, camping rough meets with little objection from the locals, a reflection of their friendly attitude towards outsiders. For **food**, *Manolis* does excellent grills and has a fascinating gyrating clay oven in the courtyard; *Iy Okeanidha* has good mezédhes such as chickpea balls and cheesy aubergine patties; while *To Tsikali* behind the monastery is cheaper but less varied.

Now that there are regular buses (8 daily in high season, 2 daily at other times) the kaïkia no longer run from Kamáres. It is possible to walk to Platýs Yiálos in ninety minutes, but the path is not well marked. At the far end of the bay a traditional pottery still functions.

Mílos

Mílos has always derived prosperity from its strange geology. Minoan settlers were attracted by obsidian, and other products of its volcanic soil made the island – along with Náxos – the most important of the Cyclades in the ancient world. Today the quarrying of barite, perlite and porcelain brings in a steady revenue, but has left deep and unsightly scars on the landscape. The rocks, however, can be beautiful in situ: on the left as your ferry enters Mílos Bay, two outcrops known as the Arkoúdhes (Bears) square off like sumo wrestlers. Off the north coast, accessible only by excursion boat, the Glaroníssia (Seagull Isles) are shaped like massed organ pipes, and there are more weird formations on the southwest coast at Kléftiko. Inland, too, you frequently come across strange, volcanic outcrops, and thermal springs burst forth.

The landscape has been violated, but as with most weathered volcanic terrain, Mílos is incredibly fertile; away from the summits of **Profítis Ilías** in the southwest and lower hills in the east, a gently undulating countryside is intensively cultivated to produce grain, hay and orchard fruits. The island's domestic architecture, with its lava-built, two-up-and-two-down houses, is reminiscent of Níssyros, while parts of the coast, with their sculpted cliffs and inlets, remind some visitors of Cyprus.

Yet the drab whole is less than the sum of the often interesting parts; Mílos is not and never will become another Santoríni, despite a similar geological history, and is probably the better for it. The locals are reconciled to a very short tourist season lasting from late June to early September, and make most of their money during late July and August, when prices are rather high.

Adhámas

The main port of **ADHÁMAS**, known as Adhámandas to locals, was founded by Cretan refugees fleeing a failed rebellion in 1841. Despite sitting on one of the Mediterranean's best natural harbours (created by a volcanic cataclysm similar to, but earlier than, Thíra's), Adhámas is not a spectacularly inviting place, though it's lively enough and has all the requisite facilities.

Most hotel **accommodation** manages to be simultaneously noisy, viewless and relatively expensive. Exceptions are the *Delfini* (☎0287/22 001; ④), a short way inland from the first beach north of the harbour, the smart, central, double-glazed *Portiani Hotel* (☎0287/22 940; ⑤) and the luxury *Santa Maria Village* (☎0287/21 949; ⑥), 300m behind the beach. Rooms are concentrated on the conical hill above the harbour and on or just off the main road to Pláka, and range from real cheapies with shared facilities, like those of Anna Gozadhinou (☎0287/22 364; ②), to smart rooms with TV and all mod cons, like *Falasistra* (☎0287/23 570; ⑤). During high season the highly organized

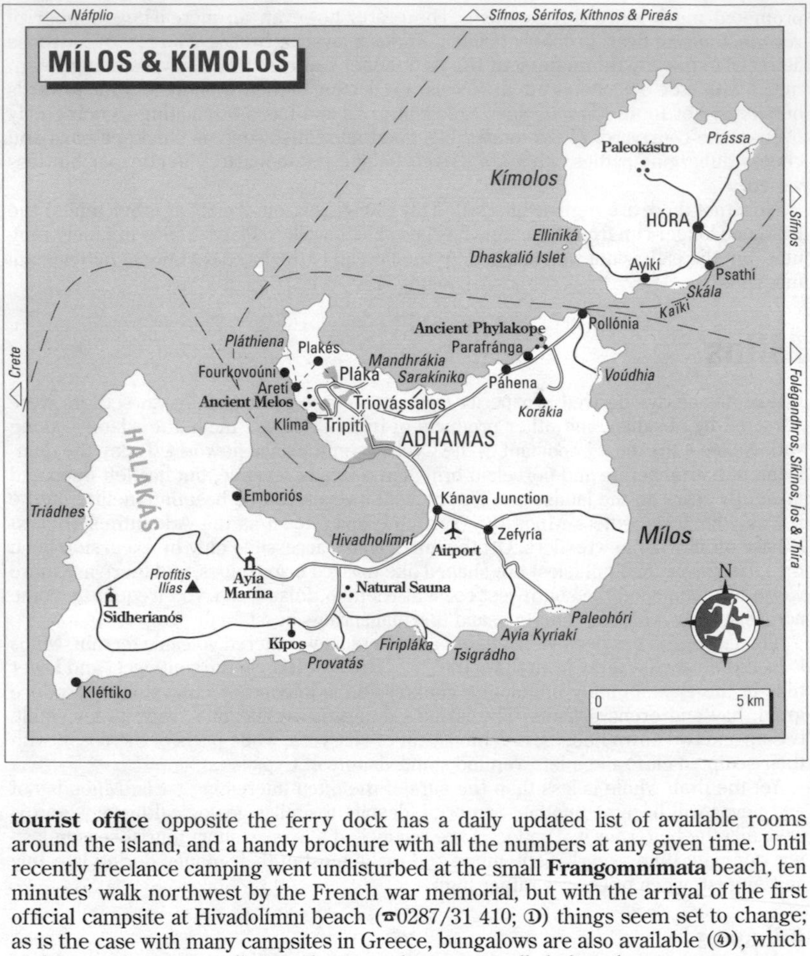

tourist office opposite the ferry dock has a daily updated list of available rooms around the island, and a handy brochure with all the numbers at any given time. Until recently freelance camping went undisturbed at the small **Frangomnímata** beach, ten minutes' walk northwest by the French war memorial, but with the arrival of the first official campsite at Hivadolímni beach (☎0287/31 410; ①) things seem set to change; as is the case with many campsites in Greece, bungalows are also available (④), which in this case is just as well since the grounds are not well sheltered.

Of the three adjacent **tavernas** along the seafront towards the long tamarisk-lined beach south of town, *Navagio* is the best value, while close to the jetty *Flisvos* is reasonable. Just off the main street inland, *Ta Pitsounakia* is a good cheap psistariá with a pleasant courtyard. Apart from the obvious string of cafés along the main seafront drag, *Akri*, above the jetty is a trendier **bar**, with a pleasant veranda. *Notos Club*, on the way to the first beach north, plays rock music, and *Viagra*, above the far end of the beach, goes on until sunrise playing a mixture of cheesy summer hits and Greek pop.

On the quayside, several travel agencies such as the efficient Vichos Tours have information about coastal boat-trips, sell maps of the island and rent out mopeds. Apricot Tours (☎0287/23 595), up the stairs behind the taxi rank, is particularly friendly and helpful. Otherwise, Adhámas is the hub of the island's **bus services**, which run hourly to Pláka, nine times daily in high season to Pollónia, seven times daily to Paleohóri via Zefíria and to Provatás. Some visitors arrive by plane from Athens: the

airport is 5km southeast of the port, close to Zefíria. There are several banks, a post office and a taxi rank with a posted list of fixed rates. The **Mining Museum of Mílos** (daily 9.30am–1pm & 5pm–8pm; free), housed in a new building towards the south beach, charts the mining history of Mílos. An unmissable day out is the **boat tour** round the island on one of three boats; weather permitting, these normally leave at 9am and make several stops at inaccessible swimming spots like the magnificent Kléftiko, as well as taking in late lunch on Kímolos.

The northwestern villages and ancient Melos

The real appeal of Mílos resides in an area that has been the island's focus of habitation since Classical times, where a cluster of villages huddle in the lee of a crag 4km northwest of the harbour.

PLÁKA (MÍLOS) is the largest of these communities and is the official capital of the island, a status borne out by the presence of the hospital and **post office.** There is also a **motorbike rental** outfit near the archeological museum. **Accommodation** in Pláka is slowly improving, and as well as the three or four modern blocks overlooking the busy approach road, which until recently served as the main accommodation option, there are several room outfits scattered around the village. *Moraitis* (☎0287/41 353; ④) consists of newly refurbished rooms in the house where the Venus de Milo was allegedly hidden following its discovery in 1820 (see archeological museum below). *Vourakis* (☎0287/21 702;④) has rooms with great views, a bit of a trek above the village towards the church, and Maria Kentrota (☎0287/21 572; ③) has a couple of charming, if a little basic, studios close to the archeological museum. A number of ouzeris have opened up in recent years, making it a real **eating** paradise: highly recommended are *Arhondoula*, *Dhiporto* and *To Kastro* up in the centre of the village, as well as *Plakiani Gonia* on the approach road.

The attractive village of **TRYPITÍ** (meaning "perforated" in Greek), which takes its name from the cliffside tombs of the ancient Melian dead nearby, covers a long ridge a kilometre south of Pláka. Despite semi-desolation (many houses are for sale), it probably makes the best base if you're after a village environment, with its three choices of modest **rooms**, two of which are just down the steep street from the tiny platía below the main church. Here also are a couple of café-bars, of which *To Mayeriko* also does simple **meals** and has a fantastic view of the vale of Klíma (see below); more elaborate and expensive fare is available at the *Methismeni Politia* ouzerí, at the top of the road to the catacombs, and at *Ta Glaronisa* fish taverna, along the main village street. From Trypití, it's possible to walk more or less directly down to Adhámas via Skinópi on the old *kalderími*, which begins on the saddle linking Trypití with the hamlet of Klimatovoúni.

TRIOVÁSSALOS and its twin **PÉRAN TRIOVÁSSALOS** are more workaday, less polished than Pláka or Trypití. There are "rooms to rent" signs out here as well, but they'll inevitably be noisier. Péran also offers the idiosyncratic taverna *O Hamos* (which means "a mess") and a naive pebble mosaic in the courtyard of **Áyios Yeóryios church**; created in 1880, the mosaic features assorted animal and plant motifs.

Local sites – and the coast

Pláka boasts **two museums** of moderate interest. Behind the lower car park, at the top of the approach boulevard through the newer district, the **archeological museum** (Tues–Sun 8am–2.30pm; 500dr) contains numerous obsidian implements, plus a whole wing of finds from ancient Phylakope (see p.113) whose highlights include a votive lamp in the form of a bull and a rather Minoan-looking terracotta goddess. Labelling is scant, but isn't really needed for a plaster cast of the most famous statue in the world, the Venus de Milo, the original of which was found on the island in 1820 and appropriated by the French; her arms were knocked off in the melée surrounding her abduction. Up in a mansion of the old quarter, the **folklore museum** (Tues–Sun 10am–1pm; 500dr, Sun free) offers room re-creations but is otherwise a Greek-labelled jumble of impedimenta pertaining to milling, brewing, cheese-making, baking and weaving, rounded off by old engravings, photos and mineral samples.

A stairway beginning near the police station leads up to the old Venetian **Kástro**, its slopes clad in stone and cement to channel precious rainwater into cisterns. The enormous chapel of **Panayía Thalassítra** looms near the summit, where the ancient Melians made their last stand against the Athenians before being massacred in 416 BC. Today it offers one of the best views in the Aegean, particularly at sunset in clear conditions.

From the archeological museum, signs point you towards the **early Christian catacombs** (Tues–Sun 8am–8pm; free), 1km south of Pláka and just 400m from Trypití village; steps lead down from the road to the inconspicuous entrance. Although some 5000 bodies were buried in tomb-lined corridors which stretch some 200m into the soft volcanic rock, only the first 50m are illuminated and accessible by boardwalk. They're worth a look if you're in the area, but the adjacent ruins of **ancient Melos**, extending down from Pláka almost to the sea, justify the detour. There are huge Dorian walls, the usual column fragments lying around and, best of all, a well-preserved Roman **amphitheatre** (unrestricted access) some 200m west of the catacombs by track, then trail. Only seven rows of seats remain intact, but these evocatively look out over Klíma to the bay. Between the catacombs and the theatre is the signposted spot where the Venus de Milo was found; promptly delivered to the French consul for "safekeeping" from the Turks, this was the last the Greeks saw of the statue until a copy was belatedly forwarded from the Louvre in Paris.

At the very bottom of the vale, **KLÍMA** is the most photogenic of several fishing hamlets on the island, with its picturesque boathouses tucked underneath the principal living areas. There's no beach to speak of, and only one place to stay – the impeccably sited, if a little basic *Panorama* (☎0287/21 623; ④), with an acceptable balcony taverna.

Pláthiena, 45 minutes' walk northwest of Pláka, is the closest proper beach, and thus is vastly popular in summer. There are no facilities, but the beach is fairly well protected and partly shaded by tamarisks. Head initially west from near the police station on the marked footpath towards **ARETÍ** and **FOURKOVOÚNI**, two more cliff-dug, boathouse-hamlets very much in the Klíma mould. Although the direct route to Pláthiena is signposted, it's no longer to go via Fourkovoúni; both hamlets are reached by side-turnings off the main route, which becomes a jeep track as you approach Fourkovoúni. By moped, access to Pláthiena is only from Plakés, the northernmost and smallest of the five northwestern villages.

The south

The main road to the south of the island splits at **Kánava junction**, an unrelievedly dreary place at first glance owing to the large power plant here. But opposite this, indicated by a rusty sign pointing seaward, is the first of Mílos's **hot springs**, which bubble up in the shallows and are much enjoyed by the locals.

Taking the left or easterly fork leads to **ZEFYRÍA**, hidden among olive groves below the bare hills; it was briefly the medieval capital until an eighteenth-century epidemic drove out the population. Much of the old town is still deserted, though some life has returned, and there's a magnificent seventeenth-century church.

South of here it's a further 8km down a winding road to the coarse-sand beach of **Paleohóri**. Actually a triple strand totalling 800m in length, it's indisputably the island's best; clothing's optional at the westerly cove, where steam vents heat both the shallow water and the rock overhangs onshore. There are a number of places to stay, such as the inland *Broutsos* (☎01/34 78 425; ④) and the purpose-built rooms at the *Artemis* restaurant (☎0287/31 221; ④) nearer the beach, but the cheapest are Panayiota Vikelli's rooms (☎0287/31 228; ③). Apart from the *Artemis*, there are a couple of other tavernas including *Pelagos*, which has a large raised patio.

The westerly road from Kánava junction leads past the airport gate to **Hivadholímni**, considered to be the best beach on Mílos bay itself. Not that this is saying much: Hivadholímni is north-facing and thus garbage-prone, with shallow sumpy water offshore, although there is a taverna, a disco-bar and a sizable community of campers during the summer. It's better to veer south to **Provatás**, a short but tidy beach, closed off by colourful cliffs on the east. Being so easy to get at, it hasn't escaped some development: there are two rooms establishments plus, closer to the shore, a newer, luxury complex, *Golden Milos Beach* (☎0287/31 307; ⑥). The best value for food and accommodation is the *Maistrali* (☎0287/31 206; ③).

Some 2km west of Provatás, you'll see a highway sign for **Kípos.** Below and to the left of the road, a small **medieval chapel** dedicated to the Kímisis (Assumption) sits atop foundations far older – as evidenced by the early Christian reliefs stacked along the west wall and a carved, cruciform baptismal font in the *ieron* behind the altar screen. At one time a spring gushed from the low tunnel-cave beside the font – sufficiently miraculous in itself on arid Mílos. Several kilometres before Provatás, a road forks east through a dusty white quarry to the trendy and popular beach of **Firipláka**, beautifully set but sadly dominated in high summer by a noisy canteen pumping out techno. Further east, **Tsigrádho** beach is accessible by boat, or by the novel means of a rope hanging down a crevice in the cliff-face.

For the most part **Hálakas**, the southwestern peninsula centred on the wilderness of 748-metre Profítis Ilías, is uninhabited and little built upon, with the exception of the **monastery of Sidherianós**. The roads are memorable, if a little tiring, and several spots are worth making the effort to see. **Emboriós** on the east side of the peninsula has a fine little beach and a great local taverna with a few cheap rooms (☎0287/21 389; ③). On the mostly rugged west coast, **Triádhes** is one of the finest and least spoilt beaches in the Cyclades, but you'll have to bring your own provisions. **Kléftiko** in the southwest corner is only reachable by boat, but repays the effort to get there with its stunning rock formations, semi-submerged rock tunnels and colourful coral.

The north coast

From either Adhámas or the Pláka area, good roads run roughly parallel to the **north coast** which, despite being windswept and largely uninhabited, is not devoid of interest. **Mandhrákia**, reached from Péran Triovássalos, is another boathouse settlement, and **Sarakíniko**, to the east, is a sculpted inlet with a sandy sea-bed and a summer beach café. About 8km from Adhámas, the little hamlet of **Páhena**, not shown on many maps, has a cluster of rooms and a small beach – the best-value rooms are *Terry's* (☎0287/22 640; ③). About a kilometre beyond this, the remains of three superimposed Neolithic settlements crown a small knoll at **Fylakopí** (ancient Phylakope); the site was important archeologically, but hasn't been maintained and is difficult to interpret. Just before the site is another one of Milos's coastal wonders: the deep-sea inlet of **Papafránga**, set in a ravine and accessible through a gap in the cliffs.

Pollónia

POLLÓNIA, 12km northeast of Adhámas, must be the windiest spot on the island, hence the name of its longest-lived and best **bar**, *Okto Bofor* (meaning "Force 8 gales"), near the church. The second resort on Mílos after Adhámas, it is, not surprisingly, immensely popular with windsurfers, and the new diving centre has further increased its popularity among watersports enthusiasts. Pollónia is essentially a small harbour protected by a storm-lashed spit of land on the northeast, where self-catering units are multiplying rapidly, fringed by a long but narrow, tamarisk-fringed beach to the rear, and closed off on the south by a smaller promontory on which the tiny original settlement huddles. Besides the town beach, the only other convenient, half-decent beach is at **Voúdhia**, 3km east, where you will find more of the island's hot springs, although it is effectively spoiled by its proximity to huge mining works, which lend it the desolate air of a *Mad Max* location.

On the quay are several **tavernas** and a couple of café/snack bars. The best tavernas are *Kapetan Nikolaos* (aka *Koula's*; open year-round) and *Araxovoli*, which has a good selection of seafood. Inland and south of here you'll find a concentration of **accommodation**, more simple rooms and fewer apartments, most with the slight drawback of occasional noise and dust from quarry trucks. Among the highest-quality units here are the *Kapetan Tasos Studios* (☎0287/41 287; ⑤), with good views of the straits between Mílos and Kímolos. *Flora* (☎0287/41 249; ④), on the road towards the spit, is a more reasonable option, as are *Efi* rooms (☎0287/41 396; ④), above the far end of the beach. *Andreas* (☎0287/41 262; ⑤) has triple studios with stunning views and easy access to the quiet neighbouring bay. Pollónia has no bank or post office, but the friendly Axios Rent A Car office (☎0287/41 442) can change money and advise you on accommodation matters. A **motorbike rental** place and a well-stocked **supermarket** complete the list of amenities. There is a huge map fixed on a metal frame near the bus stop, which shows all the facilities and gives telephone numbers.

Getting to Kímolos (see below) may be the main reason you're here. Either the *Tria Adhelfia* or one other kaïki makes the trip daily year-round at 6.45am and 2pm, returning from Kímolos an hour later; during high season, there are five crossings a day.

Kímolos

Of the three islets off the coast of Mílos, Andímilos is home to a rare species of chamois, Políegos has more ordinary goats, but only **Kímolos** has any human habitation. Volcanic like Mílos, with the same little lava-built rural cottages, it profits from its geology and used to export chalk (*kimolía* in Greek) until the supply was exhausted. Fuller's earth is still extracted locally, and the fine dust of this clay is a familiar sight on the island, where mining still outstrips fishing and farming as an occupation. Rugged and barren in the interior, it has some fertile land on the southeast coast where wells provide water, and this is where the population of about eight hundred is concentrated.

Kímolos is sleepy indeed from September to June, and even in August sees hardly any visitors. This is probably just as well, since there are fewer than a hundred beds on the whole island, and little in the way of other amenities.

Psathí and Hóra

Whether you arrive by ferry, or by kaïki from Pollónia, you'll dock at the hamlet of **PSATHÍ**, pretty much a non-event except for the excellent *To Kyma* **taverna** midway along the beach. The laissez-faire attitude towards tourism is demonstrated by the fact that there are no rooms here, but, equally, nobody minds if you sleep on the small beach. **Ferry tickets** are sold only outside the expensive café at the end of the jetty, an hour or so before the anticipated arrival of the boat; the *Tria Adhelfia* kaïki comes and goes unremarked from the base of the jetty five times a day in summer. There is no bus on the island, but a licence has been obtained for a taxi, so now only a driver is required.

Around the bay there are a few old windmills and the dazzlingly white **HÓRA** perched on the ridge above them. Unsung – and neglected, although there are plans to reconstruct it and build government rooms – is the magnificent, two-gated **kástro**, a fortified core of roughly the same design as those at Andíparos and Síkinos; the perimeter houses are intact but its heart is a jumble of ruins. Just outside the kástro on the north stands the conspicuously unwhitewashed, late-sixteenth-century church of **Khryssóstomos**, the oldest and most beautiful on the island. It takes fifteen minutes to walk up to the surprisingly large town, passing the adequate *Villa Maria* (☎0287/51 392; ③), about five minutes along the way and nearer to Psathí. Further accommodation is available in Hóra itself, where Margaro Petraki (☎0287/51 314; ②), has rooms tucked away in the rather unglamorous maze of backstreets, as does Nikos Ventouris (☎0287/51 329; ②) above his kafenío nearby. Sofia Ventouris (☎0287/51 219; ④) has a few new studios with sea views, close to the church. The aptly named *Panorama*, near the east gate of the kástro, is the most elaborate and consistently open **taverna**. *Meltémi* (☎0287/51 360; ③), to the west of the village, is a good, new taverna which also has some rooms. There are a couple of basic psistariés, as well as *1860*, a surprisingly sophisticated **café-bar**. Self-catering is an easy proposition – and may be a necessity before June or after August – with a well-stocked supermarket, produce stalls and a butcher. Finally, there are a couple of boat agencies, and a **post office** in the west of the village. The small **archeological museum** (Tues & Fri 8am–2pm, Wed, Thur, Sat, Sun 8am–1pm), currently on the road into Hóra, is due to move to more spacious premises near the church; its collection comprises pottery from the Geometric to the Roman period.

Around the island

During summer at least, the hamlet of **ALYKÍ** on the south coast is a better bet for staying than Psathí and Hóra; it only takes about thirty minutes to walk there on the paved road that forks left just before the *Villa Maria*. Alykí is named after the salt pan which sprawls between a rather mediocre beach with no shade or shelter, and has a pair of **rooms** – *Sardis* (☎0287/51 458; ④) and *Passamihalis* (☎0287/51 340; ②) – and simple **tavernas**. You can stroll west one cove to **Bonátsa** for better sand and shallow water, though you won't escape the winds. Passing another cove you come to the even more attractive beach of Kalamítsi, with better shade and the good little taverna and rooms of *Ventouris* (③). To the east, between Alykí and Psathí, the smaller, more secluded beach of **Skála** is better for camping.

The 700m coarse-sand beach of **Elliniká** is 45 minutes' walk west of Alykí: starting on the road, bear left – just before two chapels on a slope – onto a narrower track which runs through the fields at the bottom of the valley. Divided by a low bluff, the beach is bracketed by two capes and looks out over Dhaskalió islet; it tends to catch heavy weather in the afternoon, and there are no facilities here.

Another road leads northeast from Hóra to a beach and radioactive springs at **Prássa**, 7km away. The route takes in impressive views across the straits to Políegos, and there are several shady peaceful coves where you could camp out. Innumerable goat tracks invite exploration of the rest of the island; in the far northwest, on Kímolos's summit, are the ruins of an imposing Venetian fortress known as **Paleókastro**. The local community has plans to open an official campsite at Klíma Bay 2km northeast of Hóra, once it has relocated the rubbish dump that currently befouls the place.

Ándhros

Ándhros, the second largest and northernmost of the Cyclades, has a number of fine features to offer the visitor, although you have to search them out. Thinly populated but prosperous, its fertile, well-watered valleys have attracted scores of Athenian holiday villas whose red-tiled roofs and white walls stand out among the greenery. Some of the

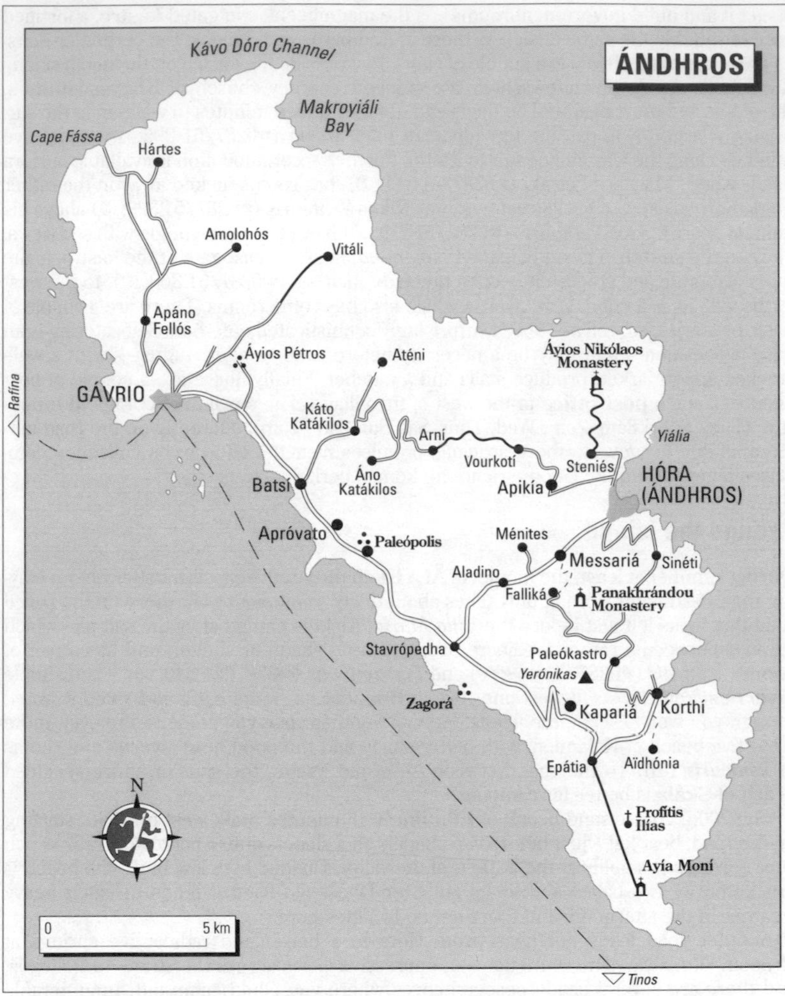

more recent of these have robbed many of the villages of life and atmosphere, turning them into scattered settlements with no nucleus, and have created a weekender mentality manifest in noisy Friday and Sunday evening traffic jams at the ferry dock. The island neither needs nor welcomes independent travellers, and it can be almost impossible to get a bed in between the block-bookings during high season. On the positive side, the permanent population is distinctly hospitable; traditionally working on ships, they are only too happy to practise their English on you. Together with some of the more idiosyncratic reminders of the Venetian period, such as the *peristereónes* (pigeon towers) and the *frákhtes* (dry-stone walls, here raised to the status of an art form), it is this friendliness that lends Ándhros its charm.

Ferries connect the island with Rafína on the mainland, only an hour from Athens on the bus, and you can loop back onto the central Cycladic routes via Mýkonos, Tínos or Sýros. The bus service is poor, and you'd be well advised to consider renting a bike to tour the sights – otherwise you'll face a lot of walking.

Northern and western Ándhros

All ferries and catamarans arrive at the main port, **GÁVRIO**. No longer the nonedescript place it once was, Gávrio is moving into the last few stages of its painfully slow transformation from scruffy port to moderately attractive holiday resort. Few venture onto the adjacent windswept beach; however, there are plenty more attractive alternatives just to the south, where you'll find some of the area's better accommodation. A converted dovecote houses a sporadically functioning **tourist office**, and there are half a dozen ferry **ticket agents**. There's also a **bank**, and a **post office** on the waterfront.

The cheapest **accommodation** is in the basic *Galaxy* (☎0282/71 228; ②), which serves as a late-arrival fall-back. There are more room and studio outfits along and above the main coastal road leading out of Gávrio to Batsí: *Aktion* (☎0282/71 607; ④) is fairly representative, and *Andros Holiday Hotel* (☎0282/71 384; ⑥) is a good upmarket choice. **Restaurants** worth trying include the good if basic estiatório, *Tria Asteria*; the *Vengera* taverna 100m inland with its nice leafy courtyard; and the smart *Trehandiri* ouzerí opposite the catamaran dock. **Nightlife** revolves around a string of cafés and bars along the harbourfront, of which *Marlin* is a popular newcomer. Alternatively, there are one or two lively venues on Áyios Pétros beach several kilometres south, including *Marabou* taverna which frequently features live guitar music. Along the same stretch the excellent *Yiannouli* taverna is worth checking out for lunch.

The road north begins behind the *Hotel Gavrion Beach*. Around 3km northwest are two beaches named **Fellós**: one with holiday villas and a taverna, the other hidden beyond the headland and popular with freelance campers. Beyond Ápano Fellós, the countryside is empty except for a few hamlets inhabited by the descendants of medieval Albanians who settled here and in southern Évvia several hundred years ago.

Most traffic heads 8km south down the coast, past, the lively Khryssí Ammos beach, and the *Perakkis Hotel* above (☎0282/71 456; ⑥), to **BATSÍ**, the island's main package resort, with large hotels and bars around its fine natural harbour. The beautiful though crowded beach curves round the port, and the sea is cold, calm and clean (except near the taxi park). **Hotels** range from the basic but comfortable *Chryssi Akti* (☎0282/41 236; ④) to the upmarket *Aneroussa Beach Hotel* (☎0282/41 045; ④), south of town past the Stivári area towards Áyia Marína beach (a picturesque cove with *Yiannoulis* fish taverna and studios (☎0282/41 963; ③)). Besides these there are plenty of other rooms, and good food can be had at *Stamatis*, an established taverna with a nice atmosphere, or at *Ta Delfinia,* which has a pleasant, sheltered balcony – both are near the harbour. For something a little different have a shrimp feast at *Restaurant Sirocco*, on the inland path above the village. Further out at **Stivári**, a pleasant café-taverna, *Stivari Gardens*, is run by an Englishwoman, who also has a few rooms (③). As well as several café-bars, of which *Capriccio* and *Select* are the most "in", there are half a dozen or so loud indoor **bars** featuring the standard foreign/Greek musical mix, although *Diva* plays some psychedelic sounds. If a full-blown *bouzoúki* night is what you are after try *Arpa* next door to *Stamatis.* Finally, there are two banks, with cash dispensers, where you can change money.

From Batsí you're within easy walking distance of some beautiful inland villages. At **KÁTO KATÁKILOS**, one hour inland, there are a couple of seasonal **tavernas** including *O Gregos*; a rough track leads to **ATÉNI**, a hamlet in a lush, remote valley, as yet unvisited by the dreaded donkey safaris. **ÁNO KATÁKILOS** has a couple of under-visited tavernas with fine views across the village. A right-hand turning out of Katákilos heads up the mountain to **ARNÍ**, whose lone taverna is often shrouded in mist. Another rewarding trip is to a well-preserved, 20-metre-high **Classical tower** at **Áyios Pétros**, 5km from Gávrio or 9km coming from Batsí.

South of Batsí along the main road are Káto and Áno Apróvato. **Káto** has rooms, including *Galini* (☎0282/41 472; ③), a taverna and a path to a quiet beach, while nearby is the largely unexplored archeological site of **Paleópolis**. Áno has the excellent taverna *To Balkoni tou Egeou*, which can be most easily visited on one of the "Mezédhes Nights" organized from Batsí, though for a more authentic evening you may be better off making your own way there.

Hóra and around

A minimal bus service links the west coast with **HÓRA** or **ÁNDHROS TOWN**, 35km from Gávrio. With its setting on a rocky spur cutting across a huge bay, the capital is the most attractive place on the island. Paved in marble and schist from the still-active local quarries, the buildings around the bus station are grand nineteenth-century affairs, and the squares with their ornate wall fountains and gateways are equally elegant. The hill quarters are modern, while the small port acts as a yacht supply station, and below are the sands of Parapórti – a fine beach, if a little exposed to the *meltémi* winds in summer.

The few **hotels** in town are on the expensive side and tend to be busy with holidaying Greeks: try the *Aigli* (☎0282/22 303; ④), opposite the big church on the main walkway. Most rooms are clustered behind the long **Nimbório** beach north of town, and range from cheap family guesthouses like those of *Firiou* (☎0282/22 921; ②) and good clean rooms like those of *Villa Stella* (☎0282/22 471; ④) to modern apartments such as the *Alkioni Inn* (☎0282/24 522; ⑤). The *Paradise Hotel* (☎0282/22 187, *marlos@mail.otenet.gr*; ⑥), with its swimming pool and tennis court, is the most upmarket choice. For **eating**, most cafés are up in Hóra: *Plátanos* do a generous mezédhes selection which can be enjoyed with an oúzo under the plane trees; the appropriately named *O Stathmos* right by the bus station is good; and there's a decent psistariá on the main drag. The nicest taverna is *O Nonas*, tucked away at the town end of the beach behind the ugly *Xenia* hotel; *Nostos*, a smart new pizzeria nearby on the seafront, is another popular choice. Up in Hóra there's the *Rock Café* for a **drink**, but Nimboúrio beach is the epicentre of nightlife with the two-storey *Veyera*, a thumping disco halfway along, and the huge *Kavo* right at the end, which plays Greek music till after 4am. There's a post office and bank around town, a couple of travel agents and three moped rentals behind the beach.

From the square right at the end of town you pass through an archway and down to windswept **Platía Ríva**, with its statue of the unknown sailor scanning the sea. Beyond lies the thirteenth-century Venetian **kástro**, precariously joined to the mainland by a narrow-arched bridge, which was damaged by German munitions in World War II. The **Modern Art Museum** (Wed–Mon 10am–2pm, also 6–8pm in summer; 1000dr) has a sculpture garden and a permanent collection that includes works by Picasso and Braque, as well as temporary exhibits. Don't be discouraged by the stark modern architecture of the **Archeological Museum** (Tues–Sun 8.30am–2.30pm; 500dr); it proves to be well laid out and labelled, with instructive models. The prize items on view are the fourth-century "Hermes of Ándros", reclaimed from a prominent position in the Athens Archeological Museum, and the "Matron of Herculaneum".

Hiking inland and west from Ándhros, the obvious destination is **MÉNITES**, a hill village just up a green valley choked with trees and straddled by stone walls. The church of the **Panayía** may have been the location of a temple of Dionysos, where water was turned into wine; water still flows continuously from the local rocks. Nearby is the medieval village of **MESSARIÁ**, with the deserted twelfth-century Byzantine church of **Taxiárhis** below and the pleasantly shady *Platanos* taverna. The finest monastery on the island, **Panakhrándou**, is only an hour's (steep) walk away, via the village of Falliká; reputedly tenth-century, it's still defended by massive walls but occupied these days by just three monks. It clings to an iron-stained cliff southwest of Hóra, to which you can return directly with a healthy two- to three-hour walk down the creek valley, guided by red dots.

Hidden by the ridge directly north of Hóra, the prosperous nineteenth-century village of **STENIÉS** was built by the vanguard of today's shipping magnates; just below, at Yiália, there's a small pebble beach with a taverna. Nearby on the road to Strapouriés is a wonderful taverna, *Bozakis*, which boasts a view all the way down to the coast and excellent food. Beyond Steniés is **APIKÍA**, a tidy little village which bottles Sariza-brand mineral water for a living; there are a few **tavernas**, including *O Tassos* which has a lovely garden setting and specialities such as goat and rabbit. There are a very limited number of **rooms** here, as well as the " luxury" hotel *Pigi Sariza* (☎0282/23 799 or 23 899; ⑥), which is getting a bit tatty around the edges. The road is now asphalted up to Vourkotí and even past this point is quite negotiable via Arní to the west coast. There are some stunning views all along this road but bike riders need to take care when the *meltémi* is blowing – it can get dangerously windy.

Southern Ándhros

On your way south, you might stop at **Zagorá**, a fortified Geometric town – unique in having never been built over – that was excavated in the early 1970s. Located on a desolate, flat-topped promontory with cliffs falling away on three sides, it's worth a visit for the view alone. With your own transport, the sheltered cove of Sinéti south of Hóras is also worth a detour.

The village of **KORTHÍ**, the end of the line, is a friendly village which is slowly waking up to its tourist potential. Set on a large sandy bay, cut off from the rest of the island by a high ridge and so relatively unspoiled, it is pleasant enough to merit spending the night at *Villa Aristidou* (☎0282/62 122; ③) or at the austere-looking *Hotel Korthion* (☎0282/61218; ③). There are also several good seafood **restaurants**, and a number of pleasant café-bars including *Erolo Cafe* on the seafront. You could also take in the nearby convent of **Zoödhóhou Piyís** (open to visitors before noon), with illuminated manuscripts and a disused weaving factory.

To the north is **PALEÓKASTRO**, a tumbledown village with a ruined Venetian castle – and a legend about an old woman who betrayed the stronghold to the Turks, then jumped off the walls in remorse, landing on a rock now known as "Old Lady's Leap". In the opposite direction out of Korthí are **AÏDHÓNIA** and **KAPARIÁ**, dotted with pigeon towers (*peristereónes*) left by the Venetians.

Tínos

Tínos still feels one of the most Greek of the larger islands. A few foreigners have discovered its beaches and unspoiled villages, but most visitors are Greek, here to see the church of **Panayía Evangelístria**, a grandiose shrine erected on the spot where a miraculous icon with healing powers was found in 1822. A Tiniote nun, now canonized as Ayía Pelayía, was directed in a vision to unearth the relic just as the War of Independence was getting underway, a timely coincidence which served to underscore the links between the Orthodox Church and Greek nationalism. Today, there are two major annual pilgrimages, on March 25 and August 15, when, at 11am, the icon bearing the Virgin's image is carried in state down to the harbour over the heads of the faithful.

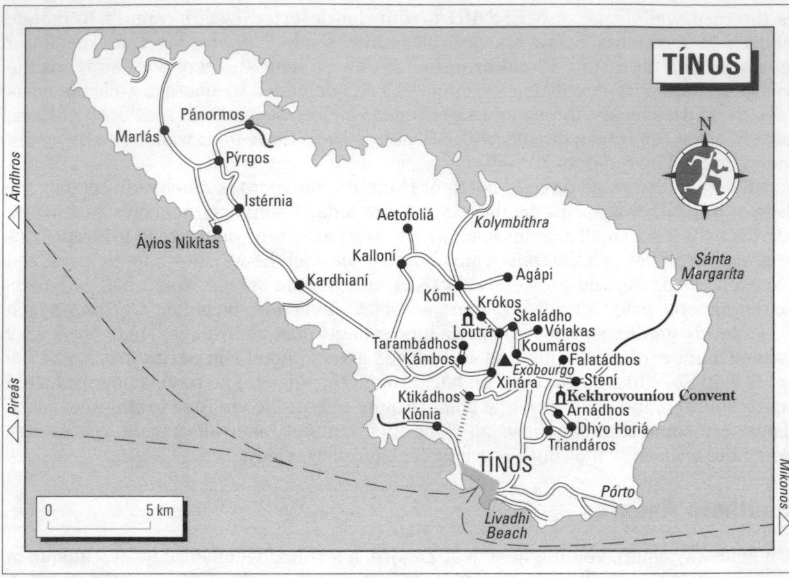

The Ottoman tenure here was the most fleeting in the Aegean. **Exóbourgo**, the craggy mount dominating southern Tínos and surrounded by most of the island's sixty-odd villages, is studded with the ruins of a Venetian citadel which defied the Turks until 1715, long after the rest of Greece had fallen. An enduring legacy of the long Venetian rule is a persistent **Catholic minority**, which accounts for almost a half of the population, and a sectarian rivalry said to be responsible for the numerous graceful belfries scattered throughout the island – Orthodox and Catholic parishes vying to build the tallest. The sky is pierced, too, by distinctive and ornate dovecotes, even more in evidence here than on Ándhros. Aside from all this, the inland village architecture is striking and there's a flourishing folk-art tradition which finds expression in the abundant local marble. The islanders have remained open and hospitable to the relatively few foreigners and the steady stream of Greek visitors who touch down here, and any mercenary inclinations seem to be satisfied by booming sales in religious paraphernalia to the faithful.

Tínos Town and the southern beaches

At **TÍNOS Town**, trafficking in devotional articles certainly dominates the streets leading up from the busy waterfront to the Neoclassical **church** (daily 8am–8pm) which towers above. Approached via a massive marble staircase, the famous **icon** inside is all but buried under a dazzling mass of gold and silver *támmata* (votive offerings); below is the crypt (where the icon was discovered) and a mausoleum for the sailors drowned when the Greek warship *Elli*, at anchor off Tínos during a pilgrimage, was torpedoed by an Italian submarine on August 15, 1940. Museums around the courtyard display more objects donated by the faithful (who inundate the island for the two big yearly festivals), as well as icons, paintings and work by local marble sculptors.

The shrine aside – and all the attendant stalls, shops and bustle – the port is none too exciting, with just scattered inland patches of nineteenth-century buildings. You might make time for the **Archeological Museum** (Tues–Sun 8.30am–3pm; 500dr) on the way up to the church, whose collection includes a fascinating sundial from the local Roman sanctuary of Poseidon and Amphitrite (see p.122).

Practicalities

Ferries dock at any of three different **jetties**; which one depends on weather conditions. There are at least two boats a day from Piraeás and Sýros, and four from Rafína and Ándhros going on to Mýkonos, as well as a useful hydrofoil, and less frequent ferry connections to Páros, Náxos and Santoríni. When you're leaving, ask your ticket agent which jetty to head for. **Buses** leave from a small parking area in front of a cubbyhole-office on the quay, to Pánormos, Kallоní, Stení, Pórto and Kiónia (timetables available here; no buses after 7.30pm). A **moped** is perhaps a more reliable means of exploring – Vidalis, Zanáki Alavánou 16, is a good rental agency.

Windmills Travel (☎0283/23 398, *tinos@windmills-travel.com*), on the front towards the new jetty, can help with information as well as hotel and **tour bookings**; they even have a book exchange. In season an excursion boat does day-trips taking in Delos (see p.129) and Mýkonos (Tues–Sun; 5000dr round trip); this makes it possible to see Delos without the expense of staying overnight in Mýkonos, but only allows you two and a half hours at the site. The **tourist police** are located on the road to the west of the new jetty.

To have any chance of securing a reasonably priced **room** around the pilgrimage day of March 25 (August 15 is hopeless), you must arrive several days in advance. At other times there's plenty of choice, though you'll still be competing with out-of-season pilgrims, Athenian tourists and the sick and the disabled seeking a miracle cure. Of the hotels, the *Eleana* (☎0283/22 561; ③), east of the quay about 400m inland at the edge of the bazaar, is a good budget option. The conspicuous waterfront *Yannis Rooms* (☎0283/22 515; ③) is just in front of the reasonable *Thalia* (☎0283/22811; ④), all the way around the bay from the old jetty. Slightly pricier options include the *Avra* (☎0283/22 242; ③), a Neoclassical relic on the waterfront, and the *Favie Souzane* just inland (☎0283/22 693 or 22 176; ④). *Hotel Tinion* (☎0283/22 261; ⑤) is a stylish 1920s hotel near the post office. The *Vyzantio*, Zanáki Alavánou 26 (☎0283/22 454; ④), on the road out towards Pórto and the villages, is not especially memorable but it and the *Meltémi* (☎0283/22 881; ④) at Filipóti 7, near Megaloháris, are the only places open out of season. Finally, there is a smart hotel with swimming pool near the beginning of the beach road east of the promontory – *Aeolos Bay Hotel* (☎0283/23 410; ④). Otherwise, beat the crowds by staying at *Tinos Camping*, which also has a few nice rooms to let (☎0283/22 344; ②); follow the signs from the port – it's a ten-minute walk. A farmers' **market** for locally produced fruit and vegetables takes place every morning in the Palládha area (towards the new jetty between the bars and the waterfront).

As usual, most seafront **restaurants** are rather overpriced and indifferent, with the exception of a friendly psitopolió right opposite the bus terminal, and the smarter *Xinari* restaurant and pizzeria on Evangelístrias. A cluster of places around the bazaar just to the left of Megaloháris as you face the church include *Palea Pallada* and *Peristereonas*, both of them reasonable. Tucked away in a small alley near the seafront off Evangelistriás, *Pigada* does a fine clay-pot moussaka, as well as some more unusual dishes, while *1000 + 1 Yevsis*, further inland on Nikoláou Loúvari, is a basic estiatório with reasonable prices. Wash down your meal with the island's very good barrelled retsina, which is available just about everywhere.

There are quite a few **bars**, mostly in a huddle near the new quay. *Fevgatos* has a pleasant atmosphere, *Koutsaros* on the corner plays rock music, and *Kala Kathoumena* is pretty lively with a mixture of international hits and Greek music. At 3am all bars in Tinos Town close, and for those not ready to hit the sack, the *Paradise* and *Vegera* club duplex on the main road out of town to Amphitrite stay open until dawn, the former playing mainly Greek music and the latter favouring trance.

Nearby beaches

Kiónia, 3km northwest (hourly buses), is the site of the **Sanctuary of Poseidon and Amphitrite** which was discovered in 1902; the excavations yielded principally columns (*kiónia* in Greek), but also a temple, baths, a fountain and hostels for the ancient pilgrims. The **beach** is functional enough, lined with rooms to rent and snack bars, but it's better to walk past the large *Tinos Beach Hotel* (☎0283/22 626; ⑥), the last stop for the bus, and follow an unpaved road to a series of sandy coves beyond.

The beach beyond the headland east of town starts off rocky but improves if you walk 500 metres further along. Further east, **Pórto** (six buses daily) boasts two good beaches, with a couple of good tavernas as well as rooms at the reasonably priced restaurant belonging to *Akti Aegeou* (☎0283/24 248; ⑥), on the first beach of Áyios Pandelímon, as well as the smart studios of *Porto Raphael* (☎0283/22 403; ④), above Áyios Ioánnis. *Porto Tango* (☎0283/24 410; ⑥) is an excellent upmarket hotel here, with a lovely pool setting.

Northern Tínos

A good beginning to a foray into the interior is to take the stone stairway – the continuation of Odhós Ayíou Nikoláou – that passes behind and to the left of the Evangelístria. This climbs for ninety minutes through appealing countryside to **KTIKÁDHOS**, a fine village with a good sea-view taverna, *Iy Dhrosia*. You can either flag down a bus on the main road or stay with the trail until Xinára (see "Around Exóbourgo" below).

Heading northwest from the junction flanked by Ktikádhos, Tripótamos and Xinára, there's little to stop for – except the fine dovecotes around Tarambádhos – until you reach **KARDHIANÍ**, one of the most strikingly set and beautiful villages on the island, with its views across to Sýros from amid a dense oasis. Nestled in the small sandy bay below is a fine little restaurant by the name of *Anemos*, which serves octopus stew and other dishes at good prices. Kardhianí has been discovered by wealthy Athenians and expatriates, and now offers the exotic *To Perivoli* taverna. **ISTÉRNIA**, just a little beyond, is not nearly so appealing but there is some accommodation on offer, including the *Lameras Hotel* (☎0283/31215; ③). The *Tavsternia* taverna commands stunning panoramic views and there are a few cafés, perched above the turning for **Órmos Isternían,** a comparatively small but overdeveloped beach.

Five daily buses along this route finish up at **PÝRGOS**, a few kilometres further north and smack in the middle of the island's marble-quarrying district. A beautiful village, its local artisans are renowned throughout Greece for their skill in producing marble ornamentation; ornate fanlights and bas-relief plaques crafted here adorn houses throughout Tínos. Pýrgos is also home to the School of Arts, and **the Museum of Tinian Artists** (daily 11am–2pm & 5.30–6.30pm; 300dr) contains numerous representative works from some of the island's finest artists. There are two **kafenía** and a **snack bar** on the attractive shady platía, and one acceptable **taverna** opposite the bus station. Pýrgos is popular in summer, and if you want to stay there are some new **studios** for rent on the main road coming into the village; alternatively ask the locals on the platía.

The marble products were once exported from **PÁNORMOS** (Órmos) harbour, 4km northeast, with its tiny but commercialized beach; there's little reason to linger, but if you get stuck there are rooms and some tavernas.

Around Exóbourgo

The ring of villages around **Exóbourgo** mountain is the other focus of interest on Tínos. The fortified pinnacle itself (570m), with ancient foundations as well as the ruins of three Venetian churches and a fountain, is reached by steep steps from **XINÁRA** (near the island's major road junction), the seat of the island's Roman Catholic bishop. Most villages in north central Tínos have mixed populations, but Xinára and its immediate neighbours are purely Catholic; the inland villages also tend to have a more sheltered position, with better farmland nearby – the Venetians' way of rewarding converts and their descendants. Yet **TRIPÓTAMOS**, just south of Xinára, is a completely Orthodox village with possibly the finest architecture in this region – and has accordingly been pounced on by foreigners keen to restore its historic properties.

At **LOUTRÁ**, the next community north of Xinára, there's an Ursuline convent and a good **folk art museum** (summer only 10.30am–3.30pm; free) in the old Jesuit monastery here; to visit, leave the bus at the turning for Skaládho. From Krókos, which has a scenically situated restaurant *O Krokos*, it's a forty-minute walk to **VÓLAKAS** (Vólax), one of the most remote villages on the island, a windswept oasis surrounded by bony rocks. Here, half a dozen elderly Catholic basketweavers fashion some of the best examples of that craft in Greece. There is a small **folklore museum** (free) which you have to ask the lady living in the house opposite the entrance to open, and the charming outdoor **Fontaine Theatre** which in August hosts visiting theatre groups from all over Greece. Accommodation is hard to come by; however there are a couple of places to eat, including the recommended *O Rokos* taverna.

At Kómi, 5km beyond Krókos, you can take a detour for **KOLYMBÍTHRA**, a magnificent double beach: one part wild, huge and windswept (temporary residence to pink flamingos migrating to Africa during May), the other sheltered and with a couple of tavernas including *Kolibithra Beach* (☎0283/51213; ④), which also has rooms. The bus to Kalloní goes on to Kolymbíthra twice a day in season; out of season you'll have to get off at Kómi and walk 4km.

From either Skaládho or Vólakas you go on to Koúmaros, where another long stairway leads up to Exóbourgo, or skirt the pinnacle towards Steni and Falatádhos which appear as white speckles against the fertile Livádha valley. From Steni you can catch the bus back to the harbour (seven daily). On the way down, try and stop off at one of the beautiful settlements just below the important twelfth-century **convent of Kekhrovouníou**, where Ayía Pelayía had her vision. Particularly worth visiting are **DHÝO HORIÁ**, which has a fine main square where cave-fountains burble, and **TRIANDÁROS**, which has two reasonable **eating** places: *Iy Lefka* and *Eleni's* (a tiny place at the back of the village). If you have your own transport, there are quite wide and fairly negotiable tracks down to some lovely secluded bays on the east of the island from the area of Steni. One such is **Sánta Margaríta**; given the lack of tourist development here, it's a good idea to take something to drink.

This is hardly an exhaustive list of Tiniot villages; armed with a map and good walking shoes for tackling the many old trails that still exist, you could spend days within sight of Exóbourgo and never pass through the same hamlets twice. Take warm clothing out of season, especially if you're on a moped, since the forbidding mountains behind Vólakas and the Livadhéri plain keep things noticeably cool.

Mýkonos

Originally visited only as a stop on the way to ancient Delos, **Mýkonos** has become easily the most popular (and the most expensive) of the Cyclades. Boosted by direct air links with Britain and domestic flights from Athens, it sees an incredible 800,000 tourists pass through in a good year, producing some spectacular overcrowding in high summer on Mýkonos's 75 square kilometres. But if you don't mind the crowds, or – and this is a much more attractive proposition – you come out of season, the prosperous capital is still one of the most beautiful of all island towns, its immaculately whitewashed houses concealing hundreds of little churches, shrines and chapels.

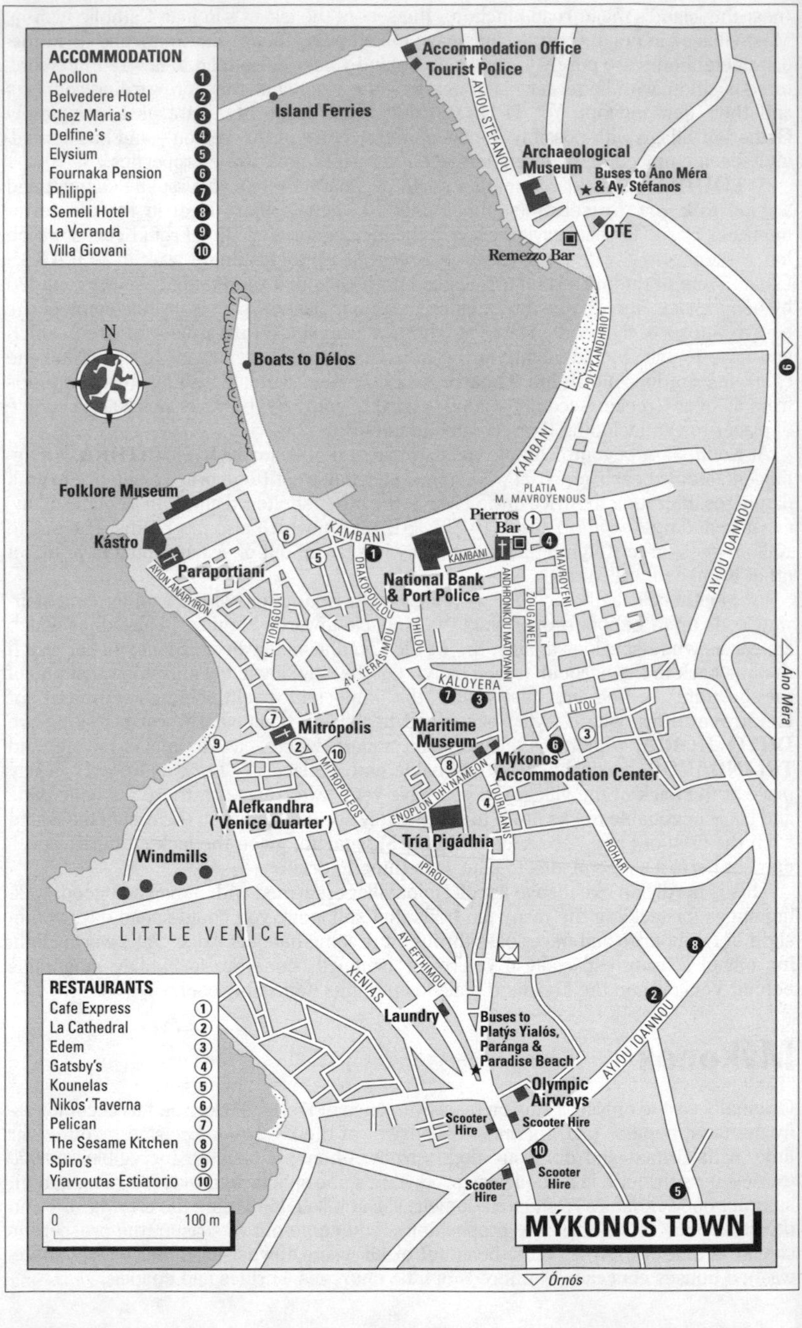
ACCOMMODATION
Apollon 1
Belvedere Hotel 2
Chez Maria's 3
Delfine's 4
Elysium 5
Fournaka Pension 6
Philippi 7
Semeli Hotel 8
La Veranda 9
Villa Giovani 10
Accommodation Office
Tourist Police
Island Ferries
AYIOU STEFANOU
Archaeological Museum
Buses to Áno Méra & Ay. Stéfanos
OTE
Remezzo Bar
N
Boats to Délos
POLYKANDHRIOTI
9
KAMBANI
PLATIA M. MAVROYENOUS
Folklore Museum
Kástro
Paraportianí
AYION ANARYIRON
Pierros Bar
KAMBANI
DRAKOPOULOU
National Bank & Port Police
ANDHRONIKOU MATOYANNI
ZOUGANELI
MAVROYENI
AYIOU IOANNOU
K. YIORGOULI
AY. YERASIMOU
DHILOU
KALOYERA
Áno Méra
LITOU
Mitrópolis
Maritime Museum
Mýkonos Accommodation Center
MITROPOLEOS
ENOPLON DHYNAMEON
TOURLIANIS
Alefkandhra ('Venice Quarter')
Tría Pigádhia
ROHARI
Windmills
IPIROU
LITTLE VENICE
AY. EFTHIMOU
XENIAS
RESTAURANTS
Cafe Express 1
La Cathedral 2
Edem 3
Gatsby's 4
Kounelas 5
Nikos' Taverna 6
Pelican 7
The Sesame Kitchen 8
Spiro's 9
Yiavroutas Estiatorio 10
Laundry
Buses to Platýs Yialós, Paránga & Paradise Beach
AYIOU IOANNOU
Olympic Airways
Scooter Hire
Scooter Hire
Scooter Hire
Scooter Hire
0
100 m
MÝKONOS TOWN
Órnós

The sophisticated nightlife is pretty hectic, amply stimulated by Mýkonos's former reputation as *the* gay resort of the Mediterranean – a title shared in recent years with places like Ibiza and Sitges in Spain; whatever, the locals take this comparatively exotic clientele in their stride. Unspoiled it isn't, but the island does offer excellent (if crowded) beaches, picturesque windmills and a rolling arid interior. An unheralded Mýkonian quirk is the widespread legality of scuba diving, a rarity in Greece, and dive centres have sprung up on virtually every beach.

Mýkonos Town

Don't let the crowds put you off exploring **MÝKONOS TOWN**, the archetypal postcard image of the Cyclades. Its sugar-cube buildings are stacked around a cluster of seafront fishermen's dwellings, with every nook and cranny scrubbed and shown off. Most people head out to the beaches during the day, so early morning or late afternoon are the best times to wander the maze of narrow streets. The labyrinthine design was intended to confuse the pirates who plagued Mýkonos in the eighteenth and early nineteenth centuries, and it still has the desired effect.

You don't need any maps or hints to explore the convoluted streets and alleys of town; getting lost is half the fun. There are, however, a few places worth seeking out. Coming from the ferry quay you'll pass the **Archeological Museum** (Tues–Sat 9am–3.30pm, Sun 10am–3pm; 500dr) on your way into town, which displays some good Delos pottery; the town also boasts a **marine museum** displaying various nautical artefacts, including a lighthouse re-erected in the back garden (Tues–Sun 8.30am–3pm; 350dr). Alternatively, behind the two banks there's the **library**, with Hellenistic coins and late medieval seals, or, at the base of the Delos jetty, the **Folklore Museum** (Mon–Sat 4–8pm, Sun 5–8pm; free), housed in an eighteenth-century mansion and cramming in a larger-than-usual collection of bric-a-brac, including a vast four-poster bed. The museum shares the same promontory as the old Venetian kástro, the entrance to which is marked by Mýkonos's oldest and best-known church, **Paraportianí**, which is a fascinating asymmetrical hodge-podge of four chapels amalgamated into one.

The shore leads to the area known as "Little Venice" because of its high, arcaded Venetian houses built right up to the water's edge. Its real name is **Alefkándhra**, a trendy district packed with art galleries, chic bars and discos. Away from the seafront, behind Platía Alefkándhra, are Mýkonos's two **cathedrals**: Roman Catholic and Greek Orthodox. Beyond, the famous **windmills** look over the area, a little shabby but ripe for photo opportunities. Instead of retracing your steps along the water's edge, follow Énoplon Dhinaméon (left off Mitropóleos) to **Tría Pigádhia** fountain. The name means "Three Wells", and legend has it that should a maiden drink from all three she is bound to find a husband.

Arrival and information

There is some accommodation information at the **airport**, but unless you know where you're going it's easier to take a taxi for the 3km into town, and sort things out there. The vast majority of visitors arrive by boat at the new northern **jetty**, where a veritable horde of room-owners pounces on the newly arrived. The scene is actually quite intimidating, and so, if you can avoid the grasping talons, it is far better to go a hundred metres further where a row of offices deal with official hotels, rented rooms and camping information, or into town to the extremely helpful Mykonos Accommodation Centre on the corner of Énoplon Dhinaméon and Malamatenías (☎0289/23 160, *mac@mac.myk.forthnet.gr*).

The harbour curves around past the dull, central Polikandhrióti beach, south of which is the **bus station** for Toúrlos, Áyios Stéfanos, Elía and Áno Méra. The **tourist**

police are located at the harbour. A second **bus terminus**, for beaches to the south, is right at the other end of the town, in the Lákka area where the **post office and** Olympic Airways office are. Buses to all the most popular beaches and resorts run frequently, until the early hours. **Taxis** go from Platía Mavroyénous on the seafront, and their rates are fixed and quite reasonable; try Mykonos Radio Taxi (☎0289/22 400). It is also here that the largest cluster of **motorbike rental** agencies is to be found; prices vary little.

Accommodation

Accommodation **prices** in Mýkonos rocket in the high season to a greater degree than almost anywhere else in Greece. One **hotel** that comes recommended despite its unattractive location is *Villa Giovani* (☎0289/22 485; ⑤), on Ayíou Ioánnou, the busy main road above the bus station. **In town**, try *Delfines* on Mavroyénous (☎0289/22 292; ⑤), *Apollon* on Kambáni (☎0289/22 223; ⑤), *Chez Marias* at Kaloyéra 27 (☎0289/22 480; ⑥) or the *Philippi* at Kaloyéra 25 (☎0289/22 294, *chrico@otenet.gr*; ④). There are plenty of very expensive splurge hotels like *Semeli Hotel* (☎0289/27 466; ⑥) on Ayíou Ioánnou, which has a pool, whirlpool and very tastefully decorated rooms, or the *Belvedere Hotel* (☎0289/25 122, *belvedere@myk.forthnet.gr*; ⑥) next door. *La Veranda* (☎0289/23 670; ⑥) is a hidden gem, located on the hillside above town, with rooms set around a small pool. Unsurprisingly, most accommodation is extremely gay-friendly; *Elysium* (☎0289/23 952; ⑥) is almost exclusively gay, and *Fournakia Pension* (☎0289/23 160; ⑤) has clean, modern rooms close to *Pierro's Bar*. There are two **campsites**: *Mykonos Camping* (☎0289/24 578) above Paránga Beach is smaller and has a more pleasant setting than nearby *Paradise Camping* on Paradise Beach (☎0289/22 852, *PARADISE@paradise.myk.forthnet.gr*); however, the latter also has bungalows (③). Both are packed in season, and dance music from the 24-hour bars on Paradise Beach makes sleep difficult. The campsite restaurants are best avoided. Hourly bus services to Paránga and Paradise Beach continue into the early hours but can get very overcrowded.

Eating and nightlife

Even **light meals** and **snacks** are expensive in Mýkonos, but there are several bakeries – the best is *Andhrea's*, just off Platía Mavroyénous – and plenty of supermarkets and takeaways in the backstreets, including *Three Wells* on Énoplon Dhinaméon.

The area around Alefkándhra is a promising place to head for a full **meal**: *La Cathedral*, by the two cathedrals on the platía, has standard fare; *Pelican*, behind the cathedrals, is pricey but well sited; and *Kostas*, also nearby, has competitive prices, a good wine list including barrelled wine (not easily found on Mýkonos) and friendly service. Less than fifty metres further along Mitropóleos, the small *Yiavroutas Estiatorio* is probably the least expensive and most authentically Greek place on the island, again with good barrelled wine. *Kounelas* is a good fish taverna with more reasonable prices than *Spiro's* on the seafront. *Edem*, close to Panakhrándou, offers poolside dining. *El Greco* at Tría Pigádhia is expensive but romantic, and *Gatsby's* on Tourlianís is a popular gay restaurant with an adventurous menu. *The Sesame Kitchen* on Énoplon Dhinaméon is an acceptable vegetarian restaurant; however, most of the smarter restaurants in Mýkonos do cater well for vegetarians anyway. Just behind the town hall is *Nikos' Taverna* – crowded, reasonable and recommended. For **late-night** snacks, most of the cafés on Kambani stay open until the small hours, and *Cafe Express* is open all night.

Nightlife in town is every bit as good as it's cracked up to be – and every bit as pricey. *Remezzo* (near the OTE) is one of the oldest bars, now a bit over the hill but a lively spot nonetheless, and a good place to have a drink before moving onto *Mercedes Club* next door; both are popular with young Athenians. *Skandinavian Bar-Disco* is a cheap-and-cheerful party spot, as is the nearby *Irish Bar*, and there are more sophisticated bars on Andhroníkou Matoyiánni and Énoplon Dhinaméon. *Caprice* and *Kastro's*, both around Little Venice, are ideal for sunset cocktails; the latter plays classical music and is popular with an older gay crowd. *La Mer* is a popular disco-bar playing a lively mix of Greek and dance music, while *Porta* is a popular gay haunt. *Pierro's* and *Icarus* (upstairs), just off Platía Mavroyénous, become the focal point of gay activity later on, the latter having great drag shows and welcoming proprietors. *Cavo Paradiso*, near *Paradise Camping*, is the after-hours club where die-hard party animals of all persuasions come together.

The beaches

The closest **beaches** to town are those to the north, at **Toúrlos** (only 2km away but horrid) and **Áyios Stéfanos** (4km, much better), both developed resorts and connected by a very regular bus service to Mýkonos Town. There are tavernas and rooms to let (as well as package hotels) at Áyios Stéfanos, away from the beach; *Mocambo Lido* taverna at the far end of the bay has a pleasant setting and good food.

Other nearby destinations include southwest peninsula resorts, with undistinguished beaches tucked into pretty bays. The nearest to town, 1km away, is **Megáli Ámmos**, a good beach backed by flat rocks and pricey rooms, but nearby Kórfos Bay is disgusting, thanks to the town dump and machine noise. Buses serve **Ornós**, an average beach, and **Áyios Ioánnis**, a dramatic bay with a tiny, stony beach, which achieved its moment of fame as a location for the film *Shirley Valentine*. The taverna *To Iliovasilema* has an excellent selection of fish and is highly recommended, if a little pricey.

The south coast is the busiest part of the island. Kaïkia ply from town to all of its beaches, which are among the straightest on the island, and still regarded to some extent as family strands by the Greeks. You might begin with **Platýs Yialós**, 4km south of town, though you won't be alone: one of the longest-established resorts on the island, it's not remotely Greek any more, the sand is monopolized by hotels, and you won't get a room to save your life between June and September. **Psaroú**, next door to the west, is very pretty – 150m of white sand backed by foliage and calamus reeds, crowded with sunbathers. Facilities here include a diving club (☎0289/23 579), waterskiing and windsurfer rental, but again you'll need to reserve well in advance to secure a room between mid-June and mid-September.

Just over the headland to the east of Platýs Yialós is **Paránga Beach**, which is actually two beaches separated by a smaller headland. The highly recommended *Nicolas* taverna and rooms (☎0289/23 566; ④) on the first beach is worlds apart from its noisy neighbour which is home to a loud beach bar and *Mykonos Camping*. A dusty footpath beyond Platýs Yialós crosses the fields and caves of the headland across the clifftops past Paranga, and drops down to **Paradise Beach**, a crescent of golden sand that is packed in season. Behind are the shops, self-service restaurants and noisy 24-hour beach bars of *Paradise Camping*. The next bay east contains **Super Paradise** (officially "Plindhrí") beach, accessible by footpath or by kaïki. One of the most fun beaches on the island, it has a decent taverna and two bars at opposite ends of the beach pumping out cheesy summer hits. One half of the beach is very mixed, getting progressively more gay as you walk away from where the kaïkia dock towards the beach bar perched in the hills, below which the beach is almost exclusively gay and nudist.

Probably the **best beach** on Mýkonos, though, is **Eliá**, the last port of call for the kaïkia. A broad, sandy stretch with a verdant backdrop, it's the longest beach on the island, though split in two by a rocky area. Almost exclusively nudist, it boasts a couple of restaurants, including the excellent *Matheos*. If the crowds have followed you this far, one last escape route is to follow the bare rock footpath over the spur (look for the white house) at the end of Eliá Beach. This cuts upwards for grand views east and west and then winds down to **Kaló Livádhi** (seasonal bus service), a stunning beach adjoining an agricultural valley scattered with little farmhouses; even here there's a restaurant (a good one at that) at the far end of the beach. **Lía**, further on, is smaller but delightful, with bamboo windbreaks and clear water, plus another taverna.

The rest of the island

If time is limited, any of the beaches above will be just fine. There are others, though, away from Mýkonos Town, as well as a few other destinations worth making the effort for.

East of Eliá, roughly 12km by road from the town, **Ayía Ánna** boasts a shingle beach and taverna, with the cliffs above granting some fine vistas. **Tarsaná**, on the other side of the isthmus, has a long, coarse sand beach, with watersports, a taverna and smart bungalows on offer. **Kalafáti**, almost adjacent, is more of a tourist community, its white-sand beach supporting a few hotels, restaurants and a disco. There's a local bus service from here to Áno Méra (see below), or you can jump on an excursion boat to **Tragoníssi**, the islet just offshore, for spectacular coastal scenery, seals and wild birds. The rest of the east coast is difficult – often impossible – to reach: there are some small beaches, really only worth the effort if you crave solitude, and the region is dominated by the peak of Profítis Ilías, sadly spoiled by a huge radar dome and military establish-

ment. The **north coast** suffers persistent battering from the *meltémi*, plus tar and litter pollution, and for the most part is bare, brown and exposed. **Pánormos Bay** is the exception to this – a lovely, relatively sheltered beach. Despite a good restaurant, a relaxed beach bar and the rather conspicuous *Albatros Club Hotel* (☎0289/25 130; ⑥), Pánormos remains one of the least crowded beaches on the island.

From Pánormos, it's an easy walk to the only other settlement of any size on the island, **ÁNO MÉRA**, where you should be able to find a **room**. The village prides itself on striving to maintain a traditional way of life, the result however being rather pseudo and wishy-washy; the so-called traditional kafenío has long since ditched Greek coffee for cappuccino and traditional sweets for "ice-cream special". There are, however, several acceptable **tavernas** on the platía, of which *Tou Apostoli to Koutouki* is most popular with locals, and a large **hotel** – *Hotel Ano Mera* (☎0289/71 276; ⑥). The red-roofed church near the square is the sixteenth-century **monastery of Panayía Tourlianí**, where a collection of Cretan icons and the unusual eighteenth-century marble baptismal font are worth seeing. It's not far, either, to the late twelfth-century **Paleokástro monastery** (also known as Dárga), just north of the village, in a magnificent green setting on an otherwise barren slope. To the northwest are more of the same dry and wind-buffeted landscapes, though they do provide some enjoyable, rocky walking with expansive views across to neighbouring islands – head to Áyios Stéfanos for buses back to the harbour.

Delos (Dhílos)

The remains of **ancient Delos**, Pindar's "unmoved marvel of the wide world", though skeletal and swarming now with lizards and tourists, give some idea of the past grandeur of this sacred isle a few sea-miles west of Mýkonos. The ancient town lies on the west coast on flat, sometimes marshy ground which rises in the south to **Mount Kýnthos**. From the summit – an easy walk – there's a magnificent view across the Cyclades: the name of the archipelago means "those [islands] around [Delos]".

The first excursion boats to Delos leave Mýkonos daily at 8.30am (1900dr round trip), except Mondays when the site is closed. You have to return on the same boat but in season each does the trip several times and you can choose what time you leave. The last return is usually about 3pm, and you'll need to arrive early if you want to make a thorough tour of the site. In season a daily kaïki makes return trips from the beaches (3000dr) with pick-up points at Platýs Yialós and Órnos, but only allows you three hours on the island. It's a good idea to bring your own food and drink as the tourist pavilion's snack bar is a rip-off.

Some history

Delos's ancient fame was due to the fact that Leto gave birth to the divine twins Artemis and Apollo on the island, although its fine harbour and central position did nothing to hamper development. When the Ionians colonized the island around 1000 BC it was already a cult centre, and by the seventh century BC it had become the commercial and religious centre of the **Amphictionic League**. Unfortunately Delos also attracted the attention of Athens, which sought dominion over this prestigious island; the wealth of the Delian Confederacy, founded after the Persian Wars to protect the Aegean cities, was harnessed to Athenian ends, and for a while Athens controlled the Sanctuary of Apollo. Athenian attempts to "purify" the island began with a decree that no one could die or give birth on Delos – the sick and the pregnant were taken to the islet of Rheneia – and culminated in the simple expedient of banishing the native population.

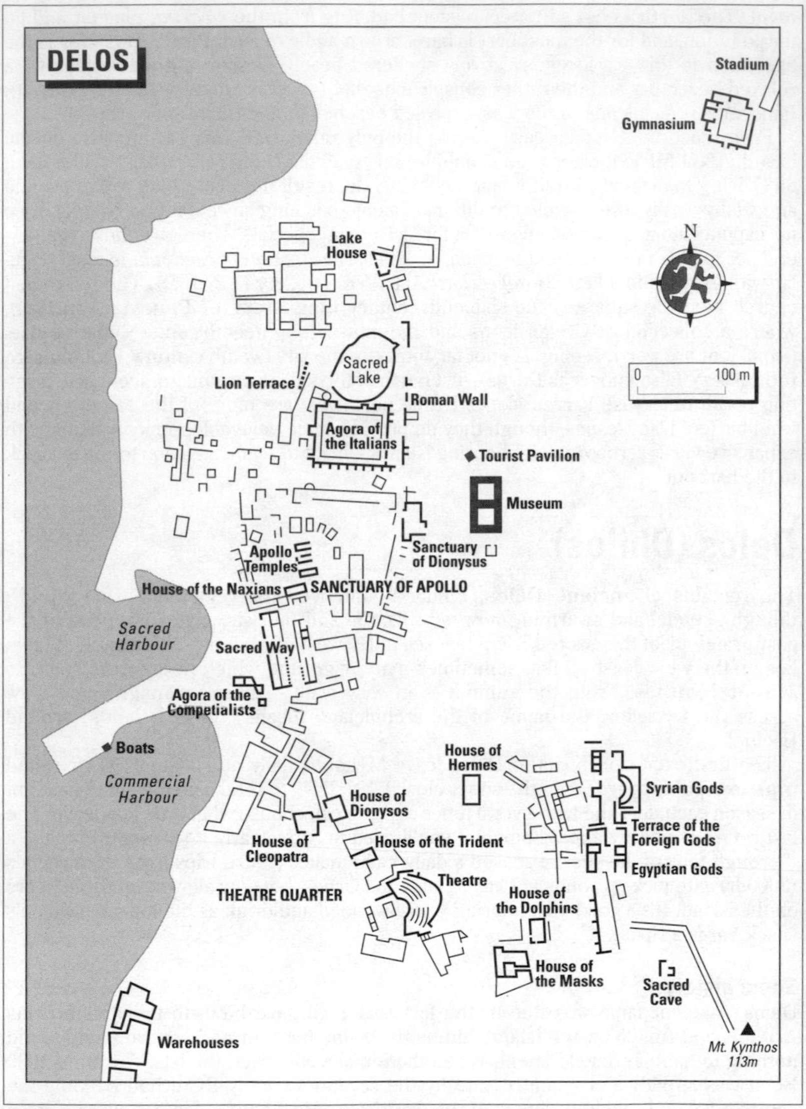

Delos reached its peak in the third and second centuries BC, after being declared a free port by its Roman overlords. In the end, though, its undefended wealth brought ruin: first Mithridates (88 BC), then Athenodorus (69 BC) plundered the treasures and the island never recovered. By the third century AD, Athens could not even sell it, and for centuries, every passing seafarer stopped to collect a few prizes.

The site

Tues–Sun 8.30am–3pm; 1500dr.

As you land, the Sacred Harbour is on your left, the Commercial Harbour on your right; and straight ahead is the **Agora of the Competialists**. Competialists were Roman merchants or freed slaves who worshipped the Lares Competales, the guardian spirits of crossroads; offerings to Hermes would once have been placed in the middle of the *agora*, their position now marked by a round and a square base. The **Sacred Way** leads north from the far left corner; it used to be lined with statues and the grandiose monuments of rival kings. Along it you reach three marble steps which lead into the **Sanctuary of Apollo**; much was lavished on the god, but the forest of offerings has been plundered over the years. On your left is the Stoa of the Naxians, while against the north wall of the House of the Naxians, to the right, a huge statue of Apollo stood in ancient times. In 417 BC the Athenian general Nikias led a procession of priests across a bridge of boats from Rheneia to dedicate a bronze palm tree; when it was later blown over in a gale it took the statue with it. Three **Temples of Apollo** stand in a row to the right along the Sacred Way: the Delian Temple, that of the Athenians and the Porinos Naos, the earliest of them, dating from the sixth century BC. To the east towards the museum you pass the **Sanctuary of Dionysos**, with its marble phalluses on tall pillars.

The best finds from the site are in Athens, but the **museum** still justifies a visit. To the north stands a wall that marks the site of the **Sacred Lake** where Leto gave birth, clinging to a palm tree. Guarding it are the superb **lions**, their lean bodies masterfully executed by Naxians in the seventh century BC; of the original nine, three have disappeared and one adorns the Arsenale at Venice. On the other side of the lake is the City Wall, built in 69 BC – too late to protect the treasures.

Set out in the other direction from the Agora of the Competialists and you enter the residential area, known as the **Theatre Quarter**. Many of the walls and roads remain, but there is none of the domestic detail that brings such sites to life. Some colour is added by the mosaics: one in the **House of the Trident**, and better ones in the **House of the Masks**, most notably a vigorous portrayal of Dionysos riding on a panther's back. The **theatre** itself seated 5500 spectators, and, though much ravaged, offers some fine views. Behind the theatre, a path leads past the **Sanctuaries of the Foreign Gods** and up **Mount Kýnthos** for more panoramic sightseeing.

Sýros

Don't be put off by first impressions of **Sýros**. From the ferry it looks grimly industrial, but away from the Neórion shipyard things improve quickly. Very much a working island with only a very recent history of tourism, it is probably the most Greek of the Cyclades; there are few holiday trappings and what there is exists for the benefit of the locals. You probably won't find, as Herman Melville did when he visited in 1856, shops full of ". . . fez-caps, swords, tobacco, shawls, pistols, and orient finery . . .", but you're still likely to appreciate Sýros as a refreshing change from the beautiful people. Of course, outsiders do come to the island; in fact there's a thriving permanent foreign community, and the beaches are hardly undeveloped, but everywhere there's the underlying assumption that you're a guest of an inherently private people.

Ermoúpoli

The main town and port of **ERMOÚPOLI** was founded during the War of Independence by refugees from Psará and Híos, becoming Greece's chief port in the

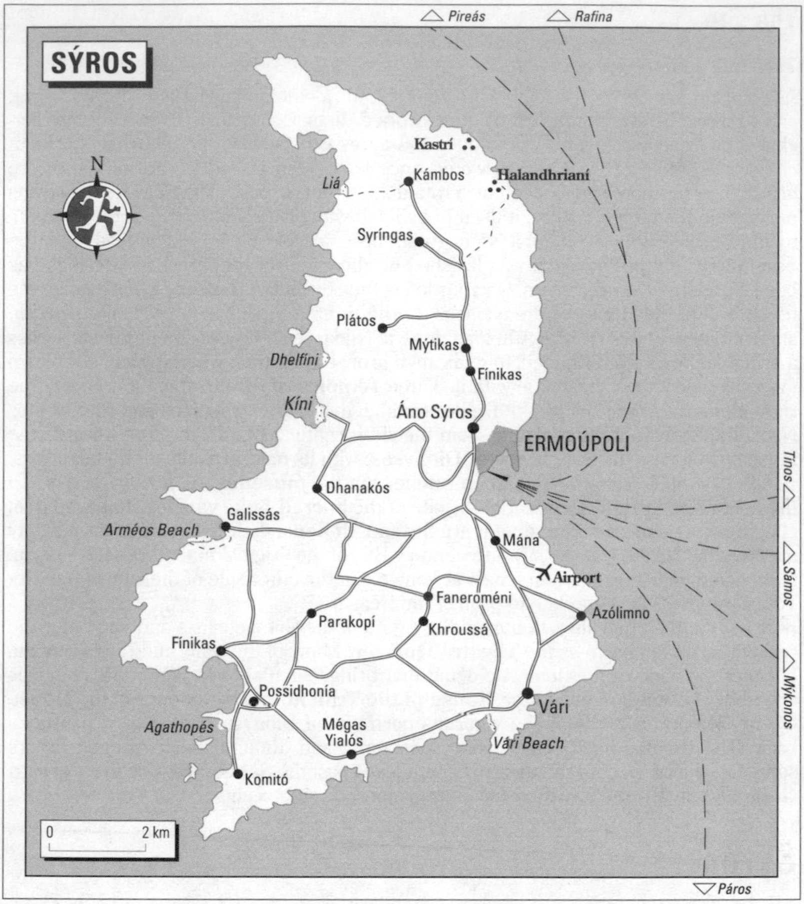

nineteenth century. Although Pireás outstripped it long ago, Ermoúpoli is still the largest town in the Cyclades, and the archipelago's capital. Medieval Sýros was largely a Catholic island, but an influx of Orthodox refugees during the War of Independence created two distinct communities; now almost equal in numbers, the two groups today still live in their respective quarters, occupying two hills that rise up from the sea.

Ermoúpoli itself, the **lower town**, is worth at least a night's stay, with grandiose buildings a relic of its days as a major port. Between the harbour and **Áyios Nikólaos**, the fine Orthodox church to the north, you can stroll through its faded splendour. The **Apollon Theatre** is a copy of La Scala in Milan and once presented a regular Italian opera season; today local theatre and music groups put it to good use. The long, central **Platía Miaoúli** is named after an admiral of the revolution whose statue stands there, and in the evenings the population parades in front of its arcaded kafenía, while the children ride the mechanical animals. Up the stairs to the left of the town hall is the small **Archeological Museum** (Tues–Sun 8.30am–3pm; free), with three rooms of finds from Sýros, Páros and Amorgós. To the left of the clocktower more stairs climb up to **Vrondádho**, the hill that hosts the Orthodox quarter. The wonderful church of the **Anástasis** stands atop the hill, with its domed roof and great views over Tínos and Mýkonos – if it's locked, ask for the key at the priest's house.

On the taller hill to the left is the intricate medieval quarter of **Áno Sýros**, with a clutch of Catholic churches below the cathedral of St George. There are fine views of the town below, and, close by, the **Cappuchin monastery of St Jean**, founded in 1535 to do duty as a poorhouse. It takes about 45 minutes of tough walking up Omírou to reach this quarter, passing the Orthodox and Catholic cemeteries on the way – the former full of grand shipowners' mausoleums, the latter with more modest monuments and French and Italian inscriptions (you can halve the walking time by taking a short cut on to the stair-street named Andhréa Kárga, part of the way along). Once up here it's worth visiting the local art and church exhibitions at the Vamvákeris **museum** (daily 10.30am–1pm & 7–10pm; 500dr), and the Byzantine museum attached to the monastery.

Arrival, facilities and accommodation

The **quayside** is still busy, though nowadays it deals with more tourist than industrial shipping; Sýros is a major crossover point on the ferry-boat routes. Also down here is the **bus station**, along with the **tourist police** and several **bike rental** places, of which Apollon on Andíparou, one block behind the seafront, is recommended. Between them shops sell the *louhoúmia* (Turkish delight) and *halvadhópita* (sweetmeat pie) for which the island is famed. **Odhós Hlíou**, the market street, is especially lively on Saturday when people come in from the surrounding countryside to sell fresh produce.

Keeping step with a growing level of tourism, **rooms** have improved in quality and number in recent years; many are in garishly decorated, if crumbling, Neoclassical mansions. Good choices include *Kastro* rooms, Kalomenopóulou 12 (☎0281/88 064; ③), *Dream*, on the seafront near the bus station (☎0281/84 356; ④), and *Paradise*, Omírou 3 (☎0281/83 204; ④). Particularly recommended are the traditionally decorated rooms of *Villa Nefeli*, Parou 21 (☎0281/87 076; ③), and *Sea Colours Apartments* (☎0281/88 716; ④), located at Áyios Nikólaos beach, a quieter corner of town. A notch up in price and quality is the well-sited *Hotel Hermes* (☎0281/83 011; ⑥) on Platía Kanári, overlooking the port or, for a slice of good-value opulence, try the *Xenon Ipatias* (☎0281/83 575; ④), beyond Áyios Nikólaos and above *Sea Colours Apartments*. Team Work agency (☎0281/83 400, *teamwork@otenet.gr*), on the waterfront, is a useful source of information and able to help with your accommodation needs. Alternatively, you can try the kiosk belonging to the Rooms and Apartments Association of Sýros (☎0281/87 360) along the waterfront – turn right after disembarking.

Eating, drinking and nightlife

The most authentic and reasonably priced of the harbour **eateries** are the *Yiannena Estiatorio* on Platía Kanári and the popular *Psaropoula Ouzeri*. On or near Platía Miaoúli, the *Manousos* taverna is a good traditional place, as is *Archontariki*. *Ambix*, near where the ferries dock, is a good Italian restaurant; for snacks resist the neon glare of the popular *Goody's* hamburger-joint and have a *yíros* at the more authentic *Fresh Corner* nearby. In Áno Sýros, the *Thea* taverna, signposted in Greek from the car park, is fine and affords the views its name would suggest; *Iy Piatsa* ouzerí is also worth a try.

Incidentally, Sýros still honours its contribution to the development of **rembétika**; *bouzoúki*-great Markos Vamvakaris hailed from here, and a platía in Áno Sýros has been named after him. **Taverna-clubs** such as *Xanthomalis* (up in Áno Sýros) with music on weekends, now take their place beside a batch of more conventional disco-clubs down near the Apollon Theatre. There are several other (often expensive) *bouzoúki* bars scattered around the island, mostly strung along routes to beach resorts. The seafront has a rash of lively **bars**: the *Cotton Club* café seems to be the focal point of activity in this area. There's a more interesting cluster around the Platía Miaoúli: *Clearchos* piano bar is rather smooth, *Agora* has imaginative decor, good DJs and a lovely garden, and *Piramatiko* is heaving, playing a loud and varied mix from indie to house. The big

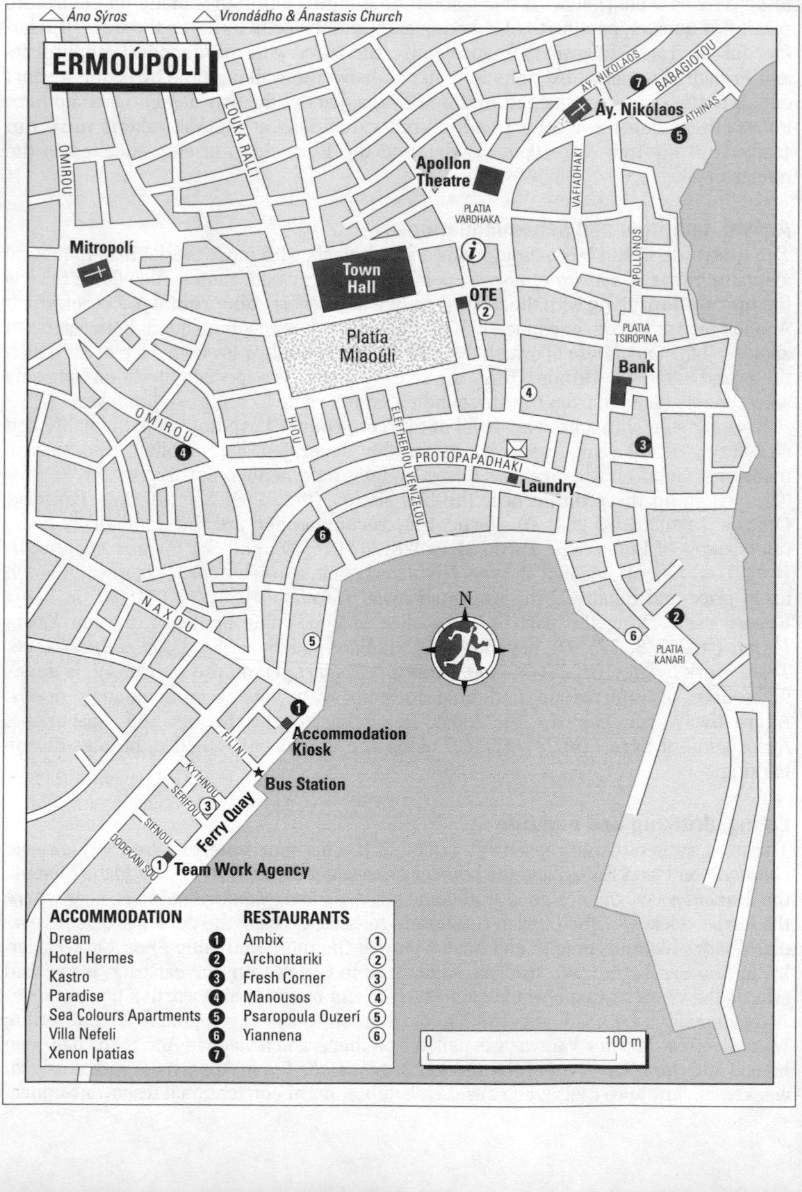

venue for night-owls is *Rodo,* a huge club in a converted warehouse out past the Neórión shipyard opposite the turning to Vári. Finally, the *Aegean Casino* on the seafront features live music at the restaurant, and is open till 6am for those who have money to burn (and are sufficiently well-dressed).

Around the island

The main loop road (to Gallissás, Fínikas, Mégas Yialós, Vári and back), and the road west to Kíni, are good: **buses** ply the routes hourly in season, and run until late. Elsewhere, expect potholes – especially to the **north** where the land is barren and high, with few villages. The main route north from Áno Sýros has improved and is quite easily negotiable by bike; en route, the village of **Mýtikas** has a decent taverna just off the road. A few kilometres further on the road forks, with the left turn leading, after another left, to the small settlement of **Syríngas**, where there's an interesting cave to explore. Straight on leads to **Kámbos**, from where a path leads down to Liá Beach; the right fork eventually descends to the northeast coast after passing an excellent kafenío, *Sgouros,* with views across to Tínos.

The well-trodden route **south** offers more tangible and accessible rewards. Closest to the capital, fifteen minutes away by bus, is the twin-beach coastal settlement of **KÍNI**. Good accommodation includes the *Sunset Hotel* (☎0281/71 211; ④–⑤), with the excellent *Zalounis* taverna just below and, just away from the seafront, the *Hotel Elpida* (☎0281/71 224; ③). **GALISSÁS**, a few kilometres south, but reached by different buses, has developed along different lines. Fundamentally an agricultural village, it's been taken over since the mid-1980s by backpackers attracted by the island's only **campsites** (both have good facilities and send minibuses to all boats, but *Camping Yianna* (☎0281/42 418) has the advantage over the newer *Two Hearts* (☎0281/42 052) of being closer to the sea) and a very pretty beach, more protected than Kíni's. This new-found popularity has created a surplus of unaesthetic **rooms**, which at least makes bargaining possible, and six bona fide hotels, of which the cheapest are *Petros* and *Semiramis* (☎0281/42 067; both ③), though the *Benois* (☎0281/42 833; ⑤) is decent value, with buffet breakfast included. Amongst the many **eating** choices, *To Iliovasilema*, next to *Benois,* is an acceptable fish taverna, and *Cavos,* part of a luxury complex, the *Dolphin Bay Hotel* (☎0281/42 924, *dolphinbay@syr.forthnet.gr*, ⑥), has great views overlooking the bay. Galissás's identity crisis is exemplified by the proximity of bemused, grazing dairy cattle, a heavy-metal music pub and upmarket handicrafts shops. Still, the people are welcoming, and if you feel the urge to escape, you can rent a moped, or walk ten minutes past the headland to the nudist beach of **Arméos**, where there's fresh spring water. Note that buses out are erratically routed; to be sure of making your connection you must wait at the high-road stop, not down by the beach. **Dhelfíni** just to the north is also a fine beach, though it's slowly falling prey to the developers under the translated name of Dolphin Bay (not to be confused with aforementioned hotel).

A pleasant forty-minute walk or a ten-minute bus ride south from Galissás brings you to the more mainstream resort of **FÍNIKAS**, purported to have been settled originally by the Phoenicians (although an alternative derivation could be from *fínikas,* meaning "palm tree" in Greek). The beach is narrow and gritty, right next to the road but protected to some extent by a row of tamarisk trees; the pick of the hotels is the *Cyclades* (☎0281/42 255; ④), and there is an acceptable restaurant just in front, while the *Amaryllis* rooms (☎0281/42 894; ④) are slightly cheaper. The fish taverna *O Barpalias* on the seafront is recommended.

Fínikas is separated by a tiny headland from its neighbour **POSSIDHONÍA** (or Delagrazzia), a nicer spot with some idiosyncratically ornate mansions and a bright blue church right on the edge of the village. It's worth walking ten minutes further south, past the naval yacht club and its patrol boat to **Agathopés**, with a sandy beach and a little islet just offshore. Komitó, at the end of the unpaved track leading south from Agathopés, is nothing more than a stony beach fronting an olive grove. **Accommodation** around Possidhonía ranges from the smart *Possidonion* hotel (☎0281/42 100; ④) on the seafront to basic rooms inland, while *Meltémi* is a good seafood taverna.

The road swings east to **MÉGAS YIALÓS**, a small resort below a hillside festooned with brightly painted houses. The long, narrow beach is lined with shady trees and there are pedal boats for hire. Of the **room** set-ups, *Mike and Bill's* (☎0281/43 531; ③) is a reasonable deal, and the pricier *Alexandra Hotel* (☎0281/42 540; ⑥), on the bay, enjoys lovely views. **VÁRI** is more – though not much more – of a town, with its own small fishing fleet. Beach-goers are in a goldfish bowl, as it were, with tavernas and **rooms** looming right overhead, but it is the most sheltered of the island's bays, something to remember when the *meltémi* is up. The *Kamelo* hotel (☎0281/61 217; ⑤) provides the best value and has TV in all the rooms. The adjacent cove of **AKHLÁDHI** is far more pleasant and boasts two small good-value hotels, including the *Emily* (☎0281/61400; ④), on the seafront, and has one taverna.

Páros and Andíparos

Gently and undramatically furled around the single peak of Profítis Ilías, **Páros** has a little of everything one expects from a Greek island – old villages, monasteries, fishing harbours, a labyrinthine capital – and some of the best nightlife and beaches in the Aegean. Parikía, the hóra, is the major hub of inter-island ferry services, so that if you wait long enough you can get to just about any island in the Aegean. However, the island is almost as touristy and expensive as Mýkonos: in peak season, it's touch-and-go when it comes to finding rooms and beach space. At such times, the attractive inland settlements or the satellite island of **Andíparos** handle the overflow. Incidentally, the August 15 festival here is one of the best such observances in Greece, with a parade of flare-lit fishing boats and fireworks delighting as many Greeks as foreigners, but it's a real feat to secure accommodation around this time.

Parikía and around

PARIKÍA sets the tone architecturally for the rest of Páros, with its ranks of typically Cycladic white houses punctuated by the occasional Venetian-style building and church domes. But all is awash in a constant stream of ferry passengers, and the town is relentlessly commercial. The busy waterfront is jam-packed with bars, restaurants, hotels and ticket agencies, while the maze of houses in the older quarter behind, designed to baffle both wind and pirates, has surrendered to an onslaught of chi-chi boutiques.

Just beyond the central clutter, though, the town has one of the most architecturally interesting churches in the Aegean – the **Ekatondapilianí**, or "The One-Hundred-Gated". What's visible today was designed and supervised by Isidore of Miletus in the sixth century, but construction was actually carried out by his pupil Ignatius. It was so beautiful on completion that the master, consumed with jealousy, is said to have grappled with his apprentice on the rooftop, flinging them both to their deaths. They are portrayed kneeling at the column bases across the courtyard, the old master tugging at his beard in repentance and his rueful pupil clutching a broken head. The church was substantially altered after a severe earthquake in the eighth century, but its essentially Byzantine aspect remains, its shape an imperfect Greek cross. Enclosed by a great wall to protect its icons from pirates, it is in fact three interlocking churches; the oldest, the chapel of Áyios Nikólaos to the left of the apse, is an adaptation of a pagan

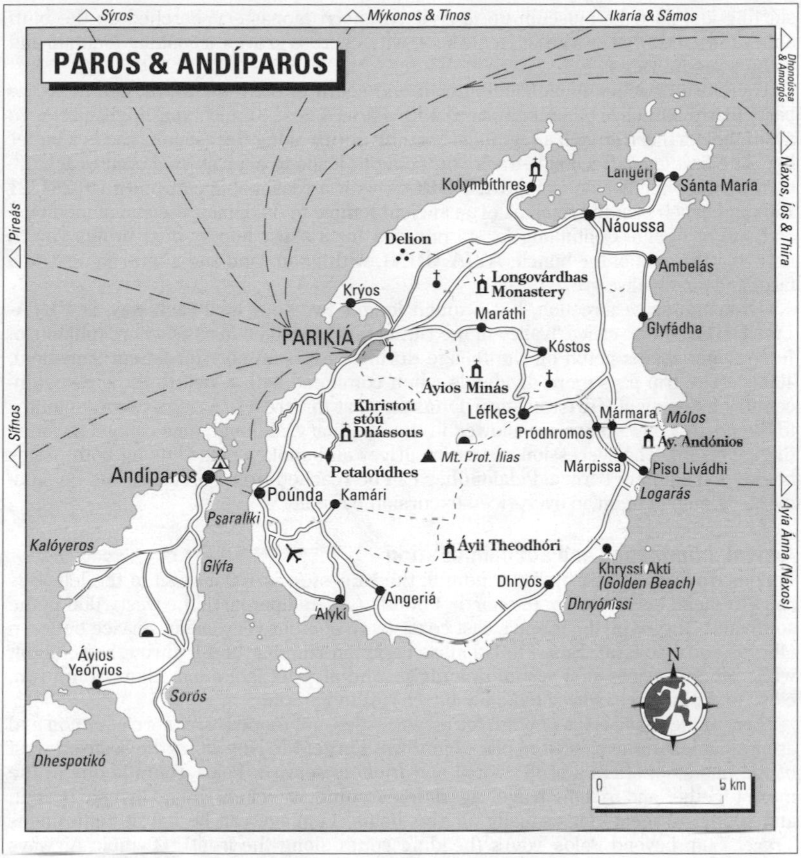

building dating from the early fourth century BC. To the right of the courtyard, the **Byzantine Museum** (daily 9am–1pm & 5.30–9.30pm; 500dr, free on Tues) displays a collection of icons. Behind Ekatondapilianí, the **Archeological Museum** (Tues–Sun 8am–2.30pm; 500dr) has a fair collection of antique bits and pieces, its prize exhibits being a fifth-century winged Nike and a piece of the *Parian Chronicle*, a social and cultural history of Greece up to 264 BC engraved in marble.

These two sights apart, the real attraction of Parikía is simply to wander the town itself. Arcaded lanes lead past Venetian-influenced villas, traditional island dwellings and the three ornate wall-fountains donated by the Mavroyénnis family in the eighteenth century. The town culminates in a seaward Venetian **kástro**, whose surviving east wall incorporates a fifth-century BC round tower and is constructed using masonry pillaged from a temple of Athena. Part of the base of the temple is still visible next to the beautiful, arcaded church of Áyios Konstandínos and Áyia Eléni which crowns the highest point, from where the fortified hill drops sharply to the quay in a series of hanging gardens.

If you're staying in town, you'll want to get out into the surroundings at some stage, if only to the beach. The most rewarding **excursion** is the hour's walk along the road starting just past the museum up to **Áyii Anáryiri** monastery. Perched on the bluff above town, this makes a great picnic spot, with cypress groves, a gushing fountain and some splendid views.

There are **beaches** immediately north and south of the harbour, though none are particularly attractive when compared with Páros's best. In fact, you might prefer to avoid the northern stretch altogether; heading **south** along the asphalt road is a better bet. The first unsurfaced side-track you come to leads to a small, sheltered beach; fifteen minutes further on is **PARASPÓROS**, with a reasonable **campsite** (☎0284/21 100) and beach near the remains of an ancient temple to Asklepios, the god of medicine and son of Apollo. Continuing for 45 minutes (or a short hop by bus) brings you to arguably the best of the bunch, **AYÍA IRÍNI**, with good sand and a taverna next to a farm and shady olive grove.

Off in the same direction, but a much longer two-hour haul each way, is **PETALOÚDHES**, the so-called "Valley of the Butterflies", a walled-in oasis where millions of Jersey tiger moths perch on the foliage during early summer (June–Sept 9am–8pm; 400dr). The trip pays more dividends when combined with a visit to the eighteenth-century nunnery of **Khristoú stoú Dhássous**, at the crest of a ridge twenty minutes to the north. Only women are allowed in the sanctuary, although men can get as far as the courtyard. The succession of narrow drives and donkey paths linking both places begins just south of Parikía. Petaloúdhes can be reached from Parikía by bus (in summer), by moped or on an overpriced excursion by mule.

Arrival, information and accommodation

Ferries **dock** in Parikía by the windmill; the **bus stop** is 100m or so to the left. Bus routes extend to Náoussa in the north, Poúnda (for Andíparos) in the west, Alikí in the south and Dhrýos on the island's east coast (with another very useful service between Dhrýos and Náoussa). Buses to Náoussa carry on running hourly through the night, while other services stop around midnight. The **airport** is around 12km from town, close to Alykí – from where ten daily buses run to Parikía.

Most of the island is flat enough for bicycle rides, but mopeds are more common and are available for rent at several places in town; Forget-Me-Not, along the seafront west of the bus stop, offers a professional and friendly service. Polos Tours is one of the more together and friendly **travel agencies**, issuing air tickets when Olympic is shut, and acting as agents for virtually all the boats. Luggage can be left at Santorineos Travel, 50m beyond Polos Tours (heading south along the front). Olympic Airways itself is at the far end of Odhós Probóna, while the **tourist police** occupy a building at the back of the seafront square.

As for **accommodation**, Parikía is a pleasant and central base, but absolutely mobbed in summer. You'll be met off the ferry by locals offering rooms, even at the most unlikely hours; avoid persistent offers of rooms or hotels to the north as they'll invariably be a long walk away from town. One of the best deals to be had is at the *Pension Festos* on the back streets inland, managed by young Brits (☎0284/21 635; ① per person); it has beds in shared rooms, making it a good choice for single travellers. Another budget option includes *Kouala Camping* (☎0284/22081), along the seafront west of the bus stop, with good facilities, if a little noisy. Popular **hotels** include *Dina*, (☎0284/21 325; ④), near Platía Veléntza, and *Hotel Oasis* (☎0284/21 227; ④), on Prombóna, very close to the harbour. *Hotel Kypreou* (☎0284/21 383; ⑤) is a small family-run hotel on Prombóna, which, like *Oasis*, stays open through the winter. The smart, family-run *Hotel Argonauta* (☎0284/21440; ④), close to the National Bank, is highly recommended, and also has a pleasant restaurant. Irini Triandafilou (☎0284/23 022; ③) has a few basic rooms within the kástro, some with good sea views, and *Argonauta Appartments* (☎0284/23888; ④) have some smart accommodation in the Livádhia area in the north of town.

Eating, drinking and nightlife

Many Parikía **tavernas** are run by outsiders operating under municipal concession, so year-to-year variation in proprietors and quality is marked. However, the following seem to be long-established and/or good-value outfits. Rock-bottom is the *Koutouki Thanasis*, which serves oven food for locals and bold tourists and lurks in a back street to the left of the town hall. Also in the picturesque backstreets are *Kyriakos Place* on Lohágou Grivári, which has seats out under a fine tree, and the *Garden of Dionysos*. In the exotic department, *May Tey* serves average Chinese food at moderate markup, while Italian dishes can be found at *La Barca Rossa* on the seafront or *Cavo D'Oro* in the Livádhia area. *Trata* behind the post office is recommended for fish, and *Le Coq Fou*, on the same road as *Dionysos*, is a good breakfasting spot, serving excellent crepes. There are a couple of specialist eating places: *The Happy Green Cow*, a friendly café with vegetarian and vegan food behind the National Bank, and *Wired Café* (*stnicolas@bigfoot.com*), an Internet café, on the market street running behind the kástro (2400dr per hour).

Parikía has a wealth of **pubs**, **bars** and low-key **discos**, not as pretentious as those on Mýkonos or as raucous as the scene on Íos, but certainly everything in between. The most popular cocktail bars extend along the seafront, all tucked into a series of open squares and offering competing but staggered (no pun intended) "Happy Hours", so that you can drink cheaply for much of the evening. A rowdy crowd favours the conspicuous *Saloon D'Or*, while the *Pirate Bar* features jazz and blues, and *Havanna* nearby plays a lively Latin mix. *Evinos* and *Pebbles* are more genteel, the latter pricey but with good sunset views and the occasional live gig. The "theme" pubs are a bit rough and ready for some: most outrageous is the *Dubliner Complex*, comprising four bars, a snack section, disco and seating area.

Finally, a thriving cultural centre, *Arhilohos* (near Ekatondapilianí) caters mostly to locals, with occasional **film** screenings – there are also two open-air cinemas, *Neo Rex* and *Paros*, where foreign films are shown in season.

Náoussa and around

The second port of Páros, **NÁOUSSA** was once an unspoiled, sparkling labyrinth of winding, narrow alleys and simple Cycladic houses. Alas, a rash of modern concrete hotels and attendant trappings have all but swamped its character, though down at the small harbour, fishermen still tenderize octopuses by thrashing them against the walls. The local festivals – an annual Fish and Wine Festival on July 2, and an August 23 shindig celebrating an old naval victory over the Turks – are also still celebrated with enthusiasm; the latter tends to be brought forward to coincide with the August 15 festival of the Panayía. Most people are here for the local beaches (see p.140) and the relaxed nightlife; there's really only one sight, a **museum** (daily 9am–1.30pm & 7–9pm; free) in the monastery of Áyios Athanásios, with an interesting collection of Byzantine and post-Byzantine icons from the churches and monasteries around Náoussa.

Despite encroaching development, the town is noted for its nearby beaches and is a good place to head for as soon as you reach Páros. **Rooms** are marginally cheaper here than in Parikía; track them down with the help of the **tourist office** which is just over the bridge, west from the harbour. The *Sea House* (☎0284/52 198; ④) on the rocks above Pipéri beach was the first place in Náoussa to let rooms and has one of the best locations, and the *Manis Inn* (☎0284/51 744, *manisinn@otenet.gr*; ⑥) is an upmarket hotel with pool behind Pipéri Beach; out of season you should haggle for reduced prices at the *Madaki* (☎0284/51 475; ④), just over the bridge west of the harbour, and at the basic, but well-located *Stella* (☎0284/52 198; ④), inland, behind the old harbour. There are two **campsites** in the vicinity: the relaxed and friendly *Naoussa* (☎0284/51 565), out of town towards Kolymbíthres (see p.140), and the newer *Surfing Beach*

(☎0284/51 013) at Sánta Mariá, northeast of Náoussa; both run courtesy minibuses to and from Parikía.

Most of the harbour **tavernas** are surprisingly good, specializing in fresh fish and seafood; *O Barbarossas* ouzerí is the best of these. There are more places to eat along the main road leading inland from just beside the little bridge over the canal. *Glaros*, with good barrelled unresinated wine, and the *Vengera* opposite stay open until the early morning hours. **Bars** cluster around the old harbour: *Linardo* and *Agosta* play dance music, *Camaron* plays mainly Greek music, and *Café Sante*, inland, off the main drag, is a cool spot playing easy-listening, and mellower dance grooves. There are several big clubs around the bus station, including *Slalom* and *Nostos,* popular with a younger late-night crowd.

Local beaches

Pipéri Beach is couple of minutes' walk west of Náoussa's harbour; there are other good-to-excellent beaches within walking distance, and a summer kaïki service to connect them. To the west, an hour's tramp brings you to **Kolymbíthres** (Basins), where there are three tavernas and the wind- and sea-sculpted rock formations from which the place draws its name. A few minutes beyond, **Monastíri** Beach, below the abandoned Pródhromos monastery, is similarly attractive, and partly nudist. If you go up the hill after Monastíri onto the rocky promontory, the island gradually shelves into the sea via a series of flattish rock ledges, making a fine secluded spot for diving and snorkelling, as long as the sea is calm. Go northeast and the sands are better still, the barren headland spangled with good surfing beaches. **Langéri** is backed by dunes; the best surfing is at **Sánta María**, a trendy beach connected with Náoussa by road, which also has a couple of tavernas, including the pleasant *Aristofanes*; and **Platiá Ámmos** perches on the northeastern tip of the island.

The northeast coast and inland

AMBELÁS hamlet marks the start of a longer trek down the **east coast**. Ambelás itself has a good beach, a small taverna and some rooms and hotels, of which the *Hotel Christiana* (☎0284/51 573; ⑤) is good value, with great fresh fish, local wine in the restaurant and extremely friendly proprietors. From here a rough track leads south, passing several undeveloped stretches on the way: after about an hour you reach **Mólos Beach**, impressive and not particularly crowded. **MÁRMARA**, twenty minutes further on, has rooms to let and makes an attractive place to stay, though the marble that the village is built from and named after has largely been whitewashed over.

If Mármara doesn't appeal, then serene **MÁRPISSA**, just to the south, might – a maze of winding alleys and ageing archways overhung by floral balconies, all clinging precariously to the hillside. There are rooms here too: *Hotel Afendakis* (☎0284/41141; ④) is clean and modern, and you can while away a spare hour climbing up the conical Kéfalos hill, on whose fortified summit the last Venetian lords of Páros were overpowered by the Ottomans in 1537. Today the monastery of **Áyios Andónios** occupies the site, but the grounds are locked; to enjoy the views over eastern Páros and the straits of Náxos fully, pick up the key from the priest in Máripissa before setting out (ask in the mini-market of his whereabouts). On the shore nearby, **PÍSO LIVÁDHI** was once a quiet fishing village, but has been ruined by rampant construction in the name of package tourism. The main reason to visit is to catch a (seasonal) kaïki to Ayía Ánna on Náxos; if you need to **stay** overnight here, *Hotel Andromache* (☎0284/41 387 or 42 565; ⑥) is a good place behind the beach, as is the more reasonably priced *Akteon Hotel* (☎0284/ 41873; ④) at **Logarás Beach** next door. The *Captain Kafkis Camping* (☎0284/41 479) – a small quiet site – is out of town on the road up to Márpissa.

Inland

The road runs west from Píso Livádhi back to the capital. A medieval flagstoned path once linked both sides of the island, and parts of it survive in the east between Mármara and the villages around Léfkes. **PRÓDHROMOS**, encountered first, is an old fortified farming settlement with defensive walls girding its nearby monastery, while **LÉFKES** itself, an hour up the track, is perhaps the most beautiful and unspoiled settlement on Páros. The town flourished from the seventeenth century on, its population swollen by refugees fleeing from coastal piracy; indeed it was the island's hóra during most of the Ottoman period. Léfkes' marbled alleyways and amphitheatrical setting are unparalleled and, despite the few rooms, a disco (*Akrovatis*), a taverna on the outskirts and the presence of two oversized hotels – the *Hotel Pantheon* (☎0284/41 646; ④), a large 1970s hotel at the top of the village, and *Lefkes Village* (☎0284/41 827 or 42 398; ⑥), a beautiful hotel on the outskirts, with stunning views – the area around the main square has steadfastly resisted change; the central kafenío and bakery observe their siestas religiously.

Thirty minutes further on, through olive groves, is **KÓSTOS**, a simple village and a good place for lunch in a taverna. Any traces of path disappear at **MARÁTHI**, on the site of the ancient marble quarries which once supplied much of Europe. Considered second only to Carrara marble, the last slabs were mined here by the French in the nineteenth century for Napoleon's tomb. From Maráthi, it's easy enough to pick up the bus on to Parikía, but if you want to continue hiking, strike south for the monastery of **Áyios Minás**, twenty minutes away. Various Classical and Byzantine masonry fragments are worked into the walls of this sixteenth-century foundation, and the friendly custodians can put you on the right path up to the convent of **Thapsaná**. From here, other paths lead either back to Parikía (two hours altogether from Áyios Minás), or on up to the island's summit for the last word in views over the Cyclades.

The south of the island

There's little to stop for south of Parikía until **POÚNDA**, 6km away, and then only to catch the ferry to Andíparos (see below). What used to be a sleepy hamlet is now a concrete jungle, and neighbouring **ALYKÍ** appears to be permanently under construction. The **airport** is close by, making for lots of unwelcome noise; the sole redeeming feature is an excellent beachside restaurant, by the large tamarisk tree. The end of the southern bus route is at Angeriá, about 3km inland of which is the **convent of Áyii Theodhóri**. Its nuns specialize in weaving locally commissioned articles and are further distinguished as *paleomeroloyítes*, or old-calendarites, meaning that they follow the medieval Orthodox (Julian) calendar, rather than the Gregorian one.

Working your way around the **south coast**, there are two routes east to Dhryós. Either retrace your steps to Angeriá and follow the (slightly inland) coastal road, which skirts a succession of isolated coves and small beaches; or keep on across the foothills from Áyii Theodhóri – a shorter walk. Aside from an abundant water supply (including a duck pond) and surrounding orchards, **DHRYÓS** village is mostly modern and characterless, lacking even a well-defined platía. Follow the lane signed "Dhrýos Beach", however, and things improve a bit.

Between here and Píso Livádhi to the north are several sandy coves – Khryssí Aktí (Golden Beach), Tzirdhákia, Mezádha, Poúnda and Logarás – prone to pummelling by the *meltémi*, yet all favoured to varying degrees by campers and by windsurfers making a virtue out of necessity. **KHRYSSÍ AKTÍ** is now thoroughly overrun with tavernas, room complexes and the whole range of watersports; there are also tavernas at Logarás, but other facilities are concentrated in Dhrýos, which is still the focal point of this part of the island.

Andíparos

Andíparos was once quiet and unspoiled, but now the secret is definitely out. The waterfront is lined with new hotels and apartments, and in high season it can be full of the same young, international crowd you were hoping to leave behind on Páros. It has, however, kept its friendly small island atmosphere and still has a lot going for it, including good sandy beaches and an impressive cave, and the rooms and hotels are less expensive than on Páros.

Most of the population of eight hundred live in the large low-lying northern **village**, across the narrow straits from Páros, the new development on the outskirts concealing an attractive traditional settlement around the kástro. A long, flagstoned pedestrian street forms its backbone, leading from the jetty to the Cycladic houses around the outer wall of the kástro, which was built by Leonardo Loredano in the 1440s as a fortified settlement safe from pirate raids: the Loredano coat of arms can still be seen on a house in the courtyard. The only way into the courtyard is through a pointed archway from the platía, where several cafés are shaded by a giant eucalyptus. Inside, more whitewashed houses surround two churches and a cistern built into the surviving base of the central tower.

Andíparos's **beaches** begin right outside town: **Psaralíki** just to the south with golden sand and tamarisks for shade is much better than Sifnéïko (aka "Sunset") on the opposite side of the island. Villa development is starting to follow the newly paved road down the east coast, but has yet to get out of hand. **Glýfa**, 4km down, is another good beach and, further south, **Sorós** has rooms and tavernas. On the west coast there are some fine small sandy coves at Áyios Yeóryios, the end of the road, and a long stretch of sand at Kalóyeros. Kaïki make daily trips round the island and, less frequently, to the uninhabited islet of Dhespotikó, opposite Áyios Yeóryios.

The great **cave** (summer daily 10.45am–3.45pm; 600dr) in the south of the island is the chief attraction for day-trippers. In these eerie chambers the Marquis de Nointel, Louis XIV's ambassador to Constantinople, celebrated Christmas Mass in 1673 while a retinue of five hundred, including painters, pirates, Jesuits and Turks, looked on; at the exact moment of midnight explosives were detonated to emphasize the enormity of the event. Although electric light and cement steps have diminished its mystery and grandeur, the cave remains impressive. Tour buses (700dr return) and public buses (220dr one-way) run from the port every hour in season; out of season, bus services and opening hours are reduced and in winter you'll have to fetch the key for the cave from the mayor or village council (☎0284 61 218).

Practicalities

To get here, you have a choice of **boats** from Parikía (hourly; 40min), arriving at the jetty opposite the main street, or the car ferry from Poúnda (half-hourly; 10min), arriving 150m to the south. In season there's no need to use the car ferry unless you take a moped over or miss the last boat back to Parikía; the car ferry keeps running until midnight. The service to Parikía is reduced out of season and runs only once a day in winter.

There are plenty of **hotels** along the waterfront, including *Anargyros* (☎0284/61 204; ③), which has good, basic rooms. More upmarket places to the north of the jetty include *Mantalena* (☎0284/61 206; ④) and *Artemis* (☎0284/61 460; ④), while inland there are some cheaper rooms as well as the *Hotel Galini* (☎0284/61 420; ④) to the left of the main street. The popular **campsite** (☎0284/61 221) is a ten-minute walk north-east along a track, next to its own nudist beach; the water here is shallow enough for campers to wade across to the neighbouring islet of Dhipló. For peace and quiet with a degree of comfort try *Studios Delfini* (☎093/275 911; ④) at Áyios Yeóryios, a long stretch of beach with several tavernas, of which *Captain Pipinos* is recommended.

The best of the waterfront **tavernas** is *Anargyros*, below the hotel of the same name. *Klimataria*, 100m inland to the left off the main street, has tables in a pleasant, shady garden, and *To Kastro* is one of the better restaurants outside the kástro. There are plenty of **bars** in the same area but the locals usually stick to the excellent *To Kendro* sweetshop in the eucalyptus-filled platía; *Café Margarita* is a pleasant street-side hang-out on the way up to this platía. For quiet music and views of the mountains try *Café Yam*, an outdoor café-bar near the *Klimataria*. A short-schedule **bank**, a **post office**, a cinema and several **travel agents** round up the list of amenities.

Náxos

Náxos is the largest and most fertile of the Cyclades, and with its green and mountainous highland scenery seems immediately distinct from many of its neighbours. The difference is accentuated by the **unique architecture** of many of the interior villages: the

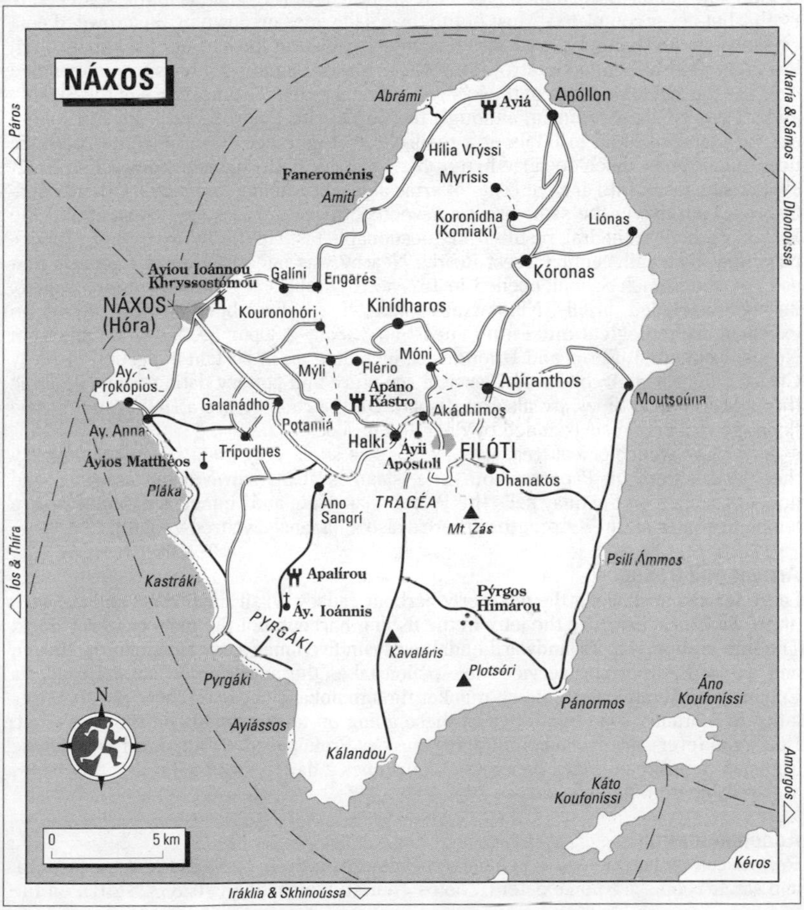

Venetian Duchy of the Aegean, which ruled from the thirteenth to the sixteenth century, left towers and fortified mansions scattered throughout the island, while medieval Cretan refugees bestowed a singular character upon Náxos's eastern settlements.

Today Náxos could easily support itself without tourists by relying on its production of potatoes, olives, grapes and lemons, but it has thrown in its lot with mass tourism, so that parts of the island are now almost as busy and commercialized as Páros in season. But the island certainly has plenty to see if you know where to look: the highest mountains in the Cyclades, intriguing central valleys, a spectacular north coast and marvellously sandy beaches in the southwest.

Náxos Town

A long causeway, built to protect the harbour to the north, connects **NÁXOS TOWN** (or Hóra) with the islet of Palátia – the place where, according to legend, Theseus abandoned Ariadne on his way home from Crete. The huge stone portal of a **temple of Apollo** still stands there, built on the orders of the tyrant Lygdamis in the sixth century BC, but never completed. Most of the town's life goes on down by the crowded port esplanade or just behind it; back streets and alleys behind the harbour lead up through low arches to the fortified **kástro**, from where Marco Sanudo and his successors ruled over the Cyclades. Only two of the kástro's original seven towers – those of the Sanudo and Glezos families – remain, although the north gate (approached from Apóllonos) survives as a splendid example of a medieval fort entrance. The Venetians' Catholic descendants, now much declined in numbers, still live in the old mansions which encircle the site, many with ancient coats of arms above crumbling doorways. Other brooding relics survive in the same area: a seventeenth-century Ursuline convent and the Roman Catholic cathedral, restored in questionable taste in the 1950s, though still displaying a thirteenth-century crest inside. Nearby was one of Ottoman Greece's first schools, the French School; opened in 1627 for Catholic and Orthodox students alike, its pupils included, briefly, Nikos Kazantzakis. The school building now houses an excellent **archeological museum** (Tues–Sun 8.30am–2.30pm; 500dr), with finds from Náxos, Koufoníssi, Keros and Dhonoússa, including an important collection of Early Cycladic figurines. Archaic and Classical sculpture and pottery dating from Neolithic through to Roman times are also on display. On the roof terrace a Hellenistic mosaic floor shows a nereid surrounded by deer and peacocks.

As well as archeological treasures, Náxos has some very good sandal-makers: try the Markos store on Papavassilíou. The island is also renowned for its wines and liqueurs; a shop on the quay sells the Prombonas white and vintage red, plus *kítron*, a lemon firewater in three strengths (there's also a banana-flavoured variant).

Arrival and transport

Large **ferries** dock along the northerly harbour causeway; all small boats and the very useful *Skopelitis* ferry use the jetty in the fishing harbour, not the main car-ferry dock. The **bus station** is at its landward end: buses run five times a day to Apóllon (1100dr), and one of the morning services to Apóllon takes the newly paved coastal road via Engarés and Abrámi, and is much quicker though not any cheaper. There are six buses a day to Apíranthos via Filóti, two of these going on to Moutsoúna on the east coast. Buses run (every 30min; 8am–midnight) to Áyios Prokópios, Ayía Ánna and as far as the Maragás campsite on Pláka beach, and four times a day to Pirgáki. Printed timetables are available from the bus station.

Accommodation

Rooms can be hard to come by and somewhat overpriced in the old quarter of Hóra, and single rooms are non-existent. Naxos Tourist Information (☎0285/25 201), on the seafront near the jetty, is a wealth of information. If you come up with nothing after an hour of hunting, the southern extension of town offers better value, although there's significant night-time noise from the clubs and discos. *Bourgos Rooms* (☎0285/25 979; ④) comprise good new rooms near the kástro, behind *Panorama* (see below); or try *Iliada Studios* (☎0285/23 303 or 24 277, *ILIADA@naxos-island.com*; ⑤) on the cliffs beyond Grotta Beach, with good views over the town and out to sea. *Studios Irene* (☎0285/23 169; ③) consists of good-value, comfortable rooms in the Kristós area, a slightly calmer part of town.

Hotel choices include the *Panorama* on Amfitrítis (☎0285/24 404; ⑤), the nearby *Anixis* (☎0285/22 112; ④), *Hotel Pantheon* (☎0285/24 335; ④), with a few rooms in a traditionally furnished house on Apóllonos, or, as a last resort, the bargain *Dionyssos* (☎0285/22 331; ①) near the kástro, which also has dorm beds (①). Upmarket choices include the traditional *Chateau Zevgoli* (☎0285/22 993; ⑤), with tastefully decorated, air-conditioned rooms near the kástro, and *Hotel Galaxy* (☎0285/22 422; ⑥), an upmarket beach hotel with a pool, behind Áyios Yeóryios beach. *Hotel Anna* (☎0285/22 475; ③), towards the Grótta area, is not particularly remarkable; however it stays open through the winter.

Eating, drinking and nightlife

One of the best quayside breakfast bars is the *Bikini* creperie. Further along to the south are a string of relatively expensive but simple oven-food **tavernas** – *Iy Kali Kardhia* is typical, serving acceptable casserole dishes washed down with barrelled wine. *Iy Platia* on the main square, towards the new south district, serves traditional fare and is popular with Greeks, while the nearby *Cafe Picasso* serves up Mexican food (supper only) for a mixed crowd. On the front *Karnayio* is a good, if a little pricey, fish taverna; *Cafe En Plo* and *Musique Café* are two reasonable places in the middle of the quay, both popular with locals. A hidden gem is *To Roupel*, a good old kafenío in the backstreets between the front and the kástro, with the *Manolis Garden Taverna* nearby one of the most pleasant of the kástro tourist eateries. *Elli Cafe Bar Restaurant* behind Grótta beach is a little more expensive but serves imaginative food, and *Portokali Club* on the headland to the south of town is a club, café and restaurant with good views over Áyios Yeóryios bay.

Much of the evening action goes on at the south end of the waterfront, and slightly inland in the new quarter. **Nightlife** tends more towards drinking places, though there is the lively *Ocean Club*, subsisting on pop-chart fodder, *Ole Club* towards the middle of the quay for dance music and *Vegerra*, a lively cocktail bar behind *Karnayio*. *Lakrindi Jazz Bar*, a tiny place on Apóllonos between the front and the kástro, is recommended. There's also an open air cinema, the Ciné Ástra, on the road to the airport at the southern end of town. It's a fair walk out but the Ayía Ánna bus stops here.

The southwestern beaches

The **beaches** around Náxos Town are worth sampling. For some unusual swimming just to the **north** of the port, beyond the causeway, **Grótta** is easiest to reach. Besides the caves for which the place is named, the remains of submerged Cycladic buildings are visible, including some stones said to be the entrance to a tunnel leading to the unfinished temple of Apollo. The finest spots, though, are all **south** of town, the entire southwestern coastline boasting a series of excellent **beaches** accessible by regular bus. **ÁYIOS YEÓRYIOS**, a long sandy bay fringed by the southern extension of the hotel "colony", is within walking distance. There's a line of cafés and tavernas at the northern end of the beach, and a windsurfing school, plus the first of four **campsites**, whose touts you will no doubt have become acquainted with at the ferry jetty. This first campsite, *Camping Naxos* (☎0285/23 500), isn't recommended; *Maragas* and *Plaka* have far more attractive locations on Pláka beach (see below). A word of warning for campers: although this entire coast is relatively sheltered from the *meltémi*, the plains behind are boggy and you should bring along mosquito repellent.

Buses take you to **ÁYIOS PROKÓPIOS** beach, with plenty of reasonably priced hotels, rooms and basic tavernas, plus the relaxed *Apollon* campsite (☎0285/24 117) nearby. *Hotel Lianos Village* (☎0285/23 366, *lianos-village@nax.forthnet.gr*; ⑥) is an upmarket choice with a pleasant pool setting; of the restaurants *Pizzeria Promponas* has a varied menu and nice setting. Rapid development along this stretch means that this resort has blended into the next resort of **AYÍA ÁNNA** (habitually referred to as "Ayi'Ánna"), further along the busy road; here you will find accommodation of similar price and quality. The seaview *Hotel Ayia Anna* (☎0285/42 576; ③) and adjacent *Gorgona* taverna are recommended, as is *Bar Bagianni* on the road from Áyia Ánna to Áyios Prokópios, a colourful and popular bar which serves vegetarian food. Moving along the coast, away from the built-up area, the beach here is nudist.

Beyond the headland stretch the five kilometres of **PLÁKA** beach, a vegetation-fringed expanse of white sand. Things are not so built up here, and parts of the beach are nudist (past Pláka campsite). There are two suitably laid-back and friendly **campsites** here: *Maragas* campsite (☎0285/24 552) which also has double rooms (②), and the newer *Pláka* campsite (☎0285/42 700), a little further along, which is small and quiet with a few cheap bungalows (①). The *Hotel Orkos Village* (☎0285/75 321, *orkos@nax.forthnet.gr*; ⑥) comprises apartments in an attractive location, on a hillside above the coast between Pláka beach and Mikrí Vígla.

For real isolation, go to the other side of Mikrí Vígla headland, along a narrow footpath across the cliff-edge, to **KASTRÁKI** beach; towards the middle of the beach *Areti* (☎0285/75 292; ⑤) has apartments and a restaurant. A few people camp around the taverna on the small headland a little further down. In summer this stretch, all the way from Mikrí Vígla down to Pyrgáki, attracts camper vans and windsurfers from all over Europe. On the Alíko promontory to the south of Kastráki there is a small nudist beach.

From Kastráki, it's a couple of hours' walk up to the Byzantine castle of **Apalírou** which held out for two months against the besieging Marco Sanudo. The fortifications are relatively intact and the views magnificent. **Pyrgáki** beach has a couple of tavernas and a few rooms; four kilometres further on is **Ayiássos** beach.

The rest of the **southern coast** – indeed, virtually the whole of the southeast of the island – is remote and mountain-studded; you'd have to be a dedicated and well-equipped camper/hiker to get much out of the region.

Central Náxos and the Tragéa

Although buses bound for Apóllon (in the north) link up the central Naxian villages, the core of the island – between Náxos Town and Apíranthos – is best explored by moped or on foot. Much of the region is well off the beaten track, and can be a rewarding excursion if you've had your fill of beaches; Christian Ucke's *Walking Tours on Naxos*, available from bookshops in Náxos Town, is a useful guide for hikers.

Once out of Hóra, you quickly arrive at the neighbouring villages of **GLINÁDHO** and **GALANÁDHO**, forking respectively right and left. Both are scruffy market centres: Glinádho is built on a rocky outcrop above the Livádhi plain, while Galánadho displays the first of Náxos's fortified mansions and an unusual "double church". A combined Orthodox chapel and Catholic sanctuary separated by a double arch, the church reflects the tolerance both by the Venetians during their rule and by the locals to established Catholics afterwards. Continue beyond Glinádho to **TRÍPODHES** (ancient Biblos), 9km from Náxos Town. Noted by Homer for its wines, this old-fashioned agricultural village has nothing much to do except enjoy a coffee at the shaded kafenío. The start of a long but rewarding walk is a rough road (past the parish church) which leads down the colourful Pláka valley, past an old watchtower and the Byzantine church of **Áyios Matthéos** (mosaic pavement), and ends at the glorious Pláka beach (see above).

To the east, the twin villages of **SANGRÍ**, on a vast plateau at the head of a long valley, can be reached by continuing to follow the left-hand fork past Galanádho, a route which allows a look at the domed eighth-century church of **Áyios Mámas** (on the left), once the Byzantine cathedral of the island but neglected during the Venetian period and now a sorry sight. Either way, **Káto Sangrí** boasts the remains of a Venetian castle, while **Áno Sangrí** is a comely little place, all cobbled streets and fragrant courtyards. Thirty minutes' stroll away, on a path leading south out of the village, are the partially reconstructed remains of a Classical temple of Demeter.

The Tragéa

From Sangrí the road twists northeast into the **Tragéa** region, scattered with olive trees and occupying a vast highland valley. It's a good jumping-off point for all sorts of exploratory rambling, and **HALKÍ** is a fine introduction to what is to come. Set high up, 16km from the port, it's a noble and silent town with some lovely churches. The **Panayía Protóthronis** church, with its eleventh- to thirteenth-century frescoes, and the romantic **Grazia (Frangopoulos) Pýrgos**, are open to visitors, but only in the morning. Tourists wanting to stay here are still something of a rarity, although you can usually get a room in someone's house by asking at the store. *Yiannis* taverna is the focal point of village activity and has a good selection of fresh mezédhes to enjoy with a glass of oúzo. Nearby is the distillery and shop of *Vallindras Naxos Citron*, whose charming proprietors explain the proccess of producing this speciality citrus liqueur (*kítron*), followed by a little tasting session. The olive and citrus plantations surrounding Halkí are criss-crossed by paths and tracks, the groves dotted with numerous Byzantine chapels and the ruins of fortified *pyrgi* or Venetian mansions. Between Halkí and Akadhimí, but closer to the latter, sits the peculiar twelfth-century "piggyback" church of **Áyii Apóstoli**, with a tiny chapel (where the ennobled donors worshipped in private) perched above the narthex; there are brilliant thirteenth-century frescoes as well.

The road from Halkí heads north to **MONÍ**. Just before the village, you pass the sixth-century monastery of **Panayía Dhrossianí**, a group of stark grey stone buildings with some excellent frescoes; the monks allow visits at any time, though you may have to contend with coach tours from Náxos Town. Moní itself enjoys an outstanding view of the Tragéa and surrounding mountains, and has four tavernas, plus some rooms. The main road leads on to Kinídharos, with an old marble quarry above the village, a few kilometres beyond, a signpost points you down a rough track to the left, to **FLÉRIO** (commonly called Melanés). The most interesting of the ancient marble quarries on Náxos, this is home to two famous **koúri**, dating from the sixth century BC, that were left recumbent and unfinished because of flaws in the material. Even so, they're finely detailed figures, over five metres in length. One of the statues lies in a private, irrigated orchard; the other is up a hillside some distance above, and you will need to seek local guidance to find it.

From Flério you could retrace your steps to the road and head back to Hóra via Mýli and the ruined Venetian castle at Kouronohóri, both pretty hamlets connected by footpaths. If you're feeling more adventurous, ask to be directed south to the footpath which leads over the hill to the Potamiá villages. The first of these, **ÁNO POTAMIÁ**, has a fine taverna and a rocky track back towards the Tragéa. Once past the valley the landscape becomes craggy and barren, the forbidding Venetian fortress of **Apáno Kástro** perched on a peak just south of the path. This is believed to have been Sanudo's summer home, but the fortified site goes back further, if the Mycenaean tombs found nearby are any indication. From the fort, paths lead back to Halkí in around an hour.

Alternatively, you can continue further southwest down the Potamiá valley towards Hóra, passing first the ruined **Cocco Pýrgos** – said to be haunted by one Constantine Cocco, the victim of a seventeenth-century clan feud – on the way to **MÉSO POTAMIÁ**, joined by some isolated dwellings with its twin village **KÁTO POTAMIÁ**, nestling almost invisibly among the greenery flanking the creek.

At the far end of the gorgeous Tragéa valley, **FILÓTI**, the largest village in the region, lies on the slopes of Mount Zás (or Zeus) which, at 1000m, is the highest point in the Cyclades. Under the shade of the plane trees on the main platía are several pleasant kafenía, as well as *Babulas Grill-Restaurant* (☎0285/31 426; ②) which has the best rooms in the village. To get an idea of the old village, climb the steps up the hill starting at the platía. A turning at the southern end of the village is signposted to the **Pýrgos Himárou**, a remote 20-metre Hellenistic watchtower, and **Kalándou** beach on the south coast; beyond the turning the road is unpaved. There are no villages in this part of the island, so bring supplies if you're planning to camp. From the village, it's a round-trip walk of two to three hours to the summit of Zás, a climb which rewards you with an astounding panorama of virtually the whole of Náxos and its Cycladic neighbours. From the main Filóti–Apóllon road, take the side-road towards Dhánakos until you reach a small chapel on the right, just beside the start of the waymarked final approach trail.

APÍRANTHOS, a hilly, winding 10km beyond, shows the most Cretan influence of all the interior villages. There are four small **museums** and two Venetian fortified mansions, while the square contains a miniature church with a three-tiered belltower. Ask to be pointed to the start of the spectacular path up over the ridge behind; this ends either in Moní or Kalóxilos, depending on whether you fork right or left respectively at the top. Cafés and tavernas on the main street look out over a terraced valley below. Rooms are available but are not advertised – ask in the cafés or in the embroidery shop. Apíranthos is a good quiet place to stay for a few days, and being high in the mountains is noticeably cooler and greener than the coast.

Apíranthos has a beach annexe of sorts at **Moutsoúna**, 12km east. Emery mined near Apíranthos used to be transported here by means of an aerial funicular and then shipped out of the port. The industry collapsed in the 1980s, and the sandy cove beyond the dock now features a growing colony of holiday villas. An unpaved road heads south along the coast to a remote sandy beach at **Psilí Ámmos** – ideal for self-sufficient campers, but you must take enough water. From here a track carries on to **Pánormos** beach in the southeastern corner of the island.

Northern Náxos

The route through the mountains from Apíranthos to Apóllon is very scenic, and the road surface is in good condition all the way. Jagged ranges and hairpin bends confront you before reaching Kóronos, the halfway point, where a road off to the right threads through a wooded valley to **Liónas**, a tiny and very Greek port with a pebble beach. You'd do better to continue, though, past Skadhó to the remote, emery-miners' village of **KOMIAKÍ** which is a pleasing, vine-covered settlement – the highest village in the island and the original home of *kítron* liqueur.

Back on the main road, a series of slightly less hairy bends leads down a long valley to **APÓLLON** (Apóllonas), a small resort with two beaches: a tiny and crowded stretch of sand backed by cafés and restaurants, and a longer and quieter stretch of shingle, popular mainly with Greek families. If you are staying, try the friendly rooms of *Maria* (☎0285/67 106; ②) behind the harbour. The only major attraction is a **koúros**, approached by a path from the main road just above the village. Lying in situ at a former marble quarry, this largest of Náxos's abandoned stone figures is just over ten metres long, but, compared with those at Flério, disappointingly lacking in detail. Here since 600 BC, it serves as a singular reminder of the Naxians' traditional skill; the famous Delian lions (see p.131) are also made of Apollonian marble. Not surprisingly, bus tours descend upon the village during the day, and Apóllon is now quite a popular little place. The local festival, celebrated on August 28–29, is one of Náxos's best.

From Náxos Town there is now a daily bus service direct to Apóllon (taking about an hour). It's easy to make a round trip by bus of the north coast and inland villages in either direction. The coastal road is spectacularly beautiful, going high above the sea for most of the way – it's more like parts of Crete or the mainland than other islands. Ten kilometres past the northern cape sprouts the beautiful **Ayiá** *pýrgos*, or tower, another foundation (in 1717) of the Cocco family. There's a tiny hamlet nearby, and, 7km further along, a track leads off to **Abrámi** beach, an idyllic spot with a highly recommended family-run taverna and **rooms** to let, *Pension and Restaurant Efthimios* (☎0285/63 244; ③). Just beyond the hamlet of Hília Vrýssi is the abandoned **monastery of Faneroménis**, built in 1606. Carrying on along the coastal road you will reach Engarés valley, at the foot of which is another quiet beach, **Amití**, which can be reached via one of two dirt tracks, the most obvious being the one leading down from Galíni, only 6km from Hóra. On the final stretch back to the port you pass a unique eighteenth-century Turkish fountain-house and the fortified monastery of **Ayíou Ioánnou Khryssostómou**, where a couple of aged nuns are still in residence. A footpath from the monastery and the road below lead straight back to town.

Koufoníssi, Skhinoússa, Iráklia and Dhonoússa

In the patch of the Aegean between Náxos and Amorgós there is a chain of six small islands neglected by tourists and by the majority of Greeks, few of whom have heard of them. **Kéros** – ancient Karos – is an important archeological site but has no permanent population, and **Káto Koufoníssi** is inhabited only by goatherds. However, the other four islands – **Áno Koufoníssi**, **Skhinoússa**, **Iráklia** and **Dhonoússa** – are all inhabited, served by ferry and can be visited. Now increasingly discovered by Greeks and foreigners alike, the islets' popularity has hastened the development of better facilities, but they're still a welcome break from the mass tourism of the rest of the Cyclades, especially during high season. If you want real peace and quiet – what the Greeks call *isyhiá* – get there soon.

A few times weekly in summer a Pireás-based **ferry** – usually the *Olympia Express* or the *Naias Express* – calls at each of the islands, linking them with Náxos and Amorgós and (usually) Páros, and Sýros. A kaïki, the *Express Skopelitis*, is a reliable daily fixture, leaving Náxos in mid-afternoon for relatively civilized arrival times at all the islets.

Koufoníssi and Kéros

Ano Koufoníssi is the most populous island of the group; there is a reasonable living to be made from fishing and, with some of the best beaches in the Cyclades, it is attracting increasing numbers of Greek and foreign holidaymakers. Small enough to walk round in a morning, the island can actually feel overcrowded in July and August.

The old single-street village of **HÓRA**, on a low hill behind the harbour, is being engulfed by new room and hotel development, but still has a friendly, small-island atmosphere. A map by the jetty shows where to find all the island's **rooms**: *To Limani* (☎0285/71 851 or 71 450; ③) is a café with rooms near the harbour; the popular restaurant and pension *Iy Melissa* (☎0285/71 454; ③) is another good choice. The most upmarket options include *Hotel Aigaion* (☎0285/74 050 or 74 051; ⑥), by the village beach, or *Villa Ostria* (☎0285/71 671; ⑤), on the hillside to the east of the village. *To*

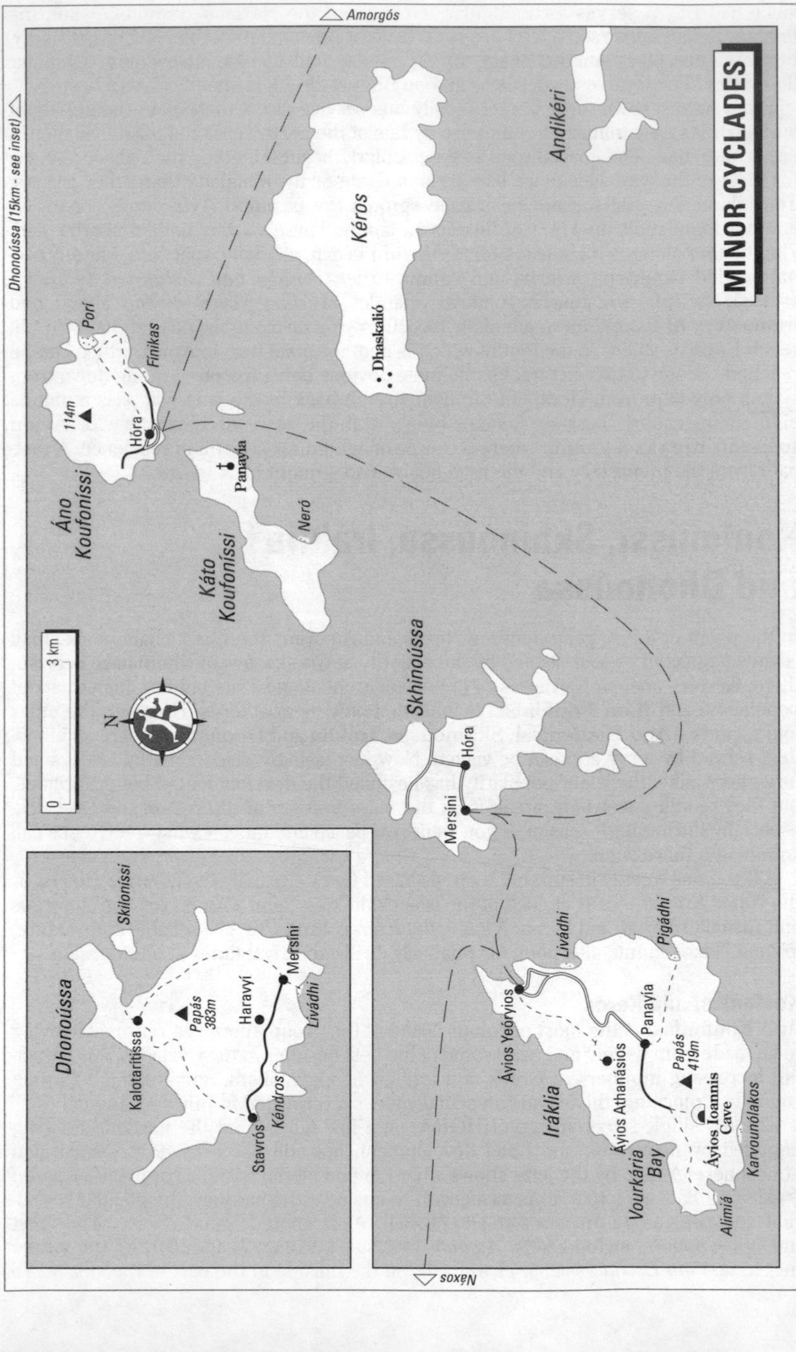
MINOR CYCLADES
Amorgós
Dhonoússa (15km - see inset)
Andikéri
Kéros
Dhaskalió
Porí
Fínikas
114m
Hóra
Áno Koufoníssi
Panayía
Neró
Káto Koufoníssi
0
3 km
N
Skhinoússa
Hóra
Mersíni
Livádhi
Pigádhi
Áyios Yeóryios
Panayía
Áyios Athanásios
Papás 419m
Iráklia
Áyios Ioannis Cave
Karvounólakos
Vourkária Bay
Alimiá
Náxos
Dhonoússa
Skilonissi
Kalotarítissa
Papás 383m
Haravyí
Mersíni
Livádhi
Kéndros
Stavrós

Akroyiali (☎0285/71 685; ④) is on the front just beyond the beach; Yeofyia Kouveou has beautifully situated rooms at *Hondros Kavos* (☎0285/71 707; ③), outside the village to the east; and the *Petros Club* (☎0285/71 728; ⑤) is in a quiet position inland, with excellent views.

Koufoníssi is noted for its fish **tavernas**; *To Nikitouri*, up in Hóra, has very personable Greek-American management, and the *Karnayio* ouzerí on the bay to the west of the harbour is cheaper than most and has a fine array of seafood. The nearby *To Steki Tis Marias* is a good breakfast place with a few rooms; ③, and has views over the narrow channel to Káto Koufoníssi. The most popular nightspot is *Soroccos*, a lively café-bar on the front, while good alternatives include *Ta Kalamia*, with a quieter choice of music; *Nikitas*; and *Skholeio*, a creperie and bar. *To Palio Fanari*, to the west of the village, is the club favoured by locals, playing a mix of dance and Greek music. The OTE office and ticket agency are on the main street, and money, unusually, of late, can be changed at the somewhat improvised "post office" (limited hours).

All the good beaches are in the southeast of the island, starting at **Fínikas**, a ten-minute walk from the village, where there are rooms, an acceptable taverna and a **campsite** (☎0285/71 683) with rather poor facilities. Fínikas is the first of a series of small bays and coves of gently shelving golden sand, some with low cliffs hollowed out into sea-caves. Further east, a path round a rocky headland leads to **Porí**, a much longer and wilder beach, backed by dunes and set in a deep bay. It can be reached more easily from the village by following a track heading inland through the low scrub-covered hills.

KÁTO KOUFONÍSSI, the uninhabited island to the southwest, has a seasonal taverna and some more secluded beaches; a kaïki shuttles people across until late in the evening. A festival is held here on August 15, at the church of the Panayía. The island of **Kéros** is harder to reach, but if there is a willing group of people keen to visit the ancient site, a boat and boatmen can be hired at around 15,000dr for the day.

Skhinoússa

A little to the southwest, the island of **Skhinoússa** is just beginning to awaken to its tourist potential. Boats dock at the small port of Mersíni, which has one pension (☎0285/71 157; ④) and a couple of cafés; a road leads up to **HÓRA**, the walk taking just over ten minutes. As you enter the village, the well-stocked shop of the Grispos family is one of the first buildings. Yiorgos Grispos is a mine of information and is personally responsible for the island's map and postcards, as well as being the boat/hydrofoil agent, having a metred phone and selling the Greek and foreign press.

Accommodation is mostly in fairly simple rooms, such as *Pension Meltemi* (☎0285/71 195; ⑤), *Anesis* (☎0285/71180; ③) and the pleasant *Provaloma* (☎0285/71 936; ③), which also has a taverna. The rooms belonging to Anna (☎0285/71 161; ③) are particularly recommended, as is the modern *Hotel Sunset* (☎0285/71 948; ③) which enjoys stunning views of the harbour. The main concentration of **restaurants**, cafés and bars is along the main thoroughfare, including the popular *Bar Ostria* and a lively ouzerí.

There are no fewer than sixteen beaches dotted around the island, accessible by a lacework of trails. **Tsigoúri Beach** is a ten-minute walk from Hóra; largely undeveloped except for the new *Tsigouri Beach Villas* (☎0285/71 175; ③), this was traditonally the beach where freelance campers congregated. The arrival of this new hotel, complete with taverna (great views) may, however, put a damper on things; the only other beach with any refreshments is **Almyrós**, which has a simple canteen.

Iráklia

In an attempt to accommodate increasing visitor numbers, **Iráklia** (pronounced Irakliá by locals), the westernmost of the minor Cyclades, is losing its charm as the number of purpose-built rooms increases.

Ferries and hydrofoils call at **ÁYIOS YEÓRYIOS**, a small but sprawling settlement behind a sandy tamarisk-backed beach. Irini Koveou (☎0285/71 488; ③) has a café-restaurant and rooms opposite the harbour, and more rooms and places to eat can be found along the old road to Livádhi beach. *Anna's Place* (☎0285/71 145; ③) consists of rooms with shared cooking facilities, and *Mestrali* (☎0285/71 807; ③) has newer rooms as well as its own café-cum-taverna. Theofanis Gavalas (☎0285/71 565; ②), Dhimítrios Stefanídhis (☎0285/71 484; ③), Alexandra Tournaki (☎0285/71 482; ②) and Angelos Koveos (☎0285/71 486; ②) all have rooms nearby. *O Pefkos* is a pleasant **taverna**, with tables shaded by a large pine tree, while the café/shop *Melissa* acts as the main ticket agency for ferries. The recommended *Perigiali* taverna also has a small shop selling maps showing the route to a fine **cave** on the far side of the island.

Livádhi, the best beach on the island, is a fifteen-minute walk past a taverna, whose friendly and animated proprietor usually meets ferries at the dock. There is shade, but bring refreshments, since locals seem unsure whether or not the lone taverna on the far side of the beach will reopen. The village of Livádhi, deserted since 1940, stands on the hillside above, its houses ruined and overgrown; among the remains are Hellenistic walls incorporated into a later building, and fortifications from the time of Marco Sanudo. Marietta Markoyianni (☎0285/71 252; ②) has the only rooms on the beach; *Zografos Rooms* (☎0285/71 946; ④), above the road to Panayía, has fine views but is rather remote.

PANAYÍA or **HÓRA**, an unspoiled one-street village at the foot of Mount Papás, is another hour's walk inland along the newly paved road. It has a bakery/mini-market, two café/shops and the excellent and cheap *O Kritikos* ouzerí, but no rooms. A track to the east heads down to Pigádhi, a rocky beach with sea urchins, at the head of a narrow inlet. To the west a track from the near-deserted hamlet of **Áyios Athanásios** leads back to the port.

The **cave of Áyios Ioánnis** lies behind the mountain, at the head of a valley leading to Vourkária bay. From Panayía, follow a signposted track west before zigzagging up to a saddle well to the north of the summit, with views over Skhinoússa, Koufoníssi, Kéros, Náxos and Amorgós; the path drops down to the south around the back of the mountain. A painted red arrow on the left indicates the turning to the cave, just over an hour from Panayía. A church bell hangs from a cypress tree above the whitewashed entrance; inside there's a shrine, and the cave opens up into a large chamber with stalactites and stalagmites. It can be explored to a depth of 120m and is thought to be part of a much larger cave system, yet to be opened up; a festival is held here every year on August 18.

The main trail continues beyond the cave to a small sandy beach at **Alimiá** but this can be reached more easily with the beach boat from Áyios Yeóryios. In season the boat sails daily to either Skhinoússa, Alimiá or the nearby pebble beach of Karvounólakos.

Dhonoússa

Dhonoússa is a little out on a limb compared with the others, and ferries and hydrofoils call less frequently. Island life centres on the pleasant port settlement of **STAVRÓS**, spread out behind the harbour and the village beach.

Rooms, most without signs, tend to be booked up by Greek holidaymakers in August; try Mihalis Prasinos (☎0285/51 578; ④ – based on four people sharing), with rooms along a lane behind the church; Dhimitris Prasinos (☎0285/51 579; ③), with rooms open year-round near the *Iliovasilema* restaurant; or Nikos Prasinos (☎0285/51 551; ④), who has good new studios above the rocks west of the harbour. *Ta Kymata* is the most popular of the four tavernas but *Meltemi* is also good, as is the friendly *Aposperitis*, right on the village beach. Nikitas Roussos (☎0285/51 648) has a **ticket agency** above the harbour and can change money and book rooms.

The hills around Stavrós are low and barren and scarred by bulldozed tracks, but a little walking is repaid with dramatic scenery and a couple of fine beaches. Campers and nudists head for **Kéndros**, a long and attractive stretch of sand fifteen minutes to the east, although shade is limited and there are no facilities. A road has been built on the hillside above, replacing the donkey track to the farming hamlets of Haravyí and Mersíni; these have more hens and goats in the streets than people, and there are no cafés, shops or rooms. **Mersíni** is an hour's walk from Stavrós and has a welcome spring beneath a plane tree, the island's only running water. A nearby path leads down to Livádhi, an idyllic white sand beach with tamarisks for shade. In July and August there's a daily beach boat from the port.

KALOTARÍTISSA in the north can still only be reached on foot or by boat – a track heading inland from Stavrós climbs a valley west of Papás, the island's highest point, before dropping down rapidly to the tiny village with a simple **taverna** and one room to rent (☎0285/51 562; ②). There are two small pebble beaches and a path that continues above the coast to Mersíni. It takes four to five hours to walk round the island.

Amorgós

Amorgós, with its dramatic mountain scenery and laid-back atmosphere, is attracting visitors in increasing numbers; most ferries and hydrofoils call at both Katápola in the southwest and Eyiáli in the northeast. The island can get extremely crowded in midsummer, the numbers swollen by French paying their respects to the film location of Luc Besson's *The Big Blue*, although few actually venture out to the wreck of the *Olympia*, at the island's west end, which figured so prominently in the movie. In general it's a low-key, escapist clientele, happy to have found a relatively large, interesting and uncommercialized island with excellent walking.

The southwest

KATÁPOLA, set at the head of a deep bay, is actually three separate hamlets: **Katápola** proper on the south flank, **Rahídhi** on the ridge at the head of the gulf and

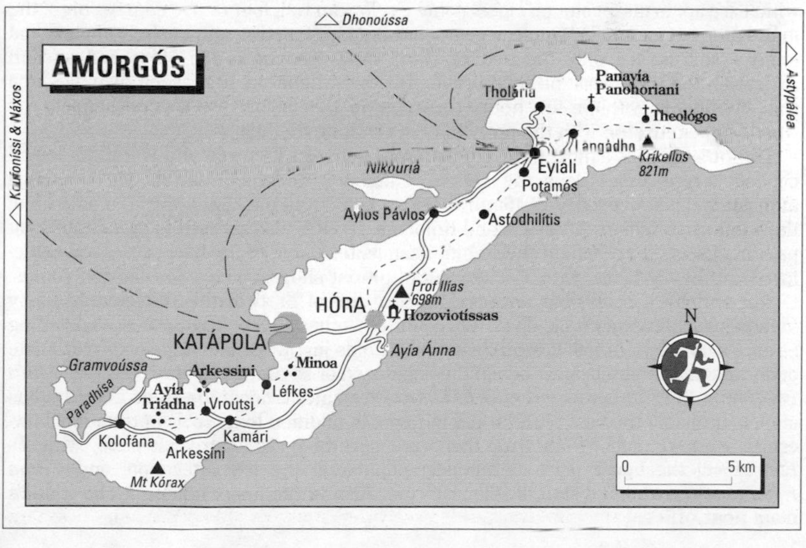

Xilokeratídhi along the north shore. There is a beach in front of Rahídhi, but the beach to the west of Katápola is better, though not up to the standards of Eyiáli. In season there is also a regular kaïki to nearby beaches at **Maltézi** and **Plákes** (400dr return) and a daily kaïki to the islet of **Gramvoússa** off the western end of Amorgós (2000dr return).

There are plenty of small **hotels** and **pensions** and, except in high summer when rooms are almost impossible to find, proprietors tend to meet those boats arriving around sunset – though not necessarily those that show up in the small hours. A good clean place next to the beach at the western end of Katápola is *Eleni Rooms* (☎0285/71 543 or 71 628; ④). *Dhimitri's Place* in Rahídhi (☎0285/71 309; ②) is a compound of interconnecting buildings in an orchard, where shared cooking facilities add to the laid-back atmosphere. On the same road, *Angeliki Rooms* (☎0285/71 280; ③) is well run, friendly and good value, as Angeliki doesn't put up her prices for August; the smart *Hotel Minoa* (☎0285/71 480; ⑤) on the waterfront is noisier than its sister hotel will be when it opens up, round the corner, in the near future. *Panayiotis Rooms* (☎0285/71 890; ③) in Xilokeratídhi is also good value. There is another cluster of hotels behind the port, past *Hotel Anna* (☎0285/71 218; ③), of similar price and quality (③–④), including *Pension Big Blue. Hotel Anna* itself is a little old-fashioned; however, it has a lovely setting and basic cooking facilities, and you can enjoy breakfast in the beautiful garden.

In Katápola proper, *Mourayio* is the most popular **taverna** in town; alternatively try the *Akrogiali* taverna. What **nightlife** there is focuses on a handful of cafés and pubs. A bar called *Le Grand Bleu* in Xilokeratídhi regularly shows *The Big Blue* on video but there are other less obvious and less expensive places to drink, such as *The Moon Bar* next door, or *Ippokampos*, a café and bar on the front at Rahídhi.

Prekas is the one-stop **boat ticket agency**, and there are several **moped rental** outlets including the friendly Corner Rentabike, though the local bus service is more than adequate and walking trails delightful. The **campsite** (☎0285/71 802;) is well signed between Rahídhi and Xilokeratídhi; in the latter district are four **tavernas**, of which the first is a friendly fish taverna, and of the others around the corner *Vitzentzos* is by far the best.

Steps, and then a jeep track, lead out of Katápola to the remains of **ancient Minoa**, which are apt to disappoint up close: some Cyclopean wall four or five courses high, the foundations of an Apollo temple, a crumbled Roman structure and bushels of unsorted pottery shards. It's only the setting, with views encompassing Hóra and ancient Arkessíni, that's the least bit memorable. Beyond Minoa the track soon dwindles to a trail, continuing within a few hours to Arkessíni (see below) via several hamlets – a wonderful **excursion** with the possibility of catching the bus back.

The **bus** shuttles almost hourly until 11pm between Katápola and Hóra, the island capital; several times daily the service continues to Ayía Ánna via Hozoviotíssas monastery, and once a day (9.45am) there's a run out to the "Káto Meriá", made up of the hamlets of Kamári, Arkessíni and Kolofána. **HÓRA**, also accessible by an hour-long path beginning from behind the Rahídhi campsite, is one of the best-preserved settlements in the Cyclades, with a scattering of tourist shops, cafés, tavernas and rooms. Dominated by a rock plug wrapped with a chapel or two, the thirteenth-century Venetian fortifications look down on countless other bulbous churches – including Greece's smallest, **Áyios Fanoúrios**, which holds just three worshippers – and a line of decapitated windmills beyond. Of the half-dozen or so **places to stay**, *Pension O Ilias* (☎0285/71 277; ③) is recommended. *Liotrivi* restaurant, down the steps from the bus stop, is probably the best place to **eat** in town. In addition to the pair of traditional tavernas, *Kastanis* and *Klimataria*, there are several noisy bistro-café-pubs, with *To Plateaki* in the upper plaza perennially popular in the late afternoon, and *Giulia Kafeneon*, near the bus stop, livelier later on. Also in the upper square is the island's main **post office**.

From the top of Hóra, next to the helipad, a wide cobbled *kalderími* drops down to two major attractions, effectively short-cutting the road and taking little longer than the bus to reach them. Bearing left at an inconspicuous fork after fifteen minutes, you'll come to the spectacular **monastery of Hozoviotíssas** (daily 8am–1pm & 5–7pm; donation), which appears suddenly as you round a bend, its vast wall gleaming white at the base of a towering orange cliff. Only four monks occupy the fifty rooms now, but they are quite welcoming, considering the number of visitors who file through; you can see the eleventh-century icon around which the monastery was founded, along with a stack of other treasures. The foundation legend is typical for such institutions in outlandish places: during the Iconoclastic period a precious icon of the Virgin was committed to the sea by beleaguered monks at Hózova, somewhere in the Middle East, and it washed up safely at the base of the palisade here. The view from the *katholikón's* terrace, though, overshadows all for most visitors, and to round off the experience, visitors are ushered into a comfy reception room and treated to a sugary lump of *loukoúmi*, a fiery shot of *kítron* and a cool glass of water.

The right-hand trail leads down, within forty minutes, to the pebble **beaches** at **Ayía Ánna**. Skip the first batch of tiny coves in favour of the path to the westernmost bay, where naturists cavort, almost in scandalous sight of the monastery far above. As yet there are no tavernas here, nor a spring, so bring food and water for the day.

For alternatives to Ayía Ánna, take the morning bus out toward modern Arkessíni, alighting at **Kamári** hamlet (where there's a single taverna) for the twenty-minute path down to the adjacent beaches of **Notiná**, **Moúros** and **Poulopódhi**. Like most of Amorgós's south-facing beaches, they're clean, with calm water, and here, too, a freshwater spring dribbles most of the year. The road is paved as far as **Kolofána**, where there is one place with rooms. From here unpaved roads lead to the western tip of the island, and remote beaches at Káto Kámbos and at Paradhísa, facing the islet of Gramvoússa.

Archeology buffs will want to head north from Kamári to Vroútsi, start of the overgrown hour-long route to **ancient Arkessini**, a collection of tombs, six-metre-high walls and houses out on the cape of Kastrí. The main path from Minoa also passes through Vroútsi, ending next to the well-preserved Hellenistic fort known locally as the "Pýrgos", just outside modern **ARKESSÍNI**. The village has a single taverna with rooms, and, more importantly, an afternoon bus back to Hóra and Katápola.

The northeast

The energetically inclined can walk the four to five hours from Hóra to Eyiáli. On the Hóra side you can start by continuing on the faint trail just beyond Hozoviótissas, but the islanders themselves, in the days before the road existed, preferred the more scenic and sheltered valley route through Terláki and Rikhtí. The two alternatives, and the modern jeep road, more or less meet an hour out of Hóra. Along most of the way, you're treated to amazing views of **Nikouriá islet**, nearly joined to the main island, and in former times a leper colony. The only habitations en route are the summer hamlet of **Asfodhilítis**, with well water but little else for the traveller, and **Potamós**, a double village you encounter on the stroll down towards Eyiáli bay.

EYIÁLI (Órmos), smaller than Katápola, is a laid-back beachside place in a 1970s time-warp. The road inland, behind the harbour, leads to a group of **hotels** of similar price and quality. *Nikitas* (☎0285/73 237; ③) is the most pleasant, in that it stands on its own in a field, commanding unobstructed sea views. Above is a row of hotels including *Pension Christine* (☎0285/73 236; ③), *Akrogiali* (☎0285/73 249; ④) and *Hotel Pelagos* (☎0285/73 206; ③). Along the beach is the *Lakki* (☎0285/73 244; ④) and behind this the pleasant *Pension Askas* (☎0285/73 333; ④) – both of which have their own shaded tavernas. Next to *Pension Askas* there is a very friendly official **campsite**, *Amorgos*

Camping (☎0285/ 73 500). Overlooking the bay on the road up to Tholária is a luxury hotel with a swimming pool, the *Aegialis* (☎0285/73 393; ⑥). For **eating out**, try *To Limani* (aka *Katerina's*) on the single inland lane, packed until midnight by virtue of its excellent food and barrel wine. Other good options are the *Amorgialos* kafenío, right by the harbour which serves up octopus, and *Delear*, a smart beach bar with live music some evenings and rather pricey drinks. A few seasonal music **bars**, such as *Blé Café*, attempt to compete with *Katerina's*. The *Corte Club* at the *Aegialis* hotel is a typical holiday resort disco playing the usual mix of northern European dance music and Greek pop. For a more active adventure you can take advantage of the new **diving** centre, Dive Ventures (☎0285/73 611), which organizes daily boat and shore dives.

The main Eyiáli **beach** is more than serviceable, getting less weedy and reefy as you stroll further north, the sand interrupted by the remains of a Roman building jutting into the sea. A trail here leads over various headlands to an array of clothing-optional bays: the first sandy, the second mixed sand and gravel, the last shingle. There are no facilities anywhere so bring along what you need.

Eyiáli has its own **bus service** up to each of the two villages visible above and east, with eight departures daily up and down (a timetable is posted by the harbour bus stop in town), but it would be a shame to miss out on the beautiful **loop walk** linking them with the port. A path starting at the far end of the beach heads inland and crosses the road before climbing steeply to **THOLÁRIA**, named after vaulted Roman tombs found around Vígla, the site of ancient Eyiáli. Vígla is on a hill opposite the village but there is little to see beyond the bases of statues and traces of city walls incorporated into later terracing. Another path winds down behind the hill to a tiny pebble beach at Mikrí Vlihádha far below. There are a few **taverna-cafés**, including a handsome wooden-floored establishment near the church, and there are now several places to stay, including some comfortable **rooms** (reserve through *Pension Lakki* in Eyiáli), the large and upmarket *Vigla* (☎0285/73 288; ⑤) and the *Thalassino Oneiro* (☎0285/73 345; ③), which has a fine restaurant and an extremely friendly owner. **LANGÁDHA** is another hour's walk along a path starting below Tholária; to the left of the trail is the chapel of Astrátios with an altar supported by the capital of a Corinthian column. Past here there are views down to the inlet of Megáli Vlihádha and, on a clear day, across to Ikaría in the north. The path descends through the village of Stroúmbos, abandoned apart from three or four houses restored as holiday homes, and into a small gorge before climbing the steps up to Langádha. The place is home to a sizable colony of expatriates – something reflected in the German-Greek cooking at the beautifully located *Nikos*' **taverna** at the lower end of the village, which also runs the attached *Pagali* hotel (☎0285/73 310; ④). The *Loza* taverna, at the top of the village also runs a more straightforward pension with rooms (☎0285/73 315; ③).

Beyond Langádha, another rocky path leads around the base of the island's highest peak, the 821-metre-high **Kríkellos**, passing on the way the fascinating church of **Theológos**, with lower walls and ground plan dating to the fifth century. Somewhat easier to reach, by a slight detour off the main Tholária–Langádha trail, are the church and festival grounds of **Panayía Panohorianí** – not so architecturally distinguished but a fine spot nonetheless.

Íos

No other island is quite like **Íos**, nor attracts the same vast crowds of young people, although attempts are being made to move the island's tourism upmarket; the island now enforces Greece's early closing laws (3am except Fri & Sat), and bars no longer stay open all night. The only real villages – **Yialós**, **Hóra** and **Mylopótamos** – are in one small corner of the island, and until recently development elsewhere was restrict-

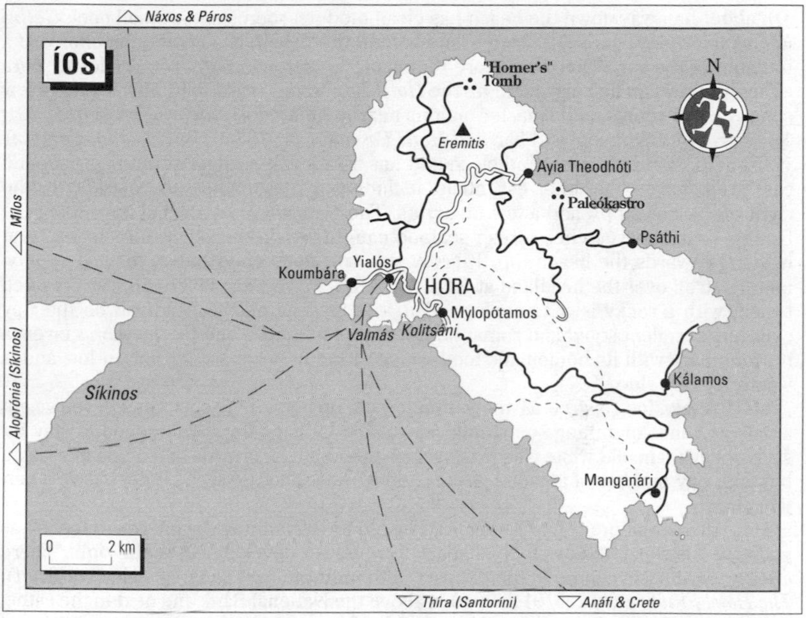

ed by poor roads. As a result there are still some very quiet beaches with just a few rooms to rent. Yialós has one of the best and safest natural harbours in the Cyclades and there is talk of building a new yacht marina.

Most visitors stay along the arc delineated by the port – at Yialós, where you'll arrive (there's no airport), in Hóra above it or at the beach at Mylopótamos; it's a small area, and you soon get to know your way around. **Buses** constantly shuttle between Koumbára, Yialós, Hóra and Mylopótamos, with a daily service running roughly from 8am to midnight; you should never have to wait more than fifteen minutes during high season, but at least once try the short walk up (or down) the stepped path between Yialós and Hóra. Various travel offices run their own buses to the beaches at Manganári and Ayía Theodhóti; they sell return tickets only, and are a bit expensive. To rent your own transport, try Jacob's Car and Bike Rental (☎0286/91 047) in Yialós and Vangelis Bike Rental (☎0286/91 919) in Hóra.

Despite its past popularity, **sleeping on the beach** on Íos is really worth avoiding these days. Crime and police raids are becoming more frequent as the island strains under the sheer impact of increasing youth tourism, and the police have been known to turn very nasty. They prefer you to sleep in the official campsites and, given the problem of theft, you should probably take their advice.

Yialós and Hóra

From **YIALÓS** quayside, **buses** turn around just to the left, while Yialós **beach** – surprisingly peaceful and uncrowded – is another five minutes' walk in the same direction. You might be tempted to grab a room in Yiálos as you arrive: owners meet the ferries, hustling the town's **accommodation**, and there are also a couple of kiosks by the jetty that will book rooms for you. *Hotel Mare Monte* (☎0286/91 585;

④), about half-way down the beach has clean modern rooms and a small pool; *Galini Rooms* (☎0286/91 115; ⑤), down a lane behind the beach, is a good quiet choice, if a little out of the way. There are more rooms on the stepped path from Yialós to Hóra although they can be noisy at night: the *Hotel-Bar Helios* (☎0286/91 500; ④) has a few simple, older rooms, and smarter options nearby include *Armadoras* (☎0286/91 201; ⑤), with a pleasant pool and bar, and *Hotel Poseidon* (☎0286/91 091; ⑤). *Ios Camping* (☎0286/91 329) is friendly and clean and has a rather luxurious swimming pool and café area. Yialós has other essentials, including a reasonable supermarket (to the right of the bus stop), and a few **tavernas**. The *Octopus Tree*, a small kafenío by the fishing boats, serves cheap fresh seafood caught by the owner, while on the front heading towards the beach the *Waves Restaurant* does good Indian food. A twenty-minute stroll over the headland at **KOUMBÁRA**, there's a smaller and less crowded beach, with a rocky islet to explore. *Philippos* taverna on the headland on the way over has excellent squid and romantic views across Yialós, and the *Polydoros* taverna in Koumbára with its homemade food is one of the better places to eat on Iós, and is worth the bus ride.

HÓRA (aka Íos Town) is a twenty-minute walk up behind the port, though you've got a better chance of getting something reasonable by haggling if you intend to stay for several days. The old white village is overwhelmed by the crowds of tourists in season, but with any number of arcaded streets and whitewashed chapels, it does have a certain charm.

Hóra divides naturally into two parts. The old town climbing the hillside to the left as you arrive is separated by an open space from newer development to the right. There are plenty of basic **rooms** in the old part (although the bars can make sleep difficult): *The Hotel Filippou* (☎0286/91 290; ③) is above the National Bank and next to the cathedral; Yannis Stratis (☎0286/91 494; ②) has a few very simple rooms next door; and *Markos Pension* (☎0286/91 059; ④; ask for the ten percent discount for *Rough Guide* readers), with a poolside bar, is one of the best choices in the new part. *Katerina Rooms* (☎0286/91 997; ④), just out of town down a path past the *Iós Club*, is quiet and has fine views over the port, and the friendly *Four Seasons Pension* (☎0286/91 308; winter 0286/92 081; ④), up a turning by Vangelis Bike Rental, is also well away from the noise of the bars and clubs.

What Hóra is still really about, though, is **nightlife**. Every evening the streets throb to music from ranks of competing discos and clubs – mostly free, or with a nominal entrance charge, though drinks tend to be expensive. Most of the smaller **bars** and pubs are tucked into the thronging narrow streets of the old village on the hill, offering something for everyone – unless you just want a quiet drink. A welcome exception to the techno-pop dancing fodder can be found at the *Ios Club*, perched right up on the hill, which plays quieter music, has reasonable food and is a good place to watch the sunset; *Pegasus* and *Super Fly* are also recommended. The larger **dancing clubs**, including the *Mojo*, which plays techno and trance music, and *Disco Scorpion* are to be found on the main road to Mylopótamos.

Eating is a secondary consideration but there are plenty of cheap and cheerful psistariés and takeaway joints: sound choices include the Italian restaurant *Pinocchio*, and the *Lord Byron* mezedhopolí in an alley near the cathedral – it's open year round and tries hard to recreate a traditional atmosphere, with old rembétika music and some good, unusual Greek food.

Culturally things are improving with the recent opening of the **Archeological Museum of Ios** (Tues–Sun 8am–2pm; 500dr), which is hoped will attract a more diverse range of visitors to the island. The outdoor theatre of Odysseus Elytis, behind the windmills, provides a beautiful setting in which to enjoy concerts and plays, details of which can be found from the travel agent/information booth next to the archeological museum.

Around the island

The most popular stop on the island's bus routes is **MYLOPÓTAMOS** (universally abbreviated to Mylópotas), the site of a magnificent beach and a mini-resort. Due to the large number of young travellers in Íos, camping is a popular option. *Far Out* (☎0286/91 468), towards the far end of the beach, consists of a camping ground (2000dr) and bungalows; it has an attractive setting and is very popular but can get very noisy and crowded. *The Purple Pig* (☎0286/91 302, *purplpig@otenet.gr*), a friendly Australian-run **backpackers' complex**, by the road up to Hóra, has clean bungalows, good camping facilities (2000dr) and plenty of other pleasurable distractions, including its own club and a poolside bar. Up the road at the far end of the beach, *Gorgona* (☎0286/91 307; ④) and *Dracos* (☎0286/91 281 or 91 010; ④) have reasonable rooms, but *Dracos* also has a good taverna on its own little quay, serving freshly caught fish. The *Far Out Village* (☎0286/92 305; *farout@otenet.gr*; ⑤), next to the camping site of the same name, the *Far Out Hotel* (☎0286/91 446 or 91 702; ⑤), on the road down from Hóra, and the luxurious *Ios Palace Hotel* (☎0286/91 269; ⑥), above the near end of the beach, are the most upmarket choices. The *Harmony Restaurant* on the rocks beyond the *Ios Palace* is one of the better places to eat, serving pizzas and Mexican food. The restaurants and self-service cafés behind the beach are uninspiring, and only the *Faros Café* rates a mention for staying open through the night to cater for the crowds returning from Hóra in the early hours. Mylopótamos itself has surprisingly little in the way of nightlife.

From Yialós, daily boats depart at around 10am (returning in the late afternoon) to **Manganári** on the south coast, where there's a beach and a swanky hotel; you can also get there by moped. There's an expensive speedboat (4000dr return) from Yialós to Manganári, but most people go by bus (1500dr return). These are private buses run by travel agencies, leaving Yialós about 11am, calling at Hóra and Mylopótamos and returning later in the afternoon. Predominantly nudist, Manganári is the beach to come to for serious tans, although there's more to see, and a better atmosphere at **Ayía Theodhóti** up on the east coast. There's a paved road across the island to Ayía Theodhóti – the daily excursion bus costs 1000dr return. A couple of kilometres south of Ayía Theodhóti is a ruined Venetian castle which encompasses the ruins of a marble-finished town and a Byzantine church. In the unlikely event that the beach – a good one and mainly nudist – is too crowded, try the one at **Psáthi**, 14km to the southeast. Frequented by wealthy Athenians, this small resort has a couple of pricey tavernas, making it better for a day-trip than an extended stay. The road is very poor and not really safe for mopeds, although there are plans to improve it. Another island beach is at **Kálamos**; get off the Manganári bus at the turning for Kálamos, which leaves you with a 4km walk.

"**Homer's**" **tomb** is the only cultural diversion on the island. The story goes that, while on a voyage from Sámos to Athens, Homer's ship was forced to put in at Íos, where the poet subsequently died. The tomb can be reached by moped along a safe new unpaved road (turning left from the paved road to Ayía Theódhoti 4.5km from Hóra). The town itself has long since slipped down the side of the cliff, but the rocky ruins of the entrance to a tomb remain, as well as some graves – one of which is claimed to be Homer's, but which in reality probably dates only to the Byzantine era.

Síkinos

Síkinos has so small a population that the mule ride or walk up from the port to the village was only replaced by a bus late in the 1980s and, until the new jetty was completed at roughly the same time, it was the last major Greek island where ferry passengers were still taken ashore in launches. With no dramatic characteristics, nor any nightlife

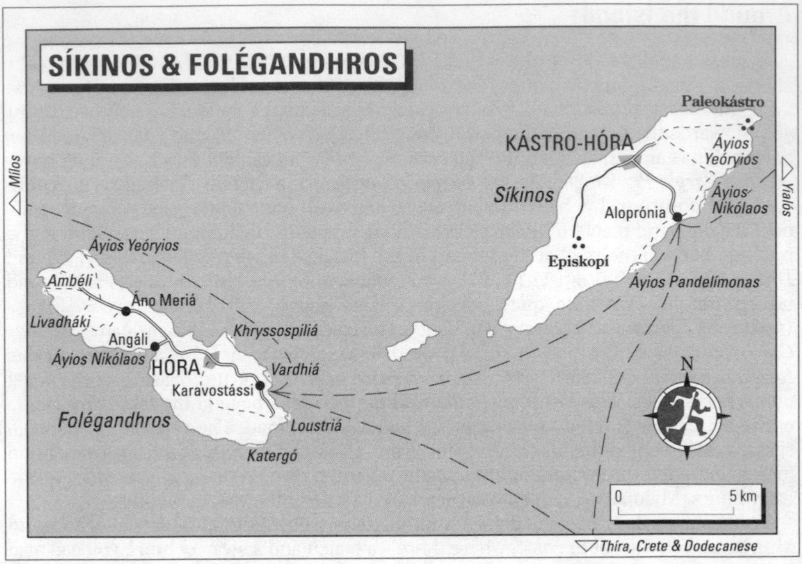

to speak of, few foreigners make the short trip over here from neighbouring Íos and Folégandhros or from sporadically connected Páros, Náxos, or Thíra. There is no bank on the island, but there is a **post office** up in Kástro-Hóra, and you can sometimes change cash at the store in Aloprónia.

Aloprónia and Kástro-Hóra

Such tourist facilities as exist are concentrated in the little harbour of **ALOPRÓNIA**, with its long sandy beach and the recent additions of an extended breakwater and jetty. More and more formal **accommodation** is being built here, but it's still possible to camp or just sleep out under the tamarisks behind the beach. For rooms, try *Flora* (☎0286/51 214; ②), near the main road leading to Hóra, *Loukas* (☎0286/51 076; ①–④), who has rooms and studios around town to suit most budgets, or the recommended *The Rock* (☎0286/51 135; ③), above the *Vrachos Rock Cafe*; alternatively, the comfortable and traditional *Hotel Kamares* (☎0286/51 234; ③) has a nicer setting than the conspicuous *Porto Sikinos* luxury complex (☎0286/51 247; ⑥). *To Meltemi* **taverna** on the quay is the locals' hangout, while the fancier *Ostria* is affiliated with the *Hotel Kamares* and the *Loukas* provides standard fare. The *Vrachos Rock Cafe* above the quay plays a more varied music selection than its name would suggest and attracts a good mix of people, while *Vengera* music bar on the opposite side of the bay is a smoother joint.

The double village of **KÁSTRO-HÓRA** is served by the single island bus, which shuttles regularly from early morning till quite late in the evening between the harbour and here, though the route should soon be extended to Episkopí with the completion of the new road. On the ride up, the scenery turns out to be less desolate than initial impressions suggest. Draped across a ridge overlooking the sea, Kástro-Hóra makes for a charming day-trip, and the lovely oil-press **museum** (July to mid-Sept 6.30–8.30pm; free), run privately by a Greek-American is definitely not to be missed. A partly ruined monastery, **Zoödhóhou Piyís** ("Spring of Life", a frequent name in the

Cyclades), crowns the rock above; the architectural highlight of the place, though, is the central quadrangle of **Kástro**, a series of ornate eighteenth-century houses arrayed defensively around a chapel square, their backs to the exterior of the village. The quality of rooms has improved, and both Markos Zagoreos (☎0286/51 263; ②) and Haroula (☎0286/51 212; ②) have competitive prices – the former has great views. A good selection of food is available, along with fine local wine, at both *Klimataria* and *To Steki tou Garbi* next door. The kafenía up here are very traditional affairs and you might feel more welcome at *Kastro* or *Platía*, two newly opened cafe-bars.

Around the island

West of Kástro-Hóra, an hour-plus walk (or mule ride) takes you through a landscape lush with olive trees to **Episkopí**, where elements of an ancient temple-tomb have been ingeniously incorporated into a seventh-century church – the structure is known formally as the Iróön. Ninety minutes from Kástro-Hóra, in the opposite direction, lies **Paleokástro**, the patchy remains of an ancient fortress. The beaches of **Áyios Yeóryios** and **Áyios Nikólaos** are reachable by a regular kaïki from Aloprónia; the former is a better option because it has the daytime *Almira* restaurant. It is possible to walk to them, but there is no real path at the later stages. A more feasible journey by foot is the pebble beach at **Áyios Pandelímonas**: just under an hour's trail walk southwest of Aloprónia, it is the most scenic and sheltered on the island, and is also served by a kaïki in season.

Folégandhros

The cliffs of **Folégandhros** rise sheer in places over 300m from the sea – until the early 1980s as effective a deterrent to tourists as they always were to pirates. It was used as an island of political exile right up until 1974, but life in the high, barren interior has been eased since the junta years by the arrival of electricity and the construction of a lengthwise road from the harbour to Hóra and beyond. Development has been given further impetus by the recent exponential increase in tourism and the mild commercialization this has brought.

A veritable explosion in accommodation for most budgets, and slight improvement in ferry arrival times, means there is no longer much need for – or local tolerance of – sleeping rough on the beaches. The increased wealth and trendiness of the heterogeneous clientele is reflected in fancy jewellery shops, an arty postcard gallery and a helipad. Yet away from the showcase Hóra and the beaches, the countryside remains mostly pristine, and is largely devoted to the spring and summer cultivation of barley, the mainstay of many of the Cyclades before the advent of tourism. Donkeys and donkey paths are also still very much in evidence, since the terrain on much of the island is too steep for vehicle roads.

Karavostássi and around

KARAVOSTÁSSI, the rather unprepossessing port whose name simply means "ferry stop", serves as a last-resort base; it has several **hotels** but little atmosphere. Best value if you do decide to stay is *Hotel Aeolos* (☎0286/41 205; ④), while the *Poseidon* (☎0286/41 272; ⑤) throws in breakfast at its decent restaurant *To Kati Allo*, which means "Something Else". The new *Vrahos Hotel* (☎0286/41 304; ④) has some nice rooms on the far side of the bay. *Iy Kali Kardhia* **taverna** above the harbour is recommended, and there are a couple of pleasant beach bars including the *Smyrna Ouzeri*, housed in a converted boathouse. There are many buses a day in summer to Hóra, and three of those go on to Áno Meriá; if you're feeling adventurous try Jimmy's motorbike rental (☎0286/41 448), which is cheaper than its counterparts in Hóra.

The closest **beach** is the smallish, but attractive enough, sand and pebble **Vardhiá**, signposted just north over the headland. Some twenty minutes' walk south lies **Loustriá**, a rather average beach with tamarisk trees and the island's official **campsite**, *Livadi Camping* (☎0286 41 304), which is good and friendly, although the hot water supply can be erratic.

Easily the most scenic beach on Folégandhros, a 300m stretch of pea-gravel with an offshore islet, is at **Katergó**, on the southeastern tip of the island. Most people visit on a boat excursion from Karavostássi or Angáli, but you can also get there on foot from the hamlet of Livádhi, a short walk inland from Loustriá. Be warned, though, that it's a rather arduous trek, with some nasty trail-less slithering in the final moments.

Hóra

The island's real character and appeal are to be found in the spectacular **HÓRA**, perched on a clifftop plateau some 45 minutes' walk from the dock; an hourly high-season **bus** service (6 daily spring/autumn) runs from morning until late at night. Locals and foreigners – hundreds of them in high season – mingle at the cafés and tavernas under the almond, flowering judas and pepper trees of the two main platías, passing the time unmolested by traffic, which is banned from the village centre. Toward the cliff-edge, and entered through two arcades, the defensive core of the medieval **kástro** is marked by ranks of two-storey houses, whose repetitive, almost identical stairways and slightly recessed doors are very appealing.

From the square where the bus stops, a zigzag path with views down to both coastlines climbs to the crag-top, wedding-cake church of **Kímisis Theotókou**, nocturnally illuminated to grand effect. Beyond and below it hides the **Khryssospiliá**, a large cave with stalactites, accessible only to proficient climbers; the necessary steps and railings have crumbled away into the sea, although a minor, lower grotto can still be visited.

Practicalities

Hóra's **accommodation** seems slightly weighted to favour hotels over rooms, with concentrations around the bus plaza at the eastern entrance to the village and at the western edge. Many of the tavernas and shops advertise rooms in their windows; otherwise try the purpose-built complex run by Irini Dekavalla (☎0286/41 235; ④), east of the bus stop. The nearby *Hotel Polikandia* (☎0286/41 322; ⑤) has an engaging proprietress and lower rates off season. The most luxurious facilities are at the cliff-edge *Anemomilos Apartments* (☎0286/41 309; ⑥), immaculately appointed and with stunning views; the new *Meltemi* (☎0286/41 328; ④), just opposite, has clean, comfortable rooms. The only hotel within Hóra is the *Castro* (☎0286/41 230; ⑤), with three rather dramatic rooms looking directly out on an alarming drop to the sea. At the western edge of Hóra near the police station, a dense cluster of rooms tend to block each other's views; the least claustrophobic is the recently rennovated *Odysseas* (☎0286/41 276; ⑤), which also manages some attractive apartments near the *Anemomilos*, the *Folgeandros Apartments* (☎0286/41 239; ⑤). By the roadside on the way to Áno Meriá, the *Fani-Vevis* (☎0286/41 237; ④), in a Neoclassical mansion overlooking the sea, seems to function only in high season; one hundred metres beyond are some smart new studios managed by *Iy Kali Kardhia* (see p.161) (☎0286/41 274; ⑥).

Hóra's dozen or so **restaurants** are surprisingly varied. The *Folegandhros* ouzerí in water-cistern plaza, is fun, if a bit eccentrically run. Breakfast can be enjoyed on the adjacent Platía Kondaríni at *Iy Melissa*, which does good fruit and yoghurt, omelettes and juices. *Iy Piatsa* has a nightly changing menu of well-executed Greek dishes, while their neighbour and local hangout *O Kritikos* is notable only for its grills. *Iy Pounda* near the bus stop is the most traditional place and has a small garden, while *Apanemo* at the far end of town has good food and a quieter setting, despite its proximity to the main bar area. Self-catering is an attractive option, with two well-stocked fruit shops and two supermarkets. Hóra is inevitably beginning to sprawl unattractively at the edges, but this at least means that the burgeoning **nightlife** – two dancing bars and a quantity of musical pubs and ouzeris – can be exiled to the north, away from most accommodation. *Avli* and *Greco* are two lively bars and both play up-to-date sounds, while *Kellari* is a rustic and charming wine bar where the atmosphere is more relaxed. A **post office** (no bank or OTE) completes the list of amenities, though the single **ferry agent** also does money exchange, as does the friendly and competent Italian-run Sottavento agency, which offers a wide range of services.

The rest of the island

Northwest of Hóra a narrow, paved road threads its way towards **ÁNO MERIÁ**, the other village of the island; after 4km you pass its first houses, clustered around the three churches of Áyios Pandelímonas, Áyios Yeóryios and Áyios Andhréas. Four tavernas operate in high season only: *Barba Kostas* is at the beginning of the village, *O Mimis* is about halfway along, *Iy Sinandisi* is at the turning for Áyios Yeóryios beach, while *Iliovasilema*, at the far end of the sprawling village, completes the list. Several rooms are also available; including *Stella's* (☎0286/41 329; ②) and *Irini's* (☎0286/41 344; ②).

Up to six times a day in high season a **bus** trundles out here to drop people off at the footpaths down to the various sheltered beaches on the southwest shore of the island. Busiest of these is **Angáli** (aka Vathý), with four rather basic room outfits including *Vangelis* (0286/41 105; ②) and *Panagiotis* (☎0286/41 116; ③) and two equally simple summer-only tavernas, reached by a fifteen-minute walk along a dirt road from the bus stop.

Nudists are urged to take the paths which lead twenty minutes east or west to **Firá** or **Áyios Nikólaos** beaches respectively; the latter in particular, with its many tamarisks, coarse sand and view back over the island, is Katergó's only serious rival in the best-beach sweepstakes. At Áyios Nikólaos, a lone taverna operates up by the namesake chapel; Firá has no facilities at all. From the *Iliovasilema* taverna, a motorable track continues north to a point from where a 500-metre path takes you down to the pleasant little bay of **Ambéli**.

Thíra (Santoríni)

As the ferry manoeuvres into the great caldera of **Thíra**, the land seems to rise up and clamp around it. Gaunt, sheer cliffs loom hundreds of feet above, nothing grows or grazes to soften the view, and the only colours are the reddish-brown, black and grey pumice striations layering the cliff-face. The landscape tells of a history so dramatic and turbulent that legend hangs as fact upon it.

From as early as 3000 BC the island developed as a sophisticated outpost of Minoan civilization, until around 1550 BC when catastrophe struck: the volcano-island erupted, its heart sank below the sea, and earthquakes reverberated across the Aegean. Thíra was destroyed and the great Minoan civilizations on Crete were dealt a severe blow. At this point the island's history became linked with legends of Atlantis, the "Happy Isles Submerged by Sea". Plato insisted that the legend was true, and Solon dated the cataclysm to 9000 years before his time – if you're willing to accept a mistake and knock off the final zero, a highly plausible date.

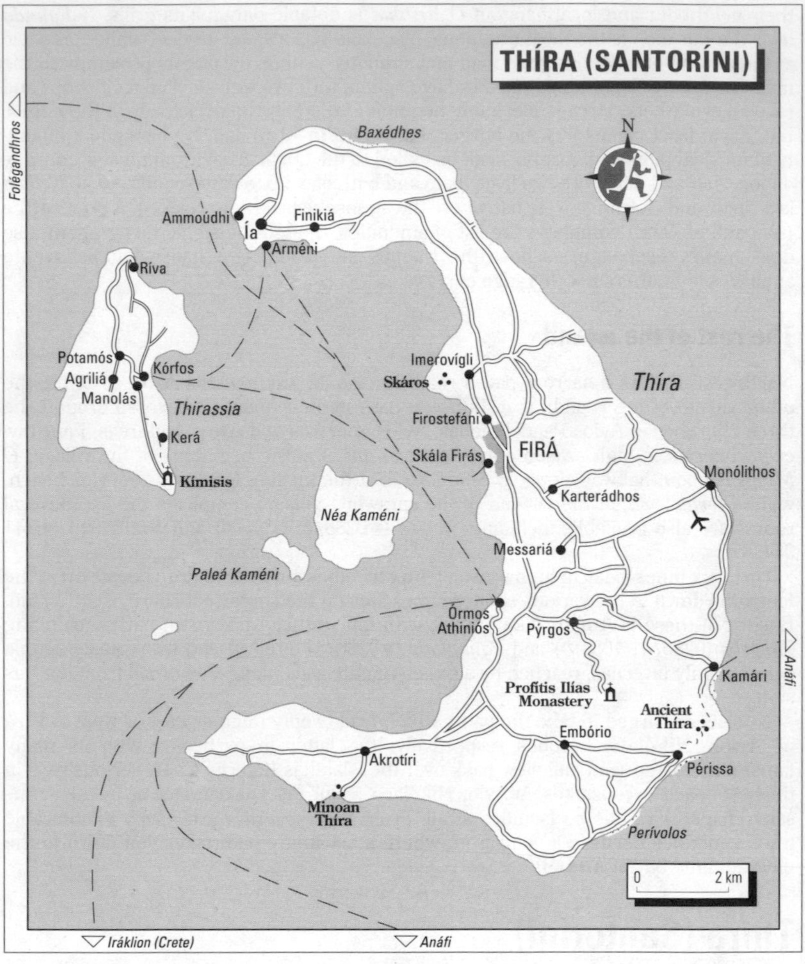

These apocalyptic events, though, scarcely concern modern tourists, who are here mostly to stretch out on the island's dark-sand beaches and absorb the peculiar, infernal atmosphere; as recently as a century ago, Thíra was still reckoned to be infested with vampires. Though not nearly so predatory as the undead, current visitors have in fact succeeded in pretty much killing off any genuine island life, creating in its place a rather expensive and stagey playground.

Arrival and departure

Ferries dock at the somewhat grim port of **Órmos Athiniós**; **Skála Firás** and **Ía** in the north are reserved for local ferries, excursion kaïkia and cruise ships. **Buses**, astonishingly crammed, connect Athiniós with the island capital Firá, and, less frequently, with the main beaches at Kamári and Périssa; disembark quickly and take whatever's going, if you want to avoid a long walk. You're also likely to be accosted at Athiniós by people offering rooms all over the island; it may be a good idea to pay attention to them, given the scramble for beds in Firá especially. If you alight at Skála Firás, you have the traditional route above you – 580 mule-shit-splattered steps to Firá itself. It's not that difficult to walk, but the intrepid can also go up by mule or by cable car (summer only 6.40am–10pm, every 20min; 800dr). The **airport** is located towards the other side of the island, near Monólithos; there is a regular shuttle-bus service to the Firá bus station, which runs until 10pm.

When it comes to **leaving** – especially for summer/evening ferry departures – it's best to buy your ticket in advance. Note, too, that although the bus service stops around midnight, a shared taxi isn't outrageously expensive. Incidentally, **ferry information** from any source is notoriously unreliable on Thíra, so departure details should be quadruple-checked. If you do get stranded in Athiniós waiting for a ferry connection, there's no place to stay, and the tavernas are pretty awful. With time on your hands, it's well worth zigzagging the 3500m up to the closest village, **MEGALOHÓRI**. Between Megalohóri and Pýrgos village, near the junction of the main and Athiniós road, is *Hotel Zorbas* (☎0286/31 433; ④), and at the centre of Megalohóri, the *Yeromanolis* is a surprisingly reasonable and tasty grill which offers the increasingly rare homemade Santoríni wine.

Firá

Half-rebuilt after a devastating earthquake in 1956, **FIRÁ** (also known as Thíra or Hóra) still lurches dementedly at the cliff's edge. With a stunningly attractive setting, it appears on postcards and tourist brochures and, naturally, you pay the price for its position. Busy with day-trippers in summer at least, initial impressions of Firá are of gross commercialism, and it is perhaps best avoided in season.

However, Firá's clifftop position does justify a visit, and you should also make time for the **Archeological Museum** (Tues–Sun 8am–2.30pm; 800dr), near the cable car to the north of town, whose collection includes a curious set of erotic Dionysiac figures. The interesting **Museum Megaro Ghyzi** (Mon–Sat 10.30am–1.30pm & 5–8pm, Sun 10.30am–4.30pm; 500dr) is in an old mansion owned by the Catholic diocese of Santoríni and restored as a cultural centre. It has a good collection of old prints and maps as well as photographs of the town before and after the 1956 earthquake.

Practicalities

Caldera-side hotels and studios in **Firá** itself are expensive but there are plenty of rooms without caldera views at the back of town. *Villa Haroula* (☎0286/24 226; ⑥) is a good smart hotel on the road down to *Santorini Camping* (☎0286/22 944), at the back of town, which stays open with heating through the winter. Along the same road *Pension Petros* (☎0286/22 573; ④) and *Pension Soula* (☎0286/ 23 473; ⑤) are two reasonable, if not very exciting alternatives. Otherwise there is the *International Youth Hostel* (☎0286/22 387), in the northern part of town, between Erythroú Stavroú and 25-Martíou, with dorm beds and double rooms; it's a good budget option although it can be a bit noisy at night. *Camping Caldera View* (☎0286/82 010) is probably the most pleasant **campsite** in Thíra, in between Firá, the port and the nearest beach.

FIROSTEFÁNI, between Firá and Imerovígli, is the best bet for reasonably priced rooms with views over the caldera. Rooms in Firostefáni of varying prices and standards include *Apartments Gaby* (☎0286/22 057; ④), *Hotel Mylos* (☎0286/23 884; ④), *Kafieris Hotel* (☎0286/22 189; ④) and the rooms of Ioannis Roussos (☎0286/22 611 or 22 862; ④). For something smarter, *Manos Apartments* (☎0286/23 202; ⑥) is highly recommended. You might try **KARTERÁDHOS**, a small village about twenty minutes' walk south of Firá, where there are rooms and the pleasant *Hotel Albatross* (☎0286/23 435, fax 23 431; ⑥), or Messariá, another 2km further, with some more expensive hotels.

Firá's **restaurants** are primarily aimed at the tourist market, but there are a few worth trying: the *Flame of the Volcano* is the last of the caldera-side restaurants heading north past the cable-car station (towards Firostefáni) and is better and more reasonably priced than most, although you are still paying extra for the view. *Nikolas* on Erythroú Stavroú is an old-established and defiantly traditional taverna but it can be hard to get a table. Otherwise try *Koutouki* on 25-Martíou, *Mama's Cyclades*, a little further up on the same road, or *Aktaion* in Firostefáni. As for **nightlife**, *Enigma*, a soul disco, occupying a converted house and garden, and *Kyra Thira*, a good jazz bar, are both on Erythroú Stavroú (walking south from the *International Youth Hostel*), along with various other clubs. The best bars from which to admire the caldera are *Franco's*, a rather exclusive and pricey cocktail bar, and the more laid-back *Tropical*, just above, for easy listening which gets funkier as the night progresses.

Nomikos Travel (☎0286/23 660) on 25-Martíou, opposite the OTE, is friendly and organizes excursions and trips to ancient Thira and Thirassía in conjunction with Kamari Tours (☎0286/31 390). **Buses** leave Firá from just south of Platía Theotokopoúlou to Périssa, Perívolos, Kamári, Monólithos, Akrotíri, Athiniós and the airport. **Taxis** (☎0286/22 555) go from near the bus station. If you want to see the whole island in a couple of days a rented **moped** is useful; Moto Chris at the top of the road that leads down to *Santorini Camping* is recommended.

The north

Once outside Firá, the rest of Santoríni comes as a nice surprise, although development is beginning to encroach. The volcanic soil is highly fertile, with every available space terraced and cultivated: wheat, tomatoes (most made into paste), pistachios and grapes are the main crops, all still harvested and planted by hand. The island's *vysándo* and *nikhtéri* wines are a little sweet for many tastes but are among the finest produced in the Cyclades.

A satisfying – if demanding – approach to Ía, 12km from Firá in the northwest of the island, is to walk the stretch from **IMEROVÍGLI**, 3km out of Firá, using a spectacular footpath along the lip of the caldera; the walk takes around two hours. Imerovígli is crowded with luxury, caldera-side **apartments** such as *Chromata* (☎0286/24 850; ⑥) and *Astra* (☎0286/23 641; ⑥), requiring reservations well in advance; *Katerina* (☎0286/22 708; ⑤) is a more moderately priced hotel, with caldera views from the large balcony/bar area only. *Altana* between *Katerina* and *Chromata* is a small caldera-side **café** whose position and relaxed atmosphere make for a pleasing breakfast spot. Continuing to Ía, you'll pass Toúrlos, an old Venetian citadel on Cape Skáros, on the way.

ÍA (Oía) was once a major fishing port of the Aegean, but it has declined in the wake of economic depression, wars, earthquakes and depleted fish stocks. Partly destroyed in the 1956 earthquake, the town has been sympathetically reconstructed, its pristine white houses clinging to the cliff-face. Apart from the caldera and the village itself there are a couple of things to see, including the **Naval Museum** (daily except Tues 9am–1pm & 5–8pm) and the very modest remains of a Venetian castle. With a **post office**, a couple of travel agencies and several **bike-rental** offices (of which Motor Fun is particularly good), Ía is a fine, and quieter, alternative to Firá. Much of the town's **accommodation** is in its restored old houses, including the troglodytic *Hotel Lauda* (☎0286/71 204; ④), the *Hotel Anemones* (☎0286/71 342; ④) and the *Hotel Fregata* (☎0286/71 221; ④). The highly recommended *Chelidonia Villas* (☎286/71 287; ⑥) are attractive restored cliff-side houses.

Quite near the bus terminal, also reachable by the main road that continues round to the back end of the village, is an excellent new hostel – the *Oia Youth Hostel* (☎0286/71 465), with a terrace and shady courtyard, a good bar, clean dormitories and breakfast included. Generally, the further you go along the central ridge towards the new end of Ía, the better value the **restaurants**; the *Anemomilos* and *Laokastri* are two such examples. The more centrally located *Skala* has standard fare, but you pay that little bit extra for the caldera-side location. **Nightlife** revolves around sunset-gazing, for which people are coached in from all over the island, creating traffic chaos; when this pales, there's *Petra* and *Alitana*, two bars located on the road leading down to the youth hostel, both playing easy listening in pleasant garden surroundings.

Below the town, 200-odd steps switchback hundreds of metres down to two small harbours: **Ammoúdhi**, for the fishermen, and **Arméni**, where the excursion boats dock. Both have excellent fish tavernas. *Sunset* taverna at Ammoúdhi is recommended, and at Arméni there is a taverna which specializes in grilled octopus lunches. **FINIKIÁ**, 1km east of Ía, is a very quiet and traditional little village. The reopening of the village taverna looks dubious, and accommodation is not in abundance. *Lotza Rooms* (☎0286/ 71 051; ③) are located in an old house in the middle of the village, while *Hotel Finakia* (☎0286/71 373; ⑤), above the village near the main road, is a smarter option. Just north of Ía is **Baxédhes** beach, a quiet alternative to Kamári and Périssa (see below), with a few tavernas including the *Paradhisos*, which has good food and reasonable prices.

The east and south

Beaches on Santoríni, to the east and south, are bizarre – long black stretches of volcanic sand which get blisteringly hot in the afternoon sun. They're no secret, and in the summer the crowds can be a bit overpowering. Closest to Firá, **MONÓLITHOS** has a couple of tavernas but is nothing special. Further south, **KAMÁRI** has surrendered lock, stock and barrel to the package-tour operators and there's not a piece of sand that isn't fronted by concrete villas.

Nonetheless it's quieter and cleaner than most, with some beachfront **accommodation**, including *Hotel Nikolina* (☎0286/31 702; ③), with basic but cheap rooms towards the southern end of the beach, as well as the *White House* (☎0286/31 441; ④) and the friendly *Sea Side Rooms* (☎0286/33 403; ③) further along the beach. *Rose Bay Hotel*(☎0286/33 650; ⑥) is a far pricier option, with a pleasant pool setting, set back away from the noisy beach thoroughfare. *Kamari Camping* (☎0286/31 453), a fifteen-minute walk on the road out of Kamári, is a small municipal-run site with limited facilities and no points for a warm welcome.

Psistaria O Kritikos, a taverna-grill frequented by locals rather than tourists, is one of the best places to **eat** on the island. It's a long way out of Kamári on the road up to Messariá, and too far to walk, but the bus stops outside. There are plenty of cafés and restaurants behind the beach, though many are expensive or uninspired. *Saliveros*, in front of the *Hotel Nikolina*, has taverna food at reasonable prices, and *Almira*, next to *Sea Side Rooms*, is a smarter restaurant and only a little more expensive. Kamári is a family resort with little in the way of clubs and nightlife, but there is a good open-air **cinema** near the campsite, and in summer buses run until 1am, so there's no problem getting back to Firá after seeing a film.

Things are scruffier at **PÉRISSA**, around the cape. Despite (or perhaps because of) its attractive situation and abundance of cheap rooms, it's noisy and crowded with backpackers. *Camping Perissa Beach* (☎0286/81 343) is right behind the beach and has plenty of shade but is also next to a couple of noisy late-night bars. There is also a youth hostel on the road into Périssa: *Anna* (☎0286/82 182) has dorm beds as well as a few simple studios closer to the beach. There are plenty of cheap rooms in the same area and some upmarket hotels behind the beach, including the smart and expensive *Hotel Veggara* (☎0286/82 060; ⑥). The beach itself extends almost 7km to the west, sheltered by the occasional tamarisk tree, with beach bars dotted along at intervals; *Wet Stories*, about ten minutes' walk from Périssa village, has a fun atmosphere and a varied snack selection.

Kamári and Périssa are separated by the Mésa Vounó headland, on which stood **ancient Thíra** (Tues–Sun 9am–3pm), the post-eruption settlement dating from the ninth century BC. Excursion buses go up from Kamári (5000dr), staying two hours at the site (ask at Kamári Tours behind the beach) but you can walk the **cobbled path** starting from the square in Kamári by the Argo General Store. The path zigzags up to a whitewashed church by a **cave**, containing one of Thíra's few freshwater springs, before crossing over to meet the road and ending at a saddle between Mésa Vounó and Profítis Ilías, where a refreshments van sells expensive drinks. From here, the path to the site passes a chapel dating back to the fourth century AD before skirting round to the Temenos of Artemidoros with bas-relief carvings of a dolphin, eagle and lion representing Poseidon, Zeus and Apollo. Next, the trail follows the sacred way of the ancient city through the remains of the agora and past the theatre. Most of the ruins (dating mainly from Hellenistic and Roman times) are difficult to place, but the site is impressively large and the views are awesome. The site can also be reached by a path from Périssa, and either way it's less than an hour's walk.

Inland along the same mountain spine is the monastery of **Profítis Ilías**, now sharing its refuge with Greek radio and TV pylons and the antennae of a NATO station. With just one monk remaining to look after the church, the place only really comes to life for the annual Profítis Ilías festival, when the whole island troops up here to celebrate. The views are still rewarding, though, and from near the entrance to the monastery an old footpath heads across the ridge in about an hour to ancient Thíra. The easiest ascent is the thirty-minute walk from the village of Pýrgos.

PÝRGOS itself is one of the oldest settlements on the island, a jumble of old houses and alleys that still bear the scars of the 1956 earthquake. It climbs to another Venetian fortress crowned by several churches and you can clamber around the battlements for sweeping views over the entire island and its Aegean neighbours. By way of contrast **MESSARIÁ**, a thirty-minute stroll north, has a skyline consisting solely of massive church domes that lord it over the houses huddled in a ravine.

Akrotíri

Evidence of the Minoan colony that once thrived here has been uncovered at the other ancient site of **Akrotíri** (Tues–Sat 8.30am–3pm; 1500dr), at the southwestern tip of the island. Tunnels through the volcanic ash uncovered structures, two and three storeys high, first damaged by earthquake then buried by eruption; Professor Marinatos, the excavator and now an island hero, was killed by a collapsing wall and is also buried on the site. Only a small part of what was the largest Minoan city outside of Crete has been excavated thus far. Lavish frescoes adorned the walls, and Cretan pottery was found stored in a chamber; most of the frescoes are currently exhibited in Athens.

Akrotíri itself can be reached by bus from Firá or Périssa; the excellent *Glaros* taverna, on the way to Kókkini Ámmos beach, has excellent food and barrelled wine. Kókkini Ámmos is about 500m from the site and is quite spectacular with high reddish-brown cliffs above sand the same colour (the name means "red sand"). There's a drinks stall in a cave hollowed into the base of the cliff. It's a better beach than the one below the site, but gets crowded in season.

The Kaméni islets and Thirassía

From either Firá or Ía, boat excursions and local ferries run to the charred volcanic islets of **Paleá Kaméni** and **Néa Kaméni**, and on to the relatively unspoiled islet of

Thirassía, which was once part of Santoríni until shorn off by an eruption in the third century BC. At Paleá Kaméni you can swim from the boat to hot springs with sulphurous mud, and Néa Kaméni, with its own mud-clouded hot springs, features a demanding hike to a volcanically active crater.

The real attraction though, is **Thirassía**, the quietest island in the Cyclades. The views are as dramatic as any on Santoríni, and tourism has little effect on island life. The downside is that there is no sandy beach, no nightlife and nowhere to change money.

Most tour boats head for **Kórfos**, a stretch of shingle backed by fishermen's houses and high cliffs. It has a few tavernas, including *Tonio* which stays open when the day-trippers have gone, but no rooms. From Kórfos a stepped path climbs up to **MANOLÁS**, nearly 200m above. Donkeys are still used for transport, and stables can be seen in both villages. Manolás straggles along the edge of the caldera, an untidy but attractive small island village that gives an idea of what Santoríni was like before tourism arrived there. It has a bakery, a couple of shops and a few tavernas, including the friendly *Panorama*, that opens only for the midday rush: the **restaurant** at the *Hotel Cavo Mare* (☎0286/29 176; ⑤) wins out by giving diners the use of the swimming pool. Dhimítrios Nomikós has **rooms** (☎0286/29 102; ③) overlooking the village from the south.

The best **excursion** from Manolás is to follow the unmade road heading south; about halfway along you pass the church of Profítis Ilías on a hilltop to the left. From here an old and overgrown trail descends through the deserted caldera-side village of **Kerá**, before running parallel with the road to the **monastery of the Kímisis** above the southern tip of the island. Minoan remains were excavated in a pumice quarry to the west of here in 1867, several years before the first discoveries at Akrotíri, but there is nothing to be seen today.

Ferries run to Thirassía four times a week in season and three times a week through the winter. There is no problem taking a car or rental bike over, but fill up with petrol first. Day-trips take in Néa Kaméni and Paleá Kaméni but are expensive (6000dr) and only stay two or three hours on Thirassía.

Anáfi

A ninety-minute boat ride to the east of Thíra, **Anáfi** is the last stop for ferries and hydrofoils and something of a travellers' dead end, with only the occasional high season ferry on to Astypálea in the Dodecanese. Not that this is likely to bother most of the visitors, who intentionally come here for weeks in mid-summer, and take over the island's beaches with a vengeance.

At most other times the place seems idyllic, and indeed may prove too sleepy for some: there are no bona fide hotels, mopeds, discos or organized excursions, and donkeys are still the main method of transport in the interior. Anáfi, though initially enchanting, is a harsh place, its mixed granite/limestone core overlaid by volcanic rock spewed out by Thíra's eruptions. Apart from the few olive trees and vines grown in the valleys, the only plants that seem to thrive are prickly pears.

The harbour and Hóra

The tiny harbour hamlet of **ÁYIOS NIKÓLAOS** has a single taverna, *To Akroyiali*, with a few rooms (☎0286/61 218; ②), while *Dave's Cafe*, with straw umbrellas above the beach, is a colourful English-run drinking spot. Jeyzed Travel (☎0286/61 253, fax 61 352) can provide information as well as issuing ferry tickets, changing money and booking rooms. In August there are enough Greek visitors to fill all the rooms on the island, so it's a good idea to book ahead. Most places to stay are in Hóra. In season a bus runs from the harbour every two hours or so from 9am to 11pm.

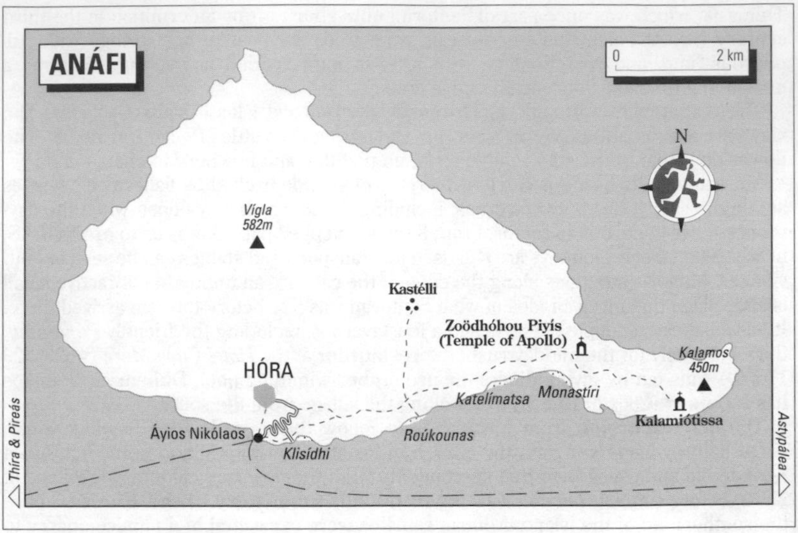

HÓRA itself, adorning a conical hill overhead, is a stiff, 25-minute climb up the obvious old mule path which shortcuts the modern road. Exposed and blustery when the *meltémi* is blowing, Hóra can initially seem a rather forbidding ghost town. This impression is slowly dispelled as you discover the hospitable islanders taking their coffee in sheltered, south-facing terraces, or under the anti-earthquake barrel vaulting that features in domestic architecture here.

The modern, purpose-built **rooms** run by Kalliopi Halari (☎0286/61 271; ②) and Voula Loudharou (☎0286/61 279; ②), and those run by Margarita Kollidha (☎0286/61 292; ③) at the extreme east edge of the village, are about the most comfortable – and boast stunning views south to the islets of Ftená, Pahiá and Makriá, and the distinctive monolith at the southeastern corner of Anáfi. Evening **diners** seem to divide their custom between the simple, welcoming *To Steki*, with reasonable food and barrel wine served on its terrace, and the more upmarket *Alexandhra's* on the central walkway. *Armenaki* is a lively new taverna/ouzerí which hosts regular *bouzoúki* nights. Otherwise nightlife revolves around the two bars: *Mylos Bar*, housed in a converted windmill in the village, and *Mantres* on the main road between the port and Hóra. Several shops, a bakery and a **post office** round up the list of amenities.

East along the coast: beaches and monasteries

The glory of Anáfi is a string of south-facing beaches starting under the cliffs at Áyios Nikólaos. Freelance campers head for **KLISÍDHI**, a short walk to the east of the harbour, where 200m of tan, gently shelving sand is pounded by gentle surf, and splendidly malopropic signs announce that "Nubbism is not allowed". Above the calamus-and-tamarisk oasis backing the beach there are two cafés and a taverna, including the *Kafestiatorion tis Margaritas*, with popular rooms (☎0286/61 237; ③). The *Villa Apollon* on the hillside above has the island's most upmarket accommodation (☎0286/61 348; ③). Klisídhi can be reached by road but it's quicker to take the cliff-top path starting behind the power station at the harbour. East of here the beaches can only be reached by foot or boat.

From a point on the paved road just east of Hóra, the **main path** skirting the south flank of the island is signposted: "Kastélli – Paleá Hóra – Roúkouna – Monastíri". The primary branch of this trail roller-coasters in and out of several agricultural valleys that provide most of Anáfi's produce and fresh water. Just under an hour along, beside a well, you veer down a side trail to **Roúkounas**, easily the island's best beach, with some 500m of broad sand rising to tamarisk-stabilized dunes, which provide welcome shade. A single taverna, *Tou Papu*, operates up by the main trail in season; the suggestively craggy hill of **Kastélli**, an hour's scramble above the taverna, is the site both of ancient Anaphi and a ruined Venetian castle.

Beyond Roúkounas, it's another half hour on foot to the first of the exquisite half-dozen **Katelímatsa** coves, of all shapes and sizes, and 45 minutes to **Monastíri** beach – all without facilities, so come prepared. Nudism is banned on Monastíri, because of its proximity to the monasteries.

The monasteries

Between Katelímatsa and Kálamos, the main route keeps inland, past a rare spring, to arrive at the **monastery of Zoödhóhou Piyís**, some two hours out of Hóra. A ruined temple of Apollo is incorporated into the monastery buildings to the side of the main gate; according to legend, Apollo caused Anáfi to rise from the waves, pulling off a dramatic rescue of the storm-lashed Argonauts. The courtyard, with a welcome cistern, is the venue for the island's major festival, celebrated eleven days after Easter. A family of cheesemakers lives next door and can point you up the start of the spectacular onward path to **Kalamiótissa**, a little monastery perched atop the abrupt pinnacle at the extreme southeast of the island. It takes another hour to reach, but is eminently worthwhile for the stunning scenery and views over the entire south coast. Kalamiótissa comes alive only during its 7–8 September festival; at other times, you could haul a sleeping bag up here to witness the amazing sunsets and sunrises, with your vantage point often floating in a sea of cloud. There is no water up here, so bring enough with you. It's a full day's outing from Hóra to Kalamiótissa and back; you might wish to take advantage, in at least one direction, of the excursion **kaïki** that runs from Áyios Nikólaos to Monastíri (6 times daily in high season). There is also a slightly larger mail and supplies boat (currently Mon & Thurs 11am) which takes passengers to and from Thíra (Athiniós), supplementing the main-line ferries to Pireás.

travel details

Ferries

Most of the Cyclades are served by mainline ferries from **Pireás**, but there are also boats which depart from **Lávrio** (for Kéa) and **Rafína**, which has become increasingly important of late, as work proceeds on the new international airport at nearby Spáta. At the moment there are daily services from Rafína to Ándhros, Tínos and Mýkonos, with less frequent sailings to Sýros, Páros, Náxos and Amorgós, and the North and East Aegean. All three ports are easily reached by bus from Athens. From June to September there are also a few weekly sailings from Thessaloníki to the most popular islands.

The frequency of sailings given below is intended to give an idea of services from April to October, when most visitors tour the islands. During the winter expect departures to be at or below the minimum level listed, with some routes cancelled entirely. Conversely, routes tend to be more comprehensive in spring and autumn, when the government obliges shipping companies to make extra stops to compensate for numbers of boats still in dry dock.

The long-awaited computerized booking system is now in operation, and all agents are required to issue computerized tickets. This move was designed to conform to EU regulations and prevent the overcrowding of ferries so common in the past. It means that in high season, certain popular routes may be booked up days in advance, so if you're visiting a few islands it is important to check availability on arrival in Greece, and book your outward and final pre-flight tickets well ahead. There is not usually so much problem with space between islands as there is to and from Pireás.

Amorgós 6–8 ferries weekly to Náxos and Páros, one of these continuing to Rafína rather than Pireás; 3–4 weekly to Sýros; 2–3 weekly to Tínos and Mýkonos; 2–3 weekly to Ándhros, Koufoníssi, Skhinoússa, Iráklia and Dhonoússa; 2–3 weekly to Astypálea.

Anáfi 6–8 weekly to Pireás (12hr 30min), mostly via Thíra (1hr 30min), Íos, Náxos, Páros; 1 weekly to Astypálea; 1 weekly to Sýros, Síkinos and Folégandhros; 2 weekly mail boats to Thíra (2hr).

Ándhros At least 3 daily to Rafína (2hr), Tínos (2hr) and Mýkonos; 4 weekly to Sýros; 2 weekly to Amorgós and Náxos; 1–4 weekly to Paros.

Dhonoússa 3–4 weekly to Amorgós; 2–3 weekly to Náxos, Koufoníssi, Skhinoússa, Iráklia, and Páros; 1 weekly to Pireás, Mýkonos, Tínos and Sýros; 2 weekly to Astypálea.

Íos At least 3 daily to Pireás (10hr), Páros (5hr), Náxos (3hr) and Thíra (several of which continue to Anáfi); 4–5 weekly to Síkinos and Folégandhros; 1 weekly to Crete; 1 weekly to Mílos, Kímolos, Sérifos and Sífnos; 2–3 weekly to Sýros and Kássos; daily to Mýkonos.

Kéa 1–3 daily to Lávrio (1hr 30min); 4 weekly to Kýthnos; 2 weekly to Sýros.

Kímolos 2 daily kaïkia to Mílos (Pollónia) year-round, 5 in summer; 2–5 weekly to Mílos (Adhámas), Sífnos, Sérifos, Kýthnos and Pireás (7hr); 2 weekly to Folégandhros, Síkinos and Thíra.

Koufoníssi, Skhinoússa, Iráklia 2–3 weekly Náxos; 1–2 weekly to Páros, Sýros and Tínos and Mýkonos; 1 weekly to Dhonoússa, Amorgós and Pireás.

Kýthnos 4–12 weekly to Pireás (3hr 15min); 4–10 weekly to Sérifos, Sífnos, Kímolos and Mílos; 3–4 weekly to Thíra and Folégandhros; 1–2 weekly to Síkinos, Sýros, Íos and Kéa.

Mílos At least daily to Pireás (8hr); Sat–Thurs to Sífnos (2hr), Sérifos and Kýthnos; 2–5 daily kaïkia or 4–6 weekly ferries to Kímolos; 2–3 weekly to Folégandhros, Síkinos, Íos and Thíra; 2 weekly to Sýros; 2 weekly to Crete (Iráklion or Sitía); 2 weekly to Kássos and Kárpathos; 1 weekly to Hálki and Rhodes.

Mýkonos At least 2 daily to Pireás (5hr), Rafína (3hr 30min), Tínos (1hr), Ándhros (2hr 30min) and Sýros (2hr); 2–3 weekly to Amorgós; 2 weekly to Crete (Iráklion), Skiáthos and Thessaloníki; 1–2 weekly to Dhonoússa, Koufoníssi, Skhinoússa and Iráklia; 1 weekly to Pátmos and Foúrni; 3–4 weekly to Ikaría and Sámos; daily to Íos, Náxos and Páros; daily (except Monday) excursion boats to Delos.

Náxos At least 3 daily to Pireás (8hr), Páros (1hr), Íos and Thíra; 6–8 weekly to Sýros; 5–7 to Amorgós; 3 weekly to Crete (Iráklion); 5–6 weekly to Amorgós; 4–5 weekly to Tínos; 5 weekly to Síkinos and Folégandhros; 2 weekly to Ándhros and Rafína; 3 weekly to Anáfi; 3–4 weekly to Rhodes; 2–6 weekly to Ikaría and Sámos; 4 weekly to Astypálea; 1–2 weekly to Kássos and Kárpathos; 1 weekly to Kós and Foúrni; 2–3 weekly to Skiáthos and Thessaloníki; 3–4 weekly to Iráklia, Skhinoússa, Koufoníssi and Dhonoússa.

Páros At least 3 daily to Pireás (7hr), Andíparos, Náxos, Íos, Thíra; 6–8 weekly to Sýros and Tínos; 4 weekly to Iráklion (Crete); 3–6 weekly to Ikaría and Sámos; 4–6 weekly to Síkinos, Folégandhros and Amorgós; 4 weekly to Rafína and Ándhros; 2–3 weekly to Skiáthos and Thessaloníki; daily to Rhodes; 4–6 weekly to Anáfi; 1–2 weekly to Foúrni, Kós, Kássos and Kárpathos; 4 weekly to Astypálea; 2–4 weekly to Koufoníssi, Skhinoússa, Iráklia and Dhonoússa; 1 weekly to Vólos; 1 weekly to Pátmos and Kálymnos; 3–6 weekly to Ikaría and Sámos; at least 1 daily to Mýkonos; at least hourly (from Parikía) to Andíparos in summer, dropping to 3 weekly in winter. There is also a car ferry from Poúnda to Andíparos at least hourly throughout the year.

Sérifos and Sífnos 5–12 weekly to Pireás (4hr 30min), Kýthnos and each other; 5–10 weekly to Mílos; 2–5 weekly to Kímolos; 2–3 weekly to Folégandhros, Síkinos, and Thíra; once weekly to Íos; 2 weekly to Sýros; 1–2 weekly to Crete from Sífnos only; twice weekly from Sífnos to Páros.

Síkinos and Folégandhros 6 weekly between each other, and to Pireás (10hr); 2 weekly to Sýros, Kýthnos, Sérifos, Sífnos, Mílos and Kímolos; 3–6 weekly to Íos, Thíra, Páros and Náxos.

Sýros At least 2 daily to Pireás (4hr), Tínos (1hr), Mýkonos (2hr), Náxos, and Páros; at least 2 weekly to Rafína (3hr 30min) and Ándhros; 3 weekly to Amorgós and the islets behind Náxos; 2–4 weekly to Íos and Thíra; 1 weekly to Síkinos and Folégandhros; 2 weekly to Ikaría, Sámos and Astypálea; 2 weekly to Kéa, Kýthnos, Sérifos, Sífnos, Mílos and Kímolos; 1 weekly to Pátmos, Léros and Lipsí; 2–4 weekly to Skiáthos and Thessaloníki.

Thíra At least 3 daily to Pireás (10–12hr), Páros, Íos and Náxos; 5–6 weekly to Iráklion, Crete (5hr) and Thessaloníki; 6–8 weekly to Síkinos and Folégandhros; 4–6 weekly to Anáfi and Sífnos; daily to Mýkonos; 6–8 weekly to Sýros; 3–5 weekly to Tínos and Skiáthos; 2–4 weekly to Mílos and Kímolos; 1–2 weekly to Kárpathos, Kássos and Sérifos; 2 weekly to Rhodes; 1 weekly to Vólos; 4–6 weekly to Thirassía (plus lots of expensive daily excursion boats in season); 2 weekly mail boats to Anáfi.

Tínos At least 2 daily to Pireás (5hr), Rafína (4hr), Ándhros, Sýros and Mýkonos; 3–4 weekly to Páros and Náxos; 3 weekly to Thíra and Iráklion (Crete); 2–4 weekly Skiáthos and Thessaloníki; 3 weekly to Amorgós; 1 weekly to Íos, Koufoníssi, Skhinoússa, Iráklia and Dhonoússa; also excursion boats calling at Delos and Mýkonos, 1 daily except Monday.

Other services

To simplify the lists above, certain strategic **hydrofoil** and **small-boat services** have been omitted. Of these, the *Express Skopelitis* plies daily in season between Mýkonos and Amorgós, spending each night at the latter and threading through all of the minor isles between it and Náxos, as well as Náxos and Páros (Píso Livádhi), in the course of a week. For anyone familiar with the old *Skopelitis*, the *Express* is a slight improvement in that refreshments are available on board; however this "newer" boat is as overcrowded and unreliable as her long-lost sister. The Seajet catamaran – a small-capacity (and expensive) jet-boat (☎01 414 12 50 for details) – operates daily during summer out of Rafína and connects Sýros, Ándhros, Tínos, Mýkonos, Páros, Náxos and Thíra. Cycladic routes are pretty well mapped out by the three hydrofoil companies – Minoan Flying Dolphins, Speed Lines and Cruises (Santorini Dolphin) and Dolphin Sea Line, with regular services from Zéa (Pireás), Thíra and Rafína respectively. Hydrofoil travel is expensive; however when time is an issue, or for more regular connections to some of the less commonly serviced routes such as the minor islets around Náxos, these handy flying machines are a welcome addition to the conventional fleet.

Flights

There are **airports** on **Páros**, **Mýkonos**, **Thíra**, **Sýros**, **Mílos** and **Náxos**. In season, or during storms when ferries are idle, you have little chance of getting a seat with Olympic Airways at less than three days' notice. Olympic's Athens–Mílos route is probably the best value for money; the other destinations seem deliberately overpriced, in a usually unsuccessful attempt to keep passenger volume manageable. Air Manos has recently introduced June–Sept flights to Thíra, Sýros and Mýkonos. Expect off-season (Oct–April) frequencies to drop by at least eighty percent.

Flights are on Olympic unless otherwise stated.

Athens–Mílos (1–2 daily; 45min)

Athens–Mýkonos (5–6 daily on Olympic; 5 weekly on Air Manos; 45min)

Athens–Náxos (1–2 daily; 45min)

Athens–Páros (3–4 daily; 45min)

Athens–Sýros (1–2 daily on Olympic; 3–4 weekly on Air Manos; 35min)

Athens–Thíra (5–6 daily on Olympic; 6 weekly on Air Manos; 50min)

Mýkonos–Rhodes (2 weekly; 1hr)

Mýkonos–Sámos (2 weekly on Air Manos; 45min)

Mýkonos–Thessaloníki (3 weekly; 1hr 15min)

Mýkonos–Thíra (3–5 weekly; 30min)

Thíra–Iráklion (Crete) (2 weekly; 40min)

Thíra–Rhodes (5 weekly; 1hr)

Thíra–Sámos (2 weekly on Air Manos; 1hr 20min)

Thíra–Thessaloníki (3weekly; 1hr 30min)

CHAPTER THREE

CRETE

Crete (Kríti) is a great deal more than just another Greek island. In many places, especially in the cities or along the developed north coast, it doesn't feel like an island at all, but rather a substantial land in its own right – a mountainous, wealthy and surprisingly cosmopolitan one. But when you lose yourself among the mountains, or on the lesser-known coastal reaches of the south, it has everything you could want of a Greek island and more: great beaches, remote hinterlands and hospitable people.

In **history**, Crete is distinguished above all as the home of Europe's earliest civilization. It was only at the beginning of this century that the legends of King Minos and of a Cretan society that ruled the Greek world in prehistory were confirmed by excavations at **Knossós** and **Festós**. Yet the **Minoans** had a remarkably advanced society, the centre of a maritime trading empire as early as 2000 BC. The artworks produced on Crete at this time are unsurpassed anywhere in the ancient world, and it seems clear that life on Crete in those days was good. This apparently peaceful culture survived at least three major natural disasters. Each time the palaces were destroyed, and each time they

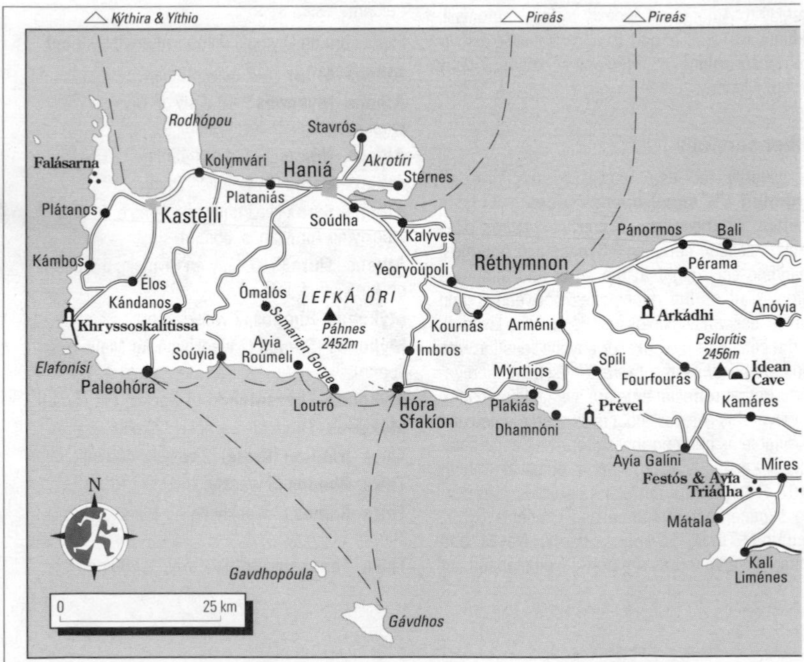

were rebuilt on a grander scale. Only after the last destruction, probably the result of an eruption of Thíra (Santoríni) and subsequent tidal waves and earthquakes, do significant numbers of weapons begin to appear in the ruins. This, together with the appearance of the Greek language, has been interpreted to mean that Mycenaean Greeks had taken control of the island. Nevertheless, for nearly 500 years, by far the longest period of peace the island has seen, Crete was home to a culture well ahead of its time.

The Minoans of Crete probably came originally from Anatolia; at their height they maintained strong links with Egypt and with the people of Asia Minor, and this position as meeting point and strategic fulcrum between east and west has played a major role in Crete's subsequent history. Control of the island passed from Greeks to Romans to Saracens, through the Byzantine empire to Venice, and finally to Turkey for more than two centuries. During World War II, the island was **occupied** by the Germans and attained the dubious distinction of being the first place to be successfully invaded by paratroops.

Today, with a flourishing **agricultural economy**, Crete is one of the few islands which could probably support itself without tourists. Nevertheless, **tourism** is heavily promoted. The northeast coast in particular is overdeveloped, and though there are parts of the south and west coasts that have not been spoiled, they are getting harder to find. By contrast, the high mountains of the interior are still barely touched, and one of the best things to do on Crete is to **rent a vehicle** and explore the remoter villages.

Where to go

Every part of Crete has its loyal devotees and it's hard to pick out highlights, but generally if you want to get away from it all you should head west, towards **Haniá** and the

ACCOMMODATION PRICE CODES

Throughout the book we've used the following **price codes** to denote the cheapest available double room in each establishment in high season. Out of season, rates can drop by more than fifty percent, especially if you are staying for three or more nights. Single rooms, where available, cost around seventy percent of the price of a double.

Rented private rooms on the islands usually fall into the ② or ③ categories, depending on their location and facilities, and the season; a few in the ④ category are more like plush self-catering apartments. They are not generally available from late October through to the beginning of April, when only hotels tend to remain open.

① Up to 6000dr	④ 12,000–16,000dr
② 6000–9000dr	⑤ 16,000–20,000dr
③ 9000–12,000dr	⑥ 20,000dr and upwards

Note: Youth hostels typically charge 2000–2500dr for a dormitory bed.

For more accommodation details, see pp.44–47.

smaller, less well-connected places along the south and west coasts. It is in this part of the island that the White Mountains rise, while below them yawns the famous **Samarian Gorge**. The far east, around **Sitía**, is also relatively unscathed.

Whatever you do, your first main priority will probably be to leave **Iráklion** (Heraklion) as quickly as possible, having paid the obligatory, and rewarding, visit to the **Archeological Museum** and nearby **Knossós**. The other great Minoan sites cluster around the middle of the island: **Festós** and **Ayía Triádha** in the south (with Roman **Górtys** to provide contrast), and **Mália** on the north coast. Almost wherever you go, though, you'll find a reminder of the island's history, whether it's the town of **Gourniá** near the cosmopolitan resort of **Áyios Nikólaos**, the exquisitely sited palace of **Zákros** in the far east, or the lesser sites scattered around the west. Unexpected highlights include Crete's Venetian forts at **Réthymnon** and **Frangokástello**; its hundreds of frescoed Byzantine churches, most famously at **Kritsá**; and, at Réthymnon and Haniá, the cluttered old Venetian and Turkish quarters.

Climate

Crete has by far the longest summers in Greece, and you can get a decent tan here right into October and swim at least from May until November. The one seasonal blight is the *meltémi*, a northerly wind which regularly blows harder here and more continuously than anywhere else in Greece – the best of several reasons for avoiding an **August** visit.

IRÁKLION, KNOSSÓS AND CENTRAL CRETE

Many visitors to Crete arrive in the island's capital, **Iráklion** (Heraklion), but it's not an outstandingly beautiful city, nor one where you'll want to stay much longer than it takes to visit the **Archeological Museum** and nearby **Knossós**. Iráklion itself, though it has its good points – superb fortifications, a fine market, atmospheric old alleys and some interesting lesser museums – is for the most part an experience in survival: despite a recent makeover of central areas by the city hall it remains modern, raucous, traffic-laden and overcrowded.

The area immediately around the city is less touristy than you might expect, mainly because there are few decent beaches of any size on this central part of the coast. To

PETER WILSON

Harbour, Éyina

MARC S. DUBIN

Drydock for kaïkia, Parikía, Páros

MARC S. DUBIN

Church in Kástro, Síkinos

ROB STEINBERGER

The clear waters of Delos

ROB STEINBERGER

The Sanctuary of Dionysos, Delos

MARC S. DUBIN

Stairpath to Hóra, Sérifos

PETER WILSON

Large storage jar, Malia palace, Crete

PETER WILSON

West beach, Paleohóra, Crete

PETER WILSON

A windmill at Toploú Monastery, Crete

PETER WILSON

Venetian houses, Réthymnon, Crete

the west, mountains drop straight into the sea virtually all the way to Réthymnon, with just two significant coastal settlements – **Ayía Pelayía**, a sizable resort, and **Balí**, which is gradually becoming one. Eastwards, the main resorts are at least 30km away, at **Hersónissos** and beyond, although there is a string of rather unattractive developments all the way there. Inland, there's agricultural country, some of the richest on the island, Crete's best vineyards, and a series of wealthy but rather dull villages. Directly behind the capital rises **Mount Ioúktas** with its characteristic profile of Zeus; to the west the Psiloritis massif spreads around the peak of **Mount Ídha** (Psiloritis), the island's highest mountain. On the south coast there are few roads and little development of any kind, except at **Ayía Galíni** in the southwest, a nominal fishing village long since swamped with tourists, and **Mátala**, which has thrown out the hippies that made it famous and is now crowded with package-trippers. **Léndas** has to some extent occupied Mátala's old niche.

Despite the lack of resorts, there seem constantly to be thousands of people trekking back and forth across the centre of the island. This is largely because of the superb archeological sites in the south: **Festós**, second of the Minoan palaces, with its attendant villa at **Ayía Triádha**, and **Górtys**, capital of Roman Crete.

Iráklion

The best way to approach **IRÁKLION** is by sea: that way you see the city as it should be seen, with Mount Ioúktas rising behind and the Psiloritis range to the west. As you get closer, it's the city walls that first stand out, still dominating and fully encircling the oldest part of town; finally you sail in past the great **fort** defending the harbour entrance. Unfortunately, big ships no longer dock in the old port but at great modern concrete wharves alongside, which neatly sums up Iráklion itself. Many of the old parts have been restored from the bottom up, but they're of no relevance to the dust and noise that characterizes much of the city today. In recent times, however, Iráklion's administrators have been giving belated attention to dealing with some of the image problems, and large tracts of the centre – particularly the focal Platía Eleftherías – have been landscaped and refurbished with the aim of presenting a less daunting prospect to the visitor.

Orientation, arrival and information

Virtually everything you're likely to want to see in Iráklion lies within the walled city, and even here the majority of the interest falls into a relatively small sector, the northeastern corner. The most vital thoroughfare, **25-Avgoústou**, links the harbour with the commercial city centre. At the bottom it is lined with shipping and travel agencies and rental outlets, but as you climb these give way to banks, restaurants and stores. **Platía Venizélou** (or Fountain Square), off to the right, is crowded with cafés and restaurants; behind Venizélou lies **El Greco Park** (actually a rather cramped garden), with more bars, while on the opposite side of 25-Avgoústou are some of the more interesting of Iráklion's older buildings. Further up 25-Avgoústou, **Kalokerinoú** leads down to Haniá Gate and westwards out of the city; straight ahead, **Odhós 1821** is a major shopping street, and adjacent 1866 is given over to the animated **market**. To the left, Dhikeosínis heads for the city's main square, **Platía Eleftherías**, paralleled by the touristy pedestrian alley, Dhedhálou, the direct link between the two squares. The newly revamped Eleftherías is very much the traditional centre of the city, both for

The telephone code for Iráklion is ☎081

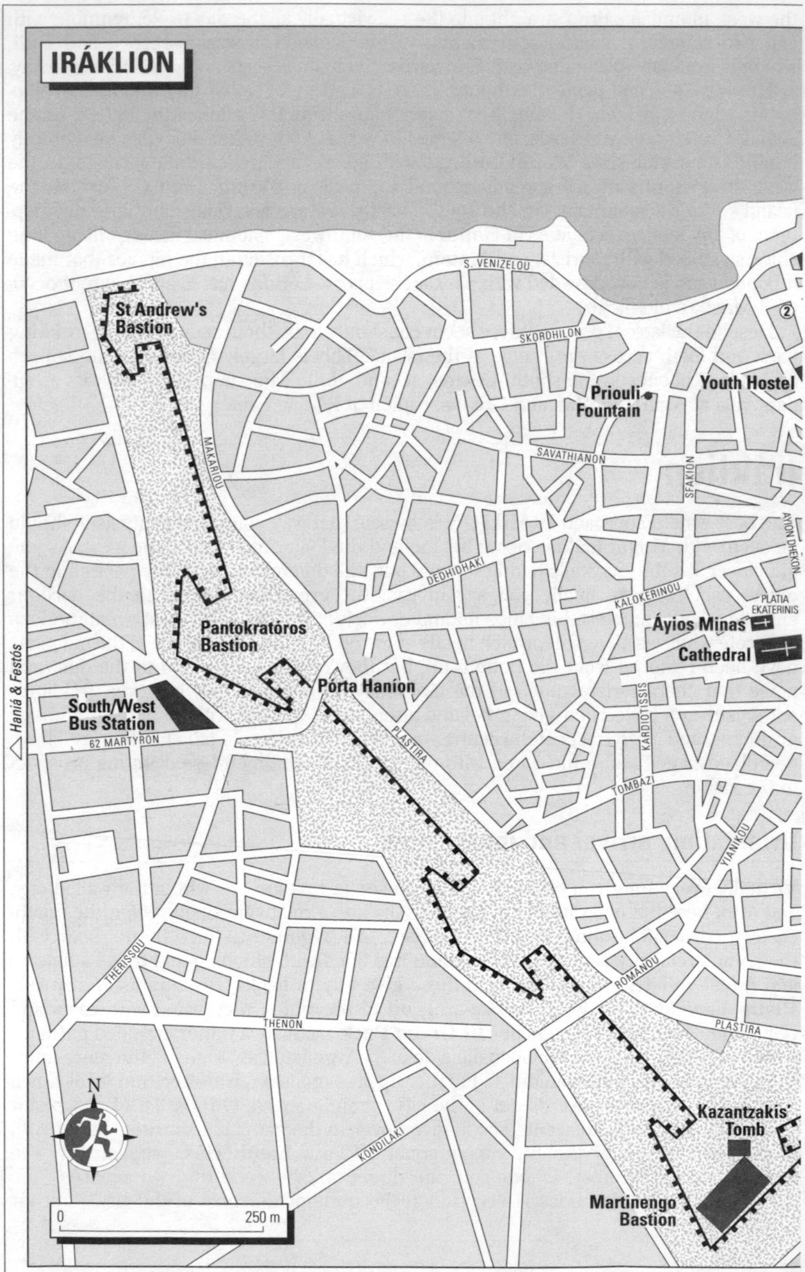
IRÁKLION
S. VENIZELOU
St Andrew's Bastion
SKORDHILON
Youth Hostel
Priouli Fountain
MAKARIOU
SAVATHIANON
SFAKION
AYION DHEKON
DEDHIDHAKI
KALOKERINOU
PLATIA EKATERINIS
Áyios Minas
Cathedral
Pantokratóros Bastion
Pórta Haníon
Haniá & Festós
South/West Bus Station
62 MARTYRON
PLASTIRA
KARDIOTISSIS
TOMBAZI
YIANIKOU
THERISSOU
ROMANOU
THENON
PLASTIRA
N
Kazantzakis' Tomb
KONDILAKI
Martinengo Bastion
0
250 m

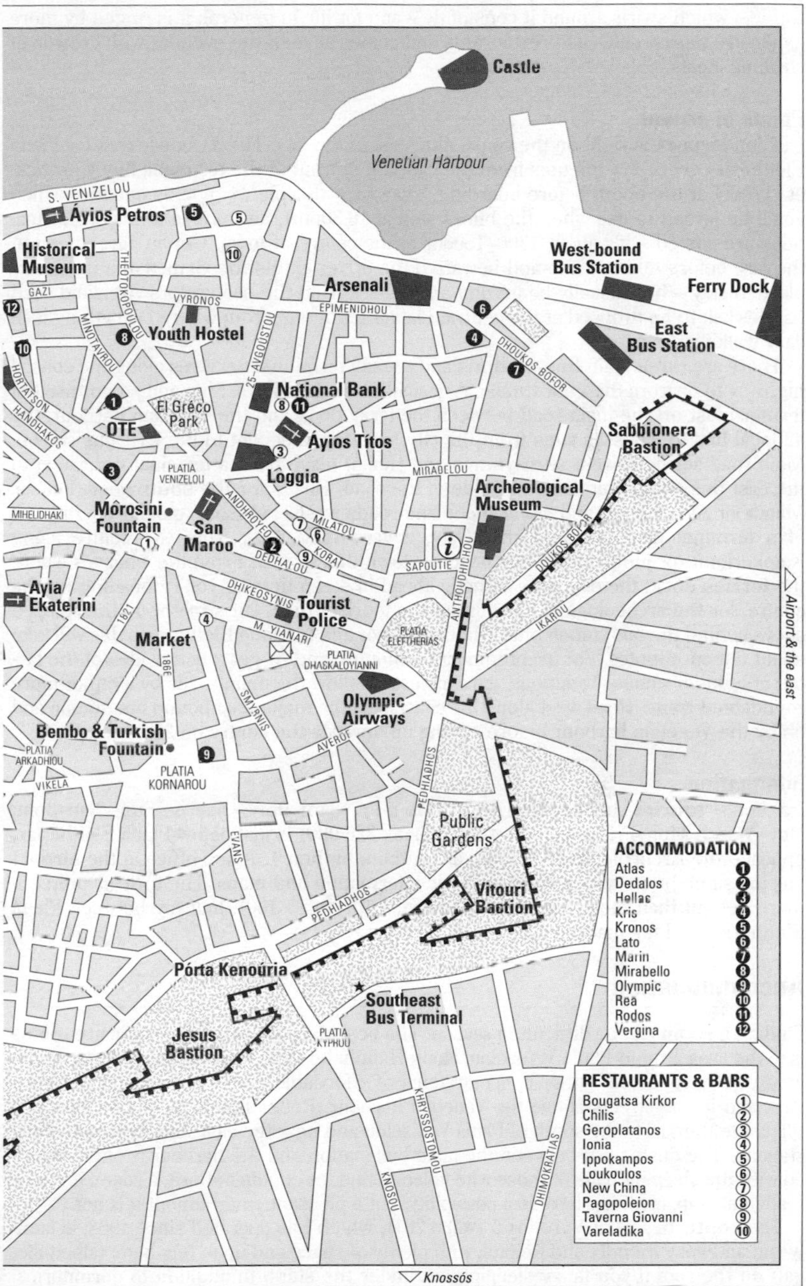

Castle
Venetian Harbour
S. VENIZELOU
Áyios Petros
Historical Museum
West-bound Bus Station
Ferry Dock
Arsenali
GAZI
VYRONOS
EPIMENIDHOU
THEOTOKOPOULOU
MINOTAVROU
Youth Hostel
25-AVGOUSTOU
East Bus Station
DHOUKOS BOFOR
HORTATSON
HANDHAKOS
National Bank
El Gréco Park
OTE
Áyios Títos
Sabbionera Bastion
PLATIA VENIZELOU
Loggia
MIRABELLOU
Archeological Museum
MIHELIDHAKI
Môrosini Fountain
San Maroo
ANDHROYEO
MILATOU
KORAI
DEDHALOU
SAPOUTIE
ANTHOUDHICHOU
DOUKOS BOFOR
DHIKEOSYNIS
Ayia Ekaterini
Tourist Police
M. YIANARI
1821
Market
1866
PLATIA ELEFTHERIAS
PLATIA DHASKALOYIANNI
IKAROU
Airport & the east
SMYRNIS
Olympic Airways
AVEROF
Bembo & Turkish Fountain
PLATIA ARKADHIOU
PLATIA KORNAROU
VIKELA
PEDHIADHOS
Public Gardens
EVANS
PEDHIADHOS
Vitouri Baction
Pórta Kenoúria
Southeast Bus Terminal
Jesus Bastion
PLATIA KYPHUU
KHRYSSOSTOMOU
KNOSOU
DHIMOKRATIAS
Knossós
ACCOMMODATION
Atlas 1
Dedalos 2
Hellas 3
Kris 4
Kronos 5
Lato 6
Marin 7
Mirabello 8
Olympic 9
Rea 10
Rodos 11
Vergina 12
RESTAURANTS & BARS
Bougatsa Kirkor 1
Chilis 2
Geroplatanos 3
Ionia 4
Ippokampos 5
Loukoulos 6
New China 7
Pagopoleion 8
Taverna Giovanni 9
Vareladika 10

traffic – which swirls around it constantly – and for life in general; it is ringed by more expensive tourist cafés and restaurants and comes alive in the evening with crowds of strolling locals.

Points of arrival

Iráklion **airport** is right on the coast, 4km east of the city. The #1 bus leaves for Platía Eleftherías every few minutes from the car park in front of the terminal; buy your ticket (170dr) at the booth before boarding. There are also plenty of taxis outside (which you'll be forced to use when the buses stop at 10.30pm), and prices to major destinations are posted – it's about 1200–1500dr to the centre of town. Get an agreement on the fare before taking a cab and beware if the driver extols the virtues of a particular place to stay – he'll usually be getting a kick-back from the proprietors. To avoid such hassles ask to be dropped at the central Platía Eleftherías, from where everything is in easy walking distance.

There are three main **bus stations** and a small terminus. Services along the coastal highway to or from the **east** (Mália, Áyios Nikólaos, Ierápetra, Sitía and so on) use the terminal just off the main road between the ferry dock and the Venetian harbour; the #2 local bus to Knossós runs from the city bus stop, adjacent to the east bus station. Main road services **west** (Réthymnon and Haniá) leave from a terminal right next to the east bus station on the other side of the road. Buses for the **southwest** (Festós, Mátala or Ayía Galíni) and along the inland roads west (Týlissos, Anóyia) operate out of a terminal just outside Haniá Gate, a very long walk from the centre along Kalokerinoú (or jump on any bus heading down this street). From the wharves where the **ferries** dock, the city rises directly ahead in steep tiers. If you're heading for the centre, for the archeological museum or the tourist office, cut straight up the stepped alleys behind the bus station onto Dhoúkos Bofór and to Platía Eleftherías; this will take about fifteen minutes. For accommodation though, and to get a better idea of the layout of Iráklion's main attractions, it's simplest to follow the main roads by a rather more roundabout route. Head west along the coast, past the major east-bound bus station and on by the Venetian harbour before cutting up towards the centre on 25-Avgoústou.

Information

Iráklion's **tourist office** (April–Oct Mon–Fri 8am–9pm, Sat & Sun 9am–3pm; Nov–March Mon–Fri 8am–3pm; ☎228 225, fax 226 020) is just below Platía Eleftherías, opposite the Archeological Museum at Zanthoudhídhou 1. A sub-office at the **airport** has the same hours and is good for basic information and maps. The **tourist police** – more helpful than most – are at Dhikeosýnis 10 (☎283 190), halfway between Platía Eleftherías and the market.

Accommodation

Finding a **room** can be difficult in season. The best place to look for inexpensive rooms is in the area around Platía Venizélou, along Hándhakos and towards the harbour to the west of 25-Avgoústou. Other concentrations of affordable places are around El Greco park and in the streets above the Venetian harbour. Better hotels mostly lie closer to Platía Eleftherías, to the south of Platía Venizélou and near the east- and west-bound bus stations. The dusty park between the main bus station and the harbour is often crowded with the sleeping bags of those who failed to find, or couldn't afford, a room; if you're really hard up, crashing here is a possibility, but a pleasant environment it is not.

The **youth hostel** at Výronos 5 (☎286 281), which has operated since 1963, is family run and very friendly and helpful, with plenty of space and up to fifty beds (albeit illegal) on the roof if you fancy sleeping out under the stars. In addition to dormitories, family and double rooms are also available; there are hot showers, breakfast and TV. There are no **campsites** near Iráklion. The nearest sites are both found to the east of the city – *Creta Camping* at Goúves (16km) and *Caravan Camping* at Hersónissos (28km).

Atlas, Kandanoléon 11 (☎288 989). A rather run-down old pension in a convenient but noisy alley between Platía Venizélou and El Greco Park. There's a pleasant roof garden, and freshly squeezed orange juice for breakfast. ①.

Dedalos, Dhedhálou 15 (☎241 812, fax 224 391). Very centrally placed on the pedestrianized alley between Venizélou and Eleftherías. Decent balcony rooms with private bath. ③.

Hellas, Hándhakos 24 (☎280 858, fax 284 442). Hostel-type place with simple doubles, and dormitory rooms favoured by younger travellers. Also has a roof garden and snack bar. ①.

Kris, Dhoúkos Bofór 2, near the Venetian harbour (☎223 221). Apartment-style rooms with kitchenette, fridge, great balcony views and friendly female proprietor. ③.

Kronos, Agaráthou 2, west of 25-Avgoústou (☎282 240, fax 285 853). Pleasant, friendly and modern hotel with seaview and baths in all rooms. ③.

Lato, Epomenídhou 15 (☎228 103, fax 240 350). Stylish and luxurious hotel where the air-con rooms have mini-bar, TV and seaview balcony with breakfast included. ⑥.

Marin, Dhoúkos Bofór 10, (☎224 736, fax 224 730). Comfortable and good-value rooms with bath, overlooking the Venetian harbour; get a balcony room at the front for a great view. Very convenient for the bus stations and the Archeological Museum. ②.

Mirabello, Theotokopoúlou 20 (☎285 052, fax 225 852). Good-value, family-run place with some rooms en-suite in a quiet street close to El Greco Park. ③.

Olympic, Platía Kornárou (☎288 861, fax 222 512). Overlooking the busy platía and the famous Bembo and Turkish fountains. One of the many hotels built in the 1960s, but one of the few that has been refurbished. ④.

Rea, Kalimeráki 1 (☎223 638, fax 242 189). A friendly, comfortable and clean pension in a quiet street. Some rooms with washbasin, others with own shower. ②.

Rodos, Platía Áyios Títos (☎228 519). Homely no-frills double and triple rooms place, on a picturesque square with a great breakfast bar next door. ①.

Vergina, Hortátson 32 (☎242 739). Basic but pleasant rooms (with washbasins) in quiet street around a courtyard with a giant banana tree. ①.

The Town

From the port, the town rises overhead, and you can cut up the stepped alleys for a direct approach to Platía Eleftherías (Liberty Square) and the Archeological Museum. The easiest way to the middle of things, though, is to head west along the coast road, past the main bus stations and the *arsenáli*, and then up 25-Avgoústou, which leads into Platía Venizélou. This is crowded with Iraklian youth, patronizing outdoor cafés (marginally cheaper than those on Eleftherías), and with travellers who've arranged to meet in "Fountain Square". The recently restored Morosini fountain itself is not particularly spectacular at first glance, but on closer inspection is really a very beautiful work; it was built by Venetian governor Francesco Morosini in the seventeenth century, incorporating four lions which were some three hundred years old even then. From the platía you can strike up Dhedhálou, a pedestrianized street full of tourist shops and restaurants, or continue on 25-Avgoústou to a major traffic junction. To the right, Kalokerinoú leads west out of the city, the market lies straight ahead, and Platía Eleftherías is a short walk to the left up Dhikeosínis.

Platía Eleftherías and the Archeological Museum

The recently revamped **Platía Eleftherías**, with seats shaded by palms and eucalyptuses is very much the traditional heart of the city: traffic swirls around it constantly, and on summer evenings strolling hordes jam its expensive cafés and restaurants. Most of Iráklion's more expensive shops are in the streets leading off the platía.

The **Archeological Museum** (Mon 12.30–7pm, Tues–Sun 8am–7pm; 1500dr) is nearby, directly opposite the EOT office. Almost every important prehistoric and Minoan find on Crete is included in this fabulous, if bewilderingly large, collection. The museum tends to be crowded, especially when a guided tour stampedes through, but it's worth taking time over. You can't hope to see everything, nor can we attempt to describe it all (several good museum guides are sold here; the best probably being the glossy one by J.A. Sakellarakis), but highlights include the **mosaics** in Room 2 (galleries are arranged basically in chronological order), the famous **inscribed disc** from Festós in Room 3 (itself the subject of several books), most of Room 4, especially the magnificent bull's head **rhyton** (drinking vessel), the **jewellery** in Room 6 (and everywhere) and the engraved **black vases** in Room 7. Save some of your time and energy for upstairs, where the **Hall of the Frescoes**, with intricately reconstructed fragments of the wall paintings from Knossós and other sites, is especially wonderful.

Walls and fortifications

The massive **Venetian walls**, in places up to fifteen metres thick, are the most obvious evidence of Iráklion's later history. Though their fabric is incredibly well preserved, access is virtually nonexistent. It is possible, just, to walk along them from St Anthony's bastion over the sea in the west, as far as the tomb of Nikos Kazantzakis, Cretan author of *Zorba the Greek*, whose epitaph reads: "I believe in nothing, I hope for nothing, I am free." At weekends, Iraklians gather here to pay their respects and enjoy a free view of the soccer matches played by the island's first-division team, OFI Crete, in the stadium below. If the walls seem altogether too much effort, the **port fortifications** are very much easier to see. Stroll out along the jetty (crowded with courting couples after dark) and you can get inside the sixteenth-century **castle** (Mon–Sat 8am–6pm, Sun 10am–3pm; 500dr) at the harbour entrance, emblazoned with the Venetian Lion of St Mark. Standing atop this, you can begin to understand how Iráklion (or Candia as it was known until the seventeenth century) withstood a 22-year siege before finally falling to the Ottomans. On the landward side of the port, the Venetian **arsenáli** (arsenals) can also be seen, their arches rather lost amid the concrete road system all around.

Churches, icons and the historical museum

From the harbour, 25-Avgoústou will take you up past most of the rest of what's interesting. The **church of Áyios Títos**, on the left as you approach Platía Venizélou, borders a pleasant little platía. It looks magnificent principally because, like most of the churches here, it was adapted by the Turks as a mosque and only reconsecrated in 1925; consequently it has been renovated on numerous occasions. On the top side of this platía, abutting 25-Avgoústou, is the Venetian **city hall** with its famous loggia, again almost entirely rebuilt. Just above this, facing Platía Venizélou, is the **church of San Marco**, its steps usually crowded with the overflow of people milling around in the platía. Neither of these last two buildings has found a permanent role in its refurbished state, but both are generally open to house some kind of exhibition or craft show.

Slightly away from the obvious city-centre circuit, but still within the bounds of the walls, there are a couple of lesser museums worth seeing if you have the time. First of these is the excellent collection of **icons** in the **church of Ayía Ekateríni** (Mon–Sat 9am–1.30pm, Tues, Thurs & Fri also 5–7pm; 500dr), an ancient building just below the undistinguished cathedral, off Kalokerinoú. The finest here are six large scenes by Mihaïl Damaskinos (a near-contemporary of El Greco) who fused Byzantine and Renaissance influences. Supposedly both Damaskinos and El Greco studied at Ayía Ekateríni in the sixteenth century, when it functioned as a sort of monastic art school.

The **historical museum** (Mon–Fri 9am–1pm; 500dr) is some way from here, down near the waterfront opposite the stark *Xenia* hotel. Its display of folk costumes and jumble of local memorabilia includes the reconstructed studies of both Nikos Kazantzakis and Emanuel Tsouderos (Cretan statesman and Greek prime minister). There's enough variety to satisfy just about anyone, including the only El Greco painting on Crete, *View of Mount Sinai and the Monastery of St Catherine*.

The beaches

Iráklion's **beaches** are some way out, whether east or west of town. In either direction they're easily accessible by bus: #6 west from the stop outside the *Astoria* hotel in Platía Eleftherías; #7 east from the stop opposite this, under the trees in the centre of the platía.

Almyrós (or Ammoudhári) to the west has been subjected to a degree of development, comprising a campsite, several medium-size hotels and one giant one (the *Zeus Beach*, in the shadow of the power station at the far end), which makes the beach hard to get to without walking through or past something built up.

Amnissós, to the east, is the better choice, with several tavernas and the added amusement of planes swooping in immediately overhead to land. This is where most locals go on their afternoons off; the furthest of the beaches is the best, although new hotels are encroaching here, too. Little remains here to indicate the once-flourishing port of Knossós aside from a rather dull, fenced-in dig. If you're seriously into antiquities, however, you'll find a more rewarding site in the small villa, known as **Nírou Háni** (Tues–Sun 8.30am–3pm; free) at **Háni Kokkíni**, the first of the full-blown resort developments east of Iráklion.

Eating

Big city as it is, Iráklion disappoints when it comes to eating. The cafés and tavernas of platías **Venizélou** and **Eleftherías** are essential places to sit and watch the world pass, but their food is expensive and mediocre. One striking exception is *Bougatsa Kirkor*, by the Morosini fountain in Venizélou, where you can sample authentic *bougátsa*; alternatively, try a plate of *loukoumádhes*, available from a number of cafés at the top of Dhikeosínis. The cafés and tavernas on **Dhedhálou**, the pedestrian alley linking the two main platías, are very run of the mill, persistent waiters enticing you in with faded photographs of what appears to be food.

A more atmospheric option is to head for the little alley, **Fotíou Theodhosáki**, which runs through from the market to Odhós Evans. It is entirely lined with the tables of rival taverna owners, certainly authentic and catering for market traders and their customers as well as tourists. Compared with some, they often look a little grimy, but they are by no means cheap, which can come as a surprise. Nearby, at the corner of Evans and Yiánari, is the long-established *Ionia* taverna, which is the sort of place to come to if you are in need of a substantial, no-nonsense feed, with a good range of Greek dishes.

A relaxed lunchtime venue in the **centre** of town is *Geroplatanos* with tables on the leafy Platía Ayíou Títou beside the church of the same name. Across from here is a stylish new bar *Pagopoleion* (Ice Factory), good for breakfast, snacks and meals. It's the creation of photographic artist Chrissy Karelli, who has preserved a strident inscription on one wall, left by the Nazi occupiers who used local labour to run what was then Iráklion's only ice factory. Still near the centre, just off Eleftherías at **Platía Dhaskaloyiánni** (where the post office is), are some inexpensive and unexceptional tavernas; by day the platía is however a pleasant and relaxing venue, if not for a meal then to sit at one of its cafés, which transform themselves into more raucous and crowded music bars after dark. Nearer Venizélou, try exploring some of the backstreets to the east, off Dhedhálou and behind the loggia. The *Taverna Giovanni*, on the alley Koráï parallel to Dhedhálou, is one of the better tavernas in Iráklion, although the pricey food and an expensive wine list seem aimed more at Iráklion's smart set than the casual visitor. Should you have a craving for non-Greek food, there is Italian at the equally expensive *Loukoulos* and Chinese at the *New China Restaurant*, both with leafy courtyards and in the same street as the *Taverna Giovanni*. More reasonable prices are on offer at the excellent new taverna *Vareladika*, Monís Agaráthou 13, close to the Venetian harbour which offers a wide range of Cretan specialities in a stylish setting. Mexican tacos and beers are on offer at *Chilis*, Hándhakos 71 on the west side of the central zone – an area with many lively bars and cafés.

The **waterfront** is dotted with fish tavernas with little to recommend them. Instead, turn left at the bottom of 25-Avgoústou and cross the road to *Ippokampos*, which specializes in excellent-value fish dishes and mezédhes at moderate prices. It is deservedly popular with locals and is often crowded late into the evening: you may have to wait in line or turn up earlier than the Greeks eat. Even if you see no space it is worth asking as the owner may suddenly disappear inside the taverna and emerge with yet another table to carry further down the pavement.

For **snacks** and **takeaways**, there's a whole group of *souvláki* stalls clustering around the top of 25-Avgoústou at the entrance to El Greco Park, which is handy if you need somewhere to sit and eat. For *tyrópita* and *spanakópita* (cheese or spinach pies) and other pastries, sweet or savoury, there are no shortage of zaharoplastía and places such as *Everest* – just north of the Morosini fountain – which does takeaways of these as well as a whole bunch of other savouries. If you want to buy your own food, the **market** on Odhós 1866 is the place to go; it's an attraction in itself, and does a great line in modestly priced Cretan herbs (including saffron) to take home.

Drinking, nightlife and entertainment

Iráklion is a bit of a damp squib as far as **nightlife** goes, certainly when compared with many other towns on the island. If you're determined, however, there are a few city-centre possibilities, and plenty of options if all you want to do is sit and **drink**. In addition, there are a number of **cinemas** scattered about: check the posters on the boards by the tourist police office.

Bars

Bars tend to fan out into the streets around Hándhakos; among a number of new-style places, *Jasmin*, Ayiostefanitón 6, is tucked in an alley on the left mid-way down Hándhakos, and serves a variety of teas (including the Cretan *dhíktamo* – a panacea used by the ancients) with easy jazz and rock as background music. At the beginning of Hándhakos is *Tasso's*, a popular hangout for young hostellers, lively at night and with good breakfasts to help you recover in the morning. *Utopia*, also on Hándhakos and the nearby *Bonsai* and *Kallioton* are more places to try in an area that is fast becoming Iráklion's major focus for younger revellers.

Another animated place nearer the centre is Platía Koráï behind Dhedhálou (up from the *Giovanni* restaurant listed above), where there are several pricey bars (including the trendy *Flash* and *Notos*) with outdoor tables, which are popular with students in term time. Enjoy a game of backgammon here during the day or early evening; later it can get extremely lively with many more distractions. In and around **Platía Venizélou** (Fountain Square), there are many bars, again some are very fashionable, with *De Facto* being one of the most popular. This is one of the new breed of kafenío emerging in Iráklion, attracting younger people: the drinks are **cocktails** rather than *rakí*, the music is Western or modern Greek, and there are prices to match. Another is *Rebels*, Perdhikári 3 at the junction with Koráï, which has a good atmosphere with a cluster of similar places nearby; there are similar bars along Kandanoléon, off El Greco Park.

Clubs and discos

For **discos** proper, there is a large selection, even if they are all playing techno at the moment, interspersed with Greek music (not the Greek music you get for tourists). *Genesis* is the most popular, down towards the harbour at the bottom of Dhoúkos Bofór, below the Archeological Museum. The nearby *Kastro* has nightly *lýra* and *bouzoúki* entertainment which you can take in for the price of a drink, although many locals take advantage of their restaurant to have a meal as well. Another cluster of nightclubs can be found on Ikárou, about a twenty-minute walk or easy taxi ride away. Retrace your steps towards the Archeological Museum, but before emerging onto Platía Eleftherías turn left downhill and follow the main road, Ikárou. Here you'll find the *Minoica*, the *Korus Club* and the *Athina*, all playing similar music and popular with young Iraklians.

Listings

Airlines Air Greece, Dhedhálou 36 (☎330 074); Cronus Air, at the airport (☎222 217); Olympic, Platía Eleftherías (☎229 191). Charter airlines flying in to Iráklion mostly use local travel agents as their representatives.

Airport For airport information call ☎245 644. Bus #1 runs from Platía Eleftherías to the airport every few minutes; buy a ticket (170dr) from the booth outside the *Astoria Hotel* first.

Banks There are now 24hr cash dispensers all over town, but the main bank branches are on 25-Avgoústou.

Car and bike rental 25-Avgoústou is lined with rental companies, but you'll often find cheaper rates on the backstreets; it's always worth asking for discounts. Good places to start include: Blue Sea, Kosmá Zótou 7, near the bottom of 25-Avgoústou (☎241 097) for bikes; Motor Club, Platía Ánglon 1 at the bottom of 25-Avgoústou facing the port (☎222 408), Eurocreta, Sapotié 2 (☎226 700) near the Archeological Museum, and Ritz in the *Hotel Rea*, Kalimeráki 1 (☎223 638), are worth trying for cars; Sun Rise, 25-Avgoústou 46 (☎221 609), does both cars and bikes.

Ferry tickets Available from Minoan Lines, 25-Avgoústou 78 (☎229 646; handles the islands and Athens), ANEK Lines, 25-Avgoústou 33 (☎222 481; Athens only), or any of the travel agents listed on p.186.

Hospital Most central is the hospital on Apollónion, southwest of Platía Kornárou, between Albér and Moussoúrou.

Laundry Washsalon, Hándhakos 18 (Mon–Sat 8am–8pm) is reliable and also does service washes (2000dr for 6kg). The new Laundry Perfect at Malikoúti 32, north of the Archeological Museum, will do the same for 1800dr.

Left luggage Offices in the east-bound and southwest bus stations (daily 6am–8pm; 300dr per bag per day), as well as a commercial agency at Hándhakos 18 (open 24hrs; large locker 450dr per day). You can also leave bags at the youth hostel (even if you don't stay there) for 500dr per bag per day. If you want to leave your bag while you go off on a bike for a day or two, the rental company should be prepared to store it.

Newspapers and books For English-language newspapers and novels, as well as local guides and maps, Dhedhálou is the best bet, where Bibliopoleio (no. 6) stocks a wide selection of books in English. Planet International Bookstore, behind Platía Venizélou at the corner of Hándhakos and Kydhonías, has the island's biggest stock of English-language titles.

Pharmacies Plentiful on the main shopping streets – at least one is open 24hr on a rota basis: the others will have a sign on the door indicating which it is. There are traditional herbalists in the market.

Post office Main office in Platía Dhaskaloyiánnis, off Eleftherías (Mon–Fri 7.30am–8pm). There's also a temporary office (a van) at the entrance to El Greco Park (daily 7.30am–2pm).

Taxis Major taxi ranks in Platía Eleftherías and by the Morosini Fountain (Platía Kalergón), or call ☎210 102 or 210 168. Prices displayed on boards at ranks.

Telephones The OTE head office is on the west side of El Greco Park; it's open 8am–11pm, but most overseas destinations can now be phoned from street booths using a phone card (*telekárta*) obtainable from a *períptero* (kiosk).

Toilets In El Greco Park and the public gardens near the cathedral, or at the bus stations and the Archeological Museum (no need to pay entrance charge to use them).

Travel agencies Budget operators and student specialists include the extremely helpful Blavakis Travel, Platía Kallergón 8, just off 25-Avgoústou by the entrance to El Greco Park (☎282 541), and Prince Travel, 25-Avgoústou 30 (☎282 706). For excursions around the island, villa rentals and so on, the bigger operators are probably easier: Irman Travel, Dhedhálou 26 (☎242 527), or Creta Travel Bureau, Epimenídhou 20–22 (☎227 002). The latter is also the local American Express agent.

Knossós

KNOSSÓS, the largest of the **Minoan palaces**, reached its cultural peak more than three thousand years ago, though a town of some importance persisted here well into the Roman era. It lies on a low, largely man-made hill some 5km southeast of Iráklion; the surrounding hillsides are rich in lesser remains spanning 25 centuries, starting at the beginning of the second millennium BC.

Barely a hundred years ago the palace existed only in mythology. Knossós was the court of the legendary King Minos, whose wife Pasiphae bore the Minotaur, half-bull, half-man. Here the labyrinth was constructed by Daedalus to contain the monster, and youths were brought from Athens as human sacrifice until Theseus arrived to slay the beast, and with Ariadne's help, escape its lair. The discovery of the palace, and the interplay of these legends with fact, is among the most amazing tales of modern archeology. Heinrich Schliemann, the German excavator of Troy, suspected that a major Minoan palace lay under the various tumuli here, but was denied the necessary permission to dig by the local Ottoman authorities at the end of the last century. It was left for Sir Arthur Evans, whose name is indelibly associated with Knossós, to excavate the site, from 1900 onwards.

The #2 local **bus** sets off every ten minutes from the Iráklion's city bus stands (adjacent to the east-bound bus station), runs up 25-Avgoústou (with a stop by Platía Venizélou) and out of town on Odhós 1821 and Evans. At Knossós, outside the fenced site, stands the *caravanserai* where ancient wayfarers would rest and water their animals. Head out onto the road and you'll find no lack of watering holes for modern travellers either – a string of rather pricey tavernas and tacky souvenir stands. There are several **rooms** for rent here, and if you're really into Minoan culture, there's a lot to be said for staying out this way to get an early start. Be warned, though, that it's expensive and unashamedly commercial.

The site

Daily: April–Sept 8am–7pm; Oct–March 8.30am–3pm; 1500dr.

As soon as you enter the **Palace of Knossós** through the West Court, the ancient ceremonial entrance, it is clear how the legends of the labyrinth grew up around it. Even with a detailed plan, it's almost impossible to find your way around the site with any success. The best advice is not to try; wander around for long enough and you'll eventually stumble upon everything. If you're worried about missing the highlights, you can always tag along with one of the constant guided tours for a while, catching the patter and then backtracking to absorb the detail when the crowd has moved on. Outside the period December to February you won't get the place to yourself, whenever you come, but exploring on your own does give you the opportunity to appreciate individual parts of the palace in the brief lulls between groups.

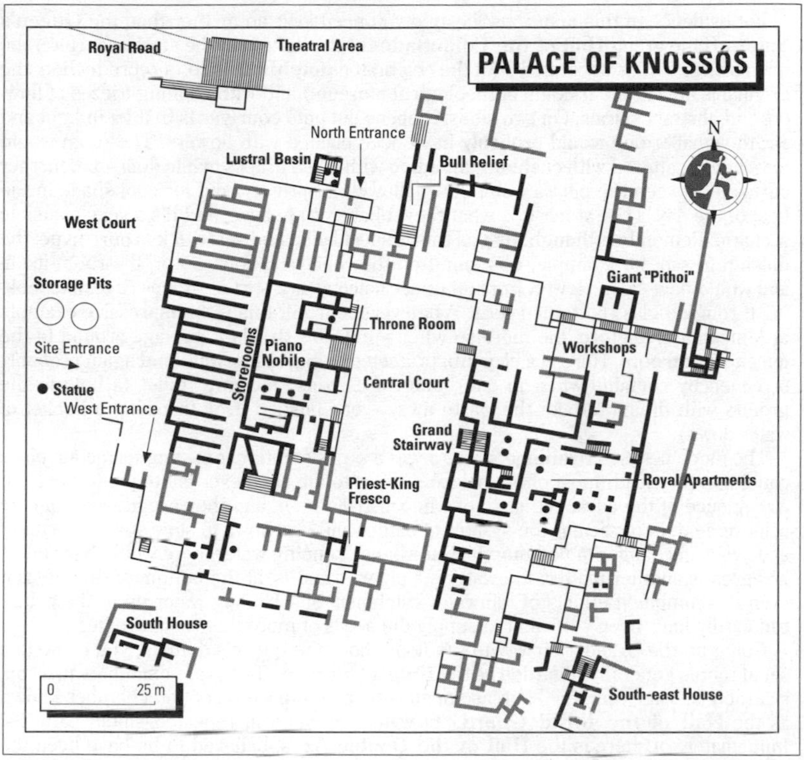

Knossós was liberally "restored" by Evans, and these restorations have been the source of furious controversy among archeologists ever since. It has become clear that much of Evans's upper level – the so-called *piano nobile* – is pure conjecture. Even so, his guess as to what the palace might have looked like is certainly as good as anyone else's, and it makes the other sites infinitely more meaningful if you have seen Knossós first. Without the restorations, it would be almost impossible to imagine the grandeur of the multistorey palace or to see the ceremonial stairways, strange, top-heavy pillars and gaily painted walls that distinguish the site. For some idea of the size and complexity of the palace in its original state, take a look at the cutaway drawings (wholly imaginary but probably not too far off) on sale outside.

Royal Apartments

The superb **Royal Apartments** around the central staircase are not guesswork, and they are plainly the finest of the rooms at Knossós. The **Grand Stairway** itself is a masterpiece of design: not only a fitting approach to these sumptuously appointed chambers, but also an integral part of the whole plan, its large well bringing light into the lower storeys. Light wells such as these, usually with a courtyard at the bottom, are a constant feature of Knossós and a reminder of just how important creature comforts were to the Minoans, and of how skilled they were at providing them.

For evidence of this luxurious lifestyle you need look no further than the **Queen's Suite**, off the grand **Hall of the Colonnades** at the bottom of the staircase. Here, the main living room is decorated with the celebrated **dolphin fresco** (a reproduction; the original is now in the Iráklion archeological museum) and with running friezes of flowers and abstract spirals. On two sides, it opens out onto courtyards that let in light and air; the smaller one would probably have been planted with flowers. The room would have been scattered with cushions and hung with plush drapes, while doors and further curtains between the pillars would have allowed for privacy, and for cool shade in the heat of the day. This, at least, is what they'd have you believe, and it's a very plausible scenario. Remember, though, that all this is speculation and some of it is pure hype; the dolphin fresco, for example, was found on the courtyard floor, not in the room itself, and would have been viewed from an upper balcony as a sort of *trompe l'oeil*, like looking through a glass-bottomed boat. Whatever the truth, this is an impressive example of Minoan architecture, the more so when you follow the dark passage around to the queen's **bathroom**. Here is a clay tub, protected behind a low wall (and again probably screened by curtains when in use), and the famous "flushing" toilet (a hole in the ground with drains to take the waste away – one flushed it by throwing a bucket of water down).

The much perused **drainage system** was a series of interconnecting terracotta pipes running underneath most of the palace. Guides to the site never fail to point these out as evidence of the advanced state of Minoan civilization, and they are indeed quite an achievement, in particular the system of baffles and overflows to slow down the runoff and avoid any danger of flooding. Just how much running water there would have been, however, is another matter; the water supply was, and is, at the bottom of the hill, and even the combined efforts of rainwater catchment and hauling water up to the palace can hardly have been sufficient to supply the needs of more than a small elite.

Going up the Grand Stairway to the floor above the queen's domain, you come to a set of rooms generally regarded as the **King's Quarters**. These are chambers in a considerably sterner vein; the staircase opens into a grandiose reception chamber known as the **Hall of the Royal Guard**, its walls decorated in repeated shield patterns. Immediately off here is the **Hall of the Double Axes**, believed to be have been the ruler's personal chamber, a double room that would allow for privacy in one portion while audiences were held in the more public section. Its name comes from the double-axe symbol carved into every block of masonry.

The Throne Room and the rest of the palace

Continuing to the top of the Grand Stairway, you emerge onto the broad **Central Court**, a feature of all the Minoan palaces. Open now, this would once have been enclosed by the walls of the buildings all around. On the far side, in the northwestern corner of the courtyard, is the entrance to another of Knossós's most atmospheric survivals, the **Throne Room**. Here, a worn stone throne – with its hollowed shaping for the posterior – sits against the wall of a surprisingly small chamber; along the walls around it are ranged stone benches, suggesting a king ruling in council, and behind there's a reconstructed fresco of two griffins. In all probability in Minoan times this was the seat of a priestess rather than a ruler (there's nothing like it in any other Minoan palace), and its conversion into a throne room seems to have been a late innovation wrought by the invading Mycenaeans, during their short-lived domination prior to the palace's final destruction in the fourteenth century BC. The Throne Room is now closed off with a wooden gate, but you can lean over this for a good view, and in the antechamber there's a wooden copy of the throne on which everyone perches to have their picture taken.

The rest you'll see as you wander, contemplating the legends of the place which blur with reality. Try not to miss the giant *pithoi* in the northeast quadrant of the site, an area known as the palace workshops; the storage chambers which you see from behind the Throne Room, and the reproduction frescoes in the reconstructed room above it; the fresco of the Priest-King looking down on the south side of the central court, and the relief of a charging bull on its north side. This last would have greeted you if you entered the palace through its north door; you can see evidence here of some kind of gatehouse and a lustral bath, a sunken area perhaps used for ceremonial bathing and purification. Just outside this gate is the **theatral area**, an open space a little like a stepped amphitheatre, which may have been used for ritual performances or dances. From here the **Royal Road**, claimed as the oldest road in Europe, sets out. At one time, this probably ran right across the island; nowadays it ends after about a hundred yards in a brick wall beneath the modern road. Circling back around the outside of the palace, you get more idea of its scale by looking up at it; on the south side are a couple of small reconstructed Minoan houses which are worth exploring.

Beyond Knossós

If you have transport, the drive beyond Knossós can be an attractive and enjoyable one, taking minor roads through much greener country, with vineyards draped across low hills and flourishing agricultural communities. If you want specific things to seek out, head first for **MYRTIÁ**, an attractive village with the small **Kazantzakis Museum** (Mon, Wed & Sat 9am–1pm & 4pm–8pm, Tues & Fri 9am–1pm; 500dr) in a house where the writer's parents once lived. **ARHÁNES**, at the foot of Mount Ioúktas, is a much larger place that was also quite heavily populated in Minoan times. None of the three archeological sites here is open to the public, but **Anemospiliá**, 2km northwest of the town (directions from the archeological museum below), can be visited and has caused huge controversy since its excavation in the 1980s: many traditional views of the Minoans, particularly that of Minoan life as peaceful and idyllic, have had to be rethought in the light of the discovery of an apparent human sacrifice. An excellent new **archeological museum** (daily, excluding Tues, 8.30am–2.30pm; free) displays finds from here and other nearby excavations, including the strange ceremonial dagger apparently used for human sacrifice. From Arhánes you can also drive (or walk with a couple of hours to spare) to the top of Mount Ioúktas to see the imposing remains of a Minoan **peak sanctuary** and enjoy spectacular panoramic **views** towards Knossós (with which it was linked) and the northern coast beyond. At **VATHÝPETRO**, south of the mountain, is a **Minoan villa and vineyard** (daily 8.30am–3pm, but often fails to open so enquire at the museum in Arhánes; free), which once controlled the rich farmland south of Arhánes. Inside, a remarkable collection of farming implements was found, as well as a unique **wine press** which remains *in situ*. Substantial amounts of the farm buildings remain, and it's still surrounded by fertile vines (Arhánes is one of Crete's major wine-producing zones) three and a half thousand years later – making it probably the oldest still-functioning vineyard in Europe, if not the world.

Southwest from Iráklion: sites and beaches

If you take a **tour** from Iráklion (or one of the resorts), you'll probably visit the **Górtys**, **Festós** and **Ayía Triádha** sites in a day, with a lunchtime swim at **Mátala** thrown in. Doing it by public transport, you'll be forced into a rather more leisurely pace, but there's still no reason why you shouldn't get to all three and reach Mátala within the day; if necessary, it's easy enough to hitch the final stretch. **Bus services** to the Festós site are excellent, with some nine a day to and from Iráklion (fewer run on Sunday), five of which continue to or come from Mátala; there are also services direct to Ayía Galíni. If you're arriving in the afternoon, plan to visit Ayía Triádha first, as it closes early.

The route to Áyii Dhéka

The road from Iráklion towards Festós is a pretty good one by the standards of Cretan mountain roads, albeit rather dull. The country you're heading towards is the richest agricultural land on the island, and right from the start the villages en route are large and business-like. In the biggest of them, Ayía Varvára, there's a great rock outcrop known as the **Omphalos** (Navel) of Crete, supposedly the very centre of the island.

Past here, you descend rapidly to the fertile fields of the Messará plain, where the road joins the main route across the south near the village of **ÁYII DHÉKA**. For religious Cretans Áyii Dhéka is something of a place of pilgrimage; its name, "The Ten Saints", refers to ten early Christians martyred here under the Romans. In a crypt below the modern church you can see the martyrs' tombs. It's an attractive village to wander around, with several places to eat and even some **rooms** along the main road.

Górtys

Daily 8am–5pm; 800dr.

Within easy walking distance of Áyii Dhéka, either through the fields or along the main road, sprawls the site of **Górtys**, ruined capital of the Roman province that included not only Crete but also much of North Africa. After a look at the plan of the extensive site at the entrance, cutting across the fields will give you some idea of the scale of this city, at its zenith in approximately the third century AD; an enormous variety of other remains, including an impressive **theatre**, are strewn across your route. Even in Áyii Dhéka you'll see Roman pillars and statues lying around in people's yards or propping up their walls.

There had been a settlement here from the earliest times, but the extant ruins date almost entirely from the Roman era. Only now is the site being systematically excavated, by the Italian Archeological School. At the main entrance to the fenced site, alongside the road, are the ruins of the still impressive **basilica of Áyios Títos**; the eponymous saint converted the island to Christianity and was its first bishop. Beyond this is the **odeion** which houses the most important discovery on the site, the **Law Code**. These great inscribed blocks of stone were incorporated by the Romans from a much earlier stage of the city's development; they're written in an obscure early Greek-Cretan dialect, and in a style known as *boustrophedon* (ox-ploughed), with the lines reading alternately in opposite directions like the furrows of a ploughed field. At ten metres by three metres, this is reputedly the largest Greek inscription ever found. The laws set forth reflect a strictly hierarchical society: five witnesses were needed to convict a free man of a crime, only one for a slave; raping a free man or woman carried a fine of a hundred staters, violating a serf only five. A small **museum** in a loggia (also within the fenced area) holds a number of large and finely worked sculptures found at Górtys, more evidence of the city's importance.

Míres

Some 20km west of Górtys, **MÍRES** is an important market and focal point of transport for the fertile Messará plain: if you're switching buses to get from the beaches on the south coast to the archeological sites or the west, this is where you'll do it. There are good facilities including a **bank**, a few **restaurants** and a couple of **rooms**, though there's no particular reason to stay unless you are waiting for a bus or looking for work (it's one of the better places for agricultural jobs). Heading straight for Festós, there's usually no need to stop.

Festós (Phaestos)

Daily 8am–7pm; 1200dr.

The **Palace of Festós** was excavated by the Italian, Federico Halbherr (also responsible for the early work at Górtys), at almost exactly the same time as Evans was working at Knossós. The style of the excavations, however, could hardly have been more different. Here, to the approval of most traditional archeologists, reconstruction was kept to an absolute minimum – it's all bare foundations, and walls which rise at most a metre above ground level. This means that despite a magnificent setting overlooking the plain of Messará, the palace at Festós is not as immediately arresting as those at Knossós or Mália. Much of the site is fenced off and, except in the huge central court, it's almost impossible to get any sense of the place as it was; the plan is almost as complex as at Knossós, with none of the reconstruction to bolster the imagination.

It's interesting to speculate why the palace was built halfway up a hill rather than on the plain below – certainly not for defence, for this is in no way a good defensive position. Psychological superiority over the peasants or reasons of health are both possible, but it seems quite likely that it was simply the magnificent view that finally swayed the decision. The site looks over Psilorítis to the north and the huge plain, with the Lasíthi mountains beyond it, to the east. Towards the top of Psiloritis you should be able to make out a small black smudge: the entrance to the Kamáres cave (see p.200).

On the ground closer at hand, you can hardly fail to notice the strong similarities between Festós and the other palaces: the same huge rows of storage jars, the great

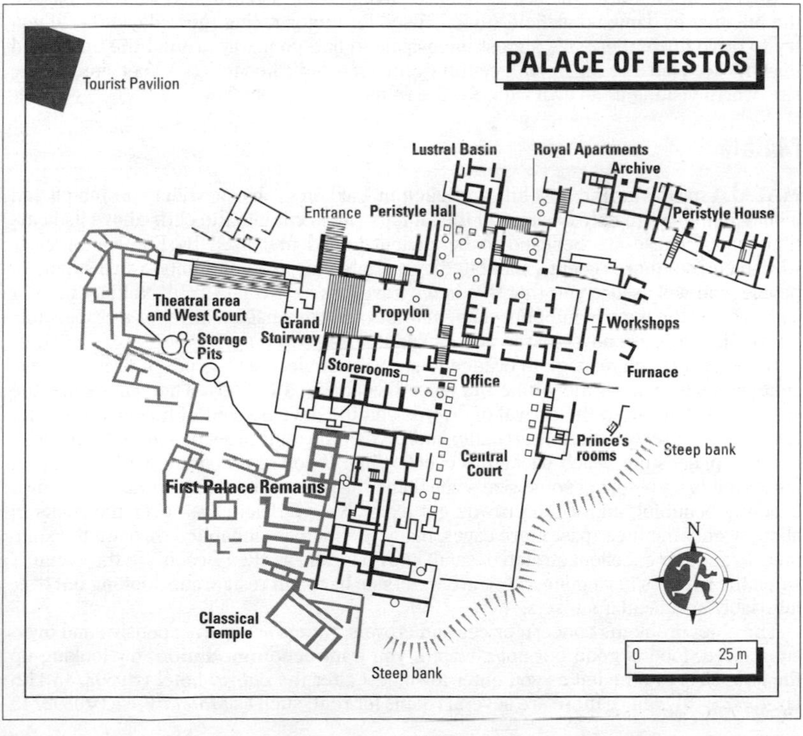

courtyard with its monumental stairway, and the theatral area. Unique to Festós, however, is the third courtyard, in the middle of which are the remains of a **furnace** used for metalworking. Indeed, this eastern corner of the palace seems to have been home to a number of craftsmen, including potters and carpenters. Oddly enough, Festós was much less ornately decorated than Knossós; there is no evidence, for example, of any of the dramatic Minoan wall-paintings.

The **tourist pavilion** at Festós serves drinks and food and also has a few beds, though these are very rarely available (thanks to advance bookings) and expensive when they are. The nearby village of **ÁYIOS IOÁNNIS**, along the road towards Mátala, has a few more **rooms**, including some at *Taverna Ayios Ioannis* (☎0892/42 006; ①), which is also a good place to eat.

Ayía Triádha

Daily 8.30am–3pm; 500dr.

Some of the finest artworks in the museum at Iráklion came from **Ayía Triádha**, about a 45-minute walk (or a short drive) from Festós. No one is quite sure what this site is, but the most common theory has it as some kind of royal summer villa. It's smaller than the palaces, but if anything even more lavishly appointed and beautifully situated. In any event, it's an attractive place to visit, far less crowded than Festós, with a wealth of interesting little details. Look out in particular for the row of **stores** in front of what was apparently a marketplace, and for the remains of the **paved road** that once led down to the Gulf of Messará. The sea itself looks invitingly close, separated from the base of the hill only by Timbáki airfield (mainly used for motor racing these days), but if you try to drive down there, it's almost impossible to find your way around the unmarked dust tracks. There's a fourteenth-century **church** – dedicated to Áyios Yeóryios – at the site, worth visiting in its own right for the remains of ancient frescoes.

Mátala

MÁTALA has by far the best-known **beach** in Iráklion province, widely promoted and included in tours mainly because of the famous **caves** cut into the cliffs above its beautiful sands. These are believed to be ancient tombs first used by Romans or early Christians, but more recently inhabited by a sizable hippie community. You'll still meet people who will assure you that this is *the* travellers' beach on Crete. Not any more it isn't. Today, the town is full of package tourists and tries hard to present a respectable image; the cliffs are now cleared and locked up every evening.

A few people still manage to evade the security, or sleep on the beach or in the adjacent campsite, but on the whole the place has changed entirely. The years since the early 1980s have seen the arrival of crowds and the development of hotels, discos and restaurants to service them; early afternoon, when the tour buses pull in for their swimming stop, sees the beach packed to overflowing. If you're prepared to accept Mátala for what it is – a resort of some size – you'll find the place more than bearable. The town beach is beautiful, and if the crowds get excessive, you can climb over the rocks in about twenty minutes (past more caves, many of which are inhabited through the summer) to another excellent stretch of sand, known locally as "Red Beach". In the evening, when the trippers have gone, there are waterside bars and restaurants looking out over invariably spectacular sunsets.

The chief problems concern prices and crowds: rooms are both expensive and oversubscribed, food is good but not cheap. If you want **accommodation**, try looking up the little street to the left as you enter town, just after the *Zafiria* hotel (☎0892/45 112, fax 45 725; ③), where there are several rooms for rent, such as *Matala View* (☎0892/45

114; ①), and *Pension Nikos* (☎0892/42 375, fax 45 120; ②). If these are full, then everywhere closer in is likely to be as well, so head back out on the main road, or try the **campsite**, *Camping of Matala* (☎0892/45 720), next to the beach above the car park; *Kommos Camping* (☎0892/45 596) is a nicer site, but a few kilometres out of Mátala and reached by heading back towards Pítsidia and turning left along a signed track. There are places to **eat and drink** all over the main part of town and a solitary summer **disco**, *Neosicos*, competes with a handful of raucous music bars to attract night owls. Also impossible to miss are most other facilities, including stores and a bookshop, currency exchange, car and bike rental, travel agents, post office and a covered market where tourist tat has almost squeezed out the fruit and veg stalls.

Around Mátala: Pitsídhia and Kalamáki

One way to enjoy a bit more peace is to stay at **PITSÍDHIA**, about 5km inland. This has long been a well-used option, so it's not quite as cheap as you might expect, but there are plenty of rooms, lively places to eat and even music bars. If you decide to stay here, the beach at **KALAMÁKI** is an alternative to Mátala. Both beaches are approximately the same distance to walk, though there is a much better chance of a bus or a lift to Mátala. Kalamáki has developed somewhat, with a number of rooms and a couple of tavernas, but it's a messy and unattractive little place. The beach stretches for miles, surprisingly wild and windswept, lashed by sometimes dangerously rough surf. At the southern end (more easily reached by a path off the Pitsídhia–Mátala road) lies **Kómmos**, once a Minoan port serving Festós and now the site of a major archeological excavation. It's not yet open to the public, but you can peer into the fenced-off area to see what's been revealed so far, which is pretty impressive: dwellings, streets, hefty stonework and even the ship sheds where repairs on the Minoan fleet were carried out.

Iráklion's south coast

South of the Messará plain are two more beach resorts, Kalí Liménes and Léndas, with numerous other little beaches along the coast in between, but nothing spectacular. **Public transport** is very limited indeed; you'll almost always have to travel via Míres (see p.190). If you have your own transport, the roads in these parts are all passable and newly sealed, but most are very slow going; the Kófinas Hills, which divide the plain from the coast, are surprisingly precipitous.

Kalí Liménes

While Mátala itself was an important port under the Romans, the chief harbour for Górtys lay on the other side of Cape Líthinon at **KALÍ LIMÉNES**. Nowadays, this is once again a major port – for oil tankers. This has rather spoiled its chances of becoming a major resort, and there are few proper facilities. Some people like Kalí Liménes: it's certainly off the beaten track and the constant procession of tankers gives you something to look at while beach lounging. There are a couple of places offering **rooms** – the best is the *Karavovrousi Beach* (☎0892/42 197; ②), a kilometre or so east of the main village where the main Míres road arrives, which also has a decent **taverna** attached. The coastline is broken up by spectacular cliffs and, as long as there hasn't been a recent oil spill, the beaches are reasonably clean and totally empty. But (fortunately) not too many share this enthusiasm.

Léndas

LÉNDAS, further east along the coast, is far more popular, with a couple of buses daily from Iráklion and a partly justified reputation for being peaceful (sullied by considerable summer crowds). Many people who arrive think they've come to the wrong place, as at first sight the village looks shabby, the beach is small, rocky and dirty, and the rooms are frequently all booked. A number of visitors leave without ever correcting that initial impression, but the attraction of Léndas is not the village at all but on the other (west) side of the headland. Here, there's a vast, excellent sandy beach, part of it usually taken over by nudists, and a number of taverna/bars overlooking it from the roadside. The beach is a couple of kilometres from Léndas, along a rough track; if you're walking, you can save time by cutting across the headland. A considerably more attractive prospect than staying in Léndas itself is **camping** on the beach to the west of the village, or with luck getting a **room** at one of the few beach tavernas – try *Tsarakis* (☎0892/95 378, fax 95 377; ②) for seaview rooms. After you've discovered the beach, even Léndas begins to look more welcoming, and at least it has most of the facilities you'll need, including a shop which will change money and numerous places to **eat and drink**.

Once you've come to terms with the place, you can also explore some less good but quite deserted beaches eastwards, and the scrappy remains of **ancient Lebena** on a hilltop overlooking them. There was an important Asclepion (temple of the god Asclepius) here around some now-diverted warm springs, but only the odd broken column and fragments of mosaic survive in a fenced-off area on the village's northern edge.

East of Iráklion: the package-tour coast

East of Iráklion, the startling pace of **tourist development** in Crete is all too plain to see. The merest hint of a beach is an excuse to build at least one hotel, and these are outnumbered by the concrete shells of resorts-to-be. It's hard to find a room in this monument to the package-tour industry, and expensive if you do.

Goúrnes and Goúves

As a general rule, the further you go, the better things get: when the road detours all too briefly inland, the real Crete of olive groves and stark mountains asserts itself. You certainly won't see much of it at **GOÚRNES**, where a former US Air Force base is now occupied by the Greek military, or at nearby Káto Goúves, where there's a **campsite**, *Camping Creta* (☎0897/41 400), which will be quiet unless and until the Greek Air Force moves in next door as planned. From here, however, you can head inland to the old village of **GOÚVES**, a refreshing contrast, and just beyond to the **Skotinó cave**, one of the largest and most spectacular on the island (about an hour's walk from the coast).

Not far beyond Goúrnes is the turning for the direct route up to the Lasíthi plateau, and shortly after that you roll into the first of the big resorts, Hersónissos or, more correctly, Límin Hersoníssou; Hersónissos is the village in the hills just behind, also overrun by tourists.

Hersónissos (Límin Hersonissou)

HERSÓNISSOS was once just a small fishing village; today it's the most popular of Crete's package resorts. If what you want is plenty of bars, tavernas, restaurants and Eurodisco nightlife, then come here. The resort has numerous small patches of sand beach between rocky outcrops, but a shortage of places to stay in peak season.

Along the modern seafront, a solid line of restaurants and bars is broken only by the occasional souvenir shop; in their midst you'll find a small pyramidal Roman **fountain** with broken mosaics of fishing scenes, the only real relic of the ancient town of Chersonesos. Around the headland above the harbour and in odd places along the seafront, you can see remains of Roman harbour installations, mostly submerged.

Beach and clubs excepted, the distractions of Hersónissos comprise **Lykhnostatis** (Tues–Sun 9.30am–2pm; 1250dr), an open-air "museum" of traditional Crete, on the coast on the eastern edge of the town; a small **aquarium** just off the main road at the west end of town, opposite the *Hard Rock Cafe* (daily 10am–9pm; 800dr); the watersports paradise *Star Water Park* (admission free, charges for individual sports) at the eastern end of the resort; and, a few kilometres inland, the slides, cascades and whirlpools of the newly opened and immense *Aqua Splash Water Park* (daily 10am–7pm; 4000dr per day, discounted rates after 2.30pm).

A short distance inland are the three **hill villages** of Koutoulafári, Piskopianó and "old" Hersónissos, which all have a good selection of tavernas, and are worth searching out for accommodation.

Practicalities

Hersónissos is well provided with all the back-up **services** you need to make a holiday go smoothly. Banks, bike and car rental and post office are all on or just off the main drag, as are the taxi ranks. **Buses** running east and west leave every thirty minutes.

Finding somewhere to stay can be difficult in July and August. Much of the **accommodation** here is allocated to package-tour operators and what remains is not that cheap. To check for availability of accommodation generally, the quickest and best option is to enquire at one of the many travel agencies along the main street, Venizélou, such as Zakros Tours at no. 46. Reasonably priced central options include the *Nancy* on Ayías Paraskevís (☎0897/22 212; ③) and *Virginia* on Máhis Krítis (☎0897/22 466; ②), but be prepared for a fair amount of noise. One place to try on the western edge as you enter the town is *Hotel Ilios* (☎0897/22 500 fax 22 582; ④), just back from the main road, which has a rooftop pool. There are two good **campsites**: one at the eastern end of town, *Caravan Camping* (☎0897/22 025 or 24 718), which also has several reed-roofed bungalows, and *Hersonissos Camping* (☎0897/22 902 or 23 792), just to the west of town. The well-run **youth hostel**, at the east end of Venizélou (☎0897/23 674), is sited opposite *Caravan Camping* (above) and serves meals.

Despite the vast number of **eating places**, there are few in Hersónissos worth recommending, and the tavernas down on the harbourfront should be avoided. One of the few Greek tavernas that stands out is *Kavouri* along Arhéou Theátrou, but it's fairly expensive, so it's better to head out of town on the Piskopianó road where, near the junction to Koutoulafári, the friendly *Fegari* taverna serves good Greek food at reasonable prices. Sitting at your table overlooking the street below you can view the steady trek of clubbers heading down the hill to the bars and nightclubs of Hersónissos. The hill villages have the greatest selection of tavernas, particularly Koutoulafári, where you can have a relaxed evening amongst the narrow streets and small platías. One in-town restaurant definitely worth a try is *Passage to India*, an authentic and extremely good Indian restaurant just off the main street near the church and the war memorial.

Hersónissos is renowned for its **nightlife**, and there's no shortage of it. Most of the better bars and clubs are along the main road. Especially popular are *It*, with up-to-the-minute chart hits, and the *Hard Rock Café*, which often puts on live music. *Aria*, a large glass-fronted disco, is the biggest on Crete and only opens during July and August when it can get the crowds to fill it. Other popular haunts include *Legend* and the beach bar-disco pub *Pirates*, both at the eastern end of town, and, towards the harbour, *Camelot* and *New York*. If you fancy a quiet drink then you have come to the wrong resort, but you could try *Kahluai Beach Cocktail Bar* or *Haris Ouzo* and *Raki Place* (beneath the *Hotel Virginia*). There is an open-air **cinema** showing original version films at the *Creta Maris* hotel at the west end of the town and close to the beach.

Stalídha

STALÍDHA is a Cinderella town, sandwiched in between its two louder, brasher and some would say uglier sisters, Mália and Hersónissos, but it is neither quiet or undeveloped. This rapidly expanding beach resort, with more than sixty tavernas and bars and a few discos, can offer the best of both worlds, with a friendlier and more relaxed setting, a better beach (and usual array of watersports) and very easy access to its two livelier neighbours. The town essentially consists of a single, relatively traffic-free street which rings the seafront for more than two miles, before the apartment blocks briefly become fewer and further, until the mass development of Mália begins.

Finding a place to stay can be difficult, since **accommodation** is almost entirely in studio and apartment blocks which are booked by package companies in high season. Out of season, however, you may well be able to negotiate a very reasonable price for a studio apartment complete with swimming pool; ask in the central travel agencies first, as they will know what is available, and expect to pay at least 8000dr for two. Finding somewhere to **eat** is less difficult as there are plenty of rather ordinary tavernas, the best and most authentic being *Maria's* and the *Hellas Taverna*, both at the western end of the resort.

Stalídha is completely overshadowed by its neighbours when it comes to **nightlife**, though you can dance at *Bells* disco, on the main coast road, or at *Rhythm*, on the beach; the music bars *Sea Wolf Cocktail Bar* and *Akti Bar* are near each other along the beach.

Mália

Much of **MÁLIA** is taken up by the package industry, so in peak season finding a place to stay is not always easy. You're best off, especially if you want any sleep, trying one of the numerous **rooms** and **pensions** signposted in the old town, such as the *Esperia* (☎0897/31 086; ②). Backtracking from here, along the main Iráklion road, there are a number of reasonably priced **pensions** on the left and right including *Hibiscus* (☎0897/31 313, fax 32 042; ③), which has rooms and studios with kitchenette and fridge around a pool in a garden behind. If you really want to be in the centre of things, try *Kostas* (☎0897/31 485; ②), a family-run pension incongruously located behind the mini-golf at the end of the beach road. Otherwise, on arrival visit one of the travel companies along the main road – for example, Stallion Travel, Venizélou 128 (☎0897/33 690) – to enquire about accommodation availability.

Eating in Mália is unlikely to be a problem as **restaurants** jostle for your custom at every step, especially along the beach road. None is particularly good. The best places are around Platía Ayíou Dhimitríou, a pleasant square beside the church in the centre of the old town to the south of the road. Try a meal at *Kalesma*, *Kalimera* or *Petros*, after an aperitif at *Bar Yiannis* just north of the church or *Ouzeri Alisabi* alongside it, where they serve local wine from the wooden barrel. There are a number of other welcoming tavernas and very pleasant bars, including the *Stone House* and *Temple*, lining, or just off, the platía.

The beach road comes into its own at night, when the profusion of **bars**, **discos** and **clubs** erupt into a pulsating cacophony. *Zoo* is a relatively new club, and once past midnight, one of the internal walls parts to reveal an even larger dance area. *Corkers* and *Highway* are the other really popular clubs in Mália. *Desire*, along the beach road, concentrates on rock and has good-quality live music some nights. Unfortunately, a good night's clubbing and dancing is frequently spoiled by groups of drunken youths pouring out of the bars and getting into brawls. The situation got so bad that tour operators threatened to pull out of the resort if action wasn't taken to deal with the hooligans – all rather ironical as it was they who were shipping them in by the plane-load on cut-price packages. Recent years have seen a police clampdown on such activities as drinking on the street, and the situation has considerably improved.

The Palace of Mália

Tues–Sun 8.30am–3pm; 800dr.

Much less imposing than either Knossós or Festós, the **Palace of Mália**, 2km east of Mália town, in some ways surpasses both. For a start, it's a great deal emptier and you can wander among the remains in relative peace. While no reconstruction has been attempted, the palace was never reoccupied after its second destruction, so the ground plan is virtually intact. It's a great deal easier to comprehend than Knossós and, if you've seen the reconstructions there, it's easy to envisage this seaside palace in its days of glory. There's a real feeling of an ancient civilization with a taste for the good life, basking on the rich agricultural plain between the Lasíthi mountains and the sea.

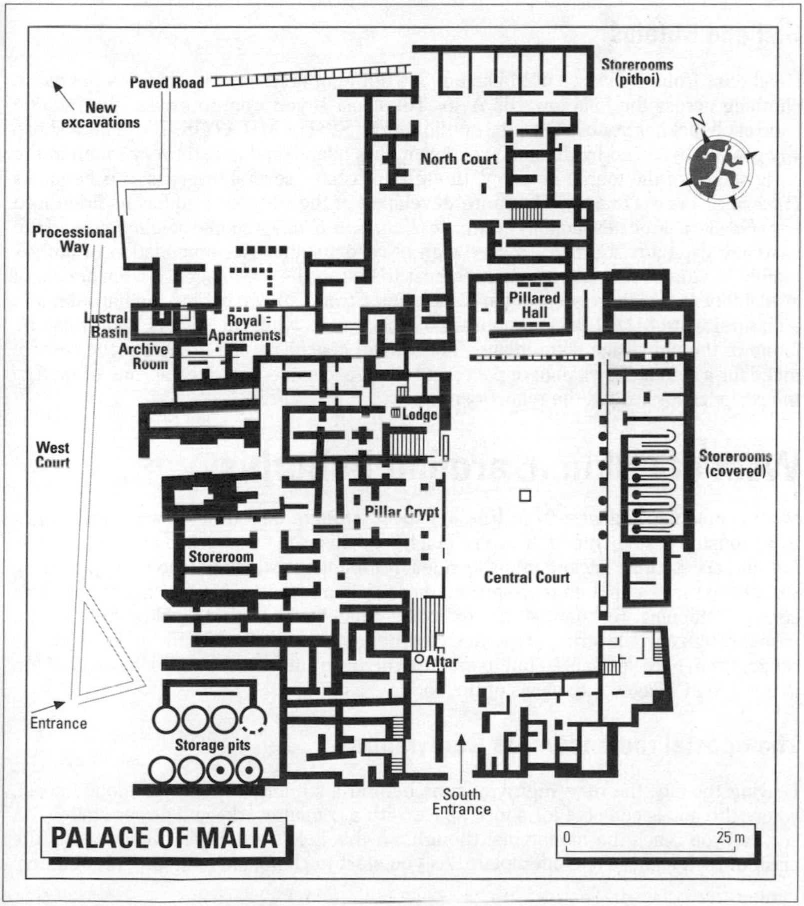

From this site came the famous **gold pendant** of two bees (which can be seen in the Iráklion museum or on any postcard stand), allegedly part of a horde that was plundered and whose other treasures can now be found in the British Museum in London. The beautiful leopard-head axe, also in the museum at Iráklion, was another of the treasures found here. At the site, look out for the strange indented stone in the central court (which probably held ritual offerings), for the remains of ceremonial stairways and for the giant *pithoi* which stand like sentinels around the palace. To the south and west, digs are still going on as a large town comes slowly to light, and these can now be seen via an overhead walkway.

Any passing **bus** should stop at the site, or you could even rent a **bike** for a couple of hours as it's a pleasant, flat ride from Mália town. Leaving the archeological zone and turning right, you can follow the road down to a lovely stretch of clean and relatively peaceful **beach**, backed by fields, scrubland and a single makeshift taverna, which serves good fresh fish. From here you can walk back along the shore to Mália or take a bus (every thirty minutes in either direction) from the stop on the main road.

Sísi and Mílatos

Head **east** from the Palace of Mália, and it's not long before the road leaves the coast, climbing across the hills towards Áyios Nikólaos. If you want to escape the frenetic pace of all that has gone before, try continuing to **SÍSI** or **MÍLATOS**. These little shore villages are bypassed by the main road as it cuts inland, and are still very much in the early stages of the tourist industry, though both have several tavernas – *Fisherman's Place* in Sísi is worth a try. The more developed of the two, Sísi also has its first disco bar (*Faros*), a large new holiday complex (*Kalimera Krita*) a couple of kilometres to the east, and even a post office – a sure sign of resort status. Accommodation in both is mainly in studios and apartments; it's best to ask in the travel agencies for details of availability. In Sísi there's also a small pension, *Elena* (②) just behind the harbour, and a **campsite** (☎0841/71 247) signposted on the way in, whilst in Mílatos, rooms can be found in the old village, 2km inland. The village beaches aren't great, but the resorts make for a refreshing change of pace, and there are some fine, deep aprons of sand in the rocky coves beyond the resort centres.

West of Iráklion: around Psiloritis

Most people heading west from Iráklion speed straight out on the new **coastal highway**, nonstop to Réthymnon. If you're in a hurry this is not such a bad plan; the road is fast and spectacular, hacked into the sides of mountains which for the most part drop straight to the sea, though there are no more than a couple of places where you might consider stopping. By contrast, the old roads inland are agonizingly slow, but they do pass through a whole string of **attractive villages** beneath the heights of the Psiloritis range. From here you can set out to explore the **mountains** and even walk across them to emerge in villages with views of the south coast.

The coastal route towards Réthymnon

Leaving the city, the **new highway** runs behind a stretch of highly developed coast, where the hotels compete for shore space with a cement works and power station. As soon as you reach the mountains, though, all this is left behind and there's only the clash of rock and sea to contemplate. As you start to climb, look out for **Paleókastro**, beside a bridge which carries the road over a small cove; the castle is so weathered as to be almost invisible against the brownish face of the cliff.

Ayía Pelayía and Fódhele

Some 3km below the highway, as it rounds the first point, lies the resort of **AYÍA PELAYÍA**. It looks extremely attractive from above but, once there, you're likely to find the narrow, taverna-lined beach packed to full capacity; this is not somewhere to roll up without a reserved room, although the Pagasimo travel agency (☎081/811 402, fax 811 424) can usually come up with something, even at the last minute. Out of season you might find a real bargain at an apartment and, despite the high-season crowds, the resort maintains a dignity long since lost in Mália and Hersónissos, and even a certain exclusivity; a couple of Crete's most luxurious hotels, including the enormous *Peninsula* (☎081/811 313, fax 811 219; ⑥), nestle on the headland just beyond the main town beach.

Not far beyond Ayía Pelayía, there's a turning inland to the village of **FÓDHELE**, allegedly El Greco's birthplace. A plaque from the University of Toledo acknowledges the claim and, true or not, the community has built a small tourist industry on that basis. There are a number of craft shops and some pleasant tavernas where you can sit outside along the river. A peaceful 1km walk (or drive) takes you to the spuriously titled "El Greco's house" and the more worthwhile and picturesque fourteenth-century Byzantine **church of the Panayía** (Mon–Fri 9.30am–5pm; free) opposite. None of this amounts to very much but it is a pleasant, relatively unspoiled village if you simply want to sit in peace for a while. A couple of **buses** a day run here from Iráklion, and there's the odd tour; if you arrive on a direct bus, the walk back down to the highway (about 3km), where you can flag down a passing service, is not too strenuous.

Balí and Pánormos

BALÍ, on the coast approximately halfway between Iráklion and Réthymnon, also used to be tranquil and undeveloped, and by the standards of the north coast it still is in many ways. The village is built around a couple of small coves, some 2km from the highway (a hot walk from the bus), and is similar to Ayía Pelayía except that the beaches are not quite as good and there are no big hotels, just an ever-growing proliferation of studios, apartment buildings, rooms for rent and a number of "modest hotels" (brochure-speak). You'll have plenty of company here; the last and best beach, known as "Paradise", no longer really deserves the name; it's a beautiful place to splash about, surrounded by mountains rising straight from the sea, but there's rarely a spare inch on the sand in high season.

Continuing along the coast, the last stop before you emerge on the flat stretch leading to Réthymnon is at **PÁNORMOS**. This makes a good stopover if you're in search of somewhere more peaceful and authentic. The small sandy beach can get crowded when boats bring day-trippers from Réthymnon, but most of the time the attractive village remains relatively unspoiled, and succeeds in clinging to its Cretan identity. There are several decent tavernas and rooms places, one large hotel and the very comfortable *Pension Lucy* (☎0834/51 212, fax 51 434; ②).

Inland towards Mount Psiloritis

Of the **inland routes**, the old main road (via Márathos and Dhamásta) is not the most interesting. This, too, was something of a bypass in its day and there are few places of any size or appeal, though it's a very scenic drive. If you want to dawdle, you're better off on the road which cuts up to **Týlissos** and then goes via **Anóyia**. It's a pleasant ride through fertile valleys filled with olive groves and vineyards, a district (the Malevísi) renowned from Venetian times for the strong, sweet Malmsey wine.

Týlissos and Anóyia

TÝLISSOS has a significant archeological site (daily 8.30am–3pm; 400dr) where three Minoan houses were excavated; unfortunately, its reputation is based more on what was found here (many pieces in the Iráklion museum) and on its significance for archeologists than on anything which remains to be seen. Still, it's worth a look, if you're passing, for a glimpse of Minoan life away from the big palaces, and for the tranquillity of the pine-shaded remains.

ANÓYIA is a much more tempting place to stay, especially if the summer heat is becoming oppressive. Spilling prettily down a hillside close below the highest peaks of the mountains, it looks traditional, but closer inspection shows that most of the buildings are actually concrete; the village was destroyed during World War II and the local men rounded up and shot – one of the German reprisals for the abduction of General Kreipe by the Cretan Resistance. The town has a reputation as a **handicrafts** centre (especially for woven and woollen goods), skills acquired both through bitter necessity after most of the men had been killed and in a conscious attempt to revive the town. At any rate it worked, for the place is thriving today – thanks, it seems, to a buoyant agricultural sector made rich by stockbreeding and the number of elderly widows keen to subject any visitor to their terrifyingly aggressive sales techniques.

Quite a few people pass through Anóyia during the day, but not many of them stay, even though there are some good pensions and rented rooms in the upper half of the town, including the flower-bedecked *Aris* (☎0834/31 460, fax 31 058; ①) and the nearby *Aristea* (☎0834/31 459; ②), which has en-suite rooms. The town has a very different, more traditional ambience at night, and the only problem is likely to be finding a **place to eat**: although there are plenty of snack bars and so-called tavernas, most have extremely basic menus, more or less limited to spit-barbecued lamb, which is the tasty local speciality served up by the grill places on the lower square.

Mount Psiloritis and its caves

Heading for the mountains, a smooth road ascends the 21km from Anóyia to an altitude of 1400m on the **Nídha plateau** at the base of Mount Psiloritis. Here, the *Taverna Nida* (☎0834/31 141; April–Sept daily; Sat & Sun only in winter) serves up hearty taverna standards and has a couple of **rooms** (①), which makes it a good base for hikes in the surrounding mountains. A short path leads from the taverna to the celebrated **Idhéon Ándhron** (Idean cave), a rival of that on Mount Dhíkti (see opposite) for the title of Zeus's birthplace, and certainly associated from the earliest of times with the cult of Zeus. There's a major archeological dig going on inside, which means the whole cave is fenced off, with a miniature railway running into it to carry all the rubble out. In short, there's not a great deal to see.

The taverna also marks the start of the way to the top of **Mount Psiloritis** (2456m), Crete's highest mountain, a climb that for experienced, properly shod hikers is not at all arduous. The route is well marked with the usual red dots, and it should be a six- to seven-hour return journey to the chapel at the summit, although in spring, thick snow may slow you down.

If you're prepared to camp on the plateau (it's very cold, but there's plenty of available water) or find rooms at the taverna, you could continue on foot next day down to the southern slopes of the range. It's a beautiful hike and also relatively easy, four hours or so down a fairly clear path to **VORÍZIA**. If you're still interested in caves, there's a more rewarding one above the nearby village of **KAMÁRES**, a climb of some three hours on a good path. Both Vorízia and Kamáres have a few **rooms** and some tavernas, at least one daily **bus** down to Míres and alternate (more difficult) routes to the peak of Psiloritis if you want to approach from this direction.

EASTERN CRETE

Eastern Crete is dominated by **Áyios Nikólaos**, and while it is a highly developed resort, by no means all of the east is like this. Far fewer people venture beyond the road south to **Ierápetra** and into the eastern isthmus, where only **Sitía** and the famous beach at **Váï** ever see anything approaching a crowd. Inland, too, there's interest, especially on the extraordinary **Lasíthi** plateau, which is worth a night's stay if only to observe its abidingly rural life.

Inland to the Lasíthi plateau

Leaving the palace at Mália, the highway cuts inland towards **NEÁPOLI**, soon beginning a spectacular climb into the mountains. Set in a high valley, Neápoli is a market town little touched by tourism. There is one excellent hotel (*Neapolis* ☎0841/33 966; ③), some rooms, a modern church and a folk museum. Beyond the town, it's about twenty minutes before the bus suddenly emerges high above the Gulf of Mirabéllo and Áyios Nikólaos, the island's biggest resort. If you're stopping, Neápoli also marks the second point of access to the **Lasíthi Plateau**.

Scores of bus tours drive up here daily to view the "thousands of white-cloth-sailed windmills" which irrigate the high plain ringed by mountains, and most groups will be disappointed. There are very few working windmills left, and these operate only for limited periods (mainly in June). This is not to say the trip is not justified, as it would be for the drive alone, and there are many other compensations. The plain is a fine example of rural Crete at work, every inch devoted to the cultivation of potatoes, apples, pears, figs, olives and a host of other crops; stay in one of the villages for a night or two and you'll see real life return as the tourists leave. There are plenty of easy rambles around the villages as well, through orchards and past the rusting remains of derelict windmills. You'll find rooms in the main town of **TZERMIÁDHO**, and at Áyios Konstandínos, Áyios Yeóryios – where you'll find a **folk museum**, and the friendly *Hotel Dias* (☎0844/31 207; ①) – and Psykhró.

Psykhró and the Dhiktean cave

PSYKHRÓ is much the most visited, as it's the base for visiting Lasíthi's other chief attraction, the birthplace of Zeus, the **Dhiktean cave** (daily 8am–6.45pm, reduced hours off-season; 800dr; watch out for slippery stones inside). In legend, Zeus's father, the Titan Kronos, was warned that he would be overthrown by a son and accordingly ate all his offspring; however, when Rhea gave birth to Zeus in the cave, she fed Kronos a stone and left the child concealed, protected by the Kouretes, who beat their shields outside to disguise his cries. The rest, as they say, is history (or at least myth). There's an obvious path running up to the cave from Psykhró and, whatever you're told, you don't have to have a guide if you don't want one, though you will need some form of illumination. On the other hand, it is hard to resist the guides, who do make the visit much more interesting, and they're not expensive if you can get a small group together (around 2000dr for two including lamps or 500–600dr each as part of a larger group). It takes a Cretan imagination to pick out Rhea and the baby Zeus from the lesser stalactites and stalagmites. One of the best guides is Petros Zarvakis, who is also a wildlife expert and leads guided hikes (April–Sept) into the mountains surrounding the plain (☎0844/31 316 for details). **Buses** run around the plateau to Psykhró direct from Iráklion and from Áyios Nikólaos via Neápoli. Both roads offer spectacular views, coiling through a succession of passes guarded by lines of ruined windmills.

Áyios Nikólaos and around

ÁYIOS NIKÓLAOS ("Ag Nik" to the majority of its British visitors) is set around a supposedly bottomless **salt lake**, now connected to the sea to form an inner harbour. It is supremely picturesque and has some style and confidence, which it exploits to the full. There are no sights as such but the excellent **archeological museum** (Tues–Sun 8.30am–3pm; 500dr) and an interesting **folk museum** (daily, excluding Sat, 10am–1.30pm & 7–9.30pm; 300dr) are both worth seeking out. The lake and port are surrounded by restaurants and bars, which charge above the odds, and whilst the

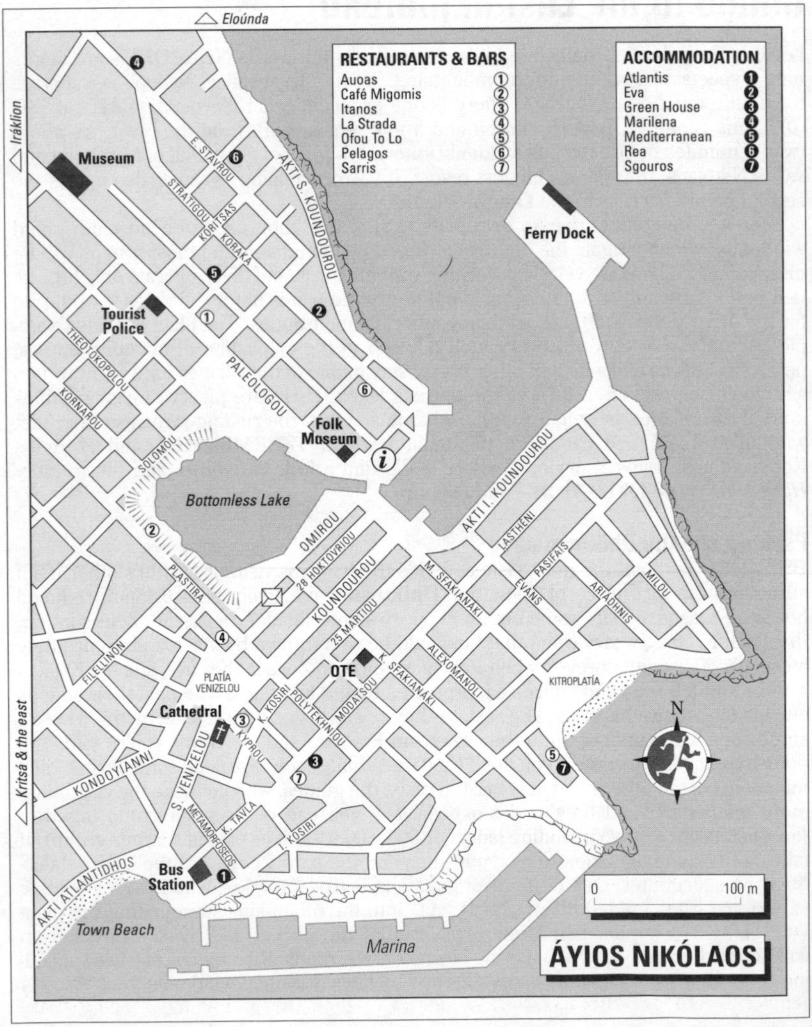

resort is still very popular, some tourists are distinctly surprised to find themselves in a place with no decent beach at all.

There are swimming opportunities further north however, where the pleasant low-key resort of **Eloúnda** is the gateway to the mysterious islet of **Spinalónga**, and some great back country to the north – perfect to explore on a scooter. Inland from Áyios Nikólaos, **Kritsá** with its famous church and textile sellers is a tour-bus haven, but just a couple of kilometres away, the imposing ruins of **ancient Lató** are usually deserted.

Áyios Nikólaos practicalities

The greatest concentration of **stores** and **travel agents** are on the hill between the bridge and Platía Venizélou. The main **ferry agent** is LANE (☎0841/26 465 or 23 090) on the corner of 25-Martíou and K. Sfakianáki. The **post office** (Mon–Fri 7.30am–8pm, Sat 7.30am–2pm) is halfway up the newly pedestrianized 28-Oktovríou on the right. The **tourist office** (daily 8.30am–9.30pm; ☎0841/22 357, fax 82 534), situated between the lake and the port, is one of the best on the island for information about accommodation. To **hire a motorbike** or mountain bike try the reliable Mike Manolis (☎0841/24 940), who has a pitch at the junction of 25-Martíou and Sfakianáki. Good **car rental** deals are available at Club Cars, 28-Oktobríou 24 (☎0841/25 868), near the post office. Various **boat trips** to points around the gulf (such as Spinalónga and Eloúnda) leave from the west side of the harbour. **Internet Café** Peripou (daily 9.30am–2am; 1000dr per hour), 28-Oktovríou 25, is Áyios Nikólaos's first of the breed should you want to pick up your emails.

Accommodation

The town is no longer packed solid with tourists, so it is much easier to find a place to stay, though in the peak season you won't have so much choice. One thing in your favour is that there are literally thousands of **rooms**, scattered all around town. The tourist office normally has a couple of boards with cards and brochures about hotels and rooms, including their prices. If the prices seem very reasonable it is because many are for the low season. There is no longer a youth hostel, and the nearest **campsite** is *Gournia Moon*, 17km away (see p.206).

Atlantis, Metamorfoseos, one block east of the bus station (☎0841/28 964). Nothing special but handy for early or late buses; there's a snack bar below for breakfast. ①.

Hotel Eva, Stratigoú Kóraka 20 (☎0841/22587). Decent simple rooms in a misnamed pension close to the centre. ①.

Green House, Modhátsou 15 (☎0841/22 025). Probably the best cheap place to stay in town; clean with shared facilities. ①.

Katerina, Stratigoú Kóraka 30 (☎0841/22 766). A pension close to the *Marilena* and another good choice in the lower price bracket. ②.

Marilena, Érythrou Stavroú 14 (☎0841/22 681, fax 22 681). One of the cheaper pensions for en-suite rooms, this is excellent value. ③.

Mediterranean, S. Dhávaki 27 (☎0841/23 611). Clean, economical rooms without bath close to the lake. ①.

Hotel Rea, Marathónos 1 (☎0841/82 023, fax 28 324). Charming old hotel at top end of this price bracket with stunning views from pleasant balcony rooms overlooking the Mirabéllo Gulf: breakfast included. ③.

Sgouros, Kitroplatía (☎0841/28 931, fax 25 568). Modern hotel overlooking one of the town's beaches, and close to plenty of tavernas. ③.

Eating

At least when it comes to eating there's no chance of missing out, even if the prices are fancier than the restaurants. There are tourist-orientated **tavernas** all around the lake and harbour and little to choose between them, apart from the different perspectives you get on the passing fashion show. Have a drink here perhaps, or a mid-morning coffee, and choose somewhere else to eat. The places around the Kitroplatía are generally fairer value, but again you are paying for the location.

Auoas, Paleológou 44. This taverna serves good, traditional Cretan dishes in and under a plant-covered trellised courtyard, where food and wine prices are among the lowest in town.

Café Migomis, Nikoláou Plastíra 22. Pleasant café high above the bottomless lake with a stunning view. Perfect place for breakfast, afternoon or evening drinks.

Itanos, Kyprou 1, off the east side of Platía Venizélou. Popular with locals, this taverna serves Cretan food and wine and has a terrace across the road opposite.

La Strada, Nikoláou Plastíra 5, just below the west side of Platía Venizélou. Authentic and good-value pizza and pasta, should you fancy a change of cuisine.

Ofou To Lo, Kitroplatía. Best of the moderately priced places on the seafront here: the food is consistently good.

Pelagos, on Stratigoú Kóraka, just back off the lake behind the tourist office. A stylish fish taverna with garden, serving excellent food reflected in the prices.

Sarris, Kýprou 15, off the east side of Platía Venizélou. Great little economical neighbourhood café-diner, especially good for breakfast and *souvláki* served on a leafy terrace.

Drinking and nightlife

After you've eaten you can get into the one thing which Áyios Nikólaos undeniably does well: **bars and nightlife**. Not that you really need a guide to this – the bars are hard to avoid, and you can just follow the crowds to the most popular places centred around the harbour and 25-Martíou. For a quieter drink you could try *Hotel Alexandros* on Paleológou (behind the tourist office), with a rooftop cocktail bar overlooking the lake, or *Zygos* on the north side of the lake which serves low priced cocktails and ices until the small hours. One curiosity worth a look in the harbour itself is *Armida*, a bar inside a beautiful century-old wooden trading vessel, serving cocktails and simple mezédhes.

Quiet drinking, however, is not what it's all about in the **disco bars**. *Lipstick*, on the east side of the harbour, as well as *Prince*, *Roxy* and *Santa Maria*, along 25-Martíou ("Soho Street") where it heads up the hill, are very popular and you'll soon be accosted by the greeters on the doors of the nearby *Aquarius*, *Charlie Chan* and *Premiere* as they all try to persuade you to help swell their takings.

The coast north of Áyios Nikólaos

North of Áyios Nikólaos, the swankier hotels are strung out along the coast road, with upmarket restaurants, discos and cocktail bars scattered between them. **ELOÚNDA**, a resort on a more acceptable scale, is about 8km out along this road. Buses run regularly, but if you feel like renting a scooter it's a spectacular ride, with impeccable views over a gulf dotted with islands and moored supertankers. Ask at the bookshop near the post office, on the central square facing the sea, about the attractive seaview *Delfinia Apartments* (☎0841/41 641, fax 41 515; ②). Or you could try the friendly *Pension Oasis* (☎0841/41 076, fax 41 128; ②), which has rooms with kitchenette just off the square, behind the church; there are quite a few similar places along the same road. Alternatively, one of the many travel agents around the main square can help with finding a room or apartment; try the friendly Olous Travel (☎0841/41 324, fax 41 132), which also gives out information and changes money or travellers' cheques. For **eating**, *Britomares*, in a plum spot in the centre of the harbour, is the town's best taverna and although **nightlife** tends to be generally low key, *Aligos* is a lively music bar and *Katafigio* on the Olous road often has *bouzoúki* nights.

Just before the village a track (signposted) leads across a causeway to the "sunken city" of **Oloús**. There are restored windmills, a short length of canal, Venetian salt pans and a well-preserved dolphin mosaic, but of the sunken city itself no trace beyond a couple of walls in about two feet of water. At any rate swimming is good, though there are sea urchins to watch out for.

From Eloúnda, kaïkia run to the fortress-rock of **Spinalónga**. As a bastion of the Venetian defence, this tiny islet withstood the Turkish invaders for 45 years after the mainland had fallen; in more recent decades, it served as a leper colony. As you watch the boat which brought you disappear to pick up another group, an unnervingly real sense of the desolation of those years descends. **PLÁKA**, back on the mainland, and 5km north of Eloúnda, used to be the colony's supply point; now it is a haven from the crowds, with a small pebble beach and a couple of ramshackle fish tavernas which can arrange a boat to take you across to Spinalónga for about 1000dr. There are boat trips daily from Áyios Nikólaos to Oloús, Eloúnda and Spinalónga, usually visiting at least one other island along the way.

Inland to Kritsá and Lató

The other excursion everyone takes from Áyios Nikólaos is to **KRITSÁ**, a "traditional" village about 10km inland. Buses run at least every hour from the bus station, and despite the commercialization it's still a good trip: the local **crafts** (weaving, ceramics and embroidery basically, though they sell almost everything here) are fair value, and it's also a welcome break from living in the fast lane at "Ag Nik". In fact, if you're looking for somewhere to stay around here, Kritsá has a number of advantages: chiefly availability of **rooms**, better prices and something at least approaching a genuinely Greek atmosphere; try *Argyro* (☎0841/51 174; ①) on your way to the village. There are a number of decent places to eat, too – try *Sygonos* near the bus stop for meals – or just to have a coffee and a cake under one of the plane trees.

On the approach road, some 2km before Kritsá, is the lovely Byzantine **church of Panayía Kyrá** (daily 8.30am–2.30pm; 800dr), inside which survives perhaps the most complete set of Byzantine frescoes in Crete. The fourteenth- and fifteenth-century works have been much retouched, but they're still worth the visit. Excellent (and expensive) reproductions are sold from a shop alongside. Just beyond the church, a surfaced road leads off towards the archeological site of **Lató** (Tues–Sun 9am–2.30pm; free), a Doric city with a grand hilltop setting. The city itself is extensive, but neglected, presumably because visitors and archeologists on Crete are more concerned with the Minoan era. Ruins aside, you could come here just for the views: west over Áyios Nikólaos and beyond to the bay and Oloús (which was Lató's port), and inland to the Lasíthi mountains.

The eastern isthmus

The main road south and then east from Áyios Nikólaos is not a wildly exciting one, essentially a drive through barren hills sprinkled with villas and skirting above the occasional sandy cove. Five kilometres beyond a cluster of development at Kaló Hório, a track is indicated on the right for the **Moní Faneroméni**. The track (though partly asphalted) is a rough one and climbs dizzily skywards for 6km, giving spectacular views over the Gulf of Mirabéllo along the way. The **view** from the monastery over the gulf must be the among the finest in Crete. To get into the rather bleak-looking monastery buildings, knock loudly. You will be shown up to the chapel, built into a cave sanctuary, and the frescoes are quite brilliant.

Gourniá, Pahiá Ámmos and Mókhlos

Back on the coast road, it's another 2km to the site of **Gourniá** (Tues–Sun 8.30am–3pm; 500dr), slumped in the saddle between two low peaks. The most completely preserved **Minoan town**, its narrow alleys and stairways intersect a throng of one-roomed houses (of which only the ground-floor walls survive – they would have had at least one upper floor) centred on a main square, and the rather grand house of what may have been a local ruler or governor. Although less impressive than the great palaces, the site is strong on revelations about the lives of the ordinary people – many of the dwellings housed craftsmen in wood, metal and clay, who left behind their tools and materials to be found by the excavators. Its desolation today (you are likely to be alone save for a dozing guard) only serves to heighten the contrast with what must have been a cramped and raucous community 3500 years ago.

It is tempting to cross the road here and take one of the paths through the wild thyme to the sea for a swim. Don't bother – the bay and others along this part of the coastline act as a magnet for every piece of floating detritus dumped off Crete's north coast. There is a larger beach (though with similar problems), and rooms to rent, in the next bay along at **PAHIÁ ÁMMOS**, about twenty minutes' walk, where there is also an excellent fish taverna, *Aiolus*; in the other direction, there's the campsite of *Gourniá Moon*, with its own small cove and a swimming pool.

This is the narrowest part of the island, and from here a fast road cuts across the isthmus to Ierápetra (p.210) in the south. In the north though, the route on towards Sitía is one of the most exhilarating in Crete. Carved into cliffs and mountain-sides, the road teeters above the coast before plunging inland at Kavoúsi. Of the beaches you see below, only **MÓKHLOS** is at all accessible, some 5km below the main road. This sleepy village has a few rooms, a hotel or two and a number of tavernas; if you find yourself staying the night, try the rooms at *Limenaria* (☎0843/94 206; ①). Nearer Sitía the familiar olive groves are interspersed with vineyards used for creating wine and sultanas, and in late summer the grapes, spread to dry in the fields and on rooftops, make an extraordinary sight in the varying stages of their slow change from green to gold to brown.

Sitía

SITÍA is the port and main town of the relatively unexploited eastern edge of Crete. It's a pleasantly scenic if unremarkable place, offering a plethora of waterside restaurants, a long sandy beach and a lazy lifestyle little affected even by the thousands of visitors in peak season. There's an almost Latin feel to the town, reflected in (or perhaps caused by) the number of French and Italian tourists, and it's one of those places that tends to grow on you, perhaps inviting a longer stay than intended. For entertainment, there's the **beach**, providing good swimming and windsurfing, and in town a mildly entertaining **folklore museum** (Tues–Sun 9.30am–2.30pm; Wed & Thurs also 6pm–8pm; 500dr), a Venetian fort and Roman fish tanks to explore, plus an excellent **archeological museum** (Tues–Sun 8.30am–3pm; 500dr). Look out, too, for the town's resident and mischievous pelican, Nikos, who has his own living quarters on the harbour quay.

Practicalities

The bus drops you at the new **bus station** (actually an office on the street) on the southwest fringe of the centre and close to the town's main **supermarket**, useful for stocking up on provisions. There are plenty of cheap pensions and **rooms** within easy walking distance, especially in the streets around the folkore museum and beyond here towards the ferry port. A good and friendly **youth hostel** (☎0843/22 693) on the main

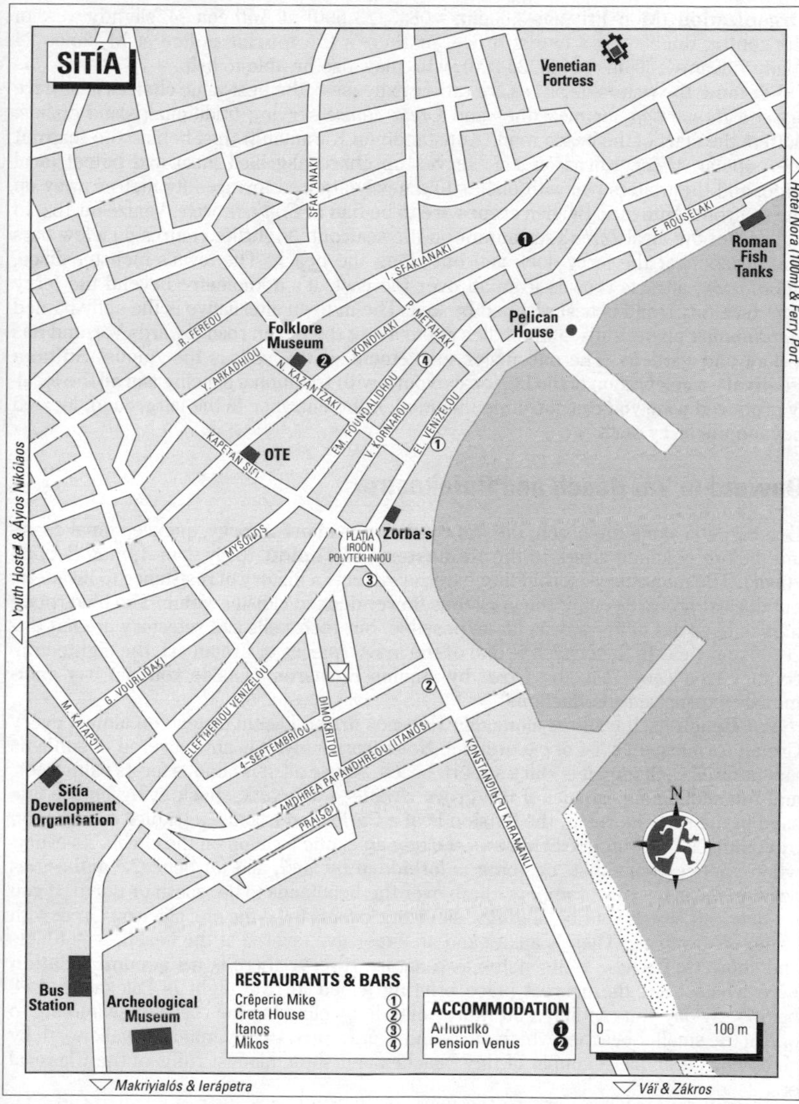

road as it enters town also has a few private rooms and a garden for tents; there's rarely any problem about sleeping on the beach (though it is worth going a little way out of town to avoid any danger of being roused by the police). For rooms, try *Pension Venus*, Kondiláki 60 (☎0843/24 307; ①), *Hotel Arhontiko*, Kondiláki 16 (☎0843/28 172; ①), and *Hotel Nora*, Rouseláki 31 (☎0843/23 017; ②), near the ferry port, for rooms with bath. If you have problems finding somewhere to stay, the **Sitía Development**

Organization (Mon–Fri 8am–3.30pm; ☎0843/23 590) at Anthéon 24, slightly west of the centre, doubles as a tourist office, or there's the **tourist police** at Mysónos 24 (daily 7.30am–2.30pm; ☎0843/24 200), who may also be able to help.

For **food**, the waterside places are rather expensive; the best-value choices near here are the *Itanos Cafe* for mezédhes and *Creta House* serving traditional island dishes, both at the start of the beach road (Konstandínou Karamanlí). Just behind the seafront the popular *Mikos*, Kornárou 117, serves up charcoal-grilled meat and potent local wine, and the waiters run with dishes to a newly aquired terrace fifty metres away on the seafront. Authentic Belgian crepes are to be had at *Creperie Mike*, Venizélou 162, to the east of the focal *Zorba's* restaurant on the seafront. **Nightlife** centres on a few bars and discos near the ferry dock and out along the beach. The town's monster disco, *Planitarion*, attracts crowds from all over the east. It's a kilometre beyond the ferry port (see map), and is best reached by taxi. The in-town alternative is the aptly named *Hot Summer* open-air disco which lies 800m along the beach road towards Váï, and has a pool and gardens. The one major excitement of the year is the August **Sultana Festival** – a celebration of the big local export, with traditional dancing and all the locally produced wine you can consume included in the entrance to the fairground, located beyond the ferry port.

Onward to Váï Beach and Palékastro

Leaving Sitía along the beach, the Váï road climbs above a rocky, unexceptional coastline before reaching a fork to the **monastery of Toploú** (daily 9am–1pm & 2–6pm; 700dr). The monastery's forbidding exterior reflects a history of resistance to invaders, but doesn't prepare you for the gorgeous flower-decked cloister within. The blue-robed monks keep out of the way as far as possible, but their cells and refectory are left discreetly on view. In the church is one of the masterpieces of Cretan art, the eighteenth-century icon *Lord Thou Art Great* by Ioánnis Kornáros. Outside you can buy enormously expensive reproductions.

Váï Beach itself features alongside Knossós or the Lasíthi plateau on almost every Cretan travel agent's list of excursions. Not surprisingly, it is now covered in sunbeds and umbrellas, though it is still a superb beach. Above all, it is famous for its palm trees, and the sudden appearance of the grove is indeed an exotic shock; lying on the fine sand in the early morning, the illusion is of a Caribbean island – a feature seized upon by countless TV-commercial makers seeking an exotic location on the cheap. As everywhere, notices warn that "camping is forbidden by law", and for once the authorities seem to mean it – most campers climb over the headlands to the south or north. If you do sleep out, watch your belongings, since this seems to be the one place on Crete with crime on any scale. There's a café and an expensive taverna at the beach, plus toilets and showers. Because of its status as a nature reserve there is **no accommodation** here whatsoever; the nearest place offering a bed for the night is Palékastro (see below). By day you can find a bit more solitude by climbing the rocks or swimming to one of the smaller beaches which surround Váï. **Ítanos**, twenty minutes' walk north by an obvious trail, has a couple of tiny beaches and some modest ruins of the Classical era.

PALÉKASTRO, some 9km south, is in many ways a better place to stay. Although its beaches can't begin to compare, you'll find several modest places with **rooms** – notably *Hotel Hellas* (☎0843/61 240, fax 61 340; ②), which provides good rooms and food – a number of reasonable restaurants, and plenty of space to camp out without the crowds. The sea is a couple of kilometres down a dirt track, effortlessly reached with a scooter hired from Motor Action (☎0843/61 276) next door to the *Hotel Hellas*. Palékastro is also the crossroads for the road south to Zákros and your own transport presents all kinds of beach and exploration possibilities.

Zákros

ÁNO ZÁKROS is a little under 20km from Palékastro. There are several tavernas and a simple hotel, the *Zakros* (☎0843/43 379, fax 93 379; ①), which has some rooms with bath and great views from its rear rooms; it also offers guests a free minibus service to the Minoan palace and beach. The Minoan palace is actually at Káto (Lower) Zákros, 8km further down towards the sea. Most buses run only to the upper village, but in summer, a couple every day do run all the way to the site. Part way along you can, if on foot, take a short cut through an impressive **gorge** (the "Valley of the Dead", named for ancient tombs in its sides) but it's usually not difficult to hitch if your bus does leave you in the village.

The **Palace of Zákros** (Tues–Sun 8.30am–2.30pm; 500dr) was an important find for archeologists; it had been occupied only once (between 1600 and 1450 BC), and was abandoned hurriedly and completely. Later, it was forgotten almost entirely and as a result was never plundered or even discovered by archeologists until very recently. The first major excavation began only in 1960; all sorts of everyday objects (tools, raw materials, food, pottery) were thus discovered intact among the ruins, and a great deal was learned from being able to apply modern techniques (and knowledge of the Minoans) to a major dig from the very beginning. None of this is especially evident when you're at the palace, except perhaps in a particularly simple ground plan, so it's as well that it is also a rewarding visit in terms of the setting. Although the site is set back from the sea, in places it is often marshy and waterlogged: partly the result of eastern Crete's slow subsidence, partly the fault of a spring which once supplied fresh water to a cistern beside the royal apartments, and whose outflow is now silted up. In wetter periods, among the remains of narrow streets and small houses higher up, you can keep your feet dry and get an excellent view down over the central court and royal apartments. If you want a more detailed overview of the remains, buy the guide to the site on sale at the entrance.

The delightful village of **KÁTO ZÁKROS** is little more than a collection of tavernas, some of which rent out rooms around a peaceful beach and minuscule fishing anchorage. It's a wonderfully restful place, but is often unable to cope with the volume of visitors seeking accommodation in high season, and as rooms are rarely to be had on spec you'd be wise to ring ahead. You should also be aware that villagers are far more hostile these days to wild camping after years of problems, and you should be sensitive to their concerns. Reliable rooms can be found at *Poseidon* (☎0843/93 316; ①), which has fine views, and the friendly *Rooms George* (☎ & fax 0843/93 201; ②), 200m behind the archeological site, is also good.

Ierápetra and the southeast coast

From Sitía, the route south is a cross-country roller-coaster ride until it hits the south coast at **MAKRYIALÓS**. This little fishing village has one of the best beaches at this end of Crete, with fine sand which shelves so gently you feel you could walk the 340km to Africa. Unfortunately, since the early 1990s it has been heavily developed, so while still a very pleasant place to stop for a swim or a bite (the *Porfiria* taverna on the sea is recommended), it's not somewhere you're likely to find a cheap room.

From here to Ierápetra there's little reason to stop; the few beaches are rocky and the coastal plain submerged under ranks of polythene-covered greenhouses. Beside the road leading into Ierápetra, are long but exposed stretches of sand, including the appropriately named "Long Beach", where you'll find a campsite, *Camping Koutsounari* (☎0842/61 213), which has plenty of shade.

Ierápetra

IERÁPETRA itself is a bustling modern supply centre for the region's farmers. It also attracts a fair number of package tourists and not a few backpackers looking for work in the prosperous surrounding agricultural zone, especially out of season. The tavernas along the tree-lined front are scenic enough and the EU blue-flagged beach stretches a couple miles east. But as a town, most people find it pretty uninspiring, despite an ongoing modernization programme which has cleaned up the centre and revamped the seafront. Although there has been a port here since Roman times, only the **Venetian fort** guarding the harbour and a crumbling minaret remain as reminders of better days. What little else has been salvaged is in the one-room **museum** (Tues–Sat 8am–3pm; 500dr) near the post office.

The town hall (*dhimarhío*) on the main square, Platía Kanoupáki, should be able to provide a town map (but not much else) which will help you find your way around. If you want to stay, head up Kazantzákis from the chaotic bus station, and you'll find **rooms** at the *Four Seasons* (☎0842/24 390; ②) or in the nearby *Cretan Villa*, Lakérdha 16 (☎ & fax 0842/28 522; ②), a beautiful 180-year-old house. More central, and also good value, is the *Hotel Ersi*, Platía Eleftherías 20 (☎0842/23 208; ②), which can also rent you a seafront apartment for not much more than the cost of a room. You'll find places to **eat** and **drink** all along the waterfront, the better places such as *Taverna Napoleon* and *Gorgona* being towards the Venetian fort. **Nightlife** centres on a clutch of disco bars and fast-food places along central Kýrba, behind the promenade. Ierapetra's **Internet café**, Orfeas (1400dr per hour), is at Koundouriótou 25, just north of the museum, and serves good breakfasts.

West from Ierápetra

Heading west from Ierápetra, the first stretch of coast is grey and dusty, the road jammed with trucks and lined with drab ribbon development. There are a number of small resorts along the beach, though little in the way of public transport. If travelling under your own steam, there is a scenic detour worth taking at Gría Liyiá: the road, on the right for Anatolí climbs to Máles, a village clinging to the lower slopes of the **Dhíkti range**. Here would be a good starting point if you want to take a walk through some stunning mountain terrain. Otherwise, the dirt road back down towards the coast (signposted Mýthi) has spectacular views over the Libyan Sea, and eventually follows the Mýrtos river valley down to Mýrtos itself.

Mýrtos and Árvi

MÝRTOS is the first resort that might actually tempt you to stop, and it's certainly the most accessible, just off the main road with numerous daily **buses** to Ierápetra and a couple direct to Iráklion. Although developed to a degree, it nonetheless remains tranquil and inexpensive, with lots of young travellers (many of whom sleep on the beach, to the irritation of locals). If you want a **room**, try *Rooms Angelos* (☎0842/51 106; ①), or *Nikos House* (☎0842/51 116; ①), though there are plenty of others. Just off the road from Ierápetra are a couple of excavated **Minoan villas** you might want to explore: Néa Mýrtos and Pýrgos.

After Mýrtos the main road turns inland towards Áno Viánnos, then continues across the island towards Iráklion; several places on the coast are reached by a series of rough sidetracks. That hasn't prevented one of them, **ÁRVI**, from becoming a larger resort than Mýrtos. The beach hardly justifies it, but it's an interesting little excursion (with at least one bus a day) if only to see the bananas and pineapples grown here and to experience the microclimate – noticeably warmer than neighbouring zones, especially in spring or autumn – that encourages them. For rooms you could try the central *Pension Gorgona* (☎0895/71 211; ②).

Beyond Árvi

Two more villages, **KERATÓKAMBOS** and **TSOÚTSOUROS**, look tempting on the map. Keratókambos has a rather stony beach and only basic rooms – the *Morning Star* taverna (☎0895/51 209; ①) is a good bet and the food is tasty too – and although popular with Cretan day-trippers it's a great place to escape the tourist grind for a spell. Tsoútsouros is developed and not really worth the tortuous thirteen-kilometre dirt road in.

If you hope to continue across the **south** of the island, be warned that there are no buses, despite completion of the road towards Mýres after years of work. It's an enjoyable rural drive, but progress can be slow; there's very little traffic if you're trying to hitch.

RÉTHYMNON AND AROUND

The relatively low, narrow section of Crete which separates the Psiloritis range from the White Mountains in the west seems at first a nondescript, even dull part of the island. Certainly in scenic terms it has few of the excitements that the west can offer; there are no major archeological sites and many of the villages seem modern and ugly. On the other hand, **Réthymnon** itself is an attractive and lively city, with some excellent beaches nearby. And on the south coast, in particular around **Plakiás**, there are beaches as fine as any Crete can offer, and as you drive towards them the scenery and villages improve by the minute.

Réthymnon

Since the early 1980s, **RÉTHYMNON** has seen a greater influx of tourists than perhaps anywhere else on Crete, with the development of a whole series of large hotels extending almost 10km along the beach to the east. For once, though, the middle of town has been spared, so that at its heart Réthymnon remains one of the most beautiful of Crete's major cities (only Haniá is a serious rival), with an enduringly provincial air. A wide sandy beach and palm-lined promenade border a labyrinthine tangle of Venetian and Turkish houses lining streets where ancient minarets lend an exotic air to the skyline. Dominating everything from the west is the superbly preserved outline of the **fortress** built by the Venetians after a series of pirate raids had devastated the town.

The town

With a **beach** right in the heart of town, it's tempting not to stir at all from the sands, but Réthymnon repays at least some gentle exploration. For a start, you could try checking out the further reaches of the beach itself. The waters protected by the breakwaters in front of town have their disadvantages – notably crowds and dubious hygiene – but less sheltered sands stretch for miles to the east, crowded at first but progressively less so if you're prepared to walk a bit.

Away from the beach, you don't have far to go for the most atmospheric part of town, immediately behind the **inner harbour**. Almost anywhere here, you'll find unexpected old buildings, wall fountains, overhanging wooden balconies, heavy, carved doors and rickety shops, many still with local craftsmen sitting out front, gossiping as they ply their trades. Look out especially for the **Venetian loggia**, which houses a shop selling

high quality and expensive reproductions of Classical art; the **Rimóndi fountain**, another of the more elegant Venetian survivals; and the **Nerandzés mosque**, the best preserved in Réthymnon but currently serving as a music school and closed to the public. Simply by walking past these three, you'll have seen many of the liveliest parts of Réthymnon. Ethnikís Andistásis, the street leading straight up from the fountain, is also the town's **market** area.

The old city ends at the Porta Guora at the top of Ethnikís Andistásis, the only surviving remnant of the city walls. Almost opposite are the quiet and shady **public gar-**

dens. These are always a soothing place to stroll, and in the latter half of July, the **Réthymnon Wine Festival** is staged here. Though touristy, it's a thoroughly enjoyable event, with spectacular local dancing as the evening progresses and the barrels empty. The entrance fee includes all the wine you can drink, though you'll need to bring your own cup or buy one of the souvenir glasses and carafes on sale outside the gardens.

The museums and fortress

A little further up the street from the Nerandzés mosque at M. Vernárdhou 28, a beautifully restored seventeenth-century Venetian mansion is the home of the small but tremendously enjoyable **Historical and Folk Art Museum** (Mon–Sat 10am–2pm, Mon & Tues also 6–8pm; 500dr). Gathered within four, cool, airy rooms are musical instruments, old photos, basketry, farm implements, an explanation of traditional bread-making techniques, smiths' tools, traditional costumes and jewellery, lace, weaving and embroidery, pottery, knives and old wooden chests. It makes for a fascinating insight into a fast disappearing rural (and urban) lifestyle, which had often survived virtually unchanged from Venetian times to the 1960s, and is well worth a look.

Heading in the other direction from the fountain you'll come to the fortress and **Archeological Museum** (Tues–Sun 8am–2.30pm; 500dr), which occupies a building almost directly opposite the entrance to the fortress. This was built by the Turks as an extra defence, and later served as a prison, but it's now entirely modern inside: cool, spacious and airy. Unfortunately, the collection is not particularly exciting, and really only worth seeing if you're going to miss the bigger museums elsewhere on the island.

The massive **Venetian fortress** (Tues–Sun 8am–8pm; reduced hours out of season; 800dr) is a must, however. Said to be the largest Venetian castle ever built, this was a response, in the last quarter of the sixteenth century, to a series of **pirate raids** (by Barbarossa among others) that had devastated the town. Inside is now a vast open space dotted with the remains of all sorts of barracks, arsenals, officers' houses, earthworks and deep shafts, and at the centre a large domed building that was once a church and later a **mosque** (complete with a surviving but sadly defaced *mihrab*). It was designed to be large enough for the entire population to take shelter within the walls, and you can see that it probably was. Although much is ruined, it remains thoroughly atmospheric, and you can look out from the walls over the town and harbour, or in the other direction along the coast to the west. It's also worth walking around the outside of the fortress, preferably at sunset, to get an impression of its fearsome defences, plus great views along the coast and a pleasant resting point around the far side at the *Sunset* taverna.

Practicalities

The **bus station** in Réthymnon is by the sea to the west of town just off Periferiakós, the road which skirts the waterfront around the fortress. The **tourist office** (Mon–Fri 8am–5.30pm, Sat 9am–2pm; ☎0831/24 143) backs onto the main town beach, close to the mobile post office (summer only). If you arrive by **ferry**, you'll be more conveniently placed, over at the western edge of the harbour. To pick up your emails head for the Galero **Internet café** (1400dr per hr), beside the Rimóndi fountain in the old town.

Accommodation

There's a great number of places to stay in Réthymnon, and only at the height of the season are you likely to have difficulty finding somewhere, though you may get weary looking. The greatest concentration of **rooms** is in the tangled streets west of the inner harbour, between the Rimóndi fountain and the museums; there are also quite a few places on and around Arkadhíou and Platía Frakidháki. The cheapest beds in town are in the **youth hostel**, Tombázi 41 (☎0831/22 848), where you can also sleep (illegally) on the roof. It's large, clean, very friendly and popular, and there's food, showers, clothes-washing facilities and even a library, with books in various languages.

There are a couple of **campsites** 4km east of town; take the bus for the hotels (marked *Scaleta/El Greco*) from the long-distance bus station to get there. *Camping Elizabeth* (☎0831/28 694) is a pleasant, large site on the beach, with all facilities. Only a few hundred metres further east along the beach is *Camping Arkadia* (☎0831/28 825), a bigger and slightly less friendly site.

Anna, Katehåki (☎0831/25 586). Comfortable pension in a quiet position on the street that runs straight down from the entrance to the fortress to Melissínou. ③.

Atelier, Himáras 32 (☎0831/24 440). Pleasant rooms close to *Rooms George*, run by a talented potter, who has her studio in the basement and sells her wares in a shop on the other side of the building. ②.

Barbara Dokimaki, Platía Plastíra 14 (☎0831/22 319). Strange warren of a rooms place, with one entrance at the above address, just off the seafront behind the *Ideon*, and another on Dambérgi; ask for the newly refurbished top-floor rooms, which have balconies. ②.

Byzantine, Vospórou 26 (☎0831/55 609). Excellent-value rooms in a renovated Byzantine palace. The tranquil patio bar is open to all, and breakfast is included in price. ③.

Ideon, Platía Plastíra 10 (☎0831/28 667, fax 28 670). Hotel with a brilliant position just north of the ferry dock; little chance of space in season, though. ⑥.

Leo, Vafé 2 (☎0831/26 197). Good hotel with lots of wood and a traditional feel; the price includes breakfast, and there's a bar. ③.

Olga's, Soulíou 57 (☎0831/53 206, fax 29 851). The star attraction at this very friendly pension on one of Réthymnon's most touristy streets is the resplendent flower-filled roof garden. ②.

Rethymnon House, V. Kornárou 1 (☎0831/23 923). Very pleasant rooms of a high standard in an old building just off Arkadhíou. Bar downstairs. ②.

Rooms George, Makedhonías 32 (☎0831/50 967). Decent rooms (some with fridge), near the Archeological Museum. ②.

Sea-Front Rent Rooms, Arkadhíou 159 (☎0831/51 981, fax 51 062). Rooms with sea views and balconies in an attractively refurbished mansion with ceiling fans and lots of wood. ②.

Zania, Pávlou Vlástou 3 (☎0831/28 169). Pension right on the corner of Arkadhíou; a well-adapted old house, but only a few rooms. ②.

Eating and drinking

Immediately behind the town beach are arrayed the most touristy **restaurants**, the vast majority being overpriced and of dubious quality. One that maintains some integrity (and reasonable prices) is the *Samaria* taverna, almost opposite the tourist office. Around the inner **harbour**, there's a second, rather more expensive group of tavernas, specializing in fish, though as often as not the intimate atmosphere in these places is spoiled by the stench from the harbour itself: *O Zefyros* is one of the less outrageously pricey and maintains reasonable standards. Not far from here and slightly west of Platía Plastíra, *Taverna Fanari* at Makedhonías 5 is a good-value little restaurant serving up tasty lamb and chicken dishes.

The cluster of kafenía and tavernas by the **Rimóndi fountain** and the newer places spreading into the surrounding streets generally offer considerably better value, and a couple of the old-fashioned kafenía serve magnificent yoghurt and honey. Places to try include *Kyria Maria* at Moskhovítou 20, tucked down an alley behind the fountain (after the meal, everyone gets a couple of María's delicious *tyropitákia* with honey on the house); *Agrimia*, a reliable standard on Platía Petiháki, slightly east of the fountain; and the *Zanfoti* kafenío overlooking the fountain which is relatively expensive, but a great place to people-watch over a coffee; and, for a slightly cheaper option *O Psaras* (the Fisherman), a simple, friendly taverna by the church on the corner of Nikifórou

Foká and Koronéou. A good lunchtime stop close to the Archeological Museum is *O Pontios*, Melissinoú 34, a simple place with tables outside and an enthusiastic female proprietor. Healthy, home-baked lunches can also be had at *Stella's Kitchen*, a simple café linked to *Olga's Pension* at Soulíou 55, where meals can be enjoyed up on the leafy roof garden. Tucked behind the church on Platía Martíron, *Mesostrati* is a pleasant little neighbourhood ouzerí/taverna serving well-prepared Cretan country dishes and having a small terrace. A noisier evening alternative is *Taverna O Gounos*, Koronéou 6 in the old town; the family who run it perform live *lyra* every night, and when things get really lively the dancing starts.

If you want takeaway food, there are numerous **souvláki** stalls, including a couple on Arkadhíou and Paleológou and another at Petikháki 52, or you can buy your own ingredients at the **market** stalls set up daily on Ethnikís Andistásis below the Porta Guora. There are small general stores scattered everywhere, particularly on Paleológou and Arkadhíou; east along the beach road you'll even find a couple of mini supermarkets. The **bakery** *I Gaspari* on Mesolongíou, just behind the Rimóndi fountain, sells the usual cheese pies, cakes and the like, and it also bakes excellent brown, black and rye bread. There's a good zaharoplastío, *N.A. Skartsilakos*, at Paleológou 36, just north of the fountain, and several more small cafés which are good for breakfast or a quick coffee.

Nightlife

Nightlife is concentrated in the same general areas as the tavernas. At the west end of Venizélou, in the streets behind the inner harbour, the overflow from a small cluster of noisy music bars – *Templum*, *252*, *Dimmam*, *Karma* and *Venetianikoa* – begins to spill out onto the pavement as party-goers gather for the nightly opening of the *Fortezza Disco* in the inner harbour, which is the glitziest in town, flanked by its competitors *Metropolis*, *NYC* and *Vitro*. Heading up Salamínos, a string of more subdued cocktail bars – *Petaloúda*, *Memphis*, *Santan* and *Pasodia* – cater for those in search of a quieter drink as does *Notas*, Himeras 27 near the *Fortezza* and facing the *Atelier* pension, which puts on live (acoustic) guitar and song every night.

Around Réthymnon

While some of Crete's most drastic resort development spreads ever eastwards out of Réthymnon, to the west a sandy coastline, not yet greatly exploited, runs all the way to the borders of Haniá province. But of all the short trips that can be made out of Réthymnon, the best known and still the most worthwhile is to the **monastery of Arkádhi**.

Southeast to Arkádhi

The **monastery of Arkádhi** (daily 8am–8pm; 300dr), some 25km southeast of the city and immaculately situated in the foothills of the Psiloritis range, is also something of a national Cretan shrine. During the 1866 rebellion against the Turks, the monastery became a rebel strongpoint in which, as the Turks gained the upper hand, hundreds of Cretan guerrillas and their families took refuge. Surrounded and, after two days of fighting, on the point of defeat, the defenders ignited a powder magazine just as the Turks entered. Hundreds (some sources claim thousands) were killed, Cretan and Turk alike, and the tragedy did much to promote international sympathy for the cause of Cretan independence. Nowadays, you can peer into the roofless vault where the explosion occurred and wander about the rest of the well-restored grounds. The sixteenth-century church survived, and is one of the finest Venetian structures left on

Crete; other buildings house a small museum devoted to the exploits of the defenders of the (Orthodox) faith. The monastery is easy to visit by public bus or on a tour.

West to Aryiroúpolis, Yeoryoúpoli and beyond

Leaving Réthymnon to the west, the main road climbs for a while above a rocky coastline before descending (after some 5km) to the sea, where it runs alongside sandy **beaches** for perhaps another 7km. An occasional hotel offers accommodation, but on the whole there's nothing but a line of straggly bushes between the road and the windswept sands. If you have your own vehicle, there are plenty of places you can stop at here for a swim, and rarely anyone else around – but beware of some very strong currents.

One worthwhile detour inland is to **ARYIROÚPOLIS**, a charming village perched above the Mousselás river valley and the seat of ancient Lappa, a Greek and Roman town of some repute. The village is famous for its **springs** which gush dramatically from the hillside and provide most of the city of Réthymnon's water supply. Among the number of **places to stay** try *Rooms Argiroupolis* (0831/81 148; ②), near the springs, while for **places to eat**, you're spoilt for choice, with five tavernas at the springs and a bar in the upper village together with a taverna (*Agnantema*) offering a spectacular terrace view over the valley. A shop under the arch in the main square can provide a village **map** detailing a surprising number of churches, caves and ancient remains to see in and around the village, including an outstanding third-century **Roman mosaic**. An interesting **folklore museum** (daily 9am–9pm; 300dr) – signed from the main square – is worth a look for its collection of tapestries, farm implements, photos and ephemera collected by the Zografakis family who have lived here for countless generations. There are numerous fine **walks** to be had in the surrounding hills, on which the proprietor of the village shop, who speaks English will advise. Although little over 20km from Réthymnon and easy to get to with your own transport, Aryiroúpolis is also served by **buses** from Réthymnon's bus station at 11.30am and 2.30pm, and in the reverse direction at 7.30am, 12.30 and 4pm (all Mon–Fri only).

Back on the coastal route, if you are looking for a place to relax for a while, probably the best base is **YEORYOÚPOLI** just across the provincial border in Haniá, where the beach is cleaner, wider and further from the road. There's been a distinct acceleration in the pace of development at Yeoryoúpoli over the last few years and it's now very much a resort, packed with rooms to rent, small hotels, apartment buildings, tavernas and travel agencies; there's even a small land train to transport visitors along the seafront and on short excursions. But everything remains on a small scale, and the undeniably attractive setting is untarnished, making it a very pleasant place to pass a few days, as long as you don't expect to find many vestiges of traditional Crete. Most of the better rooms, including *Rent Rooms Stelios* (☎0825/61 308; ②), *Irene* (☎0825/61 278; ②) and *Cretan Cactus* (☎0825/61 027; ②), are away from the main platía along the road down towards the beach. More central possibilities include *Rooms Voula* (☎0825/61 359; ①) above a gift shop to the east of the platía and the *Paradise Taverna* (☎0825/61 313; ②) off the southeast corner of the platía, which has rooms and is a good place to eat.

Within walking distance inland – though it can also be visited on the tourist train from Yeoryoúpoli – is **Kournás**, Crete's only lake, set deep in a bowl of hills and almost constantly changing colour. There are a few tavernas with rooms to rent along the shore here (bring mosquito repellent), or you could try for a bed in the nearby village of Moúri. A few kilometres uphill in Kournás village, the *Kali Kardia* taverna is a great place to sample the local lamb and sausages.

Beyond Yeoryoúpoli, the main road heads inland, away from a cluster of coastal villages beyond Vámos. It thus misses the Dhrápano peninsula, with some spectacular views over the sapphire Bay of Soúdha, several quiet beaches and the setting for the film of *Zorba the Greek*. **Kókkino Horió**, the movie location, and nearby **Pláka** are indeed postcard-picturesque (more so from a distance), but **Kefalás**, inland, outdoes both of them. On the exposed north coast there are good beaches at **Almyrídha** and **Kalýves**, and off the road between them. Both are fast developing into resorts in their own right; accommodation is mostly in apartments and rooms are scarce, although there are a few mid-range and more upmarket hotels, and a decent pension, *Katrina* (☎0825/38 775; ②), a short walk uphill from the centre of Almyrídha. With a string of good fish tavernas (try *Dimitri's* or *Manoli's*) along the beach and a pleasantly refreshing sea breeze, Almyrídha makes an enjoyable lunch stop.

South from Réthymnon

There are a couple of alternative routes south from Réthymnon, but the main one heads straight out from the centre of town, an initially featureless road due south across the middle of the island towards **Ayía Galíni**. About 23km out, a turning cuts off to the right for **Plakiás** and **Mýrthios**, following the course of the spectacular Kourtaliótiko ravine.

Plakiás and the south coast

Since the late 1980s, **PLAKIÁS** has undergone a major boom and is no longer the pristine village all too many people arriving here expect. That said, it's still quite low key, and there's a satisfactory beach and a string of good tavernas around the dock. There are hundreds of **rooms**, but at the height of summer you'll need to arrive early if you hope to find one; the last to fill are generally those on the road leading inland, away from the waterside. For rooms try *Christos Taverna* (☎0832/31 472; ①) on the seafront, or the excellent balcony rooms at *Ippokambos* (☎0832/31 525; ①) slightly inland on the road to the relaxed **youth hostel** (☎0832/31 306), which is 500m inland and signed from the seafront.

Once you've found a room there's not a lot else to discover here. You'll find every facility strung out around the waterfront, including a temporary **post office** parked by the harbour, bike rental, money exchange, supermarket and even a laundry. Places to eat are plentiful too. The attractive **tavernas** on the waterfront in the centre are a little expensive; you'll eat cheaper further inland – seek out *Taverna Medusa* at the east end of town – or around the corner from *Christos* at one of the tavernas facing west, where *Sunset* taverna is the first in line.

Mýrthios

For a stay of more than a day or two, **MÝRTHIOS**, in the hills behind Plakiás, also deserves consideration. It's no longer a great deal cheaper, but at least you'll find locals still outnumbering the tourists and something of a travellers' scene based around another popular **youth hostel** (☎0832/31 202), with a friendly taverna and several rooms for rent. The Plakiás bus will usually loop back through Mýrthios, but check; otherwise, it's less than five minutes' walk from the junction. It takes twenty minutes to walk down to the beach at Plakiás, a little longer to Dhamnóni, and if you're prepared to walk for an hour or more, there are some entirely isolated coves to the west – ask for directions at the hostel.

Dhamnóni

Some of the most tempting **beaches** in central Crete hide just to the east of Plakiás, though unfortunately they're now a very poorly kept secret. These three splashes of yellow sand, divided by rocky promontories, are within easy walking distance and together go by the name **Dhamnóni**. At the first, Dhamnóni proper, there's a taverna with showers and a wonderfully long strip of sand, but there's also a lot of new development including a number of nearby rooms for rent and a huge and ugly Swiss-owned holiday village, which has colonized half of the main beach. At the far end, you'll generally find a few people who've dispensed with their clothes, while the little cove which shelters the middle of the three beaches (barely accessible except on foot) is entirely nudist. Beyond this, **Ammoúdhi** beach has another taverna (with good rooms for rent) and a slightly more family atmosphere.

Préveli and "Palm Beach"

Next in line comes **PRÉVELI**, some 6km southeast of Lefkóyia. It takes its name from a **monastery** (daily 8am–7pm; 500dr) high above the sea which, like every other in Crete, has a proud history of resistance, in this case accentuated by its role in the last war as a shelter for marooned Allied soldiers awaiting evacuation off the south coast. There are fine views and a monument commemorating the rescue operations, but little else to see. The evacuations took place from "**Palm Beach**", a sandy cove with a small date-palm grove and a solitary drink stand where a stream feeds a little oasis. The beach usually attracts a summer camping community and is now also the target of day-trip boats from Plakiás. Sadly, these two groups between them have left this lovely place filthy, and despite an ongoing clean-up campaign it seems barely worth the effort. The climb down from the monastery is steep, rocky and surprisingly arduous: it's a great deal easier to come here by boat.

Spíli and Ayía Galíni

Back on the main road south, **SPÍLI** lies about 30km from Réthymnon. A popular coffee break for coach tours passing this way, Spíli warrants time if you can spare it. Sheltered under a cliff are narrow alleys of ancient houses, all leading up from a platía with a famous 24-spouted fountain. If you have your own transport, it's a worthwhile place to stay, peacefully rural at night but with several good **rooms** for rent. Try the *Green Hotel* (☎0832/22 225; ②) or the pleasant *Rooms Herakles* (☎0832/22 411; ②) just behind, the eponymous proprietor of which can advise on some superb **walks** in the surrounding hills.

The ultimate destination of most people on this road is **AYÍA GALÍNI**. If heading here was your plan, maybe you should think again since this picturesque "fishing village" is so busy in high season that you can't see it for the tour buses, hotel billboards and British package tourists. It also has a beach much too small for the crowds that congregate here. Even so, there are a few saving graces – mainly some excellent restaurants and bars, plenty of rooms and a friendly atmosphere that survives and even thrives on all the visitors. Out of season, it can be quite enjoyable, and from November to April the mild climate makes it an ideal spot to spend the winter. A lot of long-term travellers do just that, so it's a good place to find work packing tomatoes or polishing cucumbers. If you want somewhere to stay, start looking at the top end of town, around the main road: the good-value and friendly *Hotel Minos* (☎0832/91 292; ①), with superb views, is a good place to start, with the nearby *Hotel Hariklia* (0832/91 350, fax 91 257; ①) as a backup, but there are dozens of possibilities, and usually something to be found even at the height of summer.

The coastal plain east of Ayía Galíni, hidden under acres of polythene greenhouses and burgeoning concrete sprawl, must be among the ugliest regions in Crete, and **Timbáki** the dreariest town. Since this is the way to Festós and back to Iráklion, however, you may have no choice but to grin and bear it.

The Amári Valley

An alternative route south from Réthymnon, and a far less travelled one, is the road which turns off on the eastern fringe of town to run via the **Amári Valley**. Very few buses go this way, but if you're driving it's well worth the extra time. There's little specifically to see or do (though hidden away are a number of richly frescoed Byzantine churches), but it's an impressive drive under the flanks of the mountains and a reminder of how, in places, rural Crete continues to exist regardless of visitors. The countryside here is delightfully green even in summer, with rich groves of olive and assorted fruit trees, and if you **stay** (there are rooms in Thrónos and Yerákari), you'll find the nights are cool and quiet. It may seem odd that many of the villages along the way are modern; they were systematically destroyed by the Germans in reprisal for the 1944 kidnapping of General Kreipe.

HANIÁ AND THE WEST

The substantial attractions of Crete's westernmost quarter are all the more enhanced by its relative lack of visitors, and despite the now-rapid spread of tourist development, the west is likely to remain one of the emptier parts of the island. This is partly because there are no big sandy beaches to accommodate resort hotels, and partly because it's so far from the great archeological sites. But for mountains and empty (if often pebbly) beaches, it's unrivalled.

Haniá itself is one of the best reasons to come here, perhaps the only Cretan city which could be described as enjoyable in itself. The immediately adjacent coast is relatively developed and not overly exciting; if you want beaches head for the south coast. **Paleohóra** is the only place which could really be described as a resort, and even this is on a thoroughly human scale; others are emptier still. **Ayía Rouméli** and **Loutró** can be reached only on foot or by boat; **Hóra Sfakíon** sees hordes passing through but few who stay; **Frangokástello**, nearby, has a beautiful castle and the first stirrings of development. Behind these lie the **Lefká Óri** (White Mountains) and, above all, the famed walk through the **Gorge of Samariá**.

Haniá

HANIÁ, as any of its residents will tell you, is spiritually the capital of Crete, even if the nominal title was passed back (in 1971) to Iráklion. For many, it is also by far the island's most attractive city, especially if you can catch it in spring, when the Lefká Óri's snow-capped peaks seem to hover above the roofs. Although it is for the most part a modern city, you might never know it as a tourist. Surrounding the small outer harbour is a wonderful jumble of half-derelict **Venetian streets** that survived the wartime bombardments, and it is here that life for the visitor is concentrated. Restoration and gentrification, consequences of the tourist boom, have made inroads of late, but it remains an atmospheric place.

Arrival, information and orientation

Large as it is, Haniá is easy to handle once you've reached the centre; you may get lost wandering among the narrow alleys of the old city but that's a relatively small area, and

The phone code for Haniá is ☎0821

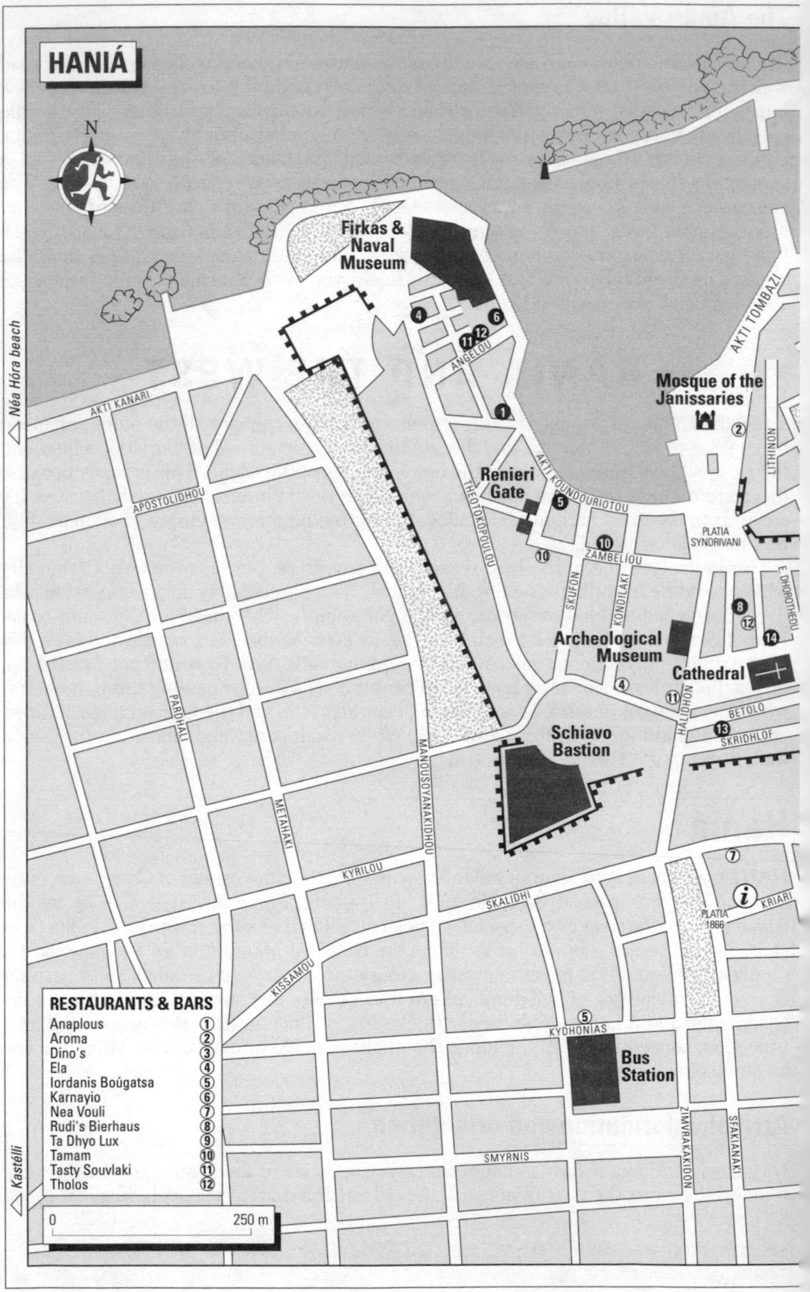
HANIÁ
N
Firkas & Naval Museum
Mosque of the Janissaries
Renieri Gate
Archeological Museum
Cathedral
Schiavo Bastion
Bus Station
PLATIA SYNDRIVANI
PLATIA 1866
AKTI TOMBAZI
AKTI KANARI
ANGELOU
AKTI KOUNDOURIOTOU
APOSTOLIDHOU
THEOTOKÓPOULOU
ZAMBELIOU
SKUFON
KONDILAKI
LITHINON
E. DHOROTHEOU
HALIDHON
BETOLO
SKRIDHLOF
PARDHALI
METAHAKI
MANOUSOYANAKIDHOU
KYRILOU
SKALIDHI
KRIARI
KISSAMOU
KYDHONIAS
ZIMVRAKAKIDON
SFAKIANAKI
SMYRNIS
Néa Hóra beach
Kastélli
RESTAURANTS & BARS
Anaplous 1
Aroma 2
Dino's 3
Ela 4
Iordanis Boúgatsa 5
Karnayio 6
Nea Vouli 7
Rudi's Bierhaus 8
Ta Dhyo Lux 9
Tamam 10
Tasty Souvlaki 11
Tholos 12
0
250 m

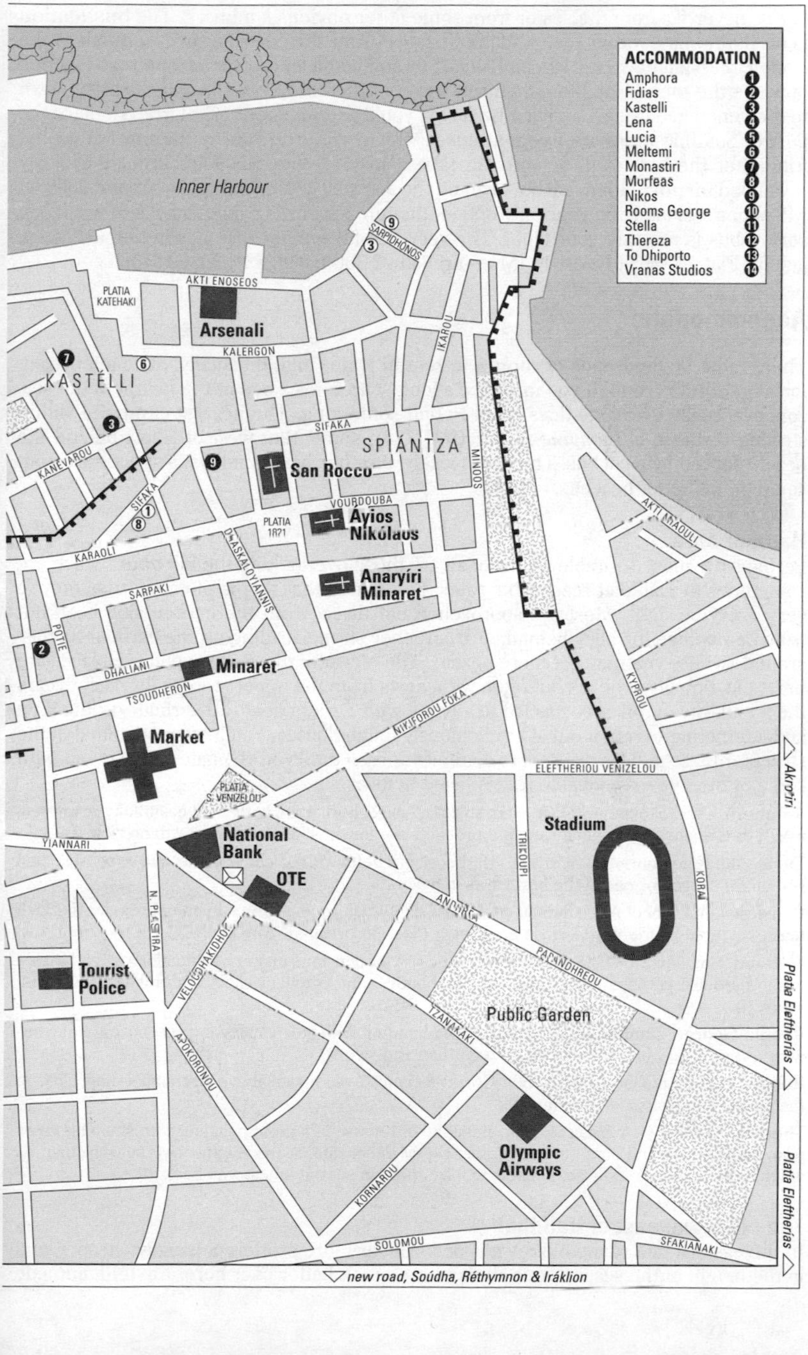
ACCOMMODATION
Amphora 1
Fidias 2
Kastelli 3
Lena 4
Lucia 5
Meltemi 6
Monastiri 7
Murfeas 8
Nikos 9
Rooms George 10
Stella 11
Thereza 12
To Dhiporto 13
Vranas Studios 14
Inner Harbour
SARPIDHONOS
AKTI ENOSEOS
PLATIA KATEHAKI
Arsenali
KALERGON
KASTÉLLI
IKAROU
SIFAKA
SPIÁNTZA
MINOOS
KANEVAROU
San Rocco
VOURDOUBA
PLATIA 1821
Áyios Nikólaos
AKTI KHAOULI
KARAOLI
DHASKALOYIANNIS
SARPAKI
Anaryíri Minaret
POTIE
DHALIANI
Minaret
TSOUDHERON
NIKIFOROU FOKA
KYPROU
Market
ELEFTHERIOU VENIZELOU
Akrotíri
PLATIA S. VENIZELOU
Stadium
National Bank
YIANNARI
OTE
TRIKOUPI
KORAI
N. PLASTIRA
ANDROGEO
PAPANDHREOU
VELOUDHAKIDHOU
Tourist Police
Platía Eleftherías
Public Garden
APOKORONOU
TZANAKAKI
Olympic Airways
Platía Eleftherías
KORNAROU
SOLOMOU
SFAKIANAKI
new road, Soúdha, Réthymnon & Iráklion

you're never far from the sea or from some other obvious landmark. The **bus station** is on Kydhonías, within easy walking distance from the centre – turn right out of the station, then left down the side of Platía 1866 and you'll emerge at a major road junction opposite the top of Halídhon, the main street of the old quarter leading straight down to the Venetian harbour. Arriving by **ferry**, you'll anchor about 10km from Haniá at the port of Soúdha: there are frequent buses which will drop you by the **market** on the fringes of the old town, or you can take a taxi (around 1500dr). From the newly revamped **airport** (15km east of town on the Akrotíri peninsula) taxis (around 2500dr) will almost certainly be your only option, though it's worth a quick check to see if any sort of bus is meeting your flight. The very helpful **tourist office** is in the new town, just off Platía 1866 at Kriári 40 (Mon–Fri 8am–2.30pm ☎92 624, fax 92 943).

Accommodation

There must be thousands of **rooms** to rent in Haniá and, unusually, quite a few comfortable **hotels**. Though you may face a long search for a bed at the height of the season, eventually everyone does seem to find something. The nearest **campsite** within striking distance is *Camping Hania* (☎31 138), some 4km west of Haniá behind the beach, served by local bus. The site is lovely, if rather basic, and just a short walk from some of the better beaches.

Harbour area

Perhaps the most desirable rooms of all are those overlooking the **harbour**, which are sometimes available at reasonable rates: be warned that this is often because they're very noisy at night. Most are approached not direct from the harbourside itself but from Zambelíou, the alley behind, or from other streets leading off the harbour further around (where you may get more peace). The nicest of the more expensive places are here, too, equally set back but often with views from the upper storeys. In recent years the popularity of this area has led to anyone with a room near the harbour tarting it up and attempting to rent it out at a ridiculously inflated price. You'll often be touted in the street for these and it's wise not to commit yourself until you've made comparisons with some of the more reasonable places listed below.

Amphora, Theotokopoúlou 20 (☎ & fax 93 224). Large, traditional hotel, and beautifully renovated; worth the expense if you get a view, but probably not for the cheaper rooms with no view. ⑥.

Lucia, Aktí Koundouriótou (☎90 302). Harbourfront hotel with balcony rooms; less expensive than you might expect for one of the best views in town. ②.

Pension Lena, Theotokopoúlou 60 (☎ & fax 72 265). Charming rooms in an old wooden Turkish house restored by friendly German proprietor. Pleasant breakfast café below. ②.

Meltemi, Angélou 2 (☎ 92 802). First of a little row of pensions in a great situation on the far side of the harbour; perhaps noisier than its neighbours, but excellent views and a good café downstairs. ③.

Rooms George, Zambelíou 30 (☎88 715). Old building with steep stairs and eccentric antique furniture; rooms vary in price according to position and size. ①.

Rooms Stella, Angélou 10 (☎73 756). Creaky, eccentric old house above a ceramics shop, close to the *Lucia*, with plain, clean rooms. ②.

Thereza, Angélou 8 (☎ & fax 92 798). Beautiful old house in a great position, with stunning views from roof terrace and some of the rooms; classy decor, too. A more expensive pension than its neighbours but deservedly so; unlikely to have room in season unless you book. ③.

The old town: east of Halídhon

In the eastern half of the old town rooms are far more scattered, usually cheaper, and in the height of the season your chances are much better over here. **Kastélli**, immediately east of the harbour, has some lovely places with views from the heights. Take one of the alleys leading left off Kanevárou if you want to try these, but don't be too hopeful since they are popular and often booked up.

To Dhiporto, Betólo 41, one block north of Skridhlóf (☎53 430). The proprietor of one of Haniá's longest established tavernas with the same name has retired and turned it into a very good-value rooms place with economical doubles and trebles. Recommended. ①.

Fidias, Kalinákou Sarpáki 8 (☎52 494). Signposted from the cathedral, this favourite backpackers' meeting place is rather bizarrely run, but is a friendly pension and has the real advantage of offering single rooms or fixing shares – but watch your baggage with strangers. ①.

Kastelli, Kanevárou 39 (☎57 057, fax 45 314). Not in the prettiest of locations, but a comfortable, modern, reasonably priced pension and very quiet at the back. All rooms come with fans and anti-mosquito machines. The owner is exceptionally helpful and also has a few apartments and a beautiful house (for up to five people) to rent. ②.

Monastiri, Ayíou Márkou 18, off Kanevárou (☎54 776). Pleasant rooms, some with a sea view in the restored ruins of a Venetian monastery. ②.

Morfeas, Isodhíon 15 (☎57 179). Between the cathedral platía and Platía Syndriváni, in the first street parallel to Halídhon. Rather dark, but good value for so central a position. ②.

Nikos, Dhaskaloyiánnis 58 (☎54 783). One of a few down here near the inner harbour; good-value, relatively modern rooms, all with shower. Same owner has economical studios nearby with kitchen and fridge. ①.

Vranas Studios, Ayíon Dhéka & Kalinákou Sarpáki, near the cathedral (☎ & fax 58 618). Pleasant, spacious studio-style rooms with TV, air-con, fridge and kitchenette. ③.

The City

Haniá has been occupied almost continuously since Neolithic times, so it comes as a surprise that a city of such antiquity should offer little specifically to see or do. It is, however, a place which is fascinating simply to wander around, stumbling upon surviving fragments of city wall, the remains of **ancient Kydonia** which are being excavated, and odd segments of Venetian or Turkish masonry.

Kastélli and the harbour

The **port** area is as ever the place to start, the oldest and the most interesting part of town. It's at its busiest and most attractive at night, when the lights from bars and restaurants reflect in the water and crowds of visitors and locals turn out to promenade. By day, things are quieter. Straight ahead from Platía Syndriváni (also known as Harbour Square) lies the curious domed shape of the **Mosque of the Janissaries**, until 1991 the tourist office, but currently without a function.

The little hill that rises behind the mosque is **Kastélli**, site of the earliest habitation and core of the Minoan, Venetian and Turkish towns. There's not a great deal left, but archeologists believe that they may have found the remains of a Minoan palace (logically, there must have been one at this end of the island) in the **excavations** being carried out – and open to view – along Kanevárou. It's also here that you'll find traces of the oldest **walls**; there were two rings, one defending Kastélli alone, a later set encompassing the whole of the medieval city. Beneath the hill, on the inner (eastern) harbour, the arches of sixteenth-century **Venetian arsenals** survive alongside remains of the outer walls; both are currently undergoing restoration.

Following the esplanade around in the other direction leads to a hefty bastion which now houses Crete's **Naval Museum** (daily 10am–4pm; 500dr). The collection is not exactly riveting, although a recently added section on the 1941 **Battle of Crete** with fascinating artefacts, and poignant photos depicting the suffering here under the Nazis, perhaps justifies the entry fee. You might want to wander in anyway for a (free) look at the seaward fortifications and the platform from which the modern Greek flag was first flown on Crete (in 1913). Walk around the back of these restored bulwarks to a street heading inland and you'll find the best-preserved stretch of the outer walls.

The old city

Behind the harbour, lie the less picturesque but more lively sections of the old city. First, a short way up Halídhon on the right, is Haniá's **archeological museum** (Tues–Sun 8am–2.30pm; 500dr) housed in the Venetian-built church of San Francesco. Damaged as it is, especially from the outside, this remains a beautiful building and it contains a fine little display, covering the local area from Minoan through to Roman times. In the garden, a huge fountain and the base of a minaret survive from the period when the Turks converted the church into a mosque; around them are scattered various other sculptures and architectural remnants.

The **cathedral**, ordinary and relatively modern, is just a few steps further up Halídhon on the left. Around it are some of the more animated shopping areas, particularly **Odhós Skrídhlof** ("Leather Street"), with streets leading up to the back of the market beyond. In the direction of the Spiántza quarter are ancient alleys with tumble-down Venetian stonework and overhanging wooden balconies; though gentrification is spreading apace, much of the quarter has yet to feel the effect of the city's modern popularity. There are a couple more **minarets** too, one on Dhaliáni, and the other in Platía 1821, which is a fine traditional platía to stop for a coffee.

The new town

Once out of the narrow confines of the maritime district, the broad, traffic-choked streets of the **modern city** have a great deal less to offer. Up Tzanakáki, not far from the market, you'll find the **public gardens**, a park with strolling couples, a few caged animals (including a few *kri-kri* or Cretan ibex) and a café under the trees; there's also an open-air auditorium which occasionally hosts live music or local festivities. Beyond here, you could continue to the **historical museum** (Mon–Fri 9am–1pm), but the effort would be wasted unless you're a Greek-speaking expert on the subject; the place is essentially a very dusty archive with a few photographs on the wall. Perhaps more interesting is the fact that the museum lies on the fringes of Haniá's desirable residential districts. If you continue to the end of Sfakianáki and then go down Iróön Polytekhníou towards the sea, you'll get an insight into how Crete's other half lives. There are several (expensive) garden restaurants down here and a number of fashionable café-bars where you can sit outside.

The beaches

Haniá's beaches all lie to the west of the city. For the packed **city beach**, this means no more than a ten-minute walk following the shoreline from the naval museum, but for good sand you're better off taking the local bus out along the coast road. This leaves from the east side of Platía 1866 and runs along the coast road as far as **Kalamáki beach**. Kalamáki and the previous stop, **Oásis beach**, are again pretty crowded but they're a considerable improvement over the beach in Haniá itself. In between, you'll find emptier stretches if you're prepared to walk: about an hour in all (on sandy beach virtually all the way) from Haniá to Kalamáki, and then perhaps ten minutes from the road to the beach if you get off the bus at the signs to *Aptera Beach* or *Camping Hania*. Further afield there are even finer beaches at **Ayía Marína** to the west, or **Stavrós** (see p.227) out on the Akrotíri peninsula (reached by KTEL buses from the main station).

Eating

You're never far from something to **eat** in Haniá: in a circle around the harbour is one restaurant, taverna or café after another. All have their own character, but there seems little variation in price or what's on offer. Away from the water, there are plenty of slightly cheaper possibilities on Kondhiláki, Kanevárou and most of the streets off Halídhon. For snacks or lighter meals, the cafés around the harbour on the whole serve cocktails and fresh juices at exorbitant prices, though breakfast (especially "English") can be good value. For more traditional places, try around the market and along Dhaskaloyiánnis (*Synganaki* here is a good traditional bakery serving *tyrópitta* and the like, with a cake shop next door). Fast food is also increasingly widespread, with numerous *souvláki* places on Karaolí; at the end of the outer harbour, near the naval museum; and around the corner of Plastíra and Yiannári, across from the **market** (see "Listings" overleaf, for details of the market and supermarkets).

Anaplous, Sífaka 37. A couple of blocks west of Platía 1821, this is a popular new open-air restaurant inside a stylishly "restored" ruin of a Turkish mansion bombed in the war. Serves both mezédhes and full meals to live guitar music.

Aroma, Aktí Tombázi 4, next to the Mosque of the Janissaries. Pleasant café with great harbour view to savour over lazy breakfasts or late drinks.

Iordanis Bougatsa, Kydhonias 96, opposite the bus station. This place serves little except the traditional creamy *bougátsa*, a sugar-coated cheese pie to eat in or take away.

Ta Dhyo Lux, Sarpidhónos. One of a line of cafés close to the harbour to sit out and be seen in the evening. Try an expensive but sublime lemon *granita*.

Dino's, inner harbour by bottom of Sarpidhónos. One of the best choices for a pricey seafood meal with a harbour view; *Apostolis*, almost next door, is also good.

Karnayio, Platía Kateháki 8. Set back from the inner harbour near the port police. Not right on the water, but one of the best harbour restaurants nonetheless.

Meltemi, Angélou 2. Slow, relaxed terrace bar beneath the rooms place of the same name; good for breakfast, and where locals (especially expats) sit whiling the day away or playing *tavli*.

Nea Vouli, Yiannári 27, just west of Platía 1866. Excellent and stylish new restaurant serving high-quality standards at modest prices.

Rudi's Bierhaus, Sífaka 24. Austrian Rudi Riegler's bar stocks more than a hundred of Europe's finest beers to accompany mezédhes.

Tamam, Zambelíou just before Renieri Gate. Young, trendy place with adventurous Greek menu including much vegetarian food. Unfortunately only a few cramped tables outside, and inside it's very hot. Slow service.

Tasty Souvlaki, Halídhon 80. Always packed despite being cramped, which is a testimonial to the quality and value of the *souvláki*. Better to take away.

Taverna Ela, top of Kondhiláki. Live Greek music to enliven your meal in yet another roofless taverna townhouse.

Tholos, Ayíon Dhéka 36. Slightly north of the cathedral, *Tholos* is another "restaurant in a ruin", this time Venetian/Turkish, with a wide selection of Cretan specialities.

Bars and nightlife

Haniá's **nightlife** has more than enough venues to satisfy the most insomniac night-owls. Most of the clubs and disco bars are gathered in the area around the inner harbour, whilst there are plenty of terrace bars along both harbourfronts, with more scattered throughout the old quarter.

The smartest and newest places are on and around **Sarpidhónos**, in the far corner of the inner harbour, a good example of which is *Fraise* on Sarpidhónos itself. Heading from here around towards the outer harbour, you'll pass others including the *Four Seasons*, a very popular bar by the port police, and then reach a couple of the older places including *Remember* and *Scorpio* behind the Plaza bar complex on the harbour. Nearby, and running along the **Aktí Miaoúli** seafront just outside the eastern wall are a string of terrace cafés, currently the place to be seen for Haniot late drinkers. At the opposite or **western end of the harbour** *Fagotto*, Angélou 16, is a pleasant, laid-back jazz bar, often with live performers. Other music bars near here are *Mythos* and *Street* on the outer harbour, playing rock and modern Greek sounds until the early hours. **Discos** proper include *Kyvotos* near the mosque, *Ariadni* on the inner harbour (opens 11.30pm, but busy later), and *Millennium*, a big, bright place on Tsoudherón behind the market, which doesn't really get going until 2am. West of here along Skalídhi (no. 39) *Titanic* is another dance place which is a late starter, and, not far away, tucked down a passage near the Schiavo Bastion (Skalídhi and Halídhon), *Game* is a new place that becomes frenetic after midnight.

A couple of venues offering more traditional entertainment are the *Café Kriti*, Kalergón 22, at the corner of Andhroyíou, basically an old-fashioned kafenío where there's **Greek music** and **dancing** virtually every night, and the *Firkas* (the bastion by the naval museum), with Greek dancing at 9pm every Tuesday – pricey but authentic entertainment. It's also worth checking for events at the open-air auditorium in the public gardens, and for performances in restaurants outside the city, which are the ones the locals will go to. Look for posters, especially in front of the market and in the little platía across the road from there.

For **films**, you should also check the hoardings in front of the market. There are open-air screenings at *Attikon*, on Venizélou out towards Akrotíri, about 1km from the centre, and occasionally in the public gardens.

Listings

Airlines Olympic, Tzanakáki 88 (Mon–Fri 9am–4pm; ☎57 701). There's a bus from here connecting with their flights. For airport information call ☎63 264.

Banks and exchange The main branch of the National Bank of Greece is directly opposite the market. Convenient smaller banks for exchange are next to the bus station, at the bottom of Kanevárou just off Platía Syndriváni, or at the top of Halídhon. There are also a couple of exchange places on Halídhon, open long hours.

Bike and car rental Possibilities everywhere, especially on Halídhon, though these are rarely the best value. For bikes, try Kavroulakis, Hálidhon 91 (☎43 342) or Summertime, Daskaloyiánnis 7, slightly northeast of the market (☎98 918); for cars, two reliable local companies are Hermes, Tzanakáki 52 (54 418) or Tellus Rent a Car, Kanevárou 9, east of Platía Syndriváni (☎50 400).

Boat trips Various boat trips are offered by travel agents around town, mostly to Soúdha Bay or out to beaches on the Rodhópou peninsula. Domenico's (☎55 019), on Kanevárou, offers some of the best of these.

Ferry tickets The agent for ANEK is on Venizélou, right opposite the market (☎27 500).

Internet Haniá has two Internet cafés: Sante on the outer harbour at Aktí Koundouriótou 55–56 (2000dr for two hours) and the more tranquil Vranas (30min 500dr), just north of the cathedral and beneath *Vranas Studios* (see p.223).

Laundry There are five laundries, the best of which is Speedy Laundry (☎88 411), junction of Koronéou and Korkidi, just west of Platía 1866; others at Kanevárou 38 (9am–10pm), Episkópou Dhorothéou 7 and Ayíon Dhéka 18; all do service washes. The *Fidias* pension also has its own economical place next door (see p.223).

Left luggage The bus station has a left luggage office open 6am–8.30pm; 300/400dr per item per day depending on size.

Market and supermarkets If you want to buy food or get stuff together for a picnic, the entertaining market is the place to head for. There are vast quantities of fresh fruit and vegetables as well as meat and fish, bakers, dairy stalls and general stores for cooked meats, tins and other standard provisions. There are also several small stores down by the harbour platía which sell cold drinks and a certain amount of food, but these are expensive (though they do open late). A couple of large supermarkets can be found on the edge of the old town, for instance Inka on Platía 1866.

Post office The main post office is on Tzanakáki (Mon–Fri 7am–8pm, Sat 8am–2pm for exchange).

Taxis The main taxi ranks are in Platía 1866. For radio taxis try ☎98 700 or ☎94 300.

Telephones Cardphones (all over town) are the best bet for overseas calls.

Tourist police Inconveniently relocated to Iraklíou 23, in the southern suburb of Koubés (☎53 333 fax 28 708), which means they'll rarely be bothered by visitors – perhaps the thinking behind the move.

Travel agencies For cheap tickets home try Bassias Travel, Halídhon 69 (☎44 295), very helpful for regular tickets too. They also deal in standard excursions. Other travel agents for tours and day trips are everywhere.

Around Haniá: the Akrotíri and Rodhópou peninsulas

Just north of Haniá, the **Akrotíri peninsula** loops around to protect the Bay of Soúdha and a NATO military base and missile-testing area. In an ironic twist, the peninsula's northwestern coastline is fast developing into a luxury suburb; the beach of Kalathás, near Horafákia, long popular with jaded Haniotes, is surrounded by villas and apartments. **STAVRÓS**, further out, has not yet suffered this fate, and its **beach** is absolutely superb if you like the calm, shallow water of an almost completely enclosed lagoon. It's not very large, so it does get crowded, but rarely overpoweringly so. There's a makeshift taverna/*souvláki* stand on the beach, and a couple of tavernas across the road, but for accommodation you need to search slightly south of here, in the area around **Blue Beach**, where there are plenty of apartment buildings.

Inland are the **monasteries** of **Ayía Triádha** (daily 6am–2pm & 5–7pm; 300dr) and **Gouvernétou** (daily 8am–12.30pm & 4.30–7.30pm; free). The former is much more accessible and has a beautiful seventeenth-century church inside its pink-and-ochre cloister, though ongoing renovations have recently caused many of the monks to relocate and on occasions make the normally peaceful enclosure more like a building site. Beyond Gouvernétou, which is in a far better state of preservation and where traditional monastic life can still be observed, you can clamber down a craggy path to the abandoned ruins of the monastery of Katholikó and the remains of its narrow (swimmable) harbour.

West to Rodhópou

The coast to the west of Haniá was the scene of most of the fighting during the German invasion in 1941. As you leave town, an aggressive diving eagle commemorates the German parachutists, and at Máleme there's a big German cemetery; the Allied cemetery is in the other direction, on the coast just outside Soúdha. There are also beaches and considerable tourist development along much of this shore. At **Ayía Marína** there's a fine sandy beach and an island offshore said to be a sea monster petrified by Zeus before it could swallow Crete. Seen from the west, its "mouth" still gapes open.

Between **Plataniás** and **Kolymvári** an almost unbroken strand unfurls, by no means all sandy, but deserted for long stretches between villages. The road here runs through mixed groves of calamus reed (Crete's bamboo) and oranges; the windbreaks fashioned from the reeds protect the ripening oranges from the *meltémi*. At Kolymbári, the road to Kastélli cuts across the base of another mountainous peninsula, **Rodhópou**.

Just off the main road here is a monastery, **Goniá** (daily 8am–12.30pm & 4–8pm; respectable dress), with a view most luxury hotels would envy. Every monk in Crete can tell tales of his proud ancestry of resistance to invaders, but here the Turkish cannon balls are still lodged in the walls to prove it, a relic of which the good fathers are far more proud than of any of the icons.

South to the Samarian Gorge

From Haniá the **Gorge of Samariá** (May–Oct; 1200dr for entry to the national park) can be visited as a day trip or as part of a longer excursion to the south. At 18km, it's Europe's longest gorge and is startlingly beautiful. In the June–Aug period (ring Haniá tourist office for other times) **buses** leave Haniá for the top at 6.15am, 7.30am, 8.30am and 1.30pm (this latter service changes to 4.30pm outside school term time), depositing you at the gorge entrance and then collecting you at the port of Hóra Sfakíon for the return trip to Haniá. Should you take the last bus you will need to spend a night at Ayía Rouméli (the end of the gorge) as you will not get through the gorge in time for the last boat. For the three early buses you'll normally be sold a return ticket (valid from Hóra Sfakíon at any time). It's well worth catching the earliest bus to avoid the full heat of the day while walking through the gorge, though be warned that you will not be alone – there are often as many as five coachloads setting off before dawn for the nail-biting climb into the White Mountains. There are also direct early-morning buses from Iráklion and Réthymnon and bus tours from virtually everywhere on the island, adding up to a couple of thousand plus walkers on most days during high season.

Despite all the crowds, the walk *is* hard work, especially in spring when the stream is a roaring torrent. Early and late in the season, there is a danger of **flash floods**, which are not to be taken lightly: in 1993, a number of walkers perished when they were washed out to sea. For this reason the first and last three weeks of the season are entirely dependent on the weather and you will only be allowed into the gorge if the authorities deem it safe. If in doubt (and to save yourself a wasted journey), phone the Haniá Forest Service (☎0821/67 140) for information. Should you arrive after 4pm you will only be allowed into the first couple of kilometres from each end of the gorge and the wardens ensure that no one remains in the gorge overnight, where camping is strictly forbidden.

Omalós

One way to avoid an early start from the north coast would be to stay at **OMALÓS**, in the middle of the mountain plain from which the gorge descends. There are some ordinary **rooms** for rent and a couple of surprisingly fancy **hotels**; try the *Neos Omalos* (☎0821/67 269 fax 67 190; ①), or *Samaria* (☎0821/67 168; ①), for a cheap and friendly no-frills alternative. But since the village is some way from the start of the path, and the buses arrive as the sun rises, it's almost impossible to get a head start on the crowds. Some people sleep out at the top (where there's a bar-restaurant in the *Tourist Lodge* and kiosks serving drinks and sandwiches), but a night under the stars here can be a bitterly cold experience. The one significant advantage to staying up here would be if you wanted to undertake some other climbs in the White Mountains, in which case there's a **mountain hut** (☎0821/54 560; ①) about ninety minutes' hike (signed) from Omalós or from the top of the gorge.

The gorge

The **gorge** itself begins at the *xylóskala*, or "wooden staircase", a stepped path plunging steeply down from the southern lip of the Omalós plain. Here, at the head of the track, opposite the sheer rock face of Mount Gíngilos, the crowds pouring out of the buses

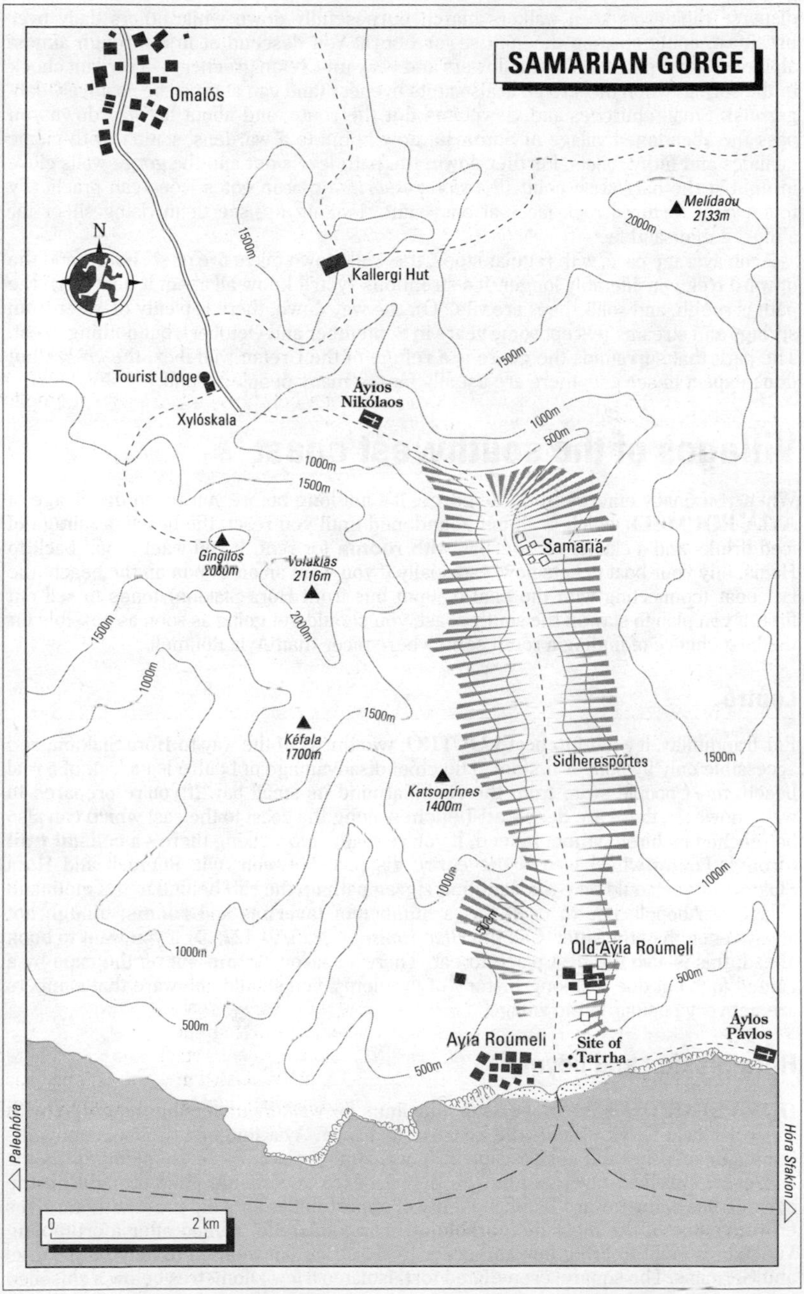
SAMARIAN GORGE
Omalós
Melídaou
2133m
Kallergi Hut
Tourist Lodge
Xylóskala
Áyios
Nikólaos
Samariá
Gíngilos
2080m
Volakias
2116m
Kéfala
1700m
Katsoprínes
1400m
Sidherespórtes
Old Ayía Roúmeli
Ayía Roúmeli
Site of
Tarrha
Áyios
Pávlos
Paleohóra
Hóra Sfakíon
0
2 km
N
500m
1000m
1500m
2000m

disperse rapidly as keen walkers march purposefully down while others dally over breakfast, contemplating the sunrise for hours. You descend at first through almost alpine scenery: pine forest, wild flowers and very un-Cretan greenery – a verdant shock in the spring, when the stream is also at its liveliest (and can at times be positively dangerous). Small churches and viewpoints dot the route, and about halfway down you pass the abandoned village of **Samariá**, now home to a wardens' station, with picnic facilities and filthy toilets. Further down, the path levels out and the gorge walls close in until at the narrowest point (the *sidherespórtes* or "iron gates") one can practically touch both tortured rock faces at once, and, looking up, see them rising sheer for almost a thousand feet.

At an average pace, with regular stops, the walk down takes five or six hours, and the upward trek considerably longer. It's strenuous (you'll know all about it next day), the path is rough, and solid shoes are vital. On the way down, there is plenty of water from springs and streams (except some years in September and October), but nothing to eat. The park that surrounds the gorge is a refuge of the Cretan wild ibex, the *kri-kri*, but don't expect to see one; there are usually far too many people around.

Villages of the southwest coast

When you finally emerge from the gorge, it's not long before you reach the village of **AYÍA ROUMÉLI**, which is all but abandoned until you reach the beach, a mirage of iced drinks and a cluster of tavernas with **rooms** for rent. If you want to get back to Haniá, buy your boat tickets now, especially if you want an afternoon on the beach; the last boat (connecting with the final 6.30pm bus from Hóra Sfakíon) tends to sell out first. If you plan to stay on the south coast, you should get going as soon as possible for the best chance of finding a room somewhere nicer than Ayía Rouméli.

Loutró

For tranquillity, it's hard to beat **LOUTRÓ**, two-thirds of the way to Hóra Sfakíon, and accessible only by boat or on foot. The chief disadvantage of Loutró is its lack of a real beach; most people swim from the rocks around its small bay. If you're prepared to walk, however, there are **deserted beaches** along the coast to the east which can also be reached by hired **canoe**. Indeed, if you're really into walking there's a **coastal trail** through Loutró which covers the entire distance between Ayía Rouméli and Hóra Sfakíon, or you could take the daunting zigzag path up the cliff behind to the mountain village of Anópoli. Loutró itself has a number of **tavernas** and **rooms**, though not always enough of the latter. Call the *Blue House* (☎0825/91 127; ①) if you want to book ahead; this is also the best place to eat. There's space to **camp** out on the cape by a ruined fort, but due to a long history of problems, you should be aware that campers are not very popular in the village.

Hóra Sfakíon and beyond

HÓRA SFAKÍON is the more usual terminus for walkers traversing the gorge, with a regular boat service along the coast to and from Ayía Rouméli. Consequently, it's quite an expensive and not an especially welcoming place; there are plenty of rooms and some excellent tavernas, but for a real beach you should jump straight on the evening bus going toward Plakiás. Plenty of opportunities for a dip present themselves en route, one of the most memorable at **Frangokástello**, named after a crumbling Venetian attempt to bring law and order to a district that went on to defy both Turks and Germans. The square, crenellated fort, isolated a few kilometres below a chiselled wall of mountains, looks like it's been spirited out of the High Atlas or Tibet. The place is said to be haunted by ghosts of Greek rebels massacred here in 1829; every May, these *dhrossoulítes* (dewy ones) march at dawn across the coastal plain and disappear into the sea near the fort. The rest of the time Frangokástello is peaceful enough, with a superb beach and a number of tavernas and rooms, but is somewhat stagnant if you're looking for things to do. Slightly further east, and less influenced by tourism or modern life, are the attractive villages of **Skalotí** and **Rodhákino**, each with basic lodging and food.

Soúyia

In quite the other direction from Ayía Rouméli, less regular boats also head to **SOÚYIA** and on to Paleohóra. Soúyia, until World War II merely the anchorage for Koustoyérako inland, is low key, with a long, grey pebble beach and mostly modern buildings (except for a church with a sixth-century Byzantine mosaic as the foundation). Since the 1990 completion of the paved road to Haniá, the village has started to expand; even so, except in the very middle of summer, it continues to make a good fall-back for finding a room or a place to camp, eating cheaply and enjoying the beach when the rest of the island is seething with tourists. Of the **rooms** places try *Hotel Santa Irene* (☎0823/51 342, fax 0821/90 047; ②), where en-suite rooms come with seafront view; for **food**, the nearby *Rembetiko* has a pleasant garden terrace.

Kastélli and the western tip

Apart from being Crete's most westerly town, and the end of the main road, **KASTÉLLI** (Kíssamos, or Kastélli Kissámou as it's variously known) has little obvious attraction. It's a busy town with a rocky beach visited mainly by people using the boat that runs twice weekly to the island of Kýthira and the Peloponnese. The very ordinariness of Kastélli, however, can be attractive: life goes on pretty much regardless of outsiders, but there's every facility you might need. The **ferry agent's office** in Kastélli is one block inland from the main square, Platía Kastellíou (Xirouxákis; ☎0822/22 655). Here there are also good value en-suite rooms at *Koutsanakis* (☎0822/23 416; ①), opposite the *Castelli Hotel*. Heading north from here brings you to the beach promenade where there are a number of **tavernas**. Nothing else is far away from the centre apart from the dock, a two-kilometre walk (or inexpensive taxi ride) from town.

A ROUND TRIP

If you have transport, a circular drive from Kastélli, taking the coast road in one direction and the inland route through Élos and Topólia, makes for a stunningly scenic circuit. Near the sea, villages cling to the high mountainsides, apparently halted by some miracle in the midst of calamitous seaward slides. Around them, olives ripen on the terraced slopes, the sea glittering far below. Inland, especially at **ÉLOS**, the main crop is the chestnut, whose huge old trees shade the village streets.

In **TOPÓLIA**, the chapel of Ayía Sofía is sheltered inside a cave which has been used as a shrine since Neolithic times. Cutting south from Élos, a paved road continues through the high mountains towards Paleohóra. On a motorbike, with a sense of adventure and plenty of fuel, it's great: the bus doesn't come this way, villagers still stare at the sight of a tourist, and a host of small, seasonal streams cascade beside or under the asphalt.

Falásarna to Elafonísi

To the west of Kastélli lies some of Crete's loneliest, and, for many visitors, finest coastline. The first place of note is ancient and modern **Falásarna**, city ruins which mean little to the non-specialist, but they do overlook some of the best beaches on Crete, wide and sandy with clean water. There's a handful of tavernas and an increasing number of rooms for rent; otherwise, you have to sleep out, as many people do. This can mean that the main beaches are dirty (try not to add to the mess), but they remain beautiful, and there are plenty of others within walking distance. The nearest real town is **Plátanos**, 5km up a paved road, along which there are a couple of daily buses.

Further south, the western coastline is still less discovered and there's little in the way of official accommodation. **Sfinári** has several houses which rent rooms, and a quiet pebble beach a little way below the village. **Kámbos** is similar, but even less visited, its beach a considerable walk down a hill. Beyond them both is the **monastery of Khryssoskalítissa**, increasingly visited by tours from Haniá and Paleohóra now the road has been sealed, but well worth the effort for its isolation and nearby beaches; the bus gets as far as Váthy, from where the monastery is another two hours' walk away.

Five kilometres beyond Khryssoskalítissa, a dusty, unpaved road bumps down to the coast opposite the tiny uninhabited islet of **Elafonísi**. You can easily wade out to the islet with its sandy beaches and rock pools, and the shallow lagoon is warm and crystal clear. It looks magnificent, but daily boat trips from Paleohóra and coach tours from elsewhere on the island have attracted a cluster of beach stalls renting loungers and selling tourist tat, which ensures that, in the middle of the day at least, it's far from deserted. To cope with the resulting sanitary problems, a single and totally inadequate Portaloo has been installed by the authorities next to the beach. If you want to stay, and really appreciate the place, there are a couple of seasonal tavernas, but bring some supplies unless you want to be wholly dependent on them.

Kándanos and Paleohóra

Getting down to Paleohóra by the main road, paved the whole way, is a lot easier, and several daily buses from Haniá make the trip. But although this route also has to wind through the western outriders of the White Mountains, it lacks the excitement of the routes to either side. **Kándanos**, at the 58-kilometre mark, has been entirely rebuilt since it was destroyed by the Germans for its fierce resistance to their occupation. The original sign erected when the deed was done is preserved on the war memorial: "Here stood Kándanos, destroyed in retribution for the murder of 25 German soldiers, and never to be rebuilt again." The pleasantly easy-going and once again substantial village had the last laugh.

When the beach at **PALEOHÓRA** finally appears below it is a welcome sight. The little town is built across the base of a peninsula, its harbour and a beach known as Pebble Beach on the eastern side, the wide sands ("Sandy Beach") on the other. Above, on the outcrop, Venetian ramparts stand sentinel. These days Paleohóra has become heavily developed, but it's still thoroughly enjoyable, with a main street filling with tables as diners spill out of the restaurants, and with a pleasantly chaotic social life. A good place to **eat** with some imaginative vegetarian specials is *The Third Eye*, just out of the centre towards Sandy Beach. There are plenty of **places to stay** (though not always many vacancies in high season) – try the basic *Dolphin Rooms* (☎0823/41 703; ①), below the Venetian fort, or *Castello Rooms* (☎0823/41 143; ②), at the south end of Sandy Beach, for a little more en-suite luxury. There's also a fair-sized **campsite** 2km north of Pebble Beach; in extremis, if you are tempted to sleep on the main Sandy Beach – one of the best on the south coast, with showers, trees and acres of sand – be prepared for trouble from police and local residents; your best bet is to get as far away from the town as possible if you want to be left in peace. When you tire of Paleohóra and the excellent **windsurfing** in the bay (boards for hire), there are excursions up the hill to Prodhrómi, for example, or along a five-hour coastal path to Soúyia.

You'll find a helpful **tourist office** (Wed–Mon 10am–1pm & 6–9pm; ☎0823/41 507) in the town hall on Venizélou in the centre of town; they have full accommodation lists and a map (though you'll hardly need this). The **banks** and **travel agents** are all nearby; the **post office** is on the road behind Sandy Beach. **Boats** run from here to Elafonísi, the island of Gávdhos and along the coast to Soúyia and Ayía Rouméli.

Gávdhos

The island of **Gávdhos**, some fifty kilometres of rough sea south of Paleohóra, is the most southerly landmass in Europe. Gávdhos is small (about 10km by 7km) and barren, but it has one major attraction: the enduring **isolation** which its inaccessible position has helped preserve. There are now a few package tours organized by travel agents in Paleohóra such as Interkreta (☎0823/41 393, fax 41 050), who can arrange a room if you want one and also provide current ferry information. There's a semipermanent community of campers through the summer, but if all you want is a beach to yourself and a taverna to grill your fish, this remains the place for you.

travel details

Flights are on Olympic unless otherwise stated

Haniá–Athens (4 daily on Olympic; 2 daily on Cronus; 2 daily on Air Greece)

Haniá–Thessaloníki (1 weekly)

Iráklion–Athens (5–7 daily on Olympic; 4 daily on Cronus; 3–4 daily on Air Greece)

Iráklion–Santorini (2 weekly)

Iráklion–Rhodes (4 weekly, summer only, on Olympic; 3 weekly on Air Greece)

Iráklion–Thessaloníki (3 weekly on Olympic; 3 weekly on Air Greece)

Sitía–Athens (1 weekly, Fri all year)

Ferries

Áyios Nikólaos and Sitía 3–4 sailings a week to Pireás (12hr), 1–3 ferries a week to Kásos, Kárpathos, Hálki and Rhodes; 1–2 weekly to Mílos.

Haniá 1 or 2 ferries daily to Pireás (12hr).

Hóra Sfakíon 5 ferries daily to Loutró/Ayía Rouméli; 3 weekly to Gávdhos in season.

Iráklion 2 ferries daily to Pireás and 3 on Tues & Wed (12hr); 3–5 ferries weekly to Thessaloníki; 1 daily ferry to Thíra (4hr), also fast boats and hydrofoils (2hr 30min); daily ferries to Páros in season; 1–2 weekly to Mýkonos and Íos; weekly to Náxos, Tínos, Skýros, Skíathos.

Kastélli (Kíssamos) 1–2 ferries weekly to Kýthira and Yíthio (8hr).

Paleohóra 3 boats a week in season to Gávdhos. Also daily sailings to Elafonísi and Soúyia.

Réthymnon daily ferries to Pireás (12hr); seasonal day-trips to Thíra.

Buses

Áyios Nikólaos–Sitía (6 daily 6.15am–6pm; 2hr).

Haniá–Hóra Sfakíon (3 daily 8.30am–2pm; 2hr).

Haniá–Paleohóra (3 daily 8.30am–3.30pm; 2hr).

Haniá–Réthymnon–Iráklion (17 daily, two via old road 5.30am–8.30pm; 3hr total).

Iráklion–Ayía Galíni (8 daily 6.30am–6.30pm; 2hr 15min).

Iráklion–Áyios Nikólaos (32 daily 6.30am–9pm; 1hr 30min).

Iráklion–Festós (8 daily 7.30am–4.30pm; 1hr 30min).

Iráklion–Ierápetra (7 daily 7.30am–5.30pm; 2hr 30min).

Kastélli–Haniá (15 daily 6am–7.30pm; 1hr 30min).

Réthymnon–Spíli–Ayía Galíni (4 daily 7am–2.15pm; 45min–1hr 30min).

CHAPTER FOUR

THE DODECANESE

The furthest Greek island group from the mainland, the **Dodecanese** (Dhodhekánisos) lie close to the Turkish coast – some, like Kós and Kastellórizo, almost within hailing distance of Anatolia. Because of this position, and their remoteness from Athens, the islands have had a turbulent history: they were the scene of ferocious battles between German and British forces in 1943–44, and were only finally included in the modern Greek state in 1948 after centuries of occupation by crusaders, Ottomans and Italians. Even now the threat (real or imagined) of invasion from Turkey is very much in evidence. When you ask about the heavy military presence, some locals answer in terms of "*when* the Turks come", rather than "*if*".

Whatever the rigours of the various occupations, their legacy includes a wonderful blend of architectural styles and of Eastern and Western cultures. Medieval Rhodes is the most famous, but almost every island has some Classical remains, a crusaders' castle, a clutch of traditional villages and abundant grandiose public buildings. For these last the Italians, who occupied the islands from 1912 to 1943, are mainly responsible. In their determination to beautify the islands and turn them into a showplace for fascism they undertook public works, excavations and reconstruction on a massive scale; if historical accuracy was often sacrificed in the interests of style, only an expert is likely to complain. A more sinister aspect of the Italian administration was the attempted forcible Latinization of the populace: spoken Greek and Orthodox observance were banned in public from 1923 to 1943. The most tangible reminder of this policy is the (rapidly dwindling) number of older people who can still converse – and write – more fluently in Italian than in Greek.

Aside from this bilingualism, the Dodecanese themselves display a marked topographic and economic schizophrenia. The dry limestone outcrops of **Kastellórizo**, **Sými**, **Hálki**, **Kássos** and **Kálymnos** have always been forced to rely on the sea for their livelihoods, and the wealth generated by this maritime culture – especially in the

ACCOMMODATION PRICE CODES

Throughout the book we've used the following **price codes** to denote the cheapest available double room in each establishment in high season. Out of season, rates can drop by more than fifty percent, especially if you are staying for three or more nights. Single rooms, where available, cost around seventy percent of the price of a double.

Rented private rooms on the islands usually fall into the ② or ③ categories, depending on their location and facilities, and the season; a few in the ④ category are more like plush self-catering apartments. They are not generally available from late October through to the beginning of April, when only hotels tend to remain open.

① Up to 6000dr	④ 12,000–16,000dr
② 6000–9000dr	⑤ 16,000–20,000dr
③ 9000–12,000dr	⑥ 20,000dr and upwards

Note: Youth hostels typically charge 2000–2500dr for a dormitory bed.
For more accommodation details, see pp.44–47.

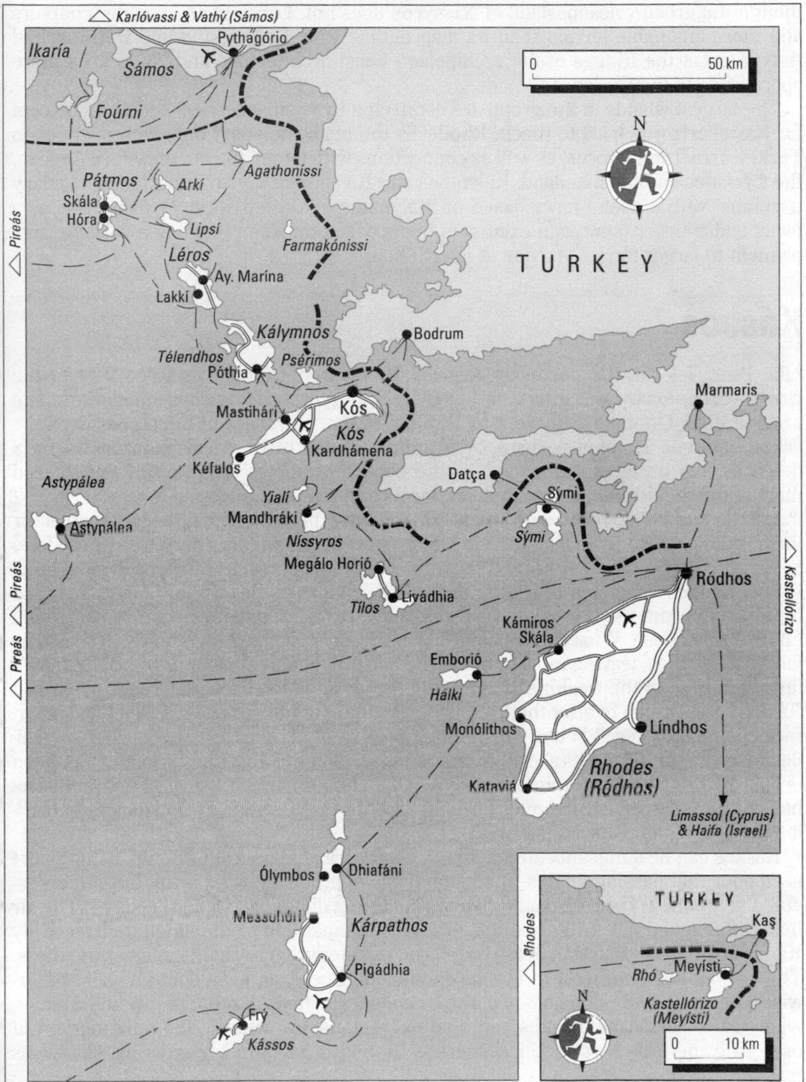

nineteenth century – fostered the growth of attractive port towns. The sprawling, relatively fertile giants, **Rhodes** (Ródhos) and **Kós**, have recently seen their traditional agricultural economies almost totally displaced by a tourist industry grown up around good beaches and nightlife, as well as the Aegean's most exciting historical monuments. **Kárpathos** lies somewhere in between, with a (formerly) forested north grafted on to a rocky limestone south; **Tílos**, despite its lack of trees, has ample water, though the green volcano-island of **Níssyros** does not. **Léros** shelters softer contours and more amenable terrain than its map outline would suggest, while **Pátmos** and **Astypálea** at the fringes of the archipelago boast architecture and landscapes more appropriate to the Cyclades.

The largest islands in the group are connected by regular ferries, and none (except for Kastellórizo) is hard to reach. Rhodes is the main transport hub, with services to Turkey, Israel and Cyprus, as well as connections with Crete, the northeastern Aegean, the Cyclades and the mainland. Kálymnos and Kós are jointly an important secondary terminus, with a useful ferry based on Kálymnos, hydrofoil services using Kós as a focus and transfer point, and excursion boats based on Kós providing a valuable supplement to larger ferries arriving at uncivil hours.

Kássos

Like Psará islet in the northeast Aegean, **Kássos** contributed its large fleet to the Greek revolutionary war effort, and likewise suffered appalling consequences. In late May 1824, an Ottoman army sent by Ibrahim Pasha, Governor of Egypt, besieged the island; on June 7, aided perhaps by a traitor's tip as to the weak point in Kássos's defences, the invaders descended on the populated north-coastal plain, slaughtered most of the inhabitants and put houses, farms and trees to the torch.

Barren and depopulated since then, Kássos attracts few visitors, despite regular air links with Rhodes and Kárpathos, and being a port of call on ferry lines from those isles to Crete. Numerous sheer gorges slash through lunar terrain, with fenced smallholdings of midget olive trees providing the only permanent relief. Springtime grain crops briefly soften the usually empty terraces, and livestock somehow survives on a thin furze of thornbush. What remains of the population is grouped together in five villages facing Kárpathos, leaving most of the island accessible only on foot or by boat. There's little sign here of the wealth brought into other islands by diaspora Greeks or – since Kássos hasn't much to offer them – tourists; crumbling houses and disused hillside terraces poignantly recall better days. A long pattern of serving as roving pilots, or residence in Egypt (Kassiots were instrumental in digging the Suez Canal), has been eclipsed by subsequent emigration to the US. Thus American logo-T-shirts and baseball caps are de rigueur summer fashion, and the conversation of vacationing expatriates is spiked with Americanisms.

Kássos can be a nuisance to reach; Frý's anchorage just west of Boúka fishing port is so poor that passing ferries won't stop if any appreciable wind is up. In such cases, you disembark at Kárpathos and fly the remaining distance in a light aircraft. The air ticket plus a taxi fare to Kárpathos airport is comparable to the amount charged by Kárpathos-based excursion boats which can manoeuvre into Boúka in most weathers. The airport lies 1km west of Frý (pronounced "free"), an easy enough walk, otherwise a cheap (500dr) ride on one of the island's three taxis. Except in July and August, when a few rental motorbikes and boat excursions are offered, the only method of exploring the island's remoter corners is by hiking along fairly arduous, shadeless tracks.

Frý and Emboriós

Most of the appeal of the capital, **FRÝ**, is confined to the immediate environs of the wedge-shaped fishing port of **Boúka**, protected from the sea by two crab-claws of breakwater and overlooked by the cathedral of Áyios Spyrídhon. Inland, Frý is engagingly unpretentious, even down-at-heel; little attempt has been made to prettify what is essentially a dusty little town poised halfway between demolition and reconstruction.

Accommodation is found at the seafront hotels *Anagenissis* (☎0245/41 323, fax 41 036; ②) and, just behind, the less expensive *Anessis* (☎0245/41 201, fax 41 730; ②). The manager of the *Anagenessis* also has a few pricier apartments, and runs the all-in-one travel agency just below (though Olympic has its own premises). Both hotels tend to be noisy owing to morning bustle on the waterfront – and the phenomenal number of small but lively **bars** in town. During high season a few **rooms** operate; these tend to be more expensive, and also located in the suburb of Emboriós, fifteen minute's walk east.

Perched overlooking the Boúka, *Iy Oraia Bouka* is easily the best of Frý's **tavernas**, and is reasonably priced. *To Meltemi* ouzerí, on the way to Emboriós, is an honourable runner-up. Shops in Frý, including two fruit stalls, are fairly well stocked for self-catering.

Frý's town **beach**, if you can call it that, is at **Ammouá** (Ammoudhiá), a thirty-minute walk beyond the airstrip along the coastal track. This sandy cove, just before the landmark chapel of Áyios Konstandínos, is often caked with seaweed and tar, but persevere five minutes more and you'll find much cleaner pea-gravel coves. Otherwise, it's worth shelling out for high-season boat excursions to far better beaches on a pair of islets visible to the northwest, **Armathiá** and **Makrá**. There are no amenities (or shade) on either islet.

The interior

Kássos's inland villages cluster in the agricultural plain just inland from Frý, and are linked to each other by road; all, except the dull grid of Arvanitohóri, are worth a passing visit, accomplishable by foot in a single day.

Larger in extent and more rural than Frý, **AYÍA MARÍNA**, 1500m inland and uphill, is most attractive seen from the south, arrayed above olive groves; one of its two belfried churches is the focus of the island's liveliest festival, on July 17. Just beyond the hamlet of Kathístres, a further 500m southwest, the cave of **Ellinokamára** is named for the Hellenistic wall partially blocking the entrance; from there a path continues another ninety minutes in the same direction to the larger, more natural cave of **Seláï**, with impressive stalactites in the rear chamber. On the opposite side of the plain, **PANAYÍA** is famous for its now-neglected mansions – many of Kássos's wealthiest ship captains hailed from here – and for the oldest surviving church on the island, the eighteenth-century **Panayía tou Yióryi**. From **PÓLIO**, 2km above Panayía and site of the island's badly deteriorated medieval castle, a track leads southeast within ninety minutes to **Áyios Mámas**, one of two important rural monasteries.

Between Ayía Marína and Arvanitohóri, a dirt track heads southwest from the paved road linking the two villages; having skirted the narrows of a fearsome gorge, you are unlikely to see another living thing aside from goats or an occasional wheeling hawk. After about an hour, the Mediterranean appears to the south, a dull expanse ruffled only by the occasional ship bound for Cyprus and the Middle East. When you finally reach a fork, adopt the upper, right-hand turning, following derelict phone lines and (initially) some cement paving towards the rural monastery of **Áyios Yeóryios Hadhión**, 11km (3hr on foot) from Frý. This is frequented only during its late-April festival time, and during mid-summer by the resident caretaker. There are a few open guest cells and cistern water here if you need to fill up canteens; the only other water en route is a well at the route's high point.

From the monastery it's another 3km – motorbikes can make it most of the way – to **Hélathros**, a lonely cove at the mouth of one of the larger, more forbidding Kassiot canyons. The sand-and-gravel beach itself is small and mediocre, but the water is pristine and – except for the occasional fishing boat – you'll probably be alone. The lower, left-hand option at the fork is the direct track to Hélathros, but this is only 2km shorter, and following severe storm damage, impassable to any vehicle and all but the most energetic hikers.

Kárpathos

A long, narrow island marooned between Rhodes and Crete, wild **Kárpathos** has always been something of an underpopulated backwater, although it is the third largest of the Dodecanese. An habitually cloud-capped mountainous spine rises to over 1200 metres, and divides the more populous, lower-lying south from an exceptionally rugged north. Despite a magnificent windswept coastline of cliffs and promontories interrupted by little beaches, Kárpathos has succumbed surprisingly little to tourism. This has much to do with the appalling road system – rutted where paved, unspeakable otherwise – the paucity of interesting villages and the often high cost of food, which offsets reasonable room prices. Most visitors come here for a glimpse of the traditional village life that prevails in the isolated north of the island, and for the numerous superb, secluded beaches. The airport receives direct international flights – typically several weekly charters from northern Europe – and visitor numbers are on the increase. Since the 1990s, package tourism has more or less dominated several resorts in the southern part of the island, pushing independent travellers up to the remote north.

Kárpathos hasn't the most alluring of interiors: the central and northern uplands were badly scorched by forest fires in the 1980s, and agriculture plays a slighter role than on any other Greek island of comparable size. The Karpathians are too well off to bother much with farming; massive emigration to America and the resulting remittance economy has transformed Kárpathos into one of the wealthiest Greek islands.

Kárpathos's four Mycenaean and Classical cities figure little in ancient chronicles. Alone of the major Dodecanese, the island was held by the Genoese and Venetians after the Byzantine collapse and so has no castle of the crusading Knights of St John, nor any surviving medieval fortresses of consequence. The Ottomans couldn't be bothered to settle or even garrison it; instead they left a single judge or *kadi* at the main town, making the Greek population responsible for his safety during the many pirate attacks.

Pigádhia (Kárpathos Town)

The island capital of **PIGÁDHIA**, often known simply as Kárpathos, nestles at the south end of scenic **Vróndi Bay**, whose sickle of sand extends 3km northwest. The town itself, curling around the jetty and quay where ferries and excursion boats dock, is as drab as its setting is beautiful; an ever-increasing number of concrete blocks contributes to the air of a vast building site, making the Italian-era port police and county governmental buildings seem like heirlooms by comparison. Although there's nothing special to see, Pigádhia does offer just about every facility you might need, albeit with a definite package-tourism slant.

Practicalities

Olympic Airways (book a week minimum in advance) is on Apodhímon Karpathíon, the "Street of the Overseas Karpathians", at the corner of Mitropolítou. The **post office** is a few paces west on Yeoryíou Loízou, while amongst several **banks** there are two cash dispensers.

To explore the island, there are regular **buses** to Pylés, via Apéri, Voládha and Óthos, as well as to Ammopí; the terminal (just a stop with a destination-placard) is at the corner of 28-Oktovriou and Dhimokratías, a couple of blocks back from the front. Set-rate, unmetered **taxis** aren't too expensive to get to these and other points (such as the airport) on the paved road system, but charge a fortune to go anywhere else. Upwards of a dozen outfits **rent cars**, though you may have to try every one to find a free vehicle, rates are vastly over the odds, and the cars themselves often well-worn

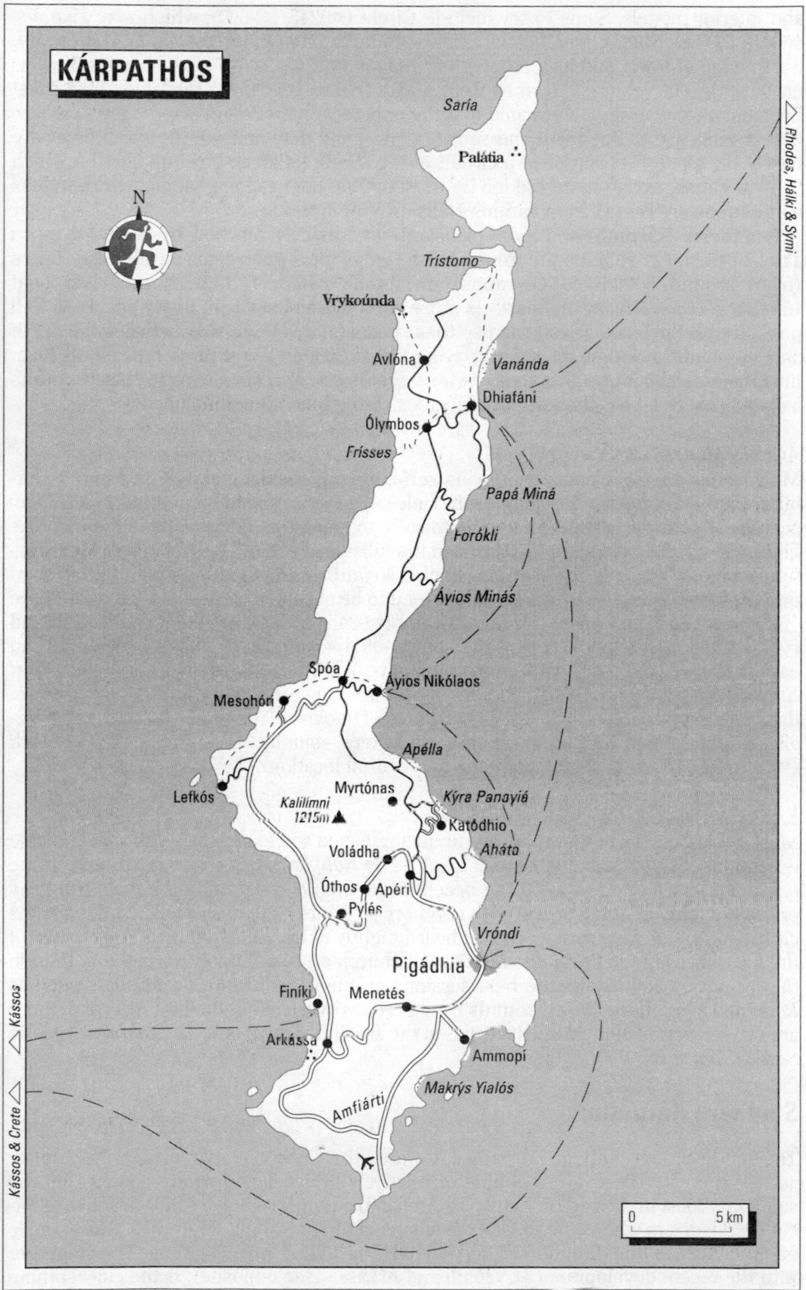
KÁRPATHOS
N
Saría
Palátia
Rhodes, Hálki & Sými
Trístomo
Vrykoúnda
Avlóna
Vanánda
Dhiafáni
Ólymbos
Frísses
Papá Miná
Forókli
Áyios Minás
Spóa
Áyios Nikólaos
Mesohóri
Apélla
Lefkós
Myrtónas
Kýra Panayiá
Kalilimni
1215m
Katódhio
Voládha
Aháta
Óthos
Apéri
Pylés
Vróndi
Pigádhia
Finíki
Menetés
Kássos
Arkássa
Ammopí
Makrýs Yialós
Amfiárti
Kássos & Crete
0
5 km

and inferior models. Some to try include Circle (☎0245/22 690), which may give discounts to *Rose Studios* (see below) clients; friendly *Panorama* (☎0245/22 702), at the north edge of town; and less courteous *Gatoulis* (☎0245/22 747), which does, however, have decent vehicles. Hermes Rent a **Motorbike** (☎0245/22 090) has the largest fleet and on-site sevice. Be warned that the only fuel on the island is to be found at several stations just to the north and south of town, and that tanks on the small bikes are barely big enough to complete a circuit of the south, let alone head up north – which is, in any case, expressly forbidden by most outfits. For seagoing jaunts, **windsurfers** and **canoes** are rented from various stalls on Vróndi beach.

Northern Kárpathos is most pleasantly and usually reached **by boat**. Olympos Travel (☎0245/22 993), on the front near the jetty, offers good deals on all-in **day-tours** (from around 5000dr to Ólymbos) on its *Karpathos I*, though the rival boat (*Chrisovalandou III*; pay on board) is more attractive and stable in heavy sea. Less well publicized is the fact that you can use these boats to travel **one-way** between the north and the south in either direction, paying about 2000dr; departures typically 8.30am northbound, 4.30pm southbound. Various agents can also offer trips to Kássos and to isolated east coast beaches without facilities (bring lunch if not included).

ACCOMMODATION

Most ferries are met by people offering **self-catering studios**, though they may be forbidden from touting on the quay itself. Unless you've arranged something in advance, you might consider such offers – the town is so small that no location is too inconvenient, though the best place to stay is on the hillside above the bus terminal. More luxurious places lie north, towards and behind **Vróndi** beach to either side of the ruined fifth-century basilica of **Ayía Fotiní**, but tend to be occupied by package groups. Three of the best hillside premises are *Rose Studios* (☎0245/22 284), well-kept studios (②) and rooms (①) run by a kindly family; the courteous *Amarillis Studios* slightly downhill and east (☎0245/22 375; ②), with enormous units; and *Elias Rooms* just above the *Hotel Karpathos* (☎0245/22 446; ①), en-suite rooms in a converted older house. Lower down, the rambling *Konaki* (☎0245/22 908; ①) on 28-Oktovríou, the upper through-road parallel to Apodhímon Karpathíon, is a backpackers' standby, while the *Karpathos* itself (☎0245/22 347; ②) is serviceable and in a central location.

EATING AND DRINKING

Most of the waterfront **tavernas** are undistinguished and expensive, with a few notable exceptions: fish aficionados should head for *Iy Kali Kardhia*, at the north end of the shore boulevard on the way to the beach, while the *To Perigiali* on the main front is a pricey but fairly genuine ouzerí with good bread, homemade desserts and frozen items clearly indicated. Live **music** can be heard nightly at the *Kafenio Life of Angels*, one of the few surviving old buildings next to the church on Apodhímon Karpathíon, though they're not by any means the best sessions on the island. More trendy bars such as *Rocks* and *Eros* offered taped sounds from perches overlooking the bay. At Vróndi there are two serviceable lunchtime tavernas at the southerly, town end: *To Limanaki* and the *Seaside Snack Bar*.

Southern Kárpathos

The southern extremity of Kárpathos, towards the airport, is extraordinarily desolate and windswept. There are a couple of relatively undeveloped sandy beaches on the southeast coast in the region known as Amfiárti, but they're only really attractive to foreign windsurfers who come to take advantage of the prevailing westerlies. Most people go no further in this direction than **AMMOPÍ**, just 7km from Pigádhia. This, together with the recent development at Vróndi and Arkássa (see opposite), is the closest thing on Kárpathos to a purpose-built beach resort. Two sand-and-gravel, tree-fringed coves fringed by a couple of **tavernas** and numbers of **hotels** and **rooms** are rapidly filling up most of the available space – recommendable among these are the *Votsalakia* (☎0245/22 204; ②) or the *Kastelia Bay* (☎0245/22 678; ②). Heading west from Pigádhia rather than south, the road climbs steeply 9km up to **MENETÉS**, an appealing ridgetop village with handsome old houses, a tiny folklore museum and a spectacularly sited church. There's a single **taverna** here (*Ta Dhyo Adhelfia*) and a World War II memorial with sweeping views north.

Beyond Menetés, you descend to **ARKÁSSA**, on the slopes of a ravine draining to the west coast, with excellent views to Kássos en route. Despite poor, tiny beaches on a mostly rocky shore, Arkássa has been heavily developed, with hotels and restaurants sprouting in clusters. Much of the **accommodation** is aimed squarely at the package market, but independent travellers could try the en-suite *Rooms Irini* (☎0245/61 263 or 61 206; ②) or the more opulent *Hotel Dimitrios* (☎0245/81 256; ③). Most **tavernas** lie north of the ravine in the village centre, for example *Petaloudha* and *Paradhisos* on the dead-end access street.

A few hundred metres south of where the ravine meets the sea, a signposted cement side road leads briefly to the whitewashed chapel of Ayía Sofía, marooned amidst various remains of Classical and Byzantine Arkessia. These consist of several mosaic floors with geometric patterns, including one running diagonally under the floor of a half-buried chapel, emerging from the walls on either side. The Paleókastro headland beyond was the site of Mycenean Arkessia.

The tiny fishing port of **FINÍKI**, just a couple of kilometres north, offers a minuscule beach, occasional excursions to Kássos, half a dozen **tavernas** and several **rooms** establishments lining the road to the jetty; prominent examples include *Taverna Flisvos* and *Giavasis Studios* (☎0245/61 365; ②). The west-coast road is now asphalted all the way to the turning for the attractive resort of **LEFKÓS** (Paraliá Lefkoú). Although this is a delightful place for flopping on the beach, only three weekly buses call, and Lefkós marks the furthest point you can reach from Pighádhia on a small motorbike and return safely without running out of fuel. However, any effort will be rewarded by the striking topography of cliffs, hills, islets and sandspits surrounding a triple bay. There are now nearly two dozen places to stay, and perhaps half as many tavernas, but package companies tend to monopolize the better **accommodation** from June to September. Exceptions include the *Akroyiali Studios* (☎0245/71 178; ②), on stonier fourth bay just south off the access road, or the *Hotel Krinos* (☎0245/71 410; ③), on the final approach just before the fishing port. Overlooking the port itself on the seaward promontory, the *Dhramoundana II* **taverna** has a well-priced menu of Greek and Western specialities, plus drinks, and may be able to help in the search for available **rooms**.

Back on the main road, you climb northeast through one of the few sections of pine forest not scarred by fire to **MESOHÓRI**. The village tumbles down towards the sea around narrow, stepped alleys, coming to an abrupt halt at the edge of a flat-topped bluff dotted with three tiny, ancient chapels and separated from the village proper by a vast oasis of orchards. These are nurtured by the fountain underneath the church of **Panayía Vryssianí**, wedged against the mountainside just east and invisible from the end of the access road. On the stair-street leading to this church are a taverna and a simple kafenío. The main road, all paved continues on to Spóa, overlooking the east coast.

Central Kárpathos

The **centre** of Kárpathos supports a quartet of villages blessed with superb hillside settings, ample running water – and a cool climate, even in August. Nearly everyone here has "done time" in North America, then returned home with their nest eggs. New Jersey, New York and Canadian car plates tell you exactly where repatriated islanders struck it rich, and it's claimed the area has the highest per capita income in Greece. West-facing **PYLÉS** is the most attractive, set above another oasis, while **ÓTHOS**, noted for its red wine and a private ethnographic museum, is the highest and chilliest, just below 1215-metre Mount Kalilímni. On the east side of the ridge you find **VOLÁDHA** with its tiny Venetian citadel and a pair of nocturnally operating tavernas. From **APÉRI**, the largest, lowest and wealthiest settlement with another pair of night-time eateries, you can drive 6km along a very rough road to the dramatic pebble beach of **Aháta**, with just a drinks-only *kantína*.

Beyond Apéri, the road up the **east coast** is extremely rough in places, passing above beaches most easily accessible by boat trips from Pigádhia. **Kýra Panayiá** is the first encountered, reached via a paved but twisty side road through Katódhio hamlet; there's a surprising number of villas, rooms and tavernas in the ravine behind the 150m of fine gravel and sheltered, turquoise water. **Apélla** is the best of the beaches you can reach by road, though there's a final short path from the single taverna-rooms (the only facility) at the road's end to the scenic 300-metre gravel strand. The end of this route is **SPÓA**, high above the shore just east of the island's spine, with a snack bar (*Fota*) at the edge of the village which might make a better meal stop than the overpriced one down at **Áyios Nikólaos**, 5km below, a small hamlet with an average beach and the overgrown ruins of a Paleo-Christian basilica to explore.

Northern Kárpathos

Although connected by dirt road with Spóa, much the easiest (and usual) way to get to northern Kárpathos is by sea. Inter-island ferries call at Dhiafáni twice a week in season, or there are smaller tour boats from Pigádhia daily. These take a couple of hours, and are met at Dhiafáni by buses for the eight-kilometre transfer up to the traditional village of Ólymbos, the main attraction in this part of the island.

Ólymbos and around

Originally founded as a pirate-safe refuge in Byzantine times, windswept **ÓLYMBOS** straddles a long ridge below slopes studded with mostly ruined windmills. Two restored ones, beyond the main church, grind wheat and barley during late summer only, though one is kept under sail most of the year. Its basement houses a small ethnographic museum (odd hours; free), while a small shop nearby sells locally produced farm products. The village has long attracted foreign and Greek ethnologists, who treat it as a living museum of peasant dress, crafts, dialect and music long since gone elsewhere in Greece. It's still a very picturesque place, yet traditions are vanishing by the year. Nowadays it's only the older women and those working in the several tourist shops who wear the striking and magnificently colourful traditional dress – an instant photo opprtunity in exchange for persistent sales pitches.

After a while you'll notice the prominent role that the women play in daily life: tending gardens, carrying goods on their shoulders or herding goats. Nearly all Ólymbos men emigrate or work outside the village, sending money home and returning only on holidays. The long-isolated villagers also speak a unique dialect, said to maintain traces of its Doric and Phrygian origins – thus "Ólymbos" is pronounced "Élymbos" locally. Live vernacular music is still heard regularly and draws crowds of visitors at festival times, in particular Easter and August 15, when you've little hope of finding a bed.

At other times, the daytime commercialization of Ólymbos makes a good reason to **stay** overnight. The *Rooms Restaurant Olymbos* (☎0245/51 252; ①), near the village entrance, has rooms with baths and traditional furnishings, while *Hotel Aphrodite*

(☎0245/51 307; ②) in the centre offers en-suite facilities and a southerly sea view. There are also several places to **eat**; one of the best and most obvious is *O Mylos*, occupying one of the restored mills and offering locally made wine and home-style specialties. *Parthenonas*, on the square by the church, is also good; try their *makaroúnes*, a local dish of homemade pasta with onions and cheese.

From the village, the west coast and tiny port and beach at **Frísses** are a dizzy, half-hour's drop by path below. Most **local hikes**, however, head north or east, many of them on waymarked paths, though you'll have to stay overnight in the area to enjoy them. The easiest option is the ninety-minute walk back down to Dhiafáni, beginning just below the two working windmills. The way is well marked, with water en route, eventually dropping to a ravine amidst extensive forest – though the last half-hour is mostly over bulldozed riverbed. You could also tackle the trail north to the ruins and beach at **Vrykoúnda** ("Vrougoúnda" in dialect), via sparsely inhabited **Avlóna**, set on a high upland devoted to grain. There's a drinks café at the edge of this hamlet, but best take food and ample water to make a day of it, as it's just under three hours' walk one way to Vrykoúnda, which offers traces of Hellenistic/Roman Brykous, the remote cave-shrine of John the Baptist on the promontory and good swimming. Trístomo, a Byzantine anchorage in the far northeast of Kárpathos, is easiest reached by the recently marked trail from Dhiafáni.

Dhiafáni

Although its popularity is growing – especially since the 1997 completion of a new dock for large ferries – rooms in **DHIAFÁNI** are still inexpensive, and the pace of life slow outside of August. There are plenty of places at which to stay and eat, shops that will change money and even a small travel agency, Orfanos Travel (☎0245/51 410), which has its own en-suite hotel (②). The obvious non-en-suite hotels opposite the quay are noisy; try instead the garrulously friendly *Pansion Delfini* (☎0245/51 391; ①), up on the southern hillside. On the front, the favourite taverna is *Anatoli*, easily recognizable by the folk reliefs that sprout from its roofline.

Boat trips are offered to various nearby **beaches**, as well as to the Byzantine site of Palátia on the uninhabited islet of **Saría** or through the narrow strait to Trístomo anchorage and the ruins of Vrykoúnda. There are several coves within walking distance. Closest is **Vanánda**, a stony beach with an eccentric campsite snack bar in the oasis behind. To get there, follow the pleasant signposted path north through the pines, but don't believe the signs that say ten minutes – it's over thirty minutes away, short-cutting the more recent road. **Papá Miná**, with a few trees and cliff-shade, lies an hour's walk away via the obvious track starting above the ferry dock.

Rhodes (Ródhos)

It's no accident that **Rhodes** is among the most visited of the Greek islands. Not only is its east coast lined with numerous sandy beaches, but the capital's nucleus is a beautiful and remarkably preserved medieval city, the legacy of the crusading Knights of St John who used the island as their main base from 1309 until 1522. Unfortunately this showpiece is jammed to capacity with over a million tourists in a good year, as against about 100,000 permanent inhabitants (including many foreigners). Of transient visitors, Germans, Brits, Swedes, Italians and Danes predominate in that order; accordingly fish fingers, smörgåsbord and pizza jostle alongside moussaka on tourist menus.

Blessed with an equable climate and strategic position, Rhodes was important from earliest times despite a lack of good harbours. The best natural port spawned the ancient town of Lindos which, together with the other city-states Kameiros and Ialyssos, united in 408 BC to found the new capital of Rhodes at the northern tip of the

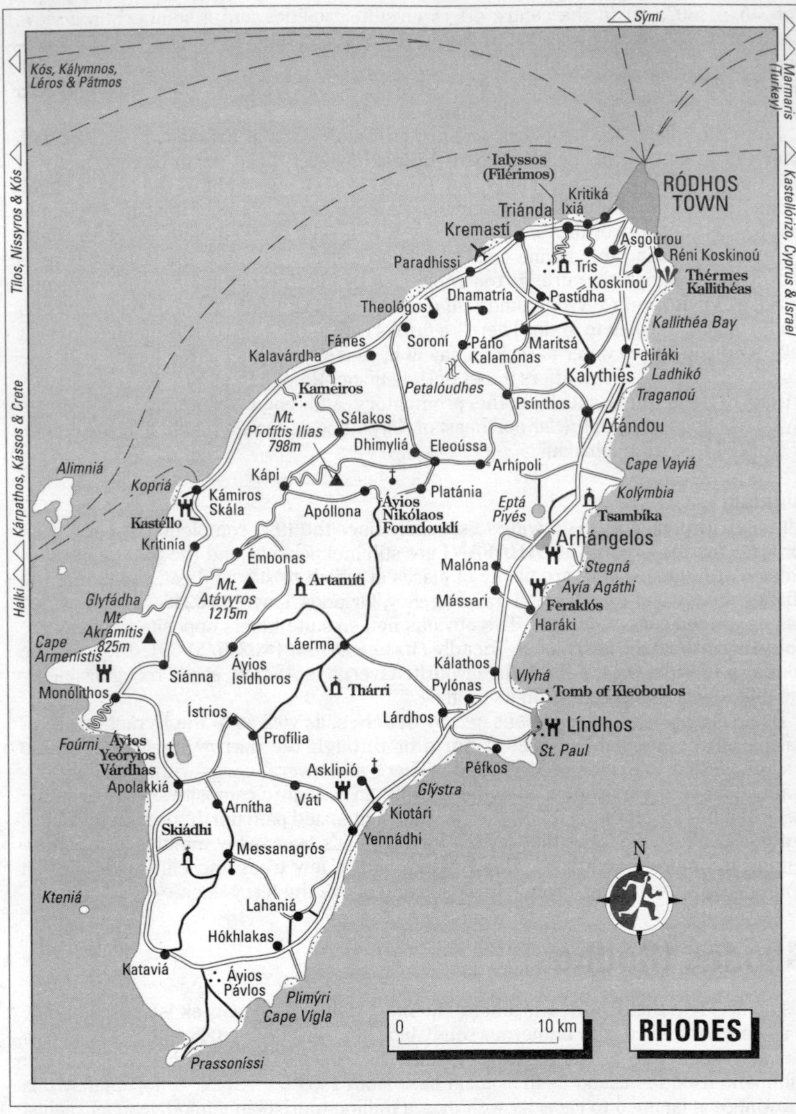

island. At various moments the cities allied themselves with Alexander, the Persians, Athenians or Spartans as prevailing conditions suited them, generally escaping retribution for backing the wrong side by a combination of seafaring audacity, sycophancy and burgeoning wealth as a trade centre. Following the failed siege of Demetrios Polyorketes in 305 BC, Rhodes prospered even more, displacing Athens as the major venue for rhetoric and the arts in the east Mediterranean. The town, which lies underneath virtually all of the modern city, was laid out by one Hippodamus in the grid layout much in vogue at the time, with planned residential and commercial quarters. Its perimeter walls totalled nearly 15km, enclosing nearly double the area of the present town, and the Hellenistic population was said to exceed 100,000, a staggering figure for late antiquity.

Decline set in when Rhodes became involved in the Roman civil wars, and Cassius sacked the city; by late imperial times, it was a backwater, a status confirmed by numerous barbarian raids during the Byzantine period. The Byzantines were compelled to cede the island to the Genoese, who in turn surrendered it to the Knights of St John. The second great siege of Rhodes, during 1522–23, saw Ottoman sultan Süleyman the Magnificent oust the stubborn knights, who retreated to Malta; the town once again lapsed into relative obscurity, though heavily colonized and garrisoned, until its seizure by the Italians in 1912.

Ródhos Town

RÓDHOS TOWN divides into two unequal parts: the compact old walled city, and the new town which sprawls around it in three directions. The latter dates from the Ottoman occupation, when Greek Orthodox natives – forbidden to dwell in the old city – founded several suburb villages or *marásia* in the environs, which have since merged. Commercialization is predictably rampant in the walled town, and in the modern district of Neohóri west of Mandhráki yacht harbour, the few buildings which aren't hotels are souvenir shops, car rental or travel agencies and bars – easily sixty to seventy in every category. To either side of this stretches the **town beach** (standing room only for latecomers), complete with deckchairs, parasols and showers, particular on the more sheltered east-facing section called **Élli**. At the northernmost point of the island an **Aquarium** (daily April–Sept 9am–9pm, Oct–March 9am–4.30pm; 600dr), officially the "Hydrobiological Institute", offers some diversion with its subterranean maze of seawater tanks. Upstairs is a less enthralling collection of half-rotten stuffed sharks, seals and even a whale. Some 200m southeast stand the **Murad Reis mosque**, an atmospherically neglected Muslim cemetery and the equally dilapidated **Villa Cleobolus**, where Lawrence Durrell lived from 1945 to 1947.

Just a few paces northwest of this, the Italian-built Albergo delle Rose (*Hotel Rodon*) was refurbished and pressed into service in 1999 as the **Playboy Casino Rhodes**, Greece's third largest, complete with "bunnies" serving drinks on the upper floors. Despite parting large sums of money from Rhodians in its first year of operation – uniquely in Greece, locals are allowed to patronize this casino – the outfit has yet to turn a profit.

The old town

Simply to catalogue the principal monuments and attractions cannot do full justice to the infinitely more rewarding **medieval city**. There's ample gratification to be derived from slipping through the eleven surviving gates and strolling the streets, under flying archways built for earthquake resistance, past the warm-toned sandstone and limestone walls painted ochre or blue, and over the *hokhláki* (pebble) pavement.

Dominating the northernmost sector of the city's fourteenth-century fortifications is the **Palace of the Grand Masters** (summer Mon noon–7pm, Tues–Fri 8am–7pm; winter Mon 12.30–3pm, Tues–Sun 8.30am–3pm; 1200dr). Largely destroyed by an ammunition depot explosion set off by lightning in 1856, it was reconstructed by the Italians as a summer home for Mussolini and Victor Emmanuel III ("King of Italy and Albania, Emperor of Ethiopia"), neither of whom ever visited Rhodes. The exterior, based on medieval engravings and accounts, is passably authentic, but inside matters are on an altogether grander scale: a marble staircase leads up to rooms paved with

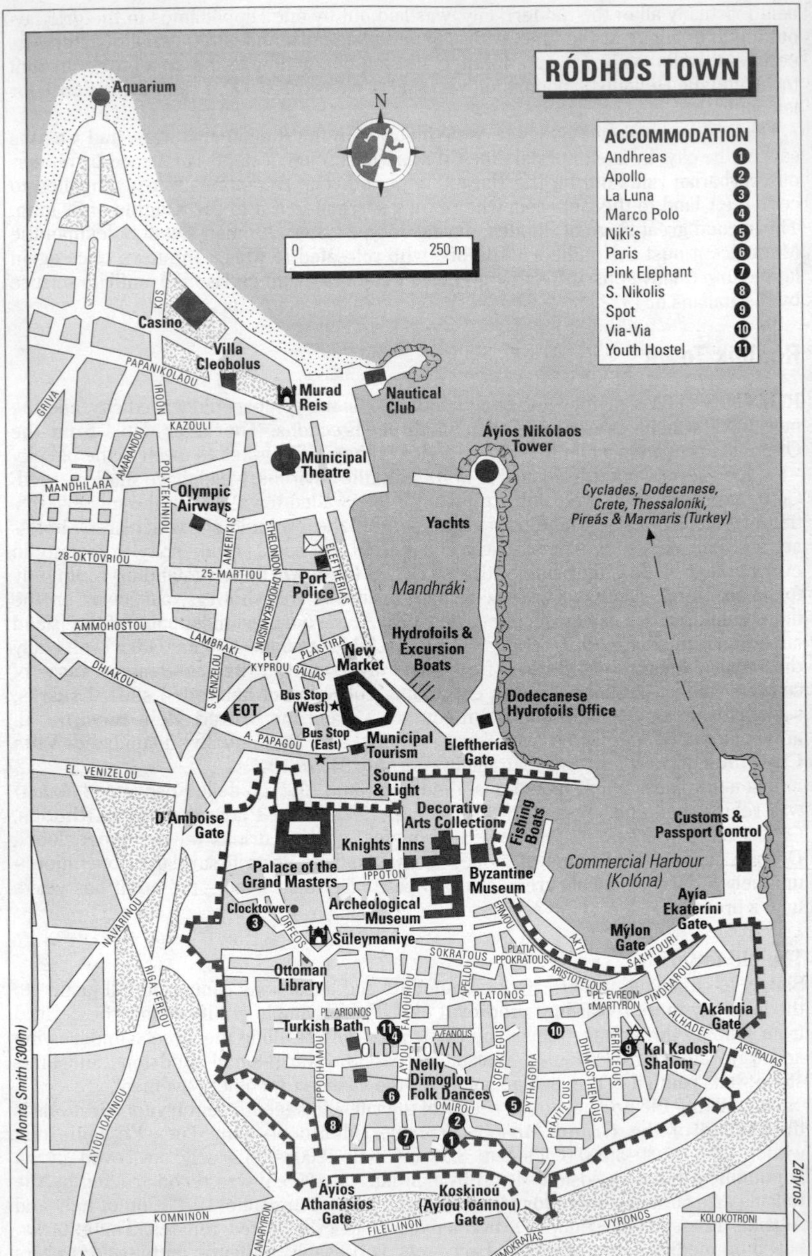
RÓDHOS TOWN
ACCOMMODATION
Andhreas 1
Apollo 2
La Luna 3
Marco Polo 4
Niki's 5
Paris 6
Pink Elephant 7
S. Nikolis 8
Spot 9
Via-Via 10
Youth Hostel 11
N
0 250 m
Aquarium
Casino
Villa Cleobolus
Murad Reis
Nautical Club
Municipal Theatre
Olympic Airways
Áyios Nikólaos Tower
Cyclades, Dodecanese, Crete, Thessaloníki, Pireás & Marmaris (Turkey)
Yachts
Mandhráki
Port Police
Hydrofoils & Excursion Boats
New Market
Bus Stop (West)
Bus Stop (East)
EOT
Municipal Tourism
Dodecanese Hydrofoils Office
Eleftherías Gate
Sound & Light
D'Amboise Gate
Decorative Arts Collection
Fishing Boats
Knights' Inns
Palace of the Grand Masters
Byzantine Museum
Customs & Passport Control
Commercial Harbour (Kolóna)
Clocktower
Archeological Museum
Süleymaniye
Ayía Ekaterîni Gate
Mýlon Gate
Ottoman Library
Turkish Bath
OLD TOWN
Nelly Dimoglou Folk Dances
Kal Kadosh Shalom
Akándia Gate
Áyios Athanásios Gate
Koskinoú (Ayíou Ioánnou) Gate
Monte Smith (300m)
Zéfyros
Líndhos & Rodhíni Park
PAPANIKOLAOU
GRIVA
KAZOULI
AMARANDOU
IROON
POLYTEKHNIOU
MANDHILARA
AMERIKIS
28-OKTOVRIOU
25-MARTIOU
ETHELONDON DHODHEKANISION
ELEFTHERIAS
AMMOHOSTOU
LAMBRAKI
PLASTIRA
PL. KYPROU
GALLIAS
DHIAKOU
S. VENIZELOU
A. PAPAGOU
EL. VENIZELOU
IPPOTON
ORFEOS
ERMOU
SOKRATOUS
PLATIA IPPOKRATOUS
ARISTOTELOUS
AKTI SAKHTOURI
PINDHAROU
PL. EVREON MARTYRON
ALHADEF
AFSTRALIAS
PLATONOS
PL. ARIONOS
FANOURIOU
APELLOU
A. FANOUS
AYIOU
SOFOKLEOUS
PYTHAGORA
DHIMOSTHENOUS
PERIKLEOUS
PRAXITELOUS
IPPODHAMOU
OMIROU
NAVARINOU
RIGA FEREOU
AYIOU IOANNOU
KOMNINON
AV. ANARYIRON
FILELLINON
DHIMOKRATIAS
VYRONOS
KOLOKOTRONI

Hellenistic mosaics from Kós, and the ponderous period furnishings rival many a northern European palace. The ground floor is home to the splendid **Medieval Exhibit** and **Ancient Rhodes, 2400 Years** gallery (same hours and admission ticket), together the best museums in town. The medieval collection highlights the importance of Christian Rhodes as a trade centre, with exotic merchandise placing the island in a trans-Mediterranean context. The Knights are represented with a display on their sugar-refining industry and a gravestone of a Grand Master; precious manuscripts and books precede a wing of post-Byzantine icons, moved here permanently from Panayía Kástrou (see below). Across the courtyard in the north wing, "Ancient Rhodes" overshadows the official archeological museum by explaining the everyday life of the ancients, arranged topically (beauty aids, toys, cookware, worship and so on); highlights include a Hellenistic floor mosaic and a household idol of Hecate, goddess of the occult. On Tuesday and Saturday afternoons, there's a supplementary tour of the **city walls** (one hour starting at 2.45pm; 1200dr), beginning from a gate next to the palace and finishing at the Koskinoú gate.

The heavily restored **Street of the Knights** (Odhós Ippotón) leads due east from the Platía Kleovoúlou in front of the Palace; the "Inns" lining it housed the Knights of St John, according to linguistic and ethnic affiliation, until the Ottoman Turks compelled them to leave for Malta after a six-month siege in which the defenders were outnumbered thirty to one. Today the Inns house various government offices and cultural institutions vaguely appropriate to their past, with occasional exhibitions, but the whole effect of the renovation is predictably sterile and stagy (nearby streets were indeed used in the 1987 filming of *Pascali's Island*).

At the bottom of the hill, the Knights' Hospital has been refurbished as the **Archeological Museum** (Tues–Sun 8am–2.30pm; 800dr), though the arches and echoing halls of the building somewhat overshadow the appallingly labelled and presented contents – largely painted pottery dating from the sixth and seventh centuries BC. Behind the second-storey sculpture garden, the Hellenistic statue gallery is more accessible; in a rear corner stands the so-called "Marine Venus", beloved of Lawrence Durrell, but lent a rather sinister aspect by her sea-dissolved face – in contrast to the friendlier *Aphrodite Bathing*. Virtually next door is the **Decorative Arts Collection** (Tues–Sun 8am–2.30pm; 500dr), gleaned from old houses across the Dodecanese; the most compelling artefacts are carved cupboard doors and chest lids painted in naïve style with mythological or historical episodes.

Across the way stands the **Byzantine Museum** (Tues–Sun 8am–2.30pm; 500dr), housed in the old cathedral of the Knights, who adapted the Byzantine shrine of Panayía Kástrou for their own needs. Medieval icons and frescoes lifted from crumbling chapels on Rhodes and Hálki, as well as photos of art still *in situ*, constitute the exhibits; it's worth a visit since most of the Byzantine churches in the old town and outlying villages are locked. Highlights of the collection are a complete cycle from the domes of Thárri monastery (see p.256) dating from 1624, removed in 1967 to reveal much older work beneath.

If instead you head south from the Palace of the Grand Masters, it's hard to miss the most conspicuous Turkish monument in Rhodes, the rust-coloured **Süleymaniye mosque**. Rebuilt in the nineteenth century on foundations three hundred years older, it's currently closed and under scaffolding like most local Ottoman monuments. The old town is in fact well sown with mosques and *mescids* (the Islamic equivalent of a chapel), many of them converted from Byzantine shrines after the 1522 conquest, when the Christians were expelled from the medieval precinct. A couple of these mosques are still used by the sizable **Turkish-speaking minority** here, some of them descended from Muslims who fled Crete between 1898 and 1913. Their most enduring civic contributions are, opposite the Süleymaniye, the **Ottoman Library** (Mon–Fri 7.30am–2.30pm & 6–9pm, Sat–Sun 8am–noon; tip to custodian), with a rich collection of early medieval manuscripts and Korans, and the imposing, still-functioning **hamam**, or Turkish bath, on Platía Ariónos up in the southwest corner of the medieval city (Tues 1–6pm, Wed–Fri 11am–6pm, Sat 8am–6pm; 500dr, 300dr Weds & Sat).

Heading downhill from the Süleymaniye mosque, **Odhós Sokrátous**, once the heart of the Ottoman bazaar, is now the "Via Turista", packed with fur and jewellery stores pitched at cruise-ship tourists. Beyond the tiled central fountain in Platía Ippokrátous, Odhós Aristotélous leads into the Platía tón Evréon Martýron (Square of the Jewish Martyrs), named in memory of the large local community that was almost totally annihilated in summer 1944. Of the four synagogues which once graced Rhodes, only the ornate, arcaded **Kal Kadosh Shalom** (daily 10am–5pm; donation) on Odhós Simíou just to the south survives. It's maintained essentially as a memorial to the approximately 1800 Jews of Rhodes and Kós sent from here to the concentration camps; plaques in French – the language of educated Ottoman Jews across the east Aegean – commemorate the dead. At the rear of the building, a one-room **museum**, set up by a Los Angeles attorney of Jewish Rhodian descent, features archival photos of the community's life on Rhodes and in its far-flung diaspora in the Americas and Africa.

About 2km southwest of Mandhráki, the sparse, unenclosed remains of **Hellenistic Rhodes** – a restored theatre and stadium, plus a few columns of an Apollo temple – perch atop Monte Smith, the hill of Áyios Stéfanos renamed after a British admiral who used it as a watchpoint during the Napoleonic wars. The wooded site is popular with joggers and strollers, but for summer shade and greenery the best spot is probably **Rodini park**, nearly 2km south of town on the road to Líndhos, and served by city bus route #3. The wooded Zimboúli ravine here, fed by natural springs, is home to ducks, peacocks and (in special pens) the native miniature Rhodian deer. Hellenistic **rock-cut tombs**, signposted via a separate side road at the south end of the park, constitute a final possible diversion.

Practicalities

All international and inter-island **ferries** dock at the middle of Rhodes' three ports, the commercial harbour; the only exceptions are local **boats** to and from Sými, all excursion craft, and the **hydrofoils**, which use the yacht harbour of Mandhráki. Its entrance was supposedly once straddled by the Colossus, an ancient statue of Apollo built to celebrate the end of the 305 BC siege; today two columns surmounted by bronze deer are less overpowering replacements.

The **airport** is 13km southwest of town, near the village of Paradhíssi; public urban buses bound for Paradhíssi, Kalavárdha, Theológos or Sálakos pass the stop on the main road opposite the northerly car-park entrance fairly frequently between 6am and midnight. A taxi into town will cost 3000–3700dr, plus bags, depending on time of day. Orange-and-white KTEL **buses** for both the west and east coasts of Rhodes leave from two almost adjacent terminals on Papágou and Avérof, just outside the Italian-built New Market (a tourist trap). Between the lower eastern station and the **taxi** rank at Platía Rimínis there's a **municipal tourist office** (June–Oct Mon–Sat 9am–9pm, Sun 9am–3pm), while some way up Papágou on the corner of Makaríou stands the **EOT office** (Mon–Fri 7.30am–3pm); both dispense bus and ferry schedules.

ACCOMMODATION

Hotels and pensions at all price levels abound in the old town, mostly in the quad bounded by Omírou to the south, Sokrátous to the north, Perikléous to the east and Ippodhámou to the west. At crowded seasons, or late at night, it's prudent to either ring ahead or be prepared to accept the offers of proprietors meeting the ferries and change base next day if necessary – as it frequently is, since standards amongst quay-touted premises tend to be low.

Andreas, Omírou 28d (☎0241/34 156, fax 74 285). Perennially popular (reservations needed), this pension is one of the more imaginative old-house restorations. Rooms in a variety of formats and plumbing arrangements (many en-suite). Terrace view-bar, email facilities, credit cards accepted. Open Mar–Oct. ③.

Apollo, Omírou 28c (☎0241/35 064). Basic but clean and friendly rooms place; the self-catering kitchen makes it good for longer stays. ①.

La Luna, Ierokléous 21 (☎ & fax 0241/25 856). Clean if plain (no en-suite) pension in a converted old Turkish house, complete with still-functioning *hamam* (Turkish bath). Garden bar for breakfast, by the citrus and banana trees. ③.

Marco Polo Mansion, Ayíou Fanouríou 42 (☎ & fax 0241/25 562, *marcopolomansion@hotmail.com*). Superb, newish (1999) conversion of an old Turkish mansion, again with a *hamam* on site, but here all rooms are en-suite and exquisitely furnished with antiques from the nearby eponymous gallery. Large buffet breakfasts provided by ebullient manageress Efi, and adjoining café after-hours. Three-day minimum stay, breakfast included. ⑥.

Niki's, Sofokléous 39 (☎0241/25 115). Rooms can be on the small side, but ground-floor units are en-suite, and upper-storey ones have fine views. There's a washing machine and common terrace, too. ②.

Paris, Ayíou Fanouríou 88, corner Omírou (☎0241/26 356). Plain but en-suite rooms with fans, the best facing a large courtyard. ③.

Pink Elephant/Roz Elefandas, officially Irodhótou 42 but actually on Timahídhas (☎ & fax 0241/22 469). Simple but clean rooms occupying several levels of a modernized old building; roof deck and card-phone that receives calls too. ②.

S. Nikolis, Ippodhámou 61 (☎0241/34 561, fax 32 034, *niholiss@hol.gr*). A variety of premises in the west of the old town. Hotel/honeymoon-suite rates ⑥ include breakfast, TV and air con, or there are self-catering apartments (④) or even a simple house pension (③). Bookings essential for hotel and apartments, accepted only with credit-card number. Open Apr–Nov.

Spot, Perikléous 21 (☎0241/34 737). Rooms are a bit dark, but clean enough, and you won't find en-suite rooms elsewhere for this price, except at *Niki's*. ②.

Via-Via, Lysipoú, alley off Pythagóra 31 (☎ & fax 0241/27 895). Efficiently French-run rooms, either shared bathrooms (②) or en-suite (③). Self-catering, roof terrace, email facility, open all year.

Youth Hostel, Eryíou 12 (☎0241/30 491). Both dorms and doubles in this courtyarded house with kitchen facilities; 2000dr for a bunk, but none-YHA-affiliated.

EATING AND DRINKING

Eating well for a reasonable price in and around Ródhos Town is a challenge, but not an insurmountable one. As a general rule, the remoter and further south you go, the better value you'll find.

Araliki, Aristofánous 45, Old Town. Bohemian expatriates and travellers tired of standard resort grub seek out this old-style kafenío on the ground floor of a medieval house. Small plates of exquisitely original mezédhes are provided by Italian proprietors Miriam, Enio and Valeria; count on 4500dr per person with drinks, which include Nissyrot *soumádha*. Open Mar–Dec daily except Sun for supper (and often lunch); also shut two random weeks July–Aug.

Dhiafani, Platía Ariónos, Old Town. Enormous salads and *mayireftá* plates, the cheapest (3000dr a head for the works) in the old town; outdoor seating opposite the *hamam*.

Khristos Ouzeri Inomayerio (O Vlahos), Klavdhíou Pépper 165, at the big bend, Zéfyros Beach, New Town. As the name implies, both ouzerí fare – marinated fish or peppers, great *tzatzíki* – accompanying a vast oúzo list, plus vegetable-strong *mayireftá* (cuttlefish with spinach) that sell out quickly. Not as cheap or big-portioned as formerly, but still worth the trek out.

Le Bistrot de l'Auberge, Praxitélous 21, Old Town. Genuine, popular, French-run bistro with excellent Frenchified food: allow 5000dr per person for three hefty courses plus wine from a well-selected Greek list, jazz soundtrack included. Summer seating in the courtyard of this restored medieval inn; inside under the arches during cooler months. Open Mar–Dec for lunch and supper daily except Mon.

O Meraklis, Aristotélous 30. A *pátsatzídhiko* (tripe-and-trotter soup kitchen) that's only open 3–7am for a motley clientele of post-club lads, Turkish stallholders, night-club singers and travellers just stumbled off an overnight ferry. Great free entertainment, including famously rude staff, and the soup – the traditional Greek hangover cure – is good too.

Metaxi Mas, Klavdhíou Pépper 116, Zéfyros Beach, New Town. No sign or menu in English – look for the elevated boat – at this somewhat pricey seafood ouzerí with various exotic titbits; count on 12,000dr per couple with booze, slightly less in a group. Daily lunch and supper except Sun lunch only.

Mikes (pronounced "mee-kess"), nameless alley behind Sokrátous 17. Inexpensive (for Rhodes, anyway) hole-in-the-wall, serving only grilled fish, salads and wine.

Palia Istoria, Mitropóleos 108, cnr Dhendhrínou, in Ámmos district of New Town. Reckoned to be the best *kultúra* taverna in town, but predictably expensive for such dishes as celery hearts in egg-lemon sauce and scallops with mushrooms and artichokes, washed down by a hundred-strong wine list. Supper only; reservations essential on ☎0241/32 421.

Sheftalies, Tsaldhári 21, New Town, south of Monte Smith past Marinopoulos Supermarket. Direct antithesis to *Palia Istoria*, since you can fill up for 2500dr. Zero atmosphere, but a genuine charcoal griller featuring the namesake *sheftaliés*, dioxin-free chicken and *kokorétsi*, plus a few daily *mayireftá* plates.

To Steno, Ayíon Anaryíron 29, New Town, 400m southwest of the Ayíou Athanasíou Gate. A genuinely welcoming ouzerí, with outdoor seating during the warmer months and limited but superb menu (chickpea soup, courgette croquettes, sausages) at eminently reasonable prices.

Stou Apostoli, Mitropóleos 49, New Town, 500m south of the stadium, past the big church. Inexpensive ouzerí housed on the ground floor of an Italian mansion; brief but well-executed menu of grilled titbits plus vegetable mezédhes.

Vassilis (Kova), Kolokotroni, 80m east of Kanadhá, south of Akándia commercial port. Another place to go when you're down to your last drachma: a friendly working man's canteen, busiest from noon to 2pm, with several *mayireftá* dishes to choose from and shady outdoor seating between the auto-repair shops.

NIGHTLIFE

The old town formerly had a well-deserved reputation for being tomb-silent at night; this has changed drastically since the late 1990s, with an entire alley (Miltiádhou) off Apéllou given over to five loud music bars and clubs, frequented almost exclusively by Greeks. This is just a mini taster for the estimated two hundred foreigner-patronized bars and clubs in Neohóri, where theme nights and various other gimmicks predominate. They are found mostly along the streets and alleys bounded by Alexándhrou Dhiákou, Orfanídhou (aka "Skandi Street", after the latter-day Vikings), Fanouráki and Nikifórou Mandhilará.

Sedate by comparison, Ministry-of-Culture-approved folk dances (May–Oct Mon, Wed, Fri 9.20pm; 2500dr) are presented with live accompaniment by the Nelly Dimoglou Company, performed in the landscaped "Old Town Theatre" off Andhroníkou, near Platía Ariónos. More of a technological extravaganza is the **Sound and Light** show, spotlighting sections of the city walls, staged in a garden just off Platía Rimínis. There's English-language narration nightly except Sunday, its screening time varying from 8.15pm to 10.15pm (1200dr).

Thanks to a large contingent from the local university, there are several year-round **cinemas** in the new town showing first-run fare indoors or open-air according to season. Choose from among the Rodon Municipal Theatre, next to the town hall in Neohóri; the Metropol, southeast of the old town opposite the stadium; and the nearby Pallas on Dhimokratías, completely refurbished in 1999.

Blue Lagoon Pool Bar, 25-Martíou 2, Neohóri. One of the better theme bars, in this case a "desert island" with palm trees, waterfalls, a shipwrecked galleon – and taped music.

Café Besara (very small sign out), Sofokléous 11-13, Old Town. Congenial breakfast café/low-key boozer run by an Australian lady, with interesting mixed clientele and live music some nights.

Christos' Garden/To Dhiporto, Dhilberáki 59, Neohóri. This combination art-gallery/bar/café occupies a carefully restored old house and courtyard with pebble-mosaic floors throughout. Incongruously classy for the area.

Colorado Entertainment Centre, Orfanídhou 57, cnr Aktí Miaouli, Neohóri. Triple venue: "pub" with live in-house band (rock covers), "club" with taped sounds, and quiet upstairs "bar".

Mango Bar, Platía Dhoriéos 3, Old Town. Piped music and a variety of drinks at this durable bar on an otherwise quiet plaza; also a good source of breakfast after 8am, served under a plane tree.

O'Reilly's, Apolloníou Rodhíou 61, Neohóri. Irish theme pub with claimed live music nightly, and Irish draught.

Resalto, Plátonos 6, opposite the mosque. Live Greek rembétika and laikó sounds, rather cheaper than nearby rival *Café Chantant*.

Rolóï, Orféos 1, Old Town. The baroque clocktower erected by Ahmet Fetih Pasha in 1857 is now the focus of possibly the most exclusive café-bar in the old town. Admission charge to climb the tower, and steeply priced drinks, but you are paying for the terrific view.

Sticky Fingers, Anthoúla Zérvou 6, Neohóri. Long-lived music bar with reasonable drinks; live rock several nights weekly from 10pm onwards.

Listings

Airlines British Airways, Platía Kýprou 1 (☎0241/27 756); Olympic, Iérou Lókhou 9 (☎0241/24 571). Air Greece and Cronus Air have no set office; most bona fide travel agents handle them.

Bookshop Second Storey Books, Amarándou 24, Neohóri, has a large stock of used English paperbacks; open all year, normal shop hours.

Car rental Prices at non-international chains are fairly standard at 13,000–14,000dr per day, but can be bargained down to about 10,000–11,000dr a day, all-inclusive, out of peak season and/or for long periods. More flexible local outfits, all in the new town, include Alexander, Afstralías 58, Akándia port (☎0241/27 547); Alamo, 28-Oktovríou 18 (☎0241/73 570); Just, Orfanídhou 45 (☎0241/31 811); Kosmos, Papaloúka 31 (☎0241/74 374); Orion, Yeoryíou Leóndos 36 (☎0241/22 137); and Payless, Íonos Dhragoúmi 29 (☎0241/26 586).

Exchange Most conventional bank branches are near Platía Kýprou in Neohóri, plus there are numerous exchange bureaux keeping long hours. At other times use the cash dispensers of the Commercial Bank (branch in the old town too), Credit Bank, Ionian Bank or National Bank (old town branch).

Ferries Tourist office handouts list the bewildering array of representatives for the several boat and hydrofoil companies which operate here; authoritative schedule information is available at the *limenarhío*, on Mandhráki esplanade near the post office.

Internet cafés The most central and competitive of several are *Rock Style*, Dhimokratías 7, opposite the stadium, and *Café Besara* (see "Nightlife" opposite).

Laundries House of Laundry, Erythroú Stavroú 2, Neohóri; Star, Kostí Palamá 4–6, behind New Market; Wash & Go, Plátonos 33, Old Town.

Motorbike rental Low-volume scooters will make little impact on Rhodes; sturdier Yamaha 125s, suitable for two people, start at about 6000dr a day. In the old town, Mandar Moto at Dhimosthénous 2, cnr Platía Evréon Martýron, has a large stable of medium-sized scooters suitable for short jaunts. Recommended outlets in Neohóri include Margaritis, Ioánni Kazoúli, with a wide range of late models up to 500cc, plus mountain bikes; or (to roll out in style) Rent a Harley at 28-Oktovríou 80 – classic models for two riders start at a whopping 33,000dr per day.

Post office Main branch with outgoing mail, poste restante and exchange windows on Mandhráki harbour, open Mon–Fri 7.30am–8pm.

Radio stations For foreign sounds, try Rodos International at 102 FM, or UK Radio at 107.5 FM.

Scuba diving Waterhoppers and Dive Med both tout for business daily at Mandhráki quay; however days out are expensive (18,000dr for two dives) and you're restricted to one small site at Thérmes Kallithéas.

Travel agencies Particularly recommended in the old town is Castellania, Evripídhou 1–3, cnr Platía Ippokrátous, which can arrange all domestic air tickets, both domestic and international ferries, and also discount scheduled and charter flights abroad. In Neohóri, Visa at Grigóri Lambráki 54 (☎0241/33 282) and Contours at Ammohóstou 9 (☎0241/36 001) are also worth contacting, while Plaza Travel at Ieroú Lóhou 7 is the main outlet for hydrofoil tickets to Marmaris in Turkey.

The east coast

Heading down the coast from the capital you have to go some way before you escape the crowds from local beach hotels, their numbers swollen by visitors using the regular buses from town or on boat tours out of Mandhráki. You might look in at the decayed, abandoned spa of **Thérmes Kallithéas**, dating in its present spectacle of enjoyable mock-orientalia from the Italian period. Located 3km south of Kallithéa resort proper, down a dirt track through pines, the buildings are set in a palm grove, though an EU-funded restoration begun in 1999 seems stalled indefinitely. Nearby are several hidden sandy coves framed by rock formations, furnished with sunbeds and (in some cases) snack bars. The former fishing village of **FALIRÁKI**, which primarily draws a youngish package clientele, is all too much in the mould of a Spanish *costa* resort, while the scenery just inland – arid, scrubby sand-hills at the best of times – has been made that much bleaker by fire damage that stretches way beyond Líndhos.

The enormous mass of **Tsambíka**, 26km south of town, is the first place at which most non-package visitors will seriously consider stopping. Actually the very eroded flank of a much larger extinct volcano, the hill has a monastery on top offering unrivalled views along some 50km of coastline. From the main highway, a steep, 1500-metre cement drive leads to a small car park and a snack bar, from which steps lead to the summit. The monastery here is unremarkable except for its September 8 festival: childless women climb up – sometimes on their hands and knees – to be relieved of their barrenness, and any children born afterwards are dedicated to the Virgin with the names Tsambikos or Tsambika, which are particular to the Dodecanese. From the top you can survey **Kolýmbia** just to the north, a small beach to one side of a tiny cove ringed with volcanic rocks, backed by a dozen, low-rise hotels. Shallow **Tsambíka** bay on the south side of the headland warms up early in the spring, and the excellent beach, though protected by the forest service from development other than a permanent taverna and a dozen *kantína* caravans, teems with people all summer.

The next beach south, gravelly **Stegná** with its summer cottages for locals, can only be reached by a steep road east from **ARHÁNGELOS**, a large village just inland overlooked by a crumbling castle. Though you can disappear into the warren of alleys between the main road and the citadel, the place is now firmly caught up in package tourism, with a full complement of banks, tavernas, mini-marts and jewellery stores.

A more peaceful overnight base on this stretch of coast would be **HARÁKI**, a pleasant if undistinguished two-street fishing port with mostly self-catering accommodation (generally ③) overlooked by the stubby ruins of **Feraklós castle**, the last stronghold of the Knights to fall to the Turks. You can swim off the town beach if you don't mind an audience from the handful of waterfront cafés and tavernas, but most people head west out of town, then north 800m to the secluded **Agáthi beach**. The best taverna near Haráki is *Efterpi*, 200m south at so-called Massári beach.

Líndhos

LÍNDHOS, the island's second-ranking tourist attraction, erupts from barren surroundings 12km south of Haráki. Like Ródhos old town, its charm is heavily undermined by commercialism and crowds: up to half a million visitors in a typical year. At midday dozens of coaches park nose-to-tail on the narrow southerly access road, with even more on the drives down to the beaches. Back in the village itself, those few vernacular houses not snapped up by package operators have, since the 1960s, been bought up and refurbished by wealthy British, Germans and Italians. The old *agorá* or serpentine high street presents a mass of fairly indistinguishable bars, creperies, mediocre restaurants and travel agents. Although high-rise hotels and all vehicular traffic have been prohibited inside the municipal boundaries, the result is a relentlessly commercialized theme park – hot and airless in August, but deserted and quite ghostly in winter.

Nonetheless, if you arrive before or after peak season, when the pebble-paved streets between the immaculately whitewashed houses are relatively empty of both people and droppings from the donkeys shuttling up to the acropolis (see below), you can still appreciate the beautiful, atmospheric setting of Líndhos. The most imposing fifteenth- to eighteenth-century **captains' residences** are built around *hokhláki* courtyards, their monumental doorways often fringed by intricate stonework, with the number of braids or cables supposedly corresponding to the number of ships owned. A few are open to the public, most notably the **Papakonstandis Mansion**, the most elaborate and now home to an unofficial museum; entrance to the "open" mansions is free but some pressure will probably be exerted on you to buy something, especially lace and embroidery.

On the bluff looming above the town, the ancient acropolis with its 1990s-restored Doric **Temple of Athena** and imposing **Hellenistic stoa** is found inside the Knights' **castle** (summer Tues–Sun 8am–6.40pm, Mon 12.30am–6.40pm; rest of year Tues–Sun 8.30am–3pm; 1200dr) – a surprisingly felicitous blend of ancient and medieval culture. Though the ancient city of Lindos and its original temple date from at least 1100 BC, the present structure was begun by local ruler Kleoboulos in the sixth century BC and replaced by the present structure after a fourth-century fire.

Líndhos's north beach, once the main ancient harbour, is overcrowded and occasionally polluted; if you do base yourself here, cleaner, quieter **beaches** are to be found one cove beyond at Pállas beach (with a nudist annexe around the headland), or 5km north at **Vlyhá** bay. South of the acropolis huddles the small, perfectly sheltered **St Paul's harbour**, where the apostle is said to have landed in 58 AD on a mission to evangelize the island.

PRACTICALITIES

It used to be tempting fate to just turn up and hope for accommodation vacancies on spec, but since certain British tour companies pulled out of Líndhos in the late 1990s, it's something of a buyers' market. If you're not met at the bus stop under the giant fig tree by proprietors touting rooms, *Pallas Travel* (☎0244/31 494, fax 31 595) can arrange a room or even a whole villa for a small fee. The oft-cited backpackers' standbys, 1970s-vintage *Pension Electra* (☎0244/31 226; ③) and *Pension Katholiki* (☎0244/31 445; ②), next door to each other on the way to the north beaches, are both low standard (shared baths) and overpriced.

Local **restaurants** tend to be bland and exploitative, although *Agostino's* by the southerly car park possesses the important virtues of bulk Émbonas wine and real country sausages (not imported hot dogs). You may as well push the boat out at *Mavrikos* on the fig-tree square, founded in 1933 and in the same family ever since. Mezédhes are good, as are quasi-French main courses like cuttlefish in wine; dipping into the excellent (and expensive) Greek wine list as well will land you a bill of 5000–6000dr per person. If your wallet won't stretch that far, the *Panorama* up on the main road, 2km towards Vlyhá, does good fish. For snacks and desserts, try respectively *Il Forno*, an Italian-run bakery, and *Gelo Blu*, still the best of several gelaterie here despite the departure of its Italian founders. There's a unique combination laundry/second-hand bookshop up beyond Pallas Travel, open during normal shop hours, while there are currently three Internet cafés operating in Líndhos. Local **car rental** rates tend to be cheaper than in Ródhos Town, though you've less choice in models and vehicles may be less roadworthy. There are two proper **banks**, working normal hours, each with cash dispensers. And finally, Lindos Suntours (☎0244/31 333) has metred phones (call boxes tend to have huge queues) and a nice line in unclaimed one-way charter seats back to Britain.

The west coast

Rhodes' west coast is the windward flank of the island, so it's damper, more fertile and more forested; most beaches, however, are exposed and decidedly rocky. None of this has deterred development, and as in the east the first few kilometres of the busy shore road down from the capital have been surrendered entirely to tourism. From Neohóri's aquarium down to the airport, the shore is fringed by an almost uninterrupted line of Miami-Beach-style hotels, though such places as Triánda, Kremastí and Paradhíssi are still nominally villages, with real centres. This was the first part of the island to be favoured by the package operators, and tends to be frequented by a decidedly middle-aged, sedate clientele that doesn't stir much from the poolside.

There's not much inducement to stop until you reach the important archeological site of **KAMEIROS**, which together with Líndhos and Ialyssos was one of the three Dorian powers that united during the fifth century BC to found the powerful city-state of Rhodes. Soon eclipsed by the new capital, Kameiros was abandoned and only rediscovered in 1859. As a result it is a particularly well-preserved Doric townscape, doubly worth visiting for its beautiful hillside site (summer Tues–Sun 8am–6.40pm, winter 8.30am–3pm; 800dr). While none of the individual remains are spectacular, you can make out the foundations of two small temples, the re-erected pillars of a Hellenistic house, a Classical fountain, and the stoa of the upper *agora*, complete with a water cistern. Because of the gentle slope of the site, there were no fortifications, nor was there an acropolis. On the beach below Kameiros there are several tavernas, highly commercialized but acceptable while waiting for one of the two daily buses back to town (if you're willing to walk 4km back to Kalavárdha you'll have a better choice of service).

At the tiny anchorage of **KÁMIROS SKÁLA** (aka Skála Kamírou) 15km south, there are more touristy restaurants which somewht inexplicably have become the target of coach tours. Less heralded is the daily **kaïki** which leaves for the island of **Hálki** at 2.30pm, weather permitting, returning early the next morning; on Wednesdays and Sundays there are day-trips departing at 9am and returning at 4pm. For a decent **meal**, skip the circus here and proceed 400m southwest to off-puttingly named **Paralía Kopriá** (Manure Beach), where *Psarotaverna Johnny's* has superb, non-farmed fish and mezédhes, especially on Sundays when own-made *dolmádhes* and (seasonally) squash blossoms may be on the menu with the usual standards.

A couple of kilometres south of Skála, the "Kastello", signposted as **Kástro Kritinías**, is from afar the most impressive of the Knights' rural strongholds, and the paved access road is too narrow and steep for tour buses. Close up it proves to be no more than a shell, but a glorious shell, with fine views west to assorted islets and Hálki. You make a "donation" to the formidable old harpy at the car park in exchange for fizzy drinks, seasonal fruit or flowers.

Beyond Kritinía itself, a quiet hillside village with a few rooms and tavernas, the main road winds south through the dense forests below mounts Akramítis and Atávyros to **SIÁNNA**, the most attractive mountain settlement on the island, famous for its aromatic pine-sage honey and *soúma*, a grape-residue distillation similar to Italian *grappa* but far smoother. The rough-and-ready *Elektra*, whose owner spent 27 years in Connecticut, is the place to sample it, with tomato and cheese mezédhes. The tiered, flat-roofed farmhouses of **MONÓLITHOS**, 4km southwest at the end of the public bus line, are scant justification for the long trip out here, and food at the four **tavernas** is indifferent owing to the tour-group trade, but the view over the bay is striking and you could use the village as a base by staying in rooms or at the pricier *Hotel Thomas* (☎0241/22 741 or ☎0246/61 291; ②), self-catering and open most of the year. Diversions in the area include yet another **Knights' castle** 2km west of town, photogenically perched on its own pinnacle (the "monolith" of the name) but enclosing even less inside than Kastéllo Kritinías, and the sand and gravel beaches (no facilities) at

Foúrni, five paved but curvy kilometres below the castle. In the headland between the first and second beaches are some caves that were hollowed out by early Christians fleeing persecution.

The interior

Inland Rhodes is hilly, and still mostly wooded, despite the recent depredations of arsonists. You'll need a vehicle to see its highlights, especially as enjoyment resides in getting away from it all; no single site justifies the tremendous expense of a taxi or the inconvenience of trying to make the best of sparse bus schedules.

Ialyssos and the Valley of the Butterflies

Starting from the west coast highway, turn inland at the central junction in Tríanda for the five-kilometre uphill ride to the scanty acropolis of ancient **Ialyssos** (Tues–Sun 8am–6.40pm, Mon 8am–2.30pm; 800dr) on flat-topped, strategic Filérimos hill; from its Byzantine castle Süleyman the Magnificent directed the 1522 siege of Rhodes. Filérimos means "lover of solitude", after the tenth-century settlement here by Byzantine hermits. The existing **Filérimos monastery**, restored successively by Italians and British, is the most substantial structure here. As a concession to the Rhodian faithful, the church alone is usually open to pilgrims after the stated hours. Directly in front of the church sprawl the foundations of third-century **temples to Zeus and Athena**, built atop a far older Phoenician shrine. Below this, further towards the car park, lies the partly subterranean church of **Aï-Yeórgis Hostós**, a simple, barrel-vaulted structure with fourteenth- and fifteenth-century frescoes, not as vivid or well preserved as those at Thárri or Asklipió. A bit southeast of the parking area, a hillside **Doric fountain** with a columned facade was only revealed by subsidence in 1926 – and is now off-limits owing to another landslip which has covered it again. Southwest of the monastery and archeological zone, a "Way of the Cross", with the fourteen stations marked out in copper plaques during the Italian era, leads to an enormous concrete crucifix, a recent replacement of an Italian-era one; you're allowed to climb out onto the cross-arms for a supplement to the already amazing view. Illuminated at night, the crucifix is clearly visible from the island of Sými and – perhaps more pertinently – infidel Turkey across the way.

The only highly publicized tourist "attraction" in the island's interior, **Petaloúdhes** or the **"Butterfly Valley"** (May–Sept daily 8.30am–7pm; 300dr–600dr depending on butterfly numbers), reached by a seven-kilometre paved side road bearing inland from the west-coast highway between Paradhíssi and Theológos, is actually a rest stop for Jersey tiger moths (*Panaxia quadripunctaria*). Only in summer do these creatures congregate here, attracted for unknown reasons by the abundant *Liquidambar orientalis* trees. In season, the moths roost in droves on the tree trunks; they cannot eat during this final phase of their life cycle, must rest to conserve energy and die of starvation soon after mating. When sitting in the trees, the moths are a well-camouflaged black and yellow, but flash cherry-red overwings in flight.

Eptá Piyés to Profítis Ilías

Heading inland from Kolýmbia junction on the main east-coast highway, it's a four-kilometre walk or drive to **Eptá Piyés** (Seven Springs), a superb oasis with a tiny dam created by the Italians for irrigation. A shaded streamside **taverna**, immensely popular at weekend with islanders and visitors alike, serves hearty if slightly pricey fare. A trail, or a rather claustrophobic Italian aqueduct-tunnel, both lead from the vicinity of the springs to the reservoir.

Continuing inland, you reach the Italian governor's summer residence at Eleoússa after another 9km, in the shade of the dense forest at the east end of Profítis Ilías ridge.

Two other undisturbed villages, Platánia and Apóllona, nestle on the south slopes of the mountain overlooking the start of the burned area, but most people keep straight on 3km further from Eleoússa to the late Byzantine church of **Áyios Nikólaos Foundoúkli** (St Nicholas of the Hazelnuts). The partly shaded site has a fine view north over cultivated valleys, and locals descend in force for picnics on weekends. The frescoes inside, dating from the thirteenth to the fifteenth centuries, could do with a good cleaning but various scenes from the life of Christ are recognizable.

Heading west from the church along mostly paved roads gets you finally to **Profítis Ilías**, where the Italian-vintage chalet-hotels *Elafos* and *Elafina* (shut down) hide in deep woods just north of the 798-metre peak, Rhodes' third-highest point but out of bounds as a military area. However, there's good, gentle strolling below and around the summit, and a snack bar on the through road is generally open in season.

Atávyros villages

All tracks and roads west across Profítis Ilías converge upon the main road from Kalavárdha bound for **ÉMBONAS**, a large and architecturally nondescript village backed up against the north slope of 1215-metre **Mount Atávyros**. Émbonas, with its two pensions and meat-orientated tavernas, is more geared to handling tourists than you might expect, since it's the venue for summer "folk-dance tours" from Ródhos Town. The village also lies at the heart of the island's most important wine-producing districts, and CAÏR – the Italian-founded vintners' co-operative – produces a choice of acceptable mid-range varieties. However, products of the smaller, family-run Emery winery (☎0246/41 208; Mon–Fri 9am–3pm for tasting tours) at the village outskirts are more esteemed. To see what Émbonas would be like without tourists, carry on clockwise around the peak past the Artamíti monastery, to less celebrated **ÁYIOS ISÍDHOROS**, with as many vines and tavernas, a more open feel, and the **trailhead** for the five-hour return ascent of Atávyros. This path, beginning at the northeast edge of the village, is the safest and easiest way up the mountain, which has extensive foundations of a Zeus temple on top.

Thárri monastery

The road from Áyios Isídhoros to Siána is paved; not so the appalling one that curves for 12km east to Láerma, but it's worth enduring if you've any interest in Byzantine monuments. The **monastery of Thárri**, lost in pine forests five kilometres south, is the oldest religious foundation on the island, re-established as a living community of half a dozen monks in 1990 by the charismatic abbot Amfilohios. The striking *katholikón* (open daily, all day) consists of a long nave and short transept surmounted by barrel vaulting. Various recent cleanings have restored formerly damp-smudged frescoes dating from 1300 to 1450 to their former exquisite glory. The most distinct, in the transept, depict the Evangelists Mark and Matthew, plus the Archangel Gabriel, while the nave boasts various acts of Christ, including such scenes as the *Storm on the Sea of Galilee*, *Meeting the Samaritan Woman at the Well* and *Healing the Cripple*.

The far south

South of a line connecting Monólithos and Lárdhos, you could easily begin to think you had strayed onto another island. Gone are most of the five-star hotels and roads to match, and with them the bulk of the crowds. Gone too are most tourist facilities and public transport. Only one or two daily buses (in season) serve the depopulated villages here, approaching along the east coast; tavernas grace the more popular stretches of sand, but aside from the growing package enclaves of Lárdhos, Péfkos and Kiotári there are few places to stay.

Despite the shelving of plans for a second island airport in the area, new beachfront development mushrooms to either side of **LÁRDHOS**, itself solidly on the tourist circuit despite an inland position between Láerma and the peninsula culminating in Líndhos. The beach 2km away is gravelly and dull, so it's best to continue 3km to Glýstra cove, a small but delightful crescent, with umbrellas and a snack bar, which sets the tone for the coast from here on. Four kilometres east of Lárdhos, **PÉFKOS** (Péfki on some maps) began life as the garden annexe and overflow for Líndhos, but is now a burgeoning package resort in its own right; the sea is clearer than at Lárdhos, with small, well-hidden beaches which are getting harder to find with all the new development on the clifftop.

Asklipió

Nine kilometres beyond Lárdhos, a paved side road heads 3.5km inland to **ASKLIPIÓ**, a sleepy village guarded by a crumbling castle and graced by the Byzantine church of **Kímisis Theotókou** (daily 9am–6pm; free). The building dates from 1060, with a ground plan nearly identical to Thárri's, except that two subsidiary apses were added during the eighteenth century, supposedly to conceal a secret school in a subterranean crypt. The frescoes within are in better condition than those at Thárri owing to the drier local climate; they are also a bit later, though some claim that the final work at Thárri and the earliest here were executed by the same hand, a master from Híos.

The format and subject matter of the frescoes are both rare in Greece: didactic "cartoon strips" which extend completely around the church in some cases, featuring extensive Old Testament stories in addition to the more usual lives of Christ and the Virgin. There's a complete sequence from Genesis, from the Creation to the Expulsion from Eden; note the comically menacing octopus among the fishes in the panel of the Fifth Day, and Eve subsequently being fashioned from Adam's rib. A *Revelation of John the Divine* takes up most of the east transept; pebble-mosaic flooring decorates both the interior and the vast courtyard. Two adjacent buildings house separate museums: an ecclesiastical exhibit (donation requested) and a more interesting folklore gallery full of rural craft tools.

To the southern tip

Back on the coast road, the beachfront hamlet of **KIOTÁRI** has mushroomed as a package venue for Germans and Italians since the mid-1990s, when the Orthodox Church elected to sell up its vast holdings here. There's little local character remaining, so most will choose to continue 4km to **YENNÁDHI**, the only sizable settlement on this coast, with various amenities including **car rental**, **a post office**, some rooms and a few **tavernas** (best of these is *Klimis*) behind the seemingly endless sand and gravel beach. Some 10km south of Yennádhi, and 2km inland, **LAHANIÁ** village with its eponymous **hotel** (☎0244/43 089; ②) and smattering of private rooms makes another possible base. Abandoned after a postwar earthquake, since the 1980s its older houses have been mostly occupied and renovated by Germans on long-term lease agreements. On the main platía at the lower, eastern end of the village, the *Platanos* taverna has decent food and seating between the church and two wonderful fountains, one with an Ottoman inscription.

You can go directly from Lahaniá to **Plimýri**, an attractive sandy bay backed by dunes heaped up by strong afternoon winds; so far the only facility is a good-value rustic **taverna**, next to the church of Zoödhóhou Piyís which has ancient columns upholding its vaulted porch. Beyond Plimýri the road curves inland to **KATAVIÁ**, over 100km from the capital, marooned amidst grain fields; the village, like so many in the south, is three-quarters deserted, the owners of the closed-up houses off working in Australia or North America.

There are a few **rooms** to rent, a vital **filling station** and several **tavernas** at the junction that doubles as the platía – most interesting of these the brightly coloured *Martine's Bakaliko* (shut Thurs), run by folk from Lahanía, which has some vegetarian dishes and attempts to use local organic ingredients when possible.

From Kataviá a paved road leads on to **Prassoníssi**, Rhodes' southernmost extremity and a mecca for European **windsurfers**. The sandspit which tethers Prassoníssi (Leek Island) to Rhodes was partially washed away by storms early in 1998, but enough remains to create flat water on the east side and up to two-metre waves on the west, ideal for different ability levels. Of the two windsurfing centres operating here, Swiss-run Procenter (April–Oct; ☎0244/91 045, *procenter.prasonisi@EUnet.at*) is the more professional, with hourly rates from 4500dr, and a ten-hour card (valid over several days) from 37,500dr. They're geared for one-week packages, including jeeps and lodged in rooms above the *Lighthouse Restaurant*, one of a half-dozen food and accommodation outfits here; the UK agent is Sportif (☎01273/844919, *Sportif@compuserve.com*).

The far southwest

From Lahaniá it's also possible to head 9km northwest along a narrow paved road to the picturesque hilltop village of **MESSANAGRÓS**. This already existed in some form by the fifth century AD, if foundations of a ruined basilica at the village outskirts are anything to go by. A smaller thirteenth-century chapel squats amidst mosaic-floor patches of the larger, earlier church, with a *hokhláki* floor and stone barrel arches (key from the nearby kafenío).

The onward road to Skiádhi monastery, 6km distant, is shown incorrectly on most maps. Take the Kataviá-bound road initially, then bear right onto an unsigned dirt track after about 2km; the last 4km are quite badly surfaced. Known formally as Panayía Skiadhení, **Skiádhi monastery** – despite its undistinguished modern buildings – was founded in the thirteenth century to house a miraculous icon of the Virgin; in the fifteenth century a heretic stabbed the painting, and blood flowed from the wound in the Mother of God's cheek. The offending hand was, needless to say, instantly paralysed; the fissure, and intriguing brown stains around it, are still visible. The immediate surroundings of the monastery are rather dreary since a fire in 1992, but the views west are stunning. Tiny Khténia islet is said to be a petrified pirate ship, rendered into stone by the Virgin in answer to prayers from desperate locals. Except on September 7–8, the festival of the icon, you can stay the night on arrangement with the caretaker.

West of Kataviá, the completely paved island loop road emerges onto the deserted, sandy southwest coast; Skiádhi can more easily be reached from this side as well. If freelance camping and nudism are your thing, this is the place to indulge, though you'll need to be completely self-sufficient, and only strong swimmers should venture far offshore here.

The nearest village is nondescript, agricultural **APOLAKKIÁ**, 7km north of the Skiádhi turning and equipped with a bona fide **hotel**, **tavernas** and shops. Northwest the road leads to Monólithos, while the northeasterly bearing leads quickly and pleasantly back to Yennádhi via Váti. Due north, just below an irrigation reservoir, the tiny frescoed chapel of **Áyios Yeóryios Várdhas** (unlocked) is worth the short detour if you have your own transport.

Hálki

Hálki, a tiny (20 square kilometres), waterless, limestone speck west of Rhodes, is a fully fledged member of the Dodecanese, though all but about three hundred of the former population of three thousand have emigrated (mostly to Rhodes or to Florida) in the wake of a devastating sponge blight during the early 1900s. Despite a renaissance through tourism in recent years, the island is tranquil compared with its big neighbour, with a slightly weird, hushed atmosphere. The big event of the day is the arrival of the regular afternoon kaïki from Kámiros Skála on Rhodes.

Hálki first attracted outside attention in 1983, when UNESCO designated it the "isle of peace and friendship", and the seat of regular international youth conferences. Some 150 crumbling houses were to be restored at UNESCO's expense as accommodation for delegates, but by 1987 just one hotel had been completed, and the only sign of "peace and friendship" was a stream of UNESCO and Athenian bureaucrats staging musical binges under the rubric of "ecological seminars". Confronted with an apparent scam, the islanders sent UNESCO packing and contracted two UK package operators to complete restorations and bring in paying guests.

Emborió

The skyline of **EMBORIÓ**, the port and only habitation, is pierced by the tallest free-standing clocktower in the Dodecanese and the belfry of Áyios Nikólaos church. Emborió's restored houses are pretty much block-booked from April to October by the tour companies mentioned; independent travellers will be lucky to find anything at all on spec, even early or late in the season. Non-package **accommodation**, all requiring advance reservations, includes the delightful, en-suite *Captain's House* (☎0241/45 201; ③), with the feel of a French country hotel, whose English manageress can point you in likely directions if she's full; *Pension Keanthi* (☎0241/45 334; ④) near the school, with high-ceiling rooms and stone walls; or the hillside rooms at *Pension Argyrenia* (☎0241/45 205; ③), below the municipal cistern. Of the half-dozen **tavernas** along the field-stoned, pedestrianized waterfront, *Mavri Thalassa* near the fish depot is one of the best for portion size and freshness, with a stress on seafood, while *Houvardas*, near the opposite end of the quay has proven reliable for *mayireftá* over the years. Amongst several bars and cafés, the standout must be the 1999-opened sweet shop near the base of the jetty, with puddings and own-made ice cream to die for. There's a **post office**, four well-stocked stores, two good bakeries cranking out a range of bread and pies, plus two **travel agencies** which sell boat tickets, change money (there's no bank) and at slow times just might be able to find you a vacancy amongst the studios they manage on behalf of the UK companies.

The rest of the island

Three kilometres west lies the old pirate-safe village of **HORIÓ**, abandoned in the 1950s but still crowned by the Knights' castle. Except during the major August 14–15 festival, the church here is kept securely locked to protect its frescoes. Across the valley, the little monastery of **Stavrós** is the venue for the other big island bash on September 14. There's little else to see or do inland, though you can spend three hours **walking** across the island on the 1998-vintage dirt track, the extension of the cement "Tarpon Springs Boulevard" donated by the expatriate community in Florida. At the end of the road you'll come to the monastery of **Ayíou Ioánnou Prodhrómou**; the caretaking family there can put you up in a cell (except around August 29, the other big festival date), but you'll need to bring supplies. The terrain en route is monotonous, but compensated by views over half the Dodecanese and Turkey.

Longish but narrow **Póndamos**, fifteen minutes' walk west of Emborió, is the only sandy beach on Hálki, and even this has had to be artificially supplemented. The sole facility is the somewhat pricey *Nick's Pondamos Taverna*, serving lunch only. Small and pebbly **Yialí**, west of and considerably below Horió via a jeep track, lies an hour's hike away from Póndamos. A thirty-minute walk north of Emborió lies **Kánia**, with a rocky foreshore and a rather industrial ambience from both power lines and the island's only petrol pump to one side.

Since these three coves are no great shakes, it's worth signing on at Emborió quay for **boat excursions** to more remote beaches. More or less at the centre of Hálki's southern shore, directly below Horió's castle, **Trahiá** consists of two coves to either side of an isthmus. North-coast beaches figuring as excursion-boat destinations include the pretty fjord of **Aréta**, **Áyios Yeóryios** just beyond, and the remote double bay of **Dhýo Yialí**. Of these, Aréta is the most attractive, and the only one accessible overland (in about two hours) by experienced hillwalkers equipped with the *Chalki, Island of Peace and Friendship* map based on the old Italian topographical survey products.

Alimniá (Alimiá) islet

One of the more promoted local boat excursions visits **Alimniá (Alimiá) islet**, roughly halfway between Hálki and Rhodes. Despite more well-water and greenery and a better harbour than Hálki's, the deserted village here, overlooked by a few palm trees and yet another Knights' castle, was completely abandoned by the 1960s. The locals were initially deported during World War II after they admitted to assisting British commandos sent in April 1944 to sabotage the enemy submarines who used the deep harbour here. The seven commandos themselves were captured here by the Nazis, bundled off first to Rhodes, then to Thessaloníki, where six were summarily executed as spies rather than regular prisoners of war; Kurt Waldheim allegedly countersigned their death sentences.

Interesting history acknowledged, Alimniá is probably not a place you'd want to be stuck for an entire day. Excursions on offer are pricey (about 6500dr), beach space very limited, the castle a long, hot walk up and the crumbling village behind its salt marsh unedifying. If you snorkel in the outer bay beyond little Áyios Mínas monastery, you might glimpse outlines of the Italian-built submarine pens to one side of the deep bay. The former inhabitants only show up to graze livestock, or on the date of the annual festival (Áyios Yeóryios).

Kastellórizo (Meyísti)

Kastellórizo's official name, Méyisti (biggest), seems more an act of defiance than a statement of fact. While the largest of a tiny group of islands, it is actually the smallest of the Dodecanese, over seventy nautical miles from its nearest Greek neighbour (Rhodes) but barely more than a nautical mile off the Turkish coast at the narrowest straits. At night its lights are quite outnumbered by those of the Turkish town of Kaş, across the bay, with whom Kastellórizo generally has excellent relations.

Less than a century ago there were almost 14,000 people here, supported by a fleet of schooners that transported goods, mostly timber, from the Greek towns of Kalamaki (now Kalkan) and Andifelos (Kaş) on the Anatolian mainland opposite. But the withdrawal of autonomy after the 1908 "Young Turk" revolution, the Italian seizure of the other Dodecanese in 1912 and an inconclusive 1913–1915 revolt against the Turks sent the island into decline. A French occupation of 1915–21 prompted destructive shelling from the Ottoman-held mainland, a harbinger of worse to come (see below). Shipowners failed to modernize their fleets upon the advent of steam power, preferring to sell ships to the British for the Dardanelles campaign, and the new frontier between the island and republican Turkey, combined with the expulsion of all Anatolian Greeks in 1923, deprived any remaining vessels of their trade. During the 1930s the island enjoyed a brief renaissance when it became a major stopover point for French and Italian seaplanes, but events at the close of World War II put an end to any hopes of the island's continued viability.

When Italy capitulated to the Allies in the autumn of 1943, a few hundred Commonwealth commandos occupied Kastellórizo, departing of their own accord in spring 1944 – leaving the island deserted and vulnerable to the attentions of pirates. In early July, a harbour fuel dump caught (or was set on) fire and an adjacent arsenal exploded, taking with it more than half of the two thousand houses on Kastellórizo. Even before these events most of the population had left for Rhodes, Athens, Australia (especially Perth) and North America. Today there are fewer than two hundred people living permanently on Kastellórizo, largely maintained by remittances from over 30,000 emigrants and by subsidies from the Greek government, which fears that the island will revert to Turkey should their numbers diminish any further.

Yet Kastellórizo may have a future of sorts, thanks to expat "Kassies" who have begun renovating their crumbling ancestral houses as a retirement or holiday home. Each summer, the population is swelled by returnees of Kassie ancestry, some of whom celebrate traditional weddings in the **Áyios Konstandínos** cathedral at Horáfia, which incorporates ancient columns from Patara in Asia Minor. Access has also improved since the 1980s: an airport (domestic flights only) was completed, the harbour dredged to accommodate larger ferries, and the island designated an official port of entry to Greece, which has appealed to both yachtics and conventional travellers crossing from Turkey.

Perhaps the biggest recent boost for Kastellórizo was its role as location for the 1990 film *Mediterraneo*, which has resulted in a tidal wave of Italian visitors (though the island in fact gets a broad spectrum of tourists). You will either love it and stay a week, or crave escape after a day; detractors dismiss Kastellórizo as a human zoo maintained by the government for the edification of nationalists, while partisans celebrate an atmospheric, barely commercialized outpost of Hellenism.

Kastellórizo Town

The current population is concentrated in the northern town of **KASTELLÓRIZO** – supposedly the finest natural harbour between Beirut and Fethiye on the Turkish coast – and its little "suburb" of **Mandhráki**, just over the fire-blasted hill with its half-ruined castle of the Knights. Its keep now houses the local **museum** (Tues–Sun 7am–2.30pm; free), with displays including plates from a Byzantine shipwreck, frescoes rescued from decaying churches and a reconstruction of an ancient basilica on the site of today's gaudy Ayíou Yeoryíou Santrapé church at Horáfia. Just below and beyond the museum, in the cliff-face opposite Psorádhia islet, is Greece's only **Lycian house-tomb**; it's signposted from the shoreline walkway, up some steps beside the first wooden lamp standard.

Most of the town's surviving mansions are ranged along the waterfront, their tiled roofs, wooden balconies and long, narrow windows having obvious counterparts in the originally Greek-built houses of Kalkan and Kaş just across the water. Just one street back, however, many properties are derelict – abandonment having succeeded where the World War I shelling, a 1926 earthquake and the 1944 explosions failed; sepia-toned posters and postcards on sale of the town in its prime are poignant evidence of its later decline.

Practicalities

Kastellórizo is not really geared up for large numbers of visitors, though **pensions** in the old houses have been upgraded of late to en-suite status. If you're not met off the boat, the best budget en-suite options include the restored mansion-pension of Damian Mavrothalassitis (☎0241/49 208; ②); the nearly adjacent *Kristallo* (☎0241/41 209; ②); and the waterfront *Mediterraneo* (☎0241/49 368; ②), on the northwest quay. Relative luxury is available, for a price, at the *Hotel Meyisti* (☎0241/49 272, fax 49 221; ④; April–Oct), on the opposite side of the bay from the ferry jetty, beyond the *Mediterraneo*.

Apart from fish, goat meat and various fig-based sweets, plus whatever can be smuggled over from Kaş, Kastellórizo has to import foodstuffs and drinking water from Rhodes; prices when eating out can consequently be higher than usual, with the further pretext of the island's celebrity status. The two most prominent waterfront **tavernas** have had a long and pernicious acquaintance with the yacht trade – best to continue to the *Sydney* for reliably fresh and affordable seafood and meat grills. Another good quayside choice is *Kas-Bar*, just left of the Italian market arcade, where a mother and son team serve up fine grills, vegetable dishes and cold mezédhes nightly except perhaps Thursday in off-season. Two to recommend inland are *Iy Orea Meyisti*, run by Savvas Mavrothalassitis and his wife, and *Ta Platania*, opposite Áyios Konstandínos in Horáfia, good for daily-changing *mayireftá* and frequently homemade desserts. **Nightlife** mostly occurs in *barákia* along the quay, though English Kassie Mariana Ftiara's *The Magic Shop*, inland in the ground floor of her restored house, is perhaps the best with its range of drinks and light snacks in an oriental ambience.

The **post office** sits behind *Hotel Meyisti*; there's a single, short hours bank. Most ferry companies are represented by one of several grocery stores, while the only travel agency, grumpy DiZi Travel, is the Olympic Airways representative; at busy times, you should book return flights immediately on arrival if you've not done so in Ródhos Town. A public transfer van shuttles between town and airstrip at flight times.

It is usually possible to arrange a ride over **to Turkey** on one of five local boats, and possibly one of the three Kaş-based boats which appear regularly. The standard day-return fee is 4000dr, and you may have to leave your passport with the authorities the night before. Since Kastellórizo is a legal port of entry to Greece, they technically cannot prevent EU nationals arriving **from Kaş**, which is also an officially entry–exit point for Turkey.

The rest of the island

Kastellórizo's austere hinterland is predominantly bare rock, flecked with stunted vegetation; incredibly, two generations ago much of the countryside was carefully tended, producing wine of some quality and in quantity. A rudimentary road system links points between Mandhráki and the airport, but there aren't many specific places to go along it and no scooters for rent. Karstic cliffs drop sheer to the sea, offering no anchorage for boats except at the main town, Mandhráki and Návlakas fjord (see below).

Rural monasteries and ruins

Heat permitting, you can hike up the obvious, zigzag stair-path, then south through desolate fire-charred scrub to the rural **monastery of Áyios Yeóryios toú Vouniоú**, forty minutes away. The sixteenth to eighteenth-century church boasts fine rib-vaulting and a carved *témblon*, but its highlight is a crypt, with the frescoed, subterranean chapel of **Áyios Harálambos** off to one side; access is via a steep, narrow passage descending from the church floor – bring a flashlight and grubby clothes, and get the key first from the keeper, who lives behind the *Little Paris* taverna. Alternatively, a fifteen-minute track-walk west of the port leads to the peaceful monastery of **Ayías Triádhas**, perched on the saddle marked by the OTE tower, and an army strongpoint (off-limits) – one of many sprung up here since the Ímia crisis (see p.474).

The onward path arrives after 25 minutes at the ancient citadel of **Paleókastro**, where you'll find masonry from Classical to medieval times, a warren of vaulted chambers, tunnels, cisterns plus another, ruined monastery with a *hokhláki* courtyard. From any of the heights above town there are tremendous views north over sixty kilometres of Anatolian coast.

The shoreline and Rhó

Swimming is complicated by a total absence of beaches and an abundance of sea urchins and razor-sharp limestone reefs; the safest entry near town lies beyond the graveyard at Mandhráki, or at the tiny inlet of **Áyios Stéfanos**, a forty-minute walk north of town along the obvious trail beginning behind the post office. Once away from the shore, you're rewarded by clear waters with a rich variety of marine life. From Áyios Yeóryios toú Vounoú, you can continue 45 minutes further on foot, partly on a French-built *kalderími*, to the multi-lobed fjord of **Návlakas**, a favourite mooring spot for yachts and fishing boats. The French built the cobbled way to facilitate offloading supplies here during World War I, safe from Ottoman artillery. Uniquely on Kastellórizo, this bay is sea-urchin-free, with freshwater seeps keeping the temperature brisk; there's superb snorkelling to 25-metre depths off the south wall.

Over on the southeast coast, accessible only by a 45-minute boat ride from town, the grotto of **Perastá** deserves a look for its stalactites and strange blue-light effects; the low entrance, negotiable only by inflatable raft, gives little hint of the enormous chamber within, where seals occasionally are glimpsed. Two-hour raft trips (2000dr minimum per person) visit only the cave, or for 5000dr minimum on a larger kaïki, you can take it in as part of a five-hour tour that includes Rhó islet.

Should you make the trip out to **Rhó**, the tomb of *Iý Kyrá tís Rhó* (**The Lady of Rhó**), aka Dhespina Akhladhiotis (1893–1982) – who resolutely hoisted the Greek flag each day on that islet in defiance of the Turks on the mainland – is the first thing you see when you dock at the sandy, northwestern harbour. From here a path heads southeast for 25 minutes to the islet's southerly port, past the side trail up to the intact Hellenistic fortress on the very summit. The islet has no facilities – just a few soldiers to prevent Turkish military landings or poachings of the hundreds of goats – so bring your own food and water.

Sými

Sými's most pressing problem, lack of water, is in many ways also its saving grace. As with so many dry, rocky Dodecanese, water must be imported at great expense from Rhodes, pending completion of a reservoir in the distant future. As a result the island can't hope to support more than a handful of large hotels; instead, hundreds of people are shipped in daily during the season from Rhodes, relieved of their money and sent back. This arrangement suits both the islanders and those visitors lucky enough to stay longer; many foreigners return regularly, or even own houses here.

Once beyond the inhabited areas, you'll find a surprisingly attractive island that has retained some of its original forest cover of junipers, valonea oaks and even a few pines – ideal walking country in spring or autumn (though not midsummer, when temperatures are among the highest in Greece). Another prominent feature of the landscape are dozens of tiny monasteries, usually locked except on their patron saint's day, though their cisterns with a can on a string to fetch water are usually accessible.

Sými Town

SÝMI, the island's capital and only proper town, consists of **Yialós**, the excellent natural port, and **Horió**, on the hillside above. Incredibly, less than a hundred years ago the place was richer and more populous (25,000) than Rhodes, its wealth generated by shipbuilding and sponge-diving, skills nurtured since pre-Classical times. Under the Ottomans, Sými, like most of the smaller Dodecanese, enjoyed considerable autonomy in exchange for a yearly tribute in sponges to the sultan; but the Italian-imposed frontier, the 1919–22 Greco-Turkish war, the advent of synthetic sponges and the gradual replacement of the

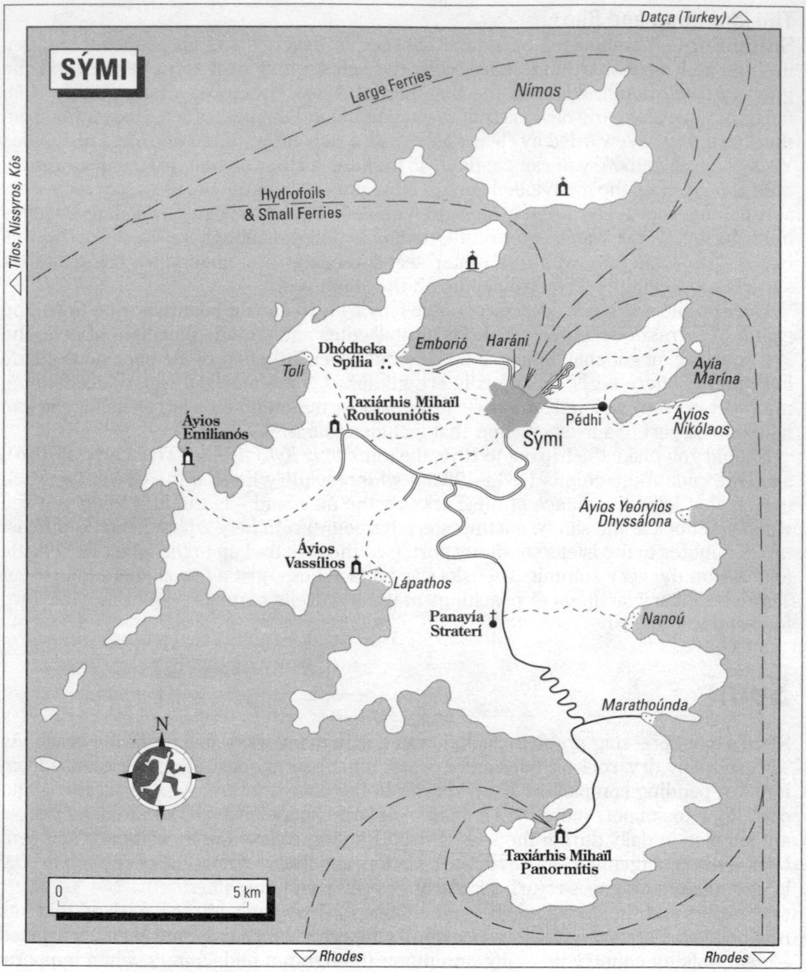

crews by Kalymniots spelt doom for the local economy. Vestiges of past nautical glories remain in still-active boatyards at Pédhi and Haráni, but today the souvenir-shop sponges come entirely from overseas, and the recent boom notwithstanding, a significant fraction of the magnificent nineteenth-century mansions stands roofless and empty.

The approximately three thousand remaining Symiotes are scattered fairly evenly throughout the mixture of Neoclassical and more typical island dwellings; despite the surplus of properties many outsiders have preferred to build anew, rather than restore derelict shells accessible only by donkey or on foot. As on Kastellórizo, a wartime ammunition blast – this time set off by the retreating Germans – levelled hundreds of houses up in Horió. Shortly afterwards, the official surrender of the Dodecanese to the Allies was signed here on May 8, 1945: a plaque marks the spot at the present-day *Restaurant Les Catherinettes*.

At the lively **port**, an architecturally protected area since the early 1970s, spice and sponge stalls plus a few jewellery shops are thronged with Rhodes-based trippers between 11am and 3pm, and exhaust fumes from four or five excursion boats envelop the quay. But one street back from the water the more peaceful pace of village life takes over, with sheep and chickens roaming free-range. Two massive stair-paths, the Kalí Stráta and Katarráktes, effectively deter many of the day-trippers and are most dramatic towards sunset; large ruins along the lower reaches of the Kalí Stráta are lonely and sinister after dark, though these too are now scheduled for restoration.

A series of blue arrows through Horió leads to the excellent local **museum** (Tues–Sun 10am–2pm; 500dr). Housed in a fine old mansion at the back of the village, the collection concentrates on Byzantine and medieval Sými, with exhibits on frescoes in isolated, locked churches and a gallery of medieval icons, as well as antiquarian maps and the inevitable ethnographic wing. The nearby **Hatziagapitos Mansion** has been refurbished as an annexe; there, wonderful carved wooden chests are the main exhibits, along with fragmentary wall-paintings. On the way back to central Horió, the nineteenth-century pharmacy, with its apothecary jars and wooden drawers labelled for exotic herbal remedies, is worth a look.

At the very pinnacle of things, a **castle of the Knights** occupies the site of Sými's ancient acropolis, and you can glimpse a stretch of Cyclopean wall on one side. A dozen churches grace Horió; that of the Ascension, inside the fortifications, is a replacement of the one blown to bits when the Germans detonated the munitions cached there. One of the bells in the new belfry is the nose-cone of a thousand-pound bomb, hung as a memorial.

Practicalities

Excursion boats run daily to Sými from Mandhráki in Ródhos Town, but you'll come under considerable pressure at the quay to buy an expensive (approximately 5000dr) return ticket – not what you want if you're off island-hopping. Instead, take the islanders' own craft – the *Symi I*, the catamaran *Symi II* or the hydrofoil *Aigli* – which between them provide an *epivatikó* (normal passenger) service at 2000–3000dr per person. The *Symi I* or *II* departs Rhodes four days weekly at 6pm, returning the next day at 6–6.30am, while the hydrofoil follows a far more variable service six days weekly, though typically it leaves Mandhráki at 2.30 or 6pm, returning 7am. A few times a week there are mainline ferries as well in either direction. ANES, the outlet for *Symi I/Symi II/Aigli* tickets, maintains a booth on the quay; Sunny Land, in the marketplace lanes, is the agent for most inter-island **ferries** except for DANE Lines.

There's no official tourism bureau but the island's English-language advertiser-newsletter, *The Symi Visitor* (free), is literate and has current island gossip with informative features. The **post office** in the Italian "palace" is open standard hours; of the two **banks**, the Ioniki/Ionian is more efficient and has a cash dispenser. During the season a small green bus shuttles between Yialós and Pédhi via Horió on the hour (returning at the half-hour) until 11pm. There are also four **taxis**, and a few pricey outlets for **motor-scooter hire** (5000dr and up daily), though this is a perfect island for boat and walking excursions. A **laundry** operates in the grid of market lanes, resorted to by those whose hosts forbid clothes-washing in rooms.

ACCOMMODATION

Accommodation for independent travellers is somewhat limited, though the situation isn't nearly so bad as on Hálki; proprietors tend not to meet arriving boats. Studios, rather than simple rooms, predominate, and package operators control most of these. Despite asphyxiating summer heat, air conditioning and ceiling fans are rarely found – go for north-facing and/or balconied units when possible. If you're planning in advance, the BBC-award-winning *www.symi-island.com* site is worth consulting; there's visual information on lodging, and you can make bookings either through the site or by phone (UK: ☎01782/815231, Sými: ☎0241/72 693).

Albatros, marketplace (☎0241/72 784 or 71 829). Partial sea views from this exquisite small hotel; pleasant second-floor breakfast salon, air con. ④. The same family have five apartments at *Villa Thalassa* on the south quay opposite the clock tower, with either air con or balconies, all suitable for families or groups of four. ⑥.

Anastasia, behind the post office (☎0241/71 364). Pleasantly set hotel though with limited views, this has parquet-floored rooms plus a couple of studios, with some package allotment however. ④.

Fiona, at the top of the Kalí Stráta (☎0241/72 088 or 72 755). Mock-traditional hotel building whose large airy rooms have double beds and stunning rooms; breakfast in mid-air on common balcony. ④. Managed by affable returned Greek-Australian Nikos Halkitis and family, who also offer *The Cottages*, four studio units in two adjacent old houses in Horió. ⑤.

Jean Manship, c/o Jean & Tonic Bar (☎0241/71 819 8pm–1am Greek time, fax 72 172). Jean has two traditional houses in Horió, both suitable for couples and with stunning views. ④.

Katerina Tsakiris Rooms (☎0241/71 813). Just a handful of very simple en-suite rooms with common kitchen and grandstand view; reservations essential. ③.

Kokona, at the rear of the marketplace, by the clinic (☎0241/71 451). En-suite if plain hotel, the upstairs rooms with balconies (though no sea views). ③.

Les Catherinettes, above eponymous restaurant, north quay (☎0241/72 698, *marina-epe@rho.forthnet.gr*). Creaky but spotless pension in a historic building with painted ceilings and sea-view balconies for most rooms. ④.

Rooms Egli, base of the Kalí Stráta (☎0241/71 392). Basic (non-en-suite), but clean enough rooms, and usually has vacancies when everyone else is full. ②.

Taxiarhis Apartments, edge of Horió overlooking Pédhi (☎0241/72 012). Secluded, well-designed row of studios with common areas, though some German package groups. ⑤.

EATING

You're best off avoiding most **eateries** on the north and west quays of the port, where menus, prices and attitudes have been terminally warped by the day-trip trade. Away from these areas, you've a fair range of choice among *kultúra* tavernas, old-style *mayireftá* places, a few genuine ouzeris and even a traditional kafenío or two.

To Amoni, far side of main platía, Yialós. An excellent, inexpensive, authentic ouzerí, where big helpings of liver, sausage and seafood titbits accompany the usual fried vegetarian starters and mainland bulk wine. Open most of the year; seating indoors and out.

Dhimitris, south quay, on the way out of town. Excellent, family-run seafood-stressing ouzerí with exotic items such as *hokhliόalo* (sea snails), *foúskes* (mock oysters), *spinόalo* (pinna-shell flesh) and the indigenous miniature shrimps, along with the more usual plates and lots of vegetarian starters. Nov–May this outdoor premises moves inside to *Tasty*, in the bazaar next to *O Meraklis*.

Ellinikon, off main square, Yialós. The more reasonable (6000–7000dr a head) of the *kultúra* tavernas, with own-made pasta and desserts, plus 140 varieties of Greek wine (their main selling point).

Elpidha, north quay. This landmark with wooden chairs, a hundred paces in from the clocktower, is a hallowed snack and drinks café and marvellous people-watching vantage.

O Ilios, west quay. British-run, with "English" or healthy full breakfasts, plus vegetarian meals and own-made cakes all hours. Also does picnic hampers for beach outings – notify them the previous day.

To Klima, near top of Kalí Stráta, Horió. British-run place that's an excellent source of breakfast (after 9.30am); also does Indian food on Saturday nights, and an all-you-can eat buffet on Sundays – Greek food at other times.

O Meraklis, rear of the bazaar. Polite service and fair portions of well-priced *mayireftá* and mezédhes make this a reliable bet April–Dec. Sample meal: beans, beets, dips, and roast lamb with potatoes as a tender main course.

Mythos, south quay near taxi rank. Professionally run, Athens-style ouzerí where your host reels off the plates of the day; moderately pricey.

Pahos, west quay, beside *O Ilios* (no sign). The old-boys' kafenío, in operation since World War II, and a classic spot for a sundown oúzo.

Syllogos, top of Kalí Stráta in Horió. Aspires to be a *kultúra* taverna, and popular with Greeks and Italians in summer; recipes aren't that imaginative, but ingredients are fresh and presentation home-style.

Yiorgos, by Kalí Stráta in Horió. Jolly, supper-only institution since 1977, with seating on a pebble-mosaic courtyard; service is slipshod, but excellent-value food such as feta-stuffed peppers, spinach-rice, chicken in mushroom-wine sauce, and grilled fish when available.

DRINKING

Nightlife is long and occasionally loud, with a number of bars owned by expatriates. Up in Horió, convivial *Jean & Tonic* is the heart and soul of nightlife, catering to a mixed clientele until the small hours most of the year; a short way down the Kalí Stráta, *Kali Strata* is a low-key place with unbeatable views and excellent wide-ranging music. Down at Yialós, *Vapori*, the oldest bar on the island, and former adjacent rival *Mina's* have merged, welcoming customers with desserts and breakfast as well as drinks. However, the local nickname for their noisy alley is still "the Gaza Strip", and some prefer *Katoi* on the south quay, a no-touts, no-hassle, low-key bar.

Around the island

Sými has no big sandy beaches, but there are plenty of pebbly stretches at the heads of the deep, protected bays which indent the coastline. **PÉDHI**, a 45-minute walk from Yialós, retains some of its former identity as a fishing hamlet, with enough water in the plain behind – the island's largest – to support a few vegetable gardens. The beach is poor, though, and patronage from yachts and the giant *Pedhi Beach* hotel (packages only) has considerably bumped up prices at the four local **tavernas**, of which the most reasonably priced and authentic is *Iy Kamares* at the far south end. Many will opt for another twenty minutes of walking via a rough but obvious path along the south shore of the almost landlocked bay to **Áyios Nikólaos**. The only all-sand beach on Sými, this offers sheltered swimming, tamarisks for shade and a mediocre taverna. Alternatively, a paint-splodge-marked path on the north side of the inlet leads in just over half an hour to **Ayía Marína**, where there's a minuscule beach, a shingle and sunbed lido, another snack bar and a monastery-capped islet to which you can easily swim.

Around Yialós, you'll find tiny **NOS (Navtikós Ómilos Sýmis)** "beach" ten minutes past the boatyards at Haráni, but there's sun here only until lunchtime and it's usually packed with day-trippers. You can continue along the cement-paved coast road, or cut inland from the Yialós platía past the abandoned desalination plant, to appealing **Emborió** (Nimborió) bay, with a poor **taverna** (*Metapontis*) and an artificially sand-strewn beach a bit beyond. Inland from this are Byzantine mosaic fragments under a protective shelter, and, nearby, a catacomb complex known locally as **Dhódheka Spília**.

Plenty of other, more secluded coves are accessible by energetic walkers with sturdy footwear, or those prepared to pay a modest sum for the taxi-boats (daily in season 10am–1pm, returning 4–5pm; one-way fares available to the nearer bays cited above). These are the best way to reach the southern bays of **Marathoúnda** and **Nanoú**, and the only method of getting to the spectacular, fjord of **Áyios Yeóryios Dhyssálona**. Dhyssálona lacks a taverna and lies in shade after 1pm, while unalluring Marathoúnda consists of coarse, slimy pebbles, making Nanoú the most popular destination for day-trips. The 200-metre beach there consists of gravel, sand and small pebbles, with a scenic backdrop of pines and a reasonable taverna (squid, chips and salad) behind. It's also possible to reach Nanoú overland, by taking a motor scooter to Panayía Straterí chapel and then descending a scenic gorge for some 45 minutes.

For more hiking adventures, you can cross the island from Horió in ninety minutes to **Áyios Vassílios**, the most scenic of the gulfs with its Lápathos beach; in about the same time to **Tolí**, a deserted, west-facing cove, also accessible from Emborió; or in three hours, partly through forest, to **Áyios Emilianós** at the island's extreme west end, where a little monastery is tethered to the body of Sými by a causeway. On the way to the latter you should look in at the monastery of **Taxiárhis Mihaïl Roukouniótis** (daily 9am–2pm & 4–8pm) Sými's oldest, with naive eighteenth-century frescoes and a peculiar ground plan: the current *katholikón* is actually superimposed on a lower, thirteenth-century structure abandoned after being burnt and pillaged by pirates during the 1400s, though a fine fresco of St Lawrence (Áyios Lavréntios) survives behind the altar screen. Resident, trilingual Father Amfilohios will be able to tell you about anything else you might possibly wish to know about the place.

The Archangel is also honoured at the huge monastery of **Taxiárhis Mihaïl Panormítis** near the southern tip of the island, Sými's biggest rural attraction and generally the first port of call for the excursion boats from Rhodes. These allow only a quick thirty-minute tour; if you want more time, you'll have to come by scooter from Yialós (though the someday-to-be-paved road down from the central escarpment is terrible, with nine hairpin bends), or arrange to stay the night (2000dr minimum donation) in the *xenónas* set aside for pilgrims. There are large numbers of these in summer, as Mihaïl has been adopted as the patron of sailors in the Dodecanese.

Like many of Sými's monasteries, Panormítis is of recent (eighteenth-century) vintage and was thoroughly pillaged during the last war, so don't expect too much of the building or its treasures. An appealing pebble-mosaic court surrounds the central *katholikón*, tended by the monk Gabriel, lit by an improbable number of oil lamps and graced by a fine *témblon*, though the frescoes are recent and mediocre. One of the two small museums (400dr admits to both) contains a strange mix of precious antiques, exotic junk (stuffed crocodiles and koalas, elephant tusks), votive offerings, models of ships and a chair piled with messages-in-bottles brought here by Aegean currents – the idea being that if the bottle or toy boat arrived, the sender got their prayer answered. There's a small beach, a shop/kafenío, a bakery and a **taverna** (*Panormio*) popular with passengers of the many yachts calling in. Near the taverna stands a memorial commemorating three Greeks, including the monastery's abbot, executed in February 1944 by the Germans for aiding British commandos.

Tílos

The small, blissfully quiet island of **Tílos**, with an official population of about three hundred (dwindling to eighty in winter), is one of the least frequented of the Dodecanese, though it can be visited on a day-trip by hydrofoil once or twice a week. Why anyone would want to come for just a few hours is unclear: while it's a great place to rest on the beach or go walking, there is nothing very striking at first glance. After a few days, however, you may have stumbled on several of the seven small castles of the Knights of St John which stud the crags, or found some of the inconspicuous medieval chapels clinging to the hillsides.

Tílos shares the characteristics of its closest neighbours: limestone mountains resembling those of Hálki, plus volcanic lowlands, pumice beds and red-lava sand as on Níssyros. Though rugged and scrubby on its heights, the island has ample water – from springs or pumped up from the agricultural plains – and clusters of oak and terebinth near the cultivated areas. From many points on the island you've startling views across to Kós, Sými, Turkey, Níssyros, Hálki, Rhodes and even (weather permitting) Kárpathos.

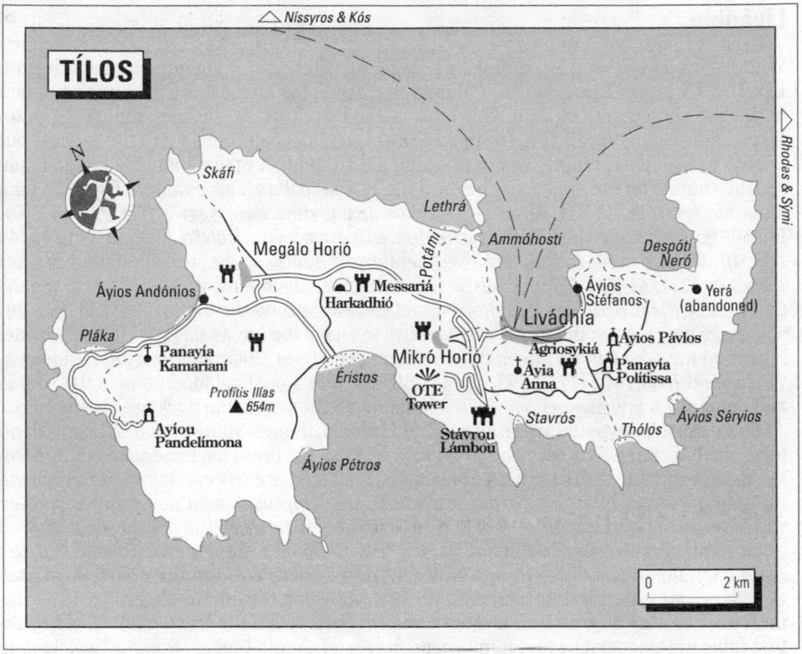

Since the mid-1990s, however, development on Tílos has threatened to reverse the conditions which many visitors have historically come to enjoy; besides the Dodge-City atmosphere of Livádhia (see p.270), a hyperactive bulldozing programme has scarred virtually every mountain in the east of the island. A 1998-vintage road from the telecom-tower hill, heading east along the summit ridge, is intended to facilitate proposed fish farms at Thólos and Áyios Séryios, which will finish those coves as leisure beaches. Other manic schemes proposed for the immediate future include a road down the pristine Potámi ravine to Lethrá beach (to serve a proposed taverna), and around the coast past Áyios Stéfanos towards a planned mega-hotel. The long-running foreigners' interest group, FOTA (Friends of Tílos Association), has effectively decided not to stick its neck out on these issues and to emphasize its role as the expatriates' social-events co-ordinating committee, leaving activist environmental campaigns to new rival organization Tilos 2000 (57 Avenue Jules Malou, Brussels B1040, ☎32/2/646 7098, *nigel.gardner@spp.cec.be*, or c/o Nigel Gardner, Megálo Horió, Tílos).

Tílos's main necessary road, widened in 1999 but awaiting new asphalt, runs 7km from Livádhia, the port village, to Megálo Horió, the capital and only other significant habitation. A public **minibus** links the two, and services are theoretically scheduled to coincide with ferry arrivals; at other times the bus makes up to six runs daily along the Livádhia–Éristos stretch. There are also two **taxis**, or you can rent **scooters** from two outlets in Livádhia. The new filling station lies between Livádhia and Megálo Horió. Non-wheeled transport includes **boat trips** (offered through Blue Sky Restaurant or David's Bikes, summer only) and your own two feet – many visitors come specifically to **walk**, assisted by the extremely accurate map prepared by Baz "Paris" Ward and sold locally.

Livádhia

With its unpaved streets, unfinished building sites and higgledy-piggledy layout, **LIVÁDHIA** makes a poor introduction to the island, but it remains the better equipped of the two settlements to deal with tourists, and is closer to the best remaining path-hikes. If they have vacancies, **room** and **hotel** owners sometimes meet the ferries, but in peak season it's certainly worth phoning ahead. Budget options include several consecutive outfits on the shore just beyond the Italian "palace", for example *Paradise* (aka *Stamatia's*; ☎0241/44 334; ②) or two studios next door at *Paraskevi* (☎0241/44 280; ②). Inland, go for either the 1994-refurbished and good-value *Hotel Livadhia* (☎0241/44 266; ②), with en-suite rooms and two "penthouse" units, or the well-appointed *Studios Irinna* (☎0241/44 305; ②), above the ironmonger's which runs it. More luxury means the friendly *Eleni Beach* on the shore about halfway around the bay (☎0241/44 062; ③), with large airy rooms; the *Faros* at the extreme end of the bay (☎0241/44 068; ②), widely praised for calm and its hospitable managing family; or, 200m inland from mid-beach, the top-end *Irini* (☎0241/44 293, fax 44 238; ③), with a pool, all mod cons in the rooms and generally a few on-spec vacancies in amongst the Laskarina package clients here.

There must be twenty **tavernas** around Livádhia, though some churn out lazy, bland food (such as tinned carrots and peas in your rice) for timid package patrons. Among the more authentic spots for a no-nonsense Greek feed are *Irinna*, doling out *mayireftá* right on the shore near the *Paradise*; *Zorba's* (aka *Vangelis's*), east along the bay, often with live music and dance at weekends; *Kritikos Psistaria* in the village centre, well regarded by carnivores; and inland on the way to *Zorba's*, the *Pantelis Souvla Maria's Pizza* (sic), doing just those things superbly, despite zero atmosphere courtesy of plastic chairs and a purple bug-zapper. The best place for reliably fresh grilled fish with mezédhes is *Blue Sky*, an unmissable eyrie perched above the ferry dock. For **breakfast** (plus evening snacks and homemade desserts), Anglo-Italian *Joanna's Café*, just up from Kritikos, is hard to beat, also with a long list of strong cocktails. *Omonia* – under the trees strung with fairy lights, near the post office – is the enduringly popular "traditional" alternative for a sundowner or breakfast. Livelier organized **nightlife** in or near Livádhia is limited to three bars: *Cafe Ino* on the shore near Irinna for the trendy set, the new *La Luna* at the far east end of bay (nightly in summer, weekends otherwise) and a durable music pub in Mikró Horió (see below).

There's a **post office**, but no bank or cash dispenser, so come with sufficient Greek cash or submit to the mercies of Stefanakis Travel, the sole ferry agency, which also has a metered phone in the unlikely event that both village card-phones are out of order. A **bakery** and several well-stocked **supermarkets** round out the roster of amenities.

Around the island

From Livádhia you can trail-walk an hour north along the obvious path to the pebble bay of **Lethrá**, or in about the same time south on separate itineraries to the secluded coves of **Stavrós** or **Thólos**. The track to the former begins between the *Tilos Mare Hotel* and the *Castellania Apartments*, becoming a trail at the highest new house in the village; once up to the saddle with its new road, there's a sharp drop (some of it cross-country, but cairned) to the beach. The latter route begins by the cemetery and the chapel of **Áyios Pandelímon** with its Byzantine *hokhláki* court, then curls around under the seemingly impregnable castle of **Agriosykiá**; from the saddle overlooking the descent to Thólos, a route marked with cairns leads northwest to the citadel in twenty minutes. It's less than an hour's walk west, with some surviving path sections shortcutting the road curves, up to the ghost village of **Mikró Horió**, whose 1200 inhabitants left for Livádhia during the 1950s. The only intact structures are the church (locked except for the August 15 festival) and an old house which has been restored as a long-hours **music pub**, which operates only during July and August, with a variable formula of Greek/foreign music, and a shuttle van laid on from the port.

Megálo Horió and Éristos

The rest of Tílos's inhabitants live in or near **MEGÁLO HORIÓ**, which has an enviable perspective over the vast agricultural *kámbos* stretching down to Éristos (see below), and is overlooked in turn by the vast castle of the Knights, which encloses a sixteenth-century chapel. The castle was built on the site of ancient Tílos – with recycled masonry evident – and is reached by a stiff, thirty-minute climb that begins on the lane behind the Ikonomou supermarket before threading its way through a vast jumble of cisterns, house foundations and derelict chapels – the remains of the much large medieval Megálo Horió. Two more flanking fortresses stare out across the plain: the easterly one of **Messariá** helpfully marks the location of the **Harkadhió** cave where Pleiocene midget-elephant bones were discovered in 1971. A signposted 500-metre track goes there from the road, ending near a spring and modern amphitheatre (to be used in a new summer festival) just below the cave-mouth, which was hidden for centuries until a World War II artillery barrage exposed it. The bones themselves have been transferred to a tiny, not very compelling **museum** in Megálo Horió, on the ground floor of the town hall (open Mon–Fri 8am–2.30pm on application upstairs to the warden).

Your choices for **accommodation** in the village are the *Pension Sevasti* (☎0241/44 237; ①) at the lower end of town, the central *Miliou Apartments* (☎0241/44 204; ②) or (best) *Studios Ta Elefandakia* (☎0241/44 213; ②), among attractive gardens by the car park. Of the two **tavernas**, the *Kali Kardhia*, next to the *Pension Sevasti*, is more reliably open and has the best view; there's a traditional **kafenío** by the church, and futher up the Athenian-run *Kafenio Ilikati* (May–Sept only), with cakes and drinks.

South of and below Megálo Horió, signs direct you towards the three-kilometre paved side road to the long, pink-to-grey-sand **Éristos** beach, reputedly the island's best, though summer rubbish piles from campers can be disconcerting. Discreet nudism at either end goes unremarked. About halfway down the road on the right amongst the orchards is *Taverna-Rooms Tropikana* (☎0241/44 020; ①), nothing special in either respect, but the most reliable all-season venue for a snack near the beach; its perennial rival on the far side of the access road is the *Navsika*, also with simple rooms (☎0241/44 306; ①). If you ring ahead, one or other may send a van to fetch you from the ferry dock.

The far northwest

The main road beyond Megálo Horió hits the coast again at dreary **Áyios Andónios**, whose single **hotel/taverna**, the *Australia* (☎0241/44 296; ②) sees little trade outside high season. At low tide on the exposed, average beach you can find more lava-trapped skeletons strung out in a row – human this time, presumably tide-washed victims of a Nissyrian eruption in 600 BC, and discovered by the same archeologists who found the miniature pachyderms.

There's better swimming at isolated **Pláka** beach, 2km west of Áyios Andónios, where people camp rough despite a total lack of facilities. The paved road finally ends 8km west of Megálo Hório at the fortified monastery of **Ayíou Pandelímona**, founded in the fifteenth century for the sake of its miraculous spring. Now the place is usually deserted except from July 25 to 27, when it hosts the island's major festival. Its tower-gate and oasis setting more than two hundred forbidding metres above the west coast are the most memorable features, though an eminently photogenic inner courtyard boasts a *hokhláki* surface, and the church a fine marble floor. On the *katholikón* wall, an early eighteenth-century fresco shows the founder-builder holding a model of the monastery, while behind the ornate altar screen hides another fresco of the Holy Trinity.

To guarantee access, you should visit with the regular Sunday-morning minibus tour from Megálo Horió (fare 1000dr; 1hr to look around), or contact Pandelis Yiannourakis, the key-keeper, in Megálo Horió (☎0241/44 213). To vary the return, you can walk back much of the way on a signposted path; it's shown correctly on Baz Ward's map, and ends at the minor monastery of Panayía Kamarianí near Áyios Andónios.

Níssyros

Volcanic **Níssyros** is noticeably greener than its southern neighbours Tílos and Hálki, and unlike them has proven wealthy enough to retain over eight hundred of its population year-round (down, though, from 10,000 in 1900). While remittances from abroad (particularly Astoria, New York) are significant, most of the island's income is derived from the offshore islet of Yialí, where a vast lump of **pumice** is slowly being quarried away by Lava Ltd. The concession fee collected from Lava by the municipality has engendered a huge public payroll and vast per-capita sums available to spend. Under the circumstances, the Nissyrians bother little with agriculture other than keeping cows and pigs; the hillside terraces meticulously carved out for grain and grapes lie fallow, and wine is no longer made locally.

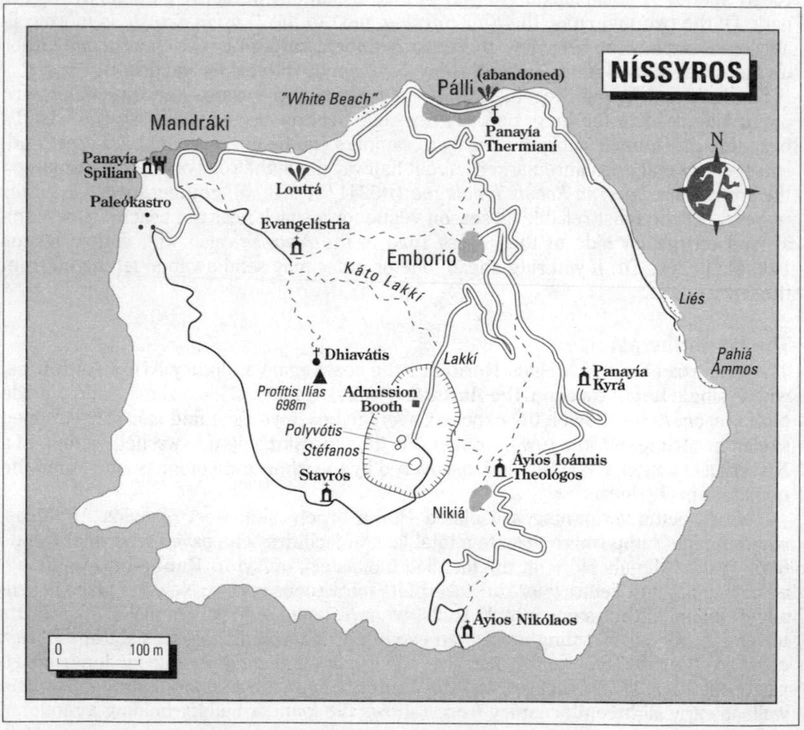

The main island's peculiar geology is potentially a source of other benefits: DEI, the Greek power company, spent the years between 1988 and 1992 sinking exploratory **geothermal** wells and attempting to convince the islanders of the benefits of cheap electricity.

In 1993, a local referendum went massively against the project, and DEI, together with its Italian contractor, took the hint and packed up. The desalination plant, reliant on an expensive fuel-oil generator, scarcely provides enough fresh water to spur a massive growth in package tourism. The relatively few tourists (mostly German) who stay the night, as opposed to the day-trippers from Kós, still find peaceful villages with a minimum of concrete eyesores and a friendly tight-knit population. Níssyros also offers good **walking** opportunities through a countryside planted with oak or terebinth, on a network of trails finally being marked and maintained with EU money; wherever you stroll you'll hear the contented grunting of pigs as they gorge themselves on acorns from the many oak trees. Autumn is a wonderful time, especially when the landscape has perked up after the first rains, and the late-January almond-blossoming is one of the island's glories.

Mandhráki

MANDHRÁKI is the deceptively large port and island capital, with blue patches of sea visible and audible at the end of narrow streets lined with tightly-packed houses whose brightly painted balconies and shutters are mandated by law. Except for the tattier fringes near the ferry dock, where multiple souvenir shops and bad tavernas pitched at day-trippers leave a poor first impression, the bulk of the place is cheerful and villagey, arrayed around the community orchard or *kámbos* and overlooked by two ancient fortresses.

Into a corner of the first of these, the fourteenth-century Knights' castle, is wedged the little monastery of **Panayía Spilianí**, built on this spot in accordance with instructions from the Virgin, who appeared in a vision to one of the first Christian islanders. The monastery's prestige grew after raiding Saracens failed to discover the vast quantities of silver secreted here in the form of a rich collection of Byzantine icons. During 1996–97, the Langadhaki area just below was rocked by a series of earthquakes, damaging a score of venerable houses, and rendering the small **folklore museum** homeless – it's now temporarily on the shore (daily 11am–2pm & 5–8pm; 200dr), but hardly worth the admission fee for a couple of mannequins in traditional dress. A new combination archeological-ethnographical-historical museum is being built on the *kámbos* with money donated by the Nissyrian founder of the Vitex paint company.

As a defensive bastion, the seventh-century BC Doric **Paleókastro** (unrestricted access), twenty minutes' well-signposted walk out of the Langadháki district, is infinitely more impressive than the Knights' castle, and ranks as one of the more underrated ancient sites in Greece. You can clamber up onto the massive, Cyclopean-block walls by means of a broad staircase beside the still-intact gateway.

Practicalities

You'll see a handful of port **hotels** on your left as you disembark; cheapest of these is the waterfront *Three Brothers* (☎0242/31 344; ①) and the *Romantzo* (☎0242/31 340; ①) across the way, which also runs the *Studios Volcano* (②) in town. For more comfort, try the municipally run *Xenon* (☎0242/31 011; ②) just beyond. In the town proper, the main budget option is the small, simple, hillside *Hotel Ypapandi* (☎0242/31 485 or visit *Taverna Panorama*; ①), near Mandhráki's most comfortable accommodation, the *Hotel Porfyris* (☎0242/31 376; ③), also overlooking the sea and *kámbos*, with gardens and a large swimming pool. There's little actually on the shore aside from *Studios Sunset-Iliovasilema* (☎0242/31 159; ③), adequate and quiet, near the converted windmill.

Culinary **specialities** include pickled caper greens, honey, *pittiá* (chickpea croquettes), and *soumádha*, an almond-syrup drink widely sold in recycled wine bottles. When eating out, it's best to give all of the commercialized, shoddy shoreline **tavernas** a miss – *Manolis* is the honourable exception, often with fresh fish – in favour of more genuine haunts inland. Top of the heap is evening-only, musical ouzerí *Iy Fabrika*, with indoor/outdoor tables by season and family recipes from founder Patti preserved by new owner Manolis, also the miners' chef on Yiali. Runners-up include *Panorama*, with bean and mushroom salad and suckling pig on offer, or *Irini* on lively, ficus-shaded Platía Ilikioméni, with more involved *mayireftá* unavailable elsewhere. Two resolutely simple spots are the summer-only *Panayiotis* (no sign) in Langadháki, with mezédhes served at a half-dozen outside tables, or *Taverna Nissiros*, the oldest eatery in town, always packed despite predictably average grill quality. Focuses of **nightlife** are Platía Ilikioméni and a string of *barákia* on the shore west of *Manolis*.

The most useful of three **travel agencies** is Dhiakomihalis, which acts as a representative for most ferries and hydrofoils, rents cars and exchanges money (albeit for stiff commissions – there's a post office but no bank). Kentris, near the town hall, does G&A ferries and Olympic Airways tickets. At the base of the jetty is the **bus stop**, with (theoretically) up to five daily departures to the hill villages and seven to Pálli; otherwise, there are two set-rate **taxis** and three outlets for **scooter rental**, among which Alfa provides the best service – rates begin at 3000dr per day.

Beaches and Pálli

Beaches on Níssyros are in even shorter supply than water, so much so that the tour company here can successfully market excursions to a sandy cove on **Áyios Andónios** islet, opposite the Yialí mines. Closer at hand, the short, black-rock beach of **Hokhláki**, behind the Knights' castle, is unusable if the wind is up, and the town beach of **Miramáre** at the east edge of the harbour would be a last resort in any weather. It's best to head east along the main road, passing the refurbished spa of **Loutrá** (hot mineral water only by doctor's prescription) and the smallish **"White Beach"** (properly Yialiskári), 2km along and dwarfed by an ugly eponymous hotel (☎0242/31 498; ④), unwelcoming and generally filled by tour groups.

A kilometre or so further, 4km in total from Mandhráki, the fishing village of **PÁLLI** makes a more attractive base and excellent hangout at lunchtime, when the port fills with trippers. Tavernas here are multiplying, but stick with the two long-term favourites: the less expensive *Ellinis*, with spit-roasted meat by night, grilled fish in season and simple rooms upstairs (☎0242/31 453; ①), or the adjacent *Afroditi* (aka *Nikos & Tsambika*), with big portions to match bumped-up prices, Cretan bulk wine and excellent own-made desserts. They've also a house to rent, all or in part (☎0242/31 242; ③ for the entire house). A scooter-rental outlet, an excellent bakery cranking out brown bread and fine pies (branch in Mandhráki), and modest nightlife make Pálli also worth considering as a base. A tamarisk-shaded, dark-sand beach extends east of Pálli, improving as it goes, to the abandoned Pantelídhi spa, behind which the little grotto-chapel of **Panayía Thermianí** is tucked inside the vaulted remains of a Roman baths complex. To reach Níssyros's best beaches, continue in this direction for an hour on foot (or twenty minutes by bike along the road), past an initially discouraging seaweed- and cowpat-littered shoreline, to the delightful cove of **Liés** (snack bar June 15–Sept 15), where the track ends. Walking a further fifteen minutes along a trail over the headland brings you to the idyllic, 350-metre expanse of **Pahiá Ámmos**, with grey-pink sand heaped in dunes, shade at the far end and a large summer colony of free campers.

The interior

Its central, dormant **volcano** gives Níssyros its special character and fosters the growth of the abundant vegetation – and no stay would be complete without a visit. When excursion boats arrive from Kós, an agency coach and usually one of the public buses are pressed into service to take customers into the interior. Tours tend to monopolize the crater floor between 11am and 2pm, so if you want solitude, use early morning or late afternoon scheduled buses to Nikiá (two daily continue to the crater floor), a scooter or your own two feet to get there.

The road up from Pálli winds first past the virtually abandoned village of **EMBORIÓ**, where pigs and cows far outnumber people, though the place is slowly being bought up and restored by Athenians and foreigners. New owners are often surprised to discover natural saunas, heated by volcano steam, in the basements of the crumbling houses; at the outskirts of the village there's a public **steam bath** in a grotto, its entrance outlined in white paint. If you're descending to Pálli from here, an old cobbled way starting at the sharp bend below the sauna offers an attractive short cut of the four-kilometre road, while another *kalderími* drops from behind *To Balkoni tou Emboriou* **taverna** (Easter–Sept, limited menu) to within a quarter-hour's walk to the craters.

NIKIÁ, the large village on the east side of the volcano's caldera, is with seventy inhabitants more of a going concern, and its spectacular situation 14km from Mandhráki offers views out to Tílos as well as across the volcanic caldera. There are three places to **drink** (and, modestly, **eat**) here: *Porta* and *Platia* on or near the engagingly round *hokhláki* plaza, or *Nikia*, at the entrance to the village. By the bus turnaround area, signs point to the 45-minute **trail** descending to the crater floor; a few minutes downhill, you can detour briefly to the eyrie-like **monastery of Áyios Ioánnis Theológos**, which only comes to life at the September 25 festival. To **drive** directly to the volcanic area you must use the road which veers off just past Emborió.

However you approach the **volcano**, a sulphurous stench drifts out to meet you as fields and scrub gradually give way to lifeless, caked powder. The sunken main crater of **Stéfanos** is extraordinary, a moonscape of grey, brown and sickly yellow; there is another, less-visited double crater (dubbed **Polyvótis**) to the west, equally dramatic, with a clear trail leading up to it from the access road. The perimeters of both are pocked with tiny blowholes from which jets of steam puff constantly and around which form little pincushions of pure sulphur crystals. The whole floor of the larger crater seems to hiss, and standing in the middle you can hear something akin to a huge cauldron bubbling away below you. According to legend this is the groaning of Polyvotis, a Titan crushed here by Poseidon under a huge rock torn from Kós. When there are tour groups around, a small, tree-shaded snack bar operates in the centre of the wasteland, and a booth on the access road sporadically charges admission (500dr) to the volcanic zone.

Since the 1991 destruction of the old direct *kalderími* between the volcano and Mandhráki, finding pleasant options for **walking** back to town requires a bit of imagination and possession of Beate and Jürgen Franke's locally available, GPS-drawn topographical map. First choice involves backtracking along the main crater access road for about 1km from the admission booth to find the start of a clear, crudely marked path which passes the volcanic gulch of **Káto Lákki** and the monastery of **Evangelístria** on its two-hour-plus course back to the port. You can lengthen the trip by detouring from Evangelístria south to **Profítis Ilías**, the island's summit – a two-hour detour round-trip, with the route recently cleaned and well marked with cairns or white paint. An alternative approach to Evangelístria requires returning to Emborió and leaving from the top of the village, near the cemetery and small castle, on a 45-minute course to the monastery – an enjoyable link, despite haphazard 1998 marking and cleaning.

Kós

After Rhodes, **Kós** is the second largest and most popular island in the Dodecanese, and there are superficial similarities between the two. Here also the harbour is guarded by an imposing castle of the Knights of St John; the streets are lined with grandiose Italian public buildings; and minarets and palm trees punctuate extensive Hellenistic and Roman remains. Although its hinterland for the most part lacks the wild beauty of Rhodes' interior, acre for acre Kós is the most fertile of the Dodecanese, blessed with rich soil and abundant ground water.

Mass tourism has largely displaced the old agrarian economy amongst the population of about 27,000, and outside the main town and Kardhámena this is very much a family-holiday isle, where you can turn the kids loose on push-bikes. Except for Kós Town and Mastihári, there aren't many independent travellers, and from early July to early September you'll be lucky to find any sort of room at all without reservations far in advance, or a pre-booked package. The tourist industry is juxtaposed rather bizarrely with cows munching amidst baled hay, and Greek army tanks exercising in the volcanic badlands around the airport. All these peculiarities acknowledged, Kós is still definitely worth a few days' time while island-hopping: its handful of mountain villages are appealing, the tourist infrastructure excellent (including such amenities as regular city buses and cycle paths) and swimming opportunities are limitless – virtually the entire coast is fringed by beaches of various sizes, colours and consistencies.

Kós Town

The town of **KÓS**, home to most of the island's population, spreads in all directions from the harbour, with little charm aside from its scattered ancient and medieval antiquities. Apart from the Knights' castle, the first thing you see on arrival, its attraction lies in the wealth of Hellenistic and Roman remains, many of which were only revealed by an earthquake in 1933, and excavated subsequently by the Italians, who also planned and laid out the "garden suburb" extending east of the central grid. Elsewhere, vast areas of open space alternate with a hotchpotch of Ottoman monuments and later mock-medieval or Art Deco buildings.

The **castle** (Tues–Sun 8.30am–2.30pm; 800dr) is reached via a causeway over its former moat, now filled in and planted with palms (hence the avenue's Greek name, Finíkon). The existing double citadel, which was built in stages between 1450 and 1514, replaced an original fourteenth-century fort deemed not capable of withstanding advances in medieval artillery. A fair proportion of ancient Koan masonry has been recycled into the walls, where the escutcheons of several Grand Masters of the Knights of St John can also be seen.

Immediately opposite the castle entrance stands the riven trunk of Hippocrates' plane tree, its branches now propped up by scaffolding instead of the ancient columns of yore; at seven hundred years of age, it's not really old enough to have seen the great healer, though it has a fair claim to being one of the oldest trees in Europe. Adjacent are two Ottoman fountains (a dry hexagonal one and a working one in an ancient sarcophagus) and the eighteenth-century **mosque of Hassan Pasha**, also known as the Loggia Mosque after the portico on one side; its ground floor – like that of the **Defterdar mosque** on Platía Eleftherías – is taken up by rows of shops.

Opposite the latter stands the Italian-built **Archeological Museum** (Tues–Sun 8.30am–2.30pm; 800dr), with a predictable Latin bias in the choice of exhibits. Four rooms of statuary are arrayed around an atrium with a mosaic of Hippocrates welcoming Asklepios to Kós; the most famous item, purportedly a statue of Hippocrates, is indeed Hellenistic, but most of the other highly regarded works (such as Hermes seated with a lamb) are Roman.

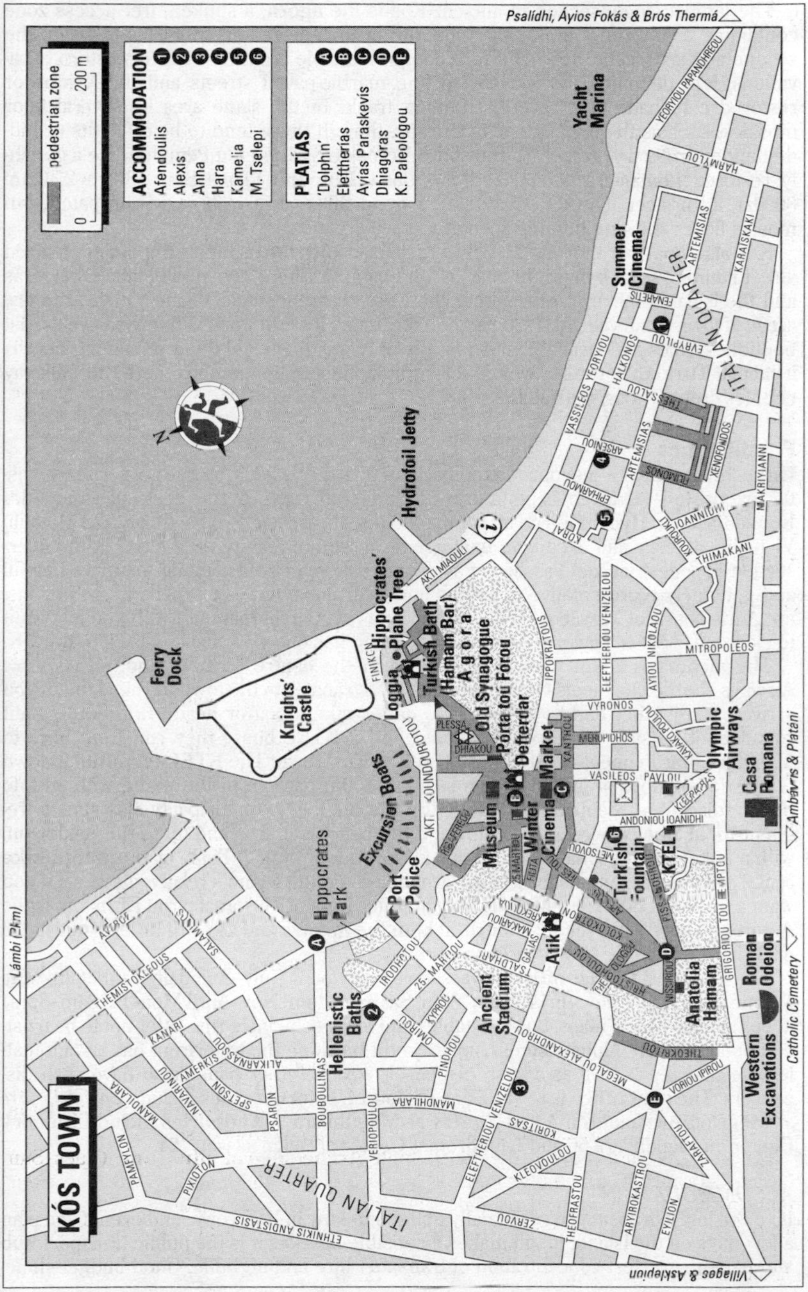
KÓS TOWN
0
200 m
pedestrian zone
ACCOMMODATION
Afendoulis 1
Alexis 2
Anna 3
Hara 4
Kamelia 5
M. Tselepi 6
PLATÍAS
'Dolphin' A
Eleftherías B
Ayías Paraskevís C
Dhiagóras D
K. Paleológou E
Psalídhi, Áyios Fokás & Brós Thermá
Lámbi (3km)
Ambávris & Platáni
Catholic Cemetery
Villages & Asklepíon
Ferry Dock
Knights' Castle
Hippocrates' Plane Tree
Loggia
Turkish Bath (Hamam Bar)
Agora
Old Synagogue
Pórta toú Fórou
Old Defterdar
Market
Museum
Winter Cinema
Excursion Boats
Port Police
Hippocrates Park
Hellenistic Baths
Ancient Stadium
Atiki
Turkish Fountain
KTEL
Olympic Airways
Casa Romana
Roman Odeion
Anatolia Hamam
Western Excavations
Hydrofoil Jetty
Yacht Marina
Summer Cinema
ITALIAN QUARTER
ITALIAN QUARTER
AKTÍ MIAOÚLI
AKTÍ KOUNDOURIÓTOU
VASSILÉOS YEORYÍOU
IPPOKRÁTOUS
ELEFTHERÍOU VENIZÉLOU
MITROPÓLEOS
THIMAKANI
MAKRIYIÁNNI
XENOFÓNDOS
ARTEMISÍAS
HARMYLOU
YEORYÍOU PAPANDHRÉOU
KARAISKÁKI
EVRYPILOU
HALKONOS
ARSENÍOU
EPIHARMOU
KORAÍ
THESSALOÚ
FILÍNONOS
IOANNÍDOU
KOUROÚKLI
AYÍOU NIKOLÁOU
VYRONOS
MERÓPIDHOS
VASILÉOS PÁVLOU
ANDONÍOU IOANÍDHI
GRIGORÍOU TOU E'
THEOKRÍTOU
MEGÁLOU ALEXÁNDHROU
VORÍOU IPÍROU
ZARAFTOU
ARYIROKÁSTROU
EVÍLION
THEÓFRASTOU
ZÉRVOU
ETHNIKÍS ANDÍSTASIS
KLEOVOÚLOU
KORÍTSAS
MANDHILARA
PINDHOU
OMÍROU
KÝPROU
25 MARTÍOU
IRODHÓTOU
BOUBOULÍNAS
VERIOPOÚLOU
PSARÓN
SPETSÓN
ALIKARNASSOÚ
AMERIKÍS
NAVARÍNOU
KANARI
THEMISTOKLÉOUS
SALAMÍNOS
PAMFÝLON
PIXIOTON
MANDILARA
PLÉSSA
DHIAKOU
XÁNTHOU
METSOVOU
KOLOKOTRÓNI
FINÍKON
NISSÍRIOU

The largest single section of ancient Kós is the **agora**, a sunken, free-access zone containing a confusing jumble of ruins, owing to repeated earthquakes between the second and sixth centuries AD. More comprehensible are the so-called western excavations, lent definition by two intersecting marble-paved streets and the **Xystos** or restored colonnade of a covered running track. In the same area lie several floor mosaics, such as the famous one of Europa, though these tend to be off-limits or hidden under protective gravel. To the south, across Grigoríou toú Pémptou, are a garishly restored Roman-era odeion and the **Casa Romana** (Tues–Sun 8.30am–2.30pm; 800dr), a third-century AD house built around three atria with suriviving patches of mosaic floors showing hunting scenes and sea creatures.

Kós also boasts a thoroughly commercialized **old town**, lining the pedestrianized street running from behind the market on Platía Eleftherías as far as Platía Dhiagóras and the isolated minaret overlooking the western archeological zone. One of the few areas of town to survive the 1933 earthquake, today it's crammed with expensive tourist boutiques, cafés and snack bars. About the only genuinely old thing remaining here is a capped **Turkish fountain** with an calligraphic inscription, found where the walkway cobbles cross Odhós Venizélou.

Practicalities

Large **ferries** anchor just outside the harbour at a special jetty by one corner of the castle; **excursion boats** to neighbouring islands sail right in and dock all along Aktí Koundouriótou. **Hydrofoils** tie up south of the castle at their own berth, on Aktí Miaoúli. Virtually all ferry and excursion boat agents sit within 50m of each other at the intersection of pedestrianized Vassiléos Pávlou and the waterfront. Among the more helpful and genuinely representative of ferries and hydrofoils, not just expensive excursions, are Adris Nissia at Vassiléos Pávlou 2, and Exas at Andóni Ioannídhi 4. If you just want to clear out, Aeolos Travel at Artemisías 25 often has one-way charters back to the UK.

The **airport** is 26km west of Kós Town in the centre of the island; an Olympic Airways shuttle bus meets Olympic flights for a transfer to the town terminal, but if you arrive on any other flight you'll have to either take a taxi or head towards the giant roundabout outside the airport gate and find a KTEL bus – they run from here to Mastihári, Kardhámena and Kéfalos as well as Kós Town. The **KTEL terminal** in town is a series of stops around a triangular park 400m back from the water, with an info booth adjacent at Kleopátras 7 (tickets on the bus). The municipality also runs a frequent **local bus** service, DEAS, through the beach suburbs and up to the Asklepion, with a ticket and information office at Aktí Koundouriótou 7. Push- or **mountain-bike** rental are popular options for getting around, given the island's relative flatness; if you want a **motor scooter**, try Moto Harley at Kanari, corner Neomartýrou Khrístou, while Autorent/Helen's in Psalídhi suburb, at both the *Ramira* and *Okeanis* hotels (☎0242/28 882), is reputable for good-condition **cars**.

The municipal **tourist office** at Vassiléos Yeoryíou 3 (July–Aug daily 7am–9pm; May & June, Sept & Oct Mon–Fri 7.30am–8pm, Sat 8am–3pm; Nov–April Mon–Fri 8am–3pm) keeps stocks of local maps, bus timetables and ferry schedules (the latter not to be trusted implicitly). The Alpha Pisteos/Alpha Credit **bank** on the waterfront has an automatic note-changer as well as a cash dispenser; several other banks also have cash dispensers. The **post office** is at Vassiléos Pávlou 14; **Internet cafés** include *Café del Mare* at Megálou Alexándhrou 4 and *Taurus* at Mandhilará 9. **Laundries** include Laundry Center on Mandhilará 56 and Laundromat Center at Alikarnassoú 124.

ACCOMMODATION

If you're just in transit, you're virtually obliged to **stay** in Kós Town, and even if you plan a few days on the island, it still makes a sensible base, as it is the public transport hub and has the greatest concentration of transport hire and nightlife. Good budget choices in the centre include the deservedly popular *Pension Alexis* (☎0242/25 594; ②), Irodhótou 9 at the corner of Omírou, across from the Roman *agora*, with wood-floored, non-en-suite rooms and a self-catering kitchen; the same welcoming family has the *Hotel Afendoulis* (☎0242/25 321; April–Nov; ③), about 600m south at Evripýlou 1, with large, balconied en-suite rooms and breakfast included. If they're full, try the nearby *Hotel Kamelia* at Artemisías 3 (☎0242/28 983; ③), claimed open all year, with winter heating; the rear rooms have an orchard view. Other quiet possibilities include the simple but en-suite *Hara* at Hálkonos 6 (☎0242/22 500; ②), the *Pension Anna* at Venizélou 77 (☎024/223 030; ③) or the self-catering rooms let by Moustafa Tselepi (☎0242/28 896; ④) at Venizélou 29, on the corner of Metsóvou. For more comfort and a small private beach, the *Hotel Theodhorou Beach*, 1200m from the centre at the end of town towards Psalídhi (☎0242/22 280; ④) has generous-sized rooms and attractive common areas not completely monopolized by packages. The well-appointed **campsite** lies another 1300m out towards Cape Psalídhi, and can be reached by either the DEAS bus service or its own minibus (which meets ferrries), but is open only during the summer.

EATING, DRINKING AND NIGHTLIFE

Despite an overwhelming first impression of Euro-bland cuisine, it's easy to **eat** well and even reasonably as long as you search inland, away from the harbour. The *Australia-Sydney* on Vassiléos Pávlou opposite the post office is a cheap and cheerful hole-in-the wall with a limited menu of daily dishes where two can eat for about 5000dr; the *Hellas* at Psarón 7, corner of Amerikís, offers more bog-standard *mayireftá*, plus *kléftiko*, in a slightly fancier environment; while *Noufara* at Kanári 45 is carnivore heaven with roast chicken, *kondosoúvli* and the like. Moving up in the world, the nearby *Nikolaos O Psaras*, corner Alikarnassoú and Avérof, is the most genuine fish taverna in town, though expect price hikes since it was refurbished and expanded in 1999. The best one of a number of *kultúra* tavernas is *Petrino* at Theológou 1, open all year with indoor/outdoor seating on Avérof at the corner of Alikarnassoú. Other recommendations are the *Olympiadha* at Kleopátras 2, near Olympic Airways, and *To Kokhili* ouzerí at Alikarnassoú 64, corner of Amerikís. Equal to any of these is *Ambavris* (May–Oct), 800m south out of town by the road from near Casa Romana, in the eponymous village; the "Greek (medley) Plate" in large quantity is a good choice, and again vegetarians will be happy, but expect to wait for a table in summer. For **breakfast** or **dessert**, *Fresko Gelateria-Café*, corner Kleopátras and Ioannídhi, serves crepes and waffles in the morning and sticky cakes or decadent own-made ice cream later on. For a quiet **drink** in atmospheric surroundings, there's the *Anatolia Hamam*, housed partly in a former Ottoman mansion off Platía Dhiagóras (though eating isn't suggested); durable music bars include *Jazz Opera* at Arseníou 5, with varied music for an older crowd, or *Beach Boys* at Kanári 57, with a tiny dance floor and cheapish drinks. If you prefer loud techno and house, look no further than the "Pub Lanes", officially Nafklírou and Dhiákou; every address is a bar, whose identity tends to change each season, so just choose according to the crowd and the noise level. Otherwise there is one active **cinema**, the Orfeas, with summer and winter (Oct–May) premises as shown on the map; the indoor premises also hosts concerts and other special events.

The Asklepion and Platáni

Native son **Hippocrates** is justly celebrated on Kós; not only does he have a tree, a street, a park, a statue and an international medical institute named after him, but the **Asklepion** (Tues–Sun 8.30am–2.30pm; 800dr) 4km south of town, one of just three in Greece, is a major tourist attraction. DEAS buses run to the site via Platáni 8am–2pm and to Platáni only 2–10pm; otherwise it's a 45-minute walk. There is a small snack bar at the Asklepion, or pause for lunch in Platáni (see below) en route.

HIPPOCRATES

Hippocrates (c. 460–370 BC) is generally regarded as the father of scientific medicine, though the Hippocratic oath probably has nothing to with him and is in any case much altered from its original form. Hippocrates was certainly born on Kós, probably at Astypalia near present-day Kéfalos, but otherwise details of his life are few and disputed; what seems beyond doubt is that he was a great physician who travelled throughout the Classical Greek world, but spent at least part of his career teaching and practising at the Asklepion on his native island. A vast number of medical writings have been attributed to Hippocrates, only a few of which he could have actually written; *Airs, Waters and Places*, a treatise on the importance of environment on health, is widely thought to be his, but others were probably a compilation from a medical library kept on Kós. This emphasis on good air and water, and the holistic approach of ancient Greek medicine, now seems positively contemporary.

The Asklepion was actually founded just after the death of Hippocrates, but it's safe to assume that the methods used and taught here were his. Both a temple to Asklepios (god of medicine, son of Apollo) and a renowned curative centre, its magnificent setting on three artificial hillside terraces overlooking Anatolia reflects early recognition of the importance of the therapeutic environment. Until recently, a fountain provided the site with a constant supply of clean, fresh water, and extensive stretches of clay piping are still visible, embedded in the ground.

Today very little remains standing above ground, owing to the chronic earthquakes and the Knights' use of the site as a quarry. The lower terrace in fact never had many structures, being instead the venue for the observance of the *Asklepieia* – quadrennial celebrations and athletic/musical competitions in honour of the healing god. Sacrifices to Asklepios were conducted at an **altar**, the oldest structure on the site, whose foundations can still be seen near the middle of the second terrace. Just to its east, the Corinthian columns of a second-century AD **Roman temple** were partially re-erected by nationalistically minded Italians. A monumental **staircase** leads from the altar to the second-century BC Doric temple of Asklepios on the topmost terrace, the last and grandest of a succession of the deity's shrines at this site.

About halfway to the Asklepion, the village of **PLATÁNI** (also Kermetés, from the Turkish name *Germe*) is, along with the Kós Town, the remaining place of residence for the island's dwindling community of ethnic Turks. Until 1964 there were nearly three thousand of them, but successive Cyprus crises and the worsening of relations between Greece and Turkey prompted mass emigration to Anatolia, and a drop in the Muslim population to currently under a thousand. Near or at the main crossroads junction, with a working Ottoman fountain, are a number of excellent Turkish-run tavernas: *Arap* (summer only), the slightly less touristy *Sherif* (ditto) and *Gin's Palace* (all year), each offering Anatolian-style mezédhes (fried vegetables with yoghurt, *bourekákia*, and so on) and kebabs better than most places in Kós Town.

Just outside Platáni on the road back to the port, the island's **Jewish cemetery** lies in a dark conifer grove, 300m beyond the Muslim graveyard. Dates on the Hebrew-Italian-script headstones stop after 1940, after which none of the local Jews were allowed the luxury of a natural death prior to their deportation in summer 1944. Their former synagogue, a wonderfully orientalized Art Deco specimen at Alexándhrou Dhiákou 4, was refurbished in 1991 as a municipal events hall.

Eastern Kós

If you're looking for anything resembling a deserted **beach** near the capital, you'll need to make use of the DEAS bus line connecting the various resorts to either side of town, or else rent a vehicle; pedal-bikes can take advantage of the cycle paths extending as far east as Cape Psalídhi. Closest is **Lámbi**, 3km north towards Cape Skandhári with its military watchpoint, the last vestige of a vast army camp which has deferred to the demands of tourism.

The far end of the city bus line beginning at Lámbi is Áyios Fokás, 8km southeast, with the unusual and remote **Brós Thermá** 5km further on, easiest reached by rented vehicle (though the final kilometre of dirt track was storm-damaged in 1999). Here **hot springs** issue from a grotto and flow through a trench into a shoreline pool protected by boulders, heating the seawater to an enjoyable temperature. Winter storms typically disperse the boulder wall, rebuilt every spring, so that the pool changes from year to year. A taverna above the lower parking area is currently shut but may of course reopen.

Tingáki and Marmári

The two neighbouring beach resorts of Tingáki and Marmári are separated from each other by the salt marsh of **Alykí**, which retains water until June after a wet winter. Between January and April Alykí is host to hundreds of migratory birds, and most of the year you'll find tame terrapins to feed near the outlet to the warm, shallow sea. There's almost always a breeze along this coast, which means plenty of windsurfers for hire at either resort. The profiles of Kálymnos, Psérimos and Turkey's Bodrum peninsula all make for spectacular scenery. If you're aiming for either of these resorts from town, especially on a bike of any sort, it's safest and most pleasant to go by the obvious **minor road** which takes off from the southwest corner of town; the entire way to Tingáki is paved, and involves the same distance as using the main trunk road and marked turnoff. Similarly, a grid of paved rural lanes links the inland portions of Tingáki and Marmári.

TINGÁKI, a busy beachside resort popular with Brits, lies 12km west of the harbour. Oddly, there's very little accommodation near the beach in the dozen or so medium-sized hotels and more numerous studios; most of these are scattered inland through fields and cow pastures. One of the better choices, if heavily subscribed to by packages, is the family-orientated *Hotel Constatinos Ilios* (☎0242/29 411; ③), a well-designed bungalow complex. The best local taverna here is *Ambeli* (supper only), well signposted 2.5km east of the main beachfront crossroads. The beach itself is white sand, long and narrow – it improves, and veers further out of earshot from the frontage road, as you head southwest.

MARMÁRI, 15km from town, has a smaller built-up area than Tingáki, and the beach itself is broader, especially to the west where it forms little dunes. Most hotels here are monopolized by German tour groups, but you might hit on an on-spec vacancy at the 1997-built *Esperia* on the main access road down from the island trunk road (☎0242/42 010; ④), in grassy surroundings. Just inland on the same street stands a pair of adjacent noteworthy **tavernas**: *Apostolis* and the currently superior *Dimitris*, offering *mezedhákia*, seafood and meat grills at reasonable prices and usually open weekends November to April.

The Asfendhioú villages

The main interest of inland Kós resides in the villages on **Mount Dhíkeos**, a handful of settlements collectively referred to as **Asfendhioú**, nestled amidst the island's only natural forest. Together they give a good idea of what Kós looked like before tourism and ready-mix concrete arrived, and all are now severely depopulated by the mad rush to the coast. They are accessible via the curvy side road from Zipári, 8km from Kós Town; a badly marked but paved minor road to Lagoúdhi; or by the shorter access road for Pylí.

The first Asfendhioú village you reach up the Zipári road is Evangelístria, where a major crossroads by the parish church and the recommendable *Asfendhiou* taverna leads to Lagoúdhi and Amanioú (west), Asómati (east) and Ziá (uphill). **ZIÁ**'s spectacular sunsets make it the target of up to six evening tour buses daily, though the village has barely a dozen families still resident, and its daytime tattiness seems to increase by the year. Best of the dozen **tavernas** here is the *Olympiada*, at the start of the pedestrian walkway up to the church, open all year with such dishes as chickpeas, bulgur pilaf, *spédzofaï* and good bulk wine; runner up, close to said church and the abandoned school, is *Iliovasilema/Sunset*, with an unbeatable, car-free situation and simple grills. Ziá is also the trailhead for the ascent of 846-metre Dhíkeos peak, a two-and-a-half-hour round-trip, initially on track but mostly by path. The route is fairly obvious, and the views from the pillbox-like summit chapel of Metamórfosis are ample reward for the effort. Up top, you can also ponder the esoteric symbolism of a giant crucifix fashioned of PVC sewer pipe and filled with concrete.

Heading east from Ziá or Evangelístria, roads converge at **ASÓMATI**, home to about thirty villagers and numbers of outsiders restoring abandoned houses; the evening view from the church of Arhángelos with its pebble mosaic rivals that of Zía, though there are no reliable facilities here. **ÁYIOS DHIMÍTRIOS**, 2km beyond along an exceedingly rough track, is marked by its old name of Haïhoúdhes on some maps, and is today completely abandoned except for a single house next to the attractive church; you can continue from here on 3.5km of more rough road to the junction with the paved road linking Plátani with the municipal rubbish tip.

Pylí

PYLÍ can be reached via the paved road through Lagoúdhi and Amanioú, or from the duck-patrolled Linopótis pond on the main island trunk road. In the upper of its two neighbourhoods, 100m west of the pedestrianized square and church, the simple *Iy Palia Piyi* taverna serves inexpensive but appetizing grills and mezédhes in a superb setting, beside a giant cistern-fountain (*piyí*), decorated with carved lion-head spouts. Pylí's other attraction is the so-called **Harmýlio** (Tomb of Harmylos), signposted near the top of the village as "Heroon of Charmylos". This consists of a subterranean, niched vault (fenced off), probably a Hellenistic family tomb; immediately above, traces of an ancient temple have been incorporated into the medieval chapel of Stavrós.

Paleó (medieval) **Pylí**, roughly 3km southeast of its modern descendant, was the Byzantine capital of Kós. Head there via Amanioú, keeping straight at the junction where signs point left to Ziá and Lagoúdhi. In any case, the castle should be obvious on its rock, straight ahead; the deteriorating road ends next to a spring, opposite which a stair-path leads within fifteen minutes to the roof of the fort. En route you pass the remains of the abandoned town tumbling southward down the slope, as well as three fourteenth-century chapels often locked to protect fresco fragments within.

Western Kós

Near the arid, desolate centre of the island, well sown with military installations, a pair of giant, adjacent roundabouts by the airport funnels traffic northwest towards Mastihári, northeast back towards town, southwest towards Kéfalos, and southeast to Kardhámena.

Mastihári and Andimáhia

The least developed, least "packaged" and least expensive of the northern shore resorts, **MASTIHÁRI** has a shortish, broad beach extending west, and a less attractive one at **Troúllos**, 1.5km east. At the end of the west beach, inside a partly fenced enclosure, lie remains of the fifth-century basilica of **Áyios Ioánnis**, one of several on the island. If you want to **stay**, quieter digs overlooking the west beach include the simple *Hotel Kyma* (☎0242/59 045; ②) or the *Hotel Fenareti* (☎0242/59 024) further up the grade, with rooms (②) and studios (③) in a peaceful garden environement. *O Makis*, one street inland from the quay, and *Kali Kardia*, at the base of the jetty, are the best of a half-dozen tavernas, both well regarded for fresh fish, mezédhes and (at *Kali Kardia*) *mayireftá*. Mastihári is also the port for small ro-ro **ferries** to Kálymnos; there are three well-spaced departures in each direction most of the year, timed more or less to coincide with Olympic Airways' flight schedules – though KTEL buses to or from Kós Town don't (perhaps deliberately) dovetail well.

The workaday village of **ANDIMÁHIA**, 5km southeast of Mastihári, straggles over several ridges; the only concession to tourism is a much-photographed windmill on the main street, operating sporadically as a working museum with its unfurled sails. If open, for a token fee you can climb up to the mast loft and observe its workings. East of Andimáhia, reached via a marked, three-kilometre side road, an enormous, triangular **Knights' castle** overlooks the straits to Níssyros. Once through the imposing north gateway (unrestricted access), you can follow the well-preserved west parapet, and visit two interior chapels: one with a fresco of Áyios Khristóforos (St Christopher) carrying the Christ Child, the other with fine rib-vaulting.

Kardhámena

KARDHÁMENA, on the southeast coast 31km from Kós Town, is the island's largest package resort after the capital itself, with locals outnumbered twenty to one in season by visitors (mostly Brits) intent on getting as drunk as possible as cheaply as possible. Runaway local development has banished whatever redeeming qualities the place may once have had, reducing it to a seething mass of offlicences, bars, trinket shops and excursion agencies. Pubs named the *Black Swan* or *Slug and Lettuce* dispense imported beer, plus you can even find fish and chips. A hefty sand beach stretches to either side of the town, hemmed in to the east with ill-concealed military bunkers and a road as far as Tolári, home to the massive *Norida Beach* all-inclusive complex.

Kardhámena is most worth knowing about as a place to catch a **boat to Níssyros**. There are supposedly two daily sailings in season: the morning tourist excursion kaïki at approximately 9.30am, and another, far less expensive, barely publicized one – the *Chrissula* – at 2.30pm, but in practice the afternoon departure (typically Mon, Wed, Thurs & Fri) can occur any time between 1.30pm and 6.30pm, depending on when the Nissyrians have finished their shopping.

Outside high season, there are generally a few **rooms** not taken by tour companies, and prices are not outrageous. For more comfort, the *Hotel Rio* (☎0242/91 627; ③) gets good reviews, and like most accommodation here is underpriced for its class. **Tavernas** are not very numerous, and predictably poor, though the longest-lived and most reasonable one is *Andreas*.

South-coast beaches

The thinly populated portion of Kós southwest of the airport and Andimáhia boasts the most scenic and secluded beaches on the island, plus a number of minor ancient sites. Though given fanciful names and shown as separate extents on tourist maps, the south-facing **beaches** form essentially one long stretch at the base of a cliff. **Magic**, officially Poléni, is the longest, broadest and wildest. **Sunny**, easily walkable from Magic, has a few sunbeds and a taverna. **Banana** (Langádha) is the cleanest and most picturesque, with junipers tumbling off its dunes. **Paradise**, often dubbed Bubble Beach because of volcanic gas vents in the tidal zone, is small and oversubscribed, with wall-to-wall sunbeds.

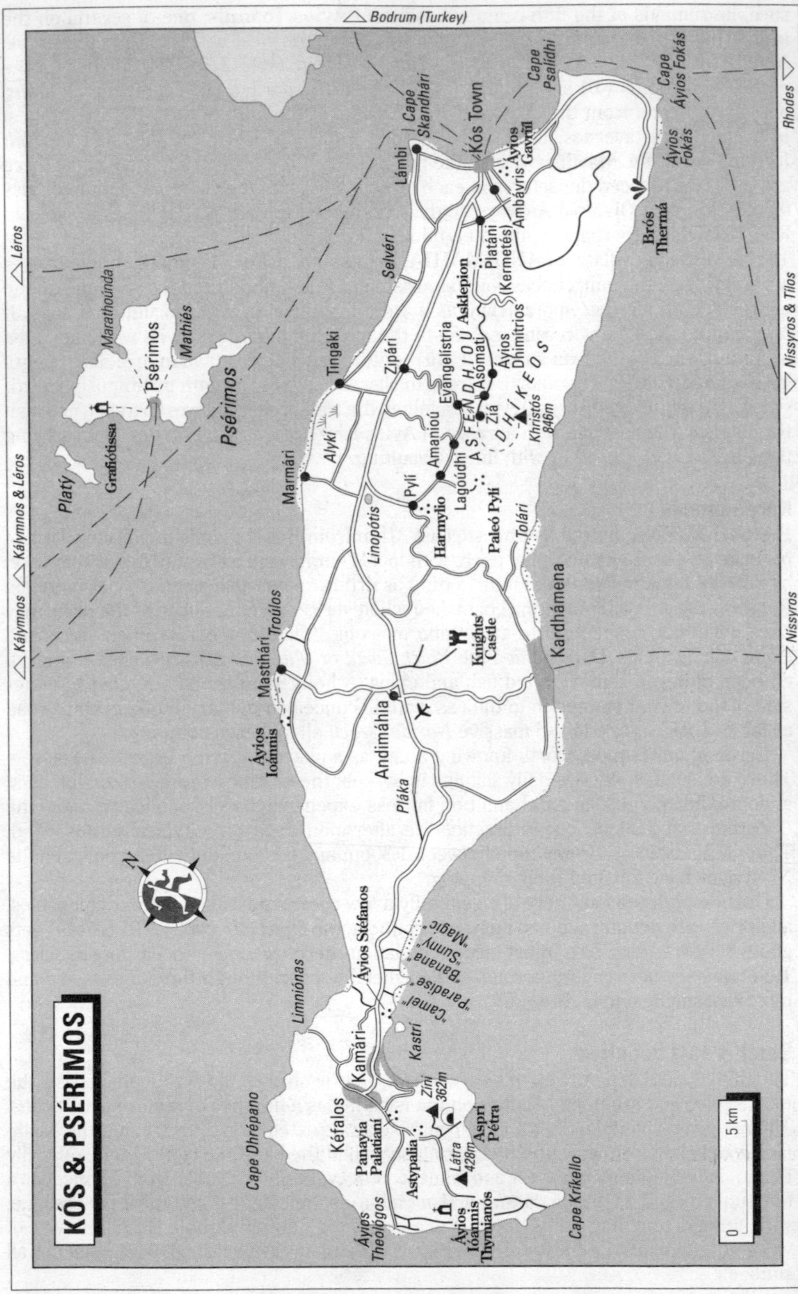

KÓS & PSÉRIMOS
Bodrum (Turkey)
Léros
Kálymnos & Léros
Kálymnos
Rhodes
Níssyros & Tílos
Níssyros
Cape Psalídhi
Cape Áyios Fokás
Áyios Fokás
Brós Thermá
Cape Skandhári
Kós Town
Lámbi
Áyios Gavriíl
Ambávris
Platáni (Kermetés)
Asklepion
Áyios Dhimítrios
Asómati
Selvéri
Tingáki
Zipári
Evangelístria
ASFENDHIOÚ
DHÍKEOS
Ziá
Khristós 846m
Amanioú
Lagoúdhi
Pylí
Paleó Pylí
Harmylío
Alykí
Marmári
Linopótis
Tolári
Kardhámena
Knights' Castle
Troúlos
Mastihári
Áyios Ioánnis
Andimáhia
Pláka
Psérimos
Marathoúnda
Mathiés
Grafiótissa
Platý
Áyios Stéfanos
Limniónas
"Camel"
"Paradise"
"Banana"
"Sunny"
"Magic"
Kástri
Kamári
Kéfalos
Zíni 362m
Aspri Pétra
Panayía Palatianí
Astypalia
Látra 428m
Cape Dhrépano
Cape Kríkello
Áyios Theológos
Áyios Ioánnis Thymianós
0
5 km
N

Uninterrupted beach resumes at **Áyios Stéfanos**, overshadowed by a huge Club Med complex, and extends 5km west to Kamári (see below). A marked public access road leads down to the beach just west of a small peninsula, crowned with the exquisite remains of two triple-aisled, sixth-century basilicas. Though the best preserved on the island, several columns have been toppled since the 1980s, and wonderful bird mosaics languish under a permanent layer of "protective" gravel. The basilicas overlook tiny but striking Kastrí islet with its little chapel; in theory it's an easy swim (sometimes wading) across from the westerly beach, with some of the best snorkelling on Kós around the rock formations, but you must run the gauntlet of boats from the local water-ski school.

The far west

Essentially the shore annexe of Kéfalos (see below), **KAMÁRI** is a sprawling package resort of rapidly multiplying breeze-blocks, pitched a few notches above Kardhámena; it's a major watersports centre and an alternative departure point for Níssyros (up to five days weekly in season). One independent hotel that can be recommended is the simple *Maria* (☎0242/71 308; ②), on the seafront west of the main road up to **KÉFALOS**, 43km from Kós Town. Squatting on a bluff looking down the length of the island, this is the end of the line for buses: a dull village but worth knowing about for its post office and as a staging point for expeditions into the rugged peninsula terminating dramatically at Cape Kríkello.

Main highlights of a half-day tour here, beginning along the widened ridge road south, are: a Byzantine church incorporating an ancient temple, 1km beyond the village; the late Classical theatre (unrestricted access), with two rows of seats remaining, of **ancient Astypalia**, 500m further at the side-path signposted "Palatia"; and the cave of **Asprí Pétra** (inhabited during the Neolithic period), marked rather vaguely off the ridge road and requiring a half-hour walk to reach. An improved, soon-to-be-paved road west from just after Astypalia leads to an often windy beach and small chapel at **Áyios Theológos**, 7km from Kéfalos; the *Sunset Wave* taverna is a reliable option for lunch, though quality varies. Keeping to the main paved road until the end of the line brings you to the appealing (but usually locked) monastery of **Áyios Ioánnis Thymianós**, also 7km from the village.

About 1.5km north of Kéfalos on the road tracing the island's summit ridge, a paved side road covers the 2.7 km to **Limniónas**, the only north-facing beach and fishing anchorage on this part of Kós. Of the two fish tavernas here whose signs guide you from the upper road, *Limionas* – the one nearer the jetty – is preferable. Two compact sandy beaches sit either side of the peninsula.

Psérimos

PSÉRIMOS could be an idyllic little island were it not so close to Kós and Kálymnos. Throughout the season, both of these larger neighbours dispatch daily excursion boats, which compete strenuously to dock at the undersized harbour; in mid-summer, day-trippers blanket the main sandy beach stretching around the bay in front of the thirty-odd houses of the single village. Even during May or late September you're guaranteed at least a hundred outsiders daily (nearly double the permanent population), and not surprisingly the islanders are apt to respond in a surly fashion to visitors. There are a couple of other, less attractive beaches to hide away on during the day: **Mathiés** (sand), a thirty-minute walk east, or **Marathoúnda** (pebble), a 45-minute walk north. Nowhere on Psérimos, including the monastery of Grafiótissa, is much more than an hour's walk away.

Even during the season there won't be too many other overnighters, since there's a limited number of **rooms** available. Pick of the several small pensions is *Tripolitis*

(☎0243/23 196; ②) over the *Saroukos* taverna, and rooms managed by Katerina Xyloura (☎0243/23 497; ②) above her taverna on the eastern side of the harbour. There's just one small **store**, and most of the island's supplies are brought in daily from Kálymnos. **Eating out** however, won't break the bank, and there's often fresh fish in the handful of **tavernas**.

Virtually all boats based at Kós harbour operate triangle tours (approximately 6000dr), which involve departure between 9.30am and 10am, followed by a stop for swimming on either Platý islet or adjacent Psérimos, lunch in Póthia, the port of Kálymnos, and another swimming stop at whichever islet wasn't visited in the morning. If you want to spend the entire day on Psérimos, you're much better off departing Póthia at 9.30am daily on the tiny *Pserimos*, returning at 4pm (2000dr round-trip). The islanders themselves use either this boat to haul supplies or their own small craft to visit Kálymnos for shopping on Monday, Wednesday and Friday (returning early afternoon).

Astypálea

Geographically, historically and architecturally, **Astypálea** (alias Astropália) would be more at home among the Cyclades – on a clear day you can see Anáfi or Amorgós in the west far more easily than any of the other Dodecanese (except western Kós), and it looks and feels more like these than its neighbours to the east. Despite an evocative butterfly shape, Astypálea does not immediately impress you as the most beautiful of islands. The heights, which offer modest walking opportunities, are bleak and covered in thornbush. Yet the herb *alisfakiá*, brewed as a tea, flourishes too, and somehow hundreds of sheep survive – as opposed to snakes, which are (uniquely in the Aegean) entirely absent. Lush citrus groves and vegetable patches in the valleys signal a relative abundance of water, hoarded in a reservoir. The various beaches along the generally featureless coastline often have reef underfoot and suffer periodic dumpings of seaweed.

In antiquity the island's most famous citizen was Kleomedes, a boxer disqualified from an early Olympic Games for causing the death of his opponent. He came home so enraged that he demolished the local school, killing all its pupils. Things have calmed down a bit in the intervening 2500 years, and today Astypálea is renowned mainly for its honey and fish; the abundant local catch has only been shipped to Athens since the late 1980s, a reflection of the traditionally poor ferry links in every direction. These have improved recently with the introduction of extra services towards Piréas via select Cyclades, and high-season links with Rhodes via a few intervening islets, but outside July or August you still risk being marooned here for a day or two longer than intended. There is, curiously, no package tourism here since Laskarina Holidays deleted the island from their list in 1995, frustrated by chronically unreliable connections to Kós and its airport.

Despite this relative isolation, plenty of people find their way to Astypálea during the short, intense midsummer season, when the 1100 permanent inhabitants are all but overrun by upwards of 7000 guests a day. Most arrivals are Athenians or Italians, supplemented by large numbers of yachties and foreign owners of holiday homes in the understandably popular Hóra. At such times you won't find a bed without reserving well in advance, and camping rough is expressly frowned upon.

Skála and Hóra

The main harbour of **SKÁLA** or Péra Yialós dates from the Italian era (Astypálea was the first island the Italians occupied in the Dodecanese) and most of the settlement

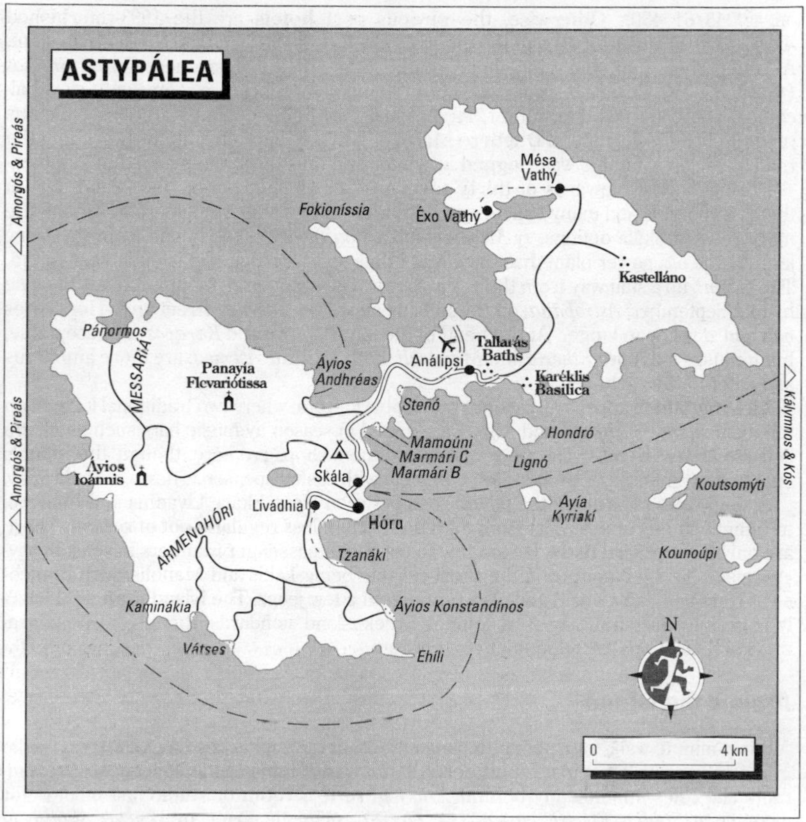

between the quay and the line of nine windmills is even more recent. Its only real bright spot is a 1998-inaugurated **archeological museum** (Tues–Sun 8.30am–2.30pm; free), a single well-lit room crammed with the best local finds spanning all historical periods from the Bronze Age to medieval times.

As you climb up beyond the port towards **HÓRA**, however, the neighbourhoods get progressively older and more attractive, their steep streets enlivened by the *poúndia*, or colourful wooden balconies of the whitewashed houses. The whole culminates in the thirteenth-century **kástro**, one of the finest in the Aegean, erected not by the Knights but by the Venetian Quirini clan and subsequently modified by the Ottomans after 1537. Until well into this century over three hundred people lived inside the *kástro*, but depopulation and World War II damage have combined to leave only a desolate shell today. The fine rib vaulting over the entrance supports the church of Evangelístria Kastrianí, one of two intact here, the other being Áyios Yeóryios (both usually locked).

Skála, and to a lesser extent Hóra, have **accommodation** ranging from spartan, 1970s-vintage rooms to new luxury studios; proprietors meet ferries if they have vacancies. Owing to harbour noise – particularly the sound of ferries dropping anchor at 3am – you might prefer more atmospheric rooms or restored villas (③–④) up in Hóra if uninterrupted sleep is a priority; enquire at the antique shop on the quay or ring ahead on ☎0243/61 430). Otherwise, the obvious port **hotels** are the 1993-refurbished *Astynea* (☎0243/61 040; ②) and the elderly *Paradisos* (☎0243/61 224; ②), both en-suite. A better choice, on the east shore of the bay, are the misnamed *Karlos Studios* (☎0246/61 330; ④, but ② spring and autumn), actually enormous rooms with view balconies, above its own restaurant. A seasonal **campsite** operates amongst calamus reeds and tamarisks behind Dhéftero Marmári bay (see opposite), about 4km along the road to Análipsi, but it's waterlogged in winter and thus mosquito-plagued in summer.

During August, upwards of thirty **tavernas** set up shop across the island, few of them memorable and many concerned primarily with turning a quick profit. Among the more reliable Skála options, *Iy Monaxia* (aka *Viki's*), one block inland from the ferry jetty by the old power plant, has excellent home-style cooking and is open year-round. The *Galini*, up a stairway from the *Hotel Astynea*, is a good grill, though it tends to close by mid-September; *Astropalia*, on the hillside above the one-way street up to Hóra, does fish and stays open longer. At the head of the bay, *Albatros* and *Karavos* are acceptable, but for just a tad more *Etherio* and *Maïstrali*, both near the *Astynea*, are more ambitious and cater to the yacht set.

Most **nightlife** happens up in more atmospheric Hóra, where two traditional kafenía on the main square – *Aigaion* and *Myli* – are joined in season by music bars such as *Kastro* and the newer *Artemis*. The **post office** and most shops are here, though the island's only **bank** (Emboriki/Commercial), complete with cash dispenser, is down at Skála quay.

A single **bus** runs along the paved road between Hóra, Skala, Livádhia and Analípsi, frequently in July and August from 8am until 11pm, less regularly out of season. There are only three official **taxis**, far too few to cope with passenger numbers in season; several places rent out **scooters**, the most reliable being Lakis and Manolis, with branches at Hóra and Skála dock, and also renting out a few jeeps. The island **map** sold locally is grossly inaccurate, even by lenient Greek-island standards, though in compensation rural junctions are adequately signposted.

Around the island

A thirty-minute walk (or a short bus journey) from the capital lies **LIVÁDHIA**, a fertile green valley with a popular, good beach but a rather ramshackle collection of restaurants and cafés immediately behind. You can **rent a room** or studio just inland– for example at *Studios Electra* (☎0243/61 270; ③), near the water, or *Venetos Studios & Bungalows* (☎0243/61 490; ③), on the westerly hillside. Among the half-dozen **tavernas**, *Iy Kalamia* and *To Yerani* are commendable, especially the latter which stays open into October and keeps simple rooms adjacent (☎0243/61 484; ②).

If the busy beach here doesn't suit, continue southwest fifteen minutes on foot to three small single coves at **Tzanáki**, packed out with naturists in mid-summer. The third bay beyond, more easily reached by motorbike, is **Áyios Konstandínos**, a partly shaded, sand and gravel cove with a good seasonal taverna. Around the headland, the lonely beaches of **Vátses** and **Kaminákia** are more usually visited by excursion boat from Skála, subject to weather and captain's whim. By land, Vátses has the easier dirt road in, some twenty minutes by scooter from Livádhia, but it's prone to surf and seaweed; the track to Kaminákia is atrocious but the sheltered, clean scenic cove with a seasonal *kantína* makes the effort worthwhile.

A favourite outing in the west of the island is the two-hour walk or 45-minute motorbike trip from Hóra to the oasis of **Áyios Ioánnis**, 10km distant. Proceed northwest along the initially paved road beginning from the fifth or sixth windmill, then keep left when a side-track goes right to Panayía Flevariotíssas monastery. Beyond this point the main track, briefly dampened by a spring seeping across the road surface, curls north towards farming cottages at Messariá before reaching a junction with gates across each option. Take the left-hand one, and soon the walled orchards of the uninhabited farm-monastery of Áyios Ioánnis come into view. From the balcony of the church, a steep, faint path leads down to the base of a ten-metre waterfall; bathing pools here come and go depending on silt deposit.

Northeast of the harbour, are three coves known as **Próto** (First), **Dhéftero** (Second) and **Tríto** (Third) **Mármari**, and marked as **Marmári A'**, **B'** and **C'** respectively on some maps. The first is home to the power plant and boatyards, the next hosts the campsite (see opposite), while the third, reasonably attractive, also marks the start of the path east to the perfectly decent coves of unfortunately named **Mamoúni** ("Bug" or "Critter" in Greek). Beyond Tríto Marmári, the middle beach at **Stenó** ("narrow", after the isthmus here) with clean sand and a seasonal *kantína*, is the best.

ANÁLIPSI, widely known as Maltezána after medieval Maltese pirates, is a ten-kilometre bus trip or taxi ride from town. Although the second-largest settlement on Astypálea, there's surprisingly little for outsiders save a narrow, sea-urchin-speckled beach (there are better ones east of the main bay) and a nice view south to some islets. Despite this, blocks of **rooms** sprout in ranks well back from the sea, spurred by the proximity of the airport, 700m away. Among a handful of tavernas, the most dependable are *Analipsi*, by the jetty, or the more ambitious-menued *Porto Stampalia*, inland. Behind calamus reeds and eucalyptus near the fishing jetty lie the best-preserved mosaic floors on the island: those of the Byzantine **Tallarás baths**, with somewhat crude figures of zodiacal signs, the seasons personified, and a central androgynous figure (Time or Fortune) holding the cosmic orb.

The motorable road ends at Méso Vathý, from where an appalling track (or occasional kaïki) continues to **ÉXO VATHÝ**, a sleepy fishing village with a single reasonable taverna and a superb small-craft harbour. Following several accidents, this is no longer the **backup ferry port** in winter, when Skála is buffeted by the prevailing southerlies; foot passengers (but no vehicles) are transferred ashore to the unlit quay at **Áyios Andhréas**, just west of Tríto Marmári.

Kálymnos

Most of the 16,000-strong population of **Kálymnos** lives in or around the large port of Póthia, a wealthy but not conventionally beautiful town famed for its sponge industry. Unfortunately, almost all of the eastern Mediterranean's sponges were devastated by a viral disease in 1986, and only three or four of the fleet of thirty odd boats are still in use. In response to this catastrophe, the island has recently established a tourist industry – so far confined to one string of beach resorts – and has also retrofitted most of its sponge boats for deep-sea fishing. Warehouses behind the harbour still process and sell sponges all year round, though most of these are imported from Asia and America. There are also still numbers of elderly gentlemen about who rely on two canes, walking frames or even wheelchairs, stark evidence of the havoc wrought in their youth by nitrogen embolism (the "bends"), long before divers understood its crippling effects. The departure of the remaining sponge fleet, usually just after Easter, is preceded by a festive week known as *Yprogrós*, with food, drink and music; the fleet's return, approximately six months later, has historically also been the occasion for more uproarious, male-orientated celebration in the port's bars.

Kálymnos essentially consists of two cultivated and inhabited valleys sandwiched between three limestone ridges, harsh in the full glare of noon but magically tinted towards dusk. The climate, especially in winter, is alleged to be drier and healthier than that of neighbouring Kós or Léros, since the quick-draining limestone strata, riddled with many caves, doesn't retain as much moisture. The rock does, however, admit seawater, which has tainted Póthia's wells; drinking water must be brought in by tanker truck from Vathý, and there are potable springs at Dámos and Hóra.

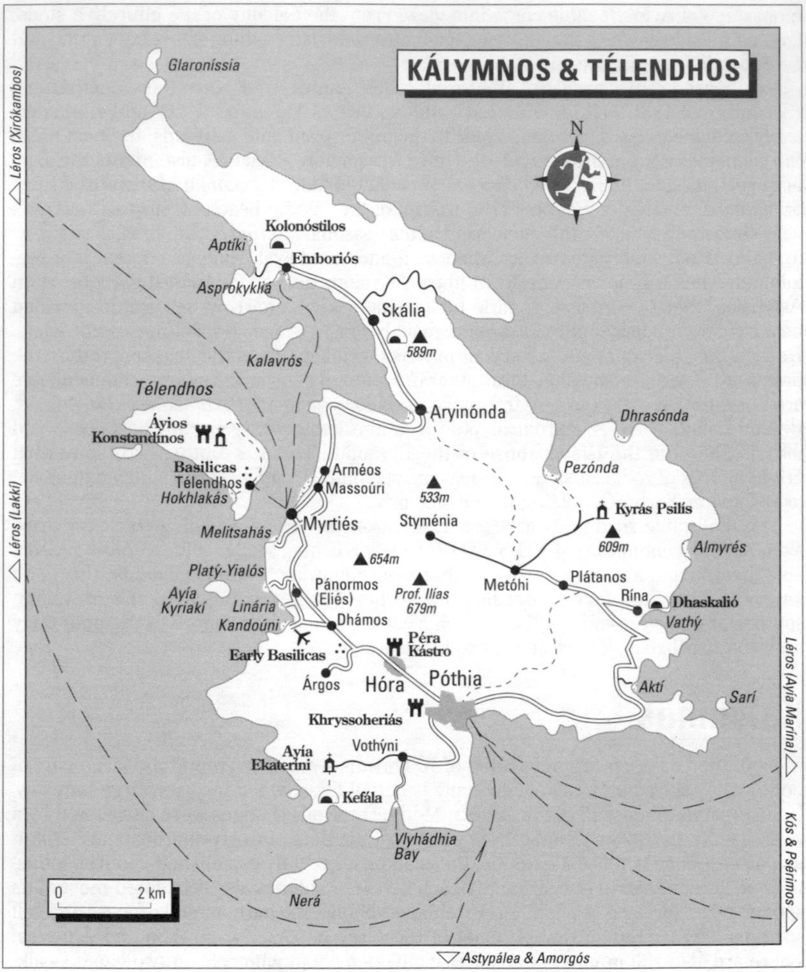

Since Kálymnos is the home port of the very useful local namesake ferry (see p.306), a minor hub for Dodecanese Hydrofoils, and moreover where the long-distance ferry lines from the Cyclades and Astypálea join up with the main Dodecanesian routes, many travellers arrive unintentionally, and are initially most concerned with how to move on quickly. Yet Kálymnos has sufficient attractions to justify a stay of several days while island-hopping – or even longer, as the package industry at the western beaches suggests.

Póthia

PÓTHIA (sometimes pronounced Pothiá), without being obviously picturesque, is colourful and authentically Greek, its houses marching up the valley inland or arrayed in tiers up the sides of the mountains framing it. Your first and overwhelming impression will be of the phenomenal amount of noise engendered by motorbike traffic and the cranked-up sound systems of the dozen waterfront cafés. This is not entirely surprising, since with about 11,000 inhabitants, Póthia ranks as the third largest city in the Dodecanese after the main towns of Rhodes and Kós.

Perhaps the most rewarding way to acquaint yourself with Póthia is by wandering the backstreets, where elegant Neoclassical houses are surrounded by surprisingly large gardens, and craftsmen ply their trade in a genuine workaday bazaar. During the Italian occupation, many local houses were painted blue and white to irritate the colonial overlords, and though the custom has all but died out, the Greek national colours are still evident amongst more traditional pink and ochre buildings.

Of the two local museums, priority should be given to the **Municipal Nautical and Folklore Museum** (Mon–Fri 8am–1.30pm, Sat–Sun 10am–12.30pm; 500dr), on the seaward side of Khristós cathedral. A large photo in the foyer shows Póthia as it was in the 1880s, with no quay, jetty, roads or sumptuous mansions, and with most of the population still up in Hóra, while other photos document sponge-fishing and the Allied liberation of 1945. Three-dimensional exhibits include horribly primitive divers' breathing apparatuses, and "cages" designed to keep propellers from cutting air lines, a constant fear. The local **archeological museum** (Tues–Sun 8.30am–2pm; free guided tours only) is installed in a grand former residence of the Vouvallis family of sponge magnates. A rather eclectic collection, including a kitsch-furnished Second Empire parlour and small troves from the island's several caves, it's not exactly required viewing.

Practicalities

Accommodation is rarely a problem, since pension proprietors usually meet the ferries (though many of the premises touted are substandard, or remote, or both). The town's best, and quietest **hotel**, near the Vouvalis museum, is the *Villa Themelina* (☎0243/22 682; ③), housed in a nineteenth-century mansion plus modern studio annexes ⑤, with gardens and a large swimming pool. The high-ceiling, bug-screened, wood-floored rooms in the main house make this Kálymnos's most elegant accommodation. Next niche down, on the west quay but fairly quiet, is occupied by the *Arhondiko* (☎0243/24 061), a refurbished mansion with plain rooms at ② and "luxury" ones (balcony, TV, fridge) at ③; all have heating/air conditioning. Two places in Amoudhára district (west of the harbour) are worth contacting in advance: the en-suite *Pension Greek House* (☎0243/29 559; ②; open most of year) with volubly friendly management and kitsch decor; and considerably above this, the well-signposted *Hotel Panorama* between the *Hotel Porfyris* and Platía Ilikioméni (☎0243/23 138; April–Oct; ③), with balconied view rooms.

When **eating out**, the obvious strategy involves following the waterfront northeast past the Italian-built municipal "palace" to a line of fish **tavernas** and **ouzeris**, where the local speciality is octopus croquettes, more tender than you'd expect. However, recent years have seen touts multiply and prices climb here, so even though the locals still patronize places like *Burba Petros*, you might consider *mayireftá* at *Xefteris*, well signposted inland from Khristós cathedral, with courtyard seating, or *Navtikos Omilos*, at the base of the ferry jetty opposite Áyios Nikólaos church. This has a limited menu of seafood and grills, but portions are large and there's a pleasant terrace. Sticky-cake fans will want to attend the traditional *Zaharoplastiki O Mihalaras* back on restaurant row, while four paces west from here, just before the municipal "palace", *Apothiki* is an old warehouse refurbished as a musical bar for some years now. A summer cinema, Cine Oasis, operates behind the traditional, column-facaded café-tearoom *Ai Musai*, on the front.

All **boat** and **hydrofoil** agents, including the headquarters of the *Nissos Kalymnos*, plus a fairly useless municipal tourist information bureau (sporadic Mon–Fri hours), line the waterfront as you bear right out of the pier-area gate. Olympic Airways has an office at Patriárhou Maxímou 17, 200m inland from the quay, and the new airport near Árgos village may commence operations in 2000. Finally, waterfront branches of the National/Ethniki and Ionian/Ioniki **banks** both have cash dispensers.

Around the island

Buses run as far as Emborió in the northwest and Vathý in the east, from a stop beside the municipal "palace", with schedules helpfully posted and departures in season fairly frequent. Tickets must be bought beforehand from authorized kiosks, and cancelled on board. Otherwise, you can use shared **taxis** from Platía Kýprou (more than KTEL rates, less costly than a normal taxi), or rent a **scooter** from reputable Scootermania, just back from the waterfront, near where it bends south. Avis **car** rental is represented locally (☎0243/28 990), though the island's compact enough that only families would need one.

The castles and basilicas

Heading northwest across the island, the first place you reach after just over a kilometre along is a castle of the Knights of St John, **Kástro Khryssoheriás**, in the suburb of Mýli. From the whitewashed battlements there are wonderful views southeast over town to Kós, and north towards Hóra and Péra Kástro. The former Kalymnian capital of **HÓRA** (aka Horió), 1.5km further along the main road, is still a village of nearly three thousand inhabitants, and guards a critical pass in local geography, focus of settlement in every era. Steep steps lead up from its eastern edge to the Byzantine citadel-town of **Péra Kástro** (daily May–Oct 10am–2pm; tip to guide), appropriated by the Knights of St John and inhabited until late in the eighteenth century. Inside the imposing gate the former heaps of rubble are slowly being re-pieced together; a guided tour by the warden visits five well-maintained, whitewashed chapels, containing late medieval fresco fragments.

Some 200m past the turning for Árgos en route to the northwest coast from Horió, you can detour briefly left to visit two early Byzantine basilicas which are fairly representative, and among the easiest to find, of a vast number on the island. The more impressive of the two, accessed by whitewashed steps on the left just as the highway begins to descend, is that of **Khristós tís Ierousalím**, probably dating from the late fourth century, with its apse fully preserved; the three-aisled **Limniótissa** church in an adjacent field is larger but considerably less intact.

West coast resorts

From the basilicas, the road dips into a tree-shaded valley leading to the consecutive **beach resorts** of Kandoúni, Myrtiés and Massoúri, collectively referred to as "Brostá" by islanders. **KANDOÚNI**, some 200m of brown, hard-packed sand favoured by the locals, is the shore annexe of the rich agricultural valley-village of **Pánormos** (aka Eliés). Accommodation closest to the water here is monopolized by tour companies, and for both bathing and staying you're better off at **Linária**, the north end of the same bay. A smaller cove set apart from Kandoúni proper by a rock outcrop, this has better sand and the possibility of staying at *Skopellos Studios* (☎0243/47 155; ③), on the slope below the church. For eating, there are two worthy options: *Ouzeri Giannis/Ta Linaria* on the shore, with leisurely service but abundant portions of grills and seafood, or *To Steki tis Fanis* in an old mansion up on the hillside, offering local specialities such as *merziméli* (salad with barley rusks) and *mourí* (baked lamb in a clay pot).

The next beach north, **Platý-Yialós**, though again a bit shorter than Kandoúni, is arguably the best on the island: cleaner than its southern neighbours, more secluded, and placed scenically at the base of a cliff, opposite Ayía Kyriakí islet. A lone taverna (*Kyma*), right behind the sand at road's end, will do for lunch. There are two worthwhile choices for **staying** on spec: the 1970s-vintage rooms at *Pension Platy-Gialos* (☎0243/47 029; ②), actually overlooking Linária, simple but en-suite, or the mammoth *Mousselis Studios* (☎0243/47 757; ③), with so many units (and on-site snack bar) that they usually have stray vacancies even in summer.

The main road climbs from Pánormos up to a pass, where the *Hotel Kamari* (☎0243/47 278; ③) is another non-packaged possibility, with views from most rooms, before descending in zigzags to meet the sea again 8km from Póthia at **MYRTIÉS**. Together with **MASSOÚRI** (1km north) and **ARMÉOS** (2km north and end of the line for most buses), it sees the lion's share of Kálymnos tourism: all too many neon-lit music bars, "special menus", souvenir shops and the other accoutrements of the package trade. The beach at Myrtiés is narrow, pebbly and cramped by development, though it does improve as you approach Massoúri. The closest all-sand beach to Myrtiés lies 500m south, at **Melitsahás** cove, which also has the only really passable local **taverna** at its fishing anchorage, *Iy Dhrossia*, fish specialists claiming to be open all year. Most local **accommodation** is block-booked by overseas companies; a remote exception enjoying spectacular views is *Studios Nikis* (☎0243/47 201; ②), up on the higher one-way bypass road between Myrtiés and Massoúri. Possibly this coast's most appealing feature is its position opposite the evocatively shaped islet of Télendhos (see below), which frames some of the most dramatic sunsets in Greece. It's also possible to go from Myrtiés directly to Xirókambos on Léros aboard the daily early afternoon **kaïki**.

Some 5km beyond Massoúri, **ARYINÓNDA** has a clean pebble beach backed by a single **rooms** outfit (*Arginonta Beach*, ☎0243/40 000; ②), with a friendly proprietor, and several **tavernas**. It is also the trailhead for the spectacular two-and-a-half-hour walk inland and over two gentle passes to Metóhi in the Vathý valley. From the bus-stop area and small spring, head southwest on a path between rock walls which soon climbs the south flank of the ravine here, sporadically marked by paint dots. Don't believe sources which show the route emerging at Styménia, and be aware that plans are afoot to bulldoze a road from just above the *Arginonta Beach* to Styménia, which may disrupt the first half-hour or so of the trail. You'll need a sunhat, stout shoes and a litre or so of water, as the next source is in Plátanos hamlet, beyond Metóhi.

The end of the bus line, **EMBORIÓ**, 20km from the port, offers a gravel and sand beach, which improves as you head west, **accommodation** (much of it taken up by Laskarina Holidays) and a number of **tavernas**, including the long-running *Harry's Paradise*, with attached garden apartments (☎0243/47061; ④), and *Akti Emborios*, closer to the sea. If the twice-daily bus service fails you, there is usually a shuttle boat back to Myrtiés.

Télendhos

The trip across the strait to the striking, volcanic-plug islet of **TÉLENDHOS** is arguably the best reason to come to Myrtiés; little boats shuttle to and fro constantly throughout the day and late into the night. According to local legend, Télendhos is a petrified princess, gazing out to sea after her errant lover; the woman's head profile is most evident at dusk. The hardly less pedestrian geological explanation has the islet sundered from Kálymnos by a cataclysmic earthquake in 554 AD; traces of a submerged town are said to lie at the bottom of the straits.

Home to about fifteen families, Télendhos is car-free and blissfully tranquil, though even here package tourism has arrived in a modest way. For cultural edification you'll find the ruined thirteenth-century **monastery of Áyios Vassílios** and an enormous, 1997-excavated basilica of Ayía Triádha up on the ridge, part way along the ten-minute path to **Hokhlakás** pebble beach, which is small but very scenic, with sunbeds for hire. Accommodation and food can be basic or worse; we've had complaints about *Pension/Restaurant Uncle George*, the obvious place by the jetty. Best perhaps to veer off south to adjacent *Pension Studios Rita* (☎0243/47 914; ②), with rooms and renovated-house studios managed by the namesake dessert café, *Zorba's*, or to *Barba Stathis* tavernas en route to Hokhlakás; or north (beyond Áyios Vasílios) to the Greek-Australian-run *On the Rocks*, which doubles as a decent taverna with homemade desserts, and has a bar that's the heart and soul of local **nightlife**. At one corner of the premises you can visit yet another Byzantine monument, the chapel and sauna of Áyios Harálambos. If you want more (relative) luxury on Télendhos, you'll have to squeeze in between packages at the *Hotel Porto Potha* (☎0243/47 321, fax 48 108; ③), set rather bleakly at the very edge of things but with a large pool.

Vathý

Heading east from Póthia, the first four kilometres (power plant, rubbish tip, multiple gasworks and quarries) seem vastly unpromising, until you round a bend and the ten-kilometre ride ends dramatically at **VATHÝ** a long, fertile valley, carpeted with orange and tangerine groves, whose colour provides a startling contrast to the lifeless greys higher up on Kálymnos. At the simple fjord port of **RÍNA**, more ruined basilicas flank the bay; near the southerly one is the best accommodation option, the helpful *Rooms Manolis* (☎0243/41 300; ②). Some of the five tavernas are pricier than you'd expect, owing to patronage from the numerous yachts which call here; currently the best choice, with shambolic service but good grilled fish, is *The Harbor*, first place on the right at road's end.

The steep-sided inlet has no beach to speak of, so people swim off the artificial lido on the far right; the closest reachable overland are **Aktí**, about 3km back towards Póthia, a functional pebble strand with sunbeds and a single snack bar, and **Pezoúnda**, a little further north, reached by track (and then walking) from Metóhi hamlet. Boat excursions sometimes visit the stalactite cave of **Dhaskalió**, inhabited in Neolithic times, out towards the fjord mouth on its north flank, and the remoter, tiny beaches of **Almyrés** and **Dhrasónda**, accessible only by sea.

It's possible to **walk** back to Póthia along the old direct *kalderími* which existed before the coastal highway – a two-hour jaunt which begins in Plátanos hamlet. The route is tricky to find in this direction, however, so most people start in Póthia, at the church of Ayía Triádha behind the *Villa Themelina* hotel – the way is marked initially by red paint splodges.

The southwest

Some 6km southwest of Póthia, the small bay of **Vlyhádhia** is reached via a narrow ravine draining from the nondescript village of Vothýni. The sand and pebble beach here isn't really worth a special trip, unless you're interested in **scuba**, since the Vlyhádhia area is one of the limited number of legal diving areas in Greece. Stavros Valsamidhes, the local divemaster, has also assembled an impressive **Museum of Submarine Finds** (Mon–Sat 9am–7pm, Sun 10am–2pm; free), which in addition to masses of sponges and shells offers a reconstructed ancient wreck with amphorae and World War II debris. Depending on your ability, dives (arrange in advance on ☎0243/50 662; 10,000dr for one dive, 18,000dr for two) may visit ancient wrecks *in situ*, as well as seal caves.

Póthia-based kaïkia make well-publicized excursions to the cave of **Kefála** just west of Vlyhádhia, the most impressive of half a dozen caverns around the island. You have to walk thirty minutes from where the boats dock, but the vividly coloured formations repay the effort; the cave was inhabited before recorded history, and later served as a sanctuary of Zeus (who is fancifully identified with a particularly imposing stalagmite in the biggest of six chambers).

Léros

Léros is so indented with deep, sheltered anchorages that during World War II it harboured, in turn, the entire Italian, German and British Mediterranean fleets. Unfortunately, many of these magnificent fjords and bays seem to absorb rather than reflect light, and the island's relative fertility can seem scraggly and unkempt when compared with the crisp lines of its more barren neighbours. These characteristics, plus the island's lack of spectacularly good beaches, meant that until the late 1980s just a few thousand foreigners (mostly Italians who grew up on the island), and not many more Greeks, came to visit each August.

Such a pattern is now history, with German, Dutch, Danish and British package operators at the vanguard of those "discovering" Léros and the company of islanders unjaded by mass tourism. Foreign visitor numbers have, however, levelled out of late,

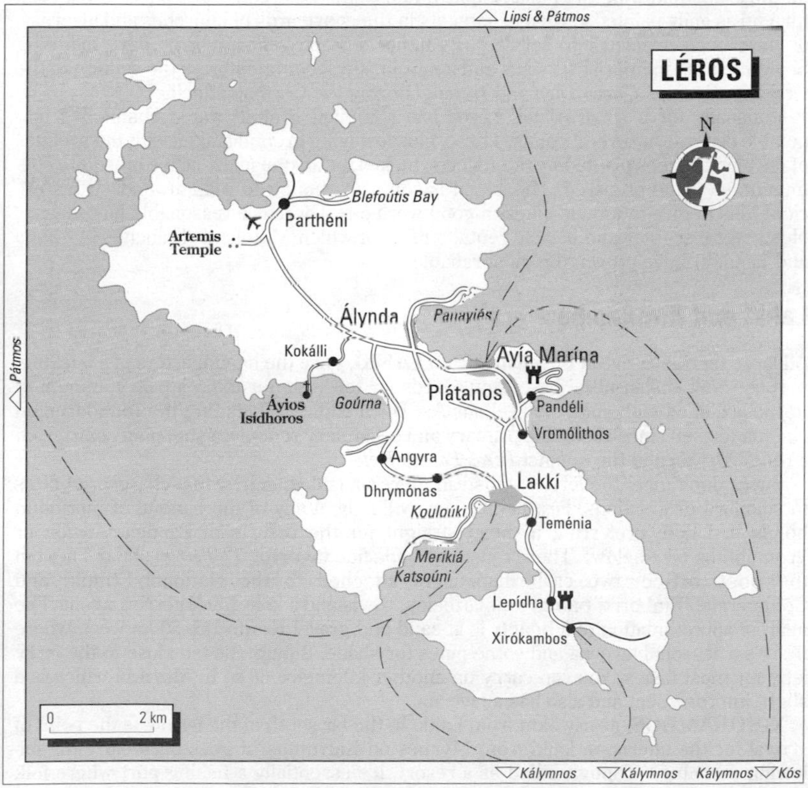

with matters unlikely to change until and unless the tiny airport is expanded to accommodate jets.

Not that Léros needs, or strenuously encourages, mass tourism; various prisons and sanatoriums have dominated the Lerian economy since the 1950s, directly or indirectly employing about a third of the population. During the junta era, the island hosted a notorious detention centre at Parthéni, and today the mental hospital on Léros remains the repository for many of Greece's more intractable psychiatric cases; another asylum is home to hundreds of mentally handicapped children. The island's domestic image problem is compounded by its name, the butt of jokes by mainlanders who pounce on its similarity to the word *lerá*, connoting rascality and unsavouriness.

In 1989, a major scandal emerged concerning the administration of the various asylums, with EU maintenance and development funds found to have been embezzled by administrators and staff, and the inmates kept in degrading and inhumane conditions. Since then, an influx of EU inspectors, foreign psychiatrists and extra funding have resulted in drastic improvements in patient treatment, including the establishment of halfway houses across the island.

More obvious is the legacy of the **Battle of Léros** on November 12–16, 1943, when overwhelming German forces displaced a Commonwealth division which had landed on the island following the Italian capitulation. Bomb nose-cones and shell casings still turn up as gaily painted garden ornaments in the courtyards of churches and tavernas, or have been pressed into service as gateposts. Each year for three days following September 26, memorial services and a naval festival commemorate the sinking of the Greek battleships *Queen Olga* and *Intrepid* during the German attack.

Unusually for a small island, Léros has abundant ground water, channelled into potable cisterns at several points. These, plus low-lying ground staked with the avenues of eucalyptus trees planted by the Italians, makes for an unusually active mosquito contingent, so come prepared. The island is compact enough to walk around, with sufficient hills to give mountain-bikers a good work-out. There is a reasonable bus service, plus several scooter and bicycle rental outfits, of which Motoland (branches at Álinda and Pandéli) have proven the most reliable.

Lakkí and Xirókambos

All large **ferries** arrive at the main port of **LAKKÍ**, once the headquarters of a bustling, purpose-built Italian naval base. Boulevards far too wide for today's paltry amount of traffic are lined with some marvellous Art Deco edifices, including the round-fronted cinema (closed since 1985), the primary and secondary schools, a shopping centre with a round atrium and the defunct *Leros Palace Hotel*.

Buses don't meet the ferries – instead there's a taxi squadron that charges set fares to standard destinations. Few people stay willingly at any of the handful of moribund hotels in Lakkí, preferring to head straight for the resorts of Pandéli, Álynda or Vromólithos (see below). There's just one bona fide **taverna**, *To Petrino*, inland next to the **post office**, two cash dispensers attached to the National/Ethniki and Commercial/Emboriki **banks** and Gribelos, the island's sole G&A Ferries agent. The nearest approximation of a **beach** is at sand and gravel **Kouloúki**, 500m west, where there's a seasonal taverna and some pines for shade, though it's too close to the ferry jetty for most tastes. You can carry on another kilometre or so to **Merikiá** which is a slight improvement and also has a taverna.

XIRÓKAMBOS, nearly 5km from Lakkí in the far south of the island, is the point of arrival for the afternoon kaïki from Myrtiés on Kálymnos (it goes back early the following morning). Though billed as a resort, it's essentially a fishing port where folk also happen to swim – the beach here is poor to mediocre, improving as you head west.

Accommodation is available at *Villa Maria* (☎0247/22 827; ②) on the beach or, for a higher standard, the *Hotel Efstathia* (☎0247/24 099; ③), actually studio apartments with huge, well-furnished doubles as well as family fourplexes, plus a large pool. **Meals** can be had at *Taverna Tzitzifies*, just by the jujube trees at the east end of things, where the road hits the shore. The island's **campsite** is in an olive grove at the village of **LEPÍDHA**, 750m back up the road to Lakkí; just north of the site, an access drive on the far side of the road leads up a tiny acropolis with stretches of ancient masonry and sparse patches of early Christian mosaics.

Pandéli and Vromólithos

Just less than 3km north of Lakkí, Pandéli and Vromólithos together form the fastest-growing resort on the island – and are certainly two of the more attractive and scenic places to stay, if not eat.

PANDÉLI is still very much a working port, the cement jetty benefiting local fishermen as well as increasing number of yachts which call here. A negligible beach is compensated for by a relative abundance of non-package **accommodation**, such as the *Pension Happiness* (☎0247/23 498; ②) where the road down from Plátanos meets the sea, or, for a higher standard, the *Niki Studios* (☎0247/25 600; ②) at the base of the road to the castle, airy, Aussie-run and with partial sea views. Up on the ridge dividing Pandéli from Vromólithos, the *Pension Fanari* (☎0247/23 152; ②) would seem a good choice for its calm setting below the road and views across to the castle, but hot-water provision was defective at our stay. Further south along the ridge road, the basic *Hotel Rodon* (☎0247/23 524; ②) is another possibility, though a potentially noisy ouzerí operates right next door, as does the musical *Beach Bar*, perched on a rock terrace below, facing Vromólithos. The other long-lived local **bar** is the civilized *Savana*, at the opposite end of Pandéli, beyond the row of waterfront **tavernas** which, alas, have in recent years become tourist traps of the first order. They get less expensive and less pretentious as you head east towards *Maria's*, an unchanging local institution, decked out in coloured lights and whimsically painted gourds; avoid the lousy *mayireftá* here and stick with the generally reliable seafood.

VROMÓLITHOS boasts the best easily accessible **beach** on the island, car-free and hemmed in by hills studded with massive oaks. The shoreline is gravel and coarse sand, and the sea here is clean, but as so often on Léros you have to cross a nasty, sharp reef at most points before reaching deeper water. Two **tavernas** behind the beach trade more on their location than their cuisine, but the standard of **accommodation** here is higher than at Pandéli, with the result that much of it tends to be monopolized by package companies. One that isn't is the delightful, en-suite *Pension Margarita* (☎0247/22 889; ②), slightly inland but with a fine sea view and kitchen facilities.

Plátanos and Ayía Marína

The Neoclassical and vernacular houses of **PLÁTANOS**, the island capital 1km west of Pandéli, are draped gracefully along a saddle between two hills, one of them crowned by the inevitable Knights' castle. Known locally as the **Kástro**, this is reached either by a paved but potholed road peeling off the Pandéli road, or via a more scenic stair-path from the central square; the battlements, and the views from them, are dramatic, especially near sunrise or sunset. The medieval church of **Panayía tou Kástrou** inside the gate houses a small museum (daily 8.30am–12.30pm, also Wed, Sat & Sun 3.30–7.30pm; token admission), though its carved *témblon* and naive oratory are more remarkable than the sparse exhibits, which incongruously include a certified chunk of the Berlin Wall.

Except for *Hotel Eleftheria* (☎0247/23 550; ②), with a peaceful hillside location, Plátanos is not really a place to stay or eat, although it's well sown with **shops** and **services**. The latter include Olympic Airways, south of the turning for Pandéli, a **post office**, down the road towards Ayía Marína, and two **banks** (one with a cash dispenser). The single **bus** (schedule posted at the stop, opposite the island's main **taxi** rank) plies four to six times daily between Parthéni in the north and Xirókambos in the south.

Plátanos merges seamlessly with **AYÍA MARÍNA**, 1km north on the shore of a fine bay, still graced by a small, Italian-built public market building. If you're travelling to Léros on an excursion boat or hydrofoil, this will be your port of entry. Although there's no accommodation here, it's arguably the best place to **eat** on the island. Just west of the police station, on the water, *Mezedhopolio Kapaniri* is a good, reasonable ouzerí, at its best after dark, featuring plenty of fried vegetable first courses. Just inland opposite the *Agrotiki Trapeza* in a little alley, the *Kapetan Mihalis* ouzerí claims to be open all day and offers a range of inexpensive local specialities, including various fish marinated in salt (*pastós*). Further west, there's the simple but adequate *Lemonis* grill by the waterside and the 1999-opened *Ouzeri Neromylos*, out by the marooned windmill.A semblance of **nightlife** is provided by a half-dozen bars, such as *Remezzo* near the Agricultural Bank, and *Harama* on the quay.

Álynda and the north

ÁLYNDA, 3km northwest of Ayía Marína, ranks as the longest-established resort on Léros, with development just across the road from a long, narrow strip of pea-gravel beach. It's also the first area for accommodation to open in spring, and the last to shut in autumn. Many of the half-dozen **hotels** and **pensions** here are block-booked by tour companies, but you may have better luck at two outfits overlooking the war cemetery: *Hotel Gianna* (☎247/23 153; ③), with fridge-equipped rooms plus a few studios, or the nearby *Studios Diamantis* (☎247/23 213; ③) just inland, with large balconied units but somewhat unpleasant management. At Krithóni, 1.5km south, more comfort is available at the island's top-flight accommodation: the *Crithoni's Paradise* (☎0247/25 120, fax 24 680; ⑥), a mock-traditional low-rise complex with buffet breakfast, a large pool and all mod cons in the rooms. **Restaurant** options aren't brilliant, except for *To Steki* next to the war cemetery, open year round with good grills and rich mezédhes attracting a local clientele.

The **Allied War Graves Cemetery**, mostly containing casualties of the November 1943 battle, occupies a walled enclosure at the south end of the beach; immaculately maintained, it serves as a moving counterpoint to the holiday hubbub outside. The other principal sight at Álynda is the privately run **Historical and Ethnographic Museum** (May–Sept only, daily 10am–noon & 6–9pm; 500dr), housed in the unmistakable castle-like mansion of Paris Bellinis (1871–1957). Most of the top floor is devoted to the Battle of Léros: relics from the sunken *Olga*, a wheel from a Junkers bomber, a stove made from a bomb casing. There's also a rather grisly mock-up clinic (mostly gynecological tools) and assorted rural impedimenta, costumes and antiques.

Alternative beaches near Álynda include **Panayiés**, a series of gravel coves (one naturist) at the far northeast of the bay, and **Goúrna**, the turning for which lies 1km or so off the trans-island road. The latter, Léros's longest sandy beach is hard-packed and gently shelving; it's also wind-buffeted, bereft of any nearby facilities, and permanently fringed by an impromptu car park and construction rubble. A separate road beyond the Goúrna turning leads to **Kokálli**, no great improvement beach-wise, but flanked to one side by the scenic islet of **Áyios Isídhoros**, which is tethered to the mainland by a causeway, its eponymous chapel perched on top.

Seven kilometres from Álynda along the main route north, a marked side-track leads left to the purported **Temple of Artemis**, on a slight rise just west of the airport runway. In ancient times, Léros was sacred to the goddess, and the temple here was supposedly inhabited by guinea fowl – the grief-stricken sisters of Meleager, metamorphosed thus by Artemis following their brother's death. All that remains now are some jumbled, knee-high walls, which may in fact have been an ancient fortress, but the view is superb. The onward road skims the shores of sumpy, reed-fringed Parthéni bay, with its dreary army base (formerly the political prison), until the paved road ends 11km along at **Blefoútis**, a rather more inspiring sight with its huge, virtually landlocked bay. The beach (the rough Lerian norm) has tamarisks to shelter under and an adequate taverna, *Iy Thea Artemi*, for *kalamári*-and-chips-type lunch.

Pátmos

Arguably the most beautiful and certainly the best known of the smaller Dodecanese, **Pátmos** has a distinctive, immediately palpable atmosphere. It was in a cave here that St John the Divine (in Greek, *O Theológos* or "The Theologian"), received the New Testament's Book of Revelation and unwittingly shaped the island's destiny. The monastery honouring him, founded here in 1088 by the Blessed Khristodhoulos (1021–93), dominates Pátmos both physically – its fortified bulk towering high above everything else – and, to a considerable extent, politically. While the monks inside no longer run the island as they did for more than six centuries, their influence has nonetheless stopped Pátmos going the way of Rhodes or Kós.

Despite vast numbers of visitors and the island's firm presence on the cruise, hydrofoil and yacht circuits, tourism has not been allowed to take Pátmos over completely. While there are a number of clubs and even one disco around Skála, drunken rowdiness is virtually unknown, and this is one island where you do risk arrest for nudism on all but the most isolated beaches. Package clients have only since the 1990s begun to outnumber independent visitors, and are pretty much confined to Gríkou and a handful of larger hotels at Skála and Kámbos. Day-trippers still exceed overnighters, and Pátmos seems an altogether different place once the last cruise ship has gone at sunset. Away from Skála, development is appealingly subdued if not deliberately retarded, thanks to the absence of an airport.

Skála and around

SKÁLA, with most of the island's population of about three thousand, seems initially to contradict any solemn, otherworldly image of Pátmos. The waterside, with its ritzy cafés and clientele, is a bit too sophisticated for such a small town, and some of the service staff a bit world-weary. During peak season, the quay and commercial district heave by day with hydrofoil and cruise-ship passengers souvenir-hunting or being shepherded onto coaches for the ride up to the monastery; after dark there's still a considerable traffic in well-dressed cliques of visitors on furlough from the cruise ships which weigh anchor after midnight. In winter (which here means October), Skála assumes a ghost-town air as most shops and restaurants close, their owners and staff back in Rhodes or Athens.

Melóï Beach lies 1.5km to the north (see p.301), one of the most convenient and popular coves on the island; Hóra, a bus or taxi ride up the mountain, is a more attractive base but has few rooms. Yet given time – especially in spring or autumn – Skála reveals some more enticing corners in the residential fringes to the east and west, where vernacular mansions hem in pedestrian lanes creeping up the hillsides. The modern town dates only from the 1820s, when the Aegean had largely been cleared of pirates, but at the summit of the westerly rise, **Kastélli**, you can see the extensive foundations of the island's ancient acropolis.

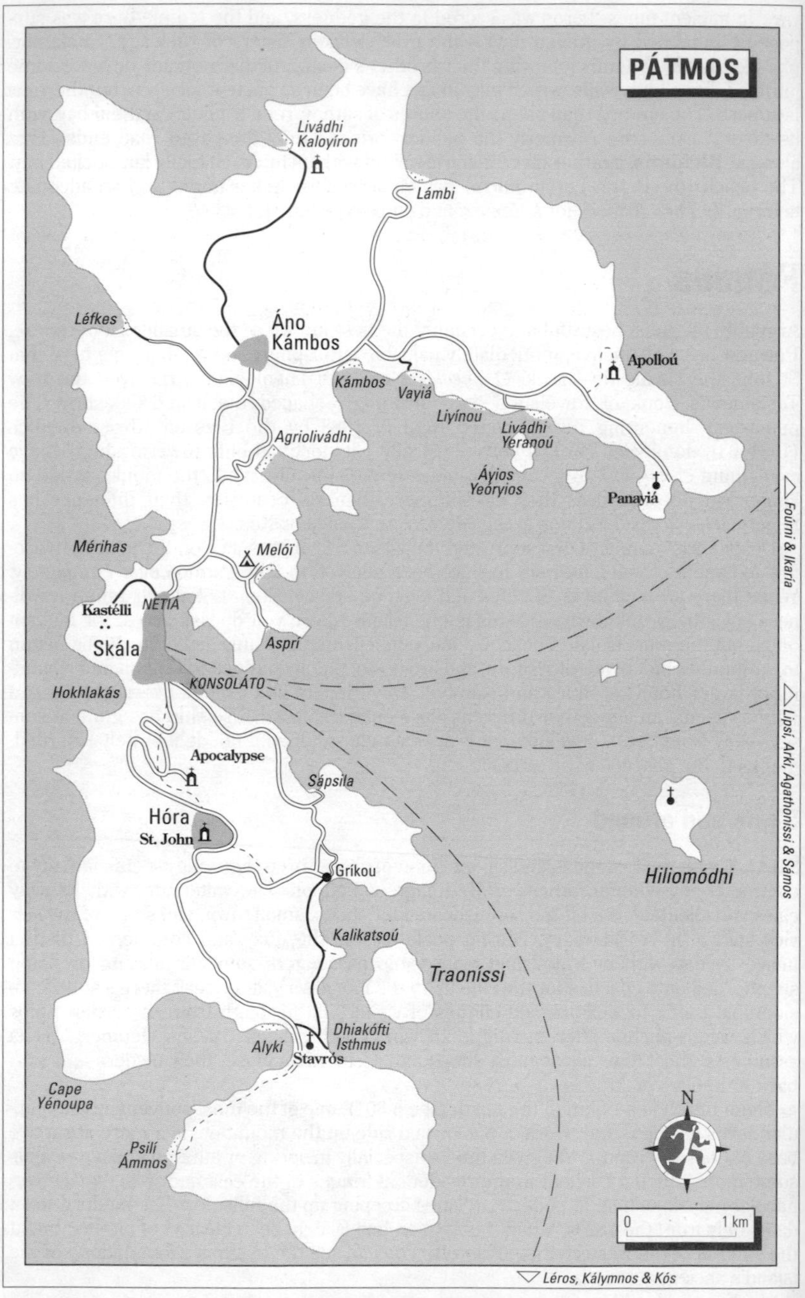
PÁTMOS
Livádhi Kaloyíron
Lámbi
Léfkes
Áno Kámbos
Apolloú
Kámbos
Vayiá
Liyínou
Livádhi Yeranoú
Agriolivádhi
Áyios Yeóryios
Panayiá
Foúrni & Ikaría
Mérihas
Melóï
Kastélli
NETIA
Skála
Aspri
Hokhlakás
KONSOLÁTO
Lipsí, Arkí, Agathoníssi & Sámos
Apocalypse
Sápsila
Hóra
St. John
Gríkou
Hiliomódhi
Kalikatsoú
Traoníssi
Dhiakófti Isthmus
Alykí
Stavrós
Cape Yénoupa
Psilí Ámmos
N
0
1 km
Léros, Kálymnos & Kós

Practicalities

Almost everything of interest can be found within, or within sight of, the Italian-built municipal "palace": large ferries anchor opposite, the port police occupy the east end, the **post office** one of its corners, while the fairly helpful municipal **tourist information** office (Mon–Sat 9am–1pm) takes up the back. Two banks each have cash dispensers. **Motorbike rental** outfits are common, with lowish rates (3000dr a day) owing to the modest size of the island. **Excursion boats** to Psilí Ámmos, Lipsí and Arkí/Maráthi all leave at about 10am from just in front of Astoria Travel and Apollon Travel, the two most reliable places handling Samos Hydrofoil tickets. G&A Ferries and the *Nissos Kalymnos*/DANE have separate agencies on, or just off, the central square.

ACCOMMODATION

Accommodation touts meet all ferries and hydrofoils, and their offerings tend to be a long walk distant and/or inland – not necessarily a bad thing, as no location is really remote, and anywhere near the waterfront, which doubles as the main road between Gríkou and Kámbos, will be noisy. Pátmos vernacular architecture is quite distinctive, but you wouldn't know it from most lodgings, bland if inoffensive rooms thrown up during the 1980s, with institutional (one might even say monastic) furnishings.

Establishments worth reserving in advance (they'll often then send a van to fetch you) are scattered across several districts. In **central Skála**, good hotel choices include the 1970s-vintage but quiet *Dhiethnes* (☎0247/31 357; ③), back in the fields, or the *Galini*, in a quiet cul-de-sac off the Hóra road (☎0247/31 240; ④).

Konsoláto district, east of the centre near the fishing anchorage, has more high-quality digs, though the worst noise from fishing boats and cruisers coming and going at 4am. Here you'll find the *Captain's House* (☎0247/31 793, fax 32 277; ④), with friendly management, better-than-average furnishings and car rental available, and the **Byzance** a few steps inland (☎0247/31 052; ④), with premises spread over two buildings – go for the larger rooms with balconies looking onto a garden. Some 150m further towards Gríkou, the *Blue Bay* (☎0247/31 165; ④) is not as well appointed but has calm, unbeatable sea views and Skála's only **Internet café** in its favour.

Netiá, the unglamorous area northwest between the power plant and Mérihas cove, is actually a good choice as a base. Various members of a Greek-Australian family run clustered establishments: the *Hotel Australis* (☎0247/31 576; ③), with full breakfast for the price and myriad small kindnesses that guarantee repeat clientele; and the adjacent *Villa Knossos* (☎0247/32 189; ③), whose rooms all have attractive terraces, or the simpler *Pension Sydney* (☎0247/31 139; ③). But the best standard in this area is provided by the *Hotel Asteri* (☎0247/32 465; ④), unimprovably set on a knoll overlooking the bay, in a well-landscaped environment that's also a working farm – guests have own-produced honey, eggs and tomatoes at breakfast.

Pebbly **Hokhlakás** bay, just a ten-minute walk southwest of the central market street, is perhaps the quietest district, with wonderful sunset views. Comfortable options here include the hillside *Summer* (☎0247/31 769; ④); the *Maria* down in the flatlands (☎0247/31 201; ④), where air conditioning and big sea-view balconies make up for tiny bathrooms; the budget en-suite rooms, right on the water, above the *Cactus Restaurant* (☎0247/33 059; ②); or Skála's top accommodation, the *Romeos* (☎0247/31 962; ⑤) on the southerly slope, with a pool, large common areas, and sizable units numerous enough that there's usually a vacancy. Hokhlakás isn't very swimmable; if you're keen to stay nearer a proper beach, there's a well-run, pleasantly set **campsite** (*Stefanos-Flowers*) at **MELÓÏ**, just down the slope from Pátmos's most exclusive digs: the *Porto Scoutari Hotel* (☎0247/33 124, fax 33 175; ⑥), a self-catering bungalow complex open all year, furnished with mock antiques and original art, and arrayed around a pool and sea views. Melóï has an excellent *mayireftá* taverna, *Melloi* (alias *Stefanos*): excellent, reasonably priced and open early or late in the season.

EATING AND DRINKING

Restaurant options are surprisingly limited in Skála; there are altogether too many *souvláki/yíros* joints and not enough good-value sit-down places. Easily the town's best is seafood-only *Ouzeri To Hiliomodhi*, just off the start of the Hóra road, with its vegetarian mezédhes and delicacies such as limpets (served live, be warned), grilled octopus and salted anchovies. Honourable mentions go to *Iy Kalia Kardhia*, well on the way to Hokhlakás, with grilled fish and meat served to a local crowd, and *Cactus* on the beach at Hokhlakás, doing nouvelle-minceur Italian snacks (don't show up too hungry) accompanied by Italian wines and apperitifs. Aside from that, you're best off heading 2km southeast to Sápsila bay, where *Benetos* (June–Sept; reserve on ☎0247/33 089) has since 1998 established a reputation as one of the best spots on the island for seafood and generic Mediterranean dishes. Back in town, the most reliable **breakfast** venue is the second, smaller platía beyond the main one, where *La Frianderie* serves hot drinks and croissants under medieval arches, and the adjacent bakery turns out terrific turnovers. The biggest and most durable **café-bar** is the wood-panelled, barn-like *Café Arion* on the waterside, where local youth play cards; others include open-air *Kafe Aman* in Konsoláto, with music and snacks, or indoor *Pepe Nero*, with a Greek soundtrack.

The monasteries and Hóra

Top of your sightseeing agenda is likely to be the monastery of St John, sheltered behind massive defences in the hilltop capital of Hóra. There is a regular KTEL bus up, or a forty-minute walk by a beautiful old cobbled path. To find its start, proceed through Skála towards Hokhlakás, and once past *Iy Kali Kardhia* bear left onto a lane starting opposite an ironmonger's; follow this uphill to its end on the main road – immediately opposite you'll see the cobbled path. Just over halfway, you might pause at the **monastery of the Apocalypse** (Mon, Wed, Fri & Sat 8am–1.30pm, Tues & Thurs 8am–1.30pm & 4–6pm, Sun 8am–noon & 4–6pm; free) built around the cave where St John heard the voice of God issuing from a cleft in the rock, and where he sat dictating his words to a disciple. In the cave wall, the presumed nightly resting place of the saint's head is fenced off and outlined in beaten silver.

This is merely a foretaste of the **monastery of St John** (Mon, Wed, Fri & Sat 8am–1.30pm, Tues & Thurs 8am–1.30pm & 4–6pm, Sun 8am–noon & 4–6pm; free daily 8am–2pm & Mon, Tues, Thurs & Sun 4–6pm). In 1088, the soldier-cleric Ioannis "The Blessed" Khristodhoulos was granted title to Pátmos by Byzantine Emperor Alexios Komnenos; within three years he and his followers had completed the essentials of the existing monastery, the threats of piracy and the Selçuk Turks dictating a heavily fortified style. A warren of interconnecting courtyards, chapels, stairways, arcades, galleries and roof terraces, it offers a rare glimpse of a Patmian interior; hidden in the walls are fragments of an ancient Artemis temple which stood here before being destroyed by Khristodhoulos. Off to one side, the **treasury** (same hours; 1200dr) justifies its hefty entrance fee for some with its magnificent array of religious treasure, mostly medieval icons of the Cretan school, but pride of place goes to an unusual mosaic icon of Áyios Nikólaos, and the eleventh-century parchment chrysobull (edict) of Emperor Alexios Komnenos, granting the island to Khristodhoulos.

Hóra

The promise of security afforded by St John's stout walls spurred the growth of **HÓRA** immediately outside the fortifications. It remains architecturally homogeneous, with cobbled lanes sheltering dozens of shipowners' mansions from the island's seventeenth- to eighteenth-century heyday. High, windowless walls and imposing wooden doors betray nothing of the opulence within: painted ceilings, pebble-mosaic terraces, flagstoned kitchens, and carved furniture. Inevitably touristic tattiness disfigures the main approaches to the monastery gate, but away from the principal thoroughfares are lanes that rarely see traffic, and by night, when the monastery ramparts are floodlit to startling effect, it's hard to think of a more beautiful Dodecanesian village. Neither should you miss the **view** from Platía Lódza (named after the remnant of an adjacent Venetian *loggia*), particularly at dawn or dusk. Landmasses to the north, going clockwise, include Ikaría, Thýmena, Foúrni, Sámos with the brooding mass of Mount Kérkis, Arkí, and the double-humped Samsun Dağı (ancient Mount Mykale) in Turkey.

Among several tavernas in Hóra, *Vangelis* on the inner square has a wonderful old jukebox, friendly service and view seating on various levels, but alas the cooking has declined of late; you'll probably eat better across the way at *Olympia* (which keeps unpredictable hours), or at *Balkoni* near the monastery. Again on the square, *Kafeteria Stoa* is minimally touristy despite its showcase interior, still functioning as the village kafenío. There are, however, very few places to **stay**; foreigners here are mostly long-term occupants, who have bought up and restored almost a third of the crumbling mansions since the 1960s. Getting a short-term room can be a pretty thankless task, even in spring or autumn; the best strategy is to contact *Vangelis* taverna early in the day, or phone ahead for reservations to Yeoryia Triandafyllou (☎0247/31 963; ③) or Marouso Kouva (☎0247/31 026; ③).

The rest of the island

Pátmos, as a locally published guide once memorably proclaimed, "is immense for those who know how to wander in space and time". Lesser mortals may find it easier to get around on foot, or by bus. There's still scope for **walking** despite a dwindling network of paths; otherwise a single **bus** offers surprisingly reliable service between Skála, Hóra, Kámbos and Gríkou – the main stop, with a posted timetable, is right in front of the main ferry dock.

After its extraordinary atmosphere and magnificent scenery, **beaches** are Patmos's principal attraction. From Hóra, a paved road (partly shortcut by a path) winds east to the sandiest part of rather overdeveloped and cheerless **GRÍKOU**, the main venue for Patmian package tourism – and shut tight as a drum come late September. The beach itself, far from the island's best, forms a narrow strip of hard-packed sand giving way to large pebbles towards the south. En route you pass the hillside *Flisvos* (aka *Floros*) taverna, going since the 1960s with a limited choice of inexpensive *mayireftá*, served on the terrace; they also have simple rooms (②) and fancier apartments (④) – reserve on ☎0247/31 380. Another good **accommodation** option here, open late in the year and not monopolized by packages, is the hillside *Hotel Golden Sun* (☎0247/32 318; ④), with most rooms facing the water.

From Hóra, you can ride a scooter over as far as the Dhiakoftí isthmus, beyond which a thirty-minute walk southwest leads to **Psilí Ámmos** beach. This is the only pure-sand cove on the island, with shade lent by tamarisks, nudism galore at the far south end and a good lunchtime **taverna** that occasionally does roast goat, freshly shot on the surrounding hills. There's also a summer kaïki service here from Skála, departing by 10am and returning at 5pm.

More good beaches are to be found in the north of the island, tucked into the startling eastern shoreline (west-facing bays are uniformly unusable); most are accessible from side roads off the main route north from Skála. **Melóï** is handy and quite appealing, with tamarisks behind the slender belt of sand, and good snorkelling offshore. The first beach beyond Méloï, **Agriolivádhi (Agriolívadho)**, has mostly sand at its broad centre, kayak rental, and two tavernas: one at mid-beach, the other (*O Glaros*, doing fish) on the south hillside. Hilltop Kámbos is the only other real village on the island, the focus of scattered farms in little oases all around; **Kámbos** beach, 600m downhill, is popular with Greeks, and the most developed remote resort on the island, with seasonal watersports facilities and tavernas (best of these *Ta Kavourakia*), though its appeal is diminished by the road just inland and a rock shelf in the shallows.

East of Kámbos are several less frequented coves, including pebble **Vayiá**, nudist **Liyínou** and sand and gravel **Livádhi Yeranoú**, the latter with more tamarisks, an excellent namesake taverna doing simple but clean grills and salads, and an islet to swim out to. From lower Kámbos you can also journey north to the bay of **Lámbi**, best for swimming when the prevailing wind is from the south, and renowned for an abundance of multicoloured volcanic stones – as well as one of the best beach **tavernas** on the island, *Lambi-Leonidas*, open May to October, with a wide range of fish, mezédhes and grilled meat.

Lipsí

Of the various islets to the north and east of Pátmos, **LIPSÍ** is the largest, most interesting and most populated, and the one that has the most significant summer tourist trade. The presence of a British package company, and the island's appearance on both main-line and off-line ferry routes, mean that it's unwise to show up in peak season without a reservation (though rooms proprietors meet arrivals at other times).

During quieter months, however, Lipsí still makes an idyllic halt, its sleepy pace making plausible a purported link between the island's name and that of Calypso, the nymph who legendarily held Odysseus in thrall. Deep wells provide water for many small farms, but there is only one flowing spring, and pastoral appearances are deceptive – four times the relatively impoverished full-time population of about six hundred live overseas (many in Tasmania, for some reason). Most of those who remain cluster around the fine harbour, as does most of the food and lodging.

A prime **accommodation** choice in all senses is Nikos' and Anna's welcoming *Apartments Galini* (☎0247/41 212, fax 41 012; ②), the first building you see above the ferry jetty; Nikos may take guests for fishing trips on request. Other good options not monopolized by package clients include *Rena's Rooms* (☎0247/41 363 or 41 120; ②), overlooking Liendoú beach, the *Flisvos Pension* at the east end of the port (☎0247/41 261; ②); the *Glaros* (☎0247/41 360; ②) on the hillside behind the *Kalypso Hotel/Restaurant*; and *Studios Paradise* (☎0247/41 125; ③), up on the ridge north of the *Dhelfini* restaurant which manages it. Top of the heap is the 1997-built *Aphrodite Hotel* (☎0247/41 000 or 41 394; ④), a studio-bungalow complex designed to accommodate package clients, though they're not adverse to walk-ins at slow times.

Among eight or so **tavernas**, mostly on or just behind the quay, *To Dhelfini* next to the police station and *O Yiannis* next to the eponymous rooms are the best all-rounders, with a good range of grilled items, appetizers and often local bulk wine (white or rosé). *Barbarosa*, on the slope near *Rena's Rooms*, does good vegetable-based *mayireftá*; while *Fish Restaurant* on the quay is reliably fresh. On the waterfront to either side of the *Kalypso*, kafenía and ouzeris with idiosyncratic decor (especially *Asprakis*) offer mezédhes outdoors – an atmospheric and almost obligatory pre-supper ritual. Later on, *The Rock* is the clear winner amongst a handful of **bars** for a congenial crowd and good taped music. Two licensed **travel agents** (Paradhisis and Laid Back) organize excursions and change money, though there's a free-standing Emboriki/Commercial cash dispenser near the former. The **post office** is up a stairway on the attractive cathedral platía, opposite a hilariously indiscriminate **ecclesiastical museum** (theoretically Mon–Fri 9.30am–1.30pm & 4–8pm, Sat/Sun 10am–2pm) featuring such "relics" as oil from the sanctuary on Mount Tabor and water from the Jordan River, as well as archeological finds and two letters from Greek revolutionary hero Admiral Miaoulis.

The island's **beaches** are rather scattered, though none is more than an hour's walk distant. Closest to town, and sandiest, are **Liendoú** and **Kámbos**, but many visitors prefer the attractive duo of **Katsadhiá** and **Papandhriá**, adjacent sand and pebble coves 2km south of the port, with an extremely basic taverna, *Andonis* (May–Sept), just inland from a musical café-bar, *Dilaila* (June–Sept), which dominates the main bay here and runs an informal pine-grove campsite (free but you must buy a snack from them daily).

An hour's walk along the paved road leading west from town brings you to protected **Platýs Yialós**, a small, shallow, sandy bay with a single taverna (June–Sept). During these months a pair of adapted transit vans provides a **minibus** service from the port to all the points cited above; otherwise you can rent a **scooter** from one of two outlets and point them towards isolated east-coast beaches. Of these, **Hokhlakoúra** consists of rather grubby shingle with no facilities, though nearby **Turkómnima** is better. A final ten-minute path scramble gets you from a rough track's end to **Monodhéndhri**, on the northeast coast, notable only for its lone juniper tree and nudist practice – though there's a superior, nameless cove just to the right.

A growing network of roads, paved or otherwise, rather limit opportunities for genuine path-**walks** through the undulating countryside, dotted with blue-domed churches. The most challenging route heads west from the pass between Kámbos and Platýs Yialós to the bay of **Kímisi** (3hr round-trip), where Filippos the octogenarian religious hermit dwells in a tiny monastery above the shore, next to the single island spring. A particularly ugly road has been bulldozed in from the north to disturb his solitude, and partly paved.

Arkí, Maráthi and Agathónissi

About two-thirds the size of Lipsí, **Arkí** is considerably more primitive, lacking drinking water, dynamo electricity (there are solar panels), ferry anchorage or much in the way of a village centre. Just 45 permanent inhabitants eke out a living here, mostly engaged in fishing, though catering for yacht parties attracted here by the superb anchorage is increasingly important. Arkí is an elective, once-weekly stop on the *Nissos Kalymnos* and Miniotis Lines routes: if you want to disembark here, you must warn the captain well in advance, so he can radio for the shuttle service from the island. Most visitors arrive by the more reliable supply boat from Pátmos, which actually docks at the quay. Of the three tavernas around the round harbourside platía, the better two – *Nikolas* (☎0247/32 477) and *O Trypas* ☎0247/32 230) – each control a handful of rooms (②), but avoid August when Italians and Greeks snap up every vacancy in advance. *Nikolas* is more food-orientated, with homemade puddings, while *O Trypas* doubles as the happening music pub, courtesy of the owner's enormous collection of CDs and tapes.

You can swim at the "Blue Lagoon" of **Tiganákia** at the southeast tip of the island – Paradise Travel's excursions stop there – but there are no real beaches to speak of on Arkí. The nearest sandy, tamarisk-shaded one is just offshore on the islet of **Maráthi**, where another pair of **tavernas** cater to day-trippers who come at least several times a week from Pátmos or Lipsí. *Marathi* (☎0247/31 580; ②), run by the engagingly piratical Mihalis Kavouras, is the more traditional, cosy outfit, with waterside seating and simple, adequate rooms; *Pantelis* (☎0247/32 609; ③) is plusher but more commercially minded, and only open June to October.

The small, steep-sided, waterless islet of **Agathoníssi (Gaïdharo)** is too remote – much closer to Turkey than Pátmos, in fact – to be a target of day excursions, though a few are advertised on Sámos. Intrepid German and Italian backpackers (some of whom return annually) form its main clientele, along with a steady trickle of yachts.

Even though hydrofoil connections dovetail well with appearances of the *Nissos Kalymnos*, you should count on staying two to three days, especially if the wind's up. Despite the lack of springs (cisterns are ubiquitous, topped up by tanker shipments from Rhodes), the island is greener and more fertile than apparent from the sea; mastic, carob and scrub oak on the heights overlooks two arable plains in the west. Just 140 people live here, down from several hundred before the last war, but those who've opted to stay seem determined to make a go of raising goats or fishing, and there are virtually no abandoned or neglected dwellings.

Most of the population lives in the hamlet of **MEGÁLO HORIÓ**, just visible on the ridge above the harbour of **Áyios Yeóryios**, and level with tiny **Mikró Horió**. Except for two café-restaurants (*Dhekatria Adherfia* being the more reliable) and the *Katsoulieri Pension* (☎0247/29 035; ②) in Megálo Horió, all amenities are in the port. Here the choice is between *Rooms Theoloyia Yiameou* (☎0247/29 005; ②), the vine-patioed *Hotel Maria Kamitsi* (☎0247/29 003; ②) or *George's Rooms* behind and inland (☎0247/29 064; ②). Worthy **eating/drinking** options in Áyios Yeóryios include *George's* (he of the rooms) near the jetty, local hangout *Limanaki* and the combination breakfast-café and bar, *Yetousa* (incidentally the ancient name for the islet).

With no wheeled transport for hire, exploring involves **walking** along the cement- or dirt-road network, or following a limited number of tracks and paths. If you don't swim at the port, which has the largest beach, you can walk twenty minutes southwest along a track to shingle-gravel **Spiliás**, or continue another quarter-hour along a faint path over the ridge to **Gaïdhourávlakos**, where nudists enjoy a gravel and sand cove. Bays in the east of the island, all served by the paved road system (occasionally shortcut by trails), tend to be dominated by fish farms; **Pálli** is the most pristine of these, though usually visited by boat trip. At **Thóli** in the far southeast, an hour-plus trek away, you can see an arcaded Byzantine structure, probably a combination granary and trading post, and by far the most venerable sight on Agathoníssi.

travel details

To simplify the lists below, several companies/boats have been left out. DANE or G&A provide a once-weekly link between Rhodes, Kós, Sámos and Thessaloníki, while NEL plies once weekly between Rhodes, Kós, Sámos, Híos, Lésvos, Límnos and Alexandhroúpoli.

The small, slow but reliable **Nissos Kalymnos** (cars carried) is the most regular lifeline of the smaller islands (aside from Kárpathos and Kássos) – it visits them all twice a week between mid-March and mid-January. This ship can be poorly publicized on islands other than its home port; if you encounter difficulties obtaining information, you should phone the central agency on Kálymnos (☎0243/29 612). Specimen schedules, observed for some years now, are as follows:

Mid-March to April, and mid-Sept to mid-Jan: Mon and Fri 7am, leaves Kálymnos for Kós, Níssyros, Tílos, Sými, Rhodes; out to Kastellórizo late afternoon, turns around at midnight. Tues and Sat 9am, departs Rhodes for Sými, Tílos, Níssyros, Kós, Kálymnos, with a Tues evening return trip to Astypálea. Wed and Sun departs Kálymnos 7am for Léros, Lipsí, Pátmos, Arkí (Wed only), Agathónissi, Pythagório (Sámos), returning from Sámos at 2.30pm bound for Kálymnos via the same islands. Thurs 7am from Kálymnos to Astypálea.

May to mid-June: Mon and Fri 7am, leaves Kálymnos for Kós, Níssyros, Tílos, Sými, Rhodes; out to Kastellórizo late afternoon, turns around at midnight. Tues and Sat 9am, departs Rhodes for Sými, Tílos, Níssyros, Kós, Kálymnos, with an evening return trip both days to Astypálea. Wed and Sun departs Kálymnos 7am for Léros, Lipsí, Pátmos, Arkí (Wed only), Agathónissi, Pythagório (Sámos), returning from Sámos at 2.30pm bound for Kálymnos via the same islands. Thurs, idle.

Mid-June to mid-Sept: Mon and Thurs 7am, leaves Kálymnos for Kós, Níssyros, Tílos, Sými, Rhodes; out to Kastellórizo late afternoon, turns around at midnight. Tues and Fri 9am, departs Rhodes for Sými, Tílos, Níssyros, Kós, Kálymnos, with an evening return trip both days to Astypálea. Wed and Sun departs Kálymnos 7am for Léros, Lipsí, Pátmos, Arkí (Wed only), Agathónissi, Pythagório (Sámos), returning from Sámos at 2.30pm bound for Kálymnos via the same islands. Sat, idle.

Large ferries

Be aware that the following frequencies are only valid for the period mid-June to mid-September; in spring or autumn some of the more esoteric links, such as Astypálea to Tílos/Níssyros, or Lipsí to Sými, will not be operating.

Agathoníssi 1 weekly on Miniotis Lines to Arkí, Lipsí, Pátmos, Sámos (Pythagório).

Astypálea 3–5 weekly to Amorgós, Náxos, Páros & Pireás, 1 to Mýkonos and Sýros, on one of 3 companies; 1–2 weekly to Kós, Kálymnos, Rhodes, Níssyros and Tílos on DANE or G&A.

Hálki 1–2 weekly to Rhodes Town, Kárpathos (both ports), Kássos, Crete and Mílos, all subject to cancellation in bad weather. Once-daily kaïki (6am) to Rhodes (Kámiros Skála).

Kálymnos Similar ferry service to Kós, plus at least 1 weekly to Astypálea, Amorgós (both ports), Náxos, Páros, Sýros; 3 daily ro-ro ferries, well-spaced, to Mastihári; daily morning kaïki to Psérimos; and a daily kaïki (1pm) from Myrtiés to Xirókambos on Léros.

Kárpathos (both ports) and Kássos 2–3 weekly with each other, Crete (Áyios Nikólaos and/or Sitía), Mílos and Rhodes Town, on LANE; 1–2 weekly to Hálki on LANE.

Kastellórizo (Méyisti) 1–2 weekly to Rhodes; 1–2 weekly to Pireás indirectly, via select Dodecanese and Cyclades.

Kós 7–14 weekly to Rhodes and Pireás on G&A or DANE; at least daily to Kálymnos, Léros and Pátmos on G&A or DANE; 1 weekly to Tílos, Níssyros and Sými on DANE or G&A; 1 weekly on G&A or DANE to Astypálea, Sými, Níssyros, Tílos; 3 daily ro-ro ferries year-round from Mastihári to Kálymnos; 1–2 daily from Kós Town to Kálymnos; 4 weekly islanders' kaïkia from Kardhámena to Níssyros.

Léros 7–14 weekly to Pireás, Pátmos, Kálymnos, Kós and Rhodes on G&A or DANE; seasonal daily excursion boats from Ayía Marína to Lipsí and Pátmos (2pm), and from Xirókambos to Myrtiés on Kálymnos (7.30am).

Lipsí 1 weekly to Léros, Kálymnos, Kós, Pátmos, Tílos, Níssyros on DANE or G&A; 1 weekly to Sámos (Vathý) on Nomicos Lines.

Níssyros and Tílos Same as for Sými, plus excursion boats between Níssyros and Kós as follows: to Kardhámena daily at 3.30–4pm; to Kéfalos 4 weekly at 4pm; 4–6 weekly to Kós Town (all of these are seasonal and expensive). The islanders' much cheaper "shopping" kaïki, the *Chrissula*, leaves 4–5 times weekly at 7am.

Pátmos Similar ferry service to Léros, with the addition of 1 weekly to Foúrni, Arkí, Lipsí, Sámos (Pythagório); seasonal tourist boats to Sámos (Pythagório), Lipsí, Arkí and Maráthi on a daily basis; Mon–Thur only to Arkí in low season.

Rhodes 10–12 weekly to Kós and Pireás on G&A or DANE; 7–10 weekly to Kálymnos on G&A or DANE; daily to Léros and Pátmos; 2 weekly to Kárpathos, Kássos, Hálki, Crete (Sitía or Áyios Nikólaos) on LANE; 1–2 weekly to Sými, Lipsí, Tílos, Níssyros, Astypálea on G&A or DANE; 2–3 weekly to Santoríni, Náxos, Páros.

Sými 1–2 weekly to Rhodes, Tílos, Níssyros, Kós, Kálymnos, Léros, Lipsí, Pátmos and Pireás on G&A Ferries or DANE; at least daily catamaran or hydrofoil run by ANES to Rhodes.

Hydrofoils

Two hydrofoil companies, Dodecanese Hydrofoils and Samos Hydrofoils, serve the Dodecanese between mid-May and mid-October, operating out of Rhodes, Kós, Kálymnos and Sámos.

Dodecanese Hydrofoils have three craft, whose schedules are accordingly more complicated; in peak season, there is a daily link Kós–Rhodes and back, usually south in the morning and north in the evening; another craft leaves Kálymnos early in the morning for Kós and a selection of islands north to Pythagório on Sámos; while the third hydrofoil leaves Rhodes at 8am for Kós, returning in the evening; another leaves Kálymnos or Kós at 7 or 8am for Sámos (Pythagório) via select islands, returning at 2.30pm; while the third craft tends to serve a changing cast among the small Dodecanese between Kálymnos and Rhodes, including, once or twice weekly, Hálki, Sými, Tílos, Níssyros and even Astypálea, though some of these runs can get completely booked by transfers of package tour groups. For current routes and schedules, phone ☎0242/25 920.

Samos Hydrofoils, with their GM Caterpillar engines, tend to be more reliable than the Russian-powered Dodecanese Hydrofoils, which did, however, go under new, improved management in 1999. Typically, one craft of Sámos Hydrofoils leaves that island at 7am, reaching Kós along a varying itinerary by 11am or noon, returning via the same islands at 1 or 2pm. Their other craft, based in Kós, departs northward between 7.30am and 8.30am, reaching Pythagório at about 11am and returning via the same ports of call between 1.30pm and 2.30pm. Two to four days weekly, remote or minor ports such as Foúrni, Ikaría, Agathoníssi and Lipsí are served. For precise routes and schedules, ring ☎0273/27 337.

Flights

Note: All are on Olympic Aviation/Olympic Airways unless stated otherwise.

Kárpathos 1–2 daily to Rhodes; 4 weekly to Kássos; 3 weekly to Athens on Olympic, 2 weekly to Athens on Air Manos.

Kássos 1–2 weekly to Kárpathos; 4 weekly to Rhodes.

Kastellórizo (Meyísti) 1 daily to Rhodes June–Sept, 3 weekly otherwise.

Kós 2–3 daily to Athens.

Léros 1 daily to Athens.

Rhodes On Olympic, 5 daily to Athens; 4 weekly to Iráklion; 4–5 weekly to Santoríni; 2 weekly to Thessaloníki; 2 weekly to Mýkonos. On Air Greece, 2 daily to Athens; 3 weekly to Iráklion; 1 daily to Thessaloníki. On Cronus Air, 2 daily to Athens.

International ferries

Kós 2–14 weekly to Bodrum, Turkey (45min), one of the most expensive island–Anatolia services despite the short distance. Greek boat leaves 9am, returns 4pm; £36/$60 return, Greek tax inclusive, £26/$44 one-way; no cheap day-return, no Turkish port tax. Turkish boat, departing 4.30pm, is cheaper at 15,000dr return, 10,000dr one-way, tax inclusive, and provides the only service in winter.

Rhodes Daily in summer to Marmaris, Turkey (1hr) by Greek hydrofoil; £20/$34 one-way, £24/$40 return, plus $10 Turkish port tax. Two to three days weekly a small Turkish ferry (cars carried) puts in appearances. Also 2–3 weekly to Limassol, Cyprus (18hr) and Haifa, Israel (39hr).

CHAPTER FIVE

THE EAST AND NORTH AEGEAN

The seven substantial islands and four minor islets scattered off the north Aegean coast of Asia Minor and northeastern Greece form a rather arbitrary archipelago. Although there are some passing similarities in architecture and landscape, the strong individual character of each island is far more striking. Despite their proximity to modern Turkey, members of the group bear few signs of an Ottoman heritage, especially when compared with Rhodes and Kós. There's the occasional mosque, often shorn of its minaret, but by and large the enduring Greekness of these islands is testimony to the 4000-year Hellenic presence in Asia Minor, which ended only in 1923. This heritage is regularly referred to by the Greek government in an intermittent propaganda war with Turkey over the sovereignty of these far-flung outposts. Tensions here are occasionally worse than in the Dodecanese, aggravated by potential undersea oil deposits in the straits between the islands and the Anatolian mainland. The Turks have also persistently demanded that Límnos, astride the sea lanes to and from the Dardanelles, be demilitarized, but so far Greece has shown no signs of giving in.

The heavy military presence can be disconcerting, and despite the growth of tourism, large tracts of land remain off-limits as military reserves. But as in the Dodecanese, local tour operators do a thriving business shuttling passengers for inflated tariffs between the easternmost islands and the Turkish coast with its amazing archeological sites and busy resorts. Most of these islands' main ports and towns are not quaint, picturesque spots, but urbanized administrative, military and commercial

ACCOMMODATION PRICE CODES

Throughout the book we've used the following **price codes** to denote the cheapest available double room in each establishment in high season. Out of season, rates can drop by more than fifty percent, especially if you are staying for three or more nights. Single rooms, where available, cost around seventy percent of the price of a double.

Rented private rooms on the islands usually fall into the ② or ③ categories, depending on their location and facilities, and the season; a few in the ④ category are more like plush self-catering apartments. They are not generally available from late October through to the beginning of April, when only hotels tend to remain open.

① Up to 6000dr	④ 12,000–16,000dr
② 6000–9000dr	⑤ 16,000–20,000dr
③ 9000–12,000dr	⑥ 20,000dr and upwards

Note: Youth hostels typically charge 2000–2500dr for a dormitory bed.
For more accommodation details, see p.44–47.

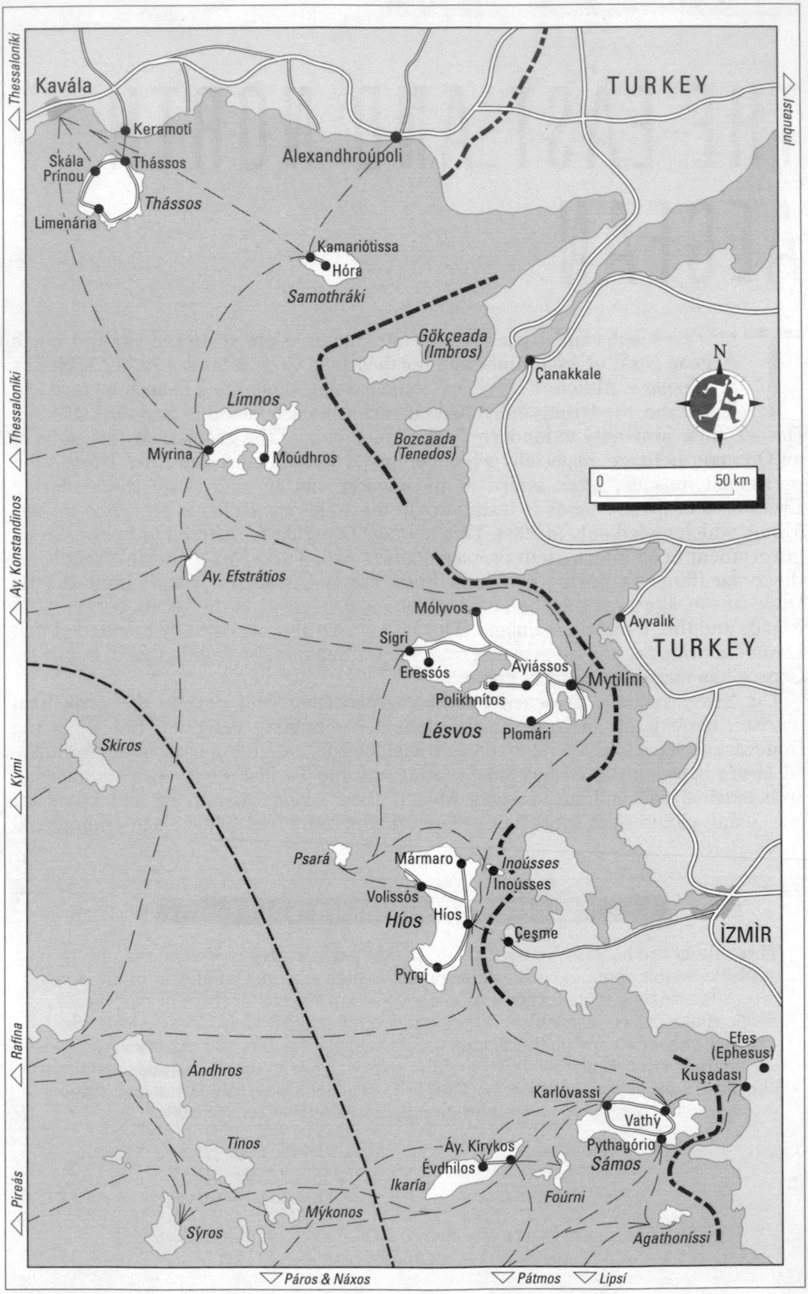

Thessaloníki
Kavála
TURKEY
Istanbul
Keramotí
Skála Prínou
Thássos
Alexandhroúpoli
Thássos
Limenária
Kamariótissa
Hóra
Samothráki
Gökçeada (Imbros)
N
Çanakkale
Límnos
Thessaloníki
Bozcaada (Tenedos)
Mýrina
Moúdhros
0
50 km
Ay. Konstandínos
Ay. Efstrátios
Mólyvos
Ayvalık
Sígri
TURKEY
Eressós
Ayiássos
Mytilíni
Polikhnítos
Lésvos
Plomári
Skíros
Kými
Psará
Mármaro
Inoússes
Inoússes
Volissós
Híos
Híos
Çeşme
İZMİR
Pyrgí
Rafína
Efes (Ephesus)
Ándhros
Kuşadası
Karlóvassi
Vathý
Tínos
Pythagório
Áy. Kírykos
Évdhilos
Sámos
Pireás
Ikaría
Foúrni
Mýkonos
Sýros
Agathoníssi
Páros & Náxos
Pátmos
Lipsí

centres. In most cases you should suppress any initial impulse to take the next boat out, and press on into the interiors.

Sámos is the most visited island of the group, but if you can leave the crowds behind, is still arguably the most verdant and beautiful. **Ikaría** to the west remains relatively unspoiled, if a minority taste, and nearby **Foúrni** is a haven for determined solitaries, as are the Híos satellites **Psará** and **Inoússes**, neither of which have any package tourism. **Híos** itself offers far more cultural interest than any of its southern neighbours, but its natural beauty has been ravaged by fires, and the development of tourism was until the late 1980s deliberately retarded. **Lésvos** may not impress initially, though once you get a feel for its old-fashioned, Anatolian ambience, you may find it hard to leave. By contrast virtually no foreigners and few Greeks visit **Áyios Efstrátios**, and with good reason. **Límnos** to the north is a bit livelier, but its appeal is confined mostly to the area around the attractive port town. To the north, Samothráki and Thássos are totally isolated from the others, except via the mainland ports of Kavála or Alexandhroúpoli, and remain easier to visit from northern Greece. **Samothráki** has one of the most dramatic seaward approaches of any Greek island, and one of the more important ancient sites. **Thássos** is more varied, with sandy beaches, mountain villages and minor archeological sites.

Sámos

The lush and seductive island of Sámos was formerly joined to Asia Minor, until sundered from Mount Mykale opposite by Ice Age cataclysms; the resulting 2500-metre strait is now the narrowest distance between Greece and Turkey in the Aegean, except at Kastellórizo. There's little tangible evidence of it today, but Sámos was also once the wealthiest island in the Aegean and, under the patronage of the tyrant Polykrates, home to a thriving intellectual community: Epicurus, Pythagoras, Aristarchus and Aesop were among the residents. Decline set in as the star of Classical Athens was in the ascendant, though Sámos's status was improved somewhat in early Byzantine times when it constituted its own *theme* (imperial administrative district). Towards the end of the fifteenth century, the Genoese abandoned the island to the mercies of pirates; following their attacks, Sámos remained almost uninhabited until 1562, when an Ottoman admiral received permission from the sultan to repopulate it with Greek Orthodox settlers recruited from various corners of the empire.

The heterogeneous descent of today's islanders largely explains an enduring identity crisis and a rather thin topsoil of indigenous culture. Most of the village names are either clan surnames, or adjectives indicating origins elsewhere – constant reminders of refugee descent. Consequently there is no genuine Samiote music, dance or dress, and little that's original in the way of cuisine and architecture. The Samiotes compensated somewhat for their deracination by fighting fiercely for independence during the 1820s, but, despite their accomplishments in sinking a Turkish fleet in the narrow strait and annihilating a landing army, the Great Powers handed the island back to the Ottomans in 1830, with the consoling proviso that it be semi-autonomous, ruled by an appointed Christian prince. This period, referred to as the *Iyimonía* (Hegemony), was marked by a mild renaissance in fortunes, courtesy of the hemp and tobacco trades. However, union with Greece, the ravages of a bitter World War II occupation and mass emigration effectively reversed the recovery until tourism appeared on the horizon during the 1980s.

Today the Samian economy is increasingly dependent on package **tourism**, far too much of it in places; the eastern half of the island, and much of the south coast, has pretty much surrendered to the onslaught of holidaymakers, although the more rugged northwestern part has retained much of its undeveloped grandeur. The rather

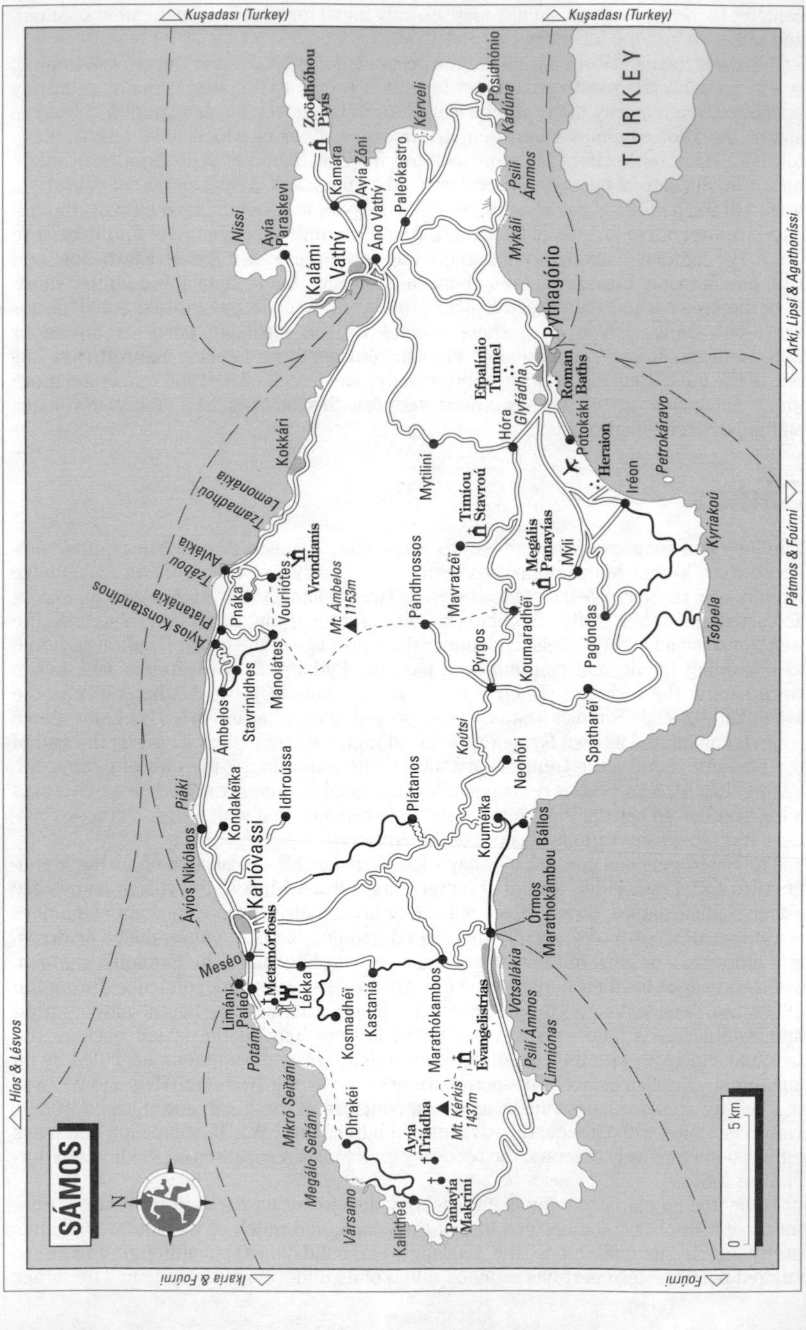
SÁMOS
N
Kuşadası (Turkey)
Kuşadası (Turkey)
TURKEY
Híos & Lésvos
Ikaria & Foúrni
Foúrni
Pátmos & Foúrni
Arkí, Lipsí & Agathonissi
Karlóvassi
Vathý
Pythagório
Kalámi
Ayía Paraskeví
Nissí
Kamára
Zoödhóhou Piyís
Ayía Zóni
Áno Vathý
Paleókastro
Kérveli
Posidhónio
Kadúna
Psilí Ámmos
Mykáli
Evpalínio Tunnel
Roman Baths
Glyfádha
Hóra
Potokáki
Heraion
Iréon
Petrokáravo
Mytilíni
Timíou Stavroú
Kokkári
Lemonákia
Tzamadhoú
Aviákia
Tzábou
Platanákia
Áyios Konstandínos
Vrondianís
Vourliótes
Pnáka
Manolátes
Stavrinídhes
Ámbelos
Mt. Ámbelos 1153m
Pándhrossos
Mavratzéï
Megális Panayías
Mýli
Kyriakoú
Tsópela
Pagóndas
Koumaradhéï
Pýrgos
Spatharéï
Koútsi
Neohóri
Plátanos
Idhroússa
Kondakéïka
Piáki
Áyios Nikólaos
Metamórfosis
Meséo
Limáni
Paleó
Potámi
Lékka
Kosmadhéï
Kastaniá
Marathókambos
Ormos Marathokámbou
Koumëika
Bállos
Votsalákia
Psilí Ámmos
Limniónas
Evangelistrías
Mt. Kérkis 1437m
Mikró Seïtáni
Megálo Seïtáni
Dhrakéï
Ayía Triádha
Panayía Makriní
Kallithéa
Vársamo
0
5 km

sedate, couples-orientated clientele is overwhelmingly German, Scandinavian, Swiss and Dutch, with a small number of Brits. The absence of an official campsite on such a large island, tame nightlife a world away from that in the Cyclades and phalanxes of self-catering villas hint at the sort of custom expected.

Getting there and getting around

Sámos **airport** lies 14km southwest of Vathý and 3km west of Pythagório. There are no fewer than three **ferry ports**: Karlóvassi in the west, plus Vathý and Pythagório in the east, making it a major hub for travel in every direction. All ferries between Pireás, the Cyclades, Ikaría and Sámos call at both Karlóvassi and Vathý, as do the smaller Miniotis Line ferries linking the island with Híos and, at high season, Foúrni and Ikaría. Vathý also receives the weekly G&A or NEL sailing between northern Greece and the Dodecanese, via most intervening islands, the weekly DANE ferry between Thessaloníki and Rhodes, plus hydrofoils and small ferries from Kuşadası. Pythagório siphons off a bit of the Turkey shipping in high season, and additionally sees two regular weekly ferry connections from as far south as Kós in the Dodecanese, plus a seasonal Miniotis service to Lipsí and Agathonísi. Both ports have hydrofoil services: Vathý is the home base of Samos Hydrofoils, Pythagório the northerly touch-point for Dodecanese Hydrofoils, both lines extending down to Kós.

The **bus terminals** in Pythagório and Vathý lie within walking distance of the ferry dock; at Karlóvassi, you must make your own way the 3km into town from the port. There is no airport bus service; **taxi** fares to various points are stipulated, and in high season taxis to the airport or docks must be booked several hours in advance. The KTEL service itself is excellent along the Pythagório–Vathý and Vathý–Kokkári–Karlóvassi via routes, but poor otherwise; with numerous car and motorbike rental outlets, it's easy to find a good deal outside July or August.

Vathý

Lining the steep northeastern shore of a deep bay, beachless **VATHÝ** is a busy provincial town which grew from a minor anchorage after 1830, when it replaced Hóra as the island's capital. It's an unlikely and somewhat ungraceful resort, which has seen several hotel bankruptcies of late, and minimally interesting for the most part – although the pedestrianized bazaar, tiers of surviving Neoclassical houses and the hill suburb of **ÁNO VATHÝ**, a separate community of tottering, tile-roofed houses have some attraction – and the only real highlight is the excellent **archeological museum** (Tues–Sun 9am–2.30pm; 800dr), set behind the small central park beside the restored Neoclassical town hall. One of the best provincial collections in Greece is housed in both the old Paskhallion building and a modern wing across the way, specially constructed to house the star exhibit: a majestic, five-metre-tall *kouros*, discovered out at the Heraion sanctuary (see p.318). The *kouros*, the largest free-standing effigy to survive from ancient Greece, was dedicated to Apollo, but found together with a devotional mirror to Mut (the Egyptian equivalent of Hera) from a Nile workshop, one of only two discovered in Greece to date.

In the compelling **small-objects collection** of the Paskhallion, more votive offerings of Egyptian design prove trade and pilgrimage links between Sámos and the Nile valley going back to the eighth century BC. The Mesopotamian and Anatolian origins of other artwork confirm the exotic trend, most tellingly in a case full of ivory miniatures: Perseus and Medusa in relief, a kneeling, perfectly formed mini-*kouros*, a pouncing lion and a drinking horn with a bull's head. The most famous local artefacts are the dozen or so bronze griffin-heads, for which Sámos was the major centre of production in the seventh century BC; mounted on the edge of bronze cauldrons, they were believed to ward off evil spirits.

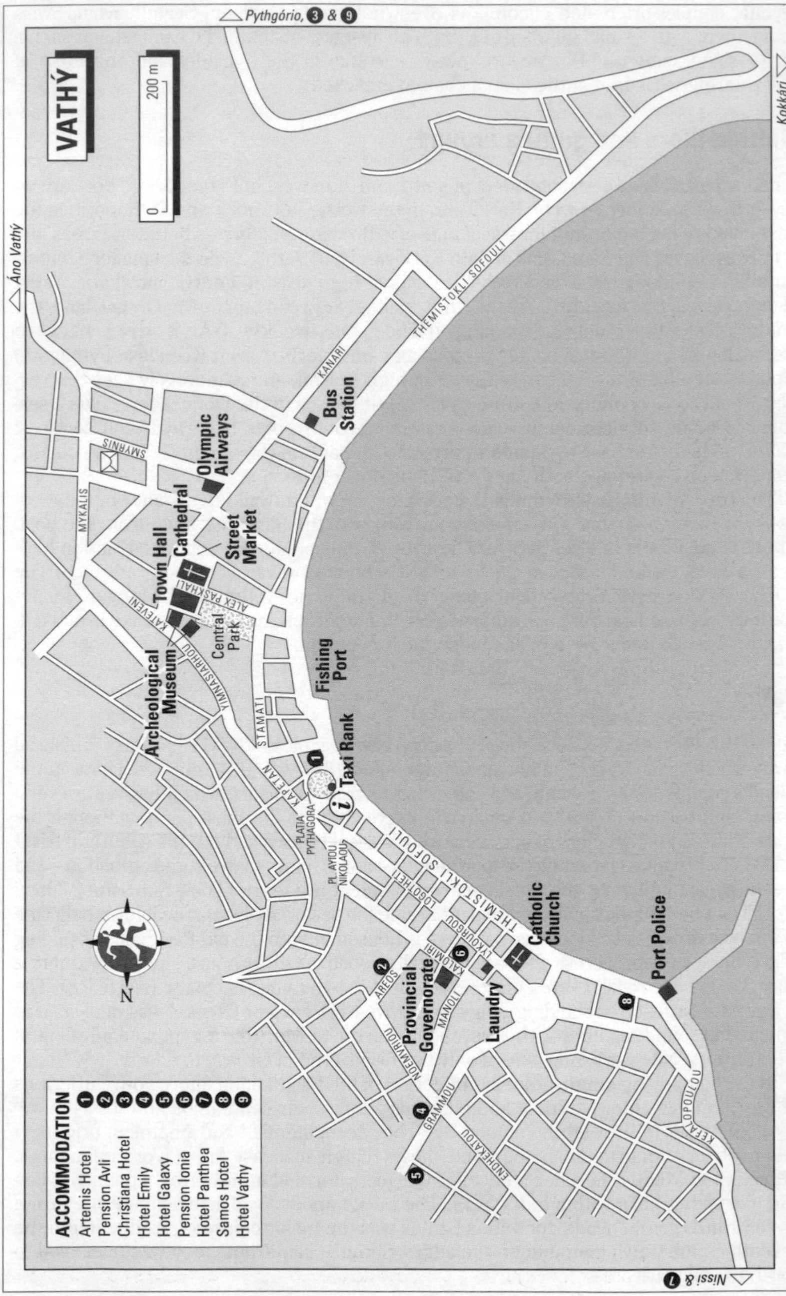
VATHÝ
0
200 m
Pythgório, 3 & 9
Áno Vathý
Kokkári
Nissi & 7
N
THEMISTOKLI SOFOULI
KANARI
Bus Station
Olympic Airways
SMYRNIS
MYKALIS
Town Hall
Cathedral
Street Market
ALEX PASKHALI
KATEVENI
Central Park
Archeological Museum
YIMNASIARHOU
STAMATI
Fishing Port
Taxi Rank
KAPETAN
PLATIA PYTHAGORA
PL. AYIOU NIKOLAOU
LOGOTHETI
THEMISTOKLI SOFOULI
Catholic Church
Port Police
LYKOURGOU
KALOMIRI
Provincial Governorate
MANOLI
Laundry
AREOS
NOEMVRIOU
GRAMMOU
ENDHEKATOU
KEFALOPOULOU
ACCOMMODATION
Artemis Hotel 1
Pension Avli 2
Christiana Hotel 3
Hotel Emily 4
Hotel Galaxy 5
Pension Ionia 6
Hotel Panthea 7
Samos Hotel 8
Hotel Vathy 9

Practicalities

From the **ferry dock** the shore boulevard – Themistoklí Sofoúli – describes a 1300-metre arc around the bay. About 400m along is the traffic circle of Platía Pythagóra, distinguished by its lion statue; some 800m along there's a major turning inland to the **KTEL** terminal, a chaos of buses at a perennially cluttered intersection by the ticket office. The **tourist information** office is at 25-Martíou 4 (May–Oct Mon–Fri 9am–2pm; winter sporadic hours), worth a stop for leaflets, comprehensive bus and ferry schedules and accommodation listings.

The most useful waterfront **ferry/travel agents** for independent travellers are Pythagoras Tours (☎0273/27 337) under the old Catholic church, handling G&A and NEL boats, plus any hydrofoils to Híos; Samos Tours-Horiatopoulos, opposite the jetty, have helpful, native-English-speaking staff and sell most other boat tickets except Agapitos and NEL Lines; By Ship (☎0273/27 337) sells tickets for DANE and Nomikos ferries, as well as being the main agent for Air Manos and Samos Hydrofoils. At present Miniotis Lines representation is in flux; try Nautica or Soutos, both near the *Samos Hotel*. Vathý is chock-a-block with **bike** and **car rental** franchises, which keeps rates reasonable, especially off-season. For motorbikes, try Aramis (☎0273/22 682 at Themistoklí Sofoúli 5, with a large fleet and recovery service, while for mountain bikes stop at Yiannis at no. 12 (☎0273/23 756). For cars, the preferred outlets are Budget at Themistoklí Sofoúli 31 (☎0273/28 856), Holiday Autos (☎0273/28 833) on Sofoúlis, with branches island wide, or the similarly far-flung Autoplan, a division of Samina Tours (☎0273/23 555). Other amenities include the **post office** on Smýrnis, inland from the Olympic terminal, four waterfront **banks** with cash dispensers and a self-serve **laundry** on pedestrianized Lykoúrgou Logothéti.

ACCOMMODATION

Most **accommodation** available to independent travellers clusters in the hillside district of Katsoúni, more or less directly above the ferry dock; except in August, you'll have little trouble finding affordable vacancies. Budget choices include the rock-bottom, waterfront *Hotel Artemis* (☎0273/27 792; ②) just off "Lion Square"; the *Pension Ionia* (☎0273/28 782; ②), inland at Manoli Kalomíri 5; and the *Pension Avli* (☎0273/22 939; ① non-ensuite, ② en-suite), a wonderful period piece up a nearby stair-street at Aréos 2, the former convent school of the French nuns who ran the Catholic church until 1973.

None of these outfits are palaces by any means; for more luxury start at the surprisingly affordable *Hotel Galaxy* (☎0273/22 665; ③–④), at Angéou 1 near the top of Katsoúni, set in garden surroundings and with a small pool, though you'll have to dodge package allotments. If they're full, try the sympathetic *Emily*, just downhill at the top of Grámmou (☎0273/24 691; ③), a small, personable outfit with a roof garden. The *Samos Hotel* (☎0273/28 377; ③) right by the ferry dock, drops its rates to ② off-season, and is open all year, if a bit noisy. Further afield and a taxi ride uphill, the *Christiana* (☎0273/27 149; ④), the only hotel in Áno Vathý, has a ravine setting, large pool and tie-in (ie discounts) with Budget Car Rental. Some 400m away in Neápoli district near the cemetery, the *Vathy* (☎0273/28 124; ③) is another good choice for its balconied rooms with bay view, small pool and friendly family management. Finally, in Kalámi district 3km north of town, the tiny *Panthea* (☎0273/22 225; ③) enjoys a rural setting, though you'll need transport and advance booking to squeeze in between packages.

Eating and drinking

The only waterfront **tavernas** worth a second glance, at extreme opposite ends of town, are *To Kalami* in the namesake suburb, just before the *Hotel Panthea*, with surprisingly good *mayireftá* and grills, and the pricier *Apanemia Ouzeri*, at the far southwest end of the shore boulevard, with interesting and rather rich recipes – go hungry.

Inland, at the Plátanos junction en route to Áno Vathý, *Ta Kotopoula* is a congenial all-round taverna featuring chicken (as in the name) and mezédhes, open most of the year – most others are shut November to April. Vathý's **nightlife** revolves around its waterfront bars, the longest lived of these being *Escape*, on a sea-view terrace at Kefalopoúlou 9 (north of the jetty). The Cine Olympia, inland on Yimnasiarhou Kateveni, is plushly fitted and operates all year with a variable programme of films. There are also two **Internet cafés**: Dhiavlos at Emmanouíl Sofoúli 15, near Olympic Airways, and NetCafe at Themistoklí Sofoúli 175, at the south end of the front.

Around Vathý

The immediate environs of Vathý offer some modest beaches and small hamlets, though you'll usually need your own transport to visit. Two kilometres east and uphill spreads the vast inland plateau of **Vlamarí**, devoted to vineyards and supporting the hamlets of Ayía Zóni and Kamára; from the latter you can climb up a partly cobbled path to the clifftop **monastery of Zoödhóhou Piyís**, for superb views across the end of the island to Turkey.

Heading north out of Vathý, the narrow road ends after 7km at the pebble bay and fishing port of **AYÍA PARASKEVÍ** (or Nissí), with good swimming. Of two tavernas here, *Nissi/O Glaros*, is one of the best this end of the island, with grilled meats and seafoods, well-selected *vegetarian* mezédhes and cheerful terrace service; there's live music at weekends, and it's open weekends in winter.

As you head southeast from Vathý along the main island loop road, the triple chapel at **Trís Ekklisíes** marks an important junction, with another fork 100m along the left-hand turning. Bearing left twice takes you through the hilltop village of Paleókastro, 3km beyond which is another junction. Forking left yet again, after another 3km you reach the quiet, striking bay of **Kérveli**, with a small beach, a pair of tavernas (the friendly *Sea and Dolphins* has good mezédhes and *soúma*, the local spirit) by the water and another characterful favourite with simple grills only, *Iy Kryfi Folia*, about 500m uphill along the access road. Taking the right forks leads to **Posidhónio**, with an even smaller beach and another pair of tavernas (the right-hand one takes its cooking more seriously). Turning right at the junction before Paleókastro leads to the beaches of Mykáli and Psilí Ámmos, the only spots in this section with a bus service. **Mykáli**, a kilometre of windswept sand and gravel, has been encumbered with three package hotels; the best place to try on spec here is *Villa Barbara* (☎0273/25 192; ④), apartments behind the *Sirenes Beach* hotel. **Psilí Ámmos**, further east around the headland, is a crowded, sandy cove backed by several commercial tavernas; if you swim to the islet beware of strong currents which sweep through the narrow straits.

Pythagório and around

Most traffic south of Vathý heads for **PYTHAGÓRIO**, the island's premier resort, renamed in 1955 to honour native son Pythagoras, ancient mathematician, philosopher and mystic. Until then it was known as Tigáni (Frying Pan) – in mid-summer you'll learn why. The sixth-century BC tyrant Polykrates had his capital here, now subject to excavations which have forced modern Pythagório to expand northeast and uphill. The village core of cobbled lanes and thick-walled mansions abuts a small **harbour**, fitting almost perfectly into the confines of Polykrates' ancient port, but today devoted almost entirely to pleasure craft and overpriced cocktail bars.

Sámos's most complete **castle**, the nineteenth-century *pýrgos* of local chieftain Lykourgos Logothetis, overlooks both the town and the shoreline. Logothetis, together with a certain "Kapetan Stamatis" and Admiral Kanaris, chalked up decisive victories over the Turks in the summer of 1824. The final battle was won on Transfiguration Day (6 August), and accordingly the church inside the castle precinct is dedicated to this festival. More antiquities include the fairly dull **Roman baths**, signposted as "Thermai", 400m west of town (Tues–Sun 8.30am–2.45pm; free) and a minuscule **archeological collection** in the town hall on Platía Irínis (Tues–Thur & Sun 9am–2pm, Fri–Sat 10am–2pm; free). Considerably more interesting is the **Efpalínio tunnel** (Tues–Sun 8.45am–2.30pm; 500dr), a 1040-metre aqueduct bored through the mountain just north of Pythagório at the behest of Polykrates. To get there, take the signposted path from the shore boulevard at the west end of town, which meets the vehicle access road towards the end of a twenty-minute walk.

Further subterranean experience can be had at the monastery of **Panayía Spilianí**, high on the hillside over town. Though most of this has been insensitively restored and touristified, behind the courtyard lies a cool, hundred-metre-long grotto, at one end of which is a shrine to the Virgin (open daylight hours; free). This was the presumed residence of the ancient oracular priestess Fyto, and a pirate-safe hideout in medieval times.

Practicalities

If there are any **accommodation** vacancies – and it's best not to assume this in mid-season – rooms proprietors meet incoming ferries and hydrofoils. The **tourist information booth** (daily June–Sept 8am–10pm; ☎0273/61 389), on the main thoroughfare Lykoúrgou Logothéti, can help in finding rooms and sells tickets for the *Nissos Kalymnos* ferryboat. Quietly located at the seaward end of Odhós Pythagóra, south of Lykoúrgou Logothéti, the modest *Tsambika* (☎0273/61 642; ②) or the more comfortable *Dora*, a block west (61 456; ③ includes breakfast) are two pensions worth considering. Some 50m inland from the north side of the harbour past the customs house, *Lambis Rooms* on Odhós Íras (☎0273/61 396; ②)is another backpackers' transit stop. Another peaceful area is the hillside north of Platía Irínis, where *Studios Galini* (☎0273/61 167; winter ☎01/98 42 248; ④) has high-quality self-catering units with ceiling fans, balconies and kind English-speaking management.

Eating out can be frustrating in Pythagório, with value for money often a completely alien concept. Away from the water, the *Platania* taverna, under two eucalyptus trees opposite the town hall, is relatively the least touristy option, and okay for a pre-ferry lunch; for waterside dining, you're best off at the far east end of the quay, where the *Remataki* ouzerí features vegetarian dishes such as *anginares ala políta*, and is the only spot the locals themselves will be seen in. Night-owls gather at either *Disco Labito* near the eponymous hotel, or the *Mythos Club* on Platía Irínis. The all-year Cine Rex in Mytiliní village, 7km northwest, is inexpensive with standard first-run fare.

If none of this appeals, the outbound **bus stop** lies just west of the intersection of Lykoúrgou Logothéti and the road to Vathý, with better than average fast food (a creperie, a simple grill) available just adjacent. Two **banks** (both with cash dispensers) and the **post office** are also on Lykoúrgou Logothéti. The flattish country to the west is ideal for cycling, a popular activity, and if you want to rent a **motorbike**, several outfits on Logothéti will oblige you.

Around Pythagório

The main local beach stretches for several kilometres west of the Logothetis "castle", punctuated about halfway along by the end of the airport runway, and the cluster of nondescript hotels known as **POTOKÁKI**. Just before the turnoff to the heart of the beach sprawls the ultra-luxurious *Doryssa Bay* complex, which includes a meticulously concocted fake village, guaranteed to confound archeologists of future eras. No two of the units, joined by named lanes, are alike, and there's even a platía with an expensive café. If you don't mind the hotel crowds and low-flying jets, the sand-and-pebble **beach** here is well groomed and the water clean; you'll have to head out to the end of the road for more seclusion.

The Potokáki access road is a dead end, with the main island loop road pressing on past the turnoff for the airport and Iréon hamlet. Under layers of alluvial mud, plus today's runway, lies the processional Sacred Way joining the ancient city with the **Heraion**, the massive shrine of the Mother Goddess (Tues–Sun 8.30am–2.45pm; 800dr). Much touted in tourist literature, this assumes humbler dimensions – one surviving column and assorted foundations – upon approach. Yet once inside the precinct you sense the former grandeur of the temple, never completed owing to Polykrates' untimely death at the hands of the Persians. The site chosen, near the mouth of the still-active Imvrassós stream, was Hera's legendary birthplace and site of her trysts with Zeus; in the far corner of the fenced-in zone you glimpse a large, exposed patch of the paved Sacred Way.

The modern resort of **IRÉON** nearby is a nondescript grid of dusty streets behind a coarse-shingle beach, attracting a slightly younger and more active clientele than Pythagório. Here you'll find more non-package rooms and two small hotels: *Venetia* (☎0273/61 195; ②) and *Heraion* (☎0273/61 180; ②), both within sight of the water. The oldest and most authentic **taverna** is the *Ireon*, at the far west end by the fishing harbour.

Southern Sámos

Since the circum-island bus only passes through or near the places below once or twice daily, you really need your own vehicle to explore them. Some 5km west of Hóra, a well-marked side road leads up and right to **MAVRATZÉÏ**, one of two Samian "pottery villages"; this one specializes in the *Koúpa tou Pythagóra* or "Pythagorean cup", supposedly designed by the sage to leak over the user's lap if they are over-filled. Slightly more practical wares can be found in **KOUMARADHÉÏ**, back on the main road, another 2km along.

From here you can descend a paved road to the sixteenth-century monastery of **Megális Panayías** (theoretically daily 9am–noon & 5–7pm; ring keeper on ☎61 449 to check), containing the finest frescoes on the island. This route continues to **MÝLI**, submerged in citrus groves and also accessible from Iréon. Four kilometres above Mýli sprawls **PAGÓNDAS**, a large hillside community with a splendid main square and an unusual communal fountain house on the south hillside. From here, a scenic paved road curls 9km around the hill to **SPATHARÉÏ** – its surroundings devastated by fire in 1993 – but set on a natural balcony offering the best sea views this side of the island. From Spatharéï, the road loops back 6km to **PÝRGOS**, lost in pine forests at the head of a ravine and the centre of Samian honey production; the most reliable local **taverna** (June–Oct) lies 3km west, in the plane-shaded Koútsi ravine.

The rugged and beautiful coast south of the Pagóndas–Pýrgos route is largely inaccessible, glimpsed by most visitors for the first and last time from the descending plane bringing them to Sámos. **Tsópela**, a highly scenic sand and gravel cove at a gorge mouth, is the only beach here with marked track access and a good seasonal taverna; you'll need a sturdy motorcycle (not a scooter) or jeep to get down there. The western reaches of this shoreline, which suffered comprehensive fire damage in 1994, are approached via the small village of **KOUMÉÏKA**, with a massive inscribed marble fountain and a pair of kafenía on its square. Below extends the long, pebble bay at **Bállos**, with sand, a cave and naturists at the far east end. Bállos itself is merely a sleepy collection of summer houses, several simple places to **stay** and a few **tavernas**. Returning to Kouméïka, the dubious-looking side road just before the village marked "Velanidhiá" is in fact partly paved and usable by any vehicle – a very useful short cut if you're travelling towards the beaches beyond Órmos Marathokámbou (see p.322).

Kokkári and around

Leaving Vathý on the north coastal section of the island loop road, there's little to stop for until you reach **KOKKÁRI**, the third major Samian tourist centre after Pythagório and the capital. Sadly, while lower Vathý and Pythagório had little beauty to sacrifice, much has been irrevocably lost here. The town's profile, covering two knolls behind twin headlands, remains unaltered, and several families still doggedly untangle their fishnets on the quay, but in general its identity has been altered beyond recognition, with constant inland expansion over vineyards and the abandoned fields of boiling onions that gave the place its name. Since the exposed, rocky beaches here are buffeted by near-constant winds, the promoters have made a virtue of necessity by developing the place as a successful windsurfing resort.

Practicalities

As in Vathý and Pythagório, a fair proportion of Kokkári's **accommodation** is block-booked by tour companies; establishments not completely devoted to such trade include *Lemos* (☎0273/92 250; ④), near the north end of the west beach, and the more modest *Vicky* (☎0273/92 231; ③), facing the same strand. For a guaranteed view of the fishing port, try the *Pension Alkyonis* (☎0273/92 225; ②). Otherwise Yiorgos Mihelios has a wide range of rooms and flats to rent (☎0273/92 456; ②–④), including the *Pension Green Hill*. If you get stuck, seek assistance from the seasonal **EOT post** (☎0273/92 217), housed in a portacabin near the main church.

Most **tavernas** line the north waterfront, and charge above the norm, though they're steadily losing ground to breakfast or cocktail bars. At the far east end of things, *Ta Adhelfia /The Brothers* is a civil, good-value place strong on grilled fish and meat, but with a few oven dishes daily; *Karyatidha*, two doors along, is another good all-rounder, while *Piccolo Porto* still further west does excellent Italian dishes, including wood-fired pizzas. Most (noisy) **bars** ring the little square just west of where the concreted stream (with its family of ducks) meets the sea, but there's also the more elaborate disco the *Cabana Beach Club* on the west beach.

Other amenities include an Emboriki/Commercial Bank **cash dispenser** on the through road, a **post office** in a portacabin on a seaward lane and a long-hours, self-service **laundry** next to that.

West of Kokkári: the coast

The closest sheltered beaches are thirty to forty minutes' walk away to the west, all with sunbeds and permanently anchored umbrellas. The first, **Lemonákia**, is a bit too close to the road, with an obtrusive café; 1km beyond, the graceful crescent of **Tzamadhoú** figures in virtually every EOT poster of the island. With path-only access, it's a bit less spoiled, and each end of the beach (saucer-shaped pebbles) is by tacit consent a nudist zone. There's one more pebble bay, 7km west beyond Avlákia, called **Tzábou**, but it's not worth a special detour when the prevailing northwest wind is up.

The next spot of any interest along the coast road is **Platanákia**, essentially a handful of undistinguished tavernas and rooms for rent at a bridge by the turning for Manolátes (see p.320). Platanákia is actually the eastern suburb of **ÁYIOS KONSTANDÍNOS**, whose surf-pounded esplanade has been prettified. However, there are no usable beaches within walking distance, so the collection of warm-toned stone buildings, with few modern intrusions, constitutes a peaceful alternative to Kokkári. In addition to modest 1970s **hotels**, such as the *Four Seasons* (①) or the *Atlantis* (☎0273/94 329; ①) just above the highway, there's a new generation of more modern rooms below the road, such as *Maria's* (☎0273/94 460; ③). **Eating** out, look no further than the excellent *To Kyma* at the east end of the quay, with good bulk wine and *mayireftá*, or (even better) the *Aeolos* at the far west end of the esplanade (June-Sept), with terrific fish and a few well-chosen baked dishes.

Once past "Áyios", as it's locally abbreviated, the mountains hem the road in against the sea, and the terrain doesn't relent until **Kondakéïka**, whose diminutive shore annexe of **Áyios Nikólaos** has an excellent venue for fish meals in *Iy Psaradhes*, its terrace lapped by the waves. There's also the reasonable beach of **Piáki**, ten minutes' walk east past the last studio units, evidence of a mild explosion in package development here since 1995.

Hill villages

Inland between Kokkári and Kondakéïka, an idyllic landscape of pine, cypress and orchards is overawed by dramatic mountains, so far little burned. Despite destructive nibblings by bulldozers, some of the trail system linking the various **hill villages** is still intact, and walkers can return to the main highway to catch a bus home. Failing that, most of the communities can provide a bed at short notice.

The monastery of **Vrondianís** (Vrónda), directly above Kokkári, is a popular destination, although since the army now uses it as a barracks, the place only really comes alive during its annual festival (7–8 September). **VOURLIÓTES**, 2km west of the monastery, has beaked chimneys and brightly painted shutters sprouting from its typical tile-roofed houses. On the photogenic central square, the oldest and arguably best of several tavernas is *The Blue Chairs*, serving two local specialities: *revithokeftédhes* (chickpea patties) and the homemade *moskháto* dessert wine.

MANOLÁTES, further uphill and an hour-plus walk away via a deep river canyon, also has several simple tavernas (the pick of these being hospitable *Loukas* at the top of the village, with the best views on the island), and is the most popular trailhead for the five-hour round-trip up **Mount Ámbelos** (Karvoúnis), the island's second highest summit. From Manolátes you can no longer easily continue on foot to Stavrinídhes, the next village, but should plunge straight down, partly on a cobbled path, through the shady valley known as **Aïdhónia** (Nightingales), towards Platanákia. Manolátes has accommodation, *Studios Angela* at the edge of town (☎0273/94 478; ③), but by far the most characterful base in the area is down in Aïdhónia at the *Hotel Aidonokastro* (☎0273/94 404, mobile 093/7069784; ④). Here the kindly, English-speaking Yannis Pamoukis has renovated half the abandoned hamlet of **Valeondátes** as a unique cottage-hotel, each former house comprising a pair of two- or four-person units with traditional touches.

Karlóvassi

KARLÓVASSI, 35km west of Vathý and the second town of Sámos, is decidedly sleepier and more old-fashioned than the capital, despite having roughly the same population. Though lacking in distinction, it's popular as a base for exploring western Sámos's excellent beaches and walking opportunies. The name, despite a vehement denial of Ottoman legacy elsewhere on Sámos, appears to be a corruption of the Turkish for "snowy plain" – the plain in question being the conspicuous saddle of Mount Kérkis overhead. The town divides into four straggly neighbourhoods: Néo, well inland, whose untidy growth was spurred by the influx of post-1923 refugees; Meséo, across the usually dry riverbed, tilting appealingly off a knoll towards the shore; and postcardworthy Paleó (or Áno), above Limáni, the small harbour district.

Most tourists stay at or near **Limáni**, the part of town with most of the tourist facilities. Hotels tend to have road noise and not much view; **rooms**, all in the inland pedestrian lane behind the through road, are quieter – try those of Vangelis Feloukatzis (☎0273/33 293; ②). The port itself is an appealing place with a working boatyard at the west end and all the **ferry-ticket agencies** grouped at the middle; often a shuttle-bus service operates from Néo Karlóvassi, timed to boat arrivals and departures. Tavernas and bars are abundant on the quay, though the only remarkable ones are *Rementzo*, tellingly the locals' hangout, and the more touristy *Boussoulas* next door, which does however stay open year-round, with consistent quality. There's also an enjoyable summer cinema on the through road.

Immediately overhead is the partly hidden hamlet of **Paleó**, its hundred or so houses draped on either side of a leafy ravine. The only facilities are the sporadically functioning café *To Mikro Parisi*. **Meséo**, just east, is a conceivable alternative base to Limáni, with the *Hotel Aspasia* (☎0273/32 363; ④), well sited 100m west of the wood-fired bakery, with a pool and air-conditioning. Following the street linking the central square to the waterfront, you pass one of the improbably huge, turn-of-the-century churches, topped with twin belfries and a blue-and-white dome, which dot the coastal plain here. Just at the intersection with the shore road you'll find the friendly, good-value *To Kyma* ouzerí (April–Oct), much improved under new management since 1998, and the best place in town to watch the sunset over a selection of mezédhes.

Néo has little to recommend it besides a wilderness of derelict stone-built warehouses and mansions down near the river mouth, reminders of the long-vanished leather industry which flourished here during the first half of this century. However, if you're staying at Limáni, you'll almost certainly visit one of the three **banks** (cash dispensers), the **post office** or the **bus stop** on the main lower square. There are virtually no **eateries** except the popular, year-round *Dionysos Psistaria*, on the west side of town at the start of the Marathókambos road.

Western Sámos

Visitors tolerate dull Karlóvassi for the sake of western Sámos's excellent **beaches**. Closest of these is **Potámi**, forty minutes' walk away via the coast road from Limáni or an hour by a more scenic, high trail from Paleó. This broad arc of sand and pebbles gets crowded at summer weekends, when virtually the entire population of Karlóvassi descends on the place. Near the end of the trail from Paleó stands *To Iliovasilema*, a friendly fish taverna; there are also a very few **rooms** signposted locally, and many folk camp rough along the lower reaches of the river which gives the beach its name.

A streamside path leads twenty minutes inland, past the eleventh-century church of **Metamórfosis** – the oldest on Sámos – to a point where the river disappears into a small gorge (a new, guard-railed but still perilous stairway takes you up and left here). Otherwise, you must swim and wade 100m in heart-stoppingly cold water through a sequence of fern-tufted rock pools before reaching a low but vigorous waterfall; bring shoes with good tread and perhaps even rope if you want to explore above the first cascade. You probably won't be alone until you dive in, since the canyon is well known to locals and tour agencies. Just above the Metamórfosis church, a clear if precipitous path leads up to a small, contemporaneous **Byzantine fortress**. There's little to see inside other than a subterranean cistern and badly crumbled lower curtain wall, but the views out to sea and up the canyon are terrific, while in October the place is carpeted with pink autumn crocuses.

The coast beyond Potámi ranks among the most beautiful and unspoiled on Sámos; since the early 1980s it has served as a protected refuge for the rare monk seal. The dirt track at the west end of Potámi bay ends after twenty minutes on foot, from which you backtrack 100m or so to find the side trail running parallel to the water. After twenty minutes along this you'll arrive at **Mikró Seïtáni**, a small pebble cove guarded by sculpted rock walls. A full hour's walk from the trailhead, through partly fire-damaged olive terraces, brings you to **Megálo Seïtáni**, the island's finest beach, at the mouth of the intimidating Kakopérato gorge. You'll have to bring food and water, though not necessarily a swimsuit – there's no dress code at either of the Seïtáni bays.

Southwestern beach resorts

Heading south out of Karlóvassi on the island loop road, the first place you reach is **MARATHÓKAMBOS**, a pretty, amphitheatrical village overlooking the eponymous gulf; there's a taverna or two, but no short-term accommodation. Its port, **ÓRMOS MARATHOKÁMBOU**, 18km from Karlóvassi, has recently emerged as a tourist resort, though some character still peeks through in its backstreets. The port has been improved, with kaïkia offering day-trips to Foúrni and the nearby islet of Samiopoúla, while the pedestrianized quay has become the focus of attention, home to several **tavernas** – best of these, by a nod, *Kyra Katina*, with a good range of seafood if somewhat obsequious service. Among the few non-packaged **accommodation** outfits, try *Studios Avra* (☎0273/37 221; ②), unimprovably perched above the jetty.

The beach immediately east from Órmos is hardly the best; for better ones continue 2km west to **VOTSALÁKIA** (officially signposted as "Kámbos"), Sámos' fastest-growing resort, straggling a further 2km behind the island's longest (if not its most beautiful) beach. But for most, Votsalákia is still a vast improvement on the Pythagório area, and the mass of 1437-metre Mount Kérkis overhead rarely fails to impress (see below). As for **accommodation**, Emmanuil Dhespotakis (☎0273/31 258; ③) has numerous premises towards the quieter, more scenic western end of things. Also in this vicinity is *Loukoullos*, an unusual **ouzerí-taverna** overlooking the sea. Other facilities include branches of nearly all the main Vathý travel agencies, offering **vehicle rental** (necessary, as only two daily buses call here) and money exchange.

If Votsalákia doesn't suit, you can continue 3km past to the 600-metre beach of **Psilí Ámmos**, more aesthetic and not to be confused with its namesake beach in the southeast corner of Sámos. The sea shelves very gently here, and cliffs shelter clusters of naturists at the east end. Surprisingly there is still little development: just two small studio complexes in the pines at mid-beach, and two tavernas back up on the road as you approach, either of these fine for a simple lunch. Access to **Limniónas**, a smaller cove 2km further west, passes the *Limnionas Bay Hotel* (☎0273/37 057; ④), much the highest standard accommodation locally with its tiered units arrayed around a garden and pool. Yachts and pleasure kaïkia occasionally call at the protected bay, which offers decent swimming away from a rock shelf at mid-strand, especially at the east end where there's a simple **taverna**.

Mount Kérkis and around

Gazing up from a supine seaside position, you may be inspired to climb **Mount Kérkis**. The classic route begins at the west end of the Votsalákia strip, along the bumpy jeep track leading inland towards Evangelistrías convent. After thirty minutes on the track system, through fire-damaged olive groves and past charcoal pits (a major local industry), the path begins, more or less following power lines up to the convent. A friendly nun may proffer an oúzo in welcome and point you up the paint-marked trail, continuing even more steeply up to the peak. The views are tremendous, though the climb itself is humdrum once you're out of the trees. About an hour before the top there's a chapel with an attached cottage for sheltering in emergencies, and just beyond, a welcome spring. All told, it's a seven-hour outing from Votsalákia and back, not counting rest stops.

Less ambitious walkers might want to circle the flanks of the mountain, first by vehicle and then by foot. The road beyond Limniónas to Kallithéa and Dhrakéï, truly back-of-beyond villages with views across to Ikaría, is paved as far as Kallithéa, making it possible to venture out here on an ordinary motorbike. The bus service is better during the school year, when a vehicle leaves Karlóvassi (1pm, Mon–Fri) bound for these remote spots; during summer it only operates two days a week (currently Mon & Fri).

From **DHRAKÉÏ**, the end of the line with just a pair of very simple kafenía to its credit, a track, then trail, descends ninety minutes through partly burned forest to

Megálo Seïtáni, from where it's easy enough to continue on to Karlóvassi within another two-and-a-half hours. People attempting to reverse this itinerary often discover to their cost that the bus (if any) returns from Dhrakéï early in the day, at about 2.30pm, compelling them to stay at one of two rather expensive **rooms** establishments (summer only) in **KALLITHÉA**, and dine there at either the simple psistariá on the square or a newer, more varied taverna on the western edge of the village. From Kallithéa, a newer track (from beside the cemetery) and an older trail both lead up within 45 minutes to a spring, rural chapel and plane tree on the west flank of Kérkis, with path-only continuation for another thirty minutes to a pair of cave-churches. **Panayía Makriní** stands detached at the mouth of a high, wide but shallow grotto, whose balcony affords terrific views of Sámos's west tip. By contrast, **Ayía Triádha**, a ten-minute scramble overhead, has most of its structure made up of cave wall; just adjacent, another long, narrow, volcanic cavern can be explored with a torch some hundred metres into the mountain.

After these subterranean exertions, the closest spot for a swim is **Vársamo** (Válsamo) cove, 4km below Kallithéa and reached via a well-signposted dirt road. The beach here consists of multicoloured volcanic pebbles, with two caves to shelter in and a single taverna just inland.

Ikaría

Ikaría, a narrow, windswept landmass between Sámos and Mýkonos, is little visited and invariably underestimated by travel journalists who haven't even bothered to show up; the name supposedly derives from the legendary Icarus, who fell into the sea just offshore after the wax bindings on his wings melted. For years the only substantial tourism was generated by a few **hot springs** on the south coast, some reputed to cure rheumatism and arthritis, some to make women fertile, though others are so highly radioactive that they've been closed for some time.

Ikaría, along with Thessaly on the mainland and Lésvos, has traditionally been one of the Greek Left's strongholds. This tendency dates from the long decades of right-wing domination in Greece, when (as in past ages) the island was used as a place of **exile** for political dissidents. Apparently the strategy backfired, with the transportees favourably impressing and proselytizing their hosts; at the same time, many Ikarians emigrated to North America, and ironically their regular capitalist remittances help keep the island going. It can be a bizarre experience to be treated to a monologue on the evils of US imperialism, delivered by a retiree in perfect Alabaman English.

These are not the only Ikarian quirks, and for many the place is an acquired taste, contrasting strongly (for better or worse) with Sámos. Except for forested portions in the west (now being steadily burned off to create land for hotels), it's not a strikingly beautiful island, with most of the terrain consisting of scrub-covered schist put to good use as building material. The mostly desolate south coast is fringed by steep cliffs, while the north face is less sheer but nonetheless furrowed by deep canyons creating hairpin bends extreme even by Greek-island standards. Neither are there many picturesque villages, since the rural schist-roofed houses are generally scattered so as to be next to their famous apricot orchards, vineyards and fields.

Until the mid-1990s, the Ikarians resisted most attempts to develop their island for conventional tourism: charter flights still don't land here, since the northeastern airport can't accommodate jets. Long periods of punitive neglect by Athens (and provincial HQ Sámos) have made the locals profoundly self-sufficient and idiosyncratic, and tolerant of the same in others. Local pride dictates that outside opinion matters not a bit, and locals often seem to have little idea what "modern tourists" expect. This lack of obsequiousness, and a studied eccentricity, are often mistaken for hostility.

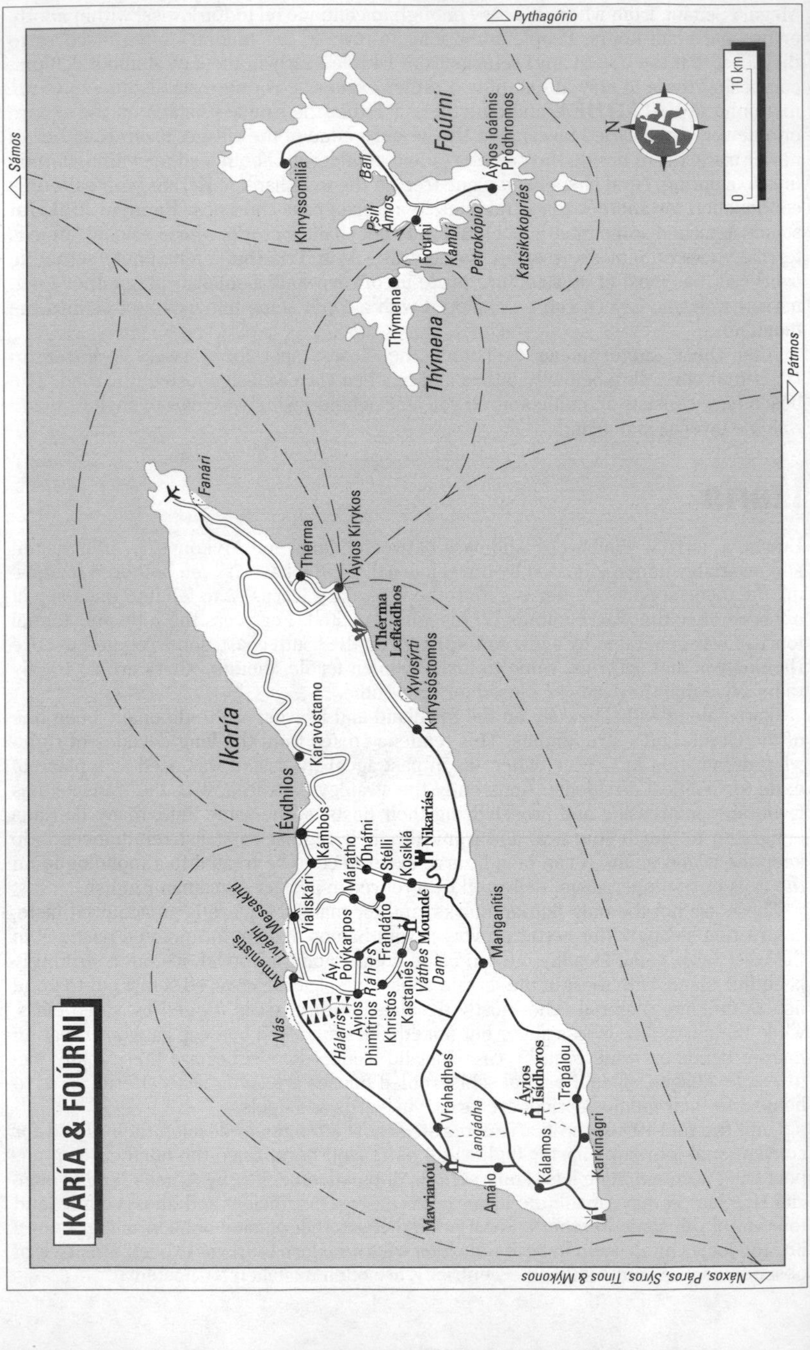
IKARÍA & FOÚRNI
Ikaría
Sámos
Pythagório
Pátmos
Náxos, Páros, Sýros, Tínos & Mýkonos
Foúrni
Thýmena
Khryssomiliá
Balí
Psilí Ámos
Foúrni
Kambí
Petrokópio
Áyios Ioánnis Pródhromos
Katsikokopriés
Thýmena
Fanári
Thérma
Áyios Kírykos
Thérma Lefkádhos
Xylosýrti
Khryssóstomos
Karavóstamo
Évdhilos
Kámbos
Dháfni
Máratho
Stélli
Kosikiá
Nikariás
Yialiskári
Messakhti
Livádhi
Armenistis
Áy. Polýkarpos
Frandáto
Moundé
Ráhes
Áyios Dhimítrios
Khristós
Kastaniés
Váthes Dam
Manganítis
Nás
Hálaris
Vráhadhes
Langádha
Áyios Isídhoros
Trapálou
Kálamos
Karkinágri
Amálo
Mavrianoú
N
0
10 km

Áyios Kírykos

Roughly half of passing ferries call at the south-coast port and capital of **ÁYIOS KÍRYKOS**, about 1km southeast of the island's main thermal resort. Because of the spa trade, beds are at a premium in town; arriving in the evening from Sámos, accept any reasonable offers of rooms at the jetty, or – if in a group – proposals of a taxi ride to the north coast, which shouldn't cost more than 7500dr per vehicle to Armenistís. A cream and green **bus** sets out across the island from the main square (daily, in theory 10am, & 1.30pm on Mon, Wed & Fri to Armenistís; Mon–Fri noon to Évdhilos only).

The baths (daily 8am–1pm) in **Thérma** are rather old-fashioned stone tubs, with preference given to those under medical care. A better bet for a less formal soak are the more natural, shoreline hot springs at **Thérma Lefkádhos**, 3km southwest of Áyios Kírykos, below a cluster of villas. Here the seaside spa is derelict, leaving the water to boil up right in the shallows, mixing with the sea between giant volcanic boulders to a pleasant temperature.

Practicalities

Hydrofoils, the Miniotis Lines boats and the kaïki for Foúrni use the small east jetty; large ferries dock at the main west pier. There are several **hotels**, such as the *Isabella* (☎0275/22 839; ③), or the friendly, basic but spotless *Akti* (☎0275/22 694; ②), on a knoll east of the hydrofoil and kaïki quay, with views of Foúrni from the garden. Otherwise, **pensions** and **rooms** are not especially cheap: directly behind the base of the ferry jetty and a little to the west there's the well-appointed *Pension Maria-Elena* (☎0275/22 543; ②), with sea views. Both the studios (☎0275/22 276; ③) above the *Snack Bar Dedalos* and the prominently marked, clean *dhomátia* run by Ioannis Proestos (☎0275/23 496; ②), get noise from the several kafenía and snack bars below.

Eating out, you've even less choice than in lodging. Give the obvious quayside eateries a miss in favour of the grilled dishes served up at the *Tzivaeri* ouzerí, just inland from Ioannis Proestos's rooms, or *Iy Klimataria* just around the corner for year-round *mayireftá*. Glitz is all the rage on the front, with *Casino* the last remaining traditional kafenío. There are two **banks** with cash dispensers, a **post office** adjacent on the road out and three ferry/hydrofoil **agents**. You can **rent** motorbikes and cars here, too, but both are cheaper in Armenistís.

Évdhilos and around

The twisting, 41-kilometre road from Áyios Kírykos to Évdhilos is one of the most hair-raising on any Greek island, and the long ridge extending the length of Ikaría often wears a streamer of cloud, even when the rest of the Aegean is clear. Karavóstamo, with its tiny, scruffy port, is the first substantial north coast place, beyond which a series of three beaches leads up to **ÉVDHILOS**. Although this is the island's second town and a ferry stop almost every day in summer, it's far less equipped to deal with visitors than Áyios Kírykos. There are two **hotels**, the *Evdoxia* on the slope southwest of the harbour (☎0275/31 502; ④) and the low-lying *Atheras* (☎0275/31 434; ④) with a small pool – plus a few **rooms**, best of these ones run by Apostolos Stenos (☎0275/31 365; ③) just west of town. Among several waterfront **restaurants**, the nameless kafestiatório between *O Flisvos* and the *Blue Nice* travel agency is the most reliable and reasonable option. A **post office** up towards the *Evdoxia*, and a good town **beach** to the east, are also worth knowing about.

KÁMBOS, 2km west, offers a small hilltop museum with finds from nearby **ancient Oinoe**; the twelfth-century church of Ayía Iríni lies just below, with the remains of a fourth-century Byzantine basilica serving as the entry courtyard. Lower down still are the sparse ruins of a Byzantine palace (just above the road) used to house exiled nobles, as well as a large sandy beach. **Rooms** are available from the store run by Vassilis Dhionysos (☎0275/31 300; ③), which also acts as the unofficial and enthusiastic tourist office for this part of Ikaría, keeping the keys for church and museum.

Starting from the large church in Évdhilos, you can also visit the Byzantine **castle of Nikariás** (Koskiná), just over 15km south. The road signposted for Manganítis is paved until Kosikiá, just over 9km away, and for 2km more to the marked side track, along which you can get a bike or jeep to within a short walk of the tenth-century castle, perched on a distinctive conical hill, with an arched gateway and a fine vaulted chapel.

Armenistís and around

Most people carry on to **ARMENISTÍS**, 57km from Áyios Kírykos, and with good reason: this little resort lies below Ikaría's finest (though rapidly dwindling) forest, with two enormous, sandy beaches battered by near-constant surf – **Livádhi** and **Messakhtí** – five and fifteen minutes' walk to the east respectively. Campers in the river-mouth greenery behind each stretch set the tone for the place, though an official campsite functions behind Livádhi in peak season, and the islanders' tolerance doesn't extend to nude bathing, as signs advise you.

A dwindling number of older buildings, plus fishing boats hauled up in a sandy cove, lend Armenistís the air of a Cornish fishing village; it's a tiny place, reminiscent of similar youth-orientated spots in southern Crete, though gentrification has definitely set in. Several "music bars", often with live Greek gigs, operate seasonally behind the nearer beach and at the quay's north end, but for most visitors **nightlife** is mostly about extended sessions in the tavernas and cafés overlooking the anchorage. Along the shore lane, the adjacent *Paskhalia* and *Delfini* **tavernas** are the best, the former offering full breakfasts as well as good-value, en-suite **rooms** (☎0275/71 302; winter 01/24 71 411; ②). On the hill to the south the *Armena Inn* (☎0275/71 320; ②) is of a similar standard. For more luxury, there are two adjacent hotels about 700m east of the main junction here, both with pools and hosting the local package custom: the *Cavos Bay* (☎0275/71 381; ⑤) and the smaller *Daidalos* (☎0275/71 390; ④). Better than either, just above Messakhtí, is the *Messakhti Village* complex (☎0275/71 331; ④), with a large pool (necessary here, as the deep water off the beach is often unsafe due to undertow) and fine common areas and private terraces making up for the rather plain rooms. Just east of here is the fishing settlement of **YIALISKÁRI**, which has a handful of tavernas and half a dozen rooms looking out to a picturesque church on the jetty.

Among the four travel agencies/car rental/money exchange outfits in Armenistís, Marabou is about the most helpful, offering mountain bikes as well as walking tours of western Ikaría; Glaros has reasonably maintained scooters. The sole drawback to staying in Armenistís is getting away, since both taxis and buses are elusive. Theoretically, **buses** head for Áyios Kírykos daily at 2 or 3pm, usually with a change or layover in Évdhilos, and out of school term only at 7am most days, but all these departures are unreliable even by Ikarian standards and should be double-checked. If you've a ferry to catch, it's far easier on the nerves to pre-book a taxi.

Ráhes

Armenistís is actually the shore annexe of four inland hamlets – Áyios Dhimítrios, Áyios Polýkarpos, Kastaniés and Khristós – collectively known as **RÁHES**. Despite the modern, mostly paved access roads through what's left of the pines (trails shortcut them), the settlements retain a certain Shangri-La quality, with the older residents speaking a positively Homeric dialect. On an island not short of foibles, Khristós is particularly strange inasmuch as the locals sleep much of the day, but shop and eat from early afternoon to the small hours; in fact most of the villages west of Évdhilos adhere to this schedule, defying central government efforts to bring them in line with the rest of Greece.

Near the small main square of Khristós, paved in schist and studded with gateways fashioned from the same rock, there's a **post office** and a **hotel/restaurant** (☎0275/71 269; ③), but for lunch you'll have to scrounge something at one of two unmarked tavernas or the more prominent kafenía. The slightly spaced-out demeanour of those serving – plus numbers of old boys shambling around in dirty clothes, with their flies unzipped – may be attributable to over-indulgence in the excellent home-brewed **wine** which everyone west of Évdhilos makes. The local festival is August 6, though better ones take place further southwest in the woods at Langádha valley (August 14–15) or at Áyios Isídhoros monastery (May 14).

Nás

By tacit consent, Greek or foreign hippies and naturists have been allowed to shift 3km west of Armenistís to **Nás**, a tree-clogged river canyon ending in a small but sheltered sand and pebble beach. This little bay is almost completely enclosed by weirdly sculpted rock formations, and as signs warn you, it's unwise to swim outside the cove's natural limits. The crumbling foundations of the fifth-century temple of **Artemis Tavropoleio** (Patroness of Bulls) overlook the permanent deep pool at the mouth of the river. If you continue inland along this past colonies of freelance campers, you'll find secluded rock pools for freshwater dips. Back at the top of the stairs leading down to the beach from the road are several tavernas (best view at *O Nas*, but better food at *Astra*), most offering **rooms**.

Satellite islands: Thýmena and Foúrni

The straits between Sámos and Ikaría are speckled with a mini-archipelago, though the only islets permanently inhabited are Thýmena and Foúrni. More westerly **Thýmena** has one tiny hillside settlement; a regular kaïki calls at the quay below on its way between Ikaría and Foúrni, but there are no tourist facilities, and casual visits are explicitly discouraged. Foúrni is home to a huge fishing fleet and one of the more thriving boatyards in the Aegean; thanks to these, and the improvement of the jetty to receive car ferries, its population is stable, unlike so many small Greek islands. The islets were once the lair of Maltese pirates, and indeed many of the islanders have a distinctly North African appearance.

The above-cited **kaïki** leaves Ikaría at about 1pm several days weekly, stays overnight at Foúrni and returns the next morning. Another twice-weekly kaïki from Karlóvassi, and the larger car ferries which appear every few days, are likewise not tourist excursion boats but exist for the benefit of the islanders. The only practical way to visit Foúrni on a day-trip is by using one of the summer morning hydrofoils out of Sámos (Vathý or Pythagório).

Foúrni

Apart from the remote hamlet of **Khryssomiliá** in the north, where the island's longest (and often roughest) road goes, most of Foúrni's inhabitants are concentrated in the **port** and Kambí hamlet just to the south. The harbour community is larger than it seems from the sea, with a friendly ambience reminiscent of 1970s Greece. Among several **rooms** establishments, the most popular are the restored mansion-premises run by Manolis and Patra Markakis (☎0275/51 268; ②), immediately to your left as you disembark. If they're full you can head inland to the modern blocks of Evtyhia Amoryianou (☎0275/51 364; ②), whose father Nikos Kondylas meets most boats and is a mine of information about the island.

Of four waterfront **tavernas**, the local favourite is *Rementzo*, better known as *Nikos*'; if you're lucky the local *astakós* or Aegean lobster may be on the menu until mid-August. For breakfast and desserts, repair to the tamarisk terrace at the Markakis family's *To Arhondiko tis Kyras Kokonas*, under their inn. The central "high street", field-stoned and mulberry-shaded, ends well inland at a little platía with traditional kafenía under each of two plane trees; between them stands a Hellenistic sarcophagus found in a nearby field, and overhead is a conical hill, site of the ancient acropolis. There's a **post office**, an Ioniki/Ionian Bank **cash dispenser**, plus several surprisingly well-stocked shops.

A fifteen-minute trail-walk south from the school, skirting the cemetery and then slipping over the windmill ridge, brings you to **KAMBÍ**, a scattered community overlooking a pair of sandy, tamarisk-shaded coves which you'll share with chickens and hauled-up fishing boats. There are three cheap and sustaining tavernas, the *Kambi* with tables on the sand and seven **rooms** that are admittedly spartan but have arguably the best views on the island. A path continues to the next bay south, which like Kambí cove, is a preferred anchorage for wandering yachts.

Heading north from the harbour via steps, then a trail, you'll find another **beach**: **Psilí Ámmos** in front of a derelict fish-processing plant, with shade at one end. At the extreme north of the island, remote **KHRYSSOMILIÁ** is still best approached by the taxi-boat *Evangelistria* rather than the atrocious eighteen-kilometre road. The village, split into a shore district and a hillside settlement, has a decent beach flanked by better but less accessible ones. Simple **rooms** and **meals** can be arranged on the spot, though the locals can be less than welcoming to outsiders. The hamlet and monastery of **Áyios Ioánnis Pródhromos** in the far south of Foúrni is probably a better day-trip target on foot or by motor-scooter (now available for rent), with some good, secluded beaches just below.

Híos

"Craggy Híos", as **Homer** aptly described his putative birthplace, has a turbulent history and a strong identity. It has always been relatively prosperous, in medieval times through the export of mastic **resin** – a trade controlled by Genoese overlords between 1346 and 1566, and later by the **Ottomans**, who dubbed the place Sakız Adası (Resin Island). Since union with Greece in 1912, several shipping dynasties have emerged here, continuing the pattern of wealth. Participation in the maritime way of life is widespread, with someone in almost every family spending time in the merchant navy.

The more powerful ship-owning families and the military authorities did not encourage tourism until the late 1980s, but the worldwide shipping crisis and the saturation of other, more obviously "marketable" islands eroded their resistance. Increasing numbers of foreigners are discovering a Híos beyond its rather daunting port capital: fascinating villages, important Byzantine monuments and a respectable, if remote, complement of beaches. While unlikely ever to be dominated by tourism, the local scene has a distinctly modern flavour – courtesy of numerous returned Greek-Americans and Greek-Canadians – and English is widely spoken.

Unfortunately, the island has suffered more than its fair share of **catastrophes** during the past two centuries. The Turks perpetrated their most infamous, if not their worst, anti-revolutionary atrocity here in March 1822, massacring 30,000 Hiots and enslaving or exiling even more. In 1881, much of Híos was destroyed by a violent **earthquake**, and throughout the 1980s the natural beauty of the island was markedly diminished by devastating forest fires, compounding the effect of generations of tree-

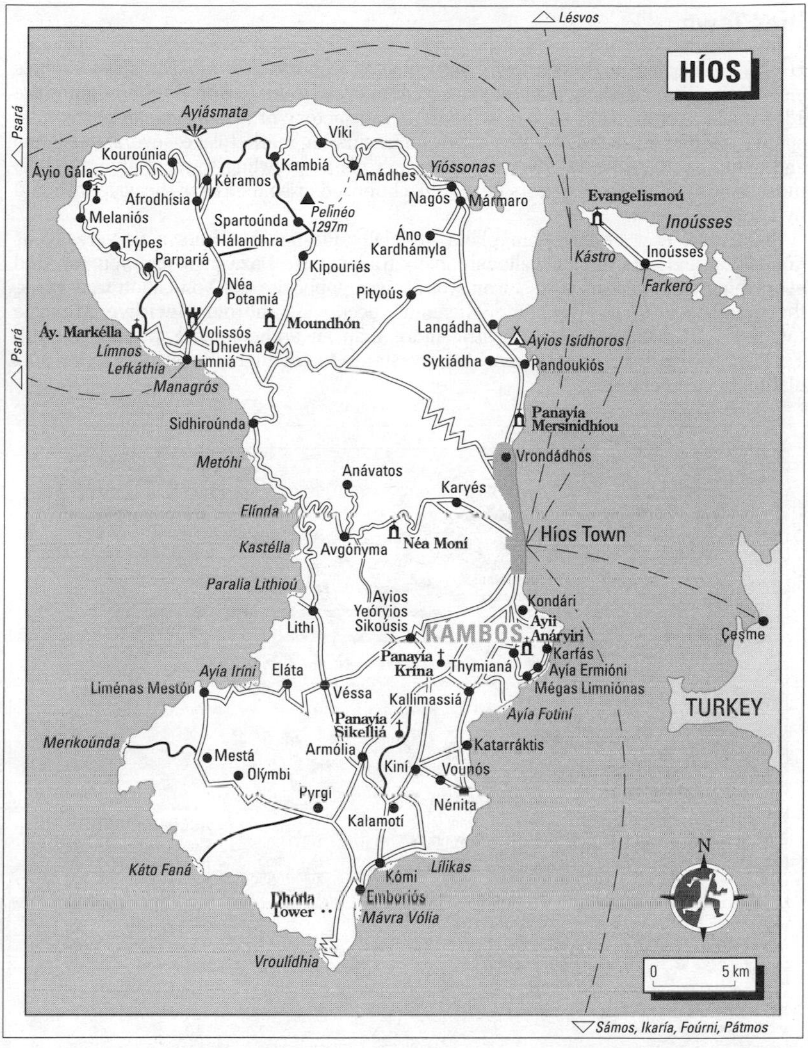

felling by boat-builders. Nearly two-thirds of the majestic pines are now gone, with substantial patches of woods persisting only in the far northeast and the centre of Híos.

In 1988 the first charters from northern Europe were instituted, signalling potentially momentous changes for the island. But there are still only 6000 guest beds on Híos, the vast majority of them in the capital or the nearby beach resort of Karfás. Further expansion, however, is hampered by the lack of direct flights from most countries, and the refusal of property owners to part with land for the extension of the airport runway.

Híos Town

HÍOS, the harbour and main town, will come as a shock after modest island capitals elsewhere; it's a bustling, concrete-laced commercial centre, with little predating the 1881 quake. Yet in many ways it is the most satisfactory of North Aegean ports; time spent exploring is rewarded with a large and fascinating marketplace, several museums and some good, authentic tavernas. Although it's a sprawling town of about 30,000, most things of interest to visitors lie within a hundred or so metres of the water, fringed by Leofóros Egéou.

South and east of the main platía, officially Plastíra but known universally as Vounakíou, extends the marvellously lively tradesmen's **bazaar**, where you can find everything from parrots to cast-iron woodstoves. Opposite the Vounakíou **taxi rank**, the grandiosely titled "Byzantine Museum", occupying the old **Mecidiye Mosque** (Mon–Fri 10am–2pm; 500dr), is little more than an archeological warehouse, with Turkish, Jewish and Armenian marble gravestones testifying to the island's varied population in past centuries.

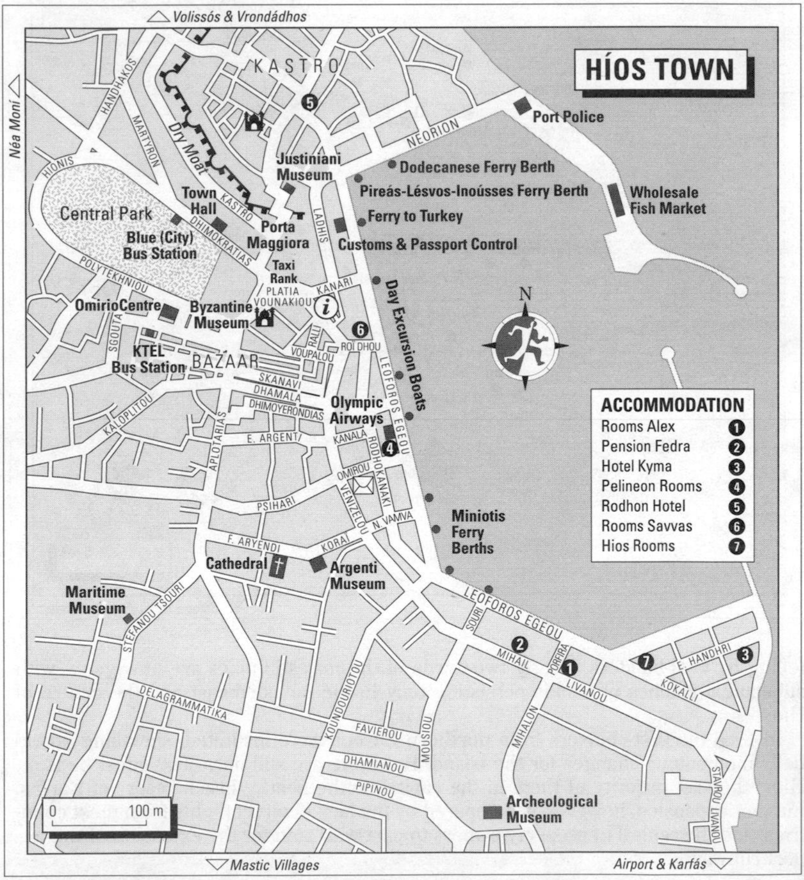

Until the 1881 earthquake, the Genoese **Kástro** was completely intact; thereafter developers razed the seaward walls, filled in much of the moat to the south and made a fortune selling off the real estate thus created around present-day Platía Vounakíou. Today the most satisfying entry to the citadel is via Porta Maggiora behind the town hall. The top floor of a medieval mansion just inside is home to the **Justiniani Museum** (Tues–Sun 9am–3pm; 500dr, 300dr Sun), with a satisfying (and periodically changing) collection of unusual icons and mosaics rescued from local churches. The small dungeon adjacent briefly held 75 Hiot hostages before their execution by the Ottomans in 1822. The old residential quarter inside the surviving castle walls, formerly the Muslim and Jewish neighbourhoods, is well worth a wander; among the wood and plaster houses you'll find assorted Ottoman monuments in various states of decay: a cemetery, a small minaretless mosque, a *hamam* (Turkish bath) and several inscribed fountains.

Further afield, three other museums beckon. The **Maritime Museum** at Stefánou Tsoúri 20 (Mon–Sat 10am–1pm; free) consists principally of model ships and oil paintings of various craft, Greek and foreign, all rather overshadowed by the mansion containing them. In the foyer is enshrined the knife and glass-globe grenade of Admiral Kanaris, who partly avenged the 1822 massacre by ramming and sinking the Ottoman fleet's flagship. In the centre of town, the **Argenti Folklore Museum** (Mon–Fri 8am–2pm, also Fri 5–7.30pm, Sat 8am–12.30pm; 400dr), on the top floor of the Koráï Library at Koráï 2, features ponderous genealogical portraits of the endowing family, an adjoining wing of costumes and rural impedimenta, plus multiple replicas of Delacroix's *Massacre at Hios*, a painting which did much to arouse sympathy for the cause of Greek independence. The **Archeological Museum** on Mihálon (Tues–Sun 8.30am–3pm; 500dr) finally re-opened in late 1999 after an eight-year overhaul – collection unreviewed, but probably worth a look.

Arrival, information and services

Ferries large and small dock at various points as shown on the town map. The **airport** lies 4km south along the coast at Kondári; any blue urban bus labelled "KONDÁRI KARFÁS" departing from the terminal on the north side of the park passes the airport gate. **Ferry** agents cluster to either side of the customs building, towards the north end of the waterfront Egéou and its continuation Neoríon: NEL is a few paces south of customs (☎0271/23 971), while Miniotis Lines, at Neoríon 21–23 (☎0271/24 670) or Egéou 11 (☎0271/21 463), operates small ferries to many neighbouring islands, as well as representing G&A boats. The Turkish evening ferry to Çeşme, as well as the most regular boat to Inoússes (see p.340), are handled by Faros Travel at Egéou 18 (☎0271/27 240). The helpful municipal **tourist office** (May–Sept Mon–Fri 7am–2.30pm & 7–10pm, Sat 10am–1pm, Sun 7–10pm; Oct–April Mon–Fri 7am–2.30pm; ☎0271/44 389) is at Kanári 18, near the Ionian Bank.

The standard green and cream **KTEL buses** leave from a parking area beside their ticket office on the south side of the park, behind the Omirio Cultural Centre. While services to the south of Híos are adequate, those to the centre and northwest of the island are almost non-existent, and to explore there you'll need to rent a powerful **motorbike** or a car, or share a **taxi** – they're bright red here, not grey as in most of Greece. Three independent **car rental** agencies sit in a row at Evyenías Handhrí 5–7, behind the *Chandris Hotel*; of these, John Vassilakis Rent a Car (☎0271/29 300), with a branch at Mégas Limniónas, can be particularly recommended. The **post office** is on Omírou, while numerous **banks** all have cash dispensers. A final Hiot idiosyncrasy is afternoon **shopping hours** limited to Monday and Thursday in summer.

Accommodation

Híos Town has a fair bit of affordable accommodation, rarely completely full. Most places line the water or the perpendicular alleys and parallel streets behind, and almost all are plagued by traffic noise to some degree – we've listed the more peaceful establishments.

Fedra, Mihaíl Livanoú 13 (☎0271/41 130). Well-appointed pension in an old mansion, with stone arches in the downstairs winter bar; in summer the bar operates outside, so ask for a rear room to avoid nocturnal noise. ④.

Hios Rooms, Kokáli 1, cnr Egéou (☎0271/27 295). Clean if creaky upper-floor rooms, relatively quiet for a seafront locale; enquire at shop below, or at the Hadzelenis Tourist Information Office on the quay. ①.

Kyma, east end of Evyenías Handhrí (☎0271/44 500). En-suite hotel rooms in a Neoclassical mansion or a modern extension, but splendid service and big breakfasts provided by Theo and Güher really make the place. The old wing saw a critical moment in modern Greek history in September 1922, when Colonel Nikolaos Plastiras commandeered it as his HQ after the Greek defeat in Asia Minor, and announced the deposition of King Constantine I. ④.

Pelineon Rooms, Omírou 9, cnr Egéou (☎0271/28 030). Choose between light, airy and noisy seaview rooms (most en-suite), or quiet, poky ones in back. ②.

Rodhon, Zaharíou 17 (☎0271/24 335). The owners can be crotchety, and the rooms are non-en-suite, but it's just about the only place inside the kástro, and very quiet. ②.

Rooms Alex, Mihaïl Livanoú 29 (☎0271/26 054). The friendly proprietor often meets late-arriving ferries; otherwise ring the bell. There's a roof garden above the well-furnished rooms (TV, fans), some en-suite. ②.

Rooms Savvas, Roïdhou 15 (☎0271/24 892). Modern pension tucked onto a tiny plaza just inland from the water; rear rooms unfortunately overlook the public toilets, but all are en-suite and well equipped. ③.

Eating

Eating out in Híos Town can be more pleasurable than the fast-food joints, touristy tavernas and *barákia* on the waterfront would suggest; it is also usually a lot cheaper than on neighbouring Sámos or Lésvos.

Agrifoglio, Stávrou Livanoú 2 (start of road to Karfás). The place for an Italian blowout; all the pasta standards.

O Hotzas, Yeoryíou Kondhíli 3, corner Stefánou Tsoúri, off ma Oldest taverna in town, much improved recently, with vegetarian dishes (*mavromátika*, cauliflower), sausages, baby fish and *mydhopílafo* (rice and mussels) among the offerings to be washed down by good retsina. Supper only, garden in summer; shut Sun.

Kronos, Filíppou Aryéndi 2, cnr Aplotariás. Own-made ice creams and nothing but, purveyed since 1929; limited seating or take away.

Ta Mylarakia, by three restored windmills in Tambákika district, on the road to Vrondádhos (☎0271/40 412). A large, well-priced seafood selection, every kind of Hiot oúzo and atmospheric waterside seating make reservations advisable in summer. Lunch in summer, supper most of the year.

Ouzeri Theodhosiou, junction Egéou and Neoríon. The genuine article, with a large, reasonable menu, though it's best to wait until the ferries which dock immediately opposite have departed. Supper only; shut Sun.

Drinking, nightlife and entertainment

Cine Kipos, in central park from June to mid-September only. Quality/art-house first-run fare, two screenings nightly; watch for flybills around town or enquire at Pension Fedra.

Iviskos, about halfway along Egéou. This tasteful café is the most popular daylight hangout on the quay, with a range of juices, coffees and alcoholic drinks.

To Loukoumi, alley off Aplotariás 27/c. Old warehouse refitted as a café (8am–2pm), ouzerí (7pm–2am) and occasional events centre. Well executed and worth checking out. Shut Sun and September.

Omirio, south side of the central park. Cultural centre and events hall with frequently changing exhibitions; foreign musicians often come here after Athens concerts to perform in the large auditorium.

Beaches near Híos Town

Híos Town itself has no beaches worth mentioning; the closest decent one is at **KARFÁS**, 7km south beyond the airport and served by frequent blue buses. Once there you can **rent bikes** at Rabbit Motos, or **cars** at MG (☎0271/31 432), both uphill from the bus sto Most Hiot hotels are planted here, to the considerable detriment of the 500-metre-long beach itself, sandy only at the south end, where all watersports are offered. The main bright spot is a unique **pension**, *Markos' Place* (☎0271/31 990; April–Nov; ②), installed in the disestablished **monastery of Áyios Yeóryios and Áyios Pandelímon**, on the hillside south of the bay. Markos Kostalas, who leases the premises from Thymianá municipality, has created a unique environment much loved by special-activity groups. Guests are lodged in the former pilgrims' cells, with a kitchen available; individuals are more than welcome (there are several single "cells"), though advance reservations are advisable. Two nearby **eating** options are refreshingly at odds with the package ethos here. Amidst it all, on the lane leading to the *Karatzas Hotel*, the *Fakiris Market Taverna* uniquely offers home-marinated aubergine or artichokes and red-pepper dip along with well-executed seafood and pork-based *bekrí mezé* at non-touristy prices; it's open off-season weekends as well. Some 3km back towards town at Kondári, at the end of a side road leading from a right-angle turn to the scrappy beach, *To Tavernaki* has personable service, large portions, magnificent fish and starters, excellent chips or whole-grain bread and decent bulk wine. It's open daily for lunch and supper, though may miss out lunch during slow seasons.

Some 2km further along the coast from Karfás, **AYÍA ERMIÓNI** is not a beach but a fishing anchorage surrounded by a handful of tavernas (*Mayeftiko Akroyialì*, below the church, is adequate, with waterside seating) and apartments to rent. The nearest beach is at **Mégas Limniónas**, a few hundred metres further, smaller than Karfás but more scenic where low cliffs provide a backdro *Taverna Angyra* is about the best eating place here, with a good line in mezédhes and a well-chosen wine list. Both Ayía Ermióni and Mégas Limniónas are served by extensions of the blue-bus route to either Karfás or Thymianá, the nearest inland village.

The coast road loops up to Thymianá, from where you can (with your own transport only) continue 3km south towards Kalimassiá to the turning for **Ayía Fotiní**, a 700-metre pebble beach with exceptionally clean water. There's no shade, however, unless you count shadows from the numerous blocks of rooms contracted out to Scandinavian tour operators; a few tavernas cluster around the point where the side road meets the sea.

Southern Híos

Besides olive groves, the gently rolling countryside in the south of the island is also home to the **mastic bush** (*Pistacia lentisca*), found across much of Aegean Greece but only here producing an aromatic resin of any quality or quantity. For centuries it was used as a base for paints, cosmetics and the chewable jelly beans, which became a somewhat addictive staple in the Ottoman harems. Indeed, the interruption of the flow of mastic from Híos to Istanbul by the revolt of spring 1822 was one of the root causes of the brutal Ottoman reaction.

The wealth engendered by the mastic trade supported twenty *mastihohoriá* (mastic villages) from the time the Genoese set up a monopoly in the substance during the fourteenth and fifteenth centuries, but the end of imperial Turkey and the development of petroleum-based products knocked the bottom out of the mastic market. Now it's just a curiosity, to be chewed – try the sweetened *Elma* brand gum – or drunk as a liqueur called *mastíha*, though it has had medicinal applications since ancient times. These days, however, the *mastihohoriá* live mainly off their tangerines, apricots and olives.

The towns themselves, the only settlements on Híos spared by the Ottomans in 1822, are architecturally unique, laid out by the Genoese but retaining a distinct Middle Eastern feel. The basic plan consists of a rectangular warren of tall houses, with the outer row doubling as the town's perimeter fortification, and breached by a limited number of arched gateways.

The mastic villages

ARMÓLIA, 20km from town, is the smallest and least imposing of the mastic villages. Its main virtue is its pottery industry; the best workshop, selling useful kitchen ware as opposed to kitsch souvenirs, is Yeoryios Sfikakis, the third outfit on the right as you head southwest. **PYRGÍ**, 5km further south, is the most colourful of these communities, its houses elaborately embossed with *xystá*, geometric patterns cut into whitewash, revealing a layer of black volcanic sand underneath; strings of sun-drying tomatoes add a further splash of colour in autumn. On the northeast corner of the central square the twelfth-century Byzantine church of **Áyii Apóstoli** (Tues–Thurs & Sat 10am–1pm), embellished with much later frescoes, is tucked under an arcade. Of late, vast numbers of postcard racks and boutiques have sprung up on every main thoroughfare, detracting somewhat from the atmosphere. Pyrgí has a handful of **rooms**, many of them bookable through the Women's Agricultural and Tourist Cooperative (☎0271/72 496; ②). In the medieval core you'll find a bank, a post office and a few *souvláki* grills, but no real tavernas. **OLÝMBI**, 7km further west along the bus route serving Armólia and Pyrgí, is the least visited of the mastic villages, but not devoid of interest. The characteristic tower-keep, which at Pyrgí stands half-inhabited away from the modernized main square, here looms bang in the middle of the platía, its ground floor occupied by two **eateries**: *Kyra Maria's* (no sign), with simple mezédhes, and *Estiatorio Pyrgos*, with more elaborate main dishes.

Sombre, monochrome **MESTÁ**, 4km west of Olýmbi, is considered the finest example of the genre; despite more snack bars and trinket shops than strictly necessary on the outskirts, Mestá remains just the right side of twee as most people here still work the land. From its main square, dominated by the **church of the Taxiárhis** (the largest on the island), a bewildering maze of cool, shady lanes with anti-seismic buttressing and tunnels, leads off in all directions. Most streets end in blind alleys, except those leading to the six gates; the northeast one still has its original iron grate. If you'd like to stay, there are half a dozen **rooms** in restored traditional dwellings managed by Dhimitris Pipidhis (☎0271/76 319; ③); alternatively, three separate premises managed by Anna Floradhi (☎0271/76 455; ②) are somewhat less elaborate. Of the two **tavernas** on the main platía, *O Morias sta Mesta* is renowned for tasty rural specialities like pickled *krítamo* (rock samphire) and locally produced raisin wine: heavy, semi-sweet and sherry-like. However, portions have shrunk of late, and *Mesaionas* – whose tables share the square – is better value and has perhaps the more helpful proprietor.

The south coast

One drawback to staying in Mestá is a lack of nearby beaches; the closest candidate is surf-battered, facility-less **Merikoúnda**, 4km west of Mestá by dirt track. Reached by a seven-kilometre side road starting just west of Pyrgí, the little cove of **Káto Faná** is also bereft of amenities (save for a spring), but more sheltered; by the roadside 400m above the shore, the fragmentary remains of an Apollo temple surround a medieval chapel.

Pyrgí is actually closest to the two major beach resorts in this corner of the island. The nearest, 6km distant, is **EMBORIÓS**, an almost landlocked harbour with four passable **tavernas** (*Porto Emborios* has the edge with homemade desserts and *atherína*-and-onion fry-up); there's a scanty, British-excavated acropolis on the hill to the northeast, vaguely signposted 1km along the road to Kómi. For swimming, follow the road to its end at an oversubscribed car park and the beach of **Mávra Vólia**, then continue by flagstoned walkway over the headland to two more dramatic pebble (part nudist) strands of red and black volcanic stones, twice as long and backed by impressive cliffs.

If you want sand you'll have to go to **KÓMI**, 3km northeast, also accessible from Armólia via Kalamotí; there are just a few tavernas (most reliable of these being the *Bella Mare*), café-bars and summer apartments behind the pedestrianized beachfront. The bus service is fairly good in season, often following a loop route through Pyrgí and Emboriós.

Central Híos

The portion of Híos extending west and southwest from Híos Town matches the south in terms of interesting monuments, and good roads make touring under your own power an easy matter. There are also several beaches on the far shore of the island which, though not the best on Híos, are fine for a dip at the end of the day.

The Kámbos

The **Kámbos**, a vast fertile plain carpeted with citrus groves, extends southwest from Híos Town almost as far as the village of Halkió. The district was originally settled by the Genoese during the fourteenth century, and remained a preserve of the local aristocracy until 1822. Exploring it by bicycle or motorbike is less frustrating than going by car, since the web of poorly marked lanes sandwiched between high walls guarantee disorientation and frequent backtracking. Behind the walls you catch fleeting glimpses of ornate old mansions built from locally quarried sandstone; courtyards are paved in pebbles or alternating light and dark tiles, and most still contain a pergola-shaded irrigation pond filled by a *mánganos*, or donkey-powered water-wheel, used before the age of electric pumps to draw water up from wells up to 30m dee

Many of the sumptuous three-storey dwellings, constructed in a hybrid Italo-Turco-Greek style, have languished in ruins since 1881, but a few have been converted for use as unique **accommodation**. The best marked and best publicized are *Mavrokordatiko* (☎0271/32 900; ④), about 1500m south of the airport, with breakfast served by the *mánganos* courtyard, or the *Hotel Perivoli* (☎0271/31 513, fax 32 042; ⑤) slightly inland, with blue urban buses bound for Thymianá passing just 200m to the east. The rooms, no two alike, have fireplaces and (in most cases) en-suite baths and sofas, and it also has a highly regarded garden restaurant with two menus: Italian haute cuisine or post-modern Greek. There's a set price for the multi-plate, vegetarian or carniverous offerings, so best go in a group of four for good value.

Not strictly speaking in Kámbos, but most easily reached from it en route to the *mastihohoriá*, is an outstanding rural Byzantine monument. The thirteenth-century **church of Panayía Krína**, isolated amidst orchards and woods, is well worth the challenge of a maze of dirt tracks beyond Vavýli village, 9km from town. It's currently closed for snail's-pace restoration, but a peek through the apse window will give you a fair idea of the finely frescoed interior, sufficiently lit by a twelve-windowed drum. Some of the late medieval frescoes have been removed, and may be displayed in Híos Town's Justiniani Museum (see p.331). The alternating brick and stonework of the exterior alone justifies the trip here, though architectural harmony is marred by the later addition of a clumsy lantern over the narthex.

Néa Moní

Almost exactly in the middle of the island, the **monastery of Néa Moní** was founded by the Byzantine Emperor Constantine Monomahos ("The Dueller") IX in 1042 on the spot where a wonder-working icon had been discovered. It ranks among the most beautiful and important monuments on any of the Greek islands; the mosaics, together with those of Dháfni and Ósios Loukás on the mainland, are among the finest surviving art of their age in Greece, and the setting – high up in still partly forested mountains 15km west of the port – is no less memorable.

Once a powerful and independent community of six hundred monks, Néa Moní was pillaged in 1822 and most of its residents put to the sword; since then many of its outbuildings have languished in ruins, though a recent EU grant has prompted massive restoration work. The 1881 tremor caused comprehensive damage, while exactly a century later a forest fire threatened to engulf the place until the resident icon was paraded along the perimeter wall, miraculously repelling the flames. Today the monastery, with its giant refectory and vaulted water cisterns, is inhabited by just two elderly, frail nuns and a couple of lay workers.

Bus excursions are provided by the KTEL on Tuesday and Friday mornings, continuing to Anávatos, Lithí and Armólia; otherwise come by motorbike, or walk from Karyés, 7km northeast, to which there is a regular blue-bus service. **Taxis** from town, however, are not prohibitive, at about 5000dr round-trip per carload, including a wait while you look around.

Just inside the main gate (daily 8am–1pm & 4–8pm) stands a **chapel/ossuary** containing some of the bones of those who met their death here in 1822; axe-clefts in children's skulls attest to the savagery of the attackers. The **katholikón**, with the cupola resting on an octagonal drum, is of a design seen elsewhere only in Cyprus; the frescoes in the exonarthex are badly damaged by holes allegedly left by Turkish bullets, but the **mosaics** are another matter. The narthex contains portrayals of the various saints of Hios sandwiched between *Christ Washing the Disciples' Feet* and the *Betrayal of Christ*, in which Judas's critical kiss has unfortunately been obliterated, but Peter is clearly visible lopping off the ear of the high priest's servant. In the dome of the sanctuary (currently hidden by scaffolding), which once contained a complete life-cycle of Christ, only the *Baptism*, part of the *Crucifixion*, the *Descent from the Cross*, the *Resurrection* and the Evangelists *Mark* and *John* survived the earthquake.

The west coast

With your own transport, you can proceed 5km west of Néa Moní to **AVGÓNYMA**, a cluster of dwellings on a knoll overlooking the coast; the name means "Clutch of Eggs", an apt description when it's viewed from the ridge above. Since the 1980s, the place has been almost totally restored as a summer haven by descendants of the original villagers, though the permanent population is just seven. A returned Greek-American family runs a reasonable, simple-fare **taverna**, *O Pyrgos*, in an arcaded mansion on the main square; *To Arhondiko*, serving more involved mezédhes on its view terrace at the village entrance, is the alternative. The classiest **accommodation** option here is *Spitakia*, a cluster of small restored houses for up to five people (☎0271/20 513 or 43 051; fax 43 052; ④).

A paved side road continues another 4km north to **ANÁVATOS**, whose empty, dun-coloured dwellings, soaring above pistachio orchards, are almost indistinguishable from the 300-metre-high bluff on which they're built. During the 1822 insurrection, some four hundred inhabitants and refugees threw themselves over this cliff rather than surrender to the besieging Ottomans, and it's still a preferred suicide lea Anávatos can now only muster five souls, and given a lack of accommodation (there's one small snack bar) plus an eerie, traumatized atmosphere, it's no place to be stranded at dusk.

West of Avgónyma, the main road descends 6km to the coast in well-graded loops. Turning right (north) at the junction leads first to the beach at **Elínda**, alluring from afar but rocky and murky up close; it's better to continue towards more secluded coves

EITAN SIMANOUR

Platía Ippokrátous, Rhodes

PETER WILSON

Mosaics in a cloister, Filérimos, Rhodes

PETER WILSON

Ruined windmill, Váti, Rhodes

MARC S. DUBIN

Flagstone colours, Sými

MARC S. DUBIN

Kaïki-building, Pátmos, Dodecanese

MATTHEW HANCOCK

Taverna terrace

MARC S. DUBIN

View of Kástro and Hóra, Astypálea

MARC S. DUBIN

Mermaid Madonna Chapel, Lésvos

MARC S. DUBIN

Tomatoes drying, Híos

MARC S. DUBIN

A ferry at Foúrni

CHARLES BOWMAN

Wild flowers, Thássos

MICHAEL JENNER

Monastery steps, Níssyros

MICHAEL JENNER

Orthodox priest

MARC S. DUBIN

Monastery roofs, Evangelístria, Skiáthos

CHARLES BOWMAN

Shipwreck Bay, Zákynthos

MARC S. DUBIN

Bright walls, Gáïos, Paxí

to either side of Metóhi, or below **SIDHIROÚNDA**, the only village hereabouts, which enjoys a spectacular hilltop setting overlooking the coast.

All along this coast, as far southwest as Liménas Mestón, are round **watchtowers** erected by the Genoese to look out for pirates – the first swimmable cove you reach by turning left from the junction has the name **Kastélla**, attractive for swimming but with rough track access. A sparse weekday-only bus service resumes 9km south of the junction at **LITHÍ**, a friendly village of whitewashed buildings perched on a wooded ledge overlooking the sea. There are tavernas and kafenía near the bus turnaround area, but must visitors head 2km downhill to **Paralía Lithíou**, a popular weekend target of Hiot townies for the sake of its large but hard-packed, wind-swept beach. You may **stay** and **eat** at *Kyra Despina* (☎0271/73 373; ③), open most of the year, and apparently improved since the demise of the eponymous founder.

Some 5km south of Lithí, the valley-bottom village of **VÉSSA** is an unsung gem, more open and less casbah-like than Mestá or Pyrgí, but still homogeneous. Its honey-coloured buildings are arrayed in a vast grid punctuated by numerous belfries; there's a simple taverna (*Snack Bar Evanemos*) installed in a tower-mansion on the main road, and you can stay at a restored inn, *To Petrino* (☎0271/25 016 or 41 097; ③).

Northern Híos

Northern Híos never really recovered from the 1822 massacre, and the desolation left by fires in 1981 and 1987 will further dampen inquisitive spirits. Since the early 1900s the villages have languished all but deserted much of the year, which means correspondingly sparse bus services. About one-third of the former population now lives in Híos Town, venturing out here only during major festivals or to tend smallholdings; others, based in Athens or the US, visit their ancestral homes for just a few intense weeks in mid-summer, when marriages are arranged between local families.

The road to Kardhámyla

Blue city buses run north from Híos Town up to **VRONDÁDHOS**, an elongated coastal suburb that's a favourite residence of the island's many seafarers. Homer is reputed to have lived and taught here, and in terraced parkland just above the little fishing port and pebble beach you can visit his purported lectern, more probably an ancient altar of Cybele. Accordingly many of the buses out here are labelled "DHASKALÓPETRA", the Teacher's Rock.

Some 15km out of town, just past the tiny bayside hamlet of Pandoukiós, a side road leads to stony **Áyios Isídhoros** cove, home to the rather inconveniently located island **campsite**, *Chios Camping* (☎0271/74 111), though the site itself is shaded and faces Inoússes islet across the water. **LANGÁDHA**, just beyond, is probably the first point on the eastern coast road where you'd be tempted to stop, though there is no proper beach nearby. Set at the mouth of a deep valley, this attractive little harbour settlement looks across its bay to a pine grove, and beyond to Turkey. There are a couple of rooms outfits, but most evening visitors come for the sustaining seafood at two adjacent tavernas on the quay: *Tou Kopelou*, better known as Stelios's, and *Paradhisos*.

Just beyond Langádha an important side road leads 5km up and inland to **Pityoús**, an oasis in a mountain pass presided over by a tower-keep; continuing 4km more brings you to a junction allowing quick access to the west of the island and the Volissós area (see p.338).

Kardhámyla and around

Most traffic proceeds to **ÁNO KARDHÁMYLA** and **KÁTO KARDHÁMYLA**, the latter 37km out of the main town. Positioned at opposite edges of a fertile plain rimmed by mountains, they initially come as welcome relief from Homer's crags. Káto, better known as **MÁRMARO**, is larger, indeed the island's second town, with a bank, post office and filling station. However, there is little to attract a casual visitor other than some Neoclassical architecture: the port, mercilessly exposed to the *meltémi*, is strictly businesslike, and there are few tourist facilities. An exception is *Hotel Kardamyla* (☎0272/23 353; ⑤), co-managed with Híos Town's *Hotel Kyma*. It has the bay's only pebble beach, and its restaurant is a reliable source of lunch if you're touring. *Iy Vlyhadha*, facing the eponymous bay west over the headland, is an excellent independent **taverna** with locally produced suckling pig and squid.

For better swimming head west 5km to **Nagós**, a gravel-shore bay at the foot of an oasis, which is where the summertime bus service terminates. Lush greenery is nourished by active springs up at a bend in the road, enclosed in a sort of grotto overhung by tall cliffs. The place name is a corruption of *naos*, after a large Poseidon temple that once stood near the springs, but centuries of orchard-tending, antiquities-pilfering and organized excavations after 1912 mean that nothing remains visible. Down at the shore the swimming is good, if a bit chilly; there are two mediocre tavernas and a few rooms to rent. Your only chance of relative solitude in July or August lies 1km west at **Yióssonas**; this is a much longer beach, but less sheltered, rockier and with no facilities.

Volissós and around

VOLISSÓS, 42km from Híos Town by the most direct road (45km via the easier Avgónyma route), was once the market town for a dozen remote hill villages beyond, and its old stone houses still curl appealingly beneath the crumbling hilltop Byzantine fort. The towers were improved by the Genoese, from whose era also dates the utterly spuriouus "House of Homer" signposted near the top of town. Volissós can seem depressing at first, with the bulk of its 250 mostly elderly permanent inhabitants living in newer buildings around the main square, but opinions improve with longer acquaintance.

Grouped around the platía you'll find a **post office** (but no bank), two well-stocked shops and three mediocre **tavernas**; far better ones are found up in Pýrgos district, where *Pyrgos* (aka *Vasilis*, disguised by day as a machine shop) and the vegetarian *Kafenio E*, run by Nikos Koungoulios, are your options; reservations (☎0274/21 480) are advised for the latter. A filling station operates 2.5km out of town, the only one hereabouts; you should plan on overnighting since the bus only comes out here on Sundays on a day-trip basis, and on Monday, Wednesday and Friday in the afternoon. This should cause no dismay, since the area has the best beaches, and some of the most interesting **accommodation**, on Híos. Some sixteen old houses, mostly in Pýrgos district, have been meticulously restored by Stella Tsakiri and Argyris Angelou (☎0274/21 421 or 21 413, fax 21 521; ③) and usually accommodate two people – all have terraces, fully equipped kitchens and features such as tree trunks upholding sleeping lofts. Larger families or groups should try for three equally impressive, interlinkable units managed by Elysian Holidays (☎0274/21 128, fax 21 013; ④), very high up near the castle.

LIMNIÁ, (sometimes Limiá), the port of Volissós, lies 2km south, with kaïki skippers coming and going from Psará (mid-June to mid-Sept, Mon, Wed & Fri mid-morning). The best **tavernas** here are the long-established *Ta Limnia* on the jetty, for *mayireftá*, and summer-only *To Limanaki* at the rear of the cove, best for fish. At Limniá you're not far from the fabled beaches either. A 1.5 kilometre walk southeast over the headland brings you to **Managrós**, a seemingly endless sand and pebble beach; nearest **lodgings** are the bungalows of Marvina Alvertou (☎0274/21 335; ③). More intimate, sandy **Lefkáthia** lies just a ten-minute stroll along the cement drive threading over the headland north of the harbour; amenities are limited to a seasonal snack shack on the sand, and Ioannis Zorbas' apartments (☎0274/21 436; ③), beautifully set in a garden where the concrete track joins an asphalt road down from Volissós. This is bound for **Límnos** (not to be confused with Limniá), the next protected cove 400m east of

Lefkáthia, where *Taverna Akroyiali* provides salubrious food and professional service, and the spruce *Latini Apartments* (☎0274/21 461, fax 21 871; ③) are graced with multiple stone terraces.

Ayía Markélla, 5km further northwest of Límnos, stars in many local postcards: a long, stunning beach fronting the monastery of Híos's patron saint, the latter not especially interesting or useful for outsiders, since its cells are reserved for Greek pilgrims. In an interesting variation on the expulsion of the money-changers from the temple, only religious souvenirs are allowed to be sold in the holy precincts, while all manner of plastic junk is on offer just outside. There's the *Taverna Krokos* to hand as well, and around July 22 – the local saint's festival and biggest island bash – the "No Camping" signs are doubtless unenforced.

The dirt road past the monastery grounds is passable to any vehicle, with care, and emerges up on the paved road running high above the northwest coast. Turn left and proceed to the remote village of **ÁYIO GÁLA**, whose claim to fame is a **grotto-church** complex, built into a stream-lapped palisade at the bottom of the village. Signs ("Panayía Ayiogaloúsena") point to a lane crossing the water, but for access, except at the festival on August 23, you'll need to find the key-keeper (ask at the central kafenío), and descend to the complex from a flight of stairs starting beside a eucalypt. Of the two churches inside the cavern, the larger one near the mouth of the complex dates from the fifteenth century but seems newer owing to a 1993 external renovation. Inside, however, a fantastically intricate *témblon* vies for your attention with a tinier, older chapel, built entirely within the rear of the cavern. Its frescoes are badly smudged, except for a wonderfully mysterious and mournful Virgin, surely the saddest in Christendom, holding a knowing Child.

Satellite islands: Psará and Inoússes

There's a single settlement, with beaches and an isolated rural monastery, on both of Híos's satellite isles, but each is surprisingly different from the other, and of course from their large neighbour. Inoússes, the nearer and smaller islet, has a daily kaïki service from Híos Town in season; Psará has less regular services subject to weather conditions (in theory 3 weekly), and is too remote to be done justice on a day-trip.

Psará

The birthplace of revolutionary war hero Admiral Kanaris, **Psará** devoted its merchant fleets – the third largest in 1820s Greece after those of Ídhra and Spétses – to the cause of independence, and paid dearly for it. Vexed beyond endurance, the Turks landed overwhelming forces in 1824 to stamp out this nest of resistance. Perhaps 3000 of the 30,000 inhabitants escaped in small boats which were rescued by a French fleet, but the majority retreated to a hilltop powder magazine and blew it (and themselves) up rather than surrender. The nationalist poet Dhionysios Solomos immortalized the incident in famous stanzas:

On the Black Ridge of Psará,
Glory walks alone.
She meditates on her heroes
And wears in her hair a wreath
Made from a few dry weeds
Left on the barren ground.

Today, it's a sad, stark place fully living up to its name ("the grey things" in Greek), which never really recovered from the holocaust. The Turks burned whatever houses and vegetation the blast had missed, and the permanent population barely exceeds four hundred. The only positive recent development was a 1980s revitalization project instigated by a French-Greek descendant of Kanaris and a Greek team. The port was improved, mains electricity and pure water provided, a secondary school opened, and cultural links between France and the island established, though so far this has not been reflected in increased tourist numbers.

Arrival can be something of an ordeal: the regular small ferry from Híos Town can take up to four hours to cover the 57 nautical miles of habitually rough sea. Use the port of Limniá to sail in at least one direction if you can; this crossing takes half the time at just over half the price.

Since few buildings in the east-facing harbour community predate this century, it's a strange hotchpotch of ecclesiastical and secular architecture that greets the eye on disembarking. There's a distinctly southern feel, more like the Dodecanese or the Cyclades, and some peculiar churches, no two alike in style.

If you **stay overnight**, there's a choice between a handful of fairly basic rooms and three more professional outfits: *Psara Studios* (☎0274/61 233; ④) and *Apartments Restalia* (☎0274/61 000; ④), both a bit stark but with balconies and kitchens, or the EOT *xenónas* (☎0274/61 293; ③) in a restored prison. For **eating**, the best and cheapest place is the EOT-run *Spitalia*, housed in a restored medieval hospital at the north edge of the port. A **post office**, bakery and shop complete the list of amenities; there is no full-service bank.

Psará's **beaches** are decent, improving the further northeast you walk from the port. You quickly pass Káto Yialós, Katsoúni and Lazarétta with its off-putting power station, before reaching **Lákka** ("narrow ravine"), fifteen minutes along, apparently named after its grooved rock formations in which you may have to shelter; much of this coast is windswept, with a heavy swell offshore. **Límnos**, 25 minutes from the port along the coastal path, is big and attractive, but there's no reliable taverna here, or indeed at any of the other beaches. The only other thing to do on Psará is to walk north across the island to the **monastery of the Kímisis (Assumption)**; uninhabited since the 1970s, this comes to life only on August 1, when its revered icon is carried in ceremonial procession to town and then back on the eve of August 5.

Inoússes

Inoússes has a permanent population of about three hundred – less than half its prewar figure – and a very different history from Psará. For generations this medium-sized islet has provided the Aegean with many of her wealthiest shipping families: various members of the Livanos, Lemos and Pateras clans (with every street or square named for the last-named family) were born here. This helps explain the large villas and visiting summer yachts in an otherwise sleepy Greek backwater – as well as a **maritime museum** (sporadic hours) near the quay, endowed by various shipping magnates. At the west end of the quay, the bigwigs have also funded a large nautical academy, which trains future members of the merchant navy.

Only on Sundays can you make an inexpensive **day-trip** to Inoússes from Híos with the locals' ferry *Inousses*; on other days of the week this arrives at 3pm, returning early the next morning. On weekdays during the tourist season you must participate in the pricey excursions offered from Híos, with return tickets running up to three times the cost of the regular ferry.

Two church-tipped islets, each privately owned, guard the unusually well-protected harbour; the **town** of Inoússes is surprisingly large, draped over hillsides enclosing a ravine. Despite the wealthy reputation, its appearance is unpretentious, the houses displaying a mix of vernacular and modest Neoclassical style. There is just one, fairly comfortable **hotel**, the *Thalassoporos* (☎0272/51 475; ④), on the main easterly hillside lane. **Eating out** is similarly limited to a simple ouzerí just below the nautical academy, or the good-value *Taverna Pateronissia*, conspicuous at the base of the disembarkation jetty. Otherwise, be prepared to patronize one of the three shops (one on the waterfront, two up the hill). Beside the museum is a **post office** and a **bank**.

The rest of this tranquil island, at least the southern slope, is surprisingly green and well tended; there are no springs, so water comes from a mix of fresh and brackish wells, as well as a reservoir. The sea is extremely clean and calm on the sheltered southerly shore; among its beaches, choose from **Zepága**, **Biláli** or **Kástro**, respectively five, twenty and thirty minutes' walk west of the port. More secluded **Farkeró** lies 25 minutes east: first along a cement drive ending at a seaside chapel, then by path past pine groves and over a ridge. As on Psará, there are no reliable facilities at any of the beaches.

At the end of the westerly road, beyond Kástro, stands the somewhat macabre convent of **Evangelismoú**, endowed by the Pateras family. Inside reposes the mummified body of the lately canonized daughter, Irini, whose prayers to die of cancer in place of her terminally ill father Panagos were answered early in the 1960s on account of her virtue and piety; he's entombed here also, having outlived Irini by some years. The abbess, presiding over some twenty nuns, is none other than the widowed Mrs Pateras; only women are allowed admission, and even then casual visits are not encouraged.

Lésvos (Mytilíni)

Lésvos, the third largest Greek island after Crete and Évvia, is not only the birthplace of Sappho, but also of Aesop, Arion and – more recently – the Greek primitive artist Theophilos, the Nobel laureate poet Odysseus Elytis and the novelist Stratis Myrivilis. Despite these artistic associations, Lésvos may not at first strike the visitor as particularly beautiful or interesting; much of the landscape is rocky, volcanic terrain, dotted with thermal springs and alternating with vast grain fields, salt pans or even near-desert. But there are also oak and pine forests as well as vast olive groves, some of these over five hundred years old. With its balmy climate and suggestive contours, the island tends to grow on you with prolonged acquaintance.

Lovers of medieval and Ottoman **architecture** certainly won't be disappointed. Castles survive at the main town of Mytilíni, at Mólyvos, Eressós and near Ándissa; most of these date from the late fourteenth century, when Lésvos was given as a dowry to a Genoese prince of the Gateluzzi clan following his marriage to the niece of one of the last Byzantine emperors. Apart from Crete and Évvia, Lésvos was the only Greek island where Turks settled significantly in rural villages (they usually stuck to the safety of towns), which explains the odd Ottoman bridge, shed-like mosque or crumbling minaret often found in the middle of nowhere. Again unusually for the Aegean islands, Ottoman reforms of the eighteenth century encouraged the emergence of a Greek Orthodox land- and industry-owning aristocracy, who built rambling mansions and tower-houses, a few of which survive.

Social and economic idiosyncrasies persist: anyone who has attended one of the extended village *paniyíria*, with hours of music and tables in the streets groaning with food and drink, will not be surprised to learn that Lésvos has the highest alcoholism rate in Greece. Breeding livestock, especially horses, is disproportionately important, and traffic jams caused by mounts instead of parked cars are not unheard of – signs reading "Forbidden to Tether Animals Here" are still common.

Historically, the olive plantations, oúzo distilleries, animal husbandry and fishing industry supported those who chose not to emigrate, but with these enterprises relatively stagnant, mass-market tourism has made visible inroads. However, it still accounts for just five percent of the local economy, there are still few large hotels outside the capital or Mólyvos, villa-type accommodation just barely outstrips rooms, and the first official campsites only opened in 1990. Tourist numbers have in fact levelled

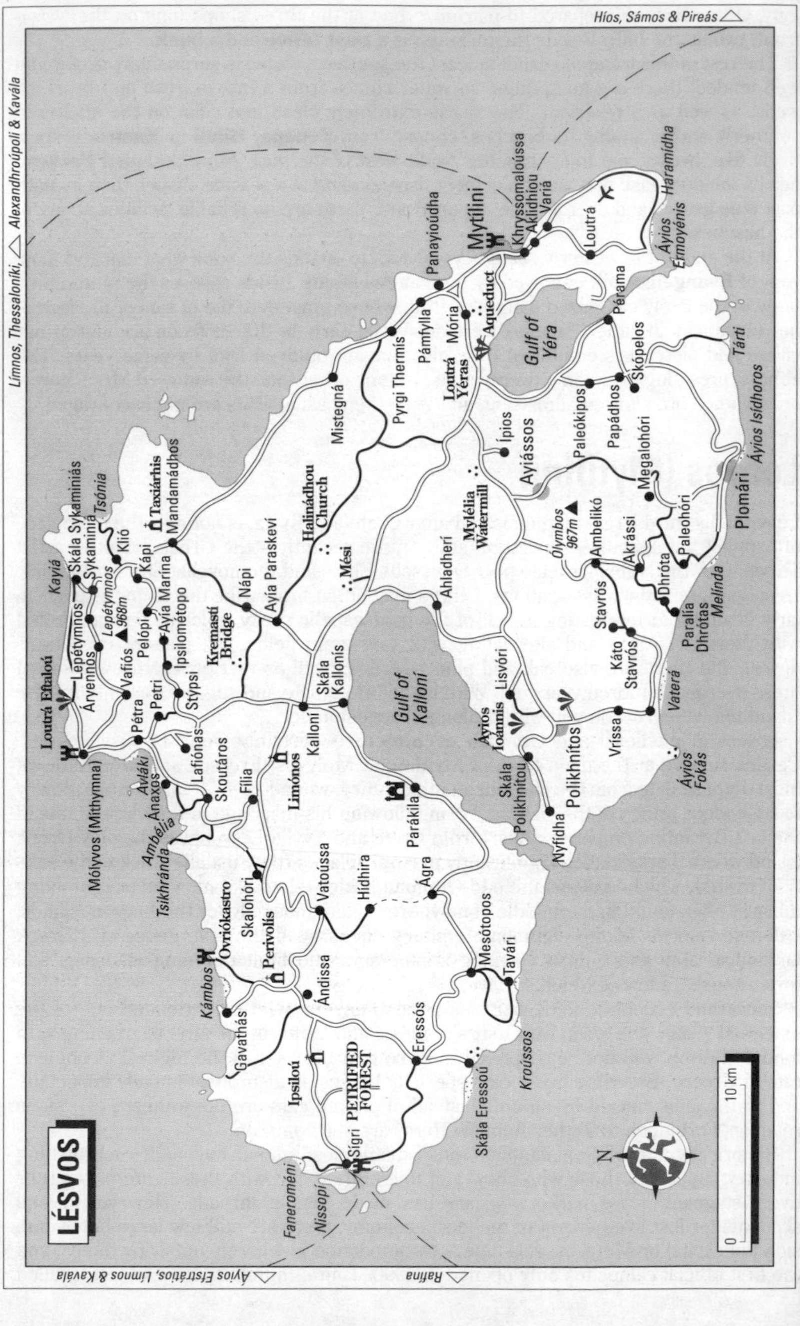
LÉSVOS
Híos, Sámos & Pireás
Límnos, Thessaloníki, Alexandhroúpoli & Kavála
Áyios Efstrátios, Límnos & Kavála
Rafína
Mytilíni
Khryssomaloússa
Aklidhíou
Variá
Haramídha
Áyios Ermoyénis
Loutrá
Pérama
Gulf of Yéra
Aqueduct
Panayioúdha
Pámfylla
Mória
Loutrá Yéras
Pyrgi Thermís
Mistegná
Skópelos
Papádhos
Paleókipos
Tárti
Áyios Isídhoros
Megalohóri
Ípios
Ayiássos
Mylélia Watermill
Plomári
Paleohóri
Ólymbos 967m
Ambelikó
Akrássi
Dhróta
Melínda
Paralía Dhrótas
Ahladherí
Stavrós
Káto Stavrós
Vaterá
Vrísa
Áyios Fokás
Polikhnítos
Lisvóri
Áyios Ioánnis
Skála Polikhnítou
Nyfídha
Gulf of Kalloní
Mési
Halinádhou Church
Skála Sykaminiás
Tsónia
Taxiárhis
Mandamádhos
Kápi
Klió
Sykaminiá
Kayiá
Lepétymnos 968m
Ayía Marína
Pelópi
Ipsilométopo
Stýpsi
Kremastí Bridge
Ayía Paraskeví
Nápi
Skála Kallonís
Kalloní
Limónos
Fília
Skoutáros
Lafiónas
Pétra
Petrí
Vafiós
Árvennos
Lepétymnos
Loutrá Eftaloú
Mólyvos (Míthymna)
Avláki
Ánaxos
Ambélia
Tsikhránda
Ovriókastro
Skalohóri
Vatoússa
Hídhira
Parákila
Ágra
Mesótopos
Tavári
Perivolís
Ándissa
Kámbos
Gavathás
Eressós
Skála Eressoú
Kroússos
Ipsiloú
PETRIFIED FOREST
Sígri
Faneroméni
Nissopí
N
0
10 km

out in recent years, the result of stalled plans to expand the airport, unrealistic hotel pricing and the dropping of the island from several tour operators' programmes.

Public **buses** tends to radiate out from the harbour for the benefit of working locals, not day-tripping tourists. Carrying out such excursions from Mytilíni is next to impossible anyway, owing to the size of the island – about 70km by 45km at its widest points – and a few appalling roads (others have been improved, along with their signposting). Moreover, the topography is complicated by the two deeply indented gulfs of Kalloní and Yéra, with no bridges across their mouths, which means that going from A to B involves an obligatory change of bus at either the port capital, on the east shore, or the town of Kalloní, in the middle of the island. It's best to decide on a base and stay there for a few days, exploring its immediate surroundings on foot or by rented vehicle.

Mytilíni Town

MYTILÍNI, the port and capital, sprawls between and around two bays divided by a fortified promontory, and in Greek fashion often doubles as the name of the island. Most visitors are put off by the combination of urban bustle and slight seediness, and contrive to leave as soon as possible; the town returns the compliment by in fact being a fairly impractical and expensive place to base yourself.

Nonetheless, Mytilíni has enough to justify a layover of a few hours. On the promontory sits the Byzantine-Genoese-Ottoman **fortress** (Tues–Sun 8.30am–2.45pm; 600dr), comprising ruined structures from all these eras and an Ottoman inscription above a Byzantine double-headed eagle at the south gate. Further inland, the town skyline is dominated in turn by the Germanic spire of **Áyios Theodhóros** and the mammary dome of **Áyios Therápon**, the pair of them expressions of the post-Baroque taste of the nineteenth-century Ottoman Greek bourgeoisie. They stand more or less at opposite ends of the bazaar, whose main street, Ermoú, links the town centre with the little-used north harbour of Páno Skála. On its way there Ermoú passes half a dozen expensive but rather picked-over antique shops near the roofless Yeni Tzami, an occasional exhibition venue. Between Ermoú and the castle lies a maze of atmospheric lanes lined with grandiose Belle Epoque mansions and elderly vernacular houses.

The excellent **Archeological Museum** (Tues–Sun 8.30am–3pm; 600dr) is housed partly in the mansion of a large estate just behind the ferry dock. Among the more compelling of the well-labelled exhibits are a complete set of mosaics from a Hellenistic dwelling, rather droll terracotta figurines, votive offerings from a sanctuary of Demeter and Kore excavated in the castle and Neolithic finds from present-day Thermí. A specially built annexe at the rear contains stone-cut inscriptions of various edicts and treaties, and – more interesting than you'd think – *stelae* featuring ***nekródhipna***, or portrayals of funerary meals. Yet another annexe for the overflow, 150m up the hill at the base of 8-Noemvríou, is not yet operational.

There's also a worthwhile **Byzantine Art Museum** (summer only Mon–Sat 10am–1pm; 400dr) just behind Áyios Therápon, containing various icons rescued from rural churches, plus a canvas of the *Assumption* by Theophilos (see p.346).

Practicalities

There's no bus link with the **airport**, so a shared taxi for the 7km into Mytilíni is the usual method; Olympic Airways is southwest of the main harbour at Kavétsou 44. As on Híos, there are two bus stations: the *astykó* (blue bus) service departing from the middle of the quay, the *iperastikó* (standard KTEL) buses leaving from a small station near Platía Konstandinopóleos at the southern end of the harbour. If you're intent on getting over to Ayvalık in Turkey, book tickets through either Dimakis Tours at

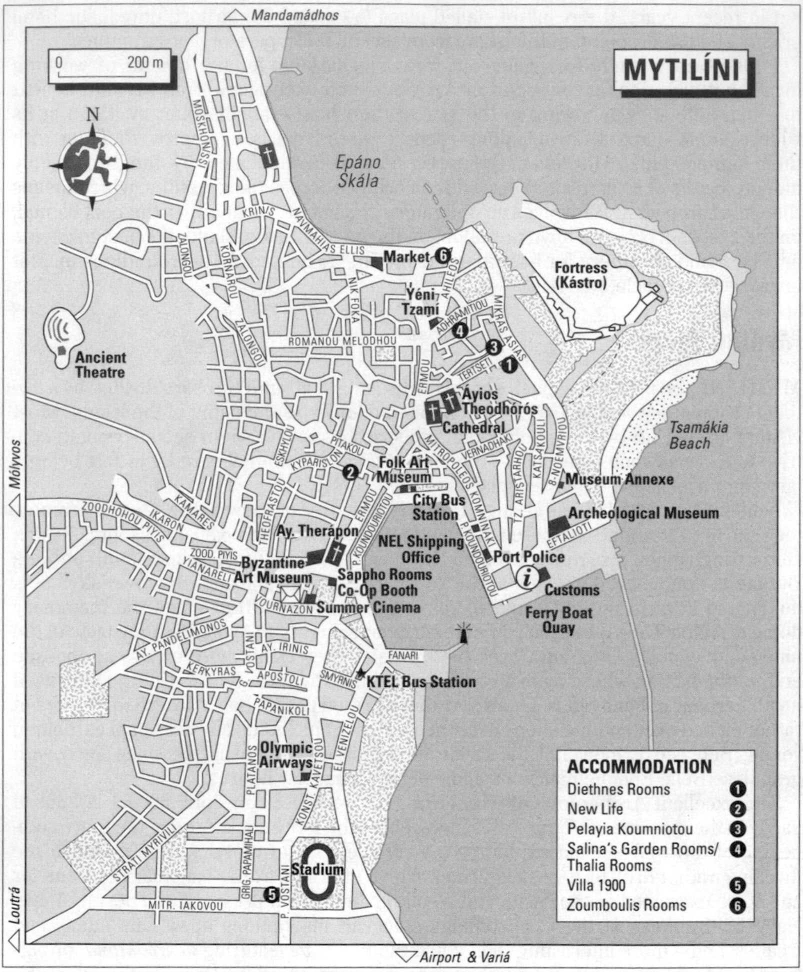

Koundouriótou 73 (☎0251/27 865) or Picolo Travel at no. 73a (☎0251/27 000). NEL Ferries has its own agency at no. 47 (☎0251/28 480), while G&A ferries are handled by Picolo Travel.

Car rental is best arranged through reputable chain franchises like Payless at Koundouriótou 49 (☎0251/43 555), Budget, next door (☎0251/25 846), Thrifty at no. 69 (☎0251/41 464) or Just at no. 47 (☎0251/43 080) – though it's generally cheaper to rent at the resort of your choice. Other amenities include the **post office** on Vournázon, behind the central park, and four banks with cash dispensers: the Ethniki/National, Alpha Pisteos/Alpha Credit – both on Koundouriótou – and the Emboriki/Commercial on Ermoú, plus a free-standing booth on the quay. Before leaving town, you might stop at the jointly housed tourist police/EOT office (daily 8.30am–6pm; ☎0251/22 776), behind the customs building, in order to get hold of their excellent town and island maps, plus other brochures. If they're shut, try the EOT regional headquarters 300m away at Aristárhou 6 (Mon–Fri 8am–2.30pm).

ACCOMMODATION

Finding **accommodation** can be difficult: the waterfront hotels are noisy and exorbitantly priced, with few single rooms to speak of. If you need to stay, hunting for better-value rooms has been eased by the formation of the "Sappho's Rented Rooms Association" (☎0251/43 375, booth by the park), with most of the 22 affiliated premises located between the castle and Ermoú. Yeoryíou Tertséti street in particular has two possibilities: the friendly if basic *Pelayia Koumniotou* at no. 6 (☎0251/20 643; ②) or the fancier, en-suite *Vetsikas/Dhiethnes* at no. 1 (☎0251/24 968; ③). Two other quiet establishments sit between the north harbour and fortress: *Salina's Garden Rooms*, behind the Yeni Tzami at Fokéas 7 (☎0251/42 073; ②), co-managed with the *Thalia Rooms* across the street (☎0251/24 640; ②). *Zoumbouli Rooms*, facing the water on Navmahías Ellís (☎0251/29 081; ③), are en-suite, but may get more noise from traffic and the bar below. Moving slightly upmarket, there's *New Life* at the end of Olýmbou, a cul-de-sac off Ermoú (☎0251/46 100), offering antique-furnished rooms in an old mansion, or *Villa 1900*, another restored mansion in the south of town at P. Vostáni 24 (☎0251/43 437; ③), whose en-suite units have fridges, air conditioning and sometimes ceiling murals.

EATING, DRINKING AND NIGHTLIFE

Dining options in Mytilíni are limited, especially since the demise of several more characterful places in the 1990s and the multiplication of fast-food joints in their stead. The obvious, if blatantly touristy, venue for a seafood blowout is the line of three fish tavernas on the southerly quay known as Fanári; *Stratos* at the far end is marginally the best, and the only one that doesn't tout aggressively. Having got this far, you may as well keep going to the end of the jetty and the square lighthouse building which houses a characterful fishermen's kafenío with excellent mezédhes; the only similar establishment left in town is a no-name ouzerí on Thássou, between Ermoú and the front.

If you're stuck here involuntarily, awaiting a dawn-departing ferry, some consolation can be derived from the town's decent **nightlife and entertainment**. *Hott Spott* is a fairly accurate self-description of the durable café-bar at Koundouriótou 63, near the NEL agency; nearby at no. 59, *Papagallino* also does crepes, and has a magnificent interior atrium. Formal live events constitute the Lesviakó Kalokéri, held in the castle from June to August, while the summer cinema Pallas is between the post office and the park on Vournázon.

Around Mytilíni

Beyond the airport and Krátigos village, the paved road becomes dirt up to **Haramídha**, 14km from town and the closest decent beach (the fee-entry town "beach" at Tsamákia is mediocre); the eastern bay has a few tavernas. The double cove at **Áyios Ermoyénis**, 4km west, is more scenic but crowded at weekends, and has no taverna or accommodation. The latter is directly accessible from Mytilíni via Loutrá village. For other pleasant immersions near Mytilíni, make for **Loutrá Yéras**, 8km along the main road to Kalloní. These public baths (daily: June–Aug 8am–7pm; Sept–May 10am–6pm; 500dr) are just the thing if you've spent a sleepless night on a ferry, with ornate spouts that feed 38°C water to marble-lined pools in vaulted chambers; there are separate facilities for each sex.

The Variá museums

The most rewarding single targets near Mytilíni are a pair of museums at **VARIÁ,** 5km south of town (half-hourly buses). The **Theophilos Museum** (Tues–Sun 9am–2pm & 5–8pm; 500dr includes key-catalogue) honours the painter, born here in 1873, with four rooms of wonderful, little-known compositions specifically commissioned by his patron Thériade (see below) during the years leading up to his death in 1934. A wealth of detail is evident in elegiac scenes of fishing, reaping, olive-picking and baking from the pastoral Lésvos which Theophilos obviously knew best; there are droll touches also, such as a cat slinking off with a fish in *The Fishmongers*. In classical scenes – *Sappho and Alkaeos*, a landscape series of Egypt, Asia Minor and the Holy Land, and historical episodes from wars historical and contemporary – Theophilos was clearly on shakier ground. In *Abyssinians Hunting an Italian Horseman*, the subject has been conflated with New World Indians chasing down a conquistador.

The adjacent, imposing **Thériade Museum** (Tues–Sun 9am–2pm & 5–8pm; 500dr) is the brainchild of another native son, Stratis Eleftheriades (1897–1983). Leaving the island at an early age for Paris, he gallicized his name to Thériade and went on to become a renowned avant-garde art publisher, convincing some of the leading artists of the twentieth century to participate in his ventures. The displays consist of lithographs, engravings, wood-block prints and watercolours by the likes of Miró, Chagall, Picasso, Matisse, Le Corbusier, Léger, Rouault and Villon, either annotated by the painters themselves or commissioned as illustrations for the works of prominent poets and authors – an astonishing collection for a relatively remote Aegean island.

Southern Lésvos

The southernmost portion of the island is indented by two great inlets, the gulfs of **Kalloní** and **Yéra**, the first curving in a northeasterly direction, the latter northwesterly, creating a fan-shaped peninsula at the heart of which looms 967-metre Mount Ólymbos. Both shallow gulfs are almost landlocked by virtue of very narrow outlets to the open sea. This is the most verdant and productive olive-producing territory on Lésvos, and the stacks of pressing-mills stab the skyline.

Plomári and around

Due south of Mount Ólymbos, at the edge of the "fan", **PLOMÁRI** is the only sizable coastal settlement in the south, and indeed the second largest town on Lésvos. It presents an unlikely juxtaposition of scenic appeal and its famous oúzo industry, courtesy of several nearby distilleries. Despite a lack of good beaches within walking distance, it's besieged in summer by hordes of Scandinavian tourists, but you can usually find a **room** (they are prominently signposted) at the edge of the old, charmingly dilapidated town, or (better) 1km west in **Ammoudhélli** suburb, which has a small gravel beach. Three specific outfits above Platía Beniamín include *Pension Lida I* and *II* (☎0252/32 620; ③), in adjacent old mansions, and *Pension Kamara* (☎0252/31 901; ③). Rustling up a decent meal may present more difficulties, with the dinner-only *Platanos* taverna at the central plane tree often unbearably busy, and nothing special at that. Ammoudhélli can offer *To Ammoudhelli*, a seafood and grills ouzerí perched over the water, and *Mama Katerina* on the opposite side of the road.

Áyios Isídhoros, 3km east, is where most tourists actually stay; pick of the hotels here, not completely overrun with package tours, is the *Pebble Beach* (☎0252/31 651; ④), with most of the large rooms overlooking a slightly reefy section of beach. Eating out here, try the adjacent *Iy Mouria* or *Mamas Papas* (sic), where the road turns inland to cross the creek draining to the long, popular pebble beach.

Melínda, another 700-metre sand and shingle beach at the mouth of a canyon, lies 6km west of Plomári on a partly paved road (closed to four-wheelers until mid-2000). Here you'll find three inexpensive **taverna-rooms** outfits, of which *Maria's* (☎0252/93 239; ②) is an endearingly ramshackle place with simple but reasonably priced food and lodging; *Melinda* (aka Dhimitris Psaros; ☎0252/93 234; ②) at the west end of the strand has a more elaborate menu and en-suite rooms. Even more unspoiled (thanks partly to a dreadful seven-kilometre side road in, being paved in 1999), Tárti, some 22km in total from Plomári, is a 400-metre-wide cove where Lésvos hoteliers and restaurant owners take *their* holidays. Of the three tavernas, the one closest to road's end is the best and cheapest; rooms also line the final stretch of road should you want to stay.

The **bus** into Plomári travels via the attractive villages of Paleókipos and Skópelos (as well as Áyios Isídhoros); the road north from Plomári to Ayiássos has paving and public transport only as far as Megalohóri.

Ayiássos and Mylélia

AYIÁSSOS, nestled in a remote, wooded valley under the crest of Mount Ólymbos, is the most beautiful hill town on Lésvos, its narrow cobbled streets lined by ranks of tiled-roof houses. On the usual, northerly approach, there's no clue of the enormous village until you see huge knots of parked cars at the southern edge of town (where the bus leaves you after the 26-kilometre run from Mytilíni).

Don't be put off by the endless ranks of kitsch wooden and ceramic souvenirs, aimed mostly at Greeks, but continue past the central **church of the Panayía Vrefokratoússa**, originally built in the twelfth century to house an icon supposedly painted by the Evangelist Luke, to the **old bazaar**, with its kafenía, yoghurt shops and butchers' stalls. With such a venerable icon as a focus, the local August 15 *paniyíri* is one of the liveliest in Greece, let alone Lésvos. Ayiássos also takes Carnival very seriously; there's a club dedicated to organizing it, opposite the post office.

The best **restaurants are** *Dhouladhelli*, on your left as you enter the village from the extreme south (bus stop) end, or *Dhayielles*, 70m further along and less subscribed to by Greek coach groups. At either of these spots you can eat for a fraction of the prices asked at the coastal resorts. There are a very few rooms available; ask at the *Anatoli* grill, between the two aforementioned restaurants.

If you're headed for Ayiássos with your own transport, you might visit the **Mylélia water mill**, whose access track takes off 1km west of the turning for Ípios village. The name means "place of the mills", and there were once several hereabouts, powered by a spring up-valley at Karíni. The last survivor (open daily 9am–6pm), restored to working order, has not been twee-ified in the least; the keeper will show you the millrace and paddle-wheel, as well as the flour making its spasmodic exit, after which you're free to buy gourmet pastas at the adjacent shop.

Vaterá, Skála Polikhnítou – and spas en route

A different bus route from Mytilíni leads to Vaterá beach via the inland villages of **Polikhnítos** and **Vríssa**. If you're after a hot bath, the small, vaulted **spa-house** 1.5km east of Polykhnítos has been restored by an EU programme (Mon–Sat 7–11am & 5–7pm, Sun 7–11am; 500dr); there are separate, pink-tinted chambers for each sex. Alternatively there are more **hot springs** at **Áyios Ioánnis** (token admission), fairly well signposted 3km below the village of Lisvóri. Flanking the eponymous chapel are two pools housed in unlocked, whitewashed, vaulted chambers (500dr fee payable when adjacent snack bar attended); the left-hand one's nicer, and there's no gender segregation or dress code.

VATERÁ itself, 9km south of Polikhnítos, is a huge, seven-kilometre-long sand beach, backed by vegetated hills; the sea here is delightfully calm and clean. If you intend to stay here you'll probably want your own transport, as the closest shops are 4km away at Vríssa, and the bus appears only a few times daily. Development straggles for several kilometres to either side of the central T-junction, consisting mostly of seasonal villas and apartments for locals; at the west end of the strip is one of the very few consistently attended and professionally run hotels, the Greek- and American-run *Vatera Beach* (☎0252/61 212, fax 61 164, *hovatera@otenet.gr*; ④). It also has a good attached restaurant with shoreline tables from where you can gaze on the cape of **Áyios Fokás** 3km to the west, where only foundations remain of a temple of Dionysos and a superimposed early Christian basilica. The little tamarisk-shaded anchorage here has an acceptable fish **taverna**, *Akrotiri/Agelerou*; it's better than most eateries east of the T-junction at Vaterá, many of them only operating July and August, but not so good as the half-dozen tavernas at **SKÁLA POLIKHNÍTOU**, 4km northwest of Polikhnítos itself, where *Ta Asteria* and *Exohiko Kendro Tzitzifies* can both be recommended, staying open most of the year. Skála itself is pleasantly workaday, with no beach to speak of but one unusual accommodation option: "Soft Tourism" run by Lefteris and Erika (☎0252/42 678; ②), who also have the concession to run the Polikhnítos spa. They generally have special-interest groups April-to-June and September, but welcome independent travellers during July and August.

East from Vaterá, an intermittently paved road leads via Stavrós, and then either Ambelikó or Akrássi to either Ayiássos or Plomári within ninety minutes. When leaving the area going north towards Kalloní, the short cut via the naval base at Akhladherí is well worth using, and completely paved despite tentative depiction on local maps.

Western Lésvos

The main road west of Loutrá Yéras is surprisingly devoid of settlement, with little to stop for before Kalloní other than the traces of an ancient **Aphrodite temple** at **Mési** (Messon), 1km north of the main road, and signposted just east of the Akhladherí turnoff. At the **site** (Tues–Sun 8.30am–3pm; free) just eleventh-century BC foundations and a few column stumps remain, plus the ruins of a fourteenth-century Genoese-built basilica wedged inside; it was once virtually on the sea but a nearby stream has silted things up in the intervening millennia. All told, it's not worth a special trip, but certainly make the short detour if passing by. With more time and your own transport, you can turn northeast towards **Ayía Paraskeví** village, midway between two more important monuments from diverse eras: the Paleo-Christian **basilica of Halinádhou**, and the **medieval bridge** of Kremastí.

KALLONÍ itself is an unembellished agricultural and market town more or less in the middle of the island, but you may spend some time here since it's the intersection of most bus routes. Some 3km south lies **SKÁLA KALLONÍS**, a somewhat unlikely package resort backing a long but coarse beach on the lake-like gulf. It's mainly distinguished as a bird-watching centre, attracting hundreds of twitchers for the spring nesting season in the adjacent salt marshes. Pick of the handful of hotels is the human-scale bungalow complex *Malemi* (253/22 594; ④), with attractive grounds and a pool. Restaurants are generally unrecommendable except for the *Medusa*, serving succulent seafood (including the gulf's celebrated *sardhélles pastés*, or salt-cured sardines) within sight of the fishing fleet.

Inland monasteries and villages

West of Kalloní, the road winds 4km uphill to the **monastery of Limónos**, founded in 1527 by the monk Ignatios, whose actual cell is maintained in the surviving medieval north wing. It's a huge, rambling complex, with just a handful of monks and lay workers to maintain three storeys of cells around a vast, plant-filled courtyard. The *katho-*

likón, with its carved-wood ceiling and archways, is built in Asia Minor style and is traditionally off-limits to women; a sacred spring flows from below the south foundation wall. A former abbot established a **museum** (daily 9am–3pm, sometimes later as funding permits; 200dr) on two floors of the west wing; the ground-floor ecclesiastical collection is interesting enough, though the upstairs ethnographic gallery (officially shut for "repairs") is better. If denied access, you may have to content yourself with an overflow of farm implements stashed in a corner storeroom below, next to a chamber where giant *pithária* (urns) for grain and olive oil are embedded in the floor.

The main road beyond passes through **VATOÚSSA**, a landlocked and beautiful settlement in the heart of the westerly landmass; besides unspoilt architecture it can offer two sterling examples of the endangered traditional oúzo-mezédhes kafenío in the upper platía: *Tryfon* and *Mihalis*.

Some 8km beyond Vatoússa, a short track leads down to the sixteenth-century **monastery of Perivolís** (daily 8am–one hour before sunset; donation, no photos), built in the midst of a riverside orchard (*perivóli*). Feeble electric light is available to view the narthex's fine if damp-damaged frescoes. In an apocalyptic panel worthy of Bosch (*The Earth and Sea Yield up their Dead*) the Whore of Babylon rides her chimera and assorted sea-monsters disgorge their victims; just to the right, towards the main door, the Three Magi approach the Virgin enthroned with the Christ Child. On the north side you see a highly unusual iconography of *Abraham, the Virgin, and the Penitent Thief of Calvary in Paradise*, with the Four Rivers of Paradise gushing forth under their feet; just right are assembled the Hebrew kings of the Old Testament.

ÁNDISSA, 3km further on, nestles under the west's only pine grove; at the edge of the village a sign implores you to "Come Visit Our Square", not a bad idea for the sake of several kafenía sheltering under three enormous plane trees. For more substantial fare, however, follow the paved road from directly below Ándissa 6km north to **GAVATHÁS**, a fishing hamlet with a narrow, partly protected beach (there's a bigger, surf-buffeted one at Kámbos just to the east) and a few places to eat and stay – the best of these are *Rooms Restaurant Paradise* (☎0253/56 376 or, in winter, call the proprietors in New Jersey ☎302/535-6376; ③); both serve with good fish and locally grown vegetables.

Just west of Ándissa there's an important junction. Keeping straight leads you past the still-functioning **monastery of Ipsiloú**, founded in 1101 atop the extinct volcano of Órdhymnos. The *katholikón*, tucked in one corner of a large, irregular courtyard, has a fine wood-lattice ceiling but had its frescoes repainted to detrimental effect in 1992; more intriguing are portions of Iznik tile stuck in the facade, and the handsome double gateway. Upstairs you can visit a fairly rich **museum** of ecclesiastical treasure (sporadically open; small donation). Ipsiloú's patron saint is John the Theologian, a frequent dedication for monasteries overlooking apocalyptic landscapes like the surrounding parched, boulder-strewn hills.

Signposted just west is the paved, five-kilometre side road to the main concentration of Lésvos's rather overrated **petrified forest** (daily 8am–sunset; 500dr), a fenced-in "reserve" which is toured along 3km of walkways. For once, contemporary Greek arsonists cannot be blamed for the state of the trees, created by the combined action of volcanic ash from Órdhymnos and hot springs some fifteen to twenty million years ago. The mostly horizontal sequoia trunks average a metre or less in length, save for a few poster-worthy exceptions; another more accessible (and free) cluster is found south of Sígri (see below), plus there are a fair number of petrified logs strewn about the courtyard of Ipsiloú.

Sígri

SÍGRI, near the western tip of Lésvos, has an appropriately end-of-the-line feel; the bay here is guarded both by an Ottoman castle, and the long island of Nissopí, which protects the place somewhat from prevailing winds. Accordingly it's an important NATO naval base, with the few weekly NEL **ferries** to Rafína, Áyios Efstrátios and Límnos obliged to dodge numbers of battleships anchored here. The eighteenth-century **castle** sports the sultan's monogram over the entrance, something rarely seen outside Istanbul, and a token of the high regard in which this productive island was held. A vaguely Turkish-looking **church** is in fact a converted mosque, while the town itself presents a drab mix of vernacular and cement dwellings. The town beach, south of the castle headland, is narrow and hemmed in by the road; there are much better beaches at **Faneroméni**, 3.5km north by coastal dirt track from the northern outskirts of town, plus another 2km south, just below the fifteen-kilometre dirt track to Eressós; neither beach has any facilities.

Most **accommodation** is monopolized by British tour companies, but you might try *Nelly's Rooms and Apartments* (☎0253/54 230; ②), overlooking the castle, or the nearby *Rainbow Studios* (☎253/54 310; ②). Among several tavernas, *Galazio Kyma* – the white building with blue trim, opposite the jetty – gets first pick of the fishermen's catch, but is no longer as cheap as it was.

Skála Eressoú

Most visitors to western Lésvos park themselves at the resort of **SKÁLA ERESSOÚ,** accessible via the southerly turning between Ándissa and Ipsilоú. The three-kilometre beach here runs a close second in quality to Vaterá's, and consequently the place is beginning to rival Plomári and Mólyvos for numbers of visitors, who form an odd mix of Brits, Scandinavians, Greek families, neo-hippies and lesbians (of whom, more below). Behind stretches the largest and most attractive agricultural plain on Lésvos, a welcome green contrast to the volcanic ridges above.

There's not much to Skála – just a roughly rectangular grid of perhaps five streets by eight, angling up to the oldest cottages on the slope of **Vígla hill**. The waterfront pedestrian zone (officially Papanikolí) is divided by a café-lined round platía at mid-waterfront dominated by a bust of **Theophrastos**, the renowned botanist who hailed from ancient Eressós. This was not, as you might suppose, on the site of the modern inland village, but atop Vígla hill at the east end of the beach; some of the remaining citadel wall is still visible from a distance. On top, the ruins prove scanty, but it's worth the scramble up for the views – you can discern the ancient jetty submerged beyond the modern fishing anchorage.

Another famous reputed native of ancient Eressós was **Sappho** (c. 615–562 BC), the ancient poetess and reputed lesbian.There are usually appreciable numbers of gay women here paying homage, particularly at the two hotels (see below) devoted to their exclusive use, and in the clothing-optional zone of the beach west of the river mouth. The river itself is home to about a hundred terrapins who have learned to come ashore for bread-feedings and – beware – finger-nippings. Ancient Eressós endured into the Byzantine era, the main legacy of which is the **basilica of Áyios Andhréas** behind the modern church, merely foundations and an unhappily covered floor mosaic; the adjacent museum of local odds and ends is even less compelling.

Skála has countless **rooms and apartments**, but ones near the sea fill early in the day or are block-booked by tour companies; in peak season often the best and quietest you can hope for is something inland overlooking a garden or fields. Late in the day it's wise to entrust the search to an agency, such as Krinellos (☎0253/53 246), just off the round "square"; you pay a small commission but it saves trudging about for vacancies. There are just three bona fide hotels, and two of these – the remote *Antiopi* (☎0253/53 311; ②–③) and the seafront *Sappho the Eressia* (☎0253/53 233; ③) – are run exclusively by and for lesbians. Straights have to make do with the central, inland *Galini* (☎0253/53 138; ②); there is no longer a campsite.

Most **tavernas**, with elevated wooden dining platforms, crowd the beach; none is bad – they wouldn't survive the intense competition – but perhaps the best are two outfits at the far west end of the front. *Adonis* is a good full-on taverna with meat and fish dishes, while adjacent *Blue Sardine* is an excellent seafood ouzerí with good bread, clearly identified frozen items, unusual salads and extra touches to the fish. On the east side of the platía, Canadian-run *Yamas* is the place for pancake breakfasts, veggie burgers, wholemeal bread and decadent chocolate desserts; nearby Austrian-run *Margaratiri* is a Viennese-themed chocolate-coffee-and-Kuchen dessert café, expensive but worth it. The gay women's contingent currently favours *Dhekati Mousa/Tenth Muse*, on the Theophrastos platía; a summer cinema further inland rounds up the nightlife. Skála has a post office and a coin-op laundry near the church, but no bank or cash dispenser; come prepared or pay travel agency commissions.

If you're returning to the main island crossroads at Kalloní, you can complete a loop from Eressós along the western shore of the Gulf of Kalloní via the hill villages of Mesótopos and Ágra; this route is now entirely paved, notwithstanding obsolete maps showing it as a track.

Northern Lésvos

The main road north of Kalloní winds up a piney ridge and then down the other side into increasingly attractive country, stippled with poplars and blanketed by olive groves. Long before you can discern any other architectural detail, the cocks'-comb silhouette of **Mólyvos castle** indicates your approach to the oldest established tourist spot on Lésvos.

Mólyvos (Míthymna)

MÓLYVOS (officially Míthymna), 61km from Mytilíni, is arguably the most beautiful village on Lésvos. Tiers of sturdy, red-tiled houses, some standing defensively with their rear walls to the sea, mount the slopes between the picturesque harbour and the **Genoese castle** (Tues–Sun 8.30am–3pm; 500dr), which provides interesting rambles around its perimeter walls and views of Turkey across the straits. Closer examination reveals a score of weathered Turkish fountains along flower-fragrant, cobbled alleyways, a reflection of the fact that before 1923 Muslims constituted over a third of the local population and owned most of the finest dwellings. You can try to gain admission to the **Krallis and Yiannakos mansions**, or the **municipal art gallery** occupying the former residence of local author Argyris Eftaliotis, which hosts changing exhibits. The small **archeological museum** (Tues–Sun 8.30am–3pm; free), in the basement of the town hall, features finds from the ancient town, including blue Roman beads to ward off the evil eye (belief in this affliction is age-old and pan-Mediterranean). Archival photos depict the Greek conquest of the island in November–December 1912, with Ottoman POWs being dispatched afterwards from Mólyvos port to Anatolia. Barely excavated **ancient Mithymna** to the northwest is of essentially specialist interest, though a necropolis has been unearthed next to the bus stop.

Modern dwellings and hotels have been banned from the municipal core, but this has inevitably sapped all the authentic life from the upper bazaar; just one lonely tailor still plies his trade amongst duplicate souvenir shops, and the last locals' ouzerí shut in 1989 (though the *Salguimi* tries gamely to re-create a traditional kafenío ambience). Cast as an upmarket resort in the early 1980s, Mólyvos is now firmly MOR, with the usual silly T-shirts and other shoddy souvenirs to remind you that you're strolling through a stage-set, however tasteful, for mass tourism.

PRACTICALITIES

The **town beach** is mediocre, improving somewhat as you head towards the southern end and a clothing-optional zone. Advertised **boat excursions** to bays as remote as

Ánaxos and Tsónia (see opposite) seem a frank admission of this failing; there are also six to eight daily minibus shuttles in season, linking all points between Ánaxos and Eftaloú.

The main sea-level thoroughfare, straight past the tourist office, heads towards the harbour; along or just below it stand a number of bona fide **hotels** or **pensions.** These include the *Amfitriti* (☎0253/71 741; ④), with its own pool in a calm garden setting; the *Hermes* very near the beach (253/71 250; ③), with large airy rooms; and the durable *Sea Horse* (☎0253/71 320; ④) down at the fishing harbour, fine if you're not interested in making an early night of it in season. For rooms, seek out the modern studio units of Khryssi Bourdhadonaki (☎0253/72 193; ③), towards Ayía Kyriakí; those of Panayiotis Baxevanellis (☎0253/71 558 or *El Greco* cake-shop; ③), with a preponderance of double beds and a common kitchen; *Studios Voula* below the castle parking lot (☎0253/72 017 or 71 305), studios (③) or a restored four-person house (④), both with knockout views; and the quiet, simple rooms of Varvara Kelesi (☎0253/71 460; ②), way up by the castle. Otherwise, rooms can be reserved through the municipal tourist office by the bus stop (daily: summer theoretically 8am–3pm & 6.30–8.30pm; spring and autumn 8.30am–3pm). The official campsite, *Camping Methymna*, lies 2km northeast of town on the Eftaloú road.

The sea-view tavernas along the lower market lane of 17-Noemvríou are all much of a muchness, where you pay primarily for the view; it's far better to either head for outlying villages (see below) or descend to the fishing port, where *The Captain's Table* (green chairs) combines the virtues of fresh seafood, meat grills and vegetarian mezédhes. On the far side of the Turkish fountain here, 1999-opened *Onar* has some unusual dishes such as stuffed squid, while *To Khtapodhi*, in the old customs house by the port entrance, has fairly consistent quality and treats such as *sardhélles pastés*. Many consider the five-kilometre trip east to Vafiós worth it to patronize either *Taverna Vafios* or *Taverna Ilias*, especially the latter with its wonderful bread and bulk wine – but avoid deep-fried dishes at either place. Also highly recommended, and open most of the year, is *Iy Eftalou*, 4km northeast near the eponymous spa (see below), where the food (mostly grills) and tree-shaded setting are splendid. For dessert, try the pudding and cake shop *El Greco* on the lower market lane, where the proprietor Panayiotis is a wonderful raconteur (in several languages).

Midsummer sees a short **festival of music and theatre** up in the castle, and there's also a well-regarded summer **cinema** next to the taxi rank. Night-owls are well catered for with a selection of music bars: the sedate, retro *Skala* near the harbour; disco-ey young things' hangout *Congas Bar* below the shore road; and the all-season *Gatelousi Piano Bar* near the *Olive Press Hotel*, a more genteel branch of state-of-the-art outdoor disco *Gatelousi*, 3km towards Pétra, the place to be seen on a Saturday night (June–Aug only). Around the tourist office you'll find an automatic money-changing machine and a cash dispenser, plus numerous motorbike and car rental places. The main post office is near the top of the upper commercial street, with a seasonal branch on the shore road Mihaïl Goútou.

Pétra and Ánaxos

Since there are political and practical limits to the expansion of Mólyvos, many package companies have shifted emphasis to **PÉTRA**, 5km due south. The place has sprawled untidily behind its broad sand beach and seafront square, but the core of old stone houses, many with Levantine-style balconies overhanging the street, remains. Pétra takes its name from the giant **rock monolith** located some distance inland and enhanced by the eighteenth-century **church of the Panayía Glykofiloússa**, reached via 103 rock-hewn steps. Other local attractions include the sixteenth-century **church of Áyios Nikólaos**, with three phases of well-preserved frescoes, and the intricately decorated **Vareltzídhena mansion** (closed indefinitely for restoration).

There are a few small **hotels**, the best of these being the *Michaelia* (☎0253/41 573; ④) on the shore road towards Ánaxos – and a Women's Agricultural Tourism Cooperative (☎0253/41 238 or 41 340, fax 41 309), formed by Pétra's women in 1984 to offer something more unusual for visitors. In addition to operating an excellent, inexpensive restaurant on the square, with both grills and *mayireftá* served at rooftop seating, they arrange rooms (②) in a number of scattered premises. Aside from the co-operative's eatery, most tavernas lack distinction, except for the *Pittakos* ouzerí (dinner only) 100m south of the square. You're probably better off out of town – either at the *Taverna Petri* in the *Petrí* village 3km inland, with superb home-recipe *mayireftá* and a view terrace, or at Avláki, 1.5km southwest en route to Ánaxos, where there's an excellent, signposted eponymous taverna (really an ouzerí) behind a tiny beach.

ÁNAXOS, 3km south of Pétra, is a higgledy-piggledy package resort fringing by far the cleanest beach in the area: a kilometre of sand cluttered with sunbeds, pedalos and unmemorable snack bars. From anywhere along here you enjoy beautiful sunsets between and beyond three offshore islets.

Around Mount Lepétymnos

East of Mólyvos, the villages of 968-metre **Mount Lepétymnos**, marked by tufts of poplars, provide a day's rewarding exploration. The first stop, though not exactly up the hill, might be **Loutrá Eftaloú**, some thermal baths 5km along the road passing the campsite. Unfortunately the Ottoman domed structure is kept locked from June to September, when you're obliged to patronize the sterile modern tub-rooms (daily 10am–5pm; 300dr). Nearby, there are a considerable number of fancy hotels and bungalow complexes, friendliest, best value and least packaged of which is the *Eftalou* (☎0253/71 584; ④), with a pool, well-tended garden and loyal repeat clientele.

The main road around the mountain first heads 6km east to **VAFIÓS**, with its two aforementioned tavernas (see opposite), before curling north around the base of the peaks. This route is now entirely paved, but twice-daily bus service back towards Mytilíni does not resume until Áryennos, 6km before the exquisite hill village of **SYKAMINIÁ (Sykamiá)**, birthplace of the novelist Stratis Myrivilis. Below the "Plaza of the Workers' First of May", with its two traditional kafenía and views north to Turkey, one of the imposing basalt-built houses is marked as his childhood home. A marked trail shortcuts the twisting road down to **SKÁLA SYKAMINIÁS**, easily the most picturesque fishing port on Lésvos. Myrivilis used it as the setting for his best-known book, *The Mermaid Madonna*, and the tiny rock-top chapel at the end of the jetty will be instantly recognizable to anyone who has read the novel.

On a practical level, Skála has a few pensions, such as the central *Gorgona* (☎0253/55 301; ③), and four **tavernas**, the best and longest-lived of these being *Iy Skamnia* (aka *Iy Mouria*), with seating under the mulberry tree in which Myrivilis used to sleep on hot summer nights. In addition to good seafood, you can try the late summer island speciality of *kolokytholoúloudha yemistá* (stuffed squash blossoms). The only local beach, however, is the extremely stony one of **Kayiá** 1.5km east, so Skála is perhaps better as a lunch stop rather than a base.

Continuing east from upper Sykaminiá, you soon come to **KLIÓ**, whose single main street (marked "*kentrikí agorá*") leads down to a platía with a plane tree, fountain, kafenía and more views across to Turkey. The village is set attractively on a slope, down which a six-kilometre dirt road, marked in English or Greek and better than maps suggest, descends to **Tsónia beach**, 600m of beautiful pink volcanic sand.

South of Klió, the route forks at Kápi, from where you can complete a loop of the mountain by bearing west along a mostly paved road. **PELÓPI** is the ancestral village of unsuccessful 1988 US presidential candidate Michael Dukakis, and sports a former mosque, now used as a warehouse, on the main square. **IPSILOMÉTOPO,** 5km further along, is punctuated by a minaret (but no mosque) and hosts revels on July 17, the feast of Ayía Marína. By the time you reach sprawling **STÍPSI**, you're just 4km shy of the main Kalloní–Mólyvos road; it's also not a bad start-point for rambles along Lepétymnos's steadily dwindling network of trails. In recent years donkey-trekking has become more popular than walking, and you'll see outfit advertising throughout the north of the island.

Mandamádhos and Taxiárhis monastery

The main highway south from Klió and Kápi leads back to the capital through **MANDAMÁDHOS**. This attractive inland village is famous for its pottery, including the Ali Baba style *pithária* (olive oil urns) seen throughout Lésvos, but more so for the "black" icon of the Archangel Michael, whose enormous **monastery of Taxiárhis** (daily: summer 6am–10pm; winter 6.30am–7pm), in a valley just northeast, is the powerful focus of a thriving cult. The image – supposedly made from a mixture of mud and the blood of monks slaughtered in a massacre – is really more idol than icon, both in its lumpy three-dimensionality and in the former rather pagan manner of veneration. First there was the custom of the coin-wish, whereby you pressed a coin to the Archangel's forehead – if it stuck, your wish would be granted. Owing to wear and tear on the image, the practice is now forbidden, with supplicants referred to an alternative icon by the main entrance.

It's further believed that while carrying out his various errands on behalf of the faithful, the Archangel gets through more footwear than Imelda Marcos. Accordingly the icon used to be surrounded not by the usual *támmata* (votive medallions) but by piles of miniature gold and silver shoes. The ecclesiastical authorities, embarrassed by such "primitive" practices, removed all the little shoes in 1986. Since then, a token substitute has reappeared: several pairs of tin slippers which can be filled with money and left in front of the icon. Just why his devotees should want to encourage these perpetual peripatetics is unclear, since in Greek folklore the Archangel Michael is also the one who fetches the souls of the dying, and modern Greek attitudes towards death are as bleak as those of their pagan ancestors.

Límnos

Límnos is a sizable agricultural and garrison island whose remoteness and peculiar ferry schedules have until now protected it from the worst excesses of the holiday trade. Most summer visitors are Greek, and as a foreign traveller, you're still likely to find yourself an object of curiosity and hospitality, though the islanders are becoming increasingly used to numbers of German and British visitors. Accommodation tends to be comfortable if a bit overpriced, with a strong bias towards self-catering units.

Among young Greek males, Límnos has a dire reputation, largely due to its unpopularity as an army posting; there is a conspicuous **military presence**, with the islanders making a reliable living off the soldiers and family members coming to visit them. In recent years, the island has been the focus of disputes between the Greek and Turkish governments; Turkey has a long-standing demand that Límnos should be demilitarized, and Turkish aircraft regularly overfly the island, prompting immediate responses from the Greek Air Force squadron here.

The bays of **Bourniá** and **Moúdhros**, the latter one of the largest natural harbours in the Aegean, almost divide Límnos in two. The west of the island is dramatically bare and hilly, with abundant basalt put to good use as street cobbles and house masonry. Like most volcanic islands, Límnos produces excellent wine from westerly vineyards – good dry whites and rosés, plus excellent retsina – plus oúzo at Kondiás. The east is low-lying and speckled with marshes popular with duck-hunters, where it's not occupied by cattle, combine harvesters and vast corn fields.

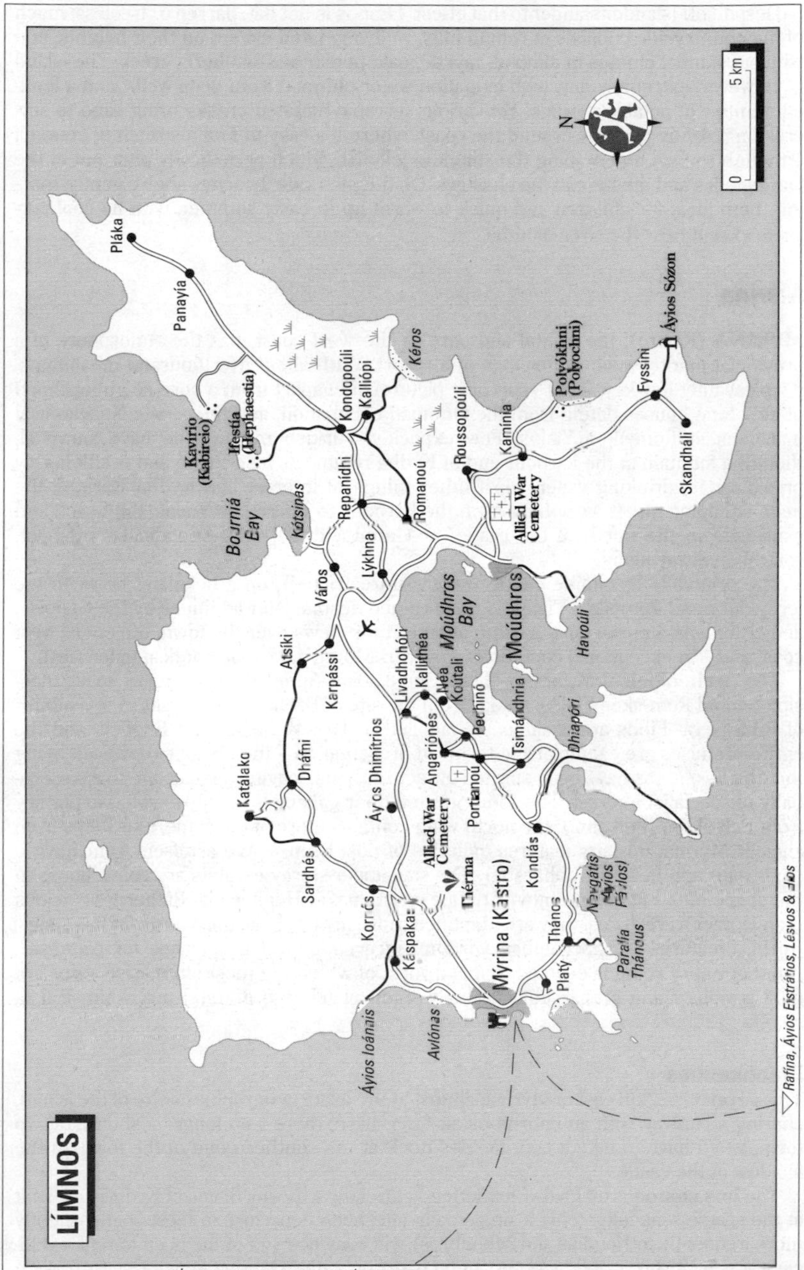
LÍMNOS
Kavála, Thessaloníki or Alexandhroúpoli
Rafína, Áyios Efstrátios, Lésvos & Híos
N
0
5 km
Pláka
Panayía
Kavirio (Kabireio)
Ifestía (Hephaestia)
Kondopoúli
Kalliópi
Kéros
Boúrnia Bay
Kótsinas
Repanídhi
Romanoú
Roussopoúli
Kamínia
Polyókhni (Polyochni)
Fyssíni
Áyios Sózon
Skandháli
Allied War Cemetery
Moúdhros
Moúdhros Bay
Havoúli
Lýkhna
Város
Atsíki
Karpássi
Livadhohóri
Kallithéa
Néa Koútali
Pedhinó
Tsimándhria
Dhiapóri
Katálako
Dhháfni
Áyios Dhimítrios
Angariónes
Allied War Cemetery
Portianoú
Thérma
Sardhés
Kondiás
Kornós
Kaspakás
Mýrina (Kástro)
Thános
Platý
Nevgátis
Áyios Pávlos
Paralía Thánous
Áyios Ioánnis
Avlónas

Despite off-islander slander to that effect, Límnos is not flat, barren or treeless; much of the countryside consists of rolling hills, well vegetated except on their heights, and with substantial clumps of almond, myrtle, oak, poplar and mulberry trees. The island is, however, extremely dry, with irrigation water pumped from deep wells, and a limited number of potable springs. Yet various terrapin-haunted creeks bring sand to several long, sandy beaches around the coast, where it's easy to find a stretch to yourself – though there's no escaping the stingless jellyfish which periodically pour out of the Dardanelles and die here in the shallows. On the plus side, beaches shelve gently, making them ideal for children and quick to warm up in early summer, with no cool currents except near the river mouths.

Mýrina

MÝRINA (Kástro), the capital and port on the west coast, has the atmosphere of a provincial market town rather than of a resort. With about five thousand inhabitants, it's pleasantly low key, if not especially picturesque, apart from a core neighbourhood of old stone houses dating from the Ottoman occupation, and the ornate Neoclassical mansions at Romeïkos Yialós. Few explicitly Turkish monuments have survived, though a fountain at the harbour end of Kýdha retains its inscription and is still highly prized for its drinking water. Most other things of interest line Kydhá/Karatzá, the main shopping street stretching from the harbour to Romeïkós Yialós, the beach and esplanade to the north of the castle, or Garoufalídhou, its perpendicular offshoot, roughly halfway along.

The originally Byzantine **castle** (access unrestricted), on a headland between the ferry dock and Romeïkós Yialós, is quite ruined despite later additions by the Genoese and Ottomans, but warrants a climb at sunset for views over the town, the entire west coast and – in exceptional conditions – over to Mount Áthos, 35 nautical miles west.

The **Archeological Museum** (Tues–Sun 8.30am–3pm; 600dr) occupies an old mansion behind Romeïkós Yialós, not far from the site of Bronze Age Myrina in the suburb of Rihá Nerá. Finds are assiduously labelled in Greek, Italian and English, and the entire premises are exemplary in terms of presentation – the obvious drawback being that the best items have been spirited away to Athens, leaving a collection that's essentially of specialist interest. The south ground-floor gallery is mainly devoted to pottery from Polyókhni (Polychni); the north wing contains more of the same, plus items from ancient Myrina; upstairs features galleries of post-Bronze Age artefacts from Kavírio (Kabireio) and Ifestía (Hephaestia). The star upper-storey exhibits are votive lamps in the shape of sirens, found in an Archaic sanctuary at Hephaestia. Rather less vicious than Homer's creatures, they are identified more invitingly as the "muses of the underworld, creatures of superhuman wisdom, incarnations of a nostalgia for paradise". Another entire room is devoted to metalwork, of which the most impressive items are gold jewellery and bronze objects, both practical (cheese graters) and whimsical (a snail).

Practicalities

The **airport** is 22km east of Mýrina, almost at the exact geographic centre of the island, sharing a runway with an enormous air-force base; there's no longer a shuttle bus to town, you'll have to take a taxi. Ferries dock at the southern end of the town, in the shadow of the castle.

The **bus station** is on Platía Eleftheríou Venizélou, at the north end of Kydhá. One look at the sparse schedules (only a single daily afternoon departure to most points, slightly more frequently to Kondiás and Moúdhros) will convince you of the need to rent a vehicle. Cars, motorbikes and bicycles can be had from either Myrina Rent a Car (☎0254/24

476), Petridou Tours (☎0254/22 039), Holiday (☎0254/24 357 or mobile ☎ 093/2481056) or Auto Europe (☎0254/23 777); rates for bikes are only slightly above the island norm, but cars are expensive. A motorbike is generally enough to explore the coast and the interior, as there are few steep gradients but many perilously narrow village streets.

All three banks have cash dispensers; the post office and Olympic airlines terminal are adjacent to each other on Garoufalídhou, with a laundry across the way by the Hotel Paris.

ACCOMMODATION

Despite Límnos's upmarket reputation, you may still be met off the boat with offers of a **room**. Otherwise, try the *Hotel Lemnos* (☎0254/22 153; ④), by the harbour; the secluded *Studios Despina* (☎0254/23 352; ③) on a cul-de-sac leading north from Garoufalídhou, with spotless, well-furnished apartments in a garden setting; or the quiet *Hotel Ifestos* in Andhróni district (☎0254/24 960, fax 23 623; ④).

Romeïkós Yialós has several **pensions** housed in its restored houses, though all are affected by evening noise from the bars below; best value of the bunch is *Kosmos* at no. 21 (☎0254/22 050; ④). One block inland at Sakhtoúri 7, the *Pension Romeïkos Yialos* (☎0254; 23 787; ④) in a stone mansion is quieter. Just north of Romeïkós Yialós, the areas of Rihá Nerá and Áyios Pandelímonas are likely bets for self-catering units; the best positioned are the hilltop *Afroditi Apartments* at Áyios Pandelímonas (☎0254/23 489; ⑤), best bookable through Sunvil Holidays in Britain. Finally, the *Akti Myrina* (☎0254/22 310, fax 22 352; winter ☎01/41 37 907) is a self-contained luxury complex of 110 wood and stone bungalows at the north end of Romeïkós Yialós, with all conceivable diversions and comforts. It's ferociously expensive – £180/$290 double half-board minimum in July – but costs considerably less if booked through one of several British tour operators offering it.

There's no official campsite on Límnos, though Greek caravanners and campers tend to congregate at the north end of Platý beach (see below).

EATING AND DRINKING

About halfway along Kydhá, *O Platanos* serves traditional oven food on an atmospheric little square under two plane trees, while *Avra*, on the quay next to the port police, makes a good choice for a pre-ferry meal or an evening grill. Seafood is excellent on Límnos due to its proximity to the Dardanelles and seasonal fish migrations; accordingly there are no fewer than six tavernas arrayed around the little fishing port. There's little to distinguish their prices or menus, though *O Glaros* at the far end is considered the best – and works out slightly more expensive.

Not too surprisingly given the twee setting, the restaurants and bars along Romeïkós Yialós are pretty poor value, except for a drink in sight of the castle. The tree-shaded tables of *Iy Tzitzifies* on the next bay north are a better option for beachfront dining.

Western Límnos

As town **beaches** go, Romeïkós Yialós is not at all bad, but if you're looking for more pristine conditions, head 3km north past the *Akti Myrina* to Avlónas, unspoiled except for the *Porto Marina Palace* luxury complex flanking it on the south. Some 6km from town you work your way through **KÁSPAKAS**, its north-facing houses in pretty, tiled tiers, before plunging down to **Áyios Ioánnis**. Here, the island's most unusual taverna features seating in the shade of piled-up volcanic boulders, with a sandy beach just north of the fishing anchorage. If it's shut, *Taverna Iliovasilemata* to the south is welcoming, with good (if slightly pricey) fish.

PLATÝ, 2km southeast of Mýrina, is a village of some architectural character, home also to three tavernas. Best of these, 100m south of the pair on the main square, is the

Zimbabwe, where the quality of the food (and the prices) belie its humble appearance. The long sandy beach, 700m below, is popular and usually jellyfish-free; except for the unsightly luxury compound at the south end, the area is still resolutely rural, with sheep parading to and fro at dawn and dusk. The low-rise *Plati Beach Hotel* (☎0254/24 301, fax 23 583; ③) has an enviable position in the middle of the beach, but is often full of package clients; there are basic rooms available at *Tzimis Taverna* (☎0254/24 142; ②), which divides the lunchtime trade with its neighbour *Grigoris* near the south end of the beach. Both lose out in the evenings to the village-centre tavernas, or the nearby poolside bar/restaurant attached to the tastefully landscaped *Villa Afroditi* (☎0254/23 141; winter ☎01/96 41 910; ⑥), co-managed with the *Afroditi Apartments* in town (and also offered advantageously through Sunvil), with one of the best buffet breakfasts in Greece.

THÁNOS, 2km further southeast, seems a bigger version of Platý village, with a few tavernas and "rooms" signs in evidence; **Paralía Thánous**, 1km on a rough track below the village, is perhaps the most scenic of the southwestern beaches, with two tavernas, one (*O Nikos*) renting studio-apartments (☎0254/22 787; ③). Beyond Thános, the road curls over to the enormous beach at **Nevgátis** (Áyios Pávlos), flanked by weird volcanic crags on the west and reckoned to be the island's best. Despite this, there's only a seasonal drinks stall on the sand and a full-service taverna across the road.

Some 3km further along (11km from Mýrina), **KONDIÁS** is the island's third largest settlement, cradled between two hills tufted with Limnos's only pine forest. Stone-built, red-tiled houses combine with the setting to make Kondiás the most attractive inland village, though facilities are limited to a few noisy rooms above one of two kafenía. Eating is better at the two simple tavernas of **Dhiapóri**, 2km east, the shore annexe of Kondiás; the beach is unappealing, with the main interest lent by the narrow isthmus dividing the bays of Kondiás and Moúdhros.

Eastern Límnos

The shores of **Moúdhros bay,** glimpsed south of the trans-island road, are muddy and best avoided. The bay itself enjoyed considerable importance during World War I, culminating in the Ottoman surrender aboard the British warship HMS *Agamemnon* here on October 30, 1918. The port of **MOÚDHROS**, the second largest town on Límnos, is a dreary place, with only a wonderfully kitsch, two-belfried church to recommend it. The closest decent beach is at **Havoúli**, 4km south by dirt track and still far from the open sea. Despite this, there are three hotels here; best of these is *To Kyma* (☎0254/71 333; ⑤), whose moderately priced restaurant is well placed for a lunch break if you're visiting the archeological sites and beaches of eastern Límnos.

About 800m along the Roussopoúli road, you pass an **Allied military cemetery** (unlocked) maintained by the Commonwealth War Graves Commission; its neat lawns and rows of white headstones seem incongruous in such parched surroundings. In 1915, Moúdhros Bay was the principal staging area for the disastrous Gallipoli campaign. Of the roughly 36,000 Allied dead, 887 – mainly battle casualties who died after having been evacuated to the base hospital at Moúdhros – are buried here, with 348 more at another graveyard behind the church in Portianoú.

Indications of the most advanced Neolithic civilization in the Aegean have been unearthed at **Polyókhni (Polyochni)**, 3km from the gully-hidden village of Kamínia (7km east of Moúdhros). Since the 1930s, Italian excavations have uncovered four layers of settlement, the oldest from late in the fourth millennium BC, pre-dating Troy on the Turkish coast opposite; the town met a sudden, violent end from war or earthquake in about 2100 BC. The actual **ruins** (daily 9.30am–5.30pm; free) are of essentially specialist interest, though a *bouleuterion* (assembly hall) with bench seating, a mansion and the landward fortifications are labelled. During August and September the Italian excavators are about, and may be free to show you around the place. The site occupies a bluff overlooking a long, narrow rock and sand beach flanked by stream valleys.

Ifestía and Kavírio, the other significant **ancient** sites on Límnos, are reached via the village of Kondopoúli, 7km northeast of Moúdhros. Both sites are rather remote, and only reachable with your own transport. **Ifestía (Hephaestia)**, 4km from Kondopoúli by rough, signposted track, has little to offer non-specialists. **Kavírio (Kabireio)**, on the opposite shore of Tigáni Bay and accessed by the same road serving a 1996-built luxury complex, is more evocative. The **ruins** (daily 9.30am–3.30pm; free) are those of a sanctuary connected with the cult of the Samothracian Kabiroi (see p.362), though the site here is probably older. Little survives other than the ground plan, but the setting is undeniably impressive. Eleven column stumps stake out a stoa, behind eight spots marked as column bases in the *telestirio* or shrine where the cult mysteries took place. More engaging, perhaps, is a nearby sea grotto identified as the Homeric **Spiliá toú Filoktíti**, where the Trojan war hero Philoctetes was abandoned by his comrades-in-arms until his stinking, gangrenous leg had healed. Landward access to the cave is via steps leading down from the caretaker's shelter.

The beach at **Kéros**, 2.5km by dirt road below **KALLIÓPI** (two snack bar/tavernas), is the best in this part of the island. A 1500-metre stretch of sand with dunes and shallow water, it attracts a number of Greek tourists and Germans with camper vans and windsurfers; a small drinks *kantína* operates near the parking area in season.

On the other side of Kondopoúli, reached via Repanídhi village, the pleasant if somewhat hard packed beach of **Kótsinas** is set in the protected western limb of Bourniá Bay. The nearby anchorage offers a pair of tavernas and, up on a knoll overlooking the jetty, a corroded, sword-brandishing statue of Maroula, a Genoese-era heroine who delayed the Ottoman conquest by a few years, and a large **church of Zoödhóhou Piyís** (the life-giving spring). This is nothing extraordinary, but beside it 62 steps lead down through an illuminated tunnel in the rock to the brackish spring in question, oozing into a cool, vaulted chamber.

Áyios Efstrátios (Aï Strátis)

Áyios Efstrátios is without doubt one of the quietest and most isolated islands in the Aegean. Historically, the only outsiders to stay here were compelled to do so – it served as a place of exile for political prisoners under both the Metaxas regime of the 1930s and the various right-wing governments that followed the civil war. It's still unusual for travellers to show up on the island, and, if you do, you're sure to be asked why you've come.

You may initially ask yourself the same question, for **ÁYIOS EFSTRÁTIOS** village – the only habitation on the island – must be one of the ugliest in Greece. Devastation caused by an earthquake in early 1968, which killed half the population, was compounded by the reconstruction plan: the contract went to a company with junta connections, who prevented the survivors from returning to their old homes and used army bulldozers to raze even those structures that could have been repaired. From the hillside, some two dozen surviving houses of the old village overlook its replacement, whose grim rows of prefabs constitute a sad monument to the corruption of the junta years. If you're curious, there's a pre-earthquake photograph of the village in the kafenío by the port.

Architecture apart, Áyios Efstrátios still functions as a traditional fishing and farming community, with the prefabs set at the mouth of a wooded stream valley draining to the sandy harbour beach. Tourist amenities consist of just two basic tavernas, plus a growing number of **pensions** where you shouldn't have much trouble finding a bed except in season. Best of these, in one of the surviving old houses, is the *Xenonas Aï-Stratis*

(☎0254/93 329; ③); Popi Panera (☎0254/93 209; ③) has more conventional rooms in one of the prefabs.

As you walk away from the village – there are few cars and no real roads – things improve rapidly. The landscape, dry hills and valleys scattered with a surprising number of oak trees, is deserted apart from wild rabbits, sheep, an occasional shepherd, and some good beaches where you can camp in seclusion. **Alonítsi**, on the north coast – a ninety-minute walk from the village following a track up the north side of the valley – is a two-kilometre stretch of sand with rolling breakers and views across to Límnos.

South of the village, there's a series of greyish sand beaches, most with wells and drinkable water, although with few real paths in this part of the island, getting to them can be something of a scramble. **Lidharío**, at the end of an attractive wooded valley, is the first worthwhile beach, but again it's a ninety-minute walk, unless you can persuade a fisherman to take you by boat. Some of the caves around the coast are home to the rare Mediterranean monk seal, but you're unlikely to see one.

Ferries between Límnos and Kavála to Rafína call at Áyios Efstrátios every two or three days throughout the year; in summer a small Límnos-based ferry, the *Aiolis*, calls twice a week. Despite recent harbour improvements, this is still a very exposed anchorage, and in bad weather you could end up stranded here far longer than you bargained for. If an indefinite stay does not appeal, it's best to visit from Límnos on the day-trip offered by the *Aiolis* (usually on Sunday).

Samothráki (Samothrace)

After Thíra, **Samothráki** has the most dramatic profile of all the Greek islands. Originally colonized by immigrants from Thrace, Anatolia and Lésvos, it rises abruptly from the sea in a dark mass of granite, culminating in 1611-metre Mount Fengári. Seafarers have always been guided by its imposing outline, and in legend its summit provided a vantage point for Poseidon to watch over the siege of Troy. The forbidding coastline provides no natural anchorage, and landing is still very much subject to the vagaries of the notoriously bad local weather. Yet despite these difficulties, for over a millennium pilgrims journeyed to the island to visit the **Sanctuary of the Great Gods** and to be initiated into its mysteries. The Sanctuary remains the outstanding attraction of the island, which, too remote for most tourists (except during July and August), combines earthy simplicity with natural grandeur.

Kamariótissa and Hóra

Ferries and hydrofoils dock at the somewhat shabby and uninteresting port of **KAMARIÓTISSA**, where you're unlikely to want to stay long. There are nonetheless three hotels behind the tree-lined seafront and various rooms for rent in the maze of streets behind. As on most islands with a short season, accommodation is pricey for what you get, and bargaining is usually unproductive, especially in midsummer. Turning left as you step ashore, the first – and cheapest – **hotel** is the spartan *Kyma* (☎0551/41 263; ②, or ③ en-suite); rooms overlooking the water can get noise from the *barákia* which constitute Samothráki's main nightlife. Calmer, but ridiculously pricey, is the *Niki Beach* (☎0551/41 545; ④) at the far north end of the quay. The seafront is also lined with tavernas, but the best one – *Orizontas*, with quick-served *mayireftá* and bulk wine – is slightly inland on the Hóra road.

Motorbikes and **cars** are in short supply, so it's worth grabbing one immediately on disembarkation – or reserving a bike in advance from Hanou Brothers (☎0551/41 511) or a car from Niki Tours (☎0551/41 465). The latter is also the Olympic Airways and main ferry/hydrofoil agent. As with lodging, rented transport is expensive by

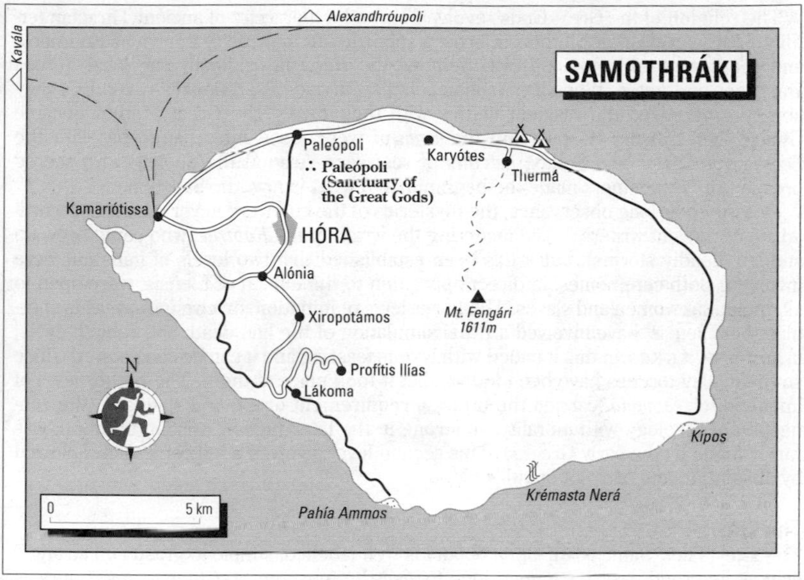

island standards, but if you've the means go for a car, as island roads are dangerously windswept for those on bikes. Note that there is only one fuel pump on the entire island, 1km above the port en route to Hóra. Kamariótissa also has a bank but no post office.

Buses travel eight times daily in season (but only twice weekly in winter) along the north coast to Thermá via Paleópoli (the site of the Sanctuary) or Karyótes, or directly inland seven times daily to **HÓRA**, the largest village and island capital. Far larger than implied by the portion visible from the sea, its attractive, whitewashed Thracian-style houses lie around a hollow in the western flanks of Mount Fengári, dominated by the Genoese Gateluzzi fort, of which little survives other than the gateway. Hóra has no reliable short-term accommodation, though asking for unadvertised rooms in the various kafenía along the winding commercial street can be productive. On the atmospheric, irregularly shaped platía, the *Iy Platia* ouzeri and the more down-to-earth *To Kastro* taverna between them provide the best (and not vastly overpriced) suppers on the island, with such delicacies as stuffed squid and *mýdhia saganáki*. There have been mutterings of moving the administrative capital down to Kamariótissa, but until further notice the island's **post office** is here.

The Sanctuary of the Great Gods

A wide but rough track leads north from Hóra to the hamlet of Paleópoli (see p.363), and, in a stony ravine between it and the plunging northeastern ridge of Mount Fengári, lie the remains of the **Sanctuary of the Great Gods.** From the late Bronze Age until the early Byzantine era, the mysteries and sacrifices of the cult of the Great Gods were performed on Samothráki, indeed in ancient Thracian dialect until the second century BC. The island was the spiritual focus of the northern Aegean, and its importance in the ancient world was comparable (although certainly secondary) to that of the Mysteries of Eleusis.

The religion of the Great Gods revolved around a hierarchy of ancient Thracian fertility figures: the Great Mother Axieros, a subordinate male deity known as Kadmilos, and the potent and ominous twin demons the *Kabiroi*, originally the local heroes Dardanos and Aeton. When the Aeolian colonists arrived (traditionally c. 700 BC) they simply syncretized the resident deities with their own – the Great Mother became Cybele, her consort Hermes and the *Kabiroi* were fused interchangeably with the *Dioskouroi* Castor and Pollux, patrons of seafarers. Around the nucleus of a sacred precinct the newcomers made the beginnings of what is now the Sanctuary.

Despite their long observance, the mysteries of the cult were never explicitly recorded, since ancient writers feared incurring the wrath of the *Kabiroi* (who could brew up sudden, deadly storms), but it has been established that two levels of initiation were involved. Both ceremonies, in direct opposition to the elitism of Eleusis, were open to all, including women and slaves. The lower level of initiation, or *myesis*, may, as is speculated at Eleusis, have involved a ritual simulation of the life, death and rebirth cycle; in any case, it's known that it ended with joyous feasting and it can be conjectured, since so many clay torches have been found, that it took place at night. The higher level of initiation, or *epopteia*, carried the unusual requirement of a moral standard (the connection of theology with morality, so strong in the later Judeo-Christian tradition, was rarely made by the early Greeks). This second level involved a full confession followed by absolution and baptism in bull's blood.

The site

The **site** (Tues–Sun 8.30am–3pm; 600dr) is well labelled, simple to grasp and strongly evokes its proud past. It's a good idea to visit the museum first (open same hours as site; 600dr), with exhibits spanning all eras of habitation, from the Archaic to the Byzantine. Highlights among these include a frieze of dancing girls from the propylon of the temenos, entablatures from different parts of the Sanctuary and Roman votive offerings such as coloured glass vials from the necropolis of the ancient town east of the Sanctuary.

The **Anaktoron**, or hall of initiation for the first level of the mysteries, dates in its present form from Roman times. Its inner sanctum was marked by a warning stele (now in the museum), and at the southeast corner you can make out the **Priestly Quarters**, an antechamber where candidates for initiation donned white gowns. Next to it is the **Arsinoeion**, the largest circular ancient building known in Greece, used for libations and sacrifices. Within its rotunda are the walls of a double precinct (fourth century BC) where a rock altar, the earliest preserved ruin on the site, has been uncovered. A little further south, on the same side of the path, you come to the **Temenos**, a rectangular area open to the sky where the feasting probably took place, and, edging its rear corner, the conspicuous **Hieron**. Five columns and an architrave of the facade of this large Doric edifice (which hosted the higher level of initiation) have been re-erected; dating in part from the fourth century BC, it was heavily restored in Roman times. The stone steps have been replaced by modern blocks, but Roman benches for spectators remain in situ, along with the sacred stones where confession was heard.

To the west of the path you can just discern the outline of the theatre, while just above it, tucked under the ridge is the **Nymphaeum (Fountain) of Nike**, famous for the exquisitely sculpted marble centrepiece – the *Winged Victory of Samothrace* – which once stood breasting the wind at the prow of a marble ship. It was discovered in 1863 by a French diplomat in the Ottoman empire and carried off to the Louvre, with a copy belatedly forwarded to the local museum. Due west of the theatre, occupying a high terrace, are remains of the main stoa; immediately north of this is an elaborate medieval fortification made entirely of antique material.

The rest of the island

The only accommodation near the site itself is in the tiny hamlet of **PALEÓPOLI,** where the old and basic *Xenia Hotel* (☎0551/41 166 or 41 230; ③) tries hard to compete with the *Kastro Hotel* (☎0551/41 001; ⑤), which comes with pool and restaurant; there are also some basic but en-suite rooms (②) down on the seashore below the *Kastro*. Four kilometres east, near Karyótes, is the much smaller *Elektra* (☎0551/98 242; ④); despite the family management, the lack of a restaurant means you may prefer to be nearer the action – such as it is – in Thermá (Loutrá), a further 2km east.

With its running streams, giant plane trees and namesake hot springs, **THERMÁ** is one of the better places to stay on Samothráki, although it's packed in late July and August, mainly with an odd mixture of foreign hippies and elderly Greeks here to take the waters. These are dispersed in three facilities: the sterile, junta-era main baths (daily 8am–1pm & 5–7pm; 500dr); the *psarováthres* or "fish ponds", a trio of pleasantly rustic open-air pools with a wooden sun-shade; and a small cottage with a very hot pool (keys from the warden of the main baths). The latter two facilities are reached by a dirt road starting above and to the right as you face the "improved" spa. For a cold-water contrast, the low waterfalls and rock pools of **Gría Váthra** are signposted 1.5km up the paved side road leading east from the main Thermá access drive. Thermá is also the base of choice for the tough, six-hour climb up 1611-metre **Fengári**, highest peak in the Aegean islands; the path starts at the top of the village, beside a concrete water tank and huge open-boled plane tree. Tell your accommodation proprietors that you're going, but no one else, as the police may try to stop you – army teams have been summoned on occasion to rescue ill-prepared climbers on what can be an unforgiving mountain.

Thermá is a rather dispersed place, with a small half-built jetty which will probably never receive any hydrofoils. Accommodation includes the *Kaviros Hotel* (☎0551/98 277; ④), just east of the "centre", and – further downhill, 700m from the beach – the *Mariva Bungalows* (☎0551/98 258; ④). None of the four tavernas in "central" Thermá is very inspired, a possible result (or cause) of a predominance in self-catering rooms; *Paradhisos* has the best setting and charges accordingly. At the bus stop, *Kafenio Ta Therma* doubles as the nightspot for Greek and foreign hippies; about halfway along the track to Gría Váthra, *Shelter Pub* occupies the old schoolhouse.

Beyond Thérma, on the wooded coastline, are two municipal campsites: the first, 1.5km from the village, although large, has no facilities except toilets, while the second, 3km from the village, is more expensive but has hot water, electricity, a small shop, restaurant and bar. The bus from Kamariótissa usually passes both sites.

Beaches on Samothráki's north shore are uniformly pebbly and exposed, but it's still worth continuing along the road east from Thermá. At **Cape Foniás** there's a Gateluzzi watchtower, and 45 minutes' walk inland along the stream, there are waterfalls and cold pools much more impressive than those at Gría Váthra. The road surface ends at Foniás, but you can bump along the dirt road beyond to its end, 15km from Thermá at **Kípos beach**, a long strand facing the Turkish-held island of Ímvros. There's a rock overhang for shelter at one end, a spring, shower and seasonal drinks *kantína*, but no food available.

From the warmer south flank of the island, you've fine views out to sea, as well as looming Ímvros, now officially Gökçeada. Up to three daily buses go as far as **PROFÍTIS ILÍAS**, an attractive hill village with good tavernas but no place to stay, via Lákoma. From Lákoma a wide, eight-kilometre dirt track, passable for cars, leads east to **Pahiá Ámmos**, an 800-metre sandy beach with a taverna-rooms place (☎0551/94 235; ③) at the west end. The nearest (meagre) supplies are at Lákoma, but this doesn't deter big summer crowds who also arrive by excursion kaïkia. These also continue east to **Vátos**, a secluded (nudist) beach also accessible by land, the **Kremastá Nerá** coastal waterfalls and finally Kípos beach (see above).

Thássos

Just 12km from the mainland, **Thássos** has long been a popular resort island for northern Greeks, and since the early 1990s has also attracted a cosmopolitan variety of tourists, in particular Romanians, Serbs, Bulgarians and Hungarians holidaying a tank or so of petrol away from home, plus plenty of Germans and Brits on packages. Accordingly, it's far from unspoiled, with cheerful vulgarity the key-note of vast numbers of rural *bouzoúkia* (music halls) and tavernas which lay on music at weekends, though these haven't completely swamped the ordinary rural industries.

Thássos still makes a substantial living from the pure-white marble which constitutes two-thirds of the landmass, found only here and quarried at forty sites (legal and unlicensed) in the hills between Liménas and Panayía. Olives, honey, fruit and nuts (often

sold candied) are also important products. *Tsípouro* rather than wine is the main local tipple; pear extract, onions or spices like cinnamon or anise are added to homemade batches.

Inhabited since the Stone Age, Thássos was settled by Parians in the seventh century BC, attracted by gold deposits between modern Liménas and Kínyra. Buoyed by revenues from these, and from silver mines under Thassian control on the mainland opposite, the ancient city-state here became the seat of a medium-sized seafaring empire. Commercial acumen did not spell military invincibility however; the Persians under Darius swept the Thassian fleets from the seas in 492 BC, and in 462 Athens permanently deprived Thássos of its autonomy after a three-year siege. The main port continued to thrive into Roman times, but lapsed into Byzantine and medieval obscurity.

The salient fact of the last few decades is a series of devastating, deliberately set **fires** between 1981 and 1993; the worst one, in 1989, began near Rahóni and burnt for three days down to Mariés. Only the northeastern quadrant of the island, plus the area around Astrís and Alykí, escaped, though the surviving forest is still home to numerous pine martens – and well-striped with preventative fire-breaks.

Thássos is just small enough to circumnavigate in one full day on a rented motorbike or car, which would give you an idea where you'd want to base yourself. The KTEL will do the driving for you – albeit with little chance for stopping – some four times daily. **Car rental** is dominated by Potos Care Rental (☎0593/23 969), with branches in all main resorts, or Rent-a-Car Thassos (☎0593/22 535), also widely represented, as are most of the major international chains. Vigorous bargaining with the local one-off outfits is often productive of 35 percent discounts on rack rates – particularly in early June or mid-September. On the other hand, don't bother showing up much before or after these dates, as most facilities will be shut, and the weather dodgy.

Liménas

LIMÉNAS (also known as Limín or Thássos) is the island's capital, though not the only port. Kavála-based ferries stop down the coast at Skála Prínou, with a KTEL bus always on hand to meet arrivals. The town, though largely modern, is partly redeemed by its picturesque fishing harbour and the substantial remains of the ancient city which appear above and below the streets.

With its mineral wealth and safe harbour, **ancient Thassos** prospered from Classical to Roman times. The largest excavated area is the *agora*, a little way back from the fishing harbour. The site (free) is fenced but not always locked, and is most enoyably seen towards dusk. Two Roman stoas are prominent, but you can also make out shops, monuments, passageways and sanctuaries from the remodelled Classical city. At the far end of the site (away from the sea) a fifth-century BC passageway leads through to an elaborate sanctuary of Artemis, a substantial stretch of Roman road and a few seats of the *odeion*. The nearby archeological museum is shut indefinitely for extensive expansion, the new wings designed to accommodate a huge backlog of finds dug up by the French Archeological School.

From a **temple of Dionysos** behind the fishing port, a path curls up to a **Hellenistic theatre**, fabulously positioned above a broad sweep of sea. It's currently open but a chaos of excavation, with summer-festival performances set to resume in the distant future. On the same corner of the headland as the theatre, you can still see the old-fashioned kaïkia being built, and gaze across to the uninhabited islet of Thasopoúla. It's possible to rent boats from the fishing harbour, self-skippered or not, to take you there and elsewhere.

From just before the theatre, the trail winds on to the **acropolis**, where a Venetian-Byzantine-Genoese fort arose between the thirteenth and fifteenth centuries, constructed from recycled masonry of an Apollo temple which stood here. You can con-

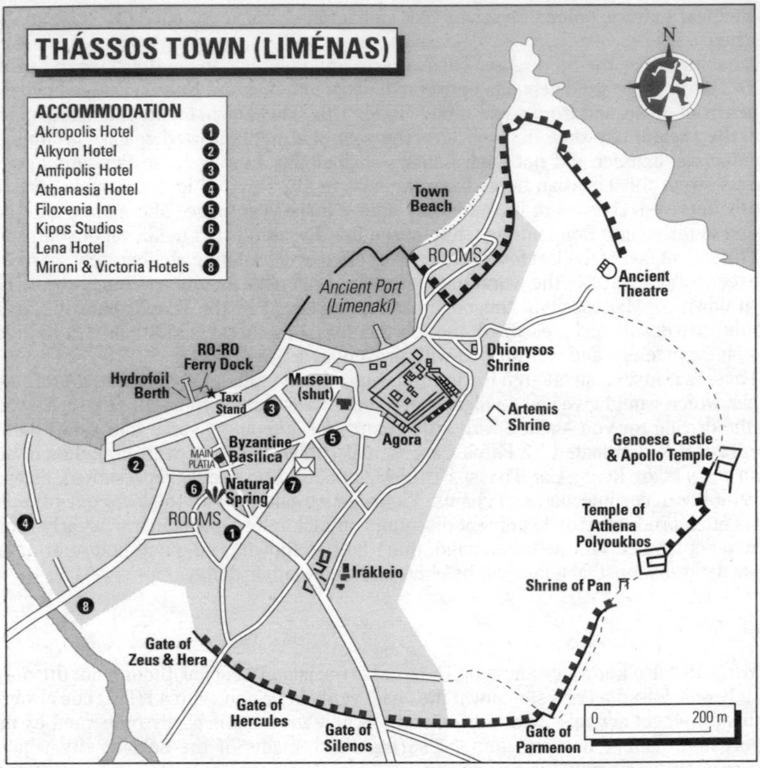

tinue, following the remains of a massive circuit of fifth-century walls to a high terrace supporting the foundations of the Athena Polyouhos (Athena Patroness of the City) temple, with Cyclopean walls. An artificial cavity in the rock outcrop just beyond was a shrine of Pan, shown in faint relief playing his pipes. From behind the summit, a rock-hewn stairway provided a discreet escape route to the Gate of Parmenon, the only gate to have retained its lintel; it's named from an ancient inscription ("Parmenon Made Me") on a nearby wall slab. From here a track, then a paved lane descend through the southerly neighbourhoods of the modern town, for a satisfying one-hour circuit.

Practicalities

Given the cheap-and-cheerful-package ethos, cuisine is not Liménas's strong point, and eateries are generally overpriced. The picturesque **tavernas** at the old harbour are predictably touristy – *Oraia Simi* is marginally the best of a mediocre bunch there – and it might be better to head for *Syrtaki*, at the far east end of the overly popular town beach. In the town centre, greasy fast food is all too abundant, though a dependable favourite for *mayireftá* is *Iy Piyi*, up at the south corner of the main square, next to the natural sunken spring of the name. Carnivores should head for *Vasilis's Grill/Veryina*, on a pedestrian lane north of the square. Finally, *Orestis*, at the northwest corner of the square near *Iy Piyi*, serves the best ice cream on the island. By contrast, there's plenty of choice in local bars. *Full Moon* and the *Café Anonymous* near the *Hotel Amfipolis* are the Anglophile watering-holes, the former more of a full-on bar and with a paperback swap-library, the latter featuring foreign beers and homemade cakes; *Platia Cafe Bar* on yet another corner of the basilica square, has good music; while *Marina's Bar* near the *Hotel Alkyon* is the best waterfront nightspot, with a mainly Greek clientele.

Mountain and motorbikes can be had from Billy's Bikes (☎0593/22 490), Thomai Tsipou (☎0593/22 815) or *Babis* (☎0593/22 129), in the lane just inland from *Hotel Alkyon*. The KTEL office is on the front, virtually opposite the ferry mooring; the service is good, with regular daily buses to Panayía and Skála Potamiás, Limenária via Potós, Theológos, Kínyra and Alykí. The taxi rank is just in front of the bus stop. Thassos Tours (☎0593/23 250), at the east end of the waterfront, is the agent for Olympic Airways (closest airport is 14km from Keramotí on the mainland). The Ethniki/National and Emboriki/Commercial banks have cash dispensers.

Accommodation

At first glance Liménas – plagued with vehicle traffic and often noisy bars – seems an unlikely resort, with many **hotels** enjoying little in the way of calm or views. Despite this, there are some worthy finds; if none from the list below suits, there are also areas in the southwest of town, plus just behind the town beach, with some relatively quiet rooms (②). The closest campsite to town is the at Nystéri cove, 2.5km west; the beach is okay, its snack bar with tables out on a lawn, but the site is small, basic and on hard ground.

Akropolis (☎0593/22 488, fax 22 441). Occupying a fine traditional house with flagstone floors and a rear garden-bar, though it can get traffic noise; worth a try now that package companies don't use it. ③.

Alkyon (☎0593/22 148, fax 23 662). Certainly the most pleasant of the harbour hotels; English tea and breakfast, plus friendly, voluble management make it a home from home for independent British travellers. Open most of the year; ask also about their cottage in Sotíros and beach villa at Astrís. ③.

Amfipolis (☎0593/23 101, fax 22 110). Housed in a folly, this is the town's most exclusive outfit – and you pay dearly for the privilege; some package commitment. ⑤.

Athanasia (☎0593/23 247). Giant and eccentrically furnished rooms with balconies; take the lane inland from behind the Xenia Hotel to reach it. Run by a friendly fisherman, this place takes the overflow from the Alkyon. ②.

Filoxenia Inn (☎0593/23 331, fax 22 231). Quietly situated behind the archeological museum, this has immaculate new rooms with fridges, dedicated breakfast areas and a garden with a small pool. ④.

Kipos Studios (☎0593/22 469). In a quiet cul-de-sac near *Iy Piyi* taverna, this has cool lower-ground floor doubles (③) and four-person galleried apartments of a fair standard (④); unfortunately, the garden of the name may soon have a pool installed to make premises attractive to package companies.

Lena (☎0593/23 565). Good-value hotel, lightly refurbished in 1998, near the post office, with English-speaking management; no packages. ③.

Myrioni (☎0593/23 256, fax 22 132). Excellent value, well run and allergic to package companies. It's co-managed with the more modest *Victoria* (③) next door, with which it shares a common breakfast room. ④.

Around the coast

Whether you plan to circumnavigate the island clockwise, or in the opposite direction, plan on a lunch stop at **Alykí**, roughly a third of the way along in the sequence described below.

Panayía, Potamiá and Mount Ipsárion

The first beach east of Liménas, Makrýammos, is a purpose-built, controlled-access compound for package tourists, so carry on to **PANAYÍA**, the attractive hillside village overlooking Potamiá Bay. It's a large, thriving place where life revolves around the central square with its large plane trees, multi-spouted fountain and slate-roofed houses. Top **accommodation** choice in all senses is the *Hotel Thassos Inn* (☎0593/61 612, fax 61 027; ④), up in the Trís Piyés district near the Kímisis church, with fine views over the rooftops and the sound of running water to lull you to sleep. Second choice, slightly lower down, is the vine-shrouded *Hotel Theo* (☎0593/61 284; ③), more old-fashioned but with a nice ground-floor bar. Down on the main road, beside the municipal car park, the newish, clean *Pension Stathmos* (☎0593/61 666; ④) is the quietest of several nearby, with stunning views out the back; there are also high-standard rooms (☎0593/61 981; ③) below the school basketball courts. Some readers have complained about high-pressure touting tactics from the hotly competing tavernas on the square; for a low-key approach, try *Iy Thea*, a view-terrace psistariá at the southeast edge of town en route to Potamiá.

POTAMIÁ, much lower down in the river valley, is far less prepossessing and thus little visited, though it has a lively winter carnival. It also offers the **Polygnotos Vayis Museum** (Tues–Sat 9am–1pm, summer also 6–9pm, Sun 10am–2pm; free), devoted to the locally born sculptor; though Vayis emigrated to America when young, he bequeathed most of his works to the Greek state. Potamiá also marks the start of the commonest route up to the 1204-metre summit of **Mount Ipsárion**. Follow the bulldozer track to the big spring near the head of the valley extending west of the village (last water here), where you'll see the first red-painted arrows on trees. Beyond this point, cairns mark the correct turnings in a modern track system; forty minutes above the spring, take an older, wide track, which ends ten minutes later at a gulch and the current trailhead. The path is steep, strenuous and unmaintained, and you'll be dependent on cairns and painted arrows. Go early in the day or season, and allow for three-and-a-half hours up from Potamiá, and nearly as much for the descent.

Skála Potamiás and Khryssí Ammoudhiá

The onward road from Potamiá is lined with *dhomátia-* and apartment-type accommodation which fill in peak season mostly with Germans, judging from the Teutonic establishment names. Just before reaching the coast at **SKÁLA POTAMIÁS** at the southern end of the bay, the road splits – the right fork leads to Skála itself and some fairly uninspired tavernas; the left-hand option brings you to sand dunes extending all the way to the far end. An honourable exception amongst the **tavernas** is *Flor International* (no sign), at the corner where the bus (hourly 7am–8pm to Liménas) turns around; the *Afrodite* next door is also acceptable for *mayireftá*. Worth a mention also is *Eric's Bar* on the approach road, where one Stratos Papafilippou has made a career of his uncanny resemblance to footballer Eric Cantona; full English breakfast (of course) available. The best places to **stay** would be either above the plane-shaded traffic turnaround area by the port – where the *Hera* (☎0593/61 467; ②), just on the left looking inland, or the *Delfini* (☎0593/61 275; ②), 200m straight back, are peaceful – or north along the shore towards the sandy beach, in rooms to either side of the *Arion* (☎0593/61 486; ③) and *Anna* (☎0593/61 070; ②) hotels, which represent the best standard hereabouts. The north end of this beach is called **Khryssí Ammoudhiá**, merely another cluster of tavernas, hotels and a campsite; a separate road (no bus service) descends the 5km from Panayía. Once there, you can choose between the self-catering *Villa Emerald*(☎0593/61 979; ⑤) or the elderly, twin premises of the *Faedra/Golden Sand* (☎0593/61 474; ③). The *Golden Beach* campsite (☎0593/61 472) is the only official one on this side of the island.

Kínyra and Alykí

The tiny hamlet of **KÍNYRA**, some 24km south of Liménas, marks the start of the depressing burnt zone which overlooks it; it's endowed with a poor beach, a couple of grocery stores and several small hotels. Those not block-booked include *Villa Athina* (☎0593/41 214; ②) at the north end of things, whose top-floor rooms see the water over the olive trees, and the welcoming *Pension Marina* (☎0593/31 384; ②). The *Faros* is about the only independent taverna here. Kínyra is convenient for the superior beaches of Loutroú (1km south) and partly nudist Paradise (3km along), officially Makrýammos Kinýron. The latter ranks as most scenic of all Thassian beaches, with still-forested cliffs inland and a namesake islet offshore beyond the extensive shallows, with much cleaner water than at Khryssí Ammoudhiá – but only a single mediocre snack bar which exploits its monopoly.

The south-facing coast of Thássos has the balance of the island's best beaches. **ALYKÍ** hamlet, 35km from Liménas, faces a perfect double bay which almost pinches off a headland. Alone of Thassian seaside settlements, it retains its original architecture as the presence of extensive antiquities here has led to a ban on any modern construction. The ruins include an ancient temple to an unknown deity, and two exquisite early Christian basilicas out on the headland, with a few columns re-erected. The sand and pebble west bay, with its four tavernas, gets oversubscribed in peak season, though you can always stalk off to the less crowded, rocky east cove, or snorkel off the marble formations on the headland's far side. Among the five **tavernas**, *O Glaros* up on the north hillside is the oldest and considered the best for reliably fresh and inexpensive fish by island regulars. The *Koala Café* down on the sand provides desserts, breakfasts and a semblance of nightlife. There are a half-dozen **rooms** establishments, closest to the water being those available through *O Glaros* (☎0593/53 047; ③), four en-suite rooms with a common kitchen, or the rustic, non-en-suite units in the cottage next door to the taverna (☎0593/53 071; ②).

Arhangélou Mihaïl to Potós

Some 5km west of Alykí, the **convent of Arhangélou Mihaïl** (open reasonable daylight hours) clings spectacularly to a cliff on the seaward side of the road. Though founded in the twelfth century above the spot where a spring had gushed forth, it has been hideously renovated by the nuns resident here since 1974. A dependency of Filothéou on Mount Áthos, its prize relic is a purported nail from the Crucifixion.

At the extreme south tip of Thássos, 9km further west, **ASTRÍS** (Astrídha) can muster two uninspiring medium-sized hotels, a few rooms and a good beach. Just 1km west is another better but crowded beach, Psilí Ámmos, with watersports on offer. A few kilometres further, **POTÓS** is the island's prime Germanophone package venue, its centre claustrophobically dense, with the few non-block-booked rooms overlooking cramped alleys. However, the kilometre-long beach to the south is still unspoiled, and on the semi-pedestrianized seafront, the original **taverna** *Iy Mouria* remains one of the cheaper and better places; next door, *Michael's Place* has great ice cream and breakfasts. There are plenty of rental outlets for cars, scooters and mountain bikes, including the headquarters of Potos Rent a Car. **Pefkári** with its manicured beach, 1km west, is essentially an annexe of Potós, with a few mid-range **accommodation** options such as *Prasino Veloudho* (☎0593/52 001, fax 51 232; ③).

Limenária and the west coast

LIMENÁRIA, the island's second town, was built to house German mining executives brought in by the Ottomans at the turn of the century. Their remaining mansions, scattered on the slopes above the harbour, lend some character, and the municipality has made a stab at prettifying the waterfront, but it remains one of the least attractive spots on Thássos, handy mainly for its banks (one with cash dispenser), post office and seasonal hydrofoil connections. At the east end of the quay, in some 1960s blocks, are a cluster of very basic hotels such as the *Sgouridis* (☎0593/51 241; ③) and the towering, non-en-suite *Papayioryiou* (☎0593/51 205; ② bathless, ③ en-suite), with mostly Greek clientele. There are also plenty of rooms on offer, and a campsite between Limenária and Pefkári: the *Pefkari* (☎0593/51 190; June–Sept). For eating and drinking, choose from among half-a-dozen each of bars and eateries along the front.

The closest good beach is **Trypití**, a couple of kilometres west – turn left into the pines at the start of a curve right. All development – mostly package villas – is well inland from the broad, 800-metre long strand, though there are umbrellas and chaise longues for rent. The perforation of the name ("pierced" in Greek) is a slender tunnel through the headland at the west end of the beach, leading to a tiny three-boat anchorage.

Continuing clockwise from Limenária to Thássos Town, there's progressively less to stop off for. The various *skáles* such as Skála Kaliráhis and Skála Sotíros are bleak, straggly and windy. **Skála Marión**, 13km from Limenária, is the exception that proves the rule: an attractive little bay, with fishing boats hauled up on the sandy foreshore, and the admittedly modern low-rise village arrayed in a U-shape all around. There are rooms available, a few tavernas, and most importantly two fine beaches to either side. **Skála Prínou** has little to recommend it, other than ferry connections to Kavála. Buses are usually timed to coincide with the ferries, but if you want to stay, there are several hotels, numerous rooms, quayside tavernas and an EOT **campsite** (☎0593/71 171; June–Sept) 1km south of the ferry dock. **Skála Rahoníou**, between here and Liménas, has more accommodation (including the *Perseus* campsite) and fish restaurants, as well as proximity to **Pahýs beach**, 9km short of Liménas, and by far the best strand on the northwest coast. Narrow dirt tracks lead past various tavernas through surviving pines to the sand, partly shaded in the morning.

The interior

Few people get around to exploring inland Thássos – with the post-fire scrub still barely waist-high, it's not always rewarding – but there are several worthwhile excursions to or around the hill villages besides the aforementioned trek up Mount Ipsárion from Potamiá (see p.368).

From Potós you can head 10km up a good road to **THEOLÓGOS**, founded in the sixteenth century by refugees from Constantinople, which was the island's capital under the Ottomans (the last Muslims only departed after 1923). Its houses, most with oversized chimneys and slate roofs, straggle in long tiers to either side of the main street, surrounded by generous kitchen gardens or walled courtyards. A stroll along the single high street, with its two kafenía, soldiers' bar, sandalmaker's and traditional baker, is rewarding and dispels the off-putting effect of vigorous advertising at the outskirts for "Greek Nights" at local tavernas. Two that eschew musical gimmicks and rely on their good fare are the long-running *Psistaria Lambiris*, near the edge of town, and *Kleoniki/Tou Iatrou*, in the very centre past the bus stop and police station. They're at their best in the evening when the *soúvles* loaded with goat and suckling pig start turning.

Despite apparent proximity on the map, there's no straightforward way from Theológos to **KÁSTRO**, the most naturally protected of the anti-pirate redoubts; especially with a car, it's best to descend to Potós and head up a rough, 17-kilometre dirt track from Limenária. Thirty ancient houses and a church surround a rocky pinnacle, fortified by the Byzantines and the Genoese, which has a sheer drop on three sides. Summer occupation by shepherds is becoming the norm after total abandonment in the last century, when mining jobs at Limenária proved irresistible, but there's only one kafenío on the ground floor of the former school, one telephone therein, far more sheep than people and no mains electricity.

From Skála Marión an unmarked but paved road (slipping under the main highway bridge to the north) proceeds 11km inland to attractive **MARIÉS** at the top of a wooded stream valley; of two tavernas here, the well-signed one to the right is more of a going concern. From Skála Sotíros, a steep road heads 3.5km up to **SOTÍROS**, the only interior village with an unobstructed view of sunset over the Aegean and thus popular with foreigners who've bought up about half of the houses for restoration. On the ridge opposite are exploratory shafts left by the miners, whose ruined lodge looms above the church. On the plane-shaded square below the old fountain, *O Platanos* taverna is congenially run by Maria and Manolis, who offer grills plus one *mayireftá* dish-of-the-day, good bulk wine and sometimes their potent, own-made *tsípouro*.

From Prínos (Kalýves) on the coast road, you've a six-kilometre journey inland to the Kazavíti villages, shrouded in greenery that escaped the fires; they're signposted and mapped officially as Megálo and Mikró Prínos but still universally known by their Ottoman name. **MIKRÓ KAZAVÍTI** marks the start of the track south for the convent of Ayíou Pandelímona. **MEGÁLO KAZAVÍTI**, 1km beyond, was once the architectural showcase of the island, a fact apparently lost on the numerous outsiders who bought holiday homes here and proceeded to do appallingly vandalistic renovations. On the magnificent platía are two decent, normal-priced **tavernas**. Some 4km up from its *skála*, **RAHÓNI** is well set at the head of its denuded valley, paired with the small village of Áyios Yeóryios across the way. The road up to the square has plenty of simple tavernas, for example *Iy Dhrosia*.

travel details

To simplify the lists that follow we've excluded three regular sailings in a generally north south direction. These are: the weekly DANE sailing between Rhodes, Kós, Sámos and Thessaloníki (23hr for the full run, usually over the weekend); the G&A sailing between the same points, usually mid-week; the NEL sailing linking Alexandhroúpoli with Límnos, Lésvos, Híos, Sámos, Kós and Rhodes (one-way trip through all ports, total 30hr).

We've also omitted the more convoluted schedules kept by the small ferries of Miniotis Lines, based on Híos. These slow and often tardy craft link Híos with Sámos (both northern ports) twice a week year-round, usually Sun or Mon, & Fri, returning Tues & Fri; from July to mid-Sept there's an extra Tues night/Weds dawn itinerary to Vathý only. Twice weekly (usually Mon/Fri), they venture from Sámos (either port) to Foúrni and Ikaría (Áyios Kírykos) and back, and once weekly (typically Tues) there's an out-and-back run from Pythagório to Agathoníssi, Arkí, Lipsí and Pátmos – these services are reliably available June to mid-Sept.

Áyios Efstrátios 3–4 weekly on NEL Lines to Límnos; 3 weekly to Rafína and Kavála; 1 weekly to Lésvos (Sígri).

Foúrni 3–4 weekly ferries to Sámos (northern ports), Páros and Pireás; morning kaïki to Ikaría on Mon, Wed, Fri; weekends only by demand; twice weekly (usually Mon and Thur) morning kaïki to Karlóvassi (Sámos)

Híos 6–11 weekly on NEL Lines to Pireás (10hr) and Lésvos (3hr 30min); 1–3 weekly to Límnos (10hr); 1 weekly summer only to Sýros or Vólos. Daily afternoon kaïki to Inoússes except Sun morning, and Thurs in off-season; 3 weekly small ferries – usually Tues, Thurs & Sat – from Híos Town to Psará (4hr), 2 weekly kaïkia on different days, mid-June to early September only, from Limniá to Psará (2hr).

Ikaría 1–3 daily from either Áyios Kírykos or Évdhilos to Sámos (both northern ports), and Pireás (at least 3 weekly services year-round); 3–5 weekly to Páros and Náxos; 3–4 weekly full-sized ferries to Foúrni, plus 3 kaïkia weekly from Áyios Kírykos to Foúrni; 1–2 weekly to Mýkonos and Sýros.

Lésvos 6–16 weekly on NEL Lines from Mytilíni to Pireás (11hr direct, 13hr 30min via Híos or Sýros); 6–10 weekly to Híos (3hr 30min); 4–6 weekly to Límnos (6hr from Mytilíni, 5hr from Sígri); 2 weekly to Thessaloníki (14hr); 1 weekly to Áyios Efstrátios (4hr) from Sígri only; 1–2 weekly to Kavála (12hr from Mytilíni, 10hr from Sígri); 1 weekly to Rafína (8hr from Sígri); 1 weekly to Psará (4hr from Sígri); 1 weekly to Vólos or Sýros (early July–early Sept only).

Límnos 4–6 weekly on NEL Lines to Lésvos (Mytilíni or Sígri); 3–4 weekly to Kavála, Áyios Efstrátios and Rafína; 1–3 weekly to Thessaloníki, Pireás, Híos. Also a small local ferry to Áyios Efstrátios 3 times weekly.

Psará 2 weekly on NEL Lines to Lésvos (Mytilíni or Sígri), 1 weekly direct to Pireás (8hr), also Límnos, Samothráki, Kavála, Alexandhroúpoli.

Sámos (Karlóvassi) As for Vathý, plus 2 weekly kaïki departures, usually early Mon and Thurs afternoon, to Foúrni.

Sámos (Pythagório) 1–2 weekly (usually Wed and Sun afternoon) with the *Nissos Kalymnos* to Agathónissi, Lipsí, Pátmos, Léros, Kálymnos, with onward connections to all other Dodecanese (see p.306 for the full schedule).

Sámos (Vathý) 1–3 daily, on G&A, Agapitos or Nomikos Lines, to Ikaría (Áyios Kírykos and/or Évdhilos) and Pireás (14hr); 3–5 weekly to Páros and Náxos; 3-4 weekly to Foúrni; 1–2 weekly to Mýkonos and Sýros; 1 weekly to Pátmos and Lipsí.

Samothráki 2–3 daily ferries to/from Alexandhroúpoli (2hr 30min) in season, dropping to 5–6 weekly out of season. Also 2 weekly late spring and early autumn, up to 4 weekly in peak season, to Kavála (and thence other North Aegean islands). At the time of writing there was weekly summer service on NEL Lines to Lésvos (Sígri) and Psará, though this may not continue in future.

Thássos 8–10 ferries daily, depending on season, between Kavála and Skála Prínou (1hr 15min; 7am–10pm, 6am–9pm to Kavála from the island); 10 daily between Keramotí and Liménas (40min; 7am–10pm, 6am–8.30pm from Thássos).

Hydrofoils

Just one company, Sámos Hydrofoils, operates in the **east Aegean**. Based on Sámos and Kós, this offers nearly daily early morning service from Vathý and Pythagório to Pátmos, Léros, Kálymnos and Kós (in the Dodecanese), returning from Kós in the late afternoon, and conversely morning service from Kós through the same ports, returning from Pythagório only at mid-afternoon. Lipsí is included 4–7 times weekly; Ikaría and Foúrni are called at 2–4 times weekly, with Agathónissi served once or twice weekly. In 1999 there were also 2 weekly links between Sámos and Híos, but historically these have been unprofitable and cannot be relied on in future. Further, if less reliable, service is provided by Dodecanese Hydrofoils (see p.307), based on Kós and Rhodes, which go northbound in the morning and head south in the afternoon; it's possible in theory to reach Rhodes the same day from Sámos, changing craft at Kós.

Thássos is served by hydrofoils from Kavála, which depart for Liménas 8–15 times daily from 7am–9pm (6am–8pm from Thássos); in summer there are also 2–3 daily departures from Kavála to the west-coast resorts of Skála Kaliráhon, Skála Marión and Limenária.

Samothráki is served by hydrofoil from Alexandhroúpoli from mid-May to mid-June and during late Sept 5-7 times weekly in the morning (1hr 10min); from mid-June through mid-Sept there are 1–2 extra daily departures between 1 and 5pm. Two to four times weekly the morning or early afternoon sailing may continue on to Límnos.

International hydrofoils

Service thrice weekly (in theory), mid-June to mid-Sept, between Vathý (Sámos) and Kuşadası (Turkey). Fares are currently a third more than for a conventional ferry (see section below), though bargains can be had in spring or autumn.

International ferries

Vathý (Sámos)–Kuşadası (Turkey) At least 1 daily, late April to late Oct; otherwise a Turkish boat only by demand in winter, usually Fri or Sat. Morning Greek boat (passengers only), afternoon Turkish boats (usually 2 in season taking 2 cars apiece). Rates are £24/US$39 one way including taxes on both the Greek and Turkish sides, £26/$43 open return; no day-return rate. Small cars £30/$45 one way. Journey time 1hr 30min. Also occasional (2–3 weekly) services in season from Pythagório.

Híos–Çeşme (Turkey) 2–12 boats weekly, depending on season. Thursday night and Saturday morning services tend to run year-round. Passenger rates on the Greek morning boat are £31/$50 one way, £41/$67 open return (no day-return fare), including Greek taxes; no Turkish taxes. Small cars £47/$77 each way, taken on either Greek or Turkish craft. Turkish afternoon boat is usually a bit cheaper. Journey time 45min.

Mytilíni (Lésvos)–Ayvalık (Turkey) 4–8 weekly May–Oct; winter link unreliable, as is the Turkish afternoon boat at any time. Passenger rates on the Greek morning boat are £33/$54 one way, £43/$70 round trip. Small cars £49/$80 each way. Journey time 1hr 30min.

Flights

NB All flights on Olympic Airways/Aviation unless otherwise specified. Frequencies are for the period May–Oct only.

Híos–Athens (4–5 daily on Olympic, 1 daily on Air Manos; 55min)

Lésvos–Athens (4–5 daily; 50min)

Lésvos–Híos (2 weekly; 30 min)

Lésvos–Thessaloníki (6 weekly; 1hr 10min–2hr)

Límnos–Athens (2–3 daily; 1hr)

Límnos–Lésvos (3 weekly; 40min)

Límnos–Thessaloníki (6 weekly; 50min)

Sámos–Athens (3–4 daily on Olympic, 1–2 daily on Air Manos; 1hr)

Sámos–Mýkonos (2 weekly on Air Manos; 40min)

Sámos–Thessaloníki (2 weekly on Olympic, 2 weekly on Air Manos; 1hr 20min)

Sámos–Thíra (2 weekly on Air Manos; 2hr)

CHAPTER SIX

THE SPORADES AND ÉVVIA

The three northern **Sporades**, Skiáthos, Skópelos and Alónissos, are scattered (as their Greek name suggests) just off the mainland, their mountainous terrain betraying their origin as extensions of Mount Pílion in Thessaly. They are archetypal holiday islands, with a wide selection of good beaches, transparent waters and thick pine forests. All are very busy in season, with Skiáthos attracting by far the most package tours.

Skiáthos has the best beaches, and is still the busiest island in the group, though these days **Skópelos** gets very crowded, too. **Alónissos** is the quietest of the three, and has the wildest scenery, so it's really more for nature lovers than night-owls. **Skýros**, further southeast, retains more of its traditional culture than the other three islands, though development is now well under way. The main town doesn't yet feel like a resort, but its main street is not without its fast food and souvenir shops. Unlike the other three islands, the best beaches are those close to the main town. To the south, the huge island of **Évvia** (or Euboea) runs for 150km alongside the mainland. It is one of the most attractive Greek islands, with a forested mountain spine and long stretches of rugged, largely undeveloped coast. Perhaps because it lacks any impressive ruins or real island feel due to its proximity to the mainland, Évvia is explored by few foreign tourists, though Athenians and Thessalians visit the island in force and have erected holiday homes around half a dozen of its major resorts.

The Sporades are well connected by **bus** and **ferry** both with Athens (via Áyios Konstandínos or Kými), Thessaloniki and Vólos, and it's easy to island-hop in the north-

ACCOMMODATION PRICE CODES

Throughout the book we've used the following **price codes** to denote the cheapest available double room in each establishment in high season. Out of season, rates can drop by more than fifty percent, especially if you are staying for three or more nights. Single rooms, where available, cost around seventy percent of the price of a double.

Rented private rooms on the islands usually fall into the ② or ③ categories, depending on their location and facilities, and the season; a few in the ④ category are more like plush self-catering apartments. They are not generally available from late October through to the beginning of April, when only hotels tend to remain open.

① Up to 6000dr	④ 12,000–16,000dr
② 6000–9000dr	⑤ 16,000–20,000dr
③ 9000–12,000dr	⑥ 20,000dr and upwards

Note: Youth hostels typically charge 2000–2500dr for a dormitory bed.

For more accommodation details, see pp.44–47.

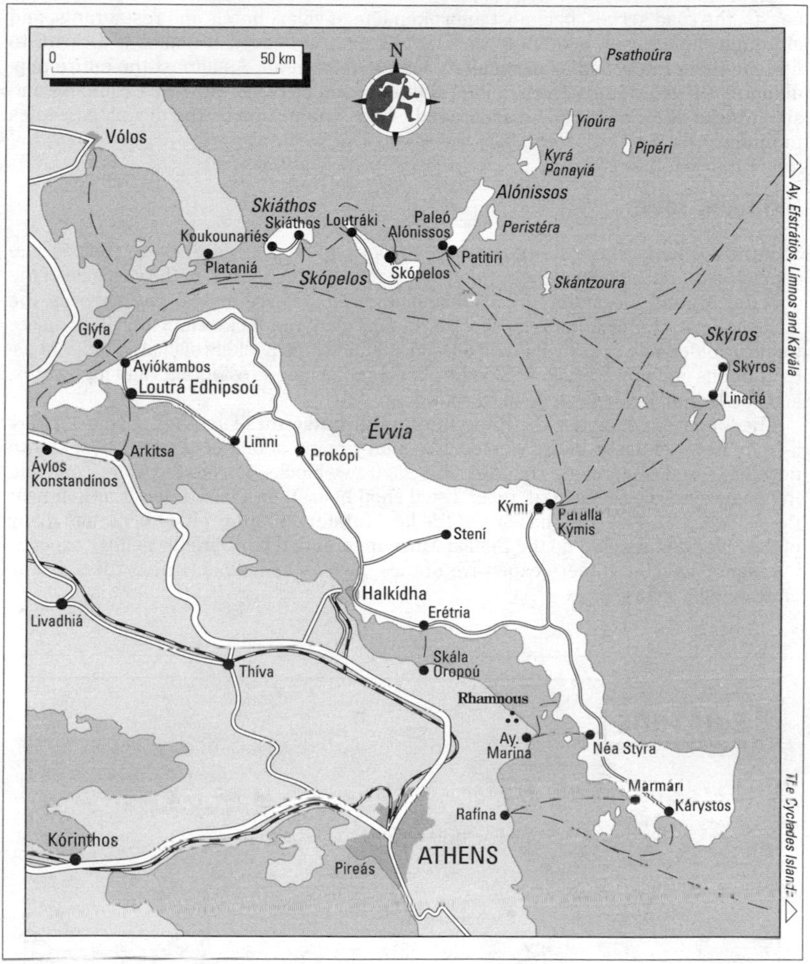

ern group. The only ferry connection to Skýros is from Kými, plus a Flying Dolphin hydrofoil service in summer from Vólos via the other Sporades. Évvia is linked to the mainland by a bridge at its capital Halkídha, and by a series of shuttle ferries. Both Skiáthos and Skýros have airports.

Skiáthos

The commercialization of **Skiáthos** is legendary among foreigners and Greeks: it's a close fourth to that of Corfu, Mýkonos and Rhodes. But if you've some time to spare, or a gregarious nature, you might still break your journey here to sample the best, if most overcrowded, **beaches** in the Sporades. Along the south and southeast coasts, the road serves an almost unbroken line of villas, hotels and restaurants, and although this doesn't take away the island's natural beauty, it makes it difficult to find anything unspoiled or particularly Greek about it all. As almost the entire population lives in Skiáthos Town, a little walking soon pays off. However, camping outside official sites is strongly discouraged, since summer turns the dry pine-needles to tinder.

Skiáthos Town

Skiáthos Town, where the ferries dock, looks great from a distance, but as you approach, tourist development becomes very apparent, especially to the east side of the port and around Alexándhrou Papadhiamándi Street, where most of the services, the tackier shops, "English" pubs and eateries are located. But tucked into the alleys on the western, older side of town, it is still possible to find some pockets of charm: older houses, gardens and flowers galore. Skiáthos boasts some good restaurants and nightclubs, and can be fun, in a crowded, boisterous way.

The few sights comprise the **Papadhiamándi museum** (Tues–Sun 9.30am–1pm & 5–8pm; free) – housed in the nineteenth-century home of one of Greece's best-known novelists – and two antique shops, Archipelago two blocks in from the waterfront, and the enduring Galerie Varsakis (open usual shop hours), on Platía Trión Ierarhón near the fishing port. The latter has one of the best **folklore displays** in Greece, and many of the older items would do the Benaki Museum proud; the proprietor neither expects, nor wants, to sell the more expensive of these, which include antique textiles, handicrafts and jewellery.

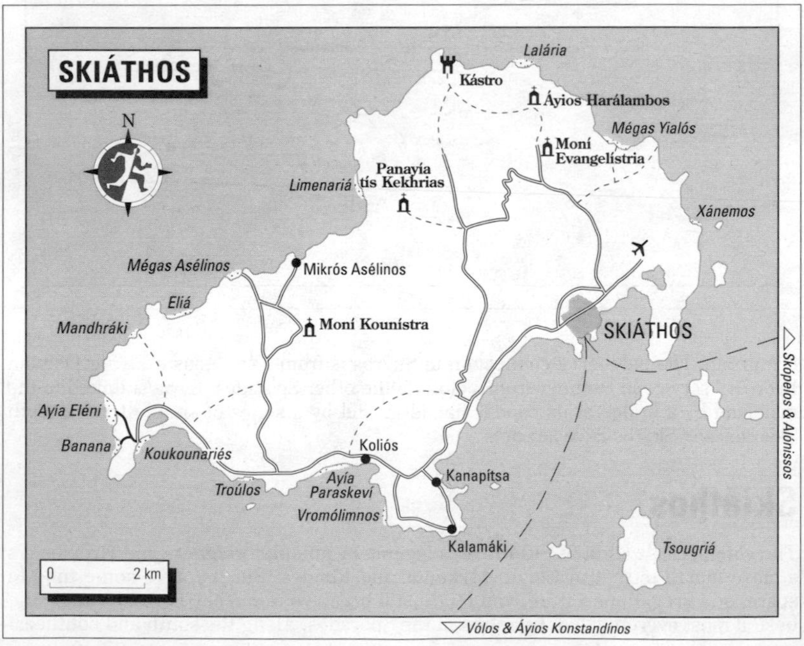

Arrival, transport and other facilities

Buses and **taxis** ply from the area around the **ferry harbour**. To Koukounariés, the bus is the cheapest option (280dr); it runs at least hourly in summer (every fifteen minutes at peak times), the last bus returning at 1am. Sharing a taxi is another option.

A large number of competing **rental outlets** in town, most on the front behind the ferry harbour, offer bicycles, mopeds, motorbikes, cars and motorboats. For bikes, good rates can be had from Makis Dimas, whose workshop is signposted at the far end of Papadhiamándi. The cheapest, small cars go for around 15,000dr a day, as do motorboats; fuel and insurance are extra. Several travel agents organize "round the island" **mule trips** (5900dr a day), and there's **horse-riding** at the Pinewood Riding Club (no phone) at Koukounariés. Most other facilities are on Alexándhrou Papadhiamándi, including the **OTE**, **post office**, **banks** and a branch of American Express.

Accommodation

Much of the island's accommodation is in Skiáthos Town. The few reasonably priced **hotels** or **pensions** are heavily booked in season, though you can usually find a room, albeit slightly more expensively than on most islands. At other times, supply exceeds demand and you can find very cheap **rooms** with a little bargaining. Try for locations in the older quarters to the west; avoid lodgings in the flatlands to the north as they tend to be noisy. There is a room-owners' association kiosk on the quay that opens fitfully in high season but at other times bookings can be made through several tourist agencies. For an honest and helpful approach, try the Mare Nostrum at Papadhiamándi 21 (☎0427/21 463) or the efficient Helotropio (☎0427/22 430, fax 21 952) on the seafront. A more direct option is Adonis Stamelos' rooms just outside town at Megáli Ámmos (☎0427/22 962; ③). Good small hotels include the *Bourtzi* (☎0427/22 694; ⑤) and *Pothos* (☎0427/21 304; ⑤), both immaculate with delightful gardens, and the *Orsa* (☎0427/22 430; ⑥), a remodelled house overlooking the sea on the west side of the port which can be booked through Heliotropio. Other fine options are the *Alkyon Hotel*, on the seafront at the commercial port end (☎0427/22 981; ⑥), or the *Meltemi Hotel*, on the front near the taxi rank (☎0427/22 493; ⑥).

The island has three official **campsites**. Koukounariés and Asélinos are fairly decent with standard facilities. Xanémos beach is 3km northeast of Skiáthos Town, right next to the airport runway, and, apart from being within walking distance of the town, has little to recommend it.

Eating, drinking and nightlife

You're spoiled for choice for **eating places**, but nothing is particularly cheap apart from the few burger/*yíros* joints. One of the best of the cheaper tavernas is *Zorba's*, opposite the taxi rank, while *Mesogeia*, above and to the west of Plátia Trión Ierarkhón, has excellent moussaka and home-cooked dishes. *Ellinikon*, up in the backstreets above the west seafront, also has home-style cooking and good wine in a secluded garden, while *Cuba*, set in a leafy square east of Papadhiamándi, has a huge range of grilled meat, fish and starters. For more elegant dining, head for *Agnantio*, at the start of the road to Evangelístria, for superlative Greek cuisine and views; *The Windmill* at the top of the hill above Áyios Nikólaos, for nouvelle cuisine and views; and *Calypso*, on the east waterfront, for genuine Italian food. Back on the west side, above the flat rocks where people sunbathe, *Tarsanas* is a converted boatbuilders' yard with a picturesque veranda – the best place in town for an evening drink as the harbour lights come on.

Nightlife centres on the clubs on or near Polytekhníou. The best places are *Borzoi*, the oldest club on the island, *Stones* and the *Apothiki Music Hall* for Greek music and a good atmosphere, while on the seafront *BBC* pulses till dawn. In the bars in the back streets around Polyteknı́ou you can hear a wider range of music; places like the *Banana* are pop-orientated and popular among British beer drinkers, the old and much loved *Kentavros* plays jazz and blues, *Adagio* has classical music in the evenings, and *Blue Chips* is a stylish upmarket place. On the east shore, the chic *Remezzo* with its maritime motifs, is a perennial favourite, while *Kavos* and *Kalua* rival it for pumping out the loudest disco sounds.

Skiáthos's outdoor **cinema** *Refresh Paradiso*, on the ring road, shows new releases in their original language. Another source of entertainment is that the little offshore Boúrtzi fortress has been transformed into an outdoor **theatre** and is home to occasional plays and musical performances during the summer.

Around the island

Other than using the buses or the various rental outlets in town (for which see above), you could also get your bearings on a **boat trip** around the island. These cost about 4500dr per person and leave at around 10am. Or try a boat trip to the islet of **Tsougriá** (opposite Skiáthos Town), where there's a good beach and a taverna. Boats leave from the fishing harbour beyond the Boúrtzi, and not the yacht anchorage to the north of the ferry harbour; east-coast boats leave from the quay area in front of the bus station.

If you're interested in seeing more of Skiáthos on foot, the locally produced guide to **walks** (by Rita and Dietrich Harkort; available in larger tourist shops) has detailed instructions and maps for trails all over the island.

Monasteries and Kástro

The **Evangelístria monastery** (daily 8am–noon & 4–8pm) is more than an hour on foot out of Skiáthos Town. Founded in the late eighteenth century, it is exceptionally beautiful, even beyond the grandeur of isolation you find in all Greek monasteries. The Greek flag was raised here in 1807, and heroes of the War of Independence such as Kolokotronis pledged their oaths to fight for freedom here. To reach the monastery, walk 500m out of the centre of town on the road towards the airport until, at the point where the asphalt veers to the right, you take a prominently signposted tarmac track that veers left; be careful to stick to the tarmac and not to wander off onto the dirt roads.

Beyond Evangelístria, a mule track continues to the abandoned **Áyios Harálambos monastery**, from where it's possible to walk across the island to the ruined capital of Kástro (see below) along another dirt road; this takes about two hours. To reach Kástro from Skiáthos Town, it's quicker to take the direct road, though in all it's still a hard five- to six-kilometre uphill slog; the turning is signposted on the road behind town, some distance beyond the turning for Evangelístria. You'll find it much easier if you do the walk in reverse. Just take a round the island kaïki ride and get off at the beach below Kástro. Another option is to ride a motorbike up the hill and then explore on foot.

Just over halfway between Evangelístria and Kástro, a well-used dirt track (signposted) turns left and heads towards the abandoned fifteenth-century monastery of **Panayía tís Kekhriás**, three hours' walk from town. It's said to be the oldest on the island and has a colony of bats inside. It's a beautiful walk (or organized donkey-ride), and there are two pebbly beaches below, one with a welcoming stream that provides a cool shower. Ignoring this excursion, the paved road continues to within a thirty-minute walk of **Kástro** – a spectacular spot, built on a windswept headland. In the past, the entrance was only accessible by a drawbridge, which has been replaced by a flight of steps. The village was built in the sixteenth century, when the people of the island moved here for security from pirate raids. It was abandoned three hundred years later in 1830, following independence from Turkey, when the population moved back to build the modern town on the site of ancient Skiáthos. The ruins are largely overgrown, and only three churches survive intact, the largest still retaining some original frescoes.

From outside the gates, a path leads down the rocks to a good pebble **beach**; with a stream running down from the hills and a daytime café (with slightly overpriced food and drinks), it makes a good place to camp. For an apparently inaccessible spot though, it does attract a surprising number of people. All the island excursion boats call here, and even when they've gone, there's little chance of having the ruins or beach to yourself.

Finally, the seventeenth-century **Kounístra monastery**, can be reached by turning right off the paved road that runs up the island from Tróulos, the last beach before Koukounariés, to the beach at Asélinos. It's a very pretty spot, with a beautiful carved icon screen, splendid icons, a grape arbour and a taverna.

The beaches

The real business of Skiáthos is **beaches**. There are reputed to be more than sixty of them, but that's hardly enough to soak up the numbers of summer visitors: at the height of the season, the local population of five thousand can be swamped by up to fifty thousand visitors. The beaches on the northeast coast aren't easily accessible unless you pay for an excursion kaïki: reaching them on foot requires treks more arduous than those described above. The bus, though, runs along the entire south coast, and from strategic points along the way you can easily reach a good number of beaches. The prevailing summer *meltémi* wind blows from the north, so the beaches on the south coast are usually better protected. Most of the popular beaches have at least a drinks/snacks stall; those at Vromólimnos, Asélinos and Troúlos have proper tavernas.

The beaches before the **Kalamáki peninsula** (where English and rich Greeks have their villas) are unexciting, but on the promontory itself are the highly-rated **Ayía Paraskeví** and **Vromólimnos beaches**, close to Kanapítsa hamlet; Vromólimnos offers windsurfing and waterskiing. For scuba enthusiasts, there is the *Dolphin Diving Centre* (☎0427/22 599) at the *Nostos* hotel, on the eastern side of the Kalamáki peninsula.

Just before Troúlos you can turn right up a paved road, which runs 4km north to **Mégas Asélinos**, a very good beach with a campsite, beach bar and a reasonable taverna. A daily bus and excursion boats stop here, so it's crowded in season. A fork in the paved road leads to Kounístra monastery (see above) and continues to **Mikrós Asélinos**, just east of its larger neighbour and somewhat quieter.

The bus only goes as far as **KOUKOUNARIÉS**, a busy resort with wooden walkways traversing the sand to a series of canteens selling drinks and light snacks, though the three beaches are excellent if you don't mind the crowds. There's a majestic sandy bay of clear, gradually deepening water, backed by acres of pines, which despite its popularity merits at least one visit if only to assess the claim that it's the best beach in Greece. The road runs behind a small lake at the back of the pine trees, and features a string of **hotels**, **rooms** and **restaurants**, as well as a good campsite. Here, the *Strofilia* apartments which sleep four (☎0427/49 251; ⑥) are particularly nicely furnished. The *Lake Hotel*, a smart new place right opposite the lake itself, is also decent value (☎0427/49 362; ⑤). Jet-skis, motorboats, windsurfing and waterskiing are all available off the beach.

"**Banana beach**" (also known as Krassá), the third cove on the far side of Poúnda headland, is one of the trendiest beaches with watersports, a couple of bars and tolerance of nude bathing. For the less adventurous, the turning for **Ayía Eléni**, 1km from the road, leads to a pleasant beach with a drinks kiosk. Further north, **Mandhráki** and **Eliá** beaches have similar facilities, and are accessible by bus.

The famed **Lalária beach**, on the northern stretch of coast, can be reached by taxi-boats from the town. Covered with smooth white stones, it's beautiful, with steep cliffs rising behind it; the swimming is excellent, but beware of the undertow. The island's three natural grottoes – Skotiní, Glazía and Halkiní – are nearby, and are included in many of the "round the island" trips. Southeast of Kástro are the greyish sands of **Mégas Yialós**, one of the less crowded beaches, and **Xánemos**, another nudist beach; both suffer from airport noise.

The only real way to get away from the crowds is to persuade a boat-owner to take you out to one of Skiáthos's **islets**. **Tsougriá**, in particular, has three beaches, with a taverna on the main one.

Skópelos

Bigger, more rugged and better cultivated than Skiáthos, **Skópelos** is almost as busy, but its concessions to tourism are lower key and in better taste than in Skiáthos. Most of the larger beaches have sunbeds, umbrellas and some watersports, but smaller, secluded coves do exist. Inland, it is a well-watered place, growing olives, plums, pears and almonds. **Glóssa** and **Skópelos**, its two main towns, are also among the prettiest in the Sporades, clambering uphill along paved steps, their houses distinguished by attractive wooden balconies and grey slate roofs. A number of **nationalities** have occupied the island at various stages of its history, among them the Romans, Persians, Venetians, French and, of course, the Turks. The Turkish admiral Barbarossa (Redbeard) had the entire population of the island slaughtered in the sixteenth century.

Loutráki, Glóssa and the west

Most boats call at both ends of Skópelos, stopping first at the small port of **LOUTRÁKI** with its narrow pebble beach, small hotels and rooms for rent. The village has been

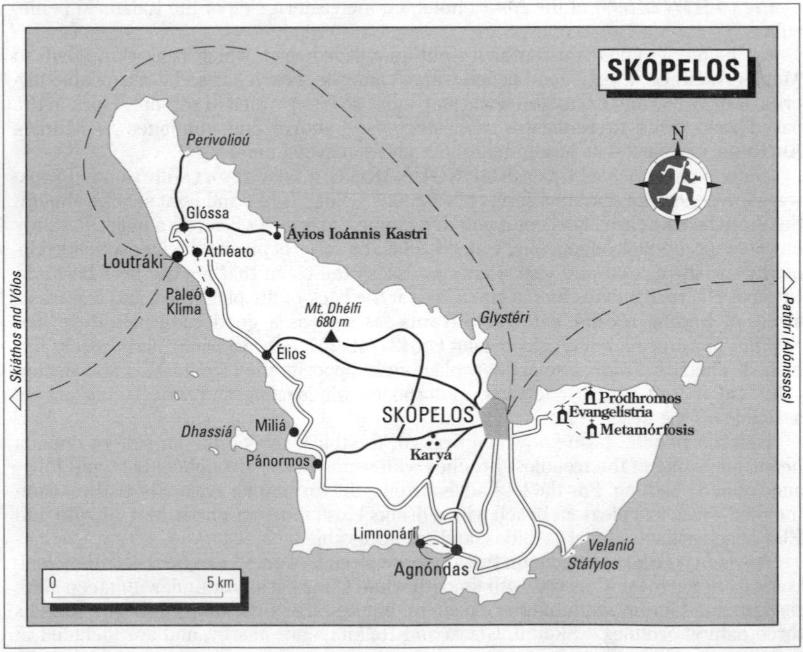

spoiled a little by development at either end, but it's not a bad place to stay if you're after peace and quiet; try *O Stelios* (☎ 0424/33 412; ③), a simple pension above the *Vrahos* taverna, the *Avra* (☎0424/33 550; ④) or any of the rooms advertised just in from the seafront. Though most of the quayside tavernas don't offer value for money, there are exceptions: the *Orea Ellas* taverna by the harbour is shaded by beautiful chestnut trees and sells a highly recommended, homemade retsina; the *Flisvos* is a friendly place with decent pasta dishes, and the small ouzerí *Boukadhoura* is good.

High above Loutráki, **GLÓSSA** would be perhaps a preferable base if it had more places to stay. It is a sizable and quite beautiful, totally Greek town, with several kafenía, a taverna and a few rooms to let, some of which are hot and musty, with erratic water pressure. *Kostas and Nina's* place (☎0424/33 686; ②) has simple, clean rooms, some with a view; they also rent out studios longer term, or you could stay at the *Selinounda Apartments* (☎0424/33 570; ③) on the road between Loutráki and Glóssa. The one central taverna, *To Agnandi*, is a lively and authentic place to eat, and full most evenings, while *Iy Kali Kardhia*, on the road out towards Élios, also serves good food in a pleasant setting. Incidentally, it's a good idea to accept offers of a taxi ride up to Glóssa from Loutráki; it's a stiff walk up even if you know the path shortcuts, and taxi drivers will know if there are any vacancies. If it's really high season, though, and even Glóssa is packed, two nearby villages, **Athéato** and **Paleó Klíma** have rooms, while Élios on the coast below has two big hotels, bungalows and rooms.

Ninety minutes' walk from Glóssa, up to the north coast, will bring you to a **beach** the locals call **Perivolioú**. The walk itself is worthwhile, passing a **monastery** next to a stone cairn containing masses of human bones and skulls. There's also a huge hollow oak tree here, in the heart of which is a small tank of drinking water. The beach, when you get there, is nothing out of the ordinary, but there's spring water for drinking and a cave for shade.

East of Glóssa, a dirt road leads to the splendidly sited church of **Áyios Ioánnis Kastrí**, perched on the top of a rock high above a small sandy cove where you can swim. A new unsightly house nearby has spoiled the isolation somewhat, but the walk from Glóssa (again, about ninety minutes) is beautiful and peaceful, with hawks and nightingales for company.

Skópelos Town

If you stay on the ferry beyond Loutráki – probably the best plan – you reach **SKÓPELOS TOWN**, sloping down one corner of a huge, almost circular bay. The best way to arrive is by sea, with the town revealed slowly as the boat rounds the final headland. Though more and more people seem to have discovered Skópelos Town, the locals are making a tremendous effort to keep it from going the way of Skiáthos. The harbour area is practically wall-to-wall tavernas and cafés, but the shops and eateries in the back alleys tend to be imaginative and tasteful, with wooden, hand-painted name signs; the two real eyesores date from the junta years. Spread below the oddly whitewashed ruins of a Venetian **Kástro**, are an enormous number of churches – 123 reputedly, though some are small enough to be mistaken for houses and most are locked except for their annual festival day. Other sights include a **folklore museum** (Wed–Fri 10am–2pm & 6–8pm, Sat 6–9pm and Sun 11am–1pm & 6–9pm) and photography exhibitions in summer.

Outside town, perched on the slopes opposite the quay, are two convents, worth visiting for their seclusion and views: **Evangelístria** (daily 8am–1pm & 4–7pm), which is within view of the town, and **Pródhromos** (daily 8am–1pm & 5–8pm). The monastery of **Metamórfosis**, also on this promontory, was abandoned in 1980 but is now being restored by the monks and is open to visitors. Access is simplest by following an old road behind the line of hotels along the bay to Evangelístria (an hour's walk). From there it's an extra half-hour's scramble over mule tracks to Pródhromos, the remotest and most beautiful of the three. Ignore the new road that goes part way – it's longer, and misses most of the beauty of the walk.

Practicalities

The **ferry quay** is at the western end of a long promenade, lined with an array of boutiques, bars, stores and restaurants. To get to the **bus station**, turn left where the quay meets the main road, and follow the sea until you pass the children's swings and the second *períptero*; at the point where the road divides around a car park. Opposite the bus station entrance, a short road leads into a maze of lanes and signposts to the **post office**. There are **banks** about 50m from the quay. Among the several **motorbike rental** outlets, friendly service can be had at Panos Bikes (☎0424/23 696), near the start of the road towards Glóssa. For around 5000dr, day-long **boat cruises** offer to take you round the island or on a tour of Alónissos and the marine park.

In the main body of the town there are dozens of **rooms** for rent. These can be arranged through the Association of Room Owners office (☎ & fax 0424/24 567; daily 9am–noon & 6–8pm), on the seafront 100m from the ferry dock. Alternatively, there are a few pleasant small hotels such as *Andromache* (inquire at Madro Travel by the quay ☎0424/22 145; ③), in a quiet old house near the post office, and the relaxed and casual *Kyr Sotos* (☎0424/22 549; ④) nearby. The old style *Georgios* (☎0424/22 308; ④), right by the quay, is a fair standby and the gaily painted *Adonis* (☎0424/22 231; ⑤), just above the mid-seafront is also good though noisy. For larger, more **expensive hotels** higher up from the port, you're unlikely to find a space without having booked through a tour operator, but if you fancy the likes of the cosy *Elli* (☎0424/22 943; ⑥) on the east side of town, the modern *Aperitton* (☎0424/22 256; ⑥) on the ring road above the town, or the neo-rustic *Dionysos* (☎0424/23 210, fax 22 954; ⑥), also on the ring road – each with a pool – ask about vacancies at Madro Travel (see above) on the quay; they're also the local Flying Dolphin agents.

There's a wide variety of **places to eat**, ranging from the acceptable to the truly excellent. Those at the near end of the harbour, like *Angelos-Ta Kymata*, *Molos* and *Klimataria*, all offer decent meals, while *Spyros* in the middle has been a reliable favourite for years. *To Aktaion* is also a good bet, with exceptionally pleasant staff and large, delicious and reasonably priced portions. At the far end of the front *Stergios* also has tasty dishes like chicken in white wine sauce. A little way inland, two *souvláki* places, both named *O Platanos*, compete for the distinction of having the best *yíros*; the one with blue chairs also has a much wider menu. And for a gourmet treat, the *Perivoli* is the place. It is located near the two *Platanos*es – above the waterfront to the east of town.

Nightlife in Skópelos is on the increase, but is more of the late-night bar than the nightclub variety, apart from the *Cocos* disco out of town. That said, *Metro, Ano Kato* and *Panselinos,* which form a cluster on Dhoulídhis street, are pretty jumping on a hot summer evening. Among bars, look out for the classy *Vengera*, in a restored house that compares favourably with the town's folk art museum, and the small, atmospheric *Nemesis*. The *bouzoúki* joint *Meintani* is housed in an old olive press near Souvlaki Square, while the *Skopelitissa* and *Anatoli* on top of the Kástro play Greek music till the early hours.

Around the rest of the island

Buses cover the island's main paved road between Skópelos Town and Loutráki via Glóssa (around 6–8 times daily 7am–10.30pm), stopping at the paths to all the main beaches and villages. **Stáfylos**, 4km south of town, is the closest beach, though rather small and rocky. It's getting increasingly crowded, but the *Terpsis* taverna, which rents

rooms, is a very pleasant spot shaded by a vast pine tree. Among the new room ventures, *Mando* (☎0424/23 917; ⑤) is friendly and quiet.

When Stáfylos gets too busy, it's better to go to **Velanió** beach, a short walk north round the coast, to have a chance of escaping the crowds. Nudity is acceptable and although the official campsite has closed, you shouldn't be hassled if you stay a night or two. There's spring water and a *kantína* too.

Further around the coast to the west, the tiny horseshoe-shaped harbour of **AGNÓNDAS** (with its two fish tavernas and rooms) is the start of a fifteen-minute path (2km by road) or half-hourly kaïki trip to **LIMNONÁRI**, 300m of fine sand set in a closed, rocky bay. The *Limnonari Beach* restaurant serves delicious spiral-shaped local *tyrópittes* and rents rooms (☎0424/23 046; ④).

PÁNORMOS is very much a full-blown, commercial resort, with rooms, tavernas, a campsite, yacht anchorage and watersports. The beach here is gravelly and steeply shelving, but there are small secluded bays close by. The thirty-room *Panormos Beach Hotel* (☎0424/22 711; ⑥) has a beautiful garden and fine views, and is lovingly looked after; beyond it, the *Adrina Beach* (☎0424/23 373; ⑥) is one of the most attractive and most expensive hotels in the Sporades. Slightly further on at **MILIÁ**, there is a tremendous, 1500m sweep of tiny pebbles beneath a bank of pines, facing the islet of Dhassía. There's one taverna and the *Milia Apartments* (☎0424/23 998; ④) in this languid setting; nudist swimming is possible at a lovely five-hundred-metre-long beach a little way north. The shore beyond is indented with many tiny coves, ranging from individual- to family-size.

Further north, **ÉLIOS**, 9km short of Glóssa, is a medium-sized, fairly new resort settled by residents of the earthquake-damaged villages above it, with nothing special to offer besides a pleasant beach. If you want to stay, try the newly done-up *Zanneta* (☎ 0424/33 140, fax 33 717; ⑤). Beyond here, the renovated village of Paleó Klíma marks the start of a beautiful forty-minute **trail** to Glóssa, via the empty hamlet of Áyii Anáryiri and the oldest village on the island, **Athéato**.

West of Skópelos Town, various jeep tracks and old paths wind through olive and plum groves toward **Mount Dhélfi** and the Vathiá forest, or skirt the base of the mountain northeast to Revýthi hill with its fountains and churches, and the site of **Karyá**, with its *sendoúkia:* ancient rock-cut tombs which may be early Christian. To the northwest of Skópelos Town, **Glystéri** is a small pebble beach with no shade, whose taverna is much frequented by locals on Sundays. A fork off the Glystéri and Mount Dhélfi tracks can – in theory – be followed across the island to Pánormos within ninety minutes; it's a pleasant walk though the route isn't always obvious.

Alónissos and some minor islets

The most remote of the Sporades, **Alónissos** is also, at first sight, the least attractive. It has an unfortunate recent history. The vineyards were wiped out by disease in 1950, and the hóra was damaged by an earthquake in 1965. Although its houses were mostly repairable, lack of water, combined with corruption and the social control policies of the new junta, were instrumental in the transfer of virtually the entire population down to the previously unimportant anchorage of Patitíri. The result is a little soulless, but what charm may be lacking in the built environment on the coast is made up for by the hospitality of the islanders.

Patitíri and the old town

PATITÍRI is not a good introduction to the island, but it's trying hard to rectify that. The port, a pretty cove flanked by pine trees, is marred by rows of flat-roofed concrete

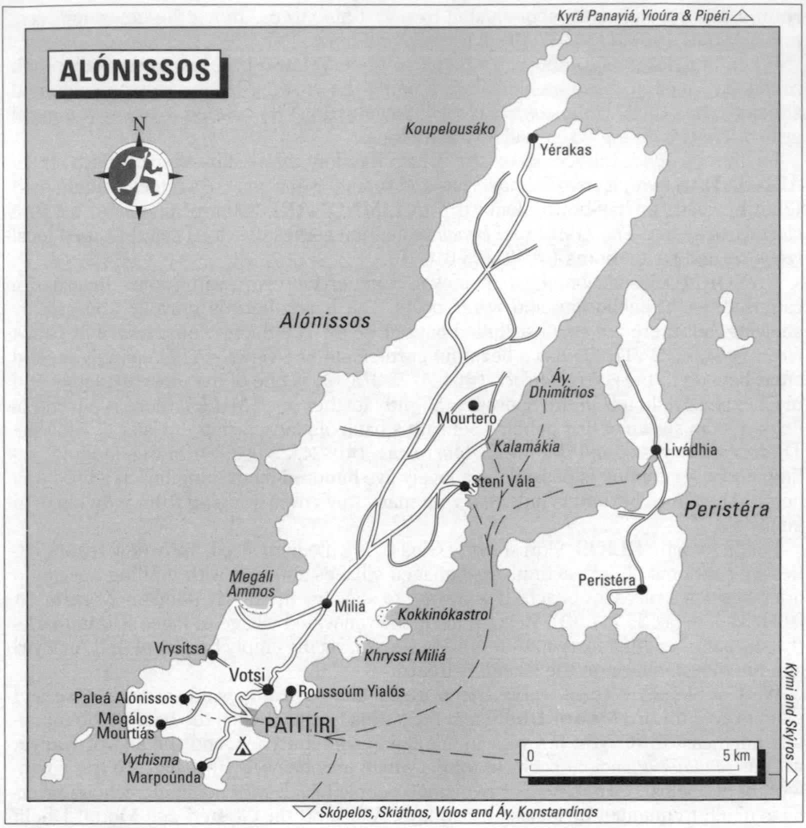

buildings rising up behind it. Nevertheless, the line of near-identical bars and restaurants that run along the waterfront is not unappealing. Alónissos attracts fewer visitors than Skíathos or Skópelos; most of those who do come stay in Patitíri, and from mid-July to the end of August it can get very crowded. It's easy, though, to pick up connections here for beaches and the old town, and there are several good hotels to choose from. The most interesting place to visit is the **Monk Seal Information Centre** (daily 10am–1pm & 7–10pm) on the first floor of a building halfway along the seafront. The displays include models, photos, video and slide shows; see box on p.386.

PALEÁ ALÓNISSOS is a fine but steep fifty-minute walk via a donkey track – signposted on the left just outside Patitíri. Alternatively, there's a frequent bus service in the mornings and afternoons. Although some houses are still derelict, much of the village has been painstakingly restored, mainly by the English and Germans who bought the properties at knock-down rates. Only a few local families continue to live here, which gives the village a rather odd and un-Greek atmosphere, but it is picturesque, and the views make the trip worthwhile.

Practicalities

All the important facilities are in Patitíri; **buses** and **taxis** congregate next door. The **post office** is on the Hóra road, while kaïkia leave from the quay beside the *Pension Flisvos* (see below). You can rent a moped or motorbike at 2 Trohi or even a car (check with Ikos Travel below) at reasonable prices. The roads between Patitíri, Stení Vála and the northernmost point on the island are paved, and the dirt roads down to the beaches are in good condition: not half as dangerous as the twisting, busy roads on Skiáthos and Skópelos. A couple of the rental places on the waterfront also rent out motorboats and dinghies.

Rooms are easy to find here, as you'll probably be approached with offers as you get off the ferry, sometimes by older women wearing traditional blue and white costumes. The local room-owners' association (☎ & fax 0424/65 577), on the front, can also find you a room (mostly ③) in Patitíri or nearby Vótsi. Other options include the *Ioulieta* pension (☎0424/65 463; ③), *Haravyi* (☎0424/65 090, fax 65 189; ④) and *Pantheon* (☎0424/65 139; ④). *Liadromia* (☎0424/65 521; ⑤) above the port, *Niirides* (☎0424/65 643; ⑤), comprising studio apartments with pool, and *Paradise* (☎0424/65 160; ⑤), on the promontory east of the port with a pool overlooking the sea, are the best in the higher price range. Ikos Travel, the Flying Dolphin agent (☎0424/65 320), can do bookings for a limited number of rooms and apartments in the old town, though accommodation here is in short supply so expect to pay well over the odds, particularly in season. Otherwise, ask around; few people put up "room for rent" signs, but try the simple and clean *Fadasia House* (☎0424/65 186; ③), at the entrance to Hóra.

The **restaurants** along the front of Patitíri are reasonably priced, but the food is nothing special. The best place for breakfast is the *To Korali*; in the evenings, try the friendly *Pension Flisvos*. For the best meal in Patitíri go two blocks up towards the post office from the waterfront to *To Kamaki*, a wonderful ouzerí with a amazing selection of seafood. Two other ouzeris worth a try on the same road are *Kala Krassa* and *Kapetan Spyros*. The *Tzimakis* grill has good food in a splendid setting on the promontary. Up in the old town, *Astrofengia* has the tastiest food, and *Paraport* at the Kástro the most spectacular views.

Nightlife is low-key. The best of the seafront bars is *Pub Dennis*, whose ice-cream concoctions are divine, though both *En Plo* and *La Vie* are popular. Club-wise, *Borio* and *Enigma* are fairly European, while *Rembetika*, on the road to the old town, specializes in Greek music.

The island's beaches

Alónissos has some of the cleanest water in the Aegean, but it's lacking in sand beaches. There's only one really sandy beach on the island (Výthisma), the rest varying from rough to fine pebbles. There's no bus, but kaïkia run half-hourly from Patitíri north to Khrissí Miliá, Kokkinókastro, Stení Vála, Kalamákia and Áyios Dhimítrios, and south around the coast to Marpoúnda, Výthisma and Megálos Mourtiás. Kaïkia also sail occasionally to Livádhia and Peristéra islet.

At Patitíri there's decent swimming from the rocks around the promontory to the north; pick your way along a hewn-out path past the hotels and you're there (ladder provided). To the north, above the headlands, Patitíri merges into two adjoining settlements, **Roussoúm Yialós** and **Vótsi**. For better beaches, you'll have to get in a boat or on a bike.

Khryssí Miliá, the first good beach, has pine trees behind the sand and a taverna; there are a couple of new hotels on the hillside above, such as the posh *Milia Bay* (☎0424/66 035; ⑥), and it can get crowded in summer. At **Kokkinókastro**, over the hill

THE MEDITERRANEAN MONK SEAL

The **Mediterranean monk seal** has the dubious distinction of being the European mammal most in danger of extinction. Fewer than eight hundred survive worldwide, the majority around the Portuguese Atlantic island of Madeira. A large colony off the coast of the West African state of Mauritania was decimated early in 1997: an estimated two hundred seals died, possibly poisoned by algae. Small numbers survive in the Ionian and Aegean seas; the largest population here, of around thirty seals, lives around the deserted islands north of Alónissos.

Monk seals can travel up to 200km a day in search of food, but they usually return to the same places to rear their **pups**. They have one pup every two years, and the small population is very vulnerable to disturbance. Originally, the pups would have been reared on sandy beaches, but with increasing disturbance by man, they have retreated to isolated sea caves, particularly around the coast of the remote islet of Pipéri.

Unfortunately, the seals compete with fishermen for limited stocks of fish, and, in the overfished Aegean, often destroy nets full of fish. Until recently it was common for seals to be killed by fishermen. This occasionally still happens, but in an attempt to protect the seals, the seas around the northern Sporades have been declared a **marine wildlife reserve**: fishing is restricted in the area north of Alónissos and prohibited within 5km of Pipéri. On Alónissos, the conservation effort and reserve have won a great deal of local support, mainly through the efforts of the Hellenic Society for the Protection of the Monk Seal (HSPMS), based at Stení Vála. The measures have been particularly popular with local fishermen, as tighter restrictions on larger, industrial-scale fishing boats from other parts of Greece should help preserve fish stocks, and benefit the fishermen financially.

Despite this, the government has made no serious efforts to enforce the restrictions, and boats from outside the area continue to fish around Pipéri. There are also government plans to reduce the prohibited area around Pipéri to 500m. On a more positive note, the HSPMS, in collaboration with the Pieterburen Seal Creche in Holland, has reared several abandoned seal pups, all of which have been successfully released in the seas north of Alónissos.

For the moment, your chances of actually seeing a seal are remote, unless you plan to spend a few weeks on a boat in the area. It's recommended that you shouldn't visit Pipéri or approach sea caves on other islands which might be used by seals, or try to persuade boat-owners to do so.

to the north, excavations have revealed the site of ancient Ikos and evidence of the oldest known prehistoric habitation in the Aegean. There's nothing much to see, but it's a beautiful spot with a good red pebble beach, and, in July and August, a daytime bar.

STENÍ VÁLA, opposite the island of Peristéra, a haven for the yachts and flotillas that comb the Sporades, has almost become a proper village, with two shops, several houses, a bar, rooms and five tavernas, one of which stays open more or less throughout the year. The Monk Seal Treatment and Rehabilitation Centre, housed in a small hut on the beach, can provide information and insight into the HSPMS's work when manned. There's a campsite (☎0424/65 258) in an olive grove by the harbour, a long pebble beach – Glýfa, where boats are repaired – and some stony beaches within reasonable walking distance in either direction. **KALAMÁKIA**, to the north, also has a couple of tavernas and a few rooms.

If you want real solitude, **Áyios Dhimítrios**, **Megáli Ámmos**, and **Yérakas** (an old shepherds' village at the northernmost point) are possibilities. However, before committing yourself to a Robinson Crusoe existence, check it out by moped or take one of the round the island trips available, and return the next day with enough food for your stay: there are no stores outside the port and Stení Vála. In the opposite direction from Patitíri, **Marpoúnda** features a large hotel and bungalow complex and a rather small beach. It's better to turn left after the campsite towards **Megálos Mourtiás**, a pebble beach with several tavernas linked by dirt track with Paleá Alónissos, 200m above. **Výthisma**, the lovely beach just before Megálos Mourtiás, can only be reached by boat, the path here having been washed out. Further north, visible from Paleá Alónissos, **Vrysítsa** is tucked into its own finger-like inlet. There's sand and a taverna, but little else.

Beyond Alónissos: some minor islets

Northeast of Alónissos, half a dozen tiny **islets** speckle the Aegean. Virtually none of these has any permanent population, or a ferry service, and the only way you can reach them – at least Peristéra, Kyrá Panayía and Yioúra – is by excursion kaïki (ask at Ikos Travel), weather permitting. No boats are allowed to take you to the other, more remote islets, as they are protected areas within the Sporades National Marine Park. But though it is possible to be left for a night or more on any of the closer islands, when acting out your desert-island fantasies, be sure to bring more supplies than you need: if the weather worsens you'll be marooned until such time as small craft can reach you.

Peristéra is the closest islet to Alónissos, to which it was once actually joined, but subsidence (a common phenomenon in the area) created the narrow straits between the two. It is graced with some sandy beaches and there is rarely anyone around, though some Alónissans do come over for short periods to tend the olive groves, and in season there are regular evening "barbecue boats" from the main island. As on Alónissos, a few unofficial campers are tolerated, but there is only one spot, known locally as "Barbecue Bay", where campfires are allowed.

Kyrá Panayiá (also known as Pelagós) is the next islet out and is equally fertile. It's owned by the Meyístis Lávras monastery of Mount Áthos and there are two monasteries here, one still inhabited. Boats call at a beach on the south shore, one of many such sandy stretches and coves around the island. There's no permanent population other than the wild goats.

Nearby **Yioúra** boasts a stalactite cave reputed to be the previous abode of Polyphemus, the Cyclops who imprisoned Odysseus, but you won't be able to check its credentials. No one is allowed within 500m of the island, since, like Pipéri, it lies inside the restricted zone of the Marine Park.

Pipéri, near Yioúra, is a sea-bird and monk-seal refuge, and permission from a ministry of the environment representative (in Alónissos) is required for visits by specialists; non-scientists are not allowed. Tiny, northernmost **Psathoúra** is dominated by its powerful modern lighthouse, the tallest in the Aegean, although here, as around many of these islands, there's a submerged ancient town, brought low by the endemic subsidence. Roughly halfway between Alónissos and Skýros, green **Skántzoura**, with a single empty monastery and a few seasonal shepherds, is a smaller version of Kyrá Panayiá.

Skýros

Despite its proximity to Athens, **Skýros** remained a very traditional and idiosyncratic island until recently. Any impetus for change had been neutralized by the lack of economic opportunity (and even secondary schooling), forcing the younger Skyrians to live in Athens and leaving behind a conservative gerontocracy. A high school was finally provided in the mid-1980s, and the island has been somewhat "discovered" since that time. It's now the haunt of continental Europeans, chic Athenians and British, many of whom check into the "New Age" Skýros Centre, to "rethink the form and direction of their lives".

Meanwhile, Skýros still ranks as one of the most interesting places in the Aegean. It has a long tradition of painted **pottery** and ornate **woodcarving**, in particular the *salonáki skyrianó* (handmade set of chairs). A very few old men still wear the vaguely Cretan traditional costume of cap, vest, baggy trousers, leggings and *trohádhia* (Skýrian sandals), but this is dying out. Likewise, just a few old women still wear the favoured yellow scarves and long embroidered skirts.

The theory that Skýros was originally two islands seems doubtful, but certainly the character of the two parts of the island is very different. The north has a greener and more gentle landscape, and away from the port and town it retains much of its original pine forest. The sparsely inhabited south is mountainous, rocky and barren; there are few trees and the landscape is more reminiscent of the Cyclades than the Sporades. Compared with Skiáthos, Skópelos and Alónissos, Skýros isn't a great place for beaches. Most **beaches** along the west coast attract a certain amount of sea-borne rubbish, and, although the scenery is sometimes spectacular, the swimming isn't that good. The beaches on the east coast are all close to Skýros Town, and the best option is probably

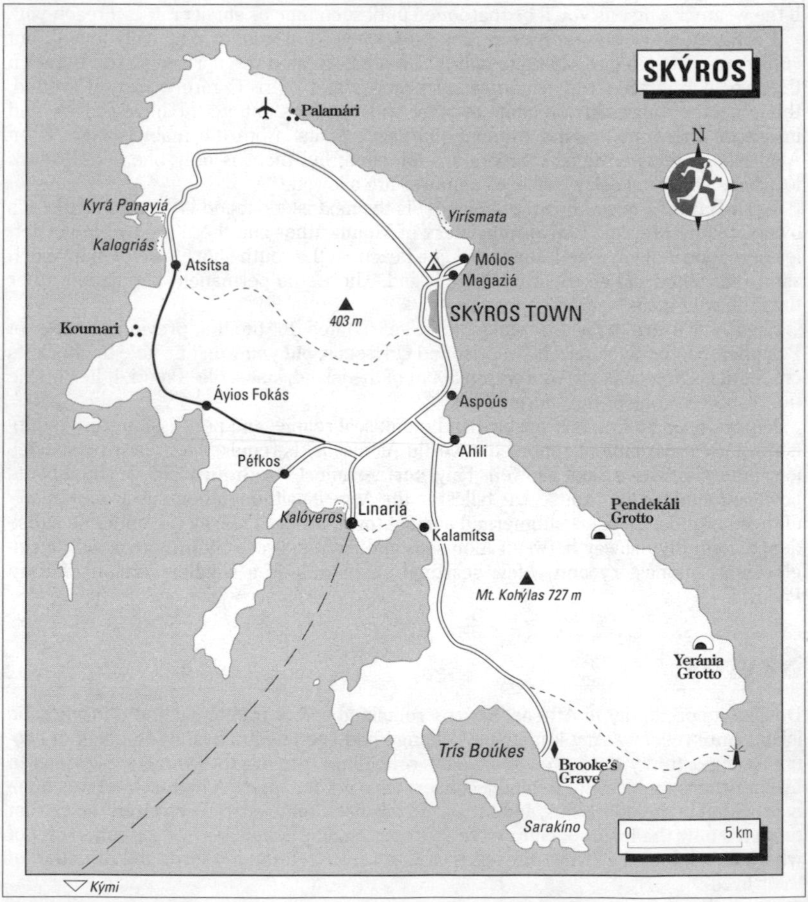

GOAT DANCES AND WILD PONIES

Skýros has some particularly lively, even outrageous, festivals. The *Apokriatiká* (pre-Lenten) Carnival here is structured around the famous **goat dance**, performed by masked revellers in the village streets. The foremost character in this is the Yéros, a menacing figure concealed by a goatskin mask and weighed down by garlands of sheep bells. Accompanying him are Korélles and Kyriés (who are transvestites, as only the men participate) and Frangi (maskers in "Western" garb). For further details, read Joy Koulentianou's *The Goat Dance of Skyros*, available in Athens and occasionally on the island.

The other big annual event takes place near Magaziá beach on August 15, when children race domesticated members of the **wild pony** herd, native to Skýros and said to be related to the Shetland pony (if so, it must be very distantly). They are thought, perhaps, to be the diminutive horses depicted in the Parthenon frieze, and at any time of the year you might find some of the tame individuals tethered and grazing near Skýros Town.

to stay here rather than heading for somewhere more isolated. The beaches at the north end have been commandeered by the big air-force base there, which otherwise keeps a low profile.

Linariá

After crossing a seemingly endless expanse of sea, the boat docks at the tiny port of **LINARIÁ**, a functional place on the island's west coast. Although most of the action is around Skýros Town, Linariá does make for a quiet alternative base and is certainly a pleasant spot to while away time waiting for the ferry. If you decide to stay, the smart *King Likomides* hotel on the harbour is very good value (☎0222/93 249, fax 93 412; ③) or cheap rooms in a family atmosphere above the bay can be rented from Khrysoula Strandzi (☎0222/96 378; ②). For eating try out the mezedhopolío next to *Kalí Kardhia* taverna, which has a wide selection of delectable dishes, the *Psariotis* ouzerí or the *Filippos* fish taverna. The splendidly situated *Kavos* bar is open day and night for drinks and snacks, while more raucous nightlife is provided by the *Castro Club* disco. In high season, kaïkia ply from Linariá to the Pentekáli and Yeránia **grottoes**, and to the islet of **Sarakíno**, which has a cave and some of the Skyrian wild ponies. There's a reasonable sandy **beach** called **Kalóyeros** a few minutes' walk along the main road from Linariá, where you can camp.

A tarmac road connects Linariá to Skýros Town, 10km away, and then continues round past the airport to Atsítsa, where the Skyros Centre has a branch; **buses** to **Skýros Town** and **Magaziá**, on the coast below, leave from the quay. Midway up the Linariá–Skýros Town route, a side road links Ahíli with Kalamítsa. Most other roads are passable by moped, apart from the direct track between Skýros Town and Atsítsa.

Skýros Town

SKÝROS TOWN (also known as Horió), with its decidedly Cycladic architecture, sits on the landward side of a high rock rising precipitously from the coast. According to legend, King Lycomedes pushed Theseus to his death from its summit. The town has a workaday atmosphere; it doesn't feel like a resort and isn't especially picturesque. The older and more intriguing parts of town are higher up, climbing towards the **Kástro**, a mainly Byzantine building, built on the site of the ancient **acropolis**. There are few traces of the acropolis, although remains of the Classical city walls survive below on the seaward side of the rock. The kástro is open to visitors; to reach its upper parts you pass through a rather private-looking gateway into the monastery, then through an attractive shaded courtyard and up a whitewashed tunnel. There's little to see at the top, apart from a few churches in various states of ruin, but there are great views over the town and the island, and the climb up takes you through the quieter and more picturesque part of town, with glimpses into traditionally decorated houses. With their gleaming copper pots, porcelain plates and antique embroideries decorating the hearth, these dwellings are a matter of intense pride among the islanders, who are often found seated in their doorways on tiny carved chairs.

At the northern end of town is the striking and splendidly incongruous **memorial to Rupert Brooke**. It takes the form of a bronze statue of "Immortal Poetry" and its nakedness caused a scandal among the townspeople when it was first erected. Brooke, who visited the south of the island very briefly in April 1915, died shortly afterwards of blood poisoning on a French hospital ship anchored offshore and was buried in an olive grove above the bay of Trís Boúkes. (The site can be reached on foot from Kalamítsa, by kaïki, or, less romantically, by taxi.) Brooke, who became something of a local hero, despite his limited acquaintance with Skýros, was adopted by Kitchener and later Churchill as the paragon of patriotic youth, in the face of his forthright socialist and internationalist views.

Just below the Brooke statue are two museums. The **Archeological Museum** (Tues–Sun 8am–2pm; 500dr) has a modest collection of pottery and statues from excavations on the island, and a reconstruction of a traditional Skýros house interior. The privately run **Faltaïts Museum** (daily 10am–1pm & 5.30–8pm/6–9pm in summer; free), in a nineteenth-century house built over one of the bastions of the ancient walls, is more interesting, with a collection of domestic items, costumes, embroideries, porcelain and rare books.

Practicalities

The **bus** from Linariá leaves you by the school, 200m below the main platía; the **post office** and **bank** are both nearby. Skýros Travel (☎0222/91 123), on the main street above the platía, can provide **information** or advice, and can find a room or hotel; in high season it's a good idea to telephone them in advance. Of the **motorbike** rental places in the area around the platía, the most prominent and efficient is Trahanas (☎0222/92 032), which also has bicycles for those with strong calf muscles.

You'll probably be met off the bus with offers of **rooms**, which it's as well to accept. If you'd like to stay in a traditional Skyrian house, those of Anna Stergiou (☎0222/91 657; ③) and Maria Mavroyiorgi (☎0222/91 440; ③) are both clean and cosy. Or you could try the pleasant *Nefeli* hotel (☎0222/91 964; ⑤) on the main road before the platía. A more basic option is the *Elena* (☎0222/91 738; ②) next to the post office, which has very cheap singles with shared bath. There's a picturesque **campsite** nearer the beach, at the bottom of the steps below the archeological museum, with basic amenities but a good bar and a friendly management.

The platía and the main street running by it are the centre of village life, with a few noisy pubs and a wide choice of kafenía, tavernas and fast-food places. There are few outstanding **places to eat**; most are overpriced, or serve undistinguished food. *Maryetis* has the best grilled fish and meat, *Sisyphos* has vegetarian specialities, and the *Sweets Workshop* does some wonderful cakes. For a special occasion, try *Kristina's* restaurant below the taxi rank (signposted); its Australian owner has an imaginative menu which has great desserts. The *Panorama*, in the lower town, towards Magaziá, is also good for its home-cooking with a view.

The town's **nightlife** is mostly bar-based until very late, when the few clubs get going. The most popular **bars** are the trendy *Kalypso* which plays jazz and blues, dance-orientated *Kata Lathos* and the rockier *Iroön* and *Rodon*. Later on, *Iy Stasis* is one of the most popular places. The best clubs include the *Skyropoula, Mylos* and the *Stone Club*.

Some bars also serve good breakfasts; here the favourite is *Anemos*, followed by *Kalypso*, which has tasty Danish pastries. Another fine spot for a drink or sweets is *O Anatolikos Anemos*, near the museum, with sweeping views across the bay.

Magaziá and Mólos and nearby beaches

A path leads down past the archeological museum towards the small coastal village of **MAGAZIÁ**, coming out by the official campsite. From Magaziá, an 800-metre-long sandy beach stretches to the adjacent village of **MÓLOS**. In recent years, a sprawl of new development between the road and the beach has more or less joined the two villages together. Despite this, the beach is good, and there are lots of **rooms** down here for the young crowd that uses the beach's watersports and volleyball facilities. *Stamatis Marmaris* (☎0222/91 672; ③) beyond Mólos, and *Manolis Balotis* (☎0222/91 386; ③) near the campsite, are both excellent choices. More upmarket hotels include the *Paliopyrgos* (☎0222/91 014, fax 92 185; ④), halfway between the beach and town with a wonderful view and the *Angela* (☎0222/91 764; ⑤), a new set of bungalows in Mólos. The beachfront **tavernas** compare favourably with those in town: on the Magaziá side *Stefanos* taverna is reliable, while the *Koufari* ouzerí near the *Xenia Hotel* has excellent food for higher prices. At Mólos try *Tou Thoma To Magazi*, the *Maryetis* garden restaurant and the ouzerí at *Balabani's Mill*, all at the end of the beach. It's worth sampling lobster in Skýros: it's a local speciality, often served as a spaghetti dish.

For quieter beaches, take the road past Mólos, or better, try the excellent and undeveloped (unofficial nudist) beach, *Papa tou Houma*, directly below the kástro. The path down to the beach is 150m beyond the *Skyropoula* disco, and isn't obvious from above. However, following the road south of here, the beaches are disappointing until **Aspoús**, which has a couple of tavernas and rooms to rent as well as the smart *Ahillion* hotel (☎0222/93 300, fax 93 303; ⑤). Further south, **Ahíli**, had one of the best beaches on the island until the construction of its new marina. Southeast of Ahíli, the coast is rocky and inaccessible, although you can take a kaïki trip down to the bay of **Trís Boúkes**, passing some picturesque sea caves on the way.

Around the rest of the island

In summer, the whimsical bus service visits the more popular beaches. But if you want to branch out on your own, hire a moped. Roads, tracks and footpaths diverge from the main circle road, leading inward and seaward. Among the most interesting places to head for is **Palamári**, the neglected site of an early Bronze Age settlement and a spectacular beach. Turn right after the road has begun to descend to the airport plain.

For a taste of the wooded interior, a hike on the dirt track from Skýros Town to **ATSÍTSA** is well worth the effort; it takes three to four hours, and is too rough for a moped. Atsítsa is an attractive bay with pine trees down to the sea (tapped by the Skyrian retsina industry), and an increasing number of rooms, in addition to the Skyros Centre buildings. The beach here is rocky and isn't great for swimming, but there are small sandy beaches fifteen and twenty minutes' walk to the north at **Kalogriás** and **Kyrá Panayiá**, with its eponymous taverna, though they are nothing out of the ordinary.

Elsewhere in the coniferous north, **Áyios Fokás** and **Péfkos** bays are easiest reached by a turning from the paved road near Linariá, while access from Atsítsa is via a reasonable dirt road. Both are in the process of being discovered by villa companies, but they have few rooms. Though quite primitive, Áyios Fokás has a very basic, excellent taverna; Péfkos has two, of which *Barba Mitsos* is the more appealing (these are only open in high season, as are all the other tavernas away from Linariá, Skýros Town, Magaziá and Mólos). The bay is beautiful, and the beach reasonable but not that clean – the beaches around Skýros Town are much better for swimming.

As for exploring the great southern mountain of **Kohýlas**, this is best attempted only if you have a four-wheel-drive vehicle, as the tracks are poor away from the main road. A good road runs south of Kalamítsa to the naval base at Trís Boúkes (where Rupert Brooke is buried), which makes getting to the southern beaches easier. Kalamítsa, just east of Linariá, lacks character, but the *Mouries* taverna between it and Linariá is worth a stop, as is the remote beach half way to Trís Boúkes, which has no facilities.

Évvia (Euboea)

Évvia is the second-largest Greek island (after Crete), and seems more like an extension of the mainland to which it was in fact once joined. At **Halkídha**, the gateway to the island, the curious old drawbridge has only a forty-metre channel to span, the island reputedly having been split from Attica and Thessaly by a blow from Poseidon's trident (earthquakes and subsidence being the more pedestrian explanations). Besides the new suspension bridge bypassing Halkídha and linking Évvia to the mainland, there are ferry crossings at no fewer than seven points along its length, and the south of the island is closer to Athens than it is to northern Évvia.

Nevertheless, Évvia *is* an island, in places a very beautiful one. But it has an idiosyncratic history and demography, and an enduringly strange feel that has kept it out of the mainstream of tourism. A marked **Albanian influence** in the south, and scattered Lombard and Venetian watchtowers give it a distinctive flavour. Indeed, the island was the longest-surviving southerly outpost of the Ottoman Turks, who had a keen appreciation of the island's wealth, as did the Venetians and Lombards before them. The last **Ottoman garrison** was not evicted until 1833, hanging on in defiance of the peace settlement that awarded Évvia to the new Greek state. Substantial Turkish communities, renowned for their alleged brutality, remained until 1923.

Economically, Évvia has always been prized. By Greek standards, it's exceptionally **fertile**, producing everything from grain, corn and cotton to kitchen vegetables and livestock. The classical name "Euboea" means "rich in cattle," but nowadays cows are few and far between; its kid and lamb, however, are highly rated, as is the local retsina. Because of the collapse of much of its mining industry, parts of the island are actively seeking foreign tourism. For the moment, however, Greeks predominate, especially in the north around the spa of **Loutrá Edhipsoú**. In July and August, Évvia can seem merely a beach annexe for much of Thessaly and Athens.

In the rolling countryside of the **north**, grain combines whirl on the sloping hay meadows between olive groves and pine forest. This is the most conventionally scenic part of the island, echoing the beauty of the smaller Sporades. The **northeast coast** is rugged and largely inaccessible, its few sandy beaches surf-pounded and often plagued by flotsam and jetsam; the **southwest** is gentler and more sheltered, though much disfigured by industrial operations. The **centre** of the island, between Halkídha and the easterly port of Kými, is mountainous and dramatic, while the far **southeast** is mostly dry and very isolated.

Public **transport** consists of seasonal hydrofoils along the protected southwest coast from Halkídha upwards, and passable bus services along the main roads to Kárystos in the southeast, and Loutrá Edhipsoú in the northwest. Otherwise, explorations are best conducted by rented car; any two-wheeler will make little impact on the enormous distances involved.

Halkídha

The heavily industrialized island-capital of **HALKÍDHA** (the ancient *Chalkis*, an appellation still used) is the largest town on Évvia, with a population of 60,000. A shipyard,

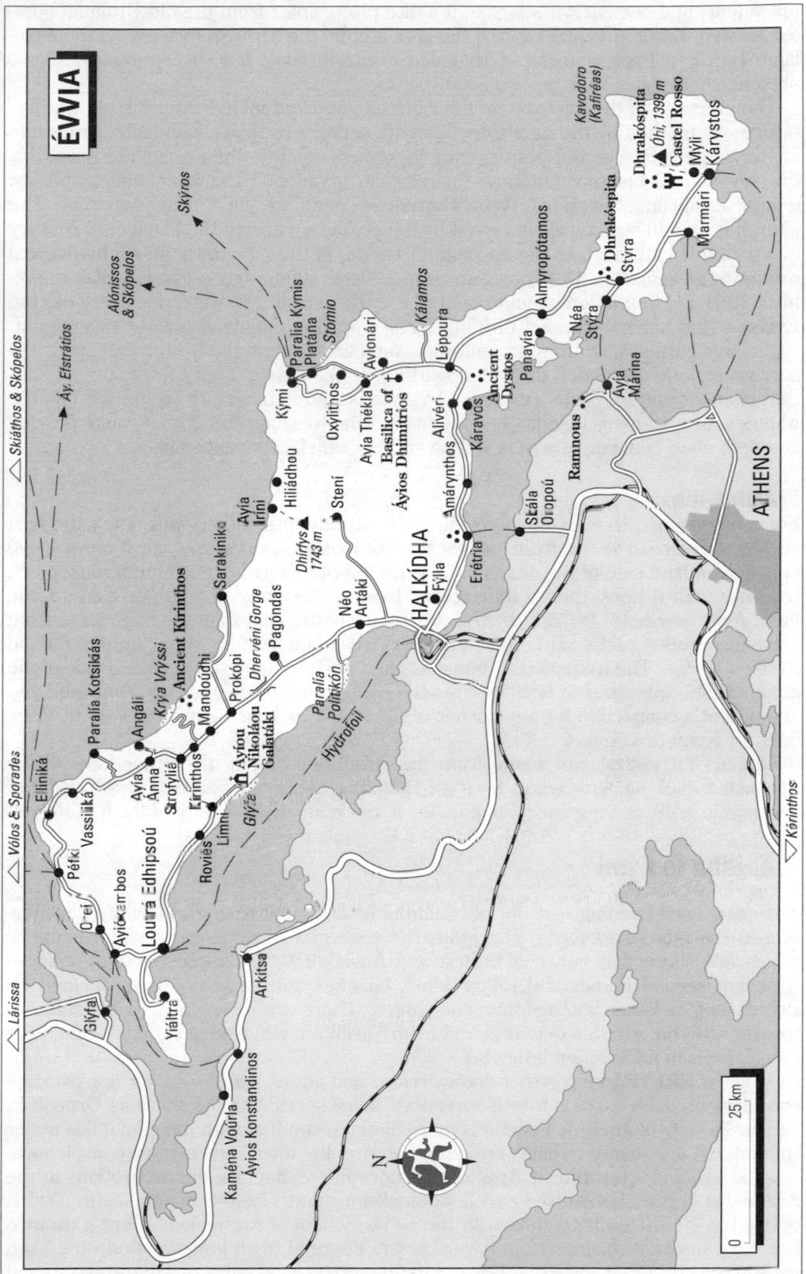
ÉVVIA
Lárissa
Vólos & Sporades
Skiáthos & Skópelos
Áy. Efstrátios
Alónissos & Skópelos
Skýros
Glýfa
Yiáltra
Ayiókambos
Oreí
Péfki
Elliniká
Vassiliká
Paralía Kotsikiás
Angáli
Ayía Ánna
Strofyliá
Kírinthos
Loutrá Edhipsoú
Roviés
Límni
Glýfa
Ayíou Nikoláou Galatáki
Mandoúdhi
Prokópi
Kryá Vrýssi
Ancient Kírinthos
Dhervéni Gorge
Pagóndas
Sarakíniko
Ayía Iríni
Hiliádhou
Dhírfys 1743 m
Kými
Paralía Kýmis
Platána
Stómio
Oxýlithos
Avlonári
Ayía Thékla
Basilica of Áyios Dhimítrios
Kálamos
Stení
Néo Artáki
Paralía Politikón
Hydrofoil
HALKÍDHA
Fýlla
Erétria
Amárynthos
Alivéri
Káravos
Lépoura
Ancient Dystos
Panayía
Almyropótamos
Néa Stýra
Stýra
Dhrakóspita
Marmári
Dhrakóspita
Óhi, 1399 m
Castel Rosso
Mýli
Kárystos
Kavodoro (Kafiréas)
Ayía Marína
Ramnous
Skála Oropoú
ATHENS
Kórinthos
Arkítsa
Áyios Konstandínos
Kaména Voúrla
N
0
25 km

rail sidings and cement works make it a dire place, apart from the old Ottoman quarter, **Kástro**, south of Venizélou, and the area around the Turkish fortress on the mainland. Hardly a trace remains of Halkídha's once-thriving Jewish community, whose presence here dates back around 2500 years.

The entrance to the kástro – on the right as you head inland from the old Euripos bridge – is marked by the handsome fifteenth-century **mosque**, nominally a museum of Byzantine artefacts, but permanently locked. Beyond lie the remains of Karababa, the seventeenth-century Ottoman fortress, an arcaded Turkish aqueduct and the unique basilican **church of Ayía Paraskeví** (shut except during services). The church is an odd structure, converted by the crusaders during the fourteenth century into a Gothic cathedral. In the opposite direction, in the new town, an **archeological museum** at Venizélou 13 (Tues–Sun 8am–2.30pm; 500dr) has a good display of prehistoric, Hellenic and Roman finds from all over the island. The waterside overlooks the **Évripos**, the narrow channel dividing Évvia from the mainland, whose strange currents have baffled scientists for centuries. You can stand on the bridge that spans the narrowest point and watch the water swirling by like a river. Every few hours the current changes and the "tide" reverses. Aristotle is said to have thrown himself into the waters in despair at his inability to understand what was happening, so if you're puzzled you're in good company; there is still no entirely satisfactory explanation.

Practicalities

For most visitors, though, such activities are strictly time-fillers, with much the best view of the place to be had from the bus, train or hydrofoil on the way out. **Trains** arrive on the mainland side of the channel, beneath the old fortress; given numerous, quick rail links with Athens, there's little reason to stay overnight. Should you want to, the basic *Kentrikon* hotel (☎0221/22 375; ②) is a far better deal than the huge waterfront establishments it backs onto. Most other services of interest lie within sight of the old Évripos bridge. The **hydrofoil** terminal sits just northeast, on the mainland side of the channel. The **bus station** is 400m from the bridge along Kótsou, then 50m right; you should get a connection for any corner of the island as long as you show up by 2pm, later for Kými or Límni.

Options for **eating out** range from the restaurants lining the waterfront, where Athenians flock on Sundays to feast on Halkídha's superior seafood, to a handful of acceptable grills serving adequate lunches in the immediate vicinity of the bus station.

Halkídha to Kými

The coast road heading east out of Halkídha is an exceptionally misleading introduction to the interior of Évvia. The industrial zone gives way to nondescript hamlets, which are succeeded between Erétria and Amárynthos by sequestered colonies of Athenian second homes and rather bleak beaches and large hotels frequented by British and German package-tour companies. There are some intriguing **Frankish towers** at **Fýlla**, worth a detour inland from Vasilikó if you have a car, and some easy connections to Athens, but little else.

Modern **ERÉTRIA** is a rather dreary resort laid out on a grid plan; for non-package travellers its main asset is a well-advertised ferry service across to Skála Oropoú in Attica. The site of **ancient Eretria** is more distinguished, though much of it lies under the town. A few scanty remains are dotted around the town centre, most conspicuously an **agora** and a **temple of Apollo**, but more interesting are the excavations in the northwest corner, behind the excellent small museum (Tues–Sun 8am–3pm; 500dr), opened in 1991 in collaboration with the Swiss School of Archeology. Here a **theatre** has been uncovered; steps from the orchestra descend to an underground vault used for sudden entrances and exits. Beyond the theatre are the ruins of a **gymnasium** and a **sanctuary**. The museum guard will be happy to unlock the fourth-century BC **House of Mosaics**, five minutes' walk from the museum. Of the numerous hotels in town the most interesting option is the municipal tourist complex *Dreams Island* (☎0229/61 224, fax 61 268; ⑤), which occupies a tiny offshore island, linked by causeway to the end of the bay.

Nine kilometres further along, **AMÁRYNTHOS** is a smaller and more pleasant resort to stay in. Though the town boasts nothing of particular interest, the seafront square is picturesque enough and there is an ample selection of good eateries, such as *Stefanos* fish taverna right by the square and *To Limenaki* a few minutes west of it. Two good accommodation options are *Iliaktidhes* (☎0229/37 605; ④), just off the main road, and *Stefania* (☎0229/36485, fax 38 384; ⑤), right on the beach.

Just before **Alivéri**, an enormous modern power plant and a virtually intact medieval castle seem incongruously juxtaposed, and more Frankish towers look down from nearby hills. Though Alivéri itself is dreary, the nearby fishing harbour of **Káravos** has several pleasant watering holes, among them the *Vlahos* taverna. Thereafter, the route heads inland. Beyond Lépoura, where the road branches north and south, the scenery improves drastically. Take the north fork towards Kými, and cross some of the most peaceful countryside in Greece. With your own vehicle you can detour east after five kilometres at Neohóri to the excellent beaches at **Kálamos** and **Korasídha**. There is a growing selection of rooms and tavernas at Kálamos.

Twelve kilometres north of Lépoura, at Háni Avlonaríou, stands the Romanesque thirteenth- or fourteenth-century **basilica of Áyios Dhimítrios**, Évvia's largest and finest (ask for the key at the café next door). **AVLONÁRI** proper, 2km east, is dominated by a hill that commands most of the island's centre. At its crown is a huge Lombard or Venetian tower, rearing above the Neoclassical and vernacular houses that tier the lower slopes. There's a single taverna below the platía, though no accommodation.

This part of Évvia is particularly well endowed with Byzantine chapels, since Avlonári was an archiepiscopal see from the sixth century onwards. Back on the road to Kými, a left fork just north of Háni Avlonaríou (the bus goes this way) leads past the hamlet of **Ayía Thékla**, where a small, shed like **chapel** of that saint, probably slightly later than Áyios Dhimítrios, hides in a lush vale below the modern church. Inside, enough fresco fragments remain with their large-eyed faces to suggest what has been lost over time. The right fork leads towards the coast and takes you past Oxýlithos, with its somewhat more elaborate chapels of **Áyios Nikólaos** and **Ayía Ánna**, both at least a hundred years older than Áyios Dhimítrios.

The road hits the coast at the fine beach of **Stómio** (known also as just Paralía, or "Beach"), some 1500m of sand closing off the mouth of a river, which is deep, swimmable and often cleaner than the sea. To the north and east you glimpse the capes enclosing the broad bay of Kými. Up on the road, there are a couple of cafés and a small pension; most facilities, however, are further round the coast at **PLATÁNA**, where another river is flanked by a line of older houses, many with rooms or flats to rent.

Despite its name, the extremely functional port of **PARALÍA KÝMIS** has no real beach, and is not a particularly congenial place to be stuck overnight waiting for a ferry or hydrofoil to the Sporades. The most substantial and traditional **taverna** is *Spanos/To Egeo*, at the south end of the front, while *To Valanti* is also reasonable and the sweet little *Rock Club* plays eclectic sounds; there are just two **hotels**, *Coralli* (☎0222/22 212, fax 23 353; ④) and *Beis* (☎0222/22 604; ④).

Most travellers get to **KÝMI** (the main ferry port to Skýros) by bus, which takes the inland route via Ayía Thékla. The upper part of town is built on a green ridge overlooking both the sea and Paralía Kými, 4km below. Note that all buses deposit you in the upper town except for the one or two daily that connect with the ferry. At the bottom of the town, on the harbour-bound road, you can visit the **Folklore Museum**, which has an improbably large collection of costumes, household and agricultural implements and old photos recording the doings of Kymians both locally and in the US, where there's a huge community. Among the emigrants was Dr George Papanikolaou, deviser of the "Pap" cervical smear test, and there's a statue honouring him up in the upper-town platía, where you might ask about **rooms**. There are some good **tavernas** like *To Balkoni*, on the main road towards the shore, with its superb view, where you can sample the products of the local vineyards.

To get up into the rugged country west of Kými, you must negotiate jeep tracks through the forest, or return to Halkídha for the bus service up to **STENÍ**, a large and beautiful village at the foot of Mount Dhírfys. The village has a few cheap psistariés and two **hotels**, the *Dirfys* (☎0228/51 217; ③) and the *Steni* (☎0228/51 221; ③). It's a good area for hiking, most notably up the peaks of Dhírfys and Xirovoúni, and beyond to the isolated beach hamlets of Hiliádhou and Ayía Iríni, though you'll need a specialist hiking guide to do this.

Southeast Évvia

The extension of Évvia southeast of Lépoura, so narrow that you can sometimes glimpse the sea on both sides, has a flavour very distinct from the rest of the island. Often bleak and windswept, it forms a geological unit with neighbouring Ándhros, with shared slates and marble. Ethnically, the south also has much in common with that northernmost Cyclade: both were heavily settled by Albanian immigrants from the early fifteenth century onwards, and Arvanítika – a **medieval dialect** of Albanian – was until recently the first language of the remoter villages here. Even non-Arvanítika speakers often betray their ancestry by their startlingly fair colouring and aquiline features. For a place so close to Athens, the south is often surprisingly untouched by modernity; some of the houses have yet to lose their original slate roofs. Others still lack electricity, and the few fields on the steep slopes are far more often worked by donkeys and horses than by farm machinery.

Immediately southeast of Lépoura, most maps persist in showing the lake of Dhýstos in bright blue. In fact, the lake area has been almost totally drained and reclaimed as rich farmland, much to the detriment of the migratory birds who used to stop off here, and to the annoyance of Greek and foreign environmentalists who would prefer that they still did so. Atop the almost perfectly conical hill in the centre of the flat basin are the sparse fifth-century BC ruins of **ancient Dystos** and a subsequent medieval citadel, hard to explore because the surroundings are so swampy.

Beyond the Dhýstos plain, the main road continues along the mountainous spine of the island to Károstos at the southern end of the paved road system and bus line. If you have your own transport, it's worth stopping off at **STÝRA**, above which are a cluster of **Dhrakóspita** (Dragon Houses), signposted at the north edge of the village and reached by track, then trail. They are so named because only mythological beings were thought capable of shifting into place their enormous masonry blocks. Their origins and uses have yet to be definitively established. The most convincing theory suggests that they are sixth-century BC temples built by immigrants or slaves from Asia Minor working in the nearby marble and slate quarries.

The shore annexe of **NÉA STÝRA**, 5km downhill from the hill village, is a fairly standard package resort, worth knowing about only for its handy ferry connection to Ayía Marína (which gives access to ancient Rhamnous) on the Attic peninsula. Much the same can be said for **MARMÁRI**, 19km south, except in this case the ferry link is with Rafína. Here the smart *Hotel Delfini* (☎0224/31 296, fax 32 300; ③) is surprisingly good value and there are a few decent places to eat; try the *Zygos* mezedhopolío, which serves cheap fish in a nice atmosphere. The road between Marmári and Kárystos is now more or less finished, completing the "superhighway" and allowing you to enjoy the nether reaches of the island as you cruise down to its last major settlement.

Kárystos and around

At first sight **KÁRYSTOS** is a rather boring grid (courtesy of nineteenth-century Bavarian town-planners), which ends abruptly to east and west and is studded with modern buildings. King Otho liked the site so much that he contemplated transferring the Greek capital here, and there are still some graceful Neoclassical buildings dating from that period. Kárystos improves with prolonged acquaintance, though you're unlikely to stay for more than a few days. What it can offer is the superb (if often windy) beach to the west, the smaller, sandier **Psilí Ámmos** ten minutes' walk to the east and a lively, genuine working-port atmosphere. Only one plot of fenced-in foundations, in the central bazaar, bears out the town's ancient provenance, and the oldest obvious structure is the fourteenth-century Venetian **Bourtzi** (locked except for occasional summer evening art exhibitions) on the waterfront. This small tower is all that remains of once-extensive fortifications. Every evening the shore road is blocked with a gate at this point to allow an undisturbed promenade by the locals. There is a small but interesting **archeological museum** (Tues–Sun 8am–3pm; 500dr) inside the Cultural Centre opposite the Bourtzi, displaying finds from the local area – mostly statues and temple carvings plus a few smaller votive objects.

PRACTICALITIES

Rafína-based **ferries** and **hydrofoils** also serve Kárystos; **buses** arrive inland, above the central platía and below the National Bank, near a tiny combination grill/ticket office labelled KTEL. This has information on the extremely infrequent (once daily at best) departures to the remote villages of the Kavodóro (Kafiréas) cape to the east. Information on the August wine festival and sightseeing in the region, including walking routes, is provided by the friendly tourist office in a kiosk near the quay.

Finding affordable **accommodation** is not a big problem. The best value is the *Als* (☎0224/22 202, fax 25 002; ③), right opposite the quay, although it may get noisy in high season. Other options are the big *Galaxy* (☎0224/22 600, fax 22 463; ④) on the west side of the waterfront, the *Karystion* (☎0224/22 391, fax 22 727; ⑤) in the park beyond the Bourtzi on the shore road and the plush new *Apollon Suite* (☎0224/22 045, fax 22 049; ⑥) on Psilí Ámmos beach. Another strategy is to follow up signs in restaurant windows advertising **rooms** inland.

By contrast, you're spoilt for choice when **eating out**, as Kárystos must have more restaurants than the rest of Évvia put together. Among the best choices are the *Kavo Doros*, a friendly and reasonable taverna on Párodos Sakhtoúri one block west of the square, which serves oven food; *Ta Kalamia*, at the west end of the esplanade by the start of the beach is a cheap, filling and popular lunchtime option; while the English-speaking *Ta Ovreïka*, in the old Jewish quarter, Sakhtoúri 114, has both Greek and international cuisine and cooked breakfasts. In the road running up from the *Als* there are several fine psistariés, serving the local lamb and goat for which Kárystos is renowned.

AROUND KÁRYSTOS

The obvious excursion from Kárystos is inland towards **Mount Óhi** (1399m) Évvia's highest peak after Dhírfys and Xirovoúni. **MÝLI**, a fair-sized village around a spring-fed oasis, 3km straight inland, makes a good first stop, with its few tavernas. Otherwise, the medieval castle of **Castel Rosso** beckons above, a twenty-minute climb up from the main church (longer in the frequent, howling gales). Inside, the castle is a total ruin, except for an Orthodox **chapel of Profítis Ilías** built over the Venetians' water cistern, but the sweeping views over the sea and the town make the trip worthwhile.

Behind, the ridges of Óhi are as lunar and inhospitable as the broad plain around Kárystos is fertile. From Mýli, it's a three-hour-plus hike up the largely bare slopes, mostly by a path cutting across the new road, strewn with unfinished granite columns, abandoned almost two thousand years ago. The path passes a little-used alpine club shelter (fed by spring water) and yet another *dhrakóspito*, even more impressive than the three smaller ones at Stýra. Built of enormous schist slabs, seemingly sprouting from the mountain, this one is popularly supposed to be haunted.

From Halkídha to Límni

The main road due north from Halkídha crosses a few kilometres of flat farmland and salt marsh on either side of the refugee settlement of Néa Artáki, after which it climbs steeply through forested hills and the **Dhervéni gorge**, gateway to the north of Évvia. With your own transport, a pleasant detour is to take the road left before Psákhna to the long pebbly beach of **Paralía Politikón**, which is dotted with places to stay or eat.

The village of **PROKÓPI** lies beyond the narrows, in a valley defined by the rich and beautiful woods that make it famous. A counterpoint, in the village itself, is the ugly 1960s pilgrimage church of **St John the Russian**, which holds the saint's relics. The "Russian" was actually a Ukrainian soldier, captured by the Turks in the early eighteenth century and taken to Turkey where he died. According to locals, his mummified body began to promote miracles, and the saint's relics were brought here by Orthodox Greeks from Cappadocian Prokópi (today Ürgüp) in the 1923 population exchange – Évvian Prokópi is still referred to by the locals as Akhmétaga, the name of the old Turkish fiefdom here that was bought by an English nobleman, Edward Noel, a cousin of Lord Byron's, right after the War of Independence. His descendants now run summer courses in various crafts, based in the manor house.

Following a shady, stream-fed glen for the 8km north of Prokópi, you suddenly emerge at Mandoúdhi, much the biggest village in the north of the island, though now squarely in the doldrums following the collapse of the local magnesite industry; ignore signs or depictions on certain maps of a beach at Paralía Mandoúdhi, which is nothing more than abandoned quarries and crushing plants. The closest serviceable beach is at **Paralía Kírinthos**, better known as **Krýa Vrýssi** (take a right-hand turning off the main road, 3km beyond Mandoúdhi). At the coast, a river and an inlet bracket a small beach, with the headland south of the river supporting the extremely sparse remains of **ancient Kirinthos**. The hamlet of Kírinthos, just past Mandoúdhi, has some visitors, owing to the craft school there.

Back on the main road, a fork at Strofiliá, 8km north of Mandoúdhi, offers a choice of routes: continue north to the coastal resorts that curl round the end of the island (see below), east to Pýli and then south to some unspoiled beaches on the way to Cape Sarakíniko, or head west for Límni.

Límni

If you're hunting for a place to stay, **LÍMNI**, on the west coast 19km from Strofiliá, is by far the most practical and attractive base north of Halkídha. The largely Neoclassical, tile-roofed town, built from the wealth engendered by nineteenth-century shipping prowess, is the most appealing on the island, with serviceable beaches and a famous convent nearby. A small **folk art museum** features pottery, coins and sculpture fragments, as well as local costumes, fabrics and furniture.

There is a regular **hydrofoil** service during summer to Halkídha and the Sporades, and buses from Halkídha stop at the north side of the quay. Límni has a **post office** and **two banks**, all inland just off the main through-road into town from Strofiliá.

As yet, Límni gets few package tours, and **accommodation** is usually available in its rooms or hotels, except during August. At the extreme south, quieter, end of the waterfront, the *Límni* (☎0227/31 316; ②) is good value, with singles and doubles; the *Plaza* (☎0227/31 235; ②), beside the bus stop, is very similar, but has no singles and gets some noise from nocturnal revels outside. Smarter rooms with TV can be rented at

Livaditis (☎0227/31 640; ④), above *Pyrofanis*, an ouzerí beyond the *Plaza*. The best **place to eat** in terms of setting, menu and popularity is *O Platanos* (under the enormous quayside plane tree) with the adjacent *Avra* not far behind. Other local favourites are *Kallitsis* inland from the waterfront, and *Lambros* and *O David* on the way to Katoúnia beach to the south of town.

Around Límni

There are no recommendable beaches in Límni itself, though if you continue 2.5km northwest from the town you reach the gravel strand of **Kohýli**, with a basic but leafy **campsite** out on the cape, 500m beyond mid-beach. Here there are some congenial places to stay, most notably *Denis House* (☎0227/31 787; ⑤) and the more luxurious *Ostria* (☎0227/32 247; ⑤), which has a pool and includes breakfast.

ROVIÉS, some 14km west of Límni, doesn't stand out, but with its medieval tower, rooms, hotels, grid of weekenders' apartments and services, it's the last place of any sort along the scenic coast road to Loutrá Edhipsoú.

The outstanding excursion from Límni is 7km south (under your own steam) to the **convent of Ayíou Nikoláou Galatáki**, superbly set on the wooded slopes of Mount Kandhíli, overlooking the north Evvian Gulf. To get there, veer up and left at the unsigned fork off the coast road; there's no formal scheme for visiting, but don't show up in the early afternoon or around sunset as the gates will be shut. Though much rebuilt since its original Byzantine foundation atop a Poseidon temple, the convent retains a thirteenth-century tower built to guard against pirates, and a crypt. One of a dozen or so nuns will show you frescoes in the *katholikón* dating from the principal sixteenth-century renovation. Especially vivid, on the right of the narthex, is the *Entry of the Righteous into Paradise*: the righteous ascend a perilous ladder to be crowned by angels and received by Christ, while the wicked miss the rungs and fall into the maw of Leviathian.

Below Ayíou Nikoláou Galatáki, and easily combined with it to make a full half-day outing, are the pebble and sand beaches of **Glýfa**, arguably the best on Évvia's southwest-facing coast. There are several in succession, leading up to the very base of Mount Kandhíli, some reachable by paths, the last few only by boat. The shore is remarkably clean, considering the number of summer campers who pitch tents here for weeks on end; a single roadside spring, 2km before the coast, is the only facility in the whole zone.

Northern coastal resorts

Returning to the junction at Strofiliá, take the main road north for 8km to **AYÍA ÁNNA** (locally and universally elided to *Ayiánna*), which has long enjoyed the unofficial status of Évvia's most **folkloric village**, by virtue of traditional costumes worn by the older women and an assiduous local ethnographer, Dimitris Settas, who died in 1989. The place itself is nothing extraordinary, and most passers-by are interested in the prominently marked turnoff for **Angáli beach**, 5km east. This is billed as the area's best, and it's sandy enough, the low hills behind lending a little drama but like this entire coast it's exposed and can gather rubbish. A frontage road, set back 200m or so, is lined by a few kilometres of anonymous villas and apartments, with the "village" at the north end. The *Agali Hotel* (☎0227/97 104, fax 97 067; ⑤) is a congenial place to stay, and there is also a campsite. Horse-riding on the beach is a well-advertised and popular diversion.

Ten kilometres north of Ayía Ánna, a side road heads downhill for 6km, past the village of Kotsikiá, to **Paralía Kotsikiás**. The small cove with its taverna and rooms serves primarily as a fishing-boat anchorage, and its tiny, seaweed-strewn beach is of little interest. **Psaropoúli beach**, 2km below Vassiliká village (13km north of the Kotsikiá turnoff), is more usable in its three-kilometre length, but like Ayía Ánna it is scruffy and shadeless, with a smattering of rooms, self-catering units and tavernas not imparting much sense of community. If you choose to stay, you can't do much better than *Motel Canadiana* (☎0226/43 274; ②), where the road down meets the seafront. **Ellinikà**, the next signposted beach, lies only 800m below its namesake village inland; it's far smaller than Angáli or Psaropoúli, but cleaner and certainly the most picturesque spot on this coast, with a church-capped islet offshore as a target to swim to. The approach driveway has a very limited number of facilities: a minimarket, one taverna and a few studios. *Motel Aigaio* (☎0226/42 262; ③) is as good as any for a stay.

Beyond Elliniká, the road (and bus line) skirts the northern tip of Évvia to curl southwest towards **PÉFKI**, a seaside resort mobbed with Greeks in summer, which straggles for some two ki lometres along a mediocre beach. The best **restaurants**, near the north end of this strip, include *Ouzeri Ta Thalassina* and *Psitopolio O Thomas*, while *Zaharoplastio O Peristeras* proffers decadent desserts. **Accommodation** is the usual Évvian mix of self-catering units and a few seaside hotels such as *Galini* (☎0226/41 208, fax 41 650; ④) and *Myrtia* (☎0226/41 202; ③), all resolutely pitched at mainlanders; the **campsite**, *Camping Pefki*, is 2km north of town behind the beach, rather pricey and geared to people with caravans. Hydrofoils for the Sporades depart from here regularly in season.

The next resort (14km southwest), **OREÍ**, is a low-key fishing village, whose cafés are favoured by those in the know as the best places to watch the sun set. It has a fine statue of a Hellenistic bull, hauled up from the sea in 1965, and is also the last **hydrofoil stop** en route to Vólos and the Sporades. Nearby Néos Pýrgos beach has a selection of rooms and restaurants. Some 7km further along the coast, **AYIÓKAMBOS** has a frequent ferry connection to Glýfa on the mainland opposite, from where there are buses to Vólos. Ayiókambos is surprisingly pleasant considering its port function, with a patch of beach, two or three tavernas and a few rooms for rent.

The trans-island bus route ends 14km south of Ayiókambos at **LOUTRÁ EDHIPSOÚ**, which attracts older Greeks, who come to bathe at the **spas** renowned since antiquity for curing everything from gallstones to depression. The spas themselves are cheap (300dr for 20min) and quite an experience. The vast number of hotels, some old and creaky, which service the summer influx means good deals can be had off-season. The classy seventy-year-old *Egli* (☎0226/22 215, fax 22 886; ③) on the seafront is a fine choice. Other decent options in the side-streets near the port are *Valar's* (☎0226/22 278, fax 23 419; ④) and the more modern *Lito* (☎0226/22 081; ③). There is an abundance of tavernas strung along the front; try the leafy restaurant of the *Egli* or the traditional *To Fagadhiko tou Barous*, which offers a wide selection of mezédhes.

There are less regimented **hot springs** at **Yiáltra**, 15km west around the head of Edhipsós bay, where the water boils up on the rocky beach, warming the shallows to comfortable bath temperature. From Loutrá Edhipsoú, the coast road heads southeast to Límni.

travel details

Alkyon Tours (in co-operation with Nomicos ferry lines), and the competing Goutos Lines, provide expensive **conventional ferry** services out of Vólos, Áyios Konstandínos and Kými, with fares steeper than those on Cyclades or Dodecanese lines. On the plus side, Alkyon maintain an Athens office (Akadhimías 97; ☎01/38 43 220) for purchase of ferry and combined bus-and-ferry tickets. Between April and October, Flying Dolphin **hydrofoils** operate between various mainland ports and the Sporades. These are pricier than the ferries but cut journey times virtually in half.

SKIÁTHOS, SKÓPELOS AND ALÓNISSOS

Ferries

Áyios Konstandínos to: Skiáthos (14 weekly; 3hr); Skópelos (10 weekly; 5hr, 6 continuing to Alónissos, 6hr).

Vólos to: Skiáthos (3–4 daily; 3hr) and Skópelos (3–4 daily; 4hr); Alónissos (at least one daily; 5hr; this is the most consistent service out of season, and is always the cheapest).

Flying Dolphins (April–Oct only)

Áyios Konstandínos to: Skiáthos, Glóssa, Skópelos and Alónissos (April, May and Oct 1–3 daily; June–Sept 3–5 daily).

Néa Moudhaniá (Halkidhikí) to: Skiáthos, Skópelos, Alónissos (June–Aug 1 daily).

Plataniás (Pílion) to: Skiáthos (June–Aug 4 weekly).

Thessaloníki to: Skiáthos, Glóssa, Skópelos and Alónissos (June–Aug 1–2 daily).

Tríkeri (Pílion) to: Vólos (April–Oct 1–2 daily); Skiáthos, Skópelos and Alónissos (April–Oct 1–2 daily).

Vólos to: Skiáthos, Glóssa and Skópelos (April, May and Oct 2–3 daily; June–Sept 4–6 daily); at least 2 daily (April–Oct) continue from Skópelos to Alónissos.

Flights

Athens to: Skiáthos (mid-June to mid-Sept 1–3 daily, otherwise 6 weekly; 40min).

SKÝROS

Ferries

Skýros is served by conventional ferry, the *Lykomides*, from **Kými** (2hr). Services are at least twice daily mid-June to mid-Sept (usually at around noon and 5pm), once daily (5pm) the rest of the year; ☎0222/96 466 for current information. There is a connecting bus service for the afternoon boat, from the Liossíon 260 terminal in Athens (departs 12.30pm).

Flying Dolphins

A **hydrofoil** (June to mid-Sept; 5 weekly) links Skýros with Skiáthos, Skópelos and Alónissos.

Flights

Athens to: Skýros (mid-June to mid-Sept 3 weekly; 35min).

ÉVVIA

Buses

Athens (Liossíon 260 terminal) to: Halkídha (every 30min 5.30am–9pm; 1hr 15min); Kými (6 daily; 3hr 30min).

Halkídha to: Kárystos (2 daily; 3hr); Límni (5 daily; 1hr 30min); Loutrá Edhipsoú (4 daily; 3hr); Kými (8 daily; 1 hr 45 min).

Trains

Athens (Istation) to: Halkídha (17 daily; 1hr 30min).

Ferries

Arkítsa to: Loutrá Edhipsoú (summer hourly, otherwise 8 daily 6.45am–11pm; 50min).

Ayía Marína to: Néa Stýra (summer 12–14 daily; 50min); Panayía (summer 3–4 daily; 50min).

Glýfa to: Ayiókambos (summer 8 daily, otherwise 4 daily; 30min).

Rafína to: Kárystos (Mon–Thurs 1 daily, Fri, Sat & Sun 2–3 daily; 1hr 30min); Marmári (4–6 daily; 1hr).

Skála Oropoú to: Erétria (summer every 30min 6am–11pm; 25min).

Flying Dolphins

Halkídha to: Límni, Loutrá Edhipsoú, Oreí, Skiáthos and Skópelos (May to mid-Oct 2 weekly; usually late afternoon).

Oreí to: Áyios Konstandinos (July to mid-Sept 2 weekly).

Péfki to: Skiáthos, Glóssa, Skópelos and Alónissos (April, May and Oct 2 weekly; June–Sept 1 daily).

Dolphin Line Hydrofoils

Rafína to: Kárystos (mid-June to late Sept 1 daily).

Tínos/Mýkonos (Cyclades) to: Kárystos (mid-June to late Sept 1 daily).

Connecting buses from Athens run to Rafína (every 30min; 1hr), Ayía Marína (5 daily, 1hr 15min) and Skála Oropoú (hourly; 1hr 30min) all from the Mavromatéon terminal, and to Arkítsa and Glýfa from the Liossíon 260 terminal.

CHAPTER SEVEN

THE IONIAN ISLANDS

The **Ionian** islands, shepherding their satellites down the west coast of the mainland, float on the haze of the Adriatic, their green, even lush, silhouettes coming as a shock to those more used to the stark outlines of the Aegean. The fertility is a direct result of the heavy rains that sweep over the archipelago – and especially Corfu – from October to March, so if you visit in the off-season, come prepared.

The islands were the Homeric realm of Odysseus, centred on Ithaca (modern Itháki) and here alone of all modern Greek territory (except for Lefkádha) the Ottomans never held sway. After the fall of Byzantium, possession passed to the **Venetians** and the islands became a keystone in that city-state's maritime empire from 1386 until its collapse in 1797. Most of the population must have remained immune to the establishment of Italian as the official language and the arrival of Roman Catholicism, but Venetian influence remains evident in the architecture of the island capitals, despite damage from a series of earthquakes.

On Corfu, the Venetian legacy is mixed with that of the **British**, who imposed a military "protectorate" over the Ionian islands at the close of the Napoleonic Wars, before ceding the archipelago to Greece in 1864. There is, however, no question of the islanders' essential Greekness: the poet Dhionyssios Solomos, author of the national anthem, hailed from the Ionians, as did Nikos Mantzelos, who provided the music, and the first Greek president, Ioannis Kapodistrias.

Today, **tourism** is the dominating influence, especially on **Corfu** (Kérkyra), which was one of the first Greek islands established on the package-holiday circuit. Its east coast is one of the few stretches in Greece with development to match the Spanish *costas*, and in summer even its distinguished old capital, Kérkyra Town, wilts beneath the onslaught. However, the island is large enough to retain some of its charms and is perhaps the most scenically beautiful of the group. Parts of **Zákynthos** (Zante) – which with Corfu has the Ionians' best beaches – seem to be going along the same tourist path,

ACCOMMODATION PRICE CODES

Throughout the book we've used the following **price codes** to denote the cheapest available double room in each establishment in high season. Out of season, rates can drop by more than fifty percent, especially if you are staying for three or more nights. Single rooms, where available, cost around seventy percent of the price of a double.

Rented private rooms on the islands usually fall into the ② or ③ categories, depending on their location and facilities, and the season; a few in the ④ category are more like plush self-catering apartments. They are not generally available from late October through to the beginning of April, when only hotels tend to remain open.

① Up to 6000dr	④ 12,000–16,000dr
② 6000–9000dr	⑤ 16,000–20,000dr
③ 9000–12,000dr	⑥ 20,000dr and upwards

Note: Youth hostels typically charge 2000–2500dr for a dormitory bed.
For more accommodation details, see pp.44–47.

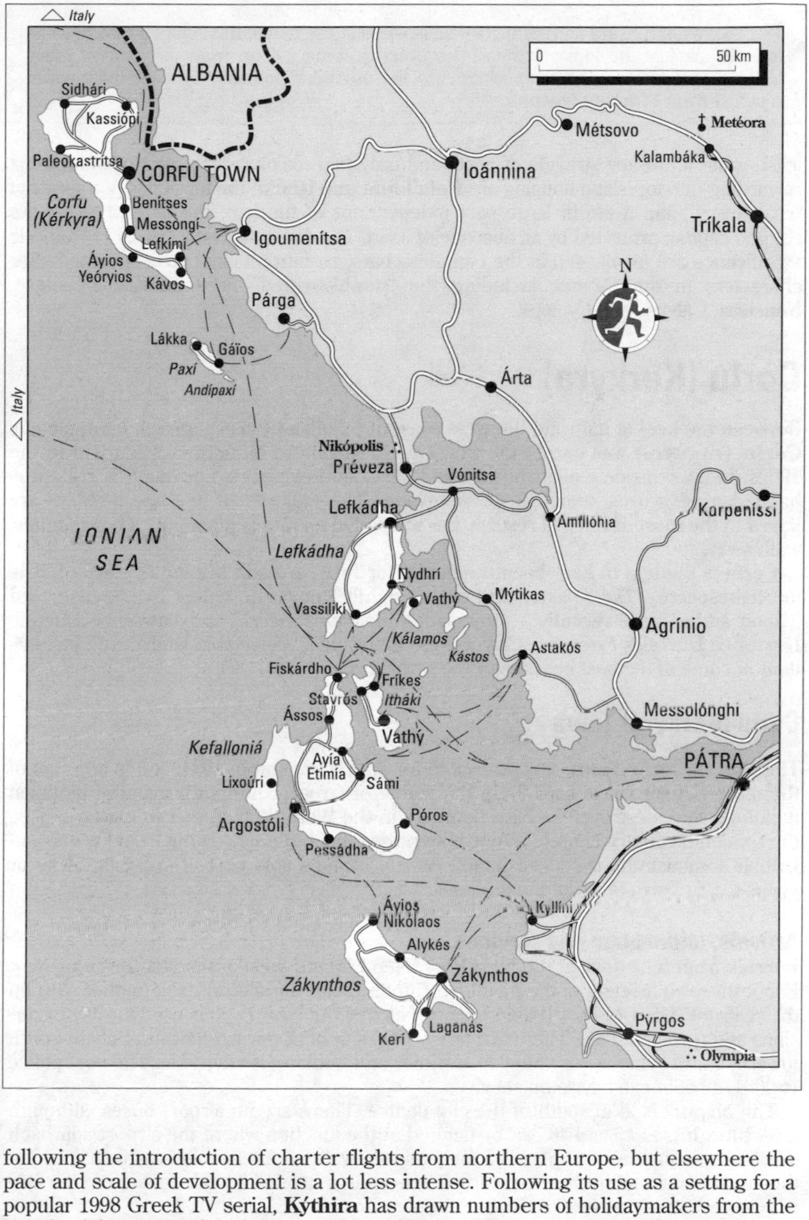

following the introduction of charter flights from northern Europe, but elsewhere the pace and scale of development is a lot less intense. Following its use as a setting for a popular 1998 Greek TV serial, **Kýthira** has drawn numbers of holidaymakers from the mainland, but its fine beaches remain largely free of foreign tourists. Little **Páxi** is a bit too tricky to reach and lacks the water to support a large-scale hotel, while **Lefkádha** – which is connected to the mainland by a causeway and "boat bridge" – has, so far at

> The islands of **Kýthira** and **Andikýthira**, isolated at the foot of the Peloponnese, are historically part of the Ionian islands. However, at some 200km from the nearest other Ionians, and with no ferry connections to the northerly Ionians, they are most easily reached from **Yíthio** or **Neápoli**.

least, quite a low-key straggle of ports and only two major resorts. Perhaps the most rewarding duo for island-hopping are **Kefalloniá** and **Itháki**, the former with a series of "real towns" and a life in large part independent of tourism, the latter, Odysseus's rugged capital, protected by an absence of sand. The Ionian islands' claims to Homeric significance are manifested in the countless bars, restaurants and streets named after characters in the *Odyssey,* including the "nimble-witted" hero himself, Penelope, Nausicaa, Calypso and Cyclops.

Corfu (Kérkyra)

Between the heel of Italy and the west coast of mainland Greece, green, mountainous **Corfu (Kérkyra)** was one of the first Greek islands to attract mass tourism in the 1960s. Indiscriminate exploitation turned parts into eyesores, but much is still uninhabited olive groves, mountain or woodland. The majority of package holidays are based in the most developed resorts, but unspoiled terrain is often only a few minutes' walk away.

Corfu is thought to have been the model for Prospero and Miranda's place of exile in Shakespeare's *The Tempest*, and was certainly known to writers like Spenser and Milton and – more recently – Lear and Miller, plus Gerald and Lawrence Durrell. Lawrence Durrell's *Prospero's Cell* evokes the island's "delectable landscape", still evident in some of the best beaches of the whole archipelago.

Corfu (Kérkyra) Town

The capital, **Corfu Town**, was renovated for an EU summit in 1994, and is now one of the most elegant island capitals in the whole of Greece. Although many of its finest buildings were destroyed by Nazi bombers in the World War II, its two massive forts, the sixteenth-century church of Áyios Spyrídhon and buildings dating from French and British administrations remain intact. As the island's sole port of entry by ferry or plane, Corfu Town is packed in summer.

Arrivals, information and services

Ferries from Italy dock at the New Port (Néo Limáni) west of the Néo Froúrio (New Fort); those connecting to the mainland (Igoumenítsa and Pátra) dock further west on the seafront. The Old Port (Paleó Limáni), east of the New Port, is used for day excursions and ferries to Paxí. There are ferry offices at both ports; ferries to Italy or south towards Pátra become very busy in summer and booking is advisable. The port police (☎0661/32 655) can advise on services.

The **airport** is 2km south of the city centre. There are no airport buses, although local **blue buses** #5 and #6 can be flagged at the junction where the airport approach meets the main road (500m). It's a forty-minute walk on flat terrain into town (right at the junction then follow the sea road). **Taxis** charge around 2000dr (but agree the fare in advance) or phone (☎0661/33 811) for a radio cab.

The **tourist office** (Mon–Fri 8am–2pm; ☎0661/37 520) on the corner of Vouleftón and Mantzárou has accommodation and transport details. The **post office** is on the corner of Alexándhras and Zafiropoúlou (Mon–Fri 7.30am–8pm).

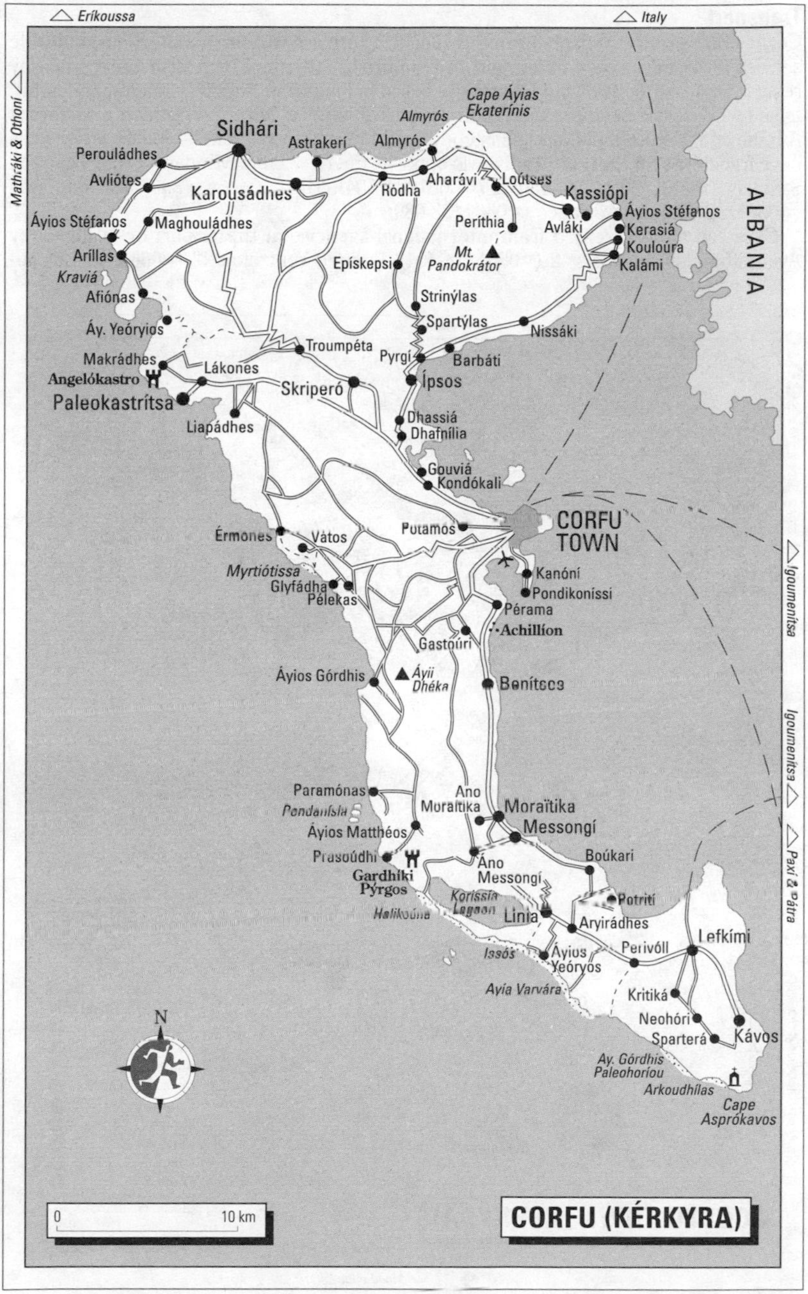
Eríkoussa
Italy
Mathráki & Othoní
ALBANIA
Cape Áyias Ekaterínis
Almyrós
Sidhári
Astrakerí
Almyrós
Peruláhdes
Avliótes
Karousádhes
Ródha
Aharávi
Loútses
Kassiópi
Áyios Stéfanos
Maghouládhes
Períthia
Avláki
Áyios Stéfanos
Kerasiá
Kouloúra
Kalámi
Arillas
Kraviá
Mt. Pandokrátor
Epískepsi
Afiónas
Strinýlas
Spartýlas
Áy. Yeóryios
Nissáki
Troumpéta
Pyrgí
Barbáti
Makrádhes
Angelókastro
Lákones
Skriperó
Ípsos
Paleokastrítsa
Liapádhes
Dhassiá
Dhafnília
Gouviá
Kondókali
CORFU TOWN
Érmones
Vátos
Putamos
Myrtiótissa
Glyfádha
Pélekas
Kanóni
Pondikoníssi
Pérama
Achillíon
Gastoúri
Áyios Górdhis
Áyii Dhéka
Benítses
Igoumenítsa
Igoumenítsa
Paxí & Pátra
Paramónas
Pondanísia
Áno Moraïtika
Moraïtika
Messongí
Áyios Matthéos
Prasoúdhi
Gardhíki Pýrgos
Áno Messongí
Boúkari
Korissía Lagoon
Halikoúna
Linia
Potrití
Aryirádhes
Lefkími
Perivóli
Issós
Áyios Yeóryos
Ayía Varvára
Kritiká
Neohóri
Kávos
Spárterá
Ay. Górdhis Paleohoríou
Arkoudhílas
Cape Asprókavos
N
0
10 km
CORFU (KÉRKYRA)

Transport

Corfu's **bus** service radiates from the capital. There are **two** terminals; the island-wide service is based on Avramíou, and the suburban system, which also serves nearby resorts such as Benítses and Dhassiá, is based in Platía San Rocco (Platía G. Theotóki). Island-wide services stop around 6pm, suburban ones at 10pm. Avramíou also serves Athens and Thessaloníki, and sells combined bus-and-ferry tickets. Major **ferry** lines have franchises on Ethnikís Andistásis opposite the New Port: Minoan (☎0661/25 000), Strintzis (☎0661/25 232), ANEK (☎0661/24 504), HML (☎0661/39 747), Ventouris (☎0661/32 664)and Adriatica (☎0661/38 089).

Cars can also be rented from international agencies at the airport or in town; try Avis, Ethnikís Andistásis 42 (☎0661/24 404), Budget, Venízelou 22 (☎0661/49 100; air-

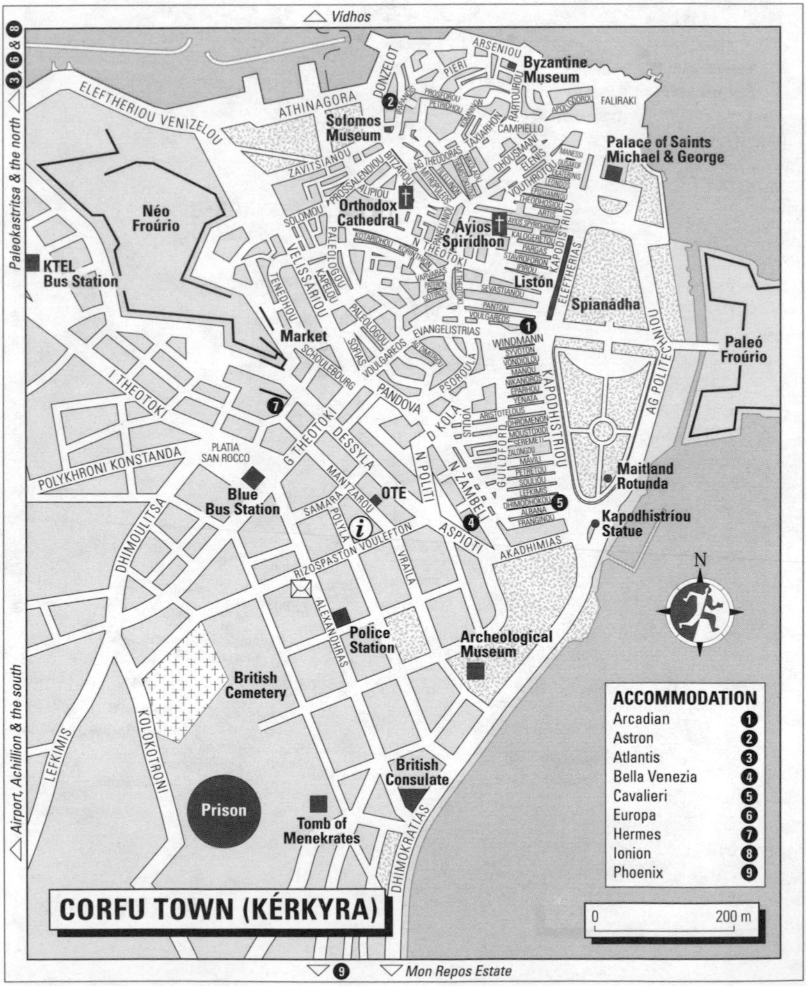

port ☎0661/44 017) or Hertz (☎0661/33 547). Among local companies, Sunrise, Ethnikís Andistásis 14, (☎0661/44 325) rents out cars, and **bikes** can be hired from Easy Rider, I. Theotóki 128 (☎0661/43 026), both in the New Port.

Accommodation

Accommodation in Corfu is busy all year round, and expensive. Room owners meet mainland and international ferries, and taxi drivers will often know of decent rooms. Budget travellers might best head straight for the nearest **campsite** at Dhassiá (see p.410).

Arcadian, Kapodhistríou 44 (☎0661/37 670, fax 45 087). Mid-range hotel in a central setting. Street noise can be a problem. ④.

Astron, Dónzelot 15 (☎0661/39 505, fax 33 708). Tastefully renovated and now decidedly upmarket place in the New Port. ⑥.

Atlantis, Xenofóndos Stratigoú 48 (☎0661/35 560, fax 46 480). Large and spacious air-conditioned hotel. ⑥.

Bella Venezia, Zambéli 4 (☎0661/46 500, fax 20 708). Smart and very good-value Neoclassical building just behind the *Cavalieri*, with all the *Cavalieri*'s comforts, but cheaper. ⑤.

Cavalieri, Kapodhistríou 4 (☎0661/39 041 or 39 336, fax 39 283). Smart and friendly, with great views and a roof bar open to the public. ⑥.

Europa, Yitsiáli 10 (☎0661/39 304). Small family hotel one block back from the Igoumenítsa ferry quay. One of the best deals around. ③.

Hermes, Markorá 14 (☎0661/39 268). Another typical lower mid-range hotel in a busy part of town. Overlooks the noisy market. ④.

Ionion, Xenofóndos Stratigoú 46 (☎0661/39 915, fax 44 690). Large, functional, friendly and very reasonably priced. Convenient New Port location. ③.

Phoenix, Khryssostómou Smýrnis 2, Garítsa (☎0661/42 290, fax 42 990). Small, stylish hotel between the airport and the seafront. Good value. ④.

The town

Corfu Town comprises a number of distinct areas. The **Campiello**, the oldest, sits on the hill above the old port, while the streets running between the Campiello and Velisaríou are what remains of the town's **Jewish quarter**. These districts form the core of the old town, and their tall, narrow alleys conceal some of Corfu's most beautiful architecture. **Mandoúki**, beyond the Old Port, is the commercial and dormitory area for the port, and is worth exploring as a living quarter of the city, away from the tourism racket. The town's **commercial area** lies inland from the Spianádha (Esplanade), roughly between Yeoryíou Theotóki, Alexándhras and Kapodhistríou streets, with shops and boutiques around Voulgaréos and Yeoryíou Theotóki and off Platía Theotóki. Tucked behind Platía San Rocco and Odhós Theotóki is the old morning **market** which sells fish and farm produce.

The most obvious sights are the forts, the **Paleó Froúrio** and **Néo Froúrio**, whose designations (*paleó* – "old", *néo* – "new") are a little misleading, since what you see of the older structure was begun by the Byzantines in the mid-twelfth century, just a hundred years before the Venetians began work on the newer citadel. They have both been modified and damaged by various occupiers and besiegers, the last contribution being the Neoclassical shrine of **St George**, built by the British in the middle of Paleó Froúrio during the 1840s. Looming above the old port, the Néo Froúrio (daily 9am–9pm; 500dr), is the more interesting of the two. The entrance, at the back of the fort, gives onto cellars, dungeons and battlements, with excellent views over town and bay; there's a small gallery and café at the summit. The Paleó Froúrio (daily 9am–9pm; 800dr) is rather dull in comparison but hosts daily *son et lumière* shows.

Just west of the Paleó Froúrio, the **Listón**, an arcaded street built during the French occupation by the architect of the Rue de Rivoli in Paris, and the green **Spianádha** (Esplanade) it overlooks, are the focus of town life. At the south end of the Spianádha, the **Maitland Rotunda** was built to honour the first British High Commissioner of Corfu and the Ionian islands. The neighbouring statue of Ioannis Kapodistrias celebrates the local hero and statesman (1776–1831) who led the diplomatic efforts for independence and was made Greece's first president in 1827. At the far northern end of the Listón, the nineteenth-century **Palace of SS Michael and George**, a solidly British edifice built as the residence of their High Commissioner (one of the last of whom was the future British prime minister William Gladstone), and later used as a palace by the Greek monarchy. The former state rooms house the **Asiatic Museum** (Tues–Sun 8am–2.30pm; free) which is a must for aficionados of Oriental culture, although at the time of writing it was being reorganized and only part of the collection was on view. Amassed by Corfiot diplomat Gregorios Manos (1850–1929) and others, it includes Noh theatre masks, woodcuts, wood and brass statuettes, samurai weapons and art works from Thailand, Korea and Tibet. Opened in 1996, the adjoining **Modern Art Museum** (same hours; 500dr) holds a small collection of contemporary Greek art. It's an interesting diversion, as are the gardens and café-bar secreted behind the palace.

In a nearby backstreet off Arseníou, five minutes from the palace, is the **museum** (Mon–Fri 5–8pm; 200dr) dedicated to modern Greece's most famous nineteenth-century poet, **Dhionysios Solomos**. Born on Zákynthos, Solomos was author of the poem *Ímnos stín Eleftheria* (*Hymn to Liberty*), which was to become the Greek national anthem. He studied at Corfu's Ionian Academy, and lived in a house on this site for much of his life.

Up a short flight of steps on Arseníou, the **Byzantine Museum** (Tues–Sun 9am–3pm; 800dr) is housed in the restored church of the Panayía Andivouniótissa. It houses sculptures and sections of mosaic floors from Paleópolis and church frescoes. There are also some pre-Christian artefacts, and a collection of icons dating from the fifteenth to nineteenth centuries. Just to the southwest is Corfu's **cathedral**, packed with icons, including a fine sixteenth-century painting of *St George Slaying the Dragon* by the Cretan artist Mihail Dhamaskinos.

A block behind the Listón, down Odhós Spyrídhonos, is the **church of Áyios Spyrídhon**, whose maroon-domed campanile dominates the town. Here you will find the silver-encrusted coffin of the island's patron saint, **Spyrídhon** – Spyros in the diminutive – after whom about half the male population is named. Four times a year (Palm Sunday and the following Saturday, August 11 and the first Sunday in November), to the accompaniment of much celebration and feasting, the relics are paraded through the streets of Corfu Town. Each of the days commemorates a miraculous deliverance of the island credited to the saint – twice from plague during the seventeenth century, from a famine of the sixteenth century and (a more blessed release than either of those for any Greek) from the Turks in the eighteenth century.

Corfu Town's **Archeological Museum** (Tues–Sun 9am–3pm; 1000dr), just south round the coast, is the best in the archipelago. The most impressive exhibit is a massive (17m) gorgon pediment excavated from the Doric temple of Artemis at Paleópolis; this dominates an entire room, the gorgon flanked by panthers and mythical battle scenes. The museum also has fragments of Neolithic weapons and cookware, and coins and pots from the period when the island was a colony of ancient Corinth.

Just south of Platía San Rocco and signposted on the corner of Methodhíou and Kolokotróni, the **British cemetery** features some elaborate civic and military memorials. It's a quiet green space away from the madness of San Rocco, and in spring and early summer is alive with dozens of species of orchids and other exotic blooms.

The outskirts

Each of the following sights on the outskirts of the city is easily seen in a morning or afternoon, and best visited from the town rather than outlying resorts.

Around the bay from the Rotunda and Archeological Museum, tucked behind Mon Repos beach, the **Mon Repos** estate (8am–8pm; free) contains the most accessible archeological remains on the island. Thick woodland conceals two **Doric temples**, dedicated to Hera and Artemis. The Neoclassical Mon Repos **villa**, built by British High Commissioner Frederic Adam in 1824 and handed over to Greece in 1864, was the birthplace of Britain's Prince Philip and is due to be opened to the public in the near future.

The most famous excursion from Corfu Town is to the islets of **Vlahérna** and **Pondikoníssi**, 2km south of town. A dedicated bus (#2) leaves San Rocco square every half-hour, or it is a pleasant walk of under an hour. Reached by a short causeway, the tiny white convent of Vlahérna is one of the most photographed images on Corfu. Pondikoníssi ("Mouse Island") can be reached by a short boat trip from the dock (500dr). Tufted with greenery and a small chapel, Vlahérna is identified in legend with a ship from Odysseus's fleet, petrified by Poseidon in revenge for the blinding of his son Polyphemus, the Homeric echoes somewhat marred by the thronging masses and low-flying aircraft from the nearby runway. A quieter destination is **Vídhos**, the wooded island visible from the old port, reached from there by a free hourly shuttle kaïki.

Four kilometres further to the south, past the resort sprawl of Pérama, is a rather more bizarre attraction: the **Achillion** (daily 9am–3pm; 800dr), a palace built in a (fortunately) unique blend of Teutonic and Neoclassical styles in 1890 by Elizabeth, Empress of Austria. Henry Miller considered it "the worst piece of gimcrackery" that he'd ever laid eyes on and thought it "would make an excellent museum for surrealistic art". The house is predictably grandiose but the gardens are pleasant to walk around and afford splendid views in all directions.

Eating and drinking

Most **restaurants** are around the old town, with some hard-to-find places favoured by locals concealed in the Campiello. Restaurants on main thoroughfares tend to be indifferent, though the *Averof*, in the old port behind Zavitsiánou, is a Corfu institution, offering above par taverna cuisine. Nearby and towards the Néo Froúrio the *Tenedos* provides tasteful live music as well as tasty food. Below the Palace of SS Michael and George, the *Faliraki* is reasonably priced for its setting and has an imaginative menu. The *Orestes*, on Xenofóndos Stratigoú in Mandoúki, is probably the best seafood restaurant in town. The *Pizzeria*, on Guildford Street, has a wide range of pizzas with a pleasing choice for vegetarians, as does *Quattro Stagione*, off the north side of N. Theotóki. One of the smartest joints in town is the *Rex*, on Zavitsiánou behind the Listón, and no one staying in Corfu Town should miss the classy *Venetian Well Bistro*, on Platía Kremastí, a tiny square a few alleys to the south of the cathedral. Another excellent choice is the municipally owned *Vidos* restaurant on the island of the same name. It allows you to eat to the gentle accompaniment of a quality duet, whilst surveying the nocturnally lit town; a free kaïki runs until 1.30am.

Nightlife

Corfu Town has plenty to offer in the way of **bars** and nightlife. On the Listón, avoid the mark-ups at the *Magnet* and follow the locals to *Koklia*, *Aegli* or *Olympia*, or drink in one of the hotels; the *Cavalieri* rooftop bar can be heaven at night. For local atmosphere, try *Dirty Dick's*, on the corner of Arseníou and Zavitsiánou, or the expat hangout *Mermaid*, on Ayíon Pantón off the Listón, which will give you a different spin on island culture.

Corfu's self-proclaimed **disco** strip lies a few kilometres north of town, en route to Kondókali. Here, at the (unofficial) *Hard Rock Café*, the *Hippodrome* disco complex (the town's biggest, with its own pool), and the bizarrely decorated *Apokalypsis* and *Coco Flash*, party animals dress up for wild and fairly expensive nights out. In some clubs, women travelling without male partners should beware *kamákia* – slang for Greek males "spearfishing" for foreign women. Corfu Town's two **cinemas** – the Pallas on Yeoryíou Theotóki and the Orfeus on the corner of Akadhimías and Aspióti – both often show English-language films.

The northeast and the north coast

The northeast, at least beyond the immediate suburbs, is the most typically Greek part of Corfu – it's mountainous, with a rocky coastline chopped into pebbly bays and coves, above wonderfully clear seas. Green **buses** between Corfu Town and Kassiópi serve all resorts, along with some blue suburban buses to Dhassiá and Ípsos.

Corfu Town to Ípsos

The landscape between Corfu Town and Kondókali is an industrial wasteland, and things don't improve much at **KONDÓKALI** itself, a small village overrun by holiday developments. The old town consists of a short street with a number of bars and traditional psistariés, the best of which are *Gerekos* and *Takis*, and an international restaurant, *Flags*.

Neighbouring **GOUVIÁ** is also Corfu's largest yachting marina. The village boasts a couple of small **hotels**, notably the *Hotel Aspa* (☎0661/91 165; ④), and some **rooms** – try Maria Lignou (☎0661/91 348; ④) or Yorgos Mavronas (☎0661/91 297 or 90 297; ④). There are a number of decent **restaurants**, including *The Captain's Table* and *Aries Taverna*, and a couple of pizzerias, *Bonito* and *Palladium*. The very narrow shingle **beach**, barely five metres wide in parts, shelves into sand; given the sea traffic the water quality is doubtful.

Two kilometres beyond Goúvia the coastline begins to improve at **DHASSIÁ** and **DHAFNÍLA**, set in two small wooded bays with pebbly beaches. Two large and expensive **hotels**, the *Dassia Chandris* and *Corfu Chandris* both (☎0661/97 100–3, fax 93 458; ⑥), dominate Dhassiá, with extensive grounds, pools and beach facilities. The more reasonable *Hotel Amalia* (☎0661/93 523; ④) has pleasant en-suite rooms and its own pool and garden. **Rooms** are scarce, although Spyros Rengis's minimarket has a few (☎0661/90 282; ③). Dhassiá does, however, have the best **campsite** on the island, *Dionysus Camping Village* (☎0661/91 417, fax 91 760); tents are pitched under terraced olive trees. *Dionysus* also has simple bungalow huts, a pool, shop, bar and restaurant, and the friendly, multilingual owners offer a ten percent discount to Rough Guide readers.

ÍPSOS, 2km north of Dhassiá, can't really be recommended to anyone but hardened bar-hoppers. There isn't room to swing a cat on the thin pebble beach, right beside the busy coast road, and the resort is pretty tacky. Most **accommodation** is pre-booked by package companies, although Ípsos Travel (☎0661/93 661) can offer rooms. *Corfu Camping Ípsos* (☎0661/93 579) has a bar and restaurant, and offers standing tents. Ípsos is also the base for one of the island's major **diving centres**, *Waterhoppers* (☎0661/93 876). **Eating** on the main drag is dominated by fast food, though a more traditional meal and a quieter setting can be found in the *Akrogiali* and *Asteria* tavernas, by the marina to the south of the strip.

North to Áyios Stéfanos

Ípsos has now engulfed the neighbouring hamlet of Pyrgí, which is the main point of access for the villages and routes leading up to **Mount Pandokrátor**; the road, signposted Spartílas, is 200km beyond the junction in Pyrgí. A popular base for walkers is the village of **STRINÝLAS**, 16km from Pyrgí. Accommodation is basic but easy to come by: the *Elm Tree Taverna*, a long-time favourite with walkers, can direct you to rooms. In summer the main routes are busy, but there are quieter walks taking in the handsome Venetian village of Epískepsi, 5km northwest of Strinýlas – anyone interested in walking the Pandokrátor paths is advised to get the **map** of the mountain by island-based cartographer Stephan Jaskulowski or Hilary Whitton-Paipeti's walking book.

The coast road beyond Ípsos mounts the slopes of Pandokrátor towards **BARBÁTI**, 4km further on. Here you'll find the best beach on this coast and ample facilities; it's a favourite with families, and much **accommodation** is pre-booked in advance. However, there are some rooms available on spec – *Paradise* (☎0663/91 320; ③) and *Roula Geranou* (☎0663/92 397; ③).

The mountainside becomes steeper and the road higher beyond Barbáti, and the population thins drastically. **NISSÁKI** is a rather spread-out village with a number of coves, the first and last accessible by road, the rest only by track – one dominated by the gigantic, expensive and rather soulless *Nissaki Beach Hotel* (☎0663/91 232; ⑥). There are a couple of shops and a bakery, and a few travel and **accommodation agencies**. The British-owned *Falcon Travel* (☎0663/91 318, fax 91 070; ⑤) rents out apartments above the first beach, a tiny, white-pebble cove with a trio of fine tavernas. The *Nissaki Holiday Center* (☎0663/91 166, fax 91 206) may have some cheaper rooms.

The two places no one visiting this coast should miss are Kalámi and neighbouring Kouloúra: the first for its Durrell connection, the latter for its exquisite bay (though neither has a beach worth mentioning). **KALÁMI** is on the way to being spoiled, but the village is still small; you can imagine how it would have been in the year Lawrence Durrell spent here on the eve of World War II. The **White House**, where Durrell wrote *Prospero's Cell*, is now split in two: the ground floor is an excellent taverna; the upper floor is let through CV Travel (see p.6). The owner of the *White House*, Tassos Athineos (☎0663/91 251), has rooms, and Yannis Vlahos (☎ and fax 0663/91 077) has rooms, apartments and studios in the bay, as do Sunshine Travel (☎0663/91 170) and Kalami Tourism Services (☎0663/91 062, fax 91 369). The **restaurant** at the White House is recommended, as is *Matella's*, the *Kalami Beach Taverna* and *Pepe's*, which is on the beach.

The tiny harbour of **KOULOÚRA** has managed to keep its charm intact, set at the edge of an unspoiled bay with nothing to distract from the pine trees and kaïkia. The fine **taverna** here has to be the most idyllic setting for a meal in the whole of Corfu.

Around the coast to Aharávi

Two kilometres beyond Kouloúra down a shady lane, the large pebble cove of **Kerasiá** shelters the family-run *Kerasia Beach Taverna*. The most attractive resort on this stretch of coast, 3km down a lane from Agnitsíni on the main road, is **ÁYIOS STÉFANOS**. Most **accommodation** here is upmarket, and the village has yet to succumb to any serious development; so far only the *Kohyli* pizzeria has rooms and apartments (☎0663/81 522; ③). Recommended are the *Garini* and *Kaporelli* **tavernas**, and the *Eucalyptus* over by the village's small beach.

A thirty-minute walk from the coastguard station above Áyios Stéfanos, along a rough track, stretches the beach of **Avláki**, a pebble bay that provides lively conditions for the **windsurfers** who visit the beach's windsurf club. There are two **tavernas**, the *Barbaro* and *Avlaki*, and some **rooms** a few hundred yards back from the beach – *Mortzoukos* (☎0663/81 196; ③), and *Tsirimiagos*, ☎0663/81 522; ④).

Further round the coast is **KASSIÓPI**, a fishing village that's been transformed into a major party resort. The Roman emperor Tiberius had a villa here, and the village's sixteenth-century church is said to stand on the site of a temple of Zeus once visited by

Nero. Little evidence of Kassiópi's past survives, apart from an abandoned Angevin kástro on the headland – most visitors come for the nightlife and the five pebbly beaches. Most **accommodation** in Kassiópi is through village agencies; the largest, Travel Corner (☎0663/81 220, fax 81 108), is a good place to start. An independent alternative, the smart *Kastro* café-pension, overlooks the beach behind the castle (☎0663/81 045; ⑤), and *Theofilos* (☎0663/81 261; ②) offers bargain rooms on Kalamíonas beach. Anglicized cuisine and fast food dominate **eating** in Kassiópi, but for something more traditional, head for the *Three Brothers* taverna on the harbour, or the neighbouring *Porto* fish restaurant. At night, Kassiópi rocks to the cacophony of its music and video bars: the flashiest is the gleaming hi-tech *Eclipse*, closely followed by the *Baron*, *Angelos* and *Jasmine*, all within falling-over distance of the small town square. The *Axis Club* boasts imported British DJs, and frolics sometimes extend onto the beach until dawn. The village is also home to one of the most reliable diving operations, Corfu Divers (☎0663/81 218), which is partly British-run.

The coastline beyond Kassiópi is overgrown and marshy until little-used **Almyrós beach**, one of the longest on the island. It is also the least developed beach, with only a few apartment buildings under construction at the hamlet of **Almyrós**. The Andinióti lagoon, smaller than Korissía (see p.416) but still a haven for birds and twitchers, backs Cape Áyias Ekaterínis to the east. With its wide main road, **AHARÁVI**, the next stop west on the main coast road, resembles an American Midwest truck stop, but the village proper is tucked behind this in a quiet crescent of old tavernas, bars and shops. Aharávi makes a quieter beach alternative to the southerly strands, and should also be considered by those seeking alternative routes up onto **Mount Pandokrátor**. Roads to small hamlets such as Áyios Martínos and Láfki continue onto the mountain, and even a stroll up from the back of Aharávi will find you on the upper slopes in under an hour. **Accommodation** isn't easy to find, but a good place to start is Castaway Travel (☎0663/63 541, fax 63 376) or HN Travel (☎0663/63 458, fax 63 454). There are a number of **restaurants** on Aharávi's main drag; go for the *Pump House* steak and pasta joint, the traditional tavernas *Chris's* and *George's*, or the *Young Tree*, which specializes in Corfiot dishes such as *sofríto* and *pastitsádha*. The bar-restaurants tend to get quite rowdy at night, although the light and airy *Captain's Bar* is a pleasant watering hole. For a quieter drink, head for the leafy awning of the friendly *Vevaiotis* kafenío in the old village.

Ródha, Sidhári and Avliótes

Just to the west, **RÓDHA** has tipped over into overdevelopment, and can't be wholeheartedly recommended for those after a quiet time. Its central crossroads have all the charm of a service station, and the beach is rocky in parts and swampy to the west. "Old Ródha" is a small warren of alleys between the main road and the seafront, where you'll find the best **restaurants** and **bars**: the *Taverna Agra* is the oldest in Ródha and is the best place for fish, and the *Rodha Star Taverna* and *New Harbour* are also good. For bars, try *Nikos* near the *Agra* and the upmarket bar-club *Skouna*. For **accommodation**, the large *Hotel Afroditi* (☎0663/63 147, fax 63 125; ④) has decently priced en-suite rooms with sea views. Both the Anglo-Greek NSK UK Travel (☎0663/63 471, fax 63 274) on the main drag and Nostos Travel on the seafront (☎0663/64 601, fax 64 602) rent rooms and handle car rental. The smart *Roda Beach Camping* (☎0663/93 120) is a little way east of the resort.

The next notable resort, **SIDHÁRI**, is expanding rapidly and is totally dominated by British package tourists; it has a small but pretty town square, with a bandstand set in a small garden, but this is lost in a welter of bars, boutiques and snack joints. The beach is sandy but not terribly clean, and many people tend to head just west to the curious coves, walled by wind-carved sandstone cliffs. However, the main reason to visit Sidhári is to reach the **Dhiapóndia islands**; day-trips to Mathráki, Othoní and Eríkoussa (see p.418) leave weekday mornings around 9am; unless you catch the 5.30am Sidhári bus from Corfu Town, your only option is to stay the night. The boats are run by Nearchos Seacruises (☎0663/95 248) and cost around 5000dr return per person. The best sources of **rooms** are Kostas Fakiolas at the *Scorpion* café-bar at the west of town (☎0663/95 046; ③) and Nikolaos Korakianitis's minimarket on the main road (☎0663/95 058; ③). The biggest accommodation agency is run by young tycoon Philip Vlasseros, whose Vlasseros Travel (☎0663/95 695) also handles car rental, excursions and horse-riding. Sidhári's **campsite**, *Dolphin Camping* (☎0663/31 846), is some way inland from the junction at the western end of town. Most **restaurants** are pitched at those looking for a great night out rather than a quiet meal in a taverna. The *Olympic* is the oldest taverna here; also recommended are the *Diamond* and *Sea Breeze* tavernas. There are no quiet bars in Sidhári, and two **nightclubs** vie for your custom, the *Remezzo* and its younger rival, *Ecstasy*.

The Sidhári bus usually continues to **AVLIÓTES**, a handsome hill town with bars and tavernas but few concessions to tourism. Avliótes is noteworthy for two reasons, however: its accessibility to the quiet beaches below the quiet village of Perouládhes, just over a kilometre away, and the fact that **Áyios Stéfanos** (see p.414) is under thirty minute's walk from here, downhill through lovely olive groves.

Paleokastrítsa and the northwest coast

The northwest conceals some of the island's most dramatic coastal scenery; the interior, violent mountainscapes jutting out of the verdant countryside. The area's honeypot attraction, **Paleokastrítsa**, is the single most picturesque resort on Corfu, but is suffering from its popularity. Further down the west coast, the terrain opens out to reveal long sandy beaches, such as delightful **Myrtiótissa** and the backpackers' haven of **Áyios Górdhis**. Public transport to the west coast is difficult: virtually all buses ply routes from Corfu Town to single destinations, and rarely link resorts.

Paleokastrítsa

PALEOKASTRÍTSA, a small village surrounded by dramatic hills and cliffs, has been identified as the Homeric city of Scheria, where Odysseus was washed ashore and escorted by Nausicaa to the palace of her father Alcinous, king of the Phaeacians. It's a stunning site though, as you would expect, one that's long been engulfed by tourism. The focal point of the village is the car park on the seafront, which backs onto the largest and least attractive of three **beaches**, home to sea taxis and kaïkia. The second beach, to the right and signed by flags for Mike's Ski Club, is stony with clear water, and the best of the three is a small unspoiled strand reached along the path by the *Astakos Taverna*. Protected by cliffs, it's undeveloped apart from the German-run Korfu-Diving Centre (☎0663/41 604) at the end of the cove. From the beach in front of the main car park, **boat trips** (2000dr for a half-hour trip, 3000dr for drop-off and later pick-up) leave for the blue grottoes, a trip worth taking for the spectacular coastal views. Boats also serve as a taxi service to three neighbouring beaches, Áyia Triánda, Platákia and Alípa, which all have snack bars.

On the rocky bluff above the village, the **Theotókou monastery** (7am–1pm & 3–8pm; free, although donations invited) is believed to have been established in the thirteenth century. There's also a museum, resplendent with icons, jewelled Bibles and other impedimenta of Greek Orthodox ritual, though the highlight is the gardens, with spectacular coastal views. Paleokastrítsa's ruined castle, the **Angelókastro**, is around 6km up the coast; only approachable by path from the hamlet of Kríni, it has stunning, almost circular views of the surrounding sea and land.

Unfortunately, perhaps due to the pressure of commerce in such a small space, there's a rather aggressive air about tourism here. **Accommodation** is at a premium, and you may be expected to commit yourself for three to seven days in some places. A good **hotel** is the small, family-run *Odysseus* (☎0663/41 209, fax 41 342; ⑤) on the road into town, and the modern *Akrotiri Beach* (☎0663/41 237, fax 41 277; ⑥) is friendly and unpretentious for such a large and expensive hotel, and accessible on foot. There are good-value **rooms** for rent above Alípa Beach on the road down into Paleokastrítsa: try Andreas Loulis at the *Dolphin Snackbar* (☎0663/41 035; ④), Spiros and Theodora Michalas (☎0663/41 485; ③), or George Bakiras at the *Green House* (☎0663/41 311; ③). Above the village, past Nikos' Bikes, the friendly Korina family also have rooms (☎0663/44 0641; ④). *Paleokastritsa Camping* (☎0663/41 204, fax 41 104), is just off the main road into town, a ten-minute walk from the centre.

There isn't a huge choice of **restaurants** in the centre of Paleokastrítsa. The *Astakos Taverna* and *Corner Grill* are two traditional places, while *Il Pirata* offers a variety of Italian and Greek dishes, including local fish and seafood, and the seafront *Smurfs* has a good seafood menu despite the shocking name. Also recommended are the very smart *St Georges on the Rock*, and the restaurant of the *Odysseus Hotel*. **Nightlife** hang-outs include the restaurant-bars in the centre, and those straggling up the hill towards Lákones. By the Lákones turning is Paleokastrítsa's one nightclub, *The Paleo Club*, a small disco-bar with a garden.

Áyios Yeóryios and Áyios Stéfanos

Like many of the west coast resorts, **ÁYIOS YEÓRYIOS**, 6km north of Paleokastrítsa, isn't actually based around a village. The resort has developed in response to the popularity of its large sandy bay, and it's a major **windsurfing** centre, busy even in low season. There are a couple of good **hotels** – the *Alkyon Beach* (0663/96 222; ⑤) and the *Chrisi Akti* (0663/96 207; ⑤) – some rooms such as *Studio Eleana* (☎0663/96 366; ③), and the *San George* campsite (☎0663/51 759) nearly a kilometre back from the beach towards Kavvadhádhes. On the way north towards Áyios Stéfanos, the pleasant sandy beach of **Aríllas** has given rise to gradual development, including several tavernas. Accommodation can be arranged through Arillas Travel (☎0663/51 280, fax 51 381) or there is the smart *Akti Arilla* hotel (☎0663/51 201, fax 51 221; ⑤).

The most northerly of the west coast's resorts, **ÁYIOS STÉFANOS** is a low-key family resort, a quiet base from which to explore the northwest and the Diapóndia islands, visible on the horizon. Day-trips to Mathráki, Othoní and Eríkoussa (see p.418) run every Thursday in season, and cost around 5000dr per person. Áyios Stéfanos's oldest **hotel**, the *Nafsika* (☎0663/51 051, fax 51 112; ③) has a large restaurant, a favourite with villagers, and gardens with a pool and bar. In recent years it has been joined by the upmarket *Thomas Bay* (☎0663/51 767, fax 51 913; ⑤) and *Romanza* hotels (☎0661/22 873, fax 41 878; ⑤). For those on a budget, Peli and Maria's gift shop offers bargain **rooms** (☎0663/51 424; ②), and the *Restaurant Evnios* (☎0663/51 766; ③) and *Hotel Olga* (☎0663/71 252; ③) have apartments above the village. A number of travel agencies handle accommodation, among them San Stefanos (☎0663/51 910, fax 51 771) in the centre. Besides the *Nafsika*, good options for **eating** include the *Golden Beach Taverna*, and the *Waves Taverna*, on the beach, while *O Manthos* taverna serves Corfiot specialities like *sofríto* and *pastitsádha*. For **nightlife**, there's a couple of lively music bars, the *Condor* and the *Athens*, plus the small *Enigma* nightclub.

Central and southern Corfu

Two natural features divide the centre and south of Corfu. The first is the **plain of Rópa**, whose fertile landscape backs on to some of the best beaches on this coast. Settlements and development stop a little to the south of Paleokastrítsa and only resume around **Érmones** and **Pélekas** – a quick bus ride across the island from Corfu Town. Down to the south, a second dividing point is the **Korissía lagoon**, the sandy plains and dunes that skirt this natural feature being great places for botanists and ornithologists. Beyond, a single road trails the interior, with sporadic side roads to resorts on either coast. The landscape here is flat, an undistinguished backdrop for a series of relatively undefiled beaches and, in the far south, **Kávos**, Corfu's big youth resort.

Érmones to the Korissía lagoon: the west coast

ÉRMONES, south of Paleokastrítsa, is one of the busiest resorts on the island, its lush green bay backed by the mountains above the Rópa River. The resort is dominated by the upmarket *Ermones Beach* **hotel** (☎0661/94 241; ⑥), which provides guests with a funicular railway down to the beach. More reasonable accommodation can be found at the *Pension Katerina* (②) and *Georgio's Villas* (③). Head for *George's* **taverna** above the beach for some of the best Greek food here: the mezédhes are often a meal in themselves. Just inland is the Corfu Golf and Country Club (☎0661/94 220), the only golf club in the archipelago, and said to be the finest in the Mediterranean.

The nearby small village of **VÁTOS** has a couple of tavernas, a disco and rooms, and is on the Glyfádha bus route from Corfu Town. Spyros Kousounis, owner of the *Olympic Restaurant and Grill* (☎0661/94 318; ③) has rooms and apartments, as does Prokopios Himarios (☎0661/94 503; ③), next to the Doukakis café-minimarket. The Myrtiótissa **path** is signposted just beyond the extremely handy, if basic, *Vatos Camping* (☎0661/94 393).

Far preferable to the gravelly sand of Érmones are the sandy beaches just south of the resort, at Myrtiótissa and Glyfádha. In *Prospero's Cell*, Lawrence Durrell described **Myrtiótissa** as "perhaps the loveliest beach in the world"; it was until recently a well-guarded secret, and though the place hasn't been entirely swamped, it's best visited at either end of the day or out of high season. Above the beach is the tiny whitewashed **Myrtiótissa monastery**, dedicated to Our Lady of the Myrtles.

The sandy bay of **GLYFÁDHA**, walled in by cliffs, is dominated by the *Louis Grand* (☎0661/94 140, fax 94 146; ⑥), a large and expensive **hotel** in spacious grounds. There's another hotel at the far north end of the beach, the *Glifada Beach* (☎0661/94 258; ④) whose owners, the Megas family, also have a fine taverna. Most of the other accommodation is block-booked – it's a very popular family beach – but the *Gorgona* pool bar and *Restaurant Michaelis* might have rooms. Nightlife centres on two music bars, the *Kikiriko* and *Aloha*.

PÉLEKAS, inland and 2km south of Glyfádha, has long been popular for its views – the **Kaiser's Throne** viewing tower, along the road to Glyfádha, was Wilhelm II's favourite spot on the island. New developments are beginning to swamp the town, but there are still some good **hotels** here, including the elegant, upmarket *Pelekas* (☎0661/94 230; ⑥) and the friendlier *Nicos* (☎0661/94 486; ④), as well as rooms at the *Alexandros* taverna (☎0661/94 215; ③). Among the **tavernas**, the *Alexandros* and *Roula's Grill House* are highly recommended. Pélekas's sandy **beach** is reached down a short path, where *Maria's Place* is an excellent family-run **taverna/rooms** place (☎0661/94 601; ③) with fish caught daily by the owner's husband. Sadly, the beach has been rather spoilt by the monstrous *Pelekas Beach* hotel that now looms over it.

Around 7km south of Pélekas, **ÁYIOS GÓRDHIS** is one of the key play beaches on the island, largely because of the activities organized by the startling **Pink Palace** complex (☎0661/53 101) which dominates the resort. It has pools, games courts, restaurants, a shop and a disco. Backpackers cram into communal rooms for up to ten (smaller rooms and singles are also available) for 6000dr a night, including breakfast and evening meal. Other accommodation is available on the beach, notably at the quieter *Michael's Place* taverna (☎0661/53 041; ③); the neighbouring *Alex-in-the-Garden* **restaurant** is also a favourite.

Inland from the resort is the south's largest prominence, the humpback of **Áyii Dhéka** (576m), reached by path from the hamlet of Áno Garoúna; it is the island's second largest mountain after Pandokrátor. The lower slopes are wooded, and it's possible to glimpse buzzards wheeling on thermals over the higher slopes.

Around 5km south by road from Áyios Górdhis, the fishing hamlet of **PENDÁTI** is still untouched by tourism. There is no accommodation here, but *Angela's* café and minimarket and the *Strofi* grill cater to villagers and the few tourists who wander in. Another 4km on, **PARAMÓNAS** affords excellent views over the coastline, which can be admired from the *Sunset* taverna, and has only a few businesses geared to tourism: the *Paramonas Bridge* restaurant (☎0663/75 761; ③) has **rooms** and **apartments** to rent, as does the *Areti Studios* (☎0661/75 838; ④) on the road in from Pendáti.

The town of **ÁYIOS MATTHÉOS**, 3km inland, is still chiefly an agricultural centre, although a number of kafenía and tavernas offer a warm if bemused welcome to passers-by: head for the *Mouria* snack bar-grill, or the modern *Steki*, which maintains the tradition of spiriting tasty mezédhes onto your table unasked. On the other side of Mount Áyios Matthéos, 2km by road, is the **Gardhíki Pýrgos**, the ruins of a thirteenth-century castle built in this unlikely lowland setting by the despots of Epirus. The road continues on to the northernmost tip of splendid and deserted **Halikoúna** beach on the sea edge of the **Korissía lagoon**, which, if you don't have your own transport, is most easily reached by walking from the village of Línia (on the Kávos bus route) via Íssos Beach; other, longer routes trail around the north end of the lagoon from Áno Messongí and Khlomotianá. Over 5km long and 1km wide at its centre, Korissía is home to turtles, tortoises, lizards, and numerous indigenous and migratory birds. For one of the quietest stays on the island, try *Marin Christel Apartments* (☎0661/75 947; ⑤) just north of Halikoúna beach or *Logara Apartments* (☎0661/76 477; ⑤) 500m inland.

Benítses to Petríti: the east coast

South of Corfu Town, there's nothing to recommend before **BENÍTSES**, a once notorious bonking-and-boozing resort, whose old town at the north end is now reverting to a quiet bougainvillea-splashed Greek village. There's really little to see here, beyond the ruins of a Roman bathhouse at the back of the village, and the tiny **Shell Museum**, part-exhibit, part-shop. **Rooms** are plentiful: try Bargain Travel (☎0661/72 137, fax 72 031; ③) and All Tourist (☎0661/72 223; ③). Visitor numbers are picking up again after a serious decline but some **hotels** can offer good deals. The *Corfu Maris* (☎0661/72 035; ④), on the beach at the southern end of town, has modern en-suite rooms with balconies and views, while the friendly *Hotel Benitsa* and neighbouring *Agis* in the centre (both ☎0661/39 269; ③) offer quiet rooms set back from the main road. Benítses has its fair share of decent if not particularly cheap **tavernas**, notably *La Mer de Corfu* and the Corfiot specialist *Spiros*, as well as the plush *Marabou*. The **bars** at the southern end of town are fairly lively, despite new rules controlling all-night partying, and the *Stadium* **nightclub** still opens occasionally. If you're looking for a quiet drink head for the north end of the village, away from the traffic.

MORAÏTIKA's main street is an ugly strip of bars, restaurants and shops, but its beach is the best between Corfu Town and Kávos. Reasonable beach-side **hotels** include the *Margarita Beach* (☎ & fax 0661/76 267; ⑤) and the *Three Stars* (☎0661/92 457; ④). The *Golden Keys* apartments (☎0661/75 778, fax 75 598; ④) are comfortable and there are **rooms** between the main road and beach, and up above the main road: try Alekos Bostis (☎0661/75 637; ③) or Kostas Vlahos (☎0661/55 350; ②). Much of the main drag is dominated by souvenir shops and minimarkets, as well as a range of **bars**, including the village's oldest, *Charlie's*, which opened in 1939. The *Islands* **restaurant** is recommended for its mix of vegetarian, Greek and international food, as is the unfortunately named beach restaurant *Crabs*, where the seafood and special salads are excellent. The village proper, **ÁNO MORAÏTIKA**, is signposted a few minutes' hike up the steep lanes inland, and is virtually unspoiled. Its tiny houses and alleys are practically drowning in bougainvillea, among which you'll find two **tavernas**: the *Village Taverna* and the *Bella Vista*, which has a basic menu but justifies its name with a lovely garden, sea views and breezes.

Barely a hundred metres on from the Moraïtika seafront, **MESSONGÍ** is disappointing: parts of the resort are sadly moribund. The sandy beach is dominated by the vast *Messonghi Beach* **hotel** complex (☎0661/76 684, fax 75 334; ⑥), one of the plushest on the island. Both the cheaper *Hotel Gemini* (☎0661/75 221, fax 75 213; ⑤) and *Pantheon Hall* (☎0661/75 802, fax 75 801; ③) have pools and gardens, and en-suite rooms with balconies. Despite several closures, Messongí still has a number of good **restaurants**: notably the *Memories* taverna, which specializes in Corfiot dishes and serves its own barrel wine, and the upmarket *Castello*. An alternative is to head for the beach-side *Almond Tree* and *Spanos* tavernas a short walk south on the road to Boúkari.

The quiet road from Messongí to **BOÚKARI** follows the seashore for about 3km, often only a few feet above it. Boukári itself comprises little more than a handful of tavernas, a shop and a few small, family-run hotels; the *Boukari Beach* is the best of the **tavernas**. The very friendly Vlahopoulos family who run the taverna also manage two small hotels nearby, the *Boukari Beach* and *Penelopi* (☎0662/51 269, fax 51 792; ④), as well as good rooms attached to the taverna (③). Boukári is out of the way, but an idyllic little strip of unspoiled coast for anyone fleeing the crowds elsewhere on the island, and inland from here is the unspoiled wooded region around **Aryirádhes**, rarely visited by tourists and a perfect place for quiet walks.

Back on the coastline, the village of **PETRITÍ** fronts onto a small but busy dirt-track harbour, but is mercifully free of noise and commerce; its beach is rock, mud and sand, set among low olive-covered hills. The *Pension Egrypos* (☎0662/51 949; ③) has **rooms** and a **taverna**. At the harbour, three tavernas serve the trickle of sea traffic: the smart *Limnopoula* guarded by caged parrots, and the more basic but friendly *Dimitris* and *Stamatis*. Some way back from the village, near the hamlet of Vassilátika, is the elegant *Regina* **hotel**, with gardens and pool (☎0662/52 132, fax 52 135; ④).

Southern Corfu

Across the island on the west coast, the beach at **ÁYIOS YEÓRYIOS** spreads as far south as Méga Hóro point, and north to encircle the edge of the Korissía lagoon, around 12km of uninterrupted sand. The village itself, however, is an unprepossessing sprawl. British package operators have arrived in force, with bars competing to present bingo, quizzes and video nights. The *Golden Sands* (☎0662/51 225; ⑤) has a pool, open air restaurant and gardens, but the best **hotel** bargain is the smaller *Blue Sea* (☎0662/51 624, fax 51 172; ③). The most likely place to head for good **rooms** is at the southern end of the strip: the *Barbayiannis* taverna-bar (☎0662/52 110; ③). Besides the *Barbayiannis*, Áyios Yeóryios has a number of good **restaurants**: *La Perla's* which serves Greek and north European food in a walled garden; the *Napoleon* psistariá; and the *Florida Cove*, with its beachcomber theme. **Nightlife** centres around music and pool bars like the *Gold Hart* and *Traxx*, although the best bar in Áyios Yeóryios is the sea-edge *Panorama*, which has views as far south as Paxí.

A few minutes' walk north of Áyios Yeóryios, **Íssos** is a far better and quieter beach; the dunes north of Íssos are an unofficial nude-bathing area. Facilities around Íssos are sparse: one **taverna**, the *Rousellis Grill* (which sometimes has rooms) a few hundred metres from the beach on the lane leading to Línia on the main road, and the *Friends* snack bar in Línia itself. An English-run **windsurfing school** operates on the beach.

Anyone interested in how a Greek town works away from the bustle of tourism shouldn't miss **LEFKÍMI**, on the island's east coast. The second largest town after Corfu, it's the administrative centre of the south of the island as well as the alternative ferry port to/from Igoumenítsa, and has some fine architecture, including two striking churches: **Áyios Theódoros**, on a mound above a small square, and **Áyios Arsénios**, with a vast orange dome that can be seen for miles. There are some **rooms** at the *Cheeky Face* taverna (☎0661/22 627; ②) and the *Maria Madalena* apartments (☎0661/22 386; ②), both by the bridge over the canal that carries the Himáros River through town. A few **bars** and **restaurants** sit on the edge of the canal – try the *River* psistariá. Away from the centre, the *Hermes* bar has a leafy garden, and there are a number of other good local places where tourists are rare enough to guarantee you a friendly welcome, including the *Mersedes* and *Pacific* bars, and, notably, the *Kavouras* and *Fontana* tavernas.

There are no ambiguities in **KÁVOS**, directly south of Lefkími: either you like 24-hour drinking, clubbing, bungee-jumping, go-karts, video bars named after British sitcoms and chips with almost everything, or you should avoid the resort altogether. Kávos stretches over 2km of decent sandy beach, with watersports galore. This is very much package-tour territory; if you want independent **accommodation**, try Britannia Travel (☎0661/61 400) and Island Holidays (☎0661/23 439), and the nearest to genuine Greek **food** you'll find is at the *Two Brothers* psistariá, at the south end of town. *Future* is still the biggest **club**, with imported north European DJs, followed by *Whispers*. Favourite **bars** include *JCs*, *Jungle*, *The Face* and *Net*, and at night the main drag is one unbroken crowd of young revellers,

Beyond the limits of Kávos, where few visitors stray, a path leaving the road south to the hamlet of Sparterá heads through unspoiled countryside; after around thirty minutes of walking it reaches the cliffs of **Cape Asprókavos** and the crumbling **monastery of Arkoudhílas**. The cape looks out over the straits to Paxí, and down over deserted **Arkoudhílas beach**, which can be reached from Sparterá, 5km by road but only 3km by the signed path from Kávos. Even wilder is **Áyios Górdhis beach**, 3km further on from Sparterá, one of the least visited on the island and not to be confused with the eponymous beach further north.

Corfu's satellite islands

Corfu's three inhabited satellite islands, **Eríkoussa**, **Othoní** and **Mathráki**, in the quintet of **Dhiapóndia islands**, are 20km off the northwest coast. Some travel agencies in the northern resorts offer **day-trips** to Eríkoussa only, often with a barbecue thrown in – fine if you're happy to spend the day on the beach. A trip taking in all three islands from Sidhári or Áyios Stéfanos is excellent value: the islands are between thirty and sixty minutes apart by boat, and most trips allow you an hour on each (longer on sandy Eríkoussa).

Locals use day-trip boats between the islands, so it's possible to pay your way between them. There is also a twice-weekly **ferry** from Corfu Town, the *Alexandros II*, which brings cars and goods to the islands, but given that it has to sail halfway round Corfu first, it's the slowest way to proceed.

Mathráki

Hilly, densely forested and with a long empty beach, beautiful **Mathráki** is the least inhabited of the three islands. The beach begins at the edge of the tiny harbour, and extends south for 3km of fine, dark-red sand, a nesting site for the endangered **loggerhead turtle** (see box on p.444). It's important therefore not to camp anywhere near the beach – and not to make any noise there at night.

A single road rises from the harbour into the interior and the scattered village of **KÁTO MATHRÁKI**, where just one friendly taverna-kafenío-shop overlooks the beach and Corfu. The views are magnificent, as is the sense of isolation. However, construction work above the beach suggests Mathráki is becoming geared towards visitors, and islander Tassos Kassimis (☎0663/71 700; ③) already rents **rooms**. The road continues to the village of **Áno Mathráki**, with its single, old-fashioned kafenío next to the church, but this is beyond walking distance on a day-visit.

Othoní

Six kilometres north, **Othoní** is the largest, and at first sight the least inviting of Corfu's satellite islands. The island has a handful of good tavernas and rooms for rent in its port, **ÁMMOS**, but the reception from islanders who aren't in the tourism trade is rather cool. Ámmos has two beaches, both pebbly, one in its harbour. The village kafenío serves as a very basic shop, and there's one smart **restaurant**, *La Locanda dei Sogni*, which also has **rooms** (☎0663/71 640; ④) – though these tend to be pre-booked by Italian visitors. Three tavernas, *New York*, *Mikros* and tiny *Rainbow*, offer decent but fairly limited menus; the owner of the *New York* also offers rooms for rent (☎0663/71 581; ③). The island's interior is dramatic, and a path up out of the village leads through rocky, tree-covered hills to the central hamlet, **Horió**, after a thirty-minute walk. Horió, like other inland villages, is heavily depopulated – only about sixty people still live on the island through the winter – but it's very attractive, and the architecture is completely traditional.

Eríkoussa

East of Othoní, **Eríkoussa** is the most popular destination for day-trippers. It's invariably hyped as a "desert island" trip, although this is a desert island with a medium-sized hotel, rooms, tavernas and a year-round community. In high season, it gets very busy: Eríkoussa has a large diaspora living in America and elsewhere who return to family homes in their droves in summer, so you may find your *yiá soú* or *kaliméra* returned in a Brooklyn accent.

Eríkoussa has an excellent golden sandy beach right by the harbour, with great swimming, and another, quieter, beach reached by a path across the wooded island interior. The island's cult following keeps its one **hotel**, the *Erikoussa* (☎0663/71 555; ④), busy through the season; rooms are en-suite with balconies and views. Simpler rooms are available from the *Anemomilos* **taverna** (☎0663/71 647, ③). If you're hoping to stay, phoning ahead is essential, as is taking anything you might not be able to buy – the only shop is a snack bar selling basic groceries.

Paxí (Paxos) and Andípaxi

Verdant, hilly and still largely unspoiled, **Paxí (Paxos)** is the smallest of the main Ionian islands. Barely 12km by 4km, it has no sandy beaches, no historical sites, only two hotels and a serious water shortage, yet is so popular it is best avoided in high season. Despite limited ferry connections with Corfu, Igoumenítsa and Párga, it still draws vast crowds, who can make its three harbour villages rather cliquey. It's also popular with yachting flotillas, whose spending habits have brought the island an upmarket reputation, and made it the most expensive place to visit in the Ionian islands (with the possible exception of Fiskárdho on Kefallonía). There is only one – rather remote – official campsite, due to reopen in 2000 after closure due to infighting, but there are pockets of unauthorized camping. Most accommodation is block-booked by travel companies, though there are local tour operators whose holiday deals are often a fraction of the price. The capital, **Gáïos**, is quite cosmopolitan, with delis and boutiques, but northerly **Lákka** and tiny **Longós** are where hardcore Paxophiles head.

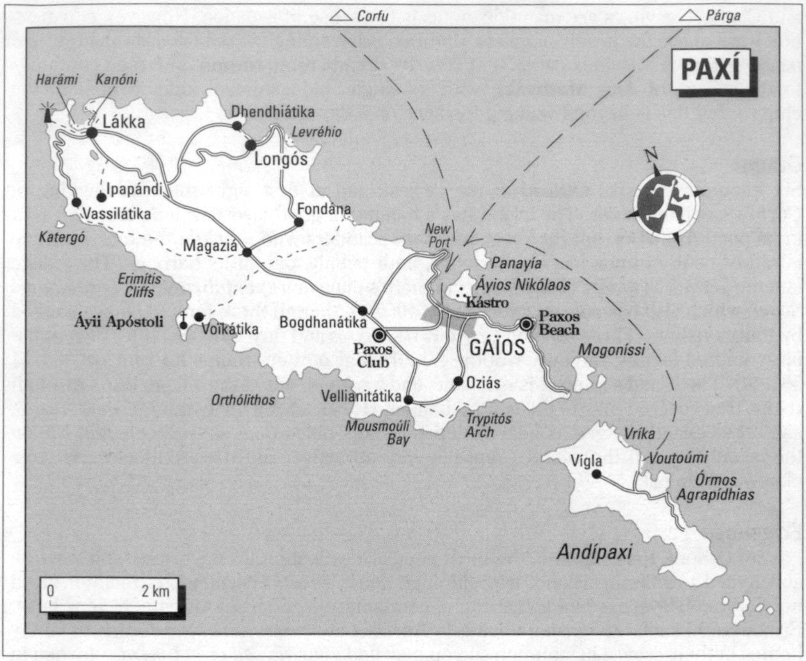

Gáïos

Most visitors arrive at **GÁÏOS**, or at the new port, 1km to the north. Gáïos is a pleasant town built around a small square on the seafront overlooking two islands, Áyios Nikólaos and Panayía. Room owners usually meet ferries, although it's advisable to phone ahead: try Gaïos Travel (☎0661/32 033, fax 32 175), run by the friendly, English-speaking Ioannis Arvanatakis, and Bouas Tours (☎0661/32 401, fax 32 610), both situated on the seafront. Paxí's two seasonal **hotels** are both near Gáïos: the *Paxos Beach Hotel* (☎0661/31 211; ⑤) which has smart en-suite bungalows on a hillside above a pebbly beach 2km south of town, and the fairly luxurious *Paxos Club Hotel* (☎0661/32 450, fax 32 097; ⑥), 2km inland from Gáïos. The island's one (basic) **campsite**, assuming it does reopen, is at Mogoníssi, 45 minutes' walk south (there's no bus), with a taverna above an imported sand beach.

Gáïos boasts a number of decent **tavernas**, the best of them being *Carcoleggio's*, 1.5km out of town towards Bogdhanátika. The menu and wine list are limited, and opening hours unpredictable, but it fills up with islanders who flock for its *souvláki*. Also recommended are the *Blue Grotto*, *Spiro's*, *Dodo's*, inland from the Anemoyiannis statue, and the *Rex* in a side-street off the town square. Of the pricey joints running down one side of the square, the *Volcano* is the best; the kafenía by the ferry ramp and at the bottom of the square are much better bargains. Trendier bars near the square include *Carnayo* and *Red Chairs*. The *Phenix* (sic) disco out by the New Port opens sporadically after midnight and has a terrace for sub-lunar fun, while the inland *Castello* is a more regular disco.

Inland are some of the island's oldest settlements, such as Oziás and Vellianitátika, in prime walking country, but with few if any facilities. Noel Rochford's book,

Landscapes of Paxos (Sunflower), lists dozens of walks, and cartographers Elizabeth and Ian Bleasdale's *Paxos Walking Map* is on sale in most travel agencies.

The rest of the island

Paxí's one main road runs along the spine of the island, with a turning at the former capital Magaziá, leading down to the tiny port of Longós. The main road continues to Lákka, the island's funkiest resort, set in a breathtaking horseshoe bay. Two buses ply the road between Gáïos and Lákka six times a day, most diverting to swing through Longós. The Gáïos–Lákka bus (35min) affords panoramic views, and the route is an excellent walk of under three hours (one way). A taxi between the two costs around 2500dr.

Approached from the south, **LÁKKA** is an unprepossessing jumble of buildings, but once in its maze of alleys and neo-Venetian buildings, or on the quay with views of distant Corfu, you do get a sense of its charm. Lákka's two **beaches**, Harámi and Kanóni, are the best on the island, although there have been complaints in high season of pollution from the yachts that cram the bay. The terraced olive grove behind Kanóni is a favourite with campers but has no facilities. **Accommodation** is plentiful (except in high season) from the island's two biggest agencies: Planos Holidays (☎0661/31 744, fax 31 010) or Routsis (☎0661/31 807, fax 31 161), both on the seafront. The latter runs two bargain rooming houses, *Ilios* and *Lefcothea* (both ②).There's an embarrassment of good tavernas; the friendly *Nionios* and its neighbour *Butterfly*, the *Nautilus*, which has the best view of any Paxiot restaurant, the more upmarket *Pergola* or the exotic *Rosa di Paxos* for a splurge. There's a similar wealth of bars: the lively *Harbour Lights*, the seafront *Romantica* cocktail bar, *Serano's* in the square, or Spyros Petrou's friendly kafenío – the hub of village life. Lákka is also best sited for **walking**: up onto either promontory, to the lighthouse or Vassilátika, or to Longós and beyond. One of the finest walks – if combined with a bus or taxi back – is an early evening visit to the **Erimítis cliffs**, near the hamlet of Voïkátika: on clear afternoons, the cliffs change colour at twilight like a seagoing Ayers Rock.

LONGÓS is the prettiest village on the island, and perfectly sited for morning sun and idyllic alfresco breakfasts. The village is dominated by the upmarket villa crowd, but the Planos office here (☎0661/31 530) is the best place to look for accommodation. It has some of the island's best restaurants: the *Nassos*, with a wide variety of fish and seafood, the seafront *Vassilis*, where you have to squeeze in for the island bus when it rumbles by, and *Kakarantzas*. *To Taxidhi* on the quay is a nice spot for coffee or an early drink, while *Malibu* and *Ores* pander to the night-owls.

Longós has a small, scruffy beach, with sulphur springs favoured by local grannies, but most people swim off Levréhio beach in the next bay south, which gets the occasional camper. (Islanders are touchy about camping for fear of fires; it's politic to ask at the beach taverna if it's acceptable to camp.) Longós is at the bottom of a steep winding hill, making **walking** a chore, but the short circle around neighbouring **Dhendhiátika** provides excellent views, and the walk to **Fondána** and **Magaziá** can be done to coincide with a bus back to Longós.

Andípaxi

A mile south of Paxí, its tiny sibling **Andípaxi** has scarcely any accommodation and no facilities beyond several beach tavernas open during the day in season. The sandy, blue-water coves have been compared with the Caribbean, but you'll have to share them with kaïkia and sea taxis from all three villages, plus larger craft from Corfu (boats from Paxí may also take you to its sea stacks and caves, the most dramatic in the Ionian islands).

Boats basically deposit you either at the sandy **Vríka beach** or the longer pebble beach of **Vatoúmi**. Vríka has a taverna at each end, of which *Spiros* (☎0662/31 172) has good food and can arrange self-catering accommodation up in **Vígla**, the island's hilltop settlement, on a weekly basis. Vatoúmi's only facility is the justifiably named *Bella Vista*, perched on a cliff high above the beach.

For a swim in quieter surroundings the trick is to head south away from the pleasure-craft moorings, although path widening has made even the quieter bays more accessible. Paths also lead inland to connect the handful of homes and the southerly lighthouse, but there are no beaches of any size on Andípaxi's western coastline and thick thorny scrub makes it difficult to approach. In low season, there's also the risk of bad weather keeping pleasure craft in port and stranding you on the island.

Lefkádha (Lefkas)

Lefkádha is an oddity. Connected to the mainland by a long causeway through lagoons, it barely feels like an island, at least on the busier eastern side – and historically in fact it isn't. It is separated from the mainland by a canal cut by Corinthian colonists in the seventh century BC, which has been re-dredged (after silting up) on various occasions since, and today is spanned by a thirty-metre boat-drawbridge built in 1986. Lefkádha was long an important strategic base, and approaching the causeway you pass a series of fortresses, climaxing in the fourteenth-century castle of **Santa Maura** – the Venetian name for the island. These defences were too close to the mainland to avoid an Ottoman tenure, which began in 1479, but the Venetians wrested back control a couple of centuries later. They were in turn overthrown by Napoleon in 1797 and then the British took over as Ionian protectors in 1810. It wasn't until 1864 that Lefkádha, like the rest of the Ionian archipelago, was reunited with Greece.

At first glance Lefkádha is not overwhelmingly attractive, although it is a substantial improvement on the mainland just opposite. The whiteness of its rock strata – *lefkás* has the same root as *lefkós*, "white" – is often brutally exposed by road cuts and quarries, and the highest ridge is bare except for ugly military and telecom installations. With the marshes and sumpy inlets on the east coast, mosquitoes can be a midsummer problem. On the other hand, the island is a fertile place, supporting cypresses, olive groves and vineyards, particularly on the western slopes, and life in the mountain villages remains relatively untouched, with the older women still wearing traditional local dress – two skirts (one forming a bustle), a dark headscarf and a rigid bodice.

Lefkádha has been the home of various literati, including two prominent Greek poets, Angelos Sikelianos and Aristotelis Valaoritis, and the short-story writer Lafcadio Hearn, son of American missionaries. Support for the arts continues in the form of a well-attended international **festival** of theatre and folk-dancing, now extended throughout the summer, with most events staged in the Santa Maura castle. On a smaller scale, frequent village celebrations accompanied by *bouzoúki* and clarinet ensure that the strong local wine flows well into the early hours.

Lefkádha remains relatively undeveloped, with just two major resorts: **Vassilikí**, in its vast bay in the south, claims to be Europe's biggest windsurf centre; **Nydhrí**, on the east coast, overlooks the island's picturesque archipelago, and is the launching point for the barely inhabited island of **Meganíssi**.

Lefkádha Town and around

Lefkádha Town sits at the island's northernmost tip, hard by the causeway. Like other southerly capitals, it was hit by the earthquakes of 1948 and 1953, and the town was devastated, with the exception of a few **Italianate churches**. As a precaution against further quakes, little was rebuilt above two storeys, and most houses acquired second storeys of wood, giving the western dormitory area an unintentionally quaint look. The town is small – you can cross it on foot in little over ten minutes – and despite the

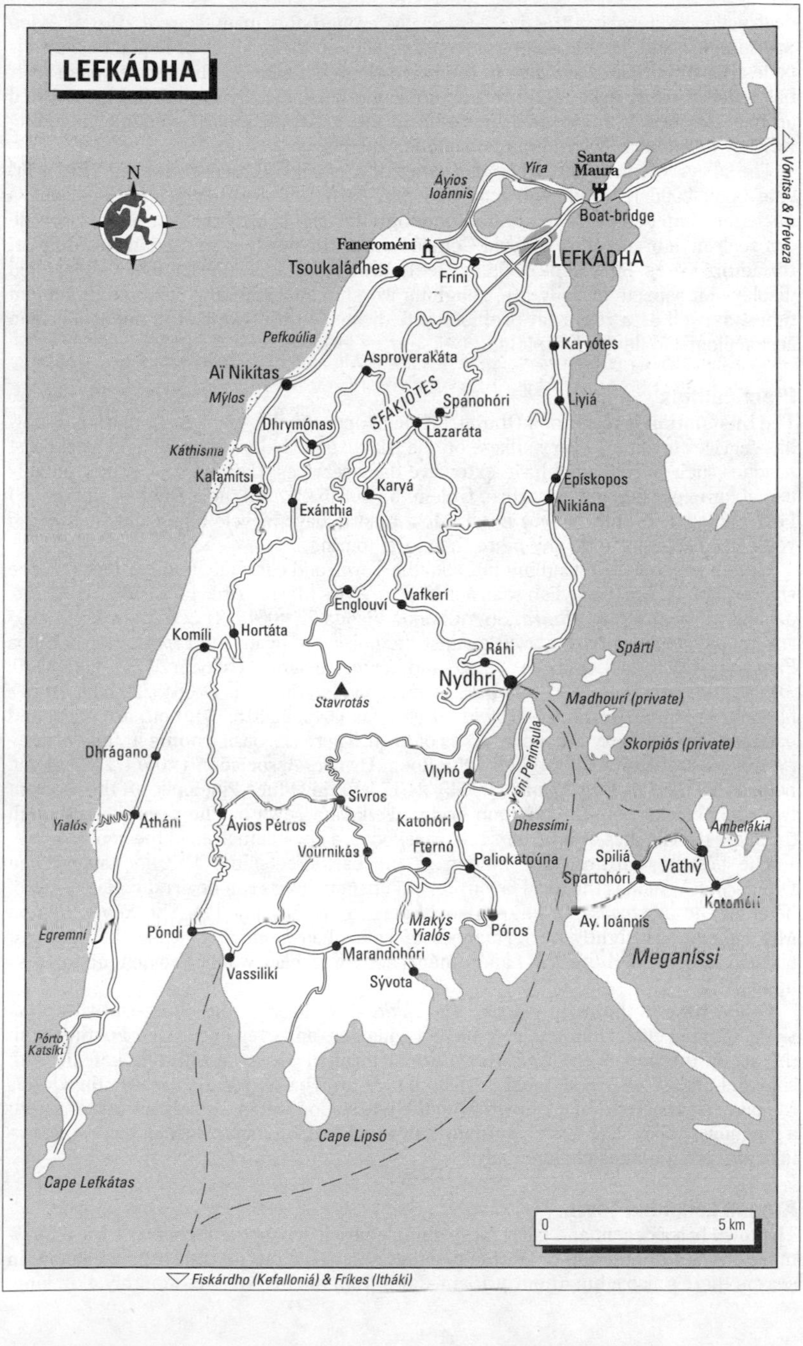
LEFKÁDHA
N
Santa Maura
Yíra
Áyios Ioánnis
Boat-bridge
Vónitsa & Préveza
Faneroméni
Tsoukaládhes
Fríni
LEFKÁDHA
Pefkoúlia
Karyótes
Asproyerakáta
Aï Nikítas
Mýlos
SFAKIOTES
Spanohóri
Liyiá
Lazaráta
Dhrymónas
Káthisma
Kalamítsi
Karyá
Exánthia
Epískopos
Nikiána
Englouví
Vafkerí
Komíli
Hortáta
Ráhi
Spárti
Nydhrí
Stavrotás
Madhourí (private)
Skorpiós (private)
Dhrágano
Vlyhó
Véni Peninsula
Yialós
Atháni
Áyios Pétros
Sívros
Katohóri
Dhessími
Ambelákia
Vournikás
Fternó
Paliokatoúna
Spiliá
Vathý
Spartohóri
Katoméri
Égremní
Póndi
Makrýs Yialós
Póros
Ay. Ioánnis
Marandohóri
Meganíssi
Vassilikí
Sývota
Pórto Katsíki
Cape Lipsó
Cape Lefkátas
0
5 km
Fiskárdho (Kefalloniá) & Fríkes (Itháki)

destruction still very attractive, especially around the main square, Platía Ayíou Spyridhónos, and the arcaded high street of Ioánnou Méla. Much of Lefkádha Town is pedestrian-only, mainly because of the narrowness of its lanes. The centre boasts over half a dozen richly decorated private family churches, usually locked and best visited around services. Many contain gems from the Ionian School of painting, including work by its founder, Zakynthian Panayiotis Doxaras.

The alleys off Ioánnou Méla also conceal a small **folklore museum** (Mon–Fri 9am–9pm; 200dr), which you may still find closed for lengthy renovations, and a museum/shop dedicated to antique phonographs and bric-a-brac. On the northwestern seafront a brand new Cultural Centre houses the newly expanded **archeological museum** (Tues–Sun 8am–2.30pm; free), which contains interesting, well-labelled displays on aspects of daily life, religious worship and funerary customs in ancient times, as well as a room on prehistory dedicated to the work of eminent German archaeologist Wilhelm Dörpfeld.

Practicalities

The **bus station** is on Odhós Dhimítri Golémi opposite the small yacht marina. It now has services to almost every village on the island, and Nydhrí, Vassilikí and west coast beaches such as Káthisma have extensive daily services. Car and motorbike rental is useful for exploring; try EuroHire, Golémi 5 (☎0645/267 76), near the bus station or I Love Santas next to the *Xenia* hotel. Most resorts have bicycle hire outlets, although you'll need stamina to do any more than local touring.

Hotels are actually dwindling in Lefkádha Town, and currently number just six. The smarter hotels, like the stylish seafront *Nirikos*, Ayías Mávras (☎0645/24 132, fax 23 756; ④) and the cosy *Santa Maura*, Spyridhónos Viánda 2 (☎0645/21 308-9, fax 26 253; ④) are in busy areas, but are glazed against the noise and heat. The *Lefkas*, Pétrou Filípa Panáyou (☎0645/23 916, fax 24 579; ⑥) and *Xenia*, Panágou 2 (☎0645/24 762, fax 25 129; ④) are both large hotels. The *Patras*, Platía Áyiou Spyridhónos (☎0645/22 359; ③) is a bargain, as is the *Byzantio*, Dörpfeld 40 (☎& fax 0645/21 315; ②); both are small and basic, and in very busy and noisy areas of town. There are basic **rooms** in the dormitory area west of Dörpfeld: the Lefkádha Room Owners Association (☎0674/21 266) can help, or try the *Pinelopis Rooms* (☎0645/24 175; ②) in Odhós Pinelópis, off the seafront two short blocks from the pontoon bridge. Lefkádha Town has no campsite, although there are decent sites at Karyótes and Epískopos, a few kilometres to the south.

The best **restaurants** are hidden in the backstreets: the *Reganto* taverna, on Dhimárhou Venióti is the local favourite, but opening hours can be erratic. If it's closed, head for the *Lighthouse*, in its own small garden on Filarmonikís. The *Romantika* on Mitropóleos has nightly performances of Lefkadhan *kantádhes*, while the smartest place in town is the *Adriatica*, Faneroménis and Merarhías, where people tend to dress up to eat.

Of the **bars** in the main square, the *Thalassina* ouzerí is the cheapest, with occasional evening entertainment from buskers, jugglers and even fire-eaters. Further from the action the best is the *Cafe Karfakis*, on Ioánnou Melá, an old-style kafenío with splendid mezédhes. The most stylish bar is the hard-to-find *Vengera*, on Odhós Maxáïra, signposted a block down from the bus station, set in a shady garden and with a hip music policy. The town's outdoor **cinema**, Eleni, on Faneroménis, has two showings and programmes change daily.

Around Lefkádha Town

The town has a decent and fairly large shingle beach across the lagoon at **Yíra**, a forty-minute walk from the top of Dörpfeld, either across the bridge or along Sikelianoú. In season there's also a bus (hourly 10am–2pm) from the bus station. Roughly 4km long, the beach is often virtually deserted even in high season; there's a **taverna** at either end, and at the western end a couple of **bars** in the renovated windmills, as well as the trendy *Club Milos*.

The uninhabited **Faneroméni monastery** (daily 8am–2pm & 4–8pm; free) is reached by any of the west-coast buses, or on foot from town (30min) through the hamlet of Fríni. There's a small museum and chapel, and an ox's yoke and hammer, used when Nazi occupiers forbade the use of bells. There are wonderful views over the town and lagoon from the Fríni road.

The island's **interior**, best reached by bus or car from Lefkádha Town, offers imposing mountainscapes and excellent walking between villages only a few kilometres apart. **KARYÁ** is its centre, with a hotel, the *Karia Village Hotel* (☎0645/41 004; ④), tucked away above the village, and some rooms: try Haritini Vlahou (☎0645/41 634; ②), the Kakiousis family (☎0645/61 136; ②), Olga Lazari (☎0645/61 547; ③) or Michael Halikias (☎0645/61 026; ③). The leafy town square has a popular taverna, *Iy Klimataria*, just off the platía and two psistariés on it, *Ta Platania*, and the smarter *O Rousos*. Karyá is the centre of the island's lace and weaving industry, with a fascinating small **museum** set in a lacemaker's home. The historic villages of **Vafkerí** and **Englouví** are within striking distance, with the west-coast hamlets of **Dhrymónas** and **Exánthia** a hike over the hills.

The east coast to Vassilikí

Lefkádha's east coast is the most accessible and the most developed part of the island. Apart from the campsites at Karyótes (*Kariotes Beach*, ☎0645/71 103) and Epískopos (*Episcopos Beach*, ☎0645/71 388), there's little point stopping before the small fishing ports of **LIYIÁ**, which has some rooms and the hotel *Konaki* (☎& fax 0645 71 127; ⑥), or **NIKIÁNA**, where you'll find the hotel *Pegasus* (☎0645/71 766, fax 25 290; ⑥) and the smarter but considerably cheaper *Ionion* (☎0645/71 721; ⑤), as well as the *Porto Fino* pension (☎ 0645/ 71 389; ③). Nikiána also has a selection of fine tavernas, notably the *Pantazis*, which also has rooms to let and the *Lefko Akroyiali*, a good fish restaurant further south. Beaches here tend to be pebbly and small.

Most package travellers will find themselves in **NYDHRÍ**, the coast's biggest resort with ferry connections to Meganíssi and myriad **boat trips** around the nearby satellite islands. The German archeologist Wilhelm Dörpfeld believed Nydhrí, rather than Itháki, to be the site of Odysseus's capital, and did indeed find Bronze Age tombs on the plain nearby. His theory identifying ancient Ithaca with Lefkádha fell into disfavour after his death in 1940, although his obsessive attempts to give the island some status over its neighbour are honoured by a statue on Nydhrí's quay. Dörpfeld's tomb is tucked away at Ayía Kyriakí on the opposite side of the bay, near the house in which he once lived, visible just above the chapel and lighthouse on the far side of the water.

Nydhrí is an average resort, with some good pebble beaches and a lovely setting, but the centre is an ugly strip with heavy traffic. The best place to stay is the *Hotel Gorgona* (☎0645/92 197, fax 92 268; ④), set in a lush garden away from the traffic a minute along the Ráhi road, which leads to Nydhrí's very own **waterfall**, a forty-five minute walk inland. There are also rooms in the centre – try Emilios Gazis (☎0645/92 703; ③) and Athanasios Konidharis (☎0645/92 749; ④). The town's focus is the Aktí Aristotéli Onássi quay, where most of the rather ritzy **restaurants** and **bars** are found. The *Barrel* and *Il Sappore* restaurants are recommended, as is the *Agra* on the beach. However, eating is better value on the noisy main drag – try *Agrabeli* or *Ta Kalamia*. Nightlife centres around bars like *No Name* and *Byblos*, and the late-night *Status* or *Sail Inn Club*.

Nydhrí sits at the mouth of a deep inlet stretching to the next village, somnolent **VLYHÓ**, with a few good tavernas and mooring for yachts. Over the Yéni peninsula across the inlet is the large **Dhessími Bay**, home to two adjacent campsites: *Santa Maura Camping* (☎0645/95 007, fax 26 087), and *Dessimi Beach Camping* (☎0645/95 374), right on the beach but often packed with outsized mobile homes.

The coast road beyond Vlyhó turns inland and climbs the foothills of Mount Stavrotás, through the hamlets of Katohóri and Paliokatoúna to **Póros**, a quiet village with few facilities. Just south of here is the increasingly busy beach resort of **MAKRÝS YIALÓS**. It boasts a handful of **tavernas**, a few rooms at *Oceanis Studios* (☎and fax 0654/95 095; ③), plus the upmarket *Poros Beach Camping* (☎0654/23 203, fax 95 152), which has bungalows (④), shops and a pool. Try the *Rouda Bay* taverna opposite the beach, which also has rooms (☎ 0645/ 95 634; ⑤).

Along the main road, walkers and drivers are recommended to take the panoramic detour to quiet **Voúrnika** and **Sývros** (the Lefkádha–Vassilíki bus also visits), which both have tavernas and some private rooms. It's around 14km to the next resort, the fjord-like inlet of **SÝVOTA**, 2km down a steep hill (bus twice daily). There's no beach except for a remote cove, but some fine fish tavernas: the *Ionion* is the most popular, but the *Delfinia* and *Kavos* are also good. Thomas Skliros (☎0645/31 151; ③) at the furthest supermarket has a few **rooms**, and there's a basic unofficial campsite by the bus stop at the edge of the village.

Beyond the Sývota turning, the mountain road dips down towards Kondárena, almost a suburb of **VASSILIKÍ**, the island's premiere watersports resort. Winds in the huge bay draw vast numbers of windsurfers, with light morning breezes for learners and tough afternoon blasts for advanced surfers. Booking your **accommodation** ahead is mandatory in high season. The *Paradise* (☎0645/32 156; ③), a basic but friendly hotel overlooking the small rocky beach beyond the ferry dock, is the best bargain. Also good value for its class is the neighbouring upmarket *Hotel Apollo* (☎0645/31 122, fax 31 142; ④). In the centre of town, the two main hotels are the smart and reasonably priced *Vassiliki Bay Hotel* (☎0645/ 31 458, fax 23 567; ⑤) and the *Hotel Lefkatas* (☎0645/31 801, fax 31 804; ⑤), a large, modern building overlooking the busiest road in town. Rooms and apartments are available along the beach road to Póndi: *Billy's House* (☎0645/31 418; ④), *Christina Politi's Rooms* (☎0645/31 440; ④) and the *Samba Pension* (☎0645/31 555; ④) are smart and purpose-built, though not particularly cheap. The largest of the three beach windsurf centres, Club Vassiliki, offers all-in **windsurf tuition** and accommodation deals. Vassilikí's only **campsite**, the large *Camping Vassiliki Beach* (☎0645/31 308, fax 31 458), is about 500m along the beach road; it has its own restaurant, bar and shop.

Vassilikí's pretty quayside is lined with tavernas and bars, notably the *Dolphin Psistaria*, the glitzier *Restaurant Miramare*, the *Penguin* and *Alexander*, which includes a Chinese menu. One of the cheapest places to drink on the entire island is *Livanakis* kafenío next to the bakery. Flyers sometimes advertise **raves** on the beach at Pórto Katsíki.

The beach at Vassilikí is stony and poor, but improves 1km on at tiny **PÓNDI**; most non-windsurfers however, use the daily kaïki trips to nearby Ayiófili or around Cape Lefkátas to the superior beaches at Pórto Katsíki and Egremní on the sandy west coast. There's a gradually increasing amount of accommodation at Póndi, some with great views of the bay and plain behind, particularly from the terrace of the *Ponti Beach Hotel* (☎0645/31 572, fax 31 576; ⑤), which is very popular with holidaying Greeks, and has a restaurant and bar open to non-residents. The *Nefeli* (☎ 0645/ 31 515; ④), right on the beach, is better value though.

The west coast

Tsoukaládhes, just 6km from Lefkádha, is developing a roadside tourism business, but better beaches lie a short distance to the south, so there's very little reason to stay here. Four kilometres on, the road plunges down to the sand-and-pebble **Pefkoúlia beach**, one of the longest on the island, with a taverna at the north end, *Oinilos*, that has rooms, and unofficial camping down at the other end, about 2km away.

Jammed into a gorge between Pefkoúlia and the next beach, Mýlos, is **AÏ NIKÍTAS**, the prettiest resort on Lefkádha, a jumble of lanes and small wooden buildings. The back of the village is a dust-blown car park, which detracts from the appeal of the pleasant, if basic, *O Aï Nikitas* **campsite** (☎0645/97 301, fax 21 173), set in terraced olive groves. The most attractive **accommodation** is in the *Pension Ostria* (☎0645/97 483, fax 97 300; ⑤), a beautiful blue and white building above the village decorated in a mix of beachcomber and ecclesiastical styles. Other options are in the alleys that run off the main drag; the best bets are the *Pansion Aphrodite* (☎0645/97 372; ③), the small *Hotel Selene* (☎0645/97 369; ④) and quieter *Olive Tree* (☎0645/97 453; ④). Best tavernas include the *Sapfo* fish taverna by the sea and the *T'Agnantia*, just above the main street.

Sea taxis (400dr one way) ply between Aï Nikítas and **Mýlos** beach, or it's a 45-minute walk (or bus ride) to the most popular beach on the coast, **Káthisma**, a shadeless kilometre of fine sand. There are two tavernas on the beach: the barn-like *Kathisma Beach* (☎ 0645/ 97 050, fax 97 335; ⑥) with smart apartments, and the *Akroyiali*. Above the beach the *Sunset* has **rooms** (☎0645/97 488; ④). Beyond Káthisma, hairpin bends climb the flank of Mount Méga towards the tiny village of **KALAMÍTSI**, where Spyros Karelis (☎0645/99 214; ②) and Spyros Veryinis (☎0645/99 411; ②) have rooms. *Hermes* (☎0645/99 417; ②), the *Blue and White House* (☎0645/99 413; ②) and *Pansion Nontas* (☎0645/99 451; ③) have larger rooms and apartments. There are also three good tavernas: the *Paradeisos* in its own garden with fountain, the more basic *Ionio* and, just north of the village, the aptly titled *Panorama View*. Three kilometres down a newly paved road is the village's quiet sandy beach, effectively the southern extension of Káthisma.

South of Kalamítsi, past the hamlets of Hortáta, which boasts the excellent *Lygos* taverna with rooms (☎ 0645/33 395; ②), and Komíli, the landscape becomes almost primeval. At 38km from Lefkádha Town, **ATHÁNI** is Lefkádha's most remote spot to stay, with a couple of good tavernas which both have rooms: the *Panorama* (☎0645/33 291; ②) and *O Alekos* (☎0656/33 484; ③).

The road continues 14km to barren **Cape Lefkátas**, which drops abruptly 75 metres into the sea. Byron's Childe Harold sailed past this point, and "saw the evening star above, Leucadia's far projecting rock of woe: And hail'd the last resort of fruitless love". The fruitless love is a reference to Sappho, who in accordance with the ancient legend that you could cure yourself of unrequited love by leaping into these waters, leapt – and died. In her honour the locals termed the place *Kávos tís Kyrás* ("Lady's Cape"), and her act was imitated by the lovelorn youths of Lefkádha for centuries afterwards. And not just by the lovelorn, for the act (known as *katapondismós*) was performed annually by scapegoats – always a criminal or a lunatic – selected by priests from the Apollo temple whose sparse ruins lie close by. Feathers and even live birds were attached to the victims to slow their descent and boats waiting below took the chosen one, dead or alive, away to some place where the evil banished with them could do no further harm. The rite continued into the Roman era, when it degenerated into little more than a fashionable stunt by decadent youth. These days, Greek hang-gliders hold a tournament from the cliffs every July. A turning before the cape leads down an asphalted road to the dramatic twin beach of **Pórto Katsíki**, where there are a couple of large canteens on the cliff above.

Lefkádha's satellites

Lefkádha has four satellite islands clustered off its east coast, although only one, **Meganíssi**, the largest and most interesting, is accessible. **Skorpiós**, owned by the

Onassis family, fields armed guards to deter visitors. **Madhourí**, owned by the family of poet Nanos Valaoritis, is private and similarly off-limits, while tiny **Spárti** is a large scrub-covered rock. Day-trips from Nydhrí skirt all three islands, and some stop to allow swimming in coves.

Meganíssi

MEGANÍSSI, twenty minutes by frequent daily ferries from Nydhrí, is a large island with few facilities but a magical, if bleak landscape, a situation that's made it a favourite with island aficionados. Ferries stop first below **SPARTOHÓRI**, an immaculate village with whitewashed buildings and an abundance of bougainvillea. The locals – many returned émigrés from Australia – live from farming and fishing and are genuinely welcoming. You arrive at a jetty on a pebble beach with a few tavernas and a primitive but free (for a night or two only) campsite behind the *Star Taverna*. The village proper boasts three restaurants: a pizza place called the *Tropicana*, which can direct you to **rooms** (☎0645/51 486; ②–③), the *Gakias* and the traditional taverna *Lakis*. Further west round the coast at Áyios Yiánnis there is a good beach with a taverna and possible future campsite.

The attractive inland village of **KATOMÉRI** is an hour's walk through magnificent country. It has the island's one **hotel**, the *Meganissi*, a comfortable place with a restaurant (☎0645/51 240, fax 51 639; ③), and a few bars. Ten minutes' walk downhill is the main port of **VATHÝ**, with some accommodation (*Different Studios*: ☎0645/22 170; ③) and the island's best restaurants, notably the waterside taverna, *Porto Vathi*, which Lefkádhans flock to on ferries for Sunday lunch. After the high-season madness of Nydhrí, Meganíssi's unspoiled landscape is a tonic, and it's easy to organize a **day-trip** from Nydhrí, getting off at Spartohóri, walking to Katoméri for lunch at the *Meganisi*, and catching a ferry back from Vathý. Paths lead from Katoméri to remote beaches, including popular **Ambelákia**, but these aren't accessible on a day-trip.

Kefalloniá

Kefalloniá is the largest of the Ionian islands – a place that has real towns as well as resorts. Like its neighbours, Kefalloniá was overrun by Italians and Germans in World War II; the "handover" after Italy's capitulation in 1943 led to the massacre of five thousand Italian troops on the island by invading German forces. These events form a key episode in Louis de Bernières' novel, *Captain Corelli's Mandolin*, a tragicomic epic of life on the island from before the war to the present day.

Until the late 1980s, the island paid scant regard to tourism; perhaps this was in part a feeling that Kefalloniá could not easily be marketed. Virtually all of its towns and villages were levelled in the 1953 earthquake, and these masterpieces of Venetian architecture had been the one touch of elegance in a severe, mountainous landscape. A more likely explanation, however, for the island's late emergence on the Greek tourist scene is the Kefallonians' legendary reputation for insular pride and stubbornness.

Having decided on the advantages of an easily exploitable industry, however, Kefalloniá is at present in the midst of a tourism boom. Long favoured by Italians, it has begun attracting British package companies, for whom a new airport terminal has been constructed, while virtually every decent beach has been endowed with restaurants. There are definite attractions here, with some beaches as good as any in the Ionian islands, and a fine (if pricey) local wine, the dry white *Rombola*. Moreover, the island seems able to soak up a lot of people without feeling at all crowded, and the magnificent scenery can speak for itself, the escarpments culminating in the 1632-metre bulk of **Mount Énos**, declared a national park to protect the fir trees (*Abies cephalonica*) named after the island.

Kefalloniá airport is 7km south of the capital, Argostóli; there are no airport buses, so you'll have to resort to an overpriced taxi. The **bus** system is basic but expanding, and with a little legwork it can be used to get you almost anywhere on the island. Key routes connect Argostóli with Sámi, Fiskárdho, Skála and Póros. There's a useful connection from Sámi to the tiny resort of **Ayía Evfimía**, which attracts many package travellers. Using a motorbike, take care as the terrain is very rough in places – although an increasing number of roads are being surfaced – and the gradients can sometimes be a bit challenging for underpowered machines. The island has a plethora of **ferry** connections, principally from Fiskárdho to Lefkádha and Itháki, and from Sámi to Lefkádha, Itháki and the mainland, as well as links to Zákynthos, Kyllíni and Pátra.

Sámi and around

Most boats dock at the large and functional port town of **SÁMI**, built and later rebuilt near the south end of the Itháki straits, more or less on the site of ancient Sami. This was the capital of the island in Homeric times, when Kefalloniá was part of Ithaca's maritime kingdom: today the administrative hierarchy is reversed, Itháki being considered the backwater. With ferries to many points of the Ionian islands, and several companies introducing direct links to Italy, the town is clearly preparing itself for a burgeoning future. The long sandy beach that stretches round the bay is quite adequate; 2km beyond ancient Sami, lies a fine pebble beach, **Andísami**.

The town has two smart **hotels**: the *Sami Beach* (☎0674/22 802, fax 22 846; ⑥), actually situated at the far end of the beach in Karavómylos, and the quieter *Pericles* (☎0674/22 780, fax 22 787; ⑤), over a kilometre along the Argostóli road, which has extensive grounds, two pools and sports facilities. The best mid-range bet is the *Ionion* (☎0674/22 035; ③), followed by the *Melissani* (☎0674/22 464; ④), both behind the seafront; on the front itself the *Kastro* (☎ 0674/22 282; ⑤) is very comfortable. The *Kyma* (☎0674/22 064; ③) on Platía Kýprou is a tarted up old-fashioned hotel and rather overpriced. Both *períptera* on the quay offer rooms, as do a variety of private homes a few blocks back from the front. Sámi's **campsite**, *Camping Karavomilos Beach* (☎0674/22 480, fax 22 932), has over 300 well-shaded spaces, a taverna, shop and bar, and opens onto the beach. It is by far the better of the island's two official sites.

Sámi doesn't have a great many **tavernas** beyond those on the seafront; visitors tend to go to the smart *Adonis Restaurant* or the *Delfinia*, but a cheaper and more genuine choice is *O Faros*, which serves a good selection of veg and meat dishes, including the famous local meat pie. Best of all, though, is *To Karnagio*, further towards the beach, where you can sample succulent grilled meat, oven dishes and good local wine. The *Riviera* and *Aqua Marina* are the favourite **bars** in the evenings, while the best place for a snack breakfast or ice cream is *Captain Jimmy's*.

The Dhrogaráti and Melissáni caves

The one good reason to stay in Sámi is its proximity to the Drogharáti and Melissáni caves; the former 5km out of town towards Argostóli, the latter 3km north towards Ayía Efimía. A very impressive stalagmite-bedecked chamber, **Dhrogaráti** (April–Oct daily 8am–9pm; 1000dr) is occasionally used for concerts thanks to its marvellous acoustics – Maria Callas once sang here. **Melissáni** (8am–sunset; 1200dr) is partly submerged in brackish water which, amazingly, emerges from an underground fault which leads the whole way under the island to a point near Argostóli. At that point, known as Katavóthres, the sea gushes endlessly into a subterranean channel – and, until the 1953 earthquake disrupted it – the current was used to drive sea mills. That the water, now as then, still ends up in the cave has been shown with fluorescent tracer dye. The beautiful textures and shades created by the light pouring through the collapsed roof of the cave make it a must.

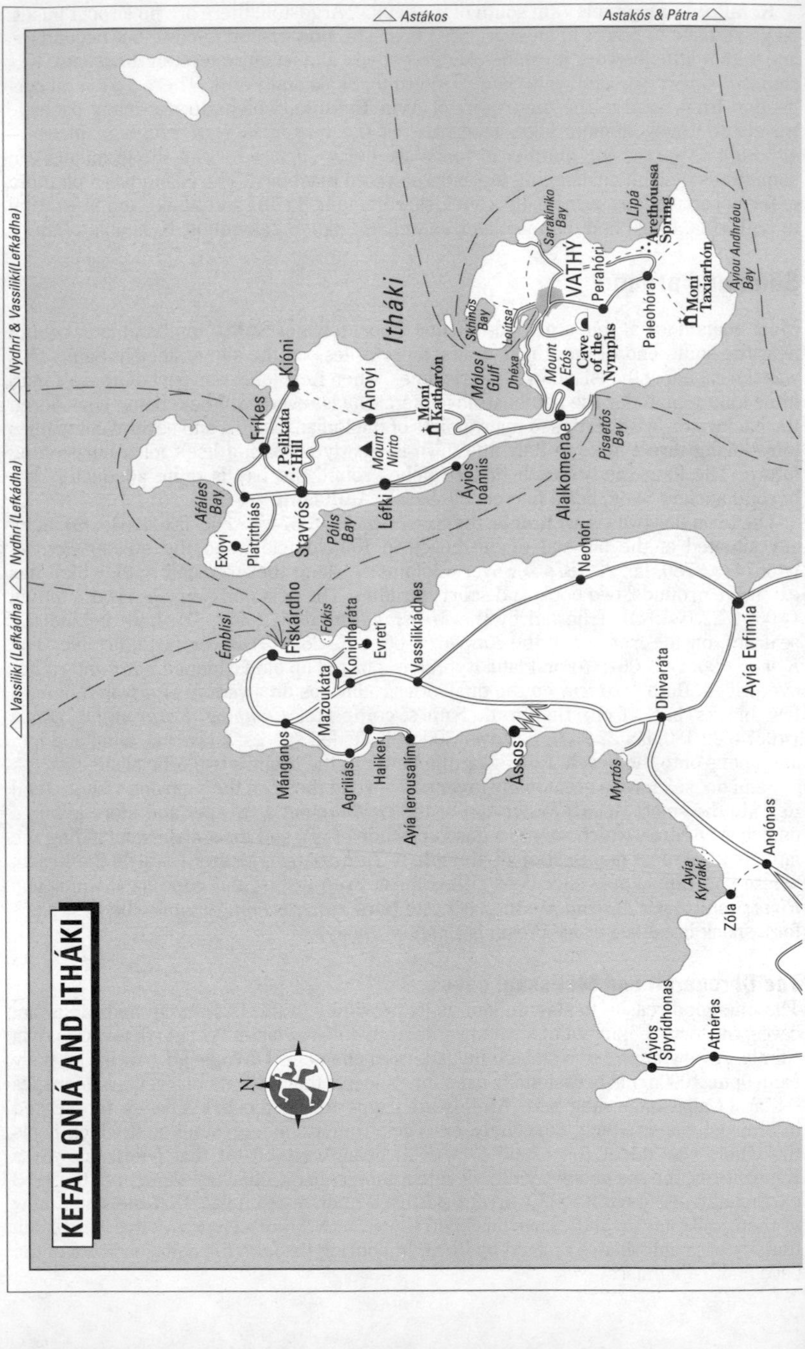
KEFALLONIÁ AND ITHÁKI
N
Astákos
Astakós & Pátra
Nydhrí & Vassilikí(Lefkádha)
Nydhrí (Lefkádha)
Vassilikí (Lefkádha)
Itháki
VATHÝ
Sarakíniko Bay
Lipá
Arethóussa Spring
Perahóri
Paleohóra
Moní Taxiarhón
Áyiou Andhréou Bay
Skhinós Bay
Loútsa
Mólos Gulf
Dhéxa
Mount Etós
Cave of the Nymphs
Pisaetós Bay
Alalkomenae
Moní Katharón
Kióni
Anoyí
Mount Níritó
Fríkes
Pelikáta Hill
Stavrós
Léfki
Áyios Ioannis
Afáles Bay
Platrithiás
Exoyí
Pólis Bay
Émblisi
Fiskárdho
Fókis
Evretí
Konidharáta
Mazoukáta
Vassilikiádhes
Neohóri
Mánganos
Agriliás
Halikerí
Ayía Ierousalím
Ássos
Myrtós
Dhivaráta
Ayía Evfimía
Angónas
Ayía Kyriakí
Zóla
Áyios Spyrídhonas
Athéras

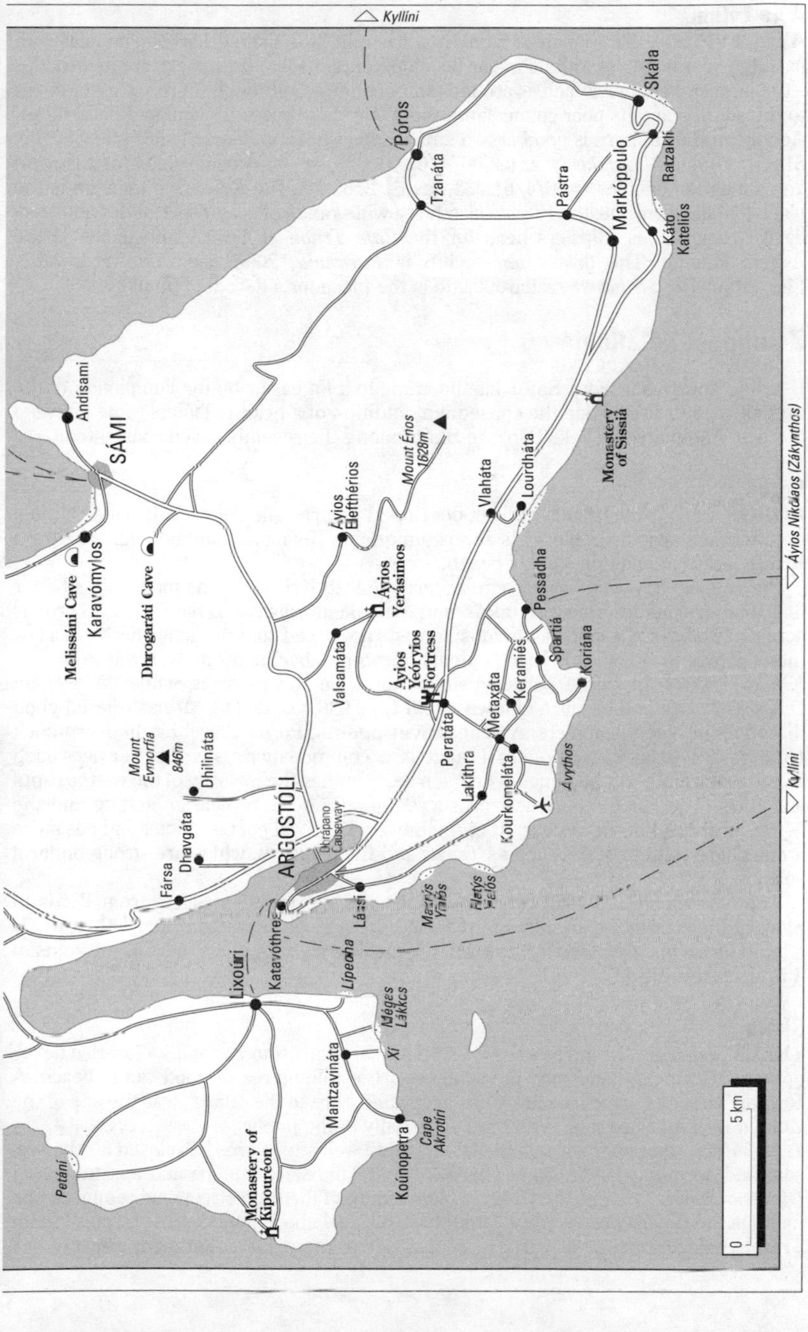
Kyllíni
Póros
Skála
Tzaráta
Markópoulo
Pástra
Ratzaklí
Káto Kateliós
Andísami
SÁMI
Monastery of Sissiá
Mount Énos 1628m
Áyios Nikólaos (Zákynthos)
Áyios Eleftérios
Vlaháta
Lourdháta
Melissáni Cave
Karavómylos
Dhrogaráti Cave
Áyios Yerásimos
Valsamáta
Pessádha
Áyios Yeóryios Fortress
Spartiá
Keramiés
Koriána
Mount Evmorfía 846m
Dhilináta
Peratáta
Metaxáta
Ávythos
Lakíthra
Kourkomeláta
Kyllíni
Dhavgáta
ARGOSTÓLI
Dhrápano Causeway
Fársa
Lássi
Makrýs Yalós
Platýs Yalós
Katavóthres
Lixoúri
Lípedha
Mégas Lákkos
Xí
Mantzavináta
Petáni
Monastery of Kipouréon
Koúnopetra
Cape Akrotíri
0
5 km

Ayía Evfimía

AYÍA EVFIMÍA, 9km north of Sámi, is a friendly little fishing harbour popular with package operators, yet with no major developments. Its two drawbacks are its beaches – the largest, Paradise Beach, is around 20m of shingle, although there are other coves to the south – and its poor connections (only two daily buses to Sámi and Fiskárdho). **Accommodation** here is good at two small, smart **hotels**: *Pilaros* (☎0674/61 800, fax 61 801; ⑥) and *Moustakis* (☎ & fax 0674/61 030; ④) or the decent-value apartments of Yerasimos Raftopoulos (☎0674/61 233, fax 61 216; ③). The *Dendrinos* **taverna** is the place for island cuisine; the *Pergola* also has a wide range of island specialities and standard Greek dishes. Hipsters head for the *Cafe Triton* at night, philhellenes to the *Asteria* kafenío. The town's night club is *Paranoia*, 700m out of town towards Fiskárdho. The *Strawberry* zaharoplastío is the place for a decadent breakfast.

Southeast Kefalloniá

Heading **southeast from Sámi** has been made a lot easier by the completion of the asphalt road to **Póros** and the consequent addition of a twice-daily bus route between the two. Another route links Póros to **Skála** along the recently paved coastal road.

Póros

PÓROS was one the island's earliest developed resorts, and shows it. Its small huddle of hotels and apartment blocks is almost unique on Kefalloniá, and not enhanced by a scruffy seafront and thin, pebbly beach.

Póros does, however, have a regular ferry link to **Kyllíni** on the mainland, a better link than the one to remote **Astakós** and a viable alternative to Sámi–Pátra. Póros is actually two bays: the first, where most tourists are based, and the actual harbour, a few minutes over the headland. There's plenty of rooms, apartments and a few **hotels**. The *Kefalos* (☎0674/72 139; ④) has en-suite rooms on the seafront, while the elegant *Odysseus Palace* in the centre of town (☎0674/72 036, fax 72 148; ⑥) has offered good discounts in recent summers. Among **travel agents**, Poros Travel by the ferry dock (☎0674/72 476, fax 72 069) offers a range of accommodation, as well as services such as car rental and ferry bookings. The main seafront has the majority of the **restaurants** and **bars**. The *Fotis Family* taverna serves good food in a pleasant setting and the *Mythos* café has Internet access. At night, however, the old port is quieter and has more atmosphere, with tavernas such as *Tzivas* and the *Dionysus*, which are strong on local seafood.

The aforementioned road twists 12km around the rocky coastline from Póros to Skála at the southern extremity of the island. It's a lovely, isolated route, with scarcely a building on the way, save for a small chapel, 3km short of Skála, next to the ruins of a **Roman temple**.

Skála

SKÁLA is also developing as a resort, but in total contrast to Póros it's a low-rise development set among handsome pines above a few kilometres of good sandy beach. A **Roman villa** and some mosaics were excavated here in the 1950s, near the site of the Golden Beach Palace rooms, and are open daily to the public.

Its faithful return crowd keep Skála busy until well after Póros has closed for the season, and accommodation can be hard to find. There are studios and apartments at *Dionysus Rooms* (☎0671/83 283; ③), a block south of the high street, and rooms can be found at the *Golden Beach Palace* (☎0671/83 327; ③) above the beach or through Etam Travel Service (☎0671/83 101, fax 83 142). The more upmarket *Tara Beach Hotel*

(☎0671/83 250, fax 83 344; ⑥) has rooms and individual bungalows in lush gardens on the edge of the beach. Skála boasts a number of good **restaurants**: the *Pines*, the *Flamingo*, and, on the beach, the *Paspalis* and *Sunset*. Drinkers head for *The Loft* cocktail **bar** and the beach-side *Pikiona* pool-bar.

Skála to Lourdháta

Some of the finest sandy beaches on the island are just beyond Skála below the village of Ratzákli, and around the growing micro-resort of **KÁTO KATELIÓS**, which already has couple of hotels: the smart *Odyssia* (☎0671/81 615, fax 81 614; ⑤) and the German-dominated *Galini Resort* (☎0671/81 582; ⑤). There are also some self-contained **apartments** available through the stylish *Arbouro* **taverna** (☎0671/81 192; ③) or the beach-side *Faros* taverna (☎0671/81 355; ③). There is now a row of around half a dozen restaurants and cafés at the seafront. However, the coast around Káto Kateliós is also Kefalloniá's key breeding ground for the **loggerhead turtle** (see box on p.444). Camping is discouraged and would, anyway, strand you miles from any facilities.

At the inland village of **MARKÓPOULO**, claimed by some to be the birthplace of homophonous explorer Marco Polo, the **Assumption of the Virgin festival** (August 15) is celebrated in unique style at the local church with small, harmless snakes with cross-like markings on their heads. Each year, so everyone hopes, they converge on the site to be grasped to the bosoms of the faithful; a few, in fact, are kept by the priests for those years when they don't naturally arrive. The celebrants are an interesting mix of locals and gypsies – some of whom come over from the mainland for the occasion. It's quite a spectacle.

The coastline is largely inaccessible until the village of **VLAHÁTA**, which has some rooms – *Maria Studios* (☎0671/31 055; ③) – and a good taverna, the *Dionysus*, but you're better off continuing to **LOURDHÁTA**, 2km to the south. It has a fine one-kilometre shingle beach and a couple of **tavernas** on a tiny plane-shaded village square – the *New World* and the *Diamond* – as well as the smarter *Spiros* steak and grill house above. *Adonis* (☎0671/31 206; ④) and *Ramona* (☎0671/31 032; ③) have **rooms** just outside the village on the approach road, while the one **hotel**, the *Lara* (☎0671/31 157, fax 31 156; ⑤), towards the beach, has en-suite rooms with sea views and a pool.

Argostóli and around

ARGOSTÓLI, Kefalloniá's capital, is a large and thriving town, virtually a city, with a marvellous site on a bay within a bay. The stone bridge, connecting the two sides of the inner bay, was initially constructed by the British in 1813. A small obelisk remains, but the plaque commemorating "the glory of the British Empire" has disappeared. The town was totally rebuilt after the earthquake but has an enjoyable street life that remains defiantly Greek, especially during the evening vólta around Platía Metaxá – the nerve centre of town.

The **Korgialenio History and Folklore Museum** (Tues–Sun 9am–2pm; 500dr), on Ilía Zervoú behind the Municipal Theatre, has a rich collection of local religious and cultural artefacts, including photographs taken before and after the 1953 quakes. Insight into how the island's nobility used to live can be gained from a visit to the new **Focas-Cosmetatos Foundation**, on Valianoú opposite the provincial government building. It contains elegant furniture and a collection of lithographs and paintings, including works by nineteenth-century British artists Joseph Cartwright and Edward Lear. The **Archeological Museum** (Tues–Sun 8.30am–2pm; 500dr), on nearby R. Vergóti, has a sizable collection of pottery, jewellery, funerary relics and statuary but at the time of writing was closed for a major refurbishment.

Practicalities

Argostóli's shiny new **Kefalloniá airport** lies 7km south of town. There are no airport buses, and suburban bus services are so infrequent or don't go close enough that a taxi (at an inflated flat rate of 3500dr) is the only dependable connection. Those arriving in Argostóli by bus from Sámi or elsewhere will wind up at the KTEL **bus station**, a minute from the Dhrápano causeway and ten minutes' walk south of the main square, **Platía Metaxá**. Argostóli's friendly **tourist office** (Mon–Fri 8am–2pm; open till 10pm in August; ☎0671/22 248 or 24 466) is on Andoníou Trítsi at the north end of the seafront, next to the port authority and has information about rooms, and can advise on transport and other resorts around the island.

Hotels around Platía Metaxá stay open year round, but tend to be pricey: the best bet here is the *Mirabel* (☎0671/25 381, fax 25 384; ⑤). A good mid-range option away from the square is the *Fokas*, Yeroulánou 1–3 (☎0671/22 566, fax 23 109; ④), whereas the *Mouikis*, Výronos 3 (☎0671/23 454; ⑥), has gone decidedly upmarket; the only budget hotel is the friendly *Chara* at the corner of G Vergóti and Dhevossétou near Dhrápano bridge (☎0671/22 427; ①). In a working town with a large permanent population, **private rooms** aren't too plentiful. Some of the best bargains can be found through waterfront tavernas, such as the *Kalafatis* (☎0671/22 627; ②–④), nearest to the Dhrápano bridge on the Metaxá waterfront, the *Tzivras* (☎0671/24 259; ②), on Vandórou, just off the centre of the waterfront, or Spyros Rouhotas' kafenío (☎0671/23 491; ③), opposite the Lixoúri ferry ramp. A number of travel agencies also offer rooms, apartments and villas: try *Filoxenos Travel* (☎0671/23 055) on R. Vergóti or *Myrtos* at A. Trítsi 75 (☎0671/25 895, fax 24 230; ③–⑤). The town's one **campsite**, *Argostoli Camping* (☎0671/23 487), lies 2km north of the centre, just beyond the Katovóthres sea mills; there's only an infrequent bus service in high season, so you'll probably have to walk and it's rather basic and limited in shade.

The *Tzivras Estiatório* (only open until 5pm) just off the seafront or *Kalafatis* **taverna** right on it are the places to try Kefallonian cuisine; the *Captain's Table* just off the platía merits a splurge and to hear Kefalloniá *kantádhes*. The *Demosthenes* opposite the *Mirabel* hotel also features gentle live music in a garden setting. Local posers hang out at the *Da Cappo* café-bar, the *Flonitiko* café and the *Koukos* club-bar, on Vasiléos Yeoryíou off the square; the *Space Girls* bar is rather more esoteric. The quay bars, particularly the kafenío by the Dhrápano bridge, are quiet, cheap and have the best views.

South of Argostóli: beaches and Áyios Yeóryios

Many package travellers will find themselves staying in **LÁSSI**, a short bus ride or twenty-minute walk from town. Lássi sprawls unattractively along a busy four-lane highway, but it does have good sandy beaches, particularly at **Makrýs Yialós** and **Platýs Yialós**, although they're right under the airport flight path. **Beaches** such as **Ávythos** are well worth seeking out, although if you're walking beyond **Kourkomeláta** there is a real if occasional risk of being attacked by farm dogs, particularly during the hunting season (Sept 25–Feb 28). There is very little accommodation in the region, and precious few shops or bars. **Pessádha** has a regular ferry link with Zákynthos in summer, but little else.

With a scooter, the best inland excursion is to **ÁYIOS YEÓRYIOS**, the medieval Venetian capital of the island. The old town here supported a population of 15,000 until its destruction by an earthquake in the seventeenth century: substantial ruins of its **castle** (Tues–Sat 8am–8pm, Sun 8am–2pm; 500dr), churches and houses can be visited on the hill above the modern village of Peratáta. Byron lived for a few months in the nearby village of Metaxáta and was impressed by the view from the summit in 1823; sadly, as at Messolóngi, the house where he stayed no longer exists. Two kilometres south of Áyios Yeóryios is a fine collection of religious icons and frescoes kept in a restored church that was part of the nunnery of Áyios Andhréas.

Mount Énos

At 15km from a point halfway along the Argostóli–Sámi road, **Mount Énos** isn't really a walking option, but roads nearly reach the official 1632-metre summit. The mountain has been declared a national park, to protect the *Abies cephalonica* firs (named after the island) which clothe the slopes. There are absolutely no facilities on or up to the mountain, but the views from the highest point in the Ionian islands out over its neighbours and the mainland are wonderful. In low season, watch the weather, which can deteriorate with terrifying speed.

Lixoúri

Half-hourly ferries (hourly in winter) ply between the capital and **LIXOÚRI** throughout the day. The town was flattened by earthquakes, and hasn't risen much above two storeys since. It's a little drab, but has good restaurants, quiet hotels and is favoured by those who want to explore the eerie quakescapes left in the south and the barren north of the peninsula. The bargain **hotel** is the *Giardino* (☎0671/92 505, fax 92 525; ②), four blocks back from the front. There are also two decent beach hotels just south of town: the *Poseidon* (☎0671/92 518, fax 91 374; ④) and *Summery* (☎0671/91 771, fax 91 062; ⑤). Two agencies offer accommodation in town: A. D. Travel (☎0671/93 142, fax 92 663; from ③) on the main road through town, and Perdikis Travel (☎0671/91 097, fax 92 503; from ③) on the quay. Among the tavernas, *Akrogiali* on the seafront draws admirers from all over the island. Nearby *Antonis* mixes traditional dishes with steaks and European food, while *Maria's* is a good basic family taverna.

Lixoúri's nearest beach is **Lípedha**, a 2km walk south. Like the **Xí** and **Mégas Lákkos** beaches (served by bus from Lixoúri and both with restaurants and accommodation), it has rich red sand and is backed by low cliffs. Those with transport can also strike out for the monastery at **Kipouréon**, and north to the spectacular beach at **Petáni**, where there are two sizable snack bars and signs of future development.

The west coast and the road north

The journey between Argostóli and Fiskárdho, by regular bus or hire vehicle, is the most spectacular ride in the archipelago. Leaving town, the road rises into the Evmorfía foothills and, beyond Agónas, clings to nearly sheer cliffs as it heads for Dhivaráta, the stop for **Mýrtos beach**. It's a four-kilometre hike down on foot (you can also drive down), with just one taverna on the beach, but from above or below, this is the most dramatic beach in the Ionian islands – a splendid strip of pure white sand and pebbles. Sadly, it's shadeless and gets mighty crowded in high season.

Six kilometres on is the turning for the atmospheric village of **ÁSSOS**, clinging to a small isthmus between the island and a huge hill crowned by a ruined fort. Accommodation is scarce – villagers invariably send you to Andhreas Rokos' rooms (☎0674/51 523; ②) on the approach road, which are great value, or you can opt for the posher *Kanakis Apartments* opposite (☎ & fax 0674/51 631; ⑥). Ássos has a small pebble beach, and three tavernas, notably the *Nefeli's Garden* and the *Platanos Grill*, on a plane-shaded village square backed by the shells of mansions ruined in the quake. It can get a little claustrophobic, but there's nowhere else like it in the Ionian islands.

Fiskárdho

FISKÁRDHO, on the northernmost tip of the island, sits on a bed of limestone that buffered it against the worst of the quakes. Two **lighthouses**, Venetian and Victorian, guard the bay, and the ruins on the headland are believed to be from a twelfth-century chapel begun by Norman invader Robert Guiscard, who gave the place his name. The nineteenth-century harbour frontage is intact, nowadays occupied by smart restaurants and chic boutiques.

The island's premier resort, Fiskárdho is very busy through to the end of October, with accommodation at a premium. None of it is cheap even when available but the best deal is at *Regina's* (☎0674/41 125; ③) at the back of the village, next to the car park. *Theodora's Café Bar* has rooms in whitewashed houses along the quay (☎0674/41 297 or 41 310; ④), and the Koria handicraft shop has rooms on the seafront (☎0674/41 270; ④). Another reasonable option is the small *Erissos* pension (☎0674/41 327; ④), just off the seafront. Further up the price range, *Fiskardhona* (☎0674/41 436; ⑤), opposite the post office, and *Philoxenia* (☎ & fax 0674/41 319; ⑤), next to *Erissos*, offer rooms in renovated traditional island homes in the village. There's a wealth of good restaurants: the *Tassia* has a vast range of seafood, and the *Captain's Table* serves succulent Greek and Kefallonian fare, while *Alexis* has a fine selection, including curries, at the most reasonable prices.. *Sirenes* is the favoured bar, although the seafront kafenío's mezédhes are the finest to be had anywhere. The dance spot is *Kastro Club* up at the back of the village. There are two good pebble beaches – **Émblisi** 1km back out of town and **Fókis** just to the south – and a nature trail on the northern headland. Daily **ferries** connect Fiskárdho to Itháki and Lefkádha in season.

Itháki

Rugged **Itháki**, Odysseus' legendary homeland, has had no substantial archeological discoveries but it fits Homer's description to perfection: "There are no tracks, nor grasslands . . . it is a rocky severe island, unsuited for horses, but not so wretched, despite its small size. It is good for goats." In Constantine Cavafy's splendid poem *Ithaca*, the island is symbolized as a journey to life:

> *When you set out on the voyage to Ithaca*
> *Pray that your journey may be long*
> *Full of adventures, full of knowledge.*

Despite the romance of its name, and its proximity to Corfu, very little tourist development has arrived to spoil the place. This is doubtless accounted for in part by a dearth of beaches, though the island is good walking country, with a handful of small fishing villages and various pebbly coves to swim from. In the north, apart from the ubiquitous drone of scooters, the most common sounds are sheep bells jangling and cocks (a symbol of Odysseus) crowing.

Its beaches are minor, mainly pebble with sandy seabeds, but relatively clean and safe; the real attractions are the interior and sites from the **Odyssey**. Some package travellers will find themselves flying into Kefalloniá and being bused to Fiskárdho (sit on the left for the bus ride of your life), for a short ferry crossing to **Fríkes** or the premier resort **Kióni**. Most visitors will arrive at **Vathý**, the capital.

Vathý

Ferries from Pátra, Kefalloniá, Astakós, Corfu and Italy land at the main port and capital of **VATHÝ** (Itháki Town), a bay within a bay so deep that few realize the mountains out "at sea" are actually the north of the island. This snug town is compact, relatively traffic-free and boasts the most idyllic seafront setting of all the Ionian capitals. Like its southerly neighbours, it was damaged by the 1953 earthquake, but some fine examples of pre-quake architecture remain here and in the northern port of **Kióni**. Vathý has a small **archeological museum** on Odhós Kallinikou (Tues–Sun

8am–2.30pm; 500dr) a short block back from the quay. There are banks, a post office, police and a medical centre in town.

Vathý has two basic but decent **hotels** which bookend the seafront: the *Odysseus* (☎0674/32 381; ④) is to the right of the ferry dock, the *Mentor* (☎0674/32 433, fax 32 293; ⑤) to its left. They have recently been usurped in comfort by the new *Captain Yiannis* (☎0674/33 173, fax 32 849; ⑤), further round the bay from the *Mentor*. Room owners meet ferries until the last knockings of the season, but you can also call ahead to Vassiliki Vlassopoulou (☎0674/32 119; ③), whose rooms are in pleasant gardens by the church above the quay. Also within easy access are those owned by Sotiris Maroulis at Odhós Odysséos 29, near the Perahóri road (☎0674/28 300; ③). Two of the town's travel agents, Polyctor Tours (☎0674/33 120, fax 33 130) and Delas Tours (☎0674/321 104, fax 33 031) on the quay have accommodation throughout the island.

Even though it's tiny, Vathý has a wealth of **tavernas** and **bars**. Many locals head off south around the bay towards *Gregory's*, popular for its lamb and fish, and the more traditional *Tziribis* and *Vlachos*. In town, *O Nikos* is an excellent restaurant in the side-streets that fills early, while *To Kohili* is the best of the half-dozen harbourside tavernas. The *Sirenes Ithaki Yacht Club* is upmarket with a nautical theme; the no-relation *Ithaki Yacht Club* on the front looks private but is actually a bar open to all. Otherwise, head for the town's ancient kafenío one street back from the front.

There are two reasonable pebble **beaches** within fifteen minutes' walk of Vathý: **Dhéxa**, over the hill above the ferry quay, which has a semi-official campsite, and tiny **Loútsa**, opposite it around the bay. Better beaches at **Sarakíniko** and **Skhinós** to the south are an hour's trek by rough track leaving the opposite side of the bay. In season, daily kaïkia ply between the quay and remote coves.

Odysseus sites

Three of the main **Odysseus** sites are just within walking distance of Vathý: the Arethoúsa Spring, the Cave of the Nymphs and ancient Alalkomenae, although the last is best approached by **bus** or **taxi** (no more than 4000dr round-trip).

The Arethóussa Spring

The walk to the **Arethóussa Spring** – allegedly the place where Eumaeus, Odysseus' faithful swineherd, brought his pigs to drink – is a three-hour round trip along a track signposted next to the seafront OTE. The unspoiled landscape and sea views are magnificent, but the walk crosses slippery inclines and might best be avoided if you're nervous of heights. The route is shadeless, so take a hat and plenty of water.

Near the top of the lane leading to the spring path, a signpost points up to what is said to have been the **Cave of Eumaeus**. The route to the spring continues for a few hundred metres, and then branches off onto a narrow footpath through gorse-covered steep cliffs. Parts of the final downhill track involve scrambling across rock fields (follow the splashes of green paint), and care should be taken around the small but vertiginous ravine that houses the **spring**. The spring is sited at the head of a small ravine below a crag known as **Korax** (the raven), which matches Homer's description of the meeting between Odysseus and Eumaeus. In summer it's just a dribble of water.

The spring is a dead end – the only way out is back the way you came. If weather and time allow, there is a small cove for swimming a short scramble down from the spring. If you're uneasy about the gradients involved, it's still worth continuing along the track that runs above it, which loops round and heads back into the village of **Perahóri** above Vathý, which has views as far as Lefkádha to the north. On the way, you'll pass **Paleóhora**, the ruined medieval capital abandoned centuries ago, but with vestiges of houses fortified against pirate attacks and some churches still with Byzantine frescoes.

The Cave of the Nymphs

The **Cave of the Nymphs** (Marmarospíli) is about 2.5km up a rough but navigable road signposted on the brow of the hill above Dhéxa beach. The cave is atmospheric, but it's underwhelming compared to the caverns of neighbouring Kefalloniá, and these days is illuminated by coloured lights. The claim that this is the *Odyssey*'s Cave of the Nymphs, where the returning Odysseus concealed the gifts given to him by King Alcinous, is enhanced by the proximity of Dhéxa beach, although there is some evidence that the "true" cave was just above the beach, and was unwittingly demolished during quarrying many years ago.

Alalkomenae and Pisaetós

Alalkomenae, Heinrich Schliemann's much-vaunted "Castle of Odysseus", is signposted on the Vathý–Pisaetós road, on the saddle between Dhéxa and Pisaetós, with views over both sides of the island. The actual site, however, some 300m uphill, is little more than foundations spread about in the gorse. Schliemann's excavations unearthed a Mycenaean burial chamber and domestic items such as vases, figurines and utensils (displayed in the archeological museum), but the ruins actually date from three centuries after Homer. In fact, the most likely contender for the site of Odysseus' castle is above the village of Stavrós (see below).

The road (though not buses) continues to the harbour of **Pisaetós**, about 2km below, with a large pebble beach that's good for swimming and popular with local rod-and-line fishermen. A couple of tavernas here largely serve the regular ferries from Sámi on Kefalloniá.

Northern Itháki

The main road out of Váthy continues across the isthmus and takes a spectacular route to the northern half of Itháki, serving the villages of **Léfki**, **Stavrós**, **Fríkes** and **Kióni**. There are only two daily **buses**, though the north of Itháki is excellent motorscooter country; the close proximity of the settlements, small coves and Homeric interest also make it good rambling country. Once a day a kaïki also visits the last two of those communities – a cheap and scenic ride used by locals and tourists alike to meet the main-line ferries in Vathý. As with the rest of Itháki there is only a limited amount of accommodation.

Stavrós and around

STAVRÓS, the second largest town on the island, discounting Perahóri, is a steep 2km above the nearest beach (Pólis Bay). It's a pleasant enough town nonetheless, with kafenía edging a small square that's dominated by a rather fierce statue of Odysseus. There is even a tiny **museum** (Tues–Sun 9.30am–2.30pm; free) off the road to Platrithiás, displaying local archeological finds. Stavrós's Homeric site is on the side of **Pelikáta Hill**, where remains of roads, walls and other structures have been suggested as the possible site of Odysseus' castle. Stavrós is useful as a base if both Fríkes and Kióni are full up, and is an obvious stopping-off point for exploring the northern hamlets and the road up to the medieval village of Anoyí (see below). Both Polyctor and Delas handle **accommodation** in Stavrós; the traditional *Petra* taverna (☎0674/31 596; ③) offers rooms, or there's the *Porto Thiaki* pension above the pizzeria. The oldest and best taverna is *Fatouros* and the *Margarita* zaharoplastío is a good place for a drink or to sample the local sweet *rovaní*.

A scenic mountain road leads 5km southeast from Stavrós to **ANOYÍ**, whose name translates roughly as "upper ground". Once the second most important settlement on the island, it is almost deserted today. The centre of the village is dominated by a free-standing Venetian campanile, built to serve the (usually locked) church of the **Panayía**, which comes alive for the annual *paniyíri* on August 14, the eve of the Virgin's Assumption; at other times enquire at the kafenío about access to the church, whose Byzantine frescoes have been heavily restored following centuries of earthquake damage. On the outskirts of the village are the foundations of a ruined **medieval prison**, and in the surrounding countryside are some extremely strange rock formations, the biggest being the eight-metre-high Iraklís (Hercules) rock, just east of the village. The **monastery of Katharón**, 3km further south along the road, has stunning views down over Vathý and the south of the island, and houses an icon of the *Panayía* discovered by peasants clearing scrubland in the area. Byron is said to have stayed here in 1823, during his final voyage to Messolóngi. The monastery celebrates its festival on 8 September with services, processions and music.

Two roads leave Stavrós heading north: one, to the right, heads 2km down to Fríkes, while the main road, to the left, loops below the hill village of **Exoyí**, and on to **Platrithiás**. Just off the start of the road up to Exoyí a signpost points about 1km along a rough track to the supposed **School of Homer**, where excavations still in progress have revealed extensive foundations, a well and ancient steps. The site is unfenced and well worth a detour for its views of **Afáles bay** as much as the remains. On the outskirts of Platrithiás a track leads down to Afáles, the largest bay on the entire island, with an unspoiled and little-visited pebble beach. The landscape around here, thickly forested in parts and dotted with vineyards, is excellent walking terrain.

Fríkes

At first sight, tiny **FRÍKES** doesn't appear to have much going for it. Wedged in a valley between two steep hills, it was only settled in the sixteenth century, and emigration in the nineteenth century almost emptied the place – as few as two hundred people live here today – but the protected harbour is a natural year-round port. Consequently, Fríkes stays open for tourism far later in the season than neighbouring Kióni, and has a better range of tavernas. There are no beaches in the village, but plenty of good, if small, pebble strands a short walk away towards Kióni. When the ferries and their cargoes have departed, Fríkes falls quiet and this is its real charm: a downbeat but cool place to lie low.

Fríkes' one **hotel** is the smart but pricey *Nostos* (☎0674/31 644, fax 31 716; ⑤). Kiki Travel (☎ & fax 0674/31 387; ③) has **rooms** and other accommodation, as do the adjacent souvenir shop (☎0674/31 735; ②) and *Ulysses* taverna (☎0674/31733; ④). Phoning ahead is advisable and in peak season chances are slim. Fríkes has a quartet of good seafront **tavernas**, the *Symposium*, the *Rementzo*, the *Penelope* and aforementioned *Ulysses* all being worth a try.

Kióni

KIÓNI sits at a dead end 5km southeast of Fríkes. On the same geological base as the northern tip of Kefalloniá, it avoided the very worst of the 1953 earthquakes, and so retains some fine examples of pre-twentieth-century architecture. It's an extremely pretty village, wrapped around a tiny harbour, and tourism here is dominated by British blue-chip travel companies and visiting yachts.

The bay has a small **beach**, 1km along its south side, a sand and pebble strand below a summer-only snack bar. Better pebble beaches can be found within walking distance towards Fríkes. While the best **accommodation** has been snaffled by the Brits, some local businesses have rooms and apartments to let, among them *Apostolis* (☎0674/31 072; ③), *Dellaportas* (☎0674/31 481, fax 31 090; ④) and *Kioni Vacations* (☎0674/31 668; ③). A quieter option, a short walk uphill on the main road in the hamlet of Ráhi, are the rooms and studios run by Captain Theofilos Karatzis and his family (☎0674/31 679; ③), which have panoramic views. Alternatively, seek out the very helpful Yiorgos Moraitis (☎0674/31 464, fax 31 702), whose boat rental company has access to accommodation in Kióni.

Kióni's **restaurants** are dotted around the picturesque harbour but compare unfavourably with those in Fríkes; the traditional *Avra* and the *Kioni* pizzeria are adequate, while the upmarket *Calypso* taverna has interesting dishes but is overpriced. Village facilities stretch to two well-stocked shops, a post office and a couple of bars and cafes.

Zákynthos (Zante)

Zákynthos, most southerly of the six core Ionian islands, currently teeters between underdevelopment and indiscriminate commercialization. Much of the island is still green and unspoiled, but the sheer intensity of business in some resorts is threatening to spill over into the quieter parts.

The island has three distinct zones: the barren, mountainous northwest; the fertile central plain; and the eastern and southern coasts which house the resorts. The big resort – rivalling the biggest on Corfu – is **Laganás**, on Laganás Bay in the south, a 24-hour party venue that doesn't give up from Easter until the last flight home in October. There are smaller, quieter resorts north and south of the capital, and the southerly Vassilikós peninsula has the best countryside and beaches, including exquisite **Yérakas**.

Although half-built apartment blocks are spreading through the central plain, this is where the quieter island begins: farms and vineyards, ancient villages and the ruins of Venetian buildings levelled in the 1948 and 1953 earthquakes. The island still produces fine wines, such as the white Popolaro, as well as sugar-shock-inducing *mandoláto* nougat, whose honey-sweetened form is best. Zákynthos is also the birthplace of *kantádhes*, the hybrid of Cretan folk song and Italian opera ballad that can be heard in tavernas in Zákynthos Town and elsewhere. It also harbours one of the key breeding sites of the endangered **loggerhead sea turtle** at Laganás Bay. The loggerhead (see box on p.444) is the subject of a continuing dispute between tourism businesses and environmentalists, which has caused an international political scandal and even provoked a bomb attack against the environmentalists.

Zákynthos Town

The town, like the island, is known as both **ZÁKYNTHOS** and Zante. This former "Venice of the East" (*Zante, Fior di Levante*, "Flower of the Levant", in an Italian jingle), rebuilt on the old plan, has bravely tried to recreate some of its style, though reinforced concrete can only do so much.

The town stretches beyond the length of the wide and busy harbour, its main section bookended by the grand **Platía Solomoú** at the north, and the church of **Áyios Dhionýsios**, patron saint of the island, at the south. The square is named after the island's most famous son, the poet Dhionysios Solomos, the father of modernism in Greek literature, who was responsible for establishing demotic Greek (as opposed to the elitist *katharévousa* form) as a literary idiom. He is also the author of the lyrics to the national anthem. There's an impressive **museum** devoted to the life and work of him and other Zakynthian luminaries in nearby Platía Ayíou Márkou (daily 9am–2pm; 800dr) which shares its collection with the museum on Corfu (see p.408), where Solomos spent most of his life. Another local man of letters, who had a museum dedicated to him by the town council in 1998, is novelist and playwright Grigorios Xenopoulos. His eponymous museum (Wed–Sun 9am–1pm; free), to be found in a small house tucked in Gaïta street not far from Áyios Dhionýsios church, displays a modest collection of manuscripts, books and photographs.

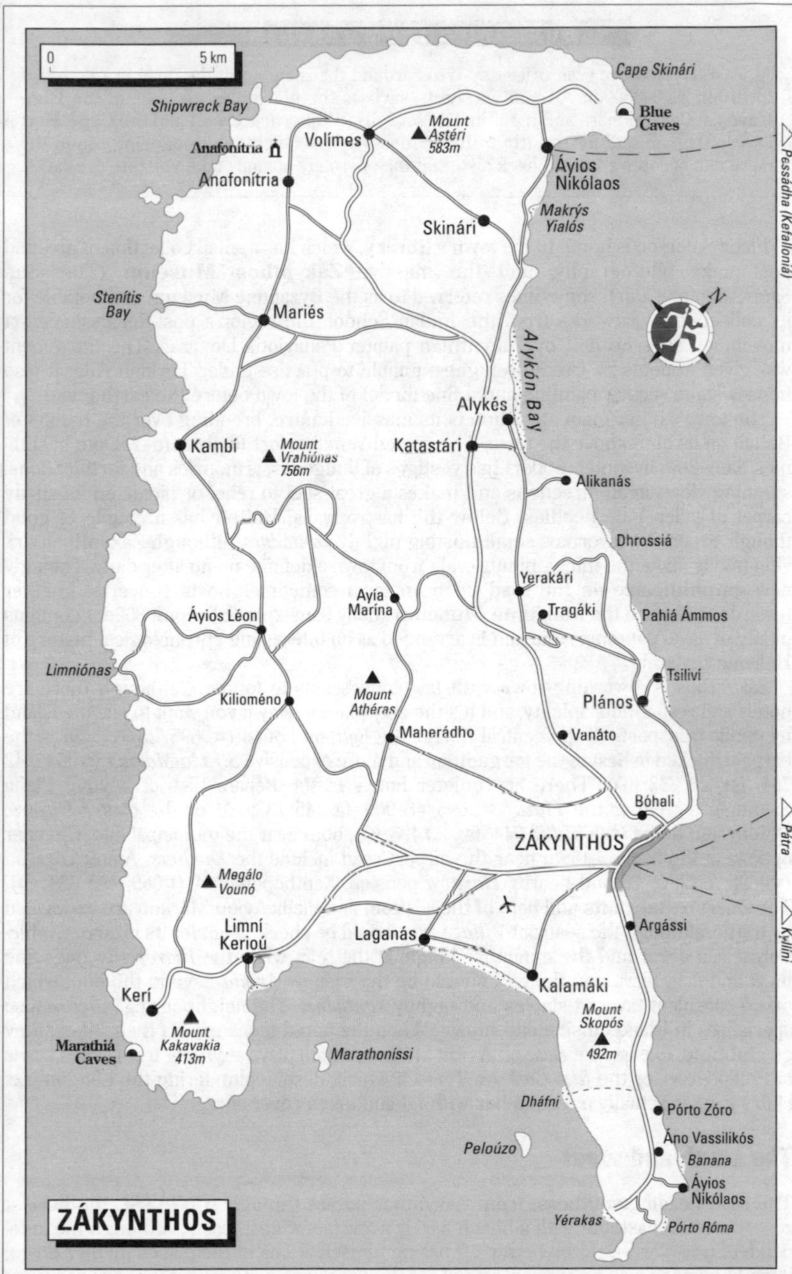
0
5 km
Cape Skinári
Blue Caves
Shipwreck Bay
Mount Astéri 583m
Volímes
Anafonítria
Anafonítria
Áyios Nikólaos
Pessádha (Kefalloniá)
Skinári
Makrýs Yialós
Stenítis Bay
Mariés
Alykón Bay
Alykés
Kambí
Mount Vrahiónas 756m
Katastári
Alikanás
Dhrossiá
Yerakári
Ayía Marína
Tragáki
Pahiá Ámmos
Áyios Léon
Limniónas
Tsiliví
Mount Athéras
Kilioméno
Plános
Maherádho
Vanáto
Bóhali
ZÁKYNTHOS
Pátra
Megálo Vounó
Kyllíni
Argássi
Limní Kerioú
Laganás
Kalamáki
Kerí
Mount Skopós 492m
Mount Kakavakia 413m
Marathiá Caves
Marathoníssi
Dháfni
Pórto Zóro
Áno Vassilikós
Peloúzo
Banana
Áyios Nikólaos
Yérakas
Pórto Róma
ZÁKYNTHOS

BOAT TRIPS FROM ZÁKYNTHOS

At least ten pleasure craft offer **day-trips** around the island from the quay in Zákynthos town for 2000–3500dr. All take in sights such as the blue-water grottoes of the **Blue Caves** at Cape Skinári, and moor in **Tó Navávio** (**Shipwreck Cove**) and the **Cape Kerí** caves. Shop around for the trip with the most stops, as eight hours bobbing round the coast can become a bore. Check also that the operators actually take you into the caves.

Platía Solomoú is home to the town's **library**, which has a small collection of pre- and post-quake photography, and the massive **Zákynthos Museum** (Tues–Sun 8am–2.30pm; 800dr), sometimes referred to as the Byzantine Museum and notable for its collection of artworks from the Ionian School, the region's post-Renaissance art movement, spearheaded by Zakynthian painter Panayiotis Doxaras. The movement was given impetus by Cretan refugees, unable to practise under Turkish rule. It also houses some secular painting and a fine model of the town before the earthquake.

The town's other main attraction is its massive **kástro**, brooding over the hamlet of Bóhali on its bluff above the town. The ruined Venetian fort (daily 8am–7.30pm in summer, 8am–2pm in winter; 500dr) has vestiges of dungeons, armouries and fortifications, stunning views in all directions and makes a great spot to relax or picnic on its shady carpet of fallen pine needles. Below the kástro walls, **Bóhali** has a couple of good though expensive tavernas, some hosting nightly *kantádhes*, although Zakynthian driving habits make the thirty-minute walk from town a definite no-no after dark. The ugly new **amphitheatre** on the road up from town sometimes hosts concerts. Further towards the kástro the **Maritime Museum** (daily 9am–2pm & 6–9pm; 800dr) contains plenty of naval paraphernalia and is arranged as an interesting chronological history of Hellenic seafaring.

Zákynthos is a working town with few concessions to tourism, although there are hotels and restaurants aplenty, and it's the only place to stay if you want to see the island by public transport. Of the central hotels, the *Egli*, on Loútzi (☎0695/28 317; ③) is the bargain, tucked in beside the gargantuan and more expensive *Strada Marina* (☎0695/42 761, fax 28 733; ⑤). There are quieter hotels in the Répara district beyond Platía Solomoú: try either the *Plaza* (☎0695/48 909, fax 45 733; ④) or the classy *Bitzaro*, Dhionysíou Róma (☎0695/23 644, fax 23 493; ⑥), both near the municipal lido. Cheaper options at the back of town near the airport road include the *Diethnes*, Ayíou Lazárou (☎0695/22 286; ③) and nearby *Haravyi* pension, Xanthopoúlou 4 (☎0695/23 629; ③). The smart **restaurants** and bars of the seafront and Platía Ayíou Márkou are bedevilled by traffic, although the seafront *Village Inn* should be checked out for its bizarre Gothic-Polynesian decor and the miniature jungle at the rear, while the *Psaropoula* does fine meat and fish. First stop though, should be the friendly *Arekia* beyond the lido, which offers succulent taverna staples and nightly *kantádhes*. The neighbouring *Alivizos* also specializes in island cuisine and music. When the bored teens get off their bikes, they go **clubbing**, to bars like *Base* on Ayíou Márkou, which plays anything from Miles Davis to Philip Glass, or the *Jazz Café*, on Tertséti which, despite plundering the London jazz club's logo, is actually a techno bar with DJ and token cover charge.

The south and west

The road heading southeast from Zákynthos passes through **ARGÁSSI**, the busiest resort on this coast, but with a beach barely a few feet wide in parts. Although the independent traveller would be better off basing himself at one of the places further down, it could be used as a jumping-off point for the Vassilikós peninsula; there are rooms at the *Pension Vaso* (☎0695/44 599; ③) and *Andro* (☎0695/22 190; ③) on the main road in the centre of the village, and the seafront boasts some smart hotels, among them the *Locanda* (☎0695/45 386; ⑤) and the *Iliessa Beach* (☎0695/45 345; ⑥). Beyond a few indigenous tavernas – try *Three Brothers* or *The Big Plate* restaurant – culture here is summed up, surreally, by an English caff that advertises a "Greek night" every Saturday. Argási is also home to some of the island's biggest and most popular discos such as *Vivlos* and *Barrage*.

The Vassilikós Peninsula

The peninsula that stretches southeast of Argássi is one of the most attractive parts of the island, with a happy blend of development and natural beauty. Various maps vaguely identify different inland spots as **Vassilikós** villages but the real interest lies in the series of small beach resorts, mainly situated on the east coast. The first two are newly-developed **Kamínia**, with the good-value *Levantino* rooms (☎0695/35 366; ③), and the more established at **Pórto Zóro**, which has a canteen and the eponymous *Porto Zoro* hotel (☎0695/35 304; ④). The only real facilities away from the coast are to be found at the sprawling village of **Áno Vassilikós**, which serves the nearby beaches of **Iónio** and **Banana**. Among accommodation possibilities on the main road are the *Vassilikos Apartments* (☎0695/35 280; ④) and *Villa Maria* (☎0695/35 316; ③). Among the **tavernas**, *O Adherfos tou Kosta* is well worth a try, as is the *Logos Rock Club*. Isolated **Áyios Nikólaos** lures day-trippers from Argási, Kalamáki and Laganás with **a free bus** service in season; its expanding *Vasilikos Beach* (☎0695/24 114; ⑤) complex has a good beach, with a fast-emerging hamlet and some rooms in the moon-like landscape behind it.

The island's star is **Yérakas**, a sublime crescent of golden sand at the very tip of the peninsula, which is also a key loggerhead turtle breeding ground, and which is therefore off-limits between dusk and dawn. There's little here beyond two tavernas back from the beach and some pleasant, if remote, cabin accommodation at *Liuba Apartments* (☎0695/35 372; ④). The beach does draw crowds, but the 6am bus out of Zákynthos Town should secure you a few hours of Yérakas to yourself. Compared with Yérakas, **Pórto Róma**, back on the east coast, is a disappointment, a small sand and pebble bay with a taverna and bar, some rooms on the approach road and occasional hardy campers, although there is a more genuinely Greek flavour to it. Beaches on the west coast, like **Dháfni**, require your own transport and have few facilities, but are worth a visit, especially in the quieter months.

Laganás and Kalamáki

The majority of the 400,000 people or so who visit Zákynthos each year find themselves in **LAGANÁS**. The nine-kilometre beach in the bay is good, if trampled, and there are entertainments from watersports to ballooning, and even an occasional funfair. Beachfront bars and restaurants stretch for over a kilometre; the bars and restaurants on the main drag another kilometre inland. Some stay open around the clock; others just play music at deafening volume until dawn. The competing video and music bars can make Laganás at night resemble the set of *Bladerunner*, but that's how its predominantly English visitors like it. If this is your bag, there's no place better; if it isn't, flee. **Accommodation** is mostly block-booked by package companies. There's a basic campsite on the southern edge of town, where there are also quietish private rooms, or you can contact the Union of Room Owners, who have an office on the main drag (daily 8.30am–2pm & 5–8pm; ☎0695/51 590). As for hotels, try the *Byzantio* (☎0695/51 136; ③), near the crossroads, *Pension Toula* (☎0695/51 560; ④), between the beach and the campsite, or *Ionis* (☎0695/51 141, fax 51 601; ⑤), on the main drag towards the beach. *Nefeli* and *Zougras* are among the more authentic **tavernas**, the former hosting nightly *kantádhes*, and respectable Chinese/Indian food can be had at *Bee Garden* or *Taj Mahal*.

LOGGERHEAD TURTLES

The Ionian islands harbour the Mediterranean's main concentration of **loggerhead sea turtles** (*Caretta caretta*). These creatures, which lay their eggs at night on sandy coves, are under direct threat from the tourist industry in Greece. Each year, many turtles are injured by motorboats, their nests are destroyed by bikes ridden on the beaches, and the newly hatched young die entangled in deckchairs and umbrellas left out at night on the sand. The turtles are easily frightened by noise and lights, too, which makes them uneasy cohabitants with freelance campers and late-night discos.

The Greek government has passed laws designed to protect the loggerheads, including restrictions on camping at some beaches, but local economic interests tend to prefer a beach full of bodies to a sea full of turtles.

On Laganás, nesting grounds are concentrated around the fourteen-kilometre bay, but Greek marine zoologists striving to protect and study the turtles are in angry dispute with locals and the burgeoning tourist industry. Other important locations include the turtles' nesting ground just west of Skála on Kefalloniá, although numbers have dwindled to half their former strength in recent years, and now only about 800 remain. Ultimately, the turtles' main hope of survival may rest in their being appreciated as a unique tourist attraction in their own right.

While capitalists and environmentalists are still at, well, loggerheads, the **World Wildlife Fund** has issued guidelines for visitors:

1. Don't use the beaches of Laganás and Yérakas between sunset and sunrise.
2. Don't stick umbrellas in the sand in the marked nesting zones.
3. Take your rubbish away with you – it can obstruct the turtles.
4. Don't use lights near the beach at night – they can disturb the turtles, sometimes with fatal consequences.
5. Don't take any vehicle onto the protected beaches.
6. Don't dig up turtle nests – it's illegal.
7. Don't pick up the hatchlings or carry them to the water, as it's vital to their development that they reach the sea on their own.
8. Don't use speedboats in Laganás Bay – a 9kph speed limit is in force for vessels in the bay.

Neighbouring **KALAMÁKI** has a better beach than Laganás, and is altogether quieter, although both resorts suffer from airport noise. There are a number of good hotels, notably the *Crystal Beach* (☎0695/42 788, fax 42 917; ⑥), and the friendly Zakyta travel agency (☎0695/27 080) can also arrange accommodation. The two *Stanis* tavernas have extensive menus of Greek and international dishes, although the beachside version is geared more to lunches and its sibling more to evening meals. Alternatives include *Afrodite* and *Merlis*. **Nightlife** centres around bars like *Al'Sandros*, and the *Vios Club* on the hillside above the village, which has a garden with breathtaking views.

Kerí

The village of **KERÍ** is hidden in a fold above the cliffs at the island's southernmost tip. The village retains a number of pre-quake, Venetian buildings, including the church of the **Panayía Kerioú**; the Virgin is said to have saved the island from marauding pirates by hiding it in a sea mist. Kerí is also famous for a geological quirk, a series of small tar pools mentioned by both Pliny and Herodotus, but these have mysteriously dried up in recent years. A rough path leaving the southern end of the village leads 1km on to the lighthouse, with spectacular views of the sea, rock arches and stacks. The beach next to **Límni Kerioú** at the southern end of Laganás bay is fast growing into a good alternative resort and is home to the *Turtle Beach Diving Centre* (☎0695/48 768).

Maherádho, Kilioméno and Kambí

The bus system does not reach the wild western side of the island, but a hire car or sturdy motorbike will get you there. **MAHERÁDHO** boasts impressive pre-earthquake architecture set in beautiful arable uplands, surrounded by olive and fruit groves. The church of **Ayía Mávra** has an impressive free-standing campanile, and inside a splendid carved iconostasis and icons by Zakynthian painter Nikolaos Latsis. The town's major festival – one of the biggest on the island – is the saint's day, which falls on the first Sunday in June. The other notable church in town, that of the Panayía, commands breathtaking views over the central plain.

KILIOMÉNO is the best place to see surviving pre-earthquake domestic architecture, in the form of the island's traditional two-storey houses. The town was originally named after its church **Áyios Nikólaos**, whose impressive campanile, begun over a hundred years ago, still lacks a capped roof. The road from Kilioméno passes through the nondescript village of Áyios Léon, from where two turnings lead through fertile land and down a newly-paved loop road to the impressive rocky coast at **Limniónas**, where there is a tiny bay and a taverna.

Further along the main road another turning leads to the tiny clifftop hamlet of **KAMBÍ**, destination for numerous coach trips to catch the sunset over the sea.. Its clifftop **tavernas** have extraordinary views over the 300-metre-high cliffs and western horizon. On an incline above the village there's an imposing concrete cross, constructed in memory of islanders killed here during the 1940s, either by nationalist soldiers or Nazis. The tiny village of **Mariés**, 5km to the north and set in a wooded green valley, has the only other coastal access on this side of Zákynthos, a seven-kilometre track leading down to the rocky inlet of **Stenítis Bay,** where there's a taverna and yacht dock, and another road to the uninspiring **Vrómi Bay**, from where speedboats run trips to Shipwreck Beach (see below).

The north

North and west from Zákynthos Town, the roads thread their way through luxuriantly fertile farmland, punctuated with tumulus-like hills. **Tsilivi**, 5km north of the capital, is the first beach resort here, which has now effectively merged with the hamlet of **PLÁNOS**. Unfortunately, this part of the coastline suffers from occasional oil pollution, with nothing but the winter storms to clear it. There's a good, basic **campsite**, *Zante Camping* (☎0695/61 710), beyond Plános, and some rooms – try *Gregory's* (☎0695/61 853; ③), *Dolphin* (☎0695/27 425; ④) or contact *Tsilivi Travel* (☎0695/44 194, fax 22 655)– but most visitors here are on package deals. *The Olive Tree* taverna is the best of a tourist-orientated bunch.

The beaches further along this stretch of coast become progressively quieter and more pleasant and they all have at least a smattering of accommodation and restaurants to choose from. Good choices include **Pahiá Ámmos**, with the *Pension Petra* (☎0695/62 410; ③) and *Porto Roulis* fish taverna, and **Dhrossiá**, where you can find the *Avouris* (☎0695/61 716; ③) and *Drosia* (☎0695/62 256; ④) apartments and eat at another fish taverna, *Andreas*.

Alykés and its bay

Ormós Alykón, 12km north of Tsiliví, is a large sandy bay with lively surf and two of the area's largest resorts. **ALIKANÁS** is a small but expanding village, much of its accommodation being overseas villa rentals and **ALYKÉS**, named after the spooky salt pans behind the village, has the best beach north of the capital. There are **rooms** on the beach (try the *Golden Dolphin* taverna), and a number of **hotels** set back from it, but with sea views – try the *Ionian Star* (☎0695/83 416, fax 83 173; ④) or the

Montreal (☎0695/83 241; ⑤), although the best deal is further back at the *Picadilly* (☎0695/83 606; ②). There are many eating joints, among the best the *Anatolikos* and *Fantasia* tavernas. Alykés is the last true resort on this coast, and the one where the bus service gives out. **Koróni**, 4km north, has sulphur springs flowing into the sea – follow the smell – which provide the odd sensation of swimming in a mix of cool and warm water. The next small beach of **Makrýs Yialós**, which has a good taverna, makeshift campsite and a diving school, makes for an extremely pleasant break on a tour of the north.

Áyios Nikólaos, 6km on, is a small working port serving daily ferries to and from Pessádha on Kefalloniá. From here another good trip is a ride by **kaïki** (1000dr) to the extreme northern tip of the island, where the **Blue Caves** are some of the more realistically named of the many contenders in Greece. They're terrific for snorkelling, and when you go for a dip here your skin will appear bright blue. The road snakes onwards through a landscape of gorse bushes and dry-stone walls until it ends at the lighthouse of **Cape Skinári**. With only a taverna and a cafeteria, and a view of the mountainous expanse of Kefalloniá, it's a good spot for unofficial camping, or you could stay in the unique setting of the converted windmill rented out by *To Faros* taverna (☎0695/31 132; ④).

Volímes, Katastári and Ayía Marína

The northern towns and villages are accessible only to those with cars or sturdy motorbikes, and although there are guided coach tours from the resorts, none is really geared to tourism. **VOLÍMES** is the centre of the island's embroidery industry – with your own transport, you could make it to the **Anafonítria monastery**, 3km south, thought to have been the cell of the island's patron saint, Dhionysios, whose festivals are celebrated on August 24 and December 17. A newly paved road leads on to the cliffs overlooking **Shipwreck Bay** (Tó Naváyio), with hair-raising views down to the shipwreck below and a fine taverna to recover your composure in. Two kilometres inland from Alykés, **KATASTÁRI** is the largest settlement after the capital. Although it's unprepared for tourism, it's the place to see Zákynthian life as it's lived away from the tourism racket. Its most impressive edifice is the huge rectangular church of Iperáyia Theotókos, with a twin belfry and small new amphitheatre for festival performances.

AYÍA MARÍNA, a few kilometres south of Katastári, has a church using an impressive Baroque altar screen, and a belfry that's being rebuilt from the remnants left after the 1953 earthquake. As in most Zákynthos churches, the bell-tower is detached, in Venetian fashion. Just above Ayía Marína is the *Parthenonas* taverna, rightly boasting one of the best views on the island. From here you can see the whole of the central plain from beyond Alykés in the north to Laganás Bay in the south.

Kýthira island

Isolated at the foot of the Peloponnese, the island of **Kýthira** traditionally belongs to the Ionian islands, and shares their history of Venetian, and later, British rule; under the former it was known as Cerigo. Administratively part of Pireás – like the Argo-Saronic islands – it is listed, confusingly, in the main Peloponnese phone directory under the village of Skála in Lakonía. For the most part, similarities end there. The island architecture, whitewashed and flat-roofed, looks more like that of the Cyclades, albeit with a strong **Venetian** influence. The landscape is different, too: wild scrub- and gorse-covered hills, or moorland sliced by deep valleys and ravines.

Depopulation has left the land underfarmed and the abandoned fields overgrown, for, since the war, most of the islanders have left for Athens or Australia, giving Kýthira a reputation of being the classic emigrant island; it is known locally as "Australian Colony" or "Kangaroo Island", and Australia is referred to as "Big Kýthira". Many of the villages are deserted, their platías empty and the schools and kafenía closed. Kýthira was never a rich island, but, along with Monemvasiá, it did once have a military and economic significance – which it likewise lost with Greek independence and the opening of the Corinth Canal. These days, tourism has brought a little prosperity (and a few luxury hotels), but most summer visitors are Greeks and especially Greek Australians. For the few foreigners who reach Kýthira, it remains something of a refuge, with its fine and remarkably undeveloped **beaches** the principal attraction. However, in 1998 a popular Greek television serial filmed on the island attracted a huge amount of domestic attention and, consequently, holidaymakers from the mainland. Much of the accommodation is now fully booked well in advance for the entire Greek school-summer-holiday period.

Arrival and getting around

Arrival on the island has changed in recent years. In 1997 a huge new all-weather **harbour** was opened at Dhiakófti, and now all hydrofoils and all ferries are docking here instead of Ayía Pelayía or Kapsáli. The airport is deep in the interior, 8km south of Potamós; taxis meet arrivals, as they do the boats. Sadly, there is no other **public transport** at the moment; although a bus has been purchased, the owner is still awaiting a permit to carry passengers. Until it is running the only alternative to pricey taxis is to hitch or, more advisedly, hire a **car** or **moped**. The roads are now well surfaced all over the island and there are reliable petrol stations at Potamós, Kondoliánika and Livádhi.

Dhiakófti

Dhiakófti, until recently an unsung and relatively inaccessible backwater towards the bottom of the northeast coast, has been catapulted into the forefront of activity by the opening of the harbour, constructed by joining the islet of Makrónisi to the shore by a causeway. There is also a nice white sandy beach, and although no major expansion has taken place yet, it seems inevitable that the developers will not be long in seizing their opportunity. For the time being there are just a couple of tavernas, including the friendly *Notaras* by the causeway, a good kafenío and a few rooms and apartments such as the *Porto Diakofti* (☎0735/33 041; ⑤–⑥; April–Oct). Transport is the main problem but there may be a branch of Panayiotis car rental soon. If there isn't, you can arrange to be brought by car by phoning their Kapsáli office, or that of Porfyra in Livádhi.

Ayía Pelayía and northern Kýthira

There's a reasonable choice of **tavernas** and **rooms** in Ayía Pelayía; the *Faros Taverna* (☎0735/33 282; ③) offers both, from its waterfront location. Best value of the upmarket hotels is *Venardos* (☎0735/34 205, fax 33 850; ⑤), which is open all year and can offer very good deals off season. The clean and comfortable *Hotel Kytherea* (☎0735/33 321; ③–④) is more luxurious, as are the more recent *Filoxenia Apartments* (☎0735/33 100, fax 33 610; ⑥; April–Oct), with striking blue shutters and an imaginative layout around small courtyards. Ferry and hydrofoil **tickets** are available from Conomos Travel (☎0735/33 490, fax 33 890), inside the tourist shop on the ground floor of the *Kytherea*. The *Paleo* ouzerí is recommended.

Potamós and around

From Ayía Pelayía, the main road winds up the mountainside towards **POTAMÓS**, Kýthira's largest village – a pleasant and unspoiled place which, if you have a rented vehicle, makes a good base for exploring the island. It has a few **rooms**, such as those at the *Pension Porfyra* (☎0735/33 329; ④) which have a fridge and TV, and *Alevizopoulos*

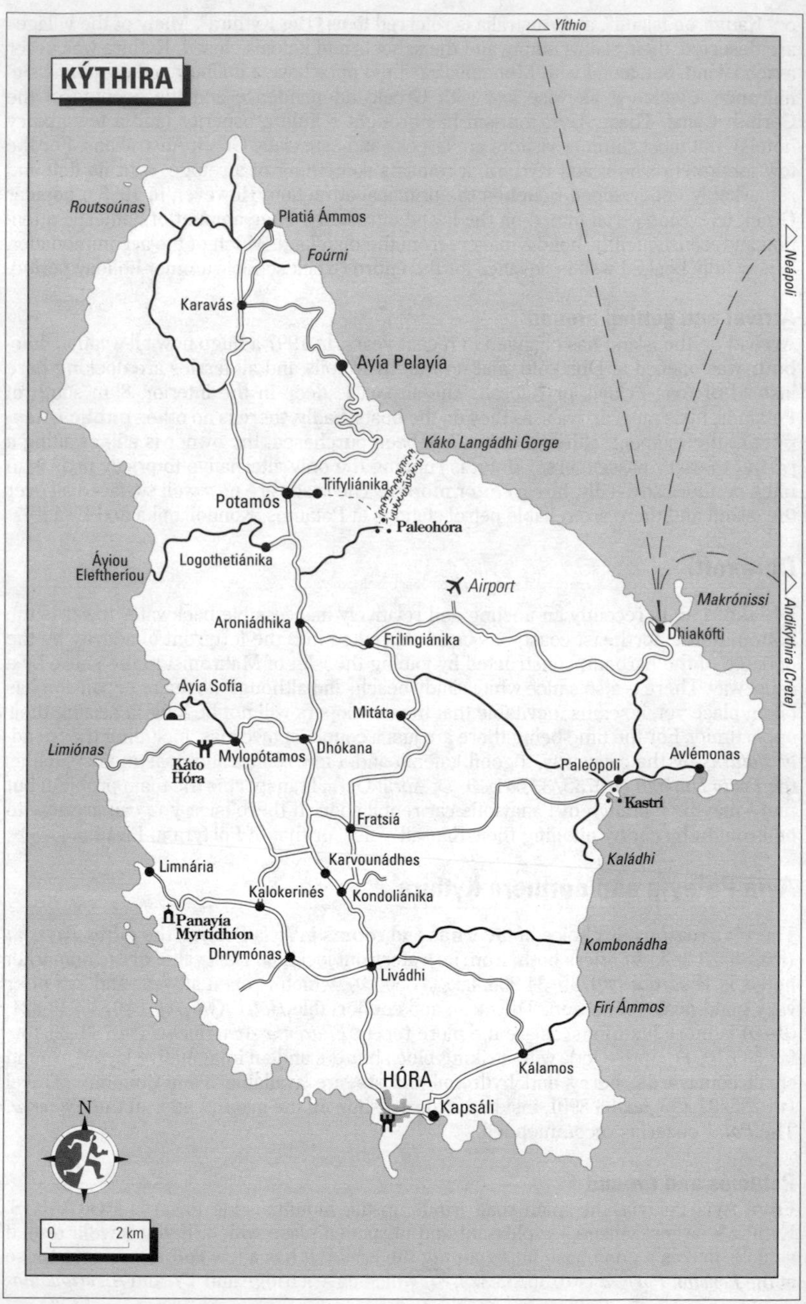
KÝTHIRA
Yíthio
Neápoli
Andikýthira (Crete)
Routsoúnas
Platiá Ámmos
Foúrni
Karavás
Ayía Pelayía
Káko Langádhi Gorge
Trifyliánika
Potamós
Paleohóra
Áyiou Eleftheríou
Logothetiánika
Airport
Makrónissi
Dhiakófti
Aroniádhika
Frilingiánika
Ayía Sofía
Mitáta
Limiónas
Káto Hóra
Mylopótamos
Dhókana
Paleópoli
Avlémonas
Kastrí
Fratsiá
Kaládhi
Limnária
Karvounádhes
Kalokerinés
Kondoliánika
Panayía Myrtidhíon
Kombonádha
Dhrymónas
Livádhi
Firí Ámmos
Kálamos
HÓRA
Kapsáli
N
0
2 km

(☎0735/33 245; ③), together with **tavernas**, a **bank**, a **post office**, Olympic Airways office (☎0735/33 688) and two petrol stations. Most of the shops on the island are here, too, as is the **Sunday market**, Kýthira's liveliest regular event.

From **Logothetiánika**, just south of Potamós, an unpaved road leads down to Ayíos Eleftheríos, where you can **swim** from the rocks on the west coast, backed by high cliffs. At Logothetiánika itself, there is a popular taverna, *Karydhies* (☎0735/33 664) with live music Thursday–Saturday, when booking is advisable.

Paleohóra

The main reason for visiting Potamós is to get to **PALEOHÓRA**, the ruined **medieval capital** of Kýthira, 3km to the east of the town. Few people seem to know about or visit these remains, though they constitute one of the best Byzantine sites around. The most obvious comparison is with Mystra: although Paleohóra is much smaller, a fortified village rather than a town, its natural setting is equally spectacular. Set on a hilltop at the head of the **Káko Langádhi gorge**, it is surrounded by a sheer 100m drop on three sides.

The site is lower than the surrounding hills and invisible from the sea and most of the island, something which served to protect it from the pirates that have plagued Paleohóra through much of its history. The town was built in the thirteenth century by Byzantine nobles from Monemvasiá, and when Mystra fell to the Turks, many of its noble families also sought refuge here. Despite its seemingly impregnable and perfectly concealed position, the site was discovered and sacked by **Barbarossa**, commander of the Turkish fleet, in 1537, and the island's seven thousand inhabitants were sold into slavery.

The town was never rebuilt, and tradition maintains that it is a place of ill fortune, which perhaps explains the emptiness of the surrounding countryside, none of which is farmed today. The hills are dotted with Byzantine **chapels**, which suggests that, in its heyday, the area must have been the centre of medieval Kýthira; it is rumoured to have once had eight hundred inhabitants and 72 churches. Now the principal remains are of the surviving churches, some still with traces of frescoes (and kept firmly locked), and the castle. The site is unenclosed and has never been seriously investigated, although excavations are now planned.

If you have your own transport, there's a rough dirt road to Paleohóra, signposted off the main road from Potamós to Aroniádhika. By foot, it's quicker and more interesting to take the path from the tiny village of Trifyliánika, just outside Potamós – look out for a rusting sign to the right as you enter the village. The path is overgrown in parts and not easy to follow; the ruins only become visible when you join the road above the gorge.

Karavás

KARAVÁS, 6km north of Potamós, is untypical of the island's villages – its architecture and the setting, in a deep wooded valley with a stream, are more reminiscent of the other Ionian islands. One of Kýthira's most pleasant villages, it would be a superb base, though there is (as yet) nowhere to stay. There is, however, a restaurant *Amir Ali*, with frequent live music.

Platiá Ámmos, at the end of the valley, is a sandy beach with a seasonal fish **taverna**. There is also an ouzerí and café and a few rooms at *Moudheas* restaurant (☎0735/33 960; ④). The little pebble beach at **Foúrni**, 2km south, is quieter and more attractive.

Kapsáli

KAPSÁLI, in addition to its harbour function, is the one place on Kýthira largely devoted to tourism. Most foreign visitors to Kýthira stay here, and it's a popular port of call for yachts heading from the Aegean to the Ionian islands and Italy. Set behind double pebble-sand bays, it is certainly picturesque. The larger of its two bays has a line of **tav-**

ernas; *To Venetsianiko*, half way along the front, has good food at reasonable prices, but the best is *Hydragogio* at the Hóra end of the beach which serves up good veggie options. For nightlife the liveliest place is *Shaker*, playing the standard mix of Greek and foreign hits.

The best **accommodation** is in high demand and expensive. Top of the tree is the *Porto Delfino* (☎0735/31 940; ⑤–⑥; April–Oct); a few hundred metres above the bay are *Kalokerines Katikies* (☎ & fax 0735/31 265; ⑥; May–Oct) and *Hotel Raïkos* (☎0735/31 629, fax 31 801; ⑤; May–Sept). The *Aphrodite Apartments* (☎0735/31 328; ⑤–⑥) have slightly more reasonable rates, as do *Megaloudis* rooms (☎0735/31 340; ④). A fairly basic **campsite** (June–Sept) nestles in the pine trees behind the village.

There's a mobile **post office** in summer, and a couple of travel agents near the harbour: Kytheros International (☎0735/31 925) arranges travel, accommodation and vehicle rental, while Roma Travel (☎0735/31 561) deals with accommodation only. Panayiotis (☎0735/31 600) and Nikos (☎0735/31 5700) both rent **cars**, **motorbikes** and **mopeds**. As well as watersports facilities the former has a friendly reliable service; you can call off season (☎0735/31 551) and get wheels when most places are closed.

Hóra

HÓRA (or Kýthira town), a steep 2km haul above Kapsáli, has an equally dramatic site, its Cycladic-style houses tiered about the walls of a Venetian castle. Within the **castle**, most of the buildings are ruined, but there are spectacular views of Kapsáli and, out to sea, to the islet of Avgó (Egg), legendary birthplace of Aphrodite. Below the castle are the remains of older Byzantine walls, and 21 Byzantine churches in various states of dereliction. A small **museum** (Tues–Sun 8.30am–2.30pm) houses modest remnants of the island's numerous occupiers, in particular Minoan finds from excavations at Paleópoli and an archaic stone lion.

Compared with Kapsáli, Hóra stays quiet and many places are closed out of season. A few **tavernas** open in summer, of which *Zorba* is by far the best, but the climb from Kapsáli discourages the crowds. Out of season, only one café/fast-food place stays open, near the square. **Accommodation** is slightly easier to find than in Kapsáli. The homeliest and best deal is the pension run by Yiorgos Pissis (☎0735/31 070; ②) with shared facilities including kitchen and some balcony views. Other options are the *Castello Studios* (☎0735/31 068; ④) and the old-style *Hotel Margarita* (☎0735/31 711; ⑤–⑥) with air-conditioning and TV in the rooms. At **MANITOHÓRI**, 2km further inland, are the *Hotel Keiti* (☎0735/31 318; ③; April–Oct) and the *Pension Kythera* (☎0735/31 563; ②–③; May–Sept). Other facilities include a couple of **banks**, **post office**, and branches of Panayiotis (☎0735/31 004) and Nikos (☎0735/31 767) vehicle rental. The only real bar is *Mercato*, which stays open in the winter and also has exhibitions of local art.

The southeast coast

The beach at Kapsáli is decent but gets very crowded in July and August. For quieter, undeveloped beaches, it's better to head out to the east coast, towards Avlémonas.

Firí Ámmos and Kombonádha

Firí Ámmos, the nearest good sand beach to Kapsáli, is popular but not overcrowded, even in summer. To get there, you can follow a paved road as far as the sleepy village of Kálamos (take the northerly side road between Kapsáli and Hóra); the beach is signposted down a dirt track on the far side of the village. Firí Ámmos can also be reached from the inland village of Livádhi, on the Hóra–Aroniádhika road – as can **Kombonádha**, the next beach north. There are summer canteens at both beaches, and the *Filio* taverna in Kálamos has good traditional food.

Paleópoli and Avlémonas

PALEÓPOLI, a hamlet of a few scattered houses, is accessible by a paved road from Aroniádhika. The area is the site of the ancient city of **Skandia**, and excavations on the headland of **Kastrí** have revealed remains of an important Minoan colony. There's little visible evidence, apart from shards of pottery in the low crumbling cliffs, but happily, tourist development in the area has been barred because of its archeological significance. Consequently, there's just one solitary **taverna**, the *Skandia* (June–Oct), on the excellent two-kilometre sand-and-pebble **beach** that stretches to either side of the headland. This place has recently been taken over by seven hippyish Anglo-Greek siblings and has great atmosphere with home cooking and frequent musical evenings.

The surrounding countryside, a broad, cultivated valley surrounded by wild hills, is equally attractive. **Paleokástro**, the mountain to the west, is the site of ancient Kýthira and a sanctuary of Aphrodite, but again, there's little to be seen today. Heading across the valley and turning right, an unpaved road leads up to a tiny, whitewashed church above the cliffs. From there, a track leads down to **Kaládhi**, a beautiful pebble beach with caves and rocks jutting out to sea.

AVLÉMONAS, 2km east of Paleópoli, is a tiny fishing port with two tavernas, of which *Sotiris* is recommended for fish, plus a few rooms including the large *Sklavos* apartments (☎0735/33 066; ⑤) and those run by Petrohilos (☎0735/33 034; ④) and his sister Mandy (☎0735/33 039; ④). There is a rather small, unimpressive Venetian fortress, the coast is rocky, the scenery bleak and exposed, and the village has something of an end-of-the-world feel.

North and west of Hóra

LIVÁDHI, 4km north of Hóra, has **rooms** and, on the main road, the newish *Hotel Aposperides* (☎0735/31656, fax 31 688; ⑤) which, together with the adequate *Toxotis* restaurant opposite, would make a good base if you had transport. Livádhi is also home to the most efficient travel agency on the island, Porfyra Travel, which is the main ANEK and Olympic agent (☎0735/31 888, fax 31888; *porfyra@kythira.com*), with exchange and car rental; they can arrange accommodation or transfers, plus group or individual hiking tours of the island. At **Katoúni** (2km out), there is an incongruous arched bridge, a legacy of the nineteenth century when all the Ionian islands were a British protectorate; it was built by a Scottish engineer. From the village, a fork heads west to Kalokerinés, and continues 3km further to the island's principal monastery, **Panayía Myrtidhíon**, set among cypress trees above the wild and windswept west coast. Beyond the monastery, a track leads down to a small anchorage at Limnária; there are few beaches along this rocky, forbidding shore. At **Káto Livádhi**, a kilometre to the east of Livádhi, there is an excellent museum of Byzantine and post-Byzantine art (Tues–Sun 8.30am–2.30pm; free) next to the large central church. It contains frescoes, painstakingly removed from island churches, dating from the sixth to the eighteenth centuries, a seventh-century mosaic floor and some portable icons. Not far away there is also a co-operative pottery workshop (open all day except 2–4pm) and, near an old bridge built by the English, a popular taverna called *Eleni*.

Mylopótamos, Káto Hóra and the Ayía Sofía cave

North of Livádhi, the main road crosses a bleak plateau whose few settlements are nearly deserted. At Dhókana it's worth making a detour off the main road for

MYLOPÓTAMOS, a lovely traditional village and an oasis in summer, set in a wooded valley occupied by a small stream. The shady *Platanos* kafenío makes a pleasant stop for a drink. *To Kamari*, in an old restored building serves snacks and drinks on a waterside terrace. Follow the sign for "Neraidha" to find a waterfall, hidden from view by lush vegetation. The valley below the falls is overgrown but contains the remains of the watermill that gave the village its name.

Káto Hóra, 500m down the road, was Mylopótamos's predecessor. Now derelict, it remains half-enclosed within the walls of a Venetian fortress. The fortress is small and has a rather domestic appearance: unlike the castle at Hóra, it was built as a place of refuge for the villagers in case of attack, rather than as a base for a Venetian garrison. All the houses within the walls, and many outside, are abandoned. Beyond here, a paved but precipitous road continues 5km through spectacular cliff-scapes to **Limiónas**, a rocky bay with a small beach of fine white sand.

The reason most visitors come to Mylopótamos is to see the **cave of Ayía Sofía**, the largest and most impressive of a number of caverns on the island. A half-hour signposted walk from the village, the cave is open regularly from mid-June to mid-September (Mon–Fri 3–8pm, Sat & Sun 11am–5pm; 800dr). When the cave is closed, you can probably find a guide in Mylopótamos; ask at the village, giving a day's notice, if possible. The cave is worth the effort to see: the entrance has been used as a church and has an iconostasis carved from the rock, with important Byzantine frescoes on it. Beyond, the cave system comprises a series of chambers which reach 250m into the mountain, although the thirty- minute guided tour (in Greek and English) only takes in the more interesting outer chambers. These include some startling formations like the "shark's teeth", but you have to ask to be shown "Aphrodite's chambers". A minute new species of disc-shaped insect has been discovered here.

Andikýthira island

The tiny island of **Andikýthira** has a once-weekly ferry from and to Ayía Pelayía, plus a once-weekly connection with Crete on the Kýthira–Kastélli–Kýthira run; theoretically it should be possible to use the latter service for a day-trip with about four and a half hours on the island. Rocky and poor, it only received electricity in 1984. Attractions include good birdlife and flora, but it's not the place if you want company. With only fifty or so inhabitants divided between two settlements – **Potamós**, the harbour, and **Sohória**, the village – people are rather thin on the ground. A resident doctor and a teacher serve the dwindling community (there are three children at the village school, as compared with nearly forty in the 1960s). The only official accommodation is the set of **rooms** run by the local community at Potamós, which also has the sole **taverna**. In Sohória the only provisions available are basic foodstuffs at the village shop.

travel details

Corfu (Kérkyra)

There are three or four daily **flights** between Corfu and Athens (1hr), and one or two daily except Sun to Thessaloníki (1hr). Several **ferries** (Port Authority ☎0661/32 655) per hour (5.15am–10pm) run between Corfu and Igoumenítsa (1hr 15min) in high season. Also 6 daily between Igoumenítsa and Lefkími (40min) Additionally, most ferries between Italy (Brindisi, Bari, Ancona and Venice) and Patra stop at Corfu; stopover is free if specified in advance and there is no problem buying Corfu–Patra tickets. You may also be able to travel between Corfu and Kefalloniá on the few Italy–Corfu–Patra ships that call there. Services to

Paxí have improved and there are now two to three daily in season, either direct or via Igoumenítsa. **Buses** to Athens via the Igoumenítsa ferry depart three times daily, once daily to Thessaloníki.

Eríkoussa, Mathráki and Othoní

A **car ferry**, the *Alexandros II*, runs from Corfu Town to all the islands twice weekly (Tues & Sat, 6.30am). The ferry leaves from near the BP station on the seafront, midway between the Old and New Ports, although it involves sailing halfway round the island. Quicker access, favoured by islanders without vehicles, is via daily excursions from **Sidhári** run by Nearchos Seacruises (☎0663/95 248).

Paxí

Ferry connections to Paxí (Port Authority ☎0662/32 259) have stabilized in the last couple of years. To Corfu, there is now one service daily throughout the year, plus one or two extra and a hydrofoil in the summer months. There are unreliable, ferries 2–3 weekly to/from Igoumenítsa. In summer two kaïkia connect daily with Párga.

Lefkádha

5 **buses** daily to and from Athens (7hr), and 5 buses daily to the Áktio ferry (30min) for Préveza, passing Áktio airport (30min). 7 **ferries** daily in season from Nydhrí to Meganíssi; daily connections (several in summer and one all year) from Nydhrí or Vassilikí to Kefalloniá (Fiskárdho and Sámi) and Itháki (Fríkes).

Kefalloniá

1–2 daily **flights** to and from Athens (45min).

Ferries in season from **Sámi** to: Pátra (2 daily; 2hr 30min); Astakós (1 daily; 3hr 30min); Vathý (Itháki; 1–2 daily; 1hr); Pisaetós (Itháki; 5 daily; 30min); Vassilikí (Lefkádha; 1 daily; 3hr). Also ferries from **Póros** to Kyllíni (3 daily; 1hr 15min). **Fiskárdho** to: Fríkes (Itháki; 1 daily; 1hr); Nydhrí (Lefkádha; 2 daily; 2hr); Vassilikí (Lefkádha; 2 daily; 1hr). **Argostóli** to: Kyllíni (2 daily; 1hr 45min); Lixoúri (every 30min; 20min). **Pessádha** to: Áyios Nikólaos (Zákynthos; 2 daily; 1hr 30min). Most routes maintain one daily service in winter – check with Port Authorities (Argostóli ☎0671/22 224; Sámi ☎0674/22 031; Póros ☎0674/72 460).

Buses 3 daily from Argostóli to Athens (6hr). 1 daily from Lixoúri, Póros and Sámi.

Itháki (Ithaca)

Seasonal **ferries** from **Fríkes** to: Fiskárdho (Kefalloniá; 1 daily; 1hr); Nydhrí (Lefkádha; 1 daily; 2hr); Vassilikí (Lefkádha; 1 daily; 1hr). **Pisaetós** to: Sámi (Kefalloniá; 5 daily; 30min). **Váthý** to: Sámi (Kefalloniá; 1–2 daily; 1hr); Astakós (2 daily; 1hr 30min); Pátra (2 daily; 5hr). **Off season**, there is one daily service on each route, weather permitting – check with Port Authority (☎0674 32 909).

Zákynthos

Ferries from: **Zákynthos Town** to: Kyllíni (5 daily all year, up to 10 in season; 1hr 30min). **Áyios Nikoláos** to: Pessádha (Kefalloniá; 2 daily May–Sept; 1hr 30min).

Buses from Zákynthos Town to Athens (3–7 daily, according to season; 6hr).

Flight (on Olympic) from Zákynthos Town to Athens (1 daily; 1hr).

Kýthira

Ferries from **Dhiakófti** to: Andikýthira island (2 weekly in season, 2hr 15min); Kastélli, Crete (once weekly in season; 4hr 15min); Neápoli, Peloponnese (4 weekly in season; 2hr 15min); Yíthio, Peloponnese (4 weekly in season; 2hr 30min).

Hydrofoils from **Dhiakófti** to: Monemvasiá, Kyparíssi, Leonídhi, Pórto Héli, Spétses, Ídhra and Pireás. For details and frequencies of services contact local agents or the Minoan Flying Dolphin's main office in Pireás (Aktí Themistokléous 8; ☎01/412 8001).

Flights from airport 8km south of Potamós to: Athens (1 daily, not Thurs; 50min).

PART THREE

THE CONTEXTS

THE HISTORICAL FRAMEWORK

This section is intended just to lend some perspective to travels around the Greek islands, and is heavily weighted towards the era of the modern, post-independence nation – especially the twentieth century. More detailed accounts of particular periods are to be found in the relevant sections of the guide.

NEOLITHIC, MINOAN AND MYCENAEAN AGES

Other than the solitary discovery of a fossilized Neanderthal skull near Thessaloníki, the earliest evidence of **human settlement** in Greece is to be found at Néa Nikomedhía, near Véria. Here, traces of large, rectangular houses dated to around 6000 BC have been excavated.

It seems that people originally came to this eastern Mediterranean territory in fits and starts, predominantly from Anatolia. These **pre-Hellenes** settled in essentially peaceful farming communities, made pottery and worshipped earth/fertility goddesses – clay statuettes of which are still found on the sites of old settlements. This simple way of life eventually disappeared, as people started to tap the land's resources for profit and to compete and trade.

MINOANS AND MYCENAEANS

The years between around **2000** and **1100 BC** were a period of fluctuating regional dominance, based at first upon sea power, with vast **royal palaces** serving as centres of administration. Particularly important were those at **Knossos** in Crete, and **Mycenae**, **Tiryns** and **Pylos** in the Peloponnese.

Crete monopolized the eastern Mediterranean trade routes during an era subsequently called the **Minoan Age**, with the palace at Knossos surviving two earthquakes and a massive volcanic eruption on the island of Thíra (Santoríni), at some undefinable point between 1500 and 1450 BC. The most obvious examples of Minoan culture can be seen in frescoes, in jewellery and in pottery, the distinctive red and white design on a dark background marking the peak period of Minoan achievement. When Knossos finally succumbed to disaster, natural or otherwise, around 1400 BC, it was the flourishing centre of **Mycenae** that assumed the leading role (and gave its name to the civilization of this period), until it in turn collapsed around 1200 BC.

This is a period whose history and remains are bound up with its legends, recounted most famously by Homer and his disciples. Knossos was the home of King Minos, while the palaces of Mycenae and Pylos were the respective bases of Agamemnon and Nestor; Menelaos and Odysseus hailed from Sparta and Ithaca. The Homeric and other legends relating to them almost certainly reflect the prevalence of violence, revenge and war as increasing facts of life, instigated and aggravated by trade rivalry. The increasing scale of conflict and militarization is exemplified in the massive fortifications – dubbed Cyclopean by later ages, after the only beings thought capable of hefting the huge stones – that were built around many of the palaces.

The Greece of these years was by no means a united nation – as the Homeric legend reflects – and its people were divided into what were in effect a series of splinter groups, defined in large part by sea and mountain barriers and by access to **pasture**. Settlements flourished according to their proximity to and prowess on the sea and the fertility of their land; most were self-sufficient, specializing in the production of particular items for **trade**. Olives, for example, were associated with the region of Attica, and minerals with the island of Mílos.

THE DORIAN AND CLASSICAL ERAS

The Mycenaean-era Greek states had also to cope with and assimilate periodic influxes of new peoples and trade. The traditional view of the collapse of the Mycenaean civilization has it that a northern "barbarian" people, the **Dorians**, "invaded" from the north, devastating the existing palace culture and inaugurating a "dark age"; a competing theory has the so-called "Sea Peoples", probably based in south-western Anatolia, conducting a series of raids over several decades. These days, archeologists see the influx more in terms of shifting trade patterns, though undoubtedly there was major disruption of the palace cultures and their sea power during the eleventh century.

Two other trends are salient to the period: the almost total supplanting of the mother goddesses by **male deities** (a process begun under the Mycenaeans), and the appearance of an **alphabet** still recognizable by modern Greeks, which replaced the so-called "Linear A" and "Linear B" Minoan/Mycenaean scripts.

CITY-STATES: SPARTA AND ATHENS

The ninth century BC ushered in the beginnings of the Greek **city-state** (*polis*). Citizens – rather than just kings or aristocrats – became involved in government, took part in community activities and organized industry and leisure. Colonial ventures increased, as did commercial dealings, and a consequent rise in the import trade was gradually to create a new class of manufacturers.

The city-state was the life of the people who dwelt within it and each state retained both its independence and a distinctive style. One result was that the sporadic attempts to unite in a league against an external enemy were always pragmatic and temporary. The two most powerful states to emerge were Athens and Sparta, who were to exist as rivals over the next five centuries.

Sparta was associated with the Dorians, who had settled in large numbers on the fertile Eurotas (Évrotas) river plain. The society of Sparta and its environs possessed a hierarchical ethos – the majority of the population, the helots, existed in a state of serfdom and worked to support the elite. Sparta was also highly militaristic, accentuated by the need to defend the exposed and fertile land on which it stood. Rather than build intricate fortifications, the people of Sparta relied upon military prowess and a system of laws decreed by the (semi-legendary) **Lycurgus**. Males were subjected to military instruction between the ages of seven and thirty. Weak babies were known periodically to "disappear". Girls too had to perform athletic feats of sprinting and wrestling, and even dwellings were more like barracks than houses.

Athens, the fulcrum of the state of Attica, was dynamic and exciting by contrast, though here too slavery was vital to the economy. Home to the administrations of **Solon** and **Pericles**, the dramatic talents of Sophocles and Aristophanes, the oratory of Thucydides and Demosthenes, and the philosophical power of Socrates and Plato, it made up in cultural achievement what it lacked in Spartan virtue. Yet Sparta did not deserve all the military glory. The Athens of the sixth and fifth centuries BC, the so-called **Classical period** in Greek history, played the major part in repelling the armies of the Persian king Xerxes at Marathon (490 BC) and Salamis (480 BC), campaigns later described by Aeschylus in *The Persians*.

Athens also gave rise to a tradition of **democracy** (*demokratia*), literally "control by the people" – although at this stage "the people" did not include either women or slaves. In Athens there were three organs of government. The Areopagus, composed of the city elders, had a steadily decreasing authority and ended up dealing solely with murder cases. Then there was the Council of Five Hundred (men), elected annually by ballot to prepare the business of the Assembly and to attend to matters of urgency. The Assembly gave every free man a political voice; it had sole responsibility for law-making and provided an arena for the discussion of important issues. It was a genuinely enfranchised council of citizens.

This was a period of intense creativity, particularly in Athens, whose actions and pretensions were fast becoming imperial in all but name. Each city-state had its **acropolis**, or high town, where religious activity was focused. In Athens, Pericles endowed the acropolis with a complex of buildings, whose climax was the temple of the Parthenon. Meanwhile, the era saw the tragedies of Sophocles performed, and the philosophies of Socrates and Plato expounded.

Religion at this stage was polytheistic, ordering eleven main gods under the aegis of Zeus. Urban temples tended to be dedicated to Zeus, Athena or Poseidon; in the countryside the proliferation of names and of sanctuary finds suggests a preference for Apollo, Hera, Dionysos and Artemis.

THE PELOPONNESIAN WAR

The power struggles between Athens and Sparta, allied with various networks of city-states, eventually culminated in the **Peloponnesian wars** of 431–404 BC. After these conflicts, superbly recorded by Thucydides and nominally won by Sparta, the city-state ceased to function so effectively.

This was in part due to drained resources and political apathy, but to a greater degree a consequence of the increasingly commercial and complex pressures on everyday life. Trade, originally spurred by the invention of **coinage** in the sixth century BC, continued to expand; a revitalized Athens, for example, was exporting wine, oil and manufactured goods, getting corn in return from the Black Sea and Egypt.

The amount of time each man had to devote to the affairs of government decreased, and a position in political life became a professional job rather than a natural assumption. Democracy had changed, while in philosophy there was a shift from the idealists and mystics of the sixth and fifth centuries BC to the Cynics, Stoics and Epicureans – followers, respectively, of Diogenes, Zeno and Epicurus.

HELLENISTIC AND ROMAN GREECE

The most important factor in the decline of the city-states was meanwhile developing outside their sphere, in the kingdom of Macedonia.

THE MACEDONIAN EMPIRE

Ruling (359–336 BC) from the Macedonian capital of Pella, **Philip II** was forging a strong military and unitary force, extending his territories into Thrace and finally establishing control over Athens and southern Greece. His son, **Alexander the Great**, in a brief but glorious thirteen-year reign, extended these gains into Persia and Egypt and parts of modern India and Afghanistan.

This unwieldy empire splintered almost immediately upon Alexander's death in 323 BC, to be divided into the three Macedonian dynasties of **Hellenistic Greece**: the Antigonids in Macedonia, the Seleucids in Syria and Persia, and the Ptolemies in Egypt. Each were in turn conquered and absorbed by the new Roman empire, the Ptolemies – under their queen Cleopatra – last of all.

ROMAN GREECE

Mainland and island Greece were subdued by the Romans over some seventy years of campaigns, from 215 to 146 BC. Once in control, however, **Rome** allowed considerable autonomy to the old territories of the city-states. Greek remained the official language of the eastern Mediterranean and its traditions and culture coexisted fairly peacefully with that of the overlords during the next three centuries.

In central Greece both **Athens** and **Corinth** remained important cities but the emphasis was shifting north – particularly to towns, such as **Salonica** (Thessaloníki), along the new Via Egnatia, a military and civil road engineered between Rome and Byzantium via the port of Brundisium (modern Brindisi in Italy). Out among the islands, Rhodes had declined since Hellenistic times but Kós, Lésvos, Thássos and Gortys on Crete remained important centres.

THE BYZANTINE EMPIRE AND MEDIEVAL GREECE

The shift of emphasis northwards was given even greater impetus by the decline of the Roman empire and its apportioning into eastern and western empires. In the year 330 AD Emperor Constantine moved his capital to the Greek city of Byzantium, and here emerged Constantinople (modern Istanbul), the "new Rome" and spiritual and political capital of the **Byzantine empire**.

While the last western Roman emperor was deposed by barbarian Goths in 476, this oriental portion was to be the dominant Mediterranean power for some seven hundred years; only in 1453 did it collapse completely.

CHRISTIANITY

Christianity had been introduced under Constantine, and by the end of the fourth century was the official state religion, its liturgies (still in use in the Greek Orthodox Church), creed and New Testament all written in Greek. A distinction must be drawn though, between perceptions of Greek as a language or culture, and as a concept. The Byzantine empire styled itself Roman, or *Romios*, rather than Hellenic, and moved to eradicate all remaining symbols of pagan Greece. The Delphic Oracle was forcibly closed, and the Olympic Games discontinued, by the emperor Theodosius at the end of the fourth century. Schools of philosophy, especially neo-Platonic ones, did however survive until 529.

The seventh century saw **Constantinople** besieged by Persians, and later Arabs, but the Byzantine empire survived, losing only Egypt, the least "Greek" of its territories. From the ninth to the early eleventh centuries it enjoyed an archetypal "golden age" in culture, confidence and security. Bound up with the Orthodox Byzantine faith was a sense of spiritual superiority, and the emperors saw Constantinople as a "new Jerusalem" for their "chosen people". It was the beginning of a diplomatic and ecclesiastical conflict with the Catholic West that was to have disastrous consequences over the next five centuries. In the meantime the eastern and western patriarchs mutually excommunicated each other.

From the seventh until the eleventh centuries **Byzantine Greece**, certainly in the islands, became something of a provincial backwater. Administration was absurdly top-heavy and imperial taxation led to semi-autonomous provinces ruled by military generals, whose lands were usually acquired from bankrupted peasants. This alienation of the poor provided a force for change, with a disaffected populace ready to turn towards or co-operate with the empire's enemies if the terms on offer were an improvement.

Waves of **Slavic raiders** needed no encouragement to sweep down from the north Balkans throughout this period. At the same time other tribal groups moved down more peaceably from **central Europe** and were absorbed with little difficulty. According to one theory, the nomadic **Vlachs** from Romania eventually settled in the Píndhos mountains, and later, from the thirteenth century onwards, immigrants from **Albania** repopulated the islands of Spétses, Ídhra, Ándhros and Évvia, as well as parts of Attica and the Peloponnese.

THE CRUSADES: FRANKISH AND VENETIAN RULE

From the early years of the eleventh century, less welcome and less assimilable Western forces began to appear. The **Normans** landed first at Corfu in 1085, and returned again to the mainland with papal sanction a decade later on their way to liberate Jerusalem.

These were only a precursor, though, for the forces that were to descend en route for the **Fourth Crusade** of 1204, when Venetians, Franks and Germans turned their armies directly on Byzantium and sacked and occupied Constantinople. These Latin princes and their followers, intent on new lands and kingdoms, settled in to divide up the best part of the empire. All that remained of Byzantium were four small peripheral kingdoms or **despotates**: the most powerful in Nicaea in Asia Minor, less significant ones at Trebizond on the Black Sea, and (in present-day Greece) in Epirus and around Mystra in the Peloponnese (known in those times as the Moreás).

There followed two extraordinarily involved centuries of manipulation and struggle between Franks, Venetians, Genoese, Catalans and Turks. The Paleologos dynasty at Nicaea recovered the city of Constantinople in 1261, but little of its former territory and power. Instead, the focus of Byzantium shifted to the Peloponnese, where the autonomous **despotate of Mystra**, ruled by members of the imperial family, eventually succeeded in wresting most of the peninsula from Frankish hands. At the same time this despotate underwent an intense cultural renaissance, strongly evoked in the churches and shells of cities seen today at modern Mystrás and Monemvassía.

TURKISH OCCUPATION

Within a generation of driving out the Franks, the Byzantine Greeks faced a much stronger threat in the expanding empire of the **Ottoman Turks**. Torn apart by internal struggles between their own ruling dynasties, the **Palaeologi** and **Cantacuzenes**, and unaided by the Catholic West, they were to prove no match for the Turks. On Tuesday, May 29, 1453, a date still solemnly commemorated by the Orthodox Church, Constantinople fell to besieging Muslim Turks.

Mystra was to follow within seven years, and Trebizond within nine, by which time virtually all of the old Byzantine empire lay under Ottoman domination. Only the **Ionian islands** and the **Cyclades**, which remained Venetian, and a few scattered and remote enclaves – like the Máni in the Peloponnese, Sfákia in Crete and Soúli in Epirus – were able to resist the Turkish advance.

OTTOMAN RULE

Under what Greeks refer to as the *turkokratía* or era of **Ottoman rule**, the lands of present-day Greece passed into rural provincialism, taking refuge in a self-protective mode of village life that was only substantially disrupted by World War II. Taxes and discipline, sporadically backed up by the massacre of dissenting communities, were inflicted by the Turkish Porte, but large areas passed into the hands of local chieftains who often had considerable independence. On the larger, more fertile islands such as Crete, Lésvos and Évvia, rule was inevitably stricter with larger garrisons and more onerous taxes; small islands too impoverished to be exploited were left pretty much to their own devices.

Greek identity, meanwhile, was preserved through the offices of the **Orthodox Church** which, despite instances of enforced conversion, the sultans allowed to continue. The **monasteries**, sometimes secretly, organized schools and became the trustees of Byzantine culture, though this had gone into stagnation after the fall of Constantinople and Mystra, whose scholars and artists emigrated west, adding impetus to the Renaissance.

As Ottoman administration became more and more decentralized and inefficient, individual Greeks rose to local positions of considerable influence, and a number of communities achieved a degree of autonomy. Sými was granted an empire-wide monopoly on sponge-diving in return for a yearly tribute to the sultan; Sámos was declared a "Muslim-free" zone and enjoyed special tax exemptions for two centuries. And on the Albanian-repopulated islands of Ídhra and Spétses, as well as Kássos and Psára, a **Greek merchant fleet** came into being in the eighteenth century, permitted to trade throughout the Mediterranean. Greeks, too, were becoming organized overseas in the sizable expatriate colonies of central Europe, which often had affiliations with the semi-autonomous village clusters of Zagória (in Epirus), Ambeláki (Thessaly) and Mount Pílion.

THE STRUGGLE FOR INDEPENDENCE

Despite these privileges, by the eighteenth century opposition to Turkish rule was becoming widespread on the mainland, exemplified most obviously by the **klephts** (brigands) of the mountains. It was not until the nineteenth century, however, that a resistance movement could muster sufficient support and firepower to prove a real challenge to the Turks. In 1770 a Russian-backed uprising had been easily and brutally suppressed, but fifty years later the situation was different.

In Epirus the Turks were overextended, subduing the expansionist campaigns of local ruler **Ali Pasha**. The French Revolution had given impetus to "freedom movements", and the Greek fighters were provided with financial and ideological underpinnings by the Filikí Etería, or "Friendly Society", a secret group recruited among the exiled merchants and intellectuals of central Europe.

This somewhat motley coalition of klephts and theorists launched their insurrection at the monastery of **Ayía Lávra** near Kalávryta in the Peloponnese, where on March 25, 1821, the Greek banner was openly raised by the local bishop, Yermanos.

THE WAR OF INDEPENDENCE

To describe in detail the course of the **War of Independence** is to provoke unnecessary confusion, since much of the rebellion consisted of local and fragmentary guerrilla campaigns. What is important to understand is that Greeks, though fighting for liberation from the Ottomans, were not fighting as and for a nation. Motives differed enormously: landowners assumed their role was to lead and sought to retain and reinforce their traditional privileges, while the peasantry saw the struggle as a means towards land redistribution.

Outside Greece, prestige and publicity for the insurrection were promoted by the arrival of a thousand or so European **Philhellenes**, almost half of them German, though the most important was the English poet, **Lord Byron**, who died while training Greek forces at Messolóngi in April 1824.

Though it was the Greek guerrilla leaders, above all **Theodhoros Kolokotronis**, "the old man of the Morea", who brought about the most significant military victories of the war, the death of Byron had an immensely important effect on public opinion in the West. Aid for the Greek struggle had come neither from Orthodox Russia, nor from the Western powers of France and Britain, ravaged by the Napoleonic Wars.

But by 1827, when Messolóngi fell again to the Turks, these three "Great Powers" finally agreed to seek autonomy for certain parts of Greece and sent a combined fleet to put pressure on the sultan's Egyptian army and fleet, then ransacking and massacring in the Peloponnese. Events took over, and an accidental naval battle in **Navarino Bay** resulted in the destruction of almost the entire Turkish-Egyptian fleet. The following spring Russia itself declared war on the Turks and the sultan was forced to accept the existence of an autonomous Greece.

At a series of conferences from 1830 to 1832, Greek independence was confirmed by the Western powers and **borders** were drawn in 1832. These included just 800,000 of the six million Greeks living within the Ottoman empire, and the Greek territories which were for the most part the poorest of the Classical and Byzantine lands, comprising Attica, the Peloponnese and the islands of the Argo-Saronic, Sporades and Cyclades. The rich agricultural belt of Thessaly, Epirus in the west, and Macedonia in the north, remained in Turkish hands. Meanwhile, the Ionian islands were controlled by a British protectorate and the Dodecanese by the Ottomans (and after 1913 by recently unified Italy).

THE EMERGING STATE

Modern Greece began as a republic and **Ioannis Kapodistrias**, its first president, concentrated his efforts on building a viable central authority and government in the face of diverse protagonists from the Independence struggle. Almost inevitably he was assassinated – in 1831, by two chieftains from the ever-disruptive Máni – and perhaps equally inevitably the three powers stepped in. They created a monarchy, gave limited aid and set on the throne a Bavarian prince, **Otho (Otto)**.

The new king proved an autocratic and insensitive ruler, bringing in fellow Germans to fill official posts and ignoring all claims by the landless peasantry for redistribution of the old estates. In 1862 he was forced from the country by a popular revolt, and the Europeans produced a new prince, this time from Denmark, who requested that Britain cede the Ionian islands as a condition of his accession to the throne. **George I**, in fact, proved more capable: he had the first railways and roads built, introduced limited land reforms in the Peloponnese, and oversaw the first expansion of the Greek borders.

THE MEGÁLI IDHÉA AND EXPANSIONIST WARS

From the very beginning, the unquestioned motive force of Greek foreign policy was the **Megáli Idhéa** (Great Idea) of liberating Greek populations outside the country and incorporating the old territories of Byzantium into the kingdom. In 1878 **Thessaly**, along with southern Epirus, was ceded to Greece by the Turks.

Less illustriously, the Greeks failed in 1897 to achieve *énosis* (union) with **Crete** by attacking Turkish forces on the mainland, and in the process virtually bankrupted the state. The island was, however, placed under a high commissioner, appointed by the Great Powers, and in 1913 did become a part of Greece.

It was from Crete, also, that the most distinguished modern Greek statesman emerged. **Eleftherios Venizelos**, having led a civilian campaign for his island's liberation, was elected as Greek prime minister in 1910. Two years later he organized an alliance of Balkan powers to fight the **Balkan Wars** (1912–13), campaigns that saw the Turks virtually driven from Europe. With Greek borders extended to include the northeast Aegean islands, northern Thessaly, central Epirus and parts of Macedonia, the Megáli Idhéa was approaching reality. At the same time Venizelos proved himself a shrewd manipulator of domestic public opinion by revising the constitution and introducing a series of liberal social reforms.

Division, however, was to appear with the outbreak of **World War I**. Venizelos urged Greek entry on the British side, seeing in the conflict possibilities for the "liberation" of Greeks in Thrace and Asia Minor, but the new king, Constantine I, who was married to a sister of the German Kaiser, imposed a policy of neutrality. Eventually Venizelos set up a revolutionary government in Thessaloníki, and in 1917 Greek troops entered the war to join the French, British and Serbians in the **Macedonian campaign**. Upon the capitulation of Bulgaria and Ottoman Turkey, the Greeks occupied **Thrace**, and Venizelos presented demands at Versailles for the predominantly Greek region of Smyrna on the Asia Minor coast.

THE KATASTROFÍ AND ITS AFTERMATH

This was the beginning of one of the most disastrous episodes in modern Greek history, the so-called **Katastrofí** ("Catastrophe"). Venizelos was authorized to move forces into Smyrna in 1919, but in Turkey itself a new nationalist movement was taking power under Mustafa Kemal, or **Atatürk** as he came to be known. In 1920 Venizelos lost the elections and monarchist factions took over, their aspirations unmitigated by the Cretan's skill in foreign diplomacy. Despite Allied support for such ventures now having completely evaporated, Greek forces were ordered to advance upon Ankara in an attempt to bring Atatürk to terms.

This so-called **Anatolian campaign** ignominiously collapsed in summer 1922 when Turkish troops forced the Greeks back to the coast and into a hurried evacuation from **Smyrna**. As they left Smyrna, the Turks moved in and systematically massacred most of the Armenian and Greek populations before burning most of the city to the ground.

Although an entire Greek army remained intact in eastern Thrace, Britain, hitherto Greece's only backer, let it be known that Greece should accept Atatürk's terms, formalized by the 1923 Treaty of Lausanne, which ordered the **exchange of religious minorities** in each country – in effect, the first large-scale regulated ethnic cleansing. Turkey was to accept 390,000 Muslims resident on Greek soil. Greece, mobilized almost continuously for the last decade and with a population of under five million, was faced with the resettlement of over 1,300,000 Christian refugees. Many of these had already read the writing on the wall after 1918 and arrived of their own accord; significant numbers were settled on Lésvos, Híos, Sámos, Évvia and Crete, as well as the mainland. The Megáli Idhéa had ceased to be a viable blueprint.

Changes, inevitably, were intense and far-reaching. The great agricultural estates of Crete, Évvia, Lésvos and Thessaly were finally redistributed, both to Greek tenants and refugee farmers, and huge shanty towns grew into new quarters around Athens, Pireás and other cities, a spur to the country's then almost nonexistent industry.

Politically, too, reaction was swift. By September 1922, a group of Venezelist army officers under **Colonel Nikolaos Plastiras**, assembled after the retreat from Smyrna, "invited" King Constantine to abdicate, and executed six of his ministers held most responsible for the debacle. Democracy was nominally restored with the proclamation of a republic, but for much of the next decade changes in government were brought about by factions within the armed forces. Meanwhile, among the urban refugee population, unions were being formed and the Greek Communist Party (KKE) was established.

VENIZELOS'S LAST GASP — AND THE RISE OF METAXAS

Elections in 1928 **returned Venizelos** to power, but his freedom to manoeuvre was restricted by the Great Crash of the following year. He had borrowed heavily abroad and was unable to renegotiate loan terms in 1931. Late 1932 saw a local crash caused by England's abandonment of the gold standard, with Greek currency heavily devalued and Venizelos forced from office. His supporters under Plastiras tried to reinstate him in March 1933, but their coup was quashed and Venizelos fled to Paris, where he died in 1936.

By 1936 the Communist Party had enough electoral support to hold the balance of power in parliament, and would have done so had not the army and the by-then restored king decided otherwise. **King George II** had been returned by a plebiscite held – and almost certainly manipulated – the previous year, and so presided over an increasingly factionalized parliament. In April 1936 he appointed **General John Metaxas** as prime minister, despite the latter's support from only six elected deputies. Immediately a series of KKE-organized strikes broke out and the king, ignoring attempts to form a broad liberal coalition, dissolved parliament without setting a date for new elections. It was a blatantly unconstitutional move and opened the way for five years of ruthless and at times absurd dictatorship.

Metaxas averted a general strike with military force and proceeded to set up a state based on **fascist** models of the era. Left-wing and trade union opponents were imprisoned or forced into exile, a state youth movement and efficient secret police set up, and rigid censorship, extending even to passages of Thucydides, imposed. It was, however, at least a Greek dictatorship, and though Metaxas was sympathetic to Nazi organization he completely opposed German or Italian domination.

WORLD WAR II AND THE GREEK CIVIL WAR

Using a submarine based on Léros in the Dodecanese, the Italians tried to provoke the Greeks into **World War II** by surreptitiously torpedoing the Greek cruiser *Elli* in Tínos harbour on August 15, 1940, but they met with no response. However, when Mussolini occupied Albania and sent an ultimatum on October 28, 1940, demanding passage for his troops through Greece, Metaxas responded to the Italian foreign minister with the apocryphal one-word answer **"óhi"** (no). (In fact, his response, in the mutually understood French, was "C'est la guerre".) The date marked the entry of Greece into the war, and the gesture is still celebrated as a national holiday. Galvanized into brief unity by the crisis, the Greeks drove the Italian forces from the country, managing to take control of the long-coveted and predominantly Greek-populated northern Epirus (southern Albania). However, the Greek army subsequently frittered away its strength in the snowy mountains of northern Epirus rather than consolidate their gains or defend the Macedonian frontier, and coordination with the British never materialized.

OCCUPATION AND RESISTANCE

In April of the following year Nazi mechanized columns swept through Yugoslavia and across the Greek mainland, effectively reversing the only Axis defeat to date, and by late May 1941, airborne and seaborne **German invasion** forces had completed the occupation of Crete and the other islands. Metaxas had died before their arrival, while King George and his new self-appointed ministers fled into exile in Cairo; few Greeks, of any political persuasion, were sad to see them go.

The joint Italian–German–Bulgarian Axis **occupation** of Greece was among the bitterest experiences of the European war. Nearly half a million Greek civilians starved to death over the winter of 1941–42, as all available food was requisitioned, principally by the Germans, to feed occupying armies. In addition, entire villages throughout the mainland and especially on Crete were burned at the least hint of resistance activity. In their northern sector, which included Thássos and Samothráki, the Bulgarians desecrated ancient sites and churches to support a future bid to annex "Slavic" Macedonia.

After the Italians capitulated in September 1943, the Jewish communities in Rhodes, Kós, Crete, Corfu, Vólos, Évvia and Zákynthos in particular were exposed to the full force of Nazi racial doctrine; in the last three places, however, co-operation between courageous church or municipal authorities and the budding Resistance (see below) ensured that most local Jews survived.

With a quisling government in Athens – and an unpopular, discredited royalist government in exile in Cairo – the focus of Greek political and military action over the next four years passed largely to the **EAM**, or National Liberation Front. By 1943 it was in virtual control of most areas of the country, including Sámos and Lésvos (but not Crete), working with the British on tactical operations, with its own army (**ELAS**) and navy and both civil and secret police forces. Initially it commanded widespread popular support, and appeared to offer an obvious framework for the resumption of postwar government.

However, most of its highest ranking members were communists, and the British prime minister, **Winston Churchill**, was determined to reinstate the monarchy. Even with two years of the war to run, it became obvious that there could be no peaceable post-liberation regime other than a republic. Accordingly, in August 1943, representatives from each of the main Resistance movements (including two noncommunist groups) flew clandestinely to Cairo to request that the king should not return unless a plebiscite had first voted in his favour. Both the Greek and British authorities refused to consider the proposal, and the best possibility of averting civil war was lost.

The EAM contingent returned divided, as perhaps the British had intended, and a conflict broke out between those who favoured taking peaceful control of any government imposed after liberation, and the hard-line Stalinist ideologues, who forbade participation in any "bourgeois" regime.

In October 1943, with fears of an imminent British landing force and takeover, ELAS launched a full-scale attack upon its Greek rivals on the mainland; by the following April, they had wiped out all but the EDES, a right-wing grouping suspected of collaboration with the Germans. ELAS's ferocity was spurred by the failure of the Egyptian conference and by half-true reports that British and American agents were being infiltrated into Greece to prevent the establishment of a communist government when the Germans began withdrawing their forces.

LIBERATION AND CIVIL WAR

In fact, as the Germans began to leave in October 1944, most of the EAM leadership agreed to join a British-sponsored "official" **interim government**. It quickly proved a tactical error, however. With almost ninety percent of the provinces under their control, the communists were given only one-third representation in Athens, and a new regular army began to form, relying on right-wing extremists rather than the ELAS officer corps. The king showed no sign of renouncing his claims, and, in November, Allied forces ordered ELAS to disarm. On December 3 all pretences of civility or neutrality were dropped; the police opened fire on an EAM demonstration in Athens, killing at least sixteen, and fighting broke out between ELAS and **British troops**, in the so-called **Dhekemvrianá** events. Though ELAS quickly quashed all opposition in the countryside, they failed to drive the British and right-wing Greeks from Athens, thus losing their best chance of seizing power. In their fury at being thwarted, ELAS rounded up their most influential and wealthiest opponents in the largest towns, and marched them out to rural areas in conditions that guaranteed their death.

A truce of sorts was negotiated at Várkiza near Athens in February 1945, but the agreement was never implemented. The army, police and civil service remained in right-wing hands, and, while collaborationists were often allowed to retain their positions, left-wing sympathizers, many of whom were not communists, were systematically excluded, the mildest aspect of what developed into a veritable "**White Terror**". The elections of 1946 were won by the right-wing parties (the Left boycotted them), followed by another rigged plebiscite in favour of the king's return. By 1947 guerrilla activity had again reached the scale of a full **civil war**, with ELAS reorganized into the Democratic Army of Greece (**DSE** in Greek).

In the interim, King George had died and been succeeded by his brother Paul (with his consort Frederika), while the **Americans** had taken over the British role, and begun implementing the cold-war **Truman doctrine**. In March 1947 they took virtual control of Greece, their first significant postwar experiment in anti-communist intervention. Massive economic and military aid was given to a client Greek government, while official decrees had to be countersigned by the American Mission chief in order to become valid.

In the mainland mountains US military advisers trained the nationalist army for **campaigns against the DSE**, and in the cities there were mass arrests, court-martials and imprisonments – an extension of the White Terror – lasting until 1951. Over three thousand executions were recorded, including a number of Jehovah's Witnesses, "a sect proved to be under communist domination", according to US Ambassador Grady. To deny the DSE local support, over 700,000 civilians were forcibly evacuated from mountain villages and dumped in squalid internment camps near towns, a move which helped destroy any hope of postwar rural existence.

In the autumn of 1949, with the Yugoslav–Greek border closed after Tito's rift with Stalin, the last DSE guerrillas finally admitted defeat, retreating into Albania from their strongholds on Mount Grámmos. Atrocities had been committed on both sides, including, from the Left, considerably more than three thousand executions, widespread vandalization of monasteries and the dubious evacuation of children from "combat areas" (as told in Nicholas Gage's virulently anti-communist book *Eleni*). Such errors, as well as the hopelessness of lightly armed guerrillas fighting an American-backed army equipped with aircraft and heavy artillery, almost certainly doomed the DSE's efforts from the start.

RECONSTRUCTION AMERICAN STYLE 1950–67

After a decade of war that had shattered much of Greece's infrastrucure, it was a demoralized country that emerged into the Western political orbit of the 1950s. Greece was also perforce American-dominated, enlisted into the Korean

War in 1950 and NATO the following year. In domestic politics, the US Embassy – still giving the orders – foisted a winner-takes-all electoral system, which was to ensure victory for the Right over the next twelve years. All leftist activity was banned; those individuals who were not herded into political "re-education" camps on barren islands, or dispatched by firing squads, legal or vigilante, went into exile throughout eastern Europe, to return only after 1974.

The American-backed, highly conservative **"Greek Rally"** party, led by General Papagos, won the first decisive post-civil-war elections in 1952. After the general's death, the party's leadership was taken over – and to an extent liberalized – by **Constantine Karamanlis**. Under his rule, stability of a kind was established and some economic advances registered, particularly after the revival of Greece's traditional German markets. However, the 1950s was also a decade that saw wholesale **depopulation** of remote villages as migrants sought work in Australia, America and Western Europe, or the larger Greek cities. This was most pronounced in the remoter islands of Kýthira, Kefalloniá, the northeast Aegean and the Dodecanese, where the longed-for union with Greece in 1948 had ironically conferred the right to emigrate, mostly denied under the Ottomans and Italians.

The main crisis in foreign policy throughout this period was **Cyprus**, where a long terrorist campaign was waged by Greek-Cypriots opposing British rule, and there were sporadic threats of a new Greco-Turkish war. An ultimately unworkable compromise was forced on the island by Britain in 1960, granting independence without the possibility of self-determination (ie union with Greece). Much of the traditional Greek–British goodwill was destroyed by the issue, with Britain seen to be acting with regard primarily for its two military bases (over which, incidentally, it still retains sovereignty).

By 1961, unemployment, the Cyprus issue and the imposition of US nuclear bases on Greek soil were changing the political climate, and when Karamanlis was again elected there was strong suspicion of a fraud arranged by the king and army. Strikes became frequent in industry and even agriculture, and both King Paul and the autocratic, fascist-inclined Queen Frederika were openly attacked in parliament and at protest demonstrations. The far Right grew uneasy about **"communist resurgence"** and, losing confidence in their own electoral influence, arranged the **assassination** of left-wing deputy **Grigoris Lambrakis** in Thessaloníki in May 1963. (The murder, and its subsequent cover-up, is the subject of Vassilis Vassilikos's thriller *Z*, filmed by Costa-Gavras.) It was against this volatile background that Karamanlis dissolved parliament, lost the subsequent elections and left the country.

The new government – the first controlled from outside the Greek Right since 1935 – was formed by **George Papandreou's Centre Union Party**, and had a decisive majority of nearly fifty seats. It was to last, however, for under two years as conservative forces rallied to thwart its progress. In this the chief protagonists were army officers and their constitutional commander-in-chief, the new king, 23-year-old **Constantine II**.

Since power in Greece depended on a pliant military as well as a network of political appointees, Papandreou's most urgent task in order to govern securely and effectively was to reform the armed forces. His first minister of defence proved incapable of the task and, while he was investigating the right-wing plot that was thought to have rigged the 1961 election, "evidence" was produced of a leftist conspiracy connected with Papandreou's son Andreas (also a minister in the government). When the allegations grew to a crisis, George Papandreou decided to assume the defence portfolio himself, a move for which the king refused to give the necessary approval. He then resigned in order to gain approval at the polls but the king would not order fresh elections, instead persuading members of the Centre Union – chief among them **Constantine Mitsotakis** – to defect and organize a coalition government. Punctuated by strikes, resignations and mass demonstrations, this lasted for a year and a half until new elections were eventually set for May 28, 1967. They failed to take place.

THE COLONELS' JUNTA 1967–74

It was a foregone conclusion that Papandreou's party would win popular support in the polls against the discredited coalition partners. And it was equally certain that there would be some sort of anti-democratic action to try and prevent it from reassuming power. Disturbed by the party's leftward shift, King Constantine was said to have briefed senior generals for a coup d'état, to take place ten days before the elections. However, he was caught by surprise, as was nearly everyone else, by the coup of April 21, 1967, staged by a group of "unknown" colonels. It was, in the words of Andreas Papandreou, "the first successful CIA military putsch on the European continent".

The colonels' junta, having taken control of the means of power, was sworn in by the king and survived the half-hearted counter-coup which he subsequently attempted to organize. It was an ostensibly fascist regime, absurdly styling itself as the true "Revival of Greek Orthodoxy" against Western "corrupting influences", though in reality its ideology was nothing more than warmed-up dogma from the Metaxas era mixed with ultra-nationalism.

All political activity was banned, independent trade unions were forbidden to recruit or meet, the press was so heavily censored that many papers stopped printing, and thousands of "communists" were arrested, imprisoned and often tortured. Among the persecuted were both the Papandreous, the composer Mikis Theodorakis (deemed "unfit to stand trial" after three months in custody) and Amalia Fleming (widow of Alexander Fleming). While relatively few people were killed outright, thousands were permanently maimed physically and psychologically in the junta's torture chambers. The best-known Greek actress, Melina Mercouri, was stripped of her citizenship in absentia, and thousands of prominent Greeks joined her in exile.

Culturally, the colonels put an end to popular music (banning, for example, bagpipes on Mýkonos lest visitors think Greece too "primitive"), and inflicted ludicrous censorship on literature and the theatre, including (as under Metaxas) a ban on production of the Classical tragedies. By contrast, chief colonel Papadapoulos's rambling, illiterate speeches became a byword for bad grammar, obfuscation and newspeak.

The colonels lasted for seven years, opposed (especially after the first two years) by the majority of the Greek people, officially excluded from the Council of Europe, but propped up and given massive aid by US presidents **Lyndon Johnson** and **Richard Nixon**. To them and the CIA the junta's Greece was an ideal client state: human rights considerations were thought trivial; orders were placed for sophisticated military technology; and foreign investment on terms highly unfavourable to Greece was made available to multinational corporations. It was a fairly routine scenario of the decade for the exploitation of an underdeveloped nation.

Opposition was voiced from the beginning by exiled Greeks in London, the United States and Western Europe, but only in 1973 did demonstrations break out openly in Greece – the colonels' secret police had done too thorough a job of infiltrating domestic resistance groups and terrifying everyone else into docility. On November 17 the students of **Athens Polytechnic** began an occupation of their buildings. The ruling clique lost its nerve; armoured vehicles stormed the Polytechnic gates and a still-undetermined number of students (estimates range from tens to hundreds) were killed. Martial law was tightened and junta chief Colonel Papadopoulos was replaced by the even more noxious and reactionary General Ioannides, head of the secret police.

THE RETURN TO CIVILIAN RULE 1975–81

The end of the ordeal, however, came within a year as the dictatorship embarked on a disastrous political adventure in **Cyprus**, essentially the last playing of the Megáli Idhéa card. By attempting to topple the Makarios government and impose *énosis* (union) on the island, they provoked a Turkish invasion and occupation of forty percent of Cypriot territory. The army finally mutinied and **Constantine Karamanlis** was invited to return from Paris to take office again. He swiftly negotiated a ceasefire (but no solution) in Cyprus, withdrew temporarily from NATO and warned that US bases would have to be removed except where they specifically served Greek interest.

In November 1974 Karamanlis and his **Néa Dhimokratía (New Democracy) Party** were rewarded by a sizable majority in **elections**, with a centrist and socialist opposition. The latter was constituted as the **Panhellenic Socialist Movement (PASOK)**, a new party led by Andreas Papandreou.

The election of Néa Dhimokratía was in every sense a safe conservative option, but to Karamanlis's enduring credit it oversaw an effective and firm return to democratic stability, even legitimizing the KKE (Communist Party) for the first time in its history. Karamanlis also held a **referendum on the monarchy**; 59 percent of Greeks rejected the return of Constantine II, so he instituted in its place a French-style presidency, a post which he himself occupied from 1980 to 1985, and again from 1990 to 1995. Economically there were limited advances, although these were more than offset by inflationary defence spending (the result of renewed tension with Turkey), hastily negotiated entrance into the EC and the decision to let the drachma float after decades of its being artificially fixed at thirty to the US dollar.

Most crucially, Karamanlis failed to deliver vital reforms in bureaucracy, social welfare and education; and while the worst figures of the junta were brought to trial and jailed indefinitely, the face of Greek political life and administration was little changed. By 1981 inflation was hovering around 25 percent, and it was estimated that tax evasion was depriving the state of one-third of its annual budget. In foreign policy the US bases remained and it was felt that Greece, back in NATO, was still acting as little more than an American satellite. The traditional Right was demonstrably inadequate to the task at hand.

PASOK 1981–89

"Change" (*Allayí*) and "Out with the Right" (*Ná Fíyi íy Dhexiá*) were the watchwords of the election campaign that swept **PASOK** and Andreas Papandreou to power on October 18, 1981.

This victory meant a chance for Papandreou to form the first socialist government in Greek history and to break a half-century monopoly of authoritarian right-wing rule. With so much at stake the campaign had been passionate even by Greek standards, and PASOK's victory was greeted with euphoria both by the generation whose political voice had been silenced in the civil war, and by a large proportion of the young. Their hopes perhaps ran naively and dangerously high.

The electoral margin, at least, was conclusive. PASOK won 174 of the 300 parliamentary seats and the Communist KKE – though not a part of the new government – returned another thirteen deputies, one of them composer Mikis Theodorakis. *Néa Dhimokratía* moved into unaccustomed opposition. There appeared to be no obstacle to the implementation of a **radical socialist programme**: devolution of power to local authorities, the effective nationalization of heavy industry, improvement of the woefully skeletal social services, a purge of bureaucratic inefficiency and malpractice, the end of bribery and corruption as a way of life, an independent and dignified foreign policy following expulsion of the US bases and finally withdrawal from NATO and the European Community.

A change of style was promised, too, replacing the country's long traditions of authoritarianism and bureaucracy with openness and dialogue. Even more radically, given that Greek political parties had long been the personal followings of charismatic leaders, PASOK was to be a party of ideology and principle, dominated by no single individual member. Or so, at least, thought some of the youthful PASOK enthusiasts.

The new era started with a bang. The wartime Resistance was officially recognized; hitherto they hadn't been allowed to take part in any celebrations, wreath-layings or other ceremonies. Peasant women were granted pensions for the first time – 3000 drachmas a month (about US$55 in 1982), the same as their outraged husbands – and wages were indexed to the cost of living. In addition, civil marriage was introduced, family law reformed in favour of wives and mothers, and equal rights legislation was put on the statute book.

These quick, low-cost and popular reformist moves seemed to mark a break with the past, and the atmosphere had indeed changed. Greeks no longer lowered their voices to discuss politics in public places or wrapped their opposition newspaper in the respectably conservative *Kathimerini*. At first there were real fears that the climate would be too much for the military and they would once again intervene to choke a dangerous experiment in democracy, especially when Andreas Papandreou assumed the defence portfolio himself in a move strongly reminiscent of his father's attempt to remove the king's appointee in 1965. But he went out of his way to soothe military susceptibilities, increasing their salaries, buying new weaponry and being fastidious in his attendance at military functions. In reality, the resistance of the Polytechnic students to the 1967–74 junta was mythologized, and PASOK activists could be counted on to form human cordons around party headquarters at the least sign of unrest in the armed forces.

THE END OF THE HONEYMOON

Nothing if not a populist, Papandreou promised a bonanza which he must have known, as an academically trained economist, he could not deliver. As a result he pleased nobody on the economic front.

He could not fairly be blamed for the inherited lack of investment, low productivity, deficiency in managerial and labour skills and other chronic problems besetting the Greek economy. However, he certainly aggravated the situation in the early days of his first term in office by allowing his supporters to indulge in violently anti-capitalist rhetoric and by the prosecution and humiliation of the Tsatsos family, owners of one of Greece's few profitable businesses (Hercules Cement), for the illegal export of capital, something of which every Greek with any savings was guilty. These were cheap victories, not backed by any rational programme of public investment, and the only nationalizations were of hopelessly lame-duck companies.

Faced with this sluggish economy and burdened with the additional charges of (marginally) improved social benefits and wage-indexing, Papandreou's government had also to cope with the effects of **world recession**, which always hits Greece with a delayed effect compared with its more advanced European partners. **Shipping**, the country's main foreign-currency earner, was devastated. Remittances from emigré workers fell off as they joined the lines of the unemployed in their host countries, and tourism diminished under the dual impact of the recession and US President Ronald Reagan's warning to Americans to stay away from the allegedly insecure and terrorist-bomb-prone Athens airport.

With huge quantities of imported goods continuing to be sucked into the country in the absence of significant domestic production, the **foreign debt** topped £10 billion in 1986, with inflation still at 25 percent and the balance of payments deficit approaching £1 billion. Greece also began to experience the social strains of unemployment for the first time. Not that it did not exist before, but it had always been concealed as underemployment because of the family and the rural structure of the economy – as well as by the absence of reliable statistics.

THE SECOND TERM

A modest spending spree transparently intended to buy votes, continued satisfaction at the discomfiture of the Right, the popularity of his Greece-for-the-Greeks foreign policy, plus some much-needed reforms, saw Papandreou through into a second term with an electoral victory in **June 1985** scarcely less triumphant than the first. But his complacent and dishonest slogan was "Vote PASOK for Even Better Days". By October PASOK had imposed a two-year wage freeze and import restrictions, abolished the wage-indexing scheme and devalued the drachma by fifteen percent. Papandreou's fat was pulled out of the fire by none other than his former bogeyman, the European Community, which offered a huge two-part loan on condition that an IMF-style **austerity programme** was maintained.

The political fallout of such classic right-wing strategies, accompanied by shameless soliciting for foreign investment, was the alienation of the communists and most of PASOK's own core constituency. Increasingly autocratic (ironic, given his earlier pledges of openness), Papandreou's response to **dissent** was to fire recalcitrant trade union leaders and expel some three hundred members of his own party. Assailed by strikes, the government veered off course completely, and in the local elections of October 1986 it lost abundant ground to *Néa Dhimokratía*, including the mayoralties of the three major cities – Athens, Thessaloníki and Pátra – the first two retained by them ever since.

Papandreou assured the nation that he had taken the message to heart, but all that followed was a minor government reshuffle and a panicky attempt to undo the ill-feeling caused by an incredible freeing of rent controls at a time when all wage earners were feeling the pinch badly. Early in 1987 he went further and sacked all the remaining PASOK veterans in his cabinet, including his son George, though this was probably a palliative to public opinion. The new cabinet was so unsocialist that even the right-wing press called it "centrist".

Similar about-faces took place in foreign policy. The first-term anti-US, anti-NATO and anti-EC rhetoric had been immensely popular, and understandable for a people shamelessly bullied by bigger powers since 1830. There was some high-profile nose-thumbing, like refusing to join EC partners in condemning Jaruzelski's Polish regime, the Soviet downing of a Korean airliner or Syrian involvement in terrorist bomb-planting.

In stark contrast to the early promises and rhetoric, the "realistic" policies that Papandreou increasingly pursued during his second term were far more conciliatory towards his big Western brothers. This was best exemplified by the fact that **US bases** remained in Greece until 1994, largely due to the fear that snubbing NATO would lead to Greece being exposed to Turkish aggression, still the only issue that unites the main parties to any degree. As for the once-reviled **European Community** (soon to be the European Union), Greece had by now become an established beneficiary, and its leader was hardly about to bite the hand that feeds.

SCANDAL

Even as late as **mid-1988**, despite the many betrayals and failings of Papandreou, it seemed unlikely that PASOK would be toppled in the following year's elections. This was due mainly to the lack of a credible alternative. Constantine Mitsotakis, a bitter personal enemy of Papandreou's since 1965, when his defection had brought down his father's government and set in train the events that culminated in the junta, was an unconvincing and unlikeable character at the helm of *Néa Dhimokratía*. Meanwhile, the liberal centrist parties had disappeared, and the main communist party, the KKE, seemed trapped in a Stalinist timewarp under the leadership of Harilaos Florakis. Only the **Ellenikí Aristerá (Greek Left)**, formerly the Euro-wing of the KKE, seemed to offer any sensible alternative programme, but they had a precariously small following.

However, a combination of spectacular blunders, plus perhaps a general shift to the Right, influenced by the cataclysmic events in Eastern Europe, conspired against PASOK. First came the extraordinary **cavortings of the prime minister** himself. Late in 1988, the seventy-year-old Papandreou was flown to Britain for open-heart surgery. He took the occasion, with fear of death presumably rocking his judgement, to make public a year-long liaison with a 34-year-old Olympic Airways hostess, **Dimitra "Mimi" Liani**. Widespread media images of an old man shuffling about after a young, large-chested blonde, to the public humiliation of Margaret, his American-born wife, and his family, were not popular. Papandreou subsequently divorced Margaret and married Mimi. His integrity was further questioned when he missed several important public engagements –

WOMEN'S RIGHTS IN GREECE

Women's right to vote wasn't universally achieved in Greece until 1956 and, until the mid-1970s, adultery was still a punishable offence, with cases regularly brought to court. The socialist party, PASOK, had a strong theoretical programme for women's rights, and their women's council review committees, set up in the early, heady days, effected a landmark reform with the 1983 Family Law. This prohibited requiring dowry (though custom still demands it) and stipulated equal legal status and shared property rights between husband and wife.

Subsequently however, the PASOK governments did little to follow through on practical issues, like improved child care, health and family planning. Contraception is not available as part of the skeletal Greek public health service, leaving many women to fall back on abortion as the preferred method of birth control – still running (as for many years past) to an estimated 70–80,000 a year.

By far the largest women's rights organization is the Union of Greek Women. Founded in 1976, this espouses an independent feminist line and is responsible for numerous consciousness-raising activities across the country, though it remains too closely linked to PASOK for the comfort of many. Indeed, Margaret Papandreou felt compelled to resign from the Union following her well-publicized divorce from Andreas, leaving it without her effective and vocal leadership. Other, more autonomous groups have been responsible for setting up advice and support networks, highlighting women's issues within trade unions and campaigning for changes in media representation.

None of this is easy in a country as socially variable as Greece. In many rural areas women rely heavily on traditional extended families for security, and are unlikely to be much affected by legislative reforms or city politics. Yet Greek men of all classes and backgrounds are slowly becoming used to the notion of women in positions of power and responsibility and are taking a substantial share in child-rearing – both postures utterly unthinkable two decades ago, and arguably one of the few positive legacies with which PASOK can at least in part be credited.

including a ceremony commemorating the victims of the 1987 Kalamáta earthquake – in order to hit the town with Mimi, reliving his youth in flashy nightspots.

The real damage, however, was done by a series of **economic scandals**. The most serious of these involved a self-made, Greek-American con-man, **Yiorgos Koskotas**, director of the Bank of Crete, who embezzled £120m (US$190m) of deposits and, worse still, slipped through the authorities' fingers on a private jet back to the US, where he had begun his career as a housepainter. Certain PASOK ministers and even Papandreou himself were implicated in the scandal. Further harm was done by allegations of illegal arms dealings and fraudulent farm-produce sales on the part of various government ministers.

United in disgust at this corruption, the other left-wing parties – KKE and Ellinikí Aristerá – formed a coalition, the **Synaspismós**, siphoning off still more support from PASOK.

THREE BITES AT THE CHERRY

In this climate of disaffection, an inconclusive result to the **June 1989 election** was no real surprise. What was less predictable, however, was the formation of a bizarre "**kathársis" (purgative) coalition** of conservatives and communists, united in the avowed intent of cleansing PASOK's increasingly Augean stables.

The Synaspismós would have formed a government with PASOK but set one condition for doing so – that Papandreou stepped down as prime minister – and the old man was having none of it. In the deal finally cobbled together between the Left and Néa Dhimokratía, Mitsotakis was denied the premiership, too, having to make way for **Ioannis Tzanetakis**, a popular former naval officer who had led a mutiny against the junta.

During the three months that the coalition lasted, the *kathársis* turned out to be largely a matter of burying the knife as deeply as possible into the ailing body of PASOK. Andreas Papandreou and three other ministers were officially accused of involvement in the Koskotas affair – though there was no time to set up their trial before the Greek people returned once again to the polls. In any case, the chief witness and protagonist in the affair, Koskotas himself, was still imprisoned in America, awaiting extradition proceedings.

Contrary to the Right's hope that publicly accusing Papandreou and his cohorts of criminal behaviour would pave the way for a *Néa Dhimokratía* victory, PASOK actually made a slight recovery in the **November 1989 elections**, though the result was again inconclusive. This time the Left resolutely refused to do deals with anyone, and the result was a consensus caretaker government under the neutral aegis of an academic named Zolotas, who was reluctantly dragged into the prime minister's office from Athens University. His only mandate was to see that the country didn't go off the rails completely while preparations were made for yet another election.

These took place in **April 1990** with the same captains at the command of their ships and with the Synaspismós having completed its about-turn to the extent that in the five single-seat constituencies (the other 295 seats are drawn from multiple-seat constituencies in a complicated system of reinforced proportional representation), they supported independent candidates jointly with PASOK. Greek communists are good at about-turns, though; after all, composer Mikis Theodorakis, musical torch-bearer of the Left during the dark years of the junta, and formerly a KKE MP, was by now standing for Néa Dhimokratía, prior to his resignation from politics altogether.

On the night, Néa Dhimokratía scraped home with a majority of one, later doubled with the defection of a centrist, and Mitsotakis finally realized his long-cherished dream of becoming prime minister. The only other memorable feature of the election was the first parliamentary representation for an independent member of the Turkish minority in Thrace, and for the Greens in Attica – a focus for many disaffected PASOK voters.

A RETURN TO THE RIGHT: MITSOTAKIS

On assuming power, Mitsotakis prescribed a course of **austerity measures** to try and revive the chronically ill economy. Little headway was made, though, given the world recession, that was hardly surprising. Greek inflation was still approaching twenty percent annually, and at nearly ten percent, unemployment remained chronic. Yet certain menial jobs went begging, taken only (since 1990) by **impoverished Albanians** who have arrived in numbers over half a million strong. They now form something of a permanent underclass, especially those who aren't ethnically Greek, and are blamed for all manner of ills. They have also prompted the first anti-immigration measures with teeth in a country whose population is more used to being on the other side of such laws.

Other conservative measures introduced by Mitsotakis included laws to combat strikes and **terrorism**. This had been a perennial source of worry for Greeks since the appearance in the mid-1970s of a group called **Dhekaeftá Novemvríou** ("November 17", the date of the colonels' attack on the Polytechnic in 1973). Since 1974 they (and more recent, copycat groups) have killed over twenty industrialists, politicians and NATO military personnel and have attacked buildings of foreign corporations in Athens; the lack of any significant arrests to date fuels continued speculation that they were a rogue faction from within PASOK itself. It hardly seemed likely that Mitsotakis's laws, however, were the solution. They stipulated that the typically long, ideologically argued statements of the group could no longer be published, which led to one or two newspaper editors being jailed for a few days for defiance – much to everyone's embarrassment. The **anti-strike laws** threatened severe penalties but were equally ineffectual, as breakdowns in public transport, electricity and rubbish collection all too frequently illustrated.

As for the Koskotas scandal, the man himself was eventually extradited and gave evidence for the prosecution against Papandreou and various of his ministers. The trial was televised and proved as popular as any soap opera, as indeed it should have been, given the twists of high drama – which included one of the defendants, Agamemnon "Menios" Koutsoyiorgas, dying in court of a heart attack in front of the cameras. The case against Papandreou gradually lost steam and he was officially acquitted (by a margin of one vote on the tribunal panel) in early 1992. The two other surviving ex-ministers, Tsovolas and Petsos, were convicted, given jail sentences (bought off with a heavy fine) and barred from public office for a time.

The great showcase trial thus went out with a whimper and did nothing to enhance Mitsotakis's position. If anything, it served to increase sympathy for Papandreou, who was felt to have been unfairly victimized. The indisputable villain of the piece, Koskotas, was eventually convicted of major fraud and is serving a lengthy sentence at the high-security Korydhallos prison.

THE MACEDONIAN QUESTION

Increasingly unpopular due to the desperate austerity measures, and perceived as ineffective on the international scene, the last thing Mitsotakis needed was a major foreign policy headache. That is exactly what he got when, in 1991, one of the breakaway republics of the former Yugoslavia named itself **Macedonia**, thereby injuring Greek national pride and sparking off vehement protests at home and abroad. Diplomatically, the Greeks fought tooth and nail against anyone's recognizing the breakaway state, let alone its use of the name "Macedonia", but their position became increasingly isolated, and by 1993 the new country had gained official recognition from both the EU and the UN – albeit under the provisional title of the Former Yugoslav Republic of Macedonia (FYROM).

Salt was rubbed into Greek wounds when the FYROM started using the "Star of Veryína" (and of the ancient Macedonian kings) as a national symbol on their new flag, allegedly printed a banknote portraying the White Tower of Thessaloníki (Solun in Macedonian) and retained passages in its constitution referring to "unredeemed" Aegean territories. Greece still refuses to call its neighbour Macedonia, instead referring to it as *Tá Skópia* after the capital – and for quite some time you couldn't go anywhere in Greece without coming across officially placed stickers proclaiming that "Macedonia was, is and always will be Greek and only Greek!"

The ongoing argument for legitimacy hinges mostly on whether the ancient Macedonian kings were pure-bred Hellenes (the Greek position), Hellenized barbarians (the neutral conclusion) or proto-Slavs (the Macedonian claim).

THE PENDULUM SWINGS BACK

In effect, the Macedonian problem more or less directly led to Mitsotakis's political **demise**. In the early summer of 1993 his ambitious foreign minister, **Andonis Samaras**, disaffected with his leader, jumped on the bandwagon of resurgent Greek nationalism to set up his own party,

Politikí Ánixi (Political Spring). His platform, still right-wing, was largely based on action over Macedonia, and during the summer of 1993 more **Néa Dhimokratía** (ND) MPs broke ranks, making *Politikí Ánixi* a force to be reckoned with. When parliament reconvened in September to approve severe new budget proposals, it became clear that the government lacked sufficient support, and early elections were called for October 1993.

Mitsotakis had also been plagued for nearly a year by accusations of phone-tapping and theft of antiquities to stock his large private collection in Crete, plus links with a nasty, complicated contracts scandal focused around the national cement company.

On October 11, Papandreou romped to election victory; ND lost in 85 percent of the constituencies and the Synaspismós was replaced as the third party in parliament by Samaras's Politikí Ánixi and the unreconstructed communists, now under Aleka Papariga. The youthful Miltiades Evert, ex-mayor of Athens, replaced Mitsotakis as head of Néa Dhimokratía, so that – along with ex-KKE head Florakis – two of the dinosaurs of post-junta politics had passed from the scene.

THE MORNING AFTER

And so a frail-looking Papandreou, now well into his seventies, became prime minister for the third time. He soon realized that the honeymoon was going to be neither as sweet nor as long as it had been in the Eighties.

PASOK immediately fulfilled two of its pre-election promises by removing restrictions on the reporting of statements by terrorist groups and de-privatizing the Athens city bus company. The new government also set about improving the health system, and began to set the wheels in motion for Mitsotakis to be tried for his purported misdemeanours, though all charges were mysteriously dropped in January 1995, prompting allegations of under-the-table dealings between Papandreou and his old nemesis.

The root of popular dissatisfaction remained **the economy**, which was still in dire straits. Nor could PASOK claim to have won any diplomatic battles over Macedonia, despite a lot of tough posturing. The only concrete move was the imposition in October 1993 of a **trade embargo** on the FYROM, which merely landed the Greeks in trouble with the European Court of Justice – and succeeded in virtually shutting down the port of Thessaloníki. By contrast, alone among NATO members, Greece was conspicuous for its open **support of Serbia** in the wars wracking ex-Yugoslavia, ostentatiously breaking that particular embargo with supply trucks to Belgrade via Bulgaria.

In autumn 1994, for the first time ever in a PASOK-sponsored reform, provincial governors were directly elected in regional elections, rather than appointed from Athens. The following spring, **presidential elections** were held in parliament to designate a successor to the 88-year-old Karamanlis, who enjoyed just three years of well-deserved retirement before his death in spring 1998. The winner, supported by Politikí Ánixi and PASOK, was Kostis Stefanopoulos, ex-head of the dissolved party **DIANA** (Democratic Renewal). A former lawyer, untainted by scandal if a bit of a nonentity, he had been nominated by Samaras and accepted by Papandreou in a deal that would allow PASOK to see out its term without ructions.

The prime recurring scandal for 1995 had to do with the high security **prison of Korydhallos**, home to Koskotas and the former junta figures – and Colombian-style rackets. Two mass breakout attempts bracketed the discovery of an extensive drug-dealing ring controlled from inside; a call girl was detected in Koskotas's cell, as were large quantities of guns, ammunition and narcotics in the office of the head warden (subsequently arrested). In November, Greece lifted its embargo on "Macedonia", opening the borders for tourism and trade in return for FYROM suitably editing its constitution and removing the offending emblem from their flag. Relations, in fact, were instantly almost normalized, with only the name still moot; current favourites are "New Macedonia" or "Upper Macedonia", though as of late 1999 the place was still being referred to as FYROM (the Former Yugoslav Republic of Macedonia) by all outsiders.

THE END OF AN ERA

However, the emerging critical issue was the 76-year-old Papandreou's obstinate clinging to power despite obvious signs of dotage. Numerous senior members of PASOK became increasingly bold and vocal in their criticism, no longer fearing expulsion or the sack as in the past.

By late 1995, Papandreou was desperately ill in intensive care at the Onassis hospital, stricken with severe lung and kidney infections and dependent on life-support machinery. As there was no constitutional provision for replacing an infirm (but alive) prime minister, the country was essentially rudderless for two months, until the barely conscious old demagogue finally faced up to his own mortality and signed a letter **resigning** as prime minister (though not as party leader) in January 1996. The "palace clique" of Mimi Liani and cohorts was beaten off in the parliamentary replacement vote in favour of the allegedly colourless but widely respected technocrat **Kostas Simitis**, who seemed to be just what the country needed after years of incompetent flamboyance.

Upon assuming office, Simitis indicated that he wouldn't necessarily play to the gallery as Papandreou had with (for a Greek politician) a remarkable statement:

> *"Greece's intransigent nationalism is an expression of the wretchedness that exists in our society. It is the root cause of the problems we have had with our Balkan neighbours and our difficult relations with Europe."*

These beliefs were immediately put to the test by a tense armed face-off with Turkey over the uninhabited Dodecanese islet of **Ímia**, which very nearly degenerated into a shooting war. Simitis eventually bowed to US and UN pressure and ordered a withdrawal of Greek naval forces, conceding "disputed" status to the tiny goat-grazing outcrop – in hindsight a wise decision, but one for which at the time he was roundly criticized in parliament by fire-eating ND MPs and the media.

Andreas finally succumbed to his illness on June 22, 1996, prompting a moving display of national mourning. Already his canonization process proceeds apace, with a spate of streets renamed to honour him in provincial towns where he was always revered.

Papandreou's demise was promptly followed by PASOK's summer conference, where Simitis ensured his survival as party leader by co-opting his main internal foe, Papandreou's former head of staff, Akis Tsohadzopoulos, with a promise of future high office (minister of defence at the time of writing). Following the summer congress, Simitis cleverly rode the wave of pro-PASOK sympathy caused by Papandreou's death and called general elections a year early in September 1996.

The results were as hoped for: 162 seats for PASOK versus 108 for Néa Dhimokratía despite a margin of only three percentage points, the winner's strength artificially inflated by a convoluted electoral law. Given that the two main parties' agendas were virtually indistinguishable, the core issues boiled down to which was better poised to deliver results – and whether voters would be swayed by ND chief Evert's strident Slav- and Turk-baiting nationalism (they weren't). The biggest surprise was the collapse of Samaras's Politikí Ánixi, which failed to clear the three-percent nationwide hurdle for parliamentary representation, but three leftist splinter parties did well: eleven seats and just over five percent for Papariga's KKE, ten seats (including one Thracian Muslim deputy) with about the same tally for the Synaspismós under new chief Nikos Konstantopoulos, and nine seats at just under five percent for the Democratic Social Movement (DIKKI), founded early in the year by rehabilitated ex-minister Tsovolas to push for 1980s-vintage leftist policies. Evert resigned as ND leader, being succeeded by Karamanlis's nephew Kostas, who is now attempting to regain the centre ground.

THE CURRENT SITUATION

Néa Dhimokratía is down but by no means out, having actually increased its strength on the mainland in the last parliamentary poll. Athens mayor Dhimitris Avramopoulos, re-elected with almost sixty percent of the vote, is widely tipped as the next ND chief. In the **June 1999** Euro-elections ND repeated their success, finishing first nationwide and sending forty percent of Greece's Euro MPs to Strasbourg.

Nonetheless, Simitis's position seems secure for the time being within the party, though elections must be called before autumn 2000. First-term problems thus far have arisen mainly from the economic squeeze caused by continuing **austerity measures**. In December 1996, farmers staged dramatic protests, closing off the country's main road and rail arteries for several weeks, before dismantling the blockades in time for people to travel for the Christmas holidays. Much of 1997 saw the teachers or students (or both) on strike over proposed educational reforms – essentially about imposing some discipline on the notoriously lax school regimens. And immediately after the 1998 regional elections, Simitis endorsed a stringent budget which has seen little support, even from within his own party.

Greece still occupies EU's economic cellar along with Eire and Portugal, though recently monitored vital signs are vastly encouraging. Simitis, by nature far more pro-European than his maverick predecessor, has devoted himself to the unenviable task of getting the Greek economy in sufficiently good shape to meet the criteria for **monetary union**. After some initial success with his "hard drachma" policy (often propping it up by dumping foreign currency reserves), he was obliged to devalue it upon Greece's **entry to the ERM** in March 1998; however, with other internationally traded currencies badly exposed in the Far East economic crises, the drachma regained its lost value by October 1998. The fact that inflation is consistently down into single figures for the first time in decades is testament to his ability as an accountant, for which he has received credit from friends and enemies alike.

Increasingly amicable relations with its Balkan neighbours – Greece is the principal foreign investor in Bulgaria and the FYROM, for example – promise to generate jobs and trim unemployment, currently just over nine percent. **Tourism** improved significantly in the islands during 1999 despite NATO's spring war against Serbia. And the *Eforía* or Greek Inland Revenue has made some highly publicized headway in curbing the largest **black economy** in the EU, by requiring meticulous documentation of transactions and by publicly "outing" the more flagrant tax-dodgers.

In September 1997, Greece received a timely boost to national morale and economic prospects with the awarding of the 2004 **Olympic Games** to Athens. Simitis sensibly warned against people treating it as an excuse merely for unbridled money-making projects, and it is to be hoped that more substantial and long-lasting benefits will arise. One can be fairly confident that both the Athens metro and the new airport at Spáta will be completed on time (2001, in theory), even if many other infrastructure improvements necessary for the games have yet to materialize.

Carrying these out has been complicated by the aftermath of the severe **earthquake** which struck northern Athens on September 7, 1999, killing scores, rendering almost one hundred thousand homeless and immobilizing two of the three national mobile phone networks. It came less than a month after the devastating tremor in northwest Turkey, and ironically may prove to be the spur for a **thaw in relations** between the two historical rivals. Greeks donated massive amounts of blood and foodstuffs to the Turkish victims, as well as being the earliest foreign rescue teams on hand in Turkey, and in turn saw Turkish disaster-relief squads among the first on the scene in Athens. Soon afterwards, Foreign Minister Papandreou announced that Greece had dropped its long-time opposition to EU financial aid to Turkey in the absence of a solution to the outstanding Cyprus and Aegean disputes, and further indicated that Greece would not at present oppose Turkish candidacy for accession to the EU.

GREEK SOCIETY TODAY

The foregoing summary of recent, salient events doesn't, however, give a full flavour of the massive, ground-level changes which have occurred in Greece since the late 1980s. First and foremost, it is a conspicuously **wealthier society** than before, with vast disparities in income, imbued with rampant Thatcherism long after that ideology has largely subsided in its homeland. Athens, Thessaloníki and Pátra have their legions of **yuppies**, addicted to gourmet wines, designer trinkets, fast cars and travel; even small-town agencies promote junkets to Bali and Cuba (the current trendy favourites). It used to be that a lifetime sinecure with the civil service was the goal for most graduates, but no more – now young people crave a **career** in the private sector, with unlimited salary prospects.

Mobile phones are common – along with Italy and Cyprus, Greece has the highest per-capita use in Europe – and the success of the two private networks has forced partly privatized OTE to offer its own mobile network at reasonable prices.

Thanks in part to PASOK's recent policies, the country is now firmly locked into the **global economy**, symbolized by the proliferation of chains such as McDonalds, Marks & Spencer and The Body Shop in most larger towns; consumer interest rates, while still high, have plunged, the Athens stock exchange burgeons, and foreign or multinational companies have flocked to invest. It is they who are funding and carrying out massive infrastructure improvements designed to long outlast the 2004 Olympics: metros in Athens and Thessaloníki, the Río-Andírrio bridge over the Gulf of Corinth, the Via Egnatia expressway across Epirus, Macedonia and Thrace. **Overseas companies** are also quietly **acquiring** more productive elements of the Greek economy; Britain's Blue Circle, for example, in 1998 purchased Hercules Cement from Italian interests, while Skymaster, a subsidiary of British Airways, is now managing troubled flag-carrier Olympic Airways prior to its eventual privatization. The imminent end to cabotage – whereby only Greek companies have been allowed to provide ferry services within Greece – should weed out the flakier steamship companies and have the others pulling their socks up, under threat of possibly being challenged by the likes of P&O or Fred Olsen.

Domestic companies have followed overseas examples and engaged in extensive **corporate takeovers**: Alpha Credit/Alpha Pisteos Bank absorbed the troubled Ionian/Ioniki Bank in early 1999 and instantly became the second largest banking group in the country, while Minoan Lines merged with Ceres Hydrofoils to form Minoan Flying Dolphins, and acquired majority interest in Air Greece, to become the largest domestic transport company. **Private airlines**, including a number of expensive executive air-taxi outfits, are all the rage, and more emerge every few months.

Greece is still infinitely richer than most of its neighbours, and this fact has attracted, besides the aforementioned Albanians, significant **immigrant communities** of Bulgarians, Poles, Arabs, Pakistanis, Africans, Filipinos, Romanians, Ukrainians, Russians and Georgians to what had hitherto been a homogenous, parochial culture. These groups, plus travel, touring bands or dance companies and programmes on the private television channels have created a taste for **exotic music and foods**. One doesn't always have to wait for the summer festivals to see name jazz, blues or soul acts in Thessaloníki or Athens, and there are now decent foreign-cuisine restaurants there as well as in some of the major resorts. All of these factors, however, have had the effect of making Greece less identifiably Greek and, it must be said, of making the Greeks themselves rather less welcoming and more self-absorbed than formerly.

MYTHOLOGY, AN A TO Z

While all ancient cultures had their **myths**, it is those from ancient Greece that have had the greatest influence on Western civilization. The Trojan War, the wanderings of Odysseus, the adventures of Herakles – these stories and many more have inspired some of the finest literature, music and art.

Homer and his followers were the first bards to codify some of the stories in around 800 BC, but they had existed in the oral tradition for many years, and it was another few centuries before Homeric epics were actually written down and other legends set forth in **Hesiod's** *Theogeny*. With the ritual enactment of the myths in their religious festivals and ceremonies, along with their representation in designs on their pots and the performances of the stories at theatre and drama competitions, Greek myth and culture became inextricably blended.

Many versions of the myths exist, some of which are contradictory and confusing. Below is a summary of the principal **gods** and **heroes**. For further reading Robert Graves's *The Greek Myths* is a good source, though maybe a little dry and academic; Pierre Grimal's *Dictionary of Classical Mythology* is a better reference, but perhaps the best starting point and a way into feeling how the myths might have been told is to read Homer's epics *The Iliad* and *The Odyssey*.

Agamemnon see Atreus, or Trojan War

Aphrodite When Kronos castrated Ouranos (see p.482) and threw his testicles into the sea off Cyprus, the water spumed and produced Aphrodite, which means "born from sea foam". Her most famous ancient shrines were at Paphos (Cyprus), Knidos on the Anatolian coast and on Lésvos. Aphrodite's magic girdle made people fall in love with the wearer, but her famed adultery with Ares ended badly when she became ensnared in the nets that Hephaistos (see p.479), her husband, had made to expose her infidelity. She restored her virginity, but later had an affair with Hermes which produced a double-sexed offspring – Hermaphroditos. She particularly favoured the mortal Paris, instigator of the Trojan War.

Apollo, the illegitimate son of Zeus and the nymph Leto, was god of the sun, of plagues and, conversely, of healing. He killed the Python snake that terrorized the land around Delphi, a location with which he subsequently had great associations (his other two main precincts were on the islet of Delos, his purported birthplace, and Letoön in Asia Minor). His shrine at Delphi was, with Olympia, considered one of the centres of the Hellenic world, and through the priestess of the oracle here, the god gave prophecies to pilgrims. A god of outstanding beauty, Apollo represented music and poetry, and was usually depicted with either a bow and arrow or a lyre, which was a gift to him from Hermes. He was not unlucky in love, but was famously spurned by Daphne (see p.478).

Ares, the god of war and the only legitimate son of Zeus and Hera, had few associations with myths or temples – not surprisingly, given Zeus' famous utterance that Ares was the most hateful of all his offspring. Usually attended by his demon henchmen Deimos (Terror) and Phobos (Fear), Ares was not, however, uniformly-victorious – in *The Iliad* he was more than once outwitted by Athena.

Argonauts, see Jason and the Argonauts

Ariadne, see Theseus, Ariadne and the Minotaur

Artemis, Apollo's twin sister, was the goddess of hunting, the moon, unmarried maidens and indeed all of nature beyond the city. Her epithet was "Mistress of the Animals" and she was attended by trains of nymphs and lions. Artemis was always described as a virgin with perpetual youth. She also had a dark aspect that involved human sacrifice at some of her rites. Furthermore, she killed the huntsman Orion who tried to rape her, and instigated the death of Actaeon who had seen her bathe naked by changing him into a stag and setting his own hounds upon him. Her most important shrines were at Brauron in Attica, at Sparta and at Ephesos in Asia Minor.

Athena did not have a conventional birth – she sprang out of the head of Zeus ready for battle with armour, helmet and spear. Hephaistos had split Zeus' forehead for the "birth" to occur, and then attempted to ravish her; she remained a virgin, but some of his semen which he flicked off her thigh fell to earth, where it grew up as her son Ericthonius-Erechteus, legendary first king of Athens. She was accordingly the protectress and namesake of that city and by extension all others, and was regarded as the goddess of both war and certain more peaceable crafts and trades vital to civilized life: olive culture, wool-gathering, spinning, ship-building, chariots and horse tackle. Her many temples are typically on city acropoles or centres; she was ever ready to intervene on behalf of favourite mortals, particularly Odysseus and Herakles.

Atlas, see Herakles

Atreus, House of A dynasty of revenge, murder, incest and tragedy. Atreus hated his younger brother Thyestes, and when their separate claims for the kingship of Mycenae were voiced, the gods marked out Atreus for the task. Atreus banished Thyestes, but learning that his wife had had an affair with him, Atreus feigned forgiveness and recalled him from exile. He then had Thyestes' sons murdered, cut up, cooked and fed to Thyestes. When Thyestes had finished eating, Atreus showed him the heads of his children, clarifying the true nature of the meal. He again banished Thyestes, who took refuge at Sikyon and, sanctioned by the gods, fathered Aegisthus by his daughter, Pelopia. Pelopia then married Atreus, her uncle, and Aegisthus (who did not know who his real father was) was brought up and cared for by Atreus. When Aegisthus came of age, Atreus instructed him to kill Thyestes, but Aegisthus found out the truth, returned to Mycenae and killed Atreus. Atreus's two sons were Agamemnon and Menelaos. Agamemnon paid for his father's crimes by dying at the hands of his wife Clytemnestra (who had committed adultery with Aegisthus while Agamemnon was fighting at Troy). She ensnared him in a net while he took a bath and stabbed him to death. She in turn was killed by her son Orestes, who was pursued by the Furies before being absolved of matricide by Athena.

Bacchus, see Dionysos

Centaurs and Lapiths The centaurs were monstrous beings with the heads and torsos of men and the lower bodies of horses. They lived a debauched life, feeding on raw flesh and enjoying the pleasures of wine, but were also considered particularly skilled in sorcery and herbal healing. There are tales of centaurs battling with Herakles on his quest to complete the twelve labours, but the most famous story is of the fight that broke out between them and the Lapiths, a race of heroes and warriors who were the descendants of the river god Pineos (the Piniós flows near Mount Olympus). Pirithous, a Lapith who partially shared descent with the centaurs, invited them all to his wedding. At the feast the centaurs tried to abduct all the women, including the bride. A bloody brawl followed, of which the Lapiths were the victors; it is depicted on the pediment reliefs at Olympia, as a metaphor for the triumph of reason over barbarism.

Daphne The nymph Daphne was one of the daughters of the river god Pineos. Apollo took a fancy to her and chased her through the woods, but just as he caught up with her, she prayed to her father to save her. He took pity and turned her into a laurel tree, and she became rooted to the spot. Apollo loved her even as a tree and made the laurel sacred, dedicating wreaths of its leaves as a sign of honour. Her name, to this day, is the Greek word for the laurel tree.

Demeter was the goddess of agriculture, in particular corn, grain and pigs, as well as of death and regeneration. Both her origins and rites were shadowy, though we do know that women were her particular devotees. She exercised her power by making the whole Earth sterile after her daughter Persephone's abduction by Hades. The mother-and-daughter duo were usually revered together, particularly at their major sanctuary at Eleusis.

Dionysos, also known as Bacchus, was the god of wine and mystic ecstasy. He was the son of Zeus by Semele, who during conception was consumed by the god in the form of a lightning-bolt; Zeus rescued the unborn child and sewed him up in his thigh for the full gestation period. On birth, he was conveyed by Hermes to a far-off realm to be reared by the nymphs, and as a small boy he was disguised as a girl to hide him from Hera. As a youth, he was abducted by pirates; Dionysos caused the ship to be overgrown with ivy and vines (henceforth his symbols) and in panic the pirates dived overboard to become the first dolphins. Thus at his festivals a commemorative miniature ship was carried or propelled on wheels, suitably decorated. In art he is often shown riding in a chariot drawn by panthers, and followed by a coterie of satyrs, sileni and mortal followers brandishing *thyrsoi* (wands topped with pine cones). Dionysos' semi-mythical women followers, the maenads (see p.481), roamed the countryside at certain seasons in a state of madness; more usually, he was revered in the form of a bearded mask on a column, the antecedent of the comic and tragic masks of theatre. He rescued Ariadne from Náxos following her abandonment there by Theseus (see p.483).

Eurydice, see Orpheus and Eurydice

Golden Fleece, see Jason and the Argonauts

Hades was the brother of Zeus and Poseidon, and when the cosmos was divided between them he was allotted the underworld. His name means "the invisible", because in the battle with Kronos and the Titans he concealed himself by wearing a magic helmet given to him by the Cyclops. To refer to him as Hades was thought to bring about his awesome anger, so the Greeks called him by his surname Pluto, which means "the rich" and alludes to the wealth that lies hidden underground. His wife was Demeter's daughter, Persephone (see p.482). Rather than temples, he had suitably mysterious oracles, most notably at Ephyra in Epirus and that of Trophonios at Levadia.

Helen was the daughter of Zeus, who appeared in the form of a swan to her mother Leda. She was believed to be the most beautiful woman in the world. Her husband Menelaos, king of Sparta, entertained the Trojans Paris and Aeneas and was foolish enough to leave them alone with her; Paris abducted her. Some sources say she went willingly, impressed by his beauty and wealth; others say she was raped. In either event her departure from Sparta was the cause of the Trojan War (see p.483).

Hephaistos was the god of fire and a master craftsman. In his workshop on volcanic Límnos, where he was especially revered, he fashioned everything from jewellery to armour. Elsewhere his cult was less elaborated, except at Athens, where he had a sumptuous temple in honour of his role in siring Erechtheus (see Athena). He was made lame, and there are two conflicting versions of how he sustained his injuries: either they were inflicted when Zeus threw him from Olympus because he had defended Hera in a quarrel, or alternatively when Hera, who bore him, tossed him down to Límnos in disappointment at her unprepossessing offspring. He was clever but very ugly, yet was married to Aphrodite (see p.477), the most beautiful of the goddesses.

Hera was Zeus' sister, wife and the most powerful of the goddesses – she wreaked her vengeance and jealousy on anyone whom Zeus seduced and the offspring of most of his encounters (see Io p.480). Zeus punished her heavily for her anger against Herakles by suspending her from her wrists from Mount Olympus, weighing her ankles down with anvils, and whipping her. Despite her vindictive and irascible Homeric portrayal, she was the protecting deity of wives and marriage. Her totems and sacrificial animals were the cow, the cuckoo and the peacock; her principal temples were on Sámos, near Argos, at modern Perahóra and at Olympia.

Herakles (Hercules) was the superhero of the ancient world. A mighty hunter and sacrificer, Herakles appealed to young men in particular. His mother was the mortal Alcmene, and his father Zeus. Jealous Hera sent two snakes to kill Herakles while he was still in his cradle, which he duly strangled, all good preparation for his twelve labours.

The labours were commanded by King Eurystheus of the Argolid, who was under the thrall of Hera. These tasks took him to the fringes of the known world, even involving his supporting it on his shoulders while Atlas took a break to lend him a hand in his final task. The labours were: to kill the Nemean lion; to kill the many-headed Hydra monster; to bring back the wild boar of Erymanthus alive; to hunt the Keryneian hind that was sacred to Artemis; to kill the man-eating birds at the lake of Stymphaleia; to clean the stables of King Augeas; to bring back the untameable Cretan bull alive; to capture the flesh-eating horses of Diomedes; to fetch the girdle of the Amazon warrior queen; to fetch the herds of Geryon from beyond the edge of the ocean; to fetch Cerberus the guard dog of the underworld gates; and finally to fetch the golden apples from the garden of the Hesperides.

Curiously for such a macho figure, Herakles spent a certain amount of time as a slave, or in drag, or both. During a fit of madness sent by Hera, he slew his wife and children at Thebes; in atonement he passed some years dressed as a woman in the court of Queen Omphale of Lydia.

His death was as dramatic as his life. Deianeira, his second wife, gave him a garment that she thought had magic powers and would prevent him from being unfaithful to her. When he put it on, it burned into his flesh and slowly and painfully killed him. Unable to bear the pain, Herakles built a funeral pyre and immolated himself. He was fully deified by Zeus – the only mortal or demigod to be so honoured.

Hermes was the son of Zeus and Maia, the daughter of Atlas. He was born in the Kyllene mountains of Arcadia, where his only major temple existed at Pheneos. A trickster figure, Hermes showed his mettle by inventing the lyre on the day of his birth, then stealing Apollo's sacred cattle, denying the deed to his brother. Zeus effected a reconciliation, and Hermes gave Apollo the lyre in exchange for the cattle and a golden staff.

Hermes was the god of commerce, thievery, herdsmen, travel and boundaries; rather than shrines he had herms, stone cairns or boundary-markers. In his role as Conductor of Souls, Hermes regularly crossed between the living and underworld. He was often depicted wearing winged shoes, a wide-brimmed hat and carrying the herald's staff which showed his position as the divine messenger.

Hippolytos and Phaedra Hippolytos, son of the hero Theseus and the Amazon Hippolyta, was an accomplished hunter who revered Artemis and scorned Aphrodite. Aphrodite sought to teach him a lesson and conspired for Phaedra, the new wife of Theseus, to fall in love with the young man. When she was spurned by Hippolytos she feared he might reveal her advances and so accused him of rape. When Theseus heard this, he called upon Poseidon to kill his son; Hippolytos was then flung from his chariot and torn apart by his horses. Phaedra in shame and remorse hanged herself.

Io, a priestess of Hera at Argos, was only one of the many mortals who caught Zeus' eye, but before he could get to know her better, Hera got wind of his interest and Zeus hastily transformed Io into a cow. Hera demanded her as a present, and placed her under the guard of Argos, the hundred-eyed monster. Hera then proceeded to torment poor Io the cow by sending a stinging gadfly to goad her on her travels. She made for the sea, first to the Ionian Sea, which was named after her, and then crossed the straits into Asia at the Bosporus (literally, the "Cow Ford"). Before settling in Egypt, she wandered all over Asia, even bumping into Prometheus, who was chained for a few centuries to the Caucasus mountain range.

Jason and the Argonauts Jason, a great Greek hero from Iolkos (present-day Vólos), was set an almost impossible task by his step-uncle Pelias to win the power that was his by birthright: to sail to the ends of the earth and bring back the Golden Fleece. He assembled his crew, assorted heroes of the ancient Greek world, and commissioned a ship, called the *Argo* after its maker Argos, which was built with the help of Athena – its prow had the remarkable gift of speech and prophecy. A long journey full of stories and surprises followed. Some of the crew didn't complete the voyage, including Herakles who missed the boat because he was searching for his favourite, Hylas, a beautiful boy who had been abducted by the nymphs. The seer Phineus gave Jason directions and advice in return for his killing the harpies that were plaguing him; in particular he told Jason how to deal with moving rocks and reefs that might smash his ship. Armed with this knowledge, Jason and the Argonauts reached their destination. On arrival in Colchis, however, the King Aeetes would not hand over the Golden Fleece until Jason had completed various labours. The king's daughter, the sorceress Medea (see opposite), fell in love with Jason and helped him with her magic powers. They stole the fleece and fled, pursued by Aeetes. Medea stalled her father by tearing up her brother Apsyrtus and casting his body parts into the sea; Aeetes had to slow down to collect the pieces. Zeus was greatly angered by this heinous crime and the *Argo* spoke to the crew telling them that they would have to purify themselves at Circe's island. After more adventures and wanderings through treacherous seas, the crew arrived at Corinth where Jason dedicated the Golden Fleece to Poseidon.

Judgement of Paris The goddess Eris (Strife) began a quarrel between Athena, Hera and Aphrodite by throwing a golden apple between them and saying that it belonged to whichever goddess was the most beautiful. All the gods were too frightened to judge the contest, so Hermes took the goddesses to the top of Mount Ida for Paris, the son of Priam of Troy, to decide. Each used bribery to win his favour: Athena offered him wisdom and victory in combat, Hera the kingdom of Asia, but Aphrodite, the winner of the contest, offered him the love of Helen of Sparta.

Kronos The Titan Kronos was the youngest son of the pre-Olympian deities Gaia and Ouranos, who seized power in the heavens by castrating his father. Once on the throne, Kronos lived in perpetual fear of the prediction that one of his offspring would one day overthrow him, and so he swallowed all of his children except Zeus (see p.483) – Zeus' mother Rhea had substituted a stone for the bundle that Kronos thought was his baby. Kronos and his Titan brothers were defeated in a cosmic battle by Zeus and his Olympian supporters.

Lapiths, see Centaurs and Lapiths

Maenads The maenads were the possessed or intoxicated female followers of Dionysos (see p.478). They wore scanty clothes, had wreaths of ivy around their heads and played upon tambourines or flutes in their processions. They had power over wild animals, and in their frenzy they believed they drank milk or honey from freshwater springs. In their orgiastic ecstasies they tore limb from limb those who offended them, did not believe or who spied upon their rites – including Orpheus (see p.482).

Medea exacted gruesome revenge on any who stood against her. She persuaded the daughters of Pelias (see Jason and the Argonauts) to cut their father up and put him in a boiling cauldron, having convinced them that if they did so she could rejuvenate him. His body parts, to their extreme disappointment, did not come back together. Akastos, Pelias's son, banished her and Jason as a punishment; they went together to Corinth, where Jason abandoned her to marry Kreusa the daughter of the local king Kreon. In revenge, Medea orchestrated a gruesome death for Kreusa, by sending her a tunic which burst into flames upon wearing, and then murdered her own two young sons by Jason.

Minotaur, see Theseus, Ariadne and the Minotaur

Mount Olympus, see Zeus

Muses The Muses were the result of nine nights of lovemaking between Mnemosyne (Memory) and Zeus. They were primarily singers and the inspiration for music (to which they gave their name), but also had power over thought in all its forms: persuasion, eloquence, knowledge, history, mathematics and astronomy. Apollo conducted their singing around the Hippocrene fountain on Mount Helicon, or on Mount Olympus itself.

Nymphs There were various subspecies of nymph: meliads were the nymphs of the ash trees; nereids lived in the springs and streams; naïads in the ocean; dryads were individual tree nymphs; oreads were the mountain nymphs; and the alseids lived in the groves. They were thought to be the daughters of Zeus and attended certain deities, particularly Artemis and Poseidon.

Odysseus Our word "odyssey" derives from Odysseus' ten-year journey home, which was no less fraught with danger, adventure and grief than the ten-year war against the Trojans which preceded it. Shipwrecked, tormented by the gods, held against his will by bewitching women, almost lured to his death by the hypnotic Sirens, witnessing his comrades devoured by the giant one-eyed Cyclops Polyphemos and all the time missing and desiring his faithful wife Penelope, Odysseus proved himself to be a great and scheming hero. At the end of his arduous journey he arrived in disguise at his palace on Ithaca to find suitors pestering his wife. He contrived a cunning trap and killed them all with the bow which only he could flex.

Oedipus was a man profoundly cursed. The Delphic Oracle said that Laius, king of Thebes, should not father any children, for if he did one would kill him. When Oedipus was born Laius abandoned the baby, piercing his ankles with a nail and tying them together: hence the name, which means "swollen foot". But the baby was discovered and brought up at the court of the neighbouring king, Polybos, at Corinth. The same oracle revealed to the adult Oedipus that he would kill his father and marry his mother. When he heard this news he resolved not to return home to Corinth, but east of Delphi he met with Laius, who was heading west to consult the oracle as to how to rid Thebes of the Sphinx. Because the road was narrow, Laius ordered Oedipus to get out of the way, and when one of the guards pushed him, Oedipus drew his sword in anger and, not knowing that Laius was his father, killed him and his entourage. He then made his way to the Thebes, where Laius had been king, and solved the riddle of the Sphinx. As a reward and in thanks, he was crowned king and offered Laius' widow Iocasta (his mother) in marriage. Plague then fell upon Thebes, because of the crimes of patricide and incest at the heart of the city. The Delphic Oracle instructed Oedipus to expel the murderer of Laius, and in his ignorance he ordered the guilty party cursed and banished. The seer and prophet Teiresias then revealed the full nature of the crime to Iocasta and Oedipus; she hanged herself and he put out his own eyes. He left the city as a vagabond accompanied by his daughter Antigone, and only at his death was granted peace. Attica, the country that received his dead body, became blessed.

Orpheus and Eurydice Orpheus was a great musician who received his lyre from Apollo himself. He played and sang so beautifully that wild beasts were charmed, trees would uproot themselves to come closer, and even the very rocks were moved. He enlisted in the crew of Argonauts and sang for them to row their oars in time. On his return from the *Argo*'s voyage he married the nymph Eurydice. She was bitten by a snake on the banks of the river Pineos and died, and Orpheus was so distraught that he went to the underworld to bring her back to life. His wish was granted by Hades on condition that during the return journey he would not look back at her. As the couple approached daylight, however, his mind became consumed with doubt and, turning around to see if she was behind him, he lost her forever. He preached that Apollo was the greatest god, much to the anger of Dionysos, who set the maenads on him. They tore him apart and cast his head, still singing, into the Thracian river Hebrus; it was finally washed up on the shores of the island of Lésvos, supposedly conferring great musical gifts on the local population.

Ouranos was the personification of the sky and by his union with Gaia (Earth) fathered many children, including Kronos (see above) and the Titans (see below). Gaia became so exhausted by her husband's continual advances that she sought protection from her sons. Kronos was the only one to assist; he cut off Ouranos's testicles with a sickle and threw them into the sea, giving rise to Aphrodite (see p.477).

Pan The patron of shepherds and flocks, Pan was the son of Hermes and a nymph and, with his beard, horns, hairy body and cloven hooves, was said to be so ugly that his own mother ran from him in fear. He had an insatiable libido, energetically pursuing both sexes. Apollo learned the art of prophecy from Pan, and hunters looked to him for guidance. He enjoyed the cool woodland shade and streams of Arcadia and relished his afternoon naps so much that he wreaked havoc if he was disturbed.

Pandora, see Prometheus

Pegasus, see Poseidon

Penelope, see Odysseus

Persephone, also known as Kore (the Maiden), was out picking flowers one day when the Earth opened up and swallowed her; she had been abducted by Hades riding his chariot. Her mother Demeter was distraught and when she found out the truth, she left Olympus in protest and made the Earth sterile so that it produced no crops. Zeus ordered Hades to return Persephone, but because she had eaten pomegranate seeds in the underworld she was bound to him. As a compromise, she would be allowed to return to Earth for two thirds of the year and had to reside with Hades for the remaining third. Thus Demeter divided the year into seasons, so that while Persephone was with Hades the Earth would be sterile and in winter, but that while she was on Earth the ground would be fertile for spring, summer and autumn.

Perseus A son of Zeus, and believed to be a direct ancestor of Herakles, Perseus was cast out to sea in a trunk with his mother Danae, because his grandfather feared a prophecy that Perseus would one day kill him. Danae and Perseus were washed up on Sérifos island, where they were discovered by a fisherman who looked after them. When Perseus came of age, the king of Sérifos demanded that he bring back the head of Medusa the gorgon, whose gaze could turn people to stone. Perseus acquired some special aids from Hermes and Athena to perform the task, including a helmet which made him invisible, and winged sandals to fly through the air. He cut off Medusa's head while looking at her reflection in Athena's polished shield. On his return flight he saw and fell in love with Andromeda, who was being offered as a sacrifice. He rescued her and returned home to find his mother had been raped by the king. He held up the gorgon's head, turned the king to stone and then presented the head as a gift to Athena, who placed it in the middle of her shield. Perseus went on to participate in the king of Larissa's celebratory games; he competed in the discus-throwing competition but his throw went off course and killed his grandfather, who was a spectator, thus fulfilling the prophecy.

Phaedra, see Hippolytos and Phaedra

Poseidon was the god of the sea, earthquakes and storms, and patron of fishermen. In the battle with Kronos and the Titans, Poseidon, the brother of Zeus, wielded the trident which he later used to shake both sea and land. After the victory he was awarded, by lot, the realm of the ocean, where he dwelt in the depths. He produced some strange offspring, including the Cyclops Polyphemos who had it in for Odysseus (see p.481), and mated with the gorgon Medusa – which resulted in the winged horse Pegasus. He quarrelled frequently with the other gods, competing with them for power over some of the major cities including Athens, Corinth and Argos. Although he helped destroy Troy in *The Iliad*, he also persecuted Odysseus mercilessly on his return home. Among his numerous temples, the most important were those at Isthmía, Soúnio and Póros near Athens; Mykale in Asia Minor; and an oracle at Cape Ténaro.

Prometheus For someone whose name means "forethought", Prometheus showed a distinct lack of it. In his desire to help mankind, he stole fire from the heavens and was immediately punished by Zeus, who bound him in chains, tied him to the Caucasus mountains and then sent an eagle to peck perpetually at his liver. Zeus then dealt with mankind by sending Pandora to Prometheus' brother Epimetheus, whose name means "afterthought". Her curiosity about the contents of his box got the better of her and, peeping inside, she unleashed all the evils and one good (hope) on the world. Prometheus gave some useful advice to Herakles when he passed by on one of his labours and Herakles repaid him by setting him free.

Theseus, Ariadne and the Minotaur Theseus' father, Aegeus of Athens, sent him as a child away from Athens for his own safety. At sixteen the hero returned, in full strength and with the weapons that his father had set aside for him. Theseus was destined for a life of action, and his greatest adventure was to kill the Minotaur on Crete. As tribute from Athens, King Minos was owed six men and six women every nine years for sacrifice to the Minotaur – a gruesome beast, half-man half-bull, born from the bestial copulation of the queen Pasiphae with the huge bull sent by Poseidon. The Minotaur was kept in the labyrinth at Crete. Ariadne, Minos's daughter, contrived to help Theseus kill the Minotaur, having fallen in love with him. She gave him a ball of thread so that he would not lose his way in the labyrinth and then accompanied him in his flight from the island, only to be abandoned later on the island of Náxos. Dionysos saw her there disconsolate on the shore, took pity on her and married her. Theseus, meanwhile, on his return to Athens forgot to change the black sails to white as a signal to his father that he was alive, and Aegeus – thinking that his son had been killed by the Minotaur – threw himself into the sea which took his name: the Aegean.

Titans The Titans were the six male children of Ouranos and Gaia. Their six sisters, who helped them father numerous gods, were called the Titanides. Kronos was the youngest Titan, and after he had overthrown his father he helped his brothers to power. The Titans lost their grip when they were toppled by the upstart Olympians, led by Zeus, in the cataclysmic battle called the Titanomachia.

Trojan War When Menelaos of Sparta realized that the Trojan Paris had made off with his wife Helen, he called on his brother Agamemnon of Mycenae. Together they roused the might of Greece to get her back. With just about every hero (Ajax, Achilles, Troilus, Hector, Paris, Odysseus, Priam, Diomedes, Aeneas) making an appearance in this epic, the story of the Trojan War is arguably the greatest tale from the ancient world. Homer's *Iliad* dealt with only one aspect of it, the wrath of Achilles. The ten-year war, fought over a woman and which sent many heroes' souls down to Hades, was finally won by the trickery of the Greeks, who used a huge wooden horse left ostensibly as a gift to the Trojans to smuggle an armed platoon inside the city walls. The cunning plan was thought to be the work of Odysseus (see p.481), who, like many of the surviving heroes, had a less than easy journey home.

Zeus was the supreme deity, king of gods and men, but he did not get to this position without a struggle. His father, the Titan Kronos, seized power in the heavens by castrating Ouranos the sky god, and in turn lived in fear that one of his own offspring would one day overthrow him. So he swallowed all of his children except Zeus, whose mother, Rhea, came to the rescue and hid him in a cave on the island of Crete, where the warrior Kouretes concealed his cries by smashing their swords and shields together. When he came of age, Zeus poisoned Kronos so that he vomited up all Zeus' siblings; with their help, and the assistance of the Cyclops, he cast Kronos and the Titans from Mount Olympus, the home of the gods. The Cyclops gave Zeus the thunderbolt as a weapon to use in the battle and it became his symbol of power, and emblem of his role as deity of weather and rain. Zeus used his position to maintain cosmic order, control the other gods and men and to get his way with whomever he fancied. Numerous myths tell of his metamorphoses to mate with a variety of mortals out of sight of his jealous wife Hera; all of his liaisons resulted in offspring, which included Herakles, Perseus and Helen (see pp.479 and 482).

MUSIC

Music is central to Greek island culture; even the most indifferent visitor will be aware of its ubiquitous presence in vehicles, tavernas, ferries and other public spaces. Like most aspects of Greece, it's an amalgamation of native and oriental styles, with occasional contributions from the West. In fact, Western music made little impression until recent decades, when aesthetic disputes arose between adherents of folk-derived styles, and the proponents of jazz/cabaret, symphonic and rock idioms.

Many older songs, invariably in Eastern-flavoured minor scales, have direct antecedents in the forms and styles of both **Byzantine religious chant** and that of the **Ottoman empire**, though some nationalistic musicologists claim their original descent from the now-lost melodies of ancient Greece. Almost all native Greek instruments are near-duplicates of ones used throughout the Islamic world, though it's an open question as to whether the Byzantines, Arabs or Persians first constructed particular instruments. To this broadly Middle Eastern base, Slavs, Albanians and Italians have added their share, resulting in an extraordinarily varied repertoire of traditional and modern pieces.

The most promising times to hear regional island music live are at the numerous summer *paniyíria* (saints'-day festivals) – or more tourist-orientated cultural programmes – when musicians normally based in Athens or city clubs during winter tour the islands. However, it's as well to know that a marked vulgarization of this type of music began during the 1960s – a trend accelerated by the 1967–74 junta – so that traditional instrumentation is now often replaced by something more appropriate to rock concerts. The musicians themselves, who have been deprived of (or actively scorn) the teachings of technique from older master players, are also not always what they could be. Furthermore, most island-based musicians are semi-professionals, required to supplement their income with another trade. All this makes recent re-releases on CD of old archival material all the more precious, and an increasing number of revival groups are attempting to recapture the musicianship, if not the ethos, of the old-timers.

Many island pieces are danceable, divided by rhythm into such categories as *kalamatianó* (a line dance), *hasaposérviko* or *syrtó*, the quintessential circle dance found across Greece. The quick-tempoed couples' dance of Crete, the *soústa*, is found with essentially the same rhythm in the eastern Aegean as *bállos*. Pieces for recitation at table or other assemblies include the slow, stately *rizítiko* of Crete, which relate, baldly or in metaphor, incidents or attitudes from the years of Ottoman rule.

CRETE, KÁSSOS, HÁLKI AND KÁRPATHOS

This arc of southern islands is one of the most promising areas in Greece for hearing live music at any time of year. The dominant instrument here is the **lýra**, a three-stringed fiddle directly related to the Turkish *kemençe*. This is played not on the shoulder but balanced on the thigh, often with tiny bells attached to the bow, which the musician can jiggle for rhythmical accent. The strings are metal, and since the centre string is just a drone, the player improvises only on the outer two. Usually the *lýra* is backed up by one or more **laoúta**, similar to the Turkish/Arab *oud* and but more closely resembling a mandolin. These are rarely used to their full potential – a *laoúto* solo is an uncommon treat – but a good player will find the harmonics and overtones of a virtuoso *lýra* piece, at the same time coaxing a pleasing, chime-like tone from his instrument.

In several places in the southern Aegean (notably northern Kárpathos) a simple bagpipe, the **askómandra** or **tsamboúna,** joins the *lýra* and *laoúto*. During the colonels' dictatorship the playing of bagpipes in the Cyclades further

DISCOGRAPHY

All of the following are available on CD unless specified otherwise; similarly, all are Greek label pressings.

If you're stopping over in Athens en route to the islands, the best record stores – Musiki Gonia, Xylouris and Metropolis – are within a few hundred metres of each other on Odhós Panepistimíou, between the university and Omónia. In the UK the best source is Trehantiri, 367 Green Lanes, London N4; (☎020/8802 6530), which also operates a worldwide mail order service. In North America, try Down Home Music, 10341 San Pablo Avenue, El Cerrito, CA (☎510/525-2129).

Anatolia tou Egeou/East of the Aegean (Verso, Athens). Dhonoússa native Nikos Ikonomidhes, now resident on Híos, leads this set of lively dance tunes on *violí*, with a few songs thrown in, all from the east Aegean islands. Marred only by a persistently heavy electric bass line.

Avthentika Nisiotika tou Peninda (Lyra CD 0168). Good Cretan and Pontic material from the 1950s, with the Dodecanese also represented, from the collection of the late Ted Petrides, musician and dance master.

Emilia Hatzidhaki *Thalassina Tragoudhia* (LP: Panvox 16311, reissued as CD by MBI). The only easily available collection dedicated to this artist, who otherwise appears only on *nisiótika* anthologies.

Kassos: Skopi tis Lyras/Lyra Tunes (Lyra 0113). A recent collection from the bleakest of the Dodecanese, whose music however tends to be more digestible than that of neighbouring Kárpathos.

Kastellorizo (Syrtos 561) and **Tradgoudhia keh Skopi tis Kalymnou** (Syrtos 564). Studio productions of musicologist Manolis Karpathios; the Kálymnos disc, with just three contemporary musicians on bagpipes, *laoúto* and fiddle, is harsh but compelling, the Kastellorizan more of the collected-and-remastered variety.

Irini Konitopoulou-Legaki *Athanata Nisiotika 1* (Tzina-Astir 1020). A 1978 warhorse, beloved of bus drivers across the islands. *Anefala Thalassina* (Lyra 4693) is far less commercial, featuring fellow Naxian lautist Dhimitris Fyroyenis; this is Irini singing her heart out, off the club stage.

Yiorgos Konitopoulos & Clan *Thalassa keh Paradhosi* (EMI 14C 064 71253). Standard taverna or party fare throughout the islands; slicker than *Athanata Nisiotika* but no worse for that.

Kritiki Mousiki Paradhosi, Iy Protomastores 1920–1953 (Aerakis, 10 Cds). For many visitors, Cretan music consists of lugubrious, monotonous sawing on the *lýra* and verses in impenetrable

northwest was banned lest tourists think the Greeks "too primitive". In Kazantzakis's classic novel (and in the movie), Zorba himself played a **sandoúri**, or hammer dulcimer, for recreation, but it was actually little known until after 1923 on most islands, being introduced by Asia Minor refugees. Today, accomplished players are few, and in *kritikí* (Cretan music) and *nisiótika* (island songs), the instrument has been relegated to a supporting role. On older Cretan recordings you may hear solos on the **voúlgari**, a stringed instrument, essentially a small *saz* (Turkish long-necked, fretted lute), which has now all but died out. Modern Cretan artists to look out for on recordings include **Kostas Moundakis**, the late acknowledged *lýra* master, the late **Nikos Xylouris**, justifiably dubbed "The Nightingale of Crete" for his soaring voice, and his younger, *lýra*-playing brother Andonis who performs under the name **Psarandonis**.

NORTHERN DODECANESE AND CYCLADES

On the northern Dodecanese islands and the Cyclades, you'll find the *lýra* replaced by a more familiar-looking **violí**, essentially a Western violin. Accompaniment was provided until recently by *laóuto* or *sandoúri*, though these days you're more likely to be confronted (or affronted) by a bass-guitar-and-drum rhythm section.

Unlike on Crete, where you can often catch reasonable music in special clubs or *kéndra*, Aegean island performances tend to use village squares or monastery courtyards as the usual, more spontaneous venue for saints'-day festivals. *Nisiótika* melodies, like much folk music the world over, rely heavily on the pentatonic scale. Lyrics, especially on the smaller islands of the central Aegean, touch on the perils of the sea, exile and – in a society where long periods dialect; this is the perfect antidote. The whole set's prohibitively pricey, and some titles are of specialist interest, but fortunately discs are available individually; go for No. 1 (Baksevanis, *lýra* and small orchestra); No. 4 (Stelios Foustalieris, the last master of the tambur-like *voúlgari*, knowledge of which died with him); No. 5 (Yiannis Demirtzoyiannis, guitarist and epic singer) and No. 6 (Yiorgis Koutsourelis, on melodic *laoúto*).

Lesvos Aiolis: Tragoudhia keh Hori tis Lesvou/Songs & Dances of Lesvos (University Press of Crete, double CD 9/10). Two decades' worth (1974–96) of field recordings of the last traditional music extant on the island, a labour of love supervised by musicologist Nikos Dhionysopoulos. Pricey, but the quality and uniqueness of the instrumental festival tunes and dances especially, and the illustrated booklet, merit the expense (typically over £20 equivalent).

Yannis Parios *Ta Nisiotika Vol 1* (Minos 430/431) & Vol 2 (Minos 1017/1018). Parios sparked a renewal of interest in *nisiotikó* – traditional island music – with the first of these two discs done a decade apart, each accompanied by members of the Konitopoulos clan. Maybe not the most authentic versions (they're essentially traditional acoustic accompaniment juxtaposed with urban-pop-style vocals) but easy on the ear, and both went platinum – Vol 1 with sales of nearly a million.

Seryiani sta Nisia Mas, Vol 1 (CD, MBI 10371). Excellent retrospective of various *nisiótika* hits and artists, mostly from the 1950s. The highlight of Vol 1 (2 doesn't exist) is Emilia Hatzidhaki's rendering of "Bratsera".

Songs and Melodies of Patmos (CD, Politistikon Idhryma Dhodhekanisou 201). Live 1995 field recordings of well-edited pieces, as raw but compelling as you'd hear them at an old-time festival. Local singers and instrumentalists on *violí, tsamboúna* and *sandoúri*.

Songs of... (Society for the Dissemination of National Music, Greece). A thirty-disc-plus series of field recordings from the 1950s through the 1970s, each covering traditional music of one region or type. All LPs contain lyrics in English, and recordings are easily available in Athens in LP, cassette or CD form, especially at the Musicological Museum on Dhioyénous 1–3 in Pláka. Best island discs to date are *Mytilene and Chios* (SDNM 110); *Mytilene and Asia Minor* (SDNM 125); *Rhodes, Chalki and Symi* (SDNM 104); and *Kassos and Karpathos* (SDNM 103).

Nikos Xylouris *O Arkhangelos tis Kritis, 1958–1968* (MBI 10376); *Ta Khronia stin Kriti* (2CD, MBI10677/78). These are the best two retrospectives of the sweet-voiced Cretan, with copious notes; the first covers his initial decade of recordings, previously unavailable, with self-accompaniment on the *lýra*.

of separation and arranged marriage were the norm – thwarted love. Though since the 1960s the **Konitopoulos clan** from Náxos has become virtually synonymous with *nisiótika*, older stars like **Anna and Emilia Hatzidhaki**, **Effi Sarri** and **Anna Karabesini** – all from the Dodecanese archipelago – offer a warmer, more innocent delivery.

NORTHEAST AEGEAN ISLANDS

There's more obvious Anatolian and Constantinopolitan influence in both the music and instrumentation of these islands. Largely because of the refugee background of its population, there is no longer an indigenous musical tradition on Sámos. Matters are better on neighbouring Ikaría, where skilled musicians still perform at the spring and summer monastery-festivals in the west of the island.

Lésvos occupies a special place in terms of island music; before the turbulent decade of 1912–22, its "mainland" was Asia Minor rather than Greece, its urban poles Smyrna and Constantinople rather than Athens. Accordingly its music is far more varied than the Aegean norm, having absorbed melodies and instrumentation from various groups who lived in neighbouring Anatolia. Lésvos is the only island with a vital tradition of brass bands, and virtually every Greek dance rhythm is represented in local music. The *vióli*, clarinet, lapdrum (*toumberléki*) or shoulder drum (*daoúli*) are also encountered at festivals here; these, or the aforementioned brass ensembles, traditionally played wedding marches or tunes marking the start of horse-racing or bull-sacrificing festivals. The keyed clarinet (*klaríno*) – as opposed to simple, single-reed, oboe-like instruments – was unknown in Greece before 1830 and (depending on whom you believe) was introduced either by the gypsies or Bavarians attached to the royal court.

IONIAN ISLANDS

By way of complete contrast and alone of all modern Greek territory, the Ionian islands – except for Lefkádha – never saw Turkish occupation and have a predominantly Western musical tradition. The indigenous song-form is Italian both in name, **kantádhes**, and instrumentation (guitar and mandolin); it's most often heard these days on **Lefkádha** and **Zákynthos**.

Marc Dubin, with George Pissalides

WILDLIFE

For anyone who has first seen the smaller Greek islands at the height of summer with their brown parched hillsides and desert-like ambience, the richness of the wildlife – in particular the flora – may come as a surprise. As winter changes to spring, the countryside (and urban waste ground) transforms itself from green to a mosaic of coloured flowers, which attract a plethora of insect life, followed by birds. Isolated areas have had many thousands of years to develop their own individual species. Overall, Greece has around six thousand species of native flowering plants, nearly four times that of Britain but in the same land area. Many are unique to Greece, and make up about one third of Europe's endemic plants.

SOME BACKGROUND

In early antiquity Greece, including the islands, was thickly forested: Aleppo and Calabrian pines grew in coastal regions, giving way to fir or black pine up in the hills and low mountains. But this **native woodland** contracted rapidly as human activities expanded. By Classical times, a pattern had been set of forest clearance, followed by agriculture, abandonment to scrub and then a resumption of cultivation or grazing. Huge quantities of timber were consumed in the production of charcoal, pottery and smelted metal, and for ships and construction work. Small patches of virgin woodland have remained on the largest islands, but even these are under threat from loggers and arsonists.

Modern Greek **farming** often lacks the rigid efficiency of northern European agriculture. Many peasant farmers still cultivate little patches of land, and even town-dwellers travel at weekends to collect food plants from the countryside. Wild greens under the generic term *hórta* are gathered to be cooked like spinach; grape hyacinth bulbs are boiled as a vegetable. The buds and young shoots of capers, and the fruit of wild figs, carobs, plums, strawberry trees, cherries and sweet chestnuts are harvested. Emergent snails and mushrooms are collected after wet weather. The more resilient forms of wildlife can coexist with these land-uses, but for many Greeks only those species that have practical application are regarded as having any value.

Despite an often negative attitude to wildlife, Greece was probably the first place in the world where it was an object of study. Theophrastos (372–287 BC) was the first recorded **botanist** and a systematic collector of general information on plants, while his contemporary, Aristotle, studied the animal world. During the first century AD the distinguished physician Dioscorides compiled a herbal that remained a standard work for over a thousand years.

Since the 1970s, tourist developments have ribboned out along coastlines, sweeping away both agricultural plots and wildlife havens as they do so. These expanding resorts increase local employment, often attracting inland workers to the coast; the generation that would have been shepherds on remote hillsides now work in bars and tavernas for the tourist. Consequently, the pressure of domestic animal grazing, particularly in the larger islands, has been significantly reduced and allows the regeneration of tree seedlings. Crete, for example, now has more woodland than at any time in the last five centuries.

FLOWERS

Whereas in temperate northern Europe plants flower from spring until autumn, the arid summers of Greece confine the main **flowering period** to the springtime, a climatic window when the days are bright, the temperatures not too high and the ground water supply still adequate. **Spring** starts in the southeast, in

Rhodes in early March, and then travels progressively westwards and northwards. Rhodes, Kárpathos and eastern Crete are at their best in March, western Crete in early April, the Peloponnese and eastern Aegean mid-April to late April, and the Ionian islands in early May, though a cold dry winter can cause several weeks' delay. In the highest island mountains the floral spring is held back until the chronological summer, with the alpine zones of central and western Crete in full flower in June.

The delicate flowers of early spring – orchids, fritillaries, anemones, cyclamen, tulips and small bulbs – are replaced as the season progresses by more robust shrubs, tall perennials and abundant annuals, but many of these close down completely for the fierce **summer**. A few tough plants, like shrubby thyme and savory, continue to flower through the heat and act as magnets for butterflies.

Once the worst heat is over, and the first showers of **autumn** arrive, so does a second "spring", on a much smaller scale but no less welcome after the brown drabness of summer. Squills, autumn cyclamen, crocus in varying shades, pink or lilac colchicum, yellow sternbergia and other small bulbs all come into bloom, while the seeds start to germinate for the following year's crop of annuals. By the new year, early spring bulbs and orchids are flowering in the south.

SEASHORE

Plants on the **beach** tend to be hardy species growing in a difficult environment where fresh water is scarce. Feathery tamarisk trees are adept at surviving this habitat, and consequently are often planted to provide shade. On hot days or nights you may see or feel them sweating away surplus saltwater from their foliage.

Sand dunes in the southern and eastern islands may support the low gnarled trees of the prickly **juniper**. These provide shelter for a variety of colourful small plants like pink campions, yellow restharrow, white stocks, blue alkanet and violet sea-lavender. The flat sandy areas or slacks behind the dunes can be home to a variety of plants, where they have not been illegally ploughed for cultivation. Open stretches of beach sand usually have fewer plants, particularly nowadays in resort areas where the bulldozed "spring cleaning" of the beach removes the local flora along with the winter's rubbish.

WATERCOURSES

Large areas of **freshwater** are scarce, particularly on the smaller islands. Many watercourses dry up completely during the hot season, and what seem to be dry river courses are often simply flood-beds, which fill irregularly at times of torrential rain. Consequently, there are few true aquatic plants compared with much of Europe. However, species that survive periodic drying-out can flourish, such as the giant reed or **calamus**, a bamboo-like grass reaching up to 6m in height and often cut for use as canes. It often grows in company with the shrubby, pink- or white-flowered and very poisonous **oleander**.

CULTIVATED LAND

Arable fields can be rich with colourful weeds: scarlet poppies, blue bugloss, yellow or white daisies, wild peas, gladioli, tulips and grape hyacinths. Small **meadows** can be equally colourful, with slower-growing plants such as orchids in extraordinary quantities. The rather dull violet flowers of the mandrake conceal its celebrated history as a narcotic and surgical anaesthetic. In the absence of herbicides, olive groves can have an extensive underflora. In the presence of herbicides there is usually a yellow carpet of the introduced, weedkiller-resistant *Oxalis pescaprae*, which now occurs in sufficient quantity to show up in satellite photographs.

LOWER HILLSIDES

The rocky earth makes cultivation on some hillsides difficult and impractical. Agriculture is often abandoned and areas regenerate to a rich mixture of shrubs and perennials – the **garigue** biome. With time, a few good wet winters and in the absence of grazing, some shrubs develop into small trees, intermixed with tough climbers – the much denser **maquis** vegetation. The colour yellow often predominates in early spring, with brooms, gorse, Jerusalem sage and the three-metre giant fennel followed by the pink and white of large rockroses (*Cistus spp*). An abundance of the latter is often indicative of an earlier fire, since they flourish in the cleared areas. Strawberry trees are also resistant to fire; they bloom in winter or early spring, producing an orange-red edible (though disappointingly insipid) fruit in the autumn. The Judas tree flowers on bare wood in spring, making a blaze of pink against the green hillsides.

A third vegetation type is **phrygana** – smaller, frequently aromatic or spiny shrubs, often with a narrow strip of bare ground between each hedgehog-like bush. Many **aromatic herbs** such as lavender, rosemary, savory, sage and thyme are natives to these areas, intermixed with other less tasty plants such as the toxic euphorbias and the spiny burnet or wire-netting bush.

Nearly 160 species of **orchid** are believed to occur in Greece; their complexity blurs species' boundaries and keeps botanists in a state of taxonomic flux. In particular, the *Ophrys* bee and spider orchids have adapted themselves, through subtleties of lip colour and false scents, to seduce small male wasps. These insects mistake the flowers for a potential mate, and unintentionally assist the plant's pollination. Other orchids mimic the colours and scents of honey-producing plants, to lure bees. Though all species are officially protected, many are still picked for decoration – in particular the giant *Barlia* orchid – and fill vases in homes, cafés, tavernas and even on graves.

Irises have a particular elegance and charm. The blue to violet winter iris, as its name suggests, is the first to appear, followed by the small blue *Iris gynandriris*. The flowers of the latter open after midday and into the night, to wither by the following morning. The widow iris is sombre-coloured in funereal shades of black and green, while the taller, white *Iris albicans*, the holy flower of Islam, is a relic of the Ottoman occupation. On the limestone peaks of Sámos, *Iris suavolens* has short stems, but huge yellow and brown flowers.

MOUNTAINS AND GORGES

The higher **mountains** of the Greek islands have winter snow cover varying with altitude, and cooler weather for much of the year, so flowering is consequently later than at lower altitudes. The **limestone peaks** of islands such as Corfu, Kefalloniá, Crete, Rhodes, Sámos and Thássos hold rich collections of attractive flowering rock plants whose nearest relatives may be from the Balkan Alps or from the Turkish mountains. Gorges are another spectacular habitat, particularly rich on Crete. Their inaccessible cliffs act as refuges for plants that cannot survive the grazing, competition or more extreme climates of open areas. Many of Greece's endemic plants – bellflowers, knapweeds and *Dianthus spp.* in particular – are confined to cliffs, gorges or mountains.

Much of the surviving **island forest** is in the mountainous areas of Kefalloniá, Évvia, Lésvos and Crete. Depending on the island, the woodland can comprise cypress (widespread at low altitudes), Greek fir (especially on Kefalloniá), oak (on Lésvos, Kéa and Crete) and a few species of pine: Calabrian or Aleppo at lower altitudes, black pine at the summits of Crete and Sámos. The cypress is native to the south and east Aegean, but in its columnar form it has been planted everywhere with a Mediterranean climate. It is sometimes said that the slim trees are the male and the broader, spreading form are female, but female cones on the thin trees prove this wrong. On Kárpathos, Sými and Crete there are extensive stands of juniper, while shady stream canyons of the largest islands shelter plane, oriental sweetgum, chestnut and poplar. The cooler shade of woodland provides a haven for plants which cannot survive full exposure to the Greek summer. Such species include the wonderful red, pink or white peonies found on Sámos, along with helleborine and bird's-nest orchids, and numerous ferns.

With altitude, the forest thins out to scattered individual hardy conifers and kermes oak, before finally reaching a limit ranging from 1000–1200m (Samothráki, Sámos) to 1400m (Kefalloniá), ending at about 1800m (Crete). Above this treeline are limited summer meadows, and then bare rock. If not severely grazed, these habitats are home to many low-growing, gnarled, but often splendidly floriferous plants.

BIRDS

Migratory species which have wintered in East Africa move north in spring through the eastern Mediterranean from mid-March to mid-May, or later, depending on the season and the weather. Some stop to breed in Greece; others move on into the rest of Europe. The southern islands can be the first landfall after a long sea-crossing, and smaller birds recuperate for a few days before moving on north. Larger birds such as storks and ibis often fly very high, and binoculars are needed to spot them as they pass over. In autumn the birds return, but usually in more scattered numbers. Although some species such as quail and turtle dove are shot, there is nothing like the wholesale slaughter that takes place in some other Mediterranean countries.

Swallows, and their relatives the martins, are constantly swooping through the air to catch insects, as are the larger and noisier swifts. Warblers are numerous, with the Sardinian warbler often conspicuous because of its black head, bright red eye and bold habits; the Rüppell's warbler is considerably rarer, and confined to thicker woodland. Other small insect-eaters include stonechats, flycatchers and woodchat shrikes.

Larger **raptors** are rare on the islands but can occur in remoter areas, particularly around mountain gorges and cliffs. Certain Dodecanese islands and Lésvos support populations of Eleonora's falcons, while peregrines visit the Ionian islands. Buzzards are perhaps the most abundant, and mistaken by optimistic bird-watchers for the much rarer, shyer eagles; vultures are also seen in passing on the largest islands. Lesser kestrels are brighter, noisier versions of the common kestrel, and often appear undisturbed by the presence of humans. Also to be seen in the mountains of larger islands are ravens, and smaller, colourful birds such as black and white wheatears, wallcreepers and the blue rock thrush.

In lowland areas, hoopoes are a startling combination of pink, black and white, particularly obvious when they fly; they're about the only natural predator of the processionary caterpillar, a major pest in pine forests (see p.29). The much shyer golden oriole has an attractive song but is rarely seen for more than a few moments before hiding its brilliant colours among the olive trees. Rollers are bright blue and chestnut, while multicoloured flocks of slim and elegant bee-eaters fill the air with their soft calls as they hunt insects. Brightest of all is the kingfisher, more commonly seen sea-fishing than in northern Europe.

In those areas of **wetland** that remain undrained and undisturbed, birds flourish. In salt marshes, coastal lagoons, estuaries and freshwater ponds, herons and egrets, ducks, ospreys, glossy ibises and spoonbills, black storks, white storks, pelicans and many waders can be seen feeding. Greater flamingos sometimes occur as lone individuals or small flocks, particularly in salt pans of the eastern Aegean.

Seashore birds are also notable; the southern Dodecanese are home to a small population of Audoin's gulls, endangered both by human activity and the more versatile yellow-legged gull. Cormorants roost on and dive off coastal cliffs from late summer onwards.

At **night**, the tiny Scops owl has a very distinct, repeated single-note call, very like the sonar beep of a submarine; the equally diminutive little owl is by contrast also visible by day, particularly on ruined houses, and has a strange repertoire of cries, chortles and a throaty hiss. Certainly the most evocative nocturnal bird is the nightingale, which requires wooded stream valleys and is most audible around midnight in May, its mating season.

MAMMALS

The island **mammal** population ranges from small rodents and shrews to hedgehogs, hares and squirrels (a very dark form of the red, seen only on Lésvos). Rats are particularly common on Corfu and Sámos. Medium-sized mammals include badgers and foxes, but one of the commonest is the fast moving, ferret-like, stone (or beech) marten, named for its habit of decorating stones with droppings to mark its territory. In the White Mountains of Crete an endemic ibex, known to Cretan hunters as the *agrími* or *krí-krí*, is occasionally seen running wild but more often as a zoo attraction. When formerly in danger of extinction, a colony of them was established on the offshore islet of Dhía, where they managed in turn to exterminate the rare local flora.

The extremely rare Mediterranean **monk seal** also breeds on some stretches of remote coast in the east Aegean and Sporades; the small world population is now highly endangered since losing many individuals – and most of its main breeding ground – to a toxic algal bloom off Morocco. If spotted, these seals should be treated with deference; they cannot tolerate human disturbance, and on present trends are unlikely to survive much into the new millennium.

REPTILES AND AMPHIBIANS

Reptiles flourish in the hot dry summers of Greece and there are many species, the commonest being **lizards**. Most of these are small, slim, agile and wary, rarely staying around for closer inspection. They're usually brown to grey, with subtle patterns of spots, streaks and stripes, though in adult males the undersides are sometimes brilliant orange, green or blue.

The more robust green lizards, with long whip-like tails, can be 50cm or more in length, but equally shy and fast-moving unless distracted by territorial disputes with each other.

On some islands, mainly in the central and eastern Aegean, lives the angular, iguana-like **agama**, sometimes called the Rhodes dragon. Occasionally reaching a robust 30cm in length, their skin is rough and grey to brown with indistinct patterning. Unlike other lizards, they will often stop to study you, before finally disappearing into a wall or under a rock.

Geckos are large-eyed nocturnal lizards, up to 15cm long, with short tails and often rough skins. Their spreading toes have claws and ingenious adhesive pads, allowing them to walk up house walls and onto ceilings in their search for insects. Groups of them lie in wait near bright lights that attract their prey, and small ones living indoors can have very pale, almost transparent skins. Not always popular locally – one Greek name for them, *miaró*, means "defiler" after their outsized faeces – they should be left alone to eat mosquitoes and other bugs. The **chameleon** is a rare, slow-moving and swivel-eyed inhabitant of eastern Crete and some eastern Aegean islands such as Sámos. Although essentially green, it has the ability to adjust its coloration to match the surroundings.

Once collected for the pet trade, **tortoises** can be found on many larger islands, though not on Crete. Usually it is their noisy progress through vegetation on sunny or wooded hills that first signals their presence. They spend their often long lives grazing the vegetation and can reach lengths of 30cm. Closely related **terrapins** are more streamlined, freshwater tortoises which love to bask on waterside mud by streams or ponds on many islands. Shy and nervous, they are usually only seen as they disappear underwater. They are scavengers and will eat anything, including fingers if handled.

Sea turtles occur mostly in the Ionian Sea, but also in the Aegean. The least rare are the loggerhead turtles (*Caretta caretta*), which nest on Zákynthos and Kefalloniá, and occasionally in Crete. Their nesting grounds are disappearing under tourist resorts, although they are a protected endangered species (see p.444).

Snakes are abundant in many islands (though Astypálea has none); most are shy and non-venomous. Several species, including the Ottoman and nose-horned **vipers**, do have a poisonous bite, though they are not usually aggressive. They are adder-like and often have a very distinct, dark zigzag stripe down the back. They are only likely to bite if a hand is put in the crevice of a wall or a rock-face where one of them is resting, or if they are attacked. Unfortunately, the locals in some areas attempt to kill any snake they see, and thus greatly increase the probability of their being bitten. Leave them alone, and they will usually do the same for you (but if the worst comes to worst, see the advice on p.29). Most snakes are not only completely harmless to humans, but beneficial in that they keep down populations of pests such as rats and mice. There are also three species of legless lizards – slow-worm, glass lizard and legless skink – all equally harmless, which suffer because they are mistaken for snakes.

Frogs and **toads** are the commonest and most obvious amphibians in most of Greece, particularly during the spring breeding season. The green toad has green marbling over a pinkish or mud-coloured background, and a cricket-like trill. Frogs prefer the wettest places, and the robust marsh frog particularly revels in artificial water storage ponds, where the concrete sides magnify their croaking impressively. **Tree frogs** are tiny jewels, usually emerald green, with huge and strident voices at night. They rest by day in trees and shrubs, and can sometimes be found in quantity plastered onto the leaves of waterside oleanders.

INSECTS

Greece teems with **insects**. Some pester, like flies and mosquitoes, but most are harmless to humans. The huge, slow-flying, glossy black carpenter bee may cause alarm by its size and noise, but is rarely a problem.

Grasshoppers and **crickets** swarm through open areas of vegetation in summer, with several larger species that are carnivorous on the smaller individuals and which can bite strongly if handled. Larger still is the grey-brown locust, which flies noisily before crash-landing into trees and shrubs. The high-pitched and endlessly repeated chirp of house crickets can drive one to distraction, as can the summer whirring of cicadas on the trunks of trees. The latter insects are giant relatives of the aphids that cluster on roses.

FLORA AND FAUNA FIELD GUIDES

In case of difficulty obtaining the titles listed below from conventional bookshops, there is one reliable mail-order outlet for wildlife field guides within the UK. **Summerfield Books**, High Street, Brough, Kirkby Stephen, Cumbria CA17 4BX (☎ & fax 017683/41577, *atkins@summerfield-books.com*) has new botanical titles and rare or out-of-print natural history books on all topics. Postage is extra, but they often have special discounts, and their catalogue descriptions are detailed.

FLOWERS

Hellmut Baumann *Greek Wild Flowers and Plant Lore in Ancient Greece* (Herbert Press, UK). Crammed with fascinating ethnobotany, plus good colour photographs.

Marjorie Blamey and Christopher Grey-Wilson *Mediterranean Wild Flowers* (HarperCollins, UK). Comprehensive field guide, with coloured drawings; recent and taxonomically up-to-date.

Lance Chilton *Plant Check-lists* (Marengo Publications, UK). Small pamphlets which also include birds, reptiles and butterflies, for a number of Greek islands and resorts. Contact the author directly at ☎01485/532 710, *Marengo@supanet.com.*

Pierre Delforge *Orchids of Britain and Europe* (HarperCollins, UK). A comprehensive guide, with recent taxonomy, though beware small inaccuracies in the translation.

Anthony Huxley and William Taylor *Flowers of Greece and the Aegean* (Hogarth Press, UK, o/p). The only volume dedicated to the islands (and mainland), with colour photos, but now slightly dated for taxonomy.

Oleg Polunin *Flowers of Greece and the Balkans* (Oxford UP, UK). Classic, older field guide (reprinted 1997), also with colour photographs, useful if Huxley and Taylor proves unfindable.

Oleg Polunin and Anthony Huxley *Flowers of the Mediterranean* (Hogarth Press, UK). The larger scope means that many Greek endemics get missed out, but recent printings have a table of taxonomic changes.

MARINE LIFE

B. Luther and K. Fiedler *A Field Guide to the Mediterranean* (HarperCollins, UK, o/p). Very thorough, includes most Greek shallow-water species.

BIRDS

Richard Brooks *Birding in Lesbos* (Brookside Publishing, UK). Superb guide which includes a list of birdwatching sites, detailed maps, colour photos and an annotated species-by-species bird list with much useful information.

George Handrinos and T. Akriotis *Birds of Greece* (A&C Black, UK). A comprehensive guide that includes island birdlife.

Heinzel, Fitter and Parslow *Collins Guide to the Birds of Britain and Europe*; **Petersen, Mountfort and Hollom** *Field Guide to the Birds of Britain and Europe* (both Collins, UK; Stephen Green Press, US). Though not specific to Greece, these two field guides have the best coverage of Greek birds outside of Lésvos.

MAMMALS

Corbet and Ovenden *Collins Guide to the Mammals of Europe* (Collins, UK; Stephen Green Press, US). The best field guide on its subject.

REPTILES

Arnold, Burton and Ovenden *Collins Guide to the Reptiles and Amphibians of Britain and Europe* (Collins, UK, Stephen Green Press, US). A useful guide, though excludes the Dodecanese and east Aegean islands.

Jiri Cihar *Amphibians and Reptiles* (Conran Octopus, UK, o/p). Selective coverage, but includes most endemic species of the Dodecanese and east Aegean isles.

INSECTS

Michael Chinery *Collins Guide to the Insects of Britain and Western Europe* (Collins, UK; Stephen Green Press, US). Although Greece is outside the geographical scope of the guide, it will provide genus identifications for most insects seen.

Lionel Higgins and Norman Riley *A Field Guide to the Butterflies of Britain and Europe* (Collins, UK; Stephen Green Press, US). A thorough and detailed field guide that illustrates nearly all species seen in Greece.

From spring through to autumn Greece is full of **butterflies**, particularly in late spring and early summer. There are three swallowtail species, named for the drawn-out corners of the hind wings, in shades of cream and yellow, with black and blue markings. Their smaller relatives, the festoons, lack the tails, but add red spots to the palette. The rarer, robust brown and orange pasha is unrelated but is Europe's largest butterfly. In autumn the black and orange plain tiger or African monarch may appear, sometimes in large quantities. In areas of deciduous woodland, look high up and you may see fast-flying large tortoiseshells, while lower down, southern white admirals skim and glide through clearings between the trees. Some of the smallest but most beautiful butterflies are the blues. Their subtle, camouflaging grey and black undersides make them vanish from view when they land and fold their wings.

Some of the Greek **hawkmoths** are equally spectacular, particularly the green and pink oleander hawkmoth. Their large caterpillars can be recognized by their tail horn. The hummingbird hawkmoth, like its namesake, hovers at flowers to feed, supported by a blur of fast-moving wings. Tiger moths, with their black and white forewings and startling bright orange hindwings, are the "butterflies" that occur in huge quantity in sheltered sites of islands such as Rhodes and Páros. The giant peacock moth is Europe's largest, up to 15cm across. A mixture of grey, black and brown, with big eye-spots, it is usually only seen during the day while resting on tree trunks.

Other insects include the camouflaged praying mantids, holding their powerful forelegs in a position of supplication until another insect comes within reach. The females are voracious, and notorious for eating the males during mating. Ant-lion adults resemble a fluttery dragonfly, but their young are huge-jawed and build pits in the sand to trap ants. Hemispherical carob beetles collect balls of dung and push them around with their back legs, while the huge longhorn beetles of the southern Ionian islands munch their way through tree trunks. Longhorns are named for their absurdly extended, whip-like antennae. Cockroaches of varying species live in buildings, particularly hotels, restaurants and bakeries, attracted by warmth and food scraps.

Corfu is famous for its extraordinary **fireflies**, which loop in quantities across meadows and marshes on May nights, speckling the darkness with bursts of cold light to attract partners. Look carefully in nearby hedges, and you may spot the less flashy, more sedentary glow-worm.

Centipedes are not often seen, but the fast-moving twenty-centimetre *Scolipendra* should be treated with respect since they can give very painful bites. Other non-vertebrates of interest include the land crabs, which are found in the south and east. They need water to breed, but can cause surprise when found walking on remote hillsides. There are plenty of genuine marine creatures to be seen, particularly in shallow seawater sheltered by rocks – sea cucumbers, sea butterflies, octopus, marine worms, starfish and sea urchins.

Lance Chilton, with Marc Dubin

BOOKS

Where separate editions exist in the UK and US, publishers are detailed below in the form "UK publisher; US publisher", unless the publisher is the same in both countries. Where books are published in one country – or Athens – only, this follows the publisher's name.

O/p signifies an out-of-print but still highly recommended book; Greek-specialist book dealers (see box below for two in London) often have stocks of these. University Press is abbreviated as UP.

Books marked * are part of a highly recommended "Modern Greek Writers" series, currently numbering over thirty titles, issued by the Athenian company Kedros Publishers.

TRAVEL AND GENERAL ACCOUNTS

MODERN ACCOUNTS

Kevin Andrews *The Flight of Ikaros* (Penguin, o/p). Intense and compelling account of an educated, sensitive archeologist loose in the backcountry during the aftermath of the civil war; a whole chapter on Páros as it was before tourism.

Gerald Durrell *My Family and Other Animals* (Penguin). Sparkling, very funny anecdotes of Durrell's childhood on Corfu – and his passion for the island's fauna: toads, tortoises, bats, scorpions, the lot.

Lawrence Durrell *Prospero's Cell* (Faber & Faber; Penguin, o/p); *Reflections on a Marine Venus* (Faber & Faber; Penguin); *The Greek Islands* (Faber & Faber, o/p; Penguin). The elder Durrell lived before World War II with Gerald and the family on Corfu, the subject of *Prospero's Cell*. *Marine Venus* recounts Lawrence's 1945–47 experiences and impressions of Rhodes and other Dodecanese islands. *Greek Islands* is a lyrical but rather dated and occasionally bilious guide to the archipelagos.

John Gill *The Stars over Paxos* (Pavilion, UK). Ex-pat's view of Paxí, with interesting statistics on olives and some acerbic asides on varieties of tourists and (other) ex-pats, amongst long-winded musings on Ionian weather, meteors and stars. Fun for the beach.

Katherine Kizilos *The Olive Grove: Travels in Greece* (Lonely Planet Journeys). Returned, ambivalent Greek-Australian's musings on the country, with a good initial section on Sýros, Thíra, Pátmos, Ikaría and Lésvos.

Elias Kulukundis *Journey to a Greek Island* (Cassell, o/p). More accurately, a journey back through time and genealogy by a diaspora Greek two generations removed from Kássos, the poorest of the Dodecanese. Worth the effort to track down.

Willard Manus *This Way to Paradise: Dancing on the Tables* (Lycabettus Press, Athens). American expatriate's memoir of four decades in Líndhos, Rhodes, before its sad descent into mass-tourist tattiness. Wonderful period detail, including hippy excesses and often hilarious cameos by the likes of S.J. Perelman, Germaine Greer and Martha Gellhorn.

Henry Miller *The Colossus of Maroussi* (Minerva, o/p; New Directions). Corfu, Crete and the soul of Greece in 1939, with Miller, completely in his element, at his most inspired.

James Pettifer *The Greeks: the Land and People since the War* (Penguin; Viking). A useful, if spottily edited introduction to contemporary Greece – and its recent past. Pettifer charts the state of the nation's politics, food, family life, religion, tourism and other topics.

SPECIALIST BOOKSHOPS

In **London**, the Hellenic Bookservice, 91 Fortess Rd, Kentish Town, London NW5 1AG (☎020/7267 9499, *www.hellenicbooks.com*, *hellenicbooks@btinternet.com*), and Zeno's Greek Bookshop, 6 Denmark St, WC2H 8LP (☎020/7836 2522), are knowledgeable and well-stocked specialist dealers in new, secondhand and out-of-print books on all aspects of Greece.

Patricia Storace *Dinner with Persephone* (Granta; Pantheon). A New York poet, resident for a year in Athens (with forays to the provinces) puts the country's psyche on the couch, while avoiding the same position with various predatory males. Storace has a sly sense of humour, and in showing how permeated – and imprisoned – Greece is by its imagined past, gets it right 95 percent of the time. Excellent.

William Travis *Bus Stop Symi* (Rapp & Whiting, o/p). Chronicles three years' residence there in the mid-Sixties; fairly insightful (if loathed on the island itself), though Travis erroneously prophesied that the place would never see tourism.

Sarah Wheeler *An Island Apart* (Abacus, UK). Entertaining chronicle of a five-month ramble through Évvia, one of the least-visited islands. Wheeler has a sure touch with Greek culture and an open approach to nuns, goatherds or academics; the sole quibble is her success in making Évvia seem more interesting than it really is.

OLDER ACCOUNTS

James Theodore Bent *Aegean Islands: The Cyclades, or Life Among Insular Greeks* (Argonaut, Chicago, US; o/p). Originally published in 1881, this remains the best account of island customs and folklore; it's also a highly readable, droll account of a year's Aegean travel, including a particularly violent Cycladic winter.

Edward Lear *The Corfu Years* (Denise Harvey, Athens). Superbly illustrated journals by the nonsense versifier and noted landscape painter, whose paintings and sketches of Corfu, Paxí and elsewhere offer a rare glimpse of the Ionian island landscape in the nineteenth century. His *The Cretan Journal* (Denise Harvey) will also be of interest.

Terence Spencer *Fair Greece, Sad Relic: Literary Philhellenism from Shakespeare to Byron* (Denise Harvey, Athens, available in UK; Scholarly Press). Greece – and incipient philhellenism – from the fall of Constantinople to the War of Independence, as conveyed by English poets, essayists and travellers.

Richard Stoneman, ed *A Literary Companion to Travel in Greece* (Getty Centre for the History of Art and the Humanities, US). Ancient and medieval authors, plus Grand Tourists – good for dipping into.

THE CLASSICS

Many of the classics make excellent companion reading for a trip around Greece – especially the historians **Thucydides** and **Herodotus**. Reading **Homer**'s *Odyssey* when you're battling with or resigning yourself to the vagaries of island ferries puts your own plight into perspective.

Most of the standard undergraduate staples are part of the **Penguin Classic** paperback series. **Routledge** also has a huge, steadily expanding backlist of Classical Studies, though many titles are expensive and quite specialized; paperback editions are indicated.

Homer *The Iliad; The Odyssey*. The first concerns itself, semi-factually, with the late Bronze Age siege by the Achaeans against Troy in Asia Minor; the second recounts the delayed return home, via seemingly every corner of the Mediterranean, of the hero Odysseus. For a verse rendition, Richard Lattimore's translation (University of Chicago, *Iliad*; HarperCollins, *Odyssey*) has yet to be bettered; for prose, the best choices are by the father-and-son team of E.V. Rieu (*Iliad*, Penguin) and D.C.H. Rieu (*Odyssey*, Penguin).

Herodotus *The Histories* (Penguin), or A.D. Godley, tr (Cambridge UP). Revered as the father of systematic history and anthropology, this fifth-century BC Anatolian writer chronicled both the causes and campaigns of the Persian Wars, as well as the contemporary, assorted tribes and nations inhabiting Asia Minor.

Ovid *The Metamorphoses*, A.D. Melville, tr (Oxford UP). Though collected by a first-century AD Roman writer, this remains one of the most accessible renditions of the more piquant Greek myths, involving transformations as divine blessing or curse.

Plutarch *The Age of Alexander*; *On Sparta*; *The Rise and Fall of Athens* (Penguin). Another ancient author, writing perhaps with benefit of hindsight – but with the detriment of shaky sources and much conjecture.

Thucydides *History of the Peloponnesian War* (Penguin). Bleak month-by-month account of the conflict, by a cashiered Athenian officer whose affiliation and dim view of human nature usually didn't get in the way of his objectivity; see the review of George Cawkwell's book overleaf for a revisionist view.

Xenophon *The History of My Times* (Penguin). Thucydides stopped his coverage of the Peloponnesian War in 411 BC; this work continues events until 362 BC.

ANCIENT HISTORY AND INTERPRETATION OF THE CLASSICS

A.R. Burn *History of Greece* (Penguin). Probably the best general introduction to ancient Greece, though for a fuller and more interesting analysis you'll do better with one of the following more specialized titles.

George Cawkwell *Thucydides and the Peloponnesian War* (Routledge). Recent, revisionist overview of Thucydides' work and relations with the main personalities of the war, challenging previous assumptions of his infallibility.

M.I. Finley *The World of Odysseus* (Penguin). Good on the interrelation of Mycenaean myth and fact.

Simon Hornblower *The Greek World 479–323 BC* (Routledge). An erudite survey of ancient Greece at its zenith, from the end of the Persian Wars to the death of Alexander, which has become a standard university paperback text.

Michael Grant and John Hazel *Who's Who in Classical Mythology* (Routledge). Gazetteer of over 1200 mythological personalities, together with historical and geographical background.

Pierre Grimal, ed *Dictionary of Classical Mythology* (Penguin). Though translated from the French, considered to still have the edge on the more recent Grant/Hazel title.

John Kenyon Davies *Democracy and Classical Greece* (Fontana; Harvard UP). Established and accessible account of the Classical period and its political developments.

Robin Lane Fox *Alexander the Great* (Penguin). An absorbing study, which mixes historical scholarship with imaginative psychological detail.

Oswyn Murray *Early Greece* (Fontana; Harvard UP). The Greek story from the Mycenaeans and Minoans through to the beginning of the Classical period.

Robin Osborne *Greece in the Making 1200–479 BC* (Routledge). Well-illustrated paperback on the rise of the city-state.

F.W. Walbank *The Hellenistic World* (Fontana; Harvard UP). Greece under the sway of the Macedonian and Roman empires.

ANCIENT RELIGION

Walter Burkert *Greek Religion: Archaic and Classical* (Blackwell). Superb overview of the deities and their attributes and antecedents, rites, the protocol of sacrifice and the symbolism of major festivals; especially good on relating Greek worship to its predecessors in the Middle East. Burkert wears his erudition lightly – you can easily skip the lengthy rear footnotes and still have an illuminating read – and states clearly when something is unknown or still speculative.

Matthew Dillon *Pilgrims and Pilgrimage in Ancient Greece* (Routledge). Pricey hardback exploring not only the main sanctuaries such as Delphi, but also minor oracles, the role of women and children, and secular festivities attending the rites.

Nano Marinatos and Robin Hagg *Greek Sanctuaries: New Approaches* (Routledge). Form and function of the temples, in the light of recent scholarship.

FOOD AND WINE

Andrew Dalby *Siren Feasts* (Routledge). Subtitled "A history of food and gastronomy in Greece", this analysis of Classical and Byzantine texts demonstrates just how little Greek cuisine has changed in three millennia; also excellent on the introduction and etymology of common vegetables and herbs.

Alan Davidson *Mediterranean Seafood* (Penguin, o/p). A 1972 classic, periodically reprinted, this amazingly erudite and witty book catalogues all known edible species, complete with legends, anecdotes, habits, local names and a suggested recipe or two for each; no photos, but useful pen-and-ink sketches.

James Davidson *Courtesans and Fishcakes* (HarperCollins, UK). The politics, class characteristics and etiquette of consumption and consummation in ancient Athens, exploring their bearing on both historical events and modern attitudes. Highly recommended.

Miles Lambert-Gócs *The Wines of Greece* (Faber & Faber). Comprehensive survey of the wines of Greece, with plenty of historical background; unfortunately, few of these grace middle-of-the-road taverna tables, and coverage ceases in 1993.

ARCHEOLOGY AND ART

John Beckwith *Early Christian and Byzantine Art* (Yale UP). Illustrated study placing Byzantine art within a wider context.

William R. Biers *Archeology of Greece: An Introduction* (Cornell UP). A recently revised and excellent standard text.

John Boardman *Greek Art* (Thames & Hudson). A very good concise introduction: part of the "World of Art" series.

Chris Hellier *Monasteries of Greece* (Tauris Parke; St Martin's). Magnificently photographed survey of the surviving, active monasteries and their treasures, with insightful accompanying essays.

Reynold Higgins *Minoan and Mycenaean Art* (Thames & Hudson). A clear, well-illustrated round-up.

Sinclair Hood *The Arts in Prehistoric Greece* (Penguin; Yale UP). Sound introduction to the subject.

Roger Ling *Classical Greece* (Phaidon, UK). Another useful illustrated introduction.

Colin Renfrew *The Cycladic Spirit* (Thames & Hudson; Abrams). A fine, illustrated study of the meaning and purpose of Cycladic artefacts.

Gisela Richter *A Handbook of Greek Art* (Phaidon; Da Capo). Exhaustive survey of the visual arts of ancient Greece.

Suzanne Slesin et al *Greek Style* (Thames & Hudson; Crown). Stunning (if sometimes contrived) designer-tweaked interiors from Corfu, Rhodes and Sérifos, among other spots.

R.R.R. Smith *Hellenistic Sculpture* (Thames & Hudson). Modern reappraisal of the art of Greece under Alexander and his successors.

David Talbot Rice *Art of the Byzantine Era* (Thames & Hudson). Talbot Rice was, with Robert Byron, one of the pioneering scholars in the "rediscovery" of Byzantine art; this is an accessible illustrated study.

Peter Warren *The Aegean Civilizations* (Phaidon, o/p; P. Bedrick Books, o/p). Illustrated account of the Minoan and Mycenaean cultures.

BYZANTINE, MEDIEVAL AND OTTOMAN HISTORY

Averil Cameron *The Mediterranean World in Late Antiquity, AD 395–600* (Routledge). Essentially the early Byzantine years.

Nicholas Cheetham *Medieval Greece* (Yale UP, o/p in US). General survey of the period and its infinite convolutions in Greece, with Frankish, Catalan, Venetian, Byzantine and Ottoman struggles for power.

John Julius Norwich *Byzantium: The Early Centuries*; *Byzantium: the Apogee* and *Byzantium: The Decline* (all Penguin; Viking-Knopf). Perhaps the main surprise for first-time travellers to Greece is the fascination of Byzantine monuments. This is an astonishingly detailed yet readable trilogy.

Vangelis Pavlidis *Rhodes 1306–1522: A Story* (Rodos Image, Rhodes). Caricature-illustrated history of the Knights of St John's occupation of Rhodes, by one of Greece's leading political cartoonists. Rigorous research and witty text illuminate a little-known era of the Dodecanese.

Michael Psellus *Fourteen Byzantine Rulers* (Penguin). A fascinating contemporary source, detailing the stormy but brilliant period from 976 to 1078.

Steven Runciman *The Fall of Constantinople, 1453* (Canto-Cambridge UP) is the standard account of the event. *The Great Church in Captivity* (Cambridge UP) follows the vicissitudes of the Orthodox Patriarchate in Constantinople up to the War of Independence. *Byzantine Style and Civilization* (Penguin, o/p in US) and *Mistra* (Thames & Hudson, o/p in US) are more slanted towards art, culture and monuments.

Kallistos (Timothy) Ware *The Orthodox Church* (Penguin). Good introduction to what is effectively the established religion of Greece, by the Orthodox bishop resident in Oxford.

MODERN GREECE

Timothy Boatswain and Colin Nicolson *A Traveller's History of Greece* (Windrush Press; Interlink). Slightly dated (coverage ceases in early 1990s), but a well-written overview of the important Greek periods and personalities.

Richard Clogg *A Concise History of Greece* (Cambridge UP). A remarkably clear and well-illustrated account of Greece, from the decline of Byzantium to 1991, with the emphasis on recent decades; there are numerous maps and lengthy feature captions to the artwork.

Douglas Dakin *The Unification of Greece, 1770–1923* (Ernest Benn, o/p; St Martin's Press, o/p). Benchmark account of the foundation of the Greek state and the struggle to extend its boundaries.

H.A. Lidderdale, trs and ed *The Memoirs of General Makriyannis, 1797–1864* (Oxford UP, o/p). The "Peasant General", one of the few honest and self-sacrificing protagonists of the Greek uprising, taught himself to write at age 32 to set down this apologia of his conduct, in vivid demotic Greek. Heartbreaking in its portrayal of the incipient schisms, linguistic and otherwise, that tore the country apart until recently.

Michael Llewellyn Smith *Ionian Vision: Greece in Asia Minor, 1919–22* (C. Hurst; University of Michigan). Standard work, by the recently retired UK ambassador to Greece, on the disastrous Anatolian campaign, which led to the exchange of populations between Greece and Turkey. Evinces considerable sympathy for the post-1920 royalists pursing an unwanted, inherited war they know is unwinnable.

Yiannis Roubatis *Tangled Webs: The US in Greece 1947–67* (Pella Publishing, US). Chronicles growing American involvement in Greece during the lead-up to the military coup.

C.M. Woodhouse *Modern Greece, A Short History* (Faber & Faber). Woodhouse was active in the Greek Resistance during World War II. Writing from a more right-wing perspective than Clogg, this history (spanning from the foundation of Constantinople in 324 to the1980s), is briefer and a bit drier, but scrupulous with facts. *The Rise and Fall of the Greek Colonels* (Granada, o/p; Watts), recounts the (horror) story of the dictatorship.

WORLD WAR II AND ITS AFTERMATH

David H. Close *The Origins of the Greek Civil War* (Longman). Excellent, readable study that focuses on the social conditions in 1920s and 1930s Greece that made the country so ripe for internecine conflict. Draws on primary sources, relatively objective (though he's no fan of the Left) and slaughters a few sacred cows on the way.

Iakovos Kambanellis *Mauthausen* (Kedros, Athens*; Central Books, London). Kambanellis, a native of Náxos, was active in the Resistance, was caught by the Germans and sent to Mauthausen, the concentration camp reserved for those who had opposed the Nazis' rise to power in any way. There are many harrowing atrocities in flashback, but the main thrust of the book is post-liberation, describing the author's awkward romance with a Lithuanian Jew, and how the idealist inmates are slowly disillusioned as they see that the "New World Order" will be scarcely different from the old.

Mark Mazower *Inside Hitler's Greece: The Experience of Occupation 1941–44* (Yale UP). Somewhat choppily organized, but the standard of scholarship is high and the photos alone justify the price, though there's not much specifically on the islands. Demonstrates how the complete demoralization of the country and the incompetence of conventional politicians led to the rise of ELAS and the onset of civil war.

George Psychoundakis *The Cretan Runner* (John Murray, o/p; Transatlantic Arts, o/p; Efstathiadis, Athens). Narrative of the invasion of Crete and subsequent resistance, by a participant who was a guide and message-runner for all the British protagonists – including Patrick Leigh Fermor, the translator of the book.

Marion Sarafis and Martin Eve *Background to Contemporary Greece, Vols 1 & 2* (Merlin, UK). Papers and panel discussion from a late 1980s conference on the civil war, with former belligerents confronting each other across podiums. Left-wing bias, but Sarafis herself – widow of the main DSE commander – is impressive, especially in Vol 1.

Adrian Seligman *War in the Islands* (Alan Sutton, UK). Collected oral histories of a little-known Allied unit: a flotilla of kaïkia organized to raid the Axis-held Dodecanese, Cyclades and northeast Aegean islands. *Boy's Own* stuff, with service-jargon-laced prose, but lots of fine period photos and detail.

C.M. Woodhouse *The Struggle for Greece, 1941–49* (Hart-Davis, o/p; Beekman). A masterly and by no means uncritical account of this crucial decade, explaining how Greece emerged without a communist government.

ETHNOGRAPHY

Juliet du Boulay *Portrait of a Greek Mountain Village* (Oxford UP, o/p in UK). An account of the village of Ambéli, on Évvia, during the 1960s. The habits and customs of an all-but-vanished way of life are observed and evoked in an absorbing narrative.

John Cuthbert Lawson *Modern Greek Folklore and Ancient Greek Religion: A Study in Survivals* (University Books, New York, o/p). Exactly as the title states, and still highly applicable a century after its writing; well worth scouring libraries and antiquarian dealers for.

Clay Perry *Vanishing Greece* (Conran Octopus; Abbeville Press). Well-captioned photos depict the threatened landscapes and relict ways of life in rural Greece, including several islands; now in paperback.

MODERN GREEK LITERATURE

Roderick Beaton *An Introduction to Modern Greek Literature* (Oxford UP). Chronological survey of fiction and poetry from independence to the early 1990s, with a useful discussion on the "language question".

FICTION

Maro Douka *Fool's Gold* (Kedros, Athens*; Central Books, London). Describes an upper-class young woman's involvement, and subsequent disillusionment, with the clandestine resistance to the junta.

Eugenia Fakinou *The Seventh Garment* (Serpent's Tail). Greek history, from the War of Independence to the colonels' junta, as told through the life stories (interspersed in counterpoint) of three generations of women. It's a rather more successful experiment than Fakinou's *Astradeni* (Kedros, Athens*; Central Books, London), in which a young girl – whose slightly irritating narrative voice is adopted throughout – leaves the island of Sými, with all its traditional values, for Athens.

Nikos Kazantzakis Whether in intricate Greek or translated into inadequate English, Kazantzakis can be hard going, yet the strength of his classics still shines through. *Zorba the Greek* is a surprisingly nihilistic work, light-years away from the two-dimensional characters of the film. On the other hand, the movie version of *The Last Temptation of Christ*, despite its shortcomings, provoked riots amongst Orthodox fanatics in Athens in 1989. *Christ Recrucified* (published in the US as *The Greek Passion*) resets the Easter drama in the milieu of Christian/Muslim relations on nineteenth-century Crete. *The Fratricides* portrays a family riven by the civil war, while *Report to Greco* – perhaps the most accessible of his works – is an autobiographical exploration of his Cretanness/Greekness (all Faber & Faber; Touchstone).

Artemis Leontis, ed *Greece: A Traveller's Literary Companion* (Whereabouts Press, San Francisco, US). An overdue idea, brilliantly executed: various regions of the country as portrayed in (very) short fiction or essays by modern Greek writers. A recommended antidote to the often condescending Grand Tourist accounts.

Stratis Myrivilis *Life in the Tomb* (Quartet; New England UP). A harrowing and unorthodox war memoir, based on the author's experience on the Macedonian front during 1917–18, well translated by Peter Bien. Completing a loose trilogy are two later novels, set on the north coast of Lésvos, Myrivilis's homeland: *The Mermaid Madonna* and *The Schoolmistress with the Golden Eyes* (Efstathiadis, Athens, Greece). Translations of these are average and heavily abridged; the volumes themselves are shabbily produced.

Alexandros Papadiamantis *The Murderess* (Writers & Readers). A landmark turn-of-the-century novel set on the island of Skiáthos, in which an old woman, appalled by the fate that awaits them in adulthood, concludes that little girls are better off dead. Also available is a collection of Papadiamantis short stories, *Tales from a Greek Island* (Johns Hopkins UP).

Nick Papandreou *Father Dancing* (Penguin). Thinly veiled *roman à clef* by the late Andreas's younger son. Papandreou Senior, not too surprisingly, comes across as a gasbag and petty domestic tyrant.

Yannis Ritsos *Iconostasis of Anonymous Saints* (Kedros, Athens*). The first three instalments of a projected nine-volume autobiographical novel. The "anonymous saints" are the characters of these vaguely sequentially vignettes. Book 1, *Ariostos the Observant*, written during World War II, is, depending on your view, either a surrealist masterpiece or self-indulgent pap; Book 2, *Such Strange Things*, and Book 3, *With a Nudge of the Elbow*, are more straightforwardly based on Ritsos's peers and life events.

Dido Sotiriou *Farewell Anatolia* (Kedros, Athens*; Central Books, London). A classic since its initial appearance in 1962 (it has now passed its 56th Greek printing), this epic chronicles the traumatic end of Greek life in Asia Minor, from World War I to the catastrophe of 1922, as narrated by a fictionalized version of the author's father; in the finale, he escapes across the narrow strait of Mykale to Sámos, as many did in those turbulent years.

Stratis Tsirkas *Drifting Cities* (Kedros, Athens*; Central Books, London). Set by turns in the Jerusalem, Cairo and Alexandria of World War II, this unflinchingly honest and humane epic of a Greek army hero secretly working for the leftist resistance got the author denounced by the Communist Party.

MODERN GREEK POETRY

With two Nobel laureates in recent years – George Seferis and Odysseus Elytis – modern Greece has an extraordinarily intense and dynamic poetic tradition. Translations of all of the following are excellent.

C.P. Cavafy *Collected Poems* (Chatto & Windus; Princeton UP). The complete works, translated by Edmund Keeley and Philip Sherrard, of perhaps the most accessible modern Greek poet, resident for most of his life in Alexandria. For some, *The Complete Poems of Cavafy* (Harcourt Brace Jovanovich), translated by Rae Dalven, or the volume done by John Mavrokordato (Chatto & Windus, UK) are superior versions.

Odysseus Elytis *The Axion Esti* (Anvil Press; Pittsburgh UP); *Selected Poems* (Anvil Press; Viking Penguin, o/p); *The Sovereign Sun* (Bloodaxe Books; Temple UP, Philadelphia, o/p). The major works in good English versions. Easier to find is *Collected Poems* (Johns Hopkins UP), which includes virtually everything except *The Axion Esti*.

Modern Greek Poetry (Efstathiadis, Athens). Decent anthology of translations, predominantly of Seferis and Elytis.

Yannis Ritsos *Exile and Return, Selected Poems 1967–1974* (Anvil Press; Ecco Press). A fine volume of Greece's foremost leftist poet, from the junta era when he was internally exiled on Sámos.

George Seferis *Collected Poems, 1924–1955* (Anvil Press, o/p; Princeton UP, o/p). Virtually the complete works of the Nobel laureate, with Greek and English verses on facing pages. More recent, but lacking the parallel Greek text, is *Complete Poems* (Anvil Press; Princeton UP).

GREECE IN FOREIGN FICTION

Louis de Bernières *Captain Corelli's Mandolin* (Minerva; Random House). Set on Kefalloniá during the World War II occupation, this is a brilliant tragicomedy by an author best known for his South American extravaganzas. It has won praise from Greek intellectuals despite its disparagement of ELAS – quite an achievement. Since appearing in 1994 it has acquired seemingly perennial best-seller status, and is soon to be a motion picture.

John Fowles *The Magus* (Vintage; Dell). Fowles's biggest and best novel: a tale of mystery and manipulation – plus Greek island life – inspired by his stay on Spétses as a teacher in the 1950s.

Mary Renault *The King Must Die*, *The Last of the Wine*, *The Mask of Apollo* (Sceptre; Random House) and others (all Penguin except *Masks*). Mary Renault's imaginative reconstructions are more than the adolescent's reading they're often taken for, with impeccable research and tight writing. The trio above retell, respectively, the myth of Theseus, the life of a pupil of Socrates and that of a fourth-century BC actor. The life of Alexander the Great is told in *Fire from Heaven*, *The Persian Boy* and *Funeral Games*, available separately or in one economical volume (all Penguin).

Evelyn Waugh *Officers and Gentleman* (Penguin). This volume of the wartime trilogy includes an account of the Battle of Crete and subsequent evacuation.

SPECIFIC GUIDES

ARCHEOLOGY

A.R. and Mary Burn *The Living Past of Greece: A Time Traveller's Tour of Historic and Prehistoric Places* (Herbert Press; HarperCollins). Unusual in extent, this covers sites from Minoan through to Byzantine and Frankish, with good clear plans and lively text.

Evi Melas, ed *Temples and Sanctuaries of Ancient Greece: A Companion Guide* (Thames & Hudson, o/p). Excellent collection of essays on the main sites, written by archeologists who have worked at them.

Alexander Paradissis *Fortresses and Castles of Greece* (Efstathiadis, Athens). Three extremely prolix volumes, widely available in Greek bookshops. Vol III covers the islands.

HIKING

Lance Chilton Various walking pamphlets (Marengo Publications, UK). Small but thorough guides to the best walks at various island charter resorts, accompanied by three-colour maps. Areas covered to date include: Áyios Yeóryios, Corfu; Yeoryioúpolis and Plakiás, Crete; Líndhos, Rhodes; Kokkári, Sámos; and Sými. Available in specialist UK shops or by mail order; catalogue from 17 Bernard Crescent, Hunstanton PE36 6ER, ☎ & fax 01485/532710, *Marengo@supanet.com*.

Marc Dubin *Trekking in Greece* (Lonely Planet; o/p). Though some sections are showing their age (the early 1990s), still an excellent walkers' guide, expanding on the hikes covered in this book. Includes day-hikes and a few longer treks on the islands, plus extensive preparatory and background information

REGIONAL GUIDES

Marc Dubin *The Rough Guide to the Dodecanese and the East Aegean* (Penguin). Exhaustive coverage of the islands described in chapters 4 and 5 of this book, by a part-time resident of Sámos.

John Fisher and Geoff Garvey *The Rough Guide to Crete* (Penguin). An expanded and practical guide to the island by two Cretophiles, who contributed the Crete chapter to this book.

Lycabettus Press Guides (Athens, Greece). This series takes in many of the more popular islands and certain mainland highlights; most, despite decade-long intervals between revisions, pay their way both in interest and usefulness – in particular those on Páros, Kós, Pátmos, Ídhra and the travels of St Paul.

Nikos Stavroulakis *Jewish Sites and Synagogues of Greece* (Talos Press, Athens). Lavishly illustrated alphabetical gazetteer of all Jewish monuments in Greece, including the islands, with town plans and full histories of the communities that created them. A few have been demolished since publication, however.

YACHTING

H.M. Denham *The Aegean* and *The Ionian Islands to the Anatolian Coast* (John Murray, UK, o/p). Long the standard references if you were out yachting; still found in secondhand bookshops, but a bit obsolete.

Rod Heikell *Greek Waters Pilot* (Imray, Laurie, Norrie and Wilson, UK). Rather better than the preceding, which it has superseded.

LANGUAGE

So many Greeks have lived or worked abroad in America, Australia and, to a much lesser extent, Britain, that you will find someone who speaks English in the tiniest island village. Add to that the thousands attending language schools or working in the tourist industry – English is the lingua franca of most resorts, with German second – and it is easy to see how so many visitors come back having learned only half a dozen restaurant words between them.

You can certainly get by this way, but it isn't very satisfying, and the willingness and ability to say even a few words will transform your status from that of dumb *turístas* to the honourable one of *xénos/xéni*, a word which can mean foreigner, traveller and guest all rolled into one.

LEARNING BASIC GREEK

Greek is not an easy language for English speakers but it is a very beautiful one, and even a brief acquaintance will give you some idea of the debt owed to it by Western European languages.

On top of the usual difficulties of learning a new language, Greek presents the additional problem of an entirely separate **alphabet**. Despite initial appearances, this is in practice fairly easily mastered – a skill that will help enormously if you are going to get around independently (see the alphabet box on p.506). In addition, certain combinations of letters have unex-

LANGUAGE LEARNING MATERIALS

TEACH-YOURSELF GREEK COURSES

Breakthrough Greece (Pan Macmillan; book and four cassettes). Excellent, basic teach-yourself course; no Greek lettering, but good for classicists who need to unlearn bad habits.

Greek Language and People (BBC Publications, UK; book and two cassettes available). More limited in scope but good for acquiring the essentials, and the confidence to try them.

Anne Farmakides *A Manual of Modern Greek* (Yale UP; McGill UP; 3 vols). If you have the discipline and motivation, this is one of the best for learning proper, grammatical Greek; indeed, mastery of just the first volume will get you a long way.

Hara Garoufalia *Teach Yourself Holiday Greek* (Hodder & Stoughton, UK; book and cassette available). Unlike many quickie courses, this provides a good grammatical foundation, but you'll need a dictionary (see below) to supplement the scanty vocabulary lists.

Niki Watts *Greek in Three Months* (Hugo, Dorling Kindersley; book and four cassettes). Delivers as promised; equals or exceeds *Breakthrough Greek*.

PHRASEBOOKS

Greek, a Rough Guide Phrasebook (Penguin, UK & US). Up-to-date and accurate pocket phrasebook not full of "*plume de ma tante*"-type expressions. The English-to-Greek section is sensibly transliterated, though the Greek-to-English part requires basic mastery of the Greek alphabet. Feature boxes fill you in on dos and don'ts and cultural know-how.

DICTIONARIES

The Oxford Dictionary of Modern Greek (Oxford UP, UK & US). A bit bulky in its wide format, but generally considered the best Greek–English, English–Greek paperback dictionary.

Collins Pocket Greek Dictionary (HarperCollins, UK & US). Very nearly as complete as the Oxford and probably better value for the money. The inexpensive *Collins Gem Greek Dictionary* (UK only) is palm-sized but exactly the same in contents – the best purse or day-pack choice.

Oxford Greek–English, English–Greek Learner's Dictionary (Oxford UP, UK & US). If you're planning a prolonged stay, this pricey, hardbound, two-volume set is unbeatable for usage and vocabulary. There's also a more portable one-volume *Learner's Pocket Dictionary*.

pected results. This book's transliteration system should help you make intelligible noises, but you have to remember that the correct **stress** (marked throughout the book with an acute accent or sometimes a dieresis) is crucial. With the right sounds but the wrong stress people will either fail to understand you, or else understand something quite different from what you intended.

Greek **grammar** is more complicated still: nouns are divided into three genders, all with different case endings in the singular and in the plural, and all adjectives and articles have to agree with these in gender, number and case. (All adjectives are arbitrarily cited in the neuter form in the following lists.) Verbs are even more complex. To begin with at least, the best thing is simply to say what you know the way you know it, and never mind the niceties. "Eat meat hungry" should get a result, however grammatically incorrect. If you worry about your mistakes, you'll never say anything.

KATHARÉVOUSSA, DHIMOTIKÍ AND DIALECTS

Greek may seem complicated enough in itself, but problems are multiplied when you consider that since the early 1800s there has been an ongoing dispute between two versions of the language: **katharévoussa** and **dhimotikí**.

When Greece first achieved independence in the nineteenth century, its people were almost universally illiterate, and the language they spoke – **dhimotikí**, "demotic" or "popular" Greek – had undergone enormous change since the days of the Byzantine empire and Classical times. The vocabulary had assimilated countless borrowings from the languages of the various invaders and conquerors, namely the Turks, Venetians, Albanians and Slavs.

The finance and inspiration for the new Greek state, as well as its early leaders, came largely from the diaspora – Greek families who had been living in the sophisticated cities of central and eastern Europe, in Constantinople or in Russia. With their European notions about the grandeur of Greece's past, and lofty conception of Hellenism, they set about obliterating the memory of subjugation to foreigners in every possible field. And what better way to start than by purging the language of its foreign accretions and reviving its Classical purity?

They accordingly set about creating what was in effect a new form of the language, *katharévoussa* (literally "cleansed" Greek). The complexities of Classical grammar and syntax were reinstated, and Classical words, long out of use, were reintroduced. To the country's great detriment, *katharévoussa* became the language of the schools and the prestigious professions, government, business, the law, newspapers and academia. Everyone aspiring to membership of the elite strove to master it and to speak it – even though there was no consensus on how many of the words should be pronounced.

The *katharévoussa/dhimotikí* debate remained a highly contentious issue until the early 1980s. Writers – from Solomos and Makriyannis in the nineteenth century to Seferis, Kazantzakis and Ritsos in the twentieth – have all championed the demotic in their literature. Advocacy of *dhimotikí* became increasingly linked to left-wing politics, while crackpot right-wing governments forcibly (re)instated *katharévoussa* at every opportunity. Most recently, the **colonels' junta** of 1967–1974 reversed a decision of the previous government to teach using *dhimotikí* in the schools, bringing back *katharévoussa*, even on sweet wrappers, as part of their ragbag of notions about racial purity and heroic ages.

Dhimotikí returned once more after the fall of the colonels and now seems here to stay. It is used in schools, on radio and TV, and after a fashion in newspapers (with the exception of the extreme right-wing *Estia*). The only institutions which refuse to bring themselves up to date are the Church and the legal professions – so beware rental contracts and official documents.

This is not to suggest that there is now any less confusion. The Metaxas dictatorship of the 1930s changed scores of village names from Slavic to Classical forms, and these official **place names** still hold sway on most road signs and maps – even though the local people may use the *dhimotikí* form. Thus you will see "Leonídhio(n)" or "Spétsai" written, while everyone actually says Leonídhi or Spétses.

DIALECTS AND MINORITY LANGUAGES

If the lack of any standard Greek were not enough, Greece still offers a rich field of linguistic diversity, both in its regional dialects and minority languages. Ancient **dialects** are alive and well in many a remote area, and some of them are quite incomprehensible to outsiders.

THE GREEK ALPHABET: TRANSLITERATION

Set out below is the Greek alphabet, the system of transliteration used in this book, and a brief aid to pronunciation.

Greek	Transliteration	Pronounced
Α, α	a	a as in f*a*ther
Β, β	v	v as in *v*et
Γ, γ	y/g	y as in yes except before consonants or α, o or οι when it's a breathy *g* as in *g*ap
Δ, δ	dh	th as in *th*en
Ε, ε	e	e as in g*e*t
Ζ, ζ	z	z sound
Η, η	i	i as in sk*i*
Θ, θ	th	th as in *th*eme
Ι, ι	i	i as in sk*i*
Κ, κ	k	k sound
Λ, λ	l	l sound
Μ, μ	m	m sound
Ν, ν	n	n sound
Ξ, ξ	x	x sound, never z
Ο, ο	o	o as in t*o*ad
Π, π	p	p sound
Ρ, ρ	r	r sound
Σ, σ, ς	s	s sound, except z before μ or γ
Τ, τ	t	t sound
Υ, υ	i	i as in sk*i*
Φ, φ	f	f sound
Χ, χ	h before vowels, kh before consonants	harsh h sound, like ch in loch
Ψ, ψ	ps	ps as in li*ps*
Ω, ω	o	o as in t*o*ad, indistinguishable from ο

Combinations and diphthongs

ΑΙ, αι	e	e as in h*ey*
ΑΥ, αυ	av/af	av or af depending on following consonant
ΕΙ, ει	i	long i, exactly like ι or η
ΕΥ, ευ	ev/ef	ev or ef, depending on following consonant
ΟΙ, οι	i	long i, exactly like ι or η
ΟΥ, ου	ou	ou as in t*ou*rist
ΓΓ, γγ	ng	ng as in a*ng*le; always medial
ΓΚ, γκ	g/ng	g as in *g*oat at the beginning of a word, ng in the middle
ΜΠ, μπ	b/mb	b at the beginning of a word, mb in the middle
ΝΤ, ντ	d/nd	d at the beginning of a word, nd in the middle
ΤΣ, τσ	ts	ts as in hi*ts*
ΤΖ, τζ	tz	j as in *j*am

Note on diereses

The dieresis is used in Greek over the second of two adjacent vowels to change the pronunciation that you would expect from the preceding table; often it can function as the primary stress in this book. In the word kaïki (caique), the presence of the dieresis changes the pronunciation from "cake-key" to "ki-ee-key" and additionally the middle "i" carries the primary stress. In the word *païdhákia* (lamb chops), the dieresis again changes the sound of the first syllable from "pay" to "pah-ee", but in this case the primary stress is on the third syllable. It is also, uniquely among Greek accents, used on capital letters in signs and personal-name spellings in Greece, and we have followed this practice.

GREEK WORDS AND PHRASES

Essentials

Yes	*Né*	Yesterday	*Khthés*	Big	*Megálo*
Certainly	*Málista*	Now	*Tóra*	Small	*Mikró*
No	*Óhi*	Later	*Argótera*	More	*Perisótero*
Please	*Parakaló*	Open	*Anikhtó*	Less	*Ligótero*
Okay, agreed	*Endáxi*	Closed	*Klistó*	A little	*Lígo*
Thank you (very much)	*Efharistó (polý)*	Day	*Méra*	A lot	*Polý*
		Night	*Níkhta*	Cheap	*Ftinó*
I (don't) understand	*(Dhén) Katalavéno*	In the morning	*Tó proï*	Expensive	*Akrivó*
		In the afternoon	*Tó apóyevma*	Hot	*Zestó*
Excuse me, do you speak English?	*Parakaló, mípos miláte angliká?*	In the evening	*Tó vrádhi*	Cold	*Krýo*
		Here	*Edhó*	With (together)	*Mazí (mé)*
		There	*Ekí*	Without	*Horís*
Sorry/excuse me	*Signómi*	This one	*Aftó*	Quickly	*Grígora*
		That one	*Ekíno*	Slowly	*Sigá*
Today	*Símera*	Good	*Kaló*	Mr/Mrs	*Kýrios/Kyría*
Tomorrow	*Ávrio*	Bad	*Kakó*	Miss	*Dhespinís*

Other Needs

To eat/drink	*Trógo/píno*	Stamps	*Gramatosímata*	Toilet	*Toualéta*
Bakery	*Foúrnos, psomádhiko*	Petrol station	*Venzinádhiko*	Police	*Astynomía*
Pharmacy	*Farmakío*	Bank	*Trápeza*	Doctor	*Iatrós*
Post office	*Tahydhromío*	Money	*Leftá/Khrimata*	Hospital	*Nosokomío*

Requests and Questions

To ask a question, it's simplest to start with *parakaló*, then name the thing you want in an interrogative tone.

Where is the bakery?	*Parakaló, o foúrnos?*	How many?	*Póssi* or *pósses?*
Can you show me the road to . . . ?	*Parakaló, o dhrómos yiá . . . ?*	How much?	*Póso?*
		When?	*Póte?*
We'd like a room for two	*Parakaló, éna dhomátio yiá dhýo átoma*	Why?	*Yiatí?*
		At what time . . . ?	*Tí óra ?*
May I have a kilo of oranges?	*Parakaló, éna kiló portokalia?*	What is/Which is . . . ?	*Tí íne/pió íne . . . ?*
		How much (does it cost)?	*Póso káni?*
Where?	*Poú?*	What time does it open?	*Tí óra aníyi?*
How?	*Pós?*	What time does it close?	*Tí óra klíni?*

Talking to People

Greek makes the distinction between the informal (*esí*) and formal (*esís*) second person, as French does with *tu* and *vous*. Young people, older people and country people nearly always use *esí* even with total strangers. In any event, no one will be too bothered if you get it wrong. By far the most common greeting, on meeting and parting, is *yiá sou/yiá sas* – literally "health to you".

Hello	*Hérite*	My name is . . .	*Me léne . . .*
Good morning	*Kalí méra*	Speak slower, please	*Parakaló, miláte pió sigá*
Good evening	*Kalí spéra*	How do you say it in Greek?	*Pos léyete stá Elliniká?*
Good night	*Kalí níkhta*		
Goodbye	*Adío*	I don't know	*Dhén xéro*
How are you?	*Ti kánis/Ti kánete?*	See you tomorrow	*Thá sé dhó ávrio*
I'm fine	*Kalá íme*	See you soon	*Kalí andhámosi*
And you?	*Ke esís?*	Let's go	*Páme*
What's your name?	*Pos se léne?*	Please help me	*Parakaló, ná mé voithíste*

contined overleaf

GREEK WORDS AND PHRASES CONTINUED

Greek's Greek

There are numerous words and phrases which you will hear constantly, even if you rarely have the chance to use them. These are a few of the most common.

Éla!	Come (literally) but also Speak to me! You don't say! etc.	*Ópa!*	Whoops! Watch it!
Oríste!	Literally, "Indicate!"; in effect, "What can I do for you?"	*Po-po-po!*	Expression of dismay or concern, like French "O la la!"
Embrós! or *Léyete!*	Standard phone responses	*Pedhí moú*	My boy/girl, sonny, friend, etc.
Ti néa?	What's new?	*Maláka(s)*	Literally "wanker", but often used (don't try it!) as an informal term of address
Ti yínete?	What's going on (here)?	*Sigá sigá*	Take your time, slow down
Étsi k'étsi	So-so	*Kaló taxídhi*	Bon voyage

Accommodation

Hotel	*Xenodhohío*	Hot water	*zestó neró*
Inn	*Xenónas*	Cold water	*krýo neró*
Youth hostel	*Xenónas neótitos*	Fan	*anamistíra*
A room . . .	*Éna dhomátio . . .*	Can I see it?	*Boró ná tó dhó?*
for one/two/three people	*yiá éna/dhýo/tría átoma*	Can we camp here?	*Boroúme na váloume ti skiní edhó?*
for one/two/three nights	*yiá mía/dhýo /trís vradhiés*	Campsite	*Kamping/Kataskínosi*
with a double bed	*mé megálo kreváti*	Tent	*Skiní*
with a shower	*mé doús*		

On the Move

Aeroplane	*Aeropláno*	Bus station	*Praktorío leoforíon, KTEL*
Bus	*Leoforío*	Bus stop	*Stási*
Car	*Aftokínito*	Harbour	*Limáni*
Motorbike, scooter	*Mihanáki, papáki*	What time does it leave?	*Ti óra févyi?*
Taxi	*Taksí*	What time does it arrive?	*Ti óra ftháni?*
Ship	*Plío/vapóri/karávi*	How many kilometres?	*Pósa hiliómetra?*
Bicycle	*Podhílato*	How many hours?	*Pósses óres?*
Hitching	*Otostóp*	Where are you going?	*Poú pás?*
On foot	*Mé tá pódhia*	I'm going to . . .	*Páo stó . . .*
Trail	*Monopáti*	I want to get off at . . .	*Thélo ná katévo stó . . .*

The dialect of Sfákia in Crete is one such, that of montane Ikaría another. Tsakónika (spoken in the east-central Peloponnese) is still another, while the dialect of the Sarakatsáni shepherds is said to be the oldest, a direct descendant of the language of the Dorian settlers.

The language of the Sarakatsáni's traditional rivals, the **Vlachs**, on the other hand, is not Greek at all, but a derivative of early Latin, with strong affinities to Romanian. In the ex-Yugoslav and Bulgarian frontier regions you can still hear Slavic **Macedonian** spoken, while small numbers of Sephardic Jews in the north speak **Ladino**, a medieval form of Spanish. Until a few decades ago **Arvanitika** – a dialect of medieval Albanian – was the first language of many villages of inland Attica, southern Évvia, northern Ándhros and much of the Argo-

The road to . . .	*O dhrómos yiá . . .*	A return ticket	*Éna isistírio mé epistrofí*
Near	*Kondá*	Beach	*Paralía*
Far	*Makriá*	Cave	*Spiliá*
Left	*Aristerá*	Centre (of town)	*Kéndro*
Right	*Dhexiá*	Church	*Ekklisía*
Straight ahead	*Katefthía*	Sea	*Thálassa*
A ticket to . . .	*Éna isistírio yiá . . .*	Village	*Horió*

Numbers

1	*énas/éna/mía*	13	*dhekatrís*	90	*eneninda*
2	*dhýo*	14	*dhekatésseres*	100	*ekató*
3	*trís/tría*	20	*íkosi*	150	*ekatón penínda*
4	*tésseres/téssera*	21	*íkosiéna*	200	*dhiakóssies/ia*
5	*pénde*		(all compounds elided	500	*pendakóssies/ia*
6	*éxi*		thus)	1000	*hílies/hilia*
7	*eftá*	30	*triánda*	2000	*dhýo hiliádhes*
8	*okhtó*	40	*saránda*	1,000,000	*éna ekatomírio*
9	*enyá*	50	*penínda*	first	*próto*
10	*dhéka*	60	*exínda*	second	*dhéftero*
11	*éndheka*	70	*evdhomínda*	third	*tríto*
12	*dhódheka*	80	*ogdhónda*		

The Time and Days of the Week

Sunday	*Kyriakí*	What time is it?	*Ti óra íne?*
Monday	*Dheftéra*	One/two/three o'clock	*Mía óra, dhýo/trís (óres)*
Tuesday	*Tríti*	Twenty minutes to four	*Tésseres pará íkosi*
Wednesday	*Tetárti*	Five minutes past seven	*Eftá ké pénde*
Thursday	*Pémpti*	Half past eleven	*Éndheka ke misí*
Friday	*Paraskeví*	In half an hour	*Sé misí óra*
Saturday	*Sávato*	In a quarter-hour	*S'éna tétarto*

Months and Seasonal Terms

January	*Yennári*	August	*Ávgoustos*
February	*Fleváris*	September	*Septémvris*
March	*Mártis*	October	*Októvris*
April	*Aprílis*	November	*Noémvris*
May	*Maïos*	December	*Dhekémvris*
June	*Ioúnios*	Summer schedule	*Therinó dhromolóyio*
July	*Ioúlios*	Winter schedule	*Himerinó dhromolóyio*

Saronic area; it is still widely spoken among the older generation. Lately the clock has been turned back as throngs of Albanian refugees circulate in most other parts of the country. In Thrace there is also a substantial **Turkish**-speaking population, as well as some speakers of **Pomak** (a relative of Bulgarian with a large Greco-Turkish vocabulary).

A GLOSSARY OF WORDS AND TERMS

ACROPOLIS Ancient, fortified hilltop.

AGORA Market and meeting place of an ancient Greek city; also the commercial "high street" of a modern village.

AMPHORA Tall, narrow-necked jar for oil or wine.

ÁNO Upper; common prefix element of village names.

APSE Polygonal or curved recess at the altar end of a church.

ARCHAIC PERIOD Late Iron Age period, from around 750 BC to the start of the Classical period in the fifth century BC.

ARCHITRAVE Horizontal masonry atop temple columns; same as ENTABLATURE.

ARHONDIKÓ A lordly stone-built mansion, as in the Venetian parts of Crete and the Ionians.

ASTYKÓ (Intra)city, municipal, local; adjective applied to phone calls and bus services.

ATRIUM Open, inner courtyard of an ancient house, usually Roman.

ÁYIOS/AYÍA/ÁYII Saint or holy (m/f/plural). Common place-name prefix (abbreviated Ag or Ay); often spelled AGIOS or AGHIOS.

BASILICA Colonnaded, "hall-" or "barn-" type church adapted from Roman models, of which only foundations remain on most islands.

BEMA Rostrum for oratory (and later the chancel) of a church.

BOULEUTERION Auditorium for meetings of an ancient town's deliberative council.

BYZANTINE EMPIRE Created by the division of the Roman empire in 395 AD, this, the eastern half, was ruled from Constantinople (modern Istanbul). In Greece, Byzantine culture peaked twice: in the eleventh century, and again at Mystra in the early fifteenth century.

CAPITAL The flared top, often ornamented, of a column.

CELLA Sacred room of a temple, housing the cult image.

CLASSICAL PERIOD Essentially from the end of the Persian wars in the fifth century BC until the unification of Greece under Philip II of Macedon (338 BC).

CORINTHIAN Decorative columns, festooned with acanthus florets; a temple built in this order.

DHIMARHÍO Town hall.

DHOMÁTIA Rooms for rent in purpose-built blocks or private houses.

DORIAN Northern civilization that displaced and succeeded the Mycenaeans and Minoans through most of Greece around 1100 BC.

DORIC Minimalist, unadorned columns, dating from the Dorian period; a temple built in this order.

DRUM Cylindrical or faceted vertical section, usually pierced by an even number of narrow windows, upholding a church cupola.

ENTABLATURE The horizontal linking structure atop the columns of an ancient temple.

EPARHÍA Greek Orthodox diocese; also the smallest subdivision of a modern province, analogous to a county.

EXEDRA Display niche for statuary.

EXONARTHEX The outer vestibule or entrance hall of a church, when a true NARTHEX is present.

FORUM Market and meeting place of a Roman-era city.

FRIEZE Band of sculptures around a temple. Doric friezes consist of various tableaux of figures (METOPES) interspersed with grooved panels (TRIGLYPHS); Ionic ones have continuous bands of figures.

FROÚRIO Medieval castle; also modern military headquarters.

GARSONIÉRA/ES Studio villa/s, self-catering apartment/s.

GEOMETRIC PERIOD Post-Mycenaean Iron Age era named for the style of its pottery; begins in the early eleventh century BC with the arrival of Dorian peoples. By the eighth century BC, with the development of representational styles, it becomes known as the ARCHAIC PERIOD.

HELLENISTIC PERIOD The last and most unified "Greek empire", created in the wake of Alexander the Great's Macedonian empire and finally collapsing with the fall of Corinth to the Romans in 146 BC. Thus "Hellenistic" refers to the art and architecture of this time.

HEROÖN Shrine or sanctuary, usually of a demigod or mortal; war memorials in modern Greece.

HOKHLÁKI Mosaic of coloured pebbles, found in church or house courtyards of the Dodecanese and Spétses.

HÓRA Main town of an island or region; literally it means "the place". An island hóra is often known by the same name as the island.

IERÓN Literally, "sacred" – the space between the altar screen and the apse of a church, reserved for priestly activities.

IKONOSTÁSIS Screen between the nave of a church and the altar, supporting at least three icons.

IONIC Elaborate, decorative development of the older DORIC order. Ionic temple columns are slimmer, with deeper "fluted" edges, spiral-shaped capitals and ornamental bases.

IPERASTYKÓ Inter-city, long-distance – as in phone calls and bus services.

JANISSARY Member of the Turkish imperial guard, often forcibly recruited in childhood from the local population.

KAFENÍO Coffee house or café; in a small village the centre of communal life and probably serving as the bus stop, too.

KAÏKI (plural KAÏKIA) Caique, or medium-sized boat, traditionally wooden and used for transporting cargo and passengers; now refers mainly to island excursion boats.

KALDERÍMI A cobbled mule-track or footpath.

KÁMBOS Fertile agricultural plain, usually near a river mouth.

KANTÍNA Shack, caravan or even a disused bus on the beach, serving just drinks and perhaps sandwiches.

KÁSTRO Any fortified hill (or a castle), but most usually the oldest, highest, walled-in part of an island HÓRA.

KATHOLIKÓN Central chapel of a monastery.

KÁTO Lower; common prefix element of village names.

KENDRIKÍ PLATÍA Central square.

KOUROS Nude Archaic or Classical statue of an idealized young man, usually portrayed with one foot slightly forward of the other.

MACEDONIAN EMPIRE Empire created by Philip II in the mid-fourth century BC.

MEGARON Principal hall or throne room of a Mycenaean palace.

MELTÉMI North wind that blows across the Aegean in summer, starting softly from near the mainland and hitting the Cyclades, the Dodecanese and Crete full on.

METOPE see FRIEZE

MINOAN Crete's great Bronze Age civilization, which dominated the Aegean from about 2500 to 1400 BC.

MONÍ Formal term for a monastery or convent.

MOREÁ(S) Medieval term for the Peloponnese; the outline of the peninsula was likened to the leaf of a mulbery tree, *moreá* in Greek,

MYCENAEAN Mainland civilization centred on Mycenae and the Argolid from about 1700 to 1100 BC.

NAOS The inner sanctum of an ancient temple; also, any Orthodox Christian shrine.

NARTHEX Western vestibule of a church, reserved for catechumens and the unbaptized; typically frescoed with scenes of the Last Judgement.

NEOLITHIC Earliest era of settlement in Greece, characterized by the use of stone tools and weapons together with basic agriculture. Divided arbitrarily into Early (*c* 6000 BC), Middle (*c* 5000 BC) and Late (*c* 3000 BC).

NÉOS, NÉA, NÉO "New" – a common prefix to a town or village name.

NOMÓS Modern Greek province – there are more than fifty of them. Village bus services are organized according to their borders.

ODEION Small, often roofed, theatre, used for musical performances, minor dramatic productions or councils.

ORCHESTRA Semi-circular area in a theatre where the chorus would sing and dance.

PALAESTRA Gymnasium for athletics and wrestling practice.

PALEÓS, PALEÁ, PALEÓ "Old" – again a common prefix in town and village names.

PANAYÍA Virgin Mary.

PANDOKRÁTOR Literally "The Almighty"; generally refers to the stern portrayal of Christ in Majesty frescoed or in mosaic in the dome of many Byzantine churches.

PANIYÍRI Festival or feast – the local celebration of a holy day.

PARALÍA Beach or seafront promenade.

PEDIMENT Triangular, sculpted gable below the roof of a temple.

PENDENTIVE Any of four triangular sections of vaulting with concave sides, positioned at a corner of a rectangular space to support a circular or polygonal dome; often adorned with frescoes of the four Evangelists.

PERÍPTERO Street kiosk.

PERISTEREÓNES Pigeon towers, especially on Ándhros and Tínos.

PERISTYLE Gallery of columns around a temple or other building.

PINAKOTHIKI Picture gallery.

PITHOS (plural PITHOI) Large ceramic jar for storing oil, grain etc. Very common in Minoan palaces and used in almost identical form in modern Greek homes.

PLATÍA Square, plaza.

PROPYLAION Monumental columned gateway of an ancient building; often used in the plural, *propylaia*.

PYRGOS Tower or bastion; also the tower-mansions found on Lésvos.

SKÁLA The port of an inland island settlement, nowadays often larger and more important than its namesake, but always younger since built after the disappearance of piracy.

SQUINCH Small concavity across a corner of a columnless interior space, which supports a superstructure such as a dome.

STELE Upright stone slab or column, usually inscribed; an ancient tombstone.

STOA Colonnaded walkway in Classical-era marketplace.

TAVERNA Restaurant; see "Eating and Drinking" in Basics, p.47, for details of the different types of specialist eating places.

TÉMBLON Wooden altar screen of an Orthodox church, usually ornately carved and painted and used to display icons; more or less interchangeable with IKONOSTÁSIS.

TEMENOS Sacred precinct, often used to refer to the sanctuary itself.

THEATRAL AREA Open area found in most of the Minoan palaces with seat-like steps around. Probably a type of theatre or ritual area, though this is not conclusively proven.

THOLOS Conical or beehive-shaped building, especially a Mycenaean tomb.

TRIGLYPH see FRIEZE

TYMPANUM The recessed space, flat or carved in relief, inside a pediment.

ACRONYMS

ANEK Anónymi Navtikí Etería Krítis (Shipping Co of Crete, Ltd), which runs most ferries between Pireás and Crete, plus many to Italy.

DANE Dhodhekanisiakí Anónymi Navtikí Etería (Dodecanesian Shipping Company Ltd), which runs many ferries between Rhodes and Pireás via intervening islands.

DIKKI Democratic Social Movement, a party leftward of PASOK.

EAM National Liberation Front, the political force behind ELAS.

ELAS Popular Liberation Army, the main resistance group during World War II and the basis of the communist army (DSE) in the civil war.

ELTA The postal service.

EOT Ellinikós Organismós Tourismoú, the National Tourist Organization.

FYROM Former Yugoslav Republic of Macedonia.

KKE Communist Party, unreconstructed.

KTEL National syndicate of bus companies. The term is also used to refer to bus stations.

LANE Lasithiakí Anónymi Navtikí Etería (Lasithian Shipping Company Ltd), based in eastern Crete, which runs ferries between Rhodes, Kárpathos, eastern Crete and Pireás.

ND New Democracy/Néa Dhimokratía (conservative) party.

NEL Navtiliakí Etería Lésvou (Lesvian Shipping Co), which runs most of the northeast Aegean ferries.

OTE Telephone company.

PASOK Pan-Hellenic Socialist Movement (socialist party).

INDEX

B

N

R

S